Emotions—
Their Parameters and Measurement

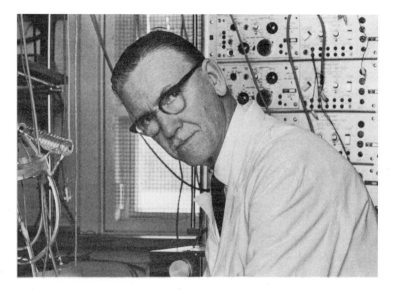

Professor Ulf von Euler

Emotions
Their Parameters and Measurement

Editor:

Lennart Levi, M.D.
Laboratory for Clinical Stress Research,
Stockholm, Sweden

Raven Press, Publishers ▪ New York

Made in the United States of America

International Standard Book Number 0-89004-019-2
Library of Congress Catalog Card Number 74-80539

ISBN outside North and South America
only: 0-7204-7528-7

The Symposium from which this book was
derived was made possible through the
generous support of F. Hoffmann-LaRoche,
Basel.

Preface

Among the most important elements in the interaction between man and his environment are his emotional reactions, which occur in response to every major environmental change and which strongly influence behavior. They are decisive elements in and determinants of our quality of life. They accompany and are thought to be part of the pathogenic mechanisms of many psychiatric and psychosomatic disorders. Briefly, then, emotional reactions affect our experiences, behavior, well-being, and health.

Most researchers and practitioners agree that emotions are of paramount importance. However, when it comes to the *measurement* of these phenomena or of their psychological and/or physiological parameters, we face a considerable diversification of opinions. Some medical and psychological circles still argue against the application of scientific methods to the study of subjective phenomena. Others, including the majority of the contributors to this volume, believe that this can be done.

Which, then, are the *concepts* of emotion, the various *parameters* of emotion, and the best available *techniques* for their measurement? The present international, interdisciplinary compilation of chapters and discussions brings together some of the best scientists and the leading schools of thought and research in this field, representing many countries, disciplines, and approaches. In addition to presenting basic scientific data, this volume also applies current knowledge to clinical medical and psychiatric work as well as today's and tomorrow's ethical implications and problems of emotion measurement and modification.

This volume is based on a recent symposium held in Stockholm under the sponsorship of the Karolinska Institutet. It was organized by this Institute's Laboratory for Clinical Stress Research and made possible through the generosity of F. Hoffmann-LaRoche of Basel, Switzerland. This work was supported in part by the Swedish Medical Research Council (project No. B74-19P-4316-01).

This meeting was held in honor of Professor Ulf S. von Euler, whose pioneering and epoch-making discoveries in the neuroendocrine field have been of decisive importance for most of the research presented in this volume and for medicine and physiology in general. We all unite in paying our respect and admiration to this great scientist and humanitarian.

Dr. Peter Blaser has been most helpful in compiling a synopsis of the discussions, Mrs. Gun Nerje has ably assisted in editing the chapters, and Mr. Björn Carlbom has retyped several of the manuscripts. The Editor sincerely hopes that the present volume not only will stimulate further research and discussions but also will lead to increased applications of these and related findings to all relevant aspects of total man's interaction with his total environment.

Lennart Levi
(November 1974)

Contents

Session 5: Measurement of Emotion in Medical Practice
Chairman: H. J. Eysenck

**Session 6: Measurement and Modification of Emotion:
Ethical Aspects**
Chairmen: Arne Engström and Stewart Wolf

Contributors

M. Åsberg
Department of Psychiatry
Karolinska Hospital
S-104 01 Stockholm 60, Sweden

Jack D. Barchas
Department of Psychiatry
Stanford University School of Medicine
Stanford, California 94305

Joseph V. Brady
Johns Hopkins University School of
    Medicine
720 Rutland Avenue
Baltimore, Maryland 21205

Sven Britton
Immunbiologiska Laboratoriet
Lilla Frescati
S-104 05 Stockholm 50, Sweden

Manfred Clynes
Sentic Research Laboratory
University of California at San Diego
La Jolla, California 92037

Leonard Cook
Department of Pharmacology
Hoffmann-La Roche Inc.
Nutley, New Jersey 07110

Börje Cronholm
Department of Psychiatry
Karolinska Hospital
S-104 01 Stockholm 60, Sweden

José M. R. Delgado
Yale University School of Medicine
333 Cedar Street
New Haven, Connecticut 06510

D. L. Ely
Department of Physiology
University of Southern California
Los Angeles, California 90007

Arne Engström
Forskningsberedningen
Utbildningsdepartementet
Fack
S-103 10 Stockholm, Sweden

Ulf S. von Euler
Department of Physiology
Karolinska Institute
S-104 01 Stockholm 60, Sweden

Hans J. Eysenck
Department of Psychology
Institute of Psychiatry
Denmark Hill
London, S. E. 5 England

Marianne Frankenhaeuser
Psychological Laboratories
University of Stockholm
Postbox 6706
S-113 85 Stockholm, Sweden

Jan E. Fröberg
Laboratory for Clinical Stress Research
Fack
S-104 01 Stockholm 60, Sweden

Joannes J. Groen
Psychiatrische Kliniek
Rijksuniversiteit Leiden "Jelgersma-
    Kliniek"
Oegstgeest, Netherlands

Beatrix A. Hamburg
Department of Psychiatry
Stanford University School of Medicine
Stanford, California 94305

David A. Hamburg
Department of Psychiatry
Stanford University School of Medicine
Stanford, California 94305

James P. Henry
Department of Physiology
University of Southern California
815 West 37th Street
Los Angeles, California 90007

Tim Hunt
Department of Psychology
University of Washington
Seattle, Washington 98195

Nicoly Ivanov
Biochemical Laboratory
Serbsky Research Institute of Forensic
  Psychiatry
Kropotkinsky pereulok, 23
Moscow, U.S.S.R.

Aubrey R. Kagan
Laboratory for Clinical Stress Research
Fack
S-104 01 Stockholm 60, Sweden

Paul Kielholz
Psychiatrische Universitätsklinik
Wilhelm-Klein-Strasse 27
CH-4052 Basle Switzerland

Heribert Konzett
Department of Pharmacology
University of Innsbruck
Peter-Mayr-Strasse 1
A-6020 Innsbruck, Austria

Edward Kostandov
Laboratory of Higher Nervous Activity
Serbsky Research Institute of Forensic
  Psychiatry
Kropotkinsky pereulok, 23
Moscow, U.S.S.R.

Malcolm H. Lader
Department of Psychiatry
De Crespigny Park, Denmark Hill
London, SE5 8 AF England

Richard S. Lazarus
Department of Psychology
University of California
Berkeley, California 94720

Lennart Levi
Laboratory for Clinical Stress Research
Fack
S-104 01 Stockholm 60, Sweden

Paul D. MacLean
Laboratory of Brain Evolution and
  Behavior
National Institute of Mental Health
Bethesda, Maryland 20014

George Mandler
Department of Psychology
University of California at San Diego
La Jolla, California 92037

John W. Mason
Walter Reed Army Institute of Research
Walter Reed Army Medical Center
Washington, D.C. 20012

Cecily de Monchaux
Department of Psychology
University of Washington
Seattle, Washington 98195

Paolo Pancheri
Istituto di Psichiatria
30, Viale dell'Università
Roma, Italy

Talcott Parsons
William James Hall 330
Harvard University
Cambridge, Massachusetts 02138

R. H. Rahe
U.S. Navy Medical Neuropsychiatric
  Research Unit
San Diego, California 92152

David M. Rioch
Institute for Behavioral Research
2429 Linden Lane
Silver Spring, Maryland 20910

Irwin G. Sarason
Department of Psychology
NI-25 University of Washington
Seattle, Washington 98195

Daisy S. Schalling
Department of Psychiatry
Karolinska Hospital
S-104 01 Stockholm 60, Sweden

Carl Wilhelm Sem-Jacobsen
EEG Research Institute Gaustad Sykehus
Gaustad Oslo 3, Norway

Jerry Sepinwall
Department of Pharmacology
Hoffmann-LaRoche, Inc.
Nutley, New Jersey 07110

Charles Shagass
Eastern Pennsylvania Psychiatric Institute
Henry Avenue and Abbotsford Road
Philadelphia, Pennsylvania 19129

Ernest B. Sigg
Department of Neuropharmacology
Hoffmann-La Roche Inc.
Nutley, New Jersey 07110

Pavel V. Simonov
*Institute of Higher Nervous Activity of
the USSR Academy of Sciences
Moscow, U.S.S.R.*

Charles D. Spielberger
*College of Social and Behavioral Sciences
Department of Psychology
University of South Florida
Tampa, Florida 33620*

P. M. Stephens
*Department of Physiology
University of Southern California
Los Angeles, California 90007*

O. B. Styri
*EEG Research Institute Gaustad Sykehus
Gaustad Oslo 3, Norway*

F. M. C. Watson
*Department of Physiology
University of Southern California
Los Angeles, California 90007*

Stewart G. Wolf
*Marine Biomedical Institute
University of Texas Medical Branch at
Galveston
200 University Boulevard
Galveston, Texas 77550*

Roy Yensen
*Department of Psychology and Sociology
Massey University
Palmerston North, New Zealand*

Emotions – Their Parameters and Measurement,
edited by L. Levi.
Raven Press, New York © 1975

The Search for Emotion

George Mandler

Department of Psychology, University of California at San Diego, La Jolla, California 92037

It is appropriate that the subject of this volume is *"parameters* of emotion" rather than *definitions* or *theories* of emotion. The only theme that could possibly hold such a divergence of opinions and competences together is the theme of parametric variations. To search for *the* definition or for *the* theory of emotion is vain – and it is that vanity that is my first theme. My second theme is the directions that this search have taken among some of our predecessors and contemporaries. My third topic is a brief consideration of the limits of an enterprise that aspires toward a theory of emotion. And in a final section I summarize my own prejudices to show how one psychologist wishes to tackle the parameters of his choice.

THE BELIEF IN FUNDAMENTAL EMOTIONS – A HUMAN VANITY

There are three major sources for the belief that the search for the complete theory of emotion is proper; all are rooted in historical notions about the nature of man. The first deals with the irreducibility of ideas and feelings, the idealism of Western philosophy; the second with the invariance of the products of evolutionary mechanism; and the third with our intuitive sense of certainty about experience, whether based on phenomenology or language analysis.

It is a refreshing and peculiarly twentieth century enterprise to ask about the *origins* of emotional feelings and experiences, to be concerned with antecedents rather than with givens. We readily forget that the psychologist-physiologist-philosopher of the nineteenth century (and his predecessors) typically inquired about the consequences of ideas (and feelings) and rarely concerned himself with the origin of ideas as such. Philosophy and psychology (such as it was) took for granted states of mind and irreducible ideas. The concern was primarily with the consequences of mental acts, with the result of feelings and affections, and with their combination. These elemental ideas and feelings were the property of rational conscious man, possibly even his birthright and distinctiveness. To ask for their origin required the postulation of processes that were nonconscious. It was easier

---

Parts of this chapter are from a manuscript for a forthcoming book on *Mind and Emotion.*

to take them for granted; and, more important, they were the mark of the philosophical idealism that dominated much of Western science.

Nowhere did this commitment to the fully fashioned psyche appear more dramatically than in the field of emotion. Contrast our two most illustrious forebears in the field, Charles Darwin and Sigmund Freud. Both were committed natural scientists, the former less a philosophical idealist than the latter, and yet it was Freud who saw emotions as emerging out of mechanisms and processes that were, in the first instance, not irreducible givens. For Darwin the *expression* of emotions was of interest, but it was the expression of something that remained an unanalyzed *a priori*. Joy, anger, pain are the ideas and feelings that *result* in expressive movement, and only rarely does Darwin even speculate about the antecedents of these feelings. When he does his observations are usually embarrassingly commonplace: "If we have suffered or expect to suffer some wilful injury from a man, or if he is in any way [*sic*] offensive to us, we dislike him; and dislike easily rises into hatred" [Darwin, 1872, p. 239].

The need to rely on some *given* emotional states that are beyond explanations is not a feature of the nineteenth century alone, but rather, often in simplified forms, has remained with us as metaphysical postulates of fundamental unanalyzed reactions. The metaphysics of *a priori* judgments or appraisals have even found their way into contemporary physiological speculations, with neurophysiological structures given the task of making *a priori* judgments (Arnold, 1960).

Another source of the belief in an unanalyzed emotional substratum is the unassailable finding that much of our expressive behavior, as so much of our other behavior, has evolutionary rather than contemporary origins—it is natured rather than nurtured. Here it was, of course, Darwin who demonstrated in detail how these expressions transcend species boundaries. Contemporary ethologists have shown us how lower animals exhibit these behaviors under specified environmental and hormonal conditions. However, the notion that these *expressions* are unavoidably tied to certain pre-wired conditions in *man* denies the plasticity of man, or even that of nonhuman primates. It is part of our humanness that we are not bound to evolutionary patterns of behavior, that we can exhibit these inherited patterns under conditions unknown to our forebears or inhibit them when their expression may be maladaptive or unavoidable in lower animals. To assert this plasticity in no way opens the backdoor to a misleading voluntarism, but it does deny the utility of using expressive behavior as the invariable demonstration of rigid stimulus-response chains or, in the modern case, of inferred internal hypothetical states. Man, in contrast to lower animals, may deliberately exhibit some emotional sign in the absence of the internal or external releasers that provide the evolutionary links to these emotional expressions. I may frown in order to frown without "wanting" to *express* anything at all.

At this point I not only want to reject the currently popular ethological journalism that tries to make laws of nakedness, apedness, territorialism, and aggression out of unsubstantiated extensions of animal behavior patterns to man, but also I need to place our inherited expressiveness into context. Expressive movements can be seen as any other indicators or behaviors that are frequently interpreted in terms of *possible* antecedent cognitive and perceptual reactions. They are not invariant, nor should they, in the most extreme popular version, be made the basis of all motivation and emotion (e.g., Tomkins, 1962, 1963).

The third major source that motivates a search for the "true" emotional theory arises out of our common language, out of folk psychology and philosophy. In the first instance it is related to the myth-making tendencies of human individuals, societies, and cultures. We shall turn first to these, and then look at the more specific constraints that the ordinary language seems to exercise on the hopes for scientific exploration of emotion.

More than any other field of knowledge psychology has been both the beneficiary and the prisoner of man's most fascinating proclivity – to explain the world around us, to understand what surrounds us, to make up stories (myths, religions, folk tales, sciences) that explain and make comprehensible the evidence of our senses, stories that in turn shape that very evidence. Over the centuries the men and women who made up the most convincing stories were elevated to a special position in the life of the mind; first they were the prophets, then the philosophers, and finally the scientists. One built on the other, first painfully clearing away the accumulated rubble of ordinary discourse, somewhere breaking through to a new way of looking at the world, a way that was somehow alien to the common language and the folk beliefs, a method or structure that in the truest sense of the word "did not make sense." The growth was slow and often misunderstood, as when Galileo first realized that mathematics was the language of science but never really used it. It took Newton not only to reach the new high ground of mathematical analysis but also to realize that common sense rejection of a concept was not relevant to the building of a system. When he postulated "attraction" in the *Principia,* he was told by his natural philosopher colleagues that this concept was a dead end, but his answer is the important one, that it might not seem reasonable but when he used it in a systematic sense in his axiomatic system it did explain the data.

The pressure on psychology to "make sense," to be consistent with "common knowledge" is infinitely stronger. It may have become even more difficult with the advent of ordinary language philosophy, which was aware of some of the rubble in the ordinary language that produced confusion and pseudo-problems, but often insisted, in unnecessary addition, that underneath the rubble – but within common sense and the ordinary language – lay the kernels of understanding of human motives and actions. Unfortunately Freud's basic insights were clouded by his system and his language, otherwise philosophers would not continue to look for the explanations of human actions in reasons and intentions and in the structure of the surface language. Freud's insight was that there are forces that act like wishes, desires, reasons, and intentions, but that are not available to inspection, to awareness, to reason. Quite rightly that formulation did not "make sense" because a wish or an intention is by definition part of the aware, sensing organism. If Freud had only changed the language and showed that these forces, by some other name, had the same *consequences* as some of our conscious wishes, desires, and intentions, much of the misunderstanding of the misnamed and misrepresented unconscious might not have further muddied the waters of an objective psychology of the past 50 years. Consider in contrast the many-faceted "unconscious" processes and mechanisms that crown our present theories of sensation, perception, cognition, learning, and syntax, without drawing the slightest concern about their "scientific" status.

Psychology's business at the present time then is still to clear away rubble, to take with it the insights of the everyday world, without its myths and fictions. The call for a psychological Newton is misplaced because it may be too early or unnecessary. Too early because too much learning is still to be done and unnecessary because psychology can build on the other sciences, not by becoming like physics (which resulted in one unfortunate turn in the road) or biology or astronomy, but because the accumulation and interpenetration of Newtonian, Mendelian, and other methods and structures may be now enough to build a psychology which will be its own master.

It seems useful not to fall into the trap of trying to explain what "emotion" *is,* that would be to follow the error of trying to explicate the common language. Nor can one yet aim for a deterministic, mathematical theory. But one can, by analyzing the system of forces and processes that make up the human organism, suggest how certain behaviors, feelings, and experiences might be produced. We cannot specify all or most of these forces or their specific structures, but we can indicate some of the subsystems that process information and show that the outcome of these forces and processes produces behaviors and experiences that, appealing to common experience, one might consider akin to what we call emotion. Thus we might start not with the aim of *explaining* emotion but rather with describing a system that has as its product some of the observations that have been called "emotion" in the common language. This outcome, if successful, would, however, be only gravy for the main dish. The system would still be viable if it makes psychological sense and explains certain human actions – that is all such an endeavor may reach for. If it also appeals to some parts of common sense and restructures it in a meaningful way, all the better. But the eventual aim is psychological theory, not an analysis of human experience expressed in phenomenal, existential, or ordinary language.

The other pitfall that ordinary language and thought impose on us is the belief in the reality of its concepts and terms. If the obvious is taken for granted (which unfortunately is not always the case in philosophy) that explanations generated by a recently evolved featherless biped cannot but be models of the world, convenient fictions that help our limited understanding, then the tendency to take folk-theories as ultimate truths must lead to holding on to distinctions and concepts that are not and cannot in principle be ultimate descriptions of the structure of reality. To take folk concepts too seriously is to confer upon man — at least historical man — a god-like status. If God created man then, so one argues, man might have god-like insights, particularly if the "insights" have been around for a few hundred years. If, however, Man created god, then he can arrogate unto himself the same characteristics of insight into ultimate truth with which he has imbued Him. Such a position implies a degree of pretentiousness about the status of this sometimes pitiful little animal that I cannot share. It also hinders the development of the kind of game-playing that I find so attractive in science: the erection and destruction of hypotheses with a claim to better and better approximations of reality but never a claim to ultimate truth. To claim that such a truth is available by a proper examination of our phenomenal selves or by the proper analysis of language is, at least, a hindrance and, at worst, a wall that keeps us from playing man's most productive game — science.

Because men and women have talked about their thoughts and emotions, both discretely and discreetly, we may assume that there may be lawful relations among events, variables, thoughts, and behaviors; but the folk psychology these thoughts express neither seeks nor cares for an unequivocal explanation. It does provide the most important starting points for science, namely the initial hypotheses and the description of the most general consistencies. But one must go beyond common experience, rather than try to imagine that because some men some time can talk about specific emotions, can make distinctions among discrete emotions, can individually and anecdotally assert some rational theory or some irrational defense, that these are therefore the necessary and sufficient building blocks of a science. Our language must be painfully built *out of* the layers of myths and pretensions and insights that make up common parlance and consciousness.

Philosophers and psychologists who have looked to ordinary language as the road to developing a satisfactory scientific language (both syntactically and semantically) often fail to apply a fundamental distinction in the primary *function* of these two languages. Common language serves first as communication, and as such it is appropriately redundant, vague, overinclusive, and ambiguous. A common language that would be nonredundant, precise, and unambiguous would require much more processing effort on the part of both speaker and listener than the organism usually has available. Scientific language on the other hand is a vehicle for description and explanation. If *it* were redundant, vague, and overinclusive, it would fail exactly on the requirements of precise definition and unequivocal explanation.

Consider the adequacy of distinguishing between heavy and light pack-

ages, loud and soft noises, and angry and joyful feelings for most communicative purposes. But the heavy-light and the loud-soft distinctions are totally
inadequate for scientific purposes. Why then should we expect angry-joyful
to be adequate?

Consider the following additional difficulties if we were to permit the common language to be our guide to the emotional states and terms that a psychological theory of emotion should be able to explain. First, there is little
disagreement that such a theory should account for such states as are commonly termed anxiety, joy, fear, euphoria, and probably even love and
disgust. But is lust an emotion, or is sexual feeling to be handled separately?
Are we to be required to explain feelings of pride? Of accomplishment? Of
empathy? Of dislike? Or, even worse, are we to construct national theories
of emotion so that a German theory may account for *Lust* and *Unlust,* for
Gemütlichkeit, or *ängstlich* (which does not strictly mean anxious), or a
French theory for feelings of *ambience.* What are the boundaries of a theory
of emotion, what terms in the ordinary language are the relevant referents
to be explained? And worse, is there even a German requirement for such a
theory, since that language has no true equivalent for the English term
emotion.

A typical argument to such protestations of confusion consists of an appeal to consensual (intuitive?) judgment. After all, it is said, we all know
what we are talking about when we talk about emotions and these counterexamples are either irrelevant or esoteric. I do not believe that a serious
theory of anything should depend on extensive intuitive judgment, nor do I
think that the counterexamples are exotic—they are necessary and useful
aspects of our flexible and redundant common language.

If you agree that none of these reasons is an adequate justification for
believing in the inevitable and necessary existence of a theory of emotions
per se, we must look elsewhere for a proper goal of the theoretical and
empirical study of emotion. None of the metapsychological arguments,
whether based on innate *a priori* ideas or feelings, on inevitable evolutionary
remnants of mating and fighting behavior, or on phenomenal or linguistic
givens, argues logically that the reality that we wish to model is best approached by a single unified theory of emotion.

One other set of observations argues similarly, although more weakly,
against a theory in which emotion or the names of discrete emotions function
as serviceable *theoretical* concepts. And that is the diversity of theoretical
work that has gone on under the banner of emotion and that is so compe-
tently demonstrated in this volume.

EMOTIONS—VARIOUSLY AND DARKLY SEEN

In this section I would like to outline briefly the major lines of thought that
are responsible for the pluralism that distinguishes the various modern ap-

proaches to the topic of emotion. I shall selectively look at some historical beginnings that might give us some understanding about the emphases that guide modern theory and research. In most of the historical cases we shall note an initial frontal attack on emotion *per se*, with a subsequent successful explication of some part of the puzzle.

I have argued before that the most efficient, reasonable, and probably most fruitful approach starts off with a theory which concerns itself primarily with a set of known or hypothesized psychological or physiological processes and determines how their interaction produces certain experiences and actions. One may rest on one's laurels when one has, by this route, advanced a satisfactory description or explanation of a reasonably large subset of those experiences and actions that common sense or *a priori* judgment vaguely defines as emotional. Such a result may be achieved deliberately—as I advocate—or accidentally; the latter when a theorist wishes to engage on the grand explication of "emotion" and arrives in fact at a subsystem. Usually his critics will find lacunae that his system fails to illuminate. So be it; within my criteria he will have gone a long way toward doing justice to the scientific enterprise. Nineteenth century psychology and physiology usually started out to "explain emotion" and ended up with a partially satisfactory subsystem.

What are the major lines of these somewhat independent developments? What significant variables have they suggested that should be included in a modern theory of man; even if today we do not insist that the purpose of such a system is to explain emotion—writ common? My survey is highly personal, selective, and certainly nonexclusive.

We have already alluded to Darwin's contribution to the evolutionary view of expressive behavior. The import of facial and other expressive movements (without stating for our purposes *what* they are expressing) has occupied us up to the present. The most recent and impressive array of evidence, old and new, has been presented by Izard (1971). There are indeed cross-cultural constancies in these expressive movements and, within important bounds, they are used as significant cognitive signs by both the viewer and the actor. But let me also remind you of Darwin's three major principles and the lines of thought they opened for succeeding scientists. His *principle of serviceable associated habits* postulates complex actions that are "of direct or indirect" service, given certain states of mind. These habits will also occur when they "may not then be of the least use" but simply because some "state of mind" similar to the originator is present. That is, expressive movements may be indices of internal states even though they may have no adaptive significance at the time whatsoever. This principle justifies the study of expressive movements *per se* rather than their functional significance.

Darwin's second *principle of antithesis* asserts that certain actions will be induced by opposing states of the mind and that these actions (or movements) may be "of no use" but will be "directly opposite in nature" to the actions and movements induced by the original state of mind..Darwin here asserts the bipolarity of certain expressive movements (reflecting the bipolarity of mind states), an assertion that has led to the respectable tradition of seeing emotions as dimensional on such bipolar axes as pleasant-unpleasant, active-quiescent, and attending-rejecting.

Finally, the third *principle of the direct action of the nervous system* states that certain expressive results are dependent solely on "excess nerve-force," independent of other factors. The lack of knowledge of the nervous system at mid-nineteenth century prevents any unequivocal interpretation of Darwin's statement. My own reading, particularly of his examples, convinces me that Darwin in the majority of cases refers to the inevitable effects of intense autonomic nervous system reactions, again a theme that is still with us today.

Next I turn to William James (1884, 1890) in contrast to Lange, of whom more later. Many of James's critics, in particular Cannon (1927), have deliberately or inadvertently restricted the Jamesian theory to visceral action. We shall simply avoid the error without arguing it. First, recall the fundamental importance of James's thought. He rejected the primacy of thought and feeling that had been with philosophy and psychology at least since the Greeks. James insisted that after the initial perceptual apprehension of an event or object it produces bodily consequences (including visceral, skeletal, and muscular) and the perception of these consequences in turn lends emotional feeling to the object or event. Apart from the revolutionary shift from the *a priori* feeling to the produced feeling, his insistence on self-perception as an important determiner of experience and action (and emotion) has stayed with us to this day and has in recent years found renewed expression in cognitive studies of emotion (Schachter and Singer, 1962) as well as in behavioristic approaches which use self-perception to explicate important social phenomena (Bem, 1967). It would be well to remember that James was falsely credited with saying that emotional feeling is defined by the perception of differing visceral patterns and these alone, an ascription that generated decades of research trying to find those particular visceral patterns that were in fact associated with each and every discrete emotion. Given what James did say, would he have approved of this search for the discrete emotion—and only in the viscera?

The man who probably would have approved was the Danish physiologist C. Lange (1885) whose major impact came in 1887 with the German translation of his work. Lange said that "we are indebted to the vasomotor system for the entire emotional part of our mental life." The psychological aspects of emotional experience of behavior, the "motor abnormalities, sensation paralysis, subjective sensations, disturbances of secretion, and intelligence" are secondary effects which "have their cause in anomalies of vascular innervation." Thus, Lange should equally be credited with the revolutionary thought that feelings could be derived from some antecedents, and he can, partly because of being linked with James, be given credit for much of the tradition of fruitful, though often misdirected, psychophysiological research.

I said misdirected research as a bridge to Walter B. Cannon who by 1927 was able to say in a tight, logical, and sparse argument, that need not be rehearsed here, that visceral patterns could not be the basis for the differentiation of emotional feeling. As I have indicated elsewhere (Mandler, 1962, 1967), there is no good evidence to the contrary. We have no replicable, documented studies that show different emotions or feeling states to be the direct *result* of specific visceral patterns. Frankenhaeuser's (1975) careful review of the evidence and her own insightful experiments support this argument convincingly and extensively. To avoid repeated misunderstanding, I should once again say that none of these remarks in the slightest way denigrates the important theoretical and empirical work on the *correlations* between feeling states and central and peripheral physiological changes. Brady (1967) as well as Frankenhaeuser (1975), among others, have shown that knowledge about these correlated changes not only produces clean and lawful generalizations but also significantly enriches our insight into possible differentiations between various feeling states such as, for example, signaled and unsignaled states of apprehension or threat (Mandler, 1967).

Three to four decades elapsed after Cannon's critique; they are interspersed with a variety of neurophysiological theories stimulated by Cannon's own work but they rarely lasted very long in the absence of adequate definition of what it was behaviorally that the physiological model was supposed to generate. At the end of this period I believe there have been several important developments, all of which, again for reasons that should be obvious by now, concentrate on one or another aspect of the "emotional" spectrum.

The work by Stanley Schachter (Schachter and Singer, 1962; Schachter, 1971), most seminal from the present perspective, once again raised the issue that divided Cannon and James (read Lange). Schachter and his associates showed in a series of ingenious experiments that emotional experience and expression was the result of undifferentiated visceral (sympathetic) arousal, combined with cognitive and social factors. The viscera were reinstated as the central antecedent factor for setting the stage for feeling states, the content of which was defined by cognitive variables. The latter are left open by Schachter—his definition of cognitions is ostensive; they are what the social environment suggests or demands as appropriate interpretations of the situation. At the same time, Lazarus and his associates (Lazarus, Averill, and Opton, 1970), working more narrowly with the negative or unpleasant end of the continuum, made the important step of defining the cognitive developments that lead to some specific cognitive apperception, stressing appraisal and reappraisal, as well as the coping mechanisms available to the organism.

If Schachter revived serious thought about a particular genus of "emotional" theory, he also left open to future developments two major areas within that approach: first, the independent specification of cognitive patterns alluded to above and second, the conditions that give rise to visceral and behavioral arousal — the evolutionary ancestors of Darwin's associated habits, antithetical reactions, and conditions for "excesses of nerve-force."

John Bowlby (1969, 1973) has contributed significantly to the modern scene in that area, using thoughtful analyses of the ethology of man to define the conditions of attachment and loss in the human infant and their development from rudimentary mechanisms derived from the history of the species. Bowlby's brilliant synthesis of modern systems analysis, careful ethological thought, and the resurrection of the most lasting and profound insights of Freud's stands as a model of theorizing. Combined with his extensive and careful observations of human infants, he has presented another theoretical approach which, in the modern tradition, illuminates emotion without letting its claim for explanation direct the theory.

As you might imagine, I consider the lesson from these historical examples to be unequivocal. Each of the investigators mentioned has illuminated part of the domain that one should consider to be the field of emotion. Some started with the express intent to "explain" emotion, letting folk-psychology guide them; whereas others might never mention such a target specifically. Each contribution helps understand part of the forest, illuminates some path, while other parts remain in darkness. I see this little history not so much as a search for emotion but as part of the more general attempt to draw a satisfactory model of the mechanisms and processes that explain human experience and behavior. And when we approach some satisfactory answer to that puzzle, we shall discover that we have explained *pari passu* all that one would want to understand about the emotions.

HOW TO STUDY EMOTION BY IGNORING IT

My major theme should be loud and clear by now: Let the intuitive and thorough investigators work on the parameters and variables that they consider important, in the event that they will illuminate, however briefly, some corner or other of the domain of emotion, however defined. The models of man that we are constructing must eventually encompass among their consequences those events that we call emotional feelings and experiences and behaviors. It is my opinion that an attempt to define emotion is obviously misplaced and doomed to failure; if we ignore the definitional problem and concentrate on the parameters, we shall find some day that the original problem which motivated us has disappeared, that it should never have existed in the first place. Much has happened in the past 100 years; the most important for the sciences of man must be our break with past myths and philosophical speculation, however much we are in debt to them. To ask today what is an emotion is old-fashioned and likely to lead to semantic hairsplitting; to construct systems that unequivocally explain, predict, and make understandable parts of the range of human experience and behavior may, in the long run, be the best or only reply.

A PERSONAL VIEW

It is presumptuous to claim that only the following section represents my personal view of our parametric puzzle. Obviously all that has gone before is a highly personal view of the goals and history of a search for emotion. But I would plead for more general assent to what has gone before than to what follows.

I have in the past expressed my debt to Stanley Schachter as a precursor to my views on visceral-cognitive interactions. Both my debt and my departures will be obvious in what follows.

In the first instance I want to outline interactions among visceral and cognitive factors that are important in the production of many significant aspects of human thought and behavior. If the suggestions to follow sound like excursions around emotion, so be it, and I might, in the process, even slip into folkpsychology and "talk about" emotions. But the intent is system construction. My description of the variables that concern me is brief, telescoped, and, for current purposes, suggestive. Herewith, then, my parameters and some of their functions.

1. Certain human behaviors and experiences follow the arousal of the autonomic nervous system (ANS), particularly the sympathetic system. However, it is now generally accepted that no clearly dichotomous statements are possible about sympathetic and parasympathetic functions.

2. The effect of ANS arousal is that of a stimulus on visceral receptors which register degrees of such arousal.

3. The conditions, mental or environmental, which lead to ANS activity are generally unknown. Lists of stimuli can be drawn up, but neither psychologists, physiologists, nor ethologists can at the present time provide us with the common element that unites these stimuli in their effect on the ANS. One of these conditions might well be the interruption of ongoing thought and plans. Blocking the execution of organized thought or action can be shown to have ANS consequences on the one hand, whereas many of the conditions of threat, loss, novelty, and frustration that have been listed as ANS activators can be subsumed under the general notion of interruption on the other (Mandler, 1964, 1972; Mandler and Watson, 1966).

4. ANS activity, apparently for good evolutionary reasons, acts as a signal that requires interpretation and analysis of the environment by the various cognitive systems (or in terms of other authors' systems, it requires appraisal). An evaluation or re-evaluation of the environment when previously appropriate actions fail (have been interrupted) seems particularly

adaptive. In part this suggestion supplements the notion of homeostasis which, in its general form, generates a psychologically and behaviorally passive organism. Mere adjustment of the internal environment to external stresses and strains is an unsatisfactory model; an effect of ANS arousal on attentional and scanning mechanisms is a reasonable mechanism to help the organism act directly on the environment. The correlation between catecholamine levels and cognitive efficiency (Frankenhaeuser, 1975) supports this view. Also of interest is the concatenation of the evolutionary primitive role of the vagus nerve in cardiovascular inhibition (e.g., Pick, 1954), the heart rate deceleration in attention, and the role of cardiovascular inhibitory processes in autonomic activation (Lacey, 1967). All of these suggest a joint evolutionary development of attentive and autonomic processes.

5. The cognitive interpretation of the situation and the self involves acquired interpretation, pre-wired automatic reactions to classes of stimuli, and reactions to the perception of the self, its state, and actions.

6. Among the classes of stimuli that may elicit automatic cognitive reactions are those expressive movements that carry with them messages arising out of the species' history. However, evaluations and re-evaluations (particularly in consciousness) may alter such interpretations.

7. Among the perceptions that produce cognitive interpretations is the class of behaviors that are appropriate or inappropriate to the situation (coping). One important such reaction is the unavailability of appropriate behavior—the cognition of helplessness, which is often coextensive with the common-sense description and experience of anxiety (Mandler, 1972; Mandler and Watson, 1966).

8. Consciousness (awareness or private experience) provides one of the systems that contributes to the plasticity of human behavior and action. Although conscious experience has generated some of the most extreme positions in psychological theory, varying from its denial by some behaviorists to an assertion of its exclusive dominance by some phenomenologists, its persistence and invariant occurrence suggest important evolutionary functions. Translating the private datum of consciousness into useful theoretical constructs remains one of the interesting tasks facing theoretical psychology. For the time being it appears reasonable to assert that some perceptions of input, some of the internal mental operations, and some outputs may at various times be represented in consciousness where planning, testing of consequences, and choices among alternative interpretations and actions can take place. It is important to add that we still tend to use ancient and philosophical interpretations of consciousness. The theoretical-analytic enterprise that properly dissects the ordinary language meaning of consciousness and constructs theoretically meaningful terms and processes (and not just a single state or mechanism) is still to be undertaken.

9. The translation of conscious content into verbal or nonverbal outputs

depends on structural characteristics of the mental system, as well as on the past history of the organism. However, no one-to-one relationship among consciousness, language, and expressive movement is either postulated or necessary.

10. One of the cognitive systems operating in human organisms is concerned with the interpretation of experiences or actions. These *hypotheses* about the system's own operations and its outputs in thought and action are not necessarily equivalent to either an accurate description of the events or to a testable theory about these events. Although many of these hypotheses apparently occur in consciousness (and thus present the problem of translation into language), they need not do so, nor is it apparently the case that these hypotheses operate exclusively on the content of consciousness. Rather, structures and processes that are not available in consciousness frequently are used in the construction of these hypotheses about the self.

The general notion arising out of these propositions is that there is a set of experiences and behaviors that are associated in particular with ANS arousal and cognition-interpretation. Clearly, other situations and events will result in some cognitive-interpretative reactions, but they are outside the immediate concern. Furthermore, the particular set of ANS-interpretative reactions which are addressed may result from specifiable environmental events, including some stimuli that produce ANS reactions and others (such as expressive movements) that result in particular cognitions. Finally, some possible interactions among these events and consciousness and self-perception are indicated.

I have tried to avoid saying two things in this brief summary: First that this is a theory of emotion and second that mental states are prior unanalyzable events. It is important to emphasize the latter: mental states are to be explained as any other part of a theoretical system; they have no special status. And this is my main point of contention with philosophers who so often are entranced by their own and other people's minds, when they admit their existence. Mind is *not* the content of mental states but rather the complete system of theory that we construct to try to understand and explain mental states and behavior.

My first disavowal is obvious. I do not claim a theory of emotion, but I do believe that many of these parameters are in fact operative when we talk about "emotions." My efforts should be impervious to examples of experiences and behaviors that are emotion in common parlance but do not fit the system. No system can or should aspire to such pretensions. I do believe, for example, that most common emotional phenomena presuppose some ANS activity (*cf.* Frankenhaeuser, 1974; Hohmann, 1966; Pátkai, 1971; Wenzel, 1972; for recent evidence). Although I am interested in the effect of variations in ANS activity, others will want to describe expressive movements, coping activities, neurophysiological models. The crucial point to be made is that we have no quarrel. A scientific model cannot and must not claim exclusivity. It can only claim competence within its own boundary conditions. Other systems may eventually relate to it, or it may be reduced to a special case of a better and more comprehensive model. As long as we do not claim omnipotence or omniscience, we can look at our models as games that scientists play. We hang on to them tenaciously because they are our brainchildren, but we must at the same time admit diversity.

I do know one fact about this chapter and about all the other chapters in this volume — they are all to one extent or another wrong. And the joy is to try to be a little less wrong next time.

SUMMARY

I first explore some of the psychological and philosophical antecedents for a search for a definitive theory of emotion. Among these are notions of irreducible *a priori* ideas and feelings, the evolutionary history of expressive movements, and the folkpsychology embedded in our language and phenomenology. Sources of current trends in parametric investigations of "emotions" are traced to Darwin, James, Lange, and Cannon. Important current revivals of these ideas are identified. The general suggestion is offered that a search for discrete emotions and a specific theory of emotions is vain and that specific investigations of important parameters that affect human experience and action are more likely to illuminate the area defined as "emotion" in the common language. A description of the parameters of special interest to the writer is offered as one example of such an approach.

REFERENCES

Arnold, M. B. (1960): *Emotion and Personality*, Columbia University Press, New York.
Bem, D. J. (1967): Self-perception: An alternative interpretation of cognitive dissonance phenomena, *Psychol. Rev. 74*, 183–200.
Bowlby, J. (1969, 1973): *Attachment and Loss*, Vols. 1 and 2, Hogarth Press, London.
Brady, J. V. (1967): Emotion and sensitivity of psychoendocrine systems. In: *Neurophysiology and Emotion*, ed. D. C. Glass, Rockefeller University Press, New York.
Cannon, W. B. (1927): The James-Lange theory of emotion: A critical examination and an alternative theory, *Am. J. Psychol. 39*, 106–124.
Darwin, C. (1872): *The Expression of the Emotions in Man and Animals*, John Murray, London.
Frankenhaeuser, M. (1975): *This volume*.
Hohmann, G. W. (1966): Some effects of spinal cord lesions on experienced emotional feelings, *Psychophysiology 3*, 143–156.
Izard, C. E. (1971): *The Face of Emotion*, Appleton-Century-Crofts, New York.
James, W. (1884): What is an emotion? *Mind, 9*, 188–205.
James, W. (1890): *Principles of Psychology*, Henry Holt, New York.
Lacey, J. I. (1967): Somatic response patterning and stress: Some revisions of activation theory. In: *Psychological Stress*, eds. M. H. Appley and R. Trumbull, Appleton-Century-Crofts, New York.
Lange, C. G. (1885): *Om Sindsbevaegelser*, Kjøbenhavn.
Lange, C. G. (1887): *Ueber Gemüthsbewegungen*, Theodor Thomas, Leipzig.
Lazarus, R. S., Averill, J. R., and Opton, E. M., Jr. (1970): Toward a cognitive theory of emotion. In: *Feelings and Emotion*, ed. M. B. Arnold, Academic Press, New York.

Mandler, G. (1962): Emotion. In: *New Directions in Psychology*, ed. R. W. Brown et al., Holt, Rinehart, & Winston, New York.

Mandler, G. (1964): The interruption of behavior. In: *Nebraska Symposium on Motivation: 1964*, ed. D. Levine, University of Nebraska Press, Lincoln.

Mandler, G. (1967): The conditions for emotional behavior. In: *Neurophysiology and Emotion*, ed. D. C. Glass, Rockefeller University Press, New York.

Mandler, G. (1972): Helplessness: Theory and research in anxiety. In: *Anxiety: Current Trends in Theory and Research*, ed. C. D. Spielberger, Academic Press, New York.

Mandler, G., and Watson, D. L. (1966): Anxiety and the interruption of behavior. In: *Anxiety and Behavior*, ed. C. D. Spielberger, Academic Press, New York.

Pátkai, P. (1971): Catacholamine excretion in pleasant and unpleasant situations, *Acta Psychol.* 35, 352–363.

Pick, J. (1954): The evolution of homeostasis, *Proc. Am. Philos. Soc.* 98, 298–303.

Schachter, S. (1971): *Emotion, Obesity, and Crime*, Academic Press, New York.

Schachter, S., and Singer, J. E. (1962): Cognitive, social and physiological determinants of emotional state, *Psychol. Rev.* 69, 379–399.

Tomkins, S. S. (1962, 1963): *Affect, Imagery, Consciousness*, Vols. 1 and 2, Springer, New York.

Wenzel, B. M. (1972): Immunosympathectomy and behavior. In: *Immunosympasectomy*, eds. G. Steiner and E. Schönbaum, Elsevier, Amsterdam.

Emotions—Their Parameters and Measurement,
edited by L. Levi.
Raven Press, New York © 1975

Toward a Behavioral Biology of Emotion

Joseph V. Brady

Johns Hopkins University School of Medicine, Baltimore, Mayland 21205

To biological and social scientists of every persuasion, the problem of emotion has traditionally presented both methodological and conceptual challenges. In recent decades the field has been cultivated assiduously, and the current lively interest in parameters of emotion is significantly reflected in this volume. It is unfortunately true, however, that dedication and industry, even of the most intense sort, does not always guarantee authentic scientific achievement. In biology, and particularly the social sciences, wide gaps frequently separate experimental operations and interpretive formulations. The quasi-technical use of the word "emotion" as a referent for a bewildering range of phenomena and experiential pseudo-phenomena, for example, continues to produce semantic and taxonomic confusion. The term itself, persistently reified as a substantive "thing" which affects and is, in turn, affected by other "things," is seldom accorded appropriate conceptual status as a construct emerging from observed relationships between specifiable antecedent conditions (biological, social) and definable consequent events (biochemical, physiological, behavioral). Within this relational context, the experimental analysis of interacting classes of "emotion" events would seem to provide a basis for defining the construct more operationally and specifying the conditions under which a unifying conceptual framework can be developed for this prominent aspect of behavioral biology.

In this regard, it appears that at least some definitional clarity is attained by dividing the vast array of "emotion" events into two reasonably exclusive categories based upon an explicitly operational criterion. Such a division is possible, for example, by distinguishing between events that occur *inside* and *outside* the skin. As a first approximation, the defining operations of the "inside" class, on the one hand, appear to include (but are not necessarily limited to) biochemical and physiological changes presumed to participate in what may be designated as the *"feelings."* The defining operations of the "outside" class, on the other hand, focus upon distinguishable *"emotional behavior"* interactions with the external environment. A similar distinction is implied in the frequent literature references to "feelings and emotions" (Reymert, 1928, 1950; Arnold, 1970) and has been explicitly framed in a recent treatment by Kantor (1966).

The validity of this somewhat simplistic dichotomy depends critically, of course, upon some further specification of these two categories of "emotion" events. It is, for example, a commonplace clinical and experimental observation (not to mention an everyday experience), that the ongoing interactions between living systems and dynamic environments are subject to abrupt and episodic changes, often disruptive in character and involving consequent alterations in the external stimulus environment. When these changes in ongoing behavior are widespread and not easily assignable to alterations in the reinforcement contingencies maintaining the affected performances, tradition often relegates them to "emotional" causes, and the more operationally oriented approach represented by the present formulation would identify such conditions as actually defining *"emotional behavior."* Concomitant with such "emotional behavior" changes, but by no means restricted to these uniquely truncated interactions, a broad range of internal changes with identifiable and measurable glandular, visceral, and proprioceptive components are frequently and prominently in evidence. The effects of these latter alterations are clearly localizable *within* the behaving organism, for the most part, and provide an operational biochemical and physiological measurement approach to defining the *"feelings"* which participate, more or less obtrusively, in virtually *all* behavioral interactions.

The discriminability of such interoceptive *"feeling"* events has, of course, been amply documented by a host of classical and instrumental conditioning studies which originated with the work of Pavlov (Razran, 1961; Hefferline and Perrera, 1963; Schuster and Brady, 1964; Slucki et al., 1965, 1969). Most recently, the direct accessibility of such visceral and glandular response systems to environmental contingency control has been dramatically confirmed by a burgeoning experimental (and clinical) literature on the analysis and application of operant autonomic learning effects (Katkin and Murray, 1968; Miller, 1969; DiCara, 1970; Benson et al., 1971; Brady et al., 1972; Bleecker and Engel, 1973; Harris and Brady, 1973; Brady, *this volume*). The range of such interoceptive conditioning effects clearly reflects the loose, flexible integration of these glandular and visceral responses with both the exteroceptive environment in general, and the verbal repertoire in particular. This characteristic flexibility is, of course, quite consistent with the proliferation of, and variability in, "feelings" which Schachter and his colleagues (Schachter and Singer, 1962; Schachter, 1964, 1970) have so convincingly related to the "cognitive" intricacies of interaction effects between current environmental stimulus situations and past history factors.

Starting with this operationalized formulation of "feelings" and "emotional behavior" components, the parameters of emotion can be further delineated within the framework of an experimental analysis which identifies two broad classes of behavioral interactions based fundamentally upon the temporal ordering of environmental stimulus events and organismic response activities. The first of these, the *respondent behavior* class, is defined by the *prior* occurrence of an environmental stimulus event which acts upon the organism and, in turn, *elicits* an "involuntary" response in *conditionable* reflex form (e.g., food → salivation). The second *operant behavior* class is represented by the more commonly observed "voluntary" performances which act upon the environment and are maintained by stimulus events which *follow emission* of the response (e.g., lever press → food). The obviously complex interrelationships between this rather traditional "two-process" behavior analysis view (Rescorla and Solomon, 1967) and the "two-factor" emotion formulation suggested above is summarized in a simplistic form in Fig. 1.

The four general classes of "biological components" which are represented in Fig. 1 presume no dependence upon the reality of "operant-respondent" distinctions other than as conventions or as a convenient shorthand for characterizing the temporal ordering of stimulus and response events. Traditional descriptions of these operant and respondent behavioral categories do, however, define relationships at some level which are at least consistent with the proposed dichotomy of "emotion" components and suggest an approach to the measurement operations which are so sorely in need of development and refinement in this area. The prominent endocrine-autonomic factors involved in respondent regulation of the internal economy, for example, bear obvious relationships to the proposed defining operations for the *"feelings,"* and reliable methods of demonstrated sensitivity (Mason, 1968) are available for performing relevant measures in relationship to behavioral interactions (Brady, 1970b). And the central focus upon skeletal-muscle responses in explicitly organized, closely integrated operant interactions with the external environment provides a consistent framework for encompassing the defining properties of *"emotional behavior"* events, and for characterizing the measurement operations which distinguish this unique transactional category (Brady, *this volume*).

Clearly, then, the "internal respondents," identified as "core" visceral and endocrine processes, and the "external operants," defined as truncated muscular skeletal performances, are represented as the principal determinants of the "emotion" process. The two other classes of interacting biological components, however, the very old "external respondents" and the very new "internal operants," must, of course, be considered as additional candidate contributors, at least at some level. Peripheral autonomic and glandular changes (e.g., sweating, blushing) have, of course, long been emphasized as psychophysiological measures of "external respondent" participation in emotional interactions, without, it would seem, providing substantial enlightenment about the process (see reviews by Lindsley, 1951; Dunbar, 1954; Fehr and Stern, 1970). The current lively interest in instrumental glandular and visceral learning, on the other hand, as reflected in the vigorous pursuit of operant control over the internal milieu, may well pro-

	RESPONDENTS	OPERANTS
I N T E R N A L	"CORE" VISCERAL AND ENDOCRINE PROCESSES	INSTRUMENTAL GLANDULAR AND VISCERAL RESPONSES
E X T E R N A L	"PERIPHERAL" AUTONOMIC AND GLANDULAR CHANGES	TRUNCATED MUSCULAR SKELETAL PERFORMANCES

		APPETITIVE OPERANTS	AVERSIVE OPERANTS
A P P E T I V E S	R E S P O N D E N T S	BEHAVIORAL FACILITATION AND PHYSIOLOGICAL INACTIVATION?	BEHAVIORAL SUPPRESSION AND PHYSIOLOGICAL ACTIVATION???
A V E R S I V E S	R E S P O N D E N T S	BEHAVIORAL SUPPRESSION AND PHYSIOLOGICAL ACTIVATION	BEHAVIORAL FACILITATION AND PHYSIOLOGICAL INACTIVATION??

FIG. 1. Categorization of interacting biological "feelings" and "emotional behavior" components.

FIG. 2. Categorization of interacting psychophysiological "appetitive" and "aversive" dimensions.

vide important insights into direct contingency relationships between "feelings," "emotional behavior," and exteroceptive environmental consequences
(Brady, *this volume*).

Having thus struggled with an *analysis* of this historical "emotion"
morass, let me not shrink from the further task of at least the limited *synthesis* suggested by these and other recent measurement and conditioning
developments. Howsoever obvious the differences between such affective
("feelings") and effective ("emotional behavior") response patterns, the
evident interrelationships between the two in complex interactional situations can not be ignored. The internal consequences of prior-occurring
"feelings" (i.e., "core" visceral and endocrine changes) may well provide
the discriminative occasion for "emotional behaviors" (i.e., truncated
muscular skeletal responses) which perturbate the ongoing organism-
environment interaction (e.g., if you make me "feel mad," you may get
"punched in the nose"). And conversely, the effects produced by abrupt and
episodic "emotional behavior" segments (i.e., truncated external operants)
most certainly generate interoceptive and proprioceptive stimuli which, in
turn, may elicit "feelings" (i.e., internal respondents) related to "core"
visceral and endocrine processes. James's classic "scared-because-you-run"
formulation of the "bear-fear emotion" provides the obvious example of
this latter relationship. Indeed, the interchangeable use of "feelings" and
"emotional behavior" terms, together with the failure to recognize this
bi-directional interaction potential, probably accounts, in large part, for
the needless polemic exchange which has characterized "emotion" controversies since at least the time of James (1894) and Cannon (1927).

Of course, the range of such interaction possibilities is expanded greatly by the numerous psychophysiological measurement dimensions that characterize the interrelationships between component affective and effective "emotion" categories. Figure 2, for example, suggests behavioral and physiological measurement parameters which may be defined to some extent at least, by experimental analysis of one such "emotion" dimension. The "appetitive-aversive" dimension of behavioral interactions is by no means, of course, the only, or even possibly the most, important biopsychological parameter to be considered. It has long played a central role in systematic treatments of affective processes, however, as the contributions of such scholars as Beebe-Center (1932) and Young (1943) eloquently testify. More importantly, it does suggest empirical measurements and analyses involving a range of presumably "emotional" response processes. Significantly, the interaction effects depicted within the "cells" of this fourfold table, although grossly overgeneralized and in need of both behavioral and physiological refinement, do provide a first-approximation psychophysiological characterization of some fundamental interrelationships. And even preliminary results emerging from the suggested experimental analysis, already well under way (Rescorla and Solomon, 1967; Hammond, 1970; Brady, 1970a, *this volume*), need be reviewed only briefly to establish the empirical basis for this hopefully unifying operational approach to the measurement of emotion parameters.

Basically, the operations to which the cells in Fig. 2 refer are combinations of operant and respondent procedures in which the measured effects of superimposing classical "Pavlovian" conditioning (e.g., presentation of a tone followed by food or shock) upon ongoing instrumental performance base lines (e.g., lever pressing for food or to avoid shock) are examined both behaviorally and physiologically with particular reference to the dichotomous "feelings" and "emotional behavior" formulation herein proposed. Of course, the most heavily worked quadrant of this unevenly plowed field is represented by the lower left cell which encompasses the so-called "conditioned suppression" model for the laboratory study of "fear" and "anxiety" (Estes and Skinner, 1941) illustrated in Fig. 3 and extensively represented in the experimental literature (Hunt and Brady, 1951; Brady, 1962; Lyon, 1967, 1968; Davis, 1968). The "conditioned emotional response" (CER), here shown in the form of intermittent performance perturbations, develops after repeated pairings of a 5-min auditory "clicker" stimulus followed by brief shock superimposed upon an ongoing lever-pressing base line maintained by an aperiodic food reward. Although the characteristically episodic disruption of ongoing lever-pressing would certainly seem to qualify this interaction effect for inclusion in the "emotional behavior" category as defined, issues have been raised concerning the role of competing reinforcement contingencies (e.g., posturing responses which may reduce shock intensity) in providing a "nonemotional" account of such

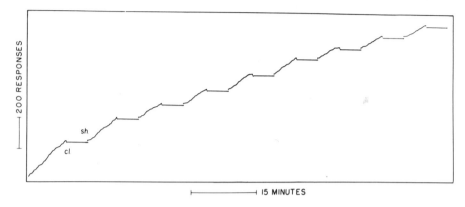

FIG. 3. Cumulative response record showing typical behavioral suppression effect of repeated clicker-shock pairings upon an ongoing appetitively maintained lever-pressing performance in a rhesus monkey.

conditioned suppression. The recent experiments of Hoffman and his collaborators (Hoffman and Barret, 1971; Stein, Hoffman, and Stitt, 1971), however, have established beyond reasonable doubt that the effects of this procedure are widespread and not easily assignable to changes in the reinforcement contingencies maintaining the affected performances.

The endocrine and autonomic "correlates" of this conditioning model have been extensively analyzed over the past decade with particular reference to the participant role of physiologically defined "feelings" components in the "emotion" complex, and I have reviewed the results of these studies elsewhere in this volume. Selected aspects of those findings provide strong support for the validity of the "separable but interacting" character of behavioral and physiological events participating in emotional transactions. Before appealing selectively to these psychophysiological measurement operations, however, some brief review of experimental progress in other related areas suggested by the dimensional cells of Fig. 2 may be in order. Several experimental reports (Walker, 1942; Estes, 1948; Herrnstein and Morse, 1957; Morse and Skinner, 1958; Brady, 1961; Trapold and Winokur, 1967; Henton and Brady, 1970; Meltzer and Brahlek, 1970; LoLordo, 1971) have now confirmed the "behavioral facilitation" ("joy"?) produced by interactions between "appetitive operants" and "appetitive respondents," as suggested in the upper left-hand cell of Fig. 2. The consequent increase in response rate during presentation of an appetitive Pavlovian conditioned stimulus superimposed upon an appetitively-maintained operant performance is illustrated typically in Fig. 4, which shows the effects of repeated pairings of a 3-min clicker followed by rewarding brain stimulation (in the septal area of the rat brain) upon an ongoing water-maintained lever-pressing performance (Brady, 1961). Although direct applications of biochemical and physiological measurement techniques to the analysis of this particular

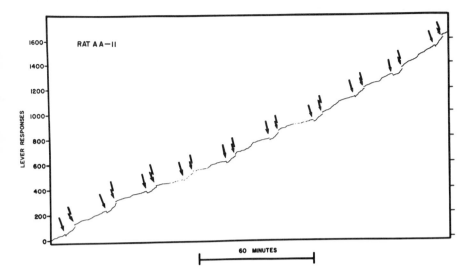

FIG. 4. Cumulative response record showing the behavioral facilitation effect of repeated pairings of a 3-min clicker presentation (beginning at each unbroken arrow) followed by rewarding brain stimulation (each broken arrow) upon an ongoing water-maintained lever-pressing performance in a laboratory rat.

"feelings" interaction have not been extensive, the tentative assignment of a "physiological inactivation" label to this cell in Fig. 2 is based upon at least some preliminary findings by Kelly (1971) related to the "contrasting cardiovascular consequences" of "conditioned elation" (upper left-hand cell, Fig. 2) and "conditioned anxiety" (lower left-hand cell, Fig. 2).

At least topographically similar "behavioral facilitation" of an instrumental shock-avoidance performance (i.e., "aversive operant") results from the superimposition of Pavlovian "fear" conditioning (i.e., "aversive respondent") upon such a base line, as suggested in the lower right-hand cell of Fig. 2 and verified experimentally by Sidman et al. (1957, 1962), Solomon and Turner (1962), Waller and Waller (1963), Belleville et al. (1963), Overmier and Leaf (1965), Rescorla and LoLordo (1965), Grossen and Bolles (1968), Kamano (1968), Pomerleau (1970) and Overmier et al. (1971). This effect is illustrated in Fig. 5, taken from Sidman (1960), showing the facilitation in lever-pressing produced by superimposing clicker-shock pairings upon a "Sidman avoidance" base line. Again, the evidence for the strongly qualified "inactivation" physiological characterization of this "feelings" ("anger-in"?) effect, suggested in the lower right-hand cell of Fig. 2, is not well documented, although some indication of attenuated hormonal and autonomic response changes are suggested by concurrent biochemical and physiological measurements performed in related emotional conditioning situations (Brady, *this volume*).

Experimental analysis of the "emotional" interaction effects suggested

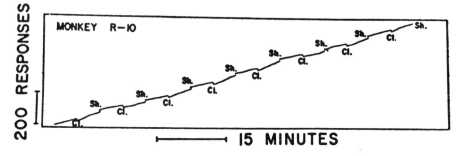

FIG. 5. Cumulative response record showing the behavioral facilitation effect of repeated pairings of a 3-min clicker presentation (beginning at each "Cl.") followed by painful foot-shock (each "Sh.") upon an ongoing shock-avoidance maintained lever-pressing performance in a rhesus monkey.

by the upper right-hand cell of Fig. 2 involving "aversive operants" and "appetitive respondents" presents some special measurement problems since the conditions maintaining the ongoing performance base line (e.g., shock avoidance) may recurrently occlude the behavioral effects of super-imposing appetitively conditioned counter-response tendencies. Several recent reports (Bull and Overmier, 1969; Grossen et al., 1969; Bull, 1970; Overmier et al., 1971; Henton, 1972; Davis and Kreuter, 1972) and the experiment illustrated in Fig. 6 do however confirm the "behavioral sup-pression" effects suggested by the characterization represented in the upper right-hand cell of Fig. 2. The food-deprived monkey whose record is shown in Fig. 6 clearly developed a decrease in the rate of the shock-avoidance-maintained lever-pressing base line during repeated presentations of a 30-sec flickering light stimulus followed by five food pellets superimposed upon the "aversive operant" performance. There are, however, some special conditions related to the obtaining reinforcement contingencies (for the instrumental avoidance base line performance) which must be con-sidered before an unequivocal "emotional" interpretation can be made of these findings, and only very limited measurements of biochemical and physiological correlates have thus far provided even a tentative basis for characterizing the suggested (and strongly qualified) "activation" hypothesis presumed to represent the "feelings" ("relief"?) aspect of this emotional interaction category. Obviously, the numerous temporal and spacial parameters that remain to be explored in defining the range of interrelation-ships and interactions between these several classes of biological events impose severe limitations on any conclusions, even tentatively drawn, from such a preliminary analysis of emotion measurement parameters.

But let me return to the more basic dichotomy between interacting but separable components of the "emotion" complex and review briefly se-lected aspects of these programmatic studies that appear to provide experi-mental support for the operational distinction between internal "feelings"

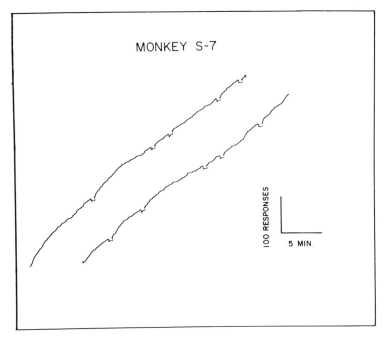

FIG. 6. Cumulative response record showing the behavior suppression effect of repeated pairings of a 30-sec flickering light (the offset sections of the record) followed by rewarding food pellets upon an ongoing shock-avoidance maintained lever-pressing performance in a rhesus monkey.

events and external "emotional behavior" interactions. Several psychophysiological studies, for example, have repeatedly documented the differential effects of a wide variety of experimental manipulations upon the distinguishable respondent and operant components of the "conditioned emotional response" model represented by the lower left-hand cell of Fig. 2 and illustrated in Fig. 3. Electroconvulsive shock treatments in both rats (Hunt and Brady, 1951; Brady and Hunt, 1955) and monkeys (Brady, 1971) have been shown to selectively attenuate the "aversive respondent" component of this emotional interaction model without materially affecting the "appetitive operant" base line. Similar differentiations between the respondent and operant components of this "conditioned emotional response" model have been suggested by studies examining the behavioral effects of limbic system lesions in rats (Brady and Nauta, 1953, 1955) and of electrical self-stimulation of the brain in monkeys (Brady and Conrad, 1960; Brady, 1960, 1961). And drug studies with both rats and monkeys maintaining stable conditioned emotional response patterns have shown that compounds such as reserpine and amphetamine can selectively alter the strength of the "aversive respondent" component of the performance while affecting the "appetitive operant" base line minimally, not at all, or even in opposite directions, depending upon experimental conditions (Brady, 1956, 1957, 1958). In fact, the attenuating effect of reserpine upon the "conditioned anxiety" model has been shown to differentiate clearly between this "aversive respondent" interaction and a topographically similar suppression of the "appetitive operant" by a stimulus associated with "discriminated punishment" (i.e., shocks produced only by lever-pressing responses during stimulus presentation). Experimental comparisons of such drug effects revealed that the behavioral suppression produced by "conditioned punishment" was essentially unaffected by the same dose of reserpine that virtually eliminated the "conditioned anxiety" response (Brady, 1959).

In general, the significance of these and other similar findings for the present behavioral biology formulation of emotion rests upon the demonstration that a range of experimental operations selectively alter (and thereby separate out) those aspects of a complex performance which appear to depend heavily upon the "internal respondent" components at least hypothetically identified with "feeling" events. These results further suggest that the differential effects may be mediated by selective changes in such internal "feeling" processes that can occur quite independently of any effects upon the externally defined "emotional behavior" components. Such an interpretive view of the emotion complex would, of course, be materially strengthened by an operational analysis of the correlated physiological processes presumed to mediate such "feeling" events, and experimental observations which have emerged from a series of studies concerned with the measurement of endocrine and autonomic participants in emotional interactions (Brady, *this volume*) can be seen to provide support for this two-factor formulation. Figure 7, for example, shows the effect of a rather basic respondent conditioning procedure with a monkey producing differential changes in circulating catecholamine secretion levels measured during exposure to brief foot shock and a stimulus (loud truck horn) paired with the electric shock. Virtually no change in either epinephrine or norepinephrine could be discerned during pre-pairing presentations of either the conditioned or unconditioned stimulus (as shown in the "before conditioning" left and middle panels of Fig. 7) despite their obviously noxious qualities. Only a few classical respondent conditioning trials were required, however, to produce the dramatically differential elevation in norepinephrine, with no change in epinephrine, during the "horn alone" presentation shown "after conditioning" in the right panel of Fig. 7 (Mason et al., 1966).

Verification of this differential hormonal accompaniment of the "aversive respondent–appetitive operant" interaction represented by the lower left-hand cell of Fig. 2 was subsequently obtained with several monkeys involving the alternating 5-min "on"–5-minute "off" clicker-shock pairings illustrated in Fig. 3. Concurrent measurements of plasma 17-OH-CS, epinephrine, and norepinephrine made during both experimental sessions of

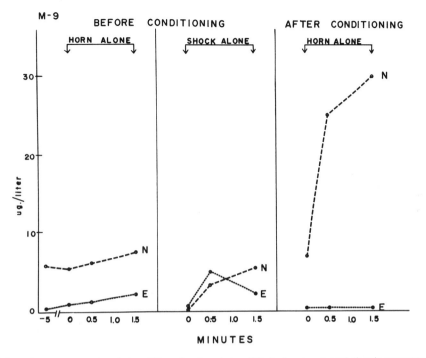

FIG. 7. Plasma norepinephrine (N) and epinephrine (E) during horn and shock presentations before and after "conditioning" pairing trials.

this type and control sessions during which no clicker presentations occurred are shown in Fig. 8. The lines connecting the open symbols represent values of the indicated measures obtained during experimental sessions including the "aversive respondent" superimposed on the "appetitive operant." The lines connecting the solid symbols show values for each measure obtained during the control sessions involving the lever-pressing performance alone. The obvious differences between the two conditions illustrate the distinguishable hormone response pattern (i.e., marked elevation in both 17-OH-CS and norepinephrine levels with no change in epinephrine) associated with the "conditioned suppression" procedure (Mason et al., 1961) and also strongly suggest a selectively close relationship between the "aversive respondent" component of the emotional interaction and the endocrine response pattern. Significantly, when the conditioned suppression was markedly attenuated by repeated doses of reserpine, administered 20 to 22 hr before such experimental sessions, the 17-OH-CS response to the auditory stimulus was also eliminated (Mason and Brady, 1956).

Even more dramatic separation of the behavioral and physiological components of this emotional interaction process has been documented in a

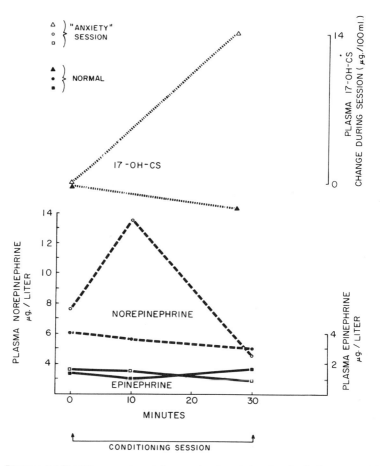

FIG. 8. Plasma 17-OH-CS, norepinephrine, and epinephrine levels during normal lever-pressing control sessions with no clicker or shock (solid symbols) and during experimental "anxiety" sessions involving repeated clicker presentations superimposed upon the ongoing lever-pressing performance (open symbols).

series of experiments (Brady et al., 1969) involving measurements of heart rate and both systolic and diastolic blood pressure recorded through chronically indwelling femoral artery catheters, with several rhesus monkeys during an extended series of experimental sessions involving superimposition of the "aversive respondent" clicker-shock pairings upon an "appetitive operant" lever-pressing performance for food. Figure 9, for example, shows the sequence of changes in the form of the autonomic response pattern typically observed in the course of 50 or more such conditioning trials and compares the direction of change for each measure on each successive trial. The behavioral suppression, shown in the bottom panel of Fig. 9 (represented in the form of percent changes in the lever-

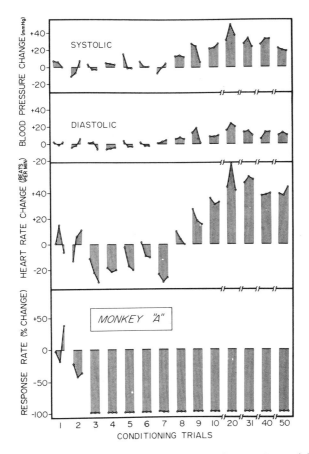

FIG. 9. Minute-by-minute changes in blood pressure, heart rate, and lever-pressing response rate for Monkey A on successive 3-min clicker-shock trials during acquisition of the conditioned emotional response. The zero points represent control values calculated from the 3-min interval immediately preceding the clicker.

pressing response rate during the clicker as compared to the pre-clicker base line), develops within three trials and remains stable thereafter. In contrast, a clearly biphasic cardiovascular pattern can be seen to accompany development and stabilization of the "conditioned emotional response," as shown in the top 3 panels of Fig. 9, again representing the values as changes during the clicker compared to pre-clicker levels for each trial. The initial decelerations in heart rate and modest decreases in blood pressure persist for the first seven or eight trials and then shift abruptly to a strong pressor pattern characterized by sharp increases in all three cardiovascular measures. Significantly, these dramatic "inside-the-skin" autonomic changes can be seen to occur in the absence of any variation in the stable "outside-the-skin" behavioral suppression pattern. And equally strong support for this "functional independence" of the two components of the "emotion" complex was obtained during subsequent phases of the study emphasizing the difference between the autonomic and behavioral changes which emerged during extinction of the "conditioned suppression" response by repeated presentation of the clicker without shock. Within seven to 10 such "clicker-alone" trials, changes in the lever-pressing rate disappeared, as shown in the bottom panel of Fig. 10. But some 30 to 40 extinction trials later, presentation of the clicker without shock continued to elicit consistent and substantial elevations in both blood pressure and heart rate (the top three panels of Fig. 10), even though the lever-pressing rates had long since ceased reflecting any change during the stimulus interval.

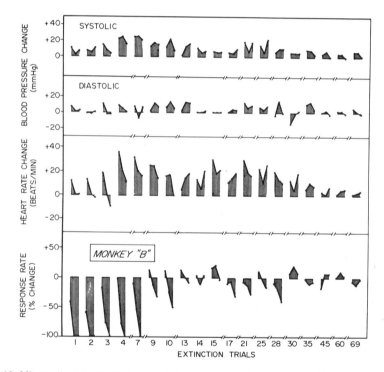

FIG. 10. Minute-by-minute changes in blood pressure, heart rate, and lever-pressing rate for Monkey B on successive 3-min presentations of the clicker alone without shock during extinction of the conditioned emotional response. The zero points represent control values calcuated from the 3-min interval immediately preceding the clicker.

Some further evidence which is at least consistent with the "interacting but separable" position herein assumed with regard to the "affective" and "effective" components of emotional response patterns has recently emerged from an experiment (Brady et al., 1970) articulating the relationship between the pattern of cardiovascular changes (Fig. 9) associated with the "conditioned suppression" procedure (Fig. 3), on the one hand, and concurrently measured skeletal muscle activity recorded electromyographically, on the other. Figure 11 illustrates the results consistently obtained with several monkeys implanted with femoral artery catheters and lumbar paraspinal muscle electrodes during a series of 50 or more clicker-shock pairings ("aversive respondent") superimposed upon an ongoing instrumental lever-pressing performance ("appetitive operant"). Development of the characteristic behavioral suppression shown in the bottom panel of Fig. 11 was accompanied by the previously documented biphasic cardiovascular pattern shown in the top three panels of Fig. 11. The initial de-

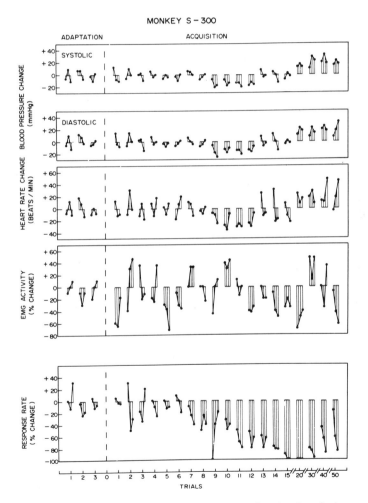

FIG. 11. Minute-by-minute changes in blood pressure, heart rate, electromyographic activity, and lever-pressing response rate for Monkey S-300 on successive 3-min clicker-shock trials during acquisition of the conditioned "anxiety" response.

crease in blood pressure and heart rate during early conditioning trials was
followed by marked and sustained elevations in all three cardiovascular
measures throughout the remaining sessions, all in the absence of any
change in the stable behavioral suppression pattern. Examination of the
concurrently recorded EMG activity (integrated electronically and sum-
mated as amplitude and frequency changes) during these same conditioning trials, as shown in the second panel from the bottom in Fig. 11 reveals, on the other hand, striking lack of any systematic pattern. Virtually
all possible combinations of cardiac and EMG activity changes (e.g., heart
rate and blood pressure increases accompanied by EMG activity decreases,
EMG activity increases accompanied by cardiac suppression) were observed in the course of the clicker-shock pairings. Figure 12, for example,

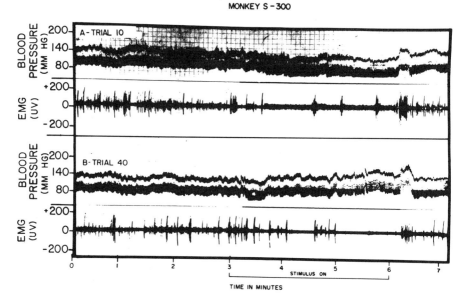

FIG. 12. Polygraph records of blood pressure changes and electromyographic activity
for Monkey S-300 during "anxiety" conditioning trials 10 and 40.

verifies the independence of these autonomic and skeletal components of the
emotional response pattern by calling attention to two conditioning trials
in particular, one (trial 10) during the early cardiac suppression stage of the
process (shown in the top panel of Fig. 12), and the other (trial 40) during
the latter, characteristically activated cardiovascular phase (shown in the
bottom panel of Fig. 12). The pattern of EMG activity during the 3-min
clicker intervals of the two trials (indicated by the bracketed line on the
abscissa of Fig. 12) is virtually indistinguishable, despite the obvious dif-

ferences in direction of the blood pressure changes between these "early" and "late" stages of behavioral suppression.

The argument in support of distinguishable and at least somewhat independently variable affective and effective components of "emotion" segments suggests the further possibility, as refinements in analytic methods emerge, of operationally defining and measuring differential "feelings" and "emotional behavior" patterns associated with a range of environmental interaction conditions. An additional extension of this analysis to encompass some observations made in the course of a series of avoidance studies, for example, may serve to illustrate the potential of such an approach. These experiments involved monkeys performing on a Sidman avoidance procedure (Sidman, 1953), which required the animal to press a lever to avoid shocks programmed to occur every 20 sec unless a lever response within that interval postponed the shock another 20 sec. The stable aversively maintained performance generated by this procedure, although lacking some of the formal features that recommend the "conditioned suppression" technique for a "two-factor" analysis of "emotion," may nonetheless be managed comfortably within an "operant-respondent" interaction framework (Kamin, 1957; Baum, 1968). The less explicit "aversive respondent" participation in a Sidman free-operant avoidance situation can readily be inferred from the conditional relationships that must be presumed to develop between even the occasional occurrence of shock, on the one hand, and the wide range of recurrent environmental stimulus events, on the other. Certainly, the pattern of hormone changes shown in Fig. 13 (Mason et al., 1961), measured during 30-min Sidman avoidance sessions (the lines connecting the solid symbols in Fig. 13), strongly suggests, by its striking similarity to the "conditioned suppression" pattern (i.e., Fig. 8) of elevated 17-OH-CS and norepinephrine levels with no change in epinephrine, that similar "aversive respondent" participation is involved.

Experimental analysis of the interaction between avoidance behavior and endocrine activity has moreover revealed a range of quantitative and qualitative relationships of direct relevance to the issues addressed by the present "emotion" formulation. Although the level of pituitary-adrenal activity has been quantitatively related to the rate of avoidance responding in the monkey (Sidman et al., 1962), hormone response levels have also been observed to vary systematically with more qualitative changes in the avoidance interaction conditions (Mason et al., 1966). Addition to the Sidman avoidance procedure of an explicit exteroceptive "warning signal," for example, programmed to occur 5 sec prior to shock whenever 15 sec of the 20-sec response-shock interval had elapsed, substantially reduced the magnitude of the 17-OH-CS elevation, as shown in Fig. 14. And similarly, dramatic changes, although opposite in sign, are documented in Fig. 15 which shows the effects upon 17-OH-CS levels of superimposing "free" shocks upon the Sidman avoidance performance. The differences between

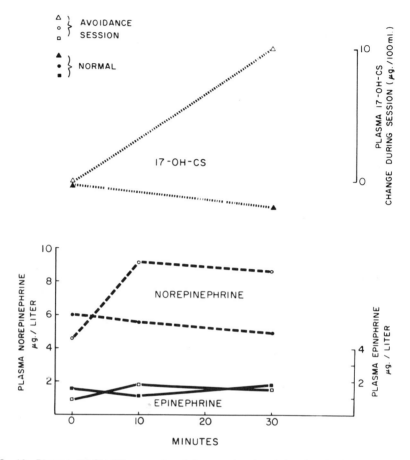

FIG. 13. Plasma 17-OH-CS, norepinephrine, and epinephrine levels during "normal" control sessions (solid symbols) and during experimental "avoidance" sessions (open symbols).

the steroid elevations observed during "regular avoidance" (the broken lines in Fig. 15), on the one hand, and "free-shock avoidance" (the solid lines in Fig. 15), on the other, were produced by disconnecting the automatic shock programmer and randomly distributing throughout the experimental session noncontingent shocks equal to the number of contingent shocks usually earned by each animal. Significantly, this "free-shock" procedure produced only minimal changes in the already high base line free-operant avoidance rate, again suggesting somewhat independently controlled altera-tions in the "internal respondent" component of the interaction.

Unique patterns of change in catecholamine levels have also been ob-served under conditions that produce little or no differential effect upon the behavioral performance base line (Mason et al., 1966), as for example, the

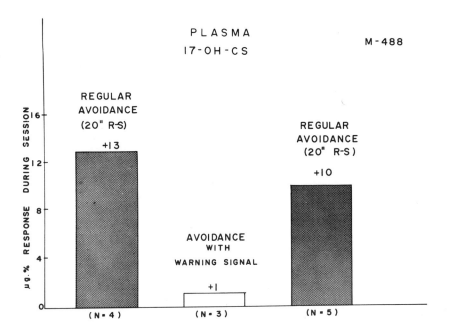

FIG. 14. Plasma 17-OH-CS levels during "regular" avoidance sessions without an exteroceptive "warning" stimulus (left and right bars) and during avoidance sessions with a "warning signal" (middle bar).

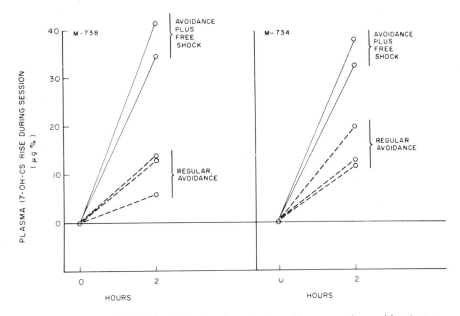

FIG. 15. Plasma 17-OH-CS levels during "regular" avoidance sessions without an exteroceptive "warning" stimulus (broken lines) and during avoidance sessions with "free shock" (solid lines).

unusual elevations in epinephrine shown in Figs. 16 and 17. The first example (Fig. 16) illustrates the elevation in epinephrine produced by the superimposition of "free shock" upon a well-established Sidman avoidance performance (right panel), even though no such epinephrine response could be elicited either by "free shock" before avoidance training (left panel) or by the regular avoidance performance (middle panel). And the second ex-

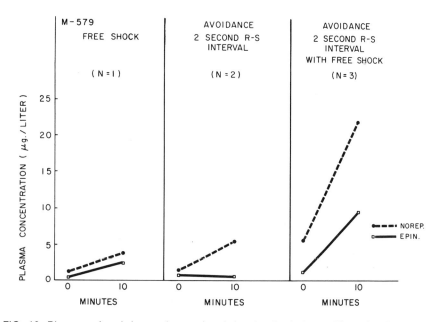

FIG. 16. Plasma epinephrine and norepinephrine levels during a "free shock" session before avoidance training (left panel), during performance sessions without an exteroceptive "warning" stimulus after avoidance training (middle panel), and during performance sessions with "free shock" after avoidance training (right panel).

ample (Fig. 17) occurred during an experiment in which the lever was abruptly removed from the monkey chair at the same time that the discriminative stimulus controlling a well-established free-operant avoidance performance was presented. The immediate and substantial, although obviously evanescent, rise in circulating epinephrine (shown in the bottom panel of Fig. 17), never before observed during performance sessions with this animal, occurred in the absence of the usual avoidance-induced norepinephrine elevation (top panel of Fig. 17). Indeed, it may not be too presumptuous to suggest that the animals participating in such interactions may well "feel" quite differently about the changing conditions that define their relationship to the environment. And these data might even further suggest that this internal difference in the "feelings" may be defined, at least in part, by the operationally measured biochemical and physiological changes

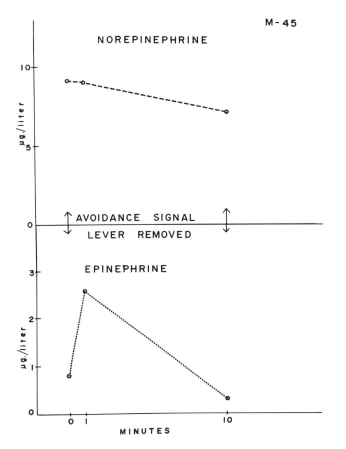

FIG. 17. Plasma epinephrine and norepinephrine levels following presentation of the "avoidance session" signal and withdrawal of the response lever.

observed to occur without apparent alteration in externally oriented behavioral interactions, emotional or otherwise.

In point of fact, some very recent studies with dogs and baboons provide additional support for the possibility of identifying and defining, to some extent at least, differential "feeling" patterns associated with topographically similar behavioral activity (Anderson and Brady, 1971; Brady et al., 1971; Findley et al., 1971). The operationally defined physiological events have focused upon cardiovascular measurements under conditions that involve comparisons of both appetitively and aversively maintained instrumental performances. Figure 18, for example, shows the reliable and stable differences in the pattern of blood pressure and heart rate changes that developed with five dogs during a 1-hr *pre-performance* interval preceding a 2-hr panel-pressing session maintained by a Sidman shock-avoidance requirement (left panel) and intermittent food-reinforcement (right panel).

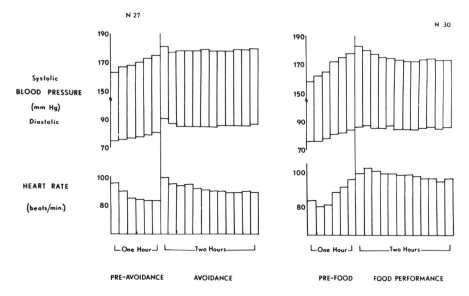

FIG. 18. Comparison of average blood pressure and heart rate values for consecutive 10-min intervals before and during 27 "avoidance" performance sessions (left panel) and 30 "food" performance sessions (right panel) with five dogs.

Both the appetitive and aversive reinforcement schedules used in this experiment were adjusted to yield comparable response rates so that topographically similar performances were required *following* the 1-hr "anticipatory" interval. The characteristic *decrease* in heart rate accompanying the blood pressure increase shown for the pre-avoidance interval (left panel, Fig. 18) contrasted sharply and reliably with the concomitant increases in both blood pressure and heart rate shown for the pre-food interval (right panel, Fig. 18). The data shown in Fig. 18 represent averages of more than 25 experimental sessions under each condition involving the five dogs. Figure 19 confirms the establishment and reversibility of this differential cardiovascular ("feelings"?) pattern in a single animal (Simon) exposed successively to both aversive and appetitive conditioning. The left panel of Fig. 19 shows Simon's typical pre-avoidance pattern (increasing blood pressure, decreasing heart rate), followed by his typical pre-food pattern (both blood pressure and heart rate increasing) in the middle panel, and a reversal to the pre-avoidance pattern (increasing blood pressure, decreasing heart rate) during a Sidman session following the block of food-maintained performances (right panel).

A related observation with the baboon is illustrated in Fig. 20, which compares blood pressure and heart rate during virtually identical lever-pulling performances, one (top panel) maintained by shock escape-avoidance, and the other (bottom panel) maintained by food reinforcement. In

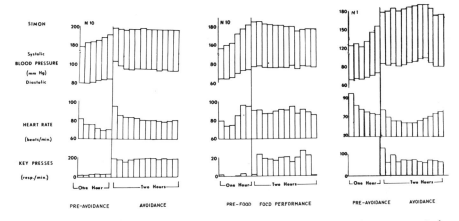

FIG. 19. Comparison of average blood pressure, heart rate, and panel response rate for consecutive 10-min intervals before and during 10 "avoidance" performance sessions (left panel), 10 "food" performance sessions (middle panel), and one additional "avoidance" performance session (right panel) following 10 "food" sessions with the same dog.

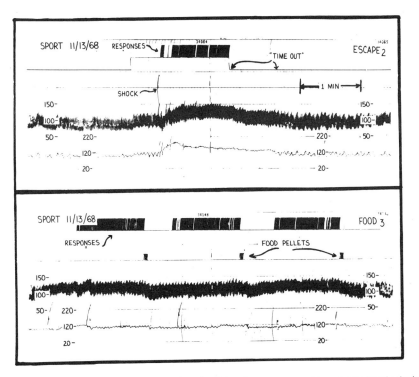

FIG. 20. Sample polygraph recording showing blood pressure and heart rate levels during "escape-avoidance" performance (top panel) and "food-maintained" performance (bottom panel) with the same baboon.

both cases a fixed ratio requirement of 150 responses on the same heavy Lindsley manipulandum was involved, although increases of the order of 20 to 40 mm Hg in blood pressure and 40 beats per minute in heart rate can be seen to characterize the avoidance "feelings" as compared to the obviously less intense cardiovascular "feelings" (modest blood pressure elevations and no heart rate increases) which accompanied the topographically similar food-maintained operant performance.

These more acute affective and effective manifestations of emotional interactions have been complemented, to some limited extent at least, by more chronic experimental observations both inside and outside the skin which may suggest some relationships to the more durable aspects of the "feelings" as they involve possibly even generalized mood states and affective dispositions. The data shown in Fig. 21 summarize for one of the three chair-restrained rhesus monkeys involved in this 18-month study (Brady, 1965) the results obtained during some 65 successive weeks of exposure to a 3-day "on"–4-day "off" Sidman avoidance schedule which required the monkey to work 72-continuous hr (day and night) followed by 96 hr of rest each week. The initial 3 months or so of this rather demanding routine produced the expected elevations in 17-OH-CS levels during the

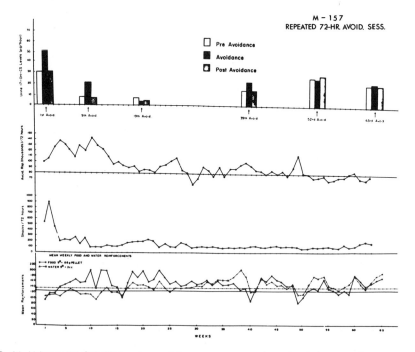

FIG. 21. Urinary 17-OH-CS levels, avoidance response rates, shock frequencies, and food and water intake levels for a monkey throughout 65 weeks of repeated exposure to a 72-hr continuous Sidman avoidance requirement.

3-day avoidance interval (the solid black bars on the top line of Fig. 21). By the 19th or 20th week, however, not only were no steroid increases discernible during the recurrent 72-hr avoidance performances, but the overall hormone levels were actually depressed during the 96-hr rest periods as well. Some 20 weeks later, around the 39th or 40th week of the study, steroid levels can be seen to have recovered somewhat, and after 1 year or more on the program, 17-OH-CS determinations revealed normal pre-experimental levels maintained unchanged throughout both work and rest periods. Despite this long-enduring cyclic variation in the "on" and "off" "internal" hormone pattern, the "external" instrumental avoidance performance remained stable over at least the last year or more of weekly sessions. The protracted sequence of independently varying endocrine activity observed with all three experimental subjects in this study suggests possible relationships involving the long-term participation of mood-determining internal respondent processes.

Of course, any such broad conjecture about enduring affective dispositions must be supported by a much more extensive assessment of endocrine, autonomic, and proprioceptive activity in relationship to long-term environmental interactions, but the biochemical and physiological technology required for operational integration with an experimental behavior analysis may be close at hand. Multiple concurrent hormone measurements in relationship to a wide range of behavioral performance situations have in fact already been undertaken and require an interpretive analysis beyond the scope of the present report. But the breadth of available biochemical, physiological, and behavioral measurement techniques has been indicated in several recent publications (Mason, 1968; Brady, 1966, 1967, 1970b) and the promise of this fruitful start has been well documented.

It may, of course, be premature to suggest that the results emerging from both these more complex psychophysiological analyses and the numerous less extensive studies described in this chapter provide support for the proposed emotion formulation in terms of separable but interacting components. Indeed, the characterization of identity relationships between distinguishable physiological and behavioral participants, on the one hand, and the rather arbitrary "feelings" and "emotional behavior" dichotomy on the other, is of course both oversimplified and somewhat artificial. Some heuristic value can be expected to derive, however, from an account of emotion events which proceeds by defining the properties of identifiable constituents and examining in detail the interrelationships between external behavioral interactions and the broader patterning or balance of biochemical and physiological processes which in concert regulate the internal milieu. In the final analysis, only a comprehensive integration of such multilevel determinants, both historical and situational, as summarized diagrammatically in Fig. 22, can provide the foundation for a meaningful behavioral biology of emotion.

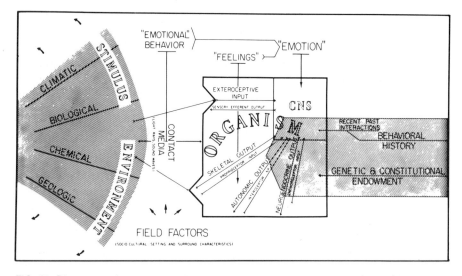

FIG. 22. Diagrammatic representation of a "behavioral universe" emphasizing organism-environmental interactions. "Emotional behavior" is represented at the interface between organism and environment, whereas "feelings" are localized within the reacting organism. The generic reference to the term "emotion" with its suggestive arrow into the CNS is meant simply to imply a *conceptual* creation of the brain, *not* the existence of a resident entity.

REFERENCES

Anderson, D. E., and Brady, J. V. (1971): Pre-avoidance blood pressure elevations accompanied by heart rate decreases in the dog, *Science 172*, 595–597.

Arnold, M. B. (1970): *Feelings and Emotion,* Academic Press, New York.

Baum, M. (1968): Dissociation of respondent and operant processes in avoidance learning, *J. Comp. Physiol. Psychol. 67*, 83–88.

Beebe-Center, J. G. (1932): *The Psychology of Pleasantness and Unpleasantness,* Van Nostrand, New York.

Belleville, R. E., Rohles, F. H., Gunzke, M. M., and Clark, F. C. (1963): Development of a complex variable schedule in the chimpanzee, *J. Exp. Anal. Behav. 63*, 348–351.

Benson, H., Shapiro, D., Tursky, B., and Schwartz, G. E. (1971): Decreased systolic blood pressure through operant conditioning techniques in patients with essential hypertension, *Science 173*, 740–742.

Bleeker, E. R., and Engel, B. T. (1973): Learned control of cardiac rate and cardiac conduction in a patient with Wolff-Parkinson-White syndrome, *N. Engl. J. Med.* (March), P 560–562.

Brady, J. V. (1956): Assessment of drug effects on emotional behavior, *Science 123*, 1033–1034.

Brady, J. V. (1957): A comparative approach to the evaluation of drug effects upon behavior. In: *Brain Mechanisms and Drug Action.* ed. W. S. Fields, C. C. Thomas, Springfield, Ill.

Brady, J. V. (1958): Perspectives in the preclinical evaluation of behavioral drugs. In: *Proceedings, Scientific and Medical Conferences,* Amer. Pharm. Manufact. Assoc., Chicago.

Brady, J. V. (1959): Animal experimental evaluation of drug effects upon behavior. In: *The Effect of Pharmacologic Agents on the Nervous System,* ed. F. Braceland, Williams and Wilkins Co., Baltimore, Md.

Brady, J. V. (1960): Temporal and emotional effects related to intracranial electrical self-stimulation. In: *Electrical Studies on the Unanesthetized Brain,* eds. E. R. Ramey and D. S. O'Doherty, Hoeber, Inc., New York.

Brady, J. V. (1961): Motivational-emotional factors and intra-cranial self-stimulation. In: *Electrical Stimulation of the Brain*, ed. D. Sheer, University of Texas Press, Austin.

Brady, J. V. (1962): Psychophysiology of emotional behavior. In: *Experimental Foundations of Clinical Psychology*, ed. A. J. Bachrach, Basic Books, New York.

Brady, J. V. (1965): Experimental studies of psychophysiological responses to stressful situations. In: *Symposium on Medical Aspects of Stress in the Military Climate*, Walter Reed Army Institute of Research, Government Printing Office, Washington, D.C.

Brady, J. V. (1966): Operant methodology and the production of altered physiological states. In: *Operant Behavior: Areas of Research and Application*, ed. W. Honig. Appleton-Century-Crofts, New York.

Brady, J. V. (1967): Emotion and the sensitivity of psychoendocrine systems. In: *Neurophysiology and Emotion*, ed. D. Glass, Rockefeller University Press, New York.

Brady, J. V. (1971): Emotion revisited, *J. Psychiat. Res. 8*, 363–384.

Brady, J. V. (1970a): Emotion: Some conceptual problems and psychophysiological experiments. In: *Feelings and Emotions*, ed. M. Arnold, Academic Press, New York.

Brady, J. V. (1970b): Endocrine and autonomic correlates of emotional behavior. In: *Physiological Correlates of Emotion*, ed. P. Black, Academic Press, New York.

Brady, J. V., and Conrad, D. (1960): Some effects of limbic system self-stimulation upon conditioned emotional behavior, *J. Comp. Physiol. Psychol. 53*, 128–137.

Brady, J. V., Findley, J. D., and Harris, A. H. (1971): Experimental psychopathology and the psychophysiology of emotion. In: *Experimental Psychopathology*, ed. H. D. Kimmel, Academic Press, New York.

Brady, J. V., Harris, A. H., and Anderson, D. E. (1972): Behavior and the cardiovascular system in experimental animals. In: *Neural and Psychological Mechanisms in Cardiovascular Disease*, ed. A. Zanchetti, Casa Editrice (Il Ponte), Milano.

Brady, J. V., Henton, W. W., and Ehle, A. (1970): Some effects of emotional conditioning upon autonomic and electromyographic activity, *Eastern Psychological Association*, Atlantic City, April.

Brady, J. V., and Hunt, H. F. (1955): An experimental approach to the analysis of emotional behavior, *J. Psychol. 40*, 313–324.

Brady, J. V., Kelly, D., and Plumlee, L. (1969): Autonomic and behavioral responses of the rhesus monkey to emotional conditioning, *Ann. N.Y. Acad. Sci. 150*, 959–975.

Brady, J. V., and Nauta, W. J. H. (1953): Subcortical mechanisms in emotional behavior: Affective changes following septal forebrain lesions in the albino rat, *J. Comp. Physiol. Psychol. 46*, 339–346.

Brady, J. V., and Nauta, W. J. H. (1955): Subcortical mechanisms in emotional behavior: The duration of affective changes following septal and habenular lesions in the albino rat, *J. Comp. Physiol. Psych. 48*, 412–420.

Bull, J. A. (1970): An interaction between appetitive Pavlovian CS's and instrumental avoidance responding, *Learning and Motivation 1*, 18–22.

Bull, J. A., and Overmier, J. B. (1969): Incompatibility of appetitive and aversive conditioned motivation, *Proc. 77th Ann. Convention, Amer. Psych. Assoc. 1*, 97–98.

Cannon, W. B. (1927): The James-Lange theory of emotions: A critical examination and alternate theory, *Am. J. Psychol. 39*, 106–124.

Davis, H. (1968): Conditioned suppression: A survey of the literature, *Psychonomic Monograph Supplements 2*, 285–291 (Whole Number 30).

Davis, H., and Kreuter, C. (1972): Conditioned suppression of an avoidance response by a stimulus paired with food, *J. Exp. Anal. Behav. 17*, 277–285.

DiCara, L. V. (1970): Learning in the autonomic nervous system, *Sci. Am. 222*, 30–39.

Dunbar, H. F. (1954): *Emotions and Bodily Changes*, Columbia University Press, New York.

Estes, W. K. (1948): Discriminative conditioning. II. Effects of a Pavlovian conditioned stimulus upon a subsequently established operant response, *J. Exp. Psychol. 38*, 173–177.

Estes, W. K., and Skinner, B. F. (1941): Some quantitative properties of anxiety, *J. Exp. Psychol. 29*, 390–400.

Fehr, F. S., and Stern, J. A. (1970): Peripheral psychological variables and emotion: The James-Lange theory revisited, *Psychol. Bull. 74*, 411–424.

Findley, J. D., Brady, J. V., Robinson, W. W., and Gilliam, W. J. (1971): Continuous cardiovascular monitoring in the baboon during long-term behavioral performances, *Comm. Behav. Biol. 6*, 49–58.

Grossen, N. E., and Bolles, R. C. (1968): Effects of a classical conditioned "fear signal" and "safety signal" on non-discriminated avoidance behavior, *Psychonom. Sci. 11*, 321–322.

Grossen, N. E., Kostansek, D. J., and Bolles, R. C. (1969): Effects of appetitive discriminative stimuli upon avoidance behavior, *J. Exp. Psychol. 81*, 340–343.

Hammond, L. J. (1970): Conditioned emotional states. In: *Physiological Correlates of Emotion*, ed. P. Black, Academic Press, New York.

Harris, A. H., and Brady, J. V. (1974): Animal learning: Visceral and atonomic conditioning, *Ann. Rev. Psychol. 25*, 107–133.

Harwood, C. T., and Mason, J. W. (1956): A systematic evaluation of the Nelson-Samuels plasma 17-hydroxycorticosteroid method, *J. Clin. Endocrin. 16*, 790–800.

Hefferline, R. F., and Perera, T. B. (1963): Proprioceptive discrimination of a covert operant without its observation by the subject, *Science 139*, 834–835.

Henton, W. (1972): Avoidance response rates during a pre-food stimulus in monkeys, *J. Exp. Anal. Behav. 17*, 269–275.

Henton, W., and Brady, J. V. (1970): Operant acceleration during a pre-reward stimulus, *J. Exp. Anal. Behav. 13*, 205–209.

Herrnstein, R. J., and Morse, W. H. (1957): Some effects of response independent positive reinforcements on maintained operant behavior, *J. Comp. Physiol. Psychol. 50*, 461–469.

Hoffman, H. S., and Barrett, J. (1971): Overt activity during conditioned suppression: A search for punishment artifacts, *J. Exp. Anal. Behav. 16*, 343–348.

Hunt, H. F., and Brady, J. V. (1951): Some effects of electroconvulsive shocks on a conditioned emotional response ("anxiety"), *J. Comp. Physiol. Psychol. 44*, 88–89.

Hunt, H. F., Jernberg, P., and Brady, J. V. (1952): The effect of electroconvulsive shocks on a conditioned emotional response: The effect of post-ECS extinction on the reappearance of the response, *J. Comp. Physiol. Psychol. 45*, 585–599.

James, W. (1894): The physiological basis of emotion, *Psychol. Rev. 1*, 516–529.

Kamano, D. K. (1968): Effects of an extinguished fear stimulus on avoidance behavior, *Psychonom. Sci. 13*, 271–272.

Kamin, L. (1957): The gradient of delay of secondary reward in avoidance learning, *J. Comp. Physiol. Psychol. 50*, 445–449.

Kantor, J. R. (1966): Feelings and emotions as scientific events, *Psychol. Rec. 16*, 377–404.

Katkin, E. S., and Murray, E. N. (1968): Instrumental conditioning of autonomically mediated behavior: Theoretical and methodological issues, *Psychol. Bull. 70*, 52–68.

Kelly, D. D. (1971): The contrasting cardiovascular consequences of monkeying around with conditioned anxiety, conditioned elation, and discriminated extinction, *Eastern Psychological Association*, 42nd Annual Meeting.

Lindsley, D. S. (1951): Emotion. In: *Handbook of Experimental Psychology*, ed. S. S. Stevens, Wiley, New York.

LoLordo, V. M. (1971): Facilitation of food-reinforced responding by a signal for response independent food, *J. Exp. Anal. Behav. 15*, 49–55.

Lyon, D. O. (1967): CER methodology, *Psychol. Rep. 20*, 206–213.

Lyon, D. O. (1968): Conditioned suppression: Operant variables and aversive control, *Psychol. Rec. 18*, 317–338.

Mason, J. W. (1968): Organization of psychoendocrine mechanisms, *Psychosom. Med. 30*, 565–569.

Mason, J. W., and Brady, J. V. (1956): Plasma 17-hydroxycorticosteroid changes related to reserpine effects on emotional behavior, *Science 124*, 983–984.

Mason, J. W., Brady, J. V., and Tolson, W. W. (1966): Behavioral adaptations and endocrine activity. In: *Proceedings of the Association for Research in Nervous and Mental Diseases*, ed. R. Levine, Williams and Wilkins Co., Baltimore.

Mason, J. W., Mangan, G., Brady, J. V., Conrad, D., and Rioch, D. (1961): Concurrent plasma epinephrine, norepinephrine, and 17-hydroxycorticosteroid levels during conditioned emotional disturbances in monkeys, *Psychosom. Med. 23*, 344–353.

Meltzer, D., and Brahlek, J. A. (1970): Conditioned suppression and conditioned enhancement with the same positive UCS: An effect of CS duration, *J. Exp. Anal. Behav. 13*, 67–73.

Miller, N. E. (1969): Learning of visceral and glandular responses, *Science 163*, 434–448.

Morse, W. E., and Skinner, B. F. (1958): Some factors involved in the stimulus control of operant behavior, *J. Exp. Anal. Behav. 1*, 103–107.

Overmier, J. B., Bull, J. A., and Pack, K. (1971): An instrumental response interaction as explaining the influences of Pavlovian CS's upon avoidance behavior, *Learning and Motivation* 2, 103–112.

Overmier, J. B., and Leaf, R. C. (1965): Effects of discriminative Pavlovian fear conditioning upon previously or subsequently acquired avoidance responding, *J. Comp. Physiol. Psychol.* 60, 213–217.

Pomerleau, O. F. (1970): The effects of stimuli followed by response-independent shock on shock-avoidance behavior, *J. Exp. Anal. Behav.* 14, 11–21.

Razran, G. (1961): The observable unconscious and the inferable conscious in current Soviet psychophysiology: Interoceptive conditioning, semantic conditioning, and the orienting reflex, *Psychol. Rev.* 68, 81–147.

Rescorla, R. A., and LoLordo, V. M. (1965): Inhibition of avoidance behavior, *J. Comp. Physiol. Psychol.* 59, 406–412.

Rescorla, R. A., and Solomon, R. L. (1967): Two-process learning theory: Relationship between Pavlovian conditioning and instrumental learning, *Psychol. Rev.* 74, 151–182.

Reymert, M. L. (ed.) (1928): *Feelings and Emotions. The Wittenberg Symposium.* Clark University Press, Worcester.

Reymert, M. L. (ed.) (1950): *Feelings and Emotions. The Mooseheart Symposium.* McGraw-Hill, New York.

Schachter, S. (1964): The interaction of cognitive and physiological determinants of emotional state. In: *Advances in Experimental Social Psychology,* ed. L. Berkowitz, Academic Press, New York.

Schachter, S. (1970): The assumption of identity and peripheralist-centralist controversies in motivation and emotion. *Feelings and Emotion,* ed. M. Arnold, Academic Press, New York.

Schachter, S., and Singer, J. (1962): Cognitive, social, and physiological determinants of emotional state, *Psychol. Rev.* 69, 379–399.

Schuster, C. R., and Brady, J. V. (1964): The discriminative control of a food reinforced operant by interoceptive stimulation, *I.P. Pavlov Journal of Higher Nervous Activity* 14, 448–458.

Sidman, M. (1953): Avoidance conditioning with brief shock and no exteroceptive warning signal, *Science 118,* 157–158.

Sidman, M. (1960): Normal sources of pathological behavior, *Science 132,* 61–68.

Sidman, M., Herrnstein, R. J., and Conrad, D. G. (1957): Maintenance of avoidance behavior by unavoidable shocks, *J. Comp. Physiol. Psychol.,* 50, 553–557.

Sidman, M., Mason, J. W., Brady, J. V., and Thach, J. (1962): Quantitative relations between avoidance behavior and pituitary-adrenal cortical activity, *J. Exp. Anal. Behav.* 5, 353–362.

Slucki, H., Adam, G., and Porter, R. W. (1965): Operant discrimination of an interoceptive stimulus in rhesus monkeys, *J. Exp. Anal. Behav.* 8, 405–414.

Slucki, H., McCoy, F. B., and Porter, R. W. (1969): Interoceptive SD of the large intestine established by mechanical stimulation, *Psychol. Rep.* 24, 35–42.

Solomon, R. L., and Turner, L. H. (1962): Discriminative classical conditioning in dogs paralyzed by curare can later control discriminative avoidance responses in the normal state, *Psychol. Rev.* 69, 202–219.

Stein, N., Hoffman, H. S., and Stitt, C. (1971): Collateral behavior of the pigeon during conditioned suppression of key pecking, *J. Exp. Anal. Behav.* 15, 83–93.

Trapold, M. A., and Winokur, S. (1967): Transfer from classical conditioning and extinction to acquisition, extinction, and stimulus generalization of a positively reinforced instrumental response, *J. Exp. Psychol.* 73, 517–523.

Walker, K. C. (1942): Effects of a discriminative stimulus transferred to a previously unassociated response, *J. Exp. Psychol. 31,* 312–317.

Waller, M. B., and Waller, D. F. (1963): The effects of unavoidable shocks on a multiple schedule having an avoidance component, *J. Exp. Anal. Behav.* 6, 29–37.

Young, P. T. (1943): *Emotion in Man and Animal,* Wiley, New York.

Emotions—Their Parameters and Measurement,
edited by L. Levi.
Raven Press, New York © 1975

The Self-Regulation of Emotion

Richard S. Lazarus

Department of Psychology, University of California, Berkeley, California 94720

INTRODUCTION

Emotion is commonly said to occur when a person (or animal) has blundered passively into a situation that is either harmful in some way or creates positive outcomes. The emotion-producing commerce with the environment results in an interruption of ongoing activity and a disturbed state of arousal and mobilization for coping with the crisis. The emotion takes over, so to speak. The person is said to be seized by the emotion against his will.

Although emotions are often unwanted intrusions (Horowitz, 1970), this focus on the person as a passive responder to emotional circumstances beyond his control and on negative emotions as unwanted intrusions that disturb ongoing functioning leads us to underemphasize the extent to which emotion in everyday life is continually being self-regulated. The major theme of this chapter is that the person is constantly guiding his thoughts and actions in such a way as to control potentially disruptive, and even positive emotional states, and that to understand the normal ebb and flow of emotional reactions and the adaptive behavior associated with them, we need to give more attention to these self-regulatory devices. Some of them are brought into play after the person has stumbled into an emotional situation; others are engaged *before* the emotion has been aroused and exert a steering function in determining consequent emotional transactions and reactions. In effect, such self-regulative activity has causal significance in emotion.

This view, whose implications I want to discuss in this paper at length, grows out of a cognitive-phenomenological approach to emotions and psychological stress that my associates and I have set forth elsewhere (e.g., Lazarus, 1966; Lazarus, Averill, and Opton, 1970). Our theoretical framework emphasizes the idea that in man emotional activity results from the person's evaluation or *appraisal* of his moment to moment transactions with the environment, transactions that can be viewed by him as benign, positive, challenging, or threatening. There are two kinds of appraisal. In *primary appraisal,* the issue to be judged is whether or not a danger (threat) has been signaled, or the situation is one of challenge, and so on; *secondary appraisal* involves evaluations by the person of the kind of adaptive action called for as well as the nature and potency of his resources for managing or coping with the threat, meeting the challenge, etc. Whether and to what extent he is threatened depends on this estimate of coping potentials, which in turn is largely based on the flow of information from the environment, and from his own experience and personal characteristics. New information can lead the person to reappraise the situation positively or negatively. Such appraisal and reappraisal activities are in the service of attempts by the person to know where he stands in any situation and to maintain mastery or control over it. The consequent emotional state at any moment, particularly in the stress emotions where the person is dealing with threatening or harmful transactions, is a product of the balance of forces between the capacity of the environmental event to harm him and the potency of his own resources to prevent, tolerate, profit from, postpone, or overcome that harm.

Because information about the potentialities for coping and about its effects alter cognitive appraisal, coping is an essential intervening factor in the ebb and flow of emotional states. If we are to understand the emotional response we must therefore also take into account the nature of coping activity and its relations to that response.

My colleagues and I have suggested a very rough and incomplete classification of coping activity which bears on the theme that coping is part of the self-regulation of emotional states. We divided coping into two main kinds of processes, namely, *direct actions* on the person-environment relationship and *intrapsychic* processes. The former are motoric and involve producing an actual change in the objective situation. The latter are internal and cognitive.

Speaking of coping processes in emotion raises an interesting theoretical question that might bear brief comment here. From an evolutionary standpoint, certain behavioral impulses, such as attack, flight, or crying and wailing, are regarded as an integral part of the emotions of anger, fear, and grief, and indeed these behaviors are primary bases of inferring arousal of the emotional state. Yet, these same behaviors are, in a sense, coping processes too in that they are instrumental in altering the plight of the person or animal, often taking him out of jeopardy. Still other forms of coping activity appear biologically to be independent of the emotion per se, that is, they are not built-in emergency reactions; examples might be rationally planned aggression or avoidance, inhibitory activities, self-deceptive defenses, attempts to present oneself in a particular light, and a host of other patterns that, while connected with an emotional transaction with the environment, are not regarded as an integral feature of an emotional response syndrome. In short, there are two large classes of coping activities, one an integral biological part of emotion in an evolutionary sense, the other an attempt to extricate oneself from a situation of jeopardy or harm. This distinction is not often made in discussions of emotion and coping, but I think that it deserves serious consideration because the rules of operation of each may be quite different.

I do not think there would be any controversy over the idea that direct actions by the person or animal alter the commerce with the environment, thereby arousing, dampening, or terminating the emotional state or changing its quality, say, from fear to relief or exultation, anger to love, grief to acceptance, depression to anger, etc. Since emotions are the result of adaptive transactions between the organism and his environment, when the nature of the transaction is changed, the emotion also will change. On the other hand, recognizing the importance of intrapsychic processes opens a messy can of worms for psychological research on emotion. For one thing, to some extent it turns the locus of the regulation of emotion from the external environment to the mental apparatus. For another, it makes it more difficult to integrate research on emotions in nonhuman animals with research in man. Nevertheless, with the phylogenetic progression from simpler animals to man, in which there is progressively less dependence on innate, tightly wired-in mechanisms and increasing dependence on learning and cognition, the regulation of emotion shifts away from built-in reactions to external releasers and toward information processing and cognitive controls. Regulation then becomes self-regulation.

There is ample evidence of the regulation of emotional reactions by environmental (especially social) events in the primates such as the chimpanzees and the baboons. The natural state of affairs appears to be that their emotions are socially regulated. Jane Van-Lawick Goodall (1971) has made an interesting observation of emotional behavior in chimpanzees that is relevant to this theme. In one passage (p. 73), for example, she describes a male chimpanzee "working himself into a frenzy of rage." And in another context she describes the aggressive behavior of a dominant male (Mike) who, in the middle of a dominance display, seized an infant (Goblin) who had gotten in his way and dragged him violently along the ground. About this latter kind of behavior Goodall makes the following interesting comment:

> It is difficult to understand Mike's behavior. Normally, small infants are shown almost unlimited tolerance from all the other members of the community; it almost seems as though the adult male may lose many of his social inhibitions during his charging display. Once I watched Rodolf pound and drag an old female during one of his displays while her screaming infant clung beneath her; then, almost before he had stopped attacking her, he turned around to embrace, pat, and kiss her.

In this description the emotion seems to represent a breakdown of the normal social controls over destructive rage. The other side of the coin, however, is the recognition that in the chimpanzee "social inhibitions" normally regulate emotional behavior, a forecast of even stronger social regulation in humans.

What might be operating in this behavioral sequence? The male chimpanzee is acting out his innately given pattern of display behavior in competitive situations with other members of his species. Such display and its accompanying emotion would never be initiated, or might be broken off in the presence of a chimpanzee of higher dominance status, or perhaps if the males toward whom the display is directed displayed vigorously in return. However, in this case cues leading to such inhibition are not forthcoming or are not strong enough to produce inhibition or the reversal of the aggressive display into subordinate fear behavior. Three processes are thus implicated in the sequence: First, each step in the mounting rage leads to the next depending on its effects on the other chimps (feedback from the environment). This is, I think, what is meant by "working himself into a rage." Second, the animal must be capable of perceiving (appraising?) the external social cues that might turn off or permit escalation of the emotional behavior. And third, there must be the capacity to inhibit a reaction that has begun. The more advanced the organism, phylogenetically, the more room there seems to be for flexible control of emotional states and behavior, and the more cognitive processes are involved in such control. The pattern is less and less a matter of the person (or animal) being passively aroused by rage-inducing cues, and more a matter of sizing up a situation (appraisal), inhibiting or redirecting the reaction, obtaining feedback from his own state and behavior, as well as from the subsequent environmental events, in a continuous process of give and take with the environment. Above all, I think there has been in man the emergence or growth of an important new set of processes involving self-control or self-regulation.

At this point it will be useful to examine some observations that highlight the ways *intrapsychic* modes of coping can regulate the emotional response. I shall consider first some anecdotal and casual impressions and then a few formal research observations.

ANECDOTAL AND CASUAL IMPRESSIONS

I have selected for comment three contexts of emotional self-regulation, namely, grief, love, and being a good loser. In each of these the focus of attention is placed on the person's management of his reaction to be in conformity to social conventions as well as internal pressures.

Grief

This is a complex emotional reaction, commonly including elements of depression, anger and bitterness, self-pity, guilt, and the agitated effort to restore the loss, elements that often seem analogous to the patterns observed in some nonhuman animals, especially primates. Grief, like most emotions, is a highly socialized reaction. The person is expected to experience and display grief appropriately, that is, in the proper degree, in the appropriate circumstances, and in the appropriate form. In our society, for example, if the person shows too much grief, he will be criticized. He should not express criticism of or anger toward the deceased, and if there is some bitterness or self-pity, this is acceptable to an extent, but it should not be extended too long. In Japan, the person learns to cover up his grief with strangers or casual acquaintances lest it produce distress in the other person and shame to the griever. This leads to the anomaly of someone from another culture seeing a person who has just experienced the death of a loved one, but who on the surface at least seems to treat the whole thing very lightly. On the other hand, in our own culture if the person gives too little evidence of grief he is also subject to social criticism and is likely to be accused of being cold or indifferent. Thus, the person may experience the cruel dilemma of struggling within himself to control and work through his grief, while being pressured by others to do just the opposite as though in a charade. He must walk a tightrope between the alternative courses.

This dilemma, interestingly, has been observed and commented on in the research literature on stress. For example, in their research with parents of children dying of leukemia at the Bethesda NIMH research hospital, Friedman et al. (1963) have poignantly described the difficulty of parents who were realistically dealing with the tragedy and yet were confronted by "concentric circles of disbelief" and denial on the part of their relatives. Friedman et al. write, "Thus, the parents were not allowed to express any feelings of hopelessness, yet, . . . they were paradoxically expected to appear grief-stricken."

Love

The self-regulation of emotion is relevant to positive emotional states as well as the stress emotions, and love provides a good illustration. As with other emotions, there is the common notion that people are "smitten" or seized by love as if this feeling was beyond the person's control. We also hold the contradictory and probably accurate view that mature people enter into loving relationships in response to a series of cues providing mutual encouragement that positive feelings are being reciprocated. Only if one's emerging feelings of love are returned does the person allow such feelings to escalate beyond tentative and well-controlled positive reactions. In the absence of encouragement, such feelings are inhibited or even shut off completely so that the person does not become trapped in a totally one-sided relationship.

Occasionally, relationships are observed where this mutuality does not occur, and where one member of the pair has strong feelings of love that the other does not share. This is the pathetic pattern of unrequited love as portrayed in the classic Somerset Maugham novel *Of Human Bondage* in which a man is all but destroyed by his love for a woman who treats him contemptuously. In common-sense thought, it is assumed that to permit feelings of love to develop without reciprocity is to behave in an immature fashion characteristic of an adolescent and ordinarily outgrown. The normal state of affairs would seem to be the close self-regulation of feelings in realistic keeping with feedback from the social object toward whom they might be directed.

The Good Loser

Typical of self-regulation of emotion is the prescribed behavior of a person who has lost in a competitive situation to which he has been strongly committed and who might well feel angry, depressed, self-pitying, etc., as a result. In our culture, we are expected to act like a good loser, meaning that we do not appear too distressed nor blame anyone, but express positive regard for the winner and equanimity at the loss. To act otherwise is to risk severe criticism, a principle dramatically evident at the end of the 1960, California gubernatorial campaign. On television after his election loss, Richard Nixon said bitterly in public to newsmen, "You won't have Dick Nixon to kick around any more," a statement he has almost surely had to regret. As a result of strong social sanctions, one is under great pressure to control his emotional response to such a loss. People are socialized from early childhood in the emotional responses considered suitable in social contexts. One of the issues we must address later concerns the degree to which this socialization process leads to self-regulation that alters the actual emotional states experienced by the person, or merely the outer behavior that the person displays to others.

While I am on the topic of culturally based self-regulation, it should be noted that variations have frequently been noted by anthropologists and sociologists in attitudes toward pain and illness (e.g., Mechanic, 1968; Zborowski, 1969), and these probably apply to emotion as well. There is, for example, the impression that some peoples (e.g., the Swiss and the British) value a controlled and unemotional pattern of behavior, while others, (e.g., Greeks and Italians) value emotionality (see also Pancheri, this volume). There is research evidence of such a difference within a culture. Thus, Lefcourt (1966) has shown that subjects who obtain high scores in repression on a personality questionnaire scale believe that displaying anxiety and emotional distress is bad and evidence of psychopathology (so they deny it in themselves), while those scoring high on sensitizing defenses and anxiety have a positive regard for emotional experience and consider it to be psychologically healthy. Lefcourt has suggested that rather than measuring actual defense preferences, such questionnaires tap variations in attitude toward emotion. In any case, his findings point to variations in the way emotion is regarded by different people within the same culture and concomitant variations in emotion-relevant self-descriptions. We might expect that such attitudinal variations among cultures and within cultures, would play an important role in the self-regulation of emotion.

FORMAL RESEARCH OBSERVATIONS

The self-regulation of emotion by coping activity has been observed in many research contexts, some of them in field study, others in the laboratory. The field study examples that I have chosen include situations of military combat, studies of imminent bereavement, and the response of medical students to an autopsy. The laboratory research is that of my own and my colleagues.

Field Studies

One of the earliest groups of researchers to see clearly the connection between coping and emotional reactions was Grinker and Spiegel (1945), who described several *denial-related* coping devices by means of which air crews kept their fears of death in control during a tour of combat duty. One way was to deny fear, a strategy that was not always successful. For example, the stressful conflict over wanting to avoid death and at the same time to be well-thought of by their combat buddies and themselves often resulted in somatic symptoms that led to their release from combat duty. By being forceably withdrawn from duty "against their will" because of the somatic symptom, they could preserve their social and self-esteem and still escape the danger.

Another common denial-related mechanism was to create the fiction that one was invulnerable, and to use magical charms to bring luck. Still another device was to maintain a detached orientation of not giving a damn, which went hand in hand with the conviction that the airman could not survive and would be killed on the next mission. Grinker and Spiegel considered this reaction to be close to a masked depression, which protected the men against overpowering anxiety. One bit of evidence supporting the inference that these attitudes (denial of vulnerability and detached, fatalistic unconcern) were defensive forms of coping with threat is the observation that toward the end of the combat tour of duty, for example, during the last few combat missions when there again are grounds for hope of survival, such men commonly again became realistic about the combat dangers with a return of intense anxiety (see especially pp. 130–132). These are excellent examples of intrapsychic (cognitive) modes of coping in a context in which nothing constructive could be done to change the actual situation (direct action), therefore the only successful modes of coping available lay in how the situation was construed (appraised) and the elements in the situation to which their attention was directed.

Equally instructive are the observations of the group of researchers, cited earlier, at the National Institute of Mental Health Hospital at Bethesda, Maryland, on parents whose children were ill with leukemia (Wolff, et al., 1964). Particularly relevant here are the comparisons between the clinical ratings of defenses (especially evidences of denial of the inevitable outcome) and the amount of 17-hydroxycorticosteroid (a stress hormone) excreted by these parents. Those who were rated as well defended showed lower hydrocortisone readings than those who acknowledged the tragic reality and were greatly distressed by it.

A paper by Lief and Fox (1963) is especially valuable here. Their analysis is based on extensive interviews with medical students observing for the first time a human dissection and a medical autopsy. Their discussion of the students' reaction to the autopsy considered both the features of the autopsy experience that tended to arouse feelings, and the intrapsychic devices used successfully in achieving detachment and the control of such feelings. Although emphasis was placed on the autopsy procedures and the setting rather than on how individuals managed their feelings, their observations help us understand also the processes of self-regulation. With respect to the *arousal of feelings,* the key factor seems to be the realization that a person is being worked on who was just alive and is now dead. Contributing to this realization are several situational factors: the body in autopsy is less covered than the cadaver in the anatomy lab; particularly arousing is the initial incision with its bleeding and the dissection of the head; knowledge of the patient's personal history makes the student more conscious of him as a real person, and this awareness is stronger if he has known the patient while he was alive, or if he is or has been in contact with the patient's family.

With respect to the *maintenance of equanimity and detachment,* one aid is the immaculate, brightly lit appearance of the operating room, and the serious, professional behavior required, which justify and facilitate a clinical and impersonal attitude toward death. Certain parts of the body are kept covered, particularly the face and genitalia, and the hands which are so strongly connected with human, personal qualities are never dissected. Once the vital organs have been taken out, the body is removed from the room, bringing the autopsy down to tissues which are more easily depersonalized. The deft touch, skill, and professional attitude of the prosector makes the procedure neater and more bloodless than might otherwise be the case, and this increases intellectual interest and makes it possible to approach the whole thing scientifically rather than emotionally. Students appear to avoid talking about the autopsy, and when they do talk about it, the discussion is impersonal and stylized. Finally, whereas in laboratory dissection humor appears to be a widespread and effective emotional control device, it is absent in the autopsy room, perhaps because the death has been too recent and would appear too insensitive. In sum, it would appear that the student who is still new to the context of the autopsy must struggle within himself to attain a balance between feeling things and looking at them objectively, a struggle in which detachment is facilitated by a number of institutional procedures probably evolved through experience in trying to cope with the emotional overtones of such situations. As we know, some individuals overdo the strategy of detachment and as physicians may appear to the patient to be cold and indifferent.

Laboratory Studies

Research from my own laboratory has also dealt with the principle that a normally stressful event can be made considerably more benign through intrapsychic mechanisms of emotional control, facilitated by situational manipulations and personality characteristics (see Lazarus, Averill, and Opton, 1970, for a review and analysis). We have repeatedly shown that by encouraging denial and intellectualization (detachment) as appraisals of disturbing events portrayed in a motion picture film, subjects show substantially lower levels of stress response, including autonomic levels of arousal (e.g., heart rate and skin conductance). Moreover, the effectiveness of these experimental inputs in lowering stress reactions seems to depend on the natural defensive dispositions of persons.

More recently, we have been able to demonstrate (cf., Monat et al., 1972) that when a person must await an inevitable harm such as a painful shock, and there is uncertainty about when during the session the shock will occur (unsignaled shock), there is a strong tendency for subjects to shift from a vigilant orientation (involving trying to get set for the shock, thinking about the shock and how it might be dealt with, wondering how to react, etc.) toward an avoidant orientation in which he seems to be trying not to think about it at all. Associated with this shift in intrapsychic coping is a progressive reduction of stress response level. It is as if not knowing when the harm will occur, the subject gives up trying to prepare himself for it, with consequent relaxation. There is a growing research literature on this problem of intrapsychic control over aversive events (reviewed recently by Averill, 1973), and considerable controversy about the conditions of cognitive control under which the stress response will be lowered or raised and the psychological mechanisms involved.

We must also distinguish between research on mechanisms of emotional self-regulation in which the focus is on situational or laboratory-induced conditions of such regulation, and studies in which the person is *left to his own devices*. With respect to the latter, there is also a growing literature of research in which patients with different coping dispositions are studied as they await surgery, and during their postsurgical recovery (e.g., Cohen and Lazarus, 1973), or in the recovery from severe burns or other illnesses (e.g., Andreason, Noyes, and Hartford, 1972), with a view to relating personality characteristics to the devices they adopt for coping with their illness and its medical intervention, and to their course of recovery. Much of this has produced complex and often contradictory findings, though again and again there is shown to be a relationship between personality, the coping mechanisms resorted to, and the outcome of these coping mechanisms for the patients' course of recovery. Much of this research is predicated on the postulated but unclear relationship between intrapsychic modes of coping with threats (and life crises) and the emotional and adaptive outcome.

One final example of formal research on the problem of the self-regulation of emotion should be considered, since it is the only experimental study explicitly designed to investigate whether and how people can alter their emotional states volitionally. Arguing that most research in the area of emotional control has been oriented to the *reduction* of stress reactions, while healthy management of one's emotional life requires also the *release* of emotional reactions, as in love, empathy, joy, distress over the suffering of others, etc., my colleagues and I (Koriat, Melkman, Averill, and Lazarus, 1972) instructed laboratory subjects to do both. In two experimental sessions they were exposed to four presentations of a film showing wood-shop accidents in which one man lacerates the tips of his fingers, another cuts off his middle finger, and a third dies after a plank of wood is thrust through his midsection by a circular saw. During the first two presentations, there were no special instructions. However, half the subjects were instructed prior to the third presentation to *detach* themselves from the emotional impact of the accidents, and before the fourth presentation they were asked to *involve* themselves more fully and emotionally in them. The other half were given reverse order instructions, that is, on the third film presentation they had to involve themselves, while on the fourth to detach themselves. They were not told how to do this, since one of the objectives of the experiment was to evaluate the cognitive devices they might use.

Among the findings of the research, two are of particular interest here. First, it was found that subjects could indeed exercise some degree of control over their emotional reactions to the accidents, as evidenced by their reported emotional state, and changes in heart rate. Second, certain strategies were reported being used most commonly in involvement, and others in detachment. The most frequently reported *involvement* device was trying to imagine that the accidents were happening to the subject himself. Other less frequent strategies included trying to relate the scenes to a similar experience he had or was a witness to, and trying to think about and exaggerate the consequences. The most popularly reported *detachment* strategy was reminding oneself that the events were dramatized for the film rather than being real, followed by the strategy of concentrating on the technical aspects of the production. Whether involvement or detachment efforts came first or second also seemed to make a difference, both in the extent of emotional reaction and the types of strategy employed. In this study, we see clearly the operation of self-generated rather than situationally induced modes of emotional control.

I have thus far avoided making explicit some of the theoretical issues or controversies inherent in this way of viewing emotion and its self-regulation by means of intrapsychic (cognitive) mechanisms, and these should now be examined carefully.

WHAT IS BEING REGULATED?

In speaking of the self-regulation of emotion I have actually meant control not only over the overt behavior associated with an emotion (e.g., the expressive gestures and postures and instrumental action) but of the entire organized state that is subsumed under the emotion construct. There will be no debate over the proposition that people often inhibit the overt behavioral expression of their anger, fear, grief, sadness, joy, love, and so on, as a result of social pressures and other concerns. This would leave the person, however, still experiencing the emotional state, presumably at the same level of intensity as when no such inhibitory process is operating.

I believe that this is common; however, my proposal goes much further; self-regulation also dampens, eliminates, or alters the quality of emotional states, depending on its successfulness. This would in fact follow from the theoretical dependence of emotions and coping processes on cognitive appraisal and reappraisal processes (that is, intrapsychic modes of coping). Thus, if a parent in the Bethesda studies, for example, successfully convinces himself that his child is not terminally ill, he will experience much less stress than found in a parent not so well defended (cf. Wolff et al., 1964). Or if a medical student watching an autopsy is able to detach himself from the emotional overtones of the situation and look upon it clinically, he will not experience the same level of emotional distress that he would in the absence of such a coping mechanism.

Still, an issue is raised here that is relevant to the assessment of emotion. The above analysis requires some empirical means of distinguishing between mere behavioral inhibition and the total regulation of the emotional state. If we look only at emotional behavior (such as avoidance, say), albeit an important source of information about the emotional state, we cannot readily tell what elements of the emotional reaction have been controlled, and it is difficult to argue that the overt behavior is tantamount to the internal state. For resolution of this issue it is essential to have multiple sources of response information from which more adequate inferences about the fate of the total emotional syndrome can be made.

The question, "What is being regulated?", points to another distinction of potential importance, namely, between efforts to cope with the person–environment transaction that has produced the emotional reaction in the first place and efforts to regulate the emotional reaction to that transaction. For example, if a student who is facing an important examination spends the anticipatory interval reading relevant books and articles, rehearsing his understanding with teachers and other students, and trying to determine the questions to be asked, etc., he is clearly coping with his problem, whether well or badly. Such coping activity is directed at the plight in which he finds himself, namely, the danger of failing the examination, and the preparatory activity is aimed at minimizing this potential harm. On the other hand, as the examination approaches, he is apt to find himself increasingly anxious (Mechanic, 1962), and this reaction of anxiety may itself be a source of embarrassment or interfere with his anticipatory coping efforts and performance. When such a student takes tranquilizers, or engages in certain other forms of coping designed to overcome the anxiety, he is attempting to regulate the emotional reaction rather than mastering the danger that brought it about in the first place. He is attacking the symptom rather than the disease, as it were. In all likelihood, the rules by which these two kinds of activity, coping with one's plight and regulating the emotional consequences of that plight, differ considerably.

THE CAUSE AND EFFECT RELATIONSHIP
BETWEEN COPING AND EMOTION

One of the central themes of this chapter is that coping often precedes an emotion. This is not to say that the usual psychological wisdom that coping follows a situation of threat or harm and is designed to take the person out of jeopardy is false. Rather, a great deal of coping also precedes the emotional arousal, and hence the cause and effect sequence can also operate in reverse of the usual direction. How could this be?

The critical point is that much of the coping is *anticipatory;* it is initiated before a confrontation with harm when something in the environment or within the person signals the future possibility or inevitability of harm. The person must then prepare in some fashion for what he anticipates will happen to master what is appraised as imminent or potential. As such, anticipatory coping activities have an impact on the nature of the future transaction if and when it does finally occur. If the preparatory activity leads to the successful prevention of the harmful event, then the emotions connected with that event will not take place, or will be different. Overcoming the danger before it materializes, for example, can lead to exhilaration rather than fear, grief, depression, etc. Thus, in basically the same way that coping after the crisis serves to alter the person-environment interaction, and hence obviates the stress emotions, anticipatory coping can also have the same effect.

There are at least two forms of anticipatory coping. First, it may be *deliberate,* analytic and reflective, the person thinking ahead and planning actively for what he judges will be required. And whether such planning is done emotionally (e.g., with anxiety, etc.) depends on secondary appraisal of the potential outcome of the coping activities, which feeds back on the primary appraisal of threat itself. Thus, if the person is totally confident that he can master the upcoming danger, he can prepare for it without stress emotion in a cold, intellectual manner.

Second, anticipatory coping may be automatized, occurring with little or no deliberation, or perhaps even without awareness of the potential dangers that are being fended off and the self-protective mechanisms involved. I think this is a most interesting and little appreciated process having great importance in stress emotions and coping. It is clearly a different kind of coping than the others I have considered here. Moreover, I can think of two ways in which such automatization can come about. The first involves the learning of cues that betoken danger, and because the person has acquired effective ways of managing the danger, or because the danger never really becomes imminent, cognitive coping processes are immediately brought into play never permitting the appraisal of threat. In effect, the threat is *short-circuited* by the coping process and never really comes into being. In such a situation, all that is required is that there be some signal (of the danger) to set the coping activity in motion. There will be no extended emotional reaction since there is no threat appraisal, the available coping process feeding back the impression of safety which is then taken into account in primary appraisal.

Second, anticipatory coping can also become established as a general lifestyle, an habitual or automatized way of relating to the environment that has adaptive significance in the face of later confrontations with harm. By virtue of the way the person orders his perceptual activity, actions, and thoughts, for example, he is, in effect, prevented from having certain emotions, and other emotions are made more likely. An example might help clarify what is meant by this. The general lifestyle characteristic of some persons might be to avoid thoughts that might generate anxiety. In other persons, the style is to seek vigilantly any information that might be relevant to their well being, and to order all such information intellectually in a detached manner. Researchers in personality believe that such processes of coping may become habits or styles of living, operating even when a threatening condition is not present (Shapiro, 1965; Schafer, 1954; Gardner, Holzman, Klein, Linton, and Spence, 1959).

In one of the few studies related to anticipatory coping, Liberty, Burnstein, and Moulton (1966) have demonstrated that occupational choices reflect the person's estimate of his ego-resources for successfully managing what is demanded in certain careers. These authors started with the observation that the most prestigious occupations generally also require the highest levels of competence; however, there are some occupations where the prestige is disproportionate to the competence required, and others were conversely the demands for competence are disproportionately higher than the prestige derived. For example, nuclear physics was ranked by students as second in required competence but sixth in prestige, while bankers are ranked third in prestige but only seventh in required competence. The student subjects were then asked to rate the degree of attractiveness to themselves of the various occupations, and also to answer a questionnaire that probed their ego resources and sense of mastery. They found that those who felt rather powerless or lacking in mastery tended to prefer occupations that required lower levels of competence in relation to the prestige involved, while those with a high sense of mastery preferred occupations that were highly challenging and demanding of competence despite the possibility of lower levels of prestige.

These data do not tell us whether or not such choices are made with insight about the self-protective processes involved, and therefore, whether they fit into the category of a deliberate, reflective mode of anticipatory coping or automatized processes of avoiding potentially traumatic situations. However, it is an excellent illustration of anticipatory coping in which the person guides his life and activities so as to prevent being confronted with harm. To the extent that these processes succeed in modifying future exposure to situations provoking stress emotions, they illustrate how in our every day activities, and even in our long term modes of living, anticipatory coping processes influence emotional states in advance by steering the person towards or away from confrontations which provoke them. In the sense noted earlier, they are important in the self-regulation of emotion.

One final point about the cause and effect relationship between coping and emotion should be considered. There is a tendency, especially in psychological research on emotion in the laboratory to focus only on the immediate stimulus situation that provokes an emotion, while forgetting what is or has been going on in the general life of the person, as if the latter did not exist and played no role. An emotion, then, becomes an immediate "figure" in the person's life, so to speak, with the "ground" simply ignored. The person is momentarily occupied by certain transactions with the environment (the figure), emotions that might well be considered in our attempts to understand emotions in nature. Perhaps the person has been struggling with multiple problems about which he may feel despair or depression much of the time, or suppressing such feelings as much as possible. He goes to work (or into our laboratories) and fulfills the day to day demands of his responsibilities against this depressive background. Although we know almost nothing about the possible interpenetrations of the figure and the ground of emotion, there may be important relationships. For example, the ongoing activities of the job (the figure) may suddenly make salient the wider problems being faced outside of the work situation in such a way as to elicit anger or depression then and there. The job is a stimulus, but only in the context of the ground with which it interacts. Or, perhaps, the job activities are sought out as ways of mastering, or at least momentarily preventing, a general sense of despair. In short, whatever the person is momentarily experiencing, be it emotional or not, happens against a background of other psychological conflicts and states even if these are tentatively pushed into the background. The background of latent emotionality is constantly lurking in the shadows and is undoubtedly a major influence on the immediate "figure" states, just as is the immediate stimulus. Perhaps this issue can be thought of as analogous to the distinction personality psychologists have been making between trait and state. It seems to me important, yet largely ignored in psychological theory and research on emotion.

WHY SELF-REGULATION?

In speaking of the control of emotion by means of intrapsychic processes, I have deliberately used the expression "self-regulation" to convey the theme that it is the person, appraising the personal and social requirements of an emotional situation, who manages his emotional reactions willfully, as it were, rather than merely passively and automatically responding to internal and environmental pressures.

The concept of self-regulation (often called self-control, and sometimes impulse-control) has a long history, especially in clinical and personality psychology. It is also a common-sense or lay concept. To some self-regulation might suggest a flirtation with the philosophical idea of free will, or a quarrel with determinism. Yet the concept does not require that such acts of will or self-control be said to occur outside of natural laws, or that we cannot discover the determinants of self-control, some of which lie within the person.

Behaviorally oriented psychologists have sometimes spoken of self-control, and when they have used such a concept, they have done so in what I consider to be a strange and contradictory way. Skinner (1953), for example, speaks of it as manipulating one's own behavior just as one might do in the case of another person, or as the environment does through its pattern of reward and punishment contingencies. To decrease an undesirable behavior in oneself, for instance, the person makes the undesirable response less probable by altering the variables of reward and punishment on which it depends. Thus, if he wishes not to overeat, he can place a time-lock device on the door of the refrigerator to eliminate snacks between meals. To prevent shopping sprees, he can leave his credit card or money at home. Thus, in this view, which has become exceedingly popular in behavior modification circles (see Hunt, 1973), the key seems to be in the environmental contingencies rather than in the person.

Although such environmental contingencies are very important, what is often missed is that an *executive agency within the person* determines which of many competing trends and impulses are to be encouraged or discouraged. Oftentimes it is not the environment that is manipulated, but what the person attends to in that environment, or how he interprets that environment. This is precisely what is meant by intrapsychic or cognitive control mechanisms, including defense mechanisms. To speak of manipulating environmental contingencies is contradictory because it makes the environment the locus of self-control rather than the person, and this emphasis distorts the meaning inherent in the term *self*-control. It is the person who makes a commitment or decision on the basis of cognitive activity, whether he is conscious of it or not. If we speak of *self*-control or *self*-regulation, this can mean only that the person chooses rather than the environment, and sometimes this choice operates against even the usual environmental pressures.

There are two modern arenas for the study of such processes. The first involves a growing body of literature on the self-control of psychophysiological reactions such as heart rate, brain-wave activity, and other somatic reactions that hitherto had been considered outside voluntary control. Self-control is studied through feedback procedures in which the person is allowed to see recorded tracings of these bodily activities and instructed to maximize certain patterns such as slowed heart rate, increased alpha rhythms, etc. A recent review of such research with heart rate and blood pressure by Blanchard and Young (1973) refers to this as the "self control of cardiac functioning." These authors suggest that such self-control has been amply demonstrated, but that the magnitude and duration of the changes have generally been small, and its generalization from the experimental laboratory to other contexts rarely demonstrated. They speak of the study of self-control as a "promise as yet unfulfilled." It might be added that little is also known about the cognitive and/or motor mechanisms by means of which such control is actually achieved. Even more relevant to the concept of the self-regulation of emotion being developed in this chapter is an older research tradition on the self-control of impulses (Block and Block, 1952; Livson and Mussen, 1957), particularly in situations that can be best characterized as involving temptations that the person seeks to resist, either for health reasons, or because of moral scruples.

A recent theoretical paper by Marston and Feldman (1972) attempts to analyze systematically the concept of self-control in the context of behavior modification techniques aimed at aiding people to stop smoking and eating, or in combating other addictions. They suggest a two-stage process by means of which a person overcomes or controls strong impulses that are regarded as undesirable for one reason or another. First there is the development of a general cognitive set in which the person comes to value the inhibition of the impulse and commits himself to make the effort. In speaking of this the authors refer to this commitment or cognitive set as *an executive response*. The second stage involves activation of specific self-controlling responses. The authors write illustratively (p. 430), ". . . the smoker strongly committed to stopping may remove all cigarettes and related stimuli from his home so that at weak moments he is not easily able to relapse." Concerned as they are with the therapeutic context, Marston and Feldman also give some attention to the conditions that lead to a change in behavior in the interest of the commitment to self-control, such as the person's evaluation of the relative importance of change in such behavior compared with the effort required, his expectations of success, the availability of organized programs or aids, and individual differences in the propensity to translate resolve into action. This all sounds to me as though they are speaking of cognitive appraisal processes and not about environmental contingencies per se. Along similar lines, Janis and Mann (1968) have attempted to analyze the components of the decision process involved in such commitments to self-control.

Although it is evident that the concept of self-control has generally been employed in the context of behavioral impulses or drives that the person is striving to inhibit, it is equally relevant to the context of emotions and may well involve similar or overlapping control devices. It is in this context that I have employed the term, self-regulation, although the meaning of the term is quite analogous to that of self-control or impulse control. In the self-regulation of emotion, just as in self-control of impulses or temptations, the person must sometimes act against certain environmental inputs or biological dispositions. In effect, he (the personality-executor) must take charge of the situation on the basis of his cognitive appraisal of the pressures and stakes in the situation having emotional potential, and of the possibilities of coping or control available to him.

All of the above considerations make attractive the proposition that emotions be viewed in the light of mechanisms of self-regulation, pointing up the idea that executive mechanisms within the personality engage in continuous processes of regulation of emotional states. Like the expressions will-power and resolve, self-regulation points to the locus of the decision process and of the management of thought and action *in the person* and nowhere else, although, as I have noted, this does not imply conscious control.

GROUP VERSUS INDIVIDUAL DATA IN EMOTION RESEARCH

The above concepts and the issues they engender have important ramifications also for the methodology of emotion research. An emotion cannot be securely tied to the stimulus situation, although it may well be responsive to it, because of the contribution of the characteristics of persons. There are major individual differences (stereotypy) in both the characteristic emotional response pattern, mode of coping, and patterns of threat appraisal. Also most of the measures from which inferences are made about emotional states are also subject to a host of irrelevant physical factors such as temperature, humidity, infection, and motor activity. Therefore, analysis of group data is apt to be quite misleading when used with human subjects to discover the rules of emotional activity. People are much geared to cognitive, subjective, and symbolic activity, and group data are likely to obscure such individual variations and their multiple determinants. This is especially apparent in ipsative research designs that use repeated observations on the same individuals, thus holding constant or making evident some of the characteristic individual trends noted above (see Opton and Lazarus, 1967, for a fuller analysis of this).

One recent research report using repeated measures on the same individuals highlights the problems created by group data (Hofer, Wolff, Friedman, and Mason, 1972). It was an attempt of the Bethesda group to do a follow-up on the coping and endocrine reactions of parents confronting the stress of having a child dying of leukemia. About 6 months after the child had died, these parents returned to the hospital for further interviews and hormonal assessment. When the data for all parents comparing the level of hormonal secretion during the child's illness and at the follow-up period were lumped together, the conclusion was that their mean hormonal values were virtually unchanged from the preloss to the postloss periods. In actuality, however, this finding resulted from two counteracting trends among the group: Parents whose level of hydrocortisone secretion had been high initially decreased, and those whose level had initially been low increased, yielding an average difference that was unchanged for the group as a whole. About this the authors write (p. 488), "Thus it would seem that any assessment of the response of the pituitary-adrenocortical axis to a life stress cannot be based on group data alone; the study of individual responses must be included for proper understanding of the dynamics of this system." The researchers attempted to explore some of the individual differences in coping that might help explain the pattern.

If we broaden our attention to the total response pattern in emotion, the problem of group data becomes even more complicated because of the complex interrelationships between coping and the various facets of the emotional response, physiological, cognitive-affective, and behavioral, and the many other factors influencing these individual facets of response. In short, if the approach to the psychodynamics of emotion suggested here is taken seriously, it is vital to tease out the sources of variation that lie in persons being studied, including cognitive coping mechanisms, as well as those produced by situations.

Programmatic Research

A theoretical outlook such as that presented above must be associated and followed up with empirical research on certain questions. These may be divided into a number of categories. For example, we need to explore the *determinants of threat appraisal* related to coping, and the way it feeds back to and modifies threat appraisal, leading to changes in the degree and quality of the emotional response. The relations between appraisal and coping must also be examined, including the *determinants of various types of coping* and their *outcomes in the emotional response.* The determinants lie in the situation, the person, and the nature of the response process, for example, the specific forms of coping employed (Lazarus, Averill, and Opton, 1974).

There remain, however, important gaps in knowledge. For example, we must be in a position ultimately to specify the particular kinds of appraisals leading to each of the emotional response syndromes we distinguish. One difficulty in doing this is that we do not have a well-established classificatory scheme for distinguishing emotional response syndromes, nor are the defining response attributes of each emotion clear or agreed upon. Moreover, emotions such as grief and depression (Sachar, Mackenzie, Binstock, and Mack, 1968) have complex patterns of reaction, involving for example, anger, depression, guilt, each traditionally distinguished as a separate emotional reaction. Or they show a sequence of reactions with the predominant affect changing from one stage to another. Thus, it makes a difference whether one studies the emotion at one particular stage or at another. It may be that we will do better to separate out the various components of a complex emotion and to study its cognitive appraisal determinants and the conditions that bring such appraisal about.

In any case, we must specify the particular appraisals characteristic of each basic emotional reaction that we are willing to recognize. My colleagues and I have made a beginning attempt at this in the case of anxiety as distinguished from fear and other emotional reactions often related to it, such as separation distress (Lazarus and Averill, 1972). Beck (1971) has attempted something similar with respect to several different emotions, drawing upon traditional clinical analyses. If my analysis has been sound, then the study of emotion in everyday life and in normal persons must be more than the study of the conditions under which the usual self-regulation of emotions has failed (as when there is overpowering anxiety, depression, grief, etc.) or when an emotion is released from such controls. It may be, as some preliminary interviews with normal people have suggested, that emotion as we see it in extreme situations or in psychopathology is not entirely like that found in normal persons in the daily course of their lives, either in quality, frequency, duration, or intensity. Clinicians typically see emotions in persons with severe problems of living, and as responses to life crises. We need more systematic information about the usual emotional life of normal persons, as well as about the devices they use in their everyday life encounters relevant to the ebb and flow of emotional reactions.

I am inclined to believe that the best strategy for such research is ideographic and naturalistic rather than nomothetic or normative and experimental. We need more study of the natural ecology of emotions. I no longer believe we can learn as much by isolating coping processes, say, or personality variables, or situational demands, from the total context of the individual person in his usual environment. We need to study given classes of normally functioning persons longitudinally, that is, day to day or week to week, as they range from one situational context to another, to analyze and put together effectively the multiple forces to which their emotional reactions respond. Such an approach has been followed in clinical studies of bereavement and loss (e.g., Friedman et al., 1963; Lindemann, 1944; etc.) or in the preparation for an important examination (e.g., Mechanic, 1962), etc. However, these researches are directed at more or less unusual situations of crisis, and they do not tell us much about the natural ecology of emotion, and its self-regulation. There is reason to believe, for example, that the incidence and combination of anger, depression, etc., will vary from one stage of life to another.

Much more attention needs to be given to the emotional life of normal individuals of diverse types over a given period of their lives, and to the way emotional situations are appraised and managed. Such research would lack some of the measurement precision and control possible in the laboratory, which is best suited for isolating variables, but it would increase our ability to uncover what has been most lacking in our understanding to date, namely, how the various individual response systems of emotion, and the mediating processes of self-regulation, are organized or integrated within the person who is struggling to manage his relations with the environment. Only when the multiple processes involved in emotion are allowed to interact normally will we be in a position to begin to understand what happens in a transaction between the person and his environment that is potentially emotional, and the complex conditions and processes that shape the outcome.

REFERENCES

Andreason, N. J. C., Noyes, R., and Hartford, C. E. (1972): Factors influencing adjustment of burn patients during hospitalization, Psychosom. Med. *34*, 517–525.

Averill, J. R. (1973): Personal control over aversive stimuli and its relationship to stress, Psychol. Bull. *80*, 286–303.

Beck, A. T. (1971): Cognition, affect, and psychopathology, Arch. Gen. Psych. *24*, 495–500.

Blanchard, E. B., and Young, L. B. (1973): Self-control of cardiac functioning: A promise as yet unfulfilled, Psychol. Bull. *79*, 145–163.

Block, J., and Block, J. (1952): An interpersonal experiment on reactions to authority, Human Relations *5*, 91–98.

Cohen, F., and Lazarus, R. S. (1973): Active coping processes, coping dispositions, and recovery from surgery, Psychosom. Med. *35*, 375–389.

Frankenhaeuser, M. (1973): Experimental approaches to the study of catecholamines and emotion, This volume.

Friedman, S. B., Chodoff, P., Mason, J. W., et al. (1963): Behavioral observations on parents anticipating the death of a child, Pediatrics, *32*, 610–625.

Gardner, R. W., Holzman, P. S., Klein, G. S., Linton, H. B., and Spence, D. P. (1959): Cognitive control: A study of individual consistencies in cognitive behavior, Psychol. Iss. *1*.

Goodall, Jane Van-Lawick (1972): *In the Shadow of Man*, Dell, New York.

Grinker, R. R., and Spiegel, J. P. (1945): *Men Under Stress*, McGraw-Hill, New York.

Hofer, M. A., Wolff, C., Friedman, S. B., and Mason, J. W. (1972): A psychoendocrine study of bereavement. Part I. 17-hydroxycorti-costeroid excretion rates of parents following death of their children from leukemia, Psychosom. Med. *34*, 481–491.

Horowitz, M. J. (1970): *Image Formation and Cognition*, Appleton-Century-Crofts, New York.

Hunt, W. A. (ed.) (1973): New approaches to behavioral research on smoking. J. Abnorm. Psychol. *81*, entire issue.

Janis, I. L., and Mann, L. (1968): A conflict-theory approach to attitude change and decision making. In: *Psychological Foundations of Attitudes* (ed. A. Greenwald et al.), Academic Press, New York.

Koriat, A., Melkman, R., Averill, J. R., and Lazarus, R. S. (1972): The self-control of emotional reactions to a stressful film, J. Personal. *40*, 601–619.

Lazarus, R. S. (1966): *Psychological Stress and the Coping Process*, McGraw-Hill, New York.

Lazarus, R. S., Averill, J. R., and Opton, E. M., Jr. (1970): Toward a cognitive theory of emotion. In: *Feelings and Emotions* (ed. M. Arnold), p. 207, Academic Press, New York.

Lazarus, R. S., and Averill, J. R. (1972): Emotion and cognition: With special reference to anxiety. In: *Anxiety: Current trends in Theory and Research* (ed. C. D. Spielberger), Vol. II, Academic Press, New York.

Lazarus, R. S., Averill, J. R., and Opton, E. M., Jr. (1974): The psychology of coping: Issues of research and assessment. In: *Coping and Adaptation* (ed. G. V. Coelho, D. A. Hamburg, and J. E. Adams), Basic Books, New York.

Lefcourt, H. M. (1966): Repression-sensitization: A measure of the evaluation of emotional expression, J. Consult. Psychol. *30*, 444–449.

Liberty, P. G., Burnstein, E., and Moulton, R. W. (1966): Concern with mastery and occupational attraction, J. Personal. *34*, 105–117.

Lief, H. I. and Fox, R. C. (1963): Training for "detached concern" in medical students. In: *The Psychological Basis of Medical Practice* (ed. H. I. Lief, V. F. Lief, and N. R. Lief), pp. 12–35, Harper & Row, New York.

Lindemann, E. (1944): Symptomatology and management of acute grief, Am. J. Psych. 101–141.

Livson, N., and Mussen, P. H. (1957): The relation of ego-control to overt aggression and dependency. J. Abnorm. Social Psychol. *55*, 66–71.

Marston, A. R., and Feldman, S. E. (1972): Toward the use of self-control in behavior modification. J. Consult. Clin. Psychol. *39*, 429–433.

Mechanic, D. (1962): *Students Under Stress*, The Free Press of Glencoe, New York.

Mechanic, D. (1968): *Medical Sociology*, The Free Press, New York.

Monat, A., Averill, J. R., and Lazarus, R. S. (1972): Anticipatory stress and coping reactions under various conditions of uncertainty, J. Personal. Social Psychol. *24*, 237–253.

Sachar, E. J., Mackenzie, J. M., Binstock, W. A., and Mack, J. E. (1968): Corticosteroid responses to the psychotherapy of reactive depressions: II. Further clinical and physiological implications, Psychosom. Med. *30*, 23–44.

Schafer, R. (1954): *Psychoanalytic Interpretation in Rorschach Testing*, Grune & Stratton, New York.

Shapiro, D. (1965): *Neurotic Styles*, Basic Books, New York.

Skinner, B. F. (1953): *Science and Human Behavior*, Macmillan, New York.

Wolff, C. T., Friedman, S. B., Hofer, M. A., et al. (1964): Relationship between psychological defenses and mean urinary 17-hydroxycorticosteroid excretion rates: Parts I and II, *Psychosom. Med. 26*, 576–609.

Zborowski, M. (1969): *People in Pain*, Jossey-Bass, San Francisco.

Emotions—Their Parameters and Measurement,
edited by L. Levi.
Raven Press, New York © 1975

Session 1: Discussion

Chairman: Aubrey R. Kagan

Delgado: I think that the problem in the search of emotion is similar to the problem of the search of the mind, or the search of man. I think that if we recognize that emotion is some kind of heterogeneous, multifunctional, polyanatomical entity, if we realize that there is a tremendous difference between maternal love, a toothache, and killing behavior, then the solution of the problem is to differentiate the attitude of the experimentalist and the attitude of the philosopher. Let us try to investigate the anatomical areas of the brain, the functional mechanisms on a very specific problem. In this way, I feel that the solution, from the experimental point of view is relatively easy.

Rioch: I would like to suggest that many of our difficulties come not from the nature of language but from the way people take language or assume it. The difference between the dirty colloquial language and scientific language is very simple. The scientist regards language as nothing except instructions. Colloquially, language is taken as description and commands.

Lazarus: Dr. Brady I would like to call your attention to an interesting parallel between what you said about the separation of what is inside the skin and behavior and what social psychologists and personality psychologists are beginning to say, and have been saying increasingly for quite a few years. The assumption has always been that attitudes cause behavior in social psychology. And it has become increasingly evident that there is a pretty big gap between attitudes and behavior. This is particularly evident in the area of prejudice, for example. You can have highly prejudiced people who behave in quite an unprejudiced way toward the objects of their prejudice. And the next question, of course, is to say something about what are the conditions that determine the continuity or discontinuity between these two very highly related events, factors within the person and presumably in the environmental situation as well.

Brady: I would simply respond that this has got to be a function of the development of an operational language. This is what I see as the two major problems in the so-called area of emotion: the problem having to do with a definition of our subject matter—what, in fact, are we talking about—and secondly, developing an operational language for dealing with that subject matter, if indeed we can identify it. This kind of collusion, if you will, is a function of an operational language.

Lazarus: I want to try to distinguish between coping and an adaptive response, or part of an emotional response which is often *thought* of as coping, but which may be tied, phylogenetically, to the emotion itself. The individual is in an immediate situation which makes demands upon him and he has to act. We act, as psychologists, as though everything is in the moment of his stimulus-response interaction, and very little of the time do we think in terms of the overall pattern of his life and this background consideration. Maybe this is analogous to the trait-state distinction that will come up again at a later point. What do we measure when we measure emotion? Do we measure what is in the foreground? Do we measure what is in the background? It seems to me that it is very important if this background material is relevant and does interpenetrate what goes on.

Parsons: I would like to make one point about Dr. Lazarus' interesting comments on the distinction between the figure and ground components of the situation. The psychologist, by the nature of his job, turns more of the focus on the individual and treats his background as more or less residual. Whereas the sociologist is concerned with collective behavior predominantly, with common features, common situations.

Brady: I find too much going on inside the head which is nonoperational, and that when you attempt to make it operational, you immediately find yourself outside the head, back in the environment, maybe not in the immediate situational environment, but at least in the historical environment.

Lazarus: There is, of course, a perpetual struggle of dispositions about how to think about psychological problems. I am very much concerned in my own research and in the thinking about this problem with what are the determinants of the appraisal process. The determinants are partly in the immediate, external situation. They are partly in the history or belief systems of the individual. For example, it would be perfectly operational if I measured beliefs of people before they entered into my research or before I observed them in the field and showed that those beliefs shape their reported appraisals (it is very hard to get at appraisals) and also correlated with the nature of the emotional response and the quality of the emotional response.

Brady: It is equally illusory to formulate beliefs as being inside the organism. In fact, an operational analysis of these will reveal that they are in fact verbal performances that correlate with other verbal performances, and that is the level with which you must deal. You can go either one way or the other: you can go toward physiology, but then you have got to identify some physiological events, or you can go toward behavior, and then you have got to identify behavioral events.

Spielberger: With regard to the usefulness of explanatory fictions in terms of the figure-ground distinction, trait is useful: not a single trait, but to conceive of human beings as consisting of a variety of dispositions which can be defined and measured.

Emotions—Their Parameters and Measurement,
edited by L. Levi.
Raven Press, New York © 1975

Sensory and Perceptive Factors in Emotional Functions of the Triune Brain

Paul D. MacLean

Laboratory of Brain Evolution and Behavior, National Institute of Mental Health, Bethesda, Maryland 20014

In the world of literature and the fine arts there are countless illustrations of the importance that introspective human beings place on the role of sensation and perception in the generation of emotional feelings. Add to this what has been written on the subject in such fields as religion, philosophy, psychology, and medicine, and the amount of information would choke the output of an ordinary computer. Imagine, however, a computer search in which the three words sensation, perception, and emotion were tied to brain function. Suddenly the outflow of substantive references would be reduced to a mere trickle!

But even this mere trickle would be more than we could cope with within the limits of this presentation. If, for example, we were to examine "first causes," we would need to analyze the extensive literature on receptors, as well as to review the effects of sensory deprivation of whatever origin on emotional experience and expression. I will therefore set arbitrary limits on the ground to be covered and deal mainly with the unanswered question of how sensory and perceptive mechanisms exert their influence on forebrain structures believed to be involved in emotion. In attempting an orderly approach to this problem, I shall deal successively with the three main evolutionary formations of the forebrain. Somewhat like an archaeological dig, I shall begin at the surface with the most recent formation and proceed toward the most ancient. For reasons to be explained, I shall focus particular attention on the limbic system, which phylogenetically represents an inheritance from lower mammals. Then in conclusion, I shall call attention to some seldom asked questions that are possibly relevant to functions of the major counterpart of the reptilian forebrain in mammals.

In constructing a piece of writing we use words both as building materials and tools for thought. Because of the lack of unanimity about the meanings for psychological terms employed in this chapter, it will be worthwhile to read the fine print of the following "contract" regarding the use of certain key words such as sensations, perceptions, and emotions.

DEFINITIONS[1]

It is the element of subjectivity that most clearly distinguishes psychological from other functions of the brain (MacLean, 1960). Even so-called unconscious processes probably require the existence of the subjective state. The case of sleep presents no exception because introspection reveals that a feeling of subjectivity is pervasive in dreaming. Subjectivity refers to the awareness associated with various forms of psychological information. A philosopher such as Kant might have called it an *a priori* "form of consciousness." To paraphrase Spencer (1896), objective psychology begins with subjective psychology. In addition to what we vaguely recognize as awareness or consciousness, introspection reveals five main classes of psychological information that will be here considered under the provisional categories of sensations, perceptions, propensions, emotions, and intellections. All these elements of the psyche are of themselves no more than information. As Wiener (1948) stated more succinctly than Berkeley and Hume, "Information is information, not matter or energy." At the same time, it is empirically established that there can be no communication of information without the intermediary of what we recognize as *behaving entities*. The statement of this invariance might be considered as a law of communication.

Information itself is regarded as orderliness, or, in other words, the order that emerges from a background of disorder. The greater the ratio of order to disorder, the greater is the amount of information. In this respect immaterial information lends itself to a quantification. (In information theory the word information is used in the strict sense to refer to a numerical quantity that is the measure of uncertainty in a communications system. In the present context it is used in the broad sense to refer to anything meaningful.)

The derivation and communication of information in animals depends upon behaving entities of the nervous system. Although introspection *per se* can give no clue as to the workings of these behaving entities (*cf.* MacKay, 1970), it is, as already stated, the first step in making an investigation. How shall we define sensations and perceptions? As a beginning, we may say that sensation represents the raw feelings which, under normal circumstances, depend upon the initiation of impulses resulting from activation of intero- and exteroceptors. In Sherringtonian terms, sensations fall into two broad classes of interoceptions and exteroceptions. They are distinguished in terms of quality (modality) and intensity. Individually, or in combination, sensations become more informative as they are appreciated in terms of time and space. In such transformation they are introspectively recognized as perceptions.

Sensing and perceiving, vis-à-vis mentation. With the exception of cer-

---

[1] This section is based on previously published material (MacLean, 1960, 1969*b*, 1970) and a book in preparation.

tain pathological conditions, it is characteristic of sensations and perceptions that they depend on incoming signals to the brain from specific afferent
systems and cease to exist after the termination of such activity. Contrast
this situation with what applies to the three other main classes of psychological information, namely, propensions, emotions, and intellections. The
latter are distinguished from sensations and perceptions by their capacity to
occur "after-the-fact." The unexplained process that makes this possible is
referred to as mentation. In terms of a behaving nervous system, one might
say that mentation involves self-regenerating neural replica of events either
as they first occurred or in some rearrangement. How the original ordering
of the events is preserved (i.e., memorized) or reordered (i.e., imagined or
conceived) remains a mystery.

Of the three psychological terms in the title of this chapter we have yet to
consider the definition of emotions. It is usual to speak of both the expressive and subjective aspects of emotion. I will use the word "affect" to refer
to the subjective state. Only we as individuals can experience affect. The
existence of affects in another individual must be inferred through some form
of verbal or nonverbal behavior. In the sense that originally inspired its use
by Descartes (1967), the word emotion is an appropriate designation for
such behavior.

The affects differ from other forms of psychological information by being
imbued with a "physical" quality that is either agreeable or disagreeable.
There are no neutral affects because, emotionally speaking, it is impossible
to feel unemotionally. As illustrated in Fig. 1, the agreeable and disagreeable
affects can be subdivided into three main categories, which I have labeled
basic, specific, and general.

The basic and specific affects are first-order affects insofar as they are
immediately dependent, respectively, on interoceptions and exteroceptions.

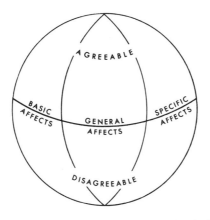

FIG. 1. A scheme for viewing the world of affects (from MacLean, 1970).

The basic affects derive from interoceptions signaling different kinds of internal states associated with basic bodily needs—namely, the needs for food, water, air, sexual outlet, sleep, and those associated with various emunctories. The specific affects apply to exteroceptions and perceptions immediately generated by activity in a specific sensory system. Some are unlearned, whereas others are conditioned. The latter include aesthetic affects identified with agreeable and disagreeable aspects of music and various art forms. Examples of unlearned specific affects are ones associated with repugnant odors, startling sounds, and intense flashes of light.

The general affects are second-order insofar as they originally derive from the first-order affects, but which through mentational processes mentioned above may persist or recur "after-the-fact." I call them general affects because they may apply to feelings aroused by other individuals, situations, or things. All the general affects may be considered from the standpoint of self-preservation and the preservation of the species. Those general affects that are informative of threats to the self or the species are disagreeable in nature, whereas those that signal the removal of threats and the gratification of needs are agreeable.

Exclusive of verbal behavior, there are six main types of animal and human behavior that we identify in varying degree with affective experience and emotional expression. These behaviors are recognized as (1) searching, (2) aggressive, (3) protective, (4) dejected, (5) gratulant, and (6) caressive. Corresponding words that would be broadly descriptive of the associated affective states are desire, anger, fear, sorrow, joy, and affection. Symbolic language and the introspective process make it possible to identify many variations of these affects, but in investigations on animals inferences about emotional states must be based largely on these six general types of behavior.

There are several behaviors that, at first, might not seem to fit these categories, but turn out to be amenable to such classification. Primary among these are obsessive-compulsive, repetitious, ritualistic, superstitious, deceitful, and imitative behaviors.

EVOLUTIONARY CONSIDERATIONS: THE TRIUNE BRAIN

Given these psychological and behavioral definitions, we next consider how the three main evolutionary formations of the forebrain participate in the sensory and perceptive aspects of emotional processes. In its evolution the primate forebrain expands along the lines of three basic patterns that may be characterized as reptilian, paleomammalian, and neomammalian (Fig. 2). There results a remarkable linkage of three cerebrotypes which are radically different in chemistry and structure and which in an evolutionary sense are eons apart. There exists, so to speak, a hierarchy of three-brains-in-one, or what I call, for short, a *triune* brain (MacLean, 1970, 1973c). It is inferred that each cerebrotype has its own special kind of intelligence, its own special memory, its own sense of time and space, and its own motor and other functions. Although the three brain types are extensively interconnected and functionally dependent, there is evidence that each is capable of operating somewhat independently.

The major counterpart of the reptilian forebrain in mammals includes the corpus striatum (caudate plus putamen) globus pallidus, and peripallidal

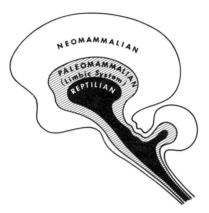

FIG. 2. In evolution the human brain expands in hierarchic fashion along the lines of three basic patterns referred to in the diagram as reptilian, paleomammalian, and neomammalian. As indicated in parenthesis, the limbic system conforms to the paleomammalian pattern. Since the limbic system has been shown to play an important role in emotional behavior, I have given particular attention to the question of how it is influenced by sensory and perceptive mechanisms. (From MacLean, 1967, *J. Nerv. Ment. Dis.* 144, 374–82.)

structures.[2] The paleomammalian brain is represented by the limbic system, a designation that I suggested in 1952. Most of the phylogenetically old cortex is contained in the limbic lobe which surrounds the brainstem (Fig. 3) and conforms somewhat like a mold to the corpus striatum (*cf*. Fig. 2 in MacLean, 1972*a*). The neomammalian brain is represented by the rapidly evolving neocortex and structures of the brainstem with which it is primarily connected.

---

[2] "Peripallidal structures" applies to the variously named structures closely associated with the globus pallidus, including the substantia innominata, basal nucleus of Meynert, nucleus of the ansa peduncularis, and entopeduncular nucleus.

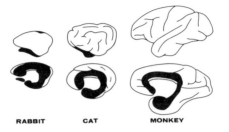

RABBIT   CAT   MONKEY

FIG. 3. The limbic lobe, which was so named by Broca because it surrounds the brainstem, contains most of the phylogenetically old cortex. Indicated by the dark shading, it is found as a common denominator in the brains of all mammals. The neocortex which undergoes great expansion relatively late in evolution is shown in white (after Mac-Lean, 1954).

ROLE OF THE NEOMAMMALIAN BRAIN

It has long been recognized from clinical observations that specific areas of the neocortex are respectively related to the somatic, auditory, and visual systems, and that these cortical areas are essential for normal sensation and perception. The evolutionary ascendency of these systems indicates that the neocortex is primarily oriented toward the external environment. As I have commented elsewhere, ". . . the signals to which these three systems are receptive are the only ones that lend themselves to electronic amplification and radiotransmission. Smells, tastes, and interoceptions have no such avenue for communication" (1972b). Anatomical and electrophysiological studies have demonstrated that an orderly projection exists between receptors and thalamus and between thalamus and neocortex, resulting in a "point-to-point," topographical relationship. The evoked potential technique has made it possible to subdivide the somatic, auditory, and visual areas into a number of subareas, with the recognition thus far of the first, second, and third visual areas; the first, second, and third auditory areas;[3] and the first, second, and supplementary somatosensory areas.

With encephalization, it is evident that in spite of the many redundancies of the nervous system, the neocortex becomes more and more crucial for sensation and perception, and that indeed there is hierarchical ordering within the neocortex itself. Higher primates, for example, are for all intents and purposes blind without the primary striate cortex. This is the extreme opposite of what Snyder and Diamond (1968) have recently observed in the tree shrew, an animal that is presumed to represent an antecedent of pri-

---

[3] Auditory "area IV" overlaps the limbic cortex of the insula (see below).

mates. "With a complete removal of the geniculo-striate system," they report, "tree shrews retain form and pattern vision as well as the capacity to localize visual objects in space." Even after removal of all the known visual areas of the neocortex, these animals are capable of differentiating between horizontal and vertical stripes.

The work of Diamond and his colleagues (Harting, Hall, Diamond, and Martin, 1973) has also added to the accumulating knowledge of the anatomical course of other than the classical sensory pathways to the neocortex. They have demonstrated a collicular-pulvinar-temporal pathway that presumably accounts for sparing of visual function in the tree shrew after ablation of the striate cortex (Snyder and Diamond, 1968). In an abstract in 1963 Myers had described collicular projections to the inferior pulvinar in the monkey. I shall refer to this pathway again when discussing limbic connections.

Electrophysiological studies have identified a number of functional properties of the neocortical sensory areas that are presumed to be involved in the perception of form. The "inhibitory surround" detected in testing receptive fields of cells in the somatosensory (Mountcastle, Davies, and Berman, 1957) and visual areas (Hubel and Wiesel, 1962), for example, is believed to be of fundamental importance in this respect. Studies of individual cells of the visual system have revealed units that respond specifically to edges, contrast, orientation, directional movement, color, etc. The findings have tended to generate a magical jargon in which reference is made to "sophisticated neurons" that are "edge detectors," "motion detectors," and the like, somewhat as though they possessed subjective properties of Leibnitz's monads and were especially constituted to recognize only one or two types of stimuli, when in actuality it is the neural network to which they belong that accounts for the selective response. Curiously enough, as Michael (1969) points out, the retinas of such animals as the frog, ground squirrel, and rabbit have the capacity for discriminative functions that take place only in the visual cortex of higher mammals—specifically the detection of edges, orientation, and direction of movement.

In neurophysiological studies of mechanisms of perception it is usually implicit that the primary goal is to learn how animals achieve the recognition of well-defined patterns, as though this aspect of perception was what mattered most to the organism. As yet, little consideration has been given to a fundamental question of the opposite sort—namely, what is it that makes an animal reactive to environmental apparitions, including ill-defined partial representations of an object or animal, that are conducive to propensive and emotional behavior, serving also, in ethological terms, as "releasers" of specific forms of behavior? Of the many examples, one of the best known is that of infants responding to crude, partial representations of the human face. I shall return to this question in discussing the limbic system and the major mammalian counterpart of the reptilian forebrain.

During neurosurgical procedures it has been learned that crude sensations may result from stimulation of the somatic, auditory, and visual cortex (*cf.* Penfield and Jasper, 1954). In attempting to locate epileptogenic foci, Penfield has found that in some individuals brain stimulation of the so-called association areas of the temporooccipital cortex may induce auditory and visual illusions or hallucinations (Penfield and Perot, 1963).

But neither clinical nor experimental observations have made it possible to trace the neural circuitry by which verbal or nonverbal information derived through the visual, auditory, and somatic systems generates affective states. Of the *specific* affects, pain has received foremost attention. In their analysis of disturbances associated with thalamic lesions, Head and Holmes (1920) noted that sometimes simple tones, like various somatic stimuli, aggravated the sense of pain on the affected side of the body. In addition, they described a curious situation that is somewhat the reverse of the one we are considering. No one seems to have recognized, they pointed out, that states of emotion may evoke different sensations on different sides of the body. "One of our patients," they continued, "was unable to go to his place of worship because he 'could not stand the hymns on his affected side.'" Cases of this kind led them to infer that the optic thalamus was the wellspring of emotion.

PROLEGOMENON TO THE CONSIDERATION OF THE LIMBIC AND REPTILIAN FORMATIONS

Von Economo (1931) singled out more ventral loci as being of primary consequence in emotional experience. In his monograph *Encephalitus Lethargica* he concluded that the tegmentum, the basal and posterior walls of the third ventricle, and the region of the aqueduct were the "favorite target" of the disease. He emphasized the relevance of these findings to the observation that among the persisting symptoms "the difficulty of arousing emotion . . . is above all a primary defect." He pointed out that some patients may feel hungry but take no pleasure in eating, or recognize the sensation of cold without experiencing the usual feeling of cold. In general, they may complain that they "feel like a spent volcano."

It is to be noted that the structures particularly mentioned by Von Economo lie in the region fed by the perforating vessels of the interpeduncular fossa (*cf.* Mettler, 1955). Thanks to recent investigations that can trace part of their "ancestry" to the man honored by this volume, it is now known that there are dopamine-containing neurons in this region that innervate the corpus striatum, including the so-called olfactory striatum. In view of the profound influence of these ascending systems on spontaneous behavior of animals, we may wonder in retrospect to what extent the emotional blunting emphasized by Von Economo was due to the destruction of dopamine-containing cells of the substantia nigra, as well as those of the network spanning the interpeduncular fossa (groups A9 and A10 of Dahlström and Fuxe, 1964). Let me give two unpublished illustrations: We have found that destruction by 6-hydroxydopamine of these cell groups in the squirrel monkey results first in catalepsy followed by a picture of parkinsonism. The cataleptic signs can be detected before the monkey fully recovers from anesthesia. In retrospect, it would appear that the catalepsy that Ingram, Barris, and Ranson (1936) observed in cats following lesions between the mammillary bodies and the third nerve may have resulted from damage of these cell groups. The incapacity produced by lesions in this region is to be contrasted with the mobilizing effect of apomorphine which is believed to act on dopamine receptors. A comparative survey has revealed that in such diverse species as the parrot, turkey, opossum, and squirrel monkey apomorphine induces aimless, increased activity. The turkey, for example, will run aimlessly in and out of the flock for 3 to 4 hr. The two opposing conditions that have been described would support other kinds of evidence that the ascending dopaminergic systems exert an "energizing" influence on an animal's behavior.

In extrapolating from animal experiments by Ranson (1939) and others, one might go further than Von Economo and say that the main avenues for the expression of the basic personality pass through the ventral diencephalon, with the lateral and the medial forebrain bundles, respectively, being two major fiber systems leading to and from striatal and limbic structures. The lateral forebrain bundle includes the ansa and fasciculus lenticularis, as well as the nigrostriatal and striatonigral pathways. The ansa lenticularis sweeps out of the rostromedial part of the globus pallidus like the swish of a mare's tail, with both compact and diffuse components coursing through the dorsolateral part of the hypothalamus and becoming partly entangled with the medial forebrain bundle. It is curious in rereading the literature to find how investigators have either discounted or overlooked the significance of the compact and widely diffuse portions of the *ansa,* as well as the fasciculus lenticularis. This may be in part due to Ranson's (1939) conclusion that these striatal connections probably did not play an important part in the emotional changes observed in rhesus monkeys with bilateral lesions of the lateral hypothalamus. Yet at the same time he pointed out that lesions of the ansa resulted in complete disappearance of the neurons in the medial segment of the globus pallidus. Parenthetically, it should be noted that the ansa is not simply a pallidofugal pathway. It is now evident that like the medial forebrain bundle, it contains ascending fibers (Carpenter and Peter, 1972). Jacobowitz and I *(unpublished),* in experimental material on the squirrel monkey, have found that it contains ascending dopamine fibers, some of which run through the hypothalamus just lateral to the fornix.

Experimental findings in animals attest to the fundamental role of the lenticular pathways in the expression of an animal's "character." In connection with investigations of brain mechanisms of species-typical behavior of the squirrel monkey (see below), I have had occasion to produce large bilateral lesions in the ventral diencephalon involving the central ansal system and part of the medial forebrain bundle. As the result of careful nursing, a number of monkeys have survived the acute post-operative period. Although there is a recovery of locomotion and an ability for self-feeding, the striking thing about these monkeys is the complete lack of what one might call their animality. They have, so to speak, a zombie-like behavior which is distressing to observe.

THE LIMBIC SYSTEM

With this background we turn next to the limbic system which represents an inheritance from lower mammals. The best evidence of the role of the limbic system in emotional behavior is derived from clinical observations. Neuronal discharges in or near the limbic cortex of the temporal lobe may trigger a broad spectrum of vivid, affective feelings. The *basic* and *general* affects are usually of the kind associated with threats to self-preservation (MacLean, 1958). More rarely, there may be affects of an agreeable or ecstatic nature, possibly reflecting a spread of the seizure to other subdivisions of the limbic system.

The *basic* affects include those of hunger, thirst, nausea, and feelings associated with the emunctories. *Specific* affects include unpleasant tastes and odors and somatic sensations such as pain and tingling (see also below). Among the *general* affects are feelings of fear, terror, sadness, wanting to be alone, familiarity, unfamiliarity, and (very rarely) anger. The feeling of fear is commonly referred to the epigastric region and may give the impression of rising in the chest to the throat. As I have emphasized elsewhere (1952), the *general* affects are usually "free-floating" insofar as they are not identified with any particular person or situation. One of the more common affective experiences is the so-called déjà vu. Significantly, as Penfield and Erickson (1941) have noted, the patient may experience *only the feeling* that accompanies the act of remembering. A similar situation applies to auras conveying eureka-type feelings expressed by such words as "This is it, the absolute truth," "This is what the world is all about" (MacLean, 1970, 1973*b*). Ironically, it would seem that the ancient limbic system provides free-floating, strong affective feelings of conviction that we attach to revelations and beliefs, regardless of whether they are true or false!

Case histories of limbic epilepsy also indicate (1) that the limbic system is basic for affective feelings of the reality of the self and of the environment (MacLean, 1972*b*) and (2) that ictal distruptions of its functions may result in changes of mood, distortions of perception, feelings of depersonalization, hallucinations, and paranoid delusions (MacLean, 1973*c*).

The affective aspects of one's experiences — as illustrated by the déjà vu — seem to be an important requisite for memory (MacLean, 1969*a*). One of the consequences of limbic seizures is the amnesia that is temporally related to the termination of the aura and the onset and duration of the automatism. Sometimes the automatism involves activities that almost certainly require a functioning neocortex.

Feelings triggered by epileptogenic foci may involve any one of the sensory systems. There may be olfactory, gustatory, visceral, and genital sensations; sounds may seem unusually loud or faint; parts of the body may seem swollen to large proportions; there may be the condition of micropsia or macropsia in which objects seem unusually small or large.

Sensations, perceptions, affect—there is no clinical entity other than limbic epilepsy that combines these three psychological aspects of our topic in its symptomatology. What is the neural basis for these and other manifestations that have been summarized?

In the "visceral brain" paper of 1949, I elaborated upon the Papez (1937) theory of emotion by suggesting that impulses from all the intero- and exteroceptive systems find their way to the hippocampus *via* the hippocampal gyrus. The hypothetical pathways were schematized in Fig. 3 of that paper. The hippocampal formation was visualized as a mechanism that combined information of internal and external origin into affective feelings that found further elaboration and expression through connections with the amygdala, septum, basal ganglia, hypothalamus, and the principle reentry circuit to the limbic lobe that has become known as "the Papez circuit."

Prior to discussing the question of inputs to the limbic cortex, two other important considerations require mention. First, the pathological studies of Sano and Malamud (1953) and of Margerison and Corsellis (1966) have revealed that Ammon's horn sclerosis is, in Malamud's words (1966), the "common denominator" in cases of psychomotor epilepsy. Since the sclerosis often extends to other medial temporal structures, Falconer, Serafetinides, and Corsellis (1964) perfer to use the term "medial temporal sclerosis." That such sclerosis or other medial temporal lesions are responsible for epileptogenic foci is strongly supported by two series of 100 cases of epilepsy in which Falconer (1970) resected the offending temporal lobe in one block, a procedure that not only affords removal of all or most of the damaged tissue but also allows complete pathological examination.

Second, it is a remarkable fact that seizure discharges originating in or near the limbic cortex have a tendency to spread in and be largely confined to the limbic system. It is probable that the hippocampus is almost always involved, with the discharge either originating in it or spreading to it from related structures. Simultaneous recordings from the neocortex may show little change during such seizures except for a generalized desynchronization. For such reasons I have referred to the potential "schizophysiology" (MacLean, 1954) of limbic and neocortical systems and suggested that this situation may partly account for conflicts between what we affectively "feel" and what we "know."

Except for olfaction with its representation in the piriform lobe, and the less certain evidence of the representation of gustatory and visceral sensation in the limbic part of the insula, it has not been at all clear how various sensory and perceptive phenomena are generated by limbic discharges. There is experimental evidence that limbic seizures do not appreciably change the bioelectrical activity of the primary sensory areas of the neocortex. Acoustic stimuli, for example, continue to be effective in evoking potentials in the auditory area during propagating hippocampal seizures (Flynn, MacLean, and Kim, 1961; Prichard and Glaser, 1966).

In the 1949 paper mentioned above, I hypothesized that somatic, auditory, and visual information was channeled to the hippocampal gyrus by transcortical connections from the primary receiving areas. Subsequently, Pribram and I reported strychnine neuronographic findings in the cat (MacLean and Pribram, 1953) and monkey (Pribram and MacLean, 1953) that would be compatible with this hypothesis. Three years ago, Jones and Powell (1970) described an experimental anatomical study in the macaque which not only revealed the possibility of stepwise cortical connections from these areas to the hippocampal gyrus, but also to the limbic cortex of the anterior cingulate gyrus and posterior orbital area (see also recent anatomical study by Van Hoesen, Pandya, and Butters, 1972).

After a brief recapitulation of earlier electrophysiological findings, I shall summarize a series of microelectrode studies that indicate, on the basis of response latencies, that visual, auditory, somatic, and visceral information reaches respective parts of the limbic lobe by rather direct subcortical pathways. At the same time, I shall mention supporting anatomical evidence.

In a study reported in 1952 (MacLean, Horwitz, and Robinson, 1952), we found that gustatory and noxious somatic stimulation resulted in rhythmically recurring olfactory-like potentials in the piriform area. Sometimes rhythmic potentials appeared in the hippocampus following olfactory or gustatory stimulation. In pursuing this lead, Green and Arduini (1954) showed that various forms of sensory stimulation evoked rhythmic theta activity in the hippocampus of unanesthetized animals. Such effects were observed in macrosmatic animals but not in primates and were regarded as nonspecific in nature.

In continuing the investigation of limbic inputs we have employed microelectrode recording of evoked unit responses in chronically prepared, awake, sitting squirrel monkeys. Such experimentation avoids the depressant effects of anesthesia on neural transmission and, in contradistinction to the technique for recording evoked slow potentials with macroelectrodes, makes it possible to be sure of the locus of the neural response. Thus far we have tested more than 7,500 cerebral units, of which about 2,500 (33%) were located in the limbic cortex. We have explored all of the cortex of the limbic lobe except for the posterior orbital and piriform areas. I shall now summarize briefly our published findings on the results of visual, auditory, and somatic stimulation.

Visual Stimulation

Virtually all photically responsive units were located in the posterior hippocampal gyrus (see Fig. 4), the parahippocampal cortex of the lingual gyrus, and the retrosplenial cortex near its junction with the striate cortex (MacLean, Yokota, and Kinnard, 1968). The conditions of the experiment made it impractical to plot receptive fields and to do more than to test with moving patterns. The regularity and character of the photic responses, as well as the latency values, were suggestive of a subcortical, rather than transcortical, pathway. Evidence in support of this inference was obtained in a neuroanatomical study in which improved techniques for demonstrating fine fibers were used to trace degeneration from lesions in the lateral geniculate body and pulvinar (MacLean and Creswell, 1970). Lesions in the ventrolateral part of the lateral geniculate nucleus resulted in degeneration in that part of the optic radiations known as Meyer's loop, which makes a temporal detour and enters the core of the posterior hippocampal gyrus. Some fibers could be traced to the photically responsive limbic cortex and adjoining neocortical areas. A coarser type of degeneration was seen in the posterior hippocampal gyrus and contiguous areas following lesions of the

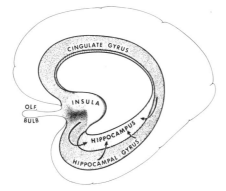

FIG. 4. Shaded areas show main areas of the limbic lobe referred to in the review of microelectrode findings on inputs from intero- and exteroceptive systems. The insular cortex overlying the claustrum is limbic by definition because it forms part of the phylogenetically old cortex surrounding the brainstem (from MacLean, 1970).

inferior pulvinar. The pulvinar projections are contained in a band of fibers just lateral to the optic radiations. These observations will recall the discussion in Section C of recently described connections between the superior colliculus and the inferior pulvinar.

About one-half the cells in the posterior hippocampal gyrus gave a sustained on-response to ocular illumination, raising the question of their possible role in states of wakefulness, alerting, and attention, or in the regulation of neuroendocrine functions affected by diurnal and seasonal changes in light.

Some cells in the retrosplenial cortex responded only to stimulation of the contralateral eye, suggesting that they may receive their innervation from the primitive temporal monocular crescent, the part of our retina through which we become aware of objects moving in from the side or rear. As witness the blinders used for horses, unexpected movements in the peripheral visual field may induce startle and alarm. I recall a patient with psychomotor epilepsy whose aura began with a feeling of fear that someone was standing behind him. If he turned to see who it was, the feeling became intensified, and he might have a generalized convulsion. He learned that by resisting the impulse to turn that he could usually prevent a generalized seizure. Horowitz, Adams, and Rutkin (1968) have reported clinical cases in which stimulation with electrodes presumably in "posterior hippocampal areas" was more apt to result in visual imagery than stimulation at other sites in the temporal lobe.

The insular cortex overlying the calustrum (Fig. 4) is by definition limbic because it forms part of the phylogenetically old cortex surrounding the brainstem. We encountered a few units in the limbic cortex of the insula, that responded with a brisk discharge to an approaching object. This finding recalls observations by Penfield and Jasper (1954) that discharges in the parainsular region may result in macropsia, a condition in which objects appear to become larger.

Somatic and Auditory Stimulation

Responses to somatic and to auditory stimulation were elicited only in the limbic cortex of the insula (Sudakov, MacLean, Reeves, and Marino, 1971). The receptive fields of the somatic units were usually large and bilateral. Units responding to auditory stimulation were located somewhat more caudally. There were two main types, one of which discharged with short latencies ranging from 7 to 15 msec. Latencies of this order suggest the possibility of direct connections from the medial geniculate body. As discussed in the original paper, both anterograde and retrograde degeneration studies indicate that the insular cortex overlying the claustrum receives projections from the medial geniculate body. The anatomical evidence is conflicting in regard to somatic projections.

Gustatory Stimulation

While exploring the insula, we also tested the responsiveness of units to gustatory stimulation. Responsive units were located anteriorly in the same region from which Benjamin and Burton (1968) recorded evoked potentials upon stimulation of the chorda tympani in the squirrel monkey. Other units in this same region were activated by mechanical stimulation of the oral cavity, including the pharynx.

Vagal Stimulation

Somewhat surprisingly, units of the cingulate cortex (see Fig. 4) are virtually unresponsive to visual, auditory, and somatic stimulation (Bachman and MacLean, 1971). In a further attempt to discover the nature of inputs to the cingulate cortex we have investigated the possibility of visceral projections by testing the effects of vagal volleys on unit activity. These experiments have been performed on awake, sitting squirrel monkeys previously prepared with electrodes chronically implanted on the cervical vagus or at the site where the vagus enters the jugular foramen (Bachman, Katz, and MacLean, 1972b). Of more than 300 units thus far tested, a little more than 20% have been responsive, with the ratio of initially excited to initially inhibited units being about 2 to 3. Most of the responsive units have been located in the middle portion of the gyrus. The response latencies of the excited units have been as short as 15 msec, suggesting a fairly direct pathway. In a parallel study we have attempted to mimic natural stimulation of visceral receptors by injecting micro-amounts of 5-hydroxytryptamine (serotonin) through an indwelling catheter in the superior vena cava (Bachman, Katz, and MacLean, 1972a). Of 82 tested units in the supracallosal cingulate cortex, 18% were affected, with two-thirds showing an increased firing rate and one-third a decrease. These units were also located in the midportion of the gyrus. The anatomical studies of Morest (1961) suggest the possibility of an ascending pathway from the nucleus solitarius to the dorsal tegmental nucleus of Gudden, from which impulses might ascend *via* the mammillary peduncle system to the anterior ventral nucleus of the thalamus and the cingulate cortex. The findings in histofluorescence studies (e.g., Fuxe, 1965; Jacobowitz and Kostrzewa, 1971; Olson and Fuxe, 1972) are not incompatible with the interesting possibility of an ascending norepinephrine system from the nucleus solitarius. The anterior ventral nucleus of the thalamus has numerous fine norepinephrine terminals, and such terminals are also found in the cingulate gyrus. In a comparative histofluorescence study including the pygmy marmoset and squirrel monkey Jacobowitz and I (unpublished) have found that the organizational pattern of all of the recognized aminergic systems have been preserved with remarkable consistency in the evolution of primates.

Among other limbic areas we hope to explore in the monkey for vagal responses are the posterior orbital and anterior insular areas which correspond to a region in the cat from which a number of investigators recorded changes in spontaneous activity (Bailey and Bremer, 1938) or evoked potentials (Dell and Olson, 1951a,b; Korn, Wendt, and Albe-Fessard, 1966) with vagal stimulation.

Sensory Integration

In prefacing the question of sensory integration I would like to emphasize that in our own experiments no hypothalamic units responded to photic and somatic stimulation, and only a few were affected by auditory stimulation (Poletti, Kinnard, and MacLean, 1973). This would suggest that sensory information affecting the hypothalamus is first integrated and processed in related structures such as the limbic cortex.

In our initial studies in monkeys anesthetized with alpha-chloralose we found a few limbic cortical units that showed convergence of sensory inputs. But it is remarkable that in the awake, sitting monkey all responsive units appear to be modality specific, indicating a high degree of selectivity. This raises the additional question as to how information reaching the limbic cortex from the intero- and exteroceptive systems is integrated and processed? Or metaphorically stated, where do the "viewers" reside in the limbic system? One likely place is the entorhinal cortex of the hippocampal gyrus which receives connections from the frontotemporal cortex (posterior orbital, anterior insular, piriform, and temporal polar areas) and from the caudally lying parahippocampal cortex (Fig. 4). The entorhinal cortex forms an extensive area in man. From the entorhinal area information would be fed forward through the perforant and alveolar pathways to the hippocampus (Fig. 4). The anterior hippocampus also receives connections from the frontotemporal region, and there are afferent connections to the posterior hippocampus from the cingulate gyrus *via* the cingulum, as well as from the lamina medullaris superficialis. These latter pathways might transmit information of vagal origin (see above). In the hippocampus the Schaffer collateral system would provide one means of interrelating information from the various sensory modalities.

The septum, which receives connections from the hypothalamus, is another presumed source of interoceptive information reaching the hippocampus. The septal projections are believed to terminate in the stratum oriens, possibly on the basal dendrites of the hippocampal pyramids, whereas the perforant pathway terminates on the apical dendrites. In an intracellular study of hippocampal neurons in the awake, sitting monkey we found that septal stimuli elicited excitatory postsynaptic potentials associated with neuronal discharge, whereas the stimulation of the olfactory bulb generated EPSP's but never spikes (Yokota, Reeves, and MacLean,

1970). In terms of classical conditioning, impulses from these respective exteroceptive inputs might be compared to unconditional and conditional stimuli. Brazier (1964) has reported photically evoked slow potentials in the hippocampus of patients undergoing diagnostic tests for epilepsy.

Limbic Outputs

It is beyond the scope of this chapter to deal with output mechanisms of the limbic system, but a few salient points deserve mention. Microelectrode studies have shown that fornix volleys or hippocampal afterdischarges inhibit unit responses in the caudal intralaminar region to potentially noxious stimuli of the fifth nerve (Yokota and MacLean, 1968). In a recent paper (Poletti et al., 1973) we have reported that hippocampal volleys elicit responses in a large proportion of units in *certain* structures of the basal forebrain, preoptic region, and hypothalamus. In each case more than 80% of the responsive units showed initial excitation. Hippocampal afterdischarges also more commonly excited than inhibited units. Following afterdischarges, units showed changes in their firing patterns that lasted from 1 to 11 min. These latter findings may help to explain the prolonged "rebound" behavioral and autonomic changes seen following hippocampal afterdischarges, including agitated states on the one hand and enhanced pleasure and sexual reactions on the other.

As seemed evident from the electrophysiological findings, a parallel neuroanatomical study showed for the first time in a primate that the fornix projects to the medial preoptic area and to the perifornical region (Poletti et al., 1973). The work of Hess and Brügger (1943) implicated the perifornical region (the so-called intermediate zone of Hess) in the expression of angry behavior. The medial preoptic area has become of increasing interest not only because of its participation in the control of gonadotropic activity and genital function but also because of its role in sexual differentiation in certain macrosmatic animals.

A few fibers could also be traced to the tuberal region where the electrophysiological study had shown a cellular response to hippocampal volleys. In view of this and other findings, attention should be called to the accumulating evidence that hippocampal stimulation, depending on the physiological state at the time, may have a facilitatory or inhibitory effect with respect to ACTH release, cardiovascular reflexes, and visceral responsiveness (see Poletti et al., 1973, for references). The results of our own microelectrode studies would indicate that in the awake, sitting monkey there is leeway for attributing a range of inhibitory, excitatory, and modulating functions to the hippocampus.

Poletti, Sujatanond, and Sweet (1972) have since shown that, following section of the fornix, hippocampal volleys were still effective in eliciting unit responses in the structures examined in the preceding study but with a longer latency. It seems probable that the impulses are transmitted *via* the amygdala, which represents one of the major avenues for projections from the frontotemporal division of the limbic system.

Clinically, as well as experimentally in animals, the hippocampal formation has been implicated in dreaming and other manifestations of REM sleep. This is a matter relevant to our topic because of the strong affective component of dreaming. The subject has recently attracted additional interest because aminergic systems have been implicated in mechanisms of sleep (see Jouvet, 1972, for review). As we reported in 1957 (Paasonen, MacLean, Giarman, 1957), the cellular parts of the hippocampus, as well as its closely associated nuclei, the amygdala and the septum, contain relatively large amounts of serotonin, and the work of Fuxe (1965) has demonstrated the presence of norepinephrine terminals in the radiate layer.

In summary, the work that has been reviewed suggests mechanisms by which information of intero- and exteroceptive systems can interact in the hippocampal formation and influence hypothalamic and other brainstem structures involved in emotional behavior.

STRIATAL COMPLEX

There remains the question of the role of the striatal complex in sensory and perceptive aspects of emotional behavior. Here we are obliged to sound even greater depths of ignorance than in the case of the neomammalian and limbic formations. Evidence has accumulated in recent years that most parts of the neocortex and limbic cortex project to the corpus striatum. The observed degeneration, however, appears to be rather scant. From an evolutionary point of view, it would appear to be of special significance that the limbic lobe conforms to the corpus striatum somewhat like a mold. The seemingly obligatory relationship between the two is reflected by the way the head of the caudate is drawn out into a long tail that is enfolded by the temporal part of the limbic lobe.

In addition to reciprocal connections with the substantia nigra, the corpus striatum (caudate plus putamen) projects to the globus pallidus which in turn establishes connections with the ventral part of the thalamus and other structures of the brainstem. Nauta and Mehler (1966) have failed to find evidence of connections of the so-called pallidohypothalamic tract with the ventromedial nucleus or other parts of the hypothalamus. The peripallidal portion of the substantia innominata, however, appears to project to the caudolateral part of the hypothalamus. Albe-Fessard, Rocha-Miranda, and Oswaldo-Cruz (1960) have reported that heterogenous afferents converge on individual neurons of the caudate nucleus of the cat. There are, however, no clear indications as to the course of ascending pathways.

Various authorities have pointed out that, despite 150 years of experimentation, remarkably little has been learned about the functions of the striatal complex. The finding that large bilateral lesions of the corpus striatum or globus pallidus in mammals may result in no apparent motor deficit is evidence against the traditional clinical view that these structures subserve purely motor functions. Perhaps because of a major interest in learning, memory, perception, and related problems, there has been a failure to ask the right questions. At our field laboratory we are investigating the role of the striatal complex in natural forms of behavior, testing the hypothesis that it is basic for species-typical, genetically constituted forms of behavior such as selecting a homesite, establishing and defending territory, hunting, homing, mating, forming social hierarchies, selecting leaders. We also hope that this work will shed light on neural mechanisms underlying compulsive, repetitious, ritualistic, deceptive, and imitative forms of behavior. The comparative approach to this work is strengthened now that developments in neurochemistry (particularly the Koelle stain for cholinesterase and the histofluorescence technique of Falck and Hillarp) have made it possible to identify corresponding structures in the striatal complex of reptiles, birds, and mammals.

In a study involving lesions in various parts of the brain in more than 90 squirrel monkeys, I (1972a, 1973a) have obtained evidence that the striatal complex is essential for the expression of the species-typical display behavior of this species, as well as the associated imitative factors.

It is relevant to mechanisms of imitation that partial representations have the capacity to trigger replicative forms of behavior. In the case of the squirrel monkey the reflection of a single eye may be enough to elicit a full display (MacLean, 1964). In reptiles and lower forms, dummies or even parts of dummies are sufficient to elicit courtship and aggressive display, as well as other patterns of behavior. In the case of domestic mammals, partial dummies are used as incitements for the purpose of collecting semen for artificial insemination. Shadowy forms or partial representations are notorious for their capacity to evoke fearful and paranoid reactions in animals and man.

As I mentioned in the introduction, workers in psychophysics seem to be interested in perceptual illusions only insofar as they help to analyze mechanisms by which subjects derive perfect images of objects regardless of size. In future neuroethological work, it is evident that more attention must be given to neural mechanisms that account for complex behavioral responses to phantoms and partial representations. As might be illustrated by several examples, the problem applies not only to the visual system, but also to other sensory systems.

Summary

In evolution, the primate forebrain has evolved and expanded along the lines of three basic patterns characterized as reptilian, paleomammalian, and neomammalian. Radically different in structure and chemistry, the three evolutionary formations comprise, so to speak, a *triune* brain. This chapter focuses on the question of how sensory and perceptive mechanisms exert their influence on forebrain structures believed to be involved in the experience and expression of emotion. Particular attention is given to recent experimental findings on inputs to the limbic system which represents an inheritance from lower mammals and which has been shown to play an important role in emotional behavior.

REFERENCES

Albe-Fessard, D., Rocha-Miranda, C. E., and Oswaldo-Cruz, E. (1960): Activités évoquées dans le noyau caudé du chat en réponse à des types divers d'afférences. II. Etude microphysiologique, *Electroencephalogr. Clin. Neurophysiol. 12*, 649–61.

Bachman, D. S., Katz, H. M., and MacLean, P. D. (1972a): Effect of intravenous injections of 5-hydroxytryptamine (serotonin) on unit activity of cingulate cortex of awake squirrel monkeys, *Fed. Proc. 31*, 303.

Bachman, D. S., Katz, H. M., and MacLean, P. D. (1972b): Vagal influence on units of cingulate cortex in the awake, sitting squirrel monkey, *Electroencephalogr. Clin. Neurophysiol. 33*, 350–351.

Bachman, D. S., and MacLean, P. D. (1971): Unit analysis of inputs to cingulate cortex in awake, sitting squirrel monkeys. I. Exteroceptive systems, *Int. J. Neuroscience 2*, 109–13.

Bailey, P., and Bremer, F. (1938): A sensory cortical representation of the vagus nerve, *J. Neurophysiol. 1*, 405–12.

Banjamin, R. M., and Burton, H. (1968): Projection of taste nerve afferents to anterior opercular-insular cortex in squirrel monkey (Saimiri sciureus), *Brain Res. 7*, 221–31.

Brazier, M. A. B. (1964): Evoked responses recorded from the depths of the human brain, *Ann. N.Y. Acad. Sci. 112*, 33–59.

Carpenter, M. B., and Peter, P. (1972): Nigrostriatal and nigrothalamic fibers in the rhesus monkey, *J. Comp. Neurol. 144*, 93–116.

Dahlström, A., and Fuxe, K. (1964): Evidence for the existence of monoamine-containing neurons in the central nervous system. I. Demonstration of monoamines in the cell bodies of brain stem neurons, *Acta Physiol. Scand. 62*, 5–55.

Dell, P., and Olson, R. (1951a): Projections thalamiques, corticales et cérébelleuses des afférences viscérales vagales, *C.R. Soc. Biol. 145*, 1084–1088.

Dell, P., and Olson, R. (1951b): Projections "secondaires" mésencéphaliques, diencéphaliques et amygdaliennes des afférences viscérales vagales, *C.R. Soc. Biol. 145*, 1088–1091.

Descartes, R. (1967): *The Philosophical Works of Descartes*, Vols. 1 and 2, translated into English by E. S. Haldane and G. R. T. Ross, Cambridge.

Falconer, M. A. (1970): Historical review: The pathological substrate of temporal lobe epilepsy, *Guy's Hosp. Rep. 119*, 47–60.

Falconer, M. A., Serafetinides, E. A., and Corsellis, J. A. N. (1964): Etiology and pathogenesis of temporal lobe epilepsy, *Arch. Neurol. 10*, 233–248.

Flynn, J. P., MacLean, P. D., and Kim, C. (1961): Effects of hippocampal afterdischarges on conditioned responses. In: *Electrical Stimulation of the Brain*, ed. D. E. Sheer, Austin.

Fuxe, K. (1965): Evidence for the existence of monoamine neurons in the central nervous system. IV. Distribution of monoamine nerve terminals in the central nervous system, *Acta Physiol. Scand. 64* (Suppl. 247), 37–84.

Green, J. D., and Arduini, A. A. (1954): Hippocampal electrical activity in arousal, *J. Neurophysiol. 17*, 533–557.

Harting, J. K., Hall, W. C., Diamond, I. T., and Martin, G. F. (1973): Anterograde degeneration study of the superior colliculus in *Tupaia glis:* Evidence for a subdivision between superficial and deep layers, *J. Comp. Neurol. 148*, 361–86.

Head, H., and Holmes, G. (1920): Part IV. The brain. Sensory disturbances from cerebral lesions. Chapt. II. Sensory disturbances associated with certain lesions of the optic thalamus. In: *Studies in Neurology*, ed. H. Head, Vol. 2, London.

Hess, W. R., and Brügger, M. (1943): Der Miktions und der Defäkationsakt als Erfolg zentraler Reizung, *Helv. Physiol. Acta 1,* 511–32.

Horowitz, M. J., Adams, J. E., and Rutkin, B. B. (1968): Visual imagery and brain stimulation, *Arch. Gen. Psychiatry 19,* 469.

Hubel, D. H., and Wiesel, T. N. (1962): Receptive fields, binocular interaction and functional architecture in the cat's visual cortex, *J. Physiol. 160,* 106–154.

Ingram, W. R., Barris, R. W., and Ranson, S. W. (1936): Catalepsy: An experimental study, *Arch. Neurol. Psychiatry 35,* 1175–1197.

Jocobowitz, D., and Kostrzewa, R. (1971): Selective action of 6-hydroxydopa on noradrenergic terminals: Mapping of preterminal axons of the brain, *Life Sci. 10,* 1329–1342.

Jones, E. G., and Powell, T. P. S. (1970): An anatomical study of converging sensory pathways within the cerebral cortex of the monkey, *Brain 93,* 793–820.

Jouvet, M. (1972): Veille, sommeil et reve: le discours biologique, *Rev. Médecine 16,* 1003–1063.

Korn, H., Wendt, R., and Albe-Fessard, D. (1966): Somatic projection to the orbital cortex of the cat, *Electroencephalogr. Clin. Neurophysiol. 21,* 209–226.

MacKay, D. M. (1970): Perception and brain function. In: *The Neurosciences,* ed. F. O. Schmitt, New York.

MacLean, P. D. (1949): Psychosomatic disease and the "visceral brain." Recent developments bearing on the Papez theory of emotion, *Psychosom. Med. 11,* 338–353.

MacLean, P. D. (1952): Some psychiatric implications of physiological studies on frontotemporal portion of limbic system (visceral brain), *Electroencephalogr. Clin. Neurophysiol. 4,* 407–418.

MacLean, P. D. (1954): The limbic system and its hippocampal formation. Studies in animals and their possible application to man, *J. Neurosurg. 11,* 29–44.

MacLean, P. D. (1958): Contrasting functions of limbic and neocortical systems of the brain and their relevance to psychophysiological aspects of medicine, *Am. J. Med. 25,* 611–626.

MacLean, P. D. (1960): Psychosomatics. *Handbook of Physiology.* In: *Neurophysiology III,* American Physiological Society, Washington.

MacLean, P. D. (1964): Mirror display in the squirrel monkey, *Saimiri sciureus, Science 146,* 940–52.

MacLean, P. D. (1969a): The internal-external bonds of the memory process, *J. Nerv. Ment. Dis. 149,* 40–47.

MacLean, P. D. (1969b): The hypothalamus and emotional behavior. In: *The Hypothalamus,* eds. W. Haymaker, E. Anderson, and W. J. H. Nauta, Springfield.

MacLean, P. D. (1970): The triune brain, emotion, and scientific bias. In: *The Neurosciences Second Study Program,* ed. F. O. Schmitt, New York.

MacLean, P. D. (1972a): Cerebral evolution and emotional processes: New findings on the striatal complex, *Ann. N.Y. Acad. Sci. 193,* 137–149.

MacLean, P. D. (1972b): Implications of microelectrode findings on exteroceptive inputs to the limbic cortex. In: *Limbic System Mechanisms and Autonomic Function,* ed. C. H. Hockman, Springfield.

MacLean, P. D. (1973a): Effects of pallidal lesions on species-typical display behavior of squirrel monkey, *Fed. Proc. 32,* 384.

MacLean, P. D. (1973b): The brain's generation gap: Some human implications, *Zygon Journal of Religion and Science 8,* 113–27.

MacLean, P. D. (1973c): A triune concept of the brain and behaviour; Lecture I. Man's reptilian and limbic inheritance; Lecture II. Man's limbic brain and the psychoses; Lecture III. New trends in man's evolution. In: *The Hincks Memorial Lectures,* eds. T. Boag and D. Campbell, Toronto.

MacLean, P. D., and Creswell, G. (1970): Anatomical connections of visual system with limbic cortex of monkey, *J. Comp. Neurol. 138,* 265–78.

MacLean, P. D., Horwitz, N. H., and Robinson, F. (1952): Olfactory-like responses in pyriform area to nonolfactory stimulation, *Yale J. Biol. Med. 25,* 159–172.

MacLean, P. D., and Pribram, K. H. (1953): Neuronographic analysis of medial and basal cerebral cortex. I. Cat, *J. Neurophysiol. 16,* 312–323.

MacLean, P. D., Yokota, T., and Kinnard, M. A. (1968): Photically sustained on-responses of units in posterior hippocampal gyrus of awake monkey, *J. Neurophysiol. 31,* 870–883.

Malamud, N. (1966): The epileptogenic focus in temporal lobe epilepsy from a pathological standpoint, *Arch. Neurol. 14,* 190–195.

Margerison, J. H., and Corsellis, J. A. N. (1966): Epilepsy and the temporal lobes: A clinical, electroencephalographic and neuropathological study of the brain in epilepsy, with particular reference to the temporal lobes, *Brain 89*, 499.

Mettler, F. A. (1955): Perceptual capacity, function of the corpus striatum, and schizophrenia, *Psychiatr. Q. 29*, 89–111.

Michael, C. R. (1969): Retinal processing of visual images, *Sci. Am. 220*, 104–114.

Morest, D. K. (1961): Connexions of dorsal tegmental nucleus in rat and rabbit, *J. Anat. 95*, 1–18.

Mountcastle, V. B., Davies, P. W., and Berman, A. L. (1957): Response properties of neurons of cat's somatic sensory cortex to peripheral stimuli, *J. Neurophysiol. 20*, 374–407.

Myers, R. E. (1963): Projections of the superior colliculus in monkey, *Anat. Rec. 145*, 264.

Nauta, W. J. H., and Mehler, W. R. (1966): Projections of the lentiform nucleus in the monkey, *Brain Res. 1*, 3–42.

Olson, L., and Fuxe, K. (1972): Further mapping out of central noradrenaline neuron systems: Projections of the "subcoeruleus" area, *Brain Res. 43*, 289–295.

Paasonen, M. K., MacLean, P. D., and Giarman, N. J. (1957): 5-Hydroxytryptamine (serotonin, enteramine) content of structures of the limbic system, *J. Neurochem. 1*, 326–333.

Papez, J. W. (1937): A proposed mechanism of emotion, *Arch. Neurol. Psychiatr. 38*, 725–43.

Penfield, W., and Erickson, T. C. (1941): *Epilepsy and Cerebral Localization*, Springfield.

Penfield, W., and Jasper, H. (1954): *Epilepsy and the Functional Anatomy of the Human Brain*, Boston.

Penfield, W., and Perot, P. (1963): The brain's record of auditory and visual experience. A final summary and discussion, *Brain 86*, 596–696.

Poletti, C. E., Kinnard, M. A., and MacLean, P. D. (1973): Hippocampal influence on unit activity of hypothalamus, preoptic region, and basal forebrain in awake, sitting squirrel monkeys, *J. Neurophysiol. 36*, 308–324.

Poletti, C. E., Sujatanond, M., and Sweet, W. H. (1972): Hypothalamic, preoptic, and basal forebrain unit responses to hippocampal stimulation in awake sitting squirrel monkeys with fornix lesions, *Fed. Proc. 31*, 404.

Pribram, K. H., and MacLean, P. D. (1953): Neuronographic analysis of medial and basal cerebral cortex. II. Monkey, *J. Neurophysiol. 16*, 324–340.

Prichard, J. W., and Glaser, G. H. (1966): Cortical sensory evoked potentials during limbic seizures, *Electroencephalogr. Clin. Neurophysiol. 21*, 180–184.

Ranson, S. W. (1939): Somnolence caused by hypothalamic lesions in the monkey, *Arch. Neurol. Psychiatr. 41*, 1–23.

Sano, K., and Malamud, N. (1953): Clinical significance of sclerosis of the cornu ammonis. Ictal "psychic phenomena," *Arch. Neurol. Psychiatr. 70*, 40–53.

Snyder, M., and Diamond, I. T. (1968): The organization and function of the visual cortex in the tree shrew, *Brain, Behav. Evol. 1*, 244–288.

Spencer, H. (1896): *Principles of Psychology*, New York.

Sudakov, K., MacLean, P. D., Reeves, A. G., and Marino, R. (1971): Unit study of exteroceptive inputs to claustrocortex in awake, sitting, squirrel monkey, *Brain Res. 28*, 19–34.

Van Hoesen, G. W., Pandya, D. N., and Butters, N. (1972): Cortical afferents to the entorhinal cortex of the rhesus monkey, *Science 175*, 1471–1473.

Von Economo, C. (1931): *Encephalitis Lethargica. Its Sequelae and Treatment*, translated by Newman, K. O., London.

Wiener, N. (1948): *Cybernetics, or Control and Communication in the Animal and the Machine*, New York.

Yokota, T., and MacLean, P. D. (1968): Fornix and fifth-nerve interaction on thalamic units in awake, sitting squirrel monkeys, *J. Neurophysiol. 31*, 358–370.

Yokota, T., Reeves, A. G., and MacLean, P. D. (1970): Differential effects of septal and olfactory volleys on intracellular responses of hippocampal neurons in awake, sitting monkeys, *J. Neurophysiol. 33*, 96–107.

Emotions—Their Parameters and Measurement,
edited by L. Levi.
Raven Press, New York © 1975

The Organization and Functions of the Central Sympathetic Nervous System

E. B. Sigg

Department of Neuropharmacology, Hoffmann-La Roche Inc., Nutley, New Jersey 07110

Emotion derives from the Latin *emovire,* meaning to move out. In a free translation emotion is understood to be the "acting out of feelings." In a physiological context it has come to mean a departure from homeostasis that is subjectively experienced by strong feelings (e.g., love, hate, desire, disgust, grief, joy, anger, fear). This "imbalance" manifests itself in neuro-muscular, visceral, and hormonal changes in preparation for overt acts which may or may not be executed. There are two categories of affective behavior: (1) the affect of "basic" needs, sometimes called primary affects, such as hunger, thirst, sex, sleep, wakefulness (in this chapter the primary affects are not elaborated on unless required for clarification of points to be made); (2) secondary affects (or emotions) which are primarily conveyed through the afferent proprioceptive, cutaneous, and sensory inputs, as reflected in our "outer" and inner "Haltung." The "external" posture is effected by the neuromuscular system. Although facial expressions (partly because of the density of facial receptors and the lack of muscle fascia) communicate an extraordinary richness of emotion, man has learned to willfully suppress most neuromuscular expression of his emotions unless he is in some extreme emotional state. In contrast, it is difficult to prevent or control the visceral (and hormonal) consequences of an emotional impact. This fact is forensically and clinically applied to lie detection and the discovery of autonomic disturbances due to vascular, neurological, and psychological disorders by measuring such sensitive parameters as the galvanic skin reflex, local blood flow by plethysmography, heart rate, and respiration.

It is usually only after a relatively sudden departure from homeostasis in either direction that man becomes aware of an autonomic disturbance. Stimuli from the milieu interieur or the environment resulting in responses which trespass homeostatic boundaries undergo a cognitive elaboration. Such stimuli must be "context sensitive" to arouse emotion. This implies complex neural processing, probably involving the neocortex. It is therefore not unexpected that there are reports that sustained control is possible over visceral responses in animals (Herd, Morse, Kelleher, and Jones, 1969; Miller, 1969) and man (Shapiro, Turshy, Gershon, and Stern, 1969) through conditioning techniques. Since the hypothesis (Cannon, 1936) that strong emotions might induce visceral pathology has received ample support, it may be possible to apply these conditionings to the treatment of emotional disorders and their antonomic sequelae.

In man, three types of response measures of affective behavior can be obtained: verbal report, physiological (visceral and somatic) response, and neurohumoral release. In animal experiments the virtual absence of verbal communication does not permit differentiation of finer emotional behavior. When an animal is presented with a "conflict" situation, its performance and autonomic responses change from control. From this we infer that the subject experiences the imposed conflict emotionally. There also are emotion-provoking life events (Holmes and Rahe, 1967) which occurs only in humans (e.g., marriage, jail sentence, being fired from job). Conversely, it is at least conceivable that there are emotions restricted to experience of animals only, thus defying our interpretation. Consequently, only the type of emotional behavior which can be readily interpreted by a response pattern more or less similar to that observed in man (e.g., fight, flight, mating) is open to a comparative analysis.

We cannot even begin to do justice to the many investigators who have elucidated the pivotal role of the autonomic nervous system in emotion. The beginning of intensive studies on anatomical substrates and physiological function underlying emotional behavior in animals was marked by the fundamental observations that reflex stimulation of nociceptive nerves induced sympathetic and somatic effects (Sherrington, 1906), that the cerebral cortex was not necessary for eliciting visceral and somatic concomitants of rage (Bard, 1928; Karplus and Kreidl, 1909), and that electrical stimulation of the diencephalon evoked the "trophotropic" and "ergotropic" syndrome (Hess, 1949; Ranson and Magoun, 1939). The technical achievement of recording preganglionic sympathetic nerve activity (Adrian, Bronk, and Phillips, 1932; Bronk, Ferguson, Margaria, and Solandt, 1936) led to the fundamental knowledge that was to be the basis for modern electrophysiological investigations on the autonomic nervous system. However, with this progress some distinct disadvantages emerged, e.g., certain electrophysiological procedures necessitate anesthesia and/or surgical manipulations (e.g., spinalization, nerve dissection for stimulation or recording) which do not permit and may well interfere with a simultaneous assessment of emotional behavior and its autonomic end organ responses. On the other hand, a more detailed physiological analysis of central functions could now be carried out. Also, it became possible to examine psychopharmacological agents used in emotional disorders in regard to their central mechanism of action uncontaminated by ganglionic or peripheral effects. This approach requires opening of normally closed feedback loops and therefore disturbs homeostasis. Information gained in such preparations has to be placed in context with results obtained from intact organisms in which positive and negative feedback are unobstructed.

It is not intended to present a complete review of studies of the sympathetic nervous system, but rather to summarize the state of the art and elucidate some of the problems that investigators must face in this field of endeavor. Many important contributions have been quoted but an equal number of significant papers have been omitted, either by ignorance or willful neglect. With these limitations in mind, we shall examine the central representation of the autonomic nervous system underlying emotional behavior. Emphasis will be placed on the physiology of the sympathetic nervous system, excluding the well-known ganglionic and peripheral aspects.

I. THE SPONTANEOUS PREGANGLIONIC ACTIVITY

The majority of the preganglionic pool of sympathetic neurons is located in the intermedio-lateral cell column (Santini and Noback, 1971). These spinal sympathetic neurons are characterized by a short (20 to 60 msec) hyperpolarization and therefore rapid recovery of their excitability (Fernandez de Molina, Juno, and Perl, 1965). The absence of collateral inhibition distinguishes them from motorhorn cells. From these neurons the preganglionic trunk is formed in which four groups of fibers can be recognized on the basis of different conduction velocities (Eccles, 1935; Grundfest, 1939). It is unusual that sympathetic neurons of the spinal cord can only be activated by electrophoretically applied 5-HT but not by acetylcholine or norepinephrine (DeGroat and Ryall, 1967).

The spontaneous unitary discharge rate in preganglionic sympathetic fibers is low and varies from 0.2 to 4 cps (Jänig and Schmidt, 1970; Kaufman and Koizumi, 1971; Koizumi and Sato, 1972). The tonic activity is greatly dependent on inputs from afferents such as the chemoreceptors (Gernandt, Liljestrand, and Zotterman, 1946), certain somatic afferents (Johansson, 1962), and some visceral afferents (Franz, Evans, and Perl, 1966). That sympathetic outflow is also dependent on supraspinal structures is indicated by the reduction of activity after spinalization.

Several different periodicities occur in sympathetic nerves. Most prominent is the cycling that occurs in phase with the respiratory cycle, in which sympathetic nerve activity increases with inspiration and decreases with expiration. This may be indicative of synaptic connections between respiratory and sympathetic neurons (Cohen and Gootman, 1970). In the splanchnic nerve (but rarely or not at all in the cervical sympathetic nerve) rhythms in a 1:1 relationship with the cardiac cycle can be seen maximally discharging in early diastole. This rhythm arises from the inhibitory influence of baroceptor input (Downing and Siegel, 1963; Koizumi, Seller, Kaufman, and Brooks, 1971). A ubiquitous 10 Hz periodicity, often synchronized with the cardiac cycle in 3:1 fashion, has been described in the splanchnic (Cohen and Gootman, 1970) and the inferior cardiac nerve (Green and Heffron, 1967). Other oscillations and irregular "bursting" have also been noted (Weidinger and Leschhorn, 1964).

Preganglionic activity includes discharges of fibers innervating different structures. Thus, the cervical sympathetic nerve carries messages to the pupil, blood vessels of the head, carotid sinus, and the nictitating membrane. On the other hand, it is generally accepted that splanchnic discharges represent predominantly vasoconstrictor fibers although nonvascular structures such as intestinal smooth muscle are also innervated by the splanchnic nerve. This assumption is based within certain limits on the linear relationship between splanchnic discharge and blood pressure. The postganglionic renal nerve also follows such a relationship. It is of functional significance to recognize not only the existence of such regional differences (Löfving, 1961) but also variations in the same nerve depending on the destination of the fibers under study.

II. INTEGRATION AT THE SPINAL AND BRAINSTEM LEVEL

It has been known for a long time that electrical stimulation of afferent nerves elicits autonomic responses such as changes in heart rate, pupil size, blood pressure, and gastrointestinal motility. The type of afferent fibers involved was analyzed with electrophysiological techniques (Johansson, 1962; Laporte, Bessou, and Bouisset, 1960). Large fiber afferents (Group I) do not contribute to a reflex vasoconstrictor response, whereas activation of intermediate fibers [mediating nociceptive and flexor reflexes (Groups II, III)] results in depressor or pressor effects depending on whether low or high frequency stimulation is employed. The C-fibers (Group IV) produce only pressor responses. The reflex transmission of these different inputs has been clarified only in recent years and is illustrated in Fig. 1.

In a lightly anesthetized cat stimulation of Group II/III fibers elicits a reflex response in preganglionic sympathetic nerves, which consists of three components, an early, a late, and an ultra-late discharge (Kaufman and Koizumi, 1971; Koizumi, Sato, Kaufman, and Brooks, 1968; Sato, 1972a,b; Sato, Tsushima, and Fujimori, 1965; Sato, Sato, Ozawa, and Fujimori, 1967). The *early* reflex, occurring with a latency of 10 to 35 msec and having a central delay of 8 to 15 msec (Beacham and Perl, 1964a,b), is segmental in character and shows a decremental response with increasing distance from the entry pool. The reflex occurs in acutely spinalized animals. It is not followed by inhibition. In chronic spinal preparations previously unexcitable muscle afferents (Group II) elicit a sympathetic efferent response. This may be due to excitability changes due to removal of supraspinal structures (Sato, Kaufman, Koizumi, and Brooks, 1969). The *late* reflex is activated by Groups II/III visceral, cutaneous, and muscle afferents (Iwamura, Uchino, Ozawa, and Kudo, 1969) and has a latency of 60 to 120 msec depending on where the recording site is located. Spinalization abolishes the late response, but it is still present in the decerebrate preparation, indicating that it involves a spino-bulbo-spinal pathway. The late reflex is more labile and more generalized than the early spinal response and, in contrast to the latter, is followed by a silent period of long duration (400 to 800 msec). The *ultra-late* reflex (Kaufman and Koizumi, 1971; Sato, 1972*a,b*), with a latency of 200 to 300 msec, involves pathways reaching into suprapontine structures, inasmuch as the reflex fails to appear after decerebration just rostral to the pons. Both late reflexes are sensitive to anesthetics and other CNS depressants.

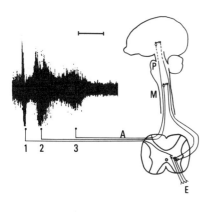

FIG. 1. Sympathetic reflex discharges in the cat. Anesthesia: chloralose, 60 mg/kg i.v., gallamine triethiodide. The potential of the ipsilateral splanchnic nerve is recorded in response to sural nerve stimulation with maximal single shocks (10 superimposed traces). The diagram represents the relay stations accounting for the early reflex (1, relay in spinal cord); the late reflex (2, relay in the medulla oblongata); and the ultra-late reflex (3, relay in the suprapontine region). Abbreviations: A, afferents; E, efferents; M, medulla oblongata; P, pons. Time scale: 100 msec. The synaptic symbols are *not* an indication of the number of synapses involved. All three pathways are multisynaptic. For clearer illustration the pathways are indicated as crossed.

A significant characteristic of sympathetic reflex function is the "silent" period which follows excitation of neurons in the supraspinal reflex. It is dependent on the reticular formation and is modulated by respiration. Its duration is from 400 to 800 msec. It is functionally important in that the silent period determines the discharge pattern and therefore the endorgan response to repetitive reflex stimuli. Thus, vascular depressor effects are related to the silent period (Fedina, Katunskii, Khayutin, and Mitsanyi, 1966). It is noteworthy that reflex responses arising from C-fibers break through the silent period. Their long latency (500 to 600 msec) would also favor a supraspinal pathway (Koizumi, Collin, Kaufman, and Brooks, 1970; Sato, 1972*b*). However, these C-reflexes can apparently be recorded in chronic spinal animals (Horeyseck and Jänig, 1972). Since the C-fibers are mediating pain responses, it is of functional significance that they be transmitted even during the block of Groups II/III input.

III. SUPRASPINAL CONTROLS

A. The Brainstem

The medulla oblongata is organized to form functional pools serving specific endorgans, to integrate somatic-autonomic mechanisms, and to provide inhibitory and facilitatory connections for input-output functions.

It is not my purpose to discuss the extensive literature on brainstem control of autonomic functions. Plots of brainstem coordinates which on stimulation evoke changes in endorgan responses (e.g., gastrointestinal motility, blood pressure, heart rate, pupil size, respiration, a.o.) indicate extensive intermingling of excitatory and inhibitory points as well as of end organ representation, so that no precise association of any function to specific nuclei or pathways can be made. Inhibitory modulation of sympathetic efferent activity, while virtually absent in the spinal cord, has been found in the brainstem. Sympathetic discharges (in renal nerve) are inhibited by stimulation of the tractus solitarius and midline areas ventral to the hypoglossal nucleus (Scherrer, 1966). The early and late reflex discharges in sympathetic efferents are also inhibited by direct midline medullar stimulation (Coote and Downman, 1969; Coote and Weber, 1969; Kirchner, Sato, and Weidinger, 1971). Recently the importance of this area in mediating powerful baroceptor influences has been recognized. Thus, medial lesions in the medulla oblongata block the pathways of baroreceptor and vagal reflexes which funnel through this medial region (Chai and Wang, 1968; Manning, 1965), whereas the excitatory input passes directly to the more laterally situated areas. Indeed, baroreceptor activation inhibits spontaneous and reflex sympathetic activity in all efferent sympathetic nerves so far studied (Koizumi et al., 1971). This is illustrated in Fig. 2 in

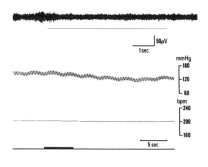

FIG. 2. Sympathetic inhibition induced by vagal afferent stimulation in the cat. Anesthesia: prehypothalamic decerebration under methoxyflurane; gallamine triethiodide, 7 mg/kg i.v. Right vagus intact; central end of cut left vagus stimulated. Top tracing: splanchnic nerve discharges; middle tracing: blood pressure; bottom tracing: heart rate. Stimulation (bar) with 12 V pulses of 0.1 msec duration at 30 Hz for 5 sec. *Note:* Lowering of blood pressure following inhibition of splanchnic discharges. Peripheral vagal effects on heart rate were blocked by gallamine; consequently, there is no change in heart rate.

which vagal afferents (containing baroreceptors) were stimulated. Slow adaptation of the receptors occurs, however, when high sinus pressures are maintained. Other viscero-visceral reflexes arising from baroreceptors in the auricles (Brooks and Lu, 1972) and in the kidneys (Beacham and Kunze, 1969), and receptors in the adrenal gland (Niijima and Winter, 1968a,b) and other areas (e.g., pulmonary arteries) may account for the fact that sinoaortic denervation does not completely abolish the depressor reflex induced by large doses of norepinephrine (Kirchner et al., 1971).

Anatomical as well as abundant electrophysiological evidence (Cottle,

1964; Rhoton, Oleary, and Ferguson, 1966; Humphrey, 1967; Crill and Reis, 1968; Miura and Reis, 1968, 1969; Sampson and Biscoe, 1968) indicates that direct projections from the carotid sinus and the aortic depressor nerves pass to the solitary tract nucleus and to the paramedian reticular nucleus. Destruction of the solitary tract nucleus abolishes all reflex blood pressure and heart rate responses to electrical or natural baroreceptor stimulation, whereas a lesion in the paramedian reticular nucleus obliterates only the depressor response to carotid sinus stimulation. Although the functional role of this dual system is not clear yet (Miura and Reis, 1972), the pathways described are of great significance. The sino-aortic inhibitory input is of particular importance, not only in the reflex regulation of respiration (Biscoe, 1971), circulation (Heymans and Neil, 1958), and the sleep-wakefulness cycle (Baust and Heinemann, 1967), but also in the modulation of emotional expression (Baccelli, Guazzi, Libretti, and Zanchetti, 1965).

Since cholinergic fibers are not involved in the depressor reflex (Uvnäs, 1960), the fibers studied are most likely of the vasoconstrictor type. No detailed knowledge is available about sudomotor, pilomotor, and cholinergic dilator nerves.

B. The Diencephalon

The designation of those parts of the "Zwischenhirn" as thalamus and hypothalamus was prophetic. In Greek, thalamus meant an inaccessible part of the house, such as the bedroom, the pantry, private armory, or the nuptial chamber. Is it therefore surprising that Hess should have found sleep, hyperphagia, and aggressive behavior, whereas MacLean, Ploog, and Robinson, (1960) described sociosexual behavior on stimulation of these regions? The hypothalamus can be functionally divided into two areas: an anterior region encompassing the trophotropic zone and a posterior area from which, together with the "ergotropic" syndrome, emotional behavior such as defensive and attack behavior can be elicited (Fig. 3) (Hess and Brügger, 1943; Hess, 1949, 1952; Hess and Akert, 1955).

Whether the response involves emotion is controversial. Masserman (1950) claimed that the aggressive behavior is not directed, is inappropriate to the environmental situation, and is entirely stimulus-bound and can be conditioned. He concluded that the hypothalamus mediated sympathetic and coordinated motor manifestations of emotion but was not concerned with emotional experience. Hess, on the other hand, was convinced that the animals' reaction did not differ from that under natural conditions. Further analysis (Bandler and Flynn, 1972) revealed two types of attack behavior: (a) an attack independent of environment, including autonomic effects, vocalization, and postural changes (Hess and Brügger, 1943; Hunsperger, 1956; Nakao, 1958; Wasman and Flynn, 1962); (b) a reflex such as head-

FIG. 3. The "trophotropic" and "ergotropic" areas of the hypothalamus. Points which on stimulation yield an increase (□) or decrease (■) in blood pressure, an increase (△) or decrease (▲) in respiration, and a widening (○) or narrowing (●) of the pupils were projected on a sagittal section 1.2 mm from the midline. The symbols were transferred from pp. 56–59 of the *Functional Organization of the Diencephalon,* by W. R. Hess (1949) to a simplified redrawing of the appropriate section of Berman's atlas, *The Brainstem of the Cat* (1968). *Note* that there is extensive overlapping of different functions. The two unlabeled outlines designate the areas from which defense reactions (anterior) and attack behavior (posterior) can be elicited. Abbreviations: AC, anterior commissure; H, hypophysis; MB, mammillary bodies; O.Ch, optic chiasma; P, pons; PC, posterior commissure; RN, red nucleus; Thal, thalamus.

turning and biting evoked by touching the area around the mouth and a jaw-opening elicited by visual presentation of a prey (MacDonnell and Flynn, 1966a,b; Bandler and Flynn, 1971). This suggested that aggression may be elicited by widening the tactile receptive field and, thereby, facilitating sensory input by means of low intensity stimulation of the hypothalamus. This finding is not unprecedented. Stimulation of the pyramidal tract also increases the area of excitatory receptive fields of neurons in the somatosensory cortex of the cat (Adkins, Morse, and Towe, 1966).

It is, however, through anatomical and electrophysiological studies that we learn more about the mechanism underlying emotional behavior. The hypothalamus receives its input from the limbic system, the thalamus, and the brainstem. Its efferents are almost reciprocally connected to the same areas. These important anatomical connections are summarized in Tables 1 and 2.

The afferent system to the hypothalamus which has its orgin in the limbic system and thalamus (Table 1) is not the subject of our discussion, although these telencephalic influences are of greatest functional significance in modulating behavioral, somatic, and autonomic functions (Gloor, 1956). Their exploration has resulted in the discovery of important *inhibitory* influences, based on the fact of two anatomically and functionally different pathways from the amygdala to the ventromedial nucleus of the hypothalamus (Dreifuss, Murphy, and Gloor, 1968). Thus, inhibition of spontaneous cell firing in the ventromedial hypothalamic nucleus by amygdaloid stimulation is mediated by bipolar cells lying at the lateral edge of this nucleus (Murphy and Renaud, 1969) and not by lateral hypothalamic stimulation, thus challenging the widely held opinion that the lateral hypothalamus controls many functions by a negative feedback arrangement with the ventromedial nucleus. The involvement of the ventromedial nucleus in

TABLE 1. *Afferents to the hypothalamus*

	Origin	Destination
From brainstem:		
1. Dorsal longitudinal fasciculus (Schütz)	Mesencephalic central gray, dorsal tegmental nucl.	Caudal and dorsal areas of hypothalamus
2. Mammillary peduncle	Ventral tegmentum and dorsal tegmental nucl.	Lateral hypothalamic nucl. Mammillary nucl.
3. Reticulo-hypothalamic pathways	a. subthalamic region b. ventromedial mid-brain tegmentum	Lateral hypothalamus Lateral preoptic area
From forebrain:		
1. Fornix		
a. precommissural	Hippocampus to septum to MFB	Lateral preoptic area
b. postcommissural	Hippocampus	Lateral and dorsal hypothalamic area; Mammillary nucl.
2. Amygdalo-fugal pathways		
a. stria terminalis	Amygdala	Lateral hypothalamus
b. ventral amygdalo-fugal pathway	Amygdala, olfactory tubercle	Lateral hypothalamus Medio-dorsal thalamic nucl.
3. Medial forebrain bundle (MFB)	Olfactory tubercle Septal area, pyriform cortex	Lateral preoptic area (and caudal to it)

feeding behavior (Anand and Brobeck, 1951), cardiovascular activity (Smith and Nathan, 1964), mating behavior (MacLean et al., 1960), gonadotropin (Sawyer, 1957), growth hormone release (Newman, Roberts, Frohman, and Bernardis, 1967), and emotional expression (Bard, 1928; Wasman and Flynn, 1962) points to the potential functional influence of this amygdaloid inhibitory system. It is supplemented by other inhibitory inputs from the dorsal hippocampus, septum, and cingular cortex. Stimulation of these areas has led to suppression of attack behavior (Egger and Flynn, 1963; Siegel and Flynn, 1968; Siegel and Skog, 1970; Siegel and Chabora, 1971) with an inhibition of a wide range of autonomic responses.

The "upstream" efferent connections of the hypothalamus leading to the septum, amygdala, and thalamus are shown in Table 2 but will not be considered further. It is surprising that, in view of the finding that the hypothalamus appears to modulate sensory input, the primary sensory representation (e.g., auditory, visual, somesthetic) of the neocortex has (anatomically) no direct access to the hypothalamus. An exception is the olfactory input which reaches the preoptic hypothalamic zone via olfactory tubercle-pyriform cortex–medial forebrain bundle. Evidence for indirect sensory input into the hypothalamus is ample. Thus, unilateral lesions in the lateral hypothalamus (in rats) cause deficits in orientation to contra-

TABLE 2. *Efferents of the hypothalamus*

	Origin	Destination
To forebrain:		
1. Medial forebrain bundle	Lateral hypothalamus	Lateral part of septum
2. Amygdalo-hypothalamic connections (ventral pathway and stria medullaris)	Lateral hypothalamic area around anterior commissure	Central amygdal. nucl. Medial part of basal nucl.
To brainstem:		
1. Medial forebrain bundle	Area lateralis to mammillary bodies	Area dorsal to mammillary bodies; central gray and nucl. centralis tegmentum superior
2. Stria medullaris	Lateral preoptic area	Lateral habenular nucl.; paramedian mesencephalic area; mediodorsal thalamic nucl.
3. Dorsal longitudinal fasciculus	Ventromedial and posterior hypothalamic nucl.	Dorsal tegmental nucl.; to visceral motor cell groups of brainstem
4. Mammillo-thalamic tract	Mammillary bodies	Anterior thalamic nucl. (to cingulate gyrus)
5. Mammillo-tegmental tract	Mammillary bodies	Dorsal and ventral nucl. of Gudden
6. Mammillo-subthalamic tract	Mammillary bodies	Via Forel's fields into subthalamic region

lateral visual, olfactory, and somatosensory stimuli or, as it is sometimes called, the syndrome of sensory neglect (Marshall, Turner, and Teitelbaum, 1971). Such lesions have a profound consequence for feeding and attack behavior, as this is the area from which overeating and killing are elicited. They confirm the finding that cutting trigeminal afferents eliminates the biting attack (MacDonnell and Flynn, 1966a) and disables rats to locate food (Welker, 1963). Hess (1943) had previously observed that hypothalamic lesions produced inattention to proprioceptive and visual stimuli opposite to the site of the lesion. These deficits are not due to motor impairment.

More directly, light-evoked potentials have been recorded in the dorsolateral hypothalamic area (Bogacz and Wilson, 1969). The responses are comparable to those ascribed to somatosensory (Feldman, Heide, and Porter, 1959), auditory (Rudomin, Malliani, Berlone, and Zanchetti, 1965), and other afferent stimulation (Norgren, 1970; Richard, 1970; Wyrwicka and Chase, 1970). Single unit studies have confirmed a rich inflow of visual, auditory, olfactory, gustatory, and somatosensory information into the posterior (Dafny and Feldman, 1970) and ventromedial areas (Campbell, Bindra, Krebs, and Ferenchak, 1969). Whether or not the different sensory modalities converge on a single unit is immaterial since intensive inter-actions can be efficiently effected through interneurons. It has also been emphasized that the neural circuits mediating such behavior as drinking, eating, and gnawing (Morgane, 1961a,b; Tenen and Miller, 1964; Coons, Levak, and Miller, 1965; Roberts and Carey, 1965; Steinbaum and Miller, 1965; Mogenson and Stevenson, 1966, 1967; Mendelson, 1967) are specific. This has been contested (Valenstein, Cox, and Kakolewski, 1968) on the basis of evidence that stimulus-bound "drinkers" (rats) appear equally motivated to get food. It seems at present reasonable to assume that there is a certain plasticity in the neural links, thus limiting a high degree of specificity. It is more significant to recognize the high degree of integration which the sensory input into the hypothalamus receives. The wide variety of emotional stimuli leading to an increase in hypothalamic activity (par-ticularly the ventromedial area) can inhibit activity generated by the internal state of the organism, e.g., eating and mating, and divert the subject to other (emotional) behavior (Krasne, 1962; Grossman, 1966). The sub-strates for conveying most of the extralemniscal sensory messages to the hypothalamus to arouse emotion are represented by the three major ascend-ing pathways: the medial forebrain bundle, the dorsal longitudinal fascicu-lus, and the diffuse reticulo-hypothalamic pathway.

At this point it should be noted that visceral afferents, representing the splanchnic and vagal input, also converge in the hypothalamus. Slower fibers of the former reach the hypothalamus via spinothalamic tract-central gray and the fasciculus longitudinalis dorsalis. The vagal fibers travel through the solitary tract to the dorsal nucleus Gudden to join the dorsal longitudinal fasciculus.

It is the "downward" influence of the hypothalamus which now has to be examined more closely in order to provide the basis for an understand-ing of the efferent mechanisms underlying emotional behavior and, in par-ticular, its autonomic manifestations. As Table 2 illustrates, there are several pathways, some spatially well separated from each other, with diffuse terminations. Figure 4 shows the extent of degeneration of a diffuse fiber system after a lesion in the hypothalamus. Functionally, this indicates a system with a great safety factor, which guarantees the successful execution of commands. Consequently, discrete medial or lateral lesions in the central gray or mesencephalic tegmentum have little effect on hypothalamic out-flow (Zanchetti, 1967). It does not, however, necessarily imply that sym-pathetic outflow is nonspecific. Sympathetic activation of multiple but selective pathways controlling the pupil and nictitating membrane have recently been described (Koss and Wang, 1972). It has also been sug-gested on the basis of regional blood flow changes during stimulation of the mesencephalon that functionally different effector organs are influenced by sympathetic activation (Löfving, 1961; Ueda, Inque, Iuzuka, Iuzuka, Ihori, and Yasuda, 1966). On the other hand, patterns of sympathetic im-

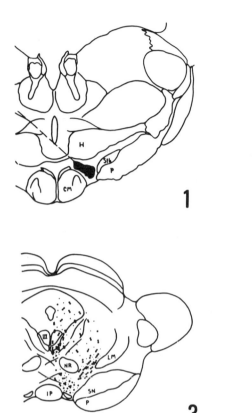

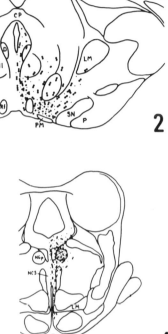

FIG. 4. Degeneration of fibers descending from a lesion site in the lateral hypothalamic area (cat). Frontal sections, rostral to caudal (1 to 4). Abbreviations: CM, corpus mammillare; CP, commissura posterior; D, nucleus Darkschewitsch; IP, interpeduncular nucleus; LM, medial lemniscus; NCS, nucleus centralis tegmenti superior (Bechterew); NGd, nucleus tegmenti dorsalis; NGp, nucleus tegmenti neutralis; NI, nucleus interstitialis; NR, red nucleus; P, cerebral peduncle; SN, substantia nigra. (Reproduced in part from Nauta, W. J. H. and Haymaker, W., with permission of the publisher.)

pulses in nerves to the heart and kidney have shown that there is no specificity in tonic sympathetic innervation (Schaefer, 1960; Weidinger and Fedina, 1960). In a more recent investigation, stimulation of discrete hypothalamic points did not demonstrate representation of functionally different, organ-specific areas. Nevertheless, the degree of contribution of stimulus effects to the four organs (heart, spleen, kidney, and skeletal muscle) varied (Ninomiya, Judy, and Wilson, 1970). It is therefore reasonable to assume that specific inputs into the sympathetic system can generate not only localized but also diffuse responses, although the latter may be quantitatively different from each other.

Bronk, Pitts, and Larrabee (1940) first described the fact that hypothalamic stimulation altered the firing rate of cardiac accelerating fibers. After a delay of some 2 sec the blood pressure usually starts to rise. During the progress of repetitive stimulation (particularly at frequencies over 20 cps), an inhibition of discharges may follow the activation which, depending on the intensity, outlasts the duration of stimulation (Fig. 5). Although

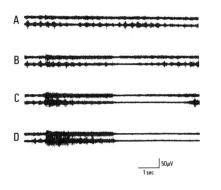

FIG. 5. Effect of hypothalamic stimulation on spontaneous cervical sympathetic and splanchnic nerve discharges (cat). Anesthesia: chloralose 30 mg/kg i.v.; decamethonium 4 mg/kg i.v. Upper trace, cervical preganglionic sympathetic nerve; lower trace, splanchnic nerve. The hypothalamus (coordinates: Fr. 9, Lat. 2, D. −2) was stimulated with 0.5 msec pulses at 50 Hz for 3 sec: A, 5 V; B, 10 V; C, 15 V; D, 20 V. *Note* that during stimulation with low intensity (A) the "bursts" in the splanchnic nerve are partially inhibited; higher intensities of stimulation lead to an increase in nerve activity followed by a progressively longer post-stimulatory inhibition in both nerves as well as inhibition during stimulation.

no systematic search for hypothalamic points eliciting inhibition without prior activation has been made by us, it appears to be a common experience that inhibition *per se* cannot be readily elicited (Pitts, Larrabee, and Bronk, 1941; Scherrer, 1962). Short trains of stimuli (and, less successfully, single stimuli) evoke potentials in respective preganglionic nerves (Fig. 6). The latencies, however, differ considerably (Koizumi et al., 1968). Single stimuli

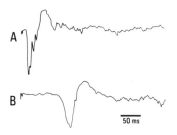

FIG. 6. Evoked responses in the cervical sympathetic and splanchnic nerve (cat). Anesthesia: chloralose 60 mg/kg i.v.; decamethonium 4 mg/kg i.v. Stimulation of hypothalamus (coordinates: Fr. 9, Lat. 2, D. −2) with pulses of 0.4 msec duration at 15 V. The average evoked response of 16 sweeps is illustrated. A, preganglionic cervical sympathetic nerve; B, splanchnic nerve. *Note* the difference in latency between the two responses and the greater temporal dispersion in the splanchnic nerve.

elicit a very short lasting post-excitatory depression followed by decaying oscillations (Gootman, 1967).

The post-stimulatory inhibition following hypothalamic stimulation is of greatest functional significance in the operation of the negative feedback loop of visceral functions. This negative feedback competes with the hypothalamic efferent discharges in a complex manner which also involves the parasympathetic system. During maintenance of homeostasis, there is generally a reciprocal relationship between parasympathetic and sympathetic activity in peripheral organs dually innervated (e.g., heart, pupil, intestines, bladder). Over several hours of observations splanchnic nerves discharge reciprocally with vagal nerves (Koizumi and Suda, 1963). When the blood pressure rises, sympathetic discharges diminish and simultaneously, although slower in reaction, vagal activity increases, and vice versa (Weidinger, Hetzel, and Schaefer, 1962). A quick saline injection into the jugular vein inhibits the cardiac sympathetic impulses but increases those in the vagus (Okada, Okamoto, and Nisida, 1961). The traditional concept of reciprocal changes in both divisions of the autonomic system has been contested and appears not always to apply. Thus, it has been found that when blood pressure rises the resulting bradycardia is mediated by the vagus with the sympathetic system playing no detectable role; vice versa, the tachycardia induced by hypotension is primarily mediated by increased sympathetic activity (Glick and Braunwald, 1965). Other deviations from the principle of reciprocity also imply simultaneous discharges in the sympathetic and parasympathetic system under certain conditions (for references see Gellhorn, 1967). However, in an emergency, emotional or physical, the sympathetic outflow has precedence over any other activity (e.g., baroreceptor reflexes; Gebber and Snyder, 1970). Consequently, heart rate and blood pressure increase. This is effectively achieved by inhibition of the negative feedback input. Thus, hypothalamic stimulation inhibits the carotid sinus reflex, the effects of which are a reduction of sympathetic vasoconstrictor tone and vagal heart slowing (Gebber and Snyder, 1970; Hilton, 1963). The mechanism by which this control takes place may be presynaptic inhibition. Primary afferent depolarization has been implicated in the increased excitability of carotid sinus afferents in response to conditioning stimuli in the posterior hypothalamus (Weiss and Crill, 1969). This interaction is complicated by the fact that only the baroceptor reflex on the heart is suppressed while the reflex modulation of the vascular bed is maintained (Djojosugito, Folkow, Kylstra, Lisander, and Tuttle, 1970). This differentiated interaction between hypothalamic activation and cardiac depression of baroreceptor reflexes helps to provide sufficient blood flow to skeletal muscles and, for the same neurogenic drive on the heart, more cardiac output and a relatively lower workload for the left ventricle is gained (Kylstra and Lisander, 1970). At this point it is necessary to consider other visceral reflex activities associated with hypothalamic excitation. The inhibition of the carotid sinus reflex has already been mentioned. The autonomic vagal efferent discharges are usually present above 140 mm Hg of arterial pressure (or after epinephrine injection) reflecting the input from sino-aortic pressure receptors. The reflex can also be recorded as an evoked potential in the vagus, appearing in response to carotid sinus nerve stimulation after a latency of 60 msec (Iriuchijima and Kumada, 1963). Both spontaneous (Fig. 7) and evoked potentials in the

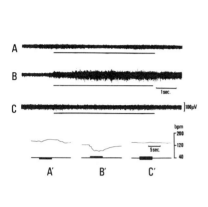

FIG. 7. The inhibitory effect of hypothalamic stimulation on the activation of autonomic vagal efferents by stimulation of the aortic depressor nerve (cat). Anesthesia: spinalized at C_1 under methoxyflurane; decamethonium 4 mg/kg i.v. Left vagus intact. Stimulation parameters (indicated by heavy bar): *Hypothalamus* at Fr. 9, Lat. −2, D. −2; 12 V, 0.1 msec, 50 Hz for 5 sec. *Aortic depressor nerve:* 20 V, 0.5 msec pulse duration, 50 Hz for 5 sec. A,A′, effect of hypothalamic stimulation on vagal outflow (A) and heart rate (A′). *Note* slight inhibition of discharge with a small increase in heart rate. B,B′, effect of aortic depressor nerve stimulation on vagal discharge (B) and heart rate (B′). *Note* increase in vagal firing and bradycardia. C,C′, effect of simultaneous stimulation of hypothalamus and aortic depressor nerve. *Note* inhibition of vagal discharge (C) and reflex bradycardia (C′).

vagus nerve are diminished during stimulation of the hypothalamus. Stimulation of the same area (and extending caudally into the mesencephalic reticular formation) also inhibits parasympathetic outflow from the pupillo-constrictor neurons as recorded by an inhibition of short ciliary nerve activity in sympathectomized cats (Fig. 8). These findings are also re-

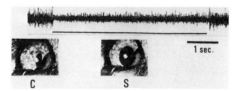

FIG. 8. Parasympathetic inhibition of ciliary nerve activity during stimulation of the mesencephalic reticular formation (cat). Anesthesia: pentobarbital 30 mg/kg i.v.; gallamine triethiodide 7 mg/kg i.v.; spinalization at C_1; bilateral cervical sympathectomy. Stimulation coordinates: Fr. 2/Lat. 2/D. ± 0. Stimulation parameters: 50 Hz, 0.01 msec. duration, 8 V for 5 sec. Photographs of the sympathectomized eye: left, control (C); right, during stimulation of MRF (S). *Note* inhibition of nerve activity and pupil dilation during stimulation.

flected in end organ responses (gastric relaxation, a rise in heart rate, and pupil dilation) of spinalized animals with intact vagi (Sigg and Sigg, 1966). It is not known whether other outflows (e.g., salivary or pelvic) are also inhibited by hypothalamic stimulation. There is evidence, at least in regard to the inhibition of parasympathetic outflow from the Edinger-Westphal nuclei, that the inhibition involves an adrenergic mechanism. This is substantiated by the finding that it is difficult to elicit pupil dilation by para-sympathetic inhibition after blocking norepinephrine synthesis or depleting amines from the brain by α-methyl-p-tyrosine or reserpine, respectively. The discovery of an abundance of fluorescent fibers in the area of the Edinger-Westphal and the vagal nuclei also lends circumstantial support to the above mentioned findings (Dahlström, Fuxe, Hillarp, and Malmfors, 1964). We have therefore proposed the theory that stimulation of the hypothalamus imposes an aminergically operated inhibitory brake on all preganglionic parasympathetic outflow. Parenthetically, the redundancy of such a mechanism is evident from its presence in the periphery where it is known that adrenergic mechanisms inhibit ganglionic transmission (e.g., in the urinary bladder; Saum and DeGroat, 1972) and may exert effects opposite to those observed from cholinergic stimulation at postsynaptic receptor sites.

IV. CHEMICAL MODULATION OF CENTRAL SYMPATHETIC FUNCTION

The chemical transmission of sympathetic impulses originating in the brainstem and diencephalon are, in contrast to the peripheral autonomic nervous system, little known. Analysis of putative transmitter substances and of histofluorescent tracing of amine-containing pathways, the effect of these substances on neural activity after electrophoretic administration, and the observation of functional changes after topical application have been the main tools of investigators.

Lesions in the medial forebrain bundle (Andén, Dahlström, Fuxe, and Larsson, 1965) and in the ventral part of the mesencephalic tegmentum (Andén, Dahlström, Fuxe, Olson, and Ungerstedt, 1966) cause a loss of nearly 75% of norepinephrine in the diencephalon of the operated side. In the hypothalamus, specifically the dorsomedial nucleus, the para- and peri-ventricular nuclei are involved. The fibers arise mostly from nuclei in the pons and medulla oblongata. The remaining terminals, still containing norepinephrine after caudal mesencephalic lesions, presumably arise from axons originating in cell bodies of the formatio reticularis mesencephali. There are also ascending 5-HT fibers to the diencephalon (Dahlström and Fuxe, 1964). These 5-HT fibers originate in the raphe nuclei and enter the median forebrain bundle. Lesions in this bundle deplete 5-HT hypothalamic neurons (Andén et al., 1965). Norepinephrine and 5-HT depletion after lesions in the medial forebrain bundle and in the midbrain tegmentum have been reported by others (Heller, Harvey, and Moore, 1962; Heller and Moore, 1965; Moore and Heller, 1967). Figure 9 illustrates the complex arrangement of several distinct aminergic pathways in the medial forebrain bundle of the cat. It indicates the presence of a dorsal and ventral norepi-nephrine bundle. The former's destination is the cortex and hippocampus,

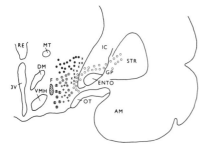

FIG. 9. Biochemically distinct pathways in the medial forebrain bundle of the cat. Frontal section at the level of the ventromedial nucleus of the hypothalamus. Abbreviations: 3 V, third ventricle; RE, nucleus reuniens; MT, tractus mammillothalamicus; DM, nucleus hypothal. dorsomedialis; VMH, nucleus hypothal. ventromedialis; F, fornix; OT, tract. opticus; ENTO, tract. entopeduncularis; IC, capsula interna; STR, neostriatum; GP, globus pallidus; AM, amygdala. ● dorsal noradrenergic system; ⊙ ventral noradrenergic system; ⊗ medial serotonergic system; + lateral serotonergic system; ○ nigrostriatal dopamine system; × mesolimbic dopamine system. (Reproduced in part from Morgane, P. J., and Stern, W. C. (1972), by permission of the publisher.)

the latter ends in hypothalamic and preoptic norepinephrine terminals, and therefore appears of importance in the regulation of autonomic functions. The finding of a dense innervation of the solitary tract nuclei and the dorsal vagal motor nuclei, as well as of the sympathetic lateral column in the spinal cord (Fuxe, 1965), points to the role of the central NE-neuron system in cardiovascular function (Bolme, Fuxe, and Lidbrink, 1972).

Cholinergic systems have also been described (Shute and Lewis, 1967). Acetylcholine axons of dorsal hypothalamic neurons reach the globus pallidus; other axons go from the supramammillary area to the mammillary bodies. An important ascending cholinergic system coming from the ventral tegmentum reaches the lateral preoptic area via the median forebrain bundle. No descending cholinergic pathways were found in the median forebrain bundle.

To relate the above findings to function is difficult. Electrophoretically applied acetylcholine, norepinephrine, and 5-HT reveal that neurons sensitive to these substances are distributed throughout the hypothalamus without regional specificity (Bloom, Oliver, and Salmoiraghi, 1963). Since endogenous amines and acetylcholinesterase are *not* similarly distributed in the hypothalamus (Shute and Lewis, 1966), it may be assumed that there are receptors for amines and acetylcholine in the hypothalamus unrelated to possible transmitter function. In this respect they resemble hypothalamic receptors for exogenous circulating hormones and temperature.

When applied in small quantities to specific hypothalamic sites, norepinephrine and acetylcholine can alter emotional behavior. The abundant literature permits us to cite only a few examples. Injection of norepinephrine into the perifornical area elicits eating in satiated rats (Slangen and Miller, 1969). Local administration into the preoptic area of 6-hydroxydopamine also induces eating in satiated rats. However, repeated injections of the latter cause less and less eating as the release of norepinephrine diminishes with the progressive depletion of the transmitter (Evetts, Fitzsimons, and Setler, 1972). Indirect evidence for a modulation of emotional behavior by norepinephrine has been obtained by administration of amine precursors and agents influencing amine metabolism. Thus, it has been demonstrated that L-DOPA produces an intense state of behavioral excitement in cats when MAO is inhibited. The observed behavior has many of the autonomic and somatic characteristics of sham rage or the defensive reaction with hissing, snarling, and tail lashing. However, the drug-excited cats are oblivious to their environment, in contrast to excitement occurring naturally or by evoked electrical brain stimulation. Measurement of the norepinephrine concentration in the brainstem indicates that the release or availability of norepinephrine is necessary for the appearance of this behavior (Reis, Moorhead, and Merlino, 1970). It does not occur if dopamine is selectively accumulated by administering L-DOPA with a decarboxylase inhibitor (Sigg, Keim, and Horst, 1973). These findings agree with the observation that prolonged intermittent stimulation of the amygdala, eliciting sham rage, is accompanied by a decrease of norepinephrine in the brain (Fuxe and Gunne, 1964; Reis and Gunne, 1965; Gunne and Lewander, 1966). Long-term stress producing aggressive behavior also affects the turnover of norepinephrine, as indicated by an increase in hypothalamic tyrosin-hydroxylase (Lamprecht, Eichelman, Thoa, Williams, and Kopin, 1972). We have previously emphasized the close relationship between behavioral and cardiovascular manifestations. When the third ventricle is perfused with desipramine, an NE-uptake inhibitor, the vasopressor response to hypothalamic stimulation is enhanced (Przuntek, Guimaraes, and Philippu, 1971). Desipramine enhances preganglionic cervical sympathetic activity evoked by hypothalamic stimulation (Sigg and Keim, 1970). Intrahypothalamic injection of norepinephrine increases body temperature in rats (Crawshaw, 1970) and alters the firing rate of temperature-sensitive interneurons (Beckman and Eisenman, 1970). Norepinephrine also causes arousal from hibernation when injected into the hypothalamus in ground squirrels (Beckman and Satinoff, 1972).

It must be pointed out that there are many controversial reports in the literature regarding the function of norepinephrine in the central nervous system. In part, this arises from the fact that the effects of peripherally administered norepinephrine are opposite to those of centrally applied norepinephrine. Circadian and seasonal rhythms for cerebral norepinephrine exist (Hökfelt, 1951; Wurtman and Axelrod, 1966), which cause different effects depending on when the drug is given. In the hypothalamus of rats, for instance, the greatest concentration of norepinephrine is reached during the middle of the dark period (Manshardt and Wurtman, 1968). These norepinephrine oscillations are of considerable functional significance. Different internal states of the hypothalamus produced by dark and light are probably responsible for opposite effects of norepinephrine on feeding behavior (Margules, Lewis, Dragovich, and Margules, 1972). The cat appears to be an exception in that these rhythms are intrinsic, e.g., they persist in constant light (Reis, Weinbren, and Corvelli, 1968). Cyclical variations in transmitter concentration may be important clinically because the timing of administration of psychotherapeutic agents may decide the effectiveness of the treatment.

Cholinergic mechanisms have also been invoked in several types of behavior. The lateral hypothalamus is known to participate in the regulation of predatory aggression (Wasman and Flynn, 1962; Roberts and Kiess, 1964; Hutchinson and Renfrew, 1966; King and Hoebel, 1968; Karli, Vergnes, and Didiergeorges, 1969). Direct carbachol stimulation of lateral (but *not* dorsal or ventral) hypothalamic sites facilitates predatory aggression by shortening attack and kill latencies (Bandler, 1969, 1970; Smith, King, and Hoebel, 1970). Furthermore, it has been suggested that the suppression of conflict behavior is mediated by a cholinergic system in the ventromedial hypothalamus (Margules and Stein, 1967). Again there are many contradictory observations due to paradoxical cases where the actions of a drug given peripherally are opposite to those observed after intracerebral application of that drug (Miller, 1965).

V. SOME PHARMACOLOGICAL CONSIDERATIONS

It is necessary to emphasize that changes in wakefulness, whether physiologically or pharmacologically induced, affect spontaneous as well as evoked sympathetic nerve activity. In decerebrate or paralyzed animals, preganglionic sympathetic nerve activity, particularly when exaggerated, is markedly depressed by halothane (Pisko, Weniger, and DeGroat, 1970), thiopental (Skovsted, Price, and Price, 1970), and pentobarbital (Elliott, 1970), and this depression is accompanied by hypotension. The clinical implication is that patients relying on high sympathetic tone may experience an extraordinary hypotension during general anesthesia. Physiological experiments carried out under general anesthesia similarly affect sympathetic nerve activity. Generalized depressant effects have also been obtained with chlorpromazine (0.2 to 1 mg/kg i.v.), perphenazine (1 mg/kg i.v.), and hydroxyzine (2 to 4 mg/kg i.v.). Of the few investigations carried out in unanesthetized animals, a study of somato-sympathetic reflexes during sleep and wakefulness in cats is particularly noteworthy (Baust, Böhmke, and Blossfeld, 1971). A progressive diminution of the cervical sympathetic evoked potential in response to sciatic stimulation was observed as the animals passed from wakefulness to sleep. Even when given in subanesthetic doses, pentobarbital and other barbiturates severely depress all (early and late) sympathetic reflexes as well as spontaneous or hypothalamically evoked sympathetic preganglionic outflow. Other CNS depressants appear to have a more selective effect. Thus potentials evoked in the cervical sympathetic nerve in response to single shocks of the hypothalamus are not significantly diminished by diazepam, whereas chlorpromazine and pentobarbital cause a marked depression (Table 3). Many of the drugs which are used clinically for mental and emotional disturbances inhibit the vasopressor response to hypothalamic stimulation. This involves, at least in part, central mechanisms since splanchnic efferent activity in

TABLE 3. *The effect of diazepam, chlorpromazine, and pentobarbital on the averaged evoked potential of the cervical sympathetic nerve elicited by hypothalamic stimulation[a]*

Dose	Percent inhibition of AEP[b] from control		
(mg/kg i.v.)	Diazepam	Chlorpromazine	Pentobarbital
0.3	8	47	—
1.0	7	70	38
3.0	9	100	63
10.0	15	—	86

[a] Species, cat; anesthesia, methoxyflurane for surgery, maintained with decamethonium 4 mg/kg i.v. Hypothalamic stimulation at coordinates Fr. 9/Lat. 2/D. −2 with single pulses of submaximal strength, 0.3 msec duration, delivered once every 3 sec (Sigg et al., 1971).

[b] Each averaged evoked potential (AEP) represents 64 single potentials. The percentage indicated is the average of three experiments.

response to stimulation of the hypothalamic defense-attack area is decreased (Fig. 10; Sigg and Sigg, 1969). When such experiments are carried out in freely moving animals, measuring blood pressure instead of splanchnic activity, the drug-induced depressant effect on the vasopressor response is considerably less impressive than in the paralyzed (or, not shown here, the anesthetized) animal (Fig. 11). This is supported by behavioral experiments in which diazepam (0.25 mg/kg p.o.), pentobarbital (10 mg/kg p.o.), and chlorpromazine (4 mg/kg p.o.) were tested in nonkiller cats for their effect on attack on rats elicited by hypothalamic stimulation. The "blind" crossover study revealed that the drugs tested did not block attacks triggered by telemetric stimulation of the lateral hypothalamus with threshold currents (MacNeil, D., *unpublished observations*). In fact, cats that were ataxic still managed to get to the rat and perform a biting attack. Other investigators who have measured "emotional" threshold responses to hypothalamic stimulation, such as hissing, have also failed to uncover significant and consistent effects with these drugs (Baxter, 1968; Dubinsky and Goldberg, 1971) unless large doses were employed (Malick, 1970). From these results it may be inferred that the action of these agents is on the input side, maybe on the ascending reticular formation, since the response to stimulation of efferent substrates of defense or attack behavior remains essentially unaltered. It may, therefore, be important to rely on an experimental design

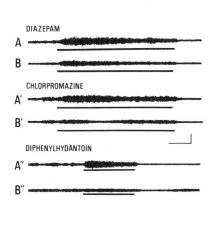

FIG. 10. Effect of diazepam, chlorpromazine, and diphenylhydantoin on hypothalamically evoked splanchnic nerve activation (cat). Anesthesia: surgery under methoxyflurane; decamethonium 4 mg/kg i.v. or gallamine triethiodide 7 mg/kg i.v. as needed; extensive local anesthesia. A,B, A'B', A"B" represent three experiments. Hypothalamic stimulation (heavy bar) at 50 Hz with pulses of 0.1 to 0.5 msec duration. Coordinates: Fr. 9/Lat. 2/D. −2. Vertical calibration: 25 μV for A and B; 50 μV for A' and B'; 150 μV for A" and B". Horizontal calibration: 1 sec for A, B, A', and B'; 1.5 sec for A" and B". A, A', A", controls; B, 10 min after i.v. injection of 0.3 mg/kg diazepam; B', 10 min after i.v. injection of 1 mg/kg chlorpromazine; B", 10 min after i.v. injection of 10 mg/kg diphenylhydantoin.

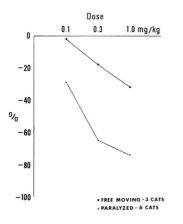

FIG. 11. The effect of diazepam on the hypothalamically evoked vasopressor response in the un-anesthetized and paralyzed cat. Hypothalamic stimulation at coordinates Fr. 9/Lat. 2/D. −2. All cats carried chronically implanted electrodes and cannulae. Three animals were anesthetized briefly with methoxyflurane and allowed to recover. Six other cats were also anesthetized but subsequently maintained under artificial respiration and 4 mg/kg i.v. decamethonium. Ordinate, percent inhibition of maximal vasopressor response; abscissa, progressive i.v. doses of diazepam (mg/kg). *Note* that the inhibition of the vasopressor response after graded doses of diazepam is greater in paralyzed cats in which compensatory feedback mechanisms must be markedly reduced.

in pharmacological studies in which emotional behavior and its autonomic concomitants are reflexly elicited through the appropriate sensory information channels.

VI. CONCLUSIONS

The fractional-analytic approach to the study of the central sympathetic system has several advantages: any part or parts of complex loops can be opened for examination with electrophysiological methods, physiological functions at the synaptic level can be investigated, and peripheral and central mechanisms can be separated. The disadvantages of such an approach, however, cannot readily be discounted. Since surgery and therefore anesthesia are usually required for an electrophysiological study of these subsystems, the behavioral equivalent and constitutional peculiarities in the intact, unanesthetized animal can at best only be inferred. Also, one cannot study parts of the sympathetic system and expect to derive the behavior of the intact system. Therefore, weighing the evidence presented here, the following conclusions may be made:

The central sympathetic system participates in the elaboration of emotions in providing multiple pathways and many levels of integration which assure, by convergency and redundancy, appropriate functional responses when the organism is thrown off balance.

At the *spinal cord level* reflexes are segmental, with short latencies, brief after-discharges and weak inhibition; they are under strong supraspinal influence. The *medulla oblongata* provides somatic-autonomic integration of more specific functions by forming functional pools (e.g., cardiovascular, respiratory). Its organization provides tonic activity and plasticity and adds strong inhibitory mechanisms. In the *hypothalamus* many afferent and efferent connections from and to the forebrain and brainstem constitute the network which involves this area in high level integrations between somatic, autonomic, and endocrine functions. This is borne out by its activation when the organism is jolted out of equilibrium by emotional or stress reactions, hemorrhage, hypoglycemia, hypoxia, fever, and related malfunctions. In contrast to the peripheral autonomic system, transmitter substances in the central sympathetic system are not well known. Undoubtedly catecholamines are important for the maintenance of normal hypothalamic function, but it appears that they contribute more to ascending arousal systems than to efferent pathways. Acetylcholine also seems to involve predominantly afferent neural systems. The significance of biogenic amines in efferent activity is more clearly represented in the brainstem-spinal pathways.

The relationship of the central sympathetic system to parasympathetic function is complex and not simply reciprocal. Unfortunately, much less is known about the electrophysiological interactions of the cranial and lumbosacral outflow of the autonomic nervous system and its significance in emotion.

Physiological and pharmacological alterations of wakefulness greatly influence an analysis of drug effects on the central sympathetic nervous system. The presence of anesthesia and/or paralyzing agents may unbalance the homeostatic system to such a degree that responses to drugs may be quantitatively as well as qualitatively different from those observed in freely moving animals. This problem is, of course, not new and has beset neuropharmacological studies for a long time.

VII. SUMMARY

The physiology of spontaneous and reflex discharges in preganglionic sympathetic nerves and their brainstem and diencephalic integration and control have been examined as a part of autonomic mechanisms accompanying emotional behavior. The modulation of sympathetic nerve activity by neurotransmitters and certain drugs influencing emotional behavior has also been briefly discussed.

ACKNOWLEDGMENT

I am greatly indebted to Dr. W. Schlosser, Dr. D. MacNeil, Mr. K. L. Keim, and Mrs. T. Sigg for their significant experimental contributions. Thanks are also due to Ms. A. DeCicco for typing the manuscript.

REFERENCES

Adkins, R. J., Morse, R. W., and Towe, A. L. (1966): Control of somatosensory input by cerebral cortex, *Science 153*, 1020–1022.

Adrian, E. D., Bronk, D. W., and Phillips, G. (1932): Discharges in mammalian sympathetic nerves, *J. Physiol. 74*, 115–133.

Anand, B. K., and Brobeck, N. R. (1951): Hypothalamic control of food intake in rats and cats, *Yale J. Biol. Med. 24*, 123–140.

Andén, N.-E., Dahlström, A., Fuxe, K., and Larsson, K. (1965): Mapping out of catecholamine and 5-HT neurons innervating the telencephalon and diencephalon, *Life Sci. 4*, 1275–1279.

Andén, N.-E., Dahlström, A., Fuxe, K., Olson, L., and Ungerstedt, U. (1966): Ascending noradrenaline neurons from the pons and the medulla oblongata, *Experientia 22*, 44–45.

Baccelli, G., Guazzi, M., Libretti, A., and Zanchetti, A. (1965): Pressoceptive and chemoceptive aortic reflexes in decorticate and decerebrate cats, *Am. J. Physiol. 208*, 708–714.

Bandler, R. J. (1969): Facilitation of aggressive behavior in rat by direct cholinergic stimulation of hypothalamus, *Nature 224*, 1035–1036.

Bandler, R. J. (1970): Cholinergic synapses in lateral hypothalamus for control of predatory aggression in rat, *Brain Res. 20*, 409–424.

Bandler, R. J., and Flynn, J. P. (1971): Visual patterned reflex present during hypothalamically elicited attack, *Science 171*, 817–818.

Bandler, R. J., and Flynn, J. P. (1972): Control of somatosensory fields for striking during hypothalamically elicited attack, *Brain Res. 38*, 197–201.

Bard, P. (1928): A diencephalic mechanism for the expression of rage, with special reference to the sympathetic nervous system, *Am. J. Physiol. 84*, 490–515.

Baust, W., Böhmke, J., and Blossfeld, U. (1971): Somato-sympathetic reflexes during natural sleep and wakefulness in unrestrained cats, *Exp. Brain Res. 12*, 361–369.

Baust, W., and Heinemann, H. (1967): Role of baroreceptors and of blood pressure in regulation of sleep and wakefulness, *Exp. Brain Res. 3*, 12–24.

Baxter, B. L. (1968): The effect of selected drugs on the "emotional" behavior elicited via hypothalamic stimulation, *Int. J. Neuropharmacol. 7*, 47–54.

Beacham, W. S., and Kunze, D. L. (1969): Renal receptors evoking a spinal vasomotor reflex, *J. Physiol. 201*, 73–85.

Beacham, W. S., and Perl, E. R. (1964a): Characteristics of a spinal sympathetic reflex, *J. Physiol. 173*, 431–448.

Beacham, W. S., and Perl, E. R. (1964b): Background and reflex discharge of sympathetic preganglionic neurons in the spinal cat, *J. Physiol. 172*, 400–416.

Beckman, A. L., and Eisenman, J. S. (1970): Microelectrophoresis of biogenic amines on hypothalamic thermosensitive cells, *Science 170*, 334–336.

Beckman, A. L., and Satinoff, E. (1972): Arousal from hibernation by intrahypothalamic injections of biogenic amines in ground squirrels, *Am. J. Physiol. 222*, 875–879.

Berman, A. L. (1968): *The Brainstem of the Cat*, University of Wisconsin Press, Madison.

Biscoe, T. J. (1971): Carotid body: Structure and function, *Physiol. Rev. 51*, 437–495.

Bloom, F. E., Oliver, A. P., and Salmoiraghi, G. C. (1963): The responsiveness of individual hypothalamic neurons to microelectrophoretically administered endogenous amines, *Int. J. Neuropharmacol. 2*, 181–193.

Bogacz, J., and Wilson, E. (1969): Visual evoked potentials at hypothalamic and tegmental areas of upper brainstem, *Electroencephalogr. Clin. Neurophysiol. 26*, 288–295.

Bolme, P., Fuxe, K., and Lidbrink, P. (1972): On the function of central catecholamine neurons, their role in cardiovascular and arousal mechanisms, *Res. Commun. Chem. Pathol. Pharmacol. 4*, 657–697.

Bronk, D. W., Ferguson, L. K., Margaria, R., and Solandt, D. T. (1936): The activity of the cardiac sympathetic centers, *Am. J. Physiol. 117*, 237–249.

Bronk, D. W., Pitts, R. F., and Larrabee, M. G. (1940): Role of the hypothalamus in cardiovascular regulation, *Res. Publ. Assoc. Nerv. Ment. Dis. 20*, 323–341.

Brooks, C. M., and Lu, H. H. (1972): *The Sinoatrial Pacemaker of the Heart*, C. C. Thomas Co., Springfield, Ill.

Campbell, J. F., Bindra, D., Krebs, H., and Ferenchak, R. P. (1969): Responses of single units of the hypothalamic ventromedial nucleus to environmental stimuli, *Physiol. Behav. 4*, 183–187.

Cannon, W. B. (1936): The role of emotion in disease, *Ann. Intern. Med. 9*, 1453–1465.

Chai, C. Y., and Wang, S. C. (1968): Integration of sympathetic cardiovascular mechanisms in medulla oblongata of the cat, *Am. J. Physiol. 215*, 1310–1315.

Cohen, M. I., and Gootman, P. M. (1970): Periodicities in efferent discharge of splanchnic nerve of the cat, *Am. J. Physiol. 218*, 1092–1101.

Coons, E. E., Levak, M., and Miller, N. E. (1965): Lateral hypothalamus: Learning of food-seeking response motivated by electrical stimulation, *Science 150*, 1320–1321.

Coote, J. H., and Downman, C. B. B. (1969): Supraspinal control of reflex activity in renal nerves, *J. Physiol. 202*, 161–170.

Coote, J. H., and Weber, W. V. (1969): Reflex discharges into thoracic white rami elicited by somatic and visceral afferent excitation, *J. Physiol. 202*, 147–159.

Cottle, M. K. (1964): Degeneration studies of primary afferents of IX and Xth cranial nerves in the cat, *J. Comp. Neurol. 122*, 329–345.

Crawshaw, L. (1970): Effects of intracerebral chemical injections on behavioral and physiological thermoregulation in rats, Ph.D. thesis, University of California.

Crill, W. E., and Reis, D. J. (1968): Distribution of carotid sinus and depressor nerves in cat brainstem, *Am. J. Physiol. 214*, 269–276.

Dafny, N., and Feldman, S. (1970): Unit responses and convergence of sensory stimuli in the hypothalamus, *Brain Res. 17*, 243–257.

Dahlström, A., and Fuxe, K. (1964): Evidence for existence of monoamine-containing neurons in the central nervous system, I. Demonstration of monoamines in cell bodies of brainstem neurons, *Acta Physiol. Scand. 62*, Suppl. 232.

Dahlström, A., Fuxe, K., Hillarp, N., and Malmfors, T. (1964): Adrenergic mechanisms in the pupillary light reflex path, *Acta Phys. Scand. 62*, 119–24.

DeGroat, W. C., and Ryall, R. W. (1967): An excitatory action of 5-hydroxytryptamine on sympathetic preganglionic neurons, *Exp. Brain Res. 3*, 299–305.

Djojosugito, A. M., Folkow, B., Kylstra, P. H., Lisander, B., and Tuttle, R. S. (1970): Differentiated interaction between the hypothalamic defence reaction and baroreceptor reflexes, I. Effects on heart rate and regional flow resistance, *Acta Physiol. Scand. 78*, 376–385.

Downing, S. E., and Siegel, J. H. (1963): Baroreceptor and chemoreceptor influences on sympathetic discharge to the heart, *Am. J. Physiol. 204*, 471–479.

Dreifuss, J. J., Murphy, J. T., and Gloor, P. (1968): Contrasting effects of two identified amygdaloid efferent pathways, *J. Neurophysiol. 31*, 237–248.

Dubinsky, B., and Goldberg, M. E. (1971): Effect of imipramine and selected drugs on attack elicited by hypothalamic stimulation in the cat, *Neuropharmacology 10*, 537–545.

Eccles, J. (1935): Action potential of superior cervical ganglion, *J. Physiol. 85*, 179–206.

Egger, M. D., and Flynn, J. P. (1963): Effects of electrical stimulation of amygdala on hypothalamically elicited attack behavior in cats, *J. Neurophysiol. 26*, 705–720.

Elliott, R. C. (1970): Action of central depressant drugs on spontaneous discharge of action potentials in superior cervical sympathetic trunk of the cat, *Neuropharmacology 9*, 129–136.

Evetts, K. D., Fitzsimons, J. T., and Setler, P. E. (1972): Eating caused by 6-hydroxydopamine-induced release of noradrenaline in the diencephalon of the rat, *J. Physiol. 223*, 35–47.

Fedina, L., Katunskii, A. Y., Khayutin, V. M., and Mitsanyi, A. (1966): Responses of renal sympathetic nerves to stimulation of afferent A and C fibers of tibial and mesenterial nerves, *Acta Physiol. Acad. Sci. Hung. 29*, 157–176.

Feldman, S., Heide, C. S. vander, and Porter, R. W. (1959): Evoked potentials in the hypothalamus, *Am. J. Physiol. 196*, 1163–1167.

Fernandez de Molina, A., Juno, M., and Perl, E. R. (1965): Antidromically evoked responses from sympathetic preganglionic neurones, *J. Physiol. 180*, 321–335.

Franz, D. N., Evans, M. H., and Perl, E. R. (1966): Characteristics of viscerosympathetic reflexes in the spinal cat, *Am. J. Physiol. 211*, 1292–1298.

Fuxe, K. (1965): Evidence for the existence of monoamine neurons in the central nervous system, III. The monoamine nerve terminal, *Z. Zellforsch. 65*, 573–596.

Fuxe, K., and Gunne, L. M. (1964): Depletion of amine stores in brain catecholamine terminals on amygdaloid stimulation, *Acta Physiol. Scand. 62*, 493–494.

Gebber, G. L., and Snyder, D. W. (1970): Hypothalamic control of baroreceptor reflexes, *Am. J. Physiol. 218*, 124–131.

Gellhorn, E. (1967): Physiological analysis of ergotropic and trophotrophic imbalances; Application to various states of consciousness. In: *Principles of Autonomic—somatic Integrations, Physiological Basis and Psychological and Clinical Implications*, University of Minnesota Press, Minneapolis.

Gernandt, B., Liljestrand, G., and Zotterman, Y. (1946): Efferent impulses in the splanchnic nerve, *Acta Physiol. Scand. 11*, 230–247.

Glick, G., and Braunwald, E. (1965): Relative roles of the sympathetic and parasympathetic nervous systems in the reflex control of heart rate, *Circ. Res. 16*, 363–375.

Gloor, P. (1956): Telencephalic influences upon the hypothalamus. In: *Hypothalamic-Hypophysial Interrelationships*, edited by W. S. Fields, C. C. Thomas Co., Springfield, Ill.

Gootman, P. (1967): Brainstem influences on efferent splanchnic discharge, Ph.D. thesis, University Microfilms, Ann Arbor, Mich.

Green, J. H., and Heffron, P. F. (1967): The interrelationship between sympathetic activity and the heart rate, *Arch. Int. Pharmacodyn. Ther. 169*, 15–25.

Grossman, S. P. (1966): The VMH: A center for affective reactions, satiety, or both?, *Physiol. Behav. 1*, 1–10.

Grundfest, H. (1939): Properties of mammalian B fibres, *Am. J. Physiol. 127*, 252–262.

Gunne, L. M., and Lewander, T. (1966): Monoamines in brain and adrenal glands of cats after electrically induced defense reaction, *Acta Physiol. Scand. 67*, 405–410.

Heller, A., Harvey, J. A., and Moore, R. Y. (1962): Demonstration of a fall in brain serotonin following central nervous system lesions in the rat, *Biochem. Pharmacol. 11*, 859–866.

Heller, A., and Moore, R. Y. (1965): Effect of central nervous system lesions on brain monoamines in the rat, *J. Pharmacol. 150*, 1–9.

Herd, J. A., Morse, W. H., Kelleher, R. T., and Jones, L. G. (1969): Arterial hypertension in the squirrel monkey during behavioral experiments, *Am. J. Physiol. 217*, 24–29.

Hess, W. R. (1943): Induzierte störungen der optischen Wahrnehmung, *Nervenarzt 16*, 57–66.

Hess, W. R. (1949): *Das Zwischenhirn*, B. Schwabe, Basel.

Hess, W. R. (1952): Experimental physiologie und psychologie, *Helv. Phys. Pharm. Acta 10*, 85–92.

Hess, W. R., and Akert, K. (1955): Experimental data on the role of the hypothalamus in mechanism of emotional behavior, *AMA Arch. Neurol. Psych. 73*, 127–129.

Hess, W. R., and Brügger, M. (1943): Das subkortikale Zentrum der affektiven Abwehrreaktion, *Helv. Phys. Pharm. Acta 1*, 35–52.

Heymans, C., and Neil, E. (1958): *Reflexogenic Areas of Cardiovascular System*, Churchill, London.

Hilton, S. M. (1963): Inhibition of baroreceptor reflexes on hypothalamic stimulation, *J. Physiol. 165*, 56P–57P.

Hökfelt, B. (1951): Noradrenaline and adrenalin in mammalian tissues, *Acta Physiol. Scand. 25*, Suppl. 92.

Holmes, T. H., and Rahe, R. H. (1967): The social readjustment rating scale, *J. Psychosom. Res. 11*, 213–218.

Horeyseck, G., and Jänig, W. (1972): Response patterns in vasoconstrictors to the skin and muscle upon stimulation of skin receptors in chronic spinal cats, *Pfluegers. Arch. 332*, R64.

Humphrey, D. R. (1967): Neuronal activity in medulla oblongata of the cat evoked by stimulation of carotid sinus nerve, In: *Baroreceptors and Hypertension*, edited by P. Kezdi, Pergamon, New York.

Hunsperger, R. W. (1956): Affektreaktionen auf elektrische Reizung im Hirnstamm der Katze, *Helv. Phys. Pharm. Acta. 14*, 70–92.

Hutchinson, R. R., and Renfrew, J. W. (1966): Stalking attack and eating behavior elicited from same sites in the hypothalamus, *J. Comp. Physiol. Psychol., 61*, 360–367.

Iriuchijima, J., and Kumada, M. (1963): Efferent cardiac vagal discharge of the dog in response to electrical stimulation of the sensory nerves, *Jap. J. Physiol. 13*, 599–604.

Iwamura, Y., Uchino, Y., Ozawa, S., and Kudo, N. (1969): Excitatory and inhibitory components of somato-sympathetic reflex, *Brain Res. 16*, 351–358.

Jänig, W., and Schmidt, R. F. (1970): Single unit responses in the cervical sympathetic trunk upon somatic nerve stimulation, *Pfluegers. Arch. 314*, 199–216.

Johansson, B. (1962): Circulatory responses to stimulation of somatic afferents, *Acta Physiol. Scand. 57*, Suppl. 198.

Karli, P., Vergnes, M., and Didiergeorges, F. (1969): Rat-mouse interspecific aggressive behavior and its manipulation by brain ablation and brain stimulation, In: *Biology of Aggressive Behavior*, edited by Sigg and Garrattini, Excerpta Med. Fdtn.

Karplus, J. P., and Kreidl, A. (1909): Gehirn und Sympathicus, Zwischenhirn basis und Hals sympathicus, *Arch. Gesamte Physiol. 129*, 138–144.

Kaufman, A., and Koizumi, K. (1971): Spontaneous and reflex activity of single units in lumbar white rami, In: *Research in Physiology, Liber Memorialis*, edited by F. F. Kao, M. Vassalle, and K. Koizumi, Anlo Gaggi, Bologna.

King, M. B., and Hoebel, B. G. (1968): Killing elicited by brain stimulation in the rat, *Comm. Behav. Biol. 2*, 173–177.

Kirchner, F., Sato, A., and Weidinger, H. (1971): Bulbar inhibition of spinal and supraspinal sympathetic reflex discharges, *Pfluegers Arch. 326*, 324–333.

Koizumi, K., Collin, R., Kaufman, A., and Brooks, C. M. (1970): Contribution of unmyelinated afferent excitation to sympathetic reflexes, *Brain Res. 20*, 99–106.

Koizumi, K., and Sato, A. (1972): Reflex activity of single sympathetic fibres to skeletal muscle produced by electrical stimulation of somatic and vago-depressor afferent nerves in the cat, *Pfluegers Arch. 332*, 283–301.

Koizumi, K., Sato, A., Kaufman, A., and Brooks, C. M. (1968): Studies of sympathetic neuron discharges modified by central and peripheral excitation, *Brain Res. 11*, 212–224.

Koizumi, K., Seller, H., Kaufman, A., and Brooks, C. M. (1971): Pattern of sympathetic discharges and their relation to baroreceptor and respiratory activities, *Brain Res. 27*, 281–294.

Koizumi, K., and Suda, I. (1963): Induced modulations in autonomic efferent neuron activity, *Am. J. Physiol. 205*, 738–744.

Koss, M. C., and Wang, S. C. (1972): Brainstem loci for sympathetic activation of the nictitating membrane and pupil in the cat, *Am. J. Physiol. 222*, 900–905.

Krasne, F. B. (1962): General disruption resulting from electrical stimulation of ventromedial hypothalamus, *Science 138*, 822–823.

Kylstra, P. H., and Lisander, B. (1970): Differentiated interaction between hypothalamic defence area and baroreceptor reflexes, II. Effects on aortic blood flow as related to workload on the left ventricle, *Acta Physiol. Scand. 78*, 386–392.

Lamprecht, F., Eichelman, B., Thoa, B. N., Williams, R. B., and Kopin, I. J. (1972): Rat fighting behavior: Serum dopamine-β-hydroxylase and hypothalamic tyrosine hydroxylase, *Science 177*, 1214–1215.

Laporte, Y., Bessou, P., and Bouisset, S. (1960): Action réflexe des différents types de fibres afferentes d'origin musculaire sur la pression sanguine, *Arch. Ital. Biol. 98*, 206–221.

Löfving, B. (1961): Cardiovascular adjustments induced from the rostral cingulate gyrus (with special reference to sympathoinhibitory mechanisms), *Acta Physiol. Scand. 53*, Suppl. 184.

MacDonnell, M. F., and Flynn, J. P. (1966a): Control of sensory fields by stimulation of the hypothalamus, *Science 152*, 1406–1408.

MacDonnell, M. F., and Flynn, J. P. (1966*b*): Sensory control of hypothalamic attack, *Anim. Behav. 14,* 399–405.

MacLean, P. D., Ploog, D. W., and Robinson, B. W. (1960): Circulatory effects of limbic stimulation, with special reference to the male genital organ, *Physiol. Rev. 40,* Suppl. 4, 105–112.

Malick, J. B. (1970): Effects of selected drugs on stimulus-bound emotional behavior elicited by hypothalamic stimulation in the cat, *Arch. Int. Pharmacodyn. Ther. 186,* 137–141.

Manning, J. W. (1965): Cardiovascular reflexes following lesions in medullary reticular formation, *Am. J. Physiol. 208,* 283–288.

Manshardt, J., and Wurtman, R. J. (1968): Daily rhythm in noradrenaline content of rat hypothalamus, *Nature 217,* 574–575.

Margules, D. L., Lewis, M. J., Dragovich, J. A., and Margules, A. S. (1972): Hypothalamic norepinephrine: Circadian rhythms and the control of feeding behavior, *Science 178,* 640–643.

Margules, D. L., and Stein, L. (1967): Neuroleptics vs. tranquilizers: Evidence from animal behavior studies of mode and site of action, In: *Neuropsychopharmacology,* edited by H. Brill, Excerpta Med. Fdtn.

Marshall, J. F., Turner, B. H., and Teitelbaum, P. (1971): Sensory neglect produced by lateral hypothalamic damage, *Science 174,* 523–525.

Masserman, J. H. (1950): In: *Feeling and Emotion,* edited by M. Reymert, McGraw-Hill Co., New York.

Mendelson, J. (1967): Lateral hypothalamic stimulation in satiated rats: Rewarding effects of self-induced drinking, *Science 157,* 1077–1079.

Miller, N. E. (1965): Chemical coding of behavior in the brain, *Science 148,* 328–338.

Miller, N. E. (1969): Psychosomatic effects of specific types of training, *Ann. N. Y. Acad. Sci. 159,* 1025–1040.

Miura, M., and Reis, D. J. (1968): Electrophysiological evidence that carotid sinus nerve fibers terminate in bulbar reticular formation, *Brain Res. 9,* 394–397.

Miura, M., and Reis, D. J. (1969): Termination and secondary projections of carotid sinus nerve in cat brainstem, *Am. J. Physiol. 217,* 142–153.

Miura, M., and Reis, D. J. (1972): Role of solitary and paramedian reticular nuclei in mediating cardiovascular reflex responses from carotid baro- and chemoreceptors, *J. Physiol. 223,* 525–548.

Mogenson, G. J., and Stevenson, J. A. F. (1966): Drinking and self-stimulation with electrical stimulation of the lateral hypothalamus, *Physiol. Behav. 1,* 251–254.

Mogenson, G. J., and Stevenson, J. A. F. (1967): Drinking induced by electrical stimulation of the lateral hypothalamus, *Exp. Neurol. 17,* 119–127.

Moore, R. Y., and Heller, A. (1967): Monoamine levels and neuronal degeneration in rat brain following lateral hypothalamic lesions, *J. Pharmacol. Exp. Ther. 156,* 12–22.

Morgane, P. J. (1961*a*): Distinct "feeding" and "hunger motivating" systems in the lateral hypothalamus of the rat, *Science 133,* 887–888.

Morgane, P. J. (1961*b*): Electrophysiological studies of feeding and satiety centers in the rat, *Am. J. Physiol. 201,* 838–844.

Morgane, P. J., and Stern, W. C. (1972): Relationship of sleep to neuroanatomical circuits, biochemistry, and behavior, In: G. Haydu, *Patterns of Integration from Biochemical to Behavioral Processes,* N. Y. Acad. Sci., *193,* 95–111.

Murphy, J. T., and Renaud, L. P. (1969): Mechanisms of inhibition in the ventromedial nucleus of the hypothalamus, *J. Neurophysiol. 32,* 85–102.

Nakao, H. (1958): Emotional behavior produced by hypothalamic stimulation, *Am. J. Physiol. 194,* 411–418.

Nauta, W. J. H., and Haymaker, W. (1969): Hypothalamic nuclei and fiber connections, In: *The Hypothalamus,* edited by W. Haymaker, E. Anderson and W. J. H. Nauta, C. C. Thomas Co., Springfield, Ill.

Newman, G., Roberts, W., Frohman, L. A., and Bernardis, L. L. (1967): Plasma growth hormone levels in rats following amygdala and pyriform cortex lesions, *Proc. Can. Fed. Biol. Soc. 10,* 41.

Niijima, A., and Winter, D. L. (1968*a*): Baroreceptors in the adrenal gland, *Science 159,* 434–435.

Niijima, A., and Winter, D. L. (1968*b*): The effect of catecholamines on unit activity in afferent nerves from the adrenal glands, *J. Physiol. 195*, 647–656.

Ninomiya, I., Judy, W. V., and Wilson, M. F. (1970): Hypothalamic stimulus effects on sympathetic nerve activity, *Am. J. Physiol. 218*, 453–462.

Norgren, R. (1970): Gustatory responses in the hypothalamus, *Brain Res. 21*, 63–78.

Okada, H., Okamoto, K., and Nisida, I. (1961): I. The activity of the cardioregulatory and abdominal sympathetic nerves of the cat in the Bainbridge reflex, *Jap. J. Physiol. 11*, 520–529.

Pisko, E., Weniger, F., and DeGroat, W. C. (1970): Effect of halothane on preganglionic and postganglionic sympathetic activity in the cat, *Brain Res. 20*, 330–334.

Pitts, R. F., Larrabee, M. G. and Bronk, D. W. (1941): An analysis of hypothalamic cardiovascular control, *Am. J. Physiol. 134*, 359–383.

Przuntek, H., Guimaraes, S., and Philippu, A. (1971): Importance of adrenergic neurons of the brain for the rise of blood pressure evoked by hypothalamic stimulation, *Naunyn. Schmiedebergs Arch. Pharmacol. 271*, 311–319.

Ranson, S. W., and Magoun, H. W. (1939): The hypothalamus, *Ergeb. Physiol. 41*, 56–163.

Reis, D. J., and Gunne, L. M. (1965): Brain catecholamines: Relation to defense reaction evoked by amygdaloid stimulation in the cat, *Science 149*, 450–451.

Reis, D. J., Moorhead, D. T., and Merlino, N. (1970): Dopa-induced excitement in the cat; Its relationship to brain norepinephrine concentrations, *Arch. Neurol. 22*, 31–39.

Reis, D. J., Weinbren, M., and Corvelli, A. (1968): A circadian rhythm of norepinephrine regionally in the cat brain; Its relationship to environmental lighting and to regional diurnal variations in brain serotonin, *J. Pharmacol. Exp. Ther. 164*, 135–145.

Rhoton, A. L., Oleary, J. L., and Ferguson, J. P. (1966): Trigeminal, facial, vagal and glossopharyngeal nerves in the monkey, *Arch. Neurol. 14*, 530–540.

Richard, P. (1970): An electrophysiological study in the ewe of the tracts which transmit impulses from the mammary glands to the pituitary stalk, *J. Endocrinol. 47*, 37–44.

Roberts, W. W., and Carey, R. J. (1965): Rewarding effect of performance of gnawing aroused by hypothalamic stimulation in the rat, *J. Comp. Physiol. Psychol. 59*, 317–324.

Roberts, W. W., and Kiess, H. O. (1964): Motivational properties of hypothalamic aggression in cats, *J. Comp. Physiol. Psychol. 57*, 187–193.

Rudomin, P., Malliani, A., Berlone, M., and Zanchetti, A. (1965): Distribution of electrical responses to somatic stimuli in the diencephalon of the cat, with special reference to the hypothalamus, *Arch. Ital. Biol. 103*, 60–89.

Sampson, S. R., and Biscoe, T. J. (1968): Electrical potentials evoked in the brainstem by stimulation of the sinus nerve, *Brain Res. 9*, 398–402.

Santini, M., and Noback, C. R. (1971): The transverse extent of the preganglionic sympathetic pool of the cat, *Brain Res. 26*, 399–401.

Sato, A. (1972*a*): Somato-sympathetic reflex discharges evoked through supramedullary pathways, *Pfluegers Arch. 332*, 117–126.

Sato, A. (1972*b*): The relative involvement of different reflex pathways in somato-sympathetic reflexes, analyzed in spontaneously active single preganglionic sympathetic units, *Pfluegers Arch. 333*, 70–81.

Sato, A., Kaufman, A., Koizumi, K., and Brooks, C. M. (1969): Afferent nerve groups and sympathetic reflex pathways, *Brain Res. 14*, 575–587.

Sato, A., Sato, N., Ozawa, T., and Fujimori, B. (1967): Further observation of the reflex potential in the lumbar sympathetic trunk, *Jap. J. Physiol. 17*, 294–307.

Sato, A., Tsushima, N., and Fujimori, B. (1965): Reflex potentials of lumbar sympathetic trunk with sciatic nerve stimulation in cats, *Jap. J. Physiol. 15*, 532–539.

Saum, W. R., and DeGroat, W. C. (1972): Parasympathetic ganglia: Activation of an inhibitory mechanism by cholinomimetic agents, *Science 175*, 659–661.

Sawyer, C. H. (1957): Triggering of the pituitary by the central nervous system, In: *Physiological Triggers*, edited by T. Bullock, Waverly, Baltimore.

Schaefer, H. (1960): Central control of cardiac function, *Physiol. Rev. 40*, Suppl. 4, 213–231.

Scherrer, H. (1962): Hypothalamic influences on electrical activity in the renal nerve of the rat, *Acta Neuroveg. 23*, 499–522.

Scherrer, H. (1966): Inhibition of sympathetic discharge by stimulation of medulla oblongata in the rat, *Acta Neuroveg. 29*, 56–74.

Shapiro, D., Tursky, B., Gershon, E., and Stern, M. (1969): Effects of feedback and reinforcement on the control of human systolic blood pressure, *Science 163*, 588–589.

Sherrington, C. S. (1906): *The Integrative Actions of the Nervous System,* C. Scribner's Sons, New Haven (Yale University Press).

Shute, C. C. D., and Lewis, P. R. (1966): Cholinergic and monoaminergic systems of the brain, *Nature 212*, 710–711.

Shute, C. C. D., and Lewis, P. R. (1967): The ascending cholinergic reticular system: Neocortical, olfactory and subcortical projections, *Brain 90*, 497–520.

Siegel, A., and Chabora, J. (1971): Effects of electrical stimulation of cingulate gyrus upon attack behavior elicited from the hypothalamus in the cat, *Brain Res. 32*, 169–177.

Siegel, A., and Flynn, J. P. (1968): Differential effects of electrical stimulation and lesions of hippocampus and adjacent regions upon attack behavior in cats, *Brain Res. 7*, 252–267.

Siegel, A., and Skog, D. (1970): Effects of electrical stimulation of the septum upon attack behavior elicited from the hypothalamus in the cat, *Brain Res. 23*, 371–380.

Sigg, E. B., and Keim, K. L. (1970): Enhancement by desipramine of hypothalamically evoked discharges in preganglionic sympathetic nerves, *Psychopharmacologia 18*, 378–386.

Sigg, E. B., Keim, K. L., and Horst, W. D. (1973): Levodopa-induced changes of brain amines and central sympathetic activity in cats, in: *Chemical Modulation of Brain Function,* edited by H. C. Sabelli, Raven Press, New York.

Sigg, E. B., Keim, K. L., and Kepner, K. (1971): Selective effects of diazepam on certain central sympathetic components, *Neuropharmacology 10*, 621–629.

Sigg, E. B., and Sigg, T. D. (1966): Adrenergic modulation of central function, in: *Proceedings of First Intl. Symposium on Antidepressant Drugs,* Milan, Excerpta Med. Intl. Congress Ser. 122.

Sigg, E. B., and Sigg, T. D. (1969): Hypothalamic stimulation of preganglionic autonomic activity and its modification by chlorpromazine, diazepam and pentobarbital, *Int. J. Neuropharmac. 8*, 567–572.

Skovsted, P., Price, M. L., and Price, H. L. (1970): Effects of short-acting barbiturates on arterial pressure, preganglionic sympathetic activity and barostatic reflexes, *Anesthesiology 33*, 10–18.

Slangen, J. L., and Miller, N. E. (1969): Pharmacological tests for the function of hypothalamic norepinephrine in eating behavior, *Physiol. Behav. 4*, 543–552.

Smith, D. E., King, M. B., and Hoebel, B. G. (1970): Lateral hypothalamic control of killing: Evidence for a cholinoceptive mechanism, *Science 167*, 900–901.

Smith, O. A., and Nathan, M. A. (1964): Effect of hypothalamic and prefrontal cortical lesions on conditioned cardiovascular responses, *Physiologist 7*, 259.

Steinbaum, E. A., and Miller, N. E. (1965): Obesity from eating elicited by daily stimulation of the hypothalamus, *Am. J. Physiol. 208*, 1–5.

Tenen, S. S., and Miller, N. E. (1964): Strength of electrical stimulation of lateral hypothalamus, food, deprivation, and tolerance for quinine in food, *J. Comp. Physiol. Psychol. 58*, 55–62.

Ueda, H., Inque, M., Iuzuka, M., Iuzuka, T., Ihori, M., and Yasuda, H. (1966): Comparison of vasoconstrictor responses in functionally different organs induced by stimulation of mesencephalic pressor area, *Jap. Heart J. 7*, 318–330.

Uvnäs, B. (1960) Central cardiovascular control, In: *Handbook of Physiology, 1. Neurophysiology II,* American Physiology Society, Washington, D.C.

Valenstein, E. S., Cox, V. C., and Kakolewski, J. W. (1968): Modification of motivated behavior elicited by electrical stimulation of the hypothalamus, *Science 159*, 1119–1121.

Wasman, M., and Flynn, J. P. (1962): Directed attack elicited from the hypothalamus, *Arch. Neurol. 6*, 220–227.

Weidinger, H., and Fedina, L. (1960): Versuche zur Tonisierung medullärer sympathischer Zentren, *Arch. Ges. Physiol. 272*, 55–56.

Weidinger, H., Hetzel, R., and Schaefer, H. (1962): Aktionsströme in zentrifugalen vagalen Herznerven und deren Bedeutung für den Kreislauf, *Pfluegers Arch. 276*, 262–279.

Weidinger, H., and Leschhorn, V. (1964): Sympathische Tonisierung und rhythmische Beutdruckschwankungen, *Z. Kreislaufforsch. 53*, 985–1002.

Weiss, G. K., and Crill, W. E. (1969): Carotid sinus nerve: Primary afferent depolarization evoked by hypothalamic stimulation, *Brain Res. 16*, 269–272.

Welker, W. I. (1963): Analysis of sniffing of the albino rat, *Behaviour 22*, 223–244.

Wurtman, R. J., and Axelrod, J. (1966): A 24-hour rhythm in the content of norepinephrine in the pineal and salivary glands of the rat, *Life Sci. 5*, 665–669.

Wyrwicka, W., and Chase, M. H. (1970): Projections from the buccal cavity to brainstem sites involved in feeding behavior, *Exp. Neurol. 27*, 512–519.

Zanchetti, A. (1967): Subcortical and cortical mechanisms in arousal and emotional behavior., in: *Brain Organization Section, Neurosciences,* Rockefeller University Press, New York.

Emotions—Their Parameters and Measurement,
edited by L. Levi.
Raven Press, New York © 1975

Vegetative System and Emotion

Malcolm Lader and Peter Tyrer

Department of Psychiatry, De Crespigny Park, Denmark Hill, London, SE 5 8 AF England

INTRODUCTION

The topic of somatic factors in emotion is a vast one. We shall concentrate on the relationship between the subjective experience of emotion and the bodily feelings and overt changes which accompany it. The problems of the mind–body relationship are thorny ones, but within the epistemological limits imposed some meaningful relationships emerge. Particular emphasis will be laid on the so-called "James-Lange Hypothesis" because of its importance in understanding subsequent approaches in this field. Recent experiments, despite their laboratory-based approach, still encounter the difficulties brought into focus by James and some of these will be outlined.

The general topic has long been of interest to writers and philosophers. Until the nineteenth century it was accepted that certain bodily changes accompanied emotional states—breathlessness, trembling, palpitations, frequency of micturition, muscle twitching, paresthesiae, difficulty in swallowing, dry mouth, diarrhea, etc.—but the mechanism of the changes was seldom considered. The simulation of emotion was a natural concern of actors and playwrights and it was appreciated that the successful imitation of an emotional state involved the faithful and convincing reproduction of these symptoms even in the absence of subjective feelings of emotion. It was not surprising that speculation was aroused concerning the importance of such symptoms in the feeling and expression of emotion, a question that must have occurred to Shakespeare from the evidence of Hamlet's lines:

"Is it not monstrous that this player here,
But in a fiction, in a dream of passion,
Could force his soul so to his own conceit,
That from her working all his visage wan'd,
Tears in his eyes, distraction in's aspect,
A broken voice, and his whole function suiting
With forms to his conceit? And all for nothing!"

Hamlet, Act II, Scene 2

THE JAMES-LANGE "THEORY" OF EMOTION

The first systematic attempts to describe the relationship between the subjective experience of emotion and the concomitant bodily feelings were made independently by William James in 1884 and C. Lange in the following year. They propounded the theory that the experience of emotion was secondary to the perception of bodily symptoms but it is interesting to note that this notion had been presaged two centuries earlier by Descartes (1648) and Malebranche (1672). Charles Darwin had also touched on the same topics that James used as the basis of his theory, and James being well acquainted with Darwin's work may have been influenced by him. Darwin (1872), in his treatise on the expression of emotion in animals and man, devoted most of his attention to the description of emotional behavior, emphasizing its adaptive nature. He stressed the similarity between such features in man and other animals to lend force to his main thesis of the close relationships that exist between man and other species. In his conclusion, he writes: "the free expression by outward signs of an emotion intensifies it. On the other hand, the repression, as far as this is possible, of all outward signs softens our emotions. He who gives way to violent gestures will increase his rage; he who does not control the signs of fear will experience fear in a greater degree; and he who remains passive when overwhelmed by grief loses his best chance of recovering elasticity of mind." Although loosely formulated and not going so far as to claim that emotional experience is dependent on the perception of bodily symptoms, these comments must certainly have influenced James as evidenced by their virtual paraphrase in the first account of his theory. Parenthetically, it is worth pointing out the similarity between these views of Darwin and the later pronouncements of psychoanalysts on the expression of emotion, mourning reactions, etc.

It is instructive to examine James's theory in further detail. Although as originally formulated the theory is more a philosophical standpoint and is incompatible with current neurophysiological knowledge, there are some aspects that still require careful attention. James argues his case cogently from the only evidence that was available and relevant introspection, and the hypothesis is stated clearly: "Common sense says, we lose our fortune, are sorry and weep; we meet a bear, are frightened and run; we are insulted by a rival, are angry and strike. The hypothesis here to be defended says that this order of sequence is incorrect, that the one mental state is not immediately induced by the other, that the bodily manifestations must first be interposed between, and that the more rational statement is that we feel sorry because we cry, angry because we strike, afraid because we tremble." He regards the whole body as "a sounding-board, which every change of consciousness, however slight, can make reverberate," and thereby claims that even the most subtle emotional changes can be accounted for by the variation in bodily symptoms. James succinctly summarizes his hypothesis: "that the bodily changes follow directly the perception of the exciting fact and that our feeling of the same changes as they occur is the emotion. Every one of the bodily changes, whatsoever it be, is felt acutely or obscurely the moment it occurs." He boldly asserts that no emotion can exist if the bodily experience of it is removed and that objectless emotion is due to derangement of bodily functions and not mental ones. Rebutting objections that deliberate inducement of bodily symptoms does not give rise to emotional states, James uses an argument that adumbrates the treatment currently termed behavior therapy. "There is no more valuable precept in moral education than this: if we wish to conquer undesirable emotional tendencies in ourselves, we must assiduously, and in the first instance cold-bloodedly, go through the outward movements of those contrary dispositions which we prefer to cultivate."

James's theory jolted both psychologists and physiologists into the objective study of emotional states and their bodily accompaniments and appeared to afford an opportunity to test their relationship using scientific methods. This was, and still is, a chimerical quest. James's hypothesis deals with the subjective elements of emotion that, together with such time-hallowed philosophical concepts as perceiving, reasoning, and willing, lie outside the epistemological boundaries of scientific endeavor and are not directly available to the laboratory investigator, the psychophysiologist. James, himself, was partly to blame for the confusion as to what physiologists, in particular, were testing, for in stating the main points of his theory he frequently blurred the distinction between the subjective experience of emotion and observed emotional behavior. However, in translating his theory into neurophysiological terms, James made no such elision: "We have a scheme perfectly capable of representing the process of the emotions. An object falls on a sense-organ and is apperceived by the appropriate cortical center; or else the latter, excited in some other way, gives rise to an idea of the same object. Quick as a flash, the reflex currents pass through their pre-ordained channels, alter the condition of muscle, skin and viscus; and these alterations, apperceived like the original object, in as many specific portions of the cortex, combine with it in consciousness and transform it from an object-simply-apprehended into an object-emotionally-felt. No new principles have to be invoked, nothing is postulated beyond the ordinary reflex circuit, and the topical centers admitted in one shape or another by all to exist." James is right about the elegant economy of this theory, which allows a parsimony of neural mechanisms in that both exteroceptive and interoceptive stimuli are apperceived similarly in the cortex. If the principle of Occum's razor were a major determinant of the acceptability of a scientific theory (which it is not!), then the theory, in these physiological terms, is most attractive. However, to discredit the *subjective* aspects of the formulation, it is necessary to show that *subjective* emotional feelings are independent of bodily symptoms. This is a daunting task as it can only be attempted in conscious man with reliance on introspection.

These considerations, in particular the need to be absolutely clear as to the distinction between introspectively felt emotional states and objectively apparent emotional behavior, must be borne in mind when evaluating theories of emotion that succeeded James's and that are more acceptable to both physiologists and psychologists. Lange (1885), whose name is always associated with James, formulated his ideas much less clearly and did not claim that the *feeling* of bodily changes is the emotion. He posed the question: "Is it possible that vasomotor disturbances, varied dilatation of the blood vessels, and consequent excess of blood, in the separate organs, are the real, primary effects of the affections, whereas the other phenomena, — motor abnormalities, sensation paralysis, subjective sensations, disturbances of secretion, and intelligence — are only secondary disturbances, which have their cause in anomalies of vascular innervation?" Lange implied that the answer was affirmative; it seems that he regarded emotion as vasomotor activity itself.

This position, which avoids subjective phenomena, perception, etc., has been revived by Wenger (1950) who pointed out the great variety of visceral patterning and the number of emotional complexes that could be related to them. This approach, however, while scientifically heuristic in evaluating the bodily changes in emotional states begs the question of the temporal relationships between physiological changes and emotional *feelings*.

It is somewhat surprising that the James theory of emotion was so readily accepted. Perhaps, James did not intend it as a formal theory but merely as a speculation for in 1890 he wrote to a friend, "It seems to me that psychology is like physics before Galileo's time — not a single elementary law yet caught a glimpse of." Nevertheless, by 1922, Dunlap in his introduction to the reprinting of James's and Lange's papers sweepingly asserts that the theory "has not only become so strongly entrenched in scientific thought that it is practically assumed today as the basis for the study of the emotional life, but has also led to the development of the hypothesis of reaction or response as the basis of all mental life." Nevertheless, opposition to the theory was growing.

THE CANNON-BARD THEORY OF EMOTION

At the turn of the century, Charles Sherrington (1900) transected the spinal cord and vagi of dogs, which destroyed any connection between the brain and the viscera — the heart, lung, stomach, gut, spleen, liver, etc. The animals continued to show emotional behavior. One of Sherrington's dogs had always been of a marked emotional temperament and the surgical operation caused no obvious change in her.

A formal rebuttal of the James theory was made by Cannon (1927) who marshaled his evidence under five headings:

(a) Total separation of the viscera from the central nervous system (CNS) does not alter emotional behavior.
(b) The same visceral changes occur in very different emotional states and in nonemotional states.
(c) The viscera are relatively insensitive structures.
(d) Visceral changes are too slow to be a source of emotional feeling.
(e) Artificial induction of the visceral changes typical of strong emotions does not produce those emotions.

Cannon was well aware that his first objection, based on the results of Sherrington and on his own experiments (Cannon, Lewis, and Britton, 1927), was invalid as "we have no real basis for either affirming or denying the presence of 'felt emotion' in these reduced animals." However, he still persisted with this as the keystone of his argument. Hebb (1958) has pointed this out by stating: "such an argument is totally irrelevant; James did not say that emotional *behavior* depends on sensation from the limbs and viscera."
The second objection is too general to be disputed and hinges on the definition of "same" and "very different." This point will be reverted to later in the discussion on autonomic patterning.
Objection (c) assumes that the sensitivity of the viscera to external noxae such as cutting or burning is related to its sensitivity to internal change. There is no reason why an internal organ should not register small changes in its function to the CNS and yet not transmit major external forces.
The speed of visceral change (objection d) is another area where relative considerations apply. Certainly, if the later reformulations of the James theory, which emphasized the role of the skeletal muscular systems are considered, then the changes that can occur are very rapid.
Objection (e) is an interesting one and will be discussed later.
However, the important feature of Cannon's thesis was not the admissibility or otherwise of his objections to the James theory but in his detailed exposition of an alternative theory, much more in line with the then current physiological thinking. This theory can be described as a "central" theory in contradistinction to the "peripheral" bias of James's and Lange's theories. Cannon regarded the thalamus as the central part of the emotional pathway, which, when "released for action" by sensory stimuli or cortical impulses, led to both the experience of emotion and its bodily changes. Thalamic neurons "not only innervate muscles and viscera but also excite afferent paths to the cortex by direct connection or by irradiation" (Cannon, 1927). Bard (1928) added further evidence that the diencephalon and associated structures were essential for the expression of emotional behavior when he

demonstrated that "sham rage," induced in cats by decortication, was abolished by extirpation of the thalamus.

Later work showed that Cannon and Bard were mistaken in attributing the chief role in emotion to the thalamus. Papez (1937) speculated that the parts of the brain collectively known as the rhinencephalon were primarily concerned with emotion rather than olfaction and this suggestion has been borne out by observations. The fornix, mammillary bodies, anterior thalamic nuclei, parahippocampal, and cingulate gyri of the brain, often known as the Papez circuit, are now collectively known as the limbic system or "visceral brain" (MacLean, 1955), which is the chief functional connection between cerebral cortex, hypothalamus, and reticular formation.

Cannon (1929, 1931) also reinterpreted the functional significance of peripheral physiological changes in emotional states. He pointed out that bodily symptoms experienced in acute emotion were the by-product of sympathetic nervous discharge. The sympathetic division of the autonomic nervous system was activated at times of "flight or fight" and the cranial and sacral (parasympathetic) division was responsible for "building up reserves and fortifying the body against times of need or stress." Thus, the peripheral bodily changes in emotion were explicable as adaptive features: it was of biological advantage to the fleeing animal pursued by a predator to have an increased cardiac output, enhanced muscle blood flow, and a faster reaction time; the subjective symptoms experienced by the animal were only a reflection of the internal physiological changes induced by sympathetic nervous and humoral discharge.

The Cannon-Bard theory accorded much more consistently with the way physiologists conceptualize the relationship between bodily and psychic events. The epistemological framework in which it fitted has provided the basis for most other more recent physiologically oriented theories of brain functioning. Psychic events are regarded as epiphenomena of neural transactions.

CURRENT THEORIES OF EMOTION

Considerations of space preclude a detailed examination of all the other models and theories of emotion—behavior and feelings—that have been put forward in the years since Cannon and Bard's formulation. In outline, these theories can be loosely grouped into psychological and physiological ones. The former include Brown and Farber's theory of frustration (1951) and motivational theories of emotion (Leeper, 1948; Webb, 1948), which were further developed by behavior theorists (Mowrer, 1950; Miller, 1951). In these theories the emphasis is laid on the external stimulus and overt response aspects of the emotion. By contrast, the physiological theories concentrate on the internal aspects and neglect the external features. These include Freeman's homeostatic theory (1948) in which emotion is considered as a result of imbalance between cortical, unlearned and conditioned stimuli, and Arnold's excitatory theory (1950) in which the autonomic symptoms of emotion are attributed a similar role to that in the James-Lange theory and are considered necessary to convert "emotional attitude" to "emotional expression."

OBSERVATIONS IN PATIENTS WITH NEUROLOGICAL LESIONS

James suggested that if a patient could be found who was anesthetic both without and within and if such a person felt no emotion, it would strengthen his theory. Such a case would be very rare as it would only arise by extensive bilateral damage to the thalami. Patients with spinal cord lesions, such as complete transection, would lose varying degrees of sensation depending on the level of the lesion. Dana (1921), a neurologist, discussed the relevance of such cases to the James theory and briefly outlined the clinical state of a patient of his who lived for a year with a lesion at the 4th cervical level with complete quadriplegia. The only skeletal muscles at her command were the cranial, upper cervical, and the diaphragm; the vagus and cranial parasympathetic system was functioning but not the sympathetic. Dana records that she showed emotions of grief, joy, displeasure, and affection with no change in personality or character.

Dana also lists other types of neurological condition such as tabes, progressive muscular atrophy, and paralysis agitans, in which emotional expression and feeling were preserved intact despite gross disabilities. He makes the telling point that: "It does not always follow that because a sensation is felt in the periphery it is due to peripheral irritation." Thalamic and midbrain lesions can cause peripheral sensations and pain.

Putting forward his own theory, Dana comes so close to the schema held explicitly or implicitly by many present-day workers that it is worth quoting *in extenso:*

"On the whole, I am led to the conclusion that emotion is centrally located and results from the action and interaction of cortex and thalamus. The bodily sensations which accompany emotion are produced by stimuli from the automatic centers in the brain-stem (acting on heart, blood vessels and glands), but they cooperate to extend and perhaps intensify the emotion. For naturally, if a man finds his heart palpitating, his hands cold and wet, his legs weak and his epigastrium calling out in distress, he will feel more alarm. On the other hand, if the automatic stimulus produced by joy at the sight of the beloved, strengthens his heart beat, raises his blood pressure, and in general improves his sense of well-being, he will feel a little happier for it."

This theory not only covers much of the later Cannon-Bard formulation but postulates a feedback from the periphery to reinforce the emotional feeling. If one extends the physiological loci from cortex and thalamus to include the limbic system, etc., then Dana's ideas, derived from his observations in the clinic, have a modern ring to them.

A more recent study (Hohmann, 1966) is noteworthy for the care with which patients with lesions at different levels of the spinal cord were selected and also for the standardization of the semistructured interview. The real problem of persuading paraplegic patients to talk freely about their emotional and sexual changes was minimized because the author-interviewer was himself a paraplegic and knew all the subjects well. Definite decreases in feelings of anger, fear, and sexual excitement were reported by the subjects, with a tendency toward this diminution in feeling being more marked, the higher up the spinal cord the site of the lesion. Despite the decrease in many emotional *feelings,* overt emotional *behavior* often continued to be displayed. A most interesting finding was that feelings of sentimentality were increased: increased weeping, feeling a lump in the throat, getting "choked up" in situations such as saying goodbye, attendance at church services, watching a "tear-jerker" movie or play, or during the expression of tender feelings. The problem of the retrospective nature of the self-observations is probably appreciable and might vitiate the findings. Nevertheless, it is hard to adapt any theory which postulates dependence of emotional feelings on the integrity of peripheral physiological mechanisms to account for the enhancement of one form of emotion *pari passu* with the decrement in other types of feeling. The psychiatrist encounters a similar sort of emotional pattern change in patients with depressive illnesses and it is possible that some of the paraplegics in Hohmann's study were chronically depressed in reaction to their personal and social disabilities.

There is another group of patients whose clinical picture throws some light on the relationship between emotional behavior and emotional feelings. Patients who have sustained bilateral damage to the pons and medulla, usually following vascular incidents such as thrombosis, often demonstrate pronounced emotional lability. They may be laughing and giggling uncontrollably one moment and sobbing inconsolably the next. Their behavior, facial appearance, speech, etc., are all consistent with their emotional response. However, if one questions such patients, their emotional feelings have been far less marked than their behavior would lead one to expect. Thus, a patient may have felt a little sad or nostalgic because a trivial incident has awakened memories but he will burst out crying and the behavior is out of all proportion. This type of emotional lability and excess illustrates yet again the dissociation that may occur between feeling and behavior.

In other types of neurological patients with emotional changes the central mechanisms subserving emotional control may be affected by the disease.

For example, the euphoria that occasionally ensues in the later stages of multiple sclerosis is probably related to plaques of demyelination in the frontal lobes. The patients feel and behave in a consistent, euphoric manner.

A condition of some relevance to this topic is familial dysautonomia. The first report of this condition appeared in 1949 and an extensive review of the features of this rare syndrome was published in 1957 (Riley, 1957). Sometimes known eponymously as the Riley-Day syndrome, the most striking manifestations are disorders of autonomic function such as diminished lacrimation, hyperhydrosis, transient skin blotching, abnormal swallowing reflex, lability of blood pressure, and instability of temperature control. These features suggest abnormalities of autonomic nervous system control but other phenomena presumably reflect much more widespread and diffuse disturbance of the CNS. These latter include poor motor coordination, relative insensitivity to pain, hypoactive deep tendon reflexes, and emotional instability often associated with severe vomiting attacks. Most cases have occurred in Jewish children.

The psychological abnormalities are difficult to characterize but fall into three main categories: behavior disturbances, intellectual abnormalities, and emotional problems. The first two aspects are usually temporary and lessen as the child grows up. Similarly, the emotional problems, mainly anxiety, restlessness and impulsiveness, also tend to lessen and may reflect the parents' concern with a physically ill child. There is no consistent evidence that the range of emotional behavior is abnormal nor that the quality of emotional experience is altered in any way. Thus, this condition really throws very little light on the psychic-somatic interactions in emotion.

RESPONSE SPECIFICITY

One of Cannon's objections to the James's hypothesis was that essentially similar somatic responses occurred in fear, rage, hunger, and other emotional states. Therefore, bodily changes would be too unsubtle to account for the wide range of emotional feelings. It is difficult to assess how valid Cannon's objection is: that we can discern different physiological patterns in ourselves accompanying different emotions is not contributory evidence because we may have learned to search for particular bodily feelings when we experience certain emotions. For example, if we are in a situation that makes us angry, we may become especially aware of a feeling of heat in the face because we have observed such a change in others and in ourselves on previous occasions. Thus, the association of "red in the face" with exasperation, "butterflies in the stomach" with anxiety, or "lightheartedness" with exhilaration may well be a learned phenomenon. Indeed, it may even be partly culture-bound in that different cultures lay varying emphases on different components of the bodily changes in emotional states.

Consequently, for elucidation of this topic, we must turn to laboratory studies that attempt to induce different emotions in subjects while monitoring physiological functions. Wolf and Wolff (1947) described changes in gastric motility, in gastric secretion, and in the appearance of the gastric mucosa in their patient Tom, who had a gastric fistula. Anger and resentment were associated with engorgement of the gastric mucosa, anxiety with inhibition of gastric function with decrease in motility and in acid output.

Ax (1953) staged an experiment in which situations were contrived to induce feelings of anxiety or anger in his normal subjects. Increases in skin conductance level and respiration rate were greater when fear was induced than when anger occurred; conversely, rises in diastolic blood pressure and skin-conductance responses were more in states of anger. The pattern for fear was interpreted as resembling that produced by injections of epinephrine; for anger, the pattern resembled that following an injection of epinephrine and norepinephrine combined.

Similar experiments were carried out by Schachter, who studied hypertensive patients as well as normal subjects. Pain induced by a cold pressor test (dipping the hand in ice-cold water) was included as well as the anger- and anxiety-inducing situations. Different patterns of physiological response were described. Other investigators have reported similar results, and the body of evidence now supports the view that different physiological systems are involved to varying extents in association with different emotions. Such a patterning would be expected on teleological grounds: as different emotions presage different behavioral responses to a situation, the physiological needs of the body would be expected to vary, and hence the preparatory bodily changes should also differ. Thus, fear is usually followed by withdrawal and flight, anger by approach and fight; the needs of the body differ somewhat according to the behavioral response.

Nevertheless, it should be emphasized that the physiological patterns described in the laboratory studies do not differ grossly one from the other. The variation between individuals and even within an individual on different occasions tends to be greater than the differences in the physiological patterns. Thus, the experimenter cannot say which emotion a subject is experiencing by evaluating his physiological response pattern.

SYMPATHOMIMETIC AGENTS AND EMOTION

There is now a large body of evidence that the sympathetic nervous system is overactive in emotional states characterized by high arousal, especially anxiety and anger. As a corollary, many investigators have administered sympathomimetic agents in attempts to induce emotional states in human subjects. The first of these studies set the pattern for much of the later work (Wearn and Sturgis, 1919). Epinephrine was administered intramuscularly (now considered a dangerous procedure) to normal controls and to army recruits suffering from the "irritable heart" syndrome, a condition probably a subvariety of anxiety neurosis, in which fatigue, dizziness, and cardiovascular symptoms (palpitations, faintness, missed beats, etc.) were prominent. Normal subjects showed an increase in heart rate and were aware of their tachycardia, but few other effects were noted. By contrast, the neurotic patients not only experienced a change in bodily symptoms but also noted subjective changes characteristic of anxiety, in some cases as acute attacks of panic. Many subsequent studies produced similar results.

In an extensive early study of the effects of epinephrine, Marañon (1924) clearly differentiated between the effects of the drug in calm and anxious subjects. In the former, the physiological changes produced by epinephrine were either noted in isolation or *"quelques fois comme simple perception subjective de certains troubles somatiques qui font naitre chez le sujet une sensation émotive indéfinie, mais percue 'en froid,' sans émotion proprement dite."* In other subjects or in the same subject on other occasions the subjective feelings were more pronounced and genuine, *"comme une émotion involuntaire complète, c'est-a-dire avec les mêmes elements somatiques que dans le cas precedent et en plus la participation psychique affective qui est le complement de ces elements."* The differences in the results of later workers are explicable in retrospect by the presence or absence of anxiety-provoking environmental cues. In a neutral setting the injection of epinephrine produced no emotional changes, "cold emotion" or "as if" emotion (Cantril and Hunt, 1932; Richter, 1940; Basowitz, Korchin, Oken, Goldstein, and Gussack, 1956; Frankenhaeuser, Jarpe, and Matell, 1961; Pollin and Goldin, 1961). In an anxiety-provoking setting, intentionally or accidentally created by the experimenters, subjects showed more evidence of anxiety and in a minority of cases panic attacks were elicited (Lindemann and Finesinger, 1938; Dynes and Tod, 1940; Richter, 1940). Patients with pre-existing neurotic anxiety were more prone to these affective changes than normal subjects.

One line of research that has aroused much interest in the past few years and has direct and close parallels to the epinephrine studies is that concerning lactate infusions. Pitts and McClure (1967) based their work on the earlier finding that exercise produces more lactate in the blood of patients with anxiety states than in control subjects. They "developed the idea that perhaps the lactate ion itself could produce anxiety attacks in susceptible persons." To test this, they performed a double-blind experiment in which the following were infused in random order intravenously into a group of 14 patients with anxiety states and into a control group of 10 normal subjects: 500 mM sodium (DL) lactate, 500 mM sodium (DL) lactate with 20 mM calcium chloride, and 555 mM glucose in 167 mM sodium chloride. These solutions are iso-osmolar and were given as 20 ml/kg body weight during a 20-minute period to each subject while symptoms were rated.

The infusion of sodium lactate produced symptoms which "were markedly similar or identical" to those experienced in their "worst attacks" by the anxious patients. Such reports were fewer from normal subjects. The anxiety symptoms caused by lactate infusion were greatly reduced in frequency when the lactate plus calcium chloride was infused, and the glucose in saline solution produced almost no symptoms in either patients or controls.

Pitts and McClure suggested that anxiety symptoms and perhaps anxiety neurosis itself were "a consequence of marked increase in lactate production in response to increased epinephrine release; the patient with anxiety neurosis would be someone especially subject to this mechanism because of chronic overproduction of epinephrine, overactivity of the central nervous system, a defect in aerobic or anaerobic metabolism resulting in excess lactate production, a defect in calcium metabolism or some combination of these." This conclusion has been very strongly attacked on biochemical grounds (Grosz and Farmer, 1969, 1972), and it is probable that a marked metabolic alkalosis is the mechanism for the anxiety symptoms produced. A similar alkalosis can result from hyperventilation. Whatever the mechanism, it is interesting that some reports replicating the original findings have reported the "cold emotion," "as if" nature of the anxious feelings engendered (Bonn, Harrison, and Rees, 1971).

BETA-BLOCKING SYMPATHOLYTIC AGENTS

The complementary experimental approach is to block peripheral physiological activity using pharmacological means. If by this means anxiety or other emotions, induced in normals or present in patients, can be abolished, both in its peripheral manifestations and in its central perceived form, it would suggest that, at the very least, feedback of peripheral physiological changes is important in the perpetuation of emotion, and perhaps even that the James hypothesis would be worth reappraisal. Muscular activity can be abolished by curare and synthetic neuromuscular-blocking agents but most work has been done with autonomic measures. With anticholinergic compounds such as atropine direct central effects are known to occur and the same problem limits the use of some sympatholytic agents. Peripheral sympathetic effects can be divided into alpha and beta effects depending on whether they are induced by norepinephrine or by isoprenaline respectively. (Epinephrine stimulates both types of receptors.) Drugs, such as propranolol, that block the beta receptors have excited some interest recently especially as anxiolytic agents. Nevertheless, the impression that one is dealing with an uncomplicated drug may be illusory.

Since the initial report that propranolol was therapeutically effective in anxious patients (Granville-Grossman and Turner, 1966), there has been speculation about the mode of action of beta adrenoceptor-blocking drugs in treating anxiety. The main possibilities are that propranolol has a central sedative effect or that it acts by peripheral beta blockade alone or by both mechanisms. Evidence for a central action has been reported in animal studies (Leszkovsky and Tardos, 1965; Bainbridge and Greenwood, 1971) and in human subjects (Gillam and Prichard, 1965; Hinshelwood, 1969). In all these studies, however, the dosage was much greater than that used in therapeutic practice. Evidence for a primary peripheral action is suggested by its effecting significant improvement in anxious patients with respect to autonomic symptoms only (Granville-Grossman and Turner, 1966), and by the absence of therapeutic effects with (+)-propranolol (Bonn and Turner, 1971) which has the same properties as the (−)-isomer with the exception of beta blockade.

Our study was designed to detect central effects in normal subjects after single doses of propranolol (120 mg) and another similar drug sotalol (240 mg) (Lader and Tyrer, 1972). We used only six subjects but a large range of measures. The subjects were each tested on three weekly occasions each time before and 1 hr and 3 hr after taking an aqueous suspension of one of the drugs or placebo. Order effects were balanced by a Williams Square design, and double-blind procedure was used. Subjects were instructed to take no alcohol or psychotropic drugs in the 24 hr before each testing.

To sample a wide range of central effects a battery of tests was carried out on each occasion using a PDP-12A laboratory computer on-line. Subjective rating scales consisted of 16 linear 100-mm scales to assess mood and eight similar scales to assess bodily symptoms. Physiological measures included the following:

(a) The electroencephalogram recorded from bipolar saline pad electrodes during a reaction time task to 32 auditory stimuli presented at random intervals. The electroencephalogram was fed into four parallel bandpass filters to give four frequency ranges: (1) 2.4 to 4 Hz; (2) 4 to 7.5 Hz; (3) 7.5 to 13.5 Hz; (4) 13.5 to 26.0 Hz. Each waveband was sampled for 5-sec epochs between the clicks and then rectified and averaged to yield the mean voltage.

(b) The mean evoked response was measured by averaging the 500-msec epochs of electroencephalogram following each of the 32 auditory click stimuli. The latencies and amplitudes of the main components of the evoked response were quantified.

(c) Power spectral analysis of a 40-sec sample of the electroencephalogram was also performed on-line by computing the auto-cross-products function followed by a Fourier analysis to yield the power spectrum between 2 and 32 Hz.

(d) Finger tremor was measured with an accelerometer, recording lasting for 40 sec, and the signals analyzed on-line to yield the power spectrum.

(e) Skin conductance (palmar-sweat-gland activity) and the number of spontaneous fluctuations in conductance were measured during the reaction-time task using a standard procedure.

(f) The radial pulse rate was taken by an independent assessor after the subject had been resting for 10 min.

Psychological measures included reaction time, key tapping, card sorting, digit symbol substitution test, and a simple copying test.

Three of the subjective mood analogue scales showed significant drug effects: the alert-drowsy, muzzy-clear-headed, and troubled-tranquil scales. Sotalol produced more drowsiness than placebo ($t = 3.65$; $p < 0.01$) and propranolol ($t = 2.57$; $p < 0.05$), and greater "muzziness" than placebo ($t = 4.92$; $p < 0.01$) and propranolol ($t = 6.05$; $p < 0.001$). Both sotalol ($t = 3.57$; $p < 0.01$) and propranolol ($t = 4.0$; $p < 0.01$) caused the subjects to feel more troubled than when on placebo. These effects were all more marked after 3 hr than after 1 hr.

None of the central physiological or behavioral measures showed significant drug effects. One of the most sensitive measures of central drug effects is the percentage of activity in the fastest waveband of the EEG (13.5 to 26.0 Hz) (Bond and Lader, 1972). Not even a trend was apparent for any drug effect as compared with placebo.

As expected there was a significant drop in pulse rate over time for both sotalol ($t = 7.17$; $p < 0.001$) and propranolol ($t = 5.05$; $p < 0.01$) as compared with placebo. No drug effects were shown with respect to tremor or skin conductance.

When one attempts to interpret the results, the same difficulties intrude as with studies involving the infusion of epinephrine and with the original James-Lange formulation. Firstly, the subjective effects could have been due to chance. Secondly, the beta-blocking agents could have had direct central effects which did not detect, although we have previously found our central measures to be very sensitive to psychotropic effects. Thirdly, the subjective effects could be mediated indirectly because of the undoubted cardiovascular changes affecting brain function. Fourthly, the subjective effects could have been secondary to the conscious perception of the peripheral physiological effects, although our subjects did not report any such awareness on the bodily symptom-rating scale.

However, a second interest was in the use of these compounds therapeutically. We carried out a sequential trial of sotalol against placebo using a double-blind crossover design (Tyrer and Lader, 1973). If the psychiatrist's rating was taken as the criterion, then the active drug showed every indication of being superior to placebo. However, if the patient's self-rating was used, then the superiority of the drug could not be unequivocally established. Examination of individual symptoms suggested that the expected lessening of such sympathetically mediated symptoms as palpitations, gastric upset, and tremor did occur. Nevertheless, the patients still felt anxious. It appeared, therefore, that many of the patients were able to distinguish between bodily symptoms of anxiety and the feeling of anxiety itself but that the psychiatrist, perhaps because of his medicophysiological orientation, overestimates the usefulness of lessening peripheral symptoms. Our conclusions were that any reinforcement of anxiety by means of peripheral mechanisms was not important in the majority of patients and that the beta-blocking agents would only be of use as additions to centrally acting anxiolytic agents in patients with marked autonomic symptoms.

Despite the problems of using alpha or beta blockers in the elucidation of emotional mechanisms, they provide an empirical approach, and the complexities are no more than those encountered when trying to control cognitive factors. Furthermore, there have been suggestions that the beta-adrenergic blocking agents have a potentially enormous role in ameliorating "the adverse effects of emotion in people" (Taggart and Carruthers, 1972). For both practical and theoretical reasons the psychophysiological study of these drugs would appear to be fruitful.

INTERACTION OF COGNITIVE FACTORS AND PHYSIOLOGICAL AROUSAL

Before attempting to draw together all the various strands into a coherent model, it is useful to outline the important and widely cited experiments of Schachter (1966). He injected small doses of epinephrine, some subjects knowing what sort of effects to expect, others remaining in ignorance. The subjects were then placed with a stooge who acted either in a euphoric way or in an angry manner. Observational ratings of the subject and his self-ratings both indicated that subjects kept ignorant of the effects of their injection showed and felt more emotional experience (euphoria or anger) than informed subjects. In a second experiment, subjects were given either a placebo injection, epinephrine, or chlorpromazine and watched a comedy film. The subjects administered epinephrine showed more amusement than those given placebo, who in turn were more amused than those given chlorpromazine, which has alpha-adrenergic blocking actions (as well as a sedative effect). Thus, awareness of physiological arousal seems to be the substrate on which cognitive clues induce a specific emotion. Although there are other tenable interpretations, a reasonable hypothesis is that an emotion is induced by the interaction of at least two states, high physiological arousal and appropriate sensory input.

CONCLUSIONS AND A MODEL OF EMOTION

We have re-examined the James hypothesis both in terms of what he originally explicitly stated and in the light of modern experimental techniques and approaches. Although the integrity of somatic responses seems unnecessary for the expression of emotional *behavior,* the evidence regarding emotional *feelings* is more equivocal. Nevertheless, the general consensus seems to acknowledge the importance of somatic responses and sensitivity in reinforcing and perpetuating emotional behavior and feelings. This does *not* imply that the *institution* of emotional feelings is dependent on peripheral somatic mechanisms.

The various ways in which somatic and psychic aspects of emotion can interact is most easily shown diagrammatically by constructing a model (Fig. 1). The model is derived from many people's ideas and work and has been presented previously in some detail by one of us with particular reference to anxiety (Lader, 1972).

The first element in the model is the physical and social environment that impinges on the subject in the form of stimuli. These stimuli may be unconditioned or may, by reason of some past contingencies, be secondarily conditioned. The sensory input interacts with factors within the individual such as personality traits and previous learning to produce in some degree a nonspecific CNS-arousal state, which results in the experience of a par-

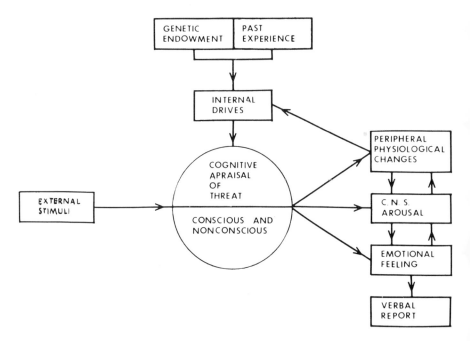

FIG. 1. A model of emotion.

ticular emotion. The interactions between sensory stimuli and individual factors may occur at a conscious level. If so, then the emotional experience will appear appropriate to the subject in his circumstances or, if inapposite, the reasons for the irrationality will be apparent. Conversely, if the interaction takes place, wholly or in part, at a nonconscious level, the emotion may appear irrational. The interactions govern both the intensity and the quality of the affect.

The stimulus–arousal interaction takes place in the CNS. As a consequence of the change in CNS activity, peripheral physiological alterations occur and are a concomitant to the felt emotion. There is also direct perception of the peripheral changes, which reinforces the emotional feeling but is not necessary to it.

In summary, the perception of the physiological changes accompanying emotion intensify it but this is not a restatement of the James-Lange hypothesis. In strict scientific terms it is still as untestable as when it was first mooted nearly 90 years ago. Meanwhile, physiological measures can be usefully employed to monitor emotional changes and it is by the interpretation of such data painstakingly garnered that light will be thrown on the mystery of the mind–body relationship.

SUMMARY

The relationship between the *feelings* of emotion and the bodily changes accompanying emotion has exerted a fascination over philosophers, psychologists, physiologists, and many other scientists. The basic enigma remains insoluble because of epistemological limitations but objective laboratory methods can be used to examine the nexus between emotional *behavior* and physiological changes. The James hypothesis has exerted an influence far in excess of its true heuristic value. Reformulations of the hypothesis have been made but recent knowledge accruing from neurological and pharmacological sources (beta-blocking agents) has still not clarified the issue.

REFERENCES

Arnold, M. B. (1950): An excitatory theory of emotion. In: *Feelings and Emotions: the Mooseheart Symposium*, pp. 11–33, McGraw-Hill, New York.

Ax, A. F. (1953): The physiological differentiation between fear and anger in humans, Psychosom. Med. *15*, 433–442.

Bainbridge, J. G., and Greenwood, D. T. (1971): Tranquillizing effects of propranolol demonstrated in rats, Neuropharmacology *10*, 453–458.

Bard, P. (1928): A diencephalic mechanism for the expression of rage with special reference to the sympathetic nervous system, Am. J. Physiol. *84*, 490–515.

Basowitz, H., Korchin, S. J., Oken, D., Goldstein, M. S., and Gussack, H. (1956): Anxiety and performance changes with a minimal dose of epinephrine, Arch. Neurol. Psych. *76*, 98–105.

Bond, A. J., and Lader, M. H. (1972): Residual effects of hypnotics, Psychopharmacologia, *25*, 117–132.

Bonn, J. A., Harrison, J., and Rees, W. L. (1971): Lactate-induced anxiety: therapeutic application, Br. J. Psych. *119*, 468–470.

Bonn, J. A., and Turner, P. (1971): D-Propranolol and anxiety, Lancet *1*, 1355–1356.

Brown, J. S., and Farber, I. E. (1951): Emotions conceptualised as intervening variables – with suggestions towards a theory of frustration, Psychol. Bull. *48*, 465–495.

Cannon, W. B. (1927): The James-Lange theory of emotion, Am. J. Psychol. *39*, 106–124.

Cannon, W. B. (1929): *Bodily Changes in Pain, Hunger, and Rage*, Branford, Boston.

Cannon, W. B. (1931): *The Wisdom of the Body*, Norton, New York.

Cannon, W. B., Lewis, J. T., and Britton, S. W. (1927): The dispensability of the sympathetic division of the autonomic system, Boston Med. Surg. J. *197*, 514.

Cantril, H., and Hunt, W. A. (1932): Emotional effects produced by injection of adrenaline, Am. J. Psychol. *44*, 300–307.

Dana, C. S. (1921): The autonomic seat of the emotions: A discussion of the James-Lange theory, Arch. Neurol. Psych. *6*, 634–639.

Darwin, C. (1872): *Expression of the Emotions in Man and Animals*, J. Murray, London.

Descartes, R. (1648): *Passions de L'âme*, Paris.

Dynes, J. B., and Tod, H. (1940): Emotional and somatic responses of schizophrenic patients and normal controls to adrenaline and doryl, J. Neurol. Psych. *3*, 1–8.

Frankenhaeuser, M., Järpe, G., and Matell, G. (1961): Effects of intravenous infusion of adrenaline and noradrenaline on certain physiological and psychological functions, Acta Physiol. Scand. *51*, 175–186.

Freeman, G. L. (1948): *Physiological Psychology*, Van Nostrand, New York.

Gillam, P. M. S., and Prichard, B. N. C. (1965): Use of propranolol in angina pectoris, Br. Med. J. *2*, 337–339.

Granville-Grossman, K. L., and Turner, P. (1966): The effect of propranolol on anxiety, Lancet *1*, 788–790.

Grosz, H. J., and Farmer, B. B. (1969): Blood lactate in the development of anxiety symptoms. A critical examination of Pitts and McClure's hypothesis and experimental study, Arch. Gen. Psych. *21*, 611–619.

Grosz, H. J., and Farmer, B. B. (1972): Pitts' and McClure's lactate-anxiety study revisited, Br. J. Psych. *120*, 415–418.

Hebb, D. O. (1958): *A Textbook of Psychology*, Saunders, Philadelphia.

Hinshelwood, R. D. (1969): Hallucinations and propranolol, Br. Med. J. *2*, 445.

Hohmann, G. W. (1966): Some effects of spinal cord lesions on experienced emotional feelings, Psychophysiology *3*, 143–156.

James, W. (1884): What is emotion? Mind *19*, 188–205.

Lader, M. (1972): The nature of anxiety, Br. J. Psych. *121*, 481–491.

Lader, M. H., and Tyrer, P. J. (1972): Central and peripheral effects of propranolol and sotalol in normal human subjects, Br. J. Pharmacol. *45*, 557–560.

Lange, C. (1885): The emotions, translated by I. A. Haupt. In: *The Emotions*, ed. K. Dunlap, Williams and Wilkins, Baltimore, 1922.

Leeper, R. W. (1948): A motivational theory of emotion to replace "emotion as disorganised response," Psychol. Rev. *55*, 5–21.

Leszkovsky, G., and Tardos, L. (1965): Some effects of propranolol on the central nervous system, J. Pharm. Pharmac. *17*, 518–520.

Lindemann, E., and Finesinger, J. E. (1938): The effect of adrenaline and mecholyl in states of anxiety in psychoneurotic patients, Am. J. Psych. *95*, 353–370.

Maclean, P. D. (1955): The limbic system ("visceral brain") and emotional behavior, Arch. Neurol. Psych. *73*, 130–134.

Malebranche, P. (1672): *Recherche de la Verité*, Paris.

Marañon, G. (1924): Contribution a l'étude de l'action émotive de l'adrenaline, Rev. Franc. Endocrinol. *2*, 301–325.

Miller, N. E. (1951): Learnable drives and rewards. In: *Handbook of Experimental Psychology*, ed. S. S. Stevens, Wiley, New York.

Mowrer, H. O. (1950): *Learning Theory and Personality Dynamics: Selected Papers*, Ronald Press, New York.

Papez, J. W. (1937): A proposed mechanism of emotion, Arch. Neurol. Psych. *38*, 725–743.

Pitts, F. N., and McClure, J. N. (1967): Lactate metabolism in anxiety neurosis, New Engl. J. Med. *277*, 1329–1336.

Pollin, W., and Goldin, S. (1961): The physiological and psychological effects of intravenously administered epinephrine and its metabolism in normal and schizophrenic men, J. Psych. Res. *1*, 50–66.

Richter, D. (1940): The action of adrenaline in anxiety, Proc. Roy. Soc. Med. *33*, 615–618.

Riley, C. M. (1957): Familial dysautonomia, Adv. Pediat. *9*, 157–190.

Schachter, J. (1957): Pain, fear, and anger in hypertensives and normotensives. A psycho-physiological study, Psychosom. Med. *19*, 17–29.

Schachter, S. (1966): The interaction of cognitive and physiological determinants of emotional state. In: *Anxiety and Behavior*, ed. C. D. Spielberger, pp. 193–224, Academic Press, New York.

Sherrington, C. S. (1900): Experiments on the value of vascular and visceral factors for the genesis of emotion, Proc. Roy. Soc. *66*, 397.

Taggart, P., and Carruthers, M. (1972): Suppression by oxprenolol of adrenergic response to stress, Lancet 2, 256–258.

Tyrer, P. J., and Lader, M. H. (1973): Clinical and physiological effects of beta-adrenergic blockade with sotalol in chronic anxiety, Clin. Pharmacol. Therapeut. *14*, 418–426.

Wearn, J. T., and Sturgis, C. C. (1919): Studies on epinephrin I. Effects of the injection of epinephrin in soldiers with "irritable heart," Arch. Intern. Med. *24*, 247–268.

Webb, W. B. (1948): A motivational theory of emotions, Psychol. Review, *55*, 329–335.

Wenger, M. A. (1950): Emotion as visceral action: an extension of Lange's theory. In: *Feelings and Emotions*, ed. M. L. Reymert, pp. 3–10, McGraw-Hill, New York.

Wolf, S., and Wolff, H. G. (1947): *Human Gastric Function,* 2nd Ed., Oxford Univ. Press, New York.

Emotions—Their Parameters and Measurement,
edited by L. Levi.
Raven Press, New York © 1975

Emotion as Reflected in Patterns
of Endocrine Integration

John W. Mason

*Walter Reed Army Institute of Research, Walter Reed Army Medical Center, Washington,
D.C. 20012*

Probably before many years have passed we shall have satisfactory tests for the internal secretion, and then shall know better
the total expression of an emotional storm in our own bodies.
(Walter Cannon, 1922)

I. SOME THEORETICAL ASPECTS OF PSYCHOENDOCRINE
STUDIES OF EMOTION

It is a basic point of biological strategy that we must derive our knowledge of the integrative mechanisms of the brain, including emotional
processes, largely in an indirect fashion, by the study of their reflections in
the output of the "effector" systems of the brain. While the skeletal-muscular
(behavioral) and autonomic effector output systems of the brain have long
been recognized, the knowledge that the endocrine apparatus is not essentially autonomous but really represents a *third effector or motor system* of
the brain (Fig. 1), is a rather recent development (Mason, 1970). Within
only the past two to three decades, the advent of specific, sensitive, and
reliable methods for the measurement of hormones in blood and urine has
permitted the development of a burgeoning field of psychoendocrine research, concerned with the central question, "What may be learned about
the functional organization of psychological processes by the study of their
reflections in endocrine activity?"

In general, the history of psychoendocrine research may be viewed as
evolving through a succession of stages of increasing insight, in which we
have moved from an initial rather narrow concern with only a few hormones
and a few psychological parameters to the recognition that we must take into
consideration a *broadening array of multiple, interdependent variables,*
from both a psychosocial and endocrine viewpoint, if we are eventually to
understand the organization of psychoendocrine relationships. The development of the psychoendocrine field has brought rather vividly into focus
again some of the unique problems inherent in the study of integrative

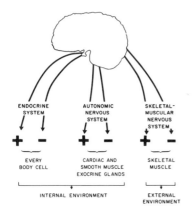

FIG. 1. The three effector or motor systems which mediate the integrative functions of the brain. The double arrows for each system indicate their similar organization on the principle of regulation by means of a balance between opposing forces (Mason, 1970).

mechanisms, which it may be useful to review briefly in the general theoretical perspective of the contrasting strategies of the "integrative" and "elementalistic" approaches in biological research.

The "elementalistic" or "analytical" or "reductionistic" approach, which has predominated in biology for about four centuries, is based upon the premise, adapted from the physical sciences by Descartes, that a full understanding of the complex living organism can eventually be achieved by breaking it down in a part-by-part analysis to the point of its smallest, ultimate, component units. The usefulness of this application of the scientific method in biology is evident in the massive knowledge gained during the long progression in study of the organism from the level of body systems, then organs, then tissues, then cells, then cytoplasm, and now down to the level of molecular biology. In general, the analytical approach encourages a tendency to focus, in piecemeal fashion, upon unit functions isolated from the whole, and from a practical standpoint, to deal with as few experimental variables as possible, often just a single independent and single dependent variable. The scientific method lends itself rather well to such reductionistic approaches in biology, requiring relatively little modification of the model which has been so fruitful in the physical sciences.

The premise underlying the "integrative" or "synthetic" approach, on the other hand, is that ultimate understanding of the living organism lies not only in knowing its ultimate component parts, but that a unique and fundamental task in biology is to determine how the many separate bodily parts or processes are integrated into the organism as a whole (Mason, 1974).

Claude Bernard, who is largely responsible for the conceptual foundation of the modern integrative approach, emphasized that these two basic strategic approaches are not antithetical, but rather are clearly complementary in principle. The integrative study of coordination of the parts obviously presupposes prior analytical characterization of the parts (Bernard, 1957).

The two approaches, therefore, go logically hand in hand, analysis first, then synthesis. It is in the complexity of the task of synthesis, however, that biology develops its unique and profound distinction from the physical sciences. The task of synthesis in biology, i.e., the understanding of the functional organization of the integrative machinery, requires, by definition, knowledge of interrelationships between many unit processes on an enormously complex scale. Tactically, it appears that such knowledge can only be gained by the experimental investigation of *many bodily processes concurrently.* From a practical standpoint, this fact raises formidable new demands for modifications of research approach, which will make the *concurrent* experimental assessment of a large number of interrelated parameters manageable. Certainly, experience in the psychoendocrine field suggests more and more that the rate at which we can make progress in the study of integrative processes, such as emotions, will be largely determined by the rate at which we can learn to develop innovative organizational and tactical approaches that will enable us to deal with a uniquely complex system of multiple, interacting, coordinated variables, within the framework of the scientific method, and on a scale well beyond that achieved so far in multidisciplinary research. The task is not just to reduce complex problems to comfortably manageable units, but to deal with complexity itself, in a manner for which the physical sciences provide few, if any, appropriate precedents.

The purpose of this chapter, then, is twofold; first, to trace the course of events in psychoendocrine research that suggests the need to deal with an increasingly broader range of complexly interrelated psychological and endocrine parameters in research on emotion; secondly, to survey some of the general biological conclusions that have emerged so far from the psychoendocrine study of emotions, particularly in the context of more general physiological knowledge of the organization of endocrine integration.

II. THE RELEVANCE OF MULTIPLE PSYCHOLOGICAL PARAMETERS IN PSYCHOENDOCRINE STUDIES OF EMOTION

Early psychoendocrine research was based upon the plausible assumption that, among various psychological parameters, affective state was most likely to be correlated with endocrine activity. It was also common for early workers to rely heavily upon *situational criteria* for the operational definition of emotional reactions in psychoendocrine studies. It was soon learned that the wide range of individual differences between subjects in psychoendocrine response to the same "stressful" life situation or laboratory stimulus, particularly in humans, required that a more direct assessment be made of the varying quality and degrees of emotional reactions occurring in each individual subject. Roughly quantitative *observer estimates of affective distress,* such as anxiety, hostility, and depression, on the basis of such methods as clinical evaluation or psychological testing, accordingly proved useful in establishing more convincingly a positive correlation between emotional and hormonal disturbances.

It next became clear, however, that many instances were observed in which superficial evaluation of overt behavioral signs of emotional state was not sufficient to provide an understanding of psychoendocrine data. In our own experience this was particularly evident in observations of the parents of leukemic children, which indicated, for example, that similar acutely disturbing occasions were associated with suppression of urinary 17-hydroxycorticosteroid (17-OHCS) levels in some subjects and elevation of such levels in other subjects (Fig. 2). Subjects who had high mean basal urinary 17-OHCS levels, such as Subjects B and D in Fig. 2, often tended to show still *higher* levels on days when events considered to be unusually distressing occurred, whereas subjects with low mean basal 17-OHCS

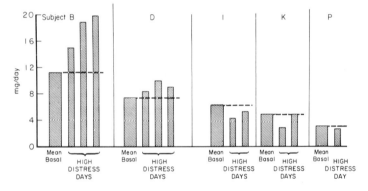

FIG. 2. Contrasting directions of change in urinary 17-OHCS levels in different persons in response to similar, distressing life events.

levels, such as Subjects I, K, and P, tended to show still *lower* levels on what appeared to be similar occasions or "high distress days."

It was only when additional attention was focused on an *evaluation of psychological defenses* in these subjects that the significance of psycho-endocrine data became greatly clarified. It was found, for example, that subjects prone to rely heavily upon the defensive mechanism of denial were likely in this situation to run low chronic mean basal corticosteroid values and to suppress corticosteroid levels even lower on acutely distressing occasions, apparently in an overcompensatory fashion. Furthermore, the overt expressions of affective state were sometimes found quite misleading. In some subjects, for example, those characterized as "suffering in silence," particularly with severe neurotic repression of affect, high chronic mean basal corticosteroid levels and spiking elevations during acutely stressful events belied the stoical, unruffled behavioral style in which external expressions of emotional distress were characteristically missing. Conversely, cases were observed in which flagrant overt signs of emotional distress were habitually displayed in an apparently histrionic or manipulative fashion and were attended by little, if any, associated disturbance in corticosteroid levels. Knowledge gained from such anecdotal observations led to the development of a relatively objective and reproducible psychiatric methodology for an overall assessment of the effectiveness of psychological defenses which, in predictive studies (Wolff, Friedman, Hofer, and Mason, 1964a; Wolff, Hofer, and Mason, 1964b; Rose, Poe, and Mason, 1968), yielded higher correlation coefficients with corticosteroid values than those obtained from the unilateral evaluation of overt affective behavior alone.

The logic of the strategy which emerged as this issue was confronted was that, if corticosteroid levels provide a sensitive index of general emotional arousal, as has been abundantly established in a large literature (Mason, 1968c), by the same token such hormonal levels should provide also a reflection, or an index, for studying the opposing psychological defensive forces that prevent, minimize, or counteract emotional arousal in the face of threat or in the face of anticipated coping activity.

In extending our studies of individual differences in effectiveness of psychological defenses to Army recruits during basic training, it further became especially clear that a particular defensive style is not necessarily invariably associated with a particular corticosteroid picture in all situations. The specific demands or conditions of the *particular psychosocial setting* or milieu must obviously be taken into account in relation to the particular defensive style, in a broader, psychodynamic view of the individual subject, as has also been emphasized in clinical studies (Sachar, 1967). A defensive style which may be effective in maintaining endocrine and physiological homeostasis during basic training, for example, may be relatively ineffective in other life settings with quite different psychosocial conditions (Poe, Rose, and Mason, 1970).

A striking correlation in these young men between parental death during childhood and chronic mean basal corticosteroid levels also emphasized the relevance of *historical or developmental variables* in psychoendocrine studies. As shown in Fig. 3, in a group of 91 Army recruits, 12 of the 14 young men who had experienced a parental death during childhood had chronic mean urinary 17-OHCS levels in the upper or lower quartiles, with a striking tendency for those with maternal deaths to be in the upper quartile and those with paternal deaths to be in the lower quartile (Poe et al., 1970). Even on a relatively short-term basis, it has also been observed that the recent prior experience of monkeys could influence not only the degree, but even the direction of cortisol response to specific emotional stimuli (Mason, Harwood, and Rosenthal, 1957b; Mason, 1968f).

Still another group of psychoendocrine observations demonstrate that both suppression and elevation of hormonal levels can occur during the

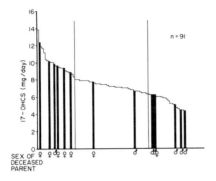

FIG. 3. Correlation between occurrence of parental death during childhood and chronic mean urinary 17-OHCS levels in army recruits.

commonplace experience of viewing different motion pictures (Wadeson, Mason, Hamburg, and Handlon, 1963; Levi, 1965). Extrapolation of these and related findings (Levi, 1972) suggests the possibility that a broad variety of *everyday mental or psychomotor activities,* including diverting or recreational activities as well as occupational activities, may be sensitively reflected in hormonal adjustments. Further exploration along these lines is needed, but tentatively, at least, the tension-building or tension-relieving effects of the particular activities subjects are engaged in while under study may represent another experimental variable to be considered in the assessment of the balance between the arousal and antiarousal forces that comprise the multiple, interacting codeterminants of psychoendocrine reactions.

Finally, in focusing on psychological determinants of endocrine activity, it must also be borne in mind that certain nonpsychological determinants such as body weight or environmental temperature, for example, may also influence chronic mean basal corticosteroid levels (Poe et al., 1970).

It is interesting that the phases of experience in psychological aspects of psychoendocrine research, which I have outlined briefly above, and at greater length elsewhere (Mason, *in press b*), fit rather closely with Cannon's conception of emotional mechanisms. Cannon cited some evidence from which he reasoned that the subjective feeling, the visceral changes, and the overt behavior, which normally comprise three integral parts of emotional reactions, may become dissociated under certain conditions (Cannon, 1922). The finding of such dissociations in recent psychoendocrine research bear out this view, and particularly emphasize the methodological corollary that it is hazardous, if not unsound, to rely upon subjective feeling state alone, visceral changes alone, or overt behavior alone in the experimental evaluation of emotional reactions. An integrated assessment of all three components together, however, appears much less likely to yield misleading conclusions.

From a practical standpoint, then, the cumulative experience so far in the psychoendocrine field suggests that simplistic or narrow methodological approaches have provided useful, but limited, insight and that it is necessary to confront the problem of dealing concurrently with an increasing range of interacting psychologic, social, and nonpsychological factors as multiple, codeterminants of hormonal levels. It appears unrealistic, as another often overlooked methodological corollary of this conclusion, for example, to expect a consistent correlation between any specific behavioral trait or test score and any specific hormonal trend to occur in all situations. It appears, rather, that the hormonal trend is a resultant of a balance of opposing and cooperating forces and can be predicted with increasing accuracy as the multiple factors involved, including affective state, defensive organization, social setting, prior experiential or developmental factors, and current activities, can all be evaluated in a psychodynamic perspective for each individual subject.

Although there are important scientific problems, such as in the need for refinements in methodology, for example, involved in effectively evaluating all these psychosocial parameters together in highly coordinated research, there are also some human and organizational problems which may ultimately prove to be even more difficult obstacles (Mason, 1970). Perhaps one of the principal problems is the disunion of the various behavioral disciplines. As a physiologist, I have been privileged over the years to collaborate with many investigators representing the major experimental and clinical behavioral disciplines. If I may venture some personal impressions emerging from this experience, I should remark first that I have been moved to admiration for the utility and the special strengths of *each* of these behavioral approaches, including behavioral conditioning, clinical psychological testing, and psychoanalytic psychiatry, in facilitating the generation and understanding of psychoendocrine data. At the same time, it has been clear that the theoretical and methodological leverage provided by any single behavioral approach alone is limited, in terms of the total research task at hand. If the approaches are taken together, however, their combined strength appears considerably greater than that of any single approach alone. As some examples, skillful psychological testing can profitably be used to provide independent and more objective evaluations of impressionistic psychiatric observations; psychiatric formulations, however subjectively based, can provide a rich source of hypotheses which may be useful in singling out the relevant developmental, social, and psychological parameters for experimental or clinical psychological studies of emotional behavior; social and clinical fields can profitably use the conditioning methodology of experimental psychology, and so on. Yet, although some encouraging, scattered efforts at such cooperation have been made, more generally, deep-rooted barriers apparently prevail between some of the behavioral disciplines in a disjunctive way which clearly works against the constructive scientific exploitation of their combined strengths. Because of the uniquely complex and difficult problems involved in the study of integrative mechanisms such as emotional processes, however, it seems to me that we especially can not afford to do anything less in this field than to use all the theoretical and methodological tools at our command for all they are worth collectively. Any future insights into the causes of this problem and any innovative measures, then, which can promote appreciation of the mutual self-interest between the various behavioral approaches and permit greater exploitation of their combined strength in complementary, supplementary, or cross-fertilizing ways seem very likely to yield significant advances in levels of insight in psychoendocrine research, if we can judge by the experience so far in this field.

III. THE RELEVANCE OF MULTIPLE ENDOCRINE PARAMETERS IN PSYCHOENDOCRINE STUDIES OF EMOTION

The first experimental observation that emotional reactions are reflected in endocrine activity was the demonstration that levels of "adrenalin," measured by an intestinal-strip bioassay, were elevated in cats frightened by a barking dog (Cannon and de la Paz, 1911). The modern era of highly refined biochemical research in psychoendocrinology, however, did not begin until about 40 years later. In the period beginning about 1946, the discoveries by Euler of the natural occurrence of norepinephrine in the body and of its role as an adrenal-medullary hormone and chemical transmitter of adrenergic nerves (Euler, 1956) made possible the reassessment and extension of Cannon's work at a new level of insight. After developing reliable methods for the measurement of urinary catecholamine levels, Euler and his associates proceeded to confirm that the sympathetic-adrenal medullary system was sensitively responsive to psychological influences (Euler and Lundberg, 1954; and Euler, Gemzell, Levi, and Strom, 1959). During the past 20 years, many other workers, particularly Levi, Frankenhaeuser, and their colleagues, have further established beyond any doubt the psychoendocrine characteristics of this system (Levi, 1972; Frankenhaeuser, 1971; Mason, 1968d). During the early 1950's, a number of workers also became interested in using newly developed biochemical methods to evaluate Selye's earlier observation that suggested that psychological stimuli could also affect secretion of adrenal cortical hormones (Selye, 1936). A considerable amount of data was soon obtained which supported the conclusion that the pituitary-adrenal cortical axis constitutes a second psychoendocrine system which sensitively reflects emotional reactions (Mason, 1968c).

During the past two decades, the great bulk of psychoendocrine research has been focused primarily on these two endocrine axes, the pituitary-adrenal cortical and sympathetic adrenal-medullary systems, as reviewed at length elsewhere (Mason, 1968c,d; Mason et al., 1968a,g). A much small amount of effort has been devoted to the pituitary-thyroid system (Mason, 1968e; Mason et al., 1968d) and still less to the various other endocrine systems (Mason, Jones, Ricketts, Brady, and Tolliver, 1968b;

Mason, Kenion, Collins, Mougey, Jones, Driver, Brady, and Beer, 1968*c;* Mason, Taylor, Brady, and Tolliver, 1968*f;* Mason, Tolson, Robinson, Brady, Tolliver, and Johnson, 1968*h;* Mason, Wherry, Brady, Beer, Pennington, and Goodman, 1968*i;* Mason, Wool, Wherry, Pennington, Brady, and Beer, 1968*k*). During our early experience in psychoendocrine research, however, we became aware of several lines of evidence and some compelling reasons which suggested that the study of endocrine regulation may be clarified greatly by an approach which considers simultaneously the full scope of relative changes of activity in the many closely interrelated neuroendocrine systems. Along with neuroanatomical and clinical lines of evidence, the steadily mounting evidence that the hormones of the many endocrine glands are *intimately interdependent* in their actions at the metabolic level, being often aligned in complex antagonistic and synergistic relationships with each other, provides a particularly compelling basis for looking at the interrelationships between these hormones at the regulatory level in terms of *patterns* of secretory change (Mason, 1968*b*).

Accordingly, as practical factors, particularly the availability of reliable new methods for assay of the various hormones has permitted, our laboratory effort has been devoted for many years to developing a broad battery of hormone assays so that we could test the hypothesis that the study of *patterns* or *profiles* of multiple endocrine secretory changes might lead to a level of understanding of integrative organization not possible with the study of single endocrine systems in isolation.

Figure 4 presents a view of the assemblage of neuroendocrine systems known at the present time, which may, on the basis of neuroanatomical

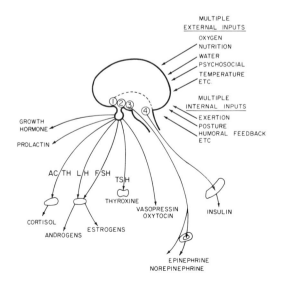

FIG. 4. The assemblage of interdependent neuroendocrine systems, with some of the multiple external and internal inputs that influence these systems.

reasoning at least, deserve close scrutiny as possible mediators of the effects of emotions and related psychological processes upon bodily functions. The relatively recent recognition of certain neurohumoral pathways and neurosecretory "releasing hormones," linking the hypothalamus to the anterior pituitary and its many hormones, has considerably extended our view of the articulations between neurons and endocrine cells beyond the previously known linkages of the posterior pituitary, sympathetic-adrenal medullary, and possibly, a vagoinsulin system (Mason, 1968b).

In reviewing some of our own research experience with this approach, I would like to emphasize that I am acting as a spokesman for a large number of investigators in both the behavioral and endocrinological fields, with whom I have collaborated in experimental studies involving both monkey and human subjects. A great debt of gratitude is particularly owed to Dr. David Rioch for his role in encouraging and supporting the development of this rather unconventional, long-term research program.

In 1968 we reported one of our initial efforts to survey the scope of psychoendocrine responses on a broader scale, using as an emotional stimulus the conditioned avoidance procedure in male rhesus monkeys (Mason, 1968a). In the avoidance procedure the monkey presses a hand lever at a moderate, continuous rate in order to avoid an unpleasant electric stimulus to the feet. Prior work had shown such a conditioned avoidance procedure to be associated with immediate, marked, and consistent plasma 17-OHCS responses in monkeys (Mason, Brady, and Sidman, 1957a). Figure 5 summarizes the results obtained when we measured concurrently some indices of activity in the pituitary-thyroidal, pituitary-gonadal, growth hormone, and insulin systems, as well as the adrenal systems. The period of the 72-hr avoidance sessions, demarcated by the vertical dotted lines, was found to be associated with a broad range of endocrine responses in normal male rhesus monkeys, involving not only the adrenal hormones, but every hormone we were able to measure at the time of this study. Urinary 17-OHCS, epinephrine, norepinephrine, plasma butanol-extractable iodine (BEI), as a thyroid index, and growth hormone levels increase, while urinary androgens, estrogens, and plasma insulin levels decrease. Inspection of the pattern of these multiple hormonal responses suggests an organization in which those hormones promoting catabolic mobilization of energy resources rise during avoidance, whereas potent anabolic hormones such as insulin and testosterone reciprocally decline initially, then secondarily rise during the aftermath when restorative processes might logically be expected to occur (Mason, 1968f). Although such an interpretation of the significance of this pattern must certainly be regarded as speculative at present, these data generally lend considerable additional support to Cannon's view of emotional arousal as being associated with organized visceral preparation for the strenuous muscular exertion of anticipated flight or struggle in threatening situations. This issue and other details of

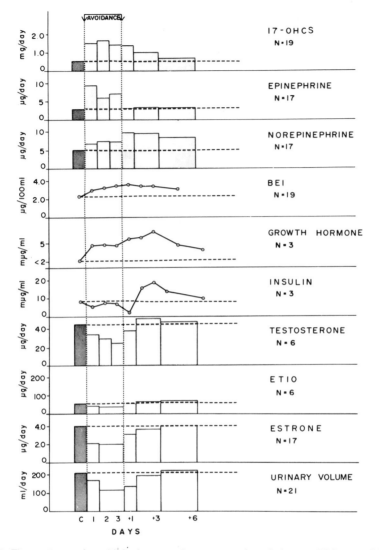

FIG. 5. The pattern of multiple hormonal responses in relation to 72-hr conditioned avoidance sessions in male rhesus monkeys.

the study summarized in Fig. 5 have been considered at some length in a recent monograph (Mason, 1968a).

Of the various possibilities for further investigations suggested by this initial study of the organization of hormonal response patterns, we have subsequently concentrated on several lines of approach. First, we have made a continuing effort to refine the endocrinological methodology of our approach, particularly with regard to the specificity and reliability of indices of pituitary-thyroidal and pituitary-gonadal activity. Secondly, we have extended this approach to the study of other emotional stimuli in the monkey and in human subjects in order to determine whether the pattern shown in Fig. 5 is a relatively fixed and common integrative response pattern associated with general emotional arousal or if variations in the response profile might be observed in different circumstances. Third, we have studied the hormonal response patterns to a variety of "physical" stimuli, such as muscular exertion, fasting, cold, heat, nutritional changes, etc., in order to determine whether specific physical stimuli evoke specific hormonal response patterns and to compare such patterns with those evoked by psychological stimuli. Fourth, we have made some preliminary, exploratory efforts to investigate the possibility that broadly viewed hormonal response patterns might at times reflect integrative disorders and play a mediating, pathogenetic role in certain medical illnesses. Of these several approaches, the first two are, of course, most directly relevant to the topic of this volume and are the principal concern of the present chapter.

During the same period in which the avoidance experiments were being conducted, an extensive series of observations were also being made on the pattern of hormonal response in the monkey to an unconditioned emotional stimulus, namely, placement in a restraining chair. Earlier observations had established that such chair restraint, which involves pillory-type confinement at the neck and waist, with freedom of the arms, legs, and some rotary trunk movement, was a potent, but transient, psychoendocrine stimulus, as judged by plasma and urinary 17-OHCS responses (Mason et al., 1957b). Figure 6 shows the pattern of hormone response to chair restraint in a male monkey, as presented in an earlier preliminary report (Mason, 1968f). It is evident that the acute response pattern is virtually identical to that observed during the initial phase of avoidance, with urinary 17-OHCS, epinephrine, norepinephrine, and plasma BEI levels rising, while urinary testosterone, estrone, and plasma insulin levels decline. As we have enlarged this series of experiments, this response pattern has been found to be as consistently reproducible for this situation as it was for the conditioned avoidance situation in the monkey. Figure 7 summarizes results of a recent series of chair restraint experiments, with mean values showing the typically organized pattern of transient 17-OHCS, epinephrine, norepinephrine, thyroid (BEI) elevation, and estrone and testosterone decrease, in male monkeys, as reported in greater detail elsewhere (Mason, 1972; Mason and Mougey, 1972; Mason, Mougey, and Kenion, 1973).

The plasma insulin and growth hormone results following chair restraint are not included in Fig. 7 because of some factors complicating the interpretation of these findings. Although mean plasma insulin levels were observed to decline sharply from 9.2 ng/ml before restraint to 1.7 ng/ml 2 hr after restraint in a series of six monkeys, an unexplained, high, prerestraint mean "fasting" plasma glucose of 148 mg/100 ml raised the question of whether

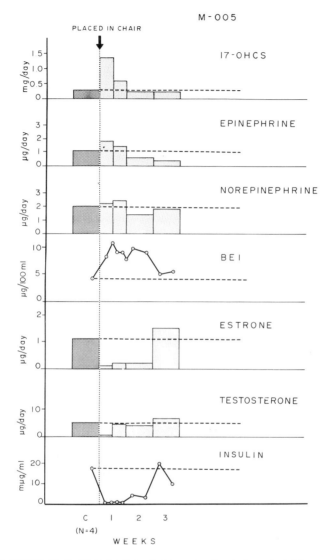

M-005

FIG. 6. The pattern of multiple hormonal responses to chair restraint in a male rhesus monkey.

the observed insulin changes might simply be a function of changing glucose levels, since the mean glucose level fell to 125 mg/100 ml 2 hr following onset of restraint. Observations in some individual animals, however, suggested that the suppression of plasma insulin levels was not determined solely by blood glucose fluctuations (Fig. 8). In these two experiments marked suppression in plasma insulin levels occurred during the 2 hr following chair restraint in spite of a marked concurrent rise in plasma glucose

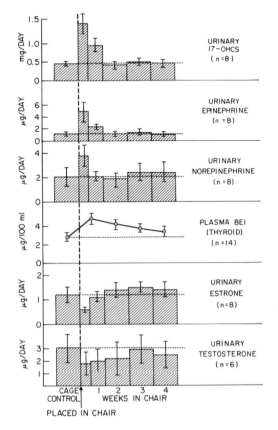

FIG. 7. The pattern of multiple hormonal responses to chair restraint in a series of male rhesus monkeys.

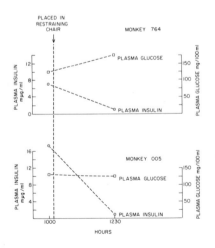

FIG. 8. Plasma insulin decrease independent of plasma glucose change following onset of chair restraint in two monkeys.

levels in Monkey 764 and in the absence of plasma glucose change in Monkey 005. Such dissociation in insulin-glucose relationships is similar to that previously observed in the more extensive series of conditioned avoidance experiments and suggests that psychological influences can preempt the regulatory effect of plasma glucose and bring about suppression of insulin levels (Mason et al., 1968*i*).

The study of plasma growth hormone responses to chair restraint was complicated by the fact that it was impossible with our standard procedure to obtain proper control, prerestraint baselines, because of the frequent occurrence of marked and very rapid growth hormone responses to the capture and venipuncture procedure itself in caged monkeys. Thus, as shown in Fig. 9, the mean value following capture and venipuncture in

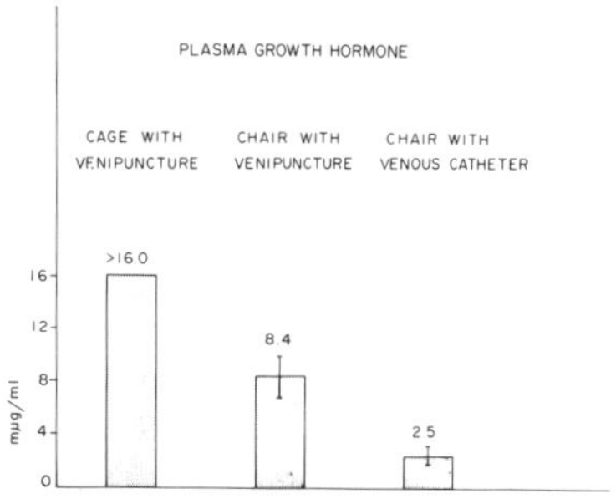

FIG. 9. "Basal" growth hormone levels in normal monkeys subjected to varying degrees of handling during blood withdrawal.

caged monkeys was greater than 16 ng/ml, as compared to a mean value of 10 ng/ml in samples obtained by the more rapid and less disturbing venipuncture procedure during chair restraint, and to a mean value of 2.5 ng/ml in samples obtained remotely through a chronic indwelling intravenous catheter without any confrontation or handling of chair-restrained animals (Mason et al., 1968*k*). The latter value compares closely with the mean basal plasma growth hormone value of about 1 ng/ml reported by Knobil (1966), using chronic indwelling venous catheters in normal rhesus monkeys. These results, although they do not permit conclusions about the effects of chair restraint as originally hoped, appear to lend further support to the conclusion that growth hormone levels are quite responsive to emotional stimuli and indicate that this system is one of the more rapidly responding and labile of the psychoendocrine systems.

Several other observations made in studies with normal human subjects suggest, however, that growth hormone responses to psychological stimuli do not always correlate in a simple or invariable manner with the responses of other endocrine systems. In a series of observations on eight normal young men, for example, in whom intravenous catheterization was performed several hours before a muscular exercise experiment, rather close correlation was observed between plasma cortisol and growth hormone responses to this procedure. As shown in Fig. 10, three of the eight subjects (Subjects A, B, and C) showed substantial plasma cortisol responses to the catheterization, whereas the mean values of the remaining five "nonresponders" declined from 9 to 7 μg%, with a relatively small standard error, during the same period. At the same time, Subjects A, B, and C were also the only three subjects to show appreciable plasma growth hormone responses to the catheterization procedure (Mason, Hartley, Mougey, Ricketts, and Jones, 1972).

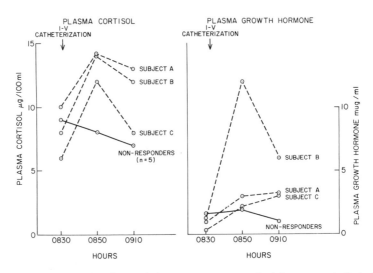

FIG. 10. Plasma cortisol and growth hormone responses to intravenous catheterization in some individual normal subjects.

On another occasion in the same subjects, however, no such similarity of response pattern was observed. A strikingly consistent elevation of plasma cortisol levels was observed during a 20-min period which represented the first experience immediately prior to the onset of an experimental session in which these young men knew that they were going to exercise on a bicycle ergometer to the point of exhaustion, as an "endurance" test. Although plasma cortisol elevations occurred in all eight subjects during this anticipatory period, as shown in Table 1, the majority of subjects failed to show plasma growth hormone elevations, although the two subjects (G and H) who showed the largest cortisol responses also showed rises in plasma growth hormone levels, so that one possible explanation to be considered may be that of threshold differences for the two systems. Dissociation between plasma cortisol and growth hormone responses to psychological stimuli has also previously been reported by others and has

TABLE 1. *Comparison of plasma cortisol, growth hormone, and free fatty acid levels in individual subjects during a 20-min period immediately prior to the onset of exhausting exercise*

	Minutes before exercise	Plasma cortisol (μg/100 ml)		Plasma growth H (nU/ml)		Plasma FFA (meq/l)	
		−20	0	−20	0	−20	0
Subject							
A		4	6	<2	<2	1.06	1.06
B		4	7	8	2	0.60	0.85
C		5	7	2	3	1.18	1.18
D		4	9	5	2	0.56	0.56
E		4	6	<2	2	1.14	1.14
F		4	8	>20	16	0.50	0.50
G		5	18	<2	3	1.60	1.60
H		7	14	2	8	1.27	1.27

prompted interest in the possibility that different psychological factors may be correlated with the two endocrine systems (Greene, Condron, Schalch, and Schreiner, 1970). Although this possibility is certainly worth further study, differences in the dynamics of the two systems and the attendant problems of designing appropriate sampling schedules, along with recent concern about the role of humoral factors in growth hormone regulation, suggest the need for caution in the design of control measures in psychoendocrine studies comparing these two endocrine systems. Recent reports of suppressing effects of free fatty acids (FFA) upon growth hormone release suggest that FFA levels should be evaluated as a possible codeterminant of growth hormonal responses in psychoendocrine experiments (Lipman, Taylor, Schenk, and Mintz, 1972). Whereas the FFA levels in the pre-exercise study (Table 1) tend to be lower in those subjects having high plasma growth hormone levels 20 min prior to exercise, they do not appear to afford an adequate basis for explaining the cortisol-growth hormone dissociation in this instance and certainly more extensive studies are needed to pursue this question further.

Although our initial experience with both conditioned avoidance and chair adaptation situations indicated that thyroid activity, as measured by BEI levels, was consistently, although modestly, increased in relation to these emotional disturbances in the monkey, some conflicting findings concerning psychological influences upon thyroid activity have been reported in the earlier psychoendocrine literature (Mason, 1968e). We have, therefore, sought opportunities to make further studies of the pituitary-thyroidal system. Since the BEI determination is generally recognized as a relatively crude index of thyroid activity which does not alone provide a basis for distinguishing between such factors as thyroid secretory rate, thyroxine-binding by plasma protein, and peripheral thyroxine turnover, all of which are codeterminants of plasma thyroid hormone level, we were particularly interested in refining our methodological approach.

The recent availability of a radioimmunoassay method for measurement of the pituitary thyroid-stimulating hormone (TSH) has provided a valuable new opportunity to circumvent some of the problems of interpreting results obtained by measurement of the target thyroid hormones alone. Accordingly, we recently measured plasma TSH levels in a series of nine monkey chair restraint experiments in which plasma BEI levels had previously been determined. As shown in Fig. 11, plasma TSH levels do rise significantly

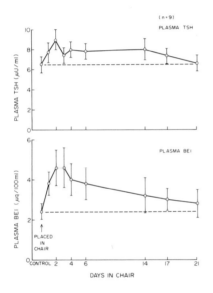

FIG. 11. Plasma TSH and BEI response to chair restraint in the monkey.

following chair restraint in the monkey and the configuration of the TSH response curve is generally similar to that for the BEI response curve over the 3-wk period, although the percentage changes are smaller for TSH levels than for BEI levels. In addition, by retrieval of frozen samples from other earlier experiments, it was possible to obtain some limited data on TSH response to conditioned avoidance sessions. In a series of 14 experiments, mean plasma TSH levels increased significantly from 10.2 to 12.3 μU/ml after 1 hr of conditioned avoidance (Mason, Wherry, Pennington, and Brady, *unpublished observations*). The study of plasma immunoreactive TSH levels in the monkey, then, tends so far to support the conclusions from earlier BEI measurements that the activity of the pituitary-thyroidal system is stimulated during two different emotionally disturbing situations in the monkey.

The occurrence of consistent plasma cortisol responses in all eight young men during the 20-min anticipatory period immediately prior to their first exhausting exercise session, as mentioned earlier, also recently provided an excellent opportunity for further studies of the pituitary-thyroidal system in the human. In these experiments we were able to measure not only plasma TSH levels, but also plasma total thyroxine levels, by a relatively specific, competitive-protein binding method, along with plasma cortisol, epinephrine, and norepinephrine levels. There are significant elevations in both plasma TSH and total thyroxine levels, as well as in cortisol and norepinephrine levels during this anticipatory period (Fig. 12). Although the hormonal elevations are generally small in magnitude, it is especially im-

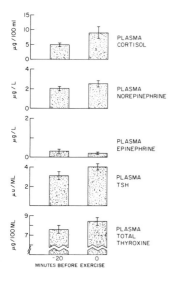

FIG. 12. The pattern of multiple hormonal responses in anticipation of exhausting exercise in normal young men (n = 8).

pressive that all eight subjects, without a single exception, showed elevations of TSH, thyroxine, cortisol, and norepinephrine levels during this period. Similarly consistent hormonal elevations were not noted in a variety of other situations involving anticipation of less strenuous exercise sessions or under control conditions (Mason et al., 1973; also *unpublished observations*). Free thyroxine levels, incidentally, did not change significantly in anticipation of exhausting exercise.

In general, then, our recent experience with plasma TSH measurements in psychoendocrine studies with both monkey and human subjects tends to confirm our earlier findings, based on BEI measurements, as well as those of other recent studies in humans (Johansson, Levi, and Lindstedt, 1970), indicating that the pituitary-thyroidal system is stimulated during emotional arousal. Pituitary-thyroidal responses, furthermore, appear to occur relatively consistently in relation to cortisol responses and do not appear to present an opportunity for possible endocrine differentiation of emotional responses, at least in the situations we have studied so far.

In this connection, however, it may be of interest to call attention to the pattern of plasma cortisol, epinephrine, and norepinephrine change during the pre-exercise session (Fig. 12). The pattern of plasma cortisol and norepinephrine increase, with little or no increase in plasma epinephrine levels in these young men anticipating exercise, is reminiscent of a pattern previously reported in several experimental situations with monkeys (Mason, Mangan, Brady, Conrad, and Rioch, 1961; Mason, Brady, and Tolson, 1966). This response pattern, referred to as "Pattern I" (Fig. 13) was ob-

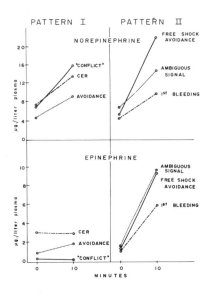

FIG. 13. Two patterns of plasma catecholamine responses in relation to different experimental situations in the monkey.

served in three conditioning situations, "conflict," "CER," and "avoidance." In "Pattern II" situations, "free-shock avoidance," "ambiguous signal," "first bleeding," marked epinephrine elevations accompanied norepinephrine elevations. In all six situations, involving both "Pattern I" and "Pattern II" responses, there were substantial plasma 17-OHCS elevations. In general, the most striking distinction between the two classes of situations appears to be the presence of a high degree of unpredictability, uncertainty, or ambiguity in the relatively rare "Pattern II" situations. Threat or unpleasant elements presumably were present in all situations, but in the "Pattern I" situations the animals knew exactly what was forthcoming, whereas in the "Pattern II" situations the animals were alerted to possible unpleasant events but did not know exactly what they would be or when to expect them. Curiosity is naturally aroused as to whether psychological correlates, such as feeling state changes, might be associated with these two different endocrinologically-defined patterns. The findings in the pre-exercise period perhaps renew some interest in pursuing this question further in the human subject with concerted attempts to test the hypotheses emerging from the monkey studies and particularly to search for possible psychological, as well as situational, correlates of the observed hormonal patterns. The pre-exercise study might be regarded as generally fitting with the "Pattern I" criteria of a situation involving rather low levels of uncertainty and ambiguity. As yet, however, we have not made any efforts to devise and study a "Pattern II" situation in human subjects, although the recent work of Frankenhaeuser (1971), which provides some support for a similar pattern of differential secretion of epinephrine in humans in relation to particular situational elements, lends encouragement for further work along these lines.

There are also some limitations to be considered in the above approach. First, the biochemical methods for plasma catecholamine methods have still not reached the high degrees of sensitivity, precision, and specificity which may be necessary for definitive physiological studies. Mean plasma epinephrine levels, for example, only rose from 0.2 $\mu g/l$ prior to exercise to 0.7 $\mu g/l$ at the point of exhaustion during the muscular exertion experiment. It may be, therefore, that relatively small changes, less than 1 $\mu g/l$, in plasma epinephrine levels may be physiologically significant in the human, although such changes may not be reliably measurable by present biochemical methods. With these reservations in mind, and considering the possibility that the "Pattern I and II" distinctions presented in Fig. 13 may represent quantitative rather than qualitative endocrinological differences, the possible differentiation of certain acute emotional reactions by their reflections in catecholamine patterns seems a promising issue for further exploration and evaluation, particularly in human subjects.

Methodological problems have also limited the rate of progress in psychoendocrine studies on the pituitary-gonadal system. Because of the complex biochemical pathways involved in the breakdown of the parent hormones secreted by the gonads and the fact that both adrenal cortical and gonadal hormones overlap considerably in the production of common steroid metabolites, the question of specificity in indices of gonadal secretion has presented a difficult problem, as reviewed by Rose (1969). In general, the techniques for assessment of gonadal secretion in the male have gradually moved through increasing degrees of specificity from measurements of the extremely crude adrenal-gonadal mixture of total 17-ketosteroids, to the major individual urinary androgen metabolites, androsterone, and etiocholanolone, to urinary estrogens derived largely from testosterone in the male, to urinary testosterone, and most recently to the radioimmunoassay of plasma testosterone levels. In addition to our previously mentioned studies of the pituitary-gonadal system in the avoidance and chair restraint situations in the monkey, we have also made some observations on this system in psychoendocrine studies of human subjects. Using a laborious gradient-elution chromatographic method for urinary androgen metabolite measurement and the Brown method for urinary estrogen measurement, the pattern of gonadal hormone response was studied in a young male student who had shown substantial adrenal and thyroid responses during the period of college final examinations. There was a progressive decrease in both urinary androsterone and estrone levels as the examination period approached and through the first examination day, during the period when urinary 17-OHCS levels were gradually rising (Fig. 14). This was followed by a sharp secondary elevation in androsterone and estrone levels

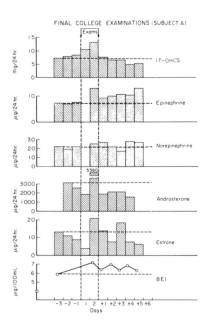

FIG. 14. The pattern of multiple hormonal responses in relation to final college examinations in a young man.

on the last examination day, when 17-OHCS levels peaked. Although not shown on the graph, the configuration of the urinary etiocholanolone response curve was closely similar to that of androsterone (Mason, Fishman, Hamburg, Tolson, *unpublished observations*). Generally, the overall pattern of rise in 17-OHCS, epinephrine, norepinephrine, and BEI levels and decline in urinary androsterone, and estrone levels seen in association with the onset of the examination period is similar to that previously observed in the psychoendocrine studies with the monkey. The sharp androgen and estrogen rise on the second examination day is unexplained, although some likely interpretations are suggested by related work. A secondary rebound elevation following initial suppression in androgen and estrogen levels was often observed in the monkey avoidance experiments (Mason et al., 1968*c,f,h*). Other possibilities, such as an overbalancing effect of adrenal cortical increase against gonadal decrease of androgen output or the occurrence of a qualitatively different emotional reaction on the second examination day, could not be evaluated further on the basis of available data in this study.

Additional early anecdotal observations were made on gonadal responses in two normal young men who showed substantial urinary 17-OHCS responses to hospital admission, i.e., admission to a normal control ward in the National Institute of Mental Health. As shown in Fig. 15, the response pattern in both subjects was characterized by elevation in urinary 17-OHCS, epinephrine, and norepinephrine levels and a decrease in urinary androsterone, etiocholanolone, and estrone levels on the first day of hospital admission, as compared to a control day after 8 days of adaptation to the hospital setting (Mason, Sachar, Fishman, Hamburg, and Handlon, 1965; also *unpublished observations;* Tolson et al., 1965). Again, the organization

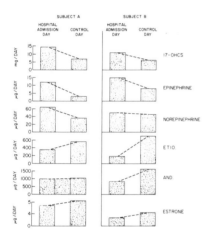

FIG. 15. The pattern of multiple urinary hormonal responses to hospital admission in two normal young men.

of the pattern resembles that observed in the monkey psychoendocrine studies.

In a relatively large series of observations on Army recruits during basic training at Ft. Dix and combat soldiers in Vietnam, additional data were obtained suggesting that gonadal hormone levels may be suppressed by psychological factors in human subjects (Rose, Bourne, Poe, Mougey, Collins, and Mason, 1969). Figure 16 shows that chronic mean urinary levels of testosterone, androsterone, and etiocholanolone are significantly lower in the Ft. Dix and Vietnam populations in "stressful" situations than in a normal population of medical center personnel. In a recent longitudinal study of young soldiers in Officer Candidate School significant suppression of plasma testosterone levels was observed during the "early, stressful part of the course" as compared with a later, more relaxed period (Kreuz, Rose, and Jennings, 1972).

A number of observations in the monkey and human, then, indicate that suppression of pituitary-gonadal activity may rather commonly accompany

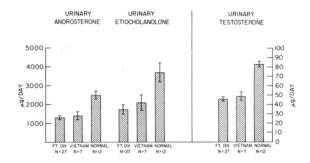

FIG. 16. Suppression of urinary testosterone, androsterone, and etiocholanolone excretion in soldiers in basic combat training (Ft. Dix) and under threat of attack (Vietnam) as compared to normal male medical center personnel.

emotional arousal or distress, as an integral part of a broad pattern of hormonal response. There are some rather intriguing preliminary data, however, which indicate that this is not an invariable phenomenon. On several occasions, a different response pattern has been observed which suggests that elevations of gonadal hormone levels can occur concurrently with elevations of the adrenal hormones. One of the first such observations was in an obese woman who was in the hospital for a routine diagnostic evaluation. On the day before she expected to be discharged, she was suddenly told by the physician that additional diagnostic tests would be required and that her return home must be postponed for a week or two. This event upset the patient greatly and she was quite angry at the disruption of family plans and the personal hardships entailed by the prolonged hospitalization. Figure 17 shows that marked elevations, from a baseline of 5 mg/day up to 11 mg/day,

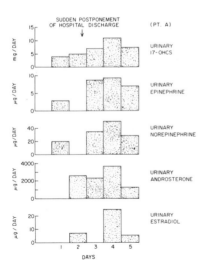

FIG. 17. The pattern of multiple hormonal responses in an obese woman following unexpected notification of postponement of hospital discharge.

in urinary 17-OHCS levels occurred during this episode, and that the peak 17-OHCS response was associated with concurrent peaking elevations of urinary androsterone and estradiol, as well as urinary epinephrine and norepinephrine levels (Mason, Fishman, *unpublished observations*).

Other episodes, in which similar response patterns were observed, occurred in the studies of normal young men during the Army basic combat training period. Figure 18 shows the response pattern of marked, concurrent, spiking elevations in urinary 17-OHCS, epinephrine, norepinephrine, androsterone, and estrone levels in a recruit (Subject A), occurring during a period when he had been singled out for humiliating harrassment by his platoon sergeant, because of his extremely poor performance in training. Although it was not possible to follow each of the 48 recruits involved in this study closely with objective, daily estimates of psychological state, it

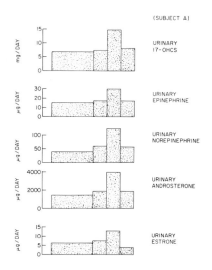

FIG. 18. The pattern of multiple hormonal responses in an army recruit during a basic training episode.

seems reasonable to assume that there was probably a substantial component of anger in the reactions of this subject to the public embarrassment to which he was subjected (Mason, Buescher, Belfer, Mougey, Taylor, Wherry, Ricketts, Young, Wade, Early, and Kenion, 1967).

Considerable emphasis was placed in basic training on competition between platoons to attain the highest score on barracks and personal inspections. On the day of such special occasions, recruits were required to perform a variety of menial, tedious, often unpleasant tasks in preparation for the inspecting officers. Figure 19 presents the hormonal response pattern in a recruit (Subject B) who showed about a twofold increase in urinary 17-OHCS levels on the day of an important inspection as compared to the preceding routine day. Again, the 17-OHCS response is accompanied by substantial concurrent elevations in urinary epinephrine, norepinephrine,

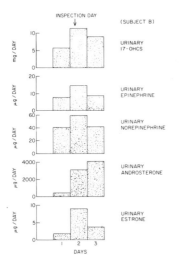

FIG. 19. The pattern of multiple hormonal responses in an army recruit in relation to platoon inspection.

androsterone, and estrone levels. Similar hormonal response patterns were observed in other subjects on occasions such as the first day of rifle training and the first forced, long march (Mason et al., 1967). In addition, such episodic spiking hormonal response patterns have been more recently observed in a group of obese patients and were found to be associated with elevations of urinary testosterone and plasma insulin levels, as well as of the androgen and estrogen urinary metabolites.

The interpretation of these data is not yet fully clear, but it appears reasonable to regard these spiking gonadal hormone elevations provisionally as probably reflecting psychoendocrine responses, although detailed psychological data were not available in most instances. The tendency for a number of these episodes involving increased gonadal hormone levels to have been associated with situations that were very likely anger-provoking may provide a clue or lead for the further, more systematic search for the possible social and psychological correlates of this endocrine response pattern. Some clinical impressions also suggest that these episodes may perhaps be particularly likely to be associated with repressed anger, so that there may be not only little or no overt expression of anger, but also little, if any, direct subjective awareness of anger or distress. If this is the case, then the problems of objective psychological evaluation are, of course, greatly multiplied. Several converging and increasingly objective approaches may be required eventually, but initially it may be particularly informative to carry out intensive, longitudinal studies of individual subjects, in whom repressed anger is a prominent clinical feature, and on whom a great deal of background historical and psychodynamic information has become available through long-term psychiatric evaluation. As psychoendocrine studies are made of such subjects through a variety of recurring life-experiences, it may be possible to utilize knowledge gained retrospectively, in the initial phase, as a basis for later prospective experiments, in which suspected relationships between hormone response pattern and psychological reactions are put to a predictive test. Such predictive studies have been useful in the past, for example, in relating basal urinary corticosteroid levels to the organization and effectiveness of psychological defenses (Wolff et al., 1964a; Rose et al., 1968). It also may well be that, even apart from the suggested hypothesis relating gonadal hormones and anger, a similar approach may be productive in the more general, extremely difficult study of neurotic processes, which has received very little systematic attention as yet in psychoendocrine research (Mason, *in press b*).

In summarizing our further experience, beyond the avoidance studies published in 1968, with the study of patterns of hormonal response to psychological influences, some additional general conclusions can perhaps be more confidently ventured. First of all, there appears to be little doubt that a broad range of hormones and endocrine systems respond *concurrently* to psychological influences, including the pituitary-thyroidal, pituitary-gonadal, growth hormone, and insulin systems, as well as the pituitary-adrenal cortical and sympathetic-adrenal medullary systems. A pattern of cortisol, epinephrine, norepinephrine, thyroxine, and growth hormone elevation with testosterone and insulin suppression has been so far the most commonly observed pattern of response to emotional stimuli and has been found to be remarkably reproducible in its entirety in both monkey and human subjects in a variety of situations. Some component hormonal changes within this pattern, however, appeared to be more consistent than others throughout our studies. Psychoendocrine responses involving cortisol, norepinephrine, and thyroxine levels tended to be among the most consistent from subject to subject and situation to situation. Epinephrine might perhaps be included in the above group, but special mention should be made of some evidence indicating that it may show relatively great quantitative, if not qualitative, variations in relation to certain psychological parameters. This finding is one of relatively few leads so far which offers some hope that psychoendocrine approaches may be useful in the differentiation of emotional states and indicates a need for further, more refined studies of catecholamine changes during acute, transient emotional reactions, particularly in human subjects.

Growth hormone responses to psychological stimuli appear to be relatively variable, both between subjects and experiences, and may provide some leverage in differentiating emotional reactions, but it is not yet clear as to the extent to which particular psychological factors versus nonpsychological factors, such as plasma free fatty acid or glucose levels, may be involved in determining the observed variability of response. In future psychoendocrine studies of the very labile growth hormone system, the rapidity of change in hormone levels within a few minutes and the question of possible refractory periods following spiking bursts of secretion will deserve close attention along with the assessment of psychological and humoral codeterminants of secretory activity in this system.

Insulin regulation has also been relatively neglected so far in psycho-endocrine research. Our own collection of data on insulin responses was limited in many of our studies because we did not want to introduce fasting as a complicating variable, as would be required to achieve stable, low base-line insulin levels prior to onset of psychological stimuli. If the insulin system were to be singled out for more detailed psychoendocrine studies, however, it should not be very difficult to deal with the complicating effects of eating or fasting, by the addition of suitable control measures. Certainly, the most common insulin response to emotional stimuli that we have so far observed has been a prompt and substantial decrease, but the possibility that insulin levels may rise in relation to psychological parameters under certain conditions is still an open question, given some preliminary support by some of our clinical data.

Although suppression of the pituitary-gonadal system has been observed under a number of emotionally disturbing conditions in both the human and monkey, there are some intriguing, although preliminary, indications that elevations of gonadal hormone levels may also occur in response to psychological influences other than sexual stimuli on some occasions, perhaps especially in relation to certain acute anger reactions. The recent availability of reliable competitive-protein binding and radioimmunoassay methods for the measurement of plasma testosterone levels should greatly expedite further psychoendocrine studies of the very tentatively suggested hypothesis that testosterone responses may yield information on the biological differentiation of emotional or related psychological states. Because of the especially prominent two-way interactions between gonadal hormones and the brain, however, special care will be required to establish independent-dependent relationships between variables in dealing with this system (Rose, 1972).

Research on psychological stimuli has so far, then, yielded only preliminary and limited indications that different, relatively specific emotional states may be correlated with different, specific patterns of multiple hormonal responses, although several promising leads along these lines appear worthy of further study. In the evaluation of differences in patterns of psycho-endocrine responses, careful attention must clearly be given to the question of whether qualitative or quantitative factors are involved, with regard to both stimuli and responses, and to the role of nonpsychological factors, as well as to the psychosocial parameters which are of primary interest. In general, however, it has been impressive how frequently a uniform pattern of acute psychoendocrine response has been observed which appears oriented, in part at least, toward mobilization of energy resources, in keeping with Cannon's notion of many visceral adjustments during emotional

reactions being concerned with preparation for the muscular e:
anticipated flight or fight, as visualized most clearly in the pr
natural situations in which the lower animals struggle to survive.

IV. PSYCHOENDOCRINE MECHANISMS IN A GENERAL PERSPECTIVE OF ENDOCRINE INTEGRATION

As a physiologist, it has been my inclination to view psychological influences on endocrine systems in a more general perspective which also considers the role of various commonplace, natural, nonpsychological stimuli upon the same endocrine systems. The integrative machinery must clearly deal routinely with all these multiple input stimuli, and often concurrently, since they are frequently present in various naturally occurring combinations. In recent years, therefore, we have also been conducting systematic studies of the patterns of multiple hormonal responses to a variety of stimuli such as muscular exercise, fasting, heat, and cold. Although it is beyond the scope of this chapter to deal in any detail with the findings in these studies, they have led to some general conclusions about the functional organization of neuroendocrine systems which may be useful in approaching future psychoendocrine research on emotions and in the clarification of controversial concepts in the "stress" field.

In attempting to study hormonal response patterns to various nonpsychological stimuli, a major obstacle soon proved to be that rigorous attention must be given to the frequent interference of attendant psychological stimuli, which have often been overlooked or underestimated in laboratory situations designed for the study of physical stimuli. The conditions to which animals or humans are subjected in the study of exercise, fasting, heat, etc., can very often *also* elicit potent psychological reactions related to pain, discomfort, or emotional arousal, particularly when elements of novelty or apprehensive anticipation are present. When such interfering independent variables are controlled or minimized, then such so-called "stressors," in Selye's terminology, as fasting or heat, for example, do not raise levels of adrenal cortical hormones in the absence of psychological stimuli (Mason, Wool, Mougey, Wherry, Collins, and Taylor, 1968*j;* Mason, 1971). A growing body of data, thus, casts serious doubt upon the concept of *absolute* "nonspecificity" of pituitary-adrenal cortical response to diverse "stressors," which has been given considerable emphasis as a basic premise of "stress" theory, as formulated by Selye (1950). A more tenable generalization in the light of current data appears to be that *psychologically induced* pituitary-adrenal cortical responses do occur in a wide variety of laboratory and life *situations* in a relatively "nonspecific" fashion, but that the pituitary-adrenal cortical system itself does not respond indiscriminately to the comprehensive range of nonpsychological stimuli or "stressors," as originally assumed in the formulation of the "nonspecificity" concept by Selye.

In evaluating data in relation to the "nonspecificity" concept it should be recognized that there are not only two polar opposites to be considered, i.e., whether a response occurs to only a *single* specific stimulus, and, thus, is *absolutely* specific, or if it occurs to *every* stimulus, and, thus, is *absolutely* nonspecific. Various intermediate degrees of *relative* "nonspecificity" must be considered. In hypothetical terms a hormone that responds to only two out of 20 stimuli can share the description "nonspecific" with a hormone that responds to 18 of the same 20 stimuli. The *degree* of "nonspecificity" of response is presumably, then, something that can be experimentally established in precise quantitative terms and is certainly an appropriate parameter to consider in the study of endocrine regulation.

From a practical, experimental standpoint, it would appear to be relatively easy to prove that a given hormone is not *absolutely specific* in its response to stimuli. This requires only the demonstration that a minimum of *two* completely different and discrete stimuli can elicit a similar response of the hormone in question. It is, however, a far different and immeasurably more difficult task to establish the other extreme of *absolute* "nonspecificity," which implies response to *all* stimuli. Enormous experimental effort would be required to move through each of the following several major stages in establishing *degrees* of response "nonspecificity": (1) to demonstrate that the response occurs in a relatively great diversity of experimental *situations;* (2) to demonstrate that the response occurs to a great diversity of *stimuli* (as independent variables are rigorously isolated in "pure" form); (3) to demonstrate that the response occurs to *all* stimuli.

It appears in the light of present knowledge that the "nonspecificity" concept was originally formulated from evidence which probably fits largely into the first of the above states of validation, since there was not rigorous isolation of independent variables in early "stress" research, particularly with regard to the common interference of psychological stimuli. What *was* demonstrated initially was that an adrenal cortical response occurred *in a wide variety of situations.* If it is to be concluded that the response, therefore, is elicited by a wide variety of *stimuli,* it must, without further data, be assumed that there is not a *single factor or stimulus* which is a component factor that the wide variety of situations share in common. Present indications are that this is not a safe assumption and that disturbing elements which elicit psychological reactions comprise a common stimulus, or stimulus class, at least, which is attendant to many situations in which physical "stressors" are studied. The more tenable conclusion, however, that *psychological reactions* occur in a wide variety of situations or to a wide variety of psychosocial stimuli, is a far different matter than the conclusion in "stress" theory than that activity of the *pituitary-adrenal cortical system* is increased by all stimuli, or by any environmental change. Certainly, it appears that the pituitary-adrenal cortical system does respond to more than one stimulus, as do other endocrine systems, but it also appears that the *degree* of its relative "nonspecificity" of response remains to be fully reevaluated with rigorous control of independent variables and special concern for the sensitivity of the system to subtle psychosocial influences (Mason, 1971).

As we became more attuned to the prevalence of psychological stimuli in laboratory experiments with conscious subjects, a picture soon began to emerge from our studies of other natural stimuli which indicated that there is actually a considerable degree of *specificity, or selectivity,* in endocrine integration. This became evident not only when interfering psychological factors were controlled, but perhaps even more so as an increasingly broadening view was obtained of the *patterning* of multiple, concurrent hormonal responses to discrete stimuli. In order to illustrate this point in a relatively simple manner, a chart focusing mainly on only the 17-OHCS, epinephrine, and norepinephrine patterns of response (" ↑ " increased levels, " ↓ " decreased levels, "0" little or no change in levels) to several, selected natural stimuli is presented in Fig. 20.

	17-OHCS	EPIN	NOREP	THYROXINE	GROWTH H	INSULIN	TESTOST	ETC
ACUTE AVOIDANCE	↑	↑	↑	↑	↑	↓	↓	
HEAVY EXERCISE	↑	↑	↑					
FASTING	0	↑	↓					
HIGH CHO DIET	↑	↓	↑					
HEAT	↓	↓	↓					
COLD	↑	↑	↑					
BED REST	0	↓	↓					
ETC								

FIG. 20. The organization of integrative patterns of hormonal responses to some natural stimuli.

First of all, by examining the columns vertically, it is evident that the levels of *none* of the three hormones, including 17-OHCS levels, are increased by *all* stimuli and that the "stress" concept of absolute *"nonspecificity"* of 17-OHCS response is not supported. Neither do any of the three hormones respond to only *one* stimulus, so that absolute *"specificity"* of response of any single hormone also does not appear to be the case. Our general experience so far in studying regulation of about 10 hormones indicates, rather, that all of them respond to multiple, discrete, natural stimuli, but that the levels of none are elevated by either *all* stimuli or only *one* stimulus. All of these hormones may be said to respond in a *relatively* "nonspecific" manner, then, as defined earlier. Judging from the literature as well as our own work, some hormones such as cortisol, thyroxine, or the catecholamines probably respond to a wider spectrum of stimuli than does aldosterone, for example, so that there may be some quantitative differences between various hormones in the degree of relative "nonspecificity" of response shown. Since response to multiple stimuli appears to be the general rule for the major endocrine systems studied so far, however, the concept of "nonspecificity" appears to be of rather limited value in distinguishing the regulation of one endocrine system from another.

In addition to the above view of the data in Fig. 20, when each line is viewed horizontally in comparison with the others, it is further evident that there are a variety of *distinctive combinations* of hormonal responses to different stimuli, even when only these three hormones are considered. Although avoidance, severe exercise, and cold, for example, do elicit a similar pattern involving elevation of all three hormones, fasting causes an increase in epinephrine, a decrease in norepinephrine, and little or no change in corticosteroid levels. A high carbohydrate (also protein and fat deficient) diet, by contrast, depresses epinephrine, while increasing corticosteroid and norepinephrine levels. Moderate heat suppresses levels of all three hormones. In bed rest, a commonplace natural stimulus on which little neuroendocrine data are available, catecholamine levels decline without associated corticosteroid changes. It should be noted, incidentally, that only the direction of initial hormonal response is indicated in Fig. 20, although there are marked quantitative differences in responses to different stimuli. The 17-OHCS response to avoidance, for example, is much greater than that to the high carbohydrate, protein and fat deficient diet in the monkey (Mason, 1974).

It has also been found that the intensity of the stimulus may affect the profile of hormonal response. Although not shown in Fig. 20, considerable evidence indicates that mild to moderate exercise elicits catecholamine increases but not increases in cortisol levels. As another example, larger growth hormone responses appear to be evoked by moderate than by mild or severe exercise (Hartley, Mason, Hogan, Jones, Kotchen, Mougey, Wherry, Pennington, and Ricketts, 1972a,b).

It also is evident as we have developed this approach that the *more hormones* measured in the response profile, the *more distinctive* the pattern becomes for each stimulus. Recent work in our laboratory by Dr. Monroe, for example, indicates that testosterone levels are increased during heavy muscular exercise, whereas the preliminary work of Dr. Ehle indicates that testosterone levels are suppressed during cold exposure, although cortisol, epinephrine, and norepinephrine elevations occur in common in both situations.

Inspection of Fig. 20 also illustrates that the *more stimuli* studied, the *more distinctive* becomes the response profile of each hormone. In comparing the main three hormonal columns vertically, it is evident that none of the hormones responds always in the same direction as either of the other two hormones, in an invariable, positively correlated relationship. Epinephrine or norepinephrine levels increase with some stimuli and decrease with others, sometimes in paired fashion, but sometimes change independently of each other. Corticosteroid levels rise, fall, or show no change depending upon the specific stimulus and are variably associated with or dissociated from catecholamine changes.

The integrative mechanisms, thus, appear to be organized to respond rather *selectively* in producing patterns of multiple hormonal changes, which differ according to the specific stimulus. The theoretical interpretation of the significance of these specific patterns of hormonal response must presumably be approached in terms of their consequences at the metabolic or homeostatic level. It may be expected that such interpretations will be largely speculative at first, but eventually they can be put to some experimental testing, particularly as both hormonal and related metabolic changes can be assessed concurrently. In viewing Fig. 20, for example, the common response pattern of increased levels of energy-mobilizing hormones and the common adaptive need for increased energy metabolism shared by severe exercise and cold provide at least circumstantial evidence for making a similar interpretation of the metabolic significance of the pattern of hormonal responses to emotional stimuli as being similarly oriented toward energy mobilization, as discussed previously (Mason, 1968*g*). As another example, the rise in levels of heat-producing hormones during cold exposure and the decrease in the same hormones during heat exposure appear to be in keeping with obvious adaptive, homeostatic needs in these environmental conditions. Such examples suggest that the interpretation of the organization of hormonal response patterns in terms of their metabolic concomitants may be a logical and illuminating approach as this work develops, but one that will be limited by existing knowledge of the range of metabolic effects of each hormone (Mason, 1968*g*).

There appears to be emerging, in fact, some dovetailing of our knowledge about the metabolic effects of hormones and about the regulation of hormone secretion. Individual hormones respond to a multiplicity of stimuli and they also individually have a multiplicity of effects at the metabolic level. In addition to having multiple metabolic effects, individual hormones appear to be aligned with each other in a complex, overlapping, staggered pattern of interpendent, often antagonistic or synergistic, relationships (Houssay, 1957). The significance of these interdependent relationships is not yet fully established, but certain case examples suggest, in a rather compelling way, that it may be through this system of interdependencies that a relative handful of hormones may become capable of effecting an enormous variety of subtly shaded, discriminating, relatively specific, integrative adjustments, as appropriate to frequently shifting specific metabolic or homeostatic needs. One such example is that of the interdependencies between insulin and growth hormone in their effects on organic metabolism. If there should be, hypothetically, a need for increased protein biosynthesis, a regulatory increase in insulin would seem especially appropriate, because of its potent anabolic effect on protein metabolism. As pointed out by Korner (1960), however, the hypoglycemia also associated with insulin release could be an undesirable, if not self-defeating, side effect. If, on the other hand, the integrative machinery were to effect a regulatory increase in growth hormone at the same time, this problem could be circumvented. Growth hormone is synergistic with insulin in its anabolic effect on protein metabolism but antagonistic in its effects on carbohydrate metabolism. Thus, in this rudimentary example, one can perhaps visualize how, in a broader and more complex way, certain of the spectrum of multiple effects of an individual hormone could be selectively enhanced or opposed by the relative integrative shifts in balance between it and the many other hormones, in accordance with their close interdependencies. From quite a different, but converging, viewpoint, then, the selectivity or patterning of the balance between the many hormones becomes a parameter of considerable, if not, key theoretical interest (Mason, 1968g).

V. SOME POSSIBLE DIRECTIONS FOR FUTURE APPROACHES

Figure 20 may perhaps be regarded as an emerging, rather skeletal, working blueprint for both a conceptual and experimental approach to the study of integrative organization of endocrine responses to emotional and other natural stimuli. The approach has some strategically advantageous practical features, including not only the objective and quantitative nature of the measurements as reflections of central integrative processes, but also the making feasible the simultaneous study of a broad array of coordinated, mediating, endocrine systems with only the intervention of collecting blood or urine samples. The enormous amount of future effort needed to develop this approach to its logical conclusion, however, is also quite evident. The number of hormones measured concurrently must eventually be made more comprehensive, hopefully as the remarkable progress of recent years in refinement of hormone assay procedures continues. In this connection, it should be borne in mind that the generalizations ventured in this chapter are derived from data obtained with a variety of hormonal indices, which still have various technical and theoretical limitations. The specificity and sensitivity of the plasma catecholamine method used, for example, are not nearly as satisfactory as those of the plasma cortisol method. Also, results obtained with plasma or urinary corticosteroid assays, such as those summarized in Fig. 20, should probably eventually be evaluated further by isotopic secretion rate or turnover studies, before we consider the direction of cortisol response to various stimuli firmly established, and so on. We are currently initiating such refined approaches whenever possible, particularly with regard to findings which appear relevant to the clarification and revision of "stress" concepts.

The number of natural, input stimuli listed in Fig. 20 must, of course, also be extended, with particular attention to isolating the input stimuli, whether psychological or physical, in as "pure" form as possible. The concept of a "nonspecific" hormonal response to any environmental change has for some time tended to diminish concern with the specific quality of discrete, input stimuli, with central receptors and tranducers, and, in fact, with the whole afferent limb of the endocrine regulatory process. It appears now that the careful isolation and identification of input stimuli should be given foremost, critical attention, and not only with regard to interfering emotional stimuli in studies of physical stimuli, as mentioned earlier. Some "stressors," such as hemorrhage, for example, are actually complex admixtures of stimuli in a physiological sense, in this case including hypoxia, dehydration, and hypovolemia, which logically should first be experimentally studied as separate, "elemental" stimuli, or separate independent variables, insofar as possible. Once the pattern of hormonal responses to the "elemental" natural stimuli are known, then the patterns of response to various natural combinations of stimuli should become more interpretable and such intriguing questions as how adaptive priorities are handled by the integrative machinery when diverse stimuli coexist may be more readily examined.

Although our studies of multiple endocrine parameters in relation to emotional and other stimuli so far might be regarded largely as basic physiological research, the implications of modern psychoendocrine approaches for medicine are worthy of brief mention. Within about two decades, we have moved, from a view of endocrine systems as governed largely by relatively simple, virtually infallible, humoral, self-regulating mechanisms, to a view in which endocrine systems represent a third effector system of the brain and are subjected to a wide range of psychological influences which profoundly affect hormonal balance in the body on both a short- and long-term basis. Outside of the concepts that hereditary defects or foreign elements, such as microorganisms or toxins, may cause disease, there is a dearth of basic hypotheses in medicine concerning disease genesis, particularly with regard to the ways in which the bodily machinery itself may be especially vulnerable to malfunction. The knowledge that the psyche is superimposed upon the humoral machinery for endocrine regulation drastically complicates our whole view of physiological homeostasis. It does not push the imagination very far to visualize that the superimposition of such complicated and idiosyncratic psychological factors, as emotions, defensive styles, and neurotic processes, on the lower physiological integrative machinery may deserve prime suspicion in our search for fallibility or disease-proneness in the human organism. Psychoendocrinology, in other words, provides still more impetus and new scientific leverage in pursuing the time-honored clinical formulation of psychosomatic medicine that the *concept of disease as resulting from integrative disorders,* rather than from regional or local disorders, may be worthy of serious consideration in medical research.

Finally, I should like to return to the basic issue of the "integrative" and

\listic" strategies in biology. Aside from theoretical differences .. ine two approaches, in practice the "integrative" approach departs irom the "elementalistic" approach largely in the number of biological parameters or variables being considered simultaneously, i.e., in the scope and complexity of the task. In confronting this problem of how to deal with complexity on such an unprecedented scale, within the framework of the scientific method, it is clear that new solutions must be sought (Mason, 1970). No one person can maintain authoritative mastery of adrenal physiology, thyroid physiology, gonadal physiology, cardiovascular physiology, etc., at the same time and on a continuing basis, any more than one person can achieve simultaneous mastery of all the behavioral disciplines relevant to studies of emotion. The only answer appears to be division of labor in an increasingly highly coordinated, cooperative manner. Our experience with interdisciplinary efforts to date, although often gratifying and productive, have generally met with only limited success, and it appears that we still have a great deal more to learn about the scientific, and particularly the practical human and organizational, factors which have proven obstacles to the effectiveness of past interdisciplinary research efforts. Ultimately, it seems very likely that advances in "integrative" research may be determined, not primarily by our rate of technological progress, but, rather, increasingly by our creative ability to develop new organizational approaches for dealing with biological complexity, in which strong emphasis is placed on the mutual self-interest among scientific specialists in pursuing cooperative rather than isolated, individual, or small group research in the traditional manner.

SUMMARY

A view is presented of psychoendocrine research on emotions as evolving through a succession of stages in which the need to consider a broadening range of multiple, interacting psychological, social, and endocrine parameters concurrently has become increasingly evident. Psychological approaches in this field have gained efficacy as an increasing number of parameters, including situational criteria, affective state, organization of psychological defenses, social milieu, and experiential or developmental history, are considered together in an integrated assessment of each individual subject. Similarly, as an increasing number of endocrine systems have been studied, it appears that not only the sympathetic-adrenal medullary and pituitary-adrenal cortical systems, but also the pituitary-thyroidal, pituitary-gonadal, growth hormone, and insulin systems can sensitively reflect emotional reactions. A conceptual and experimental approach based upon the premise that distinctive *patterns* or *profiles* of multiple, concurrent, hormonal responses to emotional and other stimuli can provide a new level of insight into the organization of endocrine integration is discussed.

REFERENCES

Bernard, C. (1957): *An Introduction to the Study of Experimental Medicine*, Dover Publications, Inc., New York.

Cannon, W. B. (1922): New evidence for sympathetic control of some internal secretions, *Am. J. Psychiatry 2*, 15–30.

Cannon, W. B. (1953): *Bodily Changes in Pain, Hunger, Fear, and Rage*, Branford, Boston.

Cannon, W. B., and de la Paz, D. (1911): Emotional stimulation of adrenal secretion, *Am. J. Physiol. 27*, 64–70.

Euler, U. S. von (1956): *Noradrenaline: Chemistry, Physiology, Pharmacology and Clinical Aspects*, Thomas, Springfield, Ill.

Euler, U. S. von, Gemzell, C. A., Levi, L., and Strom, G. (1959): Cortical and medullary adrenal activity in emotional stress, *Acta Endocrinol. 30*, 567–573.

Euler, U. S. von, and Lundberg, U. (1954): Effect of flying on the epinephrine excretion in Air Force personnel, *J. Appl. Physiol. 6*, 551–555.

Frankenhaeuser, M. (1971): Experimental approaches to the study of human behaviour as related to neuroendocrine functions. In: *Society, Stress, and Disease*, Oxford University Press, London, Vol. 1, pp. 22–35.

Greene, W. A., Conron, G., Schalch, D. S., and Schreiner, B. F. (1970): Psychologic correlates of growth hormone and adrenal secretory responses of patients undergoing cardiac catheterization, *Psychosom. Med. 32*, 599–614.

Hartley, L. H., Mason, J. W., Hogan, R. P., Jones, L. G., Kotchen, T. A., Mougey, E. H., Wherry, F. E., Pennington, L. L., and Ricketts, P. T. (1972a) Multiple hormonal responses to graded exercise in relation to physical training, *J. Appl. Physiol. 33*, 602–606.

Hartley, L. H., Mason, J. W., Hogan, R. P., Jones, L. G., Kotchen, T. A., Mougey, E. H., Wherry, F. E., Pennington, L. L., and Ricketts, P. T. (1972b) Multiple hormonal responses to prolonged exercise in relation to physical training, *J. Appl. Physiol. 33*, 607–610.

Houssay, B. C. (1957): Comments. In: *Hormonal Regulation of Metabolism*, Thomas, Springfield, Ill.

Johannson, S., Levi, L., and Lindstedt, S. (1970): Stress and the thyroid gland: A review of clinical and experimental studies, and a report of own data on experimentally induced PBI reactions in man. *Reports from the Laboratory for Clinical Stress Research*, Karolinska Institute, Stockholm, No. 17, November.

Knobil, E. (1966): The pituitary growth hormone: An adventure in physiology, *Physiologist 9*, 25–44.

Korner, A. (1960): The adrenal gland and *in vitro* protein synthesis. In: *Metabolic Effects of Adrenal Hormones* (Ciba Foundation Study Group No. 6), eds. G. E. W. Wolstenholm and C. M. O'Connor, Little, Boston, p. 38.

Kreuz, L. E., Rose, R. M., and Jennings, J. R. (1972): Suppression of plasma testosterone levels and psychological stress: A longitudinal study of young men in officer candidate school, *Arch. Gen. Psychiatry 26*, 479–482.

Levi, L. (1965): The urinary output of adrenalin and noradrenalin during pleasant and unpleasant emotional states, *Psychosom. Med. 27*, 80–85.

Levi, L., ed. (1972): Stress and distress in response to psychosocial stimuli, *Acta Med. Scand.* [*Suppl. 528*], *191*.

Lipman, R. L., Taylor, A. L., Schenk, A., and Mintz, D. H. (1972): Inhibition of sleep-related growth hormone release by elevated free fatty acids, *J. Clin. Endocrinol. 35*, 592–594.

Mason, J. W. (1968a): Organization of psychoendocrine mechanisms, *Psychosom. Med. 30*, 565–808.

Mason, J. W. (1968b): The scope of psychoendocrine research, *Psychosom. Med. 30*, 565–575.

Mason, J. W. (1968c): A review of psychoendocrine research on the pituitary-adrenal cortical system, *Psychosom. Med. 30*, 576–607.

Mason, J. W. (1968d): A review of psychoendocrine research on the sympathetic-adrenal medullary system, *Psychosom. Med. 30*, 631–653.

Mason, J. W. (1968e): A review of psychoendocrine research on the pituitary-thyroid system, *Psychosom. Med. 30*, 666–681.

Mason, J. W. (1968f): Organization of the multiple endocrine responses to avoidance in the monkey, *Psychosom. Med. 30*, 774–790.

Mason, J. W. (1968g): "Over-all" hormonal balance as a key to endocrine organization, *Psychosom. Med. 30*, 791–808.

Mason, J. W. (1970): Strategy in psychosomatic research, Presidential Address, *Psychosom. Med. 32*, 427–439.

Mason, J. W. (1971): A re-evaluation of the concept of "non-specificity" in stress theory, *J. Psychiatr. Res. 8*, 323–333.

Mason, J. W. (1972) Corticosteroid response to chair restraint in the monkey, *Am. J. Physiol. 222*, 1291–1294.

Mason, J. W. (1974): The integrative approach in medicine – Implications of neuroendocrine mechanisms, *Perspectives in Biology and Medicine*.

Mason, J. W. *(in press b):* Clinical psychophysiology: Psychoendocrine mechanisms. In: *American Handbook of Psychiatry*, Vol. 4, ed. M. Reiser.

Mason, J. W., Brady, J. V., and Sidman, M. (1957a): Plasma 17-hydroxycorticosteroid levels and conditioned behavior in the rhesus monkey, *Endocrinology 60*, 741–752.

Mason, J. W., Brady, J. V., and Tolliver, G. A. (1968a): Plasma and urinary 17-hydroxy-corticosteroid responses to 72-hour avoidance sessions in the monkey, *Psychosom. Med. 30*, 608–630.

Mason, J. W., Brady, J. V., and Tolson, W. W. (1966): Behavioral adaptations and endocrine activity. In: *Endocrines and the Central Nervous System*, ed. R. Levine, Williams & Wilkins, Baltimore, pp. 227–250.

Mason, J. W., Buescher, E. D., Belfer, M. L., Mougey, E. H., Taylor, E. D., Wherry, F. E., Ricketts, P. T., Young, P. S., Wade, J., Early, D. C., and Kenion, C. C. (1967): Pre-illness hormonal changes in Army recruits with acute respiratory infections, *Psychosom. Med. 29*, 545.

Mason, J. W., Hartley, L. H., Mougey, E. H., Ricketts, P., and Jones, L. G. (1973): Plasma cortisol and norepinephrine responses in anticipation of muscular exercise, *Psychosom. Med. 35*, 406–414.

Mason, J. W., Harwood, C. T., and Rosenthal, N. R. (1957b): Influence of some environmental factors on plasma and urinary 17-hydroxycorticosteroid levels and conditioned behavior in the rhesus monkey, *Am. J. Physiol. 190*, 429–433.

Mason, J. W., Jones, J. A., Ricketts, P. T., Brady, J. V., and Tolliver, G. A. (1968b): Urinary aldosterone and urine volume responses to 72-hour avoidance sessions in the monkey, *Psychosom. Med. 30*, 733–745.

Mason, J. W., Kenion, C. C., Collins, D. R., Mougey, E. H., Jones, J. A., Driver, G. C., Brady, J. V., and Beer, B. (1968c): Urinary testosterone response to 72-hour avoidance sessions in the monkey, *Psychosom. Med. 30*, 721–732.

Mason, J. W., Mangan, G. F., Jr., Brady, J. V., Conrad, D., and Rioch, D. M. (1961): Concurrent plasma epinephrine, norepinephrine, and 17-hydroxycorticosteroid levels during conditioned emotional disturbances in monkeys, *Psychosom. Med. 23*, 344–353.

Mason, J. W., and Mougey, E. H. (1972): Thyroid (plasma BEI) response to chair restraint in the monkey, *Psychosom. Med. 34*, 441–448.

Mason, J. W., Mougey, E. H., Brady, J. V., and Tolliver, G. A. (1968d): Thyroid (plasma butanol-extractable iodine) responses to 72-hour avoidance sessions in the monkey, *Psychosom. Med. 30*, 682–695.

Mason, J. W., Mougey, E. H., and Kenion, C. C. (1972): Urinary epinephrine and norepinephrine responses to chair restraint in the monkey, *Physiol. Behav. 10*, 801–804.

Mason, J. W., Sachar, E. J., Fishman, J. R., Hamburg, D. A., and Handlon, J. H. (1965): Corticosteroid responses to hospital admission, *Arch. Gen. Psychiatry 13*, 1–8.

Mason, J. W., Taylor, E. D., Brady, J. V., and Tolliver, G. A. (1968f): Urinary estrone, estradiol, and estriol responses to 72-hour avoidance sessions in the monkey. *Psychosom. Med. 30*, 696–709.

Mason, J. W., Tolson, W. W., Brady, J. V., Tolliver, G. A., and Gilmore, L. I. (1968g): Urinary epinephrine and norepinephrine responses to 72-hour avoidance sessions in the monkey, *Psychosom. Med. 30*, 654–665.

Mason, J. W., Tolson, W. W., Robinson, J. A., Brady, J. V., Tolliver, G. A., and Johnson, T. A. (1968h): Urinary androsterone, etiocholanolone, and dehydroepiandrosterone responses to 72-hour avoidance sessions in the monkey, *Psychosom. Med. 30*, 710–720.

Mason, J. W., Wherry, F. E., Brady, J. V., Beer, B., Pennington, L. L., and Goodman, A. C. (1968*i*): Plasma insulin responses to 72-hour avoidance sessions in the monkey, *Psychosom. Med. 30*, 746–759.

Mason, J. W., Wool, M. S., Mougey, E. H., Wherry, F. E., Collins, D. R., and Taylor, E. D. (1968*j*): Psychological versus nutritional factors in the effects of "fasting" on hormonal balance, *Psychosom. Med. 30*, 554.

Mason, J. W., Wool, M. S., Wherry, F. E., Pennington, L. L., Brady, J. V., and Beer, B. (1968*k*): Plasma growth hormone response to avoidance sessions in the monkey, *Psychosom. Med. 30*, 760–773.

Poe, R. O., Rose, R. M., and Mason, J. W. (1970): Multiple determinants of 17-hydroxy-corticosteroid excretion in recruits during basic training, *Psychosom. Med. 32*, 369–378.

Rose, R. M. (1969): Androgen responses to stress: I. Psychoendocrine relationships and assessment of androgen activity, *Psychosom. Med. 31*, 405–417.

Rose, R. M. (1972): The psychological effects of Androgens and Estrogens: A review. In: *Psychiatric Complications of Medical Drugs*, ed. R. I. Shader, Raven Press, New York.

Rose, R. M., Bourne, P. G., Poe, R. O., Mougey, E. H., Collins, D. R., and Mason, J. W. (1969): Androgen responses to stress: II. Excretion of testosterone, epitestosterone, androsterone, and etiocholanolone during basic combat training and under threat of attack, *Psychosom. Med. 31*, 418–436.

Rose, R. M., Poe, R. O., and Mason, J. W. (1968): Psychological state and body size as determinants of 17-OHCS excretion, *Arch. Intern. Med. 121*, 406–413.

Sachar, E. J. (1967): Corticosteroids in depressive illness: A reevaluation of control issues and the literature, *Arch. Gen. Psychiatry 17*, 544–553.

Selye, H. (1936): Thymus and adrenals in the response of the organism to injuries and intoxications, *Br. J. Exp. Pathol. 17*, 234–248.

Selye, H. (1950): Stress. *ACTA*, Montreal.

Tolson, W. W., Mason, J. W., Sachar, E. J., Hamburg, D. A., Handlon, J. H., and Fishman, J. R. (1965): Urinary catecholamine responses associated with hospital admission in normal human subjects, *J. Psychosom. Res. 8*, 365–372.

Wadeson, R. W., Mason, J. W., Hamburg, D. A., and Handlon, J. H. (1963): Plasma and urinary 17-OH-CS responses to motion pictures, *Arch. Gen. Psychiatry 9*, 146–156.

Wolff, C. T., Friedman, S. B., Hofer, M. A., and Mason, J. W. (1964*a*): Relationship between psychological defenses and mean urinary 17-OH-CS excretion rates: I. A predictive study of parents of fatally ill children, *Psychosom. Med. 26*, 576–591.

Wolff, C. T., Hofer, M. A., and Mason, J. W. (1964*b*): Relationship between psychological defenses and mean urinary 17-OH-CS excretion rates: II. Methodological and theoretical considerations, *Psychosom. Med. 26*, 592–609.

Emotions—Their Parameters and Measurement,
edited by L. Levi.
Raven Press, New York © 1975

Inhibitory Systems and Emotions

José M. R. Delgado

Yale University School of Medicine, New Haven, Connecticut 06510

INTRODUCTION

The existence of inhibitory functions was described long ago by Sechenov (1878) and Pavlov (1957); the study of synaptic inhibition has an abundant literature (see, for example, Eccles, 1964; Frank, 1959); and recent symposia have been devoted to inhibition (Beritoff, 1965; Diamond, Balvin, and Diamond, 1963; Florey, 1961; Roberts and Baxter, 1960; Wolstenholme and O'Connor, 1962). It is generally accepted that inhibition is as important as excitation for the normal functioning of the central nervous system (CNS) (Eccles, 1966). As indicated so vividly by Jung (1949), most neurons are firing nearly continuously, and the brain is like an enormous synaptic powder keg that would explode in epileptic convulsions in the absence of inhibitory elements. Roberts (1972) has proposed a model of the vertebrate nervous system based largely on disinhibition of inhibitory neurons, according to which genetically preprogrammed circuits are released by the inhibition of neurons that are tonically holding command neurons in check.

Serotonin-releasing neurons, located at the raphe nuclei, may inhibit noradrenergic neurons in the brainstem, regulating in this way the slow-wave sleep mechanisms (Jouvet, 1969). Inhibitory neurons utilizing gamma-amino-butyric acid (GABA) as a transmitter may be inhibited by other GABA neurons and also by adrenergic neurons. For example, in the cerebellum, the Purkinje cells are inhibited by basket and stellate cells; all three cell types are GABA-releasing neurons that may be inhibited through noradrenergic fibers originating in the locus coeruleus (Bloom, Hoffer, and Siggins, 1971). The excitatory command neurons in higher brain centers are held back by tonically active, inhibitory neurons, which presumably employ GABA as an inhibitory transmitter. In the brainstem, tonically active inhibitory GABA neurons may control the activity of an intersystem of neurons that can release dopamine, norepinephrine, or serotonin (Roberts, 1972).

These known facts and theories shed little light on the possible interrelation or independence of neuronal and behavioral inhibition (see, however, Buchwald, Hull, and Trachtenberg, 1967). The importance of inhibition on emotions is generally overlooked (Arnold, 1970; Tobach, 1969). Its role in spontaneous behavior is poorly understood, and behavioral inhibition is neglected by most textbooks of physiology and psychology. Even in this volume which deals so comprehensively with emotions, the inhibitory systems of the brain were initially left out of the program.

This lack of information and interest is partly due to methodological difficulties in the investigation of neuronal functions in awake, unrestrained animals. Recent developments, however, permit the establishment of two-way radio communication with the brain of free subjects (Delgado, 1969; Delgado, Johnston, Wallace, and Bradley, 1970) and should facilitate investigation of inhibitory mechanisms related to the emotional aspects of individual and social behavior.

The purposes of this chapter are (a) to review briefly the literature on behavioral inhibition, (b) to present experimental data on inhibitory effects evoked by electrical and chemical manipulation of the brain in awake primates, and (c) to discuss preliminary data about clinical application of inhibitory programmed stimulation of the brain in patients.

INHIBITION OF BEHAVIOR

As described earlier (Delgado, 1964), electrical stimulation of the brain may induce three types of behavioral inhibition: (a) sleep, which has a slow onset affecting all behavior, is easily interrupted by sensory stimulation, and depends primarily on environmental conditions (Hess, 1944); (b) general inhibition, which starts at the onset of stimulation, affects all behavior, reduces awareness and muscular tone, and persists in spite of sensory excitation (Akert and Anderson, 1951; Buchwald, Wyers, Lauprecht, and Heuser, 1961); (c) specific inhibition, which also starts at the onset of stimulation but affects only a determined type of behavior, such as food intake or aggressiveness (Plotnik and Delgado, 1970; Rubinstein and Delgado, 1963).

Structures with inhibitory functions include the orbitofrontal cortex, septum, caudate nucleus, putamen, pallidum, internal capsule, amygdala, hypothalamus, rostral thalamus, and cingulate gyrus (Buchwald et al., 1961; Jung, 1949; Mettler, 1945; Spehlmann, Creutzfeld, and Jung, 1960; Tokizane, Kawakami, and Gellhorn, 1957; see also review and bibliography in Delgado, 1964). The functional correlation among these structures is not well known. Buchwald et al. (1961) have postulated the existence of a "caudate loop" passing from the intralaminar nuclei to the caudate nucleus and then to the ventral anterior nucleus of the thalamus and cortex, going back to the thalamus and caudate. This system could be antagonistic to the reticular arousal system, but under some conditions, both could operate synergically. Electrically evoked inhibition may be related to blocking of corticocaudate connections (Laursen, 1962), to inhibitory influences on the lateral hypothalamus, perhaps via fornix, or to interference with the caudato-pallidal and caudatonigral pathways (Szabo, 1970). Behavioral inhibition induced by septal and caudate stimulation may depend on activation of the amygdala and hippocampus (Gloor, 1955) or the intralaminar nucleus of the thalamus (Cowan and Powell, 1955). One problem in the interpretation of the literature is the lack of precision in reported anatomical data. From its head to its tail, the caudate nucleus occupies a long stretch of brain, and even if most results have been obtained by stimulation of the head of the caudate nucleus, this area is functionally heterogeneous, and its medial part, bordering on the septum, cannot be identified with its lateral part, bordering on the internal capsule and putamen.

Another problem is that most experiments have been performed on cats or lower animals, and these findings should not be unduly generalized to higher species including man. As shown by Harman and Carpenter (see Mettler, 1952), the proportion of striatal tissue in the caudate is 83% in the fox, 81% in felines, 56% in lower primates, and 36% in higher primates. Functional identity should not be expected in different species.

It is preferable to study monkeys rather than lower animals because of their proximity to man and richer behavioral repertoire; an added anatomical benefit is that, in primates, thalamic fibers en route to the precentral gyrus do not pass close to the basal ganglia, as in the cat (Goldring, Antony, Stohr, and O'Leary, 1963). We know that cortical spindling is easier to obtain in the cat, and as indicated by Kitsikis, Horvath, and Rougeul (1968), failure to obtain spindling by excitation of thalamic and capsular points in the monkey indicates that the basal ganglia do participate in the synchronization of cortical activity. Kitsikis (1968) has also shown that thresholds for inhibitory effects of spontaneous motor activity depend on the type of movement performed.

In human patients with implanted electrodes, electrical stimulation of the frontostriatal region has produced cessation of voluntary movements and arrest of speech followed by amnesia and confusion (Delgado and Hamlin, 1960; Van Buren, 1963; van Buren, Li, and Ojemann, 1966). In monkeys and in one schizophrenic patient, Heath and Hodes (1952) observed a sleep-like effect induced by stimulation of the head of the caudate nucleus. The orbital cortex of the frontal lobes, particularly area 13, receives para-sympathetic input from the nuclei of the 9th and 10th nerves, via the anterior hypothalamus (Bailey and Bremer, 1938), and it is known that ablation of area 13 in monkeys causes restlessness and hypermotility with a peak at noon, and without affecting normal night sleep (Livingston, Fulton, Delgado, Sachs, Brendler, and Davis, 1947). Stanley-Jones (1970) has postulated that the normal function of area 13 may be "to restrain the appearance of restlessness or mania." Overactivity of area 13 would lead to depression, while underactivity would lead to mania. In summary, it is clear that behavior may be inhibited by specific areas of the brain, and it should be expected that normal functions may be regulated by a dynamic equilibrium of excitatory and inhibitory areas of the brain.

MAPPING OF INHIBITORY AREAS IN PRIMATES

The striatum (caudate nucleus, capsula interna, and putamen) is a spheriform structure that, in a 4 kg monkey, measures about 10 to 12 mm in diameter. A somatotopic localization of head and body turning has been described by Forman and Ward (1957) in the caudate nucleus of the cat. In monkeys, specific inhibition predominates in its rostral part, while general inhibition is obtained from its inferomedial part, and visceral inhibition from its central region (Rubinstein and Delgado, 1963). Most authors, however, refer to the caudate nucleus as a whole, without precise anatomical identification of the sites responsible for inhibitory effects. To obtain this information, a systematic mapping of the forebrain is necessary, using a test situation in which repeatable and reliable behavioral responses are evoked. In our laboratory, we standardized these experiments in primates as follows.

Needle guides were constructed of 15-mm lengths of stainless steel No. 21 tubing, with a small cross soldered 5 mm below the top of each guide to prevent penetration of the brain during implantation in the skull, and to facilitate its anchorage to the bone. With the animal under anesthesia and placed in a stereotaxic instrument, holes were drilled at predetermined sites on the skull and the needle guides were introduced, usually 3-mm equidistant. From 28 to 100 guides were placed, permitting the exploration of up to 2,000 cerebral points in each animal. One or more weeks after surgery, experiments were performed in the completely awake animal, placed in a plastic restraining chair. Roving electrodes were constructed of stainless-steel wire, 125 μ in diameter, insulated with teflon except at the tip, and protected inside a length of No. 26 stainless-steel tubing. These electrodes were introduced at 1-mm steps through the needle guides (Fig. 1), and each

FIG. 1. A gibbon with needle guides implanted in the skull for the systematic exploration of the brain by means of roving electrodes. The aggressive reaction of the animal, shown in A, is inhibited by stimulation of the head of the caudate nucleus, shown in B.

cerebral point was stimulated at least 3 times at 1 min intervals. At the sites of the most interesting effects, electrodes were implanted permanently.

All stimulations were cathodal, square pulses, 0.5 to 1.0 msec in pulse duration, 100 Hz, constant current, and ranged from 0.4 to 2.0 mA. Electrical activity was recorded from all points, and results mentioned here were obtained in the absence of after-discharges. Stimulation effects were photographed. The following inhibitory responses were identified.

(a) Cessation of spontaneous activity, which in the restraining chair was evident only when the animal was restless before stimulation.

(b) Hypomimic staring with closed mouth and placid facial expression, which was a typical and easily recognizable response (Fig. 1B).

(c) Slow lowering of the lead.

(d) Slow, contralateral head turning, which often accompanied inhibitory responses.

In addition, two tests were performed.

(a) Offering a small piece of appetizing fruit normally resulted in an orienting reaction followed by grabbing and eating the food. During evoked inhibition, there was a lack of interest in the fruit with diminution of the orienting reaction. If the animal was stimulated when eating, it stopped chewing.

(b) Stroking the animal's face lightly with a leather glove usually induced an offensive-defensive reaction consisting of showing the teeth, attempts to grab and pull the glove, vocalization, and biting. During evoked inhibition, however, the animal looked at the approaching glove without signs of excitment or hostility, and it was then safe to touch its mouth.

Our experimental series with needle guides included 6 rhesus monkeys and 5 gibbons (Hylobates Lar). Additional information was obtained from 16 rhesus monkeys with multilead electrode assemblies implanted in the forebrain. Results were as follows.

In all animals with needle guides, inhibitory effects were evoked while exploring the striatum. The inhibitory areas occupied a rather discrete extension of only 1 to 4 mm in depth, and the effect was lost when the tip of the roving electrode was moved 1 mm away. Bilateral explorations failed to show the expected symmetry, and although inhibitory representation was always found in both sides, its extension and location were not identical.

Coronal planes A 20 to A 30 were investigated with needle tracts 2, 6, and 10 mm lateral to the midline and penetrations of approximately 25 mm (12 mm through the striatum), representing about 400 points per animal, with a total of more than 4,400 explored points in the forebrain of the 11 animals. From all the areas studied, inhibitory results were obtained from only 7%, while from 64% there were no observable behavioral responses with intensities up to 2 mA, and detectable motor effects were evoked from only 29%. One example of the location of inhibitory points in coronal plane anterior 28 in gibbon No. 7 is shown in Fig. 2. In this case, inhibitory representation had a greater extension in the upper right side of the head of the caudate nucleus with other points in the white substance and two additional points in the left side.

For the experiments in monkeys with permanently implanted electrodes, the distance between contacts was fixed by construction at 3 mm, and in all cases, at least 2 contacts were in the head of the caudate nucleus. In five of these animals (31%), however, we failed to obtain inhibitory effects, a logical result considering the relatively small extension of inhibitory areas. This fact should be kept in mind when electrical stimulation of the brain is contemplated for therapeutic purposes in man; for example, in cases of

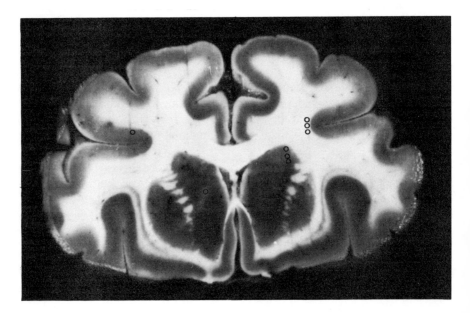

FIG. 2. Coronal section of a gibbon brain at anterior 28. The inhibitory points are marked with circles.

intractable pain. Multiplicity of implanted electrodes increases the possibility that some contacts will be in a suitable target that can then be identified functionally.

Brain mapping in the unanesthetized, alert animal is superior to other procedures performed under anesthesia with the exposed brain, using electrodes held manually and noting results in an anatomical sketch made during surgery. The present method also has limitations because the experimental set-up with an animal restrained in a chair handicaps behavioral expression and introduces a variety of psychological and physiological inhibitions. For these reasons, results of mapping must be interpreted with reservations, and for a more detailed study of behavioral inhibition, the experimental subject should enjoy freedom of movement. A compromise was reached in our experiments by performing a detailed mapping under restraint and then fixing implanted leads at the most interesting points in order to continue the study with the animals free in a large cage (see Fig. 9 and 10), where cerebral stimulations were delivered by radio.

In summary, (a) inhibitory areas were found in the striatum and white substance of the forebrain in all monkeys and gibbons with needle guides; (b) these areas were only 7% of the total number of tested points; (c) no clear, systematic anatomical distribution was found; (d) inhibitory points had bilateral representation but were not symmetrical.

FATIGABILITY, PROGRAMMED STIMULATION, AND FEEDBACK CONTROL

As indicated in previous work (Delgado, 1959), cerebral structures may be classified in three groups with respect to their fatigability. (a) In "quick fatigue," the evoked effect disappears after a few seconds of stimulation, taking about 1 min to recover the initial neuronal excitability. Motor cortex and some amygdala points are examples of this group. (b) In "slow fatigue," the response was maintained for many minutes of continuous stimulation, fading away slowly in less than 1 hr. An example was stimulation of the putamen, evoking contralateral turning of the head and body. Another example was aggressive behavior induced by hypothalamic stimulation that has persisted for more than 20 min. (c) In "no fatigue," the response was present as long as stimulation was applied. For example, pupillary constriction has been maintained day and night for 21 days during continuous stimulation of the hypothalamus (Delgado and Mir, 1966).

In our experiments in free as well as in restrained animals, behavioral inhibition evoked by stimulation of the septum, caudate, putamen, and amygdala always had quick fatigue. Usually within 60 sec, inhibition disappeared and the animal (monkey or gibbon) took food and reacted if its face was touched. The longest duration of inhibition, 280 sec, was observed in one gibbon following stimulation of the rostral head of the caudate nucleus. Recovery of initial excitability was usually complete after 2 min. These experiments were performed with intensities below 2 mA, and only 20 to 50% above inhibitory thresholds of 0.5 to 1.0 mA. By increasing the applied intensity and sending it continuously, inhibition could be prolonged, but never more than a total of 5 min.

As the inhibitory effects were short lasting, further studies were performed in an attempt to prolong the duration of behavioral inhibition by using programmed instead of continuous stimulation. The experimental design was based on previous studies in which a "smile-like" motor response evoked by stimulation of the rhinal fissure persisted for more than 500,000 times when stimulations were conveniently spaced at four times per minute (Delgado, Rivera, and Mir, 1971). In this study, the following programs were tested: (a) 5 sec on, 25 sec off; (b) 5 sec on, 10 sec off; and (c) 5 sec on, 5 sec off. With any of these programs, inhibitory responses could be elicited intermittently for over 1 hr without difficulty, demonstrating that the introduction of short rest periods avoided fatigability of effects. The problem was that the induced inhibition was so brief that activities were interrupted only during the stimulation. From the three programs, the most effective was 5 sec on, 5 sec off, which significantly reduced spontaneous and instrumental behavior. This schedule was rigid by design, and electrical stimulation was applied regardless of whether the monkey was active or resting.

Another experiment was implemented to inhibit behavior selectively by feedback, applying caudate stimulation only when the animal had performed a certain amount of spontaneous motor activity. For this purpose, the monkey free within the colony was equipped with a belt and a miniaturized transmitter with a steel ball, running freely within the emitting coil of the instrument, as sensor of the animal's mobility. This method allows the telemetric, automatic, and continuous recording of the mobility of each individual in a group. It has been used in psychiatric patients on a ward as well as in primate colonies (Kupfer, Detre, Foster, Tucker, and Delgado, 1972; see also Delgado, 1963). In the experiments described here, the console that received the signals of the animal's mobility was connected with a totalizer, which, every 25 counts, closed a circuit to activate a 1-sec radio stimulation of a preselected inhibitory point in the amygdala (see Fig. 3). In this way, no stimulations were applied when the animal was quiet, whereas the inhibitory point was stimulated with a frequency proportional to the animal's mobility.

The feedback study was performed with the experimental animal paired in the observation cage with a submissive monkey in two different 15-min situations: (a) "no demand" behavior, in which the animals were engaged in spontaneous activities, and (b) "feeding," in which 45-mg banana flavored pellets were delivered automatically through a feeder at a rate of one pellet per 15 sec. Dominance was clearly shown by the test monkey that controlled the feeding area. During each 15 min eating period, feedback brain stimulation was established for the central 5 min, and results are shown in Fig. 4. The initial 5 min of control show the cumulative curve of mobility, which is rather regular in both situations. During the second 5-min period of feedback, mobility was greatly reduced. During the third 5-min period, mobility was still below control, indicating the existence of residual inhibitory effects. With this feedback technique, the amount of stimulation necessary to inhibit spontaneous behavior was about 30 times less than in other experiments performed with fixed programs of 5 sec on, 5 sec off, demonstrating the greater efficiency of feedback stimulations.

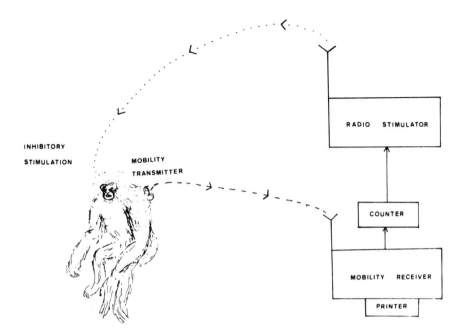

FIG. 3. Spontaneous mobility of the monkey was telemetered to a receiver that activated a counter and a radio stimulator sending signals to inhibitory points of the caudate nucleus. With this feedback stimulation, mobility was greatly reduced, and the animal's authority was lost. (In collaboration with Drs. Delgado-Garcia and Amérigo.)

SPECIFIC INHIBITION OF OFFENSIVE-DEFENSIVE RESPONSES

As mentioned in the section "Inhibition of Behavior," specific inhibition is characterized by affecting only a determined type of behavior. A clear example is the localized motor inhibition observed in man following stimulation of the motor cortex. Some patients expressed the desire to move an extremity and were unable to do so. In other cases, voluntary opposition of the thumb to the little finger has been blocked by electrical stimulation of the premotor hand area (Feindel, 1961; Penfield and Rasmussen, 1950).

Another example is the alimentary inhibition demonstrated in one of our films (Delgado, 1957; see also Delgado, 1964). In these studies, stimulation of the head of the caudate nucleus inhibited food intake specifically without modifying awareness or motor activity. When the animal was eating, stimulation stopped chewing and induced a lack of interest in food. In some cases, the animal walked away from the offered food, pushed a piece of fruit or even emptied its pouches or took from its mouth the food being chewed. These findings showed an active rejection of food and not a passive, generalized inhibition.

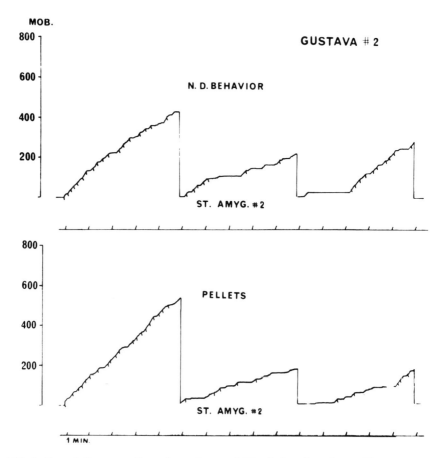

FIG. 4. Cumulative recording of monkey mobility during "no demand" spontaneous behavior (ND) and during automatic "feeding." Each experiment had three 5-min periods. During the central 5 min, programmed stimulation of the caudate nucleus was applied. Mobility was significantly reduced. (In collaboration with Drs. Delgado-Garcia and Amérigo.)

These results have been confirmed in the gibbon (Fig. 5). The voracious eating of an apple stopped as soon as the head of the caudate nucleus was radio stimulated and the piece of fruit was slowly withdrawn from the mouth. The animal remained peaceful for the duration of stimulation, resuming eating a few seconds after its cessation.

Specific inhibition of aggression without changes in general behavior has been demonstrated in the monkey (Delgado, 1964; Plotnik and Delgado, 1970). In the experiments in collaboration with Plotnik, a total of 154 areas were explored first with the animal restrained in a chair and later with the same animal paired with another monkey in a large cage. The effects of inhibitory radio stimulation were tested while the animals were engaged in

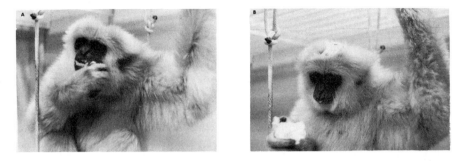

FIG. 5. Eating of pellets (A) was inhibited by radio stimulation of the caudate nucleus (B).

free behavior and also when instrumental responses were performed. In this case, the animals learned (a) to press a lever in order to obtain food (one pellet per five presses), and (b) under restraint, to avoid a 0.2-sec shock that occurred automatically every 5 sec unless the animal pressed a lever postponing the shock for 15 sec. Both instrumental responses lasted for 5 min. Additional experiments were performed by (c) restraining the dominant monkey in a chair located in front of a glassed cage where a submissive monkey had been placed. An electric shock of 0.2 could be delivered simultaneously to both animals, inducing characteristic threatening behavior in the dominant animal. In other experiments, (d) the submissive monkey was placed in the chair and electrically shocked while a 12 in. doll approached and contacted him twice. In this way, adaptation was avoided and submissive grimaces and vocalizations were reliably evoked (above 90% per 60 trials, 30 sec apart).

This combination of experiments demonstrated that programmed stimulation 5 sec on and 5 sec off, with intensities below 1.5 mA of inhibitory points located mainly in the caudate nucleus and putamen, effectively blocked grimacing, vocalizing, threatening, and other offensive-defensive behavior without modifying food intake, walking, grooming, or instrumental responses to obtain pellets and to avoid shock. Specificity of determined cerebral points to inhibit emotional responses of threatening or grimacing were thus demonstrated in the absence of disturbance of consumatory, locomotor, grooming, or learned instrumental behavior.

PARADOXICAL INHIBITION

As indicated in the previous section, inhibitory effects may be limited to a specific behavioral category without modifying other aspects of an animal's activities. In some of our experiments, however, caudate stimulation induced inhibition of food intake accompanied by an increase in walking activity. In this case, the effect could be labeled "inhibition" or "activation," depending on the type of behavior under consideration.

Monkeys Sixto (No. 4, dominant) and Petrov (No. 3, submissive) were paired in the testing cage and observed during three 15-min periods (A, B, and C). Periods A and C were "no demand," meaning that the pair engaged in spontaneous activities without performing any specific task. Period B was for "feeding," and one 45-mg banana flavored pellet was delivered every 15 sec (see Figs. 6 and 7). This situation exposed the dominant-submissive relation between the two monkeys because the boss animal took most of the pellets and dominated the feeding territory. Programmed radio stimulation of the caudate (5 sec on, 5 sec off) was applied to the dominant monkey during the central 5 min in periods A, B, and C. In this way, controls alternated with stimulation while the animals were acting spontaneously or feeding. Results, as indicated in Fig. 6, show that dominant monkey Sixto

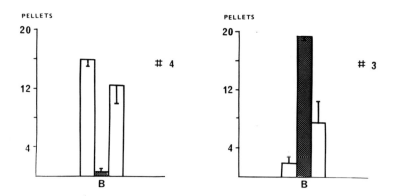

FIG. 6. Monkeys No. 4 (dominant) and No. 3 (submissive) were paired in a cage while food pellets were automatically delivered. Each bar represents the number of pellets taken during a 5-min period. The first period is control. In the second period, caudate stimulation is applied to No. 4. The third period is poststimulation control (Amérigo et al., *unpublished*).

took most of the pellets during the first 5 min of the feeding situation while submissive Petrov took only a few. During the next 5 min, radio stimulation of Sixto produced a drastic inhibition of his interest in food, and also abolished his hierarchical advantage over Petrov, who then took most of the available pellets. During the following 5 min period without stimulation, Sixto took only 13 pellets while Petrov got 7, indicating that caudate stimulation had a residual effect. The changes in Petrov following stimulation of Sixto indicate the importance of social situations in the study of brain functions.

While the inhibitory effect of caudate stimulation was clear and highly significant ($P < 0.001$), there was a paradoxical side effect: along with the decrease in food intake, there was a marked increase in walking by Sixto. During the middle 5 min of radio stimulation in periods A, B, and C, Sixto's walking increased significantly while Petrov's level of activity remained unchanged. In view of these results, the effect of caudate stimulation should be considered "behavioral activation."

It is obvious that labeling this caudate point "inhibitory" or "activator" depended on the type of test situation, and that more accurate knowledge of the functional significance of the explored structure is obtained by exploring a multiplicity of responses. In our studies, in addition to pellet taking and walking, other behavioral categories such as grooming, mounting, threatening, and escaping were also investigated, and the results will be published elsewhere (Delgado-Garcia, Amerigo, and Delgado, *unpublished*).

In summary, electrical stimulation of some caudate points produced inhibition of a specific type of behavior such as pellet taking, combined with

WALKING

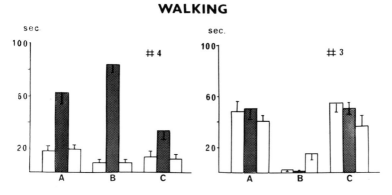

FIG. 7. Paradoxically with the inhibition of pellet taking shown in Fig. 6, caudate stimulation of monkey No. 4 during periods marked by darker bars induced an increase in walking by the stimulated animal.

activation of another activity, in this case walking. Simultaneous inhibition and activation of different kinds of behavior may be called "paradoxical inhibition," and this effect is probably determined by simultaneous stimulation of structures with different functions that are located in close anatomical proximity.

DYNAMIC EQUILIBRIUM

In previous work, we have shown that simultaneous electrical stimulation of brain structures with opposed effects may cancel both responses. For example, stimulation of two hypothalamic points that produce constriction and dilatation of the pupils resulted in a dynamic equilibrium that could be maintained without observable pupillary changes, by increasing or decreasing simultaneously the intensity of stimulation of both points (Delgado, 1959; Delgado and Mir, 1966).

A similar dynamic equilibrium has been obtained in gibbons by excitation of points located in the central gray, which increased aggressive behavior, and located in the head of the caudate nucleus, which inhibited the animal's aggressiveness. In gibbon Helmut, restrained in a chair, stimulation of the left central gray with 0.4 mA for 2 sec (cathodal, 100 Hz, 0.5-msec pulse duration) produced a reliable offensive-defensive response with restlessness, showing of the teeth, attempts to grab and bite, and vocalizations. In further experiments, stimulation of the caudate nucleus preceded the central gray stimulations by 2 sec, and both terminated simultaneously 2 sec later. Results are shown in Fig. 8. There was no change in central gray thresholds when caudate intensities were below 0.5 mA, but increase in caudate intensity resulted in a progressive rise in central gray thresholds which increased to more than twice their original value. Contralateral was more effective than ipsilateral excitation.

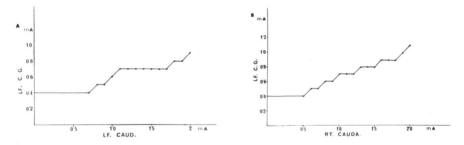

FIG. 8. Stimulation of left central gray (Lf C.G.) in a gibbon induced offensive-defensive behavior. Thresholds for this effect, expressed in the ordinate, were progressively raised by increasing intensities of caudate stimulation (caud) expressed in the abscissa. Contralateral inhibition (right caudate) was more effective than the ipsilateral side.

Similar results have been obtained with animals free in a colony cage (Fig. 9). Following stimulation of the central gray, black gibbon Gaily launched a well directed attack against blonde gibbon Coti, which reacted by defending itself and retaliating, in spite of its inferior size and strength. Usually a brief 2-sec stimulation induced threats and fights which continued for 10 to 60 sec (Fig. 9 A, B, and C), but Gaily could be immediately inhibited by caudate stimulation, which resulted in an arrest of fighting and adoption by Gaily of the innocent and peaceful posture shown in Fig. 9D. In these experiments, the aggressive response outlasted brain excitation for up to 1 min, while the inhibitory caudate stimulation had only a brief after-effect. Often fighting was resumed as soon as caudate stimulation terminated, and it was necessary to excite the caudate several times before Gaily's agonistic behavior was suppressed.

In other experiments, when caudate stimulation of sufficient intensity preceded central gray excitation, no agonistic behavior was induced, and a

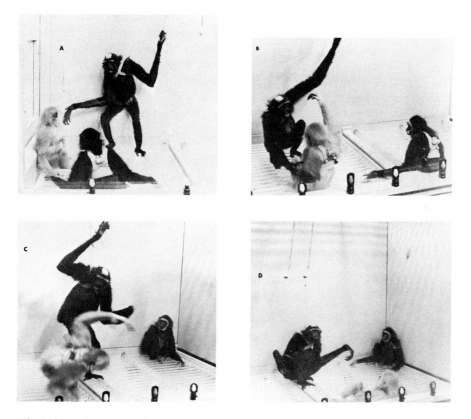

FIG. 9. Central gray stimulation induced fighting behavior as shown in A, B, and C. The attack was abruptly stopped by caudate stimulation as shown in D.

state of dynamic equilibrium could be prolonged for about 1 min until the more quickly fatiguable caudate-produced inhibition faded away and central gray aggressiveness predominated.

RELIABILITY OF RESULTS IN THE LABORATORY AND IN A FREE ECOLOGICAL SITUATION

Emotional expression and CNS functions may be handicapped when the animal is bound to a chair, and analysis of social behavior obviously requires the freedom of spontaneous activities within a group. Brain research using animal colonies in the laboratory represented considerable progress over studies in restrained animals. As mentioned in the introduction, recent developments permit two-way communication with the free experimental animal by using radio stimulation and telemetry of biological information.

In addition, individual and social behavior have been recorded, qualified, quantified, and statistically analyzed by means of computers (Amerigo, Delgado-Garcia, and Delgado, 1973; Plotnik, Mir, and Delgado, 1971). In spite of these developments, some authors consider laboratory situations highly artificial, very different from the conditions of natural life in the wild, and grossly distorting neuronal functions. The problem of ethological observations is that controlled experimentation and objective recording are not possible precisely because of the individual freedom of the animals to disappear from the field of observation.

As a compromise, in collaboration with Drs. N. S. Kline, A. H. Esser, and R. C. Carpenter, a gibbon colony was established in 1970 on the vegetated island of Hall, 1.5 acres in size and located in Harrington Sound, Bermuda. Observations have been conducted of the spontaneous activities of the gibbons (Carpenter, 1973). Their motility has been recorded by telemetry, and the behavior evoked by cerebral radio stimulation has been studied. From these results (to be published) we present a brief report here.

Gibbons Gaily (female, 5.2 kg) and Helmut (male, 6.1 kg) were studied first under restraint, then while free in a colony cage, and finally while free on the island of Hall. Effects of stimulating central gray points were rather different in the colony than on the island. In the colony, aggressive behavior was easily induced at low thresholds (0.2 to 0.4 mA) with vocalization, threats, and well organized and oriented attacks, as shown in Fig. 9 A, B, and C. Repetition of the same stimulation on the island resulted in considerable hyperactivity including vocalization, bracchiation, bipedestation, and running away. In the case of Helmut, the animal covered much more territory than usual, and after stimulation, often disappeared from the experimenters' sight. Hostility against other gibbons was not increased, while attacks against human observers were greatly augmented, being vicious and unprovoked.

Inhibitory effects evoked by caudate stimulation (tentative location, as the animal is still alive) was evident at 1 mA; it halted eating of an apple (Fig. 5), inhibited lever pressing for pellets (Fig. 10), and also arrested the animal in its tracks while free on the island (Fig. 11B). With programmed stimulation (5 sec on, 5 sec off), it was possible to keep Helmut motionless for several minutes: he sat down in the brush with the eyes sometimes closed, but remained attentive to surrounding noises and did not escape when an investigator approached to take a close up picture. In other experiments, Helmut's aggression against observers was abruptly stopped by caudate stimulation.

At present (March, 1973), the animal is in excellent condition at the Laboratory of Physiology of Madrid (Facultad de Medicina Autónoma) where he is being restudied. Inhibitory responses are being obtained at the same thresholds and with similar characteristics as following electrode implantation in the United States in August, 1970.

FIG. 10 Lever pressing for food was inhibited by caudate stimulation.

FIG. 11. With the animals free on the Island of Hall in Bermuda, radio stimulation of the central gray induced running (A) and increased aggressiveness against humans, while caudate nucleus stimulation inhibited the animal's activities (B).

BEHAVIORAL INHIBITION INDUCED BY MICROINJECTION OF PENTHOTAL

As indicated in previous sections, inhibitory effects evoked by electrical stimulation of the caudate nucleus were of short duration, and further experiments were performed in an attempt to obtain longer lasting results. The experimental design was based on previous work showing that microinjections of dibucaine into the amygdala or hippocampus of rhesus monkeys at a rate of 8 to 14 μl/hr for 1 to 4 days produced localized blocking of spontaneous electrical activity and decreased excitability lasting for up to one month, accompanied by a transitory diminution of aggressiveness (Delgado and Kitahata, 1967).

The experiments were performed in 6 rhesus monkeys equipped with chemitrodes implanted in the forebrain. They were studied first in a restraining chair and then while free in a cage where each was paired with another monkey (Lico and Delgado, *to be published*). Very small injections of 2.5% penthotal at a rate of 1 μl/10 min for 30 to 60 min, produced the following results.

In all 6 animals, about 15 min after the start of injection and before changes were noted in excitability or behavior, there was an increase in voltage and synchronization in the caudate, putamen, and pallidum that persisted for about 24 hr. Local excitability diminished progressively and was abolished several minutes after the end of injection. The cerebral area affected was about 10 mm in diameter and this effect faded as distance increased from the injection point. Some modification of excitability was also present in distant but functionally related areas after drug injection. For example, in the contralateral structure or in the intralaminar nucleus of the thalamus. Searching behavior, evoked by caudate stimulation at a threshold of 0.25 mA, after penthotal injection could not be evoked with intensitites of 3.5 mA.

In the free situation, spontaneous mobility diminished progressively in all animals after administration of 5 μl, reaching the low point in about 4 hr, and persisting for up to 8 days. Following injection, lever pressing for food was either very diminished or totally abolished, although appetite appeared normal, and the animal took food eagerly from the investigator. No impairment could be detected in the test animals' sensory perception, emotional behavior, or motor coordination, and they responded to external threats as usual by jumping and escaping.

Spontaneous social relations with the other monkey, such as grooming, sexual, or aggressive behavior, were totally absent, and the injected animal remained seated or lying down, appearing drowsy but aware of the environment. His former dominance over the control partner was lost, and the other monkey lever pressed for food and moved around in the cage without fear in each case.

These effects were found after injection into the medial forebrain bundle, medial part of the head of the caudate nucleus, and putamen. No behavioral changes were observed after injection in the white substance above the caudate or in the medial hypothalamus and intralaminar nucleus of the thalamus. Injection of ringer and electrocoagulations did not produce any of these effects.

When 2.5 μl (5% solution) of penthotal was injected together with 2.5 μl atropine (2.5 μg), none of the previous effects were observed, suggesting that results were related with activation of cholinergic pathways. Injection of 5 μl of acetylcholine (100 μg) produced results similar to those of penthotal. Histological analysis of the injection areas did not reveal any special pathology other than the usual gliosis found in needle tracts.

The very long-lasting behavioral effects of intracerebral injection of a minute dose of penthotal (5 μl) cannot be explained as a local anesthetic effect, and other mechanisms should be postulated.

INHIBITORY TRANSDERMAL STIMULATION
OF THE BRAIN IN MAN

Several investigators have used electrical stimulation of the brain for therapeutic purposes. Heath and Mickle (1960) reported immediate relief from chronic pain during septal stimulation, and in addition, the patients felt alert and well. Sem-Jacobsen and Torkildsen (1960) described stimulation of the ventromedial frontal lobe which produced relaxation, joy, and satisfaction. Gol (1967) has obtained relief from pain by septal stimulation in one terminal cancer patient, although this beneficial effect could not be repeated in other cases.

Some therapeutic failures may be explained by the limited anatomical representation of inhibitory areas, as mentioned in section B. Another problem is that for long-term stimulation, the presence of sockets on the scalp and wires piercing the skin is undesirable.

For long-term patient therapy when electrodes have been successfully located in the intended inhibitory area, we have developed a multichannel, transdermal, remote-controlled brain stimulator which has been used in monkeys, gibbons, and chimpanzees, and has recently been applied to man. The stimulator is totally subcutaneous, measures 40 mm in diameter by 12 mm thick, and is constructed with integrated circuits. Each of four channels terminates in a teflon insulated platinum wire with an exposed tip implanted stereotaxically in the brain. The stimulator has no batteries and may be used indefinitely. Power and information to activate each channel are transmitted through the intact skin by transformer action. In animals, no infections or rejections have occurred, and electronic and neurophysiological performance have been reliable for periods of up to 24 months.

The instrument has been implanted in a 30-year-old patient who suffered from a phantom limb and intolerable pain unalleviated by drugs or physical therapy. After one month of programmed stimulation of the septum, applied 3 to 5 times a week for 1 hr, the patient remained free from pain and also experienced a marked decrease in his previous spontaneous hostile behavior. At present, one year after implantation, his pain has not recurred, tolerance of the instrument is still excellent, and the patient is gainfully employed and engaged in normal activities. To our knowledge this is the first reported case of transdermal stimulation of the brain in man. For more details, a previous publication may be consulted (Delgado, Obrador, and Martin-Rodriguez, 1972).

SUMMARY

Inhibitory systems of the brain are probably as important as excitatory systems for emotional reactivity, although the study of behavioral inhibition has been neglected by most investigators. In this paper we present information about mapping of inhibitory areas in rhesus monkeys and gibbons, and data about their radio stimulation in a laboratory colony and in a free ecological situation on Hall Island, Bermuda. We also describe a lasting behavioral inhibition induced by microinjections of penthotal. Transdermal stimulation of the septum relieved pain in a patient using a totally subcutaneous, multichannel stimulator. Long term brain pacemaking is feasible with this methodology.

ACKNOWLEDGMENTS

This research was supported by grants from USPHS MH-17408, New York Foundation, International Psychiatric Research Foundation, March Foundation, Rodriguez Pascual Foundation, and Seguridad Social.

I gratefully acknowledge the collaboration of Caroline Delgado, Dr. Maria Lico, Dr. Ana Maria Sanguinetti, Dr. R. Apfelbach, Dr. José A. Amérigo, and Dr. José M. Delgado-Garcia.

REFERENCES

Akert, K., and Andersson, B. (1951): Experimenteller Beitrag zur Physiologie des Nucleus caudatus, Acta Physiol. Scand. 22, 281–298.
Amerigo, J. A., Delgado-Garcia, J. M., and Delgado, J. M. R. (unpublished): Telemetry of mobility triggering feedback stimulation of the caudate nucleus in monkeys.
Arnold, M. B. (ed.) (1970): Feelings and Emotions, Academic Press, New York.
Bailey, P., and Bremer, F. (1938): A sensory cortical representation of the vagus nerve. With a note on the effects of low blood pressure on the cortical electrogram, J. Neurophysiol. 1, 405–412.
Beritoff, J. S. (1965): Neural Mechanisms of Higher Vertebrate Behavior (trans. from Russian and ed. W. T. Liberson), Little Brown, Boston.
Bloom, F. E., Hoffer, B. J., and Siggins, G. R. (1971): Studies on norepinephrine-containing afferents to Purkinje cells of rat cerebellum. II. Sensitivity of Purkinje cells to norepinephrine and related substances administered by microiontophoresis, Brain Res. 25, 523–534.
Buchwald, N. A., Hull, C. D., and Trachtenberg, M. C. (1967): Concomitant behavioral and neural inhibition and disinhibition in response to subcortical stimulation, Exp. Brain Res. 4, 58–72.
Buchwald, N. A., Wyers, E. J., Lauprecht, C. W., and Heuser, G. (1961): The "caudate-spindle." IV. A behavioral index of caudate-induced inhibition, EEG Clin. Neurophysiol. 13, 531–537.
van Buren, J. M. (1963): Confusion and disturbance of speech from stimulation in vicinity of the head of the caudate nucleus, J. Neurosurg. 20, 148–157.
van Buren, J. M., Li, C. L., and Ojemann, G. A. (1966): The fronto-striatal arrest response in man, EEG Clin. Neurophysiol. 21, 114–130.
Carpenter, C. R. (in press): Suspensory behavior of gibbons (Hylobatidae). A photo essay.
Cowan, W. M., and Powell, T. P. S. (1955): The projection of the midline and intralaminar nuclei of the thalamus of the rabbit, J. Neurol. Psychiat. 18, 226–279.
Delgado, J. M. R. (1957): Brain stimulation in the monkey: technique and results (Motion picture), Fed. Proc. 16, 29.
Delgado, J. M. R. (1959): Prolonged stimulation of the brain in awake monkeys, J. Neurophysiol. 22, 458–475.
Delgado, J. M. R. (1963): Telemetry and telestimulation of the brain. In: Bio-Telemetry, pp. 231–249 (ed. L. Slater), Pergamon Press, New York.
Delgado, J. M. R. (1964): Free behavior and brain stimulation In: International Review of

Neurobiology, Vol. VI, pp. 349–449 (ed. C. C. Pfeiffer and J. R. Smythies), Academic Press, New York.

Delgado, J. M. R. (1969): Radio stimulation of the brain in primates and in man, Anesth. Analg. *48,* 529–543.

Delgado, J. M. R. (1970): Multichannel transdermal stimulation of the brain, Tech. Doc. Rep. #ARL-TR-70-1. Holloman Air Force Base, New Mexico, 24 pp.

Delgado, J. M. R. *(in press)* Transdermal stimulation of the brain in animals and man, Int. Res. Comm. System.

Delgado, J. M. R., and Hamlin, H. (1960): Spontaneous and evoked electrical seizures in animals and in humans. In: *Electrical Studies on the Unanesthetized Brain,* pp. 133–158, (ed. E. R. Ramey and D. S. O'Doherty), Hoever, New York.

Delgado, J. M. R. and Kitahata, L. M. (1967): Reversible depression of hippocampus by local injections of anesthetics in monkeys, EEG Clin Neurophysiol. *22,* 453–464.

Delgado, J. M. R., Johnston, V. S., Wallace, J. D., and Bradley, R. J. (1970): Operant conditioning of amygdala spindling in the free chimpanzee, Brain Res. *22,* 347–362.

Delgado, J. M. R., and Mir, D. (1966): Infatigability of pupillary constriction evoked by stimulation in monkeys, Neurology *16,* 939–950.

Delgado, J. M. R., Obrador, S., and Martin-Rodriguez, J. G. (1972): Two-way radio communication with the brain in Psychosurgical patients. Proc. int. Congr. Psychosurg. Cambridge, Eng., August.

Delgado, J. M. R., Rivera, M., and Mir, D. (1971): Repeated stimulation of amygdala in awake monkeys, Brain Res. *27,* 111–131.

Delgado-Garcia, J. M., Amerigo, J. A., and Delgado, J. M. R. *(unpublished):* Behavioral analysis of rhesus monkeys under caudate stimulation.

Diamond, S., Balvin, R. S., and Diamond, F. R. (1963): *Inhibition and Choice. An Neurobehavioral Approach to Problems of Plasticity in Behavior,* Harper & Row, New York.

Eccles, J. C. (1964): *The Physiology of Synapses,* Springer, Berlin.

Eccles, J. C. (ed.) (1966): *Brain and Conscious Experience,* Springer, New York.

Feindel, W. (1961): Response patterns elicited from the amygdala and deep temporoinsular cortex. In: *Electrical Stimulation of the Brain,* pp. 519–532, (ed. D. E. Sheer), Univ. Texas Press, Austin.

Florey, E. (ed.) (1961): Nervous inhibition. *Proceedings of the 2nd Friday Harbour Symposium,* Pergamon Press, New York.

Forman, D., and Ward, J. W. (1957): Responses to electrical stimulation of caudate nucleus in cats in chronic experiments, J. Neurophysiol. *20,* 230–244.

Frank, K. (1959): IRE Trans. Med. Electron. *ME6,* 85–88.

Gloor, P. (1955): Electrophysiological studies on the connections of the amygdaloid nucleus in the cat. II. The electrophysiological properties of the amygdaloid projection system, EEG Clin. Neurophysiol. *7,* 243–264.

Gol, A. (1967): Relief of pain by electrical stimulation of the septal area, J. Neurol. Sci. *5,* 115–120.

Goldring, S., Antony, L. V., Stohr, P. E., and O'Leary, J. J. (1963): "Caudate-induced" cortical potentials. Comparison between monkey and cat, Science *139,* 772.

Heath, R. G., and Hodes, R. (1952): Induction of sleep by stimulation of the caudate nucleus in Macacus rhesus and man, Trans. Amer. Neurol. Ass. *77,* 204–210.

Heath, R. G., and Mickel, W. A. (1960): Evaluation of seven years' experience with depth electrode studies in human patients. In: *Electrical Studies on the Unanesthetized Brain,* pp. 214–247, (ed. E. R. Ramey and D. S. O'Doherty), Hoever, New York.

Hess, W. R. (1944): Das Schlafsyndrom als Folge diencephaler Reizung, Helv. Physiol. Pharmacol. Acta *2,* 305–344.

Jouvet, M. (1969): Biogenic amines and the states of sleep, *Science 163,* 32–41.

Jung, R. (1949): Hirnelektrische Untersuchungen über den Electrokramph: Die Erregungsabläufe in corticalen und subcorticalen Hirnregionen, bei Katze und Hund, Arch. Psychiat. Nervenkr *183,* 206–244.

Kitsikis, A. (1968): The suppression of arm movements in monkeys: threshold variations of caudate nucleus stimulation, Brain Res. *10,* 460–462.

Kitsikis, A., Horvath, F. E., and Rougeul, A. (1968): Synchronized spindle activity elicited in the cortex of the monkey by basal ganglia stimulation, EEG clin. Neurophysiol., *25,* 160–169.

Kupfer, D, J., Detre, T. P., Foster, G., Tucker, G. J., and Delgado, J. M. R. (1972): The application of Delgado's telemetric mobility recorder for human studies, Behav. Biol. 7, 585–590.

Laursen, A. M. (1962): Inhibition evoked from the region of the caudate nucleus in cats, Acta Physiol. Scand. 54, 185–190.

Livingston, R. B., Fulton, J. F., Delgado, J. M. R., Sachs, Jr., E., Brendler, S. J., and Davis, G. D. (1947): Stimulation and regional ablation of orbital surface of frontal lobes, Res. Publ. Ass. Nerv. Ment. Dis. 27, 405–420.

Mettler, F. A. (1945): Effects of bilateral simultaneous subcortical lesions in the primate, J. Neuropath. Exp. Neurol. 4, 99–122.

Mettler, F. A. (1952): Discussion in Heath, R. G., and Hodes, R., Trans. Amer. Neurol. Ass. 77, 204–210.

Pavlov, I. P. (1957): Experimental Psychology, Philosophical Library, New York.

Penfield, W., and Rassmussen, T. (1950): The Cerebral Cortex of Man, Macmillan, New York.

Plotnik, R., and Delgado, J. M. R. (1970): Emotional responses in monkeys inhibited with electrical brain stimulation, Psychol. Sci. 19, 129–130.

Plotnik, R., Mir, D., and Delgado, J. M. R. (1971): Aggression, noxiousness and brain stimulation in unrestrained rhesus monkeys. In: Physiology of Aggression and Defeat, pp. 143–221 (ed. B. F. Eleftherion), Plenum Press, New York.

Roberts, E. (1972): An hypothesis suggesting that there is a defect in the GABA system in schizophrenia, Neurosci. Res. Prog. Bull. 10, 468–482.

Roberts, E., and Baxter, C. F. (eds.) (1960): Inhibition in the Nervous System and Gamma-Aminobutyric Acid, Pergamon Press, New York.

Rubinstein, E. H., and Delgado, J. M. R. (1963): Inhibition induced by forebrain stimulation in the monkey, Amer. J. Physiol. 205, 941–948.

Sechenov, I. M. (1878): Elements of Thought, in Russian. USSR Acad. Sci. Press (1943), Moscow.

Sem-Jacobsen, C. W., and Torkildsen, A. (1960): Depth recording and electrical stimulation in the human brain. In: Electrical Studies on the Unanesthetized Brain, pp. 275–290 (ed. E. R. Ramey and D. S. O'Doherty), Hoeber, New York.

Spehlmann, R., Creutzfeld, O. D., and Jung, R. (1960): Neuronale Hemmung im motorischen Cortex nach elektrischer Reizung des Caudatum, Arch. Psychiat. Zeit. Neurol. 201, 332–354.

Stanley-Jones, D. (1970): The biological orgin of love and hate. In: Feelings and Emotions, pp. 25–37 (ed. M. B. Arnold), Academic Press, New York.

Szabo, J. (1970): Projections from the body of the caudate nucleus in the rhesus monkey, Exp. Neurol. 27, 1015.

Tobach, E. (Chrmn) (1969): Experimental approaches to the study of emotional behavior, Ann. N.Y. Acad. Sci. 159, Art. 3, 621–1121.

Tokizane, T., Kawakami, M., and Gellhorn, E. (1957): On the relation between the activating and recruiting systems, Arch. Int. Physiol. Biochim. 65, 415–432.

Wolstenholme, G. E. W., and O'Connor, M., (eds.) (1962): The Nature of Sleep, CIBA Foundation Symposium, Little Brown, Boston.

Emotions – Their Parameters and Measurement,
edited by L. Levi.
Raven Press, New York © 1975

Session 2: Discussion

Chairman: John Mason

Mason: It is very reassuring for someone who has been working, like most of us have, in a specialized field and thinking that one is discovering new principles to realize that these principles have been discovered by others working in other aspects of central nervous system function. But I think it is particularly reassuring to see that a number of us working on such separate approaches, sometimes with autonomics, sometimes with purely behavioral approaches, have come to, in some areas, a consensus, and I would like to venture a view here of the way we might look at the general organization of these organ systems which indicates the similarities in principles; that the systems we have been talking about separately seem to be commonly organized. The setting: is there a stimulus that you would expect to provoke an emotional response? It provokes no behavioral response, but it provokes a hormonal response. Now, sometimes it does not provoke a hormonal response, and it provokes a behavioral response. And the question is, what is going on, what are the dynamics?

Delgado: I would agree completely about this balance of opposing forces, and perhaps a concept that we could introduce with respect specifically to emotions is the concept of tuning. In other words, rather than talking about the emotions in general or causing factors, we should talk about the emotional tuning. To give two very specific experimental examples, there is the autonomic tuning of the pupils. It has been demonstrated by some of our old experiments that you could maintain the diameter of the pupil by simultaneous stimulation of constrictor and dilator points. And you can do that through a wide range of intensity of stimulation. The pupil always is the same, but still will react to the light. In other words, the pupillary tuning has been changed. The thermostat has been changed. And a concept that I tried to introduce some time ago was something that we could call the psychostat. In other words, like a thermostat, there is a psychostat, which is a tuning.

Mason: That is very interesting. Again, there is a parallel in the psychoendocrine field.

Cook: On the same point from the pharmacological point of view, it was clear many years ago that we were well beyond the point of talking about drugs as depressants or stimulants in a general sense, but it was necessary to specify what behavior is stimulated and what behavior, specifically, is depressed because one can have concurrent increases of one pattern of behavior and decreases of another pattern.

Parsons: I would like to raise a question from my own perspective as a social scientist as to how much difference it makes whether, in consideration of the environment, the studies are made with nonhuman subjects or human subjects. The reason for concern with this problem is that the behaving organism, if human, is behaving in relation to a social-cultural environment which is, above all, symbolically structured through language and other symbolic meaning systems.

Delgado: I disagree with the thinking that only humans are suitable subjects on which to investigate the importance of social setting. In animals we certainly can investigate the role of social setting in emotional responses. But I agree that since we are all humans we should perhaps give a bit more importance to the role of social setting in human responses.

Cook: First of all, I do not doubt that environmental circumstances, social or otherwise, alter or predispose the quality of response to experimental variables, whether they are stimulation, as Dr. Delgado pointed out, or pharmacological effects. The environmental contingencies, not only social but also experimental, will change the quality. However important, I do not think that they are unique as factors in regard to altering the subject's response, in regard to experimental variables.

Kagan: It seems to me that there are three aspects of emotion: feeling, social action, and physiological change. Feeling is intrinsic and subjective, and, if we are going to measure it, we will have to measure it by subjective means. Social action is extrinsic and, to some extent, objective, but one would have to produce objective methods of measurement to measure it. The physiological change is intrinsic and I think quite a number of objective approaches to measuring it have been suggested. Each of these three fields is not just one simple thing but a system of things which might be classified into subsystems. These three aspects, which are the parameters of emotion so far discussed, are interrelated but not in any one-to-one fashion.

Brady: Dr. Lader, can you elaborate on the rationale for separating verbal from emotional behavior or other behavioral categories, as well as from the physiological changes? What about the identification of feelings with verbal behavior?

Lader: The reason that I distinguish between verbal and emotional behavior is quite simple. For example, a patient says that he is feeling extremely anxious and yet when a series of psychiatrists and psychologists rate him for anxiety they will not detect any emotional behavior. There seems to be a distinction between these two behaviors in an extreme case. There is a disassociation in an extreme case between the verbal behavior, the emotional behavior, the effect which is communicated to the rater, and the physiological activity.

Brady: But I will also suggest that the data you presented argue as strongly for verbal behavior as an unreliable measure of feelings as it does as a reliable measure.

Lader: I think it is an unreliable measure. That is just one of the points that I am making. When one is taking two of the aspects of overt behavior which one can rate, when one takes physiological measures, they are something that one can measure fairly accurately.

Brady: I suppose the issue has to do with which of the parameters accounts for most of the variance of a given parameter.

Lader: But it may be that the physiological changes that one is measuring are not relevant in that situation. I think what one has to go back to is the consistency. It is not the variance, I think, that one is interested in, but the covariance. The point that I am stressing is that you can not say that emotion is one of these facets.

Lazarus: I want to assert very firmly for the record that every measure, every index of emotion is highly unreliable. One is not more so than the other. Each is multiply determined, whether you are talking about stress disorders which are produced by a whole host of things which have nothing to do with emotion sometimes, whether you are talking about autonomic responses or endocrine responses, or whether you are talking about actions that are expressive of emotion. These are no more reliable no more dependable sources of information than is verbal behavior.

Yensen: We talked about looking at a measurement in terms of feeling, social behavior, and physiological aspects. I wonder whether this aspect of social behavior relates to aesthetic experience. One can have aesthetic experience that involves some aspect of emotion. I think that one has to try to include within the context of social behavior other behaviors that may not necessarily occur within a social setting, but that have obvious implications for a consideration of emotion.

Parsons: At least at one level, I think the conception of aesthetics has to do with cultural civilization. And our culture is learned in that sense. It has innate determinants but I would not call it an innate phenomenon. Even the experience of natural beauty is very much conditioned by social experience.

Groen: I think we all agree on what distinguishes man from the other socially living mammals, that in addition to everything else we can do in terms of communication, we have a potentiality to learn a word language. Later, we think, we read, we write in that language anything which takes place in words, and that is all our culture which is transferred in words, reading, in writing, and in thinking, that is typically human.

Emotions—Their Parameters and Measurement,
edited by L. Levi.
Raven Press, New York © 1975

Experimental Approaches to the Study of Catecholamines and Emotion*

Marianne Frankenhaeuser

Psychological Laboratories, University of Stockholm, Postbox 6706, S-113 85 Stockholm, Sweden

PERIPHERAL CATECHOLAMINES AS PARAMETERS IN BEHAVIORAL RESEARCH

The relation between sympathetic-adrenal medullary activity and emotion was first demonstrated by Walter B. Cannon and his associates at Harvard during the early part of this century. The results obtained in a series of experiments on cats led Cannon (1914, 1929) to formulate the "emergency-function" theory of adrenal medullary activity, based on the view that many of the physiological effects of epinephrine serve the goal of preparing the organism to meet threatening situations, involving fear or rage or pain.

The work by Euler (1946, 1956) and by Holtz, Credner, and Kroneberg (1947) during the 1940s showed that norepinephrine, the nonmethylated homologue of epinephrine, was the adrenergic neurotransmittor as well as an adrenomedullary hormone. These findings, together with Selye's (1950) work on pituitary-adrenocortical activity in adaptation to stress, and the concomitant advances in biochemical techniques, inspired new research efforts also in the behaviorally oriented work. Methods became available, which were sufficiently sensitive to permit the measurement of small amounts of hormones in blood plasma and in urine. The field was thus opened for new psychoendocrine approaches involving the study of human beings in different environments.

This chapter reviews the present state of knowledge, based on the study of humans, about peripheral epinephrine and norepinephrine as parameters of emotion. The twofold importance of these hormones in the study of emotion is emphasized throughout this chapter: their role as *dependent variables*, reflecting the influence of the environment, and as *independent variables*, affecting the state of the organism.

---

* This chapter is a review article and contains some findings and conclusions that have appeared in previous papers by the author. For other general surveys of similar topics see the reference section.

Secretion and Action of Catecholamines

pinephrine and norepinephrine occur in different chromaffine cells in the adrenal medulla (Hillarp and Hökfelt, 1953), the major part being located in subcellular granules (Blaschko, 1973; Blaschko and Welch, 1953; Hillarp, Lagerstedt, and Nilson, 1953). The metabolism of the catecholamines proceeds in the chromaffine cells from tyrosine, DOPA, and dopamine to norepinephrine and epinephrine.

The secreting cells of the adrenal medulla are intimately connected with preganglionic fibers of the sympathetic nervous system, and their secretory activity is controlled by stimulation through these nervous pathways. Among the stimuli known to elicit increased secretion are: cold, pain, anoxia, hypoglycemia, hypotension, hemorrhage, burns, physical exercise, psychosocial stimuli, and pharmacological agents, including drugs in common use such as caffeine, nicotine, and alcohol.

The proportion of epinephrine and norepinephrine released by the various stimuli differs characteristically: hypoglycemia, for example, raises epinephrine secretion only. Of particular importance in the present context is the greater sensitivity of epinephrine as compared with norepinephrine secretion to emotion-inducing stimuli.

Some stimuli, e.g., pain, heat, and cold, presumably induce the adrenal-medullary secretion primarily by reflex action, while reactions to psychosocial stimuli are mediated by central nervous processes. Adrenal-medullary secretion can also be elicited by electrical stimulation of different parts of the brain, both in the hypothalamic and mesencephalic regions, and in certain cortical areas.

The hormones of the adrenal medulla act on all organs of the body innervated by the sympathetic nervous system, and generally produce effects similar to sympathetic stimulation. The stimulating effect on the heart, dilation of the coronary vessels, vasodilation in the voluntary muscles, vasoconstriction in the intestinal tract, decreased peristalsis of the alimentary canal, as well as metabolic actions such as mobilization of glucose and of fat, all form part of the "emergency function" serving to increase physical effectiveness under conditions of fight and flight.

There are distinct differences between epinephrine and norepinephrine with regard to some circulatory and metabolic actions. In general, norepinephrine is more potent in raising blood pressure, and less potent in its metabolic action and in relaxing smooth muscle. However, as emphasized by Euler (1967), recent observations have brought out important similarities in action; both hormones, for example, mobilize fat and increase oxygen consumption.

When comparing the actions of the two adrenal-medullary hormones, it should also be kept in mind that the proportions of norepinephrine and epinephrine differ widely in different species. In man, as in most species, norepinephrine constitutes the relatively smaller part of the two hormones. However, adrenal-medullary secretion is often combined with increased sympathetic nervous activity in general, in which case the norepinephrine liberated directly at the nerve endings must also be taken into account.

The question of a direct action of the adrenal-medullary hormones on the central nervous system is of particular interest in the study of emotion. Although this still remains a somewhat controversial issue, the evidence now available suggests that epinephrine crosses the blood–brain barrier in the region of the hypothalamus, and acts directly on the mesencephalic reticular formation and the posterior hypothalamus (cf. reviews by Euler, 1967; Rothballer, 1959; Schildkraut and Kety, 1967). Little is known about the intracerebral concentration of epinephrine needed to achieve these effects, but it may well be that very small amounts are required.

Estimation of Catecholamines

A small fraction of the liberated amines is excreted in urine as free epinephrine and norepinephrine, and this fraction can be estimated quantitatively by spectrophotofluorimetric methods. Under normal conditions most of the epinephrine excreted in urine is derived from the adrenal medulla. With regard to norepinephrine excretion, the greater part presumably comes from the sympathetic nerve endings. The epinephrine excreted in urine represents a rough quantitative estimate of adrenal-medullary activity. With regard to norepinephrine, a large part of the amount released is reabsorbed by the nerve endings or bound to various tissues, and does not enter the bloodstream or urine. However, in spite of the methodological difficulties involved, estimates of urinary epinephrine and norepinephrine obtained by the fluorimetric technique of Euler and Lishajko (1961) show a relatively high constancy over time provided that the conditions under which urine is sampled are carefully standardized (Pátkai and Frankenhaeuser, 1964; Johansson and Post, 1972). The reliability of the fluorimetric technique, as determined by the correlation between halved urine samples analyzed by a skilled technician, is also satisfactory (Levi, 1972; Pátkai and Frankenhaeuser, 1964). An improved automated procedure has recently been developed (Andersson, Hovmöller, Karlsson, and Svensson, 1974).

Urinary catecholamines represent estimates of sympathetic-adrenal medullary activity integrated over extended time periods, usually 1 to 3 hr. Such measurements, although not reflecting momentary changes, are particularly well-suited for studying psychosocial influences of everyday life. The fact that measurements can be obtained from human beings carrying out their ordinary daily activities, adds to the usefulness of the method in behavioral research. However, catecholamine output is sensitive to a number of extraneous stimuli. The different *sources of error* have to be either eliminated or kept under control so as not to interfere with the experimental variables (for a detailed account see Levi, 1967a). Among these are a number of dietary stimuli as well as the intake of caffeine- and alcohol-containing beverages (e.g., Brohult, Levi, and Reichard, 1970; Levi, 1967b; Myrsten, Post, and Frankenhaeuser, 1971).

The tobacco-smoking habit constitutes a special problem. On the one hand, smoking should not be allowed prior to or during experimental sessions, since nicotine is a potent stimulus for epinephrine release (e.g., Frankenhaeuser, Myrsten, Waszak, Neri, and Post, 1968; Frankenhaeuser, Myrsten, Post, and Johansson, 1972). On the other hand, depriving a heavy smoker of tobacco may cause a state of physiological and psychological disequilibrium, which may in itself evoke epinephrine secretion. It is therefore advisable to avoid using heavy smokers as subjects in experiments where effects of psychosocial factors are of primary concern.

Epinephrine secretion is very sensitive to changes in the psychosocial environment, and a rise in secretion rate is likely to occur in any novel environmental setting. This particular aspect of adrenal-medullary sensitivity should also be taken into account when designing laboratory experiments, since a subject who pays his first visit to the laboratory and encounters the experimenter for the first time, usually shows a marked elevation in epinephrine output, even when he is not exposed to any experimental stressor. Basal catecholamine levels therefore cannot be obtained until after the subject has become well acquainted with the surroundings.

Other factors that have to be taken into account are physical activity, body posture, body weight, age, and sex. These variables have been given special attention in separate studies, some of which, i.e., those concerning physical activity and sex differences, will be reported in this chapter.

The diurnal rhythm of catecholamine output is of particular importance. Since epinephrine secretion displays a pronounced diurnal variation, the lowest level occurring during night and the highest generally around midday, investigations have to be designed so as to ascertain that effects of the experimental variables can be distinguished from diurnal variations. It is therefore advisable to obtain measurements under basal conditions covering the same period of the day as the experimental conditions. A further complicating factor is that individuals differ with regard to their diurnal rhythm of epinephrine secretion. Although most persons display an increase in secretion rate between early morning and midday, some persons reach their peak secretion early in the morning. Interestingly enough, interindividual differences in the diurnal rhythm of epinephrine secretion appear to be related to working habits, i.e., habitual "morning workers" and "evening workers" showing characteristic differences in epinephrine level at different times of the day (Pátkai, 1971a), although examined under identical conditions.

Marked seasonal variations do not occur under conditions of reasonably constant environmental temperature (Johansson and Post, 1972). Exposure to cold, however, is accompanied by increased catecholamine secretion (e.g., Euler, 1960).

Other possible sources of error, e.g., urine retention in the bladder after voluntary voiding, and technical mishaps associated with the collection of urine samples, have been discussed by Levi (1972, p. 33 ff.).

The numerous sources of error, together with the fact that only a small percent of the amount released is excreted as free amines, as well as the possibility that not only the release but also the turnover of catecholamines might be reflected in the urinary estimates, has led some investigators to look for other measures of adrenal-medullary activity. By measuring the major catecholamine metabolites, i.e., metanephrine, normetanephrine, 3-methoxy-4-hydroxy-phenylglycol, and 3-methoxy-4-hydroxy-phenyl-glycolic acid, additional information about sympathetic adrenal-medullary activity can be obtained. These metabolites constitute a much larger proportion of the total catecholamine release than do the free catecholamines. So far, however, little is known about the constancy of this proportion.

Methods are also available for measuring catecholamines in plasma (e.g., Häggendahl, 1963). One advantage of plasma measurements is that they permit precise timing of transient changes in hormone secretion. However, since the half-life of epinephrine in the blood is very short, the blood level is extremely sensitive to the rate of disappearance. Trying to compensate for this by drawing serial blood samples introduces a new stressor that cannot be ignored in behavioral studies. Mason (1972) and Levi (1972) have given detailed accounts of the technical problems involved in plasma-catecholamine measurements in conscious human subjects. Plasma measurements have, however, been successfully used in a series of animal studies, also reviewed by Mason (1968, 1972).

CATECHOLAMINES AS DEPENDENT VARIABLES: REFLECTING THE EMOTIONAL IMPACT OF THE ENVIRONMENT

The Influence of Psychosocial Stimuli

Catecholamine secretion varies widely under different psychosocial conditions. Under rest and inactivity, epinephrine secretion is generally low; under ordinary daily activities, secretion rises to about twice the resting level; and under moderately stressful conditions, secretion rates corresponding to between three and five times the resting levels are often noted. Severe stressors may induce a further pronounced increase to levels indicative of pheochromocytoma.

The sensitivity of the sympathetic adrenal-medullary system to psychosocial influences will be illustrated by examples from experimental in-

ons concerned with two different influences: the subject's control of
ronment, and the amount of external stimulation.

Uncertainty versus Control

Conditions characterized by novelty, anticipation, unpredictability, and
change usually produce a rise in epinephrine output, and the amount excreted in urine closely reflects the degree of arousal evoked by the stimulating condition. In the course of repeated exposure epinephrine excretion
decreases successively provided that the subject gains better control over
the situation. This is illustrated by data from an experiment by Frankenhaeuser and Rissler (1970) in which the degree of control that the subject
was allowed to exert was systematically varied. In Session I, the subject
was exposed to unpredictable and uncontrollable electric shocks. Under
these conditions, epinephrine excretion was about three times as high as
during a relaxation period (Session IV). Such a rise in epinephrine output
can be counteracted by increasing the subject's control over the situation as
was done in Sessions II and III where a choice-reaction task was performed. While in Session I the subject had to remain passive and was unable
to avoid shock, his ability to cope with the task in the two subsequent sessions influenced the amount of punishment that he received. In Session II,
the subject was often unjustly punished, whereas in Session III most shocks
could be avoided by rapid performance. As seen in Fig. 1, epinephrine output (left-hand diagram) decreased successively as the degree of control was
varied from a state of helplessness to ability to master the disturbing
influences. Norepinephrine excretion (right-hand diagram) was not much

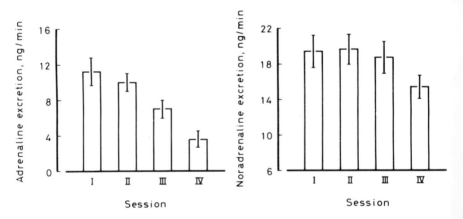

FIG. 1. Means and standard errors for epinephrine (adrenaline) and norepinephrine
(noradrenaline) excretion under four conditions. In Sessions I, II, and III, the subject's
control of the situation was successively increased. Session IV was a control condition.
Redrawn and reprinted with permission from Frankenhaeuser and Rissler (1970).

affected by degree of control, but remained slightly elevated as long as the subject was engaged in the attention-demanding activity.

It should be noted that repeated exposure to the same external situation is accompanied by decreased catecholamine secretion only insofar as the repetition is associated with a decrease in the state of subjective arousal (e.g., Frankenhaeuser, Sterky, and Järpe, 1962). Under conditions where subjective arousal remains at a high level, epinephrine output also stays high. An example is provided by results from an investigation (Bloom, Euler, and Frankenhaeuser, 1963) concerned with physiological reactions to parachute jumping, an activity which retains its stressful and threatening character even after long experience. Figure 2 shows the mean catecholamine excretion in a group of trainees performing their first jump, and in a group of officers who had previously performed between 14 and 80 jumps. It is seen that the increase in catecholamine excretion occurring under the condition involving parachute-jumping as compared with a period of ground activity, was of about the same magnitude in the officers as in the trainees.

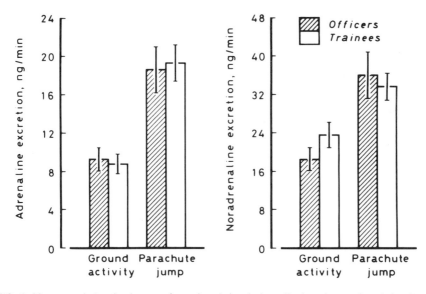

FIG. 2. Means and standard errors for epinephrine (adrenaline) and norepinephrine (noradrenaline) excretion in a group of officers and a group of paratroop trainees during periods in which either ground activity or parachute jumps were performed. Redrawn and reprinted with permission from Bloom, Euler, and Frankenhaeuser (1963).

Level of Stimulation

Conditions characterized by either stimulus excess, such as information overload, or stimulus restriction, such as monotonous work lacking in variety, represent two contrasting influences to which people living in advanced industrialized societies are commonly exposed. It is therefore of interest that catecholamine output reflects even relatively minor changes in stimulus level.

To study this problem more closely, catecholamine excretion was measured in laboratory experiments, in which some aspects of real-life environments were simulated. Data from an experiment (Frankenhaeuser, Nordheden, Myrsten, and Post, 1971) involving three levels of stimulation are shown in Fig. 3. During "understimulation" the subjects performed a prolonged visual-vigilance task while deprived of normal social and sensory inputs. During the condition of "medium stimulation" they read magazines and listened to the radio, and during "overstimulation" they performed a complex sensorimotor task while bombarded by different visual and auditory signals. Both understimulation and overstimulation evoked feelings of unpleasantness, whereas medium stimulation was perceived as "emotionally neutral." It is seen that epinephrine and norepinephrine output increased during understimulation and overstimulation as compared with the condition involving a medium or "normal" level of stimulation.

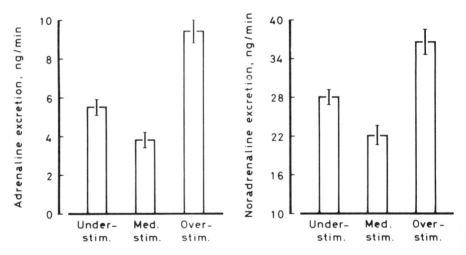

FIG. 3. Means and standard errors for epinephrine (adrenaline) and norepinephrine (noradrenaline) excretion under conditions of understimulation, medium stimulation, and overstimulation. Based on Frankenhaeuser, Nordheden, Myrsten, and Post (1971).

Effects of Physical Activity

Physical and mental strain often occur together in the same situation, for instance in physical competitions. Therefore, it has generally not been possible to distinguish between the relative influence on catecholamine output of these two kinds of stimuli. An interesting study was carried out by Elmadjian, Hope, and Lamson (1957), who measured catecholamine excretion in hockey players, some of whom took part in active competition, while others observed a game in which they did not participate. The results showed large increases in norepinephrine and smaller increases in epinephrine excretion during active play as compared with increases in epinephrine excretion alone in the physically passive condition.

The same problem was approached in a laboratory study by Frankenhaeuser and her co-workers (Frankenhaeuser, Post, Nordheden, and Sjöberg, 1969) in which a bicycle ergometer was chosen as a suitable tool for varying systematically the physical work load in an "emotionally neutral" situation. Figure 4 shows results obtained in a group of healthy male subjects who participated in a control condition and in three experimental sessions in

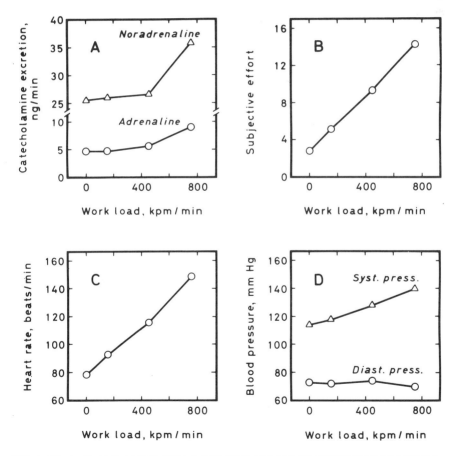

FIG. 4. Mean values for epinephrine (adrenaline) and norepinephrine (noradrenaline) excretion (A), estimates of subjective effort (B), heat rate (C), and blood pressure (D) in a control session and in three sessions involving intermittent work at different loads on a bicycle ergometer. Reprinted with permission of the publisher, Frankenhaeuser, Post, Nordheden, and Sjöberg (1969).

each of which five successive 6-min tests, involving different work loads, were performed on a bicycle ergometer. It is seen (Fig. 4A) that excretion rates of both epinephrine and norepinephrine remained close to control levels at the lower work loads, whereas the highest work load induced an increase in both catecholamines. Figure 4B shows that subjective effort increased consistently with increasing work load. When Figs. 4 A and B are compared, it is seen that catecholamine excretion remained close to baseline level at the lower work loads, where the subjective effort was judged as "extremely light," "very light," or "fairly light." When, however, in the condition involving the highest load, the subjective estimate passed the midpoint of the rating scale and approached the point defined as "laborious," a pronounced increase of both epinephrine and norepinephrine output occurred.

The increased norepinephrine output is readily identified as part of the cardiovascular-response system regulating reactions to muscular work (Figs. 4 C and D), whereas the rise in epinephrine output appears to be related to the discomfort perceived during heavy physical strain.

The Quality of Emotions

The fact that two different substances, epinephrine and norepinephrine, are involved in mediating the effects of the sympathetic adrenal-medullary system has raised the question of whether these two hormones are selectively released in different emotional states. Support for the idea of a differential release of epinephrine and norepinephrine came from several lines of research in the early 1950s, which will be briefly reviewed.

Of particular interest were studies showing that epinephrine and norepinephrine could be selectively released by electrical stimulation of specific areas in the hypothalamus (Folkow and Euler, 1954; Redgate and Gellhorn, 1953).

Among investigations concerned with emotional states in human subjects, Funkenstein's work (1956) has attracted a great deal of attention. On the basis of studies concerned with changes in blood pressure induced by injection of mecholyl or epinephrine it was suggested that epinephrine secretion was the predominant response of individuals who tended to direct their anger "inwardly" when confronted with stressful situations. Norepinephrine secretion, on the other hand, seemed associated with anger directed "outwardly." This idea appeared consistent with the results reported by Ax (1953) who, using a variety of polygraphic measurements, found that laboratory situations designed to elicit fear versus anger gave rise to different patterns of cardiovascular responses, i.e., "epinephrine-like" versus "norepinephrine-like" responses.

In general agreement with these hypothesis, some of the early studies of catecholamine excretion (Elmadjian, Hope, and Lamson, 1957; Silverman and Cohen, 1960) suggested that epinephrine was associated with anxious reactions and norepinephrine with aggressive reactions. These results appeared consistent with those of Goodall (1951) indicating that norepinephrine is predominant in the organs of aggressive animals, while epinephrine predominates in fearful, submissive animals. Investigations concerned with urinary and plasma catecholamine levels in patients with different affective disorders (reviewed by Mason, 1972) have not given consistent results.

On the basis of results obtained in plasma-catecholamine studies of monkeys, Mason and his associates (Mason, Mangan, Brady, Conrad, and Rioch, 1961) proposed that whereas epinephrine output is increased in situations characterized by novelty and uncertainty, a rise in norepinephrine occurs when conditions are familiar and stereotyped and also unpleasant. Mandler (1967) suggested an explanation in terms of "response availability" according to which epinephrine secretion would be increased in situations characterized by lack of relevant behavioral responses, whereas norepinephrine secretion would be raised under conditions that are controlled by the organism in the sense that relevant behavior is available for meeting the requirements of the situation. Referring to the different peripheral functions of the two hormones, Kety (1967) advanced the view that epinephrine is secreted primarily in situations in which either flight or fight is the appropriate response and in which epinephrine would be of use to the organism by facilitating muscular activity, whereas norepinephrine is secreted in situations where the "outcome is inevitable and unavoidable and muscular activity would be useless."

Later studies on human subjects do not support the assumption that epinephrine and norepinephrine would be selectively released in different emotional states. Instead, the results indicate that epinephrine is secreted in a variety of emotional states, including both anger and fear. Similarly, a rise in norepinephrine secretion may occur in different emotional states, but the threshold for norepinephrine release in response to psychosocial stimulation is generally much higher than for epinephrine secretion.

These conclusions are based on a series of studies from the laboratories of Frankenhaeuser (reviewed by Frankenhaeuser, 1971a,b; 1974a,b) and Levi (reviewed by Levi, 1972) during the 1960s. In these studies, the problem of a selective release of epinephrine and norepinephrine has been approached by varying systematically the stimulus content and examining, for each stimulus situation, the intensity and quality of the subjective reaction evoked as well as the amount of epinephrine and norepinephrine excreted.

An example is provided in a study by Levi (1965) showing that an increase in catecholamine output does not occur solely under conditions perceived as unpleasant or agitating, but that amusing situations, which evoke pleasant emotional states, may also be accompanied by increased catecholamine output. A further important finding is that emotionally "neutral" situations, which evoke feelings of equanimity and tranquility, may be accompanied by a decrease in sympathetic adrenal-medullary activity. This is illustrated in Fig. 5, which shows mean catecholamine-excretion rates in subjects who were shown four different films, selected with the aim of evoking feelings of either equanimity, amusement, aggressiveness, or fright. Self-estimates showed that the predominant emotional reaction induced by each film was, in fact, of the expected quality. Measurements of catecholamine excretion before, during, and after each film session showed that all the "arousing" films produced a rise in catecholamine output, irrespective of the specific quality of the emotion evoked. In contrast, the "tranquilizing" film was accompanied by a decrease in catecholamine excretion.

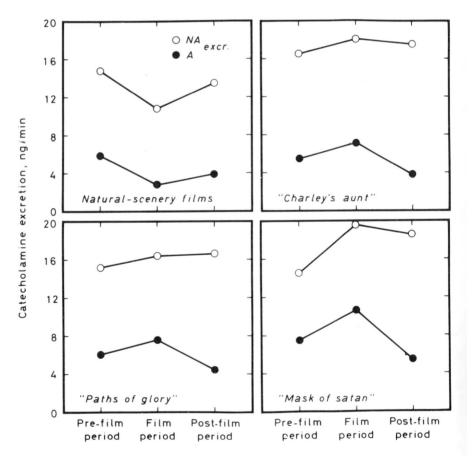

FIG. 5. Mean epinephrine (A) and norepinephrine (NA) excretion before, during, and after four film sessions. Based on Levi (1972), with the author's permission.

Similar results were obtained in a study of Pátkai (1971*b*) who designed laboratory situations so as to evoke either pleasant or unpleasant affective states (Fig. 6). The pleasant situation involved playing Bingo, the popular game of chance, with small winnings but without stakes. In one unpleasant situation the subjects watched medicosurgical films, and in another they performed tedious paper-and-pencil tests. One session was spent in neutral inactivity. The highest epinephrine excretion occurred in the game session, which was the session judged by the subjects as the most pleasant. Norepinephrine excretion did not vary between conditions.

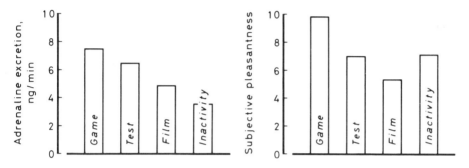

FIG. 6. Means for epinephrine (adrenaline) excretion and self-estimates of pleasantness during four sessions that involved playing a game of chance, performing psychological tests, watching a medicosurgical film, and spending the session in inactivity. Redrawn and reprinted with permission from Pátkai (1971*b*).

The outcome of the two last-mentioned studies is in general agreement with data obtained in studies concerned with the relationship between catecholamine output and personality traits, as measured by various rating techniques. According to these studies, predominantly anxious and predominantly aggressive individuals do not differ with regard to the relative rate of their epinephrine and norepinephrine output (Frankenhaeuser and Pátkai, 1965; Frankenhaeuser, Mellis, Rissler, Björkvall, and Pátkai, 1968).

Comment

It is interesting to look for a common element among the apparently diverse stimuli that elicit catecholamine secretion. The empirical data clearly show that any event perceived as emotionally arousing, regardless of whether the experience is a pleasant or an unpleasant one, will generally be accompanied by increased epinephrine output. Conversely, under conditions which are perceived as relaxing, epinephrine secretion will fall below the level typical for a given individual under conditions which he perceives as involving an "ordinary" stimulus input. Furthermore, repeated exposure to one and the same arousing stimulus is accompanied by a decrease in epinephrine secretion only if there is a concomitant decrease in subjective arousal, while a stimulus that retains its stressful character will continue to induce a high rate of epinephrine secretion.

We may thus conclude that those stimulus conditions that are perceived as deviating from the "ordinary" input level or that are in some other way incongruous with a person's expectancies based on his previous experience are likely to induce changes in catecholamine output. Conversely, stimuli that are perceived as part of the familiar environment and are not emotionally arousing will generally not affect catecholamine output.

The studies reported in this chapter clearly illustrate the part played by cognitive processes in catecholamine secretion: the brain exerts a continuous influence on sympathetic adrenal-medullary activity, and by measuring catecholamine excretion we can monitor the arousing and relaxing influences of the psychosocial environment. At present we have a fairly good understanding of these relationships, which enables us to predict how the sympathetic adrenal-medullary system will respond to specific changes in the environment. However, the mechanisms underlying individual differences in catecholamine secretion, for example, the "paradoxical" reactions, are not yet understood.

CATECHOLAMINES AS INDEPENDENT VARIABLES: AFFECTING COGNITION AND EMOTION

Catecholamine Infusions

Catecholamine infusions provide a useful technique for studying quantitative relations between different parameters of emotion. In an early study by Landis and Hunt (1932), it was shown that epinephrine in small or moderate doses gives rise to subjective emotional changes that resemble, in some respects, symptoms typical of real-life stress situations. That is, the subjects report feeling excited, restless, tense, and apprehensive. Palpitation, tremor, and dryness of the mouth are other common symptoms. Since genuine anxiety, fright, and panic are not usually experienced, it has been argued that epinephrine does not produce true emotions, but "cold" emotions, the subjects feeling *as if* they were afraid, anxious, etc., without experiencing the genuine emotion. It is possible that this is partly a question of dosage and that larger doses than those ordinarily employed in experiments with human subjects would be more likely to produce true anxiety. It is also likely that most subjects will hesitate to report a true emotion, such as fear, in the absence of a reasonable cause, no matter what they feel.

The experiment on effects of epinephrine injections by Schachter and Singer (1962) has greatly contributed to our understanding of the role of cognitive factors in the development of different emotional states. In this study it was shown that, depending upon how the external situation was manipulated, the bodily symptoms induced by an adrenaline injection were interpreted differently, and either euphoria or anger was experienced. These results are consistent with those from studies of the excretion of endogenous epinephrine in showing that an increase in circulating epinephrine is accompanied by a rise in nonspecific subjective arousal, and the affective tone is determined by the individual's cognitive appraisal of the situation.

Infusion of norepinephrine does not produce emotional reactions qualitatively different from those produced by epinephrine infusions. Results obtained by Frankenhaeuser, Järpe, and Matell (1961) showed that insofar as any emotional changes at all occurred during norepinephrine infusion, they were of the same nature as those produced by epinephrine, but much less intense. When a mixture containing equal parts of both amines was infused, subjective and physiological changes were similar to those produced by epinephrine only (Frankenhaeuser and Järpe, 1962).

By studying concomitant physiological and subjective reactions produced by epinephrine infusions, some knowledge can be gained about possible causal relationships between different parameters. Figure 7 shows dose-response curves from a study (Frankenhaeuser and Järpe, 1963) where each subject had 35-min infusions of a placebo solution and epinephrine in four different doses. The variables examined were heart rate and blood pressure, subjective stress (as measured by the method of magnitude estimation), and performance in a continuous concentration task. For all variables studied, reactions increased progressively with increasing dose of epinephrine. However, this similarity in mode of response applied only to the mean dose-response curves. For any one subject the same consistent relationship between changes in different variables could not be demonstrated. Furthermore, the time-response patterns for the various functions also differed. Thus, heart rate and blood pressure remained relatively constant during each infusion period after the first 5 to 10 min had elapsed, whereas the degree of subjective stress was markedly higher at the beginning than at the end of the infusion. This discrepancy indicates that the magnitude of the subjective response was only partly determined by that of the physiological reaction.

It should be noted that the changes in performance, although rather small, were in the direction of improvement with increasing dose. The task performed was not difficult, but it required sustained concentration. Most probably, higher doses of epinephrine, giving rise to more pronounced physiological and subjective reactions, would be accompanied by impaired performance so that an inverted-U relation between epinephrine level and performance efficiency would be obtained. The nature of the task should, of course, also be taken into account. Thus, the tremor produced by epinephrine makes tasks involving fine movements difficult to perform. However, even in such tasks, subjects have been shown to compensate to some extent for his handicap by an intense effort to concentrate (Frankenhaeuser et al.,

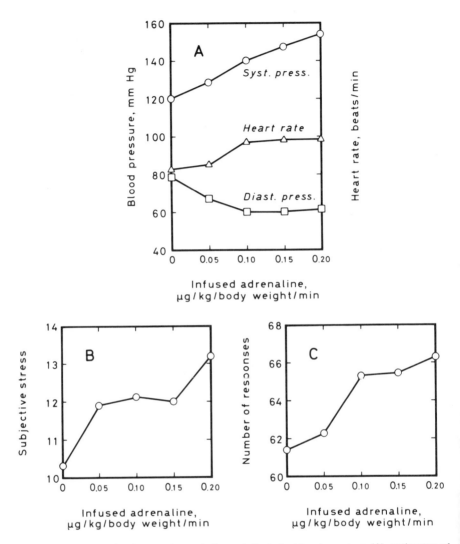

FIG. 7. Mean values for heart rate, systolic and diastolic blood pressure (A), estimates of subjective stress (B), and performance in a concentration task (C) during infusions of a placebo solution and four doses of epinephrine (adrenaline). Redrawn and reprinted with permission from Frankenhaeuser and Järpe (1963).

1961). It thus appears that such unfavorable effects of epinephrine infusions as decreased hand steadiness may be counteracted by the favorable effects of increased concentration, which enable the subjects to carry out the tasks without appreciable impairment.

Intravenously infused epinephrine produces a transient EEG activation. Interestingly enough, this effect is seen in drowsy and sleeping animals only, and it is not evident in animals which are already aroused (*cf.* Rothballer,

1967). Furthermore, whereas small doses of catecholamines administered intracerebrally or intravenously usually produce a brief arousal, larger doses may produce long-term sedation. The possible significance of these sedative effects has been discussed by Breggin (1964), who suggests that "epinephrine depression" may underlie the fatigue and exhaustion following excitement and anxiety states.

In this connection the important part played by brain norepinephrine in affective states should be recalled: drugs that increase the amount of functional norepinephrine available in the brain cause behavioral activation and tend to counteract depression, whereas, in contrast, those that reduce brain norepinephrine produce sedation and depression (see review by Schildkraut and Kety, 1967).

Catecholamines and Adjustment

The early emphasis on the "emergency function" of epinephrine has had a continuing influence on research concerned with adrenal-medullary activity. In line with this thinking, the adaptive reactions mediated by epinephrine release have commonly been regarded as part of a phylogenetically old adaptation pattern, which is obsolete in today's psychosocial environment, where fight and flight reactions are inadequate ways of dealing with stressors. Furthermore, it is claimed that increased epinephrine secretion is potentially dangerous, since, if it lasts too long or is repeated too often, it may cause functional disturbances in various organs and organ systems which, in turn, may lead to disease (cf. Levi, 1972).

These two points will be discussed in turn. First, data will be presented that show that catecholamines play important adaptive functions also in today's psychosocial environment by facilitating adjustment to cognitive and emotional pressures. Then catecholamine secretion will be considered in relation to possible harmful long-term effects involved in repeated adjustments to environmental demands.

One way of approaching these problems is to relate *interindividual differences* in catecholamine output to psychological parameters. Experimental analyses of relations between human performance and catecholamine output have given interesting results. Among normal, healthy individuals, those who have relatively higher catecholamine-excretion levels tend to perform better in terms of speed, accuracy, and endurance than those who have lower levels. Results from a series of experiments comprising different performance tasks have been reviewed by Frankenhaeuser (1971). This relationship is particularly marked in the case of epinephrine excretion, but seems to hold also for norepinephrine. An example is given in Fig. 8, which shows that performance in a learning task was consistently superior in a group of high-epinephrine subjects than in a group of low-epinephrine subjects (i.e., subjects above and below the median epinephrine-excretion value).

Individuals do not only differ in respect of their basal catecholamine level, but also with regard to the change in catecholamine output, which takes place in response to a particular stimulus. For example, some individuals respond to mental work by a large increase, whereas others show a moderate or small increase, or even a decrease. In general, "epinephrine decreasers," i.e., those whose epinephrine output decreases during strenuous mental activity as compared with passive conditions, are less efficient than "epi-

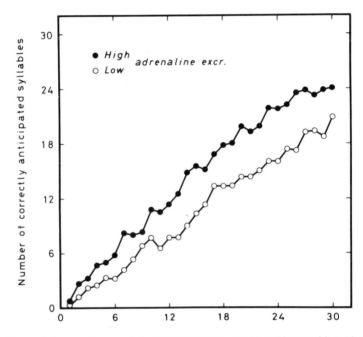

FIG. 8. Mean performance in a verbal rote-learning task in subjects with a high (above median value) and subjects with low (below median value) excretion rates of epinephrine (adrenaline). Reprinted with permission of the publisher (Frankenhaeuser and Anderson, 1974).

nephrine increasers." An example is given in a study by Johansson, Frankenhaeuser, and Magnusson (1973) as shown in Fig. 9.

Other important interindividual differences are associated with the *temporal pattern* of sympathetic adrenal-medullary activation following exposure to acute environmental pressure. There are large differences between individuals in the time taken for epinephrine secretion to return to baseline level after a brief period of exposure to environmental stress. The time course may be a significant factor in determining the relative potency of harmful versus beneficial epinephrine effects.

Recent data (Johansson and Frankenhaeuser, 1973) suggest that a rapid

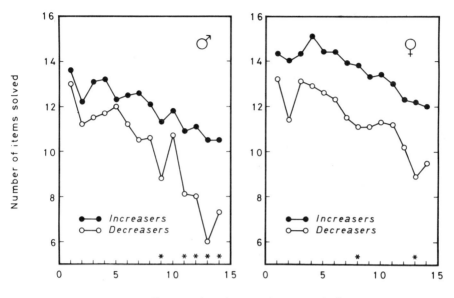

FIG. 9. Successive mean performance scores for subjects whose epinephrine (adrenaline) excretion increased, and for subjects whose epinephrine excretion decreased during an arithmetic task as compared with a preceding passive period. (*Indicates that the t-value for the mean difference between "increasers" and "decreasers" was statistically significant.) Reprinted with permission from Johansson, Frankenhaeuser, and Magnusson (1973).

return to sympathetic adrenal-medullary baselines is indicative of good adjustment. This is illustrated in Fig. 10, which shows epinephrine excretion, performance scores, and neuroticism scores in two groups of subjects, classified as rapid or slow "decreasers" depending upon the time taken for epinephrine excretion to return to baseline level after short-term exposure to a heavy mental load. The rapid "decreasers" differed significantly from the slow "decreasers" in that they had higher epinephrine output during inactivity, better performance scores in a sensorimotor task, and lower neuroticism scores as measured by the Swedish version of Eysenck's Personality Inventory. These results are in general agreement with those by Eysenck (1967) and other investigators suggesting a relationship between the speed at which autonomic equilibrium is regained and personality traits indicative of emotional stability.

In addition to the studies concerned with the relationship between cognitive efficiency and sympathetic-adrenal medullary activity in acute situations, other investigations show that consistent relationships also exist between catecholamine secretion and some enduring psychological characteristics of the individual. For example, a positive correlation has been found

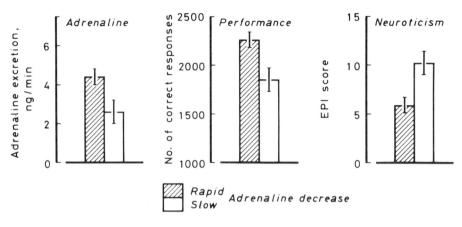

FIG. 10. Means and standard errors for epinephrine (adrenaline) excretion during inactivity, performance scores in a sensorimotor task, and neuroticism scores obtained by Eysenck's personality inventory. Redrawn and reprinted with permission from Johansson and Frankenhaeuser (1973).

in children between epinephrine excretion on the one hand and intelligence quotient and school achievement on the other (Johansson et al., 1973; Lambert, Johansson, Frankenhaeuser, and Klackenberg-Larsson, 1969). These findings indicate that relations between epinephrine and psychological functions are not restricted to efficiency in acute situations, but involve cognitive functions in general.

Furthermore, significant correlations have been found between epinephrine excretion and personality characteristics such as "ego strength" (Roessler, Burch, and Mefferd, 1967) and different indices of "emotional stability" (Johansson et al., 1973; Lambert et al., 1969). It has also been shown in a study of high-school students (Frankenhaeuser and Pátkai, 1965) that individuals with depressive tendencies, as measured by ratings, had a relatively weaker epinephrine response when required to perform under stressful conditions. The relation of norepinephrine secretion to personality traits appears similar to that of epinephrine secretion, but the data are, on the whole, less consistent.

In this connection it is interesting to recall the studies of adrenocortical function in relation to bereavement and mourning (reviewed by Mason, 1972). Among parents of leukemic children there were large individual differences in 17-hydroxy-corticosteroid excretion rates, and these differences were related to the effectiveness of psychological defenses. So far, corresponding data for catecholamine levels under chronic stress conditions are lacking. There are, however, interesting observations suggesting that a "paradoxical" epinephrine response, i.e., decreased secretion during stress exposure, is associated with poor adjustment to cognitive and emotional stressors (Johansson and Frankenhaeuser, 1973).

Sex Differences

The greater part of the investigations concerned with relationships between sympathetic- adrenal-medullary activity and behavior has been carried out on male subjects. It has generally been assumed that when catecholamine excretion is expressed in relation to body weight no differences remain in excretion rate between the sexes (e.g., Kärki, 1956). This assumption, however, has been based on data from resting and inactivity conditions, and recent investigations (Frankenhaeuser, 1972; Johansson, 1972; Johansson and Post, 1974) show that a somewhat different picture is obtained, at least with regard to epinephrine excretion, when the sexes are compared under psychosocial pressure. In Fig. 11, epinephrine excretion in a male and a female group is compared under a nonstressful condition, i.e., when the subjects carried out their daily routine activities, and under psychological stress, i.e., when they performed an intelligence test under time pressure. In the group of women, epinephrine excretion was about the same during intelligence testing as during daily routine activity. In contrast, the male subjects increased their epinephrine output significantly when they were required to perform the intelligence test.

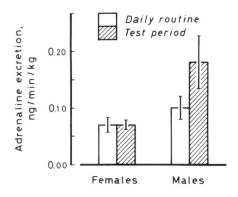

FIG. 11. Means and standard errors for epinephrine (adrenaline) excretion, expressed in relation to body weight, in adult male and female subjects during daily routine activities and during intelligence testing. Based on Johansson and Post (1972).

Similar results were obtained when 12-year-old boys and girls were compared (Fig. 12) under a "passive" condition, i.e., watching a nonengaging motion picture, and under an "active" condition, i.e. performing an attention-demanding arithmetic task. In the group of girls, epinephrine excretion was only slightly higher during the active as compared with the passive period, whereas the boys excreted significantly more epinephrine when performing the task.

In this case, as among adult males and females, there was a slight difference in performance between the sexes, in favor of the female group. Hence, a sex-linked difference in motivation does not appear to be a likely explanation of the endocrine sex difference.

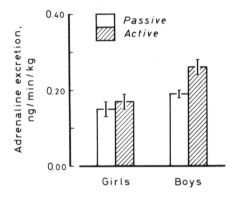

FIG. 12. Means and standard errors for epinephrine (adrenaline) excretion, expressed in relation to body weight, in 12-year-old boys and girls during a passive and an active period. Redrawn and reprinted with permission from Johansson (1972).

Another interesting example of low sympathetic adrenal-medullary reactivity in females is provided in a study by Levi (1972), which showed that male students increased their epinephrine excretion significantly during film-induced sexual arousal, while the excretion rate remained relatively unchanged in female students. In this case, however, the sex difference in hormone excretion was probably associated with a difference between the sexes in the intensity of the reactions evoked by the film, males feeling sexually more aroused than females.

It is also interesting to note that premenstrual disturbances do not appear to be accompanied by increased epinephrine excretion (Pátkai, Johansson, and Post, 1974; Silbergeld, Brast, and Noble, 1971) as might be expected in view of the sensitivity to subtle changes in emotional arousal demonstrated in studies of male subjects.

The overall picture obtained from these investigations may be tentatively interpreted as indicating that adrenal-medullary activity is a less sensitive indicator of behavioral arousal in females than in males.

Comment

The data presented in this chapter illustrate the role played by circulating catecholamines in facilitating adjustment to a variety of psychosocial conditions typical of life in advanced industrialized societies. However, our knowledge is almost entirely restricted to acute situations, and, so far, we have only a poor understanding of possible harmful consequences of repeated adjustments to environmental demands. Not until recently has interest been awakened for possible long-term risks involved in repeated, cumulative adaptive efforts, or what may be termed "the cost of adaptation."

There is a growing awareness that although human beings are highly adaptable and capable of adjusting to extreme conditions, such adjustments may have aftereffects; this means that the adaptive efforts leave the individual less able to cope with subsequent demands and less resistant to later pressures and frustrations. The aftereffects may manifest themselves as emotional maladjustments, as impairments of performance efficiency, or as somatic disturbances (*cf.* Glass and Singer, 1972).

Empirical support has been accumulating (review by Rahe, 1972) for the view that adjustments to life-changes — whether of a pleasant or an unpleasant nature — add to the wear and tear of the organism and therefore increase susceptibility to illness. It is not yet clear which role the catecholamines play in this connection. However, recent studies (Theorell, Lind, Levi, Fröberg, Karlsson, and Levi, 1972) show a distinct relationship between amount of life-change and epinephrine secretion, and some data concerning life-change and myocardial infarction (Theorell, 1970) suggest that high-epinephrine secreters may be individuals at risk.

As pointed out above, the time course of epinephrine secretion is probably a significant factor in determining the relative potency of harmful versus beneficial epinephrine effects. It appears likely that good adjustment may require efficient mechanisms for both mobilizing and demobilizing physiological resources. A rapid decrease in catecholamine secretion after cessation of a stressful stimulus probably implies an "economic" way of responding, while a slow decrease may indicate poor adjustment in the sense that the organism "overresponds" by mobilizing resources that are no longer needed.

Assuming that readiness to respond by epinephrine when confronted with threat and strain brings short-term gains but long-term risks, it is interesting to speculate about possible interpretations of the difference in adrenal-medullary reactivity between males and females. The fact that females do not mobilize epinephrine with the same readiness as males, may mean that they live more "economically." Such a sex difference in biochemical mechanisms mediating adjustment to stressful environments might contribute to the longer life-span of women, if — as some investigators believe — adrenal-medullary stimulation, when intense, frequent, or longlasting, may lead to functional disturbances and disease.

However, so far, little is known about possible long-term cumulative effects, and it still remains to be determined under what conditions catecholamine secretion serves desirable adaptive functions and when it should be regarded as a potential harmful response. There is now a great need for longitudinal studies of psychoendocrine relationships, which will eventually answer some of these questions.

ACKNOWLEDGMENTS

Financial support from the Swedish Medical Research Council (project No. 14X-997) and the Swedish Council for Social Science Research is gratefully acknowledged.

REFERENCES

Andersson, B., Hovmöller, S., Karlsson, C.-G., and Svensson, S. (1974): Analysis of urinary catecholamines: An improved auto-analyzer fluorescence method, Clin. Chim. Acta 51, 13–28.

Ax, A. F. (1953): The physiological differentiation between fear and anger in humans, Psychosomat. Med. 15, 433–442.

Blaschko, H. (1973): Catecholamine biosynthesis. In: Catecholamines, ed. L. L. Iversen, Brit. Med. Bull. 29, 105–109.

Blaschko, H., and Welch, A. D. (1953): Localization of adrenaline in cytoplasmic particles of the bovine adrenal medulla. Arch. Exp. Path. Pharmak. 219, 17–22.

Bloom, G., Euler, U. S. v., and Frankenhaeuser, M. (1963): Catecholamine excretion and personality traits in paratroop trainees, Acta Physiol. Scand. 58, 77–89.

Breggin, P. R. (1964): The psychophysiology of anxiety, J. Nerv. Ment. Dis. 139, 558–568.

Brohult, J., Levi, L., and Reichard, H. (1970): Urinary excretion of adrenal cortical and medullary hormones in man during and after one single massive dose of ethanol, and their modification by chlormethiazole, Acta Med. Scand. 188, 5–13.

Cannon, W. B. (1914): The emergency function of the adrenal medulla in pain and the major emotions, Amer. J. Physiol. 33, 356–372.

Cannon, W. B. (1929): Bodily Changes in Pain, Hunger, Fear and Rage, Branford, Boston.

Elmadjian, F. J., Hope, J., and Lamson, E. T. (1957): Excretion of epinephrine and norepinephrine in various emotional states, J. Clin. Endocrin. 17, 608–620.

Euler, U. S. v. (1946): A specific sympathomimetic ergone in adrenergic nerve fibers (sympathin) and its relation to adrenaline and noradrenaline, Acta Physiol. Scand. 12, 73–97.

Euler, U. S. v. (1956): Noradrenaline: Chemistry, Physiology, Pharmacology and Clinical Aspects, Charles C Thomas, Springfield, Ill.

Euler, U. S. v. (1960): Exposure to cold and catecholamines, Fed. Proc. 19, Suppl. 5, 79–81.

Euler, U. S. v. (1967): Adrenal medullary secretion and its neural control. In: Neuroendocrinology, Vol. 2, eds. L. Martini and W. F. Ganong, pp. 283–333, Academic Press, New York.

Euler, U. S. v., and Lishajko, F. (1961): Improved technique for the fluorimetric estimation of catecholamines, Acta Physiol. Scand. 51, 348–355.

Eysenck, H. J. (1967): The Biological Basis of Personality, Charles C Thomas, Springfield, Ill.

Folkow, B., and Euler, U. S. v. (1954): Selective activation of noradrenaline and adrenaline producing cells in the suprarenal gland of the cat by hypothalamic stimulation, Circ. Res. 2, 191–195.

Frankenhaeuser, M. (1971a): Experimental approaches to the study of human behaviour as related to neuroendocrine functions. In: Society, Stress and Disease, Vol. I, The Psychosocial Environment and Psychosomatic Diseases, ed. L. Levi, pp. 22–35, Oxford Univ. Press, London.

Frankenhaeuser, M. (1971b): Behavior and circulating catecholamines, Brain Res. 31, 241–262.

Frankenhaeuser, M. (1974a): Sex differences in reactions to psychosocial stressors and psychoactive drugs. In: Society, Stress and Disease, Vol. III, Problems Specific to the Relationship between Woman and Man, and to Family Life., ed. L. Levi, Oxford Univ. Press, London. In press.

Frankenhaeuser, M. (1974b): Sympathetic-adrenomedullary activity, behaviour and the psychosocial environment. In: Research in Psychophysiology, eds. P. H. Venables and M. J. Christie, Wiley, New York. In press.

Frankenhaeuser, M., and Andersson, K. (1974): Note on interaction between cognitive and endocrine functions, Percept. Mot. Skills 38, 557–558.

Frankenhaeuser, M., and Järpe, G. (1962): Psychophysiological reactions to infusions of a mixture of adrenaline and noradrenaline, Scand. J. Psychol. 3, 21–29.

Frankenhaeuser, M., and Järpe, G. (1963): Psychophysiological changes during infusions of adrenaline in various doses, Psychopharmacologia 4, 424–432.

Frankenhaeuser, M., Järpe, G., and Matell, G. (1961): Effects of intravenous infusions of adrenaline and noradrenaline on certain psychological and physiological functions, Acta Physiol. Scand. 51, 175–186.

Frankenhaeuser, M., Mellis, I., Rissler, A., Björkvall, C., and Pátkai, P. (1968): Catecholamine excretion as related to cognitive and emotional reaction patterns, Psychosomat. Med. *30*, 109–120.

Frankenhaeuser, M., Myrsten, A.-L., Post, B., and Johansson, G. (1971): Behavioural and physiological effects of cigarette smoking in a monotonous situation, Psychopharmacologia *22*, 1–7.

Frankenhaeuser, M., Myrsten, A.-L., Waszak, M., Neri, A., and Post, B. (1968): Dosage and time effects of cigarette smoking, Psychopharmacologia *13*, 311–319.

Frankenhaeuser, M., Nordheden, B., Myrsten, A.-L., and Post, B. (1971): Psychophysiological reactions to understimulation and overstimulation, Acta Psychol. *35*, 298–308.

Frankenhaeuser, M., and Pátkai, P. (1965): Interindividual differences in catecholamine excretion during stress, Scand. J. Psychol. *6*, 117–123.

Frankenhaeuser, M., Post, B., Nordheden, B., and Sjöberg, H. (1969): Physiological and subjective reactions to different physical work loads, Percept. Mot. Skills *28*, 343–349.

Frankenhaeuser, M., and Rissler, A. (1970): Effects of punishment on catecholamine release and efficiency of performance, Psychopharmacologia *17*, 378–390.

Frankenhaeuser, M., Sterky, K., and Järpe, G. (1962): Psychophysiological relations in habituation to gravitational stress, Mot. Skills *15*, 63–72.

Funkenstein, D. H. (1956): Nor-epinephrine-like and epinephrine-like substances in relation to human behavior, J. Ment. Dis. *124*, 58–68.

Glass, D. C., and Singer, J. E. (1972): *Urban Stress. Experiments on Noise and Social Stressors*, Academic Press, New York.

Goodall, McC. (1951): Studies of adrenaline and noradrenaline in mammalian heart and suprarenals, Acta Physiol. Scand. *24*, Suppl. 85.

Hillarp, N. A., and Hökfelt, B. (1953): Evidence of adrenaline and noradrenaline in separate adrenal medullary cells, Acta Physiol. Scand. *30*, 55–68.

Hillarp, N. A., Lagerstedt, S., and Nilson, B. (1953): The isolation of a granular fraction from the suprarenal medulla, containing the sympathomimetic catecholamines, Acta Physiol. Scand. *29*, 251–263.

Holtz, P., Credner, K., and Kroneberg, G. (1947): Über das sympathicomimetische pressorische Prinzip des Harns ("Urosympathin"), Arch. Exp. Path. Pharmak. *204*, 228–243.

Häggendahl, J. (1963): An improved method for fluorimetric determination of small amounts of adrenaline and noradrenaline in plasma and tissue, Acta Physiol. Scand. *59*, 242–254.

Johansson, G. (1972): Sex differences in the catecholamine output of children, Acta Physiol. Scand. *85*, 569–572.

Johansson, G., and Frankenhaeuser, M. (1973): Temporal factors in sympatho-adrenomedullary activity following acute behavioral activation, J. Biol. Psychol. *1*, 67–77.

Johansson, G., Frankenhaeuser, M., and Magnusson, D. (1973): Catecholamine output in school children as related to performance and adjustment, Scand. J. Psychol. *14*, 20–28.

Johansson, G., and Post, B. (1974): Catecholamine output of males and females over a one-year period, Acta Physiol. Scand. *in press*.

Kety, S. S. (1967): Psychoendocrine systems and emotion: Biological aspects. In: *Neurophysiology and Emotion*, ed. D. C. Glass, pp. 103–107, Rockefeller Univ. Press and Russell Sage Foundation, New York.

Karki, N. T. (1956): The urinary excretion of noradrenaline and adrenaline in different age groups, its diurnal variation and the effect of muscular work on it, Acta Physiol. Scand. *39*, Suppl. 132.

Lambert, W. W., Johansson, G., Frankenhaeuser, M., and Klackenberg-Larsson, I. (1969): Catecholamine excretion in young children and their parents as related to behavior, Scand. J. Psychol. *10*, 306–318.

Landis, C., and Hunt, W. A. (1932): Adrenalin and emotion, Psychol. Rev. *39*, 467–485.

Levi, L. (1965): The urinary output of adrenaline and noradrenaline during pleasant and unpleasant emotional states, Psychosomat. Med. *27*, 80–85.

Levi, L. (1967a): Some principles and sources of error in psychophysiological research. In: *Emotional Stress: Physiological and Psychosocial Reactions—Medical, Industrial and Military Implications*, ed. L. Levi, Försvarsmed., *3*, Suppl. 2, 72–90.

Levi, L. (1967b): The effect of coffee on the function of the sympathoadrenomedullary system in man, Acta Med. Scand. *181*, 431–438.

Levi, L. (1972): Stress and distress in response to psychosocial stimuli. Laboratory and real life studies on sympathoadrenomedullary and related reactions, Acta Med. Scand., Suppl. 528.

Mandler, G. (1967): The conditions for emotional behavior. In: *Neurophysiology and Emotion*, ed. D. C. Glass, pp. 96–102, Rockefeller Univ. Press and Russell Sage Foundation, New York.

Mason, J. W. (1968): A review of psychoendocrine research on the sympathetic-adrenal medullary system, Psychosomat. Med. *30*, 631–653.

Mason, J. W., Mangan, G. F., Jr., Brady, J. W., Conrad, D., and Rioch, D. McK. (1961): Concurrent plasma epinephrine and 17-hydroxycorticosteroid levels during conditioned emotional disturbances in monkeys, Psychosomat. Med. *23*, 344–353.

Myrsten, A.-L., Post, B., and Frankenhaeuser, M. (1971): Catecholamine output during and after acute alcoholic intoxication, Percept. Mot. Skills *33*, 652–654.

Pátkai, P. (1971a): Interindividual differences in diurnal variations in alertness, performance and adrenaline excretion, Acta Physiol. Scand. *81*, 35–46.

Pátkai, P. (1971b) Catecholamine excretion in pleasant and unpleasant situations, Acta Psychol. *35*, 352–363.

Pátkai, P., and Frankenhaeuser, M. (1964): Constancy of urinary catecholamine excretion, Percept. Mot. Skills *19*, 789–790.

Pátkai, P., Johansson, G., and Post, B. (1974): Variations in physiological and psychological functions during the menstrual cycle, Psychosomat. Med. *in press*.

Rahe, R. H. (1972): Subjects' recent life changes and their near-future illness susceptibility, Adv. Psychosomat. Med. *8*, 2–19.

Redgate, E. S., and Gellhorn, E. (1953): Nature of sympatheticoadrenal discharge under conditions of excitation of central autonomic structures, Amer. J. Physiol. *174*, 475–480.

Roessler, R., Burch, N. R., and Mefferd, R. B., Jr. (1967): Personality correlates of catecholamine excretion under stress, J. Psychosom. Res. *11*, 181–185.

Rothballer, A. B. (1959): The effects of catecholamines on the central nervous system, Pharmacol. Rev. *11*, 494–547.

Rothballer, A. B. (1967): Aggression, defense and neurohumors. In: *Aggression and Defense: Neural Mechanisms and Social Patterns, Brain Function*, Vol. V, eds. C. D. Clemente and D. B. Lindsley, pp. 135–170, UCLA Forum Med. Sci., No. 7, Univ. California Press, Los Angeles.

Selye, H. (1950): *Stress*, ACTA, Montreal.

Schachter, S., and Singer, J. E. (1962): Cognitive, social, and physiological determinants of emotional state, Psychol. Rev. *69*, 379–399.

Schildkraut, J. J., and Kety, S. S. (1967): Biogenic amines and emotion, Science *156*, 21–30.

Silbergeld, S., Brast, N., and Noble, E. B. (1971): The menstrual cycle: A double-blind study of symptoms, mood and behavior, and biochemical variables using Enovid and placebo, Psychosomat. Med. *33*, 411–428.

Silverman, A. J., and Cohen, S. I. (1960): Affect and vascular correlates to catecholamines, Psychiat. Res. Rep. *12*, 16–30.

Theorell, T. (1970): Psychosocial Factors in Relation to the Onset of Myocardial Infarction and to Some Metabolic Variables – a Pilot Study, Doctoral dissertation, Department of Medicine, Seraphimer Hospital, Stockholm.

Theorell, T., Lind, E., Froberg, J., Karlsson, C.-G., and Levi, L. (1972): A longitudinal study of 21 subjects with coronary heart disease: Life changes, catecholamine excretion and related biochemical reactions, Psychosomat. Med. *34*, 505–516.

Emotions – Their Parameters and Measurement,
edited by L. Levi.
Raven Press, New York © 1975

Anger and Depression in Perspective of Behavioral Biology

David A. Hamburg, Beatrix A. Hamburg, and Jack D. Barchas

Department of Psychiatry and Behavioral Science, Stanford University School of Medicine, Stanford, California 94305

INTRODUCTION

In this chapter we consider two important emotions, anger and depression, from the viewpoint of behavioral biology. In doing so, we use several of the perspectives of modern biology: evolutionary, organismic, and molecular. All of these are pertinent to the understanding of behavior, including emotions. Recent advances in all these spheres help to clarify how anger and depression have evolved, what adaptive functions they have probably served, what mechanisms underlie them, and how they can become maladaptive.

In the perspective of evolutionary biology we draw mainly upon observations of those nonhuman primates which recent work has shown to be most closely related to the human species in biochemical, physiological, and behavioral characteristics. In their natural habitats and in experimental situations they show reactions very similar to those that in man we designate anger and depression. Moreover, these reactions occur in contexts similar to some of those which precipitate anger and depression in man. By observing such responses in the natural habitats of higher primates, it has become possible to identify clues to the adaptive functions of such behavior.

The mechanisms of anger and depression are considered here primarily in terms of: (1) recent advances in understanding of biogenic amines in the brain, insofar as they appear to be involved in the neurons and circuits mediating anger and depression and (2) hormones that influence the brain mechanisms mediating these responses.

Finally, we consider genetic factors that have a bearing on anger and depression, especially through their influence on biogenic amines and steroid hormones. There is much biological variability in components underlying emotional responses. This variability has been crucial in their evolution, since it is the raw material on which natural selection acts. However, some genetically determined extremes of variability in underlying mechanisms may render the individual vulnerable to maladaptive extremes of anger or depression.

AN EVOLUTIONARY PERSPECTIVE ON ANGER AND DEPRESSION

The modern synthesis of evolution is a powerful theory which has led to many significant new observations and experiments and has been able to integrate effectively a very broad range of data from all fields of biology (Dobzhansky, 1962). Within this framework, the previously sketchy record of human evolution has been substantially enlarged (Dolhinow and Sarich, 1971). The evidence bearing on human evolution is much more abundant and enlightening than it was even 10 years ago. As a part of this development, biologists have taken increasing interest in the role of behavior in natural selection (Hinde, 1974).

In evolutionary biology, adaptation has come to be viewed as reproductive success of a population—keeping the genes of the population alive in future generations. Reproductive success of a population is positively correlated with reproductive success of individual members of that population—success in leaving progeny. In turn, reproductive success of an individual is positively correlated with behavior that is effective in relation to: (a) the physical environment, utilizing the opportunities and coping with the hazards, and (b) the social environment, knowing the rules governing interaction between members of the population and guiding behavior accordingly. When these environments are largely stable over long periods, guidelines for behavior emerge that are generally useful for the population in meeting its survival requirements and facilitating reproductive success. Such guidelines for behavior tend to be taught early in life, shaped by powerful rewards and punishments and invested with strong emotions. Such early learning of guidelines for adaptive behavior tends to induce lifelong commitments. On the average, over long time spans, they prepare the young to meet the adaptive requirements of the environment by fulfilling the roles of adult life.

In the very long course of mammalian and especially primate evolution, behavior has become a crucial way of meeting adaptive tasks which contribute to species survival: finding food and water, avoiding predators, achieving fertile copulation, caring for the young, and preparing the young to cope effectively with the specific requirements of a given environment. The contribution of behavior to adaptation is not only a function of individuals but of groups as well, especially among higher primates. Adaptive behavior functions through a social system. Recent studies tend to support the concept that, in primate evolution, social organization has functioned effectively in biological adaptation (Hamburg, 1963). Studies of nonhuman primates and of hunting-and-gathering human societies in their natural habitats—let alone agricultural and industrial societies—suggest that group living has conferred a powerful selective advantage upon the more highly developed primates.

It seems unlikely that emotional responses would be so universal in man and so important in behavior if they have not served adaptive functions in evolution. Some years ago we presented the view that emotional processes have served motivational purposes in meeting crucial adaptive tasks of the sort we have referred to above (Hamburg, 1963, 1968). We will summarize this view, extend it beyond the earlier formulation, and illustrate it with some new observations.

Natural selection favors those populations whose members, on the average over long time spans, are organized effectively to accomplish crucial adaptive tasks. This is where emotion enters. For instance, we readily consider the sexually aroused person to be reacting emotionally. By this, we usually mean that the person feels strongly a particular kind of inner experience. In this state, the probability of achieving fertile copulation is greater than in other conditions. From an evolutionary viewpoint, the individual now *wants* to do what the species has needed to have done over the long course of evolution. His emotion reflects a state of heightened motivation for a behavior pattern that has been critical in species survival.

Viewed in this way, the emotion has several components: a subjective component, an action component, and a physiologic component appropriate to the action. The term emotion usually emphasizes the subjective component, but this is in fact the subjective aspect of a motivational pattern. On the whole, these are motivational patterns that must have had selective advantage over a very long time span. There is probably substantial genetic variability in these motivational patterns, including their subjective components, just as there is genetic variability in every aspect of structure, function, and behavior. Natural selection has operated on this variability, preserving those motivational-emotional patterns that have been effective in accomplishing the tasks of survival.

It is evident that emotional responses are not limited to behavior that facilitates reproductive success of contemporary human populations. Any mechanism — structure, function, or behavior — that is adaptive on the average for populations over long time spans has many exceptions, may respond inadequately to extraordinary environmental circumstances, and may even become largely maladaptive when there are drastic changes in environmental conditions. When we consider the profound changes in human environmental conditions within very recent evolutionary times, it becomes likely that some of the mechanisms which evolved during the millions of years of mammalian, primate, and human evolution are now less useful than they once were. Since cultural change has moved much more rapidly than genetic change, the emotional response tendencies that have been built into us through their suitability for a long succession of past environments may be less suitable for the very different present environment.

This point may also be illustrated by reference to sexual behavior. We said that the emotions of sexuality are part of a strong motivational pattern that has met a long-standing need of the species to produce offspring.

Throughout most of human evolution, the production of offspring had to offset a high infant mortality rate. But with the evolutionarily recent advent of remarkable adaptive advances – effective food production, sanitation, public health, and medical care – infant mortality and other pre-reproductive mortality have diminished, although the motivation for copulation has not. Thus, in a moment of evolutionary time, a problem of population excess has arisen.

The evolutionary criterion of success in leaving progeny does not signify an endless expansion of numbers. Progeny must be able to utilize environmental opportunities and avoid catastrophes. The population size must be related to the carrying capacity of the land which in turn is related to the efficacy of technology.

The adaptive function of primate groups alerts us to look for processes in the individual that facilitate the development of interindividual bonds. We may find useful guidance in the concept that individuals seek and find gratifying those situations that have been highly advantageous in survival of the species. Tasks that must be done for species survival tend to be quite pleasurable; they are easy to learn and hard to extinguish. Their blockage or deprivation leads to anger, coping behavior, and (if prolonged) depression. Such blockage is often accompanied by physiological responses that support actions necessary to correct the situation. In the adult human a remarkable variety of coping behavior may be mobilized by such blockage or deprivation, determined in substantial part by cultural patterning (Hamburg and Adams, 1967). In view of the extreme dependence on learning in the human species, such bonds would most likely be greatly strengthened through learning. Selection may operate on differential readiness for learning responsiveness and attachment to others of the same species. For example, status orders and affiliative bonds are established very rapidly in newly formed rhesus groups (Barchas, 1971).

Another evolutionary aspect of emotion is that individuals avoid and find distressing those situations that have been highly disadvantageous in species survival. Applied to the specific issue of interindividual bonds, it seems reasonably clear that disruption of such bonds in primates is perceived as seriously threatening. It is usually felt as unpleasant and is often associated with physiological responses of alarm and mobilization. Such disruptive events usually stimulate coping behavior that tends toward restoration of strong bonds.

There are many field observations and laboratory experiments with higher primates that suggest the motivational intensity directed toward restoring the mother-infant bond when separation is threatened, and indeed in the face of all sorts of sudden, novel, presumably alarming events in the environment. In chimpanzee experiments the greater the unfamiliarity, the greater is the infant's tendency to cling to mother or mother surrogate (Mason, 1965). There are many field observations indicating that fear draws mother and infant together with maximal effectiveness (van Lawick-Goodall, 1968). The infant often clings to the mother's hair or her nipple in a frightening situation. The infant's scream is exceedingly effective in bringing the mother to him; it appears to elicit intense distress in the mother.

When separation occurs and obstacles interfere with reunion, intense and persistent aggressive behavior may occur in the course of apparent efforts on the part of both mother and offspring to restore contact. If these efforts fail, for whatever reason, they are likely to be followed by behavior that bears considerable similarity to human depression (van Lawick-Goodall, 1973). Thus, both anger and depression are linked to strong, enduring bonds characterizing mother-offspring relations in higher primates, and indeed other close relations. This is a theme we will pursue later in this chapter, sketching promising lines of inquiry into behavioral and physiological responses.

Thus, natural selection has acted to preserve those genes and genotypes that were effective in adaptation, especially by fostering behavior that can meet survival requirements (Caspari, 1958). Some of this adaptively significant behavior falls into the category we call emotional. In the case of emotions experienced as rewarding, the actions associated with the emotions have been linked with survival. This linkage may have occurred in the history of the species and be encoded in the genes or may have occurred in the history of the individual and be encoded in the brain through learning, or both. In either case, the occurrence of the emotional response conveys information. It says, in effect, "This is important." The message goes further. "This is important in a good and desirable way; it should be done again in the future."

In the case of emotions experienced as distressing, the associated actions have also been linked with survival, phylogenetically or ontogenetically or both. Once again, the message is "This is important" but the further message is different: "It is important in a bad and undesirable way, it should be avoided in the future." Thus, distressing experiences may be quite useful although unpleasant. They have a signal function which warns the organism and other individuals significant to him that something is wrong, attention must be paid, learning capacities utilized, resources mobilized to correct the situation.

Let us briefly consider anger and depression from this perspective. The angry organism is making an appraisal of his current situation, which indicates that his immediate or long-run survival needs are jeopardized: his basic interests are threatened. Moreover, his appraisal indicates that another organism (or group) is responsible for this threat. Although there are many ways he can go from this appraisal, the general tendency is to prepare for vigorous action to correct the situation, quite likely action directed against the person(s) seen as causing or at least manifesting the jeopardy to his needs. The signals are likely to be transmitted to these individuals as well as to the organism's own decision-making apparatus. The significant others are then likely to respond in a way that will ameliorate the situation. In a medium range of intensity, anger and some associated aggressive actions are likely to bring about a result desirable to the person and acceptable to his significant others. At very high intensity, the risk of serious injury becomes great for the initiator as well as for others. This behavior can readily become maladaptive.

Depressive responses have similar characteristics. However, they tend to follow a prior angry period; but the angry responses have not elicited a rewarding outcome. Then a feeling of sadness and discouragement sets in. The subject estimates the probability of effective action as low. By the term effective action we refer here to action the subject believes to be in his self-interest or group interest, even though his belief may be vaguely formulated. He may, in effect, have been prepared for this orientation through the long past experience of his species or his population or his family or his own experience or some combination of these. But, however he came to this appraisal, it is now a firm commitment, somehow bound up with his survival. How can the depressive responses be viewed as adaptive? As we saw in the case of anger, they can be adaptive in a medium range of intensity. His feeling of sadness and discouragement may be a useful stimulus to consider ways of changing his situation. If a key human relationship is in jeopardy, ways of improving that relationship, or substituting a better one, may be considered. Moreover, his state of sadness may elicit heightened interest and sympathetic consideration on the part of significant other people. Their actions as well as his own may work toward improvement of the situation. But at very high intensity, the depressive responses increase survival risks for the person: (a) in terms of his own behavior, physiology, and susceptibility to disease; (b) in terms of the response of others, which tend to become unfavorable or at least ineffective in the face of intense depression (Klerman, 1971).

So, for both anger and depression, there appears to be a curvilinear relation between intensity of the emotional response and effectiveness of behavior in adaptation. At low and moderate intensities, survival probabilities are increased; but at very high intensities they are lowered. This concept is offered as a statistical proposition covering many occasions of anger and depression on the part of many individuals in many groups. Although there are bound to be exceptions, these long-run, probabilistic relations are fundamental to the evolutionary process. We hope that examples given later in this chapter from research on human and nonhuman primates will help to clarify the concept.

In considering emotions from an evolutionary view, we assume some continuities across genera and species, as well as evolving differences. Although we cannot deal directly with the subjective experience of nonhuman animals, we can get reliable data on motivational and physiological aspects of emotional behavior. Moreover, the action patterns associated with emotions in man, e.g., anger and depression, often occur with remarkable similarity in nonhuman primates, especially those whose biological relation to man is relatively close. That is, the animal's pattern of activity closely resembles that of humans when they feel angry or depressed. In addition, these action patterns tend to occur in contexts similar to those which elicit anger or depression in humans. This point may be illustrated by brief consideration of the forms and contexts of aggressive behavior in chimpanzees.

Recent research on chimpanzee behavior, especially in the natural habitat, has revealed several similarities in the form of threat and attack patterns between chimpanzee and human behavior, especially in respect to the behavior of children and adolescents (Hamburg, 1971a; van Lawick-Goodall, 1971). These similarities are striking in the following respects: the ways in which the arms are used during threat and attack sequences, the brandishing of objects, various techniques of pounding, the hurling of objects, and screaming in the course of aggressive interactions. The net effect of these patterns, employed in various combinations and permutations, is that the aggressively displaying chimpanzee looks big and menacing, filling the air with objects. The skills of bluff and intimidation are highly developed, often going up to the brink of combat and occasionally going over it. There are also interesting similarities to human patterns of submission and reassurance which tend to reduce or regulate aggression. For example, the patterns of bowing and crouching not only are physically similar to human patterns but also tend to occur in similar contexts. The lowered body posture apparently signifies deference. Similarly, the tendencies to touch, hold, pat, cling, and embrace seem to convey reassuring messages under threat of attack in both chimpanzee and human.

These observations on the similarities in the form of threat and attack patterns raise the question whether there are also similarities in the contexts of aggressive behavior between chimpanzee and man. Of special interest in this connection are the following: whether the heavy reliance upon dominance relations in chimpanzees (and other higher primate species) is in some way a precursor of the ubiquitous status differentiations in human societies; whether the redirection of aggression downward in the dominance hierarchy is in some way related to the widespread human tendency toward the scapegoating of lower status individuals or groups; whether the turbulence in adolescent behavior, especially the male "aggression spurt," is related to similar phenomena in human adolescence. Also, there is a common conjunction of factors which, when they occur together, is quite potent in eliciting threat and attack responses: the crowding of strangers in the presence of valued resources. These factors are widespread elicitors of aggression in vertebrates, including primates, and have relevance to man (Hamburg, 1971b).

If one surveys the contexts in which aggressive behavior is most likely to occur in the natural habitats, much of the information can be condensed into two general categories: (1) defense and (2) access to valued resources. Within each of these categories, a variety of animals or objects or activities may be involved. So, behaving aggressively in contexts of defense and of access to valued resources may well have given selective advantage in the zoological sense to higher primates. In effect, such behavior, if adequately regulated, can be an enforcer of many adaptive requirements, such as those of food and water and predation.

AGGRESSIVE BEHAVIOR IN NONHUMAN PRIMATES DURING ADOLESCENCE

We wish to consider briefly a phase of the life cycle in which striking increases in aggressive behavior occur concomitantly with marked changes in endocrine function—adolescence. Several Stanford groups are investigating the psychobiology of adolescent anger and depression in chimpanzees and humans (Hamburg, 1971c).

A major reason for studying other animals is to try to understand more about the evolution and biological basis of human behavior. Man is a primate; his closest living relatives are monkeys and apes. Thus it is not surprising that behavioral and biomedical research has turned increasingly to primates in order to explore in depth the complex roots of their behavior and the possible causes, treatment, and prevention of some human disorders. There is evidence from several lines of biological research which indicates that the chimpanzee has a closer relationship to man than any other living primate. Chimpanzee behavior has been investigated in the laboratory, in artificial colonies, and in the natural habitat. The studies in the natural habitat are helpful in understanding the way that structure and behavior are adapted to environmental conditions. Such studies tend to stimulate laboratory investigations in which relevant variables can be controlled. Any research in the field, however, has certain unavoidable limitations. Thus, a combination of field and laboratory studies is useful in clarifying hormone-behavior relations during adolescence, and we have established such a program in Tanzania and California. The program in Tanzania is at the Gombe Research Center under the leadership of Dr. Jane van Lawick-Goodall. For several years, special attention has been paid to behavioral changes during adolescence. Anne Pusey is conducting a detailed, longitudinal study on this topic.

Our account of adolescent behavior is based mainly on their unique observations. One of the surprising findings of Gombe research has been the length and complexity of adolescence (van Lawick-Goodall, 1973). We find major changes in behavior during the transition from childhood to adulthood and these changes are different for the two sexes (A. Pusey, *personal communication*). Let us consider first the main changes in males.

A drastic growth spurt begins around 8 years of age, followed in a few months by an increasing frequency and vigor of charging displays. The adolescent male displays in the same sorts of contexts as adult males, e.g., when arriving at a food source or joining other groups; but some adolescents tend to display separately, further off in the undergrowth, for instance. He is unlikely to display if an adult male is nearby. He is greatly interested in the behavior of older males and is inclined to follow them through the forest, especially if he has an older brother. But he is, in early adolescence, also reluctant to leave his mother for an extended time. Often he is successful in inducing her to accompany an older brother or other male through the forest. At 8 years of age, he may still be upset when he accidentally loses his mother. He appears content to wander briefly away from her at his own initiative; but, if she goes without his seeing, he may be upset and whimper or cry out in distress.

During adolescence he becomes increasingly aggressive to females other than his mother but usually only when a superior male is not present in the group. By the time he is about 10 years old he is able to dominate many females who a few years earlier were themselves able to subdue him with ease. At the same time, he must learn to behave with increasing caution to avoid arousing the aggression of mature males, some of whom are quick to threaten him for behavior they tolerated when he was a juvenile.

At some period during his adolescence, the young male may engage in a number of status conflicts if there is another male of similar age and social rank with whom he associates quite frequently. These conflicts mainly involve bluff but may sometimes lead to physical attacks. The charging display appears to have special significance in this context. The more frequent and impressive the display, the more rapidly the adolescent may rise in the hierarchy.

He tends to observe high-ranking males with great interest, approach ambivalently, and if attacked go off alone in the forest. In such approaches he shows an exaggerated form of repetitive bowing that has been called "bobbing." He tends to sit 15 or 20 yards away from a group of adult males (or males with some females) when they are, for instance, socially grooming. He watches them carefully. Sometimes he will sit close; but, if one of the superior males makes a sudden movement, the adolescent may jump away or give a sudden whimper. Gradually he may join in a session, but it is unlikely that a high-ranking male will reciprocate. Even if the adolescent male appears increasingly fearful of high-ranking adult males, he sustains keen interest in them and over several years tends to increase the proportion of his time spent in direct association with them. During the final years of adolescence, the male gradually begins to threaten and occasionally attack the lower-ranking males of the adult male hierarchy. Sooner or later, he is able to subdue at least one of them consistently. And, in due course, he is generally accepted by most of the adult males.

The adolescent female begins to develop small, irregular swellings of the sex skin when she is about 7 years old. Throughout the next 2 years these become gradually larger. For about 6 months prior to her first "fully adult" swelling, her swelling is quite large but still does not induce adult males to mate with her. Very young, preadolescent males mate with her frequently. When she is about 9 she has her first "fully adult" swelling, i.e., the first one to attract the fully adult males. Her reaction to the overtures of the adult male varies from alarm and escape to calm acceptance. The initially fearful responses of some females are related to the fact that male courtship includes some gestures that occur also in aggressive contexts (McGinnis, 1973). Adolescent females may consort with particular males during repeated sexual cycles. Such partner preferences are not obvious in older chimpanzees because intervals between periods of sexual receptivity get longer and longer once they have started to have offspring.

Some adolescent females are fascinated by small infants and spend much time playing with, grooming, or carrying them. A female with this "maternal" approach is likely to become very preoccupied with her own infant sibling. She spends a large portion of her time in close association with her mother.

In many groups of nonhuman primates, exchange of genes between groups occurs when males from neighboring ranges change groups. Transfer of females from one group to another is known to occur occasionally among baboons and gorillas. Among chimpanzees, however, there is evidence that females, principally adolescent females, play a major role in the exchange of genes between groups. At Gombe there are a number of records of adolescent females temporarily leaving their home communities during periods of sexual receptivity and mating with males of neighboring communities. In at least two cases, young "stranger" females have gradually become integrated into our community of habituated chimpanzees, although to date no habituated adolescent female has permanently left our area. It is especially interesting that it is the adolescent female herself who initiates the change in range; she does not seem to be forced to leave her home by threatening behavior on the part of males.

Adolescence, in the champanzee as in the human, may be viewed as an extension of the period for learning, a period when some skills and behaviors learned during childhood can be practiced in the adult context so that the individual will be adequately prepared to enter social maturity. The onset of adolescence and the years immediately following are often emotionally turbulent times for chimpanzees just as they may be for humans at the same stage of the life cycle.

One group of Stanford investigators recently studied a peer group of adolescent chimpanzees in a seminatural social behavior laboratory, a 1-acre outdoor enclosure (W. McGrew, C. Tutin, P. McGinnis, P. Midgett, *personal communication*). The group consisted of three males and four females. The adolescent growth spurt in these animals was followed by striking spurts in sexual and aggressive behavior. The sexual spurt is more prominent in females, the aggressive spurt in males. Although the hormonal data are too limited for any definitive conclusion, there is some reason to believe that these "behavior spurts" are induced by the hormonal changes of puberty (Resko, 1967; McCormack, 1971). We are especially interested in the possibility that the upsurge of aggressive displays is positively correlated with the upsurge in the circulating concentration of the principal male hormone testosterone.

Adolescence is a time in both chimpanzees and humans when extensive changes in behavior occur and so do drastic changes in some physiological and biochemical systems of the body. The timing of puberty is controlled in the brain. Messages from the brain influence the pituitary gland and pituitary hormones in turn control the output of sex hormones. These sex hormones have far-reaching biochemical influences throughout the organism, including effects on cells and circuits in the brain. Although it is plausible to suppose that there are specific links between certain hormonal changes and concomitant changes in fundamental components of sexual, aggressive, and emotional behavior, virtually no well-substantiated information exists on this topic in humans, despite the fact that it has much clinical significance. The advent of precise, reliable biochemical methods for measuring the relevant hormones opens significant new opportunities. Since the endocrinology of the chimpanzee—to the extent it is presently known—is more similar to the human than that of any other species, we are studying chimpanzees to seek clues regarding hormone-behavior relations in adolescence. Clues of this sort can tell us where to look in humans for crucial points of vulnerability.

Primate field research of the past few years suggests that major behavioral changes occur in many species during adolescence. We have already described these changes in chimpanzee behavior. A general comment may be in order here regarding adolescent male behavior. In nonhuman primate societies in their natural habitats, adolescent males are the most active, exploratory, aggressive, and socially disruptive class of individuals (Washburn, Hamburg, and Bishop, 1974). In most species there are sex differences in behavior from early life, with males being more aggressive, e.g., engaging more than females in rough-and-tumble play during infancy and the juvenile years. Building on these differences at adolescence, the males play roughly and threaten adults. The adult males typically respond to these challenges by threatening, attacking, and over an extended period of time driving the adolescent males into peripheral positions. This peripheralization, while always social, is often spatial as well, e.g., on the periphery of the group. In rhesus monkeys and baboons, males commonly transfer to a different troop during periods of such turbulence (Boelkins and Wilson, 1972; C. Packer, *personal communication*). Although the turbulence and peripheralization take many forms, there is a consistent theme: the upsurge of aggressive behavior and the struggle for enhancement of dominance status in adolescent males.

Is there any reason to believe that aggressive behavior in the service of status enhancement has any adaptive utility? Why has natural selection preserved such patterns in macaques, baboons, gorillas, and chimpanzees? This is a complex subject, certainly beyond the scope of this chapter. But a recent observation of one of our captive chimpanzees groups may provide a clue (P. McGinnis, *personal communication*). In this adolescent-young adult group (with one infant), the lowest-ranking animal was an early adolescent female. Although her access to vital resources such as food was somewhat more limited than high-ranking animals, this seemed to make no practical difference over a period of several years. Then, in one sudden cold spell of exceptional severity, it made a crucial difference. On the island in southern California where the chimpanzees were living, only a few crates were available for shelter. Chimpanzees had lived there for several years with no shelter and no difficulty. In the several nights of this unusually cold episode, the chimpanzees crowded into the limited shelter available. There was simply no room for the lowest-ranking animal. So she slept at the edge of the shelter, as close as possible to the others but not, as it turned out, close enough. Before anyone realized that she was sick, she was found dead one morning and autopsy showed bilateral pneumonitis. This experience is consistent with the concept that dominance provides access to vital resources; when such resources are plentiful, dominance may make little if any practical difference, but when they are in short supply it may become highly significant in adaptation. In this and other respects, aggressive behavior (and its concomitant human experience of anger) can be an enforcer of adaptive requirements. That this may well have been the case through most of primate evolution does not mean that aggression is still adaptive under modern human conditions.

DEPRESSIVE BEHAVIOR IN NONHUMAN PRIMATES: REACTIONS TO SEPARATION AND LOSS

One of the striking findings to emerge from the study of chimpanzees in their natural habitat is the length of the period of infant and juvenile dependence on the mother (van Lawick-Goodall, 1968, 1973). The infant relies completely on his mother for food, transport, and protection until he is at least 6 months old. Weaning does not usually occur until the fifth or sixth year. Juveniles may continue to sleep in a nest with their mothers after being weaned. During the final stages of weaning, a young chimpanzee may go through a period of apparent depression. So the attachments of the early years are powerful; shifting toward a more independent life does not come easily or quickly.

The long period of dependency on the mother may be considered adaptive in the chimpanzee, as in man, in relation to social learning. Chimpanzees have an elaborate system of communication, and their behavioral repertoire includes such complex patterns as cooperative hunting and tool-using. The years in which the young chimpanzee lives under his mother's protection give it the opportunity to learn ways of coping with the characteristics of its physical and social environment that are crucial for survival.

The significance of the mother-offspring attachment was highlighted by situations in which the mother died. Four infant chimpanzees who lost their mothers were observed. Three were adopted by an older sibling. One chimpanzee lost his mother at age 3 and was adopted by a 6-year-old sister. Gradually, over several years, he developed abnormal behavior, consisting of social isolation, unusual posturing, rocking, an increase in self-grooming, and a habit of pulling out hairs and chewing them. A second infant chimpanzee was orphaned at age 3 and was adopted by an 8-year-old sister. He also developed social isolation, abnormal posturing, and a depressed appearance. A third chimpanzee was orphaned at 1 year of age. He was adopted by a brother but survived only 2 weeks. A fourth, 3 years old, was orphaned but not adopted. He showed the rapid onset of depressive symptoms and died in three months.

The most vivid instance of this kind occurred in 1972 at Gombe when the old female Flo died and her adolescent son Flint had a severe depressive reaction. We are very much indebted to Thorndahl and van Lawick-Goodall (1972) for these remarkable observations. During the last few years, Flo was regarded as a very old female. She had her last infant in 1968 and her last sexual cycle the following year. Subsequently her movements gradually slowed down, and she interacted less frequently with other chimpanzees outside her family. For the final 3 weeks of life, Flo was very weak. Her teeth were so worn that most foods were hard for her to eat and climbing tall trees was an obvious effort.

Flint was 8½ years old when his mother died and still very dependent on her; in this respect he was unusual. Although lively and intelligent, Flint was more dependent on his mother than any adolescent male we have seen. Yet, as we have noted, the mother-offspring bonds are typically still strong in adolescence. Flint had only been observed to travel independently of Flo for more than 1 hr on one occasion. He still shared her nest almost every night. He still frequently begged for a share of her food, and he constantly pressed her for social grooming. So far as we know, he was the only chimpanzee with Flo when she died. Flint was followed almost continually from the day that his mother was found dead until his own death 25 days later. During these 25 days, he became increasingly tense and apathetic. He sat for long periods in a huddled posture and lost interest in the environment. He was largely unresponsive to stimulation by other chimpanzees. He ate very little and lost one-third of his body weight over several weeks. On 16 evenings he nested alone, most in old nests which he probably shared previously with Flo. On the five occasions that he nested away from the stream with a group, he was with an older brother. He also moved with his older sister on several occasions. His eyes had a wide, frightened look which never left them. He found it increasingly difficult to travel more than short distances. Most of the remainder of his life was spent in the vicinity of the place where Flo died. Perhaps his cessation of eating and drastic weight loss heightened his vulnerability to infectious agents.

A few years earlier, at the time of weaning, Flint had shown frequent, severe "temper tantrums" — intense, rage-like episodes similar to the temper tantrums of human children. These patterns occurred often when his aged mother was unresponsive to his demands upon her. Whether he behaved in this way at the time of her death we cannot say, because she died some hours before the body was found by research workers. By the time of discovery, Flint appeared puzzled and investigated his mother's body from time to time.

In several ways these observations of reaction to interanimal loss in the natural habitat are consistent with recent laboratory investigations of a separation-induced model of depressive behavior in monkeys (Jensen and Tolman, 1962; Seay, Hansen, and Harlow, 1962; Seay and Harlow, 1965; Kaufman and Rosenblum, 1967; Mitchell, Harlow, Griffin, Moller, 1967; Spencer-Booth and Hinde, 1967; Hinde and Spencer-Booth, 1968; Rosenblum and Kaufman, 1968). In these experiments, a mother and infant are separated. Thus a strong bond is disrupted. Although there are variations, the main tendency is toward a depression-like response in both mother and infant. In the infants, typically there is initial distress: calling and searching for a day or two. This is followed by greatly diminished activity, decreased play, huddling posture, and decreased food intake. They resemble humans who report feeling depressed. There are some indications of lasting effects due to brief separation. In Hinde's experiments a 6-day separation at 32 weeks produced some lasting effects, although it takes special tests to elicit these effects more than 1 year later.

The main thrust of these path-breaking experiments was recently well stated by Hinde and Davies (1972b) as follows:

> If separated from their mothers for a few days, infant Rhesus monkeys and other macaques show increased distress calling, and reduced locomotor activity and other symptoms of behavioral depression. The symptoms may persist for weeks after reunion with the mother, and infants which have had such a separation experience differ from nonseparated controls in their responses to strange objects months and even years later.

They have extended this work by comparing mother-separated and infant-separated monkeys in a somewhat longer separation (Hinde and Davies, 1972a,b). In one set of experiments the mother was removed from the social group and kept away for 13 days. In the other set of experiments the infant was removed from the social group for 13 days. In each instance the separated monkey was returned after 13 days to the social group in the home cage.

Surprisingly, the infant-removed infants showed less distress *after reunion* than mother-removed infants. This occurs despite the fact that the infant-removed infants become markedly depressed *during* separation when they are isolated. The key factor in this result seems to be the quality of the mother-infant relation after reunion. Those mothers who are isolated from the group during separation become more disturbed than mothers who remain with the group (even though their infants are removed). This disturbance is not readily overcome on reunion. So, the mother-infant relationship proceeds more smoothly upon reunion if the mother has remained with her group while the infant was away. In our view these experiments not only highlight the crucial role of the mother-infant relationship in mediating the infant's contacts with the environment but also highlight the importance of the mother's attachments to her peers in the social group. This raises the question whether peer-separation might also precipitate depressive responses in primates. There are too few observations on separated adults or adolescents to make any definitive statement at this time (Bowden and McKinney, 1971). However, there is an interesting experiment on separation of younger age mates.

Experimental depression in nonhuman primates had always been elicited by mother-infant separation until Suomi, Harlow, and Domek (1970) measured the effects of separating infants who had become attached to each other. Starting at 3 months of age, they separated the attached infants for 4 days and reunited them for 3-day periods until a total of 20 separations had been completed over a 6-month period. With each separation experience, the infants went through stages of protest and despair, followed by reattachment when contact was again permitted. There was no evidence of adaptation over time. Each depressive episode was about equally severe. The 20 successive age-mate separations between attached peers produced a behavioral maturational arrest. Harlow and Novak (1973) summarize the main result as follows: "After separations were completed and 270 days had passed, the multiply separated peers when not subjected to further separation possessed their 90-day-old behavioral repertoire and nothing else. They sucked and clung at an infantile level, showed no interest in exploration, and bypassed any attempts at play."

REACTIONS TO SEPARATION AND LOSS IN HUMANS

Is there anything comparable to this depressive syndrome induced by separation or loss in humans? Over many years, some clinicians have made sensitive observations of personal loss, grief, and clinical depression

(Lindemann, 1944). Patients often come to medical attention in the context of an important loss. The most vivid circumstance is the grief reaction to the loss of a personally significant individual (McConville, Boag, and Purohit, 1972). The grief reaction is a specific pattern of distress in which the person's focus is on the loss. Usually, gradual recovery occurs through a difficult process of mourning over a period of months. However, some persons slide into a clinical depression, in which there is a pervasive undermining of prior interests and human relationships, with feelings of despondency.

In the past few years several research groups have undertaken systematic study of possible relations between life events and the onset of depressive episodes serious enough to come to psychiatric attention (Klerman, 1971). Some of these studies have utilized control or comparison groups. For instance, the Yale investigators obtained a control group from a random household sample. They compared these controls with 185 depressed patients. A schedule of recent life events was used in assessing the significance of separation and loss, as well as other environmental events preceding the onset of clinical depression. The depressed patients reported nearly three times as many stressful life events during the 6 months prior to the onset of the clinical depressive episodes as the control group.

In analyzing the pattern of these events, they conclude that "exits rather than entrances from the social field were followed more frequently by aggravation of symptoms, both of a psychiatric as well as medical nature. . . . The concept of the exit from the social field coincides with the psychiatric concept of separation and loss, and supports the role of these events in clinical depression." They note limitations of these findings. The separation and loss category of events accounts for only about one-quarter of the depressed patients, at least by the use of relatively gross criteria.

Clayton has obtained similar results in follow-up studies of bereaved adults. Although distress was evident, only 2% sought professional help in the acute phase (Clayton, Desmarais, and Winokur, 1968). Nevertheless, there is an increase in the amount of contact with physicians in the first year of bereavement (Clayton, 1973). Widowed persons consult physicians for psychological symptoms and receive increased numbers of tranquilizers and sedatives.

Beck and Worthen (1972) studied the life experience of 50 patients hospitalized on a general hospital short-term crisis-oriented psychiatry service. They found that clearly visible precipitating factors occurred more often in depressed than in schizophrenic patients. They conclude, "For depressed patients, there is typically a clear precipitant, and the precipitant was judged to be hazardous for ten of 21 patients."

Another recent study examined the relationship between possible precipitating events and the onset of unipolar (nonmanic) depression in 100 patients (Cadoret, Winokur, Dorzab, and Baker, 1972). The precipitating factors studied were (1) deprivation prior to age 16 as a result of loss of parents by death, separation, or divorce, (2) personal losses through death in the year before admission, (3) threatened personal losses, and (4) physical illness in the preceding 6 months. Patients whose depression occurred before age 40 had a significantly higher incidence of actual or threatened personal losses than did those whose depression began after 40. A higher proportion of patients than of age-sex matched relatives (nondepressed) reported a personal loss in a similar time period. However, the difference was modest.

In another study 225 depressive patients were selected on the basis of explicit diagnostic criteria from hospital records (Clancy, Crowe, Winokur, and Morrison, 1973). Associations were sought between precipitating factors, diagnostic groups, and clinical characteristics. Clear precipitating events were found in 35% of the depressive patients (compared with 11% of 200 schizophrenics). Overt separation and loss again constituted a clinically significant although not preponderant class of precipitating factors in depression.

A thorough study of precipitating factors in depression at the National Institute of Mental Health (NIMH) found a high frequency of stressful events (Leff, Roatch, and Bunney, 1970). Although their major finding was in threats to sexual identity, issues of interpersonal loss were prominent. The categories of stressful events uncovered were quite similar to those of Paykel's group (1969). Methodologically, the NIMH study highlights a reason why most large-sample studies tend to underestimate the occurrence of major stressful events shortly before the onset of depression. Data collected during the first week of hospitalization provided little information on environmental stress. Repeated contact with informants over 1 to 2 months was necessary to elicit the history of such recent events as a stillbirth or the death of a family member.

Parkes (1972) has recently integrated his extensive studies of grief in adult life. He describes in detail important components of the reaction to bereavement, effects of bereavement upon health, the general stress reactions and the specific "search" component that characterizes grieving, ways in which grief is avoided or postponed, the components of anger and self-reproach, and the gradual development of a modified identity. In the end, he views personal loss as one of many major transitions—one of the most difficult and yet ubiquitous of human experiences. He views psychosocial transitions as times when "we need protection, reassurance, time to recoup, and help in developing blueprints for the future."

Thus, the present evidence indicates (1) the experience of interpersonal loss elicits much distress—grief is one of the most difficult transitions of the life cycle, (2) it is a common precipitating factor in clinical depressions, (3) but such depressions need not be triggered by separation or loss, (4) separation or loss may trigger distress reactions other than depression (Holmes and Rahe, 1967), (5) most occurrences of separation and loss do not precipitate clinical depression—the best available evidence suggests that 10 to 20% of individuals confronted with separation or loss of major personal significance develop a clinical syndrome of some kind.

Bowlby (1969, 1973) has recently published two volumes of a major theoretical synthesis on attachment and loss in personality development and psychological disorders. Drawing especially upon material from ethology, developmental psychology, and clinical psychiatry, he describes in detail the process by which a human infant forms an attachment to its mother (or mother substitute), and the significance of the mother-child relationship. He emphasizes the ways in which major separation, loss or threat of loss can lead to anxiety, anger, and depression in the growing child, and indeed to lasting distortions of personality.

A few studies have explored ways of coping with separation and loss (Hamburg, Adams, and Brodie, 1974). The variety and effectiveness of such patterns in the general population are impressive. These studies highlight the question of differential susceptibility to loss and grief. What is the special vulnerability of those who become overwhelmed with despondency?

In monkeys, apes, and humans there are marked individual differences in the response to separation or loss. Some get more depressed than others, and these variations deserve biological scrutiny. Do those who get very depressed differ in some way in respect to brain amines or thyroid or adrenal function from those who were much less susceptible to the depression-like response? Both the primate separation experiments and clinical observations point the way toward a model of depression in which behavioral and biological linkages can be investigated. They highlight the question of differential susceptibility to experiences of separation and loss. Since some individuals are more vulnerable to such stresses than others, what biological factors might be relevant to these individual differences? In the remainder of this chapter we wish to consider the relevance of some hormonal and neurochemical factors to this problem. The same basic considerations apply to anger as well as to depression.

The many determinants of individual differences in stress response cannot be discussed here. It is an enormous and fascinating area, much of which remains to be explored. Some people are inclined to react with anger, others with depression. The same person may at different times respond angrily to stress on one occasion, depressively on another. We know that these and other emotional responses are mediated to a great extent by circuits of the limbic-hypothalamic-midbrain region of the brain (MacLean, 1970). These circuits are influenced significantly by steroid hormones, and transmission of impulses in these circuits depends heavily on biogenic amines in this brain region. Therefore, we shall confine our subsequent remarks largely to the possible influences of steroid hormones and biogenic amines on responses of anger and depression. Before doing so, we wish to note the important influences of the individual's prior experience on subsequent inclinations to anger and depression. We have in some respects discussed these elsewhere (Hamburg, 1969; Hamburg and Hamburg, 1973; Hamburg and van Lawick-Goodall, 1974). The fact that we do not pursue these influences here should in no way diminish the great importance we attach to them.

ENDOCRINE FACTORS RELEVANT TO DEPRESSION

The past quarter century has seen the emergence of an essentially new scientific field: neuroendocrinology. This field is concerned both with hormonal influences on the nervous system and with the brain's regulation of endocrine function (Levine, 1966; 1972). To be concise, we shall confine ourselves largely to human neuroendocrine research. The human studies have benefited from prior animal studies (Ganong and Martini, 1973). We have discussed the endocrinology of nonhuman primate and human aggressive behavior elsewhere (Hamburg, 1971c). Here we shall focus on depression.

Elevated levels of the principal hormone of the adrenal cortex, cortisol, are often observed in clinical depression. (Elevations in thyroid hormone also tend to occur when depression is severe but are less striking than the changes in adrenal steroids.) Such elevations in adrenal hormone levels may be sustained or recurrent for weeks, or even months, if the depression persists. The extent of hormone elevation is closely related to the degree of distress and, in turn, to the effectiveness of coping behavior. Adrenocortical steroids and their metabolites have been shown to be capable of affecting brain function and behavior. Variations in metabolism of these hormones may have a bearing on the individual's response to major disappointments and personal losses.

Some years ago, while studying psychological stress and endocrine functions in newly admitted psychiatric inpatients, we found high plasma 17-hydroxycorticosteroid levels in acutely depressed patients (Board, Persky, and Hamburg, 1956). Especially high corticosteroid levels were associated with intense distress and also with the development of personality disintegration. Following up this lead, the group checked the original observations by studying an additional 33 consecutively admitted depressed patients. Once again, the severely depressed patients, those suffering most intensely, had the highest elevations of plasma corticosteroids (Board, Wadeson, and Persky, 1957). These findings were confirmed and extended when Gibbons and McHugh (1962) reported a positive correlation between weekly plasma corticosteroid levels and depression ratings. The patients most severely depressed tended to have the highest levels of corticosteroids and these levels often returned to normal with clinical recovery. Subsequently, Gibbons (1964) found a two-to-threefold increase in cortisol secretory rates in two-thirds of a series of hospitalized depressed patients. Those most severely depressed tended to have the greatest increase in cortisol secretory rate. Later, a study of cortisol production showed that the change in this measure from illness to recovery correlated quite positively with changes in emotional arousal and psychotic disorganization (Sachar, Hellman, Fukushima, and Gallagher, 1970).

Thus, several laboratories confirmed and extended our (at the time) surprising finding of increased adrenocortical activity in depression and a positive correlation between the intensity of suffering and the extent of such increase. Since most of these observations dealt with a time scale of weeks, we wondered what would happen on a longer time scale. We also became curious about the possibility that the endocrine findings might, in some persons, be more than a simple reflection of emotional arousal and distress. Perhaps the high hormone levels might, over an extended period, have an effect on brain function. Also, we and others had noted that some patients had a rather low level of adrenocortical activity in the fact of personal adversity, and we wondered whether this might influence their ability to cope. For these and other reasons, we established a research unit in the late 1950's at the NIMH on the psychobiology of depression and mood disorders. That unit, under the leadership of William Bunney, has been very productive over the years (Bunney and Murphy, 1973).

We undertook longitudinal studies of urinary corticosteroids and independent daily behavioral ratings in depressed inpatients over a time span of months. We found correlations between levels of steroid excretion and behavioral variables (Bunney, Mason, and Hamburg, 1965a). On days of personal crisis, steroid excretion was clearly elevated (Bunney, Mason, Roatch, and Hamburg, 1965b). Some patients had marked elevations of steroid excretion over periods ranging up to six months. From time to time, these levels were in the range of Cushing's disease (adrenocortical hyperfunction), in one patient persistently so for months. Those depressed patients who commit suicide have been very high corticosteroid excretors in the period preceding the suicide (Bunney, Fawcett, Davis, and Gifford, 1969). About one-third of our patients showed remarkable long-term elevations. A smaller subgroup showed subnormal corticosteroid excretion. In this as in other contexts, we have sought to identify distinctive subgroups of persons prone to intense depression (or to intense anger), on the assumption that these might well have different underlying mechanisms.

Carroll and Davies effectively utilized dynamic procedures of stimulation and suppression tests in assessing functions of the hypothalamic-pituitary-adrenal system in depressed persons (Carroll and Davies, 1970; Davies, Carroll, and Mowbray, 1972). They identified a group of high cortisol secretors whose adrenal cortex is not suppressed by dexamethasone administration, unlike the normal response to this compound. They suggest that some depressives have defective regulation of hypothalamic-pituitary-adrenal control mechanisms such that they are chronically exposed to high levels of physiologically active cortisol. In our view, it is a very interesting possibility that these individuals may inherit a defective control mechanism. In the event of intense emotional distress, e.g. in response to a personal loss, the hypothalamic-pituitary-adrenal alarm system is "turned on" and thereafter it is very slow to "turn off." It is possible that the continuing exposure of the brain to high levels of cortisol may over time hinder their ability to cope. These studies may also relate to findings that suggest that brain serotonin may be involved in the regulation of the feedback inhibition of the pituitary-adrenal system (Vernikos-Danellis, Berger, and Barchas, 1973).

Thus, endocrine studies in depressed persons indicate that meaningful subgroups exist. It is at least consistent with present evidence to state that one subgroup has adrenocortical hyperfunction and another has adrenocortical hypofunction in the face of prolonged stress. The question is therefore clear whether these endocrine responses might increase vulnerability to clinical depression. One way to pursue this question is to consider evidence on the entry of corticosteroids into brain and their influence on brain function. The literature on corticosteroids and depression has been well reviewed in recent years (Fawcett and Bunney, 1967; Gibbons, 1968; Davies et al., 1972).

Corticosteroids have been found in human brain in concentrations much higher than in blood (Touchstone, Kasparow, Hughes, and Horwitz, 1966). When isotopically labeled cortisol is injected into the peripheral circulation of rats, it readily enters brain and has a prolonged half-life there, in contrast to its short half-life in the peripheral circulation (Peterson and Chaikoff, 1963). Moreover, rat brain accumulates cortisol when there is a very small increase in blood concentration, and it accumulates cortisol with each increase in blood concentration. In dogs, the brain accumulates isotopically labeled cortisol after intravenous injection and maintains high concentrations in the hypothalamus for 24 hr following the injection (Eik-Nes and Brizzee, 1965). Thus, it is plausible that substantial changes in circulating corticosteroids would lead to persistent changes in brain concentration of corticosteroids, even in humans.

Having been accumulated in brain, what functional effects might corticosteroids have there? A recent study indicates that hydrocortisone inhibits firing of single units in the midbrain raphe of rats (Foote, Lieb, Martz, and Gordon, 1972). From other evidence, these neurons are probably quite significant in emotional behavior. Phillips and Dafny (1971) studied the effect of cortisol on unit activity in unanesthetized, freely moving rats. In comparing various brain regions, they found that cortisol elicits significant changes in firing rates of most units in the midbrain, the anterior and ventromedial areas of the hypothalamus, and the hippocampus. All of these areas are known to be functionally significant in motivational-emotional patterns. The cortisol effects lasted 4 to 9 hr.

In humans, several lines of evidence show an influence of corticosteroids on brain function. High levels are associated with increased brain excitability, both in persons receiving exogenous cortisol and in patients with Cushing's disease (Hoefer and Glaser, 1950; Glaser, Kornfield, and Knight, 1955). The electroencephalogram of these patients reveals an increase in slow waves and they have a high incidence of seizures (Woodbury, 1958). Adrenocortical hypofunction is also linked to human brain abnormalities. Patients with Addison's disease show a tendency toward seizures and striking EEG changes which are reversed by the administration of cortisol (Hoffman, Lewis, and Thorn, 1942). Recently, a group of our colleagues (Kopell, Wittner, Lunde, Warrich, and Edwards, 1970) demonstrated experimentally the effect of injected cortisol on averaged evoked potentials of human brain in healthy subjects.

Henkin (1970) has studied relations between adrenocortical hormone activity and perception. He has shown effects of these hormones on the detection and integration of sensory stimuli in man, including taste detection acuity and integrative capacity, olfactory and auditory detection, and integrative acuity. He relates these findings to the modes of participation of corticosteroids in biochemical events of neural metabolism and in physiological events of conduction of neural impulses.

Altogether, these research results provide reason to believe that adrenocortical steroids have a significant role to play in brain function. Within an optimal range, they probably enhance the person's ability to cope with stress. In excess, deficiency, or distortion, they probably impair one's ability to cope. The consideration of clinical and genetic evidence may now help to clarify this point.

One of the striking biological facts about depression is the common occurrence of severe depressions in certain endocrine abnormalities (Gabrilove, 1966; Fawcett and Bunney, 1967; Smith, Barish, Correa, and Williams, 1972). Hypothyroidism, hypofunction of the adrenal cortex, and hyperfunction of the adrenal cortex are three clear examples. (Hyperthyroidism is associated with hyperirritability and excessive anger.) Intense depression often occurs in the context of major transitions in respect to female sex hormones: premenstrual, postpartum, and menopausal conditions (Hamburg, Moos, and Yalom, 1968).

Yet, most depressives do not have overt endocrine disease. But the common occurrence of severe depressions in endocrine disease might give us a clue to susceptibility to depressive experience, especially if we link endocrinology to genetics.

Some years ago, we formulated a "behavioral-endocrine-genetic" approach to stress problems, particularly in relation to adrenal cortex (Hamburg, 1967) and thyroid (Hamburg and Lunde, 1967). We chose adrenal cortex and thyroid primarily because there is more genetic-biochemical data available on the hormones of these glands than on any others and because the hormones of the adrenal cortex and thyroid are so relevant to behavior, including anger and depression. Quite recently, important new information has emerged in endocrine genetics (Rimoin and Schimke, 1971; Goldstein and Motulsky, 1974). The clinical interest in this approach is that we notice consistent individual differences in response to difficult, distressing experiences. There are many sources of consistent individual differences in stress response, but some of these must be genetic.

Our behavioral-endocrine-genetic approach examines the impact of severe psychological stress on a genetically determined peculiarity in the synthesis or transport or disposal of a hormone. The stress effect may occur in a variety of ways, especially through powerful and enduring central nervous system stimulation of the pituitary and through changes in peripheral utilization of a stress-relevant hormone. Thus, there is a conjunction of a behavioral condition, a genetic peculiarity, and a tissue response. Goiter formation is an interesting model of such processes centering on the thyroid. Stress-induced hirsutism in women partially deficient in adrenocortical biosynthetic capacity provides a similar model. The central point in these models is that a heavy functional demand impinges upon a partially deficient endocrine system. Ordinarily the responses of compensation in these complex systems are quite adequate. But compensation has its biological limits and very severe stress, including psychological stress such as interpersonal loss, is a condition in which the limits may be exceeded.

Endocrinologists have done suggestive studies in this area (Bush and Mahesh, 1959; Lloyd, Moses, Lobotsky, Klaiber, Marshall, and Jacobs, 1963; Lloyd, 1964). Each group studied a pair of identical twins. One of each twin pair developed hirsutism rapidly after a severe emotional stress. Each hirsute twin had an abnormal pattern of urinary 17-ketosteroid excretion as compared with her nonhirsute identical twin, but the difference was not very great. However, under stress the difference became much exacerbated. The results are consistent with the hypothesis that these women were partially deficient in the ability to synthesize cortisol. Under severe stress, the very high ACTH output was only able to enhance cortisol synthesis to a limited extent, but a great enhancement of adrenal androgen secretion occurred, hence the hirsutism. This may clarify the model: under ordinary conditions there was no disease. In fact, even with rather sophisticated techniques there was not much indication of a deficiency in the ability to synthesize cortisol or a tendency to oversecrete adrenal androgen. Only under very heavy functional demand did the biochemical abnormality and the disease appear.

This model can be applied to depression. To do so effectively, much will depend on improving our ability to find the partial deficiency, for example, the heterozygote. In the clinical syndrome of congenital adrenal hyperplasia, characterized by deficient cortisol synthesis, some effort has been made to identify heterozygotes. The parents both must be heterozygous, since the disease follows the transmission pattern of a single gene, autosomal recessive defect. Some of the siblings are also heterozygous. One group studied this problem by measuring urinary pregnanetriol. There was much overlap between homozygotes and heterozygotes (Childs, Grumbach, and Van Wyk, 1956). More recently a method has been developed for measuring 17-hydroxyprogesterone in blood (Strott and Lipsett, 1968). This provides a much better chance to detect the heterozygotes, because it is the compound that accumulates behind the block in the cortisol biosynthetic pathway caused by the inherited deficiency in C-21 hydroxylase. The heterozygotes are people who have only a modest and subtle limitation in their capacity to synthesize one hormone, in this case cortisol. There is a subgroup of post-partum depressives who become hirsute in connection with the depression. Their abnormality may be similar to the one described here. A similar situation exists with respect to thyroid hormone. Several heterozygotes have been biochemically characterized in respect to thyroxin synthesis. When exposed to an extraordinary demand on thyroid function, as in pregnancy, they are prone to difficulty.

If hormones and their metabolites enter brain and affect behavior, their relevance to depression is enhanced. In fact, a number of lipid-soluble steroids do enter the brain and produce changes that can be detected neurophysiologically and behaviorally. We have already considered such evidence for cortisol. Another example is progesterone (Hamburg, 1966). Indeed, some progesterone metabolites, particularly in the 5-beta-pregnane series, are very potent anesthetics, more potent than progesterone itself. This illustrates the point that metabolites, not just the hormones themselves, are sometimes psychoactive. Given an inborn error of metabolism in a steroid pathway, it is quite conceivable that brain function might be adversely affected under stress, either by an abnormal concentration of the hormone itself, or by an abnormal concentration of steroids that are metabolites of cortisol or progesterone. Gross abnormalities such as congenital adrenal hyperplasia are rare, i.e., the homozygous condition. The genes, however, are not rare. The gene frequencies in these conditions, where they have been studied, in respect to both cortisol and thyroxin, run in the order of 1:100 or 1:200 persons. There are many types of such endocrine genetic deficiencies. The real question is not whether we have the genes that involve partial deficiencies in synthesis or transport or disposal of these hormones, but whether there are some highly stressful conditions in which that fact becomes clinically significant.

Regrettably, there is so far very little investigation in patients or human populations of genetic aspects of endocrine function directly linked to emotional responses. Such genetic influences may operate at various levels of organization. We have already referred to the possibility that the defective control mechanism identified by Carroll and Davies may be inherited, but as far as we know there has been no genetic investigation. Similarly, a recently discovered inherited syndrome may provide clues to the variability of human stress responses. This is the syndrome of hereditary unresponsiveness to ACTH (Franks and Nance, 1970). Eleven sibships with adrenocortical dysfunction characterized by low cortisol production but normal aldosterone production have been described. Clinical studies have shown that the adrenal cortex is unresponsive to the pituitary hormone ACTH which is the normal stimulus for synthesis and release of cortisol. Genetic analysis indicates that the mode of inheritance may be either autosomal recessive or X-linked. The low circulating level of cortisol feeds back information to the hypothalamus, resulting in stimulation of the hypothalamic-pituitary system and high levels of ACTH, as if to compensate for the deficiency in cortisol. The ACTH molecule in these individuals appears to be biologically active, but for some unknown reason the adrenal cortex has an unusually limited capacity to respond to it. Neither do we know how this deficiency affects the ability of these individuals to cope with prolonged major stress.

In short, there are many intriguing avenues of possible endocrine-genetic influence on emotional responses such as depression and anger, but these have so far been little explored.

BRAIN AMINES AND DEPRESSION

In addition to hormonal factors relevant to differential susceptibility, recent research has drawn attention to the role of catechol and indole amines in brain. It is most appropriate to consider these compounds in this volume, since it was Professor von Euler's great work that opened up the modern era of their investigation.

We are focusing on the catecholamines (which include epinephrine, E; norepinephrine, NE; and dopamine, DA) and the indoleamine serotonin (5-hydroxytryptamine, 5-HT). We have recently reviewed the relations of biogenic amines and behavior in some detail (Barchas, Ciaranello, Stolk, Brodie, and Hamburg, 1972). Catecholamines and indoleamines are formed from amino acids. There are a number of derivatives of each of these two classes that take their names from the parent ring structure and the presence of an amino group.

These chemicals belong to a class of compounds referred to as biogenic amines. The original compounds in this class are the adrenal catecholamines — epinephrine and norepinephrine. These two compounds are viewed as hormones of the adrenal medulla and have been extensively studied biochemically, pharmacologically, and psychologically (Frankenhaeuser, *this volume*). Only small amounts of the compounds can enter the brain due to their inability to pass the blood-brain barrier. More recently, catecholamines have been found to be formed in the brain, where they are thought to function as synaptic transmitters. The principally occurring catecholamines in brain are norepinephrine and dopamine. The indoleamines are also present in high amounts in brain. Serotonin is the most extensively studied member of this group. The indoleamines, like the catecholamines, may function as synaptic transmitters in the central nervous system.

Both the catecholamines and the indoleamines are found in very discrete areas of the brain thought to be involved in emotional behaviors and are affected by many drugs known to alter behavior. This approach has received further support from investigation of changes in the concentration or utilization of these compounds in the brain as a consequence of behavioral states.

Stressful experimental procedures cause significant alterations in brain biogenic amine levels. Among these procedures are forced swimming, cold exposure, electric foot shock, and immobilization. Brain biogenic amine levels would be expected to change if (1) formation (anabolism) of the amines was increased or decreased, (2) destruction (catabolism) of the amines was enhanced or suppressed, or (3) a combination of the two processes occurred. The development of the procedures for measuring dynamic changes in brain biogenic amine metabolism revealed that most of the above stressors affecting endogenous amine levels did so by increasing the turnover and metabolism of norepinephrine, dopamine, and serotonin. Interestingly, very few instances of a stress-induced decrease in catecholamine or serotonin turnover are known, these being due to hypothermia, shock-induced aggression in rats, and social isolation in mice.

Technical difficulties have so far limited our knowledge of the effects of stress on brain amines in humans. Thus, for example, we do not know whether various types of stress alter the rate of synthesis or utilization of brain amines and whether there are times when synthesis cannot keep up with the need for these compounds. Clearly, such an issue is of great importance since there are many forms of psychiatric disorder in which an inability to respond to stress is a prominent difficulty. Genetically determined biochemical abnormalities in brain amine metabolism may well turn out to have clinical significance; we shall return to this point later.

There are several ways in which amine neuroregulatory agents in the central nervous system can be related to emotional behavior. These are being considered in human studies. The most important has been the measurement of metabolites of the neuroregulators in the spinal fluid, although the principal neuroregulators themselves are not present in spinal fluid. Serotonin and dopamine have metabolites that can be measured in the spinal fluid, 5-hydroxyindoleacetic acid, and homovanillic acid, respectively. Another approach is to search for urinary metabolites that are relatively distinctive products of a particular brain amine. There is some evidence that 3-methoxy, 4-hydroxy phenyl glycol (MHPG) may be derived in significant part from brain norepinephrine. Thus, a variety of biogenic amines and their metabolites may be measured in urine, blood, and spinal fluid — especially in relation to changes over time that may occur concomitantly with behavioral changes. For example, the same person may be studied when he is depressed and not depressed.

There is much current interest in the relationship of catecholamines to depression, especially in the catecholamine hypothesis of affective disorders. Briefly, the hypothesis relates depression to a relative deficiency of norepinephrine at certain central synapses, and relates the manic states to a relative excess of norepinephrine. In the future, it is likely that hypotheses relating neuroregulators to behavior will become much more specific, involving certain areas of brain and changes in particular processes, such as release, reuptake, or receptors.

When reserpine came into clinical use in the treatment of hypertension, two interesting facts were discovered: the drug sometimes induced depression as a side effect, and it depleted animal brains of catecholamines and indoleamines. This raised the question whether low amine levels at certain sites in the brain might play a causal role in some depressions. Many laboratory and clinical studies were then carried out, with the main trend of evidence as follows: drugs that cause depletion and inactivation of brain norepinephrine tend to cause behavioral sedation or depression; on the other hand, drugs that increase or potentiate brain norepinephrine tend to produce behavioral stimulation or excitement. The latter drugs often have an antidepressant effect in man. Hence, the catecholamine hypothesis of mood disorders has aroused much interest (Kety and Schildkraut, 1967). This hypothesis is consistent with much of the available evidence and has been a powerful stimulus to both basic research on brain biochemistry and clinical research on psychopharmacology (Brodie, Murphy, Goodwin, and Bunney, 1971).

Some investigators have pointed out that much of the evidence for the catecholamine hypothesis is indirect and could implicate other neuroregulatory agents as well. There is a competing indoleamine hypothesis which implicates serotonin. A recent symposium brings together information dealing with aspects of serotonin and behavior (Barchas and Usdin, 1973). Although it is exceedingly difficult to sort out the evidence, some of the leading investigators favor the view that serotonin systems in the brain play a crucial role in regulating responsivity to environmental stimuli. Procedures that lower brain serotonin tend to produce hyper-responsivity to both internal and external stimuli. This occurs in a variety of species including man. Such hyper-responsivity may be manifested in disturbances of sleep, increased susceptibility to convulsions, heightened sexuality, greater irritability and aggressiveness (Lipton, 1973). However, the picture of serotonin functions in brain is very complex and resolution must await further research. It may well be that balances or interactions between catecholamine- and indoleamine-mediated neurons will prove to be important in the regulation of mood and the emotional experiences of anger and depression.

Confirmation of any biochemical hypothesis ultimately requires specific demonstration of the biochemical abnormality in the human disorder (Axelrod, 1972). Workers in this field have faced the difficult problem of determining biochemical events in the human brain from measurements of available body fluids: urine is most readily available, blood next, then cerebrospinal fluid. In severe depression, the level of these metabolites may be decreased (Goodwin and Sack, 1973). This suggests an impairment in formation of norepinephrine in the brain of some depressed patients. Several years of basic research showed that one norepinephrine metabolite, MHPG, is produced preferentially, though not exclusively, by the brain (Kety, 1972a). This is not true of any other amine metabolite; the others mainly reflect events in peripheral tissues. Thus, the catecholamine hypothesis predicts that severely depressed patients should excrete less MHPG in their urine than do nondepressed persons. Norepinephrine metabolites were measured in the urine of severely depressed patients and normal individuals. The depressed patients had significantly lower levels of MHPG in urine than the controls. The groups did not differ in other amine metabolites. Maas, who has done path-breaking work in this area, has recently reviewed the topic and reported new findings (Maas, Dekirmenjian, and Jones, 1973).

Several investigators have published data indicating that, during periods of depression, patients excrete significantly less MHPG than when they are not feeling depressed. Moreover, those patients who excrete less MHPG can be identified by their emotional responses to desipramine, imipramine, or amphetamine; they become less depressed. These are all drugs that raise brain catecholamines. With the drug-induced mood elevations, there were modest increments in MHPG excretion; patients who had no mood elevation had decrements in MHPG excretion.

In an interesting case report bearing on the catecholamine hypothesis of depression (Jones, Maas, Dekirmenjian, and Fawcett, 1973), urinary MHPG and normetanephrine were measured daily in a patient with manic-depressive cycles studied longitudinally. These catecholamine metabolites were diminished during periods of depression as compared with periods of mania. Changes in MHPG preceded the emotional shifts, sometimes by several days.

Schildkraut's group has done much work on the catecholamine hypothesis. They have just reported that urinary excretion of MHPG is significantly lower in patients with manic-depressive depressions than in patients with chronic characterological depressions. Excretion of MHPG was not related to the degree of retardation, agitation, or anxiety in these patients (Schildkraut, Keeler, Papousek, and Hartmann, 1973).

These studies are consistent with the concept that a subgroup of depressed patients may be identified clinically (primary affective disorders), biochemically (low MHPG), and pharmacologically (depression-relieving response to desipramine, imipramine, and amphetamine). It is at least plausible that these persons have an abnormality in metabolism and/or disposition of norepinephrine which predisposes them to intense depression.

BRAIN AMINES AND ANGER

Just as the preceding line of inquiry is moving toward clarification of one mechanism whereby some persons are susceptible to intense depression, so too a related line of inquiry is moving toward clarification of a different mechanism whereby some persons are susceptible to intense anger. This story begins with clinical observations, made repeatedly in localities where amphetamines are widely used, of their effects upon behavior.

The psychologic effects of amphetamines at low doses in humans usually include an increase in alertness, wakefulness, and sense of well-being; however, increased irritability may occur even at low doses, and regularly occurs at moderate and high doses. In the latter case, amphetamines commonly elicit paranoid reactions (Tinklenberg, 1971). These reactions, manifested by unfounded suspiciousness, intense anger, highly aggressive behavior, and sometimes persecutory delusions, may develop gradually with oral intake or rapidly with intravenous injections of large doses. Experienced clinicians often cannot distinguish these paranoid reactions from nondrug paranoid reactions, except that they remit after amphetamine use ends. Recent studies suggest that these paranoid reactions can be largely attributed to pharmacological effects rather than to sleep disturbance or personality characteristics, although these latter can influence behavioral response to any drug (Griffith, Cavanaugh, Held, and Oates, 1972).

The amphetamine paranoid reaction has not only been observed clinically on many occasions but also has been produced experimentally in humans by two groups (Angrist and Gershon, 1970; Griffith, Cavanaugh, and Oates, 1970). In these experiments, amphetamine was given to experienced, nonschizophrenic amphetamine users. Behavioral effects included paranoid reactions, sometimes even in moderate dosage. The investigators were impressed with the similarity to spontaneously occurring paranoid reactions. Although these responses to amphetamine are complex, one major component is intense anger. In this respect, the syndrome differs considerably from those produced by other psychotomimetric drugs.

Thus, understanding the mechanism of action of amphetamine in brain could provide clues to the biochemistry and circuitry of anger and suspicion. Snyder (1972, 1973) has made significant contributions in this area. Neurochemical studies in animals indicate that amphetamine affects the metabolism of both principal brain catecholamines, norepinephrine and dopamine — each in a distinctive way, the details of which need not concern us here. Behaviorally, amphetamine produces locomotor stimulation that is probably mediated by action on norepinephrine metabolism; amphetamine also produces stereotyped behavior through an action on dopamine metabolism. Snyder and Meyerhoff (1973) point out that "it is possible, by using amphetamine isomers, to distinguish between behavioral effects mediated by norepinephrine and those mediated by dopamine neurons in the brain.

Already, this technique for pharmacological 'dissection' of the brain has been applied to humans in analyzing pathophysiological mechanisms in amphetamine psychosis; d-amphetamine is considerably more potent than l-amphetamine in affecting norepinephrine neurons, whereas the two isomers have similar potencies in affecting dopamine neurons. Assuming that these biochemical actions are responsible for the behavioral effects of amphetamine, there emerges a simple way to determine whether a particular animal or human behavior involves brain dopamine or norepinephrine. If d-amphetamine is much more potent that l-amphetamine in eliciting a behavioral effect, norepinephrine might be thought to be responsible. On the other hand, if d- and l-amphetamine have similar behavioral potencies, dopamine would be the implicated neurotransmitter." It turns out that the two isomers are about equally effective in provoking paranoid reactions in humans. Therefore, dopaminergic neurons must play a significant role in the mediation of experiences of suspicion and anger.

Kety (1972b) calls attention to the fact that those phenothiazines that are effective in treatment of schizophrenia act mainly on dopamine metabolism; a noneffective phenothiazine and sedatives do not act in this way. Since paranoid orientations, overt and covert, are so widely distributed and so behaviorally significant among schizophrenics, this is additional evidence (albeit indirect) that dopamine is probably important in mediating emotional responses pertinent to suspicion and anger. This in turn leads us to raise the question whether inherited variations in dopamine metabolism might predispose some individuals to intense suspicion and anger; just as inherited variations in norepinephrine metabolism might predispose some individuals to intense depression.

Studies in animals utilizing a variety of test situations have suggested a very powerful role of catecholamines in aggressive behavior. Catecholamines are essential for many forms of aggressive behavior, and catecholamine mechanisms are markedly altered by aggressive behavior (Reis and Gunne, 1965; Reis and Fuxe, 1969; Welch and Welch, 1969a,b,c; Eichelman, Thoa, Bugbee, and Ng, 1972; Eichelman and Thoa, 1973; Reis, 1973; Stolk, Conner, Levine, and Barchas, 1974). It is of interest that there appears to be an association between an increased level of fighting behavior and increased levels of tyrosine hydroxylase when levels of the enzyme are compared to levels of fighting behavior in different strains of mice.

Thus, to the extent that processes involving anger and depression involve catecholamines, genetic regulation of these compounds becomes of great importance.

GENETIC ASPECTS OF AMINE METABOLISM PERTINENT TO ANGER AND DEPRESSION

Do individuals inherit significant differences in the biochemistry of brain amines? It has been recognized that there may be different levels of serotonin and norepinephrine in brain in different inbred strains of mice and rats. To date there has been little investigation to determine whether there are differences in enzyme activities, metabolic pathways, utilization rates, or responses to stress in different strains, let alone of the genetic controls on those processes. There has been less genetically oriented research on amines than on the steroids we discussed earlier. We do not yet know the extent to which there can be minor or abnormal pathways in adrenal catechols or how controls on these pathways might be regulated genetically or altered by stress.

Regarding epinephrine or norepinephrine from the adrenal medulla, genetic processes might well control formation, release, or metabolism of the hormones. It has been shown in the adrenal cortex that steroids are released in differing amounts in different genetic strains (Hamburg and Kessler, 1967). Applying the same possibility to the adrenal medullary response to stress, two individuals might send the same number of nerve impulses to the adrenal medulla and yet, due to a genetic difference, one might secrete much more epinephrine than the other. If this were the case, there could be behavioral changes when the epinephrine reached various target organs, including the hypothalamus.

Strain and subline differences have been reported in the amounts of biogenic amines in brain regions of mice (Maas, 1962; 1963; Sudak and Maas, 1964*a;* Schlesinger, Boggan, and Freedman, 1965; Karczmar and Scudder, 1967) and rats (Sudak and Maas, 1964*b;* Miller, Cox, and Maickel, 1968) and in the utilization and uptake of cardiac norepinephrine in mice (Page, Kessler, and Vesell, 1970).

The known genetic variation in adrenocortical function (Badr and Spickett, 1965; Stempfel and Tomkins, 1966; Hamburg and Kessler, 1967) and in adrenocortical and adrenomedullary structure (Chai and Dickie, 1966; Shire,1970) suggested to us that the search for genetic variation in the enzymes involved in catecholamine biosynthesis would be fruitful. We have recently demonstrated that (1) significant differences exist in the activity of the enzymes involved in the synthesis of the catecholamines in inbred strains of mice, (2) this variation has a genetic basis, and (3) different regulatory mechanisms of the enzymes involved in catecholamine formation exist in different mouse strains and presumably this variation also has a genetic basis (Barchas, Ciaranello, Kessler and Hamburg, 1974*a*). Ciaranello and Axelrod (1973) have shown that two of these strains differ markedly in rate of degradation of the adrenal enzyme phenylethanolamine N-methyltransferase (PNMT). This difference is controlled by a single gene locus.

In humans, various forms of pheochromocytoma (a catecholamine-secreting tumor of the adrenal medulla) have been shown to be familial (Rimoin and Schimke, 1971). Other current work provides clues to human genetic factors pertinent to amine metabolism. If the problems we have been discussing in this chapter are to be approached in the framework of human biochemical genetics, it would be helpful to get information on enzymes important in brain amine metabolism from body fluids. Kety (1972*b*) calls attention to the possible role of the enzyme dopamine-beta-hydroxylase (DBH) in emotional responses. This enzyme operates at a crucial junction in the pathway leading to either dopamine or norepinephrine. Therefore, it is probably important in balances or interactions between these neurotransmitters in the brain. A defect in DBH could lead to an excess of dopamine or a deficiency of norepinephrine at synapses mediating emotional behavior.

Weinshilboum, working in Axelrod's laboratory, reasoned that this enzyme, which is released from sympathetic nerves, might find its way into the blood (Weinshilboum, Raymond, Elveback, and Weidman, 1973). He found that DBH activity in rat serum increases in response to stress associated with increased catecholamine excretion and decreases after a partial chemical sympathectomy induced with 6-hydroxydopamine. In humans a temperature-pain stress, the cold pressor test, increases catecholamine excretion and leads to transient increases in human serum DBH activity. Human genetic factors are significant in determining baseline DBH values. In a study of serum DBH activity in several hundred healthy children and adults, a significant sibling-sibling correlation of serum DBH values was demonstrated. In both children and adults there appears to be a bimodal distribution of serum DBH activity. If so, this should facilitate genetic analysis. These investigators also measured DBH blood levels in various diseases (Axelrod, 1972). For the present discussion, the most interesting is a genetic disease affecting the sympathetic nervous system, familial dysautonomia. This disease includes among its manifestations disorders of emotional response. Serum DBH is reduced in this disease. One quarter of the affected children have no measurable DBH. Mothers of these children have low DBH levels. These DBH studies are suggestive of the way in which future genetic and biochemical research may be linked to the analysis of emotional response tendencies, even in humans.

Valuable current analyses call attention to additional ways of relating genetics, amine metabolism, and behavior (Murphy, 1973; Matthysse and Pope, 1974). Of special interest is the opportunity to gain insight into human amine metabolism with minimum inconvenience by studying blood platelets. These cells have amine storage vesicles and can transport and store biogenic amines by mechanisms similar to those found in the nervous system. They accumulate epinephrine, norepinephrine, and dopamine against concentration gradients. There is no evidence that they contain the catechol-synthesizing enzymes tyrosine hydroxylase and DBH. However, they do contain the amine-inactivating enzyme monoamine oxidase (MAO). This MAO has more substrate and inhibitor characteristics in common with MAO in neural tissue than does plasma MAO. Studies in twins and siblings indicate that genetic factors are important in the individual variation in platelet MAO activity (Nies, Robinson, Lamborn, and Lampert, 1973).

Platelets are rich in serotonin. They share even more characteristics with serotonergic neurons than with catecholaminergic neurons. They show some effects of psychoactive drugs that are common to all neurons that contain biogenic amines.

Platelet MAO activity is diminished in severe emotional disturbances, especially in schizophrenia (Murphy and Wyatt, 1972). This is also true of discordant identical twins of schizophrenics, suggesting that it may provide a genetic marker for vulnerability to schizophrenia (Wyatt, Murphy, Belmaker, Cohen, Donnelly, and Pollin, 1973). These findings mesh with a report that urinary dopamine, norepinephrine, and epinephrine are elevated both in schizophrenics and in their nonschizophrenic identical twins (Pollin, 1972). The reduction in MAO recalls an earlier report that this enzyme is decreased in brain specimens from schizophrenics. Limbic system, hypothalamus, thalamus, striatum, pallidonigral system, and pontobulbar tegmentum were all lower relative to cerebral cortex in the schizophrenics than in the controls (Utena, Kanamura, Suda, Nakamura, Machiyama, and Takahashi, 1968).

As in the case of the behavior-endocrine-genetic approach to stress responses that we suggested some years ago, it seems desirable to view the amine systems dynamically, responding over time to loads placed upon the organism. Genetic factors in amine metabolism may make it more difficult for some persons to sustain an effective response to prolonged stress, more likely to explode in anger or slide into despondency. Our view is very similar to that of Goodwin and Bunney (1973). "Let us imagine that an individual with a strong family history of affective illness has a genetically transmitted defect in one of the systems subserving the increase in neurotransmitter amines which normally occurs in response to stress. In such an individual under chronic or recurrent stress the stores of the critical neurotransmitter amines could eventually become depleted, which according to the amine hypothesis would lead to a clinical state of retarded depression." There are a number of other possible models including alteration of synthesis, release, reuptake, or receptor mechanisms (Barchas, Ciaranello, Kessler, and Hamburg, 1974b).

Changes in catecholamine mechanisms could include relative increases or decreases of neuroregulators (Wyatt, Portnoy, Kupfer, Snyder, and Engelman, 1971) and most take into account the relative balance of the compound and different effects in different areas of the brain.

Genetically oriented research is also helping to sort out distinctive subgroups of depressive disorders (Mendlewicz, Fleiss, and Fieve, 1972; Winokur, Morrison, Clancy, and Crowe, 1973). Experience in other fields of clinical investigation suggests that reliable differentiation of subgroups can be helpful in clarifying different underlying mechanisms.

Genetically determined variation involving the biogenic amines and their physiological regulation may provide a basis for significant individual differences in emotional and endocrine responses to stressful situations.

Individuals with gene variants may, in the face of severe life stresses, be predisposed to depressive reactions or periods of labile emotion including episodes of intense anger. We consider it likely that some severe emotional disorders involving intense anger or depression may be partly based upon genetically determined alterations in normal biochemical processes. These biochemical predispositions must interact in complex ways with environmental factors such as separation, loss, or other jeopardy to crucial human relationships.

INTERACTIONS OF STRESS RESPONSE SYSTEMS

Biogenic amines at crucial sites in the brain are probably of great importance in the regulation of emotional experience. But they are not the whole story. Additional biochemical, physiological, and psychological factors must be studied in natural, experimental, and clinical settings before a comprehensive account of anger and depression can be established. Interactions among the stress-response systems may prove to be of considerable importance (Maas, 1971). We have only begun to unravel these connections. For example, there are many concomitant endocrine responses to stress, and the balance among these may be significant in adaptation (Mason, 1968).

In the past few years intriguing new data have become available on the interaction of biogenic amines, both in the periphery and in the brain, with the pituitary-adrenocortical system and the pituitary-thyroid system. We have already mentioned, in a different context, that cortisol inhibits firing of single units in the midbrain raphe (Foote, et al., 1972) which are serotonergic neurons. Similarly, injections of corticosterone have been considered by some to alter sertonin turnover in the brain (Azmtia, Algeri, and Costa, 1970).

A series of investigations in Axelrod's laboratory have demonstrated that the pituitary-adrenocortical system has a significant role in the biosynthesis of epinephrine in the adrenal medulla. The methylation of norepinephrine to epinephrine by the enzyme PNMT is controlled mainly by ACTH and corticosteroids (Wurtman and Axelrod, 1966; Axelrod and Weinshilboum, 1972).

Cortisol may influence enzymes that participate in the metabolism of norepinephrine and serotonin. Cortisol is necessary for many of the effects of epinephrine and norepinephrine, including the pressor effect of norepinephrine and the maintenance of the integrity of capillaries throughout the body (Ramey, Goldstein, and Levine, 1951; Ramey and Goldstein, 1957).

Preincubation with cortisol results in an increase in norepinephrine uptake into synaptosomes (Maas and Mednieks, 1971). When the circulating concentration of cortisol is high, as in severe stress, this mechanism could diminish the available transmitter in noradrenergic neurons. A current report indicates that ACTH can induce alterations in catecholamine metabolism in man (Hauger-Klevene and Moyano, 1973). Other examples could be given. It seems to us likely that future research will show these systems to be intimately coordinated in the organism's complex response to changing conditions.

Over the past decade, considerable evidence has accumulated on relations of pituitary-thyroid system with the autonomic nervous system, hormones of the adrenal medulla, and more recently brain amines (Ramey, 1966; Hamburg and Lunde, 1967). In general, hormones of the thyroid and the adrenal medulla tend to have a potentiating effect at the cellular level. A recent report indicates that there are probably catecholaminergic mechanisms (involving both dopamine and norepinephrine) in the hypothalamus and median eminence that are important in the regulation of TSH, thyroid-stimulating hormone (Brown, Krigstein, Dankova, and Hornykiewicz, 1972). Indeed, these catecholaminergic pathways are probably crucial for anterior pituitary function in general, including regulation of ACTH secretion.

Perhaps the most clinically significant recent observations on thyroid-amine relations are those of Prange and associates on depression (Wilson, Prange, McClane, Rabon, and Lipton, 1970; Prange, Lara, Wilson, Alltop, and Breese, 1972). They found that thyroid hormone enhances the therapeutic effect of an antidepressant, imipramine, in nonretarded depressed patients. More recently, they found that depression could be relieved by administration of the hypothalamic thyrotropin-releasing factor (called TRF or TRH). It is too early to interpret the meaning of these results, or even the range of depressive conditions to which they apply. But Prange plausibly argues that an effect on brain amines may well be involved.

EFFECTS OF EARLY EXPERIENCE ON BIOLOGICAL SYSTEMS RELEVANT TO ANGER AND DEPRESSION

We have briefly mentioned the importance we attach to early experience of the individual organism in the development of aggressive and depressive responses. To conclude, we wish to mention a few recent observations that are most provocative in this regard. If anyone had doubts of the importance of early experience in the shaping of social behavior, and especially of emotional responses to other organisms, the primate isolation-rearing experiments must have a powerful impact (Mason, 1965; Turner, Davenport, and Rogers, 1969). Among other effects, isolation-rearing produces a monkey that is highly fearful and exceedingly aggressive, both toward self and others. Moreover, the fruits of enormous efforts in long-term human longitudinal studies are now beginning to become available (Jones, Bayley, MacFarlane, and Honzik, 1971). In due course, such studies should give us a deeper understanding of environmental factors influencing the development of emotional responses and the possible setting of brain emotostats (Barchas, 1973).

Research in behavioral biology points increasingly to ways in which early experience might affect biological systems such that the organism's response to stress is modified for a long time or even permanently. Levine, one of the path-breakers in this line of inquiry, has recently reviewed evidence that early environmental stimulation can have an enduring effect on behavioral and physiological stress responses, also that early variations in steroid hormones can have lasting effects upon behavior (Levine, 1974).

It is quite possible that similar relations hold for early stress and later amine responses. A few experiments do indeed indicate that early environmental conditions of mice and rats can have an enduring effect on the response of their brain amines to stress in adult life (Welch and Welch, 1969a,b,c; Reige and Morimoto, 1970). Other studies showing effects of stress on adrenal enzymes are suggestive, even though they have not been done in a developmental context. They do clearly show that changes in environmental conditions can alter catecholamine metabolism at a molecular level (Udenfriend, 1972). During short periods of stress, norepinephrine synthesis is increased very rapidly and it disappears promptly when the stress is over. In such acute stress no changes are observed in the amounts of synthetic enzymes in the tissues. However, when powerful and enduring demands are made on the sympathetic nervous system, it responds by increasing the levels of catecholamine synthesizing enzymes in the tissues. Such responses take longer to occur and persist at least for awhile after the stress ends.

Genetic factors influence such responses. This is illustrated by a recent experiment in our laboratory (Ciaranello, Dornbusch, and Barchas, 1972). Different inbred strains responded to acute stress with differential patterns of increase of the epinephrine synthesizing enzyme PNMT. Further, there were important strain differences in the regulation of the enzyme. By analogy, it is conceivable that some persons may vary genetically in mechanisms involving catecholamine responses when faced with severe stress. We wonder what the effect of such experiences early in life would be on the ultimate fate of these individuals. Maternal manipulation can alter fetal adrenal gland PNMT (Milkovic, Deguchi, Winget, Barchas, Levine, and Ciaranello, 1974).

An ingenious experiment has shown that mice confronted chronically with the stress of intense psychosocial stimulation developed hypertension. Concomitantly, they showed increased activity of two adrenal medullary enzymes, tyrosine hydroxylase and PNMT (Axelrod, Mueller, Henry, and Stephens, 1969). These enzymes are crucial in the synthesis of catecholamines.

A recent report is consistent with the concept that chronic stress may also influence enzymes in brain amine pathways. In this study there was an increase in brain tyrosine hydroxylase that might have been stress-induced (Musacchio, Julou, Kety, and Glowinski, 1969).

Whether such effects occurring early in life might permanently alter behavioral and physiological responses to stress remains for future research to determine. At the very least, it should be clear from the research we have considered in this chapter that important new possibilities are opening up. Functional systems that form part of the emotional response mechanisms are now open to critical investigation at molecular, organismic, and evolutionary levels of behavioral biology. Over the next one to two decades, we may reasonably expect substantial progress, including an increase in our capacity to relieve some of the human suffering associated with extremes of anger and depression.

ACKNOWLEDGMENTS

We are deeply indebted to our colleagues, especially Jane van Lawick-Goodall, Anne Pusey, and Mitzi Thorndahl.

This work was made possible by generous grants from the Grant Foundation, The Commonwealth Fund, and the National Institute of Mental Health.

REFERENCES

Angrist, B. M., and Gershon, S. (1970): The phenomenology of experimentally induced amphetamine psychosis—Preliminary observations, *Biol. Psychiatry 2*, 75–107.

Axelrod, J. (1972): Biogenic amines and their impact on psychiatry, *Semin. Psychiatry 4*, 199–210.

Axelrod, J., Mueller, R. A., Henry, J. P., and Stephens, P. M. (1969): Changes in enzymes involved in the biosynthesis and metabolism of noradrenaline and adrenaline after psychosocial stimulation, *Nature 225*, 1059–1060.

Axelrod, J., and Weinshilboum, R. (1972): Catecholamines, *N. Engl. J. Med. 287*, 237–242.

Azmtia, E. C., Algeri, S., and Costa, E. (1970): *In vivo* conversion of ^{3}H-L-tryptophan into ^{3}H-serotonin in brain areas in adrenalectomized rats, *Science 169*, 201–203.

Badr, F. M., and Spickett, S. G. (1965): Genetic variation in the biosynthesis of corticosteroids in *Mus musculus*, *Nature 205*, 1088–1090.

Barchas, J. D., Ciaranello, R. D., Kessler, S., and Hamburg, D. A. (1974a): Genetic aspects of the synthesis of catecholamines. In: *Hormones, the Brain and Behavior*, edited by R. P. Michael, Karger *(in press)*.

Barchas, J. D., Ciaranello, R. D., Kessler, S., and Hamburg, D. A. (1974b): Genetic aspects of catecholamine synthesis. In: *Genetics and Psychopathology*, edited by R. Fieve, H. Brill, and D. Rosenthal, Johns Hopkins Press, Baltimore *(in press)*.

Barchas, J., Ciaranello, R., Stolk, J., Brodie, H. K. H., and Hamburg, D. (1972): Biogenic amines and behavior. In: *Hormones and Behavior*, edited by S. Levine, pp. 235–319, Academic Press, New York.

Barchas, J., and Usdin, E. (1973): *Serotonin and Behavior*, Academic Press, New York.

Barchas, P. R. (1971): Differentiation and stability of dominance and deference orders in rhesus monkeys. Unpublished doctoral thesis, Stanford University.

Barchas, P. R. (1973): Approaches to aggression as a social problem. In: *Interpersonal Behavior in Small Groups*, edited by R. Ofshe, pp. 388–401, Prentice-Hall, Englewood Cliffs, New Jersey.

Beck, J. C., and Worthen, K. (1972): Precipitating stress, crisis theory, and hospitalization in schizophrenia and depression, *Arch. Gen. Psychiatry 26,* 123–129.

Board, F., Persky, H., and Hamburg, D. A. (1956): Psychological stress and endocrine functions, *Psychosom. Med. 18,* 324–333.

Board, F., Wadeson, R., and Persky, H. (1957): Depressive affect and endocrine functions, *AMA Arch. Neurol. Psychiatry 78,* 612–620.

Boelkins, R. C., and Wilson, A. P. (1972): Intergroup social dynamics of the cayo santiago rhesus (macaca mulatta) with special reference to changes in group membership by males, *Primates 13,* 125–140.

Bowden, D. M., and McKinney, W. T. (1971): Behavioral effects of peer separation, isolation, and reunion on adolescent male rhesus monkeys, *Dev. Psychobiol. 5,* 353–362.

Bowlby, J. (1969): *Attachment and Loss. Vol. 1: Attachment,* Hogarth, London.

Bowlby, J. (1973): *Attachment and Loss. Vol. 2: Separation: Anxiety and Anger,* Hogarth Press and the Institute of Psycho-Analysis, London.

Brodie, H. K. H., Murphy, D. L., Goodwin, F. K., and Bunney, Jr., W. E. (1971): Catecholamines and mania: The effect of alpha-methyl-para-tyrosine on manic behavior and catecholamine metabolism, *Clin. Pharmacol. Ther. 12,* 218.

Brown, G. M., Krigstein, E., Dankova, J., and Hornykiewicz, O. (1972): Relationship between hypothalamic and median eminence catecholamines and thyroid function, *Neuroendocrinology 10,* 207–217.

Bunney, W. E., Fawcett, J., Davis, J., and Gifford, S. (1969): Further evaluation of urinary 17-OHCS in suicidal patients, *Arch. Gen. Psychiatry 21,* 138.

Bunney, W. E., Mason, J. W., and Hamburg, D. A. (1965a): Correlations between behavioral variables and urinary 17-hydroxycorticosteroids in depressed patients, *Psychosom. Med. 27,* 299–308.

Bunney, W. E., Mason, J. W., Roatch, J. F., and Hamburg, D. A. (1965b): A psychoendocrine study of severe psychotic depressive crises, *Am. J. Psychiatry 122,* 72–80.

Bunney, W. E., and Murphy, D. L. (1973): The behavioral switch process and psychopathology. In: *Biological Psychiatry,* edited by J. Mendels, pp. 345–367, John Wiley and Sons, New York.

Bush, I., and Mahesh, V. (1959): Adrenocortical hyperfunction with sudden onset of hirsutism, *J. Endocrinol. 18,* 1.

Cadoret, R. J., Winokur, G., Dorzab, J., and Baker, M. (1972): Depressive disease: Life events and onset of illness, *Arch. Gen. Psychiatry 26,* 133–136.

Carroll, B., and Davies, B. (1970): Clinical associations of 11-hydroxycorticoid suppression and non-suppression in severe depressive illnesses, *Br. Med. J. 1,* 789.

Caspari, E. (1958): Genetic basis of behavior. In: *Behavior and Evolution,* edited by A. Roe and G. Simpson, pp. 103–127, Yale University Press, New Haven.

Chai, C. K., and Dickie, M. M. (1966): Endocrine variations. In: *Biology of the Laboratory Mouse,* edited by E. L. Green, pp. 387, McGraw-Hill Book Company, New York.

Childs, B., Grumbach, M. M., and Van Wyk, J. J. (1956): Virilizing adrenal hyperplasia: A genetic and hormonal study, *J. Clin. Invest. 35,* 213–222.

Ciaranello, R. D., and Axelrod, J. (1973): Genetically controlled alterations in the rate of degradation of phenylethanolamine N-methyltransferase, *J. Biol. Chem. 248,* 14–21.

Ciaranello, R. D., Dornbusch, J. N., and Barchas, J. D. (1972): Rapid increase of phenylethanolamine N-methyltransferase by environmental stress in an inbred mouse strain, *Science 175,* 789–790.

Clancy, J., Crowe, R., Winokur, G., and Morrison, J. (1973): The Iowa 500: Precipitating factors in schizophrenia and primary affective disorder, *Compr. Psychiatry 14,* 197–202.

Clayton, P. J. (1973): The clinical morbidity of the first year of bereavement: A review, *Compr. Psychiatry 14,* 151–157.

Clayton, P., Desmarais, L., and Winokur, G. (1968): A study of normal bereavement, *Am. J. Psychiatry 125,* 168–178.

Davies, B., Carroll, B. J., and Mowbray, R. M. (1972): *Depressive Illness: Some Research Studies,* Charles C Thomas. Springfield.

Dobzhansky, T. (1962): *Mankind Evolving,* Yale University Press, New Haven.

Dolhinow, P., and Sarich, V. M. (1971): *Background for Man,* Little, Brown and Company, Boston.

Eichelman, B., and Thoa, N. B. (1973): The aggressive monoamines, *Biol. Psychiatry 6*, 143–164.

Eichelman, B., Thoa, N. B., Bugbee, N. M., and Ng, K. Y. (1972): Brain amine and adrenal enzyme levels in aggressive, bulbectomized rats, *Physiol. Behav. 9*, 483–485.

Eik-Nes, K. B., and Brizzee, K. R. (1965): Concentration of tritium in brain tissue of dogs given $(1,2^3H_2)$ cortisol intravenously, *Biochim. Biophys. Acta 97*, 320–333.

Fawcett, J. A., and Bunney, W. E. (1967): Pituitary adrenal function and depression, *Arch. Gen. Psychiatry 16*, 517–535.

Foote, W. E., Lieb, J. P., Martz, R. L., and Gordon, M. W. (1972): Effect of hydrocortisone on single unit activity in midbrain raphé, *Brain Res. 41*, 242–244.

Franks, R. C., and Nance, W. E. (1970): Hereditary adrenocortical unresponsiveness to ACTH, *Pediatrics 45*, 43.

Gabrilove, J. L. (1966): Neurologic and psychiatric manifestations in the classic endocrine syndromes. In: *Endocrines and the Central Nervous System*, edited by R. Levine, pp. 419–441, Williams and Wilkins Company, Baltimore.

Ganong, W. F., and Martini, L. (1973): *Frontiers in Neuroendocrinology, 1973*, Oxford University Press, New York.

Gibbons, J. L. (1964): Cortisol secretion rate in depressive illness, *Arch. Gen. Psychiatry 10*, 572–575.

Gibbons, J. L. (1968): The adrenal cortex and psychological distress. In: *Endocrinology and Human Behavior*, edited by R. Michael, pp. 220–236, Oxford University Press, London.

Gibbons, J. L., and McHugh, P. R. (1962): Plasma cortisol in depressive illness, *J. Psychiatr. Res. 1*, 162–171.

Glaser, G. H., Kornfield, D. S., and Knight, R. P. (1955): Intravenous hydrocortisone, corticoptropin and the electroencephalogram, *Arch. Neurol. Psychiatry 73*, 338–344.

Goldstein, J. L., and Motulsky, A. G. (1974): Genetics and endocrinology. In: *Textbook of Endocrinology*, edited by R. H. Williams, pp. 1004–1029, Saunders, Philadelphia.

Goodwin, F. K., and Bunney, W. E. (1973): A psychological approach to affective illness, *Psychiatric Ann. 3*, 19–55.

Goodwin, F. K., and Sack, R. L. (1973): Affective disorders: The catecholamine hypothesis revisited. In: *Frontiers in Catecholamine Research*, edited by E. Usdin and S. Snyder, Pergamon Press, New York.

Griffith, J. D., Cavanaugh, J., Held, J., and Oates, J. (1972): Dextroamphetamine – Evaluation of psychomimetric properties in man, *Arch. Gen. Psychiatry 26*, 97–100.

Griffith, J. J., Cavanaugh, J. H., and Oates, J. A. (1970): Psychosis induced by the administration of *d*-amphetamine to human volunteers. In: *Psychotomimetric Drugs*, edited by D. H. Efron, pp. 287–294, Raven Press, New York.

Hamburg, B. A., and Hamburg, D. A. (1973): Stressful transitions of adolescence: Endocrine and psychosocial aspects. In *Society, Stress and Disease, II: Childhood and Adolescence*, edited by L. Levi, Oxford University Press, London.

Hamburg, D. A. (1963): Emotions in the perspective of human evolution. In: *Expression of the Emotions in Man*, edited by P. Knapp, pp. 300–317, International Universities Press, New York.

Hamburg, D. A. (1966): Effects of progesterone on behavior. In: *Endocrines and the Central Nervous System*, edited by R. Levine, pp. 251–265, Williams and Wilkins Company, Baltimore.

Hamburg, D. (1967): Genetics of adrenocortical hormone metabolism in relation to psychological stress. In: *Behavior-Genetic Analysis*, edited by J. Hirsch, pp. 154–175, McGraw-Hill Book Company, New York.

Hamburg, D. A. (1968): Evolution of emotional responses: Evidence from recent research on nonhuman primates. In: *Animal and Human*, edited by J. Masserman, pp. 39–52, Grune and Stratton, New York.

Hamburg, D. A. (1969): A combined biological and psychosocial approach to the study of behavioral development. In: *Stimulation in Early Infancy*, edited by A. Ambrose, pp. 269–277, Academic Press, New York.

Hamburg, D. A. (1971a): Aggressive behavior of chimpanzees and baboons in natural habitats, *J. Psychiatr. Res. 8*, 385–398.

Hamburg, D. A. (1971b): Crowding, stranger contact, and aggressive behavior. In: *Society, Stress and Disease*, edited by L. Levi, Vol. 1, pp. 209–218, Oxford University Press.

Hamburg, D. A. (1971c): Recent research on hormonal factors relevant to human aggressiveness, *Inter. Soc. Sci. J. 23*, 36–47.

Hamburg, D. A., and Adams, J. E. (1967): A perspective on coping behavior, *Arch. Gen. Psychiatry 17*, 277–284.

Hamburg, D. A., Adams, J. E., and Brodie, H. K. H. (1975): Coping behavior in stressful circumstances: Some implications for social psychiatry. In: *Further Explorations in Social Psychiatry*, edited by A. H. Leighton, Basic Books *(in press)*.

Hamburg, D. A., and Kessler, S. (1967): A behavioral endocrine-genetic approach to stress problems. In: *Memoirs of the Society for Endocrinology no. 15: Endocrine Genetics*, edited by S. G. Spickett, pp. 249–270, Cambridge University Press, London.

Hamburg, D., and Lunde, D. (1967): Relation of behavioral, genetic and neuroendocrine factors to thyroid function. In: *Genetic Diversity and Human Behavior*, edited by J. Spuhler, pp. 135–170, Aldine Press, Chicago.

Hamburg, D., Moos, R., and Yalom, I. (1968): Studies of distress in the menstrual cycle and the postpartum period. In: *Endocrinology and Human Behavior*, edited by R. Michael, pp. 94–116, Oxford University Press, Oxford.

Hamburg, D. A., and Van Lawick-Goodall, J. (1974): Factors facilitating development of aggressive behavior in chimpanzees and humans. In: *Determinants and Origins of Aggressive Behavior*, edited by W. W. Hartup and J. de Wit, Mouton Publishers, The Hague, pp. 57–83.

Harlow, H. F., and Novak, M. A. (1973): Psychopathological perspectives, *Perspect. Biol. Med. 16*, 461–478.

Hauger-Klevene, J. H., and de G. Moyano, M. B. (1973): ACTH-induced alterations in catecholamine metabolism in man, *J. Clin. Endocrinol. Metab. 36*, 679–683.

Henkin, R. I. (1970): The neuroendocrine control of perception. In: *Perception and Its Disorders*, edited by D. A. Hamburg, K. H. Pribram, and A. J. Stunkard, pp. 54–107, Williams and Wilkins Company, Baltimore.

Hinde, R. (1974): *Biological Basis of Social Behavior*, McGraw-Hill, New York.

Hinde, R. A., and Davies, L. (1972a): Removing infant rhesus from mother for 13 days compared with removing mother from infant, *J. Child Psychol. Psychiatry 13*, 227–237.

Hinde, R. A., and Davies, L. (1972b): Changes in mother-infant relationship after separation in rhesus monkeys, *Nature 239*, 41–42.

Hinde, R. A., and Spencer-Booth, Y. (1968): The study of mother-infant interaction in captive group-living rhesus monkeys, *Proc. R. Soc. Lond. B. 169*, 177–201.

Hoefer, P. F. A., and Glaser, G. H. (1950): Effects of pituitary adrenocorticoptropic hormone (ACTH) therapy, *JAMA 143*, 620–624.

Hoffman, W. C., Lewis, R. A., and Thorn, G. W. (1942): The electroencephalogram in Addison's disease, *Bull. Hopkins Hosp. 70*, 335–361.

Holmes, T. H., and Rahe, R. H. (1967): The social readjustment rating scale, *J. Psychosom. Res. 11*, 213–218.

Jensen, G. D., and Tolman, C. W. (1962): Mother-infant relationship in the monkey, *Macaca nemestrina:* The effect of brief separation and mother-infant specificity, *J. Comp. Physiol. Psychol. 55*, 131.

Jones, F. D., Maas, J. W., Dekirmenjian, H., and Fawcett, J. A. (1973): Urinary catecholamine metabolites during behavioral changes in a patient with manic-depressive cycles, *Science 179*, 300–302.

Jones, M. C., Bayley, N., MacFarlane, J. W., and Honzik, M. P. (1971): *The Course of Human Development*, Xerox College Publishing, Waltham, Mass.

Karczmar, A. G., and Scudder, C. L. (1967): Behavioral responses to drugs and brain catecholamine levels in mice of different strains and genera, *Fed. Proc. 26*, 1186–1191.

Kaufman, C., and Rosenblum, L. A. (1967): The reaction to separation in infant monkeys: Anaclitic depression and conservation-withdrawal, *Psychosom. Med. 19*, 648–675.

Kety, S. S. (1972a): Projections for future research. In: *Recent Advances in the Psychobiology of Depressive Illnesses*, edited by J. Williams, M. Katz, and J. Shield, pp. 343–346, National Institute of Mental Health, Washington, D.C.

Kety, S. S. (1972b): Toward hypotheses for a biochemical component in the vulnerability to schizophrenia, *Semin. Psychiatry 4*, 233–237.

Kety, S. S., and Schildkraut, J. J. (1967): Biogenic amines and emotion, *Science 156*, 21–30.

Klerman, G. L. (1971): Depression and adaptation, presented at NIMH Conference on Psychology and Depression, Warrington, Virginia, October 8–9, 1971.

Kopell, B. S., Wittner, W. K., Lunde, D. T., Warrick, G., and Edwards, D. (1970): Cortisol effects on the average evoked potential, alpha rhythm, time estimation, and the two-flash threshold, *Psychosom. Med. 32*, 39–49.

Leff, M. J., Roatch, J. F., and Bunney, W. E. (1970): Environmental factors preceding the onset of severe depressions, *Psychiatry 33*, 293–311.

Levine, R. (1966): *Endocrines and the Central Nervous System*, Williams and Wilkins Company, Baltimore.

Levine, S. (1972): *Hormones and Behavior*, Academic Press, New York.

Levine, S. (1974): Developmental Psychobiology. In: *American Handbook of Psychiatry*, vol. 6, *New Psychiatric Frontiers*, edited by D. A. Hamburg and H. K. H. Brodie, Basic Books, New York *(in press)*.

Lindemann, E. (1944): Symptomatology and management of acute grief, *Am. J. Psychiatry 101*, 141–148.

Lipton, M. A. (1973): Summary. In: *Serotonin and Behavior*, edited by J. Barchas and E. Usdin, pp. 565–568, Academic Press, New York.

Lloyd, C. (1964): Virilization and hirsutism. In: *Human Reproduction and Sexual Behavior*, edited by C. Lloyd, Lea and Febiger, Philadelphia.

Lloyd, C., Moses, A., Lobotsky, J., Klaiber, E., Marshall, L., and Jacobs, R. (1963): Studies of adrenocortical function of women with idiopathic hirsutism: Response to 25 units of ACTH, *J. Clin. Endocrinol. Metab. 23*, 413–418.

Maas, J. W. (1962): Neurochemical differences between two strains of mice, *Science 137*, 621–622.

Maas, J. W. (1963): Neurochemical differences between two strains of mice, *Nature 197*, 255–257.

Maas, J. W. (1971): Interactions between adrenocortical steroid hormones, electrolytes, and the catecholamines. In: *Brain Chemistry and Mental Disease*, edited by B. T. Ho and W. M. McIsaac, pp. 177–195, Plenum Press, New York.

Maas, J. W., Dekirmenjian, H., and Jones, F. (1973): The identification of depressed patients who have a disorder of NE metabolism and/or disposition. In: *Frontiers in Catecholamine Research*, edited by E. Usdin and S. Snyder, pp. 1091–1096, Pergamon Press Inc., New York.

Maas, J. W., and Mednieks, M. (1971): Hydrocortisone effected increase of norepinephrine uptake by brain slices, *Science 171*, 178–179.

MacLean, P. D. (1970): The triune brain, emotion and scientific bias. In: *The Neurosciences: Second Study Program*, edited by F. O. Schmitt, pp. 336–349, Rockefeller University Press, New York.

Mason, J. W. (1968): Organization of psychoendocrine mechanisms, *Psychosom. Med. 30*, No. 5, Part II, 1–791.

Mason, W. (1965): The social development of monkeys and apes. In: *Primate Behavior*, edited by I. DeVore, Holt, Rinehart and Winston, New York.

Matthysse, S., and Pope, A. (1974): The approach to schizophrenia through molecular pathology. In: *Molecular Pathology*, edited by R. Good and S. Day, Charles Thomas, Springfield *(in press)*.

McConville, B. J., Boag, L. C., and Purohit, A. P. (1972): Mourning depressive responses of children in residence following sudden death of parent figures, *Journal of the American Academy of Child Psychiatry, 11*, 341–364.

McCormack, S. A. (1971): Plasma testosterone concentration and binding in the chimpanzee: Effect of age, *Endocrinology 89*, 1171–1177.

McGinnis, P. (1973): *Patterns of Sexual Behavior in a Community of Free-Living Chimpanzees*, Dissertation submitted for Ph.D. degree, University of Cambridge.

Mendlewicz, J., Fleiss, J. L., and Fieve, R. R. (1972): Evidence for X-linkage in the transmission of manic-depressive illness, *JAMA 222*, 1624–1627.

Milkovic, K., Deguchi, T., Winget, C., Barchas, J., Levine, S., and Ciaranello, R. (1974): The effect of maternal manipulation on the phenylethanolamine N-methyl-transferase activity and corticosterone content of the fetal adrenal gland, *Am. J. Physiol. 226*, 864.

Miller, F. P., Cox, R. H., Jr., and Maickel, R. P. (1968): Intrastrain differences in serotonin and norepinephrine in discrete areas of rat brain, *Science 162*, 463–464.

Mitchell, G. D., Harlow, H. F., Griffin, G. A., and Moller, G. W. (1967): Repeated separation in the monkey, *Psychonomic Sci. 8*, 5.

Murphy, D. L. (1973): Technical strategies for the study of catecholamines in man, In: *Fron-*

tiers in Catecholamine Research, edited by E. Usdin and S. Snyder, pp. 1077–1082, Pergamon Press Inc., New York.

Murphy, D. L., and Wyatt, R. J. (1972): Reduced monoamine oxidase activity in blood platelets from schizophrenic patients, *Nature 238,* 225–226.

Musacchio, J. M., Julou, L., Kety, S. S., and Glowinski, J. (1969): Increase in rat brain tyrosine hydroxylase activity produced by electroconvulsive shock, *Proc. Natl. Acad. Sci. 63,* 1117–1119.

Nies, A., Robinson, D. S., Lamborn, K. R., and Lampert, R. P. (1973): Genetic control of platelet and plasma monoamine oxidase activity, *Arch. Gen. Psychiatry 28,* 834–838.

Page, J. G., Kessler, R. M., and Vesell, E. S. (1970): Strain differences in uptake, pool size and turnover rate of norepinephrine in hearts of mice, *Biochem. Pharmacol. 19,* 1381–1386.

Parkes, C. M. (1972): *Bereavement: Studies of Grief in Adult Life,* International Universities Press, Inc., New York.

Paykel, E. S., Myers, J. K., Dienelt, M. N., Klerman, G. L., Lindenthal, J. J., and Pepper, M. P. (1969): Life events and depression, *Arch. Gen. Psychiatry 21,* 753–760.

Peterson, N. A., and Chaikoff, I. L. (1963): Uptake of intravenously-injected (4-^{14}C)cortisol by adult rat brain, *J. Neurochem. 10,* 17–23.

Phillips, M. I., and Dafny, N. (1971): Effect of cortisol on unit activity in freely moving rats, *Brain Res. 25,* 651–655.

Pollin, W. (1972): The pathogenesis of schizophrenia – Possible relationships between genetic, biochemical, and experimental factors, *Arch. Gen. Psychiatry 27,* 29–37.

Prange, A. J., Lara, P. P., Wilson, I. C., Alltop, L. B., and Breese, G. R. (1972): Effects of thyrotropin-releasing hormone in depression, *Lancet,* Nov. 11, 999–1002.

Ramey, E. R. (1966): Relation of the thyroid to the autonomic nervous system. In: *Endocrines and the Central Nervous System,* edited by R. Levine, pp. 309–324, Williams and Wilkins Company, Baltimore.

Ramey, E. R., and Goldstein, M. S. (1957): The adrenal cortex and the sympathetic nervous system, *Physiol. Rev. 37,* 155–195.

Ramey, E. R., Goldstein, M. S., and Levine, R. (1951): Action of norepinephrine and adrenal cortical steroids on blood pressure and work performance of adrenalectomized dogs, *Am. J. Physiol. 165,* 450–455.

Reige, W. H., and Morimoto, H. (1970): Effects of chronic stress and differential environments upon brain weights and biogenic amine levels in rats, *J. Comp. Physiol. Psychol. 71,* 396–404.

Reis, D. J. (1974): Central neurotransmitters in aggression. In: *Association for Research in Nervous and Mental Diseases Symposium on Aggression,* Vol. 52, edited by S. Frazier, pp. 119–147, Williams & Wilkins Co., Baltimore.

Reis, D. J., and Fuxe, K. (1969): Brain norepinephrine: Evidence that neuronal release is essential for sham rage behavior following brainstem transection in cat, *Proc. Natl. Acad. Sci. 64,* 108–112.

Reis, D. J., and Gunne, L. M. (1965): Brain catecholamines: Relation to the defense reaction evoked by amygdaloid stimulation in cat, *Science 149,* 450–451.

Resko, J. A. (1967): Plasma androgen levels of the rhesus monkey: Effects of age and season, *Endocrinology 81,* 1203–1212.

Rimoin, D., and Schimke, R., eds. (1971): *Genetic Disorders of the Endocrine Glands,* pp. 251–257, C. V. Mosby Co., St. Louis.

Rosenblum, L. A., and Kaufman, C. (1968): Variations in infant development and response to maternal loss in monkeys, *Am. J. Orthopsychiatry 38,* 418–426.

Sachar, E. J., Hellman, L., Fukushima, D., and Gallagher, T. F. (1970): Cortisol production in depressive illness, *Arch. Gen. Psychiatry 23,* 289.

Schildkraut, J. J., Keeler, B. A., Papousek, M., and Hartmann, E. (1973): MHPG excretion in depressive disorders: Relation to clinical subtypes and desynchronized sleep. *Science 181,* 762–764.

Schlesinger, K., Boggan, W., and Freedman, D. X. (1965): Genetics of audiogenic seizures: 1. Relation to brain serotonin and norepinephrine in mice, *Life Sci. 4,* 2345–2351.

Seay, B., Hansen, E., and Harlow, H. F. (1962): Mother-infant separation in monkeys, *J. Child Psychol. Psychiatry 3,* 123–132.

Seay, B., and Harlow, H. F. (1965): Maternal separation in the rhesus monkey, *J. Nerv. Ment. Dis. 140,* 434–441.

Shire, J. G. M. (1970): Genetic variation in adrenal structure: Quantitative measurements on the cortex and medulla in hybrid mice, *J. Endocrinol. 48,* 419–431.

Smith, C. K., Barish, J., Correa, J., and Williams, R. H. (1972): Psychiatric disturbance in endocrinologic disease, *Psychosom. Med. 34,* 69–86.

Snyder, S. H. (1972): Catecholamines in the brain as mediators of amphetamine psychosis, *Arch. Gen. Psychiatry 27,* 169–179.

Snyder, S. H. (1973): Amphetamine psychosis: A "model" schizophrenia mediated by catecholamines, *Am. J. Psychiatry 130,* 61–67.

Snyder, S. H., and Meyerhoff, J. L. (1973): How amphetamine acts in minimal brain dysfunction, *Ann. N.Y. Acad. Sci. 205,* 310–320.

Spencer-Booth, Y., and Hinde, R. A. (1967): The effects of separating rhesus monkey infants from their mothers for six days, *J. Child Psychol. Psychiatry 7,* 179–197.

Stempfel, R. S., and Tomkins, G. M. (1966): Congenital virilizing adrenocortical hyperplasia (the adrenogenital syndrome). In: *The Metabolic Basis of Inherited Disease,* edited by J. B. Stanbury, J. B. Wyngaarden, and D. S. Fredrickson, pp. 635, McGraw-Hill Book Company, New York.

Stolk, J. M., Conner, R. L., Levine, S., and Barchas, J. D. (1974): Brain norepinephrine metabolism and shock-induced fighting behavior in rats: Differential effects of shock and fighting on the neurochemical response to a common footshock stimulus, *J. Pharmacol. Exp. Ther. 190,* 193–209.

Strott, C. A., and Lipsett, M. B. (1968): Measurement of 17-hydroxyprogesterone in human plasma, *J. Clin. Endocrinol. 28,* 1426–1430.

Sudak, H. S., and Maas, J. W. (1964a): Central nervous system serotonin and norepinephrine localization in emotional and non-emotional strains in mice, *Nature 203,* 1254–1256.

Sudak, H. S., and Maas, J. W. (1964b): Behavioral-neurochemical correlation in reactive and nonreactive strains of rats, *Science 146,* 418–420.

Suomi, S. J., Harlow, H. F., and Domek, C. J. (1970): Effect of repetitive infant-infant separation of young monkeys, *J. Abnorm. Psychol. 76,* 161.

Thorndahl, M., and Goodall, J. v. L. (1972): The reaction of an adolescent chimpanzee to the death of its mother *(personal communication).*

Tinklenberg, J. R. (1971): A clinical view of amphetamines, *Am. Fam. Physician 4,* 82–86.

Touchstone, J. C., Kasparow, M., Hughes, P. A., and Horwitz, M. R. (1966): Corticosteroids in human brain, *Steroids 7,* 205–211.

Turner, C. H., Davenport, R. K., and Rogers, C. M. (1969): The effect of early deprivation on the social behavior of adolescent chimpanzees, *Am. J. Psychiatry 125,* 1531–1536.

Udenfriend, S. (1972): Molecular biology of the sympathetic nervous system, *Pharmacol. Rev. 24,* 165–166.

Utena, H., Kanamura, H., Suda, S., Nakamura, R., Machiyama, Y., and Takahashi, R. (1968): Studies on the regional distribution of the monoamine oxidase activity in the brains of schizophrenic patients, *Proc. Jap. Acad. 44,* 1078–1083.

van Lawick-Goodall, J. (1968): The behavior of free-living chimpanzees in the Gombe Stream area, *An. Behav. Mono.* 1(3), 161–311.

van Lawick-Goodall, J. (1971): Some aspects of aggressive behaviour in a group of free-living chimpanzees, *Int. Soc. Sci. J. 23,* XXIII, 89–97.

van Lawick-Goodall, J. (1973): The behavior of chimpanzees in their natural habitat, *Am. J. Psychiatry 130,* 1–12.

Vernikos-Danellis, J., Berger, P., and Barchas, J. (1973): Brain serotonin and pituitary-adrenal function, *Prog. Brain Res. 39,* 301–310.

Washburn, S. L., Hamburg, D. A., and Bishop, N. (1974): Social adaptation in nonhuman primates. In: *Coping and Adaptation,* edited by G. V. Coelho, D. A. Hamburg, and J. E. Adams, pp. 3–12, Basic Books, New York.

Weinshilboum, R. M., Raymond, F. A., Elveback, L. R., and Weidman, W. H. (1973): Dopamine B-hydroxylase activity in serum. In: *Frontiers in Catecholamine Research,* edited by E. Usdin and S. Snyder, pp. 1115–1121, Pergamon Press Inc., New York.

Welch, B. L., and Welch, A. S. (1969a): Sustained effects of brief daily stress (fighting) upon brain and adrenal catecholamines and adrenal, spleen and heart weights, *Proc. Natl. Acad. Sci. 64,* 100–107.

Welch, B. L., and Welch, A. S. (1969b): Aggression and the biogenic amine neurohumors.

In: *Aggressive Behavior,* edited by S. Garattini and E. B. Sigg, pp. 188–202, John Wiley & Sons, Inc.

Welch, B. L., and Welch, A. S. (1969c): Fighting: Preferential lowering of norepinephrine and dopamine in the brainstem, concomitant with a depletion of epinephrine from the adrenal medulla, *Commun. Behav. Biol. 3,* 125–130.

Wilson, I. C., Prange, A. J., McClane, T. K., Rabon, A. M., and Lipton, M. A. (1970): Thyroid-hormone enhancement of imipramine in nonretarded depressions, *N. Engl. J. Med. 282,* 1063–1067.

Winokur, G., Morrison, J., Clancy, J., and Crowe, R. (1973): The Iowa 500: Familial and clinical findings favor two kinds of depressive illness, *Compr. Psychiatry 14,* 99–106.

Woodbury, D. M. (1958): Relation between the adrenal cortex and the central nervous system, *Pharmacol. Rev. 10,* 275–357.

Wurtman, R. J., and Axelrod, J. (1966): Control of enzymatic synthesis of adrenaline in the adrenal medulla by adrenal cortical steroids, *J. Biol. Chem. 241,* 2301–2305.

Wyatt, R. J., Murphy, D. L., Belmaker, R., Cohen, S., Donnelly, C. H., and Pollin, W. (1973): Reduced monoamine oxidase activity in platelets: A possible genetic marker for vulnerability to schizophrenia, *Science 179,* 916–918.

Wyatt, R., Portnoy, B., Kupfer, D., Snyder, F., and Engelman, K. (1971): Resting plasma catecholamine concentration in patients with depression and anxiety, *Arch. Gen. Psychiatry 24,* 65–70.

Emotions—Their Parameters and Measurement,
edited by L. Levi.
Raven Press, New York © 1975

Electrophysiological Parameters and Methods

Charles Shagass

Temple University Medical School and Eastern Pennsylvania Psychiatric Institute, Henry Avenue and Abbotsford Road, Philadelphia, Pennsylvania 19129

INTRODUCTION

For present purposes, the term "electrophysiological" will be restricted to those electrical activities of the brain that can be recorded with electrodes placed on the intact human head. These phenomena include the electroencephalogram (EEG) and the event-related potentials (ERP). ERPs are recorded with the EEG, but they usually can be well demonstrated only by using averaging methods. The responses evoked by sensory stimuli are the best-known ERP, but there are several other kinds (Vaughan, 1969). Most of the material in this chapter concerns the EEG, although some aspects of ERP receive limited consideration. The emphasis is methodological, with an attempt to relate the material to the use of electrophysiological methods in those kinds of psychophysiological research that may be relevant to the measurement of emotional processes, e.g., studies of attention, personality, and emotional disorders.

TECHNIQUES

This section will attempt to give a brief description of recording methods, with particular attention to sources of experimental difficulty. The interested reader is referred to more detailed presentations elsewhere of EEG and ERP recording methods (Hill and Parr, 1963; Shagass, 1972*a,b*).

EEG RECORDING

Instrumentation

The conventional EEG recording instrument usually consists of several channels, each of which contains devices for amplification and display of electrical signals. Voltage amplification between 1,000 and 200,000 is required to achieve a nominal 1-V signal level over the full range of EEG phenomena. Nearly all EEG recording is done with resistance-capacitance-coupled (ac) amplifiers; these avoid the baseline drift and low-frequency noise signals associated with the theoretically more desirable direct-coupled (dc) amplifiers.

Conventional EEG apparatus generally includes the following controls: (a) lead selector switches; (b) gain or amplitude controls; (c) high-frequency filter controls; (d) low-frequency cutoff (time constant) setting. Research polygraphs generally have more numerous controls and facilities for adjustment than clinical EEG instruments. For research purposes, the technical specifications of the recording instrument may be crucial, e.g., some conventional EEG amplifiers are unsuitable for ERP recording because of restricted frequency response.

Amplitude calibration is often provided in the form of a square wave signal, generated by a battery. When the EEG is tape-recorded for later quantitative analysis, a more desirable calibration signal source is provided by one of the commercially available calibrators; these generate repetitive signals, such as square waves or sine waves, at a regular rate. Such repetitive signals can be subjected to the same processing as the EEG and may provide frequency as well as amplitude calibration.

The frequency resolution of instrumentation tape recorders is related to the recording speed; greater resolution is obtained with faster speeds. Since the common EEG signals are of relatively low frequency, a slow speed may be used in recording, but the recorder may then be sped up for playback, which can yield an important saving of processing time.

Telemetry

The need to attach the subject to the recording apparatus by lead wires introduces a serious constraint upon his activities. Telemetering equipment makes possible a greater range of movement. Several channels of EEG can be transmitted by miniaturized equipment comfortably attached to the clothing or body of the subject. It is important that materials with electrical shielding properties not be placed between the transmitter and the receiver. Telemetering equipment has been used to record the EEG of somnambulists (Gastaut and Broughton, 1965) and brain potentials associated with fairly strenuous activities, such as ball-playing (Walter, 1969). The main difficulty arises in distinguishing brain potentials from potentials of noncerebral origin.

Artifacts

Many kinds of electrodes are in use: chlorided silver disks, Bentonite paste, subcutaneous needles, etc. To keep external noise and movement artifacts to a minimum, the most important considerations are that the resistance between any pair of scalp leads should be less than 5000 ohms, and that the electrodes remain well attached and stable throughout the recording.

Important physiological artifacts include: the galvanic skin response (GSR), muscle potentials or electromyogram (EMG), eyeblinks or eye movements (electrooculogram, EOG), electrocardiogram (EKG), movements caused by pulsation of the scalp arteries, tongue movements. Most of the physiological artifacts have distinguishing characteristics, so that they may usually be identified by the trained observer. However, unless monitored and dealt with, they may lead to much error.

Muscle potentials present a particularly serious problem; they may merge into an apparent rhythmic pattern, which can easily be mistaken for brain activity, especially in frontal recordings. Filtering of high frequencies can reduce EMG activity, but desired portions of the EEG may be attenuated. The best solution is to help the subject to relax. However, it should be recognized that the degree of muscular relaxation necessary for eliminating EMG contamination of the EEG may be virtually impossible in many situations involving activity.

The EOG is generally attributed to the potential difference of about 100 mV between the cornea and the orbit; when the eyeball moves, the potential differences change, causing large deflections in recordings from near the eye. Slow changes due to eye movement are easy to recognize, but slight mystagmoid movement of the eyes may produce rhythmic voltage fluctuation that resemble brain rhythms. EOG can be monitored by electrodes placed near the eye; the ocular origin of signals can be inferred when their voltage is greatest in EOG leads.

Electrode Linkages and the Problem of the Reference Lead

Linkages between two electrodes on the scalp are designated as bipolar recordings. Unipolar (monopolar) recordings are made between an electrode on the scalp and a common (reference, indifferent) electrode, usually on the lobe of one ear or both ears connected together. The reference electrode is assumed to be relatively insensitive to potential changes within the head. The idea of the unipolar recording is that, since the reference electrode will be relatively inactive, the potential differences between the leads can be attributed to activity of a site under the scalp electrode. On theoretical grounds, the unipolar recording method is preferable to the bipolar, but it has been difficult to find a truly indifferent reference placement. Ear electrodes will frequently pick up brain activity. The obvious solution, namely, to place an indifferent electrode at a point on the body distant from the head, encounters difficulties because of the large EKG ordinarily picked up by electrodes on the body or limbs. In the noncephalic reference placement of Lehtonen and Koivikko (1971), electrodes are placed over the right sternoclavicular joint and over the spine of the seventh cervical vertebra; these are linked by a variable potentiometer, which is adjusted to greatly minimize the residual EKG. Although this noncephalic reference has a number of advantages, it usually records more artifacts than one on the ear.

Activation Methods

Liberson (1944) used the term "functional electroencephalography" to designate EEG activation procedures in general; in his opinion, the functional approach offered greater hope for psychologically relevant findings than one based on resting records. Routine clinical EEG tests have usually included maneuvers to examine alpha-rhythm responsiveness to light (opening eyes) and sensitivity to CO_2 reduction (hyperventilation). Hyperventilation generally produces increased slow activity. Intermittent photic stimulation, which is usually performed by presenting trains of brief, but intense, light flashes, is also used routinely in clinical work in an attempt to elicit convulsive activity. Photic stimulation normally causes *photic driving;* the brain rhythms follow the frequency of the train of light flashes over a variable range. Photic stimulation may also evoke photomyoclonic responses; these resemble convulsive discharges, but they reflect myoclonic twitching and do not originate in the brain (Bickford, Sem-Jacobsen, White, and Daly, 1952).

Sleep, either natural or induced by drugs, may facilitate recognition of certain epileptiform discharges, and provides another activation method, although "activation" by sleep seems a somewhat paradoxical concept (Gibbs and Gibbs, 1946). Many drugs, particularly those with convulsant properties, have been used to activate the EEG in order to bring out convulsive discharges; pentylenetetrazol (Metrazol®) is perhaps the best known of these.

EEG Analysis and Quantification

Such a great amount of information is obtained in a relatively short time in a multiple-channel EEG recording, that simple visual measurements must be restricted to small samples. Techniques for automatic quantification are needed to do justice to the data. Computer technology has made it possible to implement methods for reducing the mass of information to numerical values or forms of display that may facilitate comprehension, or at least provide more representative measurements. Various mathematical models have been proposed upon which to base analysis programs. With only one channel, such models involve the temporal analysis of the EEG. With more than one channel, the analysis can be spatial-temporal.

Perhaps the earliest approach to sophisticated quantitative EEG analysis was the Fourier transforms of Grass and Gibbs (1938); these were based on the Fourier series, which characterizes complex wave shapes as the sum of regular sine waves. With general purpose digital computers, Fourier analysis of EEG samples can be performed with relative ease. Such analysis forms the basis of the power-density spectrum, which shows the amount of energy at each of the frequencies represented in the Fourier series. Baldock and Walter (1946) described a frequency analyzer which provides information similar to that of the power-density spectrum. This type of frequency analyzer involves a series of selected center frequencies, usually ranging from 1 to 30 Hz, obtained by passing signals through a set of tuned filters. The display shows the total voltage for each frequency during the time of analysis.

The period or duration of a wave shape at certain amplitude points, such as the base line, may be its most easily described aspect. Burch, Greiner, and Correll (1955) introduced an instrument for automatic period analysis of the EEG. They analyzed the base line cross to establish each half-wave or major period. The time position of inflection points in the EEG, indicative of faster waves superimposed on the main waves, was yielded by the zero crosses of the second derivative; the time between such inflections is designated as the minor period. A histogram showing the distribution of major periods can be obtained with relative ease if an averaging computer is available. The EEG is passed through a zero-cross detector and the computer registers counts at points in memory corresponding to the duration between successive zero crosses. An averaging computer may also be used in conjunction with a zero-cross detector to record the number of zero crosses in successive, arbitrarily determined, segments of time. This type of analysis provides a time series, which shows variations in mean EEG frequency over time. A corresponding time series of amplitude may be obtained by passing the EEG through an absolute-value generator into the computer. Such an amplitude analysis can also be obtained by using the integrator described by Drohocki (1948), which summates electrical activity over wide frequency bands. The time series of frequency or amplitude may be used to show the changes produced by any experimental maneuver applied during the period of analysis.

Methods of EEG analysis that involve either auto- or cross-correlation provide sensitive measures of frequency and phase. The autocorrelation is obtained by determining the correlation between a given input and itself delayed by successive intervals. The cross-correlogram is obtained by applying the same procedure to two different inputs. A somewhat simpler approach to analysis of interarea relationships than cross-correlation is provided by the device described by Darrow and Smith (1964) for automatically scoring phase relationships between EEGs from different leads.

The analysis of spatial-temporal relationships is obviously much more complex than analyses pertaining to the description of a single channel of activity or even the relationship between two channels. Various techniques have been devised to portray spatial–temporal relationships in EEGs recorded from many locations simultaneously (e.g., Walter and Shipton, 1951;

Harris and Bickford, 1967). Although these topographic methods contain the information necessary for describing EEG activity in several dimensions, they pose extremely difficult problems for quantitative description and analysis.

RECORDING EVENT-RELATED POTENTIALS

Averaging

ERPs are usually not readily apparent in the EEG. Considering the EEG as "noise," the generally lower-amplitude ERPs are extracted by time-coherent signal averaging. By summing a number of EEG samples in fixed-time relation to an event such as a sensory stimulus or a button-press, the background EEG, which is not time coherent, tends to add to a horizontal line, while the ERP becomes more distinguishable.

Instrumentation

Given an adequate frequency range, EEG amplifiers may be used to record ERPs. The required amplifier characteristics depend upon the nature of the potential. For example, to record the very rapid early events in click-evoked responses (Jewett, Romano, and Williston, 1970), an upper frequency cutoff of at least 3 kHz is desirable. For the later events in all modalities, the upper frequency limits can be set much lower (50 to 500 Hz). Slow potential phenomena, such as the contingent negative variation (CNV), require either a dc amplifier or one with a long time constant (5 sec or more).

Averagers may be of analogue or digital type; digital devices are generally more precise. Digital averagers are either special purpose or general purpose computers; the latter may, of course, also be programmed to execute functions other than averaging. Most special purpose averaging computers are also capable of providing interval histograms. The stored average may be displayed in analogue form on the cathode-ray-oscilloscope screen or plotted on paper; the digital output can be stored on digital magnetic tape or punched paper tape. There is generally provision for selecting a wide range of analysis periods with a fixed number of data points; the temporal resolution of the signal will depend upon the analysis time selected. However, it is not usually possible to employ more than one time base; theis means that very rapid and very slow events cannot be averaged simultaneously. Analogue tape recording may be used to augment the channel capacity of the averager and multiple playbacks from tape may permit data analyses with different time bases.

Several accessory devices are either essential, or at least very useful, for recording ERP. The following may be mentioned: (a) low-level-calibration pulse generators (with Emde's (1964) calibrator, the pulse is inserted into each sweep in series with the recording electrodes); (b) timing devices for regulating the administration of stimuli and for controlling pulses that trigger the averager; (c) preset counters, which automatically terminate stimulation after a fixed number of stimuli have been administered; (d) automatic zero reset device to reduce or eliminate the effects of base line drift with long-time constant or dc amplifiers (Straumanis, Shagass, and Overton, 1969).

Stimulus Problems

Reliable recordings of sensory-evoked responses require accurately specified and standardized stimuli. It is not always possible to meet these requirements. Although physical standardization of the stimuli may be achieved, much variation may be introduced because it is necessary to repeat identical stimuli many times in the averaging sequence. Habituation may occur with simple stimuli and the meaning of complex or subtle stimuli may change as a result of repetition.

Much sensory-evoked response work has involved the use of brief stimuli that are clearly defined as to onset and serve admirably as time-defining events for averaging. These include brief, painless electrical shocks applied to the skin over a nerve, light flashes, and auditory clicks or tone pips. Such stimuli can be generated and controlled by commercially available devices.

For electrocutaneous stimulation, either a constant-voltage or a constant-current stimulus generator is required; both give equivalent results (Schwartz, Emde, and Shagass, 1964). Because of variations in electrode placement, skin thickness, etc., the effective intensity of the electrocutaneous stimulus, cannot, in practice, be established from the current or voltage of the pulse at source. In our work, we have determined a "physiological zero" by measuring the ascending and descending sensory thresholds and taking the mean of these. Stimulus strength is then given in terms of milliamps or volts above threshold. The justification for this practice is that the first measurable evoked response is found with a stimulus strength corresponding to sensory threshold (Shagass and Schwartz, 1961).

Auditory stimuli have generally been delivered either through earphones or loud speakers at a fixed distance from the subject's head. When complex auditory stimuli, such as tape-recorded words, are used to evoke responses, the averager trigger may be located at the onset time of the sound.

Light flashes may be generated by an EEG photic stimulator controlling a stroboscope lamp; less intense flashes are generated by neon lamps or glow modulator tubes, which, unlike photic stimulators, are also noiseless. A uniform surround, completely enveloping the subject's face, may be achieved by aiming the photic stimulator lamp from behind the subject onto a reflecting hemisphere of fairly large size (Dustman and Beck, 1963). In addition to intensity, some important stimulus parameters affecting visual responses include duration [there are "off" responses when flashes exceed 25 msec in duration (Efron, 1964)], color (Monnier and Rozier, 1968), and pattern and form (Spehlmann, 1965). Slide projectors with high-speed shutters can be used to deliver patterned stimuli.

Artifact

The biological artifacts encountered in EEG recording may present even more serious problems in ERP work. Bickford, Jacobson, and Cody (1964) have drawn attention to the fact that responses of muscle can be time-locked to sensory stimuli and summate to give large deflections in the ERP record. Consistent electroretinogram (ERG) and EOG effects can be produced by visual stimuli. Also, variations in pupillary diameter can effect the characteristics of visual responses. The investigator of ERP must be continuously aware of, and take measures to contend with, the possibility of contamination by such artifacts. Maneuvers to position and relax the subject may minimize artifact. Monitor recordings from leads placed near known major sources of artifact, e.g., EOG for eye movement, should also be averaged.

Quantification and Data Reduction

Hand measurements of ERPs have usually been based on visual identification of features of interest, such as peak deflections (Figs. 1 and 2). The times of occurrence of such peaks after the sensory stimulus provide latency measurements. Amplitude may be measured either as the degree of deflection from an estimate of the isoelectric line or as the amount of excursion between adjacent peaks. When the potentials are entered into a general purpose computer, other types of measurement become possible. Reliable amplitude measurements can be obtained by dividing the evoked response into fixed-time epochs, with respect to the stimulus, and computing the average deviation around the mean during such epochs (Shagass, Overton, and Straumanis, 1971). Fourier analysis can be performed in order to determine the amount of energy in the different sine-wave frequencies contributing to the complex wave form (Shagass, 1967). The similarity between the wave shapes of two averages can be estimated by computing the product-moment correlation between corresponding data points (Callaway, Jones, and Layne, 1965). The possibilities offered by computer quantification of ERPs remain to be fully explored.

NORMAL EEG RHYTHMS AND THEIR VARIATIONS

The commonly used Greek letter designations for EEG rhythms refer to frequency ranges. These ranges are usually given as follows: alpha, 8 to

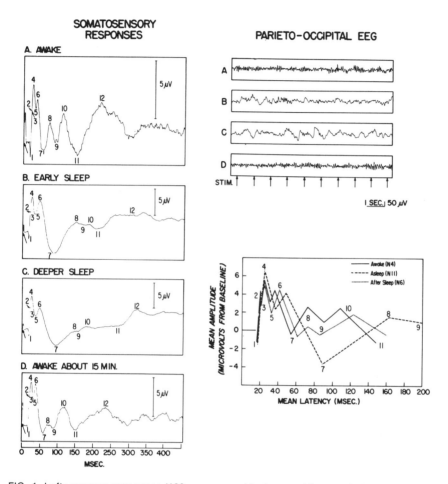

FIG. 1. Left: average responses (100 sweeps each) of one subject evoked by stimulating right median nerve at wrist with pulses of 0.1 msec duration at 1/sec rate during waking and daytime sleep. Bipolar leads 7 cm parasagittal over left hemisphere. Relative positivity at posterior electrode gives upward deflection. EEG samples at right recorded while corresponding responses were being recorded; C is slow wave sleep. Inset graphs are composite responses, based on group mean measurements of amplitudes and latencies, before, during and after sleep; note longer latencies in waking records after sleep than before, e.g., peaks 6, 7, 10.

13Hz; beta, 14 to 30 Hz; theta, 4 to 7 Hz; delta, less than 4 Hz; gamma, 35 to 50 Hz. Gamma is a controversial rhythm.

Alpha rhythm amplitude generally ranges between 25 and 100 μV and it is recorded mainly from parietal and occipital derivations. Alpha rhythm is blocked, or desynchronized, by sensory stimulation, especially visual, and during mental activity requiring attention. Alpha rhythms usually fluctuate from moment to moment and the waves may vary somewhat in shape. There appear to be several alpha generators in the brain (Walter, Rhodes, Brown, and Adey, 1966).

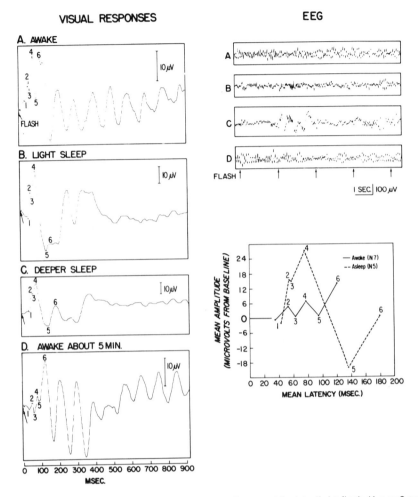

FIG. 2. Tracings at left are average responses of one subject to light flash (1 per 2 sec) during waking and daytime sleep; 100 sweeps each. Leads in midline, 3 and 12 cm above inion; relative positivity at posterior electrode gives upward deflection. EEG samples taken during corresponding averaging sequence. Inset graph is composite of waking and sleeping responses based on group means. Note amplitude increase, latency prolongation, and abolition of afterrhythm with sleep.

Beta rhythm amplitudes seldom exceed 20 μV. Beta is usually more pronounced in frontal and central areas. Beta activity predominates when the alpha rhythm is reduced. It has been thought that beta activity may be correlated with anxiety or tension, but this idea may be due more to the fact that the suppression of alpha reveals the existing beta rather than to actual augmentation of beta.

Theta rhythms are normal components of the EEG in children, but diminish in amplitude throughout the second decade. They are usually symmetrical and mainly frontal-temporal in distribution. Their amplitude is usually less than 20 μV. Delta waves are abnormal in the waking adult EEG, but waves of this frequency form a common part of the EEG in certain stages of sleep (Figs. 1 and 2).

Other EEG Waves

Also known as the wicket or comb rhythm or *rhythme en arceau,* the mu rhythm appears in the normal EEG in about 7% of subjects. It is found in the Rolandic region, sometimes near the vertex, and tends to occur in bilaterally asynchronous bursts (Gastaut, 1952). The mu frequency of 9 to 11 Hz is usually associated with beta rhythm of twice this frequency. The mu rhythm is diminished by actual movement of, or intention of moving, the contralateral limbs.

Kappa rhythm designates activity at about 10 Hz, best seen in bipolar records of temporal areas; it appears to be related to thinking, being elicited by problem solving in about 30% of normals (Kennedy, Gottsdanker, Armington, and Gray, 1948). Kappa is difficult to distinguish from eye movement, and there has been controversy about the reality of the phenomenon.

Lambda waves are single, saw-toothed waves, positive at the occiput, with a duration of about 250 msec (Evans, 1952). They are not seen when the eyes are closed or in the dark, and are best demonstrated with a well-illuminated pattern. The vertex waves described by Gastaut (1953) are sharp waves, negative at the vertex, that can be seen in the absence of overt stimulation. They may be distinguished from lambda by virtue of being maximum over the vertex and by a difference in peak polarity. Vertex waves may be induced regularly by a variety of sudden stimuli.

FACTORS INFLUENCING THE EEG

Biochemical Factors

Low oxygen level may slow EEG frequencies and oxygen excess may increase them (Engel, Romano, Ferris, Webb, and Stevens, 1944). Slow rhythms in the EEG may occur with low blood sugar. The delta response induced by hyperventilation results ultimately from CO_2 reduction, i.e., acapnia. The frequency of the alpha rhythm may also be related to body temperature, being more rapid at higher temperatures (Hoagland, 1936).

EEG changes have been associated with alterations in the functioning of various endocrine glands. In general, slow rhythms have been found in myxedema and in Addison's disease; rapid rhythms occur in hyperthyroidism (Thiebaut, Rhomer, and Wackenheim, 1958). Margerison, Anderson and Dawson (1964) showed that plasma sodium changes during the menstrual cycle were associated with changes in the amount of activity at 7 and 8 Hz in the EEG. The methodologically important point is that, in female subjects, there may be changes in EEG frequency as a function of the menstrual cycle.

Age

EEG variations with age are greatest in childhood and later life. At birth the EEG is low voltage, irregular, and arrhythmic. Occipital frequency is about 5 Hz at 6 months and increases steadily with age, following roughly an exponential curve; at about 8 years the alpha frequency approaches adult level (Lindsley, 1939). Theta rhythm is more prominent on the left than on the right side in children of all ages; up to the age of 2 or 3 years, theta is usually augmented by closing the eyes and by such emotions as laughing, crying, or hunger (Walter, 1950). Beta activity seems to be of low amplitude in normal children and to change little in frequency with age.

Alpha frequency, on the average, becomes slower with advancing years (Obrist, 1954). Beta rhythms appear to be more prominent in older subjects; increase of beta begins in middle age. The slowing of alpha may be of functional significance; Surwillo (1963a,b) found a high correlation between mean reaction time and the brain wave period ($r = 0.72$), which persisted after correction for age. Thus, older people who maintain a normal alpha frequency may also retain greater mental alertness.

Sex

Few EEG sex differences have been reported. Henry (1944) found faster alpha frequency and a higher incidence of low-voltage fast records in females than in males. There are consistent sex differences in photic driving; females show higher amplitude driving over a broad range of frequencies than do males (Shagass, 1955a).

Effects of Pharmacological Agents

Numerous drugs affect the EEG. Much relevant material may be found in *Psychopharmacology: A Review of Progress 1957–1967* (Efron, Cole, Levine, and Wittenborn, 1968). Mention may be made of the fact that barbiturates, in sedative doses, produce increased fast activity; in anesthetic doses, slow activity becomes more prominent. Most of the commonly used minor tranquilizers (e.g., meprobamate, chlordiazepoxide) have barbiturate-like effects on the EEG. Other drugs in common psychiatric use, such as the major tranquilizers and the antidepressants, also have significant EEG effects, although these may be more variable. An important aspect of drug effects on the EEG is that they may persist for a long time and their manifestations may be intermittent for a period of several weeks after administration (Ulett, Heusler, and Word, 1965).

There is evidence that commonly ingested agents, not ordinarily thought of as drugs, may also alter the EEG. Thus, Fink (1968) refers to effects of caffeine and alcohol on the EEG, and EEG differences have been found in relation to smoking. Ulett and Itil (1969) cite reports indicating that heavy cigarette smokers show less alpha and more high-frequency activity than nonsmokers and that, even after one cigarette, subjects have been found to show reduced amplitude and increased alpha frequency. In heavy cigarette smokers after 24 hr of smoking deprivation, Ulett and Itil demonstrated reduced alpha frequency and increases of both fast and slow activity. Marijuana tends to produce slowing in the EEG, but there may also be an increase of fast activity (Fink, 1968).

Considering the diversity of possible drug effects on the EEG, it becomes rather important to obtain information about the habits and recent intake of various substances by research subjects. We have found that marijuana users often do not regard marijuana as a drug, and must be specifically questioned.

INDIVIDUAL DIFFERENCES AND THE EEG

Stability of the EEG

Since so many factors can alter EEG activity, it is perhaps surprising that longitudinal studies of EEG stability indicate that, under similar conditions, adult EEG characteristics tend to be relatively stable over months and years (Davis and Davis, 1939; Johnson and Ulett, 1959). Studies of EEG similarity between identical twins indicate that a genetic factor may contribute to this stability of EEG patterning; thus Lennox, Gibbs, and Gibbs (1942) found 87% concordance between the EEGs of 53 normal twins. Evidence that conditioned EEG responses can be established suggests that experiential factors may also be of importance (Wells, 1963).

Although the EEG can show marked variations in a short time, its stability under reasonably uniform conditions seems to be sufficient to justify research attempting to relate EEG characteristics to other kinds of individual differences.

EEG and Intelligence

Attempts to correlate EEG characteristics with scores on intelligence tests have yielded variable findings. Kreezer's (1939, 1940) early work in mental retardates showed positive results in some groups, but not in others, e.g., mental age and alpha frequency were correlated in familial-type retardates, but not in Down's syndrome. Studies attempting to relate intelligence to EEG characteristics in large samples of normal adults have yielded negative results (Shagass, 1946; Gastaut, 1960). If there are any correlations between EEG and intelligence, they are probably quite low. Investigators who neglect to match normal adult subjects for intellectual level are probably on safe ground.

EEG and Personality

Emotional processes may contribute significant aspects of personality. The earliest relationship reported between EEG and personality is probably still the one most strongly supported by available evidence. Saul, Davis, and Davis (1937, 1949) studied patients in psychoanalysis (there were 136 in their 1949 sample). The subjects were assessed for the relative strength of their tendencies for activity versus passivity in habitual actions. High alpha index (percent time alpha) was found to occur together with a passive-dependent, receptive attitude toward other persons, provided this attitude was not thwarted or inhibited internally. In contrast, low alpha indices were found to be associated with a consistent, well-directed freely indulged drive to activity (excluding diffuse hypomanic activity). No pronounced shift from high to low alpha index was found in any case, even after years of psychoanalysis.

Gottlober (1938) found that high alpha index was significantly related to ratings of extraversion, but Henry and Knott (1941) failed to verify his findings. Attempts to relate the results of other personality tests, such as the Minnesota Multiphasic Personality Inventory (MMPI) and the Rorschach test, to EEG characteristics, have resulted in either negative or inconsistent findings (Werre, 1957; Gastaut, 1960).

One aspect of personality that appears related to the EEG is style of mental imagery, i.e., predominance of visual, verbal, kinesthetic, or other imagery. Golla, Hutton, and Walter (1943) classified alpha records into M, P, and R types. M type individuals (little alpha) used mainly visual imagery and thinking; P type (persistent alpha) used auditory or kinesthetic imagery; R type (responsive) used both visual and nonvisual imagery. Slatter (1960) conducted a systematic study of mental imagery; he paid careful attention to the problems of anxiety induced by task instructions and tried to avoid such reactions. He was able to classify his 60 subjects into four groups on a dimension ranging from predominant visualizers to predominant verbalizers. Slatter showed that the act of visual imagery was associated with a reduction in alpha rhythm, whereas alpha persisted during verbal imagery. The average amplitude of the resting EEG was significantly lower in subjects who habitually used visual imagery than in those who habitually used verbal imagery. Verbal imagery subjects tended to have virtually continuous alpha activity, whereas this was rare in subjects with habitual visual imagery.

Slatter's experiment is of considerable methodological importance, because the pains taken to control anxiety or tension during the experiment appear to have led to unusually clear results. Conversely, an investigator wishing to relate level of anxiety to EEG characteristics would need to institute controls for visual imagery, both in terms of the habitual imagery style of the subjects, and the imagery induced by the experimental instructions.

The degree of driving induced by intermittent photic stimulation was found to be related to "anxiety-proneness" by Ulett, Gleser, Winokur, and Lawler (1953). Although they were able to distinguish a high proportion of anxiety-prone individuals by means of photic responses in their initial studies, their results were difficult to repeat. We studied the relationship between photic driving response and affective state in psychiatric patients with anxiety or depression and a nonpatient group (Shagass, 1955a). The relative driving to flash rates of 10 and 15 Hz was expressed as a 15:10 ratio. Among female subjects, patients with anxiety showed significantly higher 15:10 ratios than control subjects who, in turn, had higher ratios than depressed patients. In longitudinal studies, variations in driving appeared to be related to life experiences of an emotional nature (Shagass, 1955b). The group results were, however, difficult to replicate in subsequent work.

The sedation threshold uses the EEG changes produced by intravenously administered amobarbital sodium to measure tolerance or sensitivity to the drug, which is given at a rate of 0.5 mg/kg every 40 sec (Shagass, 1954). The EEG index is based on changes in the amplitude of frontal 15 to 30 Hz activity and corresponds roughly to onset of dysarthria. In nonpsychotic subjects, but not in psychotics, the sedation threshold correlated well with clinical ratings of tension, which also reflected anxiety-proneness. Sedation thresholds were not only significantly higher in psychoneurotic patients than in controls, but also higher in those controls admitting to symptoms of anxiety-proneness in a clinical interview and a self-administered questionnaire (Shagass and Naiman, 1955, 1956). Sedation threshold was also found to be correlated with measurements of extraversion-introversion and with the relative predominance of hysterical or obsessional personality traits in a psychoneurotic population; thresholds were lower in hysterics or extraverts and higher in obsessionals or introverts (Shagass and Kerenyi, 1958). These results have been verified by Claridge and Herrington (1963).

Psychopathology

Comprehensive reviews of EEG findings in various psychiatric disorders are contained in the volume edited by Wilson (1965). Although there has been a consistently high incidence of EEG abnormality in brain syndromes, the findings in the "functional" disorders are more equivocal. Individuals diagnosed as having psychopathic personalities tend to have a high incidence of abnormal findings, with the occurrence of a greater than normal amount of theta activity (Knott, 1965); this finding may be age related. The reviews of

Ellingson (1954), Hill (1957), and Kennard (1965) all conclude that the incidence of abnormal findings appears to be greater in schizophrenic patients than in normals. However, the incidence of abnormality seems to vary enormously, ranging from 5 to 80% in different studies. Major problems in most of the studies are poor control of fundamental demographic variables such as age, uncertain pharmacological status of the patients, and inadequate EEG quantification.

A few of the more adequate quantitative studies will be mentioned. Kennard and her associates, using a tuned filter frequency analyzer, found less sharply defined alpha activity in schizophrenics than in nonpatients, with a greater frequency spread within the alpha range and more nonalpha activity (Kennard and Schwartzman, 1956, 1957). "Poor organization" was more common among the patients, and there was evidence of reduced synchrony between the hemispheres. Clinical improvement was associated with a shift of the frequency-analyzer graph toward the nonpatient pattern. Recently, Itil, Saletu, and Davis (1972) compared schizophrenic patients with age- and sex-matched controls; their frequency-analyzer and period-analysis data revealed significantly more activity above and below the alpha band in the patients. Although the Itil study may be, so far, the best-controlled comparison of a psychiatric-patient population with a control group, it may be noted that they applied computer quantification to only one of eight channels recorded.

Using another quantification method, Goldstein and his co-workers have shown that the temporal variability (coefficient of variation) of EEG amplitude, measured in 20-sec segments for a 10-min period, tends to be greater in normals than in chronic schizophrenic patients (Goldstein and Sugerman, 1969). Marjerrison, Krause, and Keough (1967) have essentially verified Goldstein's results.

There are still relatively few EEG studies of psychopathologic disorders that have employed adequate methods of quantification. It remains to be seen whether computer quantification will yield the consistent positive results that were denied to earlier workers who did not possess the facilities.

EEG AND AWARENESS

Reduced Awareness

The most striking behavioral correlates of the EEG are seen in relation to conditions of reduced awareness, notably sleep. The discovery of the REM stage of sleep, associated with dreaming, led to a reclassification of EEG sleep stages and much research activity (Aserinsky and Kleitman, 1955; Dement and Kleitman, 1957). Stages other than REM and stage I of sleep, which are associated with desynchronized background activity, are generally called slow-wave sleep (Figs. 1 and 2). Stage II involves a high incidence of waves in spindles of beta frequency. Stages III and IV involve slow activity in the delta frequency range.

The large volume of published EEG studies of sleep makes it impossible to consider them here, but it may be pointed out that studies of dreaming are, to an important extent, investigations of emotional states during sleep. They may provide one of the more important contributions of electrophysiology to investigation of emotional processes. The volume edited by Kales is a representative compendium of sleep research reports (Kales, 1969).

The slowing of rhythms found in nondreaming sleep is characteristic of other conditions of impaired awareness, including deliria due to such causes as cerebral arteriosclerosis or drug toxicity.

The alpha frequency of the EEG also becomes slowed under conditions of sensory deprivation. The longer the time of isolation, the greater the slowing, which may persist for hours after the subject emerges from isolation (Zubek, 1964). It appears that the maintenance of normal EEG characteristics depends upon normal sensory inputs.

Relation to Autonomic Indicators and "Arousal"

Stimulation of the reticular formation in animals produces EEG effects resembling alpha blocking in man; this analogy, with respect to EEG activation, has played an important role in the development of arousal theory. However, attempts to provide empirical support for the construct of a more-or-less unitary central activation mechanism have met with little success (Kugelmass, 1973). Sternbach (1960), reasoning that such a mechanism should be reflected in significant associations between EEG and autonomic indices of activation, attempted to correlate Wenger's estimate of relative autonomic balance with percent time alpha, and found no significant relationships; the autonomic measures included salivary output, sublingual temperature, palmar and volar forearm conductance, diastolic blood pressure, and heart rate. Stennet (1957) demonstrated an inverted-U relationship between levels of palmar conductance and alpha amplitude, but Sternbach was not able to verify this finding. Other failures to establish relationships between EEG and autonomic measures include those of Mundy-Castle and McKiever (1953) and Elliott (1964). The available evidence suggests that the central mechanisms involved in controlling the autonomic indices do not function as a unity; furthermore, those EEG phenomena which have been studied in relation to the autonomic measures are probably not immediately related to their central mechanisms.

TYPES OF ERPs

According to Vaughan (1969), ERPs can be classified into the following types: (a) sensory-evoked potentials; (b) motor potentials (associated with movement or the intention to move); (c) long latency potentials related to complex psychological variables; (d) steady potential shifts; (e) potentials of extracranial origin (biological artifacts). Some characteristics of ERP in types a, c, and d will be described here.

Sensory-Evoked Potentials

The wave shapes of these potentials are usually complex, consisting of several peaks. Figures 1 and 2 give examples of somatosensory and visual responses, elicited by electrocutaneous and flash stimuli. Response onset is usually rapid: 15 to 20 msec for somatosensory; 20 to 30 msec for visual. The responses may last from 250 to over 1,000 msec. Various schemes for designating the successive peaks or components have been proposed. Our own system of numbering consecutive peaks is indicated in Figs. 1 and 2. Although there is some degree of similarity between responses in different modalities, those in any one modality resemble one another more than they do those elicited by other kinds of stimuli.

The validity of scalp-recorded average responses as brain events is supported by the fact that they resemble responses recorded simultaneously with electrodes on the dura or on the surface of the brain (Domino, Matsuoka, Waltz, and Cooper, 1965; Giblin, 1964; Walter, 1962). Attempts have been made to relate evoked-response components to specific neurophysiological events. Goff, Rosner, and Allison (1962) suggested that the initial component of the somatosensory response (peaks 1, 2 and 3, Fig. 1) represents potentials in presynaptic thalamocortical fibers of the primary somatosensory projection pathway. They interpreted the succeeding positive component (peak 4, Fig. 1) as the corresponding postsynaptic potential. The next positive component was interpreted as reflecting extralemniscal activity, perhaps mediated by the reticular formation, and later peaks as indicative of nonspecific mechanisms. Subsequent evidence (Domino, Matsuoka, Waltz, and Cooper, 1965; Liberson, 1966) suggests that later response events may also originate in specific pathways. Cigánek (1961) interpreted the events in the first 80 msec of the visual-evoked response (peaks 1, 2, 3, Fig. 2) to be a primary response and the events from 100 to about 220 msec to be a secondary response, perhaps produced by nonspecific pathways. The late rhythmic after-activity (Fig. 2) has been called "ringing" and related to the mechanisms of alpha rhythm production.

There has been a tendency to interpret the early events in sensory evoked responses to be connected with transmission of information into the CNS, and the later events as somehow related to the "processing" of this information. The later events are particularly sensitive to psychological factors.

Amplitudes of evoked response events vary to a greater extent than do latencies. The interpretation of amplitude variations poses some difficulties, because they are determined, to an unknown extent, by nonfunctional factors, such as the thickness of the tissues intervening between the brain and the recording electrode. The variance due to these nonfunctional "neuroanatomical givens" can be minimized by using measurements which depend upon intraindividual relationships. An example of such a measure is the recovery function determination; this depends on the relationship between two responses, elicited by a pair of stimuli (Shagass and Schwartz, 1966).

Since evoked-response wave forms can vary to such a great extent as a function of numerous stimulus parameters, it is not possible to speak of *the* evoked response for any modality. In addition to variations in the nature of the stimuli, the responses recorded will obviously vary also as a function of the degree of sensitivity provided by the recording technique. For example, as usually recorded, auditory-evoked-response events begin with peaks at 30 to 50 msec (P1), followed by negative and positive peaks at 100 msec (N1) and 180 msec (P2). Events beginning about 1.5 msec after auditory clicks, and ranging from 0.5 to 1.5 μV in amplitude, can be recorded with appropriate instrumentation (Jewett, Romano, and Williston, 1970). The rate at which stimuli are presented, i.e., the repetition interval will also determine response characteristics. For example, the components from N1 of the auditory response are attenuated when repetition intervals are less than 6 sec, whereas the earliest components, which probably originate in the eighth nerve and cochlear nucleus, can sustain their amplitude with repetition intervals as fast as 200 msec.

Long-Latency Potentials

The most interesting of these is the potential described by Sutton, Braren, and Zubin (1965) with latency ranging from 300 to 500 msec, positive at the scalp in unipolar recordings. This wave, commonly known as the P3 or P300 wave, appears to be correlated with a degree of uncertainty about the stimulus, and may be elicited by the absence of an expected stimulus (Sutton, Teuting, Zubin, and John, 1967). The P3 wave is of greatest amplitude when the degree of uncertainty about a forthcoming stimulus is greatest; with unvarying stimuli, it is usually not apparent.

Contingent Negative Variation (CNV)

The CNV was described by Walter, Cooper, Aldridge, McCallum, and Winter (1964). It is most commonly recorded in a situation resembling the reaction-time experiment. An alerting or warning signal precedes delivery of an "imperative" signal to which the subject must make some kind of response, such as a button press. The interval between stimuli is usually 1 to 2 sec; a minimum of 0.5 is required for adequate CNV development. A slow potential deviation, negative at the vertex, commences about 200 msec after the alerting stimulus, and continues until the imperative stimulus is delivered and a response made. At that time, there is a precipitous shift back toward the baseline, or positivity. Ordinarily, there is a control condition, in which a similar alerting stimulus, without the same significance for responding, is administered to show absence of CNV. A motor response may not be required to demonstrate CNV; it can be exhibited when a subject anticipates seeing a picture or is instructed to "think" a word after the imperative stimulus (Cohen, 1969).

The CNV may be the most psychologically interesting of all ERP phenomena, but it is also highly subject to artifactual contamination, particularly by EOG and GSR.

FACTORS INFLUENCING EVOKED RESPONSES

Age and Sex

Age and sex differences are described in some detail in the author's monograph (Shagass, 1972b, Chap. 4). Evoked responses are generally of higher amplitude during infancy or childhood and reach their lowest amplitude between the ages of 20 and 40 years, after which amplitude once again increases. The latencies of evoked response peaks are prolonged early in life, decrease as maturation progresses, and tend to increase in later life.

Sex differences are most pronounced in latency measures, which tend to be shorter in females for both visual and somatosensory responses. The shorter somatosensory latency in females is attributable to the shorter average conduction pathway. Recent evidence suggests that, although sex differences in somatosensory response amplitudes are minimal in normal subjects, females have much larger amplitudes than males in the presence of mental illness (Shagass, Overton, and Straumanis, 1972).

Other Factors

Any of all of the factors described earlier as influencing the EEG may modify the characteristics of evoked responses. There are numerous drug effects, and endocrine influences have been demonstrated (Shagass, 1968). Fluctuations in the subject's state of alertness and attention may also be very important (Tecce, 1971). There may be significant variations with time of day (Heninger, McDonald, Goff, and Sollberger, 1969), and responses may differ with handedness (Eason, Groves, White, and Oden, 1967).

INDIVIDUAL DIFFERENCES AND EVOKED RESPONSES

Stability

Studies of stability over periods of months and years have not been reported. However, there is generally good agreement between the wave shapes of average responses recorded hours, days, or weeks apart. Thus, Dustman and Beck (1963) found median correlation coefficients of 0.88 between successive data points of visual-evoked responses recorded with intervening intervals of one week or more. Genetic factors may determine the wave shape, since the median correlation between visual responses of monozygotic twins was 0.82, whereas the medians for unrelated individuals and dizygotic twins, respectively, were 0.37 and 0.58 (Dustman and Beck, 1965). Individual stability of somatosensory and auditory responses is also high.

Evoked Responses and Intelligence

The latencies of later peaks in flash-evoked responses, occurring after about 140 msec, have been found to be correlated with intelligence test scores by several investigators (Chalke and Ertl, 1965; Ertl and Schafer, 1969; Shucard, 1969; Rhodes, Dustman, and Beck, 1969). Although significant, the correlations obtained in large samples were small; the highest was −0.36. Rhodes, Dustman, and Beck (1969) also found that, in flash responses recorded from central areas, components with latencies from 100 to 250 msec were higher in amplitude for bright children. Furthermore, the bright children had greater asymmetry than the dull, with responses from the right hemisphere consistently larger than those from the left.

Personality

In normal subjects, we have found correlations between somatosensory-response amplitude and extraversion, which appeared to be a function of age (Shagass and Schwartz, 1965). In subjects aged 15 to 19, high extraversion was accompanied by high amplitude of the initial components; in subjects aged 40 years or more, high extraversion was accompanied by lower amplitude. In psychiatric patients, somatosensory-response amplitudes were higher in those rated as psychotic than in those rated as neurotic by a set of formalized MMPI scoring rules; amplitudes were also higher in patients who were more field-dependent on the Rod-and-Frame test (Shagass and Canter, 1972). Other somatosensory-response differences between patients with more and less psychopathology on the MMPI were in the same direction as differences between patients and nonpatients.

Buchsbaum and Silverman (1968) have utilized the intensity-response function of flash-evoked responses to obtain an index of individual differences in a postulated factor of "stimulus-intensity control." They have demonstrated correlations between the slope of the intensity-response curve and Petrie's (1967) index of augmenting–reducing which is based on measurement of kinesthetic figural aftereffects. Silverman (1972) has recently reviewed the correlates of the evoked-response augmenting–reducing test.

Among other interesting findings, it appears to discriminate between depressed patients with history of manic attacks (bipolar) and those with depressions only (unipolar). Recent findings in our own laboratory suggest that there is a correlation between evoked-response-augmenting tendency and degree of extraversion.

Psychopathology

The author has reviewed at length the findings in evoked-potential studies of psychiatric patients (Shagass, 1972*b*). The most consistent positive findings have been obtained with measurements of recovery functions and indices of wave-shape stability. In general, amplitude recovery is reduced and there is greater variability, at least of the later part of the wave form, in the presence of severe psychopathology. A number of amplitude differences have also been found, but amplitude measures have given more variable results than the recovery and variability indices. The evoked-response augmenter–reducer tests have also yielded significant differences between clinical groups (Silverman, 1972). The CNV tends to be absent in psychopathic states and reduced in amplitude in schizophrenia, affective psychoses, and in conditions involving anxiety; introduction of a distraction condition produces greater CNV reduction in neurotic patients than in normals (Walter, 1970; McCallum and Walter, 1968; Small and Small, 1972). CNV tends to show a prolonged negativity after the button press in schizophrenics (Timsit, Koninckx, Dargent, Fontaine, and Dongier, 1969).

AWARENESS AND EVOKED RESPONSES

Reduced Awareness

Sensory-evoked responses show remarkable variations during sleep (Figs. 1 and 2). In general, all peak latencies become prolonged and the degree of prolongation is greater in stage IV sleep than in stage I or the REM stage. There is also a tendency for increase in the amplitude of responses, which is illustrated in composite evoked-response graphs in the figures. When the subject is awakened, the latencies of the peaks do not return immediately to those of the presleep waking state. This delayed "awakening" of the evoked responses is associated with subjective reports of "grogginess" (Shagass and Trusty, 1966).

Changes in the later components, which resemble those obtained with sleep, have been recorded in toxic deliria (Brown, Shagass, and Schwartz, 1965) and arteriosclerotic brain syndromes (Straumanis, Shagass, and Schwartz, 1965). Evoked responses become reduced in amplitude, simplified and delayed in coma (Bergamasco, Mombelli, and Mutani, 1966).

Attention and Related Phenomena

Attention has been the favorite psychological variable in ERP studies. There have been several comprehensive reviews (Callaway, 1966; Näätänen, 1967; Tecce, 1971; Dargent and Dongier, 1969; Shagass, 1972b). Several kinds of experimental maneuvers have been employed to direct attention to a stimulus, e.g., to concentrate on stimuli with certain qualities and to disregard others, to respond to some stimuli by pressing a key, hypnotic suggestion to perceive stimuli as weaker or stronger, etc. In addition, much work has been carried out with the reaction-time experiment as a way of focusing attention and obtaining a behavioral measure, i.e., reaction time, to relate to intraindividual variations in evoked-response measurements.

In general, the evidence can be summarized to indicate that the direction of attention to a stimulus tends to result in augmentation of evoked-response amplitude; this occurs in response components that peak at about 100 msec or later. Such augmentation does not seem to be evident in the earliest components. Distraction tends to reduce amplitudes of components that are augmented with directed attention. The issue of selective attention, in the sense of differential responding to one stimulus with active disregard of another, has been critically reviewed by Näätänen (1967). He concluded that the variations in evoked-response amplitude reflect a generalized anticipatory set, rather than a true selective attention, and attributed the positive results of other workers to their failure to randomize the order of stimuli, so that the subjects knew what to expect. He showed that, with randomization, differential effects tended to disappear.

In general, responses evoked by the imperative stimulus in reaction time experiments tend to be greater in amplitude when the reaction time is fastest (Morrell and Morrell, 1966; Shagass, Straumanis, and Overton, 1972). In some subjects, CNV is of greater amplitude with faster reaction times (Hillyard, 1969).

Affective Stimuli

Begleiter, Gross, and Kissin (1967) utilized conditioning procedures to endow previously meaningless figures with emotional significance that was positive, negative, or neutral. Although conditioning occurred without awareness, the visual responses associated with the three affective conditions differed significantly from one another.

Lifshitz (1966) used slides of natural scenes, repulsive medical pictures, and nude female photographs to evoke neutral, negative, and positive affective reactions in male subjects. The evoked-response patterns to the pictorial slides differed from those obtained when the slides were defocused and the responses to the three different categories of pictures differed significantly. Costell, Lunde, Kopell, and Wittner (1972) have shown that CNV can be used to distinguish the sexual interest of subjects. They showed male and female subjects pictures of male nudes, female nudes, and sexually neutral silhouettes. CNV amplitudes were greatest when pictures of the opposite sex were shown.

CONCLUDING DISCUSSION

It should be clear that EEG and ERP phenomena are sensitive to many psychological variables. In this respect, the use of electrophysiological methods in the study of emotional processes obviously offers considerable promise. However, such application of these methods imposes major requirements of technical expertise and care in experimental design. In bringing together the material presented here, I hoped to convey the nature and extent of the problems which beset the investigator in this area of research.

In concluding, it may be worthwhile to draw attention to some important conceptual issues that seem pertinent to electrophysiological investigations of emotional processes.

One issue may be expressed in the following question: Are brain potentials direct indicators of the central mechanisms that mediate emotional processes? Since the electrical signals being measured originate in the brain, there is a natural tendency to interpret them as reflecting the activity of structures in which "vital things happen," to use Grey Walter's phrase (1960). Unfortunately, such a role is not clearly established for the available electrophysiological indicators. In many ways, the brain can be regarded as not just one organ, but as a conglomerate of many organs, each one capable of interacting with the others in complex transactions. The surface potentials, which provide the subject matter of electrophysiology, are the resultant of the interactions of numerous subsystems, from molecular reactions at the synapse to transactions between large aggregates of neurons, which may be relatively distant from one another. The contribution of each subsystem to the surface potential is usually unknown. Recognition of this situation means that brain potentials cannot, a priori, be taken to reflect key central processes. If they have significance, it must be demonstrated experimentally. Even if they are found to be correlated with emotional phenomena, brain potentials could still be reflecting events that are relatively peripheral to the central mechanisms of emotion. That is, they do not necessarily possess more central significance than peripheral indicators, such as heart rate. On the other hand, the central origin of brain potentials does make it *possible* that they *may* reflect central emotional processes in a more direct way than any peripheral indicator.

A second important problem area arises from the fact that brain potentials may undergo major changes in association with many different kinds of psychological activity. As this review indicates, they may vary with alterations in alertness, attention, perception, thinking, imagery, etc., in addition to emotional state. It is almost impossible to design an experimental paradigm which can manipulate emotional reactions without also varying some of these other parameters of behavior. Consequently, the investigator who seeks electrophysiological correlates of emotion is generally confronted with substantial uncertainty about the psychological side of the correlation he has found. In essence, it is difficult to distinguish between the affective and cognitive aspects of behavior without complicated, and perhaps impossible, control experiments.

A third problem connected with the task of establishing correlates of emotion concerns the issue of specificity of emotions. Electrophysiological indicators often seem highly nonspecific, in the sense that the same changes may accompany apparently very different kinds of psychological activity. For example, the alpha rhythms of the EEG may be blocked in association with such diverse events as a change in illumination, performance of mental arithmetic, hearing a joke, or being confronted with a threat of physical injury. Although one may reasonably infer that the emotional aspects of the behavior involved in these examples differ considerably in intensity and kind, their EEG concomitants may be indistinguishable from one another. Such absence of specificity has provided one of the key observations in the development of "arousal theory." However, it should be noted that, in capitalizing on nonspecificity, the concept of central arousal really abandons any attempt to come to grips with distinctions between emotion and other aspects of behavior and between different kinds of emotional behavior. Arousal is assumed to depend on the activation of cortex by subcortical structures, such as the reticular formation, and to provide a functional substrate that makes possible an infinite variety of behavior. In this context, the electrophysiological correlates of arousal can hardly be expected to display a high degree of behavioral specificity.

SUMMARY

The use of electrophysiological methods in research of possible relevance to measurement of emotional processes was reviewed; special attention was directed to the EEG and some aspects of averaged ERPs. Techniques, artifacts, and a variety of subject factors influencing these electrophysiological phenomena were described and discussed in relation to their significance for experimental controls and design. Selected findings concerning individual differences in EEG and evoked potential measurements, and their relation to such variables as intelligence, personality, affective state, and psychiatric disorder were considered.

ACKNOWLEDGMENTS

Partial research support from the U.S. Public Health Service grant MH 12507 is gratefully acknowledged.

REFERENCES

Aserinsky, E., and Kleitman, N. (1955): Two types of ocular motility occurring in sleep, J. Applied Physiol. 8, 1–10.

Baldock, G. R., and Walter, W. G. (1946): A new electronic analyzer, Electronic Eng. 18, 339–344.

Bergamasco, B., Bergamini, L., Mombelli, A. M., and Mutani, R. (1966): Longitudinal study of visual evoked potentials in subjects in posttraumatic coma. Schweiz. Arch. Neurol. Neurochir. Psychiat. 97, 1–10.

Bickford, R. G., Jacobson, J. L., and Cody, D. T. (1964) Nature of average evoked potentials to sound and other stimuli in man, Ann. N.Y. Acad. Sci. 112, 204–223.

Bickford, R. G., Sem-Jacobsen, C. W., White, P. T., and Daly, D. (1952): Some observations on the mechanisms of photic and photo-Metrazol activation, Electroenceph. Clin. Neurophysiol. 4, 275–282.

Brown, J. D. N., Shagass, C., and Schwartz, M. (1965): Cerebral evoked potential changes associated with the Ditran delirium and its reversal in man. In: Recent Advances in Biological Psychiatry, Vol. VII, ed. J. Wortis, pp. 223–234, New York.

Buchsbaum, M., and Silverman, J. (1968): Stimulus intensity control and the cortical evoked response, Psychosom. Med. 30, 12–22.

Burch, N. R., Greiner, T. H., and Correll, E. G. (1955): Automatic analysis of electroencephalogram as an index of minimal changes in human consciousness, Fed. Proc. 14, 23.

Callaway, E. (1966): Averaged evoked responses in psychiatry, J. Nerv. Ment. Dis. 143, 80–94.

Callaway, E., Jones, R. T., and Layne, R. S. (1965): Evoked responses and segmental set of schizophrenia, Arch. Gen. Psychiat. 12, 83–89.

Chalke, F. D. R., and Ertl, J. (1965): Evoked potentials and intelligence. Life Sci. 4, 1319–1322.

Cigánek, L. (1961): The EEG response (evoked potential) to light stimulus in man, Electroenceph. Clin. Neurophysiol. 13, 165–172.

Claridge, G. S., and Herrington, R. N. (1963): An EEG correlate of the Archimedes spiral after-effect and its relationship with personality, Behav. Res. Ther. 1, 217–229.

Cohen, J. (1969): Very slow brain potentials relating to expectancy: The CNV. In: Average Evoked Potentials: Methods, Results and Evaluations, ed. E. Donchin and D. B. Lindsley, pp. 143–163, Washington, D.C.

Costell, R. M., Lunde, D. T., Kopell, B. S., and Wittner, W. K. (1972): Contingent negative variation as an indicator of sexual object preference, Science 177, 718–720.

Dargent, J., and Dongier, M. (1969): Variations Contingentes Négatives, Liège.

Darrow, C. W., and Smith, H. F. (1964): An instrument for automatic scoring of EEG phase relationships, Electroenceph. Clin. Neurophysiol. 16, 614–616.

Davis, H., and Davis, P. A. (1939): Electrical activity of the brain. Its relation to physiological states and to states of impaired consciousness, Res. Publ. Ass. Nerv. Ment. Dis. 19, 50–80.

Dement, W., and Kleitman, N. (1957): Cyclic variations in EEG during sleep and their relation to eye movements, body motility, and dreaming, Electroenceph. Clin. Neurophysiol. 9, 673–690.

Domino, E. F., Matsuoka, S., Waltz, J., and Cooper, I. S. (1965): Effects of cryogenic thalamic lesions on the somesthetic evoked response in man, Electroenceph. Clin. Neurophysiol. 19, 127–138.

Drohocki, Z. (1948): L'integrateur de l'electroproduction cerebrale pour l'electroencephalographie quantitative, Rev. Neurol. 80, 619.

Dustman, R. E., and Beck, E. C. (1963): Long-term stability of visually evoked potentials in man, Science 142, 1480–1481.

Dustman, R. E., and Beck, E. C. (1965): The visually evoked potential in twins, Electroenceph. Clin. Neurophysiol. 19, 570–575.

Eason, R. G., Groves, P., White, C. T., and Oden, D. (1967): Evoked cortical potentials: Relation to visual field and handedness, Science 156, 1643–1646.

Efron, R. (1964): Artificial synthesis of evoked responses to light flash, Ann. N.Y. Acad. Sci. 112, 292–304.

Efron, D. H., Cole, J. O., Levine, J., and Wittenborn, J. R. (1968): Psychopharmacology: A Review of Progress, 1957–1967, Washington, D.C.

Ellingson, R. J. (1954): The incidence of EEG abnormality among patients with disorders of apparently nonorganic origin: A critical review, Amer. J. Psychiat. *111*, 263.

Elliott, R. (1964): Physiological activity and performance: A comparison of kindergarten children with young adults, Psychol. Monogr. *78*, No. 10.

Emde, J. (1964): A time locked low level calibrator, Electroenceph. Clin. Neurophysiol. *16*, 616–618.

Engle, G. L., Romano, J., Ferris, E. G., Webb, J. P., and Stevens, C. D. (1944): A simple method of determining frequency spectra in the electroencephalogram, Arch. Neurol. Psychiat. *51*, 134–146.

Ertl, J. P., and Schafer, E. W. P. (1969): Brain response correlates of psychometric intelligence, Nature *223*, 421–422.

Evans, C. C. (1952): Comments on: Occipital sharp waves responsive to visual stimuli, Electroenceph. Clin. Neurophysiol. *4*, 111.

Fink, M. (1968): EEG classification of psychoactive compounds in man: Review and theory of behavioral associations. In: *Psychopharmacology: A Review of Progress, 1957–1967*, eds., D. Efron, J. Cole, J. Levine, and J. R. Wittenborn, pp. 497–508, Washington, D.C.

Gastaut, H. (1952): Étude électrocorticographique de la réactivité des rythms rolandiques, Rev. Neurol. *87*, 176–182.

Gastaut, H. (1960): Correlations between the electroencephalographic and the psychometric variables (MMPI, Rosenzweig, intelligence tests), Electroenceph. Clin. Neurophysiol. *12*, 226–227.

Gastaut, H., and Broughton, R. (1965): A clinical and polygraph study of phenomena during sleep. In: *Recent Advances in Biological Psychiatry*, ed., J. Wortis, pp. 197–221, New York.

Gastaut, Y. (1953): Les pointes négatives evoquées sur le vertex; leur signification psychophysiologique et pathologique, Rev. Neurol. *89*, 382–399.

Gibbs, E. L., and Gibbs, F. A. (1946): Diagnostic and localizing value of electroencephalographic studies of sleep, Proc. Ass. Res. Nerv. Ment. Dis. *26*, 366–376.

Giblin, D. R. (1964): Somatosensory evoked potentials in healthy subjects and in patients with lesions of the nervous system, Ann. N.Y. Acad. Sci. *112*, 93–142.

Goff, W. R., Rosner, B. S., and Allison, T. (1962): Distribution of cerebral somatosensory evoked responses in normal man, Electroenceph. Clin. Neurophysiol. *14*, 697–713.

Goldstein, L., and Sugerman, A. A. (1969): EEG correlates of psychopathology. In: *Neurobiological Aspects of Psychopathology*, eds., J. Zubin and C. Shagass, pp. 1–19, New York.

Golla, F., Hutton, E. L., and Walter, W. G. (1943): Objective study of mental imagery; physiological concomitants. Appendix on new method of electroencephalographic analysis, J. Ment. Sci. *89*, 216–223.

Gottlober, A. B. (1938): The relationship between brain potentials and personality, J. Exp. Psychol. *22*, 67–74.

Grass, A. M., and Gibbs, F. A. (1938): Fourier transform of the electroencephalogram, J. Neurophysiol. *1*, 521–526.

Harris, J. A., and Bickford, R. G. (1967): Cross-sectional plotting of EEG potential fields, Electroenceph. Clin. Neurophysiol. *23*, 88–89.

Heninger, G. R., McDonald, R. K., Goff, W. R., and Sollberger, A. (1969): Diurnal variations in the cerebral evoked response and EEG: Relations to 17-hydroxycorticosteroid levels, Arch. Neurol. *21*, 330–337.

Henry, C. E. (1944): Electroencephalograms of normal children, Monograph of the Society for Research in Child Development, Serial No. 39, Washington, D.C.

Henry, C. E., and Knott, J. R. (1941): A note on the relationship between "personality" and the alpha rhythm of the electroencephalogram, J. Exp. Psychol. *28*, 362–366.

Hill, D. (1957): Electroencephalogram in schizophrenia. In: *Schizophrenia: Somatic Aspects*, ed., D. Richter, pp. 33–51, London.

Hill, D., and Parr, G. (1963): *Electroencephalography: A Symposium on Its Various Aspects*, New York.

Hillyard, S. A. (1969): The CNV and the vertex evoked potential during signal detection: A preliminary report. In: *Average Evoked Potentials—Methods, Results, and Evaluations*, eds., E. Donchin and E. Lindsley, pp. 349–353, Washington, D.C.

Hoagland, H. (1936): Electrical brain waves and temperature, Science *84*, 139–140.

Itil, T. M., Saletu, B., and Davis, S. (1972): EEG findings in chronic schizophrenics based on digital computer period analysis and analog power spectra, Biol. Psychiat. *5*, 1–13.

Jewett, D. L., Romano, M. N., and Williston, J. S. (1970): Human auditory evoked potentials: Possible brain stem components detected on the scalp, Science *167*, 1517–1518.

Johnson, L. C., and Ulett, G. A. (1959): Stability of EEG activity and manifest anxiety. J. Comp. Physiol. Psychol. *52*, 284–288.

Kales, A. (1969): Sleep: Physiology and Pathology, Philadelphia.

Kennard, M. A. (1965): The EEG in schizophrenia. In: *Applications of Electroencephalography in Psychiatry*, ed., W. P. Wilson, pp. 168–184, North Carolina.

Kennard, M. A., and Schwartzman, A. E. (1956): A longitudinal study of changes in EEG frequency pattern as related to psychological changes, J. Nerv. Ment. Dis. *124*, 8–20.

Kennard, M. A., and Schwartzman, A. E. (1957): A longitudinal study of electroencephalographic frequency patterns in mental hospital patients and normal controls, Electroenceph. Clin. Neurophysiol., *9*, 263–274.

Kennedy, J. L., Gottsdanker, R. M., Armington, J. C., and Gray, F. E. (1948): A new electroencephalogram associated with thinking, Science *108*, 527–529.

Knott, J. R. (1965): Electroencephalograms in psychopathic personality and in murderers. In: *Applications of Electroencephalography in Psychiatry*, ed., W. P. Wilson, pp. 19–29, North Carolina.

Kreezer, G. (1939): Intelligence level and occipital alpha rhythm in the mongolian type of mental deficiency, Amer. J. Psychol. *52*, 503–532.

Kreezer, G. (1940): The relation of intelligence level and the electroencephalogram, Nat. Soc. Study Educ. *39*, part I, 130–133.

Kugelmass, S. (1973): Psychophysiological indices in psychopathological and cross-cultural research. In: *Psychopathology: Contributions from the Social, Behavioral and Biological Sciences*, eds., K. Hammer, K. Salzinger, and S. Sutton, pp. 215–225, New York.

Lehtonen, J. B., and Koivikko, M. J. (1971): The use of a non-cephalic reference electrode in recording cerebral evoked potentials in man, Electroenceph. Clin. Neurophysiol. *31*, 154–156.

Lennox, W. G., Gibbs, F. A., and Gibbs, E. L. (1942): Twins, brain waves and epilepsy, Arch. Neurol. Psychiat. *47*, 702–706.

Liberson, W. T. (1944): Functional electroencephalography in mental disorders, Dis. Nerv. Sys. *5*, 357–364.

Liberson, W. T. (1966): Study of evoked potentials in aphasics, Amer. J. Phys. Med. *45*, 135–142.

Lifshitz, K. (1966): The averaged evoked cortical response to complex visual stimuli, Psychophysiology *3*, 55–68.

Lindsley, D. B. (1939): A longitudinal study of the occipital alpha rhythm in normal children; frequency and amplitude standards. J. Genet. Psychol. *55*, 197–213.

Margerison, J. H., Anderson, W., and Dawson, J. (1964): Plasma sodium and the EEG during the menstrual cycle of normal human females, Electroenceph. Clin. Neurophysiol. *17*, 540–544.

Marjerrison, G., Krause, A. E., and Keogh, R. P. (1967): Variability of the EEG in schizophrenia: Quantitative analysis with a modulus voltage integrator, Electroenceph. Clin. Neurophysiol. *24*, 35.

McCallum, W. C., and Walter, W. G. (1968): The effects of attention and distraction on the contingent negative variation in normal and neurotic subjects, Electroenceph. Clin. Neurophysiol. *25*, 319–329.

Monnier, M., and Rozier, J. (1968): Retinal and cortical evoked responses (ON and OFF) to isoenergetic color stimuli in man. In: *Clinical Value of Electroretinography*, ISCERT Symposium, Ghent, 1966, pp. 95–109, Basel.

Mundy-Castle, A. C., and McKiever, B. L. (1953): The psychophysiological significance of the galvanic skin response, J. Exp. Psychol. *46*, 15–24.

Näätänen, R. (1967): Selective attention and evoked potentials, Ann. Acad. Sci. Fennicae, *151*, 1–226.

Obrist, W. D. (1954): The electroencephalogram of normal aged adults, Electroenceph. Clin. Neurophysiol. *6*, 235–244.

Petrie, A. (1967): *Individuality in Pain and Suffering*, Chicago.

Rhodes, L. E., Dustman, R. E., and Beck, E. C. (1969): The visual evoked response: A comparison of bright and dull children, Electroenceph. Clin. Neurophysiol. *27*, 364–372.

Saul, L. J., Davis, H., and Davis, P. A. (1937): Correlations between electroencephalograms and psychological organization of the individual, Trans. Amer. Neurol. Ass. *63*, 167–169.

Saul, L. J., Davis, H., and Davis, P. A. (1949): Psychologic correlations with the electroencephalogram, Psychosom. Med. *11*, 361–376.

Schwartz, M., Emde, J., and Shagass, C. (1964): Comparison of constant current and constant voltage stimulators for scalp-recorded somatosensory responses, Electroenceph. Clin. Neurophysiol. *17*, 81–83.

Shagass, C. (1946): An attempt to correlate the occipital alpha frequency of the electroencephalogram with performance on a mental ability test, J. Exp. Psychol. *36*, 88–92.

Shagass, C. (1954): The sedation threshold. A method for estimating tension in psychiatric patients, Electroenceph. Clin. Neurophysiol. *6*, 221–233.

Shagass, C. (1955a): Differentiation between anxiety and depression by the photically activated electroencephalogram, Amer. J. Psychiat. *112*, 41–46.

Shagass, C. (1955b): Anxiety, depression and the photically driven electroencephalogram, AMA Arch. Neurol. Psychiat. *74*, 3–10.

Shagass, C. (1967): Effects of LSD on somatosensory and visual evoked responses and on the EEG in man. In: *Recent Advances in Biological Psychiatry*, ed., J. Wortis, pp. 209–227, New York.

Shagass, C. (1968): Pharmacology of evoked potentials in man. In: *Psychopharmacology: A Review of Progress 1957–1967*, eds., D. H. Efron, J. O. Cole, J. Levine, and J. R. Wittenborn, pp. 483–492, Washington, D.C.

Shagass, C. (1972a): Electrical activity of the brain. In: *Handbook of Psychophysiology*, eds., N. S. Greenfield and R. A. Sternbach, pp. 262–328, New York.

Shagass, C. (1972b): *Evoked Brain Potentials in Psychiatry*, New York.

Shagass, C., and Canter, A. (1972): Cerebral evoked responses and psychiatry. In: *Biological Bases of Individual Behavior*, ed., V. D. Nebylitsyn, pp. 111–127, New York.

Shagass, C., and Kerenyi, A. B. (1958): Neurophysiologic studies of personality, J. Nerv. Ment. Dis. *126*, 141–147.

Shagass, C., and Naiman, J. (1955): The sedation threshold, manifest anxiety, and some aspects of ego function, AMA Arch. Neurol. Psychiat. *74*, 397–406.

Shagass, C., and Naiman, J. (1956): The sedation threshold as an objective index of manifest anxiety in psychoneurosis, J. Psychosom. Res. *1*, 49–57.

Shagass, C., Overton, D. A., and Straumanis, J. J. (1971): Evoked response findings in psychiatric illness related to drug abuse, Biol. Psychiat. *3*, 259–272.

Shagass, C., Overton, D. A., and Straumanis, J. J. (1972): Sex differences in somatosensory evoked responses related to psychiatric illness, Biol. Psychiat. *5*, 295–309.

Shagass, C., and Schwartz, M. (1961): Evoked cortical potentials and sensation in man, J. Neuropsychiat. *2*, 262–270.

Shagass, C., and Schwartz, M. (1965): Age, personality and somatosensory evoked responses, Science, *148*, 1359–1361.

Shagass, C., and Schwartz, M. (1966): Somatosensory cerebral evoked responses in psychotic depression, Brit. J. Psychiat. *112*, 799–807.

Shagass, C., and Trusty, D. (1966): Somatosensory and visual cerebral evoked response changes during sleep. In: *Recent Advances in Biological Psychiatry*, ed., J. Wortis, pp. 321–334, New York.

Shucard, D. W. (1969): Relationships among measures of the cortical evoked potential and abilities comprising human intelligence, Ph.D. thesis, University of Denver, Colorado.

Silverman, J. (1972): Stimulus intensity modulation and psychological Dis-Ease, *Psychopharmacologia 24*, 42–80.

Slatter, K. H. (1960): Alpha rhythms and mental imagery, Electroenceph. Clin. Neurophysiol. *12*, 851–859.

Small, J. G., and Small, I. F. (1972): Expectancy wave in affective psychoses. In: *Recent Advances in the Psychobiology of the Depressive Illnesses*, eds., T. A. Williams, M. M. Katz, and J. A. Shield, Jr., pp. 109–118, Washington, D.C.

Spehlmann, R. (1965): The averaged electrical responses to diffuse and to patterned light in the human, Electroenceph. Clin. Neurophysiol. *19*, 560–569.

Stennet, R. G. (1957): The relationship of alpha amplitude to the level of palmar conductance, Electroenceph. Clin. Neurophysiol. *9*, 131–138.

Sternbach, R. A. (1960): Two independent indices of activation, Electroenceph. Clin. Neurophysiol. *12*, 609–611.

Straumanis, J. J., Shagass, C., and Overton, D. A. (1969): Problems associated with application of the contingent negative variation to psychiatric research, J. Nerv. Ment. Dis. *148*, 170–179.

Straumanis, J. J., Shagass, C., and Schwartz, M. (1965): Visually evoked cerebral response changes associated with chronic brain syndrome and aging, J. Gerontology *20*, 498–506.

Sutton, S., Braren, M., and Zubin, J. (1965): Evoked-potential correlates of stimulus uncertainty, Science *150*, 1187–1188.

Sutton, S., Teuting, P., Zubin, J., and John, E. R. (1967): Information delivery and the sensory evoked potential, Science *155*, 1436–1439.

Surwillo, W. W. (1963a): The relation of simple response time to brainwave frequency and the effects of age, Electroenceph. Clin. Neurophysiol. *15*, 105–114.

Surwillo, W. W. (1963b): The relation of response-time variability to age and the influence of brain wave frequency, Electroenceph. Clin. Neurophysiol. *15*, 1029–1032.

Tecce, J. J. (1971): Attention and evoked potentials in man. In: *Attention: Contemporary Theory and Analysis*, ed., D. I. Mostofsky, pp. 331–365, New York.

Thiebaut, F., Rohmer, F., and Wackenheim, A. (1958): Contribution a l'étude electroencephalographique des syndromes endocriniens, Electroenceph. Clin. Neurophysiol. *10*, 1–30.

Timsit, M., Koninckx, N., Dargent, J., Fontaine, O., and Dongier, M. (1969): Étude de la durée des CNV chez un groupe de sujets normaux un groupe de névrosés et un groupe de psychotiques. In: *Variations Contingentes Négatives*, eds., J. Dargent and M. Dongier, pp. 206–214, Liege.

Ulett, G. A., Gleser, G., Winokur, G., and Lawler, A. (1953): The EEG and reaction to photic stimulation as an index of anxiety-proneness, Electroenceph. Clin. Neurophysiol. *5*, 23–32.

Ulett, G. A., Heusler, A. F., and Word, T. J. (1965): The effect of psychotropic drugs on the EEG of the chronic psychotic patient. In: *Applications of Electroencephalography to Psychiatry*, ed., W. W. Wilson, pp. 241–257, North Carolina.

Ulett, J. A., and Itil, T. M. (1969): Quantitative electroencephalogram in smoking and smoking deprivation, Science *164*, 969–970.

Vaughan, H. G. (1969): The relationship of brain activity to scalp recordings of event-related potentials. In: *Average Evoked Potentials*, eds., E. Donchin and D. B. Lindsley, pp. 45–75, Washington, D.C.

Walter, D. O., Rhodes, J. M., Brown, D., and Adey, W. R. (1966): Comprehensive spectral analysis of human EEG generators in posterior cerebral regions, Electroenceph. Clin. Neurophysiol. *20*, 224–237.

Walter, W. G. (1950): In: *Electroencephalography*, eds., D. Hill and G. Parr, Chap. VII, London.

Walter, W. G. (1960): Where vital things happen, Amer. J. Psychiat. *116*, 673–694.

Walter, W. G. (1962): Spontaneous oscillatory systems and alterations in stability. In: *Neural Physiopathology*, ed., R. G. Grenell, pp. 222–257.

Walter, W. G. (1969): In: *Variations Contingentes Négatives*, eds., J. Dargent and M. Dongier, pp. 70–72, Liege.

Walter, W. G. (1970): The contingent negative variation as an aid to psychiatric diagnosis. In: *Objective Indicators of Psychopathology*, eds., M. Kietzman and J. Zubin, New York.

Walter, W. G., Cooper, R., Aldridge, V. J., McCallum, W. C., and Winter, A. L. (1964): Contingent negative variation: An electric sign of sensorimotor association and expectancy in the human brain, Nature *203*, 380–384.

Walter, W. G., and Shipton, H. W. (1951): A new toposcopic display system, Electroenceph. Clin. Neurophysiol. *3*, 281–292.

Wells, C. E. (1963): Electroencephalographic correlates of conditioned responses. In: *EEG and Behavior*, ed., G. H. Glaser, New York.

Werre, P. F. (1957): The relationships between electroencephalographic and psychological data in normal adults, Thesis, University Press., Leiden.

Wilson, W. P. (1965): *Applications of Electroencephalography in Psychiatry*, North Carolina.

Zubek, J. P. (1964): Effects of prolonged sensory and perceptual deprivation, Brit. Med. Bull. *120*, 38–42.

Emotions—Their Parameters and Measurement,
edited by L. Levi.
Raven Press, New York © 1975

Conditioning and Emotion

Joseph V. Brady

Johns Hopkins University School of Medicine, Baltimore, Maryland 21205

Empirical and theoretical accounts of the relationship between conditioning and emotion have continued to maintain a strong conceptual focus upon
the interactions between psychological and physiological processes. Commonly, causal relationships between the two classes of events have been
posited with physiological changes viewed either as consequences of conditioned behavioral responses [the "classical" (Reymert, 1928) approach],
as antecedents of emotional reactions [the James (1884) formulation], or as
the concurrent result with conditioned emotional behavior of some third,
typically neural event [the Cannon (1927) "thalamic" and Lindsley (1951)
"reticular activation" theories]. A more contemporary operational approach
to the analysis of behavioral and physiological participation in emotional
conditioning is suggested by recent experimental confirmations of both
respondent and operant "learning" effects involving a broad range of visceral-autonomic functions. Within the framework of this more parsimonious
view, behavioral and physiological changes in emotional conditioning
emerge as parallel effects controlled by the same environmental stimulus
events, maintaining "causal independence," and conceptualized as interacting but separable components of the "emotion" complex (Brady, 1970*a*,
1971, *this volume*).

The available experimental evidence which bears most directly upon the
validity of this latter formulation has emerged principally from laboratory
animal studies emphasizing endocrine and autonomic participants in the
analysis of emotional conditioning situations (Brady, 1967, 1970*b*; Mason
et al., 1966; Brady et al., 1969, 1971, 1972). The basic laboratory setting
in which these studies have been conducted is illustrated in Fig. 1 and has
been previously described in considerable detail (Mason, 1958; Brady,
1965).

Briefly, the primate restraining chair situation provides for automatic and
programmable delivery of food and water, administration of mildly punishing electric shock to the feet, a hand-operated electromechanical lever
switch, and presentation of a variety of visual and auditory stimuli to the
experimental animal. Blood samples and pressure measurements are obtained through chronically indwelling catheters. Urine samples are collected
in a receptacle attached below the seat of the chair. Programming and con-

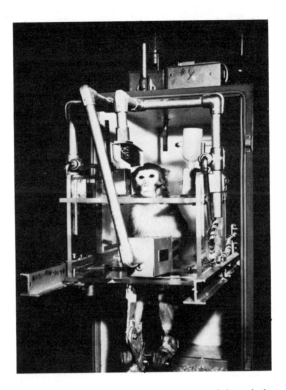

FIG. 1. Rhesus monkey in primate restraining chair.

trol of all behavioral procedures are accomplished remotely and automatically with an electromechanical system of relays, timers, counters, and recorders.

Preliminary studies readily established that neither restraint in the chain following an initial 48-hr adaptation period nor performance of lever pressing for food reward alone on several different schedules of reinforcement produced any significant endocrine or autonomic changes in monkeys maintained for prolonged intervals under such conditions. When, however, emotional conditioning procedures were superimposed upon such performance base lines, significant changes were observed. The basic procedure which provided the focus for these initial studies is a modification of the Estes-Skinner suppression technique (Estes and Skinner, 1941; Hunt and Brady, 1951) and represents a convenient laboratory model for emotional behavior within the operational framework under analysis. Conditioning trials consisting of 5-min continuous presentations of an auditory warning stimulus terminated contiguously with a brief shock to the feet are superimposed upon a lever-pressing performance for an intermittent food reward. Within a few trials, virtually complete suppression of the lever-pressing behavior occurs in response to presentation of the clicker, as illustrated in

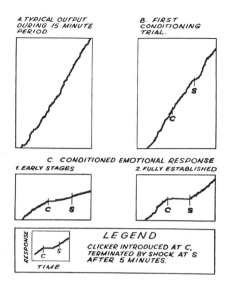

A. TYPICAL OUTPUT DURING 15 MINUTE PERIOD

B. FIRST CONDITIONING TRIAL.

C. CONDITIONED EMOTIONAL RESPONSE
1. EARLY STAGES   2. FULLY ESTABLISHED

LEGEND
CLICKER INTRODUCED AT C,
TERMINATED BY SHOCK AT S
AFTER 5 MINUTES.

FIG. 2. The conditioned emotional behavior as it appears typically in the cumulative response curve.

Fig. 2, accompanied by piloerection, locomotor agitation, and frequently urination and/or defecation.

The development of this conditioned "anxiety" response was first studied in relationship to changes in plasma 17-OH-CS levels occurring during a series of acquisition trials consisting of 30-min lever-pressing sessions with auditory stimulus and shock pairing occurring once during each session approximately 15 min after the start (Mason et al., 1966). Seven such conditioning trials were accompanied by the withdrawal of blood samples immediately before and immediately after each 30-min session and 17-OH-CS levels associated with successive stages in the acquisition of the conditioned emotional behavior were determined. Figure 3 shows the corresponding changes in lever pressing and 17-OH-CS throughout the series of seven conditioning sessions. The progressive suppression of lever pressing in response to presentation of the auditory stimulus during each successive trial is represented by the lower solid line in Fig. 3 in terms of an "inflection ratio" which provides a quantitative measure of the conditioned emotional behavior.[1] The upper broken line in Fig. 3 reflects the progressive

---

[1] The "inflection ratio" is derived from the formula $(B - A)/A$ in which "A" represents the number of lever responses emitted during the 5 min immediately preceding introduction of the auditory stimulus and "B" represents the number of lever responses emitted during the 5-min presentation of the auditory stimulus. The algebraic sign of the ratio indicates whether output increased (plus) or decreased (minus) during the auditory stimulus, relative to the output during the immediately preceding 5-min interval. The numerical value of the ratio indicates the amount of increase or decrease in output as a fraction (percentage in decimal form) of the output prior to introduction of the auditory stimulus. Complete cessation of lever pressing during the auditory stimulus yields a ratio of −1.00, and a 100% increase, a value of plus 1.00. A record showing essentially unchanged output obtains a ratio in the neighborhood of 0.00. The ratio thus indicates whether introduction of the conditioned stimulus produced an inflection in the output curve, how much of an inflection it produced, and in which direction.

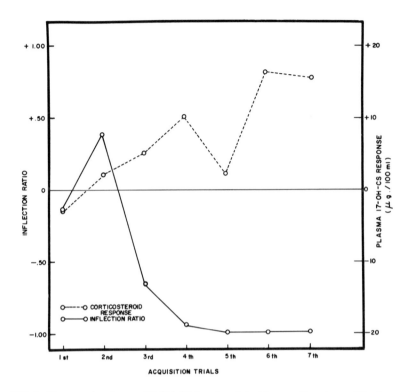

FIG. 3. Changes in plasma 17-OH-CS levels related to emotional conditioning.

increase in 17-OH-CS elevations occurring during each of the seven successive "anxiety" conditioning sessions.

This relationship between emotional behavior and the activity of the pituitary-adrenal cortical system has been further confirmed (Mason et al., 1957) in a series of experiments with monkeys in which the conditioned suppression of lever pressing had been previously established. Five such animals were studied during 1-hr lever-pressing sessions for food reward involving alternating 5-min periods of auditory-stimulus-presentation and no-auditory-stimulus, as illustrated in Fig. 4. Blood samples taken before and after several such experiments with each animal, during which *no* shock followed any of the auditory stimulus presentations, revealed substantial corticosteroid elevations related to the *conditioned* emotional behavior alone. Figure 5 shows that the rate of rise of this behaviorally-induced steroid elevation is strikingly similar to that observed following administration of large ACTH doses in these animals, although such pituitary-adrenal stimulation appears to cease shortly after termination of the emotional interaction, hormonal levels returning to normal within 1 hr. Significantly, when the conditioned "anxiety" response is markedly attenuated by repeated doses of reserpine administered 20 to 22 hr before experimental

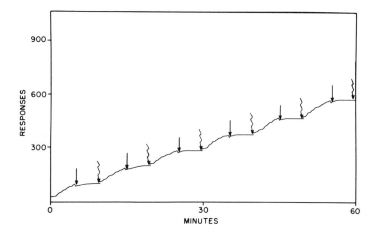

FIG. 4. Cumulative record of lever pressing with superimposed conditioned "anxiety" response in the monkey. The straight arrows indicate the onset, and the jagged arrows the termination of each 5-min clicker period. Between clicker periods the lever-pressing response rate is maintained. During clicker presentations lever pressing is suppressed.

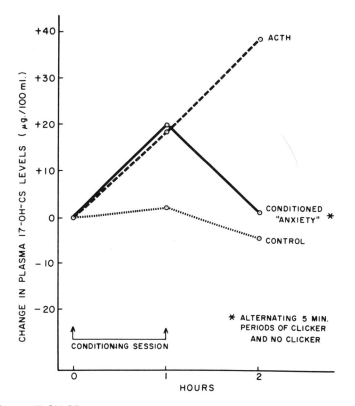

FIG. 5. Plasma 17-OH-CS response in monkeys during conditioned "anxiety" sessions as compared to control sessions and i.v. ACTH (16 mg/kg) injection.

sessions, the elevation of 17-OH-CS in response to the auditory stimulus is also eliminated (Mason and Brady, 1956).

When measurements of plasma epinephrine and norepinephrine levels were added to the corticosteroid determinations in experiments with this conditioned emotional behavior model, the potential contributions of a "hormone pattern" approach to such psychophysiological analyses became evident. Preliminary observations in the course of a rather rudimentary conditioning experiment with monkeys involving a loud truck horn and electrical foot shock suggested the differential participation of adrenal medullary systems in conditioned and unconditioned aspects of such emotional behavior patterns. Figure 7 (Brady, *this volume*)[1] shows, for example, that exposure to the horn or the shock alone *prior* to the conditioned pairing of the two produced only mild elevations in catecholamine levels. Following a series of conditioning trials, however, during which horn-sounding for 3 min was terminated contiguously with shock, presentation of the horn alone markedly increased norepinephrine levels without eliciting any epinephrine response. This hormone pattern approach has been extended in a series of experiments in which concurrent plasma epinephrine, norepinephrine, and 17-OH-CS levels were determined during monkey performance on the alternating 5-min "on"–5-min "off" conditioned "anxiety" response procedure illustrated in Fig. 4. The results summarized in Fig. 8 (Brady, *this volume*) obtained during 30-min control and experimental sessions involving recurrent emotional behavior segments confirm the differential hormone response pattern characterized by marked elevations in both 17-OH-CS and norepinephrine but little or no change in epinephrine levels (Mason et al., 1961c).

Observations of autonomic changes related to this same conditioned emotional stress model have recently been obtained with a series of monkeys catheterized for cardiovascular measurements (Brady, 1967; Brady et al., 1969). Heart rate and both systolic and diastolic blood pressure were recorded continuously during experimental sessions involving both lever pressing alone and exposure to the conditioned "anxiety" procedure. Figure 6 shows the lever-pressing performance, heart rate, and blood pressure values obtained during approximately 9 min of a 1-hr control session prior to emotional behavior conditioning. The stable lever-pressing performance was accompanied by equally stable heart rate and blood pressure values throughout the session. By contrast, Fig. 7 shows the results obtained during an early experimental session following a series of only five conditioning trials involving 3-min presentations of a clicking noise terminated contiguously with foot shock superimposed upon the lever-pressing performance. The complete suppression of lever-pressing during clicker presentation is

---

[1] For this and subsequent figures so marked see Brady, "Toward a Behavioral Biology of Emotion," *this volume.*

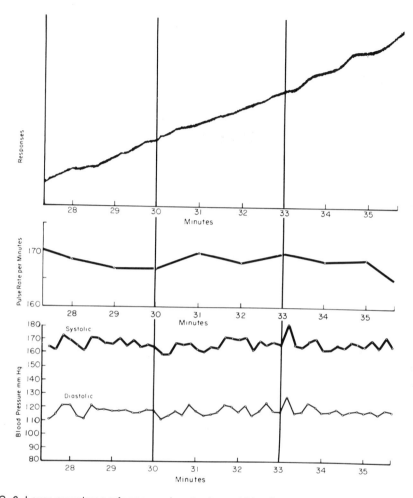

FIG. 6. Lever-pressing performance, heart rate, and blood pressure values during control session prior to emotional conditioning.

accompanied by a dramatic drop in heart rate and by a somewhat less vigorous blood pressure decrease.

Significantly, however, continued pairings of clicker and shock superimposed upon the lever-pressing performance produced abrupt reversals in the direction of these autonomic changes with cardiac acceleration and blood pressure elevation appearing and persisting in response to the clicker during the later stages of emotional conditioning. Figures 9 (Brady, *this volume*) and 8 show the sequence of changes in the form of the autonomic responses for two of a series of five such animals in the course of 50 emotional conditioning trials. Blood pressure, heart rate, and lever-pressing rate for successive conditioning trials are shown as changes during the 3-min

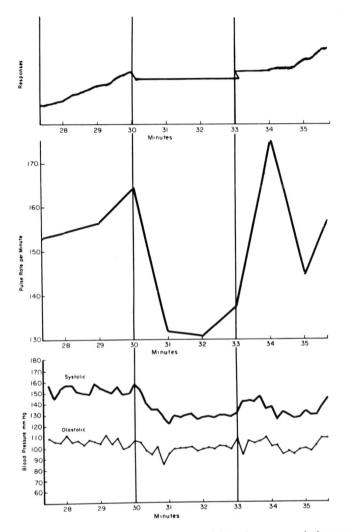

FIG. 7. Changes in lever pressing, heart rate, and blood pressure during conditioned "anxiety" sessions after emotional conditioning.

clicker period as compared to base line values (the "0" point on each graph) representing averages for each measure of the 3-min interval immediately preceding the clicker. The blood pressure and heart rate values are shown as absolute changes in millimeters of mercury and beats per minute, respectively. The lever-pressing values are shown as percent changes in response rate during the clicker as compared to the preclicker base line. Figure 9 (Brady, *this volume*) shows complete cessation of lever pressing during the clicker developing by the third conditioning trial for Monkey A and the maintenance of this behavioral suppression response throughout the entire course of 50 clicker-shock pairings. The autonomic changes can be seen to follow a more varied but nonetheless systematic course during this acquisition phase with Monkey A. A marked deceleration in heart rate first appeared during presentation of the clicker on the third conditioning trial corresponding to the initial development of complete behavioral suppression. During the next four trials, a similar decelerative change in heart rate accompanied the behavioral response with little or no change apparent in either diastolic or systolic blood pressure. During the eighth conditioning trial, however, an abrupt change in the direction of the cardiac response to the clicker was reflected in both heart rate and blood pressure measures. Increases in heart rate approximating 40 beats per minute developed in response to the clicker by the 10th conditioning trial and persisted throughout the remainder of the 50 acquisition trials. Both systolic and diastolic blood pressure showed correspondingly consistent and dramatic elevations in response to the clicker developing between the eighth and 10th conditioning trial and persisting through trial 50. Figure 8 shows a similar behavioral and autonomic response pattern for Monkey B during acquisition of the conditioned emotional response. Development of complete behavioral suppression by trial 4 is accompanied by the decelerative change in heart rate which appears repeatedly in response to the clicker through trial 7. Again, only minimal changes in blood pressure could be discerned during these early pairings of clicker and shock. And on trial 9, the cardiac accelerative response emerged precipitously in response to the clicker, persisting in the form of substantial elevations in both blood pressure and heart rate on succeeding acquisition trials.

When the conditioned "anxiety" response was extinguished by repeated presentations of clicker alone without shock during daily lever-pressing sessions with such animals following extended exposure to recurrent emotional conditioning of this type, a further divergence between autonomic and behavioral response to emotion was observed. Figure 10 (Brady, *this volume*) illustrates this characteristic difference in extinction rates for the cardiovascular and instrumental components of the conditioned emotional response with Monkey B. Although virtually complete recovery of the lever-pressing rate in the presence of the clicker can be seen to have occurred within 10 such extinction trials, both heart rate and blood pressure elevations in response to the clicker alone persisted well beyond the 40th extinction trial. Finally, reconditioning of the "anxiety" response with this same animal, as shown in Fig. 9, rapidly produced behavioral suppression accompanied immediately by the tachycardia and pressor responses. Significantly, the initial cardiac decelerative response characteristic of the early trials, during the original emotional conditioning, failed to appear during reconditioning with any of the animals.

The experimental approaches thus far described to the psychophysiological analysis of conditioning and emotion have emphasized *suppressive*

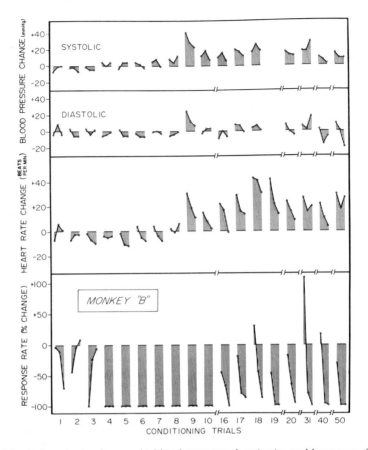

FIG. 8. Minute-by-minute changes in blood pressure, heart rate, and lever-pressing rate for Monkey B on successive 3-min clicker-shock trials during acquisition of the conditioned emotional response. The zero points represent control values calculated from the 3-min interval immediately preceding the clicker.

effects upon behavior. Under other conditions, however, a prominent consequence of such emotional conditioning is an increase in the frequency of avoidance behavior. The conditioned avoidance model that has provided the basis for extensive experimental analysis in this area has been described in previous reports on the psychophysiology of emotional behavior (Mason et al., 1957; Sidman et al., 1962; Sidman, 1953; Brady, 1965). Briefly, the basic procedure involves programming shocks to the feet of the monkey in the primate chair every 20 sec unless the animal presses the lever within that interval to postpone the shock another 20 sec. This avoidance requirement generates a stable and durable lever-pressing performance (illustrated in Fig. 10) which has been shown to be consistently associated with twofold to fourfold rises in corticosteroid levels for virtually all animals during 2-hr

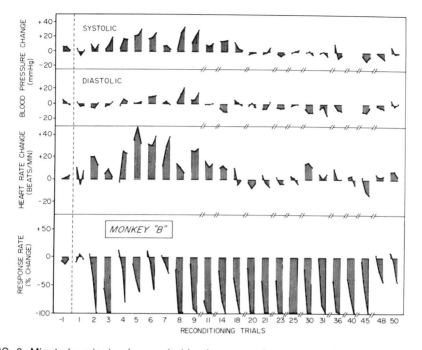

FIG. 9. Minute-by-minute changes in blood pressure, heart rate, and lever-pressing response rate for Monkey B on the last extinction trial (far left section) and on successive 3-min clicker-shock trials during reacquisition of the conditioned emotional response. The zero points represent control values calculated from the 3-min interval immediately preceding the clicker.

experimental sessions, as shown in Fig. 11, even in the absence of any shock (Mason et al., 1957; Brady, 1962, 1966). It has also been possible to demonstrate quantitative relations between the rate of avoidance responding in the monkey and the level of pituitary-adrenal cortical activity independently of the shock frequency (Sidman et al., 1962). Marked differences in the hormone response have been observed, however, when the avoidance procedure includes a discriminable exteroceptive warning signal presented 5 sec prior to administration of the shock whenever 15 sec had elapsed since the previous response. Figure 14 (Brady, *this volume*) compares the 17-OH-CS levels measured during "regular" and "discriminated" avoidance sessions with the monkey and shows the consistently reduced corticosteroid response associated with programming such a warning signal. Conversely, superimposing so-called "free" or unavoidable shocks upon a well-established avoidance base line without a warning signal has been observed to produce marked elevations in 17-OH-CS. Figure 15 (Brady, *this volume*), for example, shows that the presentation of such "free shocks" during 2-hr avoidance sessions more than doubles the corticosteroid response as compared to the regular nondiscriminated avoidance procedure.

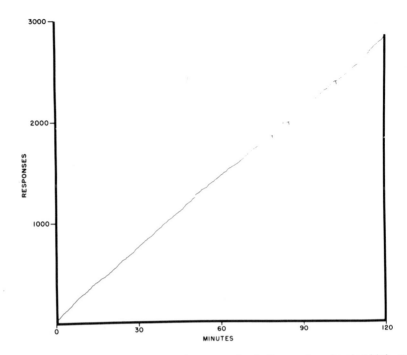

FIG. 10. Cumulative record of avoidance lever pressing in the monkey showing high, stable rate of approximately 1,500 responses/hr. The three small vertical marks on the cumulative record indicate the occurrence of shocks when 20 sec elapsed between lever responses.

   Concurrent biochemical measurements of plasma corticosteroid and catecholamine levels have also been made in the course of several avoidance experiments with the monkey and the results illustrated in Figure 13 (Brady, *this volume*) confirm the previously described emotional conditioning pattern of 17-OH-CS and norepinephrine elevations with no significant alteration in epinephrine levels. Two experimental manipulations involving the avoidance procedure, however, have been observed to produce significant variations in this hormone pattern. Figure 17 (Brady, *this volume*), for example, shows at least a modest epinephrine elevation with no change in norepinephrine accompanying presentation of the avoidance signal to a well-trained avoidance monkey following removal of the response lever from the restraining chair. Significantly, the effect occurred within 1 min of the signal presentation and could not be observed following 10 min of continued exposure. The results obtained with the second series of experiments involving such variations in catecholamine levels are illustrated in Fig. 16 (Brady, *this volume*) which shows the effects of "free shock" administration to a monkey at different stages in the course of avoidance training. The mild norepinephrine and epinephrine elevations shown at the left side of Fig. 16

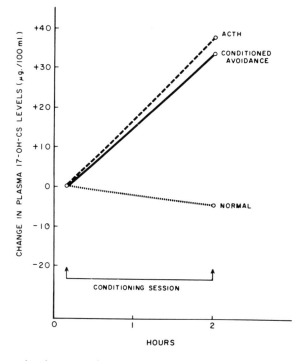

FIG. 11. Changes in plasma 17-OH-CS during 2-hr avoidance performance. The heavy dotted line labeled ACTH shows the rate of steroid rise over a 2-hr period following only one i.v. injection of 16 mg/kg ACTH. The heavy solid line labeled conditioned avoidance compares the rate of steroid elevation during a 2-hr exposure to the shock avoidance contingency with the ACTH response and the normal levels for a similar 2-hr control period represented by the smaller dotted line in the lower portion of the figure.

were obtained during an early conditioning session involving more than 100 "free shocks" before the monkey had acquired the avoidance behavior. The middle section of Fig. 16 shows the modest rise in norepinephrine levels with no change in epinephrine which accompanied later experimental sessions involving performance of the well-learned avoidance response. Finally, the right side of Fig. 16 shows the results of a series of experiments in which "free" or unavoidable shocks were programmed at the rate of one per minute (approximately, the shock frequency occurring during a typical avoidance session) with this same monkey. Significantly, dramatic elevations in both epinephrine and norepinephrine can be seen to have accompanied this procedural change even though the animal received no more shocks than during previous regular avoidance sessions.

In experiments involving more complex sequences of emotional behavior patterns with the monkey as well, it has been possible to observe differential changes in catecholamine levels under specific conditions. Figure 12, for example, summarizes the results obtained in an experiment during which

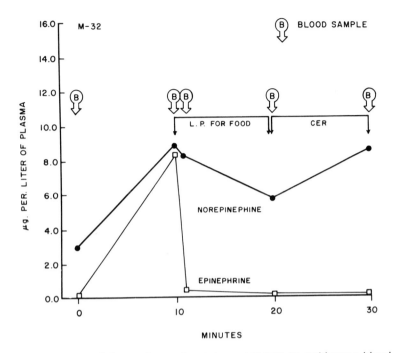

FIG. 12. Plasma epinephrine and norepinephrine responses to ambiguous blood-with-drawal signal.

the withdrawal of a blood sample 10 min prior to the start of a session produced marked elevations in both epinephrine and norepinephrine. In the course of previous conditioning trials, several different combinations of lever pressing for food alone, clicker-shock pairing alone, and both lever pressing and clicker-shock pairing concurrently (the conditioned "anxiety" procedure) had been randomly programmed in such a way that the blood-withdrawal signal could not be predictably associated with any specific component of the sequence. Under these somewhat ambiguous circumstances both epinephrine and norepinephrine levels rose significantly during the 10 min preceding the programmed session although epinephrine levels fell precipitously immediately after presentation of the first specific lever-pressing signal. In a similar experiment, illustrated in Fig. 13 involving randomly programmed 10-min component segments of "time out" (SΔ), the shock avoidance procedure described above, and a conditioned "punishment" or "conflict" situation which provided for the production of shock by each lever response emitted in the presence of a specific auditory stimulus, extremely large epinephrine and norepinephrine responses were again observed during the initial 10-min "time out" component prior to the unpredictable onset of a specifically conditioned emotional behavior signal. Interestingly, both epinephrine and norepinephrine levels can be seen to

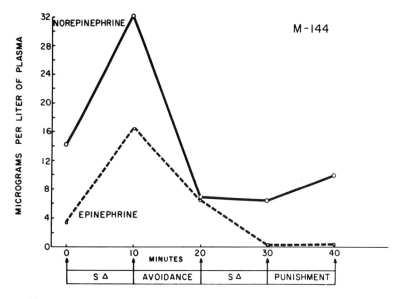

FIG. 13. Plasma epinephrine and norepinephrine responses to randomly programmed components of a multiple schedule conditioning procedure.

decline again after presentation of the first specific signal even though in this case it required participation in a shock avoidance task.

Extended exposure to continuous 72-hr avoidance sessions has recently provided the setting for an analysis of a broader spectrum of hormonal changes in relationship to emotional behavior in the rhesus monkey (Mason et al., 1961a,b,c, 1968). The pattern of corticosteroid and pepsinogen changes observed before, during, and after such a continuous 72-hr avoidance experiment, for example, is shown in Fig. 14. Although plasma 17-OH-CS levels showed the expected substantial elevation throughout the 72-hr avoidance session, plasma pepsinogen levels were consistently depressed below base line values during this same period. The postavoidance recovery period, however, was seen to have been characterized by a marked and prolonged elevation of pepsinogen levels which endured for several days beyond the 48-hr postavoidance interval required for recovery of the preavoidance corticosteroid base line. The consequences of repeated exposure to such continuous 72-hr avoidance stress over extended periods up to and, in some cases, exceeding 1 year upon patterns of thyroid, gonadal, and adrenal hormone secretion have been the focus of studies with a series of five chair-restrained rhesus monkeys (Brady, 1965). Two of the five monkeys participated in the 72-hr avoidance experiment on six separate occasions over a 6-month period with an interval of approximately 4 weeks intervening between each exposure. The remaining three animals performed on a schedule which repeatedly programmed 72-hr avoidance cycles

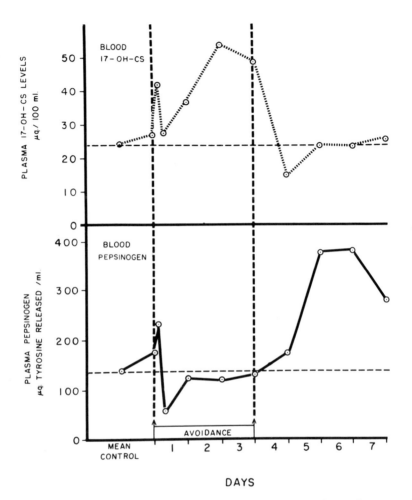

FIG. 14. Mean blood levels of 17-OH-CS and pepsinogen during 72-hr continuous avoidance sessions.

followed by 96-hr nonavoidance or "rest" cycles (3 days "on" and 4 days "off") for periods up to and exceeding 1 year.

The two animals exposed to repeated 72-hr avoidance at monthly intervals for 6 months showed a progressively increasing lever-pressing response rate for each of the six successive 72-hr avoidance sessions, as illustrated in Fig. 15. During the initial 72-hr avoidance experiment with these two animals response rates averaged 16 and 18 responses/min, respectively. Response rate values for these same monkeys during the sixth 72-hr avoidance experiment averaged 28 and 27 responses/min. In contrast, shock frequencies over this same period showed a sharp decline within the first two 72-hr avoidance sessions and remained at a stable low level (not ex-

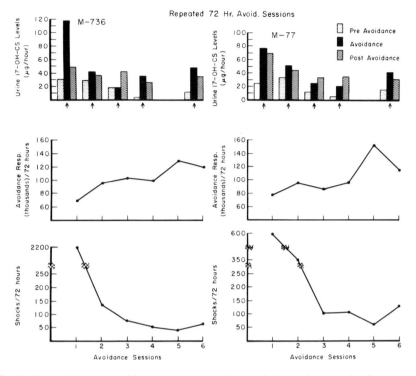

FIG. 15. Steroid levels, avoidance response rates, and shock frequencies for animals M-736 and M-77 during six monthly 72-hr avoidance sessions.

ceeding two shocks per hour for either animal) for the remaining four 72-hr avoidance cycles. Hormone changes related to the repeated 72-hr avoidance cycle showed consistent and replicable patterns over the 6-month experimental period for both animals. During the initial experimental sessions, as shown in Fig. 15, both monkeys showed approximately threefold elevations in 17-OH-CS levels during 72-hr avoidance and returned to near base line levels about 6 days afterward. The remaining four monthly experiments were characterized by substantial, although diminished steroid responses (approximately twofold elevations in 17-OH-CS levels) during avoidance with essentially the same 6-day period required for recovery of basal levels. Significant changes related to the extended avoidance performance were also observed in catecholamine, gonadal, and thyroid hormone levels with recovery cycles extending in some instances (thyroid) for 3 weeks following the 72-hr avoidance period (Mason et al., 1968).

The three remaining monkeys required to perform on the 3 days "on"–4 days "off" avoidance schedule showed an initial increase in lever-pressing response rates for approximately the first 10 avoidance sessions similar to that seen with the two animals described above. By approximately the 19th weekly session with these animals, however, lever-pressing response rates during the 72-hr avoidance period had decreased to a value well below that observed during the initial avoidance sessions, and the performance tended to stabilize at this new low level for the ensuing weeks of the experiment. In contrast, shock frequencies for all animals quickly approximated a stable low level within the first two of three exposures to the avoidance schedule and seldom exceeded a rate of two shocks per hour for the remainder of the experiment. Typically, for example, Monkey M-157 exposed to this program for some 65 weekly sessions, as illustrated in Fig. 21 (Brady, *this volume*), showed an average response rate of 23 responses/min during the initial 72-hr avoidance session, 32 responses/min during the 10th avoidance session, 19 responses/min during the 20th avoidance session, and 16, 20, and 19 responses/min during the 30th, 40th, and 50th weekly avoidance sessions respectively. The initial 72-hr avoidance sessions characterized by progressive increases in lever-pressing rate were invariably accompanied by elevations in the 17-OH-CS levels. By the 20th weekly avoidance-rest cycle, however, steroid levels had dropped below initial basal values, and no elevation in response to the 72-hr avoidance performance could be observed. By the 30th weekly session, 17-OH-CS levels had returned to their pre-experimental basal values but continued exposure to the 3-day "on"–4-day "off" schedule failed to produce any further steroid elevations in response to the 72-hr avoidance requirement up through the 65th experimental session. Figure 21 (Brady, *this volume*) also reflects the fact that following initial adjustments during the early sessions of the program, shock frequencies remained at a stable low level and normal food and water intake was maintained essentially unchanged throughout the extended course of the experiment.

The general pattern obtained with M-157 has been replicated with only minor variations in the two additional animals completing 56 and 46 weeks respectively on this same experimental program. The change in responsivity of the pituitary-adrenal system to the avoidance stress with continued exposure to this procedure over extended time periods is perhaps the most consistent and striking observation in all three monkeys and is somewhat at variance with repeated findings in many previous acute studies of a close positive relationship between steroid elevations and avoidance performance. These most recent findings, however, indicate that continued exposure to this repeated performance requirement on the time schedule programmed in this experiment produces an apparent dissociation between the avoidance behavior and the 17-OH-CS response to such emotional conditioning.

Similar divergencies involving autonomic response patterns related to aversive and appetitive behavioral conditioning procedures have been observed most recently in the course of both acute and chronic psychophysiological studies emphasizing continuous cardiovascular monitoring with dogs and baboons. The free-operant performance required of the dogs in these experiments (Anderson and Brady, 1971, 1972, 1973*a,b;* Anderson and Tosheff, 1973) was a panel press either to avoid shock or to obtain food in the specially designed restraint harness and isolation chamber (Anderson et al., 1970) shown in Fig. 16. Blood pressure and heart rate were monitored continually through chronically indwelling femoral artery catheters during a 1-hr interval before and a 2-hr interval during the panel pressing perform-

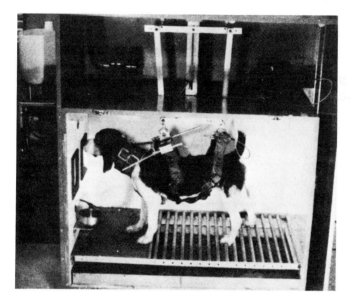

FIG. 16. Restraint harness and experimental chamber for the laboratory dog.

ance for either food or shock avoidance. Figure 18 (Brady, *this volume*) compares the concurrent changes in blood pressure and heart rate during the pre-avoidance and avoidance performances (left panel) with the concurrent changes in blood pressure and heart rate during the pre-food and food performance periods (right panel). Figure 18 (Brady, *this volume*) shows consecutive 10-min interval averages and summarizes the stable response pattern which characterized the 27 avoidance sessions on the one hand, and the 30 food sessions on the other. Progressive elevations in both systolic and diastolic blood pressure accompanied by progressive *decelerations* in heart rate were consistently observed during the preavoidance hour, while progressive increases in both heart rate and blood pressure characteristically occurred during the pre-food hour.

That these pre-performance group differences were in fact representative of the observed individual animal effects of these procedures and not related to the topography of the respective performances is illustrated in Fig. 19 (Brady, *this volume*) which shows the changes in blood pressure and heart

rate during successive exposures to both aversive and appetitive conditioning with the same dog. The left panel shows the 10-min interval averages
for blood pressure, heart rate, and panel pressing responses associated
with 10 initial avoidance sessions. The middle panel shows the changes
observed during 10 food sessions following the avoidance series, and, finally,
the right panel shows the reversal in the cardiovascular response pattern
that accompanied a single avoidance session following the food series.
Significantly, the pre-performance and performance response rates shown
in the bottom section of each panel confirm that the aversive and appetitive
conditioning situations could not be differentiated on the basis of these
behavioral characteristics alone. Of particular interest, of course, is the
divergent and sustained change in blood pressure and heart rate consistently
observed during the pre-avoidance interval. Recently, we have found that
this divergent pattern can be sustained for at least 15 hr under conditions
that generate extended delays during the pre-avoidance interval before
onset of the required shock-avoidance performance. Figure 17, for example,

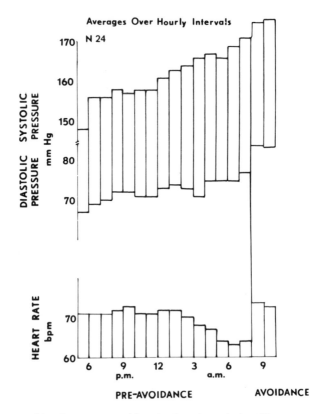

FIG. 17. Average blood pressure and heart rate values during 15 consecutive 1-hr pre-
avoidance intervals followed by two consecutive 1-hr avoidance intervals for 24 terminal
sessions.

illustrates these progressive changes in blood pressure and heart rate in the form of consecutive 1-hr interval averages for 24 sessions taken from the experimental records of three dogs during a 15-hr pre-performance interval followed by the required 2-hr shock-avoidance performance.

Distinguishable cardiovascular response patterns have also been observed in a series of chair-restrained laboratory baboons (Findley et al., 1971*b*) studied over extended periods during exposure to topographically similar aversive and appetitive behavioral conditioning procedures (Findley et al., 1971*a;* Brady et al., 1971, 1972; Brady, 1974). The baboons were monitored for more than 1 year in an experiment involving continuous recording of heart rate and both systolic and diastolic blood pressure through indwelling femoral artery catheters during shock-avoidance and food-reinforced performances within the context of a 24-hr behavior program which provided scheduled rest and sleep periods. The sequence and duration of continuously programmed behavioral events are summarized in Fig. 18. Three successive 8-hr cycles were repeated once each 24 hr with differently colored lights signaling each major activity. Beginning at 10 A.M. each day, a white light was presented for 40 min in the presence of which each block of 150 responses (FR 150) on the lever manipulandum produced six 1-g food pellets. Repetition of this 40-min food cycle on three separate occasions during each 24-hr period provided the total daily ration for the baboons.

DAILY   PROGRAM   OF   ACTIVITIES

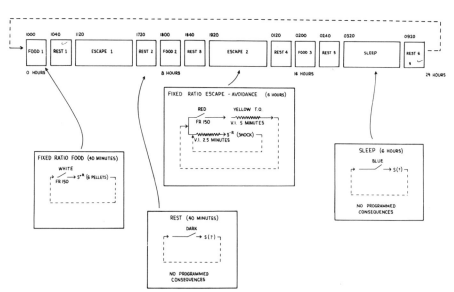

FIG. 18. Sequence of activities comprising the 24-hr behavior program.

The escape-avoidance procedure remained in effect for 6 continuous hr on two occasions during each 24-hr period. The onset of this activity cycle was signaled by a red light which reappeared intermittently on the average of once every 5 min. In the presence of the red light, shocks (10 mA for 0.25 sec) were programmed randomly on the average of once every 2.5 min independently of the animal's lever responding. Completion of 150 responses (FR 150) on the lever produced a "safe" period of variable duration (average 5 min) signaled by a yellow light. The yellow light was terminated by the reappearance of the red light signaling onset of the next escape-avoidance trial. Delivery of the independently programmed shocks occasionally occurred before the animal could complete the required FR 150 to terminate the red light and such shock delivery was accompanied by a brief flash of a separate white stimulus light. Under these conditions, however, the baboons maintained a high steady rate of lever responding which avoided all but a few shocks in the presence of the red light throughout the two 6-hr escape-avoidance intervals each day. The third 6-hr interval beginning at 3:30 A.M. each morning was provided for a sleep activity signaled by a blue light in the presence of which no contingencies were programmed. As indicated in Fig. 18, rest periods of a constant 40min duration, signaled by darkness of the work panel, were interspersed between the end of the one major activity (i.e., food, escape-avoidance, sleep) and the beginning of the next. No contingencies were programmed during these recycling rest intervals.

Both the escape-avoidance and food segments of the behavioral program generated high response rates on the required fixed ratio schedule which were topographically similar in all essential respects, as illustrated in Fig. 19. Comparisons of the acute cardiovascular changes occurring during the escape-avoidance activity with those recorded during food and sleep activities, however, revealed dramatic differences. Figure 20 (Brady, *this volume*) shows typical polygraph recordings of blood pressure and heart rate during intervals of escape-avoidance and food-maintained responding. Figure 20 (Brady, *this volume*) compares the acute changes in blood pressure and heart rate observed during an escape-avoidance performance (top panel) for one of the baboons (Sport) with those recorded during a topographically similar food-maintained performance (bottom panel) for the same animal. Although identical performance requirements (Fr 150) were programmed (top pen, each panel), the elevations in blood pressure during escape-avoidance (approximately 40 mm Hg for both systolic and diastolic, as shown on the middle pen, top panel) contrasted sharply with the more modest increases recorded during the food performance (approximately 10 to 20 mm Hg, as shown on the middle pen, bottom panel). Similarly, acute elevations in heart rate approximating 40 beats/min or more accompanied onset of escape-avoidance responding (bottom pen, top panel) while virtually no heart rate change can be observed during food activity (bottom

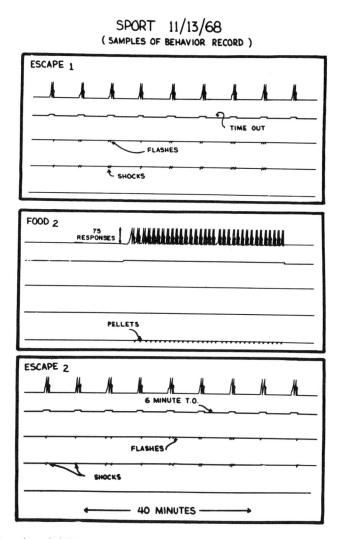

FIG. 19. Samples of daily cumulative records from "escape" and "food" portion of the program for baboon "Sport."

pen, bottom panel). Over the extended course of the experiment, literally thousands of such comparisons confirm the differential cardiovascular effects of the aversively and appetitively maintained components of this program.

Acute changes in blood pressure and heart rate of considerable interest have also been consistently observed *within* the escape-avoidance activity and in comparison with other activities. In terms of mean pressures and heart rate, highest values were generally found in escape-avoidance, lower in food, and still lower in sleep. Blood pressure and heart rate were consistently elevated during escape-avoidance in comparison with other activities, however. Specifically, with the onset of the red light, and as the animal began responding on the fixed ratio requirement, blood pressure typically rose at least 30 to 40 mm Hg and heart rate rose on the order of 60 to 80 beats/min. These acute elevations in pressure and heart rate were both reliable and clearly not directly dependent upon the delivery of electric shocks. Following completion of a typical escape from the red light, the pressure declined abruptly, predominately showing a greater decline in diastolic, and hence an increased pulse pressure. Systolic pressure, after this initial drop, generally remained stable, while diastolic gradually increased on the order of 15 to 20 mm Hg as the heart rate continued to decline to the minimum resting level found during the "safe" period. This divergence from the more usually observed positively correlated changes in blood pressure and heart rate was consistently found in both animals, and has been tentatively interpreted as reflecting peripheral changes in the cardiovascular system mediated by the central nervous system. Sample recordings illustrating these changes are shown in Fig. 20. Both the avoidance experiments

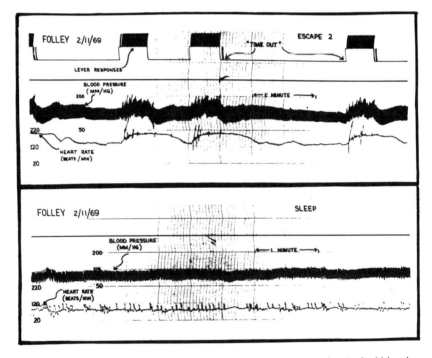

FIG. 20. Sample polygraph recording for baboon "Folley" contrasting typical blood pressure and heart rate changes during escape activity (top) with typical levels during sleep (bottom).

with dogs and these observations with baboons, indicate clearly that the divergent changes in blood pressure and heart rate are related directly to the programmed interaction contingencies, although the topographic features of the behavioral performance *per se,* may not reflect these differential psychophysiological (emotional?) response patterns.

Additional evidence for the direct influence of environmental stimulus events upon physiological response patterns characteristically associated with emotional conditioning has been developed most recently in studies of instrumental visceral-glandular learning (Miller, 1969). Significantly, the results of several experiments with both animals and men have now demonstrated that the arrangement of explicit and direct relationships between selected autonomic responses (e.g., heart rate, blood pressure) on the one hand, and the occurrence of specific environmental consequences (e.g., food-reward, shock-avoidance) on the other, can produce systematic and reliable modifications in such physiological functions (Engel and Hansen, 1966; Engel and Chism, 1967; Miller and DiCara, 1967; Plumlee, 1969; Engel and Melmon, 1968; DiCara and Miller, 1968; Benson et al., 1969; Shapiro et al., 1970; Miller et al., 1970; DiCara, 1970; Schwartz et al., 1971; Harris et al., 1971; Weiss and Engel, 1971; Schwartz, 1972). Many of the visceral-autonomic changes reported in these studies were, of course, limited in both magnitude and duration, and numerous theoretical questions have been raised concerning the role of "voluntary mediators" (e.g., respiratory and skeletal responses) in the development and maintenance of such operant physiological conditioning effects (Katkin and Murray, 1968). Recent studies in our own laboratories within the framework of this contingent model have succeeded in extending the limits of such instrumental psychophysiological procedures, however, and the results can be seen to bear importantly upon the issue of direct environmental-physiological interactions in emotional conditioning.

Chair-restrained baboons (Findley et al., 1971*a*) have served as the subjects of these experiments investigating the effects of food-reward and shock-avoidance programmed as direct environmental consequences contingent upon changes in diastolic blood pressure. Four animals were surgically prepared with indwelling femoral artery catheters and initially trained, using an operant "shaping" procedure to raise and maintain elevated diastolic blood pressure levels as high as 125 mm Hg for at least several seconds or minutes (Harris et al., 1971). Environmental stimulus changes were programmed to establish an environment in which elevated diastolic blood pressure was rewarded by both food delivery and absence of shock. Pressure levels below the specified criterion level, on the other hand, produced no food and occasionally resulted in shock. During the experiment, the duration of the interval during which the elevated blood pressure requirement was in effect increased systematically, and Fig. 21 shows a sample of four typical polygraph recordings for one baboon illustrating character-

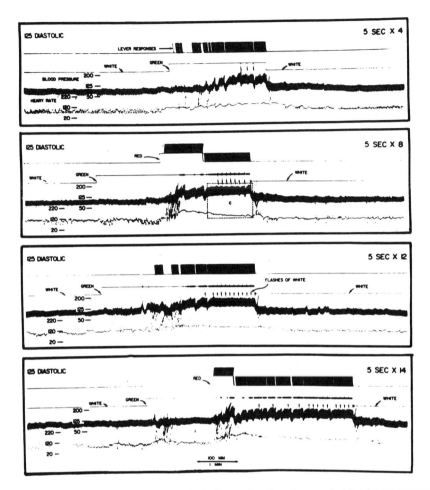

FIG. 21. Sample polygraph recordings for baboon showing changes in blood pressure and heart rate responses to four progressively higher contingency unit requirement conditions.

istically elevated blood pressure responses (125 mm Hg diastolic) during progressively longer intervals up to 60 sec and beyond. The results of this initial experiment showed clearly that substantial elevations in blood pressure could be established and maintained in baboons by operant conditioning procedures over relatively short time intervals. Under these conditions, both systolic and diastolic blood pressure levels were observed to increase 50 to 60 mm Hg above resting levels and to remain elevated for intervals up to 5 min or longer.

A subsequent study (Harris et al., 1973), currently being extended, has involved the programming of continuous 12-hr periods during which the animals are required to maintain elevated diastolic blood pressure levels in order to avoid shock and obtain food. These 12-hr "conditioning on" periods alternate with a 12-hr "conditioning off" rest period each 24 hr, and two feedback lights signal to the baboons when the diastolic blood pressure is either above or below the prescribed criterion level. More specifically, the concurrent food-reward and shock-avoidance procedure is programmed as follows. Five 1-g food pellets are delivered to the animal for every 10 min of accumulated time that the diastolic blood pressure remains above criterion level. Conversely, the animal receives a 10 mA, 0.25 sec electric shock for every 30 sec that the diastolic blood pressure falls below the criterion level. Additionally, each food reward delivery resets the shock timer (thus providing an additional 30 sec of accumulated shock-free time), and each occurrence of an electric shock resets the food timer (thus postponing the delivery of food for at least an additional 10 min of accumulated time). Initially, the criterion diastolic blood pressure was determined by the animal's pre-experimental resting base line level (approximately 75 mm Hg) with progressive increases programmed to occur at a rate approximating 5 mm Hg per week over a period of 6 to 8 weeks. Within that 1- to 2-month interval, all four baboons were maintaining diastolic blood pressure levels above 100 mm Hg for better than 95% of each daily 12-hr "conditioning on" period.

Figure 22 compares the concurrent changes in blood pressure and heart rate during the 12-hr "conditioning on"–12-hr "conditioning off" periods

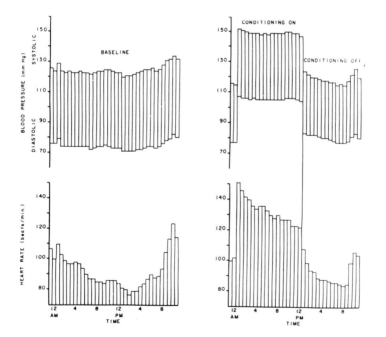

FIG. 22. Average blood pressure and heart rate values during consecutive 40-min intervals during pre-experimental base line determinations (left) compared with 12-hr "conditioning on" – 12-hr "conditioning off" sessions (right).

with the concurrent changes in blood pressure and heart rate during the pre-conditioning base line period. The data plot in Fig. 22 is in the form of averages for three to five consecutive 24-hr experimental conditioning sessions (right panel) for each of the four baboons (i.e., 16 total sessions) and three to five consecutive 24-hr pre-experimental baseline sessions (left panel) for the same four animals before conditioning (i.e., 16 total sessions). This figure shows consecutive 40-min interval averages, and summarizes in the right-hand panel the stable response pattern that developed after the baboons had been exposed to at least 40 daily 12-hr conditioning sessions. Characteristically, sustained elevations of 30 mm Hg or more in both systolic and diastolic blood pressure were maintained throughout the 12-hr "conditioning on" period accompanied by elevated but progressively decreasing heart rates over the course of the 12-hr interval. During the ensuing 12-hr "conditioning off" recovery period, heart rate continued to fall somewhat precipitously, and blood pressure returned to approximately basal levels (or slightly above) within 6 to 8 hr. In contrast, cardiovascular changes during the pre-experimental base line period, summarized in the left hand panel of Fig. 22, show only moderate fluctuations in heart rate and virtually no change in blood pressure (save the minimal diurnal variation) throughout the 24-hr interval.

That these large-magnitude, sustained elevations in blood pressure are related directly and specifically to the programmed environmental contingency requirements of the instrumental conditioning procedure is further confirmed by the results obtained with two additional baboons exposed to virtually identical experimental conditions with the exception that concurrent food-reward and shock-avoidance were made contingent upon *decreasing* diastolic blood pressure below pre-experimental base line levels. Over extended intervals (6 months or more) of daily exposure to this instrumental-blood-pressure-lowering procedure (involving electric shocks, food deprivation and reward, surgery and chronic catheterization, and chair restraint as controls for the same general laboratory conditions obtaining with the blood-pressure-raising animals in the present study), neither animal showed any change from base line blood pressure or heart rate levels.

Extended exposure to these environmental-physiological contingency arrangements with the four blood-pressure-raising baboons has continued to accentuate the divergence between maintained elevations in blood pressure and progressive decreases in heart rate during both the "conditioning on" and "conditioning off" intervals of the daily 24-hr experimental sessions. Figure 23, for example, compared the concurrent changes in blood pressure and heart rate during the 12-hr "work" periods ("conditioning on") with the changes in blood pressure and heart rate during the 12-hr "rest" periods ("conditioning off") for one of the experimental animals over the first 7 months of this study. The figure shows consecutive monthly averages for heart rate and both systolic and diastolic blood pressure during

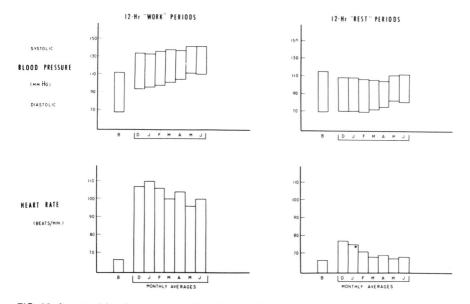

FIG. 23. Average blood pressure and heart rate values for one baboon during consecutive monthly intervals for the 12-hr "conditioning on" ("work") periods (left) compared with the 12-hr "conditioning off" ("rest") periods (right).

exposure to the alternating 12-hr "conditioning on"–"conditioning off" program and includes pre-experimental basal values for both heart rate and blood pressure. Characteristically, progressive elevations in both systolic and diastolic blood pressure can be seen to have developed in response to the experimental requirements during the 12-hr "work" periods. Heart rate, on the other hand, while substantially elevated over basal values during these 12-hr "work" periods, appears to decline over the course of the same observation interval. Similarly, divergent changes in blood pressure and heart rate can be seen to characterize the cardiovascular response pattern developing during the 12-hr "rest" periods. Blood pressure levels, initially approximating base line values over the first few months of the experiment, have shown modest but progressive elevations during the latter months of the study. In contrast, initially elevated heart rate levels during the 12-hr "rest" periods appear to have declined progressively to approximately basal values over this same interval.

The results of this extended series of conditioning studies would seem to provide at least some preliminary operational basis for defining the participant role of component physiological and behavioral processes in emotional transactions. Clearly, interrelationships between the two classes of events are prominently in evidence over the broad range of environmental interactions encompassed by the topic which provides the focus for this experimental analysis. With at least equal clarity, however, the observations emerging from these several lines of investigation argue decisively for a critical degree of independence between the separable physiological and behavioral parameters which in concert define the concept of "emotion."

REFERENCES

Anderson, D. E., and Brady, J. V. (1971): Pre-avoidance blood pressure elevations accompanied by heart rate decreases in the dog, *Science 172*, 595–597.

Anderson, D. E., and Brady, J. V. (1972): Differential preparatory cardiovascular responses to aversive and appetitive behavioral conditioning, *Cond. Reflex 7*, 82–96.

Anderson, D. E., and Brady, J. V. (1973a): Prolonged preavoidance upon blood pressure and heart rate in the dog, *Psychosom. Med. 35*, 4–12.

Anderson, D. E., and Brady, J. V. (1973b): Effects of beta blockade on cardiovascular responses to avoidance performance in dogs, *Psychosom. Med. 35*, 84.

Anderson, D. E., Daley, L. A., Findley, J. D., and Brady, J. V. (1970): A restraint system for the psychophysiological study of dogs, *Behav. Res. Instru. Meth. 2*, 191–194.

Anderson, D. E., and Tosheff, J. (1973): Cardiac output and total peripheral resistance changes during preavoidance periods in the dog. *J. Appl. Physiol. 34*, 650–654.

Benson, H., Herd, J. A., Morse, W. H., and Kelleher, R. T. (1969): Behavioral inductions of arterial hypertension and its reversal. *Am. J. Physiol. 217*, 30–34.

Brady, J. V. (1962): Psychophysiology of emotional behavior. In: *Experimental Foundations of Clinical Psychology*, ed. A. J. Bachrach, Basic Books, New York.

Brady, J. V. (1965): Experimental studies in psychophysiological responses to stressful situations. In: *Symposium on Medical Aspects of Stress in the Military Climate*, Walter Reed Army Institute of Research, Government Printing Office, Washington, D.C.

Brady, J. V. (1966): Operant methodology and the production of altered physiological states. In: *Operant Behavior: Areas of Research and Application*, ed. W. Honig, Appleton-Century-Crofts, New York.

Brady, J. V. (1967): Emotion and the sensitivity of the psychoendocrine systems. In: *Neurophysiology and Emotion*, ed. D. Glass, Rockefeller University Press, New York.

Brady, J. V. (1970a): Emotion: Some conceptual problems and psychophysiological experiments. In: *Feelings and Emotions*, ed. M. Arnold, Academic Press, New York.

Brady, J. V. (1970b): Endocrine and autonomic correlates of emotional behavior. In: *Physiological Correlates of Emotion*, ed. P. Black, Academic Press, New York.

Brady, J. V. (1971): Emotion revisited, *J. Psychiatr. Res. 8*, 343–384.

Brady, J. V. (1974): Psychophysiological syndromes resulting from overly-rigid environmental control: Concurrent and contingent animal models. In: *Symposium on Experimental Behaviour Basis of Mental Disturbance*. Ireland.

Brady, J. V., Findley, J. D., and Harris, A. H. (1971): Experimental psychopathology and the psychophysiology of emotion. In: *Experimental Psychopathology*, ed. H. D. Kimmel, Academic Press, New York.

Brady, J. V., Harris, A. H., and Anderson, D. E. (1972): Behavior and the cardiovascular system in experimental animals. In: *Neural and Psychological Mechanisms in Cardiovascular Disease*, ed. A. Zanchetti, Casa Editrice (Il Ponte), Milano.

Brady, J. V., Kelly, D., and Plumlee, L. (1969): Autonomic and behavioral responses of the rhesus monkey to emotional conditioning, *Ann. N.Y. Acad. Sci. 159*, 959–975.

Cannon, W. B. (1927): The James-Lange theory of emotions: A critical examination and alternate theory. *Am. J. Psychol. 39*, 106–124.

DiCara, L. (1970): Learning in the autonomic nervous system. *Sci. Am. 222*, 30–39.

DiCara, L. V., and Miller, N. E. (1968): Instrumental learning of systolic blood pressure responses in curarized rats: Dissociation of cardiac and vascular changes, *Psychosom. Med. 5*, 489–494.

Engel, B. T., and Chism, R. A. (1967): Operant conditioning of heart rate speeding, *Psychophysiology 3*, 418–426.

Engel, B. T., and Hansen, S. P. (1966): Operant conditioning of heart rate slowing, *Psychophysiology 3*, 176–187.

Engel, B. T., and Melmon, K. L. (1968): Operant conditioning of heart rate in patients with cardiac arrhythmias, *Cond. Reflex 3*, 130.

Estes, W. K., and Skinner, B. F. (1941): Some quantitative properties of anxiety, *J. Exp. Psychol. 29*, 390–400.

Findley, J. D., Brady, J. V., Robinson, W. W., and Gilliam, W. A. (1971a): Continuous cardiovascular monitoring in the baboon during long-term behavioral performances, *Commun. Behav. Biol. 6*, 49–58.

Findley, J. D., Robinson, W. W., and Gilliam, W. A. (1971b): A restraint system for chronic study of the baboon, *J. Exp. Anal. Behav. 15*, 69–71.

Harris, A. H., Findley, J. D., and Brady, J. V. (1971): Instrumental conditioning of blood pressure elevations in the baboon, *Cond. Reflex 6*, 215–226.

Harris, A. H., Gilliam, W., Findley, J. D., and Brady, J. V. (1973): Instrumental conditioning of large-magnitude daily 12-hour blood pressure elevations in the baboon, *Science 182*, 175–177.

Hunt, H. F., and Brady, J. V. (1951): Some effects of electroconvulsive shock on a conditioned emotional response ("anxiety"), *J. Comp. Physiol. Psychol. 44*, 88–98.

James, W. (1884): What is emotion? *Mind 19*, 188–205.

Katkin, E. S., and Murray, E. N. (1968): Instrumental conditioning of autonomically mediated behavior: Theoretical and methodological issues, *Psychol. Bull. 70*, 52–68.

Lindsley, D. B. (1951): Emotion. In: *Handbook of Experimental Psychology*, ed. S. S. Stevens, Wiley, New York.

Mason, J. W. (1958): Restraining chair for the experimental study of primates, *J. Appl. Physiol. 12*, 130–133.

Mason, J. W., and Brady, J. V. (1956): Plasma 17-hydroxycorticosteroid changes related to reserpine effects on emotional behavior, *Science 124*, 983–98.

Mason, J., Brady, J. V., Polish, E., Bauer, J. A., Robinson, J. A., Rose, R. M., and Taylor, E. D. (1961a): Patterns of corticosteroid and pepsinogen change related to emotional stress in the monkey, *Science 133*, 1596–1598.

Mason, J. W., Brady, J. V., Robinson, J. A., Taylor, E. D., Tolson, W. W., and Mougey, E. H. (1961b): Patterns of thyroid, gonadal, and adrenal hormone secretions related to psychological stress in the monkey, *Psychosom. Med. 23*, 446.

Mason, J. W., Brady, J. V., and Sidman, M. (1957): Plasma 17-hydroxycorticosteroid levels and conditioned behavior in the rhesus monkey, *Endocrinology 60*, 741–752.

Mason, J. W., Brady, J. V., Tolliver, G. A., Tolson, W., Gilmore, L., Mougey, E. H., Taylor, E., Robinson, J., Johnson, T. A., Kenyon, C., Collins, D., Jones, J., Driver, G., Beer, B., Ricketts, P., Wherry, F., Pennington, L., Goodman, A., and Wool, M. (1968): Organization of psychoendocrine mechanisms, *Psychosom. Med. 30*, 565–808.

Mason, J. W., Brady, J. V., and Tolson, W. W. (1966): Behavioral adaptations and endocrine activity. In: *Proceedings of the Association for Research in Nervous and Mental Diseases*, ed. R. Levine. Williams and Wilkins Co., Baltimore.

Mason, J. W., Mangan, G., Brady, J. V., Conrad, D., and Rioch, D. (1961c): Concurrent plasma epinephrine, norepinephrine and 17-hydroxycorticosteroid levels during conditioned emotional disturbances in monkeys, *Psychosom. Med. 23*, 344–353.

Miller, N. E. (1969): Learning of visceral and glandular responses, *Science 163*, 434–448.

Miller, N. E., and DiCara, L. (1967): Instrumental learning of heart rate changes in curarized rats: Shaping and specificity to a discriminative stimulus, *J. Comp. Physiol. Psychol. 63*, 12–19.

Miller, N. E., DiCara, L., Solomon, H., Weiss, J. M., and Dworkin, B. (1970): Learned modification of autonomic functions: A review and some new data, *Circul. Res. 26* (Suppl.), 3–11.

Plumlee, L. A. (1969): Operant conditioning of increases in blood pressure. *Psychophysiology 6*, 283–290.

Reymert, M. L. (ed.) (1928): *Feelings and Emotions. The Wittenberg Symposium*. Clark University Press, Worcester.

Schwartz, G. E. (1972): Voluntary control of human cardiovascular integration and differentiation through feedback and reward, *Science 175*, 90–93.

Schwartz, G. E., Shapiro, D., and Tursky, B. (1971): Learned control of cardiovascular integration in man through operant conditioning, *Psychosom. Med. 33*, 57.

Shapiro, D., Tursky, B., and Schwartz, G. E. (1970): Differentiation of heart rate and systolic blood pressure in man by operant conditioning, *Psychosom. Med. 32*, 417–423.

Sidman, M. (1953): Avoidance conditioning with brief shock and no exteroceptive warning signal, *Science 118*, 157–158.

Sidman, M., Mason, J. W., Brady, J. V., and Thach, J. (1962): Quantitative relations between avoidance behavior and pituitary-adrenal cortical activity, *J. Exp. Anal. Behav. 5*, 353–362.

Weiss, T., and Engel, B. T. (1971): Operant conditioning of heart rate in patients with premature ventricular contractions, *Psychosom. Med. 33*, 301–321.

Emotions—Their Parameters and Measurement,
edited by L. Levi.
Raven Press, New York © 1975

Psychophysiological Parameters and Methods

Malcolm Lader

Department of Psychiatry, De Crespigny Park, Denmark Hill, London, SE5 8 AF England

INTRODUCTION

Psychophysiology, a broad and vague entity, can be simply regarded as the use of physiological measures in a psychological, behavioral context. Although often limited in practice to variables recorded on a polygraph, it extends at least in theory to all physiological variables. I will concentrate on the measure of the palmar skin conductance. I shall also discuss, although in less detail, skin potential, salivation, gastrointestinal function, and pupillary diameter, all estimates of some aspect of autonomic functioning. After outlining the methodology of these measures, an attempt will be made to explain what these variables may be actually reflecting in central behavioral or psychological terms. However, in the introductory section, certain fundamental points will be made which, although stressed before by other authors, will bear reiterating.

Ethical Aspects

The ethical aspects of psychophysiological experimentation dictate, often to an extent barely appreciated, many of the techniques used. For example, it is fully justified in a patient with serious cardiac abnormalities to introduce a catheter into an arm vein and on through the heart into the pulmonary arteries in order to assess vascular pressures. This would not be permissible in a normal subject or a psychiatric patient in order to assess changes during "stress" because of the small but definite risk involved and because there is no direct potential benefit to the subject. Most psychophysiological techniques utilize surface electrodes rather than entering the tissues of the subject, an example being surface electromyography instead of intramuscular needle electromyography. Radioactive isotopes, about which special ethical precautions are hedged, are rarely used in psychophysiology.

Physiology and Psychophysiology

Techniques are often used or analyzed in different ways in physiology, clinical medicine, and psychophysiology. For example, the cardiologist records the wave form of the electrocardiogram from which he can detect malfunctioning of the heart. The psychophysiologist is interested in the heart rate or, as a refinement, the interbeat interval, and uses the EKG to trigger rate meters or tachographs. Another example concerns the EEG. The electroencephalographer records eight or more channels of the EEG in order to localize any abnormalities; he analyzes the recordings manually as visual inspection is the quickest and most accurate way of detecting irregularities in the wave forms. The psychophysiologist, on the other hand, may use only a few channels or even a single one; as he is often interested in such phenomena as alpha activity, he utilizes automatic methods of analysis, e.g., tuned filters, whenever he can.

Some physiological measures are relatively ignored by physiologists yet extensively used by psychophysiologists. The best example is the palmar skin conductance which is not even mentioned in many standard physiology textbooks but is the most widely used of all psychophysiological measures.

A subtle difference between physiological measures per se and physiological measures used in a psychological context concerns the general experimental approach. Physiologists usually study fairly clear phenomena and attempt to induce unequivocal changes in those phenomena, for example, the firing rate of neurons. Psychophysiologists often have to resort to complex statistical analyses to clarify the nuances of effects which they study.

BASIC TECHNICAL ASPECTS

Transducers

In general, there are two types of physiological measure: (a) those in which the bodily signal itself is an electrical potential such as the electromyogram, the EKG, and the EEG, and (b) those in which the bodily signal is nonelectrical. The latter include pressure and volume changes, movement, and temperature. It is most convenient to convert the nonelectrical signal into an electrical signal, usually a voltage. This process is termed transduction, and the device that carries it out is a transducer. Transduction into an electrical signal is a convenience not a necessity. Volume changes can be recorded using a fluid level and a float upon which is mounted a stylus writing on a smoked drum; the volume changes alter the fluid level thus transducing volume changes into vertical movements of the stylus. However, this is cumbersome compared with the use of a volumetric pressure transducer, an amplifier, and an ink-writing polygraph or analogue tape recorder. To summarize, the function of a transducer is to change one form of energy into another, in practice usually electrical. The nonelectrical signal to be converted is the transducible function; the principle by which the device works is the transducing method.

There is often a choice of transducible function and transducing method.

For example, respiration can be monitored by recording the air temperature in the nostril or the movement of a tube around the chest, both transducible functions. Temperature can be converted to a voltage signal by means of a thermocouple or a thermistor, both transducing methods. The specifications for a transducer are: (a) it should introduce minimal distortion into the signal; (b) it should be sensitive to only the physiological event of interest; (c) it should have a high efficiency and produce a good signal needing only moderate amplification. It is a further advantage if the transducer is standard, small, and inexpensive. Transducers are usually developed in physical science laboratories and may need considerable modification for use in physiological applications. Transducers utilize various principles such as the strain gauge, the piezo-electric effect, thermocouples, thermistors, photoelectric effects, and impedance changes. They are all subject to the considerations outlined above.

Electrodes

Electrical signals are picked up from the body using electrodes and a large technical literature surrounds their design, manufacture, and use. Again electrodes must transfer the signal from the biological material to the input of the amplifier without appreciably distorting the signal. Both electrical and geometrical problems are presented and the electrode must be considered in relationship to the tissue it is recording from, the contact medium between it and the tissue, and the properties of the amplifier into which it plugs. The amplifier is also an important part of the system but discussion of these complex technical matters lies outside the scope of this review.

Polygraphs

In the past, the "end-product" of a psychophysiological experiment has usually been a paper-tracing on a polygraph. The amplified voltages are applied across the coil of a galvanometer whose needle is replaced by a pen, so that the deflection of the pen is proportional to the voltage output. The advantages of the pen recorder are that a permanent record is obtained, both amplitude and temporal relationships can be studied and the mode of working can be readily understood as various test signals can be fed in and immediately seen on the pen output. The disadvantages are several: the upper frequency response is usually poor unless expensive alternatives to the ink-writing pen are used; most simple systems are curvilinear rather than rectilinear; the pens tend to clog; calibrated paper is fairly expensive.

However, the fundamental drawback of the polygraph is that its output is "static," i.e., manual intervention is necessary to extract quantitative information from the tracing. The researcher must take measurements from the record as no automatic data processing is really feasible. As a result, it usually takes longer to analyze the recording than it did to obtain it originally, especially if multichannel recording is used and if any but the sketchiest outline of the data is required. Understandably, in the more modern, sophisticated and well-funded psychophysiological laboratories, the polygraph is merely used as a monitoring instrument and the physiological variables are recorded either in a "dynamic" form on analogue or digital tape and/or processed "on-line" by means of computer techniques.

Analogue Tape Recorder

The analogue or instrumentation tape recorder resembles an audio tape recorder but is usually constructed to a higher specification. A basic difference is that instrumentation recorders used in biological applications must record frequencies down to zero, i.e., steady voltage levels. To do this, frequency modulation of a carrier-wave signal is used (FM recording). The upper frequency response depends on the precision of the engineering of the tape heads and on the tape speed but at a speed of $1\frac{7}{8}$ inches per sec (47 mm/sec) a typical frequency response on FM recording would be 0 to 300 Hz. Direct recording can be carried out for higher frequency signals using separate amplifiers.

Tape recorders have several speeds often with a range of 1 to 8 or even 1 to 32. This facility can be used in two ways. Firstly, data can be processed at a faster speed than they were originally recorded, thus saving analysis time. Secondly, events that occur very rapidly can be recorded at a fast speed and then played back at a slower speed to clarify details.

The main advantage of the analogue tape recorder over the polygraph is that the data are recorded in "dynamic" form. In other words, they can be transformed back into electrical signals for further processing which can comprise (a) recording onto a polygraph for a permanent but static record, or (b) playing back into a computer or other digital device for automatic analysis. Data can be processed and reprocessed in any number of ways and as analogue tape, especially the $\frac{1}{4}$-inch variety, is relatively inexpensive, each experiment can be stored in a convenient and compact form.

Digital Techniques

For data to be analyzed by a digital device such as a computer, they must be in digital, that is, numerical form (Zimmer, 1966) (Fig. 1). This applies to nearly all forms of analysis. Thus, in the conventional scoring of polygraphic recordings, the psychophysiologist reads off points on the tracing against the scales, amplitude and temporal, on the chart paper. With computer facilities, an appropriate voltage output of the amplifier is led into an analogue-to-digital (A/D) converter of the computer device. Sampling of the input voltage and analogue-to-digital conversion are carried out under the

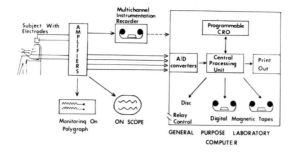

FIG. 1. Diagrammatic representation of a modern psychophysiological laboratory.

precise control of the computer program, the voltage at the instant (usually a few nanoseconds) of sampling being converted to a number that, in turn, is made available to the rest of the computer system. Since it is the voltage analogue which is actually measured, an appropriate conversion factor must be supplied separately at some stage so that the digital value corresponding to the sampled voltage can be related to the psychophysiological measure being analyzed.

Each time a sample is taken and digitized, an item of data results. As this process is repeated by the computer for the programmed number of times, the data accumulates in the computer forming a "data file." The primary form of data storage comprises a matrix of "magnetic core." Any part of core can be used at any time and data stored or retrieved ("accessed") very rapidly. In small computers, the data produced in a typical psychophysiological experiment would soon exceed the storage capacity of the magnetic core. Therefore, the data are transferred to secondary storage, usually a magnetic disc or a digital magnetic tape. Very large amounts of data (say 100,000 numbers) can easily be stored in this way, but access to the data is slower. An alternative form of data storage is paper tape in which holes are punched by a machine linked to the computer. This is relatively slow (typically, up to 100 numbers per second), but it is usually adequate for psychophysiological measures on a relatively slow time scale, e.g., the heart rate and skin conductance.

Data output can take many forms depending on the requirements of the research worker. A very useful system for monitoring and for manipulating data consists of displaying them on a cathode ray oscilloscope with provision in the program for futher processing and redisplay. The processed data are stored on disc or tape and finally analyzed using statistical programs.

Usually a computer works at its own rate: for example, programmed to square and sum 1000 numbers, this will be done as fast as possible. However, in "real-time" working, data are fed into the computer as the events governing that data occur. The upper rate of data input is limited by the speed of the input devices such as a paper-tape reader or an A/D converter. In "real-time" working, a computer may spend most of the time idling between bursts of data input. "On-line" means that the user has direct access to the computer from his terminal in contrast to "off-line" working where data accumulates away from the computer and are fed in in batches. "Real-time" working is always "on-line" but not vice versa.

Methods of Using Computer Facilities

(1) The commonest method of harnessing computer facilities in psychophysiological research is to score the paper record from a polygraph, the data being punched on cards or paper tape and analyzed by a computer. This technique is of course applicable to all forms of research, the computer acting as a large, fast calculating machine.

(2) The simplest digital method for data acquisition and manipulation is the data logger. This relatively inexpensive device consists of an A/D converter that samples one or more psychophysiological channels at preset intervals. The digital values are punched onto paper tape or stored on digital magnetic tape. The paper or magnetic tape is subsequently fed in to a computer and data manipulation, calculations, etc., are carried out. The disadvantage of the data-logging system is the need for an intermediate tangible form of the data as magnetic or paper tape. The second disadvantage, the relatively slow sampling rate, is a limiting factor only in psychophysiological experiments with rapidly changing variables such as the EEG. Even then, many loggers can digitize quickly enough onto magnetic tape.

(3) An instrumentation coupler consists of a device that samples and digitizes variables on command from a central computer and transmits the data obtained to the computer. The instrumentation coupler is an interesting new development as it utilizes the power of large computers without the need for intermediate, tangible forms of data.

(4) Special purpose computers have been used over the past 10 years to average EEG-evoked response and similar signals. The essential difference between these computers (e.g., "Computer of Average Transients," CAT) and general computers is that the program is wired in the special purpose computer so that its execution is very rapid as the computer does not interpret a long series of coded instructions as in the general computer. Consequently, a special purpose computer is capable of sampling 125 data points in a millisecond although this facility is of importance only where very transient signals are being analyzed, for example, in biophysical applications. Special purpose computers have a limited number of programs, e.g., averaging, interval and dwell histograms and correlograms, and a limited choice of parameters such as sampling speed. Also, the output of data is often cumbersome.

(5) General purpose laboratory computers have become widely available in the past few years and are ideal for psychophysiological experiments.

There are two approaches to this type of instrument. A basic small digital computer can be bought to which are added A/D converters, relay controls, etc., as required. Alternatively, the manufacturer's "package" containing all these features can be purchased complete.

Such computers are usually small in terms of core, but digital magnetic tapes or discs provide an effective and quite large "back-up" storage. Typically, one tape can store a quarter of a million numbers, which usually suffices for all but the most enthusiastic psychophysiologists. Several channels can be input via the A/D converters, and all sampled within a millisecond.

The small general purpose on-line laboratory computer is in many ways very suited to psychophysiological research. The relatively slow rate of data acquisition allows manipulations to be carried out between sampling and also the total of data accumulated is not sufficient to overload the tape or disc storage. It is, however, in the running of psychophysiological experiments that the on-line computer is most flexible. Very complex stimulus parameters can be easily programmed and "feed-back" experiments made feasible.

Stimulation Procedures

Many types of stimulation procedures have been used in psychophysiology. There are no stimulation maneuvers specific to psychophysiological research, and physiology and psychology among other disciplines have contributed stimulation procedures. The choice of stimulation procedure or whether to use one at all devolves on the particular theoretical and practical approach of the experimenter.

Firstly, he must decide whether so-called "baseline" or "background" activity levels will suffice. Although these are also euphemistically referred to as "resting" levels, the experimental situation itself—coming into a laboratory and having electrodes attached or venepunctures carried out— is a very powerful stimulation procedure. It has been shown that the initial levels of many variables are raised, often to a marked extent. This does not invalidate the use of laboratory procedures but emphasizes that on the first occasion at least, no true "resting" readings are attainable. On subsequent occasions, readings approximating more to basal values can be obtained in normals, but, in psychiatric patients, adaptation to laboratory situations may be slow or even absent. This lack of adaptation can be exploited as differences between normal subjects and psychiatric patients, such as agitated depressives, will become more and more evident on repeated testing occasions.

An alternative approach to using a stimulation procedure is to attempt to relax the individuals. This can be simple reassurance and verbal instructions, or the use of drugs to induce drowsiness or sleep. The best example of this technique is the "sedation threshold technique" (Shagass and Naiman, 1956), in which a barbiturate, usually thiopental sodium or amylobarbital sodium, is injected intravenously at a constant rate until an "end point" is reached. The "end point" can be electroencephalographic, such as the appearance of fast-wave low-voltage activity; autonomic, the disappearance of skin conductance fluctuations; neurological, the onset of slurred speech; or behavioral, the inability to do simple mental arithmetic. The amount of drug injected (mg/kg body weight) is then calculated as the variable of interest.

Stimulation procedures can be classified according to their temporal characteristics and type. Short-term stimuli can be flashes of light or auditory tones, longer-term stimuli, mental arithmetic tasks or viewing upsetting movie films. The short-term stimuli may be repeated at discrete intervals to form an habituation procedure or different types of stimuli paired as in classical respondent conditioning techniques. Long-term stimuli include "real-life" situations, such as parachute training or combat in war (Fenz and Epstein, 1967). Naturally occurring situations such as earthquakes can be utilized but there are major practical problems in systematically gathering data.

Stimuli used in psychophysiological experiments can be roughly divided into physical, physiological, pharmacological, psychological, and psychiatric. Of course, a stimulus may have elements of another type so these rubrics are not mutually exclusive. For example, viewing a horror film is psychologically disturbing but there is also the visual input, which can be quantified in physical terms. Conversely, apparently innocuous physical stimuli may have some unexpected psychological connotations, e.g., one of my patients was upset by a click stimulus because it reminded him of his hated employer who made noises by clicking his tongue.

Physical stimuli in psychophysiology consist predominantly of sensory input in the usual modalities—auditory, visual, tactile, and, occasionally, gustatory and olfactory. The advantage of this type of stimulation procedure is that the sensory input can be quantified in absolute physical terms.

Physiological stimuli utilize known bodily responses. For example, if a hand is immersed in ice-cold water, generalized vasoconstriction occurs with a rise in blood pressure—the "cold-pressor test." Similarly, adrenocortical stimulating hormone (corticotrophin, ACTH) can be injected and the adrenal response estimated.

If the substance administered is a drug, then a pharmacologically induced response may result. An example is the injection of methacholine (Mecholyl®), a cholinergic substance that has marked cardiovascular effects including a drop in blood pressure.

The stimulation procedure may be designed to elicit behavioral responses. There are a wide range of such stimuli including mental arithmetic, psychomotor tasks, memory tests, and any psychological testing procedure can be used in a psychophysiological context. Psychiatric stimuli are less commonly employed but are a subsection of such stimuli. An example is the recording of psychophysiological variables during a probing interview.

SOME AUTONOMIC MEASURES

Sweat-Gland Activity, Skin Resistance, and Skin Potential

Of all psychophysiological methods, the measurement of skin resistance is by far the most common. As will be seen later, skin resistance is essentially an indirect way of assessing sweat-gland activity. Direct methods of estimating sweating exist and will be briefly outlined first.

Estimates of Sweating

Nearly 50 years ago, Darrow (1929) estimated sweating by passing a carefully controlled flow of dry gas over an area of skin and measuring the amount of moisture picked up. The moisture content can be analyzed in a number of ways, a convenient method being thermal conductivity (Adams, Funkhouser, and Kendall, 1963).

Another approach is to count the number of active sweat glands in a measured area of skin at a particular time. In the starch-iodide technique a dilute alcoholic solution of iodine is painted on the skin and starch-containing test papers applied. Each actively secreting sweat gland is represented by a blue-black spot and the sweating can be quantified using a densitometer (optical opaqueness meter).

Direct counts can be made by illuminating the skin at an oblique angle (e.g., by a prism) and low-power microscopy, so that each active sweat gland appears as a glistening point. The skin can be photographed and counts made. Another simple method comprises painting the skin with colored liquid plastic. Active glands prevent the plastic from setting and when the plastic "skin" is peeled off, they appear as holes, which can be counted.

Although sweat-gland counts are relatively simple techniques, they can provide only intermittent readings and detailed counts are tedious.

Electrical Methods

These techniques have been widely used and all too frequently misused. The measurement technique, although simple in principle, requires great care in design and in use, and numerous sources of error can vitiate experimental findings. This complex topic is dealt with in detail in Venables and Martin (1967) and in Edelberg (1967, 1972). A particularly lucid, logical, and brief account is provided by Montagu and Coles (1966).

Resistance and Potential

Broadly speaking, there are two main ways of estimating sweat-gland activity electrically. In the first (the "exosomatic" method), discovered by Féré in 1888, a small electric current is passed between two sites on the skin and the resistance measured. Responses to stimulation are always drops in skin resistance. The second ("endosomatic") method consists of recording the naturally occurring potential difference between two skin sites (Tarchanoff, 1890). Responses in skin potential are usually biphasic, an initial negative component followed by a positive one.

Terminology

Unfortunately several terms exist for the various phenomena constituting the electrical properties of the skin. A distinction is usually made between the background skin resistance or skin potential level (often wrongly termed "basal") and changes in those levels, abrupt or gradual, following stimuli. With the exosomatic method, a further complication is that it is technically a little easier to measure the electrical resistance yet, as will be seen later, the reciprocal, conductance, is the more meaningful biological measure. It must be remembered that as sweat-gland activity increases, skin resistance drops and skin conductance rises.

Abrupt responses to stimuli are variously known as psychogalvanic reflexes (PGRs), galvanic skin responses (GSRs), and electrodermal responses (EDRs). None of these terms is satisfactory but GSR seems to have the greatest usage.

Peripheral Mechanisms

For a long time the physiological basis of the skin resistance level and GSR was unclear; two possibilities were (a) that changes in vascular tone underlay the GSR, and (b) that sweat-gland activity caused the GSR. Lader and Montagu (1962) carried out two series of studies in which skin resistance and finger pulse volume were recorded simultaneously from the same finger. In one series, atropine was introduced locally into the finger using an electric current (technique of iontophoresis) and resulted in the abolition of GSRs and the attainment of a high, steady skin resistance level, without vascular reactivity being affected. In the other series, bretylium administered iontophoretically abolished vasomotor changes without altering the GSR. As atropine blocks cholinergically innervated structures and as sweat glands are the only such structures in the fingertip it was concluded that the GSR was entirely dependent on sweat-gland activity.

Skin potential responses also appear to be dependent on sweat-gland activity as they are largely abolished by atropinization although nonsudorific factors may also operate (Venables and Martin, 1967).

The GSR seems to reflect presecretory activity of sweat-gland cell membranes rather than the actual emergence of sweat. The probable mechanism is that the stimulus "activates" the subject and produces a generalized sympathetic discharge that releases acetylcholine from the postganglionic neurons innervating the sweat glands. Depolarization and momentary breakdown of the cell membranes then occurs allowing the transient flow of ions and hence a drop in resistance.

Conductance or Resistance?

Ohm's law states that $V = IR$, where R is the resistance, I, the current through the resistor, and V, the recorded voltage across the resistor. If I is constant, the voltage recorded is directly and linearly related to the resistance. This forms the basis of the constant current method for measuring skin resistance. Ohm's law can be reformulated $I = V/R$. Therefore, if a constant voltage is applied to a resistor, the current flowing through it is proportional to I/R, the conductance. Thus, skin conductance can be measured using a constant voltage technique. Which technique and unit of measurement is preferable?

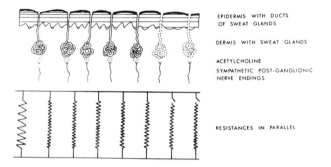

FIG. 2. Electrical representation of sweat gland activity. The upper part of the diagram shows active sweat glands plus others that become active in response to a stimulus. The lower part of the diagram shows a high-value resistor representing the resistance of the stratum corneum with smaller switched resistors representing the resistance of the individual sweat glands *in parallel.*

Darrow (1934, 1964) showed that the rate of secretion of sweat was related linearly to skin conductance. Similarly, Thomas and Korr (1957) demonstrated that conductance varies directly with the number of active sweat glands. Since sweat glands form low-resistance pathways through the high-resistance stratum corneum of the skin, they can be represented electrically as a number of switchable resistors in parallel with each other and with the high resistance of the stratum corneum (Fig. 2). The resistance across the skin cannot be calculated directly but only in terms of conductances since resistors in parallel are not additive like resistors in series. Thus the recorded conductance $G_1 = G_0 + ng$, where G_0 is the conductance of the stratum corneum; n, the number of active sweat glands; and g the mean conductance of an active sweat gland. As G_0 is negligible (about 1 μmho/cm^2, G_1 is proportional to n. If a stimulus is applied, G_1 increases to G_2 as n_1 increases to n_2. The number of additionally active sweat glands whose activity constitutes the GSR is given by $n_2 - n_1$, which is proportional to $G_2 - G_1$. Changes in resistance bear no relation to changes in sweat-gland activity.

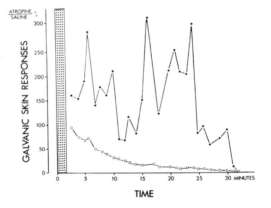

FIG. 3. Effect of atropine on the galvanic skin response. The dotted area represents the time of iontophoresis of atropine into the middle finger and of saline into the ring finger of the left hand. The lower curve represents successive GSRs of the atropinized finger quantified as change in conductance and expressed as a percentage of the equivalent GSRs of the saline control finger, similarly quantified. The upper curve represents the same GSRs quantified as change in resistance and expressed as a percentage of the equivalent saline responses, also quantified as change in resistance. Reproduced from J. Psychosom. Res. *14*, 110 (1970), by kind permission of the publishers.

This model received direct support from an experiment of Lader's (1970) in which atropine was iontophoresed into the fingertip. Atropine takes some time for its effects to become maximal, and, during this time, skin conductance drops steadily and GSR activity would be expected to fall away in a regular, monotonic fashion. GSRs were elicited from the atropinized finger and expressed as a proportion of the GSRs elicited simultaneously from a control finger treated with saline. When the GSRs were expressed as changes in conductance, a regular, monotonic decrease in the relative size of the GSRs from the atropinized finger was found (Fig. 3). Conversely, if GSRs were quantified as changes in resistance, erratic changes in the relative size of the GSRs occurred before an abrupt drop to zero.

Thus, there seems little doubt that skin conductance bears a linear relationship to sweat-gland activity whereas skin resistance is not a biologically valid unit. Nevertheless, sweat-gland activity can still be estimated by recording skin resistance and carrying out the reciprocal transformation. GSRs are quantified by measuring the resistance at the start and at the trough of the response, converting each value to conductance and then subtracting. This is not equivalent to calculating the response as a change in resistance and then taking the reciprocal: this is not a valid measure. Further transformations such as log or square root have been urged and may normalize skewed distributions. Nevertheless the important biological transformation is conductance, further transformations being *statistical* refinements.

TECHNIQUES OF MEASUREMENT

This complex topic has spawned a large technical literature summarized in Montagu and Coles (1966), Venables and Martin (1967), Edelberg (1972), and Lykken and Venables (1971). Certain technical aspects are especially important for valid recording and will be outlined (see Fig. 4).

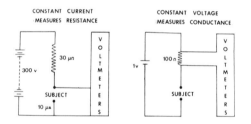

FIG. 4. Diagrammatic circuits for measuring skin resistance and skin conductance.

Constant Current Method

The electrodes are connected in series with a resistor which is large in comparison to the subject's skin resistance. For example, if a battery of 300 V is connected via a resistor of 30 megohms, then the current remains virtually constant at 10 μA regardless of fluctuations in the subject's resistance. This current will be carried by the active sweat glands, so that the fewer the active sweat glands, the greater the current through each one. It is thus impossible to establish a "safe" current density in the sense that the current will not interfere with sweat-gland function. However, under usual conditions, current densities of about 10 μA/cm^2 of skin do not appear excessive.

There are several alternative methods of delivering constant currents, transistorized circuits being particularly convenient.

Constant Voltage Method

A low voltage source (typically 1 V) is connected across the subject and the current flowing is measured by placing a small resistor in the circuit: the voltage drop across it is proportional to the current and hence the skin conductance. The resistor should be of low value, say 1,000 ohms. As the voltage across the resistor is low, fairly sensitive amplifiers are needed but are well within the capabilities of modern instruments.

Electrodes

The least complicated electrode system consists of one "active" electrode on a fingertip or palmar surface and one "inactive" electrode attached elsewhere, usually the arm. The site of attachment of the latter electrode is abraded (with an emery board) so that its resistance is negligible compared with that of the active site. In this way changes at the active site only are recorded.

The alternative is to attach two "active" electrodes to two sites, such as adjacent fingertips. The recorded conductance, G, is related to the two-site conductances G_1 and G_2 thus: $1/G = 1/G_1 + 1/G_2$. If the conductances are unequal at the two sites, then the total value is determined predominantly by the smaller of the two components and the relationship between recorded conductance and sweat-gland activity no longer holds. As differences between two palmar sites can certainly occur, it is safer to use the unipolar system despite the necessity to abrade the skin.

Polarization

Whenever a direct current flows, an electromotive force may be generated which opposes that current. In skin resistance measurement the result is an apparent gradual increase in the subject's resistance above the true reading. Nonpolarizable electrodes obviate this problem: silver–silver chloride and zinc–zinc sulfate systems can be used.

An alternative is the double-electrode system in which the current flows through one pair of electrodes and the voltage difference engendered is recorded from a second pair of electrodes. The two elements of each double electrode are in electrical contact via the contact medium. Polarization products build up on one set of electrodes but do not affect the voltage across the recording electrodes. Unfortunately, this robust system cannot be used for recording skin conductance where the current itself is measured.

Conductance or Resistance?

We have seen that conductance *units* are the appropriate biological measure but that either conductance or resistance can be recorded, with reciprocal transformation in the latter case. The recording of the skin resistance requires lower amplification and double-element electrodes are suitable. Skin conductance recording ensures a constant current through each sweat gland and no arithmetical computations are required. If good laboratory facilities are available, skin conductance recordings are preferable because a true visual representation of levels, reactivity, etc., is obtained on the polygraph record. If field studies are to be undertaken, resistance techniques have the advantage of a robust double-element electrode system. As computer analysis is now becoming commonplace, the reciprocal transformation no longer has to be done laboriously by hand.

Whichever technique is chosen, certain further precautions are essential for artifact-free recording.

Electrode Site

The active electrode must be attached either to the palmar surface of the hands or the plantar surface of the feet as these are the areas where sweat-gland activity is relatively independent of ambient temperature and humidity. The volar surface of the distal phalanx of the thumb offers a flat, extensive surface.

Site Preparation

Swabbing the skin with alcohol, ether, or carbon tetrachloride is not recommended as sweat-gland activity may be decreased by a direct local toxic action. Washing the hands with toilet soap and water is sufficient.

Site Masking

Regarding the sweat glands as resistors in parallel, the larger the area recorded from, the lower the resistance. Therefore it is essential that the recording takes place from a constant area of skin, ensured by using a masking device. Annular, self-adhesive, foam–plastic corn plasters are ideal.

Constancy of Site

As the density of sweat glands varies, the same site must be recorded from in different subjects or in the same subject on different occasions. The central whorl of the finger- or thumbprint provides a useful reference point.

Contact Medium

As the contact medium between the electrode and the skin will diffuse into the sweat-gland ducts, the contact medium should be as physiological as possible by approximating the composition of normal sweat. A contact medium containing 0.05 M sodium chloride fulfills this condition for the main electrolyte constituent of sweat.

Skin Potential

This measure has the theoretical advantage that it is more physiological because no exosomatic current is used. However, because of the biphasic responses and because skin potential levels relate to general bodily factors such as potassium concentrations, one cannot recommend the routine use of skin potential in psychophysiological measures. Its use should be left to those with particular expertise and experience.

The measurement of skin potential presents the same problems as the measurement of any other bioelectric potential. High-gain amplifiers with high-input impedance are essential as are nonpolarizable electrodes and a physiologically appropriate contact medium.

Interpretation of Recordings

The background level of skin resistance (or conductance) varies continuously and trends can be estimated by taking readings at appropriate intervals and converting to conductance levels. The variability of the background level can also be calculated.

The most common aspect of the response that is analyzed is the amplitude. Readings are taken at the onset of the response and at its peak and appropriate calculations carried out to derive the response in conductance terms. Other aspects of the response that can be analyzed are the latency (which requires a fast paper speed for accurate estimation) and the rate of recovery of the skin conductance back to its prestimulus levels. Spontaneous activity in the skin conductance can be quantified by counting the number of fluctuations above a certain criterion.

SALIVATION

Saliva is the secretion of three pairs of salivary glands, which open into the mouth through ducts: (a) the parotid glands, situated in front of and below the ear; (b) the submaxillary glands lying laterally in the floor of the mouth; and (c) the submandibular glands which are further forward (Katz, Sutherland, and Brown, 1967; Wolf and Welsh, 1972). The parotids secrete about a quarter to a third of the total saliva and the saliva secreted is serous (watery). The sublingual secretes a mucous saliva, and the submaxillary secretes saliva of intermediate composition. The innervation of the salivary glands is complex with both sympathetic and parasympathetic fibers. Parasympathetic stimulation produces an increase in the flow of saliva that becomes more concentrated; vasodilatation also occurs. Sympathetic stimulation results in vasoconstriction. Marked asymmetry is common between the glands on the two sides with respect to volume of secretion. Salivary secretion can be stimulated by chewing movements or by placing lemon juice in the mouth.

The earliest devices for recording salivary flow consisted of a cup or disc attached to the opening of the parotid duct with a tube leading to a drop counter. Various refinements have been introduced such as constant suction to attach the disc and electronic counting but the device still has the drawback that it measures salivation rate in only one gland (usually the parotid). Six suction discs would be needed to measure total flow.

A very widely used alternative method employs dental cotton-wool rolls. Three dry cylindrical rolls are placed in an air-tight plastic container which is then accurately weighed. One roll is introduced into the floor of the mouth under the front of the tongue, the other two in the floor of the mouth laterally. The rolls are left in position with the mouth closed for 2 min and then rapidly removed and replaced in the plastic container. After 2 min, the procedure is repeated and again a third time. The containers are reweighed and the mean of the three increases in weight is the salivary flow per 2 min. Care must be taken that the subject has not eaten, drunk, or smoked for at least an hour and he should lie quietly, mouth closed, for at least 15 min. With these precautions, this simple unglamorous method is surprisingly accurate and sensitive.

GASTROINTESTINAL FUNCTION

Gastric function in humans was first assessed by the subject swallowing a gastric tube, the contents of the stomach being aspirated and analyzed (Russell and Stern, 1967; Wolf and Welsh, 1972). In addition, the tube could have an inflatable balloon so that intragastric pressures could be recorded. However, such a bulky object could itself initiate contractions. More sophisticated pressure-sensitive transducers have been used but the subject must still tolerate a gastric tube.

Techniques have been developed that involve the subject swallowing a small magnet, detected externally by a magnetometer, or a steel ball-bearing, monitored with a metal detector. Radiotelemetry is a more elegant technique in which both pressure and pH can be transmitted. The radiosonde pill can be allowed to pass through the gastrointestinal tract or it can be tethered by a cord and its position determined radiographically. However, tension on the cord may cause great discomfort.

A different approach has been to attempt to record the electrical activity of the stomach using electrodes on the surface of the abdomen. Silver–silver chloride disc electrodes are used with a sensitive dc amplifier. One electrode, the reference, is attached to the leg; the active electrode is attached to the abdomen, the upper left quadrant giving the best recordings. The electrogastrogram in the human consists of waves of about 0.5 mV in amplitude occurring about once every 20 sec. This technique has still not been fully evaluated in psychophysiology.

PUPILLOGRAPHY

Techniques for the measurement of pupil size range from the most elementary to the extremely complex (Hakarem, 1967; Hess, 1972). The simplest technique employs a perspex strip in which semicircles of known dimensions have been cut. The strip is moved up and down in front of the subject's eye until a semicircle matches the pupil. To maintain constant light conditions a shaped metal tube about 30 cm long containing a small light is used. The observer presses his eyes to one end with the subject's face at the other and the perspex strip is moved up and down in front of the subject's face. Despite the primitive nature of this device, surprisingly accurate results can be obtained with even uncooperative subjects.

Another simple method consists of a black card with a series of pairs of pinholes at steadily increasing interpair distances (say from 1 to 10 mm). The subject holds the card up to one eye and looks through each pair of pinholes in turn toward a light. He sees two circles of light which overlap at those pairs a small distance apart and are separate when looking through pinhole pairs larger distances apart. One pair of pinholes will give two circles that just touch and the distance between these pinholes equals the pupillary diameter. Cooperative, trained subjects are necessary.

Several techniques depend on photography. The close-up camera is placed a standard distance from the eye and photographs of the eye are taken manually or automatically. As well as using film sensitive to light, ultraviolet and infrared systems have been used, the last enabling pupil sizes to be measured in the dark. Photographic techniques provide intermittent readings only.

In the most sophisticated technique a very narrow beam of infrared radiation is controlled electronically so that it scans the eye like the spot on a television tube. The beam is either reflected by the iris or sclera or absorbed through the pupil. The reflected radiation from the subject's eye is detected and amplified with a photomultiplier, a voltage appearing when the scan is over the iris, no voltage when the pupil is scanned. As the speed of the scan is known, the time during which no voltage is detected is proportional to the transverse diameter of the pupil.

WHAT IS BEING MEASURED?

In this final section ways will be outlined of conceptualizing psychophysiological measures in terms of the putative central processes, physiological and psychological, which those measures reflect.

Physiological Considerations

A typical psychophysiological experiment consists in the recording of one or more physiological variables while behavioral factors such as level of motivation, direction of attention, or knowledge of results are manipulated. The subjects may be normal individuals, perhaps assessed with regard to personality factors such as anxiousness or "ego strength," or psychiatric patients, e.g., schizophrenics with inherent delusional systems. The nub of the matter is that the physiological measure is being recorded and analyzed for its psychological significance. It must never be forgotten, however, that the physiological system being monitored is subserving a primary physiological function. For example, the heart pumps blood around the body and its rate increases during psychological stress situations such as a dangerous predicament. But heart rate also increases during exercise when no element of psychological stress may be apparent. Consequently, it is incorrect to assume that heart rate is an unequivocal indicator of stress. It reflects such psychological factors only when the subject is in a state of what, for lack of a better term might be called "physiological neutrality." Thus, he must be sitting or lying quietly for cardiovascular or muscular activity to be studied.

Another way of approaching this fundamental distinction between the physiological and psychological correlates of a physiological measure is in terms of the relevancy or irrelevancy of the physiological change to the direct needs of the body. If one instructs a subject to squeeze a dynamometer in his right hand, the electromyographic activity in his right forearm increases in proportion to the isometric force he exerts on the dynamometer. This muscular contraction is relevant physiological activity. The electromyographic activity also rises in his left forearm, again in proportion (approximate) to the tension in the right hand, despite the lack of useful function for that activity. This may be dubbed "irrelevant activity." Many examples in psychophysiology are not so clear cut but it is often useful to make the value judgement as to whether the physiological changes recorded are relevant or irrelevant to the changing direct physiological needs of the body.

Central Nervous System Control

Considerations of space preclude a detailed review of the central nervous system (CNS) pathways for the mediation and control of sweating, digestive tract function, and pupil size: a brief outline of the areas of brain believed to be important in the control of sweating will serve as an example.

Several studies have suggested that electrical stimulation of the premotor area 6 and posterolateral somatic area 2 results in sweat-gland responses (skin resistance or skin-potential changes) in the footpad of the cat (Darrow, 1937; Langworthy and Richter, 1930; Wang, 1957, 1958). Inhibitory influences are also exerted by the premotor area as stimulation of area 6 in cats is accompanied by a marked reduction in the amplitude of skin-potential responses to nerve stimulation (Wang, 1957, 1958, 1964). This area has major influences on autonomic activity in monkeys and in man (Bucy, 1949; Darrow, 1937), lesions of this area producing marked sweating on the contralateral side of the body.

The corticofugal pathway for control of sweat-gland activity is via the pyramidal tracts (Landau, 1953). The tracts running from the cortex to the hypothalamus exert little influence on sweating from the "emotional" areas, the palms and the soles, although control is present in thermoregulatory sweating (Wilcott, 1967). The cortical inhibition of sweat-gland responses is mediated via a medullary reticular system (Wang and Brown, 1960).

The role played by the limbic system in the control of sweating is only partly understood. In monkeys, bilateral lesions of the amygdala and lateral areas of the frontal cortex are associated with a marked diminution in the GSR to a tone. Dorsolateral frontal lesions abolished the GSR (Bagshaw, Kimble, and Pribram, 1965; Grueninger, Kimble, and Levine, 1965). As expected, the hypothalamus has intimate relationships with sweating. Stimulation of the area of the tuber cinereum results in marked footpad sweating in the cat (Celesia and Wang, 1964). Such responses have a short latency suggesting direct connections with spinal motoneurons.

The medulla contains a powerful inhibitory system for sweating activity that extends rostrally as far as the midpons (Bloch and Bonvallet, 1959; Glasser, Perez-Reyes, and Tippet, 1964). The vestibular nucleus region is also involved in control of sweating (Langworthy and Richter, 1930). Finally, motoneurons in the spinal cord form the final common pathway in the sympathetic system: The preganglionic fibers *and* the postganglionic neurons are cholinergic.

Concept of Arousal

However, it is the psychological rather than the physiological representation in the CNS which is of paramount importance to the psychophysiologist. Here, the concept of arousal has had a long and honorable influence, and, despite several severe and cogent criticisms of its validity, it still has much heuristic value. The concept of activation or arousal should be couched in behavioral and not physiological terms and it should not be confused with the diffuse mass discharge of the sympathetic nervous system described by Cannon (1915).

The concept was originally introduced by Duffy, who, over the course of more than 40 years, argued that energy must be released into various physiological systems in preparation for overt activity (Duffy, 1930, 1941, 1962, 1972). This idea had unfortunate connotations of energy mobilization, which is much better expressed in direct biochemical terms. More persuasively, Duffy argued that behavior could be regarded as projecting onto

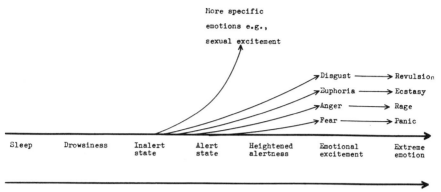

FIG. 5. The concept of arousal.

two main axes, the particular quality, i.e., characteristics of the behavioral item and the intensity or quantity of that behavior. The intensity, or activation, was regarded as present in all forms of behavior and to be marked during emotional states.

Other investigators used similar concepts. Lindsley (1951), approaching this problem using EEG measures, proposed that a continuum could be discerned in EEG patterns that corresponded to a behavioral continuum of arousal or activation. Malmo (1959) linked a similar view to activity of the ascending reticular activating system. Further, he put forward the attractive formulation that pathologically anxious patients were overaroused.

To summarize, the concept of arousal may be regarded as an *operational* construct referring to a behavioral continuum ranging from extreme drowsiness to a soporific feeling to an inalert state and on to normal conditions of wakefulness. Higher levels of arousal underly feelings of heightened awareness and emotional disquiet. At the upper end of the continuum are the high arousal states associated with emotions such as anger, anxiety, quiet, and disgust. Finally, extreme arousal is associated with powerful emotions such as rage, panic, revulsion, and horror (Fig. 5).

Many criticisms have been leveled at the concept of arousal, often on the misguided premise that a theory should explain all the experimental findings. I shall discuss two such comments.

It is manifestly impossible for a unitary, holistic concept to explain all nuances of behavior. It is therefore inevitable that many have felt it necessary to fragment the concept with such terms as "autonomic" arousal, "cortical" arousal, etc. However, this is relevant only to hypotheses regarding the central mechanisms subserving behavioral arousal. A more logical extension of the concept is into general and specific arousal. General arousal remains the concept outlined above. Specific arousal relates to the particular pattern of behavioral activity. Thus, carrying out a difficult task would involve a general level of arousal optimal to the task that would be reflected by widespread physiological activity, e.g., raised pulse rate, increased sweating, low-voltage desynchronized EEG activity. Specific arousal would be accompanied by physiological changes necessary to that task, such as EMG activity. In some ways the concepts of general and specific arousal resemble those of irrelevant and relevant activity outlined earlier. However, general arousal is not regarded as irrelevant but as necessary for the optimal performance of the on-going behavior.

In psychophysiology one is not usually particularly interested in the physiological changes accompanying specific arousal. For example, the pulse will race if one runs up several flights of stairs. This may be the prime concern of physiologists but the psychophysiologist will want to know if emotional factors are obtruding on the cardiovascular system. The pulse rate cannot tell him that because it is altered in response to the physiological needs of the body. Paradoxically, the only physiological measures that can help him are those that have either no physiological functions or strictly delimited ones. The EEG is a measure that has no function per se, but that mirrors CNS activity. Unfortunately, the actual neurophysiological basis of the EEG remains obscure but an EEG continuum corresponding to a general arousal continuum can be constructed empirically (Daniel, 1966). The widespread introduction of computers should establish this aspect of EEG studies more firmly as it will greatly increase the amount of data accruing and the sophistication with which they can be analyzed.

The palmar-skin conductance is another measure with particular application in arousal. The sweat glands that form its basis are thermoregulatory only in climatic extremes, and probably subserve functions such as grip and tactile sensitivity. Consequently, the physiological functions of these sweat glands are just those that might be expected to parallel general rather than specific arousal and the continuing popularity of palmar conductance in the psychological context supports this assumption.

The second criticism of the concept of arousal concerns the lack of correlation between physiological measures. It is argued that if the several measures used as indicators of arousal level were valid and reliable then correlations between these measures should be high. Even allowing for a certain amount of interindividual variability, the correlations have been unimpressive. However, Malmo (1959) has suggested that the crucial test of the theory of arousal is that *intra*individual correlations should be high rather than *inter*individual correlations. In other words, changes among measures within an individual should be consistent, large changes in one measure being accompanied by large changes in the other measures. Lazarus, Speisman, and Mordkoff (1963) found respectable intraindividual correlations for skin-conductance and heart-rate changes during the viewing of films.

In a study published in 1971, Mathews and I examined the relationship between several psychophysiological measures recorded from two groups of normal subjects both during repeated rest periods and during mental arithmetic and other tasks. The correlations between the measures were computed in three ways: between-subject, within-subject between-test conditions, and within-subject within-test conditions. The between-subject correlations for the rest and task situations separately are shown in Tables 1A and 1B. A very high correlation was found between the electromyographic channels and a less significant one between skin-conductance level and forearm blood flow under task conditions.

TABLE 1A. *Between-subject correlations: Group 1*

Variables	Rest				Task			
	(2)	(3)	(4)	(5)	(2)	(3)	(4)	(5)
(1) Flexor EMG	0.98[b]	−0.14	−0.25	0.01	0.98[b]	−0.29	−0.16	−0.05
(2) Extensor EMG		−0.24	−0.23	−0.05		−0.37	−0.20	−0.01
(3) SC level			0.38	0.02			0.25	0.28
(4) SC fluctuations				0.27				0.72[a]
(5) Forearm blood flow								

TABLE 1B. *Between-subject correlations: Group 2*

Variables	Rest				Task			
	(2)	(3)	(4)	(5)	(2)	(3)	(4)	(5)
(1) Fontalis EMG	−0.15	−0.21	−0.34		−0.52	−0.07	−0.16	
(2) Heart rate		−0.26	0.29			0.03	0.49	
(3) Finger pulse volume			0.27				0.49	
(4) Forearm blood flow								

[a] $p < 0.05$.
[b] $p < 0.01$.

The second group of correlations are those between the measures calculated within-subject but between-task conditions (four rest episodes, three task episodes) (Tables 2A and 2B). The cardiovascular measures tend to interrelate highly, as do the two skin conductance variables and the EMG variables. However, there are also correlations between the systems, e.g., +0.78 between forearm blood flow and skin-conductance fluctuations.

The third group of correlations within-subject, within-task were uniformly nonsignificant.

What are the implications of these and similar data? It appears that physiological measures do not show consistently high relationships between individuals. In other words, a subject who shows large pulse-rate changes may have minimal skin-conductance changes, despite both being presumed

TABLE 2A. *Within-subject, between-condition correlations: Group 1*

Variables	(2)	(3)	(4)	(5)
(1) Flexor EMG	0.37	0.19	0.47	0.40
(2) Extensor EMG		0.48	0.56	0.61
(3) SC level			0.80	0.72
(4) SC fluctuations				0.78
(5) Forearm blood flow				

TABLE 2B. *Within-subject, between-condition correlations: Group 2*

Variables	(2)	(3)	(4)	(5)
(1) Frontalis EMG	0.34	0.13	0.22	
(2) Heart rate		−0.63	0.90	
(3) Finger pulse volume			−0.58	
(4) Forearm blood flow				

$r > .26$; $p < 0.05$.
$r > .34$; $p < 0.01$.
$r > .42$; $p < 0.001$.

to be reflecting a unitary change in general arousal. I have previously suggested that physiological restraints on these physiological systems might result in marked discrepancies between measures (Lader, 1969). For example, marked vasoconstriction of the fingertip blood vessels may occur at moderate arousal levels so that a "floor" is reached and further increases in arousal are not registered (Fig. 6).

The appreciable within-individual, between-condition correlates among the measures are indicative that, within the relatively narrow arousal range in an individual at rest and undertaking mental tasks, putative physiological indices of arousal show consistent and reproducible changes. Nevertheless, the systems that I have speculated (Fig. 6) are sensitive at different ranges of the arousal continuum tend to interrelate less, e.g., EMG and skin-conductance measures.

The lack of correlation for within-task reading among the measures reflects both spontaneous fluctuations in the measure and the imprecision of the techniques.

CONCLUSIONS

The use of physiological measures in a psychological context is limited by a series of factors, the main one being that these systems have primarily physiological functions to subserve. Nevertheless, with adequate precautions and the careful choice of measure, these physiological considerations can be minimized so that valid data with reliable psychological implications

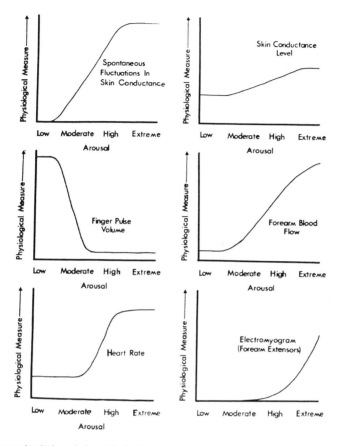

FIG. 6. Impressionistic relationship between behavioral arousal and physiological measures.

can be obtained. Among these psychophysiological measures, palmar sweat-gland activity has long enjoyed widespread usage. The electrical methods that are the most convenient ways of estimating sweat-gland activity need careful application from two points of view. Firstly, they must incorporate safeguards so that there is no interference with sweat-gland function. Secondly, the methods must use well-tried artifact-free techniques for electrodes, amplifiers, etc. The other autonomic measures outlined in this chapter are more specialized and less widely used. The recent electronic and computer revolution has altered both the details of methodology and the general strategy of psychophysiological research.

ACKNOWLEDGMENTS

Based in part on the methods chapter in a forthcoming book entitled *The Psychophysiology of Mental Illness,* to be published by Routledge, Kegan, and Paul, London.

REFERENCES

Adams, T., Funkhouser, G. E., and Kendall, W. W. (1963): Measure of evaporative water loss by a thermal conductivity cell, *J. Appl. Physiol. 18*, 1291–1293.

Bagshaw, M. H., Kimble, D. P., and Pribram, K. H. (1965): The GSR of monkeys during orienting and habituation and after ablation of the amygdala, hippocampus and inferotemporal cortex, Neuropsychologia *3*, 111–119.

Bloch, V., and Bonvallet, M. (1959): Contrôle cortico-réticulaire de l'activité électrodermale, (réponse psychogalvanique), J. Physiol. (Paris) *51*, 405–406.

Bucy, P. D., ed. (1949): *The Precentral Motor Cortex*, Univ. Illinois Press, Chicago, Ill.

Cannon, W. B. (1915): *Bodily Changes in Pain, Hunger, Fear and Rage*, Appleton-Century-Crofts, New York.

Celesia, G. G., and Wang, G. H. (1964): Sudomotor activity induced by single shock stimulation of the hypothalamus in anesthetized cats. Arch. Ital. Biol. *102*, 587–598.

Daniel, R. S. (1966): Electroencephalographic pattern quantification and the arousal continuum, Psychophysiology *2*, 146–160.

Darrow, C. W. (1929): Sensory, secretory and electrical changes in the skin following bodily excitation, J. Exp. Psychol. *10*, 197–226.

Darrow, C. W. (1934): The significance of the galvanic skin reflex in the light of its relation to quantitative measurements of perspiration, Psychol. Bull. *31*, 697–698.

Darrow, C. W. (1937): Neural mechanisms controlling the palmar galvanic skin reflex and palmar sweating, Arch. Neurol. Psych. *37*, 641–663.

Darrow, C. W. (1964): The rationale for treating the change in galvanic skin response as a change in conductance, Psychophysiology *1*, 31–38.

Duffy, E. (1930): Tensions and emotional factors in reaction, Genet. Psychol. Monographs *7*, 1–79.

Duffy, E. (1941): An explanation of "emotional" phenomena without the use of the concept "Emotion," J. Gen. Psychol. *25*, 283–293.

Duffy, E. (1962): *Activation and Behavior*, Wiley, New York.

Duffy, E. (1972): Activation. In: *Handbook of Psychophysiology*, eds. N. S. Greenfield and R. A. Sternbach, pp. 577–622, Holt, Rinehart and Winston, New York.

Edelberg, R. (1967): Electrical properties of the skin. In: *Methods in Psychophysiology*, ed. C. C. Brown, pp. 1–53, Williams and Wilkins, Baltimore.

Edelberg, R. (1972): Electrical activity of the skin. Its measurement and uses in psychophysiology. In: *Handbook of Psychophysiology*, eds. N. S. Greenfield and R. A. Sternbach, pp. 367–418, Holt, Rinehart and Winston, New York.

Fenz, W. D., and Epstein, S. (1967): Gradients of physiological arousal of experienced and novice parachutists as a function of an approaching jump, Psychosom. Med. *29*, 33–51.

Féré, C. (1880): Note sur les modifications de la résistance électrique sous l'influence des excitations sensorielles et des émotions, C. R. Séanc. Soc. Biol. (Paris) *40*, 217–219.

Glasser, R. L., Perez-Reyes, M., and Tippet, J. W. (1964): Brain-stem inhibition of electrodermal (galvanic skin) activity, Am. J. Physiol. *207*, 1133–1138.

Grueninger, W. E., Kimble, D. P., and Levine, S. (1965): GSR and corticosteroid response in monkeys with frontal ablations, Neuropsychologia *3*, 205–216.

Hakarem, G. (1967): Pupillography. In: *A Manual of Psychophysiological Methods*, eds. P. H. Venables and I. Martin, pp. 335–350, North-Holland, Amsterdam.

Hess, E. H. (1972): Pupillometrics: a method of studying mental, emotional, and sensory processes. In: *Handbook of Psychophysiology*, eds. N. S. Greenfield and R. A. Sternbach, pp. 491–534, Holt, Rinehart and Winston, New York.

Katz, R. A., Sutherland, G. F., and Brown, C. C. (1967): Measurement of salivation. In: *Methods in Psychophysiology*, ed. C. C. Brown, pp. 173–191, Williams and Wilkins, Baltimore.

Lader, M. H. (1969): Psychophysiological aspects of anxiety. In: *Studies of Anxiety*, ed. M. H. Lader, pp. 53–61, Royal Medico-Psychological Ass., London.

Lader, M. H. (1970): The unit of quantification of the G.S.R., J. Psychosom. Res. *14*, 109–110.

Lader, M. H., and Montagu, J. D. (1962): The psycho-galvanic reflex: a pharmacological study of the peripheral mechanism, J. Neurol. Neurosurg. Psych. *25*, 126–133.

Landau, W. M. (1953): Autonomic responses mediated via the corticospinal tract, J. Neurophysiol. *16*, 299–311.

Langworthy, O. R., and Richter, C. P. (1930): The influence of efferent cerebral pathways upon the sympathetic nervous system, Brain *53*, 178–193.

Lazarus, R. S., Speisman, J. C., and Mordkoff, A. M. (1963): The relationship between autonomic indicators of psychological stress: Heart rate and skin conductance, Psychosom. Med. *25*, 19–30.

Lindsley, D. B. (1951): Emotion. In: *Handbook of Experimental Psychology*, ed. S. S. Stevens, Chap. 14, Wiley, New York.

Lykken, D. T., and Venables, P. H. (1971): Direct measurement of skin conductance: A proposal for standardisation, Psychophysiology *8*, 656–672.

Malmo, R. B. (1959): Activation: a neuropsychological dimension, Psychol. Rev. *66*, 367–386.

Mathews, A. M., and Lader, M. H. (1971): An evaluation of forearm blood flow as a psychophysiological measure, Psychophysiology *8*, 509–524.

Montagu, J. D., and Coles, E. M. (1966): Mechanisms and measurement of the galvanic skin response, Psychol. Bull. *65*, 261–279.

Russell, R. W., and Stern, R. M. (1967): Gastric motility: The electrogastrogram. In: *A Manual of Psychophysiological Methods*, eds. P. H. Venables and I. Martin, pp. 219–244, North-Holland, Amsterdam.

Shagass, C., and Naiman, J. (1956): The sedation threshold as an objective index of manifest anxiety in psychoneurosis, J. Psychosom. Res. *1*, 49–57.

Tarchanoff, J. (1890): Ueber die galvanischen Erscheinungen in der Haut des Menschen bei Reizungen der Sinnesorgane und bei verscheidenen Formen der psychischen Thatigkeit, Pfluger's Arch. Gesammte Physiol. *46*, 46–55.

Thomas, P. E., and Korr, I. M. (1957): Relationship between sweat gland activity and electrical resistance of the skin, J. Appl. Physiol. *10*, 505–510.

Venables, P. H., and Martin, I. (1967): Skin resistance and skin potential. In: *Manual of Psychophysiological Methods*, eds. P. H. Venables and I. Martin, pp. 53–102, North-Holland, Amsterdam.

Wang, G. H. (1957): The galvanic skin reflex: A review of old and recent works from a physiologic point of view, Part I, Am. J. Phys. Med. *36*, 295–320.

Wang, G. H. (1958): The galvanic skin reflex: A review of old and recent works from a physiologic point of view, Part II, Am. J. Phys. Med. *37*, 35–57.

Wang, G. H. (1964): *The Neural Control of Sweating*, Univ. Wisconsin Press, Madison, Wisconsin.

Wang, G. H., and Brown, V. W. (1960): Suprasegmental inhibitions of an autonomic reflex, J. Neurophysiol. *23*, 448–452.

Wilcott, R. C. (1967): Arousal sweating and electrodermal phenomena, Psychol. Bull. *67*, 58–72.

Wolf, S., and Welsh, J. D. (1972): The gastrointestinal tract as a responsive system. In: *Handbook of Psychophysiology*, eds. N. S. Greenfield and R. A. Sternbach, pp. 419–456, Holt, Rinehart and Winston, New York.

Zimmer, H., ed. (1966): *Computers in Psychophysiology*, Charles C Thomas, Springfield, Ill.

Emotions—Their Parameters and Measurement,
edited by L. Levi.
Raven Press, New York © 1975

Cardiovascular Parameters and Methods of Measuring Emotions

Heribert Konzett

Department of Pharmacology, University of Innsbruck, Peter-Mayr-Strasse 1, A-6020 Innsbruck, Austria

OBSERVATIONS IN ANIMALS

Cats and dogs react to sudden auditory, visual, and electric cutaneous stimuli immediately with the behavioral response of alerting and with an augmentation of muscular blood flow (Abrahams, Hilton, and Zbrożyna, 1960, 1964; Uvnäs, 1966). An increase in muscular blood flow can also be elicited by electric stimulation of some points in the cortex, in the hypothalamus, and in the brainstem (Eliasson, Folkow, Lindgren, and Uvnäs, 1951; Eliasson, Lindgren, and Uvnäs, 1953; Abrahams et al., 1964; Uvnäs, 1966). Especially in cats, exceptionally in dogs, the vasodilator activation due to stimulation in the brain is associated with behavioral and autonomic responses characteristic of fear, anger, and rage, such as increased wakefulness, pupillary dilatation, piloerection, baring of the teeth, hissing and spitting, etc. The augmentation of the blood flow of the skeletal muscles is the initial and integral part of a complex pattern of cardiovascular changes, which include tachycardia, rise of arterial blood pressure, increased cardiac output, vasoconstriction in the skin and intestine, and venoconstriction. The cardiovascular system, therefore, seems to become adjusted and prepared for the needs of muscular effort during fight or flight (Eliasson et al., 1951; Abrahams et al., 1964).

OBSERVATIONS IN MAN

An increase in forearm blood flow, which is mainly due to an increase in muscular blood flow, occurs also in man during a short-lasting experimental exposure to emotionally stressing situations, e.g., mental arithmetic or alarming reports (Grant and Pearson, 1938; Abramson and Ferris, 1940; Wilkins and Eichna, 1941; Golenhofen and Hildebrandt, 1957; Blair, Glover, Greenfield, and Roddie, 1959; Brod, Fencl, Hejl, and Jirka, 1959). It is accompanied by tachycardia, rise of both systolic and diastolic blood pressure, increase in cardiac output, vasoconstriction in the intestine and skin and venoconstriction. The augmentation of the muscle blood flow is due to vasodilator activation (Blair et al., 1959). Severe emotional stress can produce fainting during which forearm blood flow even increases in spite of a remarkable fall in systolic and diastolic blood pressure (Greenfield, 1951). Electrical stimulation of the rostral hypothalamus on patients with chronically implanted electrodes caused tachycardia and anxiety (Heath and Mickle, 1960); stimulation of the amygdala caused blood-pressure rise and tachycardia with a change in emotional mood and feelings of fright (Chapman, 1960). High resting forearm blood flow and tachycardia has been found in patients with clinical and subjective ratings of anxiety (Kelly, 1966, 1970).

During states of tension and apprehension caused by the imminence of an important academic oral examination in students and before a necessary procedure involving some risk in hospitalized clinical patients, different types of cardiovascular changes have been observed in quantitative and qualitative variables; the majority of cases exhibited increased cardiac output, tachycardia, and moderate elevation of blood pressure, whereas in certain persons circulatory collapse and in others a marked rise of blood pressure with no change or fall in cardiac output occurred (Hickam, Gargill, and Golden, 1948).

CARDIOVASCULAR PARAMETERS AND METHODS

There can be no doubt that in animals and man experimentally induced emotional stress is associated with cardiovascular changes. The already mentioned cardiovascular parameters (forearm blood flow, heart frequency, systolic and diastolic blood pressure, cardiac output) and the peripheral resistance calculated as the ratio of mean arterial pressure to cardiac output are easily measurable with usual methods, e.g., EKG, directly or indirectly applied manometers, dye or other indicator dilution techniques, venous occlusion plethysmography, mercury-in-rubber strain gauge plethysmography, calorimetry (heated thermocouples), etc. The use of telemetric systems is of great importance since it allows the measurement of cardiovascular parameters during stressful situations of everyday life without incommoding the subject. With this last method, increases in heart rate have been observed, e.g., on ski jumpers waiting for the starting signal (Imhof, Blatter, Fuccella, and Turri, 1969), on pilots during the start and landing maneuvers, on parachutists during the descent before opening of the parachute, and on cosmonauts before starting (Rettenmaier, 1969).

HORMONES AND NEUROTRANSMITTERS

Besides these various physical methods, biochemical and biological assays of hormones and neurotransmitters released during emotion can add valuable information about the nature of the cardiovascular changes. Mainly catecholamines, vasopressin, and adrenocortical and thyroidal hormones have been shown to be involved in emotional stress responses (see Frankenhaeuser and Mason, *this volume*). It is therefore reasonable to evaluate different hemodynamic parameters concomitantly with the results of such assays.

Unfortunately, the existence of acetylcholine released from sympathetic cholinergic nerves innervating the muscle vessels of man has not yet been demonstrated.

THE FOREARM BLOOD FLOW: AN ESPECIALLY SENSITIVE INDICATOR OF EMOTIONAL REACTION

The question arises, whether there exists an especially sensitive cardiovascular indicator of emotion. From comparing the emotionally induced changes of the various parameters, it results that the percent increase (up to 300 to 500%) in forearm (and calf) blood flow is greater than the percent increase in other parameters, e.g., blood pressure, heart frequency, and cardiac output (Brod et al., 1959; Blair et al., 1959; Ulrych, 1969). Therefore, forearm (and calf) blood flow seems to be an especially useful indicator of emotional stress.

VENOUS OCCLUSION PLETHYSMOGRAPHY, A SIMPLE AND RELIABLE QUANTITATIVE METHOD FOR MEASURING LIMB BLOOD FLOW

The total blood flow through the forearm (and the calf) is most reliably measured by venous occlusion plethysmography (for historical notes and experimental procedure see Barcroft and Swan, 1953). The venous return from the forearm (calf) is arrested for a few seconds by means of a pneumatic cuff whereas the arterial inflow continues unchanged. The circulation to the hand (foot) is arrested by another pneumatic cuff. During the short period of inflation of the venous-collecting cuff the rate of venous collection equals the rate of arterial inflow. Records of the forearm blood flow may be obtained several times per minute; automatic filling and emptying of the venous-collection cuff can easily be arranged. The rates of blood flow are calculated in milliliters per 100 ml tissue per minute.

On the average, the muscles comprise some 60 to 80% of the forearm volume (Grant and Pearson, 1938; Abramson and Ferris, 1940). The increase in total forearm blood flow during emotion is due to an increase in blood flow through the muscle vessels and not through the skin vessels (Fencl, Hejl, Jirka, Madlafousek, and Brod, 1959).

The venous occlusion plethysmography we used, is slightly modified after Barcroft and Swan (1953). It is a simple but somewhat cumbersome method, which provides quantitative measurement of limb blood flow in man if properly used and carefully done. The mercury-in-rubber strain gauge plethysmography is easier to handle. The internal calorimetry (needle calorimeter) can also be used for indirect measurement of the blood flow in the muscle.

A STANDARDIZED AND REPRODUCIBLE STRESS PROCEDURE

For the study of emotionally induced cardiovascular changes the aim was to use mild but adequate emotional stimuli that could be repeatedly applied and would give quantitatively reproducible effects on forearm blood flow and on heart frequency as well as on systolic and diastolic blood pressure. After many trials, a combination of the Stroop procedure and mental arithmetic has proved sufficient.

Stroop introduced a method to study pairs of conflicting stimuli both being inherent aspects of the same symbols (1935). The Stroop color-word test has lately been used in various modified forms in many laboratory stress studies. The procedure is as follows: on a card the words red, blue, green, and yellow are printed in different colors; no word is printed in the color it indicates, but an equal number of times in each of the other three colors. Thus each word presents the name of one color printed in a different color. Hence a word stimulus and a color stimulus are presented simultaneously. The color-word test involves interference between color-naming and word-reading. The testcard contains a hundred words. The subjects — students from the University who volunteered for the experiments — were not informed about the procedure. They had, as a surprise, first to read aloud the words and then to name as quickly as possible the colors of the printed words.

After the 2 to 3 min necessary for the Stroop procedure the subjects had to perform some mental arithmetic for 5 to 6 min. The task was given verbally to the subjects; it consisted of repeated subtractions of a number of two digits from a number of four digits as fast as possible (e.g., $4792 - 37 = 4755 - 37 = 4718$) and of multiplications of two simple numbers of three digits (e.g., $303 \times 107 = 32,421$; $401 \times 203 = 81,403$). The total time of the whole mental stress situation was 8 to 10 min.

The color-word interference test followed by the mental arithmetic test made the blood flow of the forearm and calf, the heart rate, and the systolic and diastolic blood pressure increase (see Fig. 1). The cardiovascular pattern during such a simple experimental emotional stress situation is in principle the same as the one observed during natural stress of day-to-day life (e.g., during quiet conversation, examination, hazardous situations, etc.). It is, therefore, possible to study problems of emotional stress with this model.

An important finding was that no significant difference existed between the effect on these cardiovascular parameters when the combined Stroop

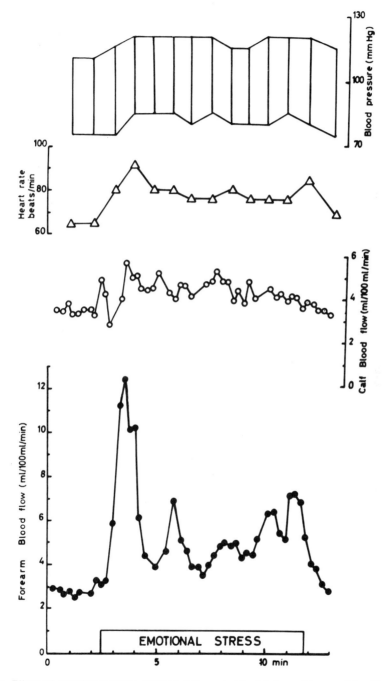

FIG. 1. Effect of emotional stress (Stroop color-word test followed by mental arithmetic test during the time represented by the rectangle) on arterial blood pressure, heart rate, calf blood flow, and forearm blood flow.

interference test and mental arithmetic task were applied twice with 1-hr or 8-hr intervals (Konzett, Strieder, and Ziegler, 1968; Konzett, Berner, and Lochs, 1973). By these experiments, a sound basis had been established for investigations, whether pharmacological agents given immediately after the first stressful situation would alter the effect on the cardiovascular parameters used during a second comparable stressful situation 1 or 8 hr later.

THE EMOTIONALLY INDUCED FOREARM BLOOD FLOW INCREASE: A SPECIFIC RESPONSE

Experiments were performed with other types of stress, e.g., application of cold or hot stress and pain production in order to test if sensory or even painful stimuli increase the forearm blood flow as well. The subjects were informed about the procedure before the experiment. Immersion of the contralateral forearm and hand in water of 4°C for 15 to 30 min did not augment the forearm blood flow although a remarkable rise of systolic and diastolic pressure occurred (Konzett and Strieder, 1970). Neither did immersion of the contralateral forearm and hand in water of 40 to 45°C for 15 to 30 min increase the forearm blood flow, although the systolic and diastolic blood pressure increased (Konzett and Strieder, 1970). Neither the application of cold nor that of hot stress changed the heart rate. However, the combined Stroop–mental-arithmetic procedure performed during the immersion of the contralateral forearm and hand in either cold or hot water elicited a remarkable increase in forearm blood flow, a tachycardia, and a further increase in systolic blood pressure.

During experimental pain induction by electrical stimulation of periosteal nerves in the tibia, no increase in forearm blood flow occurred, but there was a marked increase in pressure and a slight increase in heart rate (Steinmaurer, 1970). Even more severe pain, for example ischemic muscle pain induced by placing a tourniquet around the lower third of the thigh and by fast bending and extending of the foot during 2 min, did not increase the forearm blood flow, but produced very pronounced rises in systolic and diastolic pressure and a slight tachycardia (Steinmaurer, 1970).

From these experiments with various types of stress it can be concluded that the blood flow through the forearm does not increase uniformly as a response to stress. It seems that the forearm-blood-flow increase is a specific reaction of startling situations of some riskiness and during situational demands for mental concentration and problem-solving activity under observation and criticism.

BIOCHEMICAL CORRELATES OF EMOTIONAL STRESS

The bulk of information deals with an increased release of epinephrine mainly from the adrenal medulla and an increased release of norepinephrine mainly from sympathetic nerves during stress situations. The association of increased epinephrine excretion with apprehension and painful or unpleasant feelings on one side and the association of an increased norepinephrine excretion with anger or aggression on the other side (Funkenstein, 1956; von Euler, 1964) have recently been modified. Situations characterized by uncertainty and unpredictability produced epinephrine excretion, whereas a rise in norepinephrine excretion was correlated to unpleasant but familiar conditions (Frankenhaeuser and Rissler, 1970). In a recent experimental series in our laboratory this concept was confirmed (Konzett, Hörtnagl, Hörtnagl, and Winkler, 1971).

We found a significant increase in vasopressin excretion during emotional stress and a less-pronounced increase during pain stress. An increased vasopressin excretion coincided in our experiments with an increased epinephrine excretion (Konzett et al., 1971). Both substances may be released by a common complex central stimulation during certain stress situations. The amount of released vasopressin, however, was too small to produce an apparent action on the cardiovascular system.

PHARMACOLOGICAL STUDIES TO INTERFERE WITH THE CARDIOVASCULAR PATTERN DURING EMOTIONAL STRESS

Since the whole cardiovascular pattern is elicited centrally and integrated by diencephalic structures, it should be possible to influence it by centrally acting tranquilizers. The forearm-blood-flow increase due to emotion could be diminished by substances such as methylpentinol (Dicker and Steinberg, 1957), phenobarbital, meprobamate, chlordiazepoxide (Konzett and John, 1964), and mesoridazine (Bauer, Deisenhammer, Sporer, Winkler, and Konzett, 1967).

By means of diminution of the emotionally induced forearm blood flow as well as of the tachycardia and of the blood-pressure increase, the duration of the action of the tranquilizer mesoridazine could be determined in statistically well-controlled experiments (Bauer et al., 1967; Konzett, Berner, and Lochs, 1973). Mesoridazine (10 mg) significantly diminished the forearm-blood-flow increase during the emotionally stressing situation if given orally 1 hr before the test. There was no effect when mesoridazine was given 8 hr before the test. Therefore, the duration of action of mesoridazine in the used dose lasts more than 1 and less than 8 hr. Also dose–response relations of tranquilizers could be established by investigating their influence on the emotionally induced cardiovascular change (Bauer et al., 1967).

Furthermore, evaluation of the effect of tranquilizers on the catecholamine excretion during emotional stress has been attempted. Meprobamate in the high dose of 800 mg significantly decreased the noradrenaline excretion and slightly (not significantly) the epinephrine excretion (Frankenhaeuser and Kåreby, 1962). In a long-term study, it was found that the application of diazepam during 54 days diminished the epinephrine excretion during an emotionally stressing situation (Levi, 1968). The problem of an interference of tranquilizers with the release of catecholamines needs further investigation.

Since the emotionally induced blood-flow increase in the forearm is mediated mainly by epinephrine released from the adrenal medulla and probably partly by acetylcholine released from the sympathetic cholinergic nerves innervating the blood vessels of the skeletal muscles (Blair et al., 1959; Barcroft, Brod, Hejl, Hirsjärvi and Kitchin, 1960), antiepinephrine- and antiacetylcholine-acting substances should diminish that parameter of emotion by their peripheral action. The vasodilator effect of epinephrine on the muscle vessels and the effect of epinephrine and of norepinephrine on the heart is a so-called β-receptor action (Ahlquist, 1948). To antagonize β-receptor effects, β-receptor-blocking substances can be used. In a statistically well-controlled investigation, it has been found that oral application of 100 mg of the β-receptor-blocker Kö 592 significantly reduced the increase in blood flow through the forearm and the tachycardia. The systolic-blood-pressure increase remained unchanged whereas the diastolic-blood-pressure increase became even more pronounced (Konzett et al., 1968).

The effect of β-blocking substances on emotionally induced changes of the heart rate and of the cardiac output has also been tested in a stress situation of the professional day-to-day life on pilots during a simulated flight (Eliasch, Rosén, and Scott, 1967). The increase in heart rate and of cardiac output after application of the β-blocker propranolol was significantly less than after placebo. The emotional tachycardia of ski jumpers during the waiting on the platform before jumping was also significantly diminished by the β-receptor-blocking agent oxyprenolol (Imhof et al., 1969).

It remains to investigate the effect of an α-receptor blockade on the emotionally induced blood-pressure increase that had not been influenced by β-receptor blockade.

A reduction of the emotionally induced vasodilatation in the forearm could be achieved by intrabrachial or intravenous injection of atropine (Blair et al., 1959; Barcroft et al., 1960). This is in favor of a participation of a cholinergic nervous mechanism in the forearm vasodilatation during emotional stress.

The question arises whether a pharmacologically induced diminution of muscle blood flow, tachycardia, cardiac output, and blood pressure during emotional stress may be of value or not. It should be remembered that emotional factors can provoke coronary disease (Taggart, Gibbons, and Sommerville, 1969) or facilitate the beginning of essential hypertension (Brod, 1963). One may think that a reduced hemodynamic response to emotional stimuli may be of benefit for endangered subjects.

SUMMARY

The cardiovascular changes during an experimentally induced short-term emotional stress situation have been described. The forearm blood flow seems to be an especially sensitive and specific indicator of emotional stress. A standardized and reproducible stress procedure (Stroop color-word test and mental arithmetic test) has been used to study the interference of pharmacological agents with the stress-induced hemodynamic response.

REFERENCES

Abrahams, V C., Hilton, S. M., and Zbrożyna, A. (1960): Active muscle vasodilatation produced by stimulation of the brain stem: Its significancy in the defence reaction, J. Physiol. *154*, 491–513.

Abrahams, V. C., Hilton, S. M., and Zbrożyna, A. (1964): The role of active muscle vasodilatation in the alerting stage of the defence reaction, J. Physiol. *171*, 189–202.

Abramson, M. D., and Ferris, E. B. (1940): Responses of blood vessels in the resting hand and forearm to various stimuli, Am. Heart J. *19*, 541–553.

Ahlquist, R. P. (1948): A study of adrenotropic receptors, Amer. J. Physiol. *153*, 586–600.

Barcroft, H., Brod, J., Hejl, Z., Hirsjärvi, E. A., and Kitchin, A. H. (1960): The mechanism of the vasodilatation in the forearm muscle during stress (mental arithmetic), Clin. Sci. *19*, 577–586.

Barcroft, H., and Swan, H. J. C. (1953): *Sympathetic Control of Human Blood Vessels*, Edward Arnold & Co., London.

Bauer, G., Deisenhammer, W., Sporer, R., Winkler, H., and Konzett, H. (1967): Die Beeinflussung der emotionellen Mehrdurchblutung im Unterarm durch 1-Methyl-2-[2-(2-methyl-sulfinyl-dibenzothiazinyl-10)-äthyl-1]-piperidin (Mesoridazin), Drug Res. *17*, 194–199.

Blair, D. A., Glover, W. E., Greenfield, A. D. M., and Roddie, I. C. (1959): Excitation of cholinergic vasodilator nerves to human skeletal muscles during emotional stress, J. Physiol. *148*, 633–643.

Brod, J. (1963): Haemodynamic basis of acute pressor reactions and hypertension, Br. Heart J. *25*, 227–245.

Brod, J., Fencl, V., Hejl, Z., and Jirka, J. (1959): Circulatory changes underlying blood pressure elevation during acute emotional stress (mental arithmetic) in normotensive and hypertensive subjects, Clin. Sci. *18*, 269–279.

Chapman, W. P. (1960): Depth electrode studies in patients with temporal lobe epilepsy. In: *Electrical Studies on the Unanesthetized Brain*, ed. E. R. Ramey and D. S. O'Doherty. New York.

Dicker, S. E., and Steinberg, H. (1957): The effect of methylpentynol in man, Br. J. Pharmac. Chemother. *12*, 479–483.

Eliasch, H., Rosen, A., and Scott, H. M. (1967): Systemic circulatory response to stress of simulated flight and to physical exercise before and after propranolol blockade. Br. Heart J. *29*, 671–683.

Eliasson, S., Folkow, B., Lindgren, P., and Uvnäs, B. (1951): Activation of sympathetic vasodilator nerves to the skeletal muscles in the cat by hypothalamic stimulation, Acta Physiol. Scand. *23*, 333–351.

Eliasson, S., Lindgren, P., and Uvnäs, B. (1953): Representation in the hypothalamus and the motor cortex in the dog of the sympathetic vasodilator outflow to the skeletal muscles. Acta Physiol. Scand. *27*, 18–37.

Euler, U. S. von (1964): Quantitation of stress by catecholamine analysis, Clin. Pharmacol. Therap. *5*, 398–404.

Fencl, V., Hejl, Z., Jirka, J., Madlafousek, J., and Brod, J. (1959): Changes of blood flow in forearm muscle and skin during an acute emotional stress (mental arithmetic), Clin. Sci. *18*, 491–498.

Frankenhaeuser, M., and Kåreby, S. (1962): Effect of meprobamate on catecholamine excretion during mental stress, Percept. Mot. Skills *15*, 571–577.

Frankenhaeuser, M., and Rissler, A. (1970): Effects of punishment on catecholamine release and efficiency of performance, Psychopharmacologia *17*, 378–390.

Funkenstein, D. H. (1956): Nor-epinephrine-like and epinephrine-like substances in relation to human behavior, J. Nerv. Ment. Dis. *124*, 56–68.

Golenhofen, K., and Hildebrandt, G. (1957): Psychische Einflüsse auf die Muskeldurchblutung, Pflügers Arch. *263*, 637–646.

Grant, R. T., and Pearson, R. S. B. (1938): The blood circulation in the human limb; observations on the differences between the proximal and distal parts and remarks on the regulation of body temperature, Clin. Sci. *3*, 119–139.

Greenfield, A. D. M. (1951): An emotional faint, Lancet, *2601*, 1302–1303.

Heath, R. G., and Mickle, W. A. (1960): Evaluation of seven years' experience with depth electrode studies in human patients. In: *Electrical Studies on the Unanesthetized Brain*, ed. E. R. Ramey and S. S. O'Doherty, New York.

Hickam, J. B., Gargill, W. H., and Golden, A. (1948): Cardiovascular reactions to emotional stimuli. Effect on the cardiac output, arteriovenous oxygen difference, arterial pressure and peripheral resistance, J. Clin. Invest. *27*, 290–298.

Imhof, P. R., Blatter, H., Fuccella, L. M., and Turri, M. (1969): Beta-blockade and emotional tachycardia; radiotelemetric investigations in ski jumpers, J. Appl. Physiol. *27*, 366–369.

Kelly, D. H. W. (1966): Measurement of anxiety by forearm blood flow, Br. J. Psychiat. *112*, 789–798.

Kelly, D., Brown, C. C., and Shaffer, J. W. (1970): A comparison of physiological and psychological measurements on anxious patients and normal controls, Psychophysiology *6*, 429–441.

Konzett, H., and John, R. (1964): Neuropharmaka vom Tranquillizer-Typ und die emotionelle Reaktion der Muskelgefäße am Menschen, Drug Res. *14*, 1175–1179.

Konzett, H., Strieder, N., and Ziegler, E. (1968): Die Wirkung eines β-Rezeptorenblockers auf emotionell bedingte Kreislaufreaktionen, insbesondere auf die Durchblutung des Unterarms, Wien. Klin. Wschr. *80*, 953–959.

Konzett, H., and Strieder, K. (1970): Differentiation of stress stimuli by measuring forearm blood flow, Fed. Proc. *29*, 741, Abs. 2801.

Konzett, H., Hörtnagl, H., Hörtnagl, H., and Winkler, H. (1971): On the urinary output of vasopressin, epinephrine and norepinephrine during different stress situations, Psychopharmacologia *21*, 247–256.

Konzett, H., Berner, W., and Lochs, H. (1973): Emotionally induced cardiovascular changes in man as a means for the investigation of tranquillizing drugs, Psychopharmacologia *30*, 75–82.

Levi, L. (1968): Emotional and biochemical reactions as modified by psychotropic drugs with particular reference to cardiovascular pathology. In: *Psychotropic Drugs in Internal Medicine*, Excerpta Medica International Congress Series No. 182, pp. 206–220, Excerpta Medica, Amsterdam.

Rettenmaier, G. (1969): Biotelemetrie, Fortschr. Med. *87*, 233–236.

Steinmaurer, E. (1970): Vergleich zwischen Schmerz- und Mental Stress-Situationen in bezug auf deren physiologische und psychologische Veränderungen, dissertation, University of Innsbruck.

Stroop, J. R. (1935): Studies of interference in serial verbal reactions, J. Exp. Psychol. *18*, 643–662.

Taggart, P., Gibbons, D., and Sommerville, W. (1969): Some effects of motor-car driving on the normal and abnormal heart, Br. Med. J. *4*, 130–134.

Ulrych, M. (1969): Changes of general haemodynamics during stressful mental arithmetic and non-stressing quiet conversation and modification of the latter by beta-adrenergic blockade, Clin. Sci. *36*, 453–461.

Uvnäs, B. (1966): Cholinergic vasodilator nerves, Fed. Proc. *25*, 1618–1622.

Wilkins, R. W., and Eichna, L. W. (1941): Blood flow to the forearm and calf, Bull. Johns Hopkins Hosp. *68*, 425–429.

Emotions—Their Parameters and Measurement,
edited by L. Levi.
Raven Press, New York © 1975

Psychopharmacological Parameters of Emotion

Leonard Cook and Jerry Sepinwall

Department of Pharmacology, Hoffmann—La Roche, Inc., Nutley, New Jersey 07110

INTRODUCTION

In considering psychopharmacological parameters and methods as they relate to the issue of parameters of emotion, it is obviously necessary to acknowledge the empiricism of the available research approaches. To evaluate the effects of a pharmacological agent on emotional behavior, it would be desirable to have the facility to directly measure emotion, to classify types of emotions, and indeed, to identify emotions in animals that may have relevance or are analogous to human emotional states. When behavioral patterns and their modification due to environmental events have been studied in animals, inferences frequently have been made that a behavioral pattern change may have been due to certain motivational or emotional factors. Yet, as has been clearly pointed out by Kelleher and Morse (1968), assumptions about the nature of tranquilization due to drugs in terms of fear or anxiety have led to inconsistencies. Motivational interpretations of animal behavior are largely tautological, but they have been used in behavioral pharmacology because many drugs are considered to be useful clinically in alleviating emotional disorders. In psychopharmacology, experimental studies of behavior maintained by a variety of reinforcers and different schedules of reinforcement have made such seemingly simple motivational interpretations of drug effects untenable. However, even after acknowledging the limitations of interpreting psychopharmacological methods in regard to the issue of this volume, one must recognize that certain of these experimental methods are most valuable and used extensively in the process of identifying and predicting agents useful in humans with various types of emotional disorders. The validity or utility of such psychopharmacological methods is supported to a high degree by the correlation, albeit empirical, between drug actions in animal laboratory tests and effects in various types of emotional disorders in man. Examples of such relationships will be discussed, as well as additional questions that have arisen concerning certain preconceptions related to such laboratory methodologies.

In many instances, the strategy of designing appropriate behavioral procedures for psychopharmacological studies initially depends on the validation of the clinical effectiveness of a drug or a class of drugs; subsequent efforts are then directed to laboratory methods that offer results that correlate with the clinical findings. General classes of psychotropic drugs commonly used in various types of emotional disorders are neuroleptics (e.g., phenothiazines, haloperidol), tranquilizers (benzodiazepines, meprobamate), and barbiturates. It is presumed that their efficacy in many clinical situations may depend on actions related to emotional states. These drugs have been studied in a variety of psychopharmacological procedures, many of which have been assumed to involve emotionality in animals, and which provide measurable variables that are sensitive to such pharmacological agents. The critical issue continues to be which of the experimental parameters modified by any of these agents correlates with the reported clinically useful effects.

In discussing the role of psychopharmacological methods in the context of parameters of emotion, our experiences with two such procedures will be presented, specifically, conditioned avoidance behavior and punished (conflict) behavior. In conditioned avoidance behavior, the animal is exposed to either cued or noncued electric footshocks and has the opportunity to respond to avoid or escape these aversive stimuli. All species tested including man will predictably demonstrate such avoidance behavior. Punished behavior procedures usually involve previously established behavioral responding (e.g., for food), which is then punished (usually with electric footshock) when such responses occur. The dual processes involved, the tendency to work for food, and the suppression of such responses by punishing them if they occur, have led to considering such an experimental procedure a "conflict" situation. Furthermore, the pharmacological sensitivity of this type of procedure to agents used clinically in anxiety states has led to its frequent classification as an "anxiety" situation.

CONDITIONED AVOIDANCE BEHAVIOR

Conditioned avoidance behavior has been used in many psychopharmacological studies (Dews and Morse, 1961), and it appears that several factors may have been responsible for its extensive application, one being that neuroleptics, such as chlorpromazine and haloperidol, attentuate the conditioned avoidance response maintained by noxious stimuli (usually electric footshock). The neuroleptics can be clearly differentiated from other central nervous system (CNS) active agents such as barbiturates, benzodiazepines, or general depressants in regard to the specificity of this decrease of conditioned avoidance behavior.

One type of frequently studied conditioned avoidance response is classified as a discrete conditioned avoidance response. Although different stimulus and response modalities have been studied, a specific example of this paradigm, as described by Cook and Weidley (1957), can serve to illustrate the methodology. Rats were exposed to an auditory conditioned stimulus

(CS), which was followed after a short time by an unconditioned stimulus (US) consisting of an aversive footshock. The animals had an opportunity to avoid the US (by climbing a pole) during the duration of the CS, or to escape it by making a similar response once the unconditioned aversive stimulus was presented. Figure 1 illustrates the effects of chlorpromazine in rats trained in such a discrete conditioned pole-climb avoidance procedure. Typical of most neuroleptics, chlorpromazine specifically inhibits the conditioned avoidance behavior, while the animals still exhibit escape behavior. Generally, neuroleptics do not suppress the escape behavior until at least 10 times the avoidance suppressant dose is administered (Tedeschi, Tedeschi, Cook, Mattis, and Fellows, 1959). In contrast, agents usually classified as tranquilizers, such as chlordiazepoxide and other benzodiazepines or meprobamate, or agents such as barbiturates, significantly sup-

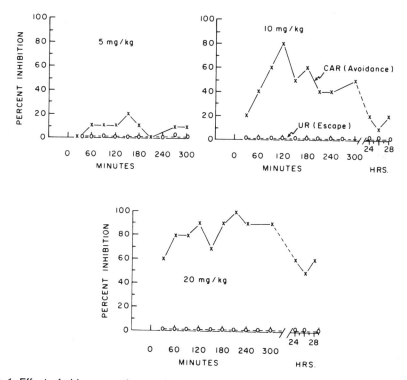

FIG. 1. Effect of chlorpromazine on discrete conditioned pole-climb avoidance response in rats. Ten Charles River (CD albino) rats were assigned to each treatment group and trained to consistently avoid or escape footshock (0.8 mA, 350 V.A.C.) before treatments. Solutions of chlorpromazine hydrochloride were administered orally at 0 time, on the abscissa. During testing, trials were spaced 30 min apart. Each point represents the percentage of animals that failed to make either the conditioned avoidance response (CAR—solid line) or the unconditioned escape response (UR——dashed line) on a given trial. Chlorpromazine was effective in selectively blocking the CAR at doses which did not alter the UR.

press the conditioned avoidance response only at doses that also disrupt the escape behavior, thus classifying such agents as nonspecific avoidance suppressants. Figure 2 presents such an effect with diazepam. Doses of diazepam that suppress the discrete pole-climb avoidance response also suppress the escape response. The differential effects of chlorpromazine and diazepam in this procedure generally are seen with other drugs in each respective category.

The effect of agents like chlorpromazine in specifically suppressing conditioned avoidance behavior is not limited to studies in rats or monkeys, and can also be demonstrated in man (Cook, 1964). Studies with humans in a continuous (Sidman) avoidance procedure were designed to compare the effects of chlorpromazine, meprobamate, chlordiazepoxide, and phenobarbital. Only chlorpromazine specifically suppressed the conditioned avoidance behavior in these human studies, thus demonstrating the species generality of the unique effects of neuroleptics on such behavior compared to other types of psychopharmacological agents.

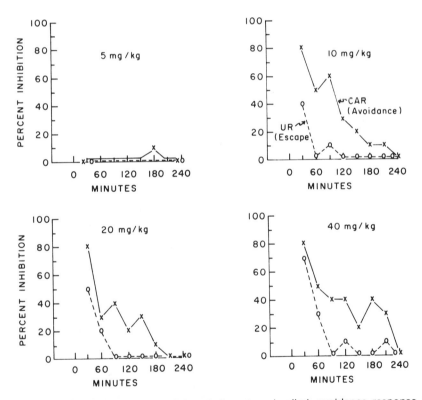

FIG. 2. Effect of diazepam on conditioned discrete pole-climb avoidance response in rats. Experimental method same as described in Fig. 1. Diazepam was suspended in 5% acacia and administered orally at 0 time, on abscissa. The UR was blocked to a significant degree at doses which blocked the CAR, thus indicating a nonselective blockade of avoidance behavior.

The role of interoceptive physiological events in behavior has been considered many times. A relevant question is whether they play any intervening role in avoidance conditioning phenomena, and whether behavior directly elicited by peripheral physiological events is affected similarly by psychopharmacological agents as is behavior directed or controlled by exteroceptive factors. The following experiment was conducted to explore this question. Infusions of *l*-epinephrine in dogs represented the conditioned stimulus in this attempt to simulate the interoceptive correlates of conditioning, and shock to the leg was used as the unconditioned stimulus (Cook and Catania, 1964). It was found that the spectrum of peripheral responses due to epinephrine could serve as an effective stimulus that controlled the development and maintenance of avoidance behavior. The effects of chlorpromazine on these possible intervening events were then examined and it was found that chlorpromazine inhibited the interoceptive conditioned avoidance response at even lower doses than it affected the exteroceptive conditioned response. Furthermore, it did this at doses that did not block the end-organ responses to the *l*-epinephrine infusion. This study showed that agents like chlorpromazine could affect behavior mediated by neurohumoral events that have frequently been associated with emotional states.

The usefulness of conditioned avoidance behavior in psychopharmacological evaluations, particularly for neuroleptics, is further supported by the reported correlation (Cook and Catania, 1964) between the effects of a series of phenothiazines in the discrete conditioned pole-climb avoidance procedure and their effects in patients diagnosed as having severe mental and emotional disorders. Table 1 presents the data that show that the rank order of relative potency of such drugs in the rat conditioned avoidance procedure correlates highly with the rank order of clinical relative potency based on an estimate of the average effective daily dose in such patients. As shown in Table 1, these average clinically effective doses, estimated from

TABLE 1. *Potency of phenothiazines on conditioned avoidance response (CAR) in rats compared with clinical potency*

Trade name	Generic name	CAR ED[50] (mg/kg,[a] p.o.)	CAR rank	Clinical daily dose[b] (mg p.o.)	Clinical rank	Clinical rank by Schiele[c]
Stelazine	Trifluoperazine	0.9	1	3–40	1	1
Trilafon	Perphenazine	1.1	2	16–64	2	2
Dartal	Thiopropazate	1.5	3	20–80	3	3–4
Vesprin	Trifluopromazine	4.0	4	50–150	5	5
Compazine	Prochlorperazine	4.2	5	30–120	4	3–4
Thorazine	Chlorpromazine	9.9	6	75–1000	6	6
Sparine	Promazine	20.3	7	300–1000	7	7

See Cook and Catania (1964).
[a] Calculated as free base.
[b] Severe mental and emotional disorders in adults based on average use.
[c] Schiele (1962).

various reports on these drugs, were supplemented with the results of Schiele (1962) who independently made a relative potency comparison in his clinical studies and reported a similar rank order. Therefore, within this phenothiazine neuroleptic series, the potency of specific suppressant effects on discrete conditioned avoidance in rats had good predictive value with regard to clinical potency. It should be pointed out that no attempt was made to relate these comparisons to degrees of clinical efficacy or possible differences in qualitative effects, nor do the results imply such a relationship.

Although the generality, consistency, and clinical predictability of the effects of neuroleptics on avoidance behavior, in particular discrete avoidance, are clearly established, the unique clinical relevance of this effect within the overall pharmacological profile of such drugs has not been firmly established. Indeed, other investigators (Gray, Osterberg, and Rauh, 1961; Irwin, 1964) have suggested that the clinical efficacy of neuroleptics can be predicted from effects produced in animals on various unconditioned or unlearned behaviors. In addition, however tempting it has been to ascribe "face validity" to behavioral patterns maintained by aversive stimuli in regard to psychopharmacological evaluations, neuroleptic agents such as chlorpromazine *also* suppress behavior maintained by appetitive reinforcement (Hanson, Witoslawski, and Campbell, 1967; Weissman, 1959). Most comparisons of the effects of neuroleptics on both types of behavior have been carried out using continuous or nondiscriminative (Sidman) avoidance behavior and various operant schedules of appetitively motivated behavior. (Continuous avoidance behavior characteristically consists of steady responding on a lever to avoid aversive shocks scheduled to occur at regular time intervals. No exteroceptive conditioned stimuli precede the shock presentations.) In both these aversively or appetitively reinforced behavioral procedures, rate of responding is the measured dependent variable. Such studies have indicated that chlorpromazine similarly decreased both types of behavior at the same dose levels (Kelleher and Morse, 1968). As Kelleher and Morse (1968) have pointed out, there are a great many difficulties involved in comparing behavioral effects of drugs on performances maintained by different types of reinforcers. The reinforcers are presented according to various schedules which frequently generate different response patterns. Studies specifically designed to make these two experimental factors (schedules of reinforcement and response patterns) similar, using either food or footshock reinforcement, have been reported (Cook and Catania, 1964). Monkeys were trained on a fixed-interval 10-min schedule either for food, or to terminate a continuously delivered pulsating electric shock. Each group maintained similar response patterns characteristic of fixed interval schedules under either food presentation or shock termination. Chlorpromazine decreased rates of responding with both reinforcers, and certain doses of amphetamine and meprobamate increased responding with both reinforcers. These results indicate that the effects of drugs are more dependent upon the schedule of reinforcement than on the type of reinforcement, "motivation," or presumed emotional factors that may be involved.

In the preceding discussion about the general response weakening tendencies of neuroleptics, all of the data pertained to experimental designs in which free operant procedures, as opposed to discrete trial tasks, were employed. Yet neuroleptics exert their most specific effects in a discrete trial paradigm. An appetitively reinforced discrete-trial test, in which both a conditioned and unconditioned response could be studied, might, therefore, provide useful information on this issue. If it were to be found in such a test that an agent like chlorpromazine produced a nonselective blockade of both the conditioned and unconditioned responses, then this would provide evidence for a unique role of discrete avoidance tests in psychopharmacological studies.

PUNISHED BEHAVIOR (CONFLICT)

Conflict behavior represents another animal model which has been employed in psychopharmacology to study processes presumably involving emotional behavior (Cook and Catania, 1964; Geller and Seifter, 1960; Miller, 1961). The basic concept consists of training an animal to work for a desirable goal object, such as food, and then introducing punishment such as electric footshock, when the animal responds to obtain the food. By pairing appetitive and aversive reinforcement, the experimenter creates a situation for the animal in which there is an inferred "conflict" between approach and avoidance tendencies or motives.

To accurately assess the effects of psychotropic agents upon such behavior, it is desirable to know their effects on food-rewarded behavior that presumably does not involve conflict. The most useful methods, therefore, are those which study both (approach–avoidance) conflict and unpunished behavior ("pure approach") within the same animals. In addition, trained animals with stable control levels of responding are used, thus making possible an experimental design in which each animal serves as its own control. A commonly employed method of this type was initially described by Geller and Seifter (1960). In some of the research to be discussed in this chapter, a modification developed by Davidson and Cook (1969) was used.

Figure 3 illustrates the multiple VI 30″ FR 10 conflict paradigm of Davidson and Cook. Rats were trained in 47-min sessions 5 days a week to press a lever to obtain food which was available intermittently during a session on two separate contingencies (left panel). During seven 5-min periods the house light was white and a variable interval (VI) 30-sec schedule of reinforcement was in effect, i.e., lever-pressing produced pellets at an average rate of one pellet every 30 sec. Alternating with the VI periods were six 2-min segments during which the house light was red and a fixed ratio (FR)

10 contingency was in effect, i.e., food was delivered for every 10th lever press. The rats developed a discrimination between the two conditions and typically responded at higher rates during the FR periods than during the VI components; maximum rates were approximately 80 to 100 responses per minute.

After the rats had been exposed to this procedure for a few weeks, the next phase of the experiment began (center panel). Electric footshock was added to the FR 10 segments but not the VI 30″ periods. Now whenever a rat completed a group of 10 responses when the red house light was on, it

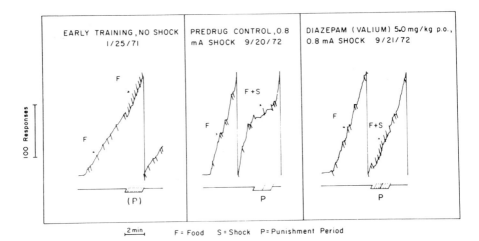

FIG. 3. Rat conflict-punishment behavior. The figure illustrates typical training sequence and diazepam effect. Shown are cumulative recordings of lever pressing responses. Recorder pen moves upward each time rat presses lever; offsets along response measure indicate food deliveries. Subjects were Charles River CD albino rats approximately 250 to 350-g body weight. Left panel: under one condition, responses occasionally produce food (F) under a variable interval 30-sec schedule; under the other condition (P) every tenth response delivers food according to a fixed ratio 10. Center panel: responding is suppressed during P stimulus condition when every tenth response now results in food *plus* footshocks (F + S). Response pattern in the unpunished variable interval condition remains unchanged. Right panel: typical effects of diazepam in restoring responding for food under punishment-conflict conditions (P) without any change in unpunished responding. Prior to diazepam treatment shown, animal had previous history of periodic treatments with various benzodiazepines.

not only received food but a 0.1-sec, 0.5–1.0 mA footshock as well. After shock was introduced, response rates were maintained during the unpunished VI periods, but punished FR rates were suppressed to less than 15 responses per minute. This suppression was designated as "conflict" behavior and psychotropic agents were studied for the ability to attenuate the conflict by increasing responding during the punishment periods. A general design feature of the psychopharmacological experiments was that treatments were administered on Thursdays and data from the preceding sessions on Monday, Tuesday, and Wednesday served as the control values against which treatment effects were assessed.

The right panel of Fig. 3 shows the characteristic effect exerted in this model by a compound with clinical antianxiety activity. Diazepam administration produced increased responding during the punishment periods so that FR response rates recovered toward the level at which they had formerly been during this rat's preshock history.

Cook and Davidson (1973) described the kinds of compounds that were active or inactive in this model (Table 2). Increases in responding during

TABLE 2. Activity of behaviorally active compounds[a]

Compound	Punishment M.E.D. (mg/kg, p.o.)	Relative potency
Effective compounds		
Chlordiazepoxide	2.2	1
Oxazepam	1.25	1.8
Diazepam	0.625	3.5
Tybamate	80	0.03
Meprobamate	62.5	0.04
Amobarbital	5	0.4
Phenobarbital	4.5	0.5
Ethanol	1000	—

	Range of doses tested (mg/kg, p.o.)
Ineffective compounds	
Iproniazid	20–120
Imipramine	0.55–17.7
Morphine	0.24–7.5 (i.p.)
Haloperidol	0.03–0.48
Diphenhydramine	0.55–17.5
d-Amphetamine	0.18–1.5
Chlorpromazine	0.27–17.9

[a] Minimum effective dose (M.E.D.) indicates the lowest dose tested which significantly ($p < .05$) attentuated effects of punishment. Potency was calculated relative to chlordiazepoxide. Compounds classified as inactive either did not affect punished behavior, or did so at only one dose level. Doses are expressed as free base. Adapted from Cook and Davidson (1973).

the punishment periods were primarily produced by several classes of agents that share the common property of being used clinically to reduce anxiety. These included benzodiazepines, carbamic acid esters, and some barbiturates. Increases in responding were obviously not due to any general stimulant property since amphetamine, for example, actually produced a greater amount of suppression during FR segments. Inactive compounds included neuroleptics, such as chlorpromazine and haloperidol, various antidepressants, an antihistaminic agent, and morphine.

Figures 4A and 4B illustrate the dose-response profiles of chlordiazepoxide and bromazepam in this procedure. Punished FR responding was increased in a dose related manner while unpunished VI behavior was only slightly changed over much of the effective anticonflict dose range. At the upper end of the range, VI responding was decreased, an effect that possibly may be related to the onset of sedative actions. Although there was less of an increase in FR responding at high doses, these response rates were still considerably higher than control levels. Thus, the effects of agents active in this procedure can be characterized on the basis of three parameters: the minimum effective anticonflict dose, the range of doses across which anticonflict activity is maintained, and the dose at which VI responding is first decreased. Occasionally, compounds that are not typically characterized as antianxiety agents, for example, trifluoperazine which is a phenothiazine

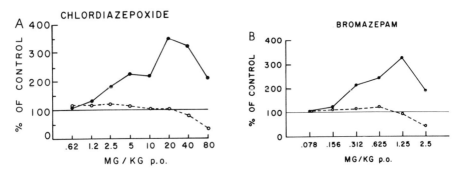

FIG. 4A. Dose response curve of chlordiazepoxide on punished fixed ratio (●——●) and unpunished variable interval (○– – –○) behavior. Doses of chlordiazepoxide hydrochloride, in water solution, were administered orally 40 to 50 min prior to testing. Effect on treatment days is expressed as a percentage of the mean baseline value for the three control days preceding each treatment. The solid horizontal line at 100 percent represents the control level. Fifteen rats served as subjects, with at least 10 rats tested at every dose level except for 80 mg/kg where only seven rats were used. The minimum effective anticonflict dose was in the range of 1.25 to 2.5 mg/kg and significant attenuation of punished behavior continued up through 40 mg/kg. Across the same dose range unpunished responding was either increased approximately 20%, unchanged, or decreased 20%. At 80 mg/kg, unpunished responding was decreased to 44% of control whereas the effects on punished responding were mixed: three rats continued to show large response increases but the other four had decreased rates.

FIG. 4B. Dose response curve of bromazepam on punished fixed ratio (●——●) and unpunished variable interval (○– – –○) behavior. Doses of bromazepam, suspended in 5% acacia, were administered orally 40 to 50 min prior to testing. Ordinate and abscissa details as in Fig. 4A. Five rats served as subjects with at least three rats tested at every dose except for 0.078 mg/kg where only two rats were used. The minimum effective anticonflict dose was 0.312 mg/kg, and unpunished responding was first depressed at 2.5 mg/kg.

neuroleptic, may produce a moderate increase in FR responding at one or two dose levels (Davidson and Cook, 1969). The smaller magnitude of their peak effects and the size of their effective dose ranges, however, appear to distinguish them from members of standard antianxiety classes of agents.

Anticonflict potency in the multiple VI/FR conflict procedure was reported by Cook and Davidson (1973) to correlate highly with clinical potency in cases of psychoneurotic disorders (Table 3). This laboratory model, therefore, not only appeared to be selective for so-called minor tranquilizers but also had predictive validity with respect to clinical application of these compounds to a certain subset of human emotional disorders. As was the case with the conditioned avoidance paradigm, the face validity of the conflict model was quite high and a convincing case could be made for interpreting anticonflict activity in terms relevant to human anxiety concepts. There are alternative explanations, however, that must be considered.

TABLE 3. Comparison of clinical potency with punishment-conflict test

	Rat-conflict			Clinical-psychoneurotics		
					Compar. studies	
	M.E.D. mg/kg p.o.	Relative potency	Rank order	Avg. daily dose, mg oral	Relative potency	Rank order
Diazepam	0.63	3.5	1	20	2	1
Chlordiazepoxide	2.2	1.0	3	40	1	2
Oxazepam	1.25	1.8	2	49	0.8	3
Phenobarbital	4.5	0.5	4	115	0.3	4
Amobarbital	5.0	0.4	5	175	0.17	5
Meprobamate	62.5	0.04	6	1410	0.03	6

Results: Rat minimum effective dose (M.E.D.) indicates lowest dose producing significant anticonflict effects. Average clinical daily dose represents dose found effective in treating psychoneurotic disorders, as estimated from over 100 studies. Relative clinical potency is based on studies in which other drugs were compared directly to chlordiazepoxide (adapted from Cook and Davidson, 1973).

Since chlordiazepoxide has been reported to increase food intake and weight gain in some conditions (Randall, 1960), the possibility has been considered that this was involved in the anticonflict effect. Direct tests of this hypothesis have shown that increases in both food deprivation and body weight loss failed to produce anything greater than a slight increase in responding during punishment periods (Cook and Davidson, 1973; Margules and Stein, 1967). One can also postulate a change in reactivity or sensitivity to shock as a mechanism to account for the reduction of suppression. Two findings have provided evidence contrary to this hypothesis: as described in Table 2, morphine was inactive at doses that are effective in analgesic tests, and, if the experimenter completely eliminates the shock in the conflict paradigm, the suppressed response pattern will recover to baseline levels relatively slowly whereas the attentuation effect of an agent like chlordiazepoxide is immediate (Cook and Davidson, 1973; Margules and Stein, 1967).

Can the suppression reducing activity of these anxiolytic agents best be explained in terms of the emotions, by using such global concepts as anxiety and conditioned fear? An important issue relevant to this question involves what might be termed a "double dissociation" between conditioned avoidance behavior and punished conflict behavior and between neuroleptics and anxiolytics. Since both types of behavior involve footshock, it might be postulated that they are both maintained by conditioned fear. Yet neuroleptics selectively block conditioned avoidance behavior but anxiolytics do not, whereas punishment induced suppression is attenuated by anxiolytics but not by neuroleptics. The contribution of emotional constructs, especially a unitary one like fear, to the interpretation of pharmacological effects in such conditions, therefore, remains open to question.

At the other extreme, it has often been suggested from an operational approach that the actions of psychotropic agents are "rate-dependent," i.e., the magnitude and quality of the pharmacological effects are dependent upon the predrug pattern of responding (Dews, 1964). One principal postulate of this hypothesis is that low predrug response rates will be increased by many psychotropic agents whereas high response rates will be increased less or will be decreased. Some investigators have attempted to apply a rate-dependency analysis to the effects of anxiolytics in the conflict paradigm (Wuttke and Kelleher, 1970). According to this interpretation, the ability of anxiolytics to increase responding that has been suppressed by punishment is merely one instance of a general tendency these agents have to increase low response rates, irrespective of how those low rates originated. It is clear that anxiolytics have increased response rates in many situations, including some which involved appetitive reinforcement only (Hanson et al., 1967; Margules and Stein, 1967).

For several reasons, however, response-contingent punishment conditions remain unique with respect to measuring what many investigators interpret as preclinical predictors of anxiolytic properties. First, under certain conditions amphetamine, chlorpromazine, and imipramine can increase low rates of responding maintained by food reinforcement, yet these agents do not typically increase low rates that have resulted from response-contingent punishment (Kelleher and Morse, 1968). Thus not all agents capable of increasing low response rates are able to increase low rates produced by punishment. Second, when a multiple or concurrent schedule is used in which each animal is exposed to both unpunished and punished segments and conditions are arranged so that matched low rates of unpunished and punished responding occur, then anxiolytics increase both rates, but they raise the punished rate to a greater extent (Cook and Catania, 1964; McMillan, 1973). Thus, even though the degree to which anxiolytics increase punished responding is inversely related to baseline rates (Cook and Davidson, 1973; McMillan, 1973), there appears to be a specific effect that these agents exert upon punished behavior that cannot entirely be explained in terms of rate-dependence.

In conflict tests, some phenomena have been observed that are relevant to the clinical application of benzodiazepine antianxiety agents and that begin to suggest something about underlying neurochemical mechanisms. A given dose of a benzodiazepine produced different profiles after what might be considered acute administration as compared with repeated treatment. This was reported by Margules and Stein (1968) who trained rats in a conflict procedure and then initiated a 22-day period of daily presession oxazepam (20 mg/kg i.p.) treatment. The first administration (which was analogous to an acute treatment) of oxazepam to rats that had never before been treated with any psychotropic agent produced the following features: there was a marked decrease in unpunished responding and only a moderate increase in responding during the punishment periods. Over the next three or four administrations the decrements in unpunished responding gradually ceased while the anticonflict effect increased to an asymptotic level. It took approximately four repeated treatments, therefore, for the characteristic features of that given dose's profile to be attained. Margules and Stein (1968) also studied effects of chronic treatment in "drug sophisticated" rats, i.e., animals with a history of periodic benzodiazepine treatments, oxazepam included. When such animals were retested with oxazepam (20 mg/kg i.p.) after a treatment-free period, they immediately showed a maximal anticonflict effect without a decrement of the unpunished response pattern. Cannizzaro et al. (1972) have reported similar results with flurazepam hydrochloride (30–100 mg/kg p.o.), even when the repeated treatments were given at 2- or 3-day intervals rather than daily. All of these investigators considered the decrease in unpunished responding to be correlated with the sedative properties of benzodiazepines. (This is an interpretation that warrants further study.) The anticonflict or response disinhibitory effects were interpreted as being masked by the initial sedative actions and as subsequently becoming apparent when tolerance to the sedative effects occurred. Furthermore, these results were considered by these authors to be analogous to similar findings observed when such agents were used to treat patients with psychoneuroses.

These interesting results lead one to assume first that some biochemical mechanisms underlying tolerance must have been primarily responsible for such findings. However, it is important to point out that the nature of a pharmacological effect may be critically determined by an interaction between drug and behavior or drug and environmental conditions. To give one example, Sparber and Tilson (1971) have reported that when rats trained to lever press for food were treated with mescaline hydrochloride (10 mg/kg i.p.) and were immediately placed in the operant conditioning chamber, lever pressing became disrupted 10 min later and this effect lasted for 25 min. However, such manipulations as briefly removing an animal from the chamber shortly after the mescaline disruption began, or keeping a rat in its home cage for 10 min after injection and then placing it into the operant chamber greatly decreased the duration of the disruptive effect. Thus, the drug effect was dependent on its interaction with the environmental setting.

To return now to the repeated-dosing benzodiazepine effects cited above, none of the experiments were designed to distinguish between behavioral and biochemical adaptation. We have begun to collect data suggesting that there may be a drug-behavior interaction that contributes to the effects of benzodiazepines in the conflict paradigm. Naive rats were trained in the multiple VI/FR conflict test and were given the usual five sessions per week. When they had reached criterion control levels, they were exposed on consecutive Thursdays to a series of six oral 40-min presession treatments, the first two of which were vehicle control (water) injections; the last four were chlordiazepoxide hydrochloride (10 mg/kg) injections. Figure 5 shows that the phenomenon reported by Margules and Stein (1968) and Cannizzaro et al. (1972) also occurred with chlordiazepoxide. Furthermore, the effect occurred even though chlordiazepoxide was given at 7-day intervals. This result, taken together with the finding that animals with a previous history of benzodiazepine treatment were immediately sensitive to the anticonflict effect and resistant to the depression of unpunished responding (Margules

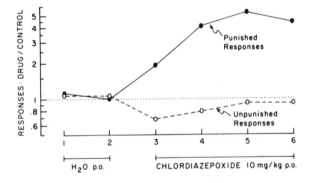

FIG. 5. Effects of chlordiazepoxide in conflict-punishment test in pharmacologically *naive* rats. Once a week, rats received either water (first two treatments) or chlordiazepoxide (last four treatments) orally 40 to 50 min prior to testing. Three rats served as subjects. Effect on treatment days is expressed as a ratio of response rate on treatment day to the mean baseline value for the three control days preceding each treatment. The dotted horizontal line at 1 represents the control level. (Note the logarithmic scale on the ordinate.) Treatment No. 3, which represented the first time these rats had ever received medication, produced a significant decrease in unpunished VI rates and only a moderate attenuation of punished FR rates. Only on the third consecutive dosing of chlordiazepoxide was VI responding no longer affected and a maximum level of FR responding attained.

and Stein, 1968), suggests that it is probably not the accumulation of either the drug or some metabolic product that accounts for the changing pharmacological effect over the first few dosings.

A second group of naive rats was trained in the conflict test until their control levels were stable, after which they were exposed to a series of six consecutive chlordiazepoxide (10 mg/kg p.o.) treatments at weekly intervals. The first two treatments, however, were given approximately 15 min *after* completion of a session whereas the last four injections were given at the usual presession pretreatment time of approximately 40 min. Figure 6 indicates that, even though the animals had received two prior administrations of the compound outside of the test situation, they still showed a marked decrease in unpunished responding and only a minimal increase in punished responding when the first presession treatment was given. It still took three presession treatments before the anticonflict effect reached its maximum. These results tentatively suggest that it is necessary for the pharmacological treatment to interact with the animal's behavior in the test situation for the ultimate nature of the treatment effect to become apparent. This is an important factor, which must be recognized in studying drugs and emotional behavior or, indeed, any behavior. It may be relevant to several clinical situations in which treatment effects take time to fully appear.

Having said this, however, it is necessary for us to add that metabolic interpretations of this phenomenon cannot be ruled out. Experiments are currently in progress to determine whether additional initial postsession treatments might modify the interaction phenomenon shown in Figs. 5 and

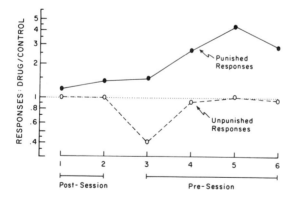

FIG. 6. Effect of chlordiazepoxide in conflict-punishment test in rats with history of two prior extrasituational chlordiazepoxide treatments. Once a week for 6 weeks, five pharmacologically naive rats received chlordiazepoxide (10 mg/kg p.o.). Ordinate details are the same as Fig. 5. The first two treatments were given 15 min *after* testing had been completed, whereas the last four were given 40 to 50 min *prior* to testing. As in Fig. 5, the first presession treatment (No. 3) was still associated with a significant decrease in unpunished VI responding. No real increase in punished FR responding was seen during this session, and it was not until the third presession treatment (treatment No. 5) that a peak in FR responding was seen.

6. Goldberg, Manian, and Efron (1967) showed that, after chlordiazepoxide was given to mice and rats at high doses for 14 consecutive days outside of the test situation, tolerance to several CNS depressant actions of this agent was demonstrated during the first testing. They attributed their results to metabolic factors. Thus, within the benzodiazepine class, the possibility remains that such a mechanism may also be operative in the conflict paradigm. Or perhaps the conflict phenomenon we have been describing for pharmacologically naive rats is determined by a combination of a drug behavior interaction and a metabolic process. The type of behavior involved, which consists of learned responses under discriminative control in the conflict method, must be important because a different type of result has been obtained with the effects of chronic benzodiazepine administration upon less complex behavior. For example, Cannizzaro et al. (1972) found that rats did not develop any tolerance to the depressant effects of flurazepam on locomotor activity even after eight repeated treatments. Goldberg et al. (1967) also found that motor activity was depressed after 14 days of chronic chlordiazepoxide treatment, although some groups showed a partial tolerance.

The initial-dose conflict phenomenon has not been reported yet for other chemical classes, such as the carbamates and barbiturates. Analogous studies with those agents should contribute useful information on this topic. One comparison between meprobamate and chlordiazepoxide that may be relevant has already been made in a different test situation using another indicator of the response disinhibitory properties of anxiolytics. The ability of these compounds to increase the low initial rates in fixed-interval food-reinforcement operant schedules in monkeys was studied during a period of chronic daily treatments. It was observed that tolerance developed over the first few daily dosings to chlordiazepoxide's response-incrementing action but not to meprobamate's similar effect (Cook, 1965). Perhaps this difference between the two classes will be found in the conflict paradigm as well.

Wise, Berger, and Stein (1972) have used the initial-dose conflict phenomenon as a point of departure for speculating about biochemical factors that may account for the antianxiety properties of benzodiazepines. Their hypothesis is based partially upon some biochemical effects observed in stressed and unstressed animals. Taylor and Laverty (1969) have reported that several benzodiazepines decreased rat-brain-norepinephrine turnover and also antagonized the increased brain-catecholamine turnover due to electrofootshock stress. Corrodi, Fuxe, Lidbrink, and Olson (1971) similarly found that the same agents blocked immobilization-stress induced increases in norepinephrine turnover and also reduced this turnover in some brain areas in unstressed rats. Chase, Katz, and Kopin (1970) found in unstressed rats that brain-serotonin turnover was also apparently reduced after diazepam treatment. These biochemical findings have been correlated with a behavioral result in the conflict paradigm, i.e., that a serotonin depletor, parachlorophenylalanine (PCPA), produced an anticonflict effect (Geller and Blum, 1970; Robichaud and Sledge, 1969). Wise et al. (1972) have postulated that the decrease in unpunished responding seen in the initial-dose phenomenon represents the sedative effect of benzodiazepines, that reduced norepinephrine turnover accounts for this effect, and that the behavioral recovery is due to a biochemical tolerance to the reduced turnover. Furthermore, the anticonflict effect represents the antianxiety activity and it is due to reduced serotonin turnover, this postulate being related to the anticonflict activity of PCPA. Wise et al. have offered some intriguing biochemical data in support of their hypothesis. They found that after six daily oxazepam (20 mg/kg i.p.) treatments the reduction in norepinephrine turnover no longer occurred whereas the serotonin turnover continued to be reduced. The effect on serotonin turnover correlates with continued anticonflict activity over the same time period (Margules and Stein, 1968).

To study this hypothesis we carried out a series of pilot experiments over a 7-month period with six rats serving as subjects. (Five of the six rats were used in more than one study.) These animals were trained in the multiple VI/FR conflict paradigm until they attained stable baseline levels, after which they were tested for responsiveness to at least several treatments of chlordiazepoxide. The four experiments to be described below essentially employed the following basic design. Chlordiazepoxide's (10 mg/kg p.o.) anticonflict effect was measured, and, at some later date, the rats were treated with a monoamine depletor, e.g., PCPA, while daily sessions were continued. On certain days after administration of the depletor, the rats were treated with chlordiazepoxide (10 mg/kg p.o.) to determine whether the response to it had been altered in any way and, if so, to assess any possible correlations with reported biochemical changes. Sufficient time, as indicated in the literature, was allowed between experiments for monoamine levels to recover to normal. Figure 7 presents the data collected in the last experiment that was carried out. In agreement with previous studies (Geller and Blum, 1970; Robichaud and Sledge, 1969), PCPA (*methyl ester hydrochloride,* 300 mg/kg p.o.) produced an immediate and significant anticonflict effect that was sustained on the two successive days. According to biochemical studies, among the various sequelae of PCPA administration at this dose is a steady fall in brain serotonin levels during this period to as low as 10% of control (Jequier et al., 1967; Koe and Weissman, 1966) and a reduction of norepinephrine levels to only 75–90% of control. At a time of maximal depletion on the third day after PCPA, chlordiazepoxide was given. The increase in punished responding due to chlordiazepoxide now seemed to be greater compared to the previous chlordiazepoxide level. Additional work will be required, however, to confirm this effect, since the number of animals involved did not permit accurate statistical testing of the difference. It appears likely that the greater chlordiazepoxide effect probably represented a simple addition with the PCPA effect. It is important to point out that in

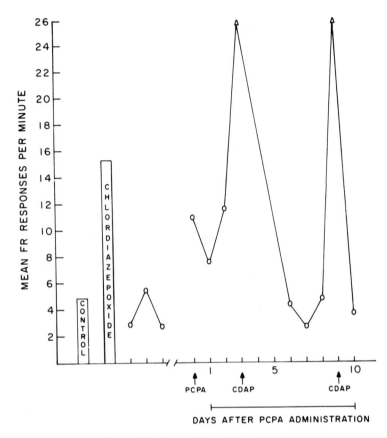

FIG. 7. Effects of chlordiazepoxide in punishment-conflict test in rats pretreated with parachlorophenylalanine (PCPA methyl ester hydrochloride, 300 mg/kg p.o.). Three rats served as subjects. Ordinate: mean punished FR responses per minute. Abscissa: the punishment attenuating effect of chlordiazepoxide hydrochloride (10 mg/kg p.o. given 40 to 50 min prior to session) was first measured (bar graphs on left). Subsequently, the rats received a single dose of PCPA (suspended in 5% acacia) approximately 40 min prior to testing, followed by chlordiazepoxide treatments 3 and 9 days later. There was a significant increase in punished responding on the PCPA day and the following 2 days as compared to the 3 control days preceding PCPA administration. The effect of chlordiazepoxide seemed to be enhanced after PCPA treatment but the sample size was too small to permit accurate statistical testing of this.

this experiment chlordiazepoxide continued to be effective in PCPA-treated animals at a time when serotonin levels were presumably very low.

In the experiment performed prior to the one just discussed, parachloromethamphetamine (PCMA hydrochloride, 3.5 mg/kg i.p.) was employed as the serotonin depletor. This agent was used because it does not affect norepinephrine levels as PCPA does, it depletes serotonin by a different mechanism, and its spectrum of additional biochemical and pharmacological effects differs considerably from PCPAs (Korf and van Praag, 1972; Miller, Cox,

Snodgrass, and Maickel 1970; Pletscher, Da Prada, Burkard, and Tranzer 1968). Figure 8 indicates that PCMAs primary effect was a typical amphetamine-like *reduction* in punished responding. Whereas PCPA produced an anticonflict effect, PCMA acted in the opposite direction. When chlordiazepoxide was given on the third day after PCMA, however, there was once again a suggestion that the response to it was slightly increased. Both of these experiments indicated, therefore, that chloridazepoxide's activity was intact in serotonin-depleted animals, that the response to it may possibly have been slightly enhanced, and that the depleting agent did not have to produce attentuation by itself for the anticonflict effect of chlordiazepoxide to occur. Additional work will be required to determine how these findings relate to a theory such as that of Wise et al. (1972).

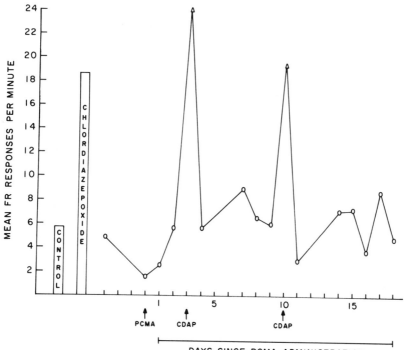

FIG. 8. Effects of chlordiazepoxide in punishment-conflict test in rats pretreated with parachloromethamphetamine (PCMA hydrobromide, 3.5 mg/kg i.p.). Four rats served as subjects. Ordinate: details as in Fig. 7. Abscissa: details as in Fig. 7, with following differences: a single treatment of PCMA (suspended in 5% acacia) was given, at point indicated, approximately 40 min prior to testing, and chlordiazepoxide hydrochloride was given 3 and 10 days later. PCMA almost completely abolished unpunished VI responding (not shown) on the treatment day and also decreased punished FR responding. When chlordiazepoxide was given after PCMA treatment, the animals showed the typical FR rate increase; during the first post-PCMA chlordiazepoxide test, this increase was slightly larger than the pre-PCMA response to chlordiazepoxide.

As a final comment on this topic, we would like to discuss two more experiments indicating that this is a complex issue and that caution is needed before ascribing results too readily to certain biochemical mechanisms. Figure 9 presents the results of the first experiment we did. Four rats received daily doses of PCPA (*free acid,* 100 mg/kg p.o. suspended in a 5% acacia solution) for three consecutive days, a regimen that has been reported to produce the typical amount of depletion (Koe and Weissman, 1966). Two of the rats received a single booster dose (100 mg/kg) 5 days later. When the three initial days of PCPA administration were compared with the three preceding control days, a significant, but small, degree of conflict attenuation was observed. The most surprising finding was that when chlordiaze-

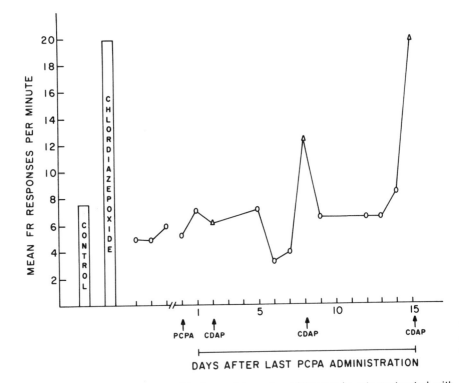

FIG. 9. Effects of chlordiazepoxide in punishment-conflict test in rats pretreated with parachlorophenylalanine (free acid, 100 mg/kg p.o. × 3 or 4). Four rats served as subject. Ordinate: details as in Fig. 7. Abscissa: details as in Fig. 7, with following differences: all rats received three consecutive daily doses of PCPA (suspended in 5% acacia) approximately 40 min prior to testing; 2 of the rats then received a booster dose 5 days later. Chlordiazepoxide hydrochloride was administered 2, 7, and 15 days following each rat's last PCPA dose. The data plotted for the PCPA day represent the mean response rates for the last PCPA day only. When the three initial PCPA days were compared with the three preceding control days, a significant, but small, increase of punished FR responding was observed. The response to chlordiazepoxide was completely blocked 2 days after the last PCPA treatment and had returned to the pre-PCPA level on the fifteenth day.

poxide (10 mg/kg p.o.) was given two days after each rat's last PCPA treatment, the anticonflict response to chlordiazepoxide was completely blocked. A graded recovery of responsiveness to chlordiazepoxide then ensued, which followed the apparent time course of serotonin repletion as reported in the literature (Jequier, 1967; Koe and Weissman, 1966).

This result was so surprising that we subsequently replicated the study using the same animals with only one change: we gave the PCPA (free acid) in one dose of 300 mg/kg p.o. instead of three or four divided doses. Whereas PCPA itself had been slightly effective in increasing punished responding in the first study, under these treatment conditions it was not active (Fig. 10). The response to chlordiazepoxide when it was given on the third day after PCPA, however, again was completely blocked, and there was a subsequent recovery like that in the first study.

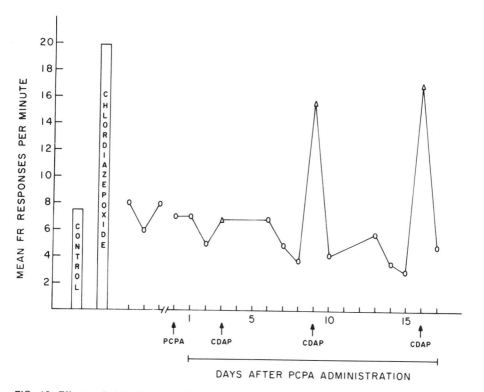

FIG. 10. Effects of chlordiazepoxide in punishment-conflict test in rats pretreated with parachlorophenylalanine (free acid, 300 mg/kg p.o.). The 4 rats used for the study depicted in Fig. 9 were also used for this study. Ordinate: details as in Fig. 7. Abscissa: details as in Fig. 7, with following differences: a single treatment of the free acid form of PCPA (suspended in 5% acacia) was given, followed by chlordiazepoxide hydrochloride administrations 2, 9, and 15 days later. PCPA itself did *not* exert an anticonflict effect. The response to chlordiazepoxide was completely blocked 2 days after the PCPA treatment and had returned to the pre-PCPA level by the fifteenth day.

Accounting for these data remains a matter that we are continuing to study. The studies using PCMA and the methyl-ester hydrochloride form of PCPA indicated that there was no absolute correlation between the depletor's effect on punished behavior and the subsequent response to chlordiazepoxide. Within the three separate experiments in which the two PCPA preparations were employed, however, when good attenuation to PCPA itself was observed, a normal or possibly enhanced sensitivity to chlordiazepoxide occurred, whereas the response to chlordiazepoxide was blocked when there was only weak attenuation or no effect produced by the PCPA. To assume that the free-acid form of PCPA was inactive in the first two experiments and was not producing any biochemical effects does not seem reasonable because one important effect was occurring, i.e., that chlordiazepoxide was now inactive in these animals and recovery of its anticonflict effects correlated with the reported recovery curves of serotonin. In addition, when the brains of untrained rats treated with 300 mg/kg p.o. of PCPA free acid or PCPA methyl-ester hydrochloride were recently assayed, it was found that both compounds were equally effective as serotonin depletors (Table 4). It seems unlikely, therefore, that serotonin depletion can be invoked as the only mechanism that may have been involved in all of these phenomena. Such a series of experiments serves to remind students of the physiological and biochemical correlates of emotional behavior that the path to improved understanding is indeed complex and is in need of patient unraveling.

DISCUSSION

Rather than attempting to survey all of the numerous procedures used in psychopharmacological studies, we have chosen to discuss two types of behavior, avoidance and conflict, at some length. This has enabled us to deal with what we consider some of the major issues involved in studying drug effects in behavioral procedures presumably involving emotional components. Although many investigators might find it convenient to apply anthropomorphic concepts in psychopharmacological approaches, a critical analysis indicates that, to date, such concepts have not contributed to any better understanding of the experimental phenomena than has an operational approach.

"Fear," for example, is a commonly employed concept or an inferred emotional state that various research workers have invoked especially in psychopharmacological studies that employ electric footshock. One can safely assume that such an environmental stimulus is aversive to or nonpreferred by animals since they will usually work to avoid it or to reduce its occurrence. It has been implied (Miller, 1964) that pharmacological attenuation of avoidance responding, as well as of other footshock-motivated behavior, is due to an effect upon conditioned fear processes assumed to be involved in such patterns of behavior. However, the available experimental

TABLE 4. *Effects of two forms of para-chlorophenylalanine (PCPA) on brain concentrations of biogenic amines*

Group[c]	Serotonin	Norepinephrine	Dopamine
	(Mean concentration (μg/g brain) $\pm$ S.D.)		
Control (acacia)	0.432 ± 0.025	0.443 ± 0.094	1.284 ± 0.505
PCPA, free acid 300 mg/kg p.o.	0.044 ± 0.010^{b} (10.1%)[d]	0.338 ± 0.070^{a} (76.4%)	0.884 ± 0.281 (68.9%)
PCPA, methyl ester HCl 300 mg/kg p.o.	0.068 ± 0.027^{b} (15.8%)	0.368 ± 0.061 (83.2%)	0.779 ± 0.271^{a} (60.6%)

We are grateful to W. Dale Horst for performing these assays.

[a] $p < 0.05$ (one-tailed "t"-test).

[b] $p < 0.005$ (one-tailed "t"-test).

[c] Each group consisted of six rats; a 5% acacia solution was used as the vehicle for both forms of PCPA.

[d] (Percent of control).

Animals were sacrificed 72 hr after treatment with PCPA or vehicle. Brains were removed and homogenized in 10 ml 0.4N perchloric acid, centrifuged and the supernatants removed for assay. The catechols were separated from noncatechols on alumina columns as described by Kopin et al. (1). Norepinephrine and dopamine were separated on dowex columns (2) and assayed fluorometrically according to Laverty and Sharman (3). Serotonin was extracted from the alumina column effluents into butanol as described by Snyder et al. (4) except that 1 ml of 0.1N HCl was substituted for 1.4 ml of 0.05M phosphate buffer in the final step of the extraction procedure. 0.5 ml of the 0.1N HCl phase was removed and reacted with O-Phthalaldehyde (OPT) in 10N HCl as indicated by Maickel et al. (5). All values have been corrected for recovery and are expressed as μg/gram of brain. 1. Kopin, I. J., Axelrod, J. and Gordon, E. (1961): The metabolic fate of ^{3}H-epinephrine and ^{14}C-metanephrine in the rat, J. Biol. Chem. *236*, 2109–2113. 2. Horst, W. D., and Jester, J. (1971): The fate of [^{14}C] L-3,4-dihydroxyphenylalanine in isolated perfused rat hearts, Biochem. Pharmacol. *20*, 2633–2638. 3. Laverty, R., and Sharman, D. F. (1965): The estimation of small quantities of 3,4-dihydroxyphenylethylamine in tissue, Brit. J. Pharmacol. *24*, 538–548. 4. Snyder, S. H., Axelrod, J., and Zweig, M. (1965): A sensitive and specific fluorescence assay for tissue serotonin, Biochem. Pharmacol. *14*, 831–835. 5. Maickel, R. P., Cox, Jr., R. H., Saillant, J., and Miller, F. P. (1968): A method for the determination of serotonin and norepinephrine in discrete areas of rat brain, Int. J. Neuropharmacol. *7*, 275–281.

evidence does not allow a conclusion that psychopharmacological agents act directly on a common unitary process of "fear." It is clear that, dependent on the experimental design and the behavioral patterns developed in such experiments, specific drugs will modify some behavioral patterns maintained by aversive footshock and not other behaviors also dependent on the same type of aversive footshock. Experimental designs and factors such as schedules of reinforcement seem to be prepotent over the reinforcement itself in regard to the effects of certain psychopharmacological agents.

We have attempted to point out that psychopharmacological agents do not act *upon* behavior. Evidence supports the concept that there are important drug-behavior *interactions* that play a major role in determining the pharmacological effect.

Studies of neurobiochemical events will hopefully contribute to a more thorough understanding of the mechanisms underlying such behavioral patterns. Studies with parachlorophenylalanine have raised interesting suggestions about the possible relationship of serotonin to conflict behavior and to the anticonflict effects of certain pharmacological agents. However, changes of serotonin levels, per se, apparently do not account for all the results discussed, and, obviously, additional studies of the overall effects of serotonin depletors are needed.

Avoidance behavior developed and maintained by epinephrine-induced physiological events was particularly sensitive to inhibition by chlorpromazine. This suggests that such conditioned interoceptive systems may play an important role in the psychopharmacological actions of this type of agent. Studies of concurrent behavioral and physiological measurements would clarify these relationships and provide additional objective criteria towards the definition of parameters of emotion.

SUMMARY

Two psychopharmacological models, conditioned avoidance and punishment-conflict procedures, are discussed in terms of their utility for studying classes of compounds, such as neuroleptics and anxiolytics, that are effective in treating emotional disorders. Although these methods have good predictive validity for identifying such agents, it does not appear at present that any unitary emotional construct, e.g., "fear," can adequately account for all of the actions of such drugs in these models.

Recently collected preliminary data are presented that suggest the possible dependence of the "anticonflict" action of benzodiazepines in pharmacologically naive animals upon an interaction between repeated treatments and behavior. Other preliminary studies are reported in which biogenic amine depletors, e.g., PCPA, were employed to investigate current hypotheses about biochemical factors which may underly punishment-conflict behavior.

ACKNOWLEDGMENTS

We thank John W. Sullivan and Edward Boff for their contributions to the performance and interpretation of experiments we have described. We also thank Elkan Gamzu for helpful comments on the manuscript and Diana Cantrella for her excellent secretarial assistance.

REFERENCES

Cannizzaro, G., Nigito, S., Provenzano, P. M., and Vitikova, T. (1972): Modification of depressant and disinhibitory action of flurazepam during short term treatment in the rat, Psychopharmacologia 26, 173–184.

Chase, T. N., Katz, R. I., and Kopin, I. J. (1970): Effects of diazepam on fate of intracisternally injected serotonin-C[14], Neuropharmacology 9, 103–108.

Cook, L. (1964): Effects of drugs on operant conditioning. In: *Ciba Foundation Symposium, Animal Behaviour and Drug Action* (ed. H. Steinberg, A. V. S. de Reuck, and J. Knight) Ciba Foundation, London.

Cook, L. (1965): Behavior changes with antipsychotic drugs in animals. In: *Neuro-Psychopharmacology*, Vol. 4 (ed. D. Bente and P. B. Bradley) Elsevier Publishing Co., Amsterdam.

Cook, L., and Catania, A. C. (1964): Effects of drugs on avoidance and escape behavior, Fed. Proc. *23*, 818–835.

Cook, L., and Davidson, A. B. (1973): Effects of behaviorally active drugs in a conflict-punishment procedure in rats. In: *The Benzodizepines* (ed. S. Garattini, E. Mussini, and L. O. Randall) Raven Press, New York.

Cook, L., and Kelleher, R. T. (1962): Drug effects on the behavior of animals, Ann. N.Y. Acad. Sci. *96*, 315–335.

Cook, L., and Weidley, E. (1957): Behavioral effects of some psychopharmacological agents, Ann. N.Y. Acad. Sci. *66*, 740–752.

Corrodi, H., Fuxe, K., Lidbrink, P., and Olson, L. (1971): Minor tranquilizers, stress and central catecholamine neurons, Brain Res. *29*, 1–16.

Davidson, A. B., and Cook. L. (1969): Effects of combined treatment with trifluoperazine-HCl and amobarbital on punished behavior in rats, Psychopharmacologia *15*, 159–168.

Dews, P. B. (1964): A behavioral effect of amobarbital,Naunyn-Schmiedebergs Arch. Exp. Path. Pharmak. *248*, 296–307.

Dews, P. B., and Morse, W. H. (1961): Behavioral pharmacology, Ann. Rev. Pharmacol. *1*, 145–174.

Geller, I., and Blum, K. (1970): The effect of 5-HTP on para-chlorophenylalanine (*p*-CPA) attenuation of conflict behavior, Eur. J. Pharmacol. *9*, 319–324.

Geller, I., and Seifter, J. (1960): The effects of meprobamate, barbiturates, *d*-amphetamine and promazine on experimentally induced conflict in the rat, Psychopharmacologia *1*, 482–492.

Goldberg, M. E., Manian, A. A., and Efron, D. H. (1967): A comparative study of certain pharmacologic responses following acute and chronic administrations of chlordiazepoxide, Life Sci. *6*, 481–491.

Gray, W. D., Osterberg, A. C., and Rauh, C. E. (1961): Neuropharmacological actions of mephenoxalone, Arch Int. Pharmacodyn. Therap. *134*, 198–215.

Hanson, H. M., Witoslawski, J. J., and Campbell, E. H. (1967): Drug effects in squirrel monkeys trained on a multiple schedule with a punishment contingency, J. Exp. Anal. Behav. *10*, 565–569.

Irwin, S. (1964): Prediction of drug effects from animals to man. In: *Ciba Foundation Symposium, Animal Behaviour and Drug Action* (ed. H. Steinberg, A. V. S. de Reuck, and J. Knight), Ciba Foundation London.

Jequier, E., Lovenberg, W., and Sjoerdsma, A. (1967): Tryptophan hydroxylase inhibition: the mechanism by which *p*-chlorophenylalanine depletes rat brain serotonin. Mol. Pharmacol. *3*, 274–278.

Kelleher, R. T., and Morse, W. H. (1968): Determinants of the specificity of the behavioral effects of drugs, Ergebnisse Physiol. *60*, 1–58.

Koe, B. K., and Weissman, A. (1966): *p*-Chlorophenylalanine: a specific depletor of brain serotonin, J. Pharmacol. Exp. Ther. *154*, 499–516.

Korf, J., and van Praag, H. M. (1972): Action of *p*-chloroamphetamine on cerebral serotonin metabolism: an hypothesis, Neuropharmacology *11*, 141–144.

Margules, D. L., and Stein, L. (1967): Neuroleptics vs. tranquilizers: evidence from animal behavior studies of mode and site of action. In: *Neuro-Psycho-Pharmacology* (ed. H. Brill), Excerpta Medica Foundation, Amsterdam.

Margules, D. L., and Stein, L. (1968): Increase of "anti-anxiety" activity and tolerance of behavioral depression during chronic administration of oxazepam, Psychopharmacologia *13*, 74–80.

McMillan, D. E. (1973): Drugs and punished responding I: rate-dependent effects under multiple schedules, J. Exp. Anal. Behav. *199*, 133–145.

Miller, F. P., Cox, R. H., Jr., Snodgrass, W. R., and Maickel, R. P. (1970): Comparative effects of *p*-chlorphenylalanine, *p*-chloroamphetamine and *p*-chloro-N-methylamphetamine on rat brain norepinephrine, serotonin and 5-hydroxy-indole-3-acetic acid, Biochem. Pharmacol. *19*, 435–442.

Miller, N. E. (1961): Some recent studies of conflict behavior and drugs, Amer. Psychologist *16*, 12–24.

Miller, N. E. (1964): The analysis of motivational effects illustrated by experiments on amylo-barbitone. In: *Ciba Foundation Symposium — Animal Behavior and Drug Action* (ed., H. Steinberg, A. V. S. de Rueck, and J. Knight) Ciba Foundation, London.

Pletscher, A., Da Prada, M., Burkard, W. P., and Tranzer, J. P. (1968): Effects of benzoquinoli-zines and ring-substituted aralkylamines on serotonin metabolism, Adv. Pharmacol. *6B*, 55–69.

Randall, L. O. (1960): Pharmacology of methaminodiazepoxide, Dis. Nerv. Syst. *21*, 7–10.

Robichaud, R. C., and Sledge, K. L. (1969): The effects of p-chlorophenylalanine on experi-mentally induced conflict in the rat, Life Sci. *8*, 965–969.

Schiele, B. C. (1962): Newer drugs for mental illness, J. Amer. Med. Assoc. *181*, 126–133.

Sparber, S. B., and Tilson, H. A. (1971): Environmental influences upon drug-induced sup-pression of operant behavior, J. Pharmacol. Exp. Ther. *179*, 1–9.

Taylor, K. M., and Laverty, R. (1969): The effect of chlordiazepoxide, diazepam and nitraze-pam on catecholamine metabolism in regions of the rat brain, Eur. J. Pharmacol. *9*, 296–301.

Tedeschi, D., Tedeschi, R., Cook, L., Mattis, P. S., and Fellows, E. J. (1959): The neuro-pharmacology of trifluoperazine: A potent psychotherapeutic agent, Arch. Int. Pharmacodyn. Therap. *122*, 129–143.

Weissman, A. (1959): Differential drug effects upon a three-ply multiple schedule of reinforce-ment, J Exp. Anal. Behav. *2*, 271–287.

Wise, C. D., Berger, B. D., and Stein, L. (1972): Benzodiazepines: Anxiety-reducing activity by reduction of serotonin turnover in the brain, Science *177*, 180–183.

Wuttke, W., and Kelleher, R. T. (1970): Effects of some benzodiazepines on punished and unpunished behavior in the pigeon, J. Pharmacol. Exp. Ther. *172*, 397–405.

Emotions—Their Parameters and Measurement,
edited by L. Levi.
Raven Press, New York © 1975

Negative Emotions and Perception

E. A. Kostandov

*Laboratory of Higher Nervous Activity, Serbsky Research Institute of Forensic Psychiatry,
Moscow, U.S.S.R.*

INTRODUCTION

The problem of the influence of emotion and motivation on the perception of external stimuli is engaging psychologists and neurophysiologists at present. McGinnies (1949) was the first to find, by tachistoscopic presentation of separate words, that the recognition threshold of unpleasant words was greater than that of neutral ones. Lazarus and McCleary (1951) elaborated conditioned defence reactions in healthy subjects to certain syllables by using cutaneous shock; this resulted in higher thresholds of recognition for these syllables than for neutral ones. Phares (1962) repeated these experiments, eliciting avoidance reactions, and demonstrated a decreased recognition threshold.

In our experiments (Kostandov, 1968) the recognition thresholds for emotional words connected with the subjects' unpleasant experiences were quite different from the thresholds for neutral words. Decreased as well as increased recognition thresholds were observed for emotional words, the latter accounting for approximately two-thirds of the cases. A particular subject's recognition threshold may be higher for one emotional word and lower for another. And the threshold for a particular word symbolizing a similar conflict situation may be high for one subject and low for another.

The subliminal presentation of an emotional word with a high recognition threshold was often associated with cortical desynchronization, galvanic-skin reaction (GSR), respiratory and cardiac reactions (i.e., the subliminal effect of an unrecognized word).

Psychologists (Eriksen, 1956; Goldiamond, 1958; Bevan, 1964; Spence, 1967) differ in opinion and offer various hypotheses and theories concerning the heightening of recognition thresholds for emotional words, which they term "emotional defense" or "psychological blindness." Little has been done to explain the neural mechanisms of these phenomena. Dixon and Lear (1964*a,b*) suggested that "emotional defense" is conditioned by preaware changes in the level of cortical activity by reticular formation. The function of the cortex in subliminal perception of a word before its conscious perception is not yet clear. Our hypothesis is that the limbic system, which sends its impulses to the neocortex, is decisively involved in changes of the recognition threshold for emotional words (Kostandov, 1970). This supposition is based on facts established by Beritoff (1965) in his experiments on animals. It is known that the limbic system integrates the whole emotional reaction with both its subjective and its objective manifestations. When the emotional stress is prolonged, a low threshold of excitation in limbic structures is observed.

The limbic system influences the perception of external stimuli. It has been studied in experiments on animals by registering evoked electrical activity. In Sierra and Fuster's (1968) experiments, using electrical stimulation of the hippocampus and amygdala, it was found that the amplitude of late evoked potentials to visual stimulus was increased. Lorens and Brown (1967), on the other hand, obtained a decreased amplitude of evoked potentials in the visual cortex when using septum stimulation and simultaneous light presentation. Posterior hypothalamus stimulation of various intensity evokes facilitation as well as inhibition of evoked visual cortical response (Baklavajian, 1967; Chi and Flynn, 1968).

Begleiter et al. (1967, 1969) observed changes in evoked potential amplitude in humans given a conditional signal for negative emotion.

The purpose of our research was:

1. To study the influence on the cortical evoked potentials of visual verbal stimuli that differ in semantic content but are constant in light intensity, the words having either neutral or emotional meaning for the subject.

2. To establish relations between time and amplitude values of evoked potentials for emotional words and the changes in the psychophysiological recognition threshold to the word.

3. To investigate the influence of benactyzine on the cortical evoked potentials to neutral and emotional words and also on the recognition threshold of these words.

Benactyzine is known to be an anticholinergic substance which according to clinical observation suppresses fear, anxiety, and tension in humans. The most suitable subjects for investigating the role of negative emotion on perception in our opinion are psychopaths in a stressful situation. In such cases the task of choosing a verbal stimulus to evoke intense negative emotions is simplified.

METHOD

The subjects were 23 adults 20 to 40 years of age, all with normal vision. They were psychopaths who had committed offenses and were under surveillance.

The experiments were carried out in a dark, soundproof room with the subjects seated in a semireclining position with the eyes open. Neutral and "conflict" words associated with the stressful situation were used as stimuli. The words, green in color, were flashed on a screen placed 1.8 m from the subject's eyes. The screen consisted of electroluminescent symbols 4×2.2 cm in size with rapid decay (1 msec). Illumination in the vicinity of the indicators was 0.1 lk $\pm$ 20%. A time relay allowing any combination of symbols to be presented on the screen was used as the control device. The time of exposure varied from 5 to 1,000 msec.

The following preliminary instruction was given to the subject: Look attentively at the screen and try to read the words that will appear there periodically for brief periods of time. As soon as you identify the word, pronounce it. The subject was given 10 min for adaptation to the dark. Then a neutral word was presented. To start with, the exposure lasted 50 msec, so that the subject could read the word. The exposures were then increased 20 to 50 msec at a time until correct recognition occurred. The recognition threshold was taken to be the minimal exposure time required for correct identification of the word. The intervals between the presentations of words lasted 20 to 60 sec. Simultaneously, the polygraph of a Nihon Kohden ME-132 registered the EEG, GSR, respiration, EKG, and the finger plethysmogram of the index finger of the left hand. The recording of EEG was monopolar. Active electrodes were placed on the vertex and inion (to 2.5 to 3 cm up and 2 cm to the left occipital tuber), the reference electrode on the ipsilateral ear lobe. The time constant for the EEG amplifier was 0.3 sec, for the GSR amplifier — 4 sec.

Having established psychophysiological word recognition thresholds in 13 subjects, the average evoked potential (AEP) was registered for the same word. The electrodes for EEG recording were also used for AEP. The potentials were put through the polygraph amplifier to be analyzed by computer (ART-1000). Analyzing time was 1,000 msec. The 50 potentials of the cortex were averaged. Time exposure of words was constant (200 msec). Flash intensity of all stimuli was the same (0.1 lk $\pm$ 20%). Each word consisted of a similar number of letters. Stimuli were presented once every 5 sec. After each session the subject gave an oral account of his sensation.

As the repetition of visual word stimuli at regular intervals gives a decreasing recognition threshold, the conditions used in our experiments were supraliminal, irrespective of their semantic content.

The AEP were photographed from an oscilloscope of ART-1000. The latencies and the amplitudes of negative wave N_{200} and positive wave P_{300} were analyzed. The amplitude was measured from peak to peak. In the trials, when only one wave was registered, the amplitude was measured from base line to peak. The amplitudes and time values were analyzed statistically. The total amount of material for analysis was 156 AEP's for neutral and 91 for emotional words.

Below are given the results of three investigations according to the plan given above. The measurements of psychophysiological threshold and the AEP registration were made before the injection of benactyzine (1.5 ml and 0.4%), after the medicine had taken effect (40 min after injection), and at the end of its effect. The interval between sessions varied from 1 to 3 days. In all three experiments each subject was presented with the same neutral and emotional stimuli.

RESULTS

Psychophysiological Word Recognition Threshold

Subjects had a range of 100 to 800 msec for the recognition threshold for neutral words. The threshold depended on the number of letters in the word. The threshold for seven to eight letter words was 100 to 200 msec higher than for four to five letter words. (The number of letters in the English words does not correspond to that of Russian.)

The threshold was quite different for emotional and neutral words with the same number of letters (Table 1). The threshold was higher for emotional words in two-thirds of the cases, that is in 62 out of 91; six subjects showed lower thresholds in 19 trials, three subjects showed similar thresholds in five trials.

Subliminal effect was observed when the threshold was high for emotional words; bioelectric and vegetative reaction occurred prior to word recognition.

The subliminal zone was wide: 90 to 820 msec. The threshold for bioelectrical and vegetative reaction was 90 msec, and emotional word threshold 820 msec. Figure 1 shows no reaction to the word "east," time exposure 180 msec (A). The same time exposure showed GSR for the emotional word "thief" (B). An exposure of 200 msec for the word "thief" (C) gave a still greater subliminal effect. Increasing the time of exposure of the emotional word evoked a decrease in reaction (D). With a time exposure of

TABLE 1. *Recognition threshold differences in neutral and emotional words*

Patient M. E.		Patient H. P.	
Exposed word	Threshold (msec)	Exposed word	Threshold (msec)
Grass	400	Armchair	500
Window	350	Plate	600
Bag	300	Bracelet	600
School	300	Syphilis	1,000
Honor	250	Tram	600
Rain	350	Snow	400
Tram	450	Beer	400
Bracelet	450	Tiger	350
Slander	1,000		
Plate	400		

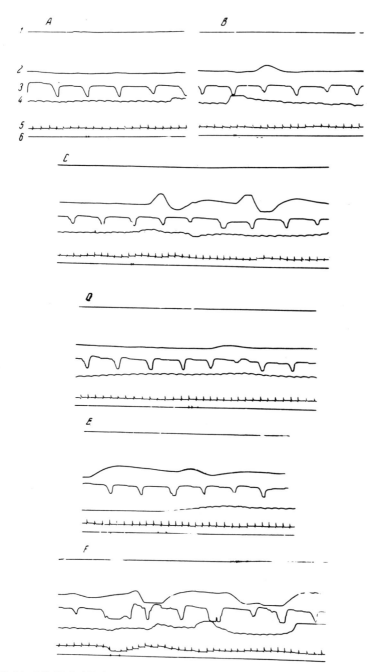

FIG. 1. Subject S. T. Subliminal effect of emotional word. 1. electromyogram of a hand; 2. galvanic skin response; 3. respiration; 4. plethysmogram; 5. electrocardiogram; 6. moment of stimulus presentation and its time exposure. A. The word "east" presented, time exposure 180 msec. The word "thief" presented (B–F): time exposure 180 msec (B), 200 msec (C), 300 msec (D), 800 msec (E), 900 msec (F).

800 msec (close to the psychophysiological threshold of 900 msec) no distinct reaction was observed (E). The subject cried, and the GSR and respiratory reactions were clearly observed (F). The increase in the emotional word threshold was in no way caused by the subject refusing to pronounce the unpleasant word. This is proved by the observed subliminal effect of the word.

AEP to Neutral Verbal Stimuli

The AEP's to visual stimuli were recorded in all subjects. Different subjects showed different wave forms. Some had AEP consisting of six to seven waves negative and positive ending in alpha-after-discharge (Fig. 2A); others consistently showed two negative and two positive components (Fig. 2B); still others showed only a slow positive wave with a latency near 300 msec (Fig. 2C).

In all cases this late positive wave was recorded from inion and vertex. The P_{300} latency was 320 ± 11.2 msec in visual cortex (occipital area), amplitude 10.9 ± 0.94 μV. In vertex the P_{300} latency was 294 ± 7.3 msec, amplitude 8.7 ± 0.43 μV. The amplitude of P_{300} in inion for neutral stimuli was significantly greater than in vertex ($p < 0.001$). Also the latency of P_{300} in vertex was shorter than in visual area; there was no significant difference between them ($p > 0.05$).

Negative wave N_{200}, preceding P_{300}, appeared with a latency of 220 ± 8 msec and an amplitude of 7.3 ± 0.9 μV. Subjects investigated on several occasions often showed varying parameters of P_{300} to neutral words (even to the same word). The same subject during one experiment showed no significant difference, even to different neutral words (Fig. 3). This made it possible to compare cortical potentials with neutral and emotional stimuli registered in the same experiment.

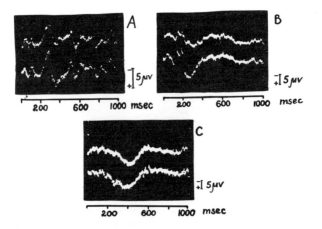

FIG. 2. Different waveforms of AEP's to visual stimuli.

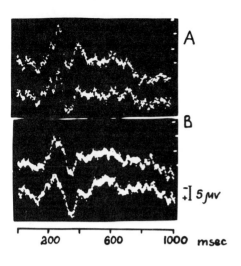

FIG. 3. AEP's to neutral words recorded during one session. Subject Sh. P. A. to the word "cabbage." B. to the word "drawing." In this and the following figures, upward deflection indicates negativity. Time analysis— 1,000 msec.

AEP to Emotional Verbal Stimuli

In the case of emotional stimuli, late positive wave P_{300} from the occipital area was recorded from 10 subjects. The wave was of greater amplitude and shorter latency than for neutral words (Figs. 4 and 5). The average amplitude component was 13.7 ± 0.82 mkv, the latency 270 ± 10.4 msec. The differ-

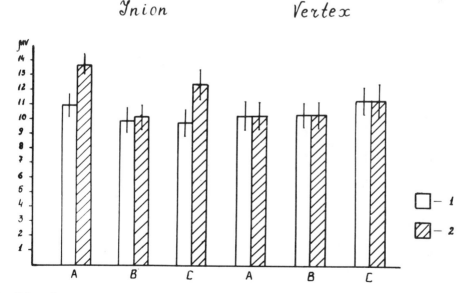

FIG. 4. Changes in P_{300} amplitude under benactyzine effect in subjects showing increased potential to emotional word. Ordinate: mean P_{300} amplitude. A. before injection; B. under benactyzine effect; C. control sessions 1 to 3 days after injection. 1. neutral word presentation; 2. emotional word presentation.

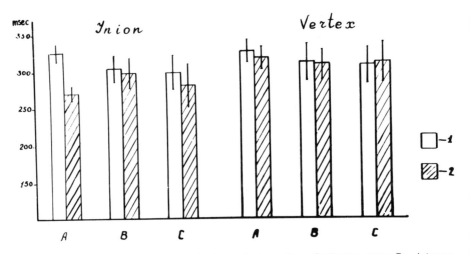

FIG. 5. Changes in P_{300} latency under benactyzine effect. Ordinate: mean P_{300} latency. Symbols same as Fig. 4.

ence in parameters of P_{300} between neutral and emotional words was significant ($p < 0.05$ and $p < 0.001$). Three subjects showed lower P_{300} to emotional words than to neutral ones. The amplitude was $10 \pm 0.45\ \mu$V for neutral and $7.6 \pm 0.62\ \mu$V for emotional, the difference being significant ($p < 0.002$). The latency to emotional words was shorter than to neutral (Fig. 6). The average latency was 287 ± 6 msec in the vertex to emotional words, similar to the latency of P_{300} to a neutral stimulus.

Figures 4–6 show that P_{300} taken from the vertex to emotional and neutral stimuli was of nearly the same latency and amplitude.

Thus emotional stimuli evoked changes in the amplitude and time param-

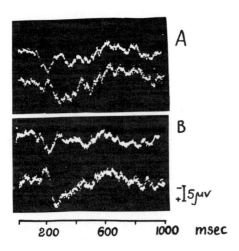

FIG. 6. Increase in amplitude and shortening of latency for P_{300} to emotional stimulus, its recognition threshold being lower. Subject B. V. A. AEP to neutral word "staircase," recognition threshold 30 msec; B. AEP to emotional word "lover," recognition threshold 15 msec.

eters of P_{300} in the occipital area. The latency became shorter and in most cases the amplitude increased; only occasionally did it decrease.

Influence of Benactyzine on AEP

No changes in the latency and amplitude of AEP to neutral words were observed after injection (Fig. 7). An insignificant slight shortening of latency and a decrease in amplitude were observed for P_{300} only in the occipital area. Emotional stimuli after injection evoked significant changes in P_{300} in the occipital region.

In cases in which the amplitude to emotional stimuli was high before injection, the administration of benactyzine decreased the amplitude. After injection, the average amplitude was 10.3 ± 0.83 μV, compared to $13.7 \pm 0.82 \mu$V before ($p < 0.01$).

This decrease in amplitude erased the differences in the amplitude of P_{300} between emotional and neutral stimuli (Fig. 7). These results were observed only during the temporary effect of benactyzine; control tests after several days gave results similar to those prior to injection.

Benactyzine also eliminated the difference in P_{300} latency in the visual area between neutral and emotional words. This reflected not only the increase of P_{300} latency to emotional stimuli but also the evoked response latency decrease to neutral words (Fig. 5).

The AEP amplitude and latency to the neutral word "cabbage" and the

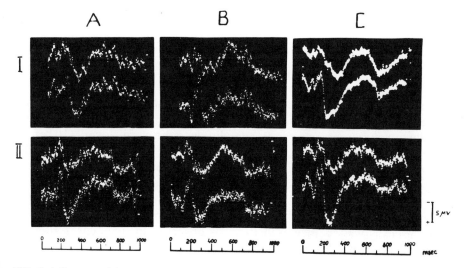

FIG. 7. Influence of benactyzine on AEP's. The P_{300} amplitude to emotional stimulus is increased. Subject S. A. I. AEP's to neutral word "cabbage"; II. AEP's to emotional word "janitor"; A. before injection; B. under effect; C. control session 1 to 3 days after injection; I. vertex; II. visual area. Upward deflection indicates negativity.

emotional word "janitor" (the subject suspecting his wife of connections with a janitor) became equal when the subject was under the effect of benactyzine. In this case, elimination of the difference was mainly the result of the decrease in electric response latency from the occipital area to the neutral word (Fig. 7).

It is of interest to study the benactyzine effect on subjects whose responses to emotional stimuli were lower than those to the neutral (Fig. 8).

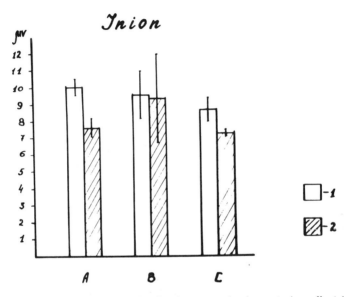

FIG. 8. Changes in P_{300} amplitude in visual area under benactyzine effect in subjects showing decreased amplitude to emotional stimulus.

Under benactyzine, the P_{300} amplitude to emotional stimuli increased, while to neutral it remained unchanged. As a result the two became equal. Benactyzine evokes an increase in P_{300} amplitude to the word "lover" (10 before injection, 13.7 under effect), becoming equal to the amplitude evoked by the neutral word "staircase" (Fig. 9). After the effect of benactyzine had ended, the amplitude to the same emotional stimulus returned to the preinjection state.

Benactyzine injection did not evoke definite changes in AEP in the vertex. Decreased as well as increased P_{300} was observed in some cases after injection. These changes were insignificant.

Figure 4 presents average P_{300} amplitudes for all subjects. No changes for neutral or emotional words were observed in the vertex under benactyzine effect. Nor were significant changes observed in latency in the vertex.

Comparisons of the amplitude and latency of the late negative wave N_{200}

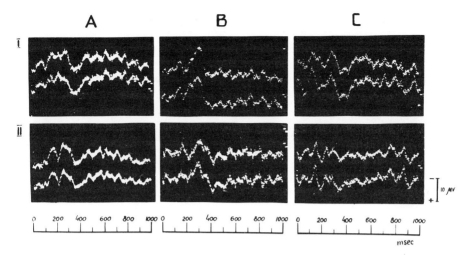

FIG. 9. Effect of benactyzine on AEP. The amplitude of P_{300} to emotional stimulus is decreased. Subject B. M. I. AEP to neutral word "staircase"; II. AEP to emotional word "lover."

before injection and during effect showed no significant differences. Benactyzine did not change the N_{200} amplitude and latency in the vertex or the occipital region for either neutral or emotional words.

Before injection, the N_{200} latency in the occipital area to emotional stimuli averaged 211 ± 11 msec and the amplitude 8.5 ± 0.9 μV; under effect, latency was 213 ± 15.9 msec and amplitude 7.6 ± 1.2 μV.

Thus benactyzine evokes significant changes only in the P_{300} component in the occipital area. These changes were expressed by the elimination of differences in the P_{300} latency and amplitude values between neutral and emotional word stimuli.

As already mentioned, the psychophysiological threshold of conscious perception of emotional stimuli differed greatly in all subjects from that for neutral words. In most cases the emotional word recognition threshold was higher. The threshold differences between neutral and emotional words were eliminated under the effect of benactyzine (Table 2).

Such an effect was noticed in only five subjects. Repeated measurements from these subjects several days later showed preinjection threshold differences. The data from these cases definitely proved the elimination of differences to be due to benactyzine. In the rest of the subjects, benactyzine either did not eliminate threshold differences or there were no control tests. In these cases it is therefore impossible to say for certain that the threshold changes were evoked by benactyzine and not be habituation as a result of repeated tests with the same words.

Thus in some subjects, benactyzine led to the elimination of differences

TABLE 2. Changes in thresholds[a] of recognition of neutral and emotional words under the influence of benactyzine

Initials of patient	B. P.	K. I.	B. M.	K. B.	L. A.	M. M.	S. A.	S. A.	T. A.	B. V.	M. E.	G. K.
Prior to be-nactyzine injection	300 / 500	250 / 1,000	550 / 400	400 / 1,000	450 / 800	400 / 1,000	500 / 550	500 / 800	300 / 600	350 / 15	500 / 150	100 / 200
After the injection of be-nactyzine	800 / 800	700 / 700	400 / 400	250 / 250	600 / 600	800 / 700	750 / 600	800 / 750	250 / 100	100 / 40	100 / 30	250 / 600
Second investiga-tion with-out be-nactyzine	250 / 350	400 / 500	400 / 350	300 / 700	200 / 400	– / –	400 / 350	– / –	300 / 300	– / –	– / –	250 / 500

[a] Number above the line stands for the threshold of recognition (in msec) of a neutral word; that under the line for an emotional word.

in the activity evoked in the visual cortex by neutral and emotional words; under the same conditions the psychophysiological thresholds for the same words were identical.

DISCUSSION

Our data show that psychophysiological threshold changes were caused by highly emotional words chosen especially for the subject. The physical energy of the stimuli was constant, but differences were observed in the amplitude and latency of AEP for emotional compared with neutral words. The changes of AEP cannot be attributed to diversion of attention or orienting reflex to the stimuli, since the subjects received preliminary instructions to count the number of neutral and emotional words presented. Nor can dilatation of the pupils have influenced the reaction to negative words: investigations by Fleming (1969) on cats and John et al. (1967) with people have shown that the amplitude and waveform of AEP's to visual stimuli are independent of pupil size.

Benactyzine is known to suppress negative emotions. Differences in AEP values were eliminated during benactyzine effect. The recognition thresholds of neutral and emotional words became equal under benactyzine effect. There is reason to suppose that changes in psychophysiological thresholds are due to emotional words.

Temporary elimination of recognition threshold differences to neutral and emotional words can be achieved with chlorpromazine, which likewise suppresses negative emotional reaction (Kostandov, 1970).

Thus the change in the perception of emotional words (called "emotional defense" or "psychogenic blindness") may be connected with the degree of its emotion. There exist many psychological hypotheses on "emotional defense" and the associated subliminal effect, but few attempts have been made to explore the neurophysiological mechanisms. Dixon and Lear (1964 *a,b*) found that alpha "blocking" could be detected on the presentation of insulting words. They supposed that the preawareness change of cortical activity originated in the reticular formation. However, the nature of the cortical process prior to word recognition has not yet been established.

Under the influence of a conflict situation, an active or passive defense reaction takes place. A complex system of temporary connections occurs in the cortex. One connection is transcortical between two groups of neo-cortex neurons, one reacting to conditioned and the other to unconditioned stimuli. Another connection is between the sensory cortex and the limbic system, the "center" of emotional behavior.

Under emotional stress, the greatest plastic structural changes in synapses evidently occur in the neuron circuits connected with emotional behavior. To facilitate the activity of these neuron circuits, the repetition of one emotional stimulus is applied.

It is conceivable that, in a state of emotional stress, the excitation threshold of temporary connections between sensory neocortex neuron circuits and limbic structures may be significantly lower than the threshold of association activity between these sensory neocortex neurons and the neurons fulfilling motor verbal function.

The hypothesis that excitation of the motor cortical region is important for conscious sensation has been tested by Sperry (1966) and Johnson and Gazzaniga (1969) in their investigations on humans with split brain. It was found that the "mute" right hemisphere "reacts" to visual and auditory speech. The absence of a motor speech center in the right hemisphere rules out verbalizing and conscious recognition. The gnostic speech zones of both hemispheres fulfill analysis and synthesis of verbal signals, but conscious recognition does not occur if the impulses from these zones are not transferred to the motor verbal region.

The impulses in response to subliminal emotional verbal stimuli come to the corresponding sensory gnostic neocortex regions; after their analysis and synthesis there, the limbic structures are excited, but the activity of the motor cortex region is absent. This results in the excitation of the paleo-cortex, hypothalamic, and brainstem mechanisms of defense and orienting reaction, with unconscious emotional reaction. Evidently this excitation of limbic structures is fulfilled by well-developed connections between the neocortex and limbic systems (Beritoff, 1968; Sager, 1968). The resulting somatovegetative and bioelectric reactions are considered to be a subliminal effect to emotional words.

Experiments on animals and humans have established that certain limbic structures, when excited, change the transmission of afferent signals (Sierra and Fuster, 1968; Lorens and Brown, 1967; Baklavajian, 1967). We observed changes in the latency and amplitude of AEP's to emotional stimuli in humans. The changes were local, occurring mostly in the occipital area, which fulfills the analysis and synthesis of visual signals. These changes were not observed in the vertex.

These facts allow us to suppose that increased (or decreased) amplitude to emotional stimuli is due to impulses from the limbic structures of the brain.

A facilitating effect from limbic structures on the cortex may act directly or through multisynaptic connections or reticular formation of brainstem and thalamus (Fuster and Docter, 1962; Lorens and Brown, 1967).

Additional excitation of the cortex takes part in the development of the late positive wave P_{300} when the stimulus is highly emotional for the subject. These word stimuli were chosen as emphasizing the stress situation of the subject, thereby eliciting negative emotions.

Our supposition is supported by pharmacodynamic experiments. Clinical data and animal experiments show that benactyzine suppresses negative emotions, supposedly inhibiting a cholinergic mechanism of the limbic system (Iluchenok and Chapligina, 1970). In our experiments it temporarily eliminated the difference in P_{300} latencies and amplitudes between neutral and emotional words. This occurred because the effect of benactyzine is chiefly confined to emotional stimuli. Evidently benactyzine blocks the impulses connected with the emotional component of verbal stimulus.

Our data do not indicate which of the limbic structures gives rise to the impulse that conditions changes in the late positive potential in the visual cortex to emotional stimulus. Benactyzine experiments have shown, however, that the changes are due to a relatively local influence on the visual cortex from the limbic system. The ascending impulses are facilitative for evoked activity in most cases, for some subjects, and for others they are inhibitative, to judge from the amplitude.

To judge from the latency of the cortex response, in all cases additional impulses evoked by emotional stimulus are facilitative, the neurons of the visual cortex being activated.

Visual emotional stimulus evokes analysis and synthesis in the cortex, leading to the stimulus and recall of unpleasant situations in the subjects memory. As a result, the corticofugal impulses give rise to additional ascending impulsation. The P_{300} values are influenced by the complex process in the neuronal circuits of the cortex-subcortex-cortex, activated by external stimulus and depending on information stored in memory.

In view of the psychological significance of the stimulus, the absence of changes in N_{200} is unexpected. This once more emphasizes the fact that only P_{300} exactly expresses functional changes in human cortex. It is of interest that benactyzine suppresses impulsation originating in that zone of the cortex, which is directly connected with the modality of emotional stimuli. Evoked activity in the vertex is in no way influenced by benactyzine. Benactyzine exerts a local influence, affecting structures that take part in mechanisms of negative emotional reactions. It is of interest that the above-mentioned benactyzine effect on the evoked activity and its elimination of psychophysiological differences in the recognition thresholds for neutral and emotional words are the same. Our experiments showed that additional impulsation, resulting from an emotional component of stimulus, influences the evoked potentials. We propose that this impulsation may also be effective in changing the recognition threshold for emotional words. With the subject in a stress situation, additional impulsation originating in the limbic system activates prior to the conscious recognition of the emotional word. The result is recognition threshold changes. Further experiments are necessary for proof.

CONCLUSION

AEP's to neutral and emotional visual stimuli were compared, the physical energy of both being constant. AEP was measured at the occipital region. The late positive component P_{300} had a shorter latency and greater amplitude to negative emotional stimuli than to neutral. Under benactyzine, differences in AEP were temporarily abolished. In the vertex there was no significant difference between the AEP to neutral and emotional words. Evidently an increase in amplitude and a shortening of latency of P_{300} in the occipital area are caused by additional "nonspecific" local impulsations from limbic structures. Experiments with benactyzine prove this supposition. Perhaps, after preliminary cortical analysis of a visual stimulus and the subject's association, there is additional impulsation caused by the emotional intensity of the word. This impulsation may be the reason for the recognition threshold changes for emotional words.

REFERENCES

Baklavajian (1967): *Vegetative Regulation of Brain Electrical Activity,* Leningrad.
Begleiter, H., Gross, M. M., and Kissin, B. (1967): *Psychophysiology 3,* 336.
Begleiter, H., Gross, M. M., Porjesz, B., and Kissin, B. (1969): *Psychophysiology 5,* 517.
Beritoff, I. (1968): In: *Structure and Function of Paleocortex.* Gagra symposium, *5,* 11.
Beritoff, I. S. (1965): *Neural Mechanisms of Behavior of Vertebrates.* Little-Brown, Boston.
Bevan, D. (1964): *Psychol. Bull. 61,* 81.
Chi, C. C., and Flynn, J. P. (1968): *Clin. Neurophysiol. 24,* 343.
Dixon, N. F., and Lear, T. E. (1964a): *Electroencephalogr. Clin. Neurophysiol. 16,* 312.
Dixon, N. F., and Lear, T. E. (1964b): *Nature, 203,* 167.
Eriksen, C. W. (1956): *Psychol. Rev., 63,* 74.
Fleming, D. E. (1969): *Electroencephalogr. Clin. Neurophysiol. 27,* 1, 84.
Fuster, J. M., and Docter, R. E. (1962): *J. Neurophysiol. 25,* 324.
Goldiamond, I. (1958): *Psychol. Bull. 55,* 373.
Iluchenok, R. U., and Chapligina, S. R. (1970): *Zh. Vyssh. Nervn. Deiat. 20,* 176.

John, E. R., Herrington, R. N., and Sutton, S. (1967): *Science 155*, 1439.
Johnson, J. D., and Gazzaniga, M. S. (1969): *Nature 223*, 5201, 71.
Kostandov, E. A. (1968): *Zh. Vyssh. Nervn. Deiat. 18*, 371.
Kostandov, E. A. (1970): *Zh. Vyssh. Nervn. Deiat. 20*, 2, 441.
Lazarus, R. S., and McCleary, R. A. (1951): *Psychol. Rev. 58*, 113.
Lorens, S. A., and Brown, T. S. (1967): *Exp. Neurol. 17*, 86.
McGinnies, E. (1949): *Psychol. Rev. 56*, 244.
Phares, E. J. (1962): *J. Psychol. 53*, 399.
Sierra, G., and Fuster, J. M. (1968): *Electroencephalogr. Clin. Neurophysiol. 25*, 274.
Spence, D. P. (1967): *Behav. Sci. 12*, 183.
Sperry, R. W. (1966): In: *Brain and Conscious Experience*, Berlin-Heidelberg-New York.

Emotions—Their Parameters and Measurement,
edited by L. Levi.
Raven Press, New York © 1975

Parameters of Action and Measuring Emotions

Pavel V. Simonov

*Institute of Higher Nervous Activity of the U.S.S.R. Academy of Sciences,
Moscow, U.S.S.R.*

INTRODUCTION

The physiology of the late 19th and early 20th century related human and animal emotional reactions mainly to humoral-vegetative processes in the organism. This trend was clearly visible in attempts to identify the role of visceral shifts in the formation of emotional coloring of stimuli influencing the organism (James-Lange theory) as well as in works discussing emotions as states of extreme mobilization of vegetative power resources (Cannon). From the late 1930's onward, however, scientists became more concerned with determining exactly which peculiarities of interaction between the organism and the environment lead to excitation of cerebral structures responsible for emotional reactions. The traditional approach to emotions as neurohumoral homeostatic and mainly vegetative processes is no longer adequate. Emotion and perception, emotion and action, emotion and *information* in general form one of the main problems in contemporary emotion physiology.

On the basis of experiments by Asratyan (1953), who investigated system approach to the activity of the cerebral hemispheres, and on studies by his other colleagues, Pavlov (1951) advanced an idea of dynamic stereotype, the steady system of "signal–response" as a result of a steadily repeated system of inner and outer signals. Pavlov related the involvement of the nervous apparatus of emotions to a process of disruption of the fixed stereotype and its substitution by a new system of adaptive action. The idea of disagreement between the model provided by the brain and the available environment was developed by other scientists.

Anokhin (1964) suggested that dissociation of "acceptor of action" (afferent model of expected results) and the afferentation about real results of adaptive act signal the involvement of a negative-emotions apparatus. Correspondence between the "acceptor of action" and the afferent signalization of achieved effect leads to the generation of positive emotions.

DEPENDENCE OF PROBABILITY OF NEED SATISFACTION ON SKILLED PERFORMANCE

We obtained relevant demonstrative data by elaborating a conditional defensive reflex in man (Simonov, 1964).

The subjects were instructed to press a key 20 sec after a short sound signal (Fig. 1). If the subject pressed the key less than 19 sec or more than 21 sec after the signal, an electric shock of 60 to 90 volts of distinct nociceptive quality was administered. After each trial the subject was told the real duration of his reaction. The degree of emotional stress was measured by the change in heart rate. Galvanic skin response (GSR) was monitored simultaneously. The increase in heart rate was estimated from the total

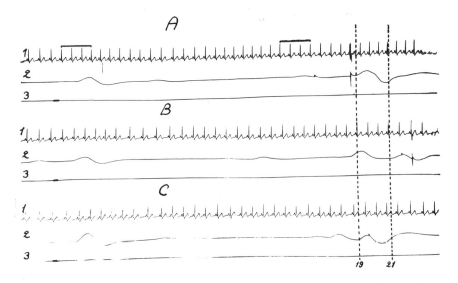

FIG. 1. Temporal conditional defensive reflex in man. A and B: wrong reactions, followed by shocks; C: right reaction. 1: ECG; 2: GSR, mark of time of reaction and shock; 3: sound signal.

duration of the first three heart beats on EEG after the sound signal (a tone) and of the last three beats before the subject's motor reaction (paper speed, 1.5 sm/sec). In the first 10 trials the subject knew that no pain shock would be administered. Then the isolated electric current was used to establish the appropriate shock intensity (not less than three times the pain threshold). The shock intensity was kept constant throughout the experiment.

The time of motor reactions in successive trials is shown as a continuous curve (B) in Fig. 2. Shocks (arrows) were delivered when the reaction did not fall within the permitted deviation (indicated by the two horizontal lines). The broken curve (A) marks the changes in the duration of the heart beats, in beats per minute, plotted against a base line representing the average pulse rate before the elaboration of the conditional reflex.

It will be seen (Table 1) that, although the two portions of the experiment contain the same number of consecutive trials (14) and the same number of pain shocks (six), the total change in heart rate is not the same in these

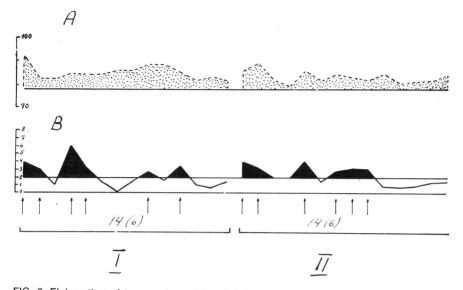

FIG. 2. Elaboration of temporal conditional defensive reflex. A: increase in heart rate as compared with the background; B: deviation of motor reaction time from the given value. Abscissa: consecutive trials in two portions of the same experiment. Arrows: shocks.

portions, indicating that the deviation does not depend solely on the number of reinforcements. As the experiments on nine subjects showed, the total increase in heart rate is proportional to the total deviation of motor reaction time from the given value, i.e., degree of perfection, accuracy, and stability of conditional defensive reflex.

This rule also holds in cases where the range of mistakes (but not their number and not the number of shocks) increased with the increase in pulse rate and where, consequently, the dynamics of vegetative shifts could not be explained by the adjustment to pain shocks throughout subsequent trials.

The experiments on animals also suggest that the brain prognosticates the probability of punishment by the degree of perfection of instrumental motor reaction. Preobrazhenskaya (1969) elaborated conditional defensive

TABLE 1. Relationship between total increase in heart rate and total mistakes

Subjects	I	II	III	IV	V	VI	VII	VIII	IX
Number of reactions	8a 8	14a 14	9a 9	9a 8	15a 15	8a 9	17a 17	9a 10	10a 10
Number of shocks	2a 2	6a 6	3a 3	3a 3	8a 8	5a 5	7a 7	7a 7	3a 3
First portion	7.5	1.56	3.28	5.4	3.08	0.48	0.66	0.42	0.73
Second portion	6.1	1.55	3.11	5.8	3.19	0.46	0.83	0.40	0.61

reflex in dogs in a situation in which lifting the foreleg to a definite level and maintaining it at this level for 10 sec enabled the dog to avoid a painful shock to the opposite hindleg. The conditional sound signal was administered 10 sec before the shock.

It was found that, long before the generation of conditional motor reactions, the combination of a sound stimulus and shock is followed by a sharp increase in thetawave regularity taken from the dorsal hippocampus and in the amplitude and percentage of theta-rhythm in a frequency spectrum of EEG activity (Fig. 3). The quantitative analysis showed that the changes in the total integrative theta-rhythm in the dorsal hippocampus (measured by integrator) correlated positively with the heart rate. Both symptoms decreased notably thoughout the stabilization of motor habit, a sound painproof for the animal. Any movement difficulties led to increased theta-rhythm.

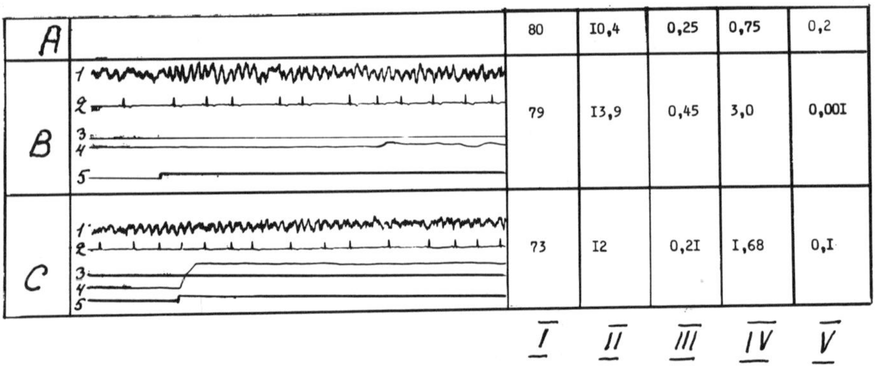

	I	II	III	IV	V
A	80	10,4	0,25	0,75	0,2
B	79	13,9	0,45	3,0	0,001
C	73	12	0,21	1,68	0,1

FIG. 3. Changes in hippocampal theta-rhythm and heart rate throughout the elaboration of an instrumental conditional reflex in dog. 1: EEG of dorsal hippocampus; 2: ECG; 3: "no shock" level; 4: lifts of the switching-off electric-current foreleg; 5: conditional signal. A: before the experiment; B: experiment No. 2; C: experiment No. 19. I: average integrated theta-rhythm; II: average pulse rate; III: coefficient of correlation; IV: Student's criterion; V: probability.

Preobrazhenskaya's studies suggest that the intensity of hippocampus theta-rhythm depends, not on the presence of motor activity *per se*, but on the effectiveness of performed motor acts in terms of their influence on the probability of reinforcement of the animal's adaptive acts.

The changes in these reflexes that result from the administration of lysergic acid diethylamide (LSD-25) can serve to illustrate that the perfection of conditional motor reaction affects the brain's estimation of the probability of punishment. Tchugunova (1968) elaborated reflexes in dogs as described above for Preobrazhenskay's studies. After the injection of small doses of LSD-25 (some 0.06 mg per 1 kg of weight), the dogs made intersignal lifts of the foreleg, imitating the movement which prevents the electric shock (Fig. 4). Later these movements became defective and

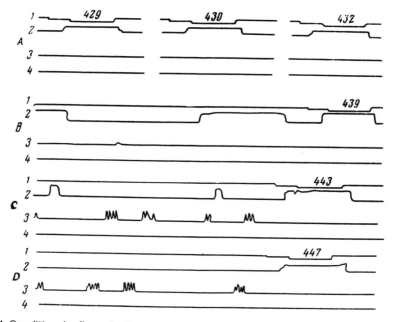

FIG. 4. Conditional reflexes in dog. A: before injection of LSD-25; B, C, and D: 21, 32, and 43 min after the injection of 0.06 mg/kg of the drug. 1: conditional signal and time of closed circuit; 2: movements with foreleg; 3: movements with hindleg; 4: shock. Numbers are times of presentation of conditional stimulus.

abortive, although the sound signal still triggered the usual instrumental reflex. It is in the background of defective defensive reactions that one obtains lifts of the hindleg (to which the shock is delivered), an effect that was not seen without the drug. On responding to a conditional signal, the dog lifts the foreleg, preventing pain stimulation, so that the lift of a hindleg is not available.

Similar results have been described by Burov (1966). He showed that, after the injection of cholinolithic amizil, the EEG activation of rats disappears in an avoidance experiment during the CS but remains if painful reinforcement is inevitable. A muscle relaxant (tricuran) added to amizil in a dose, which did not seem to suppress motor activity but evidently affected the neuronal organization, led to immediate reappearance of EEG activation. Thus the degree of emotional stress demonstrated by EEG desynchronization is determined not by the painful reinforcement *per se* but by a complicated estimation of the probability of pain avoidance.

INFORMATION THEORY OF EMOTIONS

The results of our investigations, which reveal the dependence of emotional stress on the probability of reinforcement, coupled with an analysis of numerous data from the literature, have led to the formulation of "the information theory of emotions," according to which the emotions of higher animals and of man are a special brain apparatus reflecting the value of need and the probability of its satisfaction at a given moment (Simonov, 1964, 1970). The degree of emotional stress (E) is proportional to the value of need (N), as well as to the difference between prognosticated necessary information for satisfaction (I_n) and already available information at any given moment (I_a). This rule can be expressed by the following structural formula:

$$E = -N(I_n - I_a)$$

. The term "information" is used in its pragmatic sense, i.e., the change in the probability of goal achievement resulting from a given informative message (Kharkevitch, 1960). Thus, "information" is virtually a totality of the data, habits, and skills necessary for goal achievement. Linear dependence of emotional stress on the value of need and the deficit (or growth) of pragmatic information is only one particular case of all possible relations. Moreover, the time factor, individual (typological) peculiarities of the subject, and a great variety of other factors, some of them unknown, are also involved. Finally, we should remember that the existence of several needs may often create a complex interaction of simultaneously generated emotions.

Nevertheless, the information theory of emotions appears to be quite effective in solving a variety of complex and contradictory problems. If the deficit of pragmatic information (I_n more than I_a) leads to the generation of negative emotions, actively minimized by the subject, the nervous apparatus of positive emotions is triggered when the received information exceeds the former prognosis (I_a more than I_n). Now, what is the evidence of experimental data?

A series of experiments on 17 subjects was designed to develop a model of positive emotional reaction. The subjects were instructed to differentiate between visual signals (slides).

Each slide showed five lines of zeros and ones intermixed. The subjects were informed that in the series of slide presentations there would be a cue or common sign (e.g., a pair of ones together), and that when this cue was present in any given slide, a brief tone would accompany the presentation. The subject was required to detect the cue, formulate a hypothesis, and report it to the experimenter by microphone. The duration of presentation was 10 sec. EEG, ECG, and GSR were registered throughout the experiment. The habituation of GSR to slide shifts and to the tone was done before the subject received the instructions.

It turned out that before a hypothesis about the origin of the cue has been formulated, neither a new slide nor the tone generates vegetative and EEG reactions (Fig. 5). Once a hypothesis has been formulated (Fig. 6), two situa-

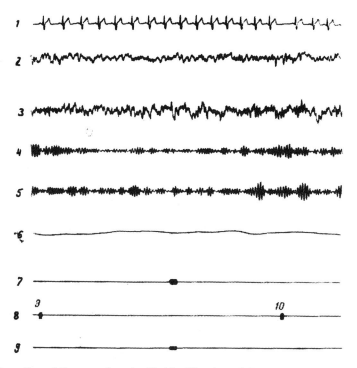

FIG. 5. A portion of the experiment with identification of the cue before a hypothesis is formulated. 1: ECG; 2, 3: EEG (frontal and parietal); 4, 5: analysis of alpha-rhythm; 6: GSR; 7: speech reactions (microphone); 8: slide changes and slide numbers; 9: tone.

tions are possible, which we consider can be regarded as experimental models of the occurrence of a negative or positive emotion.

Figure 7 illustrates the first case. The hypothesis is wrong and slide No. 25, containing the reinforced cue, does not generate GSR. When the tone tells the subject that he is wrong, GSR is registered as a result of disagreement between hypothesis and stimulus. This disagreement related to the genesis of negative emotions is discussed by Anokhin in terms of his "acceptor of action" concept. The subject changes his hypothesis and at some moment it fits reality (Fig. 8). Now, just the appearance of the "reinforced" slide 30 is enough to generate GSR, and the tone confirmation leads to even greater changes in GSR and to a long-lasting depression of alpha-rhythm.

How is this effect to be explained? We have supposed that full agreement was reached between the hypothesis ("acceptor of action," "afferent model") and the available stimulus. Actually, disagreement is involved in this case, too, but of a different kind from that used to correct a wrong hypothesis. The hypothesis, formulated in the process of repeated combinations, contains not only "the afferent model of goal," not only its semantics, but also the probability of goal achievement. The confirmation of slide 30

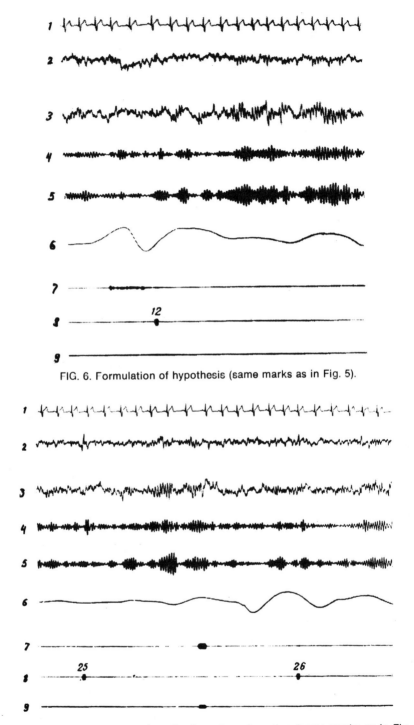

FIG. 6. Formulation of hypothesis (same marks as in Fig. 5).

FIG. 7. Disagreement between hypothesis and confirmation (same marks as in Fig. 5).

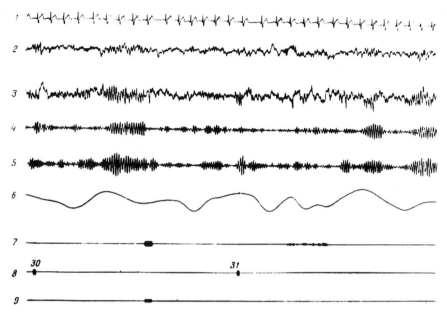

FIG. 8. Confirmation of hypothesis (same marks as in Fig. 5).

by a tone increased the probability that the hypothesis is right, and this disagreement between the prognosis and received information resulted in strong GSR as a vegetative component of positive emotional reaction. The importance of the prognosis of probability in genesis of positive emotions is also described by Feigenberg (1965).

The disagreement between the goal semantics ("acceptor of action," "neural model of stimulus," "set" etc.) and the results obtained in practice are quite sufficient for the appearance of negative emotions. Positive emotional reaction requires the prognosis of probability of goal achievement. Only in this case will positive disagreement occur, i.e., the received exceeding the expected. It is not the satisfied need (the satisfaction of need eliminates all emotions, maintained for a certain period of time by memory apparatus) but the available need together with a simultaneous increase in the probability of its satisfaction that leads to a positive emotion, actively maximized by the subject. This very circumstance pushes living beings toward the active disruption of their homeostasis, drives them toward unsatisfied needs and situations, whereas real reinforcement might surpass its prognosticated probability.

BRAIN STRUCTURES INVOLVED IN ESTIMATING THE PROBABILITY OF REINFORCEMENT

Studies by Mekhedova (1971) on dogs have shown that the probability reinforcement of a conditional signal by means of large and small portions of meat leads to salivation, which is adequate for an average quantity of food. Nevertheless, it is in this situation that the animals show maximum emotional stress, as measured by heart rate. If the prefrontal areas of the neocortex are removed, the dogs lose their ability to adequately assess the total effect of probability reinforcement. The manifestation of emotional stress also disappears.

Whereas the neocortex orients behavior on signals of highly probable events, the hippocampus provides reactions to signals with a problematic, comparatively low probability of reinforcement. In experiments by Pigareva (1974) with occasional reinforcement of conditional signals by 100 to 50% the generation of alimentary reflexes in hippocampectomized rats did not differ much from that in intact ones. When the number of reinforcements was reduced to 33 to 25%, hippocampectomized animals displayed an inability to generate conditional reflex during 9 days of experiment. Intact rats reached high levels of reaction by the 8th or 9th day. This explains why involvement of the hippocampus is essential in the early stages of the generation of conditional reflexes, whereas in later stages the activity of neocortical structures predominates.

Since competition between needs occurs, not in the sphere of needs, but at the level of their transformation into emotions, behavior may appear to be oriented on a goal that is less important but easier to achieve. In other words, the competition between needs depends not only on the value of relevant needs but also on the probability of their satisfaction. Amygdala seems to be involved in the system of brain structures, where the interaction of available emotional reactions occurs.

Pigareva (1974) has elaborated the "switching" of alimentary and defensive conditional reflexes in rats, using the method of Asratyan (1964). The same conditional signal (a bell) was reinforced by food in the morning and by pain shock in the evening. After bilateral destruction of the amygdala, the animals were still able to generate separate alimentary and defensive reflexes, but the interaction of these reflexes is seriously impaired when "switching" is attempted.

THE ROLE OF EMOTIONS IN THE ORGANIZATION
OF GOAL-ORIENTED BEHAVIOR

The appearance of negative emotions *per se* with a deficit of pragmatic information suggests their compensatory meaning. Emotion is not and cannot be a source of new information received as a result of seeking acts, reviewing memory cells and education. The role of emotion consists in compensation, the urgent substitution of deficient knowledge. This compensatory function of emotions is realized in a great variety of forms.

Since the prognosis of the real volume of power required for a forthcoming act is uncertain, as a rule, emotional activation of vegetative functions is redundant. Emotional states usually involve conjectural responses to signals with a low probability of reinforcement. When in the state of fear, animals and man often respond with a defensive reaction to any changes in environment, including stimuli they never experienced before. Many emotions are accompanied by a transition to imitative behavior. When data and time are insufficient for an independent, well-founded decision, the subject has no choice but to follow the example of other group members. The signals of emotional state serve as additional means of communication between the members of the community. It is not just a coincidence that human speech becomes more emotional as the logical arguments of an orator become weaker.

The major implication of positive emotions for the organization of behavior is that they drive living systems toward unsatisfied needs and pragmatic uncertainty. For example, when satisfying the need for food, the driving role of negative emotions disappears with variety. Positive emotions require a variety of food, resulting in a search for new types and new combinations. They serve as powerful factors for development and mastering new spheres of reality. Because of their origin and mechanisms, negative emotions are unable in principle to perform these functions, being governed by the rule of drive reduction.

A Soviet psychologist, Vygotsky (1970), writes: ". . . the way of definitions and classifications followed by psychology in the course of centuries brought psychology of feelings to the most fruitless and dull chapter of this science." The approach to emotions, which has its origin in Pavlov's system approach to the activity of cerebral hemispheres, opens new perspectives in solving the problem of emotions, hitherto "the most fruitless and dull chapter" of descriptive psychology.

SUMMARY

Experimental and theoretical arguments suggest that the degree and quality (positive or negative) of emotional reaction depend primarily on the value of the need and the probability of its satisfaction (Simonov, 1964). The assessment of this probability is performed by the brain in conformity with all habits, knowledge, and skills necessary for action directed toward satisfaction of the need. Negative emotions are brain mechanisms, compensating for the deficit of pragmatic information in the process of goal-oriented behavior. Positive emotions trigger the active creation of new goals, drive for unsatisfied needs, and pragmatic uncertainty. Thus, negative emotions primarily serve the self-preservation of living systems, and positive emotions their development. In this chapter we discuss the role of frontal areas of the neocortex, hippocampus, and amygdala in the genesis of emotional state.

REFERENCES

Anokhin, P. (1964): Emotions, *Bolshaya med. enciclopediya 33,* 339.

Asratyan, E. (1953): System approach to activity of cerebral hemispheres. In: *Fisiologiya centralnoj nervnoj systemy,* Akademiya Med. Nauk, Moskva.

Asratyan, E. (1964): *Compensatory Adaptative Reflectory Activity and Brain,* Oxford-London-Edinburg-New York.

Burov, J. (1966): *Influence of Certain Tranquillizers on Activating Brain Systems,* Moskva.

Feigenberg, M. (1965): *Interaction Between Analyzers and Their Clinical Implication,* Moskva.

Kharkevitch, A. (1960): On value of information, *Problemy kibernetiki,* No. 4, 53–57.

Mekhedova, A. (1971): On the role of frontal brain areas in elaboration of conditional reactions of adequate value and probability of reinforcement, *Journal visshej nervnoj deyatelnosti 21,* 459–464.

Pavlov, I. (1951): *Complete Works,* 3, kniga 2, 230.

Pigareva, M. (1974): The role of amygdala in conditioned switching in rats, *Journal visshej nervn. deyat. (in press).*

Prebrazhenskaya, L. (1969): Correlation between hippocampal theta-rhythm and heart rate at the early stage of elaboration of conditional defensive reflex. In: *Nervnoe napryazhenie i deyatelnost serdtsa,* edited by P. Simonov, pp. 157–184, "Nauka," Moskva.

Simonov, P. (1964): Relationship between motor and vegetative components of conditional defensive reflex in man. In: *Centr. i perif. mekhanismy dvig. deyat. zhiv. i tcheloveka,* pp. 65–66. "Nauka," Moskva.

Simonov, P. (1970): Information theory of emotions. In: *Feelings and Emotions,* edited by M. Arnold, pp. 145–149. Academic Press, New York-London.

Tchugunova, S. (1968): The influence of LSD-25 on changes in complex adaptive reflex in dogs. *Bull. Eksp. Biol. Med. 2,* 52–55.

Vigotsky, L. (1970): Spinosa and his doctrine about emotions in terms of contemporary psycho-neurology, *Voprosy philosophii, 6,* 127.

Emotions—Their Parameters and Measurement,
edited by L. Levi.
Raven Press, New York © 1975

Session 3: Discussion

Chairman: Malcolm Lader

Lader: I suppose I started off on a very simple technical procedure — examining the habituation of sweat gland response, the GSR, to repeated unconditional stimuli — because my Ph.D. supervisors said you should use some sort of conditioning paradigm. Being very young and very lazy at the time, I started to look at the literature and found that the literature on conditioning was about 10 times bigger than the literature on simple habituation. Therefore, I ended up using simple repetitive trains of stimuli. The reason the GSR was chosen is probably that it is a very deceptively simple measure to use.

Levi: We had chosen the measures we use for two reasons. One is that the catecholamines demonstrate a rather high correlation to self-rated feelings; catecholamines probably reflect some of the emotional reactions that are also reportable in simple questionnaires and magnitude estimations. The second reason is that catecholamines influence quite a number of bodily functions which probably have something to do with pathogenesis of various disorders.

Frankenhaeuser: Dr. Lader brought up the subject of why we got involved in this kind of measurement. I think Dr. Levi gave some of the reasons but I would also like to give some. To me these hormonal measurements are very interesting because they have a twofold importance: not only do they reflect what we may call the emotional impact of the environment which serves as dependent variables but they also influence the various functions of the body. There are three indices of emotion, the subjective, the behavioral, and the physiological. The interesting thing with the catecholamines is that they influence both what I call the subjective reactions of the individual and the behavioral. These measurements are of course no good if we are primarily interested in the very rapid, immediate changes, but our interest has been mainly in what might be called psychosocial influences of everyday life. For the questions that we raise, these are nearly ideal variables because our subjects can go on working and behaving in their ordinary, everyday environment, and we can get these measurements with a minimum of interference with everyday life.

Eysenck: Essentially we start out by descriptive work, analyzing certain dimensions of personality and behavior, and in doing so we come to the point at which we look for a causal theory to relate physiological underlying mechanisms to the behavioral, personality types that we discover. It becomes a question of usage as to what you regard as a physiological test and what you regard as a psychological test. You may remember T. H. Huxley's famous remark about "no psychosis without a neurosis," meaning not what you mean by it, but meaning that there are no psychical events without a neurological event underlying it and therefore any kind of psychological reaction automatically becomes a measure of a physiological reaction. From the point of view of the psychologist we tend to use physiological measures in a hypothetical deductive sense. We are looking for some causal under-structure for the kind of organization that we find in behavior and personality.

Lader: In general, what are the peripheral aspects of the technique at the recording level? What are the artifacts? How easy is it to do? How easy is it quantified?

Shagass: The problems with the EEG are legion. Apart from all the artifacts and all the things that can affect it, I think the main difficulty with the EEG in this field is that it is so sensitive to fleeting mentation. If you can not discover the stray thought that is affecting the EEG at the moment as a criterion variable, then you are in trouble as far as interpreting the meaning of the rapid fluctuations in electrical activity that are going on.

Delgado: I think that Dr. Shagass should not be so negative about his findings, which are very interesting. The contingent negative variation (CNV) seems to have reliability: there is some correlation between a test that can be performed and emotionality, and perhaps brain functions.

Shagass: Certainly the CNV is a very interesting phenomenon, but again it is a very good example of the artifacts situation. The fact that CNV was hard to distinguish from eye movement potentials was well known early. In the area of psychopathology Gary Walter has found that in a large variety of conditions the CNV is either not present at all, which he claims is the case in psychopaths, or it is markedly attentuated. For that it could be used as a diagnostic test and it has certain value. I think, however, that the issue is whether you have got a disassociation or not. If you have a psychiatric condition in which people do not attend very well, then a physiological correlative attention should be attenuated. You have an objective way of measuring something that you can ordinarily observe clinically, perhaps. I do not know what it tells you about the pathophysiology of the disorder.

Sem-Jacobsen: I would like to comment on Dr. Shagass' frustration as to what we get out of the EEG. We know that with depth recording it is easy to see the emotional state of the patient from the center part of the temporal lobe. We know that there is a lot of data down there, and, since we know these data are there, sooner or later there has to be a major effort made to get these data out without using implanted electrodes.

Clynes: Concerning the quantification of the EEG and evoked potentials, it is very interesting to observe the relationship between the various parts of the brain, particularly left and right symmetry. A form of quantification that has perhaps not been adequately used in the past but is showing some sign of promise is to correlate on line the left and right symmetrically opposite locations of particular electrodes. These show spontaneous fluctuations and sometimes will for a considerable time parallel and then change. The question is how? There is also front and back correlation. In the past it has been very difficult experimentally to induce emotions reliably in the laboratory. But, if you can, you can then observe that these correlations between left and right undergo a systematic change with various phases of emotion. Much more work needs to be done to establish this in a more reliable way.

Lader: When we are using measures, we have some sort of almost intuitive idea of which levels of emotion we think they reflect. But what is the scope of the measure? Does it reflect high or low levels of emotion? Also, what is its sensitivity, what is the slope of the measure with respect to the level of emotion? Is it highly sensitive? Are small changes in emotion intensity reflected by the physiological measure? Or is it relatively insensitive, so that it is only gross changes in emotion that can be detected?

Singer: I am very intrigued by the words "central" and "peripheral," because there is an invidious distinction between them: it is much better to be in the center than to be at the periphery, and being, I guess, a great social climber, I would very much like to get to the center. It seems like a better place to be. My difficulty in reconciling the stubborn fact that a greater portion of my variation seems to be involved in things that I naively think should be in higher cortical processes and yet I cannot find any very convenient explanation to tie into any physiological base for these.

Frankenhaeuser: I regret very much that there has been so little effort made to link peripheral measures to the central measures. It seems that very different people have been involved with these different problems, but I think that there is an increasing interest in getting this linkage. However, you said that by measuring the peripheral catecholamines we only measure what you call the peripheral expression of emotion. I am not quite sure how much you include in this, but I would like to emphasize that the measures, for instance, of epinephrine in urine do reflect the subject's cognitive evaluation of the environment, and data support this. What we are looking for is the subject's emotional subjective reactions to a situation. We can measure this very accurately by different kinds of scaling techniques or verbal techniques and then we have a quantitative relation between the subject's responses and the peripheral catecholamine measures that we get. Then also we have the other side of the story. We have the relation between the cognitive performance of the subject and these peripheral catecholamine measures. We do not know the mechanisms by which this takes place. We do not know how, in this case, epinephrine affects the central nervous system to bring out this effect. We have a positive relation between cognitive efficiency and epinephrine secretion.

Delgado: There is perhaps a misconception that physiologists try to clarify and that is the hierarchichal organization of the central nervous system with the cortex as the master control of everything. This simply is not true. I think that we should consider the central nervous system as not a dictatorial but a democratic organization, in which all levels have something to say about the final outcome of behavior. It is very important to consider the cortex as only one more stage in the organization of the brain and especially in the organization of emotions and of behavior in general, and to know that the limbic system, the reticular formation, the hypothalamus, and the thalamus play roles as important if not more important than the cortex in the final integration of the CNS.

Cook: In regard to controlling the environmental variables under which these studies are conducted, it may be equally profitable to describe these variables because, we find that the stimulus or the reinforcement which occurs is really not as important as how they occur, i.e., the schedule of reinforcement or whether a reward or an aversive stimulus is used. The schedule of reinforcement is prepotent over the reinforcement itself in regard to the drug effects. Entirely different pharmacological effects are seen. These effects are determined by the substrate systems we are discussing; there are very different effects in experiments using the same foot shock, according to whether it is avoidance in which the aversive stimuli are generating behavior, or whether it is a punishment contingency in which a shock is suppressing behavior.

Henry: I think that when you get out of the operant conditioning situation, you will find the same thing in a socially structured situation: your role is enormously important in determining how you will respond to a stimulus.

Cook: In terms of the social situation, if one uses dominance in groups of animals and measures the effect of a drug on the dominant animal and the most submissive animal in a large group, there will be various pharmacological effects. Removing the dominant animal and arranging the group structure so that the previously submissive animal has the opportunity to be dominant changes it to a different pharmacological substrate system. The environmental factors, the antecedents of these behaviors, are all-powerful determinants of some substrate system mechanism, in terms of emphasizing a social situation.

Mandler: Situational variation takes care of much more of the variants than do individual variations, contrary to the myth that psychology has been living with for at least a hundred years.

Sarason: Dr. Mandler referred to the hundred-year-old myth of personality factors and individual differences being important. . . .

Mandler: I said the myth is that they account for the major part of the variance.

Sarason: Yes, and it seems to me that you are perpetuating a more modern myth when you refer to the potency of the situational variables. The reason

I say that is due largely to recent criticisms of attempts to assess individual differences. We have done a study involving research published in the last 3 years in four psychology journals in which we calculated the percentage of the variants attributable to situations, personality variables, and the interactions between situations and personality variables, and of those three factors. The personality variables and the situational variables accounted for approximately equal and embarrassingly tiny percentages of the variants, and the interactions between personality and situational variables accounted for almost as much of the variance.

Brady: I think a major issue here has to do with how much of the personality variable is accounted for by situational variables. The issue is what are personality variables. And they to me, in an operational sense, seem to be the sum total in large part of a historical view of situational variables. In fact, personality variables are accounted for by situational variables to a considerable extent in the history of the organism.

Lazarus: If you think of the psychological processes involved in emotion on the one hand, and then you think of the physiological mechanisms on the other, the problem is that there is not a parallelism in the kinds of questions that are being asked. For example, if one were to assume that cognition is a crucial intervening step (that is, how the person or animal interprets his plight is a crucial step in the generation of an emotional response), one needs to ask at the physiological level something that is not often asked: what are the processes by which cognitive activity takes place leading to the emotional response. Most of the concern with the physiology of emotion is at the level of reaction, not at the level of mediating processes. And I think that what I would try to do is underscore a gap in the psychophysiology of emotion. I do not like to be turned off on the question of the situation because I think it is an artificial and unfortunate distinction that we make if we say let's look at the physiological reactions or mechanisms and ignore the nature of the input. The nature of the input is crucial.

Spielberger: The reason that the situation versus personality conflict is an interesting one is that these are the things that are in constant interaction, and I think that in most of the data that are being described we see the results of situation versus personality interactions. And although it is true that a personality trait reflects the past history of the individual, it does more than that. It also tells us his disposition to behave in a certain way in a certain type of situation. A personality trait implies an individual's perception of the world and his disposition to respond in certain ways to that perception.

Eysenck: I think for the last 50 years there has been a very strong tendency among psychologists and possibly among physiologists to disregard (a) individual differences and (b) the genetic component in these individual differences. I think it is tremendously important and, if we disregard that, we are never going to get any sensible answers to all these questions that we have been putting.

Wolf: Prof. Groen has published very clear-cut evidence in rats of major differences in behavior based on the genetics of these animals.

Levi: I would like to reintroduce my theme of the clinical implications of what we are discussing. We have the same position that there are genetically determined differences in the propensity to react, that there are environmentally influenced differences, the earlier environment etc., and that we can categorize individuals in accordance to their propensity to react to a certain situation.

Groen: Dr. Wolf referred to our work on the role of respectively hereditary and acquired characteristics in the development of experimental hypertension in rats. But I would like to interpret them as showing that both factors are important. These were rats that had been inbred for five generations for their propensity to develop experimental hypertension when, for instance, you clipped the renal artery or give them high salt diets or desoxycorticosterone. Some of these rats after five generations were so sensitive that just giving them 1 percent of salt in the diet would develop hypertension above 160, 180, and sometimes 190 millimeters of mercury. And other rats were so resistant that even clipping the renal artery, giving them salt, and DOPA would not develop hypertension at all. That seems to be a clear-cut example of the influence of heredity.

Lader: I will try to summarize some of the points which have been raised and some which haven't been raised. We have heard about the influence on the measures of various factors: age and sex and diurnal variation and personality. I think genetic influences are extremely important and I myself have been struck quite recently with genetic influences on anxiety in humans. It seems to be by far the most important factor in the genesis of symptoms of anxiety. We are dealing with interactions between genetic influences and environmental influences, interactions between environmental influences and variables in the subject. We are dealing with an extremely complicated subject, and probably the best way in which progress will be made will be by estimating as many parameters as possible and neglecting none.

Emotions—Their Parameters and Measurement,
edited by L. Levi.
Raven Press, New York © 1975

The Measurement of Emotion:
Psychological Parameters and Methods

Hans J. Eysenck

Department of Psychology, The Institute of Psychiatry, Denmark Hill, London, England

Historically, emotions have been considered to be characterized by three quite distinct and measurable parameters: physiological concomitants, introspective (verbal) assessment, and behavioral observation. If we consider a phobic patient who is referred for behavior therapy because of the difficulties created in his life by an overwhelming fear of cats, we can index and measure this emotion (fear) along these quite distinct lines. In the first place, we can put him in front of a cat and measure the physiological reactions (increase in heart rate, GSR response, catecholamine secretion, etc.) produced by this particular stimulus, as compared with other types of stimuli; it will usually be found that there is a marked increase in adrenergic activity. In the second place, we can ask him to fill in a "fear thermometer" on which he records his subjective feelings of fear and anxiety in relation to cats. And in the third place, we can measure his actual behavior when confronted with a cat—does he stoop to stroke the cat and pick it up; does he remain seated in his chair; does he jump up and recoil from the cat; or does he run out of the room (Eysenck and Rachman, 1965). All three types of response—physiological, introspective, behavioral—would be taken as evidence of fear, and could be made the basis of a system of measurement. Lang (1968) and Lazarus (1968) have discussed these three parameters or properties of the emotional response in detail, and cite evidence of an experimental kind to support this view. This threefold possibility of measurement may be regarded as a favorable aspect of emotion from the point of view of scientific study; we can use different lines of attack on the problem, depending on facilities, circumstances, and training. Unfortunately there is also a less favorable side to this picture; the three different types of measurement do not correlate together to any very marked extent.

There are many reasons why this is so, and we will in due course have to look at some of the causes for this discrepancy. But the fact itself is undisputed (Martin, 1972). A person may show considerable adrenergic reactivity, and yet deny that he is afraid; he may admit that he is afraid, yet bravely approach the cause of his fears, rather than run away; or he may run away, yet not show any marked physiological reaction. Clearly we need a model of emotional behavior that enables us to take all these possibilities into account; measurement that fails to pay attention to theory is little better than busy work. As T. H. Huxley once said, "They who do not go beyond fact do not get as far as fact." It will be one of the purposes of this chapter to try and indicate some of the properties that such a model of emotion would require in order to make proper measurement possible. Before turning to this task, let me just add one point, which I think is important in evaluating the failure of different types of measures to show reasonable correlations. These correlations have usually been worked out in a laboratory situation where the amount of emotion evoked was relatively small, and where the circumstances inevitably were rather artificial. This restriction of range is known, on simple psychometric grounds, to reduce the size of correlations drastically; we would be entitled to expect much higher correlations in truly fear-producing situations, as for instance in war. It is this fact that makes behavior therapy such an important test-bed of psychological theories of emotion; here we have the possibility of evoking very strong emotions under what are in fact laboratory conditions (Eysenck and Rachman, 1965). Furthermore, there are no ethical constraints of the kind that normally would force us to refrain from causing strong fears in our subjects; under the special conditions of behavior therapy, the main reason for producing these strong emotions (as for instance in "flooding" treatment) is therapeutic. We are trying to cure the patient of a very disabling type of fear response, and theory and experience show that this can often best be done by evoking this fear under controlled conditions, in order to produce experimental extinction. This situation can be used with great effectiveness to carry out measurements that may be of considerable use to the theoretician. Unfortunately these methods of treatment are too recent to have given rise to much research of the kind here envisaged, but experimentalists are invited to consider very carefully the possibilities opened up through behavior therapy for a better study of emotions arising naturally and yet under conditions that are under precise experimental control.

Behaviorists may object to our threefold division of measurable parameters of emotion, considering the very mention of introspective evidence through verbal statement or questionnaire response a throwback to the bad old days of introspectionism. This question should be regarded, like all questions in science, as a pragmatic, experimental one, rather than an issue to be settled by recourse to ancient battlecries. The question in essence is simply this: Do verbal statements concerning the strength of felt emotion have sufficient reliability and validity to be acceptable as scientific evidence? If the answer is in the affirmative, then clearly there is no problem; even a confirmed behaviorist may use verbal statements as externally observable and measurable evidence. Theoretically, we may in fact predict that such introspective statements would be likely to have better validity (and possibly even reliability) than measures of either behavior or physiological reactivity, for the following reason. Lacey's well-known law of physiological response specificity states quite clearly that measurement of single physiological indicators of emotional reaction is likely to be a fruitless endeavor, because in different people different systems mediate the main physiological response to emotion-producing situations; the cortex can integrate the differential reactivity of many physiological systems to arrive at a much better index of total emotional arousal than can the experimenter usually restricted to one, or at best two or three, different measures. Furthermore, the attachment of electrodes, and the restrictions imposed on the subject by the exigencies of laboratory measurement (even when telemetric devices are being used), constitute limitations to measurement of "natural" emotional reactions that may be insuperable. These are theoretical considerations; what does the evidence say?

Thayer (1970) reported results of a program aimed at the examination of the validity of controlled verbal reports of various emotional states. He used a difference score design in which four psychophysiological measures and verbal ratings of various emotional states were obtained in a baseline and in an activation period from 41 female subjects. Verbal reports were then correlated with individual physiological measures, as well as with composites of such measures. Two main kinds of physiological index were employed. In the first the subject's physiological change score was represented by the single system showing the greatest change; in the second, the index was weighted equally by all four physiological measures. The first index showed slightly greater correlations with verbal report than did the second, as one would have expected from Lacey's formulation of the specificity hypothesis. Skin conductance and heart rate, the best combination of the four physiological systems measures, correlated as high as 0.62 with verbal report. It should be noted that the intercorrelations between the physiological variables were quite small, lending credence to the hypothesis that the cortex acts as an integrating mechanism for information received from these various systems. Furthermore, the correlations between skin conductance and heart rate were higher than those involving the other two systems; thus the data are consistent with the postulation of a general factor of emotionality on which verbal report would have much the highest loading. (Thayer did not carry out such an analysis, but the published data are sufficient to make this statement with some degree of confidence.) Nor would it be possible to dismiss the results as a single, small scale experiment; they are a replication of an earlier study (Thayer, 1967). Bartenwerfer (1969), too, has succeeded in measuring the experience of arousal by verbal means, and has attempted to relate this measure to changes in heart rate. We may conclude that the evidence suggests that verbal report, far from being a throwback to prebehavioristic days, is in many ways the preferred method of measuring and indexing states of emotional arousal.

Physiological measures of emotion have already been adequately discussed by Lader, Mason, Delgado, Frankenhaeuser, Shagass, Konzett,

Cook, Sigg, and others; in this chapter, I shall concentrate on verbal and behavioral measures. We may begin by asking: what do we require of a theory of emotion that would permit us to make scientifically meaningful measurements? I would like to suggest an analogy with Hooke's law of elasticity: Stress $= k \times$ Strain, where k is a constant (the modulus of elasticity) that depends upon the nature of the material and the type of stress used to produce the strain. This constant k, i.e., the Stress/Strain ratio, is called Young's modulus, and is illustrated (with certain simplifications) in Fig. 1A. A and B are two metals differing in elasticity; they are stressed by increasing loads, and the elongation corresponding to each load plotted on the abscissa. It will be seen that identical loads give rise to quite divergent elongations, α and β. Figure 1B illustrates a similar analysis of human behavior (physiological, verbal, expressive) in an experimental situation productive of emotion. Again the stress (independent variable) is plotted on the ordinate, and the strain (dependent variable) on the abscissa; A and B represent an emotionally stable and an emotionally unstable individual, or group of individuals, respectively. Identical stress θ_1 gives rise to quite different strains α and β. It would require stress θ_2 to make the strain in A individuals equal to that produced by θ_1 in B individuals. Differences between θ_1 and θ_2 are the kinds of differences traditionally studied by experimental psychologists; differences between A and B are the kinds of differences traditionally studied by personality psychologists, believers in

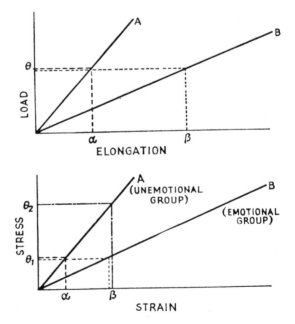

FIG. 1. Illustration of Hooke's Law (A) as applied to the measurement of emotionality (B).

the importance of constitutional factors, and clinical psychologists. Physicists have never attempted to make a choice between these two sets of variables, or to study them in isolation; it seems equally futile for psychologists to do so.

This is to my mind a very important point, and one that is crucial to the construction of any remotely adequate model of emotional behavior. If the suggestion made above is true, then it follows that we cannot make verifiable predictions from general laws without incorporating specifically a variable k, which refers to the constitution of the individual for whom the prediction is being made. Consider an experiment reported by Jensen (1962). He studied the number of errors in serial learning as a function of the rate of stimulus presentation; there were two rates, one of 2 sec and one of 4 sec. The traditional experimental psychologist would regard this problem as meaningful and soluble; either differences in rate of stimulus presentation cause a difference in the number of errors to criterion, or they do not. Jensen argued that this test imposes a stress on the subject, and that the resulting strain would be indexed in terms of an increased number of errors when the shorter rate of stimulus presentation was employed, as compared with the longer rate. (There is an obvious pressure with the quick rate of presentation, which might well increase the general stress of the test situation.) This stress would impose differential strain on individuals respectively high and low on trait anxiety, and Jensen measured this trait anxiety with the neuroticism scale of the Maudsley Personality Inventory (MPI) (Eysenck, 1959). Contrasting subjects scoring high and low respectively on this scale, he found that for low scorers (i.e., nonemotional individuals) the added stress of shortening the rate of stimulus presentation produced no effect at all; they made 63 errors on the average for the long rate and 64 errors for the short rate. But for the high scorers there was a tremendous difference; in the long rate of presentation condition, they only made 46 errors, i.e., far fewer than the unemotional subjects, while in the short rate of presentation condition they made 90 errors! In other words, the results of the experiment can only be understood in terms of the person × condition-interaction; leaving out the differential personality effect makes complete nonsense out of any simple averaging of the results. Such averaging would tell us that there was a mild and nonsignificant effect of shortening the rate of presentation, when in reality there was no effect at all for nonemotional subjects, and a very strong effect for emotional ones.

This is but one example of a general rule that I have tried to lay down in my book on the biological basis of personality (Eysenck, 1967). The general formula (Stress = k × Strain) becomes meaningless when the constant k is omitted, and when, as is the case in so much psychological experimentation, k becomes part of the error variance. The result is inevitably that the error variance becomes much the most prominent part of the total picture, a conclusion which spells failure to any expectation to formulate a proper model of emotion, or to make accurate individual predictions. The important work of Spence (Spence and Spence, 1966) is also relevant here; he has argued that anxiety, as measured verbally by the Manifest Anxiety Scale (MAS), acts as a drive, and that this makes it possible to make various experimental and behavioral predictions in terms of Hullian formulations in which drive enters into certain equations in which, together with H (habit), it determines E (excitatory potential, itself a determinant of performance). I have reviewed the large amount of literature that has grown up around these concepts in some detail (Eysenck, 1973), and there is little doubt that individual differences play a lawful role in the various tests of conditioning and learning, which Spence and his followers have used in order to test deductions from his theory. Here also results would be contradictory and meaningless if the personality variable (k) had been left out of account; the whole experimental endeavor only makes sense in terms of the interaction between personality and experimental conditions.

This, then, is the first important point in the construction of our model of emotional behavior and measurement: no model can possibly be adequate if it neglects the task of incorporating individual differences. This point is closely linked with the second point, which states that relations between emotion (arousal, drive, or whatever name is preferred for effects of activation) and performance are usually, if not always, curvilinear rather than linear. The omnipresent Yerkes-Dodson Law (Broadhurst, 1959; Wilson, 1972) not only posits the existence of this "inverted-U relation," but also relates it to the difficulty of the task; for easy tasks, the optimal drive level is high, while for difficult tasks the optimal drive level is relatively low. Spence has argued that the terms "easy" and "difficult" are not properly defined, and are in any case irrelevant; he uses the concepts of H (habit strength) as the relevant variable, and maintains that high drive facilitates performance when there are no alternative habits with higher H than the one being learned or tested. When there are alternative habits with high H that are opposed to the habit being learned or tested, then high drive lowers performance and learning. Pursuit rotor performance is "difficult" to learn, in the sense that it takes a long time to become proficient at it, yet high drive is beneficial because there are no opposing habits of high strength that might be activated by the subject's high motivation. There is no intrinsic difficulty about learning a list of paired associates such as Table–Fish, yet the high drive of the motivated subjects activates alternative habits of great strength, such as Table–Chair, and these interfere with the learning process. The work of Spence and his followers already referred to has given much support to these considerations, and for the moment at least we may accept this emendation to the Yerkes-Dodson Law.

The importance of this law for any attempts to measure behavioral effects of emotion is clear; it can account for the apparently paradoxical fact that verbal report and behavior may show no correlation. Consider a simple "inverted-U" relationship between a task, T, and drive, D. Assume for the moment that the drive in question is anxiety, and that changes in anxiety can be introspected with sufficient reliability and validity to make it possible to use these introspections, suitably psychometrized, as a measure of D. Performance on T (P_T) will at first increase with increasing D, and then decrease as D passes the point of optimal motivation. Whether we correlate introindividual differences in D (perhaps produced by instructions, or by shock stress, or in some other way) with P_T, or whether we let different individuals, having different scores on the neuroticism scale of the MPI, represent different points on the D scale, is immaterial; we will fail to discover any correlation over the whole range of D measures. If we divide up the whole range into two parts at the point where the curve relating D to P_T reaches its highest point, then we could obtain a positive correlation between D and P_T for the first part of the curve, and a negative correlation for the second part. It would be premature to assert that all the small or nonexistent correlations between D and P_T can be explained in this manner, but it seems likely that this factor is responsible for quite a large part of the apparent inconsistency.

This widespread "inverted-U" relation should be taken together with our first point, the importance of individual differences, in accounting for the great difficulties that investigators have had in replicating results and in producing deductions from theory that could be tested. Individual differences might not be so important if only we were dealing with linear relations between D and P_T; different individuals might start at different points on the D slope, and might react with different degrees of increment to experimental manipulations of D, but at least one might postulate a general law according to which P_T would increase with increases in D. When the relationship is curvilinear, however, no certain predictions can be made about individuals; an identical change in D conditions might produce an increment in P_T for a low-drive individual, and a decrement in P_T in a high-drive individual who is near or past the point of optimal motivation. Consider a study by McLaughlin and Eysenck (1967) in which D was manipulated by presenting subjects with either an easy or a difficult paired-associates learning task. Subjects were divided into high-drive and low-drive groups according to their questionnaire responses, and the prediction was made that performance would follow the "inverted-U" curve. Low-drive subjects were thought to be likely to perform poorly on the easy list, as compared to high-drive subjects, because of their poor motivation; if this motivation were to be increased by administering the difficult task, they should improve in performance compared to the high-drive subjects, who would now be handicapped by their over-high drive in an arousing situation. Results bore out the prediction—the low-drive subjects actually learned the difficult task better than the easy task, while the high-drive subjects made twice as many errors on the difficult task as on the easy one. The experiment demonstrates

quite clearly that even the direction of change cannot meaningfully be predicted by a theory that does not bear individual differences in mind; who
would have predicted that for some people making the task more difficult
would actually improve their performance?

In the studies quoted, a questionnaire (verbal assessment) was used as a
measure of D; it would of course be equally possible to use autonomic
measures. The work of Burgess and Hokanson (1964), Hokanson and Burgess (1964) and particularly Doerr and Hokanson (1965) may be quoted
as an example. In the former two studies, it was found that adult, human
subjects with characteristically low resting heart rates achieved scores on
simple performance tests that were lower than those obtained by high-heart-
rate subjects. After imposed stress, which typically increased heart rate
approximately 16 beats per minute, the low-heart-rate subjects significantly
improved in performance relative to a nonstressed control group, while
high-heart-rate subjects manifested a relative *decrement*. In the Doerr and
Hokanson study, three groups of children (ages 7, 9, and 11, respectively)
were subdivided into low, medium, and high heart rate categories on the
basis of resting heart-rate measures. The experimental variable was arousal
by a frustrating experience versus nonarousal; the number of items on a
simple coding task prior to the arousal manipulations and the number of
items completed on an alternate form after arousal served as a measure of
performance. Heart-rate recordings made at each phase of the investigation
served as an indicator of physiological strain. The results indicated as
anticipated on the basis of our general argument that high-rate subjects
showed a worsening of performance after stress, while low-rate subjects
showed an improvement; for the nonstress subjects there is no difference
in performance according to heart rate. The medium heart-rate subjects in
both groups were intermediate between the high and low groups in the stress
condition, and indistinguishable from them in the nonstress condition. Thus
it seems to make little difference whether we use verbal indicators as our
measure of D, or physiological ones; we obtain very similar results, indicating that the change which stress makes in performance depends to a very
large extent on the prior degree of arousal of the subject, i.e., his personality
makeup. No meaningful generalization is possible in this field that does not
take into account the personality variable in assessing and predicting the
effects of stress and emotional strain.

We have so far treated the terms strain, emotion, arousal, excitation,
activation, and so on as meaning essentially the same thing; unfortunately
the situation is more complicated than this. Many writers (e.g., Duffy, 1962;
Fiske and Maddi, 1961; Hebb, 1955; Lindsley, 1951; Malmo, 1959) have
postulated a hypothetical activation continuum ranging from extreme excitement to deep sleep; all these writers have recognized the importance of
studying the *intensity* of behavior as a separate dimension from its *directional* attributes. Many writers have preferred to abandon the term "emo-

tion," preferring some such concept as "arousal" or "activation." Spence and other Hullians have used the term "drive" in this connection, and Hebb has suggested the identification of the drive concept with that of arousal. The personality dimension, which may be colinear with that of drive-arousal-activation, as so conceived, has been suggested by Spence to be that of anxiety, operationally defined in terms of the MAS. I have suggested (Eysenck, 1967) that such a picture, while appealing, is grossly oversimplified, and that there are at least two independent dimensions that are involved, both on the personality side, and also on the "arousal-activation" side. I have argued that there are two major independent dimensions of personality relating to the arousal of emotion: extraversion (E) and neuroticism (N) (Eysenck and Eysenck, 1969). These dimensions recur descriptively in the majority of published analyses of personality studies, and emerge in almost identical form from the work of Cattell, Guilford, and Eysenck. In my *Biological Basis of Personality,* I have identified differences in behavior along the extrovert-introvert dimension with differential level of cortical arousal, produced by differential thresholds in the various parts of the ascending reticular activating system. It is postulated that introverts and extraverts differ both in the habitual level of arousal and in their reaction to stimulus input, introverts tending to a high level of arousal and an amplification of stimulation, and extraverts to a low level of arousal and a damping down of stimulation. Differences in behavior along the emotional-stable continuum are identified with differential thresholds of arousal in the visceral brain, i.e., the hippocampus, amygdala, cingulum, septum, and hypothalamus. N, therefore, is primarily concerned with emotional responsiveness or excitation, i.e., the adrenergic–cholinergic regulatory system.

It follows from the general scheme presented, which bears some relation to other two-arousal systems (Gellhorn and Loofbourrow, 1963; Routtenberg, 1968), that cortical arousal can be produced along two quite distinct and separate pathways. It can be produced by sensory stimulation or by the problem-solving activity of the brain, without necessarily involving the visceral brain at all. Cortical arousal can however also be produced by emotion, in which case the reticular formation is involved through the ascending and descending pathways connecting it with the hypothalamus. The fact that cortical and autonomic arousal are involved in both types of loops does not mean that these loops are identical and it is therefore dangerous to assume that indices of cortical or autonomic arousal can be used as measures of emotional involvement. As I have pointed out, "it might be true to say that emotional arousal can be indexed in terms of cortical arousal, but this proposition cannot be inverted; cortical arousal can take place without any marked degree of autonomic/emotional arousal. Thus, it is not sufficient to prove that a given change in EEG, GSR, or EMG follows upon the presentation of an emotion-producing stimulus in order to argue that these manifestations are pure measures of emotional activation. They may be measures of cortical arousal accompanying many other types of stimuli which are not emotional in nature, and which do not in any way involve the hypothalamus, the visceral brain, or the autonomic system as a whole." Thus I see a marked degree of partial independence between autonomic activation and cortical arousal; activation always leads to arousal, but arousal frequently arises from types of stimulation which does not involve activation. I have proposed that the term "activation" be used for activity mediated through the visceral brain, while the term "arousal" should be reserved for ARAS-mediated activity. Note that in ordinary, civilized life there are in the course of the day very few occasions where strong activation occurs; thus for most people the independence of the two systems is almost complete, except for rare occasions when strong emotions are involved, and activation produces arousal.

The practice of using a one-dimensional model when two dimensions are the minimum required has inevitably produced a great deal of confusion. Many measures of autonomic functioning are known to be correlated with N, as they should be according to the theory, and in addition they form a general factor which has comparatively high heritability (Eysenck, 1956); yet this should not lead us to believe that all measures of autonomic activity must show this relation. Spontaneous fluctuations on the GSR, and speed of habituation of the elicited response, are two measures which according to theory (Eysenck, 1967) should be related to arousal rather than to activation, and should consequently correlate with E rather than with N. Crider and Lunn (1970, 1971) have reported a study in which they found indeed that these two measures are highly intercorrelated (0.74), do not correlate with N, but do correlate significantly with E; introverts show greater spontaneous fluctuations and show less habituation to 90 db tones administered at 1-min intervals. The observed correlations with E were -0.45 for habituation and -0.32 for spontaneous fluctuations. (See also Mangan and O'Gorman, 1969.) In a similar way, indices on the EEG, which are usually taken as evidence of arousal, have been found to be correlated with E, rather than with N (Savage, 1964; Gale, Coles, and Blaydon, 1969). The experimental literature would be much clearer if investigators had always routinely included measures of E and N, such as the EPI (Eysenck and Eysenck, 1965), among their tests and had consistently tried to interpret their findings in terms of two, rather than one dimension. As things stand at the moment, much of the literature, particularly in the physiological field, is almost impossible to interpret. Even well-planned studies, such as those of Thayer mentioned earlier, suffer from this fatal ambiguity. Thayer uses a scale for the measurement of introspective feelings of emotional activity that might refer to arousal or to activation; without further evidence it is impossible to judge. From perusal of the contents of the scale one might be tempted to say that it is concerned with cortical arousal mediated through the ARAS, rather than with activation mediated through the limbic system, but this is mere surmise; evidence that would support or confound this hypothesis is completely missing. A similar weakness is found in the work of Spence and his associates; they use the MAS as their measure of "drive," but this too is ambiguous. The MAS has been found to correlate both with E and N (Eysenck and Eysenck, 1969), and consequently the findings reported by Spence in connection with his theory of "anxiety as a drive" might relate to "arousal as a drive" or "activation as a drive," or indeed to a combination of the two. The study by Thayer and Cox (1968), in which they used both the Thayer measure of arousal and the MAS in conjunction with several learning experiments, gave results which suggested that the active part of the MAS in mediating Spence's predictions might have been that part related to $E;$ in any case, the Thayer questionnaire of arousal gave results that were in much better accord with predictions based on Spence's theory than did the MAS. However, this may not be the correct interpretation; it is possible that the MAS acts as a "trait" measure of anxiety, and the Thayer questionnaire as a "state" measure of anxiety. In the absence of a proper measure of both E and N there is no rigorous way of answering this question.

We must now turn to the next major point in our construction of a model of emotional reactivity that would make possible proper scientific measurement of the variables in question. We have so far talked as if the concept of "stress" had some kind of universal meaning, in the sense that what constitutes a stress for one person also constitutes a stress for another. This, as we shall show, is not so; indeed, a typology of stresses seems as necessary for a proper understanding of the properties of the stress-strain relation as does a proper typology of the organisms exposed to these stresses. We may conveniently use a physical analogy here to demonstrate that the position in psychology is not very different to that in the "hard" sciences. Consider the concept of "hardness." It is not a single property but incorporates various combinations of several properties. As a result there is more than one kind of hardness. For example, *abrasion* hardness depends to a large extent on the properties of the surface so that the way the material is prepared and the effects of corrosion by the atmosphere can both be important. *Scratch* hardness involves a combination of plastic flow and fracture characteristics; here the shape of the scratching tool can also play an important part. Although plasticity, or lack of it, largely determines the *indentation* hardness, if the material is brittle it may crack or shatter. Thus lead and talc are both soft materials, but for different reasons. Lead flows readily when indented; talc offers little resistance to fracture and crumbles easily. The range of properties loosely considered as hardness is so wide that it is impossible to arrive at a concise definition that includes every characteristic. Any precise definition of hardness depends on a particular measure of assessment. Just the same is true in our measurement of emotional reactivity; while probably every organism will feel fear when threatened by death or mutilation (and even here there are obvious exceptions, such as some kinds of psychotic patients, suicides, etc.), when we turn to the milder stimuli used in the psychological laboratory, or even events occurring in life outside the laboratory, individuals differ considerably in their emotional reactions to diverse stimuli. Is it possible to organize these differences in a rational manner, as was done in relation to "hardness" by physicists who distinguish abrasion hardness, scratch hardness, indentation hardness, etc.?

I have attempted to do so with respect to one variable; possibly this might provide a useful example of the kind of thing that is required. Figure 2 shows the hypothetical model postulated here. Along the abscissa are plotted different levels of stimulation (sensory stimulation), from low (sensory deprivation) to high (painful). Along the ordinate are plotted different degrees of hedonic tone, ranging from negative (displeasure) through indifference to positive (pleasure). The relationship between these variables is known to be curvilinear, as indicated by the thick continuous inverted-U-shaped line; extreme degrees of high or low stimulation are shunned as giving rise to negative hedonic tone, while intermediate levels of stimulation are preferred, as giving rise to positive hedonic tone. Some such generalization can already be found in the writings of W. Wundt, but it does not incorporate the all-important concept of individual differences. As shown in Fig. 2, the curve for introverts is shifted toward the left, that for extraverts toward the right, in line with our theory that introverts show higher levels of arousal, and consequently have lower sensory thresholds and smaller jnds; this would lead to a "boosting" effect for the registration of all incoming sensory stimu-

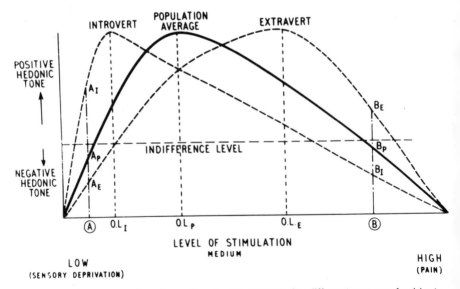

FIG. 2. Hedonic tone as a function of level of stimulation for different groups of subjects.

lation. Conversely, extraverts have low levels of arousal, and thus all incoming sensory stimulation is "damped down." Certain consequences of this hypothesis are indicated in Fig. 2. The optimal level of stimulation for introverts (OL_I) is displaced toward the left from that for the general population (OL_P), while that for extraverts is displaced in the other direction (OL_E). In the space between OL_I and OL_E, changes in strength of sensory stimulation would, therefore, have opposite effects on introverts and extraverts; an increase would make the situation more aversive to the introverts, more appealing to the extraverts. Conversely, a decrease in strength of stimulation would make the situation more aversive to the extraverts and more appealing to the introverts. Thus over a wide range of values of level of stimulation, probably including the great majority of everyday experiences of human subjects in our culture, identical stimuli may be rewarding for one group of subjects, stressful (aversive) to another.

Consider points A and B on the abscissa. These points reflect levels of stimulation that are roughly indifferent to the average person (A_P and B_P), yet point A possesses negative hedonic tone for extraverts (A_E) and positive hedonic tone for introverts (A_I). The opposite is true for point B; here introverts would have a negative feeling reaction (B_I) while extraverts would have a positive reaction (B_E). We may derive certain deductions from this model, e.g., that extraverts would be better able to tolerate pain, whereas introverts would be better able to tolerate sensory deprivation. Both these deductions have been verified several times (Eysenck, 1967), as has the hypothesis that the groups are differentiated by having high and low sensory thresholds respectively. We may convert these postulates into a behavioral test, as was done in a study quoted by Eysenck (1967). Here subjects were isolated in a bare, dark, and silent room, with instructions to push a button against a spring; their operant performance level was observed before the reinforcing condition was introduced. This consisted of 3 sec of light on and loud music, and could be produced by pushing the button harder. As predicted, introverts pushed the button less hard (to avoid stronger stimulation), while extraverts pushed it harder (to gain stimulation). The experiment was also run in reverse, i.e., with lights and music constituting the resting condition, and button pushing producing darkness and silence. Now the roles were reversed, with extraverts pushing less hard, and introverts pushing harder. There is much further evidence to support the general hypothesis outlined above, but this is not the place to review these various studies; the point to be made is simply that it is possible from the general theory to deduce the nature and direction of individual differences which would render certain stimuli stressful for one group, and rewarding for another. This type of study only constitutes a beginning, of course, but it does illustrate the way research should be moving in order to construct for us a typology of stressors.

In the absence of such a typology, how can we deal with the problem raised? Most researchers simply disregard the very existence of the problem, just as they tend to disregard the problem posed by personality and individual differences. One interesting attempt to overcome the difficulties involved is the postulation of two different kinds of anxiety by Sarason, which he calls "trait anxiety," and "state anxiety." The former refers to the habitual level of responsiveness of a person, as it might be measured by typical anxiety or neuroticism questionnaires, such as the N scale of the MPI or the EPI; thus a person who habitually worries, is anxious about many things, has variable moods, etc. would have a high score on such a scale. State anxiety refers to the specific reaction of a person to a specific situation, such as an examination; was he worried about his success, was he anxious and depressed about his actual working out of the problems, or did he feel at ease throughout? Clearly there is a connection between state and trait anxiety; a person high on N might have such a high level of intelligence, and have worked so hard beforehand, that the examination did not present any terrors to him, so that his state of anxiety would be quite low, although his trait anxiety was high. Similarly, a person low on N might be rather dull, or might have done insufficient work beforehand, so that anxiety about his success would be quite reasonable. The Thayer questionnaire mentioned earlier would appear to be to the E scale of the MPI what the Sarason state anxiety questionnaire is to the N scale; a kind of "state arousal" measure, to compare with the "trait arousal" measure which the MPI offers. It seems likely that much more consistent results would be forthcoming from attempts to measure emotional reactivity if every investigator included, besides measures of "trait arousal" and "trait activation," also measures of "state arousal" and "state activation." This would be a first step toward the recognition and possibly even solution of the problem presented by individual differences in reactivity.

Let us assume that we have worked out methods of assessing emotional reactivity, either verbally or by means of behavioral indices, or by psychophysiological methods; how do we know that we have actually succeeded in measuring what we set out to measure, rather than something else, such as intelligence or cooperation? The answer of course lies in some form of *construct validation,* i.e., in the construction of a nomological network that served to define the concept, and provides us with a system of hypothetico-deductive properties within which our attempts to measure emotion would have to fit. There are alternative ways, of course. Spence prefers an operational definition of the concept, for instance. Using this device, he simply *defines* anxiety drive in terms of a person's score on the MAS, and this enables him to rebut criticisms of the kind often elaborated by theoreticians and experimentalists, e.g., that MAS scores do not correlate with clinical evidence, or with the results of psychophysiological experiments. In a similar manner, he is able to disregard psychometric criticisms, e.g., that the MAS is not a univocal test, but consists of several orthogonal (independent) measures, or that the scale measures, not one trait (anxiety), but two (N and E). Eysenck (1973) has discussed the problem posed by operational definitions in this field, and has concluded that while philosophically and semantically Spence's position is impregnable, it is also unscientific; as Popper has often pointed out, scientific concepts and generalizations must be capable of falsification by experiment, and operational definitions are not so falsifiable. Difficult measurement problems cannot be solved by arbitrary fiat, and whereas under certain circumstances operational definitions may be acceptable, in this case they present more problems than they solve. In a sense, every experimentalist presents an operational definition of emotion in his work; yet these different measures do not correlate at all well together, suggesting that if one is an adequate definition of emotion, the others cannot be equally adequate definitions. This leaves us with the same problem we encountered at the outset — how are we to judge between different claimants? Operational definitions may be useful in cutting the Gordian knot; they do not help in unravelling it.

If we wish to go beyond operational definitions and construct a nomological network within which to define our concepts and carry out measurement, then the ideas diagrammed in Fig. 1 become very important and give us additional help in arriving at a solution. The reason for this lies in the "interchangeability principle," which is inherent in our conception. Let us return to Hooke's Law and elasticity. Suppose you had a series of weights, and a series of metal threads, each of a different alloy, but of uniform length, say 20 inches. Let us further suppose that we were required to produce a metal thread of 21 inches in length. You could achieve this result by many different combinations of weights to hang at the bottom of the metal threads in order to make them longer, and threads having different degrees of elasticity; the two concepts of "stress" (weight) and "k" (modulus of elasticity of each thread) are in some way interchangeable. Let us now consider an analogous experiment in the psychology of emotion. Rosenbaum (1953) has shown that threat of strong shock led to greater generalization of a voluntary response than did threat of weak shock. He also discovered (Rosenbaum, 1956) that anxious subjects showed greater generalization to identical stimuli than did nonanxious ones. In other words, greater generalization can be achieved either by increasing the "stress" (threat of shock), or by changes in "k" (choice of anxious or nonanxious subjects). In a very meaningful way experimental conditions and choice of subjects are interchangeable; we can trade one against the other. This is only possible if we are dealing with the same underlying concept, and it follows clearly that in this principle of "interchangeability" we have found an important aid in telling us something useful in constructing our nomological network for the identification of emotion and its measurement. If the principle were to break down for any particular measure, then we would be entitled to doubt whether what we were measuring was in fact emotion. This example also tells us that it may be possible in psychology to arrive at similar rigorous laws as in physics; we may take seriously the analogy of Hooke's Law, and attempt to do in psychology what he did in physics. It is characteristic of psychologists that they seldom attempt to imitate the successful practices of physicists, even when they assert that psychology, as a science, should in fact follow the example of the "hard sciences"; perhaps we should take the advice more seriously than we do.

There is one obvious direction in which this advice is leading, and this is indeed closely related to the topic of this chapter, i.e., the measurement of emotion. We have already noted that the three most widely used indices of emotion—physiological, verbal, behavioral—are by no means highly correlated; this is often taken to imply that the terminus *ad quem* ("emotion") either does not exist, or that there are several different varieties of concepts involved in these experiments. But this does not follow at all; what we can legitimately conclude is that our theoretical understanding of the dynamics of the measuring situation (using the term "dynamic" not in the usual Freudian sense, but simply as referring to the interplay of several factors active over time, and interacting with the concept under scrutiny) is imperfect. In other words, what is required for proper measurement is a deeper theoretical understanding; without such understanding no proper measurement is possible. Consider two simple examples. Measurement of length seems almost too simple to require any sort of theoretical underpinning, and such measurement in terms of "hands" (for height of horses) and "feet" has been commonplace for thousands of years. Yet even relatively simple and straightforward measurement requires the application of a rigid body against the length to be measured, and this requires the definition of "rigid," which is by no means simple. We also face the problem that if we measured the distance from London to Edinburgh in the summer, and again in the winter, we would get two divergent answers—because our measuring rods would have shrunk in the winter, the distance would seem greater than in the summer! Or take the case of measuring heat. Early thermoscopes of the air-water variety had an open top end, thus confounding the measurement of heat with that of barometric pressure; it was only when Pascal discovered this in his celebrated experiment on the Puy-de-Dôme that we got thermometers which measured only temperature. Measurement of emotion is still mostly in its pre-Puy-de-Dôme phase, otherwise we would not have expected the three different systems of measurement to agree any more closely than they in fact do. We have already given reasons why the verbal and the physiological measures are unlikely to agree, unless we use a multiplicity of physiological measures and integrate them in some such fashion as suggested by Lacey; we may now look at the correlation between verbal and behavioral measures.

It is clearly naive to expect two measures to show high correlation when both are affected not only by the thing they both measure, but also by other variables that may be expected to have quite different effects on them. Hull's concept E (performance) is determined by D, H, and many other variables; it would be quite unreasonable to expect these variables to affect E identically, when D was being varied. Consider a heroic warrior going to almost certain death in an attack on numerically superior enemies; his inevitable fear (introspective) clearly is at odds with his behavior (we would expect him to run away), but then his habit systems are quite different as regards verbal report of fear (it is admissible to admit some degree of fear, even in such a situation) and actual dereliction of duty (i.e., running away). In fact, a soldier would not be punished for admitting fear, but he might be shot for cowardice in the face of the enemy for running away. In other words, there are strong additional motivations that determined behavior, which are not applicable to verbal report. Or consider a young lecturer giving his first report to a scientific congress; he may well feel fear, or at least unease, and freely admit this, but he will not usually refuse to give his paper. His conduct is partly motivated by expected reinforcements (praise, better jobs, grant support for his research), which do not affect his verbal statements or emotional reaction. It will be clear why verbal and behavioral indices of emotion may be at variance, and that only a more embracing system of theoretical concepts can do justice to this complex situation. On any reasonable grounds, it would have been miraculous if the three different systems of measurement of emotion had given congruent results; we have to work toward such congruence by analyzing performance much more carefully along theoretical lines than is usually done. Spence's system of "anxiety" measurement, already mentioned, constitutes a good example of long-continued effort to do precisely this; another example is the work done in my own department on the relationship between arousal and reminiscence. Spence's work has already been discussed in considerable detail elsewhere (Eysenck, 1973); consequently I will use as my example here the phenomena of reminiscence.

Reminiscence is a much-researched phenomenon, which denotes improvement in performance, either on a verbal or a motor learning task, and takes place over a rest period interpolated between two practice periods. This phenomenon is now fairly well understood; it seems to depend on the consolidation of the memory trace, which is laid down during the first period of practice (Eysenck, 1965). As is well known, short-term memory depends on some sort of reverberating electrical circuits; in order to become permanently accessible, these must be turned into long-term memory engrams, which are believed to be of a chemical nature, involving protein synthesis. This process of turning short-term memory into long-term memory is called "consolidation," and the efficacy of this consolidation process would appear to be dependent on the degree of arousal obtaining at the time. Motor reminiscence is a fairly stable phenomenon, but verbal reminiscence is so unstable that it has been called a "now-you-see-it-now-you-don't" phenomenon, and research on it has virtually ceased. I suggested that reminiscence, being dependent on consolidation and thus on degree of cortical arousal, could be made into an index of personality and motivation (Eysenck, 1965); let us now consider the sort of theoretical considerations that must be used in order to mediate the necessary predictions. We have already noted that in theory introverts are characterized by higher arousal levels; can we predict that introverts should also show greater reminiscence? The answer is that no such direct prediction is possible, but that a more complex relationship must be postulated. This is due to what is sometimes referred to as "Walker's Law."

Walker (1968) pointed out that there was much evidence to suggest that during consolidation the neurons involved in this activity were unable to function properly as far as recall or reproduction of learned material was concerned; in other words, during consolidation there was in fact a performance deficit. There is much experimental support for this view (Kleinsmith and Kaplan, 1963, 1964; Kleinsmith, Kaplan, and Tarte, 1963; Walker and Tarte, 1963): high arousal can be shown to impede performance after a short interval (when strong consolidation processes would still be going on), but to produce strong reminiscence after a long interval (when strong consolidation processes would have ceased, producing a strong long-term memory). Conversely, low arousal produces a weak consolidation process that does not interfere much with reproduction even after a short interval, thus giving rise to high memory scores; however, after a long interval forgetting sets in (the material having only consolidated weakly) and there is little or no reminiscence. Thus after a long interval, performance is poor under conditions of low arousal. In these studies arousal was measured by a within-person technique, i.e., GSR scores were recorded after the administration of each verbal stimulus, and those stimuli that for a given person produced high arousal were compared with those producing low arousal. Under these conditions, and using different recall intervals, there was a clear crossover effect; stimuli that produced low arousal started off with high reproducibility after short intervals and went on to show poor reproducibility after long intervals, while stimuli that produced high arousal started off with poor reproducibility and went on to show high reproducibility after long intervals. Clark (1967) demonstrated a similar crossover effect when subjects were classed as high arousal or low arousal in terms of their performance on the two-flash threshold test. Taking all this work into account, and basing ourselves on the Walker theorem, we would predict that extraverts would show better recall after a short interval, introverts after a long interval; thus our prediction would be much more complex than anticipated, involving a crossover effect.

Many studies (summarized in Eysenck, 1967) have shown that extraverts show greater reminiscence after short intervals; this is true both for verbal and for motor learning. Farley (1969) has demonstrated the crossover effect with pursuit-rotor reminiscence, and McLean (1968) for paired-associate learning. Howarth and Eysenck (1968) have given a particularly clear demonstration of this effect, which is shown in Fig. 3. This shows recall scores for groups of introverts and extraverts after different recall intervals; each groups is made up of 11 subjects, and all groups are of course made up of different subjects entirely. It will be seen that extraverts, as expected, do very well shortly after learning the material (paired associates) to the agreed criterion, but as the interval increases their performance drops. Introverts, on the other hand, perform poorly shortly after learning to the same criterion, but increase in performance with increasing interval until they show considerable reminiscence after 24 hr. After 5 min, there is little difference between the two groups.

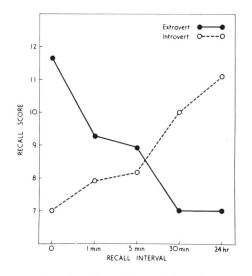

FIG. 3. Recall score as a function of recall interval for different groups of subjects.

This example will make it clear why the measurement of emotion by behavioral indices is such a complex activity. In order to use such an activity as paired-associate learning, or pursuit-rotor learning, we require (a) knowledge of the individual's habitual level of arousal, i.e., a measure of his extraversion-introversion score; (b) knowledge of his degree of arousal by each specific stimulus, using some such technique as that used by Kleinsmith and Kaplan, for instance; (c) knowledge of the general law according to which the phenomena to be quantified operate, i.e., the law of consolidation of memory traces and Walker's theorem regarding the action decrement produced by consolidation. Given all this information we may be able to relate meaningfully the verbal behavior (questionnaire score), the physiological behavior (GSR performance), and the behavioral index used (paired-associate learning reminiscence). Note that we would ideally require several experiments to be done, using different recall intervals; with just one interval the correct choice becomes crucial. There is no space to indicate the several other complexities that make this example even less simple than it would seem at first. I believe that most efforts to measure emotion, either arousal or activation, suffer from disregarding the limitations imposed on single measures, from proceeding without sufficient knowledge of the general laws that govern the behavior being used as an index of arousal or activation, and from the failure to take individual differences into account. This amounts to saying that few of the published experiments in this field can be said to tell us very much about the measurement of "emotion" in the abstract; they tend to report isolated correlations between a single measure or index and another, and while these correlations are often of interest, they do not measure up to the requirements of scientific measurement as understood in the "hard" sciences.

These considerations suggest that when measurement of emotional reaction is a requisite for a particular purpose, it is almost always necessary to use several different indices, in the hope that their agreement would validate (or their disagreement invalidate) the conclusions. Several good examples are quoted by Eysenck and Beech (1971) in their discussion of the effects of aversion therapy. Consider the treatment of a transvestite subject who is shown slides of nude women, panties, slips, skirts, and pajamas. His emotional reactions are measured along these lines: (a) penile response strength and latency; (b) latency of image of transvestite stimulus; (c) semantic differential attitude to stimulus. Treatment consisted of pairing stimuli with electric shocks, in the ordinary classical conditioning paradigm, and it was found that, on the physiological level, penile response latency increased, and strength decreased; on the behavioral level, latency of image evocation increased; and on the verbal level, attitudes grew less favorable. Thus we see that aversion therapy can be indexed along all three dimensions, with similar results; this must increase our confidence in the general conclusion that aversion therapy produced predictable changes in the emotional reactions of certain subjects to the stimuli employed. It should also be noted that these changes are quite specific; when responses to one stimulus were being extinguished, the responses to the other stimuli remained unimpaired; this specificity also tends to increase our faith in the meaningfulness of the measures taken. No single measure, along any of the three dimensions of measurement, could carry such conviction.

We may now terminate our discussion of some of the parameters that require consideration in any attempt to measure emotional arousal and activation by looking at some of the reasons why these emotional reactions produce such exceptional difficulties for measurement. It is much easier to measure intelligence, or sensory thresholds, or motor skills, than it is to measure emotional reactions. Why is this so? Probably the main reason is that emotional reactions cannot only by themselves be learned, i.e., become attached through classical conditioning to previously neutral stimuli, but can also become secondary drives and secondary reinforcements (Eysenck, 1970).

The primary drive involved in this case is pain or frustrative nonreward, probably acting through stimulation of the pain centers; neutral stimuli associated with pain give rise to anxiety/fear responses, which are very similar to responses to pain, and the proprioceptive consequences of these learned responses produce the drive stimuli (S_D) that serve the secondary drive. Anxiety may be unique in having both these functions; few other examples come to mind of secondary *drives,* although there are many studies using secondary *reinforcers.* Tokens that may be exchanged for food will act as secondary *reinforcers* for hungry chimps, but they will only cause him to work when hungry (primary drive); they will not produce a secondary hunger drive! Miller (1948, 1951) in his classical studies showed that anxiety, i.e., conditioned pain reactions, acted as a drive as well as providing reinforcement. In these studies, he demonstrated, first, that neutral stimuli become fear arousing after association with noxious stimuli and can serve as the basis for motivating an animal in a learning situation so that it strives to escape from them and, second, that reduction of the fear through cessation of the conditioned fear stimulus constitutes a reinforcing event in that it leads to the learning of those responses that it follows. To put these points very briefly, it seems that the conditioned pain reaction shares with the unconditioned pain reaction all the drive-producing and reinforcing properties which are characteristic of primary drives, and for all practical purposes it may therefore be regarded as equivalent to a primary drive.

We thus have the unusual position that emotional reactions, such as anxiety (or sexual responses) do not serve only as primary drives, with reduction or amplification serving as primary reinforcements; such emotional reactions can also become conditioned and serve as secondary drives and secondary reinforcements. This unusual situation must complicate measurement tremendously; even during the course of measurement a stimulus may change from neutral to emotionally charged, through a process of conditioning inherent in the measurement. This would not be so important if we would take seriously the usual statement of the law of extinction, according to which the unreinforced *CS* soon loses its power to evoke the *CR*. If this were so, then any fortuitous conditioning that took place would soon extinguish. However, the law of extinction unfortunately does not work in this fashion. I have suggested that while extinction does no doubt take place when the unreinforced *CS* is presented, we also observe another phenomenon, which I have labeled "incubation" or enhancement (Eysenck, 1968); in other words, we have to revise the classical law of extinction.

This revised law states, in essence, the administration of the unreinforced CS (symbolized as $\overline{CS}$), which has in the past been associated with a pain/fear/anxiety-producing UCR, has two separate and contradictory effects. (a) As traditionally suggested, $\overline{CS}$ produces extinction of the CR. (b) $\overline{CS}$ produces incubation or enhancement of the CR. Experimental conditions favorable to the production of extinction are the reverse of those favorable to the incubation of the CR; relevant here are the strength of the UCR, the duration of the $\overline{CS}$, the emotionality of the subject, etc. The outcome of the experiment depends on the interplay of these conditions, which jointly determine the strength of these two tendencies. The experimental evidence regarding this revised law has been reviewed by Eysenck (1968), who concludes that many well-designed experiments report the incubation effect, both with humans and with animals, and that there can be little doubt about its reality. A typical example is the work of Napalkov (1963); working with dogs, he found that various nocive stimuli produced increases in blood pressure of less than 50 mm, complete adaptation (habituation) occurring after some 25 applications of the UCS. A single conditioning trial, however, followed by repeated administrations of the $\overline{CS}$ (never the UCS) brought about increases in blood pressure of 30 to 40 mm at first, rising to 190 to 230; the hypertension state produced lasted over a year in some cases. Campbell et al. (1964) produced similar effects in humans. How can we account for this curious phenomenon, so contrary to established theory? Consider the usual account of aversive conditioning. A CS is followed by a UCS, say shock, which produces a great variety of UCRs; some of these, or even one of these, may then be singled out for study. After a single pairing, or after repeated pairings of CS and UCS, UCS, $\overline{CS}$ produces some, or at least segments of some, of the responses originally produced by the UCS. Fear/anxiety responses are of particular interest in this connection; they are frequently produced by nocive $UCSs$ and are readily conditioned. These CRs may be similar to the original UCRs, but they need not be; under certain conditions they may in fact be the exact opposite. Thus in rats, shock (the UCS) produces parasympathetic responses, including heart-rate decrement, but the $\overline{CS}$ produces sympathetic fear responses, including heart-rate increment (Stern and Ward, 1961, 1962; Fehr and Stern, 1965). However that may be, CS and $\overline{CS}$ acquire the function of signaling danger and coming pain, discomfort, fear, and annoyance; let us denote these nocive consequences as NRs (nocive responses). Through the intermediacy of the UCS, CS has become associated with the NRs and signals their arrival to the organism. (For reasons that will become obvious later, we prefer the term NR in this connection to the use of the terms UCR and CR. It will be argued that the classical account, which is implicitly accepted when we use the classical terms, is somewhat deficient and that a novel nomenclature will be useful in putting over a theory which departs in some ways from the usual one.) Each reinforcement (which may be defined as a NR following CS) increments the habit strength associating CS and NR; consequently each CS/UCS pairing serves to increment the CR. When we administer a $\overline{CS}$, however, so classical theory assures us, this reinforcement is missing, and consequently extinction weakens the habit strength associating CR and NR.

It is here suggested that this account is partly erroneous. $\overline{CS}$, although unaccompaned by UCS and UCR, is in fact accompanied by CR, which is a partial, possibly weak but real NR, identical in many ways with UCR, as already pointed out. Hence some reinforcement is provided, although perhaps this is so much weaker than that accompanying the UCS that its presence may not be very important under certain circumstances. Yet in principle it is always present, and its presence would theoretically lead to a strengthening of the CS/NR bond, and hence to some form of incubation. What is being suggested, in other words, is that conditioning sets in motion a positive-feedback cycle in which the CR provides reinforcement for the $\overline{CS}$. Usually the extinction process will be stronger than this form of reinforcement, leading to overall extinction, and making the action of CS/NR reinforcement unobservable, but under certain circumstances (e.g., when the UCS is exceptionally strong) the extinction process may be weaker than the CS/NR reinforcement process and observable incubation will result.

What is proposed, then, is this. As Kimble (1961, p. 426) points out, "stimuli associated with painful events come, by a process of classical conditioning, to evoke fear. The status of fear as a motive is then inferred from the fact that it has the same properties as other motives, those of providing the basis for learning and of influencing the vigor of behavior." What we propose to add is that fear, so generated, is itself a painful event, and the stimuli associated with it (i.e., $\overline{CS}$), therefore, by classical conditioning come to evoke more fear, thus producing a positive feedback. This mechanism is well known descriptively in psychiatric disorders; it resembles somewhat Seneca's famous saying about "having nothing to fear but fear itself"; this theory may account for the failure of many neurotic fears to extinguish *even though the usual conditions for extinction are present*. The theory may also suggest a firm basis for certain phenomena in the growth of neurotic fears, which otherwise would be difficult to understand. Liddell (1944) and his collaborators have shown that even with the employment of very mild shocks it was possible that where the application of a series of mild shocks would only produce habituation and ultimately extinction, the use of CS in conjunction with these self-same shocks produces stronger and stronger reactions until finally a complete experimental neurosis is in evidence? The same kind of phenomenon is often observed in human neurosis; the UCRs involved may be rather mild, but the combination of CS and $\overline{CS}$ produces a final catastrophic breakdown. These facts are difficult to understand in the absence of a theory of incubation; the cumulative addition of NRs produced by $\overline{CS}$ renders the growth in strength of anxiety reactions perfectly intelligible (Wolpe, 1958, p. 64). We must also bear in mind the important possibility that under certain circumstances, which might only too frequently occur in a real-life conditioning situations, the $\overline{CS}$ is protected from extinction, unlike the $UCR;$ Levis (1967) has provided experimental support for this view. Putting forward the view that in most situations the CS is not a single stimulus but a complex of stimuli, he pointed out that the CS may often take the form of a stimulus sequence, and that in this sequence extinction of early members of the sequence will not lead to complete extinction because of NR produced by later members of the sequence (to use our terminology). When sequential CS were actually employed in rat experiments, he was able to show that extinction was extremely slow, and proceeded very much according to theory. Clearly, whether or not these various theories are in accord with fact, the position of anxiety conditioning in real-life situations is much more complicated than the typical experimental single-stimulus conditioning set-up; animal work will have to be designed in such a way in the future that these complications can be taken into account, and evidence be secured regarding their adequacy or otherwise.

The theory of incubation may be important not only for giving a proper account of the development and preservation of neurotic anxiety in dysthymic patients, i.e., in cases of neurotic disorders of the first kind, but also in the development of disorders of the second kind (Eysenck and Rachman, 1965). Consider the experimental studies of Rachman (1966) and Rachman and Hodgson (1968) of the origins of fetishistic sexual disorders; they showed that by pairing slides of shoes and of nudes, physiological responses (penis plethysmograph) appropriate to the latter could be evoked by the former. This is in line with a simple conditioning theory of the origins of fetishism, but much is still left unexplained. In the typical fetishist, sexual responses to the fetishistic object are stronger than those of the sexual object itself, and may be indispensable for the occurrence of any response to the primary sexual object; the simple conditioning theory does not account for these facts at all. It may be suggested that sexual responses, like anxiety responses, have the property of having secondary drive properties as well as secondary reward properties; the physiological responses to the slide of the shoe are similar or identical with those of the slides of nudes, just as the physiological responses to the $\overline{CS}$ in the case of pain/anxiety are often identical with those to the primary UCS. (In fact, one might say that these drive and reinforcement properties are in fact tertiary, because responses to slides of nudes may be considered secondary and the actual touching of the genitals is primary. These fine distinctions are probably not very relevant at this stage of theory construction.) Hence we may use our paradigm of incubation of fear and extend it to the incubation of sexual responses and their enhancement upon the production of the appropriate $\overline{CS};$ in this way we can account for the observed facts of fetishistic behavior. Clearly in doing so we are progressing to a more adequate but also more complex model of conditioning, making use of Mowrer's "hope-relief" hypothesis (Gray, 1971, p. 183–192). If we consider the extinction of approach behavior in passive avoidance learning as being based on the activity of the *punishment* mechanism (i.e., through the fear-frustrative nonreward hypothesis), so we may consider active avoidance learning and positive reward learning as being based on the activity of the *reward* mechanism. Mowrer called the activity caused in the reward mechanism by secondary rewarding stimuli "hope," and the activity caused by stimuli associated with nonpunishment "relief"; hence Gray has called this compound theory the "hope-relief" hypothesis, to take its place beside the "fear-frustration" hypothesis. Such an hypothesis is of course closely linked with the neurological and physiological work of Olds and others on the reward (pleasure) and the punishment (pain) centers in the brain; Gray discusses these in some detail, a task which would not be appropriate to this chapter. (He also adds the hypothesis that pleasure centers are more readily aroused in extroverts, pain centers in the introvert; such an hypothesis, while still lacking in experimental support, cannot be ruled out and might account to some degree at least for the observed differential susceptibilities of introverts and extroverts for disorders of the first and second kinds.) Gray and Smith (1969) have constructed a detailed model for conflict and discrimination learning, which can be (and has been tested experimentally; it is in terms of some such model that we ought to be thinking in trying to account for emotional behavior, bearing in mind the complex additional drive and reinforcement variables that are involved through the mechanisms of conditioning, extinction, and incubation.

We may perhaps use the theoretical considerations outlined above to try and account for a particular example of discrepancy between verbal expression of "felt" fear on the one hand and behavior on the other. In behavior therapy, using some variety of desensitization procedure, it has often been observed that while behavioral responses suggestive of fear are much reduced, or completely abolished, yet patients still complain about "felt" fears and anxieties remaining (Lang and Lazovik, 1963; Wolpe and Lazarus, 1966; Lang, 1968; Miller and Nawas, 1969; Hart, 1966; Davidson, 1968). This "felt" fear suggests the failure to remove physiological conditioned responses by the desensitization process, and Leitenberg, Agras, Butz, and Wincze (1971) show that this is indeed true; phobic behavior was reduced but concurrent measures of heart rate either did not change or decreased only some time after the improvement in behavior took place. Thus here we have a well-documented case of dissociation between verbal/physiological responses, and behavioral measures of treatment; how can this be accounted for?

Riccio and Silvestri (1973) have discussed this problem in some detail. Basing themselves on a large amount of animal experimentation, they suggest that the *CS* in aversive conditioning has both motivational and discriminative aspects (e.g., Polin, 1959). Treatment techniques incorporating "flooding" procedures involve the extinction of both the motivational and discriminative properties of the phobic stimulus, while systematic desensitization appears to be primarily oriented toward altering its discriminative characteristics. Since desensitized patients control the termination of the fearful images, the motivational strength of these stimuli may be preserved in much the same way as they were by the patients' original avoidance responses (e.g., Solomon and Wynne, 1971). In consequence, the patients' control may serve as a discriminatively reinforced avoidance response through the action of anxiety reduction. In this way, Riccio and Silvestri attempt to account for the findings that although desensitized patients showed significant improvement on behavioral tests, they continued to report considerable fear on subjective measures taken during the behavioral test, and on those administered following treatment. On these grounds we would expect flooding procedures to be more effective in reducing both behavioral and verbal/physiological responses of fear and anxiety, and the literature (Barrett, 1969; Boulougouris et al., 1971) seems to support this statement on the whole. Exceptions (Willis and Edwards, 1969; Rachman and Hodgson, 1970) may be posited to have been due to lack of sufficient time for extinction to occur, a conclusion that would follow from the new version of the extinction law outlined above (Eysenck, 1968; see also experimental support for the posited time-linked effect of incubation in Rohrbauch and Riccio, 1970). Thus by extending the two-process theory of avoidance conditioning along these lines we are able to explain what at first sight would appear a paradoxical state of affairs, with different indices of fear/anxiety pointing in different directions. The fact that anxieties are conditioned fear responses introduces complexities into the measurement of fear reactions that can only be included in a scientific model by suitable employment of theories originating in the conditioning laboratory, and that relate to such factors as extinction, incubation, etc. It is impossible to account for the facts of human emotions without introducing these fundamental principles of conditioning, both classical and instrumental; this is the clear conclusion to which our examination of the evidence points.

It would be possible to go on almost endlessly discussing the many parameters that affect and determine the measurement of emotional reactions. I think that enough has been said to show that this is a very complex and difficult field, but that all the same there has been considerable advance in relation to the construction of a model that would prove useful in directing our activities. No realistic view of the situation could ever have encouraged the belief that some day we would emerge miraculously with a single, all-purpose test of "emotion," easy to administer and easy to interpret — analogous, perhaps, to the measurement of temperature. If we are willing to give up this chimera and buckle down to the hard task of experimental investigation of specific, definite problems, then the position is far from unpromising. Any such investigation will have to bear in mind the constraints imposed on measurement by the various parameters discussed in this chapter; nevertheless, within these constraints, we can already point to a number of findings and generalizations that are far from negligible and that bode well for future work. It would have been idle to expect more than that at such an early date in the history of measurement of the emotions.

REFERENCES

Barrett, C. L. (1969): Systematic desensitization or implosive therapy, J. Ab. Psychol. *74*, 587–592.

Bartenwerfer, N. (1969): Some practical consequences of activation theory, Zeit. Exp. Ang. Psychol. *10*, 195–222.

Boulougouris, J. C., Marks, I. M., and Marset, P. (1971): Superiority of flooding (implosive) to desensitization for reducing pathological fear, Behav. Res. Ther. *9*, 7–16.

Broadhurst, P. (1959): The interaction of task difficulty and motivation. The Yerkes-Dodson Law revived, Acta Psychol. *16*, 321–338.

Burgess, J. A., and Kokauson, J. E. (1964): Effects of increased heart rate in intelligence performance, J. Ab. Soc. Psychol. *68*, 85–91.

Campbell, D., Sanderson, R. E., and Laverty, S. G. (1964): Characteristics of a conditioned response in human subjects during extinction trials following a simple traumatic conditioning. J. Ab. Soc. Psychol. *68*, 627–639.

Clark, A. M., (1967): The relation of arousal to reminiscence, attention, withdrawal and the Hunter Prognostic Index of chronic schizophrenia, London, Ph.D. thesis.

Crider, A., and Lunn, R. (1970): Personality correlates of electrodermal lability, Psychophysiology *6*, 633–634.

Crider, A., and Lunn, R. (1971): Electrodermal lability as a personality dimension, J. Exp. Res. Personal. *5*, 145–150.

Davison, G. C. (1968): Systematic desensitization as a counterconditioning process, J. Psychol. *73*, 91–99.

Doerr, H. O., and Hokauson, J. E. (1965): A relation between heart rate and performance in children, J. Personal. Soc. Psychol. *2*, 70–76.

Duffy, E. (1962): *Activation and Behaviour*, Wiley, New York.

Eysenck, H. J. (1965): The inheritance of extraversion-introversion, Acta Psychol. *12*, 95–110.

Eysenck, H. J. (1959): *The Maudsley Personality Inventory*, Univ. London Press, London.

Eysenck, H. J. (1962): Reminiscence, drive and personality- revision and extension of a theory, Brit. J. Soc. Clin. Psychol. *1*, 127–140.

Eysenck, H. J. (1965): A three-factor theory of reminiscence, Brit. J. Psychol. *56*, 163–181.

Eysenck, H. J. (1967): *The Biological Basis of Personality*, C. C. Thomas, Springfield, Ill.

Eysenck, H. J. (1968): A theory of the incubation of anxiety/fear responses, Behav. Res. Ther. *6*, 309–321.

Eysenck, H. J. (1970): Psychological aspects of anxiety, Brit. J. Psych. Special Publication No. 3, 7–20.

Eysenck, H. J. (1973): Personality, learning and "anxiety." In: *Handbook of Abnormal Psychology*, ed. H. J. Eysenck, pp. 390–419, Pitman, London.

Eysenck, H. J., and Beech, H. R. (1971): Counter Conditioning and related methods. In: *Handbook of Psychotherapy and Behaviour Change*, eds. A. E. Bergin and S. L. Garfield, Wiley, New York.

Eysenck, H. J., and Eysenck, S. B. G. (1965): *The Eysenck Personality Inventory*, Univ. London Press, London.

Eysenck, H. J., and Eysenck, S. B. G. (1969): *Personality Structure and Measurement*, Routledge and Kegan Paul, London.

Eysenck, H. J., and Rachman, S. (1965): The causes and cures of neurosis. Routledge and Kegan Paul, London.

Farley, F. (1969): Personality and reminiscence, paper read at the International Congress of Psychology, London.

Fehr, F. S., and Stern, J. G. (1965): Heart rate conditioning in the rat, J. Psychosom. Res. *8*, 441–453.

Fiske, D. W., and Maddi, S. R. (1961): *Functions of Varied Experience*, Dosey, Homewood, Ill.

Gale, A., Coles, M., and Blaydon, J. (1969): Extraversion-introversion and the EEG, Brit. J. Psychol. *60*, 209–223.

Gellhorn, E., and Longbourrow, G. N. (1963): *Emotions and Emotional Disorders*, Harper, New York.

Gray, J. (1971): *The Psychology of Fear and Stress*, Weidenfeld and Nicolson, London.

Gray, J. A., and Smith, P. J. (1969): An arousal-decision model for partial reinforcement and discrimination learning. In: *Animal Discriminative Learning*, eds. R. M. Gilbert and N. S. Sutherland, pp. 243–272, Academic, London.

Hart, J. D. (1973): Fear reaction as a function of the assumption and success of the therapeutic role, quoted by Riccio and Silvestri.

Hebb, D. O. (1955): Drives and the C.N.S. (conceptual nervous system), Psychol. Rev. *62*, 243–254.

Hokauson, J. E., and Burgess, M. (1964): Effects of physiological arousal level, frustration and task complexity in performance. J. Ab. Soc. Psychol. *68*, 698–702.

Howarth, E., and Eysenck, H. J. (1968): Extraversion, arousal, and paired-associate recall, J. Exp. Res. Personal. *3*, 114–116.

Jensen, A. (1962): Extraversion, neuroticism and serial learning, Acta Psychologia *20*, 69–77.

Kimble, G. (1961): *Hilgard and Marquis' Conditioning and Learning*, Appleton-Century-Crofts, New York.

Kleinsmith, L. J., and Kaplan, S. (1963): Paired-associate learning as a function of arousal and interpolated interval. J. Exp. Psychol. *65*, 190–193.

Kleinsmith, L. J., and Kaplan, S. (1964): Interaction of arousal and recall interval in nonsense and syllable paired-associate learning. J. Exp. Psychol. *67*, 124–126.

Kleinsmith, L. J., Kaplan, S., and Tarte, R. D. (1963): The relationship of arousal to short and long-term recall, Can. J. Psychol. *17*, 393–397.

Lang, P. J. (1968): Fear reduction and fear behaviour: problems in treating a construct. In: *Research in Psychotherapy*, ed. J. M. Sklier, Vol. 3, American Psychological Association, Washington, D.C.

Lang, P. J., and Lazovik, S. D. (1963): Experimental desensitization of a phobia, J. Ab. Soc. Psychol. *66*, 519–525.

Lazarus, R. (1968): Emotions and adaptations: Conceptual and empirical relations, In: *Nebraska Symposium in Motivation*, pp. 175–266, ed. W. J. Arnold, Nebraska University Press, Nebraska.

Leitenberg, H., Agras, S., Butz, R., and Wincze, J. (1971): Relationship between heart rate and behavioural change during the treatment of phobias, J. Ab. Psychol. *78*, 59–68.

Levis, D. J. (1967): Implosive therapy: Part 2. The subhuman analogue, the strategy and the technique. In: *Behaviour Modification Techniques in the Treatment of Emotional Disorders*, ed. S. C. Armitage, V.A. Publications, Battle Creek.

Liddell, H. S. (1944): Conditioned reflex method in experimental neurosis. In: *Personality and the Behaviour Disorders*. ed. J. Mc V. Hunt, Ronald Press, New York.

Lindsley, D. B. (1951): Emotion. In: *Handbook of Experimental Psychology*. ed. S. S. Stevens, Wiley, New York.

McLaughlin, R. J., and Eysenck, H. J. (1967): Extraversion, neuroticism and paired-associate learning, J. Exp. Res. Personal. *2*, 128–132.

McLean, P. D. (1963): Paired-associate learning as a functional recall interval, personality and arousal. London, Ph.D. thesis.

Malmo, R. B. (1959): Activation: A neurophysiological dimension, Psychol. Rev. *66*, 367–386.

Mangan, A. L., and Gorman, J. E. (1969): Initial amplitude and rate of habituation of orienting reaction and relation to extraversion and neuroticism, J. Exp. Res. Personal. *3*, 275–282.

Martin, J. (1972): Somatic reactivity, In: *Handbook of Abnormal Psychology*, ed. H. J. Eysenck, pp. 309–361. Pitman, London.

Miller, H. R. and Nawas, M. M. (1969): Control of aversive stimulus termination in systematic desensitization, Behav. Res. Ther. *7*, 57–61.

Miller, N. (1948): Studies of fear as an acquirable drive, J. Exp. Psychol. *38*, 89–101.

Miller, N. (1951): Learnable drives and rewards. In: *Handbook of Experimental Psychology,* ed. S. S. Stevens, Wiley, New York.

Napalkov, S. V. (1967): Information process of the brain, In: *Progress in Brain Research.* Vol. 2, ed. N. Wiener and J. C. Schade, pp. 59–69, Elsevier, Amsterdam.

Polin, S. T. (1959): The effects of flooding and physical suppression as extinction techniques on an anxiety motivated locomotor response, J. Psychol. *47,* 235–245.

Rachman, S. (1966): Sexual fetishism: An experimental analogue, Psychol. Rec. *16,* 293–296.

Rachman, S., and Hodgson, R. J. (1968): Experimentally induced "sexual fetishism" replication and development, Psychol. Rec. *18,* 25–27.

Rachman, S., and Hodgson, R. J. (1970): An experimental investigation of the implosive techniques, Behav. Res. Ther. *8,* 21–27.

Riccio, D. C., and Silvestri, R. (1973): Extinction of avoidance behaviour and the problem of residual fear, Behav. Res. Ther. *11,* 1–9.

Rohrbaugh, M., and Riccio, D. C. (1970): Paradoxical enhancement of learned fear, J. Ab. Psychol. *75,* 210–216.

Rosenbaum, R. (1953): Stimulus generalization as a function of level of experimentally induced anxiety, J. Exp. Psychol. *45,* 35–43.

Rosenbaum, R. (1956): Stimulus generalization as a function of clinical anxiety, J. Ab. Soc. Psychol. *53,* 281–285.

Routtenberg, S. (1968): The two-arousal hypothesis: reticular formation and limbic system, Psychol. Rev. *75,* 51–80.

Savage, R. D. (1964): Electro-cerebral activity, extraversion and neuroticism, Brit. J. Psych. *110,* 98–100.

Solomon, R. L., and Wynne, L. C. (1954): Traumatic avoidance learning: the principle of anxiety conservation and partial irreversibility, Psychol. Rev. *61,* 353–385.

Spence, J. T., and Spence, K. W. (1966): The motivational components of manifest anxiety, drive and drive stimuli. In: *Anxiety and Behaviour,* ed. C. D. Spielberger, Academic, London.

Stern, J. G., and Ward, T. J. (1961): Changes in cardiac response of the albino rat as a function of electro-convulsive seizures, J. Comp. Physiol. Psychol. *54,* 385–391.

Stern, J. G., and Ward, T. J. (1962): Heart rate change during avoidance conditioning in the male albino rat, J. Psychosom. Res. *6,* 151–162.

Thayer, R. E. (1967): Measurement of activation through self-report, Psychol. Rep. *20,* 663–678.

Thayer, R. E. (1970): Activation states as assessed by verbal report and four psychophysiological variables, Psychophysiology *7,* 86–94.

Thayer, R. E., and Cox, S. J. (1968): Activation, manifest anxiety and verbal learning, J. Exp. Psychol. *78,* 524–526.

Walker, E. L. (1968): Action decrement and its relation to learning, Psychol. Rev. *65,* 129–142.

Walker, E. L., and Tarte, R. D. (1963): Memory storage as a function of arousal and time with homogenous and heterogeneous tests, J. Learning Verbal Behav. *2,* 113–119.

Willis, G. T. and Edwards, J. A. (1969): A study of the comparative effectiveness of systematic desensitization and implosive therapy, Behav. Res. Ther. *7,* 387–395.

Wilson, G. (1972): Abnormalities of motivation. In: *Handbook of Abnormal Psychology,* ed. H. J. Eysenck, pp. 362–389, Pitman, London.

Wolpe, J. (1958): *Psychotherapy by Reciprocal Inhibition,* Stamford University Press. Stamford, Cal.

Wolpe, J., and Lazarus, A. A. (1966): Behaviour Therapy Techniques, Pergamon Press, New York.

Emotions—Their Parameters and Measurement,
edited by L. Levi.
Raven Press, New York © 1975

Ethological Methods as Applied to the Measurement of Emotion

J. P. Henry, D. L. Ely, F. M. C. Watson, and P. M. Stephens

*Department of Physiology, University of Southern California, Los Angeles, California
90007*

PHYSIOLOGICAL CHANGES DURING EMOTIONAL STATES

The Ethological Approach

Hamburg, Hamburg, and Barchas (*this volume*) point to emotion as the subjective or "existential" aspect of important definable behavioral patterns that are accompanied by measurable physiological changes. These authors discuss the significance of emotion as an inner experience that often involves an impulse to action in a way that is critical for individual or for species survival. They draw on the now classic ethological field studies of Van Lawick-Goodall (1973) in which she observed the behavior of a group of chimpanzees living in their natural environment. Such work involves the analysis of interaction among members of a group of both sexes with their young living in an open territory unencumbered by apparatus and unaffected by handling or training.

The social ethological approach studies behavioral roles, noting the give and take and dominant and subordinate status in various social situations (Crook and Goss Custard, 1972). It studies the mother–infant relations with its behavioral evidence of the strong emotions that are involved. It records the behavior of the animals as they take care of their needs for a diet appropriate for the species, for water, and for protection from the extremes of heat, cold, damp, etc. by finding or building shelter from the environment. It observes interaction in social groups and the division of the available territory into regions that provide sufficient supplies to meet the needs of the young. Their nesting behavior and maternal- and paternal-care patterns are recorded and broken down into their various components, and their communication systems, be it by sound in the audible or ultrasonic range, by gesture, or by pheromone, are analyzed. Many of these parameters are species specific and some of the patterns are extraordinarily complex, as for example, the tree-felling and dam- and lodge-building of the beaver. Importantly, much behavior has an innate basis, and while mammals learn to fit this basis to the environment during a sensitive period of development, the nature of the stable pattern of behavior that is adopted remains peculiar to the species. The beaver is the dam-building rodent whose complex behavioral patterns will develop if given materials and running water as surely as a man born into a human culture will develop our unique capacity for speech and technological control of the environment.

Behavioral Role and Endocrine Pattern in Primates

Such an ethological approach can be applied to animals living in small groups in large cages in association with a laboratory. A good example is the work of Hinde's group at Madingley, where he has observed the consequences of social deprivation of baby rhesus monkeys and measured the frequency of interaction with mother, "aunts," peers, and males (Hinde, 1971). By dint of patient quantitative analysis of the interaction of these various components of the social nexus, they have arrived at further important conclusions, extending the work of Bowlby (1970) with man and the Harlows with monkeys (Harlow, McGaugh, and Thompson, 1971) on the importance of affectional bonds for normal social relations.

Studies using ethological methodology in which the animals are free to interact involve observation of the behavioral patterns associated with various motivational states. That such behavior is accompanied by emotional responses can be surmised from the concurrent physiological changes, for meaningful measurements can be made of the various hormone levels and indeed of a variety of physiological parameters that accompany the action. Thus Rose, Holaday, and Bernstein (1971) have recently reported on the plasma testosterone levels of a group of 34 rhesus monkeys living in a 40×40 m compound. They showed that the more aggressive animals higher in dominance rank had higher levels of testosterone than the subordinates. More recently loss of status was associated with a fall in testosterone level; and a rise in status, due to placement in a group in which a formerly low-ranking animal could be dominant, was associated with a rise in plasma level (Rose, Gordon, and Bernstein, 1972).

On the other hand, Sassenrath (1970) has recently reported on small mixed-sex groups of macaques kept in more crowded conditions for two years. She determined their rank order by testing their interaction in still smaller groups. This gave some idea of the adaptation of each individual to the social milieu of the larger home cage where they lived as a group. She found that the adrenal response to ACTH was very much higher in the most subordinate animals than it was in the dominant. She concluded that the fear-evoking component of chronic social interaction is a strong stimulus for the adrenocortical response. This is in interesting contrast to the high testosterone levels of the males who formed the confident aggressive establishment of Rose's group.

Pathophysiology of Defeat in the Tree Shrew

The physiological changes accompanying role behavior have been effectively studied by using a limited ethological approach in which only two animals were observed at a time. Von Holst (1969) has measured the extent of arousal of the sympathetic nervous system in a tree shrew that has been defeated by a dominant and is unable to withdraw from his territory. The peculiarity of which von Holst took advantage was that whenever there is strong sympathetic stimulation the hairs on the shrew's long tail will stand erect, giving it a bushy appearance. By observing the percent of the 12-hr observation time during which the tail was in this condition, he made important conclusions about consequences of the emotional state for the defeated animal. The subordinate placed in a cage that is separated only by wire mesh from the victor shows a clear-cut behavioral pattern. The subjugated animal hardly moves, spending 90% of the daily activity period lying motionless in a corner just following the movements of the victor with its head. Approach of the victor to the partition will often elicit fear squealing. The rest of the time the animal is apathetic, but the hairs on the tail and body are raised continuously. The fur becomes untidy, for he spends less than a tenth of the time normally alloted to grooming. Although the defeated animal does consume its quota of food, it eats in a stealthy way and the normal activity of marking territory with the sternal glands and urine ceases.

If the dominant is allowed to attack this defeated animal, he lies passive while being bitten on the rump, thighs, and root of the tail. The attack is not lethal and no bleeding will be elicited, yet the animal may die a few minutes after such an attack, presumably with a cardiac arrest of the type described by Richter (1957) in Norway rats that are forced to swim for their lives.

Von Holst (1972) has observed that after a couple of days to two weeks the defeated shrew will sink into a coma and die in uremia due to renal insufficiency. The histological evidence points to an acute decrease of renal blood flow with tubular necrosis and glomerular ischemia. Here then is evidence of an intense and persisting emotional state that has resulted from the confrontation between two members of the same species. Not only does the behavior of the animal betray the disturbed motivational state, but the appearance of the tail and the final death in renal failure show that the subjective and behavioral aspects of the emotion are accompanied by physiological and biochemical changes. These can be measured independently and the case is discussed in detail because such observations are not unique. Barnett (1964) has described the submissive behavior of Norway rats introduced as intruders into a caged social group dominated by an established vigorous resident male. Although their behavior is not as dramatic as that of the tree shrew, the submissive gestures suggest an intense emotional arousal when escape is found to be impossible. Here, too, the death that ensures within a few days is not due to wounds, but may be attributed to the accompanying neuroendocrine disturbances.

Status Loss and Cardiovascular Disease in a Baboon

This modified ethological approach to the generation of strong and sustained emotions combined with pathophysiological observations of the responses in various organ systems has been employed by the group at Sukhumi on the Black Sea coast, and Lapin and Cherkovitch (1971) have recently reported on the well-known observations of emotional disturbance that Miminoshvili (1956) generated in a hamadryas baboon by violating his normal social relationships. The male was separated from the females with whom he had long been associated in a free roaming group in a large open enclosure. The juveniles and females were put in one roomy cage, and the dominant male, in an adjacent one, separated only by wire mesh. His behavior indicated anxiety and alertness. He made loud vocalizations, and although after a time this agitated overt behavior subsided, it would be readily aroused when, contrary to the routine in the free state, the juveniles and females were fed first. When another male was put in with the females, the former consort's behavior became still more violent. Lapin and Cherkovitch report that, after several months, hypertension and other evidence of chronic cardiovascular disease developed. They conclude that stimuli which involve the species' preservative programs of the organism can be highly effective in inducing sustained emotional responses. Recently Kummer (1971) has pointed out that the baboons at Sukhumi are of the hamadryas species. He notes that although they have been bred in captivity for several generations, they still display the unique behavior of this species *vis-à-vis* the female. Hamadryas males will often adopt their future consorts while they are still infants, and they develop very close ties with the members of their group. The male is highly protective and possessive of his females and even during estrus this bond is not transgressed by other males. Kummer has shown by experiments that the other males are inhibited from making such approaches. Thus their behavior contrasts with that, for example, of chimpanzee males toward a female in estrus.

There must be special circumstances, as there were in the Miminoshvili experiment, for a fresh male to be induced to take over the other animal's harem. Thus an inherited pattern was being stimulated that had been strongly reinforced by the early experience of this particular baboon with that particular group of females. An attempt to reproduce the results of this experiment, which overlooked this peculiarity of the hamadryas, and used another species of primate might well not succeed in producing the sustained and intense limbic-hypothalamic responses of which the published account of the behavior of this particular animal gives evidence.

Cardiovascular Disease and Social Distress in Swine

Nevertheless, the observations of the Sukhumi workers that the chronic emotional disturbance induced in a displaced and attached baboon was associated with chronic disease of the cardiovascular system are not unique. Ratcliffe (1968) working at the Philadelphia Zoological Gardens has shown that deaths of mammals and birds from ischemic necrosis of the myocardium caused by arteriosclerotic stenosis of the intramural coronary vessels increased from less than 1% to more than 10% during 1948 to 1968. Mean age at death and diet were not relevant. He noted that 1948 was the start of the zoo management's attempts to assemble family groups. This resulted in conflicts, breeding failures, and abnormal behavior. He eventually concluded that the coronary heart disease increase was due to behavioral responses to social situations.

In an experimental follow-up of this work, he studied the psychological responses of swine to separation and pairing after the primary social bonds of grouped animals had been formed (Ratcliffe, Luginbuhl, Schnarr, and Chacko, 1969). Grouped and paired swine responded to human visitors with friendly grunts and squeals for a handout. There was give and take among the males and competition was limited to pushing and shoving. By contrast, separated swine, especially the normally sociable females, failed to respond to visitors, lying unresponsive and refusing offers of added corn. After a year of isolation the separated females showed a significantly greater development of arteriosclerosis than those that were grouped. Thus the data from this quantitative study suggest that a sustained emotional disturbance was associated with chronic pathophysiological changes.

Adrenal, Cortical, and Medullary Responses to Social Interaction in Rodents

Working in the field with freely growing, and in the laboratory with assembled populations of rats, Christian, Lloyd, and Davis (1965) have shown that adrenal weight is an index of adrenal-cortical function. They demonstrated in very extensive studies that in conditions of social interaction where population density is increased there are two basic responses that serve to control animal numbers. The one is an inhibition of the pituitary adrenal gonadal system for reproduction. An example is Rose's decrease in the testosterone level of monkeys that have lost status. The other mechanism is an activation of the pituitary adrenocortical system that increases mortality by disturbing normal defense mechanisms. This is more aroused in the young and subordinate than in older established animals. Christian points to the progressive increase in adrenal weight of defeated subordinated caged mice that are involved in fighting and he showed that corticosterone levels are elevated. Bronson and Desjardins (1971) show that short daily defeats not only cause corticosterone to rise to a peak an hour after the event, but the elevated level is sustained for as long as a day thereafter. As in the case of von Holst's tree shrews, physical contact between the fighter and the defeated mouse was not necessary. The mere threat of an attack was enough to trigger a response.

Welch and Welch (1971) have observed the fighting of pairs of grouped mice that interacted for 5 to 10 min daily for 5, 10, or 14 days. They contrasted the effects with those of grouped living. There was an increase in heart and adrenal weight. They attributed the latter to activation of the anterior pituitary adrenal-cortical axis and associated the former with the observed increase in blood pressure. They also reported an increased level of adrenal norepinephrine and epinephrine and suggested that the rate of amine biosynthesis in the adrenals is elevated in social interaction. Recent work has demonstrated that this is indeed the case (Henry, Stephens, Axelrod, and Mueller, 1971). Although the behavioral aspects of such work are limited it is a reasonable assumption that the defeated mice experience those basic emotions that would be reported by a man in the same circumstances. There is evidence that these episodes are strongly aversive and that the mood may be one of fear and depression.

Social Interaction and Endocrine Changes in Man

Commenting on their results with the formerly dominant baboon Lapin and Cherkovitch see the situation as one in which the displaced consort male had no adequate defenses and to which he inevitably reacted with intense emotional arousal. Bourne (1971), discussing the adrenal-corticosteroid responses of American soldiers in Vietnam to emotionally arousing combat situations, makes a similar point. It was when they were involved in intense personal conflict with other members of the team or with superiors with whom communication was difficult that the avoidance emotions came to the fore and corticosteroids became elevated. Furthermore, these emotions were effective in inducing neuroendocrine changes; although, as in the tree shrews and the baboons, after the first storm of affect had blown over, there was not necessarily any marked behavioral evidence of emotion. Bourne concludes that in man the available psychological defenses permit him to cope so effectively that for a meaningful study of the psysiological parameters of emotion we should focus on the reactions of the individual in highly personal conflicts with others, rather than on events where "his identity is submerged in a role in which he personally has little real investment."

Emotions: The Hypothalamus and the Limbic System

Van Lawick-Goodall's description of the behavioral responses of a young chimpanzee that has lost its mother, or of a male that is making a display to assert dominance, or of gestures of submission, and the touch and pat of reassurance are all so clearly related to the basic human gestures as described by Haas (1970) and by Eibl-Eibesfeldt (1972) that it is credible that the same emotions are being experienced and the same neuroendocrine mechanisms are being set into play.

Harlow's group has used observations of socially deprived young rhesus monkeys as a model for anaclitic depression. Their results and the carefully quantitated mother–infant observations of Hinde's group in which they study time off the mother, distance from her, time with companions, and other measures also leave no doubt that there are attachment bonds between monkey and young. These function in the same way as those studied in man by Bowlby's group in London (Bowlby, 1970) and by Ainsworth and Bell (1969) in Baltimore. The evidence for a common neurophysiological substrate for such emotion is now secure. Indeed, the major physiological textbooks include sections describing it. Ganong (1971) has a chapter on the "Neurophysiological Basis of Instinctual Behavior and Emotions" and Ruch (1965) includes one discussing the "Neurophysiology of Emotion." The small phylogenetically ancient hypothalamic area is the locus of fight-like patterns with growling, piloerection, and the other sympathetic-activated behavioral responses, and of patterns for flight with a fear-like to-and-fro darting of the eyes and turning the head from side to side. It is also the locus of rewarding sexual patterns with vocalizing and estrus crouching. In addition to this basic apparatus for drive states, Mac-Lean's (1970a) "Limbic" System is recognized as modulating such responses. This is the name given to the rhinencephalic complex of structures lying above the hypothalamus. They are largely subcortical and were once thought to be primarily concerned with olfaction. However, Kluver and Bucy (1939) had noted the profound emotional disturbances following bilateral temporal lobectomy; the operation destroyed vital limbic structures and led to loss of response to objects that previously led to fear vocalization, whereas sexual activity was intensified and indiscriminate. Their observations followed the important insight of Papez (1937) who had concluded, partly on neuroanatomic grounds, that the rhinencephalic structures were linked to the hypothalamic-, thalamic-, and limbic-cortical structures to form a neural basis for emotion and for genetically constituted forms of behavior.

Limbic-Striatal System Functions

A generation of intensive research by MacLean (1972) and others has led to the recent formulation of the added hypothesis that this limbic complex in combination with the striatum form a storage and effector mechanism basic for the ancestrally learned behavior that interests the ethologist. These areas are crucial for eliciting the basic emotions of rage, fear, attachment, and their neuroendocrine accompaniments, including the sympathoadrenal-medullary and the hypophyseal-adrenal-cortical responses. The limbic-striatal system is critical for the acts of selecting homesite, establishing and defending territory, hunting, homing, mating, rearing young, forming social hierarchies, and the like (MacLean, 1972).

MacLean (*this volume*) speaks of three brains in the mammal: one for psychophysiological drive reactions and another for emotionally-toned species and self-preservative behavior that has formed the focus of ethological interest. Superimposed on these is yet another comprising the frontal association cortex that is so large in man. This region together with the parietal and temporal cross-modal association area constitutes a new brain that in man, and only in man, attains overwhelming proportions compared with the rest of the organ. This region, which following the lead of Washburn and Hamburg (1968), might be termed a sociocultural brain appears necessary for memory, foresight, planning, inhibition of inappropriate action, and, above all, for the speech and complex technical activity that give man, the new social animal, sufficient control over the environment to undertake space travel.

Nauta (1971) points out that the frontal lobe, which is a vital part of this new brain, is in an intimate relationship with the limbic system and hypothalamus. These regions receive and process information from the internal milieu and are responsible for the homeostatic mechanisms controlling the various systems responsible for respiration, circulation, nutrition, and reproduction. The frontal cortex is the neocortical representative of the limbic system and is in reciprocal relationship with the other great new brain region, the temporoparietal cross-modal association areas.

Figure 1 presents these relationships in the form of a speculative diagram. The relatively tenuous connections of man's sociocultural brain with the affective and body economic integrative levels of the organism are symbolized by the single arrow connecting the temporoparietal region with the frontal lobe and then by another arrow connecting the frontal lobe with the limbic system and brainstem. "Valves" on these arrows symbolize the coping mechanisms or defenses that are involved in the self-regulation of the affective responses. Lazarus (*this volume*) extended his former detailed consideration of the coping process and the response to psychosocial stimulation (Lazarus, 1966) to a discussion of the control of emotion. He postulates that in addition to the self-regulatory mechanisms of emotion, which are here identified with the limbic-striatal complex, there are executive mechanisms that engage in continuous regulation of the emotional states. These defense or coping mechanisms involve cognitive control by the "sociocultural" brain. Foresight and planning inhibit inappropriate actions that might otherwise follow the various self-regulatory emotional responses; they result in responses that not only involve behavior, but also changes in the brainstem and hypothalamic sets, which in turn determine the hypophyseal and autonomic control equilibria.

These defenses or coping processes constitute a significant part of the life style of the individual. Indeed many bear the complexion of the culture in which he was raised. These processes are indicated in the diagram as valves enhancing or cutting down upon interaction between the sociocultural and the affective and body economic spheres.

MacLean (1970*b*, *this volume*) has described this interconnected but semiautonomous system complex as a triune brain. The word is etymologically correct, but its common identification with the dogma of the Trinity raises intriguing echoes. Nemiah and Sifneos (1970) have suggested that the

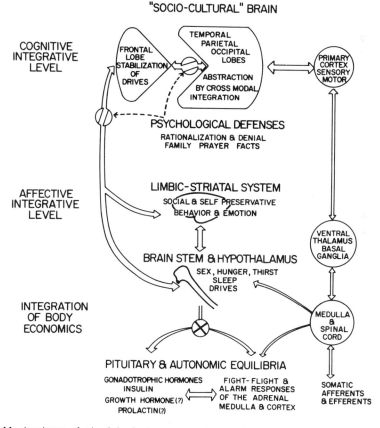

FIG. 1. Mechanisms of physiological response to psychosocial stimulation. The main current of information from the peripheral sense organs courses through the midbrain and thalamus to the primary sensory cortical projection areas. Massive neocortical crossmodal association regions provide the "semiotic" symbol-handling capacity needed for culture and technology. The frontal pole connects this "social" brain with the amygdala hippocampus, septum, and cingulate gyrus. These "limbic" structures together with the striatal storehouse of "ancestrally learned behavior" (MacLean, 1972) subserve emotion and are closely integrated with the hypothalamus that effects consummation of the basic drives. The hypothalamus together with the nonspecific reticular activating system modulates varied pituitary, vagal, and sympathetic reactions which eventually can lead to pathophysiological changes.

interaction between the sociocultural and limbic systems can be deficient, leading to runaway limbic-hypophyseal responses. Certainly the evidence just presented indicates that under the proper circumstances, emotional disturbances can lead to sustained alteration of the autonomic and endocrine equilibria, which in turn results in pathophysiological deterioration.

CONCLUSIONS

The foregoing experiments have been chosen as illustrations of ethologically based studies of the interaction of animals in groups. Observation of behavioral responses was combined in the majority of cases with various physiological or biochemical measurements. These can be related to the emotions that the animals' behavior suggests they are experiencing. In some cases the changes have been acute. In others, the social interaction has persisted for long periods and pathological disturbances were linked to the chronic emotion. Mason (*this volume*) calls attention to the need for complex experimentation in order to study the two accessible facets of the three-sided emotional phenomenon. He points to the need for simultaneous measurements of the social psychological environment that will give clues as to the predominant emotional state of the individual under study, while at the same time providing a series of physiological and/or biochemical assays that permit a determination of this latter critical aspect of the affective state. In the following section we will present an ethological methodology and the series of concurrent biochemical and physiological measures that our group has been employing to analyze the physical consequences of various emotional states in colonies of mice.

BIOCHEMICAL AND PHYSIOLOGICAL RESPONSES TO ROLE-INDUCED EMOTION IN RODENT COMMUNITIES

Observations of Calhoun and Christian

The skilled and patient observations of the ethologists have detected the basic patterns of interaction between the members of a social group. For example, Crowcroft (1966) has watched mice in large rooms furnished with multiple boxes. He has established typical characteristics such as territory formation and the patrol activity of dominant males. His delightfully written *Mice All Over* is a classic of this type of observation.

Calhoun (1962), using rooms fitted with central food and water areas and elevated nesting boxes, has been studying social interaction in the rat for many years. He has attempted to reproduce the natural habitat of the wild rat, describing in detail the mode of deterioration of closed-colony dynamics as the population increases and reproduction finally ceases. He has demonstrated the patterns of normal and abnormal behavior with the loss of parental care, disturbance of sexual behavior, and the emergence of violent aggression. Such work is difficult and time consuming, and there are limits to the possibilities of visual observation. Calhoun has realized the need for full automation and round-the-clock monitoring of his population cages.

Calhoun and Friauf have taken advantage of the functional differentiation of various areas of such cages. They have placed special portals equipped with detection devices at entrances to the feeding and nesting areas. This approach solves the problem of locating the various animals by making them announce their own "comings and goings." Their system uses passive resonant circuits enclosed in 19 × 9 mm capsules that are implanted. Because of the large number of frequencies to which the circuits can be tuned, such a system theoretically has an ultimate capability of hundreds of animals (Friauf, 1969).

Operant Conditioning and Hypertension in the Chimpanzee

Our interest in following the development of emotional disturbances in connection with environmental stimuli arose as a result of observing severe hypertension in young chimpanzees exposed to months of daily operant conditioning while they were immobilized in a seat and being trained for space flight. One in particular had diastolic pressures ranging from 90 to 130 mm Hg. With the higher values there was a reduction of renal blood flow as measured by the para-aminohippuric-acid clearance technique Fineg, 1964). When an untrained animal was exposed to the restraint and operant conditioning task with avoidance stimuli, his response was violent and highly vocal. However, despite the vigorous display of affect, the diastolic and systolic pressures during his 14-day continuous chair sessions were far lower than that of the apparently docile and unperturbed animal. Further, the untrained animal's pressure reverted to normal on release from restraint, whereas the highly trained animal had developed a fixed hypertension (Meehan, Fineg, and Wheelwright, 1963).

Hypertension and Arteriosclerosis in Colonies of Mice

The above observations prompted our group to undertake a study of the development of hypertension by psychosocial stimulation. The work has concentrated on mice. As mammals they, too, have a hypothalamus and limbic-striatal system, and if we read the biochemical and physiological changes right, they are agitated by the same basic emotions of attachment and competitive behavior as the primate; they, too, develop anxiety with loss of status due to a change in the social setting. The economic advantages include their size which permits whole colonies to be housed on 1.5 × 1.5 m shelves and their rapid maturation in 4 months with death from old age before 3 years. Finally they are available in genetically homogeneous strains having widely differing temperaments.

On starting this work we first determined that if the CBA strain, which we had selected, was housed in sibling groups of six to eight in $23 \times 11 \times 11$ cm standard caging, their systolic arterial blood pressure remained in the range of 125 ± 12 mm Hg throughout their lifespan (Henry, Meehan, Stephens, and Santisteban, 1965). Using such boxed siblings as controls, a system was devised for promoting a maximum of social disorder for long periods. This methodology was ethologically based in the sense that the animals were raised in isolation to reproduce some of the social inadequacy that has been demonstrated by Harlow with monkeys reared in isolation. By keeping them in confined isolation in glass jars only 7 cm in diameter from an early weaning at 12 to 14 days until full maturity at 4 months, they developed without attachment to their peers and with inadequate maternal associations (Fig. 2). We sought to reproduce some of the emotional lability

FIG. 2. Individual mice are maximally confined and socially deprived by being raised in glass jars with wire mesh tops. The process starts at weaning at 14 days and continues up to maturity at 4 months (Henry, Meehan, and Stephens, 1967).

and failure to inhibit inappropriate aggressive responses that are character-istic of primates that have been inadequately socialized.

At 4 months, when they had reached full maturity, the isolated animals were removed from their jars and placed in intercommunicating box sys-tems consisting of six standard cages, each of which was connected to the others and to a central food and water hexagon by narrow tubes through which the mice could just pass (Fig. 3). These population cages were stocked with equal numbers, i.e., 16 males and 16 females, making a total of 32. This does not exceed the normal capacity of the six cages involved which is 36 to 48. The sustained hypertension that rapidly develops in such colonies has been described elsewhere (Henry, Meehan, and Stephens, 1967). It persists for as long as the animals are kept in the population cage.

FIG. 3. A population cage made up of six standard 23 × 14 × 13 cm boxes. Plastic connect-ing-tubing permits passage of only one mouse at a time. Food and water are centrally located when maximum stimulation is required. In less demanding systems, six peripheral boxes provide shelter for nursing mothers and food and water are provided in all boxes.

We have also described the interstitial nephritis, aortic arteriosclerosis, intramural coronary artery sclerosis, and myocardial fibrosis that both males and females develop in such colonies (Henry, Ely, Stephens, Ratcliffe, Santisteban, and Shapiro, 1971). These lesions are in sharp contrast with minor changes that are observed in control groups of siblings living in the standard cages. These socially interacting animals are more active than controls, often having a fine tremor suggesting sustained arousal. A series of observations of the level of the adrenal enzymes tyrosine hydroxylase (TYOH) and phenylethanolamine N-methyltransferase (PNMT) were made on a number of such colonies that had interacted for 6 months. The results were contrasted with normal sibling controls of the same age living in cages and with animals that had remained isolated in glass jars. There was a gross increase in both enzymes in the groups from the population cages. By contrast there was a decrease in the isolated group. The significance of these observations was that it takes many hours to induce an increase in the level of the catecholamine-synthesizing enzymes and for these increases to return to control levels. The consequence is that this constitutes a mechanism for converting discontinuous emotional stimuli affecting the adrenal through the sympathetic into long-term changes of response capability of the gland (Henry, Stephens, Axelrod, and Mueller, 1971).

Fixed Hypertension in Mice Exposed to Psychosocial Stimulation

In recently concluded observations, 10 such colonies of former isolated animals were studied. Six for progressively longer periods of social inter-action, i.e., 2, 8, and 21 days and 2, 6, and 9 months. Four more were re-turned to isolation and hence to relief from social stimulation. The 2- and 5-month colonies were returned for 1 month, and two 9-month colonies returned to isolation of 1 and 2 months, respectively. Systolic blood pressure was measured once every 4 weeks. Figure 4 shows the values at termination. There is a return toward near normal values in the 2-month colony, but this is less marked at 5 months; and at 9 months the pressures remain elevated despite 8 weeks of isolation. Not only did the heart and adrenal weights and

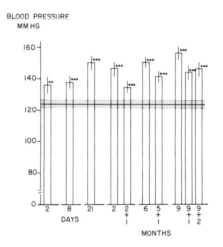

FIG. 4. *Abscissa* represents the number of days or months that the animals were exposed to social interaction in a standard population cage. The +1 and +2 represent colonies that were returned to isolation and were no longer socially stimulated for 1 and 2 months re-spectively. *Ordinate* represents the final systolic blood pressure of the males in the 10 colonies under study. The vertical lines represent standard errors of the mean. The horizontal shaded bar represents the mean and standard error for control males isolated for 6 months. The significance of the differences between the control pressures and those of the various groups was determined by paired t tests. The asterisks denote significant differences from these control values in various groups: ** $= p < 0.01$, and *** $= p < 0.001$.

the PNMT levels of the two 9-month colonies that had been returned to isolation remain grossly elevated, but there were accompanying histological changes. Figure 5 shows the incidence of myocardial fibrosis reflecting the arteriosclerotic deterioration of the intramural vessels of the various colonies. The data suggest that there are continuing progressive changes in the two 9-month colonies, despite their return to isolation (Henry, Stephens, and Santisteban, *in press*).

These observations point to the success of this ethologically based methodology in producing sustained interaction involving strong emotional arousal. By giving the formerly isolated and socially deprived animals adequate room in a complex system, they were encouraged to attempt to establish territory. By providing females in adequate numbers, the reproductive drive was activated. This in turn exacerbated emotionality as measured by physiological responses.

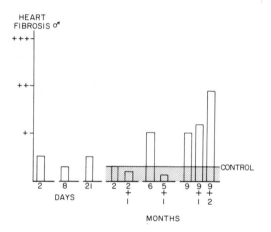

FIG. 5. The incidence of myocardial fibrosis in the 16 members of each colony of the series presented in Fig. 4. For scoring method see Henry, Ely, Stephens, Ratcliffe, Santisteban, and Shapiro (1971). The mean control score for the 2-, 6-, and 9-month groups was that for control-boxed males 6 to 13 months of age. It is represented by the shaded bar. The mean control score for the 4-month-old animals, i.e., the 2-, 8-, and 21-day groups was negligible. Abscissa is as for Fig. 4.

Magnetic Tagging to Identify Behavior Patterns in a Colony

It was noted that the incidence of high blood pressure and of pathophysiological changes, such as myocardial fibrosis, in a socially disordered colony were variable and unpredictable. The same held for the adrenal enzyme levels. It was assumed that the reason for this was that different animals adopted differing behavioral patterns. It was thought that the emotional arousal accompanying these patterns might differ, not only in intensity, but perhaps also in its nature. In one animal, agnostic behavior might predominate; in another, the pattern might be withdrawal as Calhoun (1962) has described in his deteriorating crowded rat colonies. This withdrawal might be the equivalent of the depression that Harlow has described in the rhesus monkey (Harlow, McGaugh, and Thompson, 1971) and Senay (1966) in the dog. We wished to contrast typical normal dominant and rival behavior patterns with those of the subordinates.

We have therefore undertaken a program to identify and automatically record the behavior of a group of socially interacting mice using a minicomputer to write out regular summaries of box entries and exits (Ely, 1971). A small 9 × 2 mm Alnico VIII magnet is implanted either in the back or in the belly, or two are used with one in each location. Together they provide a code, permitting identification of up to eight animals. Eight permutations are possible because the polarity can be detected as well as the dorsal or ventral location of the magnets. The Reimer and Petras (1967) cage system, which we used for this work and is illustrated in Fig. 6, differs from the

FIG. 6. A population cage based on the Reimer-Petras (1967) design. Food and water are available in each box. All boxes have a right angle to negotiate in tubular runway leading to the single entrance. The Hall effect modules are seen at the portal of each box.

previously described six-box population cage by providing eight boxes, each with a single entrance, and each connected by a short tube to a common rectangular communicating tube that joins the boxes. Hall effect detectors sensitive to changes in magnetic flux are mounted in the portals. They are both dorsally and ventrally located so that the magnet implants pass very close to them. Cards with interfacing circuitry connect the eight portals to a minicomputer. This in turn is connected to an automatic teletype. The computer, interfacing, and teletype seen in Fig. 7 are recording from a third design of population cage in which an open field area of approximately 1.5-m square replaces the rectangular tubing connecting the eight boxes (Ely, Henry, Henry, and Rader, 1972; Henry, Ely, Henry, and Rader, *in preparation*).

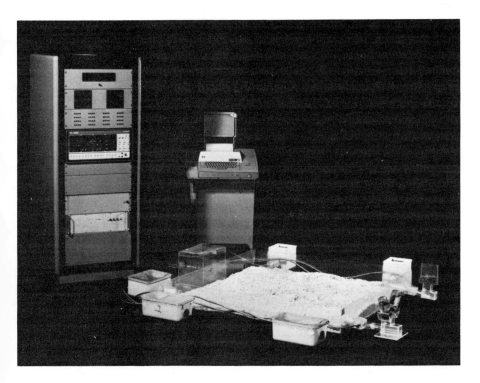

FIG. 7. The minicomputer teletype assembly is shown connected to the eight portals of a 1.5-m-square, open field cage into which eight tubes lead from eight boxes. Function is differentiated by restricting one cage each to food, water, and exercise; two to nest boxes; and assigning the remaining three as general living space.

Role Differentiation, Dominant, Rival and Subordinate Males

A monitoring system of the above type will immediately show that some animals are more active than others. The animal is usually a dominant that can be identified by its free access to all boxes, including the nesting areas, and its freedom from nicks and scars. The subordinates remain confined to one or two boxes. Dominant animals also make patrols that involve a rapid sequence of visits to four or more boxes in as many minutes. Figure 8 shows the percentage time spent in the various boxes in a Reimer-Petras eight-box population cage by the dominant, by the animal closest to him in behavior, i.e., the rival, and by the subordinates. The dominant has ready access to

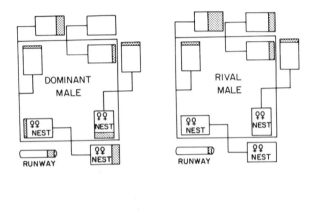

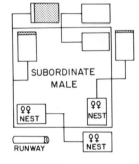

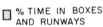

FIG. 8. Illustrating the different territorial distribution of dominants, rivals, and subordinates. The dominant animal has freedom of access to more boxes, has greatest box entry-exit and patrol activity, is free from scarring, and has access to females (Ely, 1971).

the female nest boxes (Ely, 1971). If such a closed system is stocked with normally socialized siblings and left alone, then after an initial period of fighting and role shift a single dominant usually emerges and assumes control. By using 5 males and 12 females, an uncrowded group with a normal 2:1 male-female ratio is obtained (Ely, 1971). With the passage of months there is a rise in the blood pressure of the dominant that parallels his intense entry-exit activity and his patrols. The pressure of the subordinates remains normal in a socially adjusted colony, suggesting that they accept their role and that there is little overt conflict (Fig. 9). Figure 10 supports this conclusion, for it contrasts the activity of the most dominant as opposed to the most subordinate animals in two colonies. In the case of the upper graphs, the colony consisted of socially adjusted animals. The time of night or day had no significant effect on the activity of the dominant role player as opposed to the subordinates. But in the socially disordered group made up of preisolated unsocialized animals there is a reciprocal relationship; when the dominant is active, then subordinate activity is less and vice versa. This is because in these colonies the subordinate animals avoid the dominants, waiting until they are quiet to move around the colony. These differences in

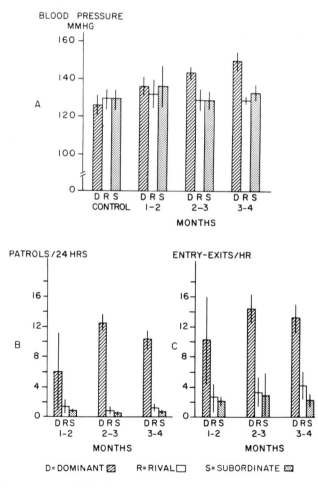

FIG. 9. Blood pressure and behavioral responses of dominants, rivals, and subordinates. Several weeks are required to achieve full role differentiation (Ely, 1971).

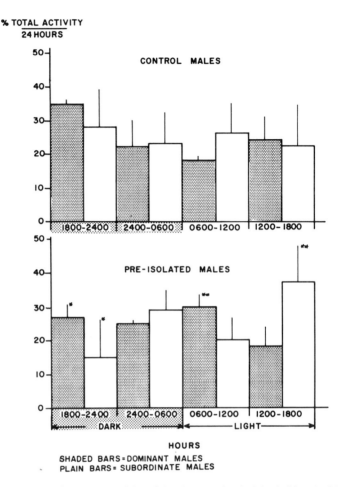

FIG. 10. Comparison of the total activity of dominant animals (shaded bars) with the subordinates (plain bars). In the normal colony (above) there is no significant difference between the activities of the two groups at any time in the 24-hr cycle. In the preisolate colony there is an inverse ratio between the two; the activities of the two groups differ significantly in three out of four occasions.

overall activity suggest that the subordinates experience more flight-avoidance emotion than the dominants.

Drug Administration and Loss of Dominance

Figure 11 gives evidence of the close interaction that goes on between members of a colony and the considerable effects that quite minor interference with the dominant may induce. In this case, the analysis made by the computer is of the entries and exits into the food and the water box, the male subordinate box, the female box, and a box containing an activity

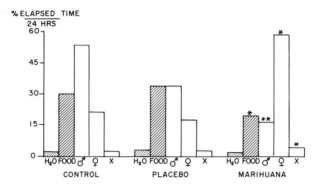

FIG. 11. The time spent in the water, food, male, female and activity areas of a functionally differentiated colony by a dominant male. The first set of histograms represent the control activity. It is compared with that for the placebo. There is no significant change when the vehicle is injected. However, when marihuana is given in a 5 mg/kg dosage, there is a significant fall in the time spent in the food box and with the males. There is also an increase in the time spent with the females and in the activity wheel, showing that the changes are not due to ataxia.

wheel. The drug marihuana ($\Delta 9$THC) was given intravenously to the dominant in a 20 mg/kg dose. There was a significant decrease in his activity in the male box, but entries into the female box increased. His food and water entries do not change significantly, showing that his drive for nutrition was not disturbed. His activity wheel usage actually increased; and open field testing confirmed there was no significant ataxia. Another striking demonstration of the effects of marihuana is shown in Fig. 12. Here the dominant's

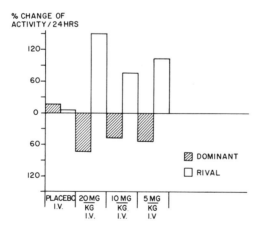

FIG. 12. Change of activity with marihuana. When the placebo is injected, there is no significant change in the overall activity of the dominant who was the recipient or of the untreated rival. However, with the initial and with progressively smaller doses of marihuana (given as $\Delta 9$THC), there was a reversal of activity with a falling off of the dominant's movements and a sharp increase in that of the rival.

activity in terms of entry-exits decreased when as little as 5 mg/kg was given by vein. At the same time, the activity of the rival which had received no injection was significantly increased as he strove to adopt the dominant-behavior pattern. Repeated tests with different animals show that sometimes the formerly dominant male recovers his role after a few days. At other times, he may not recover from a profound change to subordinate status and may even die. The high plasma corticosterone levels suggest that he is experiencing intense emotional arousal during the period of role reversal when he assumes a subordinate status.

Adrenal Medullary and Cortical Function in Intruders

It was thought that characteristic biochemical and physiological changes may accompany the emotional responses of the subordinate and that these may differ from the rival and the dominant. The changes in TYOH, PNMT, and plasma corticosterone have been measured in a group of six 1-, 3-, and 7-day male intruders placed separately one-at-a-time in a socialized colony (Fig. 13). Behaviorally, a lone intruder assumes an extremely subordinated

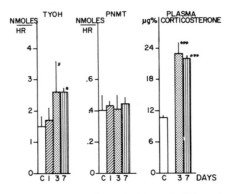

FIG. 13. The effect of introducing a single male "intruder" into the colony for 1, 3, or 7 days is determined as a mean of six experiments. TYOH increases significantly, PNMT does not change, and plasma corticosterone doubles.

role, remaining in one box where he will be repeatedly attacked by the dominant. We assume that he experiences the corresponding emotion, i.e., fear and withdrawal. The level of TYOH increases significantly over control values as the third day of interaction is exceeded. PNMT is not changed despite a week of intense social interaction. However, the plasma corticosterone shows a highly significant increase both at 3 and 7 days.

Figure 14 shows the response of the blood pressure of four sets each of six intruders. It was, however, taken on a longer time scale. By the fourth to the eighth week they were partially accepted, but the mean pressure had

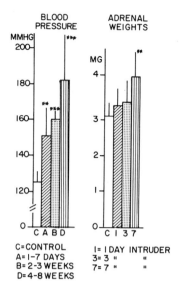

FIG. 14. In a continuation of the data shown in Fig. 13 for the experiments with intruders, the histogram on the right shows that it is not until 7 days that adrenal weight increases significantly. The histogram on the left is for weeks, instead of days, and shows the very significant rise of blood pressure up to the 180-mm-Hg range for the six animals, each of which was left alone in the colony for 1 to 2 months.

progressively risen to 180 mm Hg from a control of 125 mm Hg. The absolute adrenal weight also increased and after 7 days in the strange colony it was 25% more than in the control.

The evidence so far is one of an intense and general arousal of both the sympathoadrenal medullary (TYOH) as well as of the hypophyseal-adrenal-cortical (corticosterone) system in animals forced to intrude on a normally socialized group of animals with which they are not familiar. The blood pressure suggests that these animals are exposed to stimuli that cause intense emotional arousal.

Biochemical Differentiation of Dominants from Subordinates

We have been interested in finding the changes occurring in various parameters in dominant as compared with subordinate animals living in a socialized colony in which there is no intense interaction. Figure 15 shows the blood pressure and the adrenal weights of four dominants, three to six rivals, and six to ten subordinates in four studies, each using four 5-male–12-female colonies approximately 4 months old. The asterisks indicate the significance as measured by Student's t tests run against the dominant's values. In keeping with the separate observations shown in Fig. 9, the elevation of blood pressure of the dominant is a slow process. It does not rise

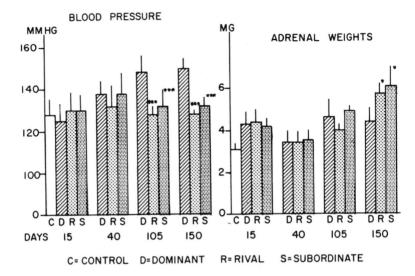

FIG. 15. The series of histograms on the left compares the systemic arterial blood pressure of the dominant, the rival, and the subordinates of four sets of four, normal, socially-adjusted colonies. Each set of four colonies was studied for 15, 40, 105, and 150 days before termination. In the last two sets of colonies, there is a significant rise of the arterial pressure of the dominant in comparison with the other two groups. The histograms on the right show that the reverse effect holds for the adrenal weights. There is an increase across-the-board compared with control values. Finally at 150 days, in these normal, now stable colonies the weight of the rival and subordinates' adrenal glands significantly exceeds that of the dominant group, despite the latter's higher blood pressure.

significantly above that of the rival or the subordinate until about the fourth month of social interaction. On the other hand, the absolute adrenal weights move in the opposite direction. It is not until 150 days that significant differentiation occurs. This time it is the subordinates that have the higher value. Thus in these normally socialized colonies, as previously reported, the dominant can be discriminated from the subordinate on the basis of adrenal weight and blood pressure (Henry, Ely, and Stephens, 1972). This discrimination can, however, only be made after several months.

Figure 16 shows the results of the assays of TYOH, the medullary enzyme that is controlled by sympathetic nervous impulses, of the PNMT that appears to be induced from the adrenal cortex, and of the plasma corticosterone that is an expression of hypophyseal-adrenal-cortical-activity.

At the 15- and 40-day stages the mean TYOH of the dominants is significantly elevated above that of the rivals and the subordinates. But after this, although at 105 days the blood pressure has now begun to separate out, the adrenal enzyme values are not differentiated. It is probable that at this stage the intensity of social interaction is less acute, since the role structure of the colony has become stable. The PNMT values are significantly elevated in all three groups, but do not differentiate between the

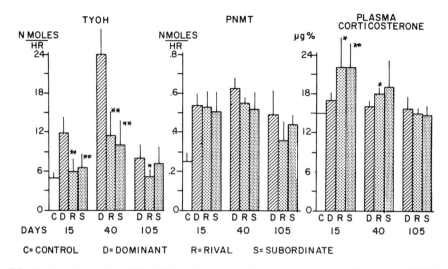

FIG. 16. A continuation of Fig. 15, the three sets of histograms compare the adrenal TYOH, PNMT, and the plasma corticosterone levels of the same groupings of four colonies with differentiated dominants, rivals, and subordinates. In those terminated at 15 and 40 days, respectively, the TYOH is significantly higher in the dominants than in the rivals and subordinates. There also is a sharp elevation of PNMT, but all the groups fall into the same general range of values. In the final set of histograms on the right, the situation once more reverses itself; at 15 days, the plasma corticosterone level for the rival and subordinate is significantly elevated above that of the group of dominants, despite their higher level of TYOH. This difference vanishes in the older more established colonies in which social interaction is less vigorous.

various roles. Finally, plasma corticosterone shows the opposite trend: that for the rival and subordinate is significantly higher than for the dominant in the 15- and 40-day studies. But here again at 105 days, as the role structure of the colony stabilizes, the values are near normal and are no longer differentiated.

It would appear that in the early stages of colony differentiation there are clear-cut differences between the biochemical picture for the dominant who shows evidence of increased sympathetic arousal as compared with the subordinate in which adrenal-cortical activity predominates. In the later stages when roles are stable, the biochemical changes vanish as the values of the various behavioral role players return to normal. Eventually chronic changes begin to develop. In the dominants there is an increase of blood pressure in place of a rise in TYOH, and in the subordinates there is an increase in adrenal weight, despite the return of the corticosterone levels to normal. These changes took 5 months to develop. This is the time at which a fixed hypertension and histopathological deterioration started to develop in the 10-colony experiment outlined above. It would be interesting to pursue these changes that occur with animals playing different roles and presumably experiencing different emotional states. It is possible that by

9 months a fixed hypertension and myocardial fibrosis of the type shown in Figs. 4 and 5 would have developed, and the intriguing question is which if any of the role players in these closed colonies of socialized colonies would be susceptible — would it be the dominants or the subordinates?

CONCLUSIONS

These observations indicate that the mouse can be used to study the parameters of emotion and that by the application of ethological methods to colonies living in population cages, the physiological consequences of emotions accompanying the dominant aggressive state can be differentiated from those associated with the subordinate fear-flight response.

SUMMARY

(1) Social ethological studies are defined and a technique is described for monitoring and environmentally stable behavior patterns of mice as they mate, establish territory, nest, raise young, and respond to the demands of a social hierarchy in a closed colony.

(2) Individual protagonists, such as dominants, rivals, and subordinates can be identified by tagging, while socially interacting within complex population cages.

(3) A computer-operated tracking system gives continuous quantitative analyses of behavior by following activity patterns of up to eight magnetically tagged individuals for periods of months.

(4) Social deprivation with consequent inadequate mutual attachment leads to chronic conflict for territory and to reproductive failure. The social disorder and accompanying sustained emotional arousal can persist for a prolonged period, significantly shortening the lifespan.

(5) Physiological measures of the chronic arousal include an elevated blood pressure, hypertrophied adrenals, increased adrenal-medullary catecholamine synthesizing enzymes, and raised plasma corticosterone levels.

(6) Pathophysiological consequences ensue after 6 months or more. They include fixed hypertension and arteriosclerosis with interstitial nephritis and myocardial fibrosis.

(7) The chronic emotional arousal of a dominant striving to maintain territory in a closed colony of normal socially adjusted animals is accompanied by an initial increase in medullary TYOH and eventually by high blood pressure. By contrast, the subordinate in the same normal colony has a higher initial plasma corticosterone and a greater eventual adrenal hypertrophy than the dominant.

(8) These quantitative techniques offer opportunities for measuring and analyzing the differing pathophysiological consequences of differing emotional states.

ACKNOWLEDGMENT

This research was supported in part by NASA grant NGL 05–018–003 and NIH grant MH 19441.

REFERENCES

Ainsworth, M. D. S., and Bell, S. M. (1969): Some contemporary patterns of mother–infant interaction in the feeding situation. in: *Stimulation in Early Infancy*, ed. A. Ambrose, pp. 133–163, London.

Barnett, S. A. (1964): *Social Stress: The Concept of Stress in Viewpoints of Biology*, Vol. 3, eds. J. D. Carthy and C. L. Dunnington, pp. 170–218, London.

Bourne, P. G. (1971): Altered adrenal function in two combat situations in Viet Nam. In: *The Physiology of Aggression and Defeat*, eds. B. E. Eleftheriou and J. P. Scott, pp. 265–290, London.

Bowlby, J. (1970): *Attachment and Loss*, Vol. 1: Attachment, London.

Bronson, F. H., and Desjardins, C. (1971): Steroid hormones and aggressive behavior in mammals. In: *The Physiology of Aggression and Defeat*, eds. B. E. Eleftheriou and J. P. Scott, pp. 43–64, New York.

Calhoun, J. B. (1962): A behavioral sink. In: *Roots of Behavior: Genetics, Instinct and Socialization in Animal Behavior*, ed. E. L. Bliss, pp. 295–315, New York.

Christian, J. J., Lloyd, J. A., and Davis, D. E. (1965): Role of endocrines in the self-regulation of mammalian populations. In: *Recent Progress in Hormone Research*, ed. G. Pincus, pp. 501–570, New York.

Crook, J. H. and Goss Custard, J. D. (1972): Social ethology. In: *Annual Review of Psychology*, Vol. 23, eds. P. H. Mussen and M. R. Rosenzweig, pp. 277–312, Palo Alto, Cal.

Crowcroft, P. (1966): *Mice All Over*, London.

Eibl-Eibesfeldt, I. (1972): *Love Not Hate: The Natural History of Behavior Patterns*, New York.

Ely, D. L. (1971): *Physiological and Behavioral Differentiation of Social Roles in a Population Cage of Magnetically Tagged CBA Mice*, Ph.D. dissertation, University of Southern California, Los Angeles.

Ely, D. L., Henry, J. A., Henry, J. P., and Rader, R. D. (1972): A monitoring technique providing quantitative rodent behavior analysis, Physiol. Behav. *9*, 675–679.

Fineg, J. (1964): *Para-Aminohippuric Acid Clearances in Young Chimpanzees*, M.S. thesis, University of Southern California, Los Angeles.

Friauf, W. S. (1969): Rats: Their comings and goings. In: *NTC 69 Record, National Telemetering Conference*, pp. 34–38, Washington, D.C.

Ganong, W. F. (1971): Neurophysiologic basis of instinctual behavior and emotions. In: *Review of Medical Physiology*, ed. W. F. Ganong, pp. 173–185, Los Altos, Cal.

Harlow, H. F., McGaugh, J. L., and Thompson, R. F. (1971): *Psychology*, San Francisco.

Hass, H. (1970): *The Human Animal*, London.

Henry, J. A., Ely, D. L., Henry, J. P., and Rader, R. D.: Minicomputer monitoring of social activity in mouse colonies, *in preparation*.

Henry, J. P., Meehan, J. P., Stephens, P., and Santisteban, G. A. (1965): Arterial pressure in CBA mice as related to age, J. Gerontol. *20*, 239–243.

Henry, J. P., Meehan, J. P., and Stephens, P. M. (1967): The use of psychosocial stimuli to induce prolonged systolic hypertension in mice, Psychosom. Med. *29*, 408–432.

Henry, J. P., Ely, D. L., Stephens, P. M., Ratcliffe, H. L., Santisteban, G. A., and Shapiro, A. P. (1971): The role of psychosocial factors in the development of arteriosclerosis in CBA mice: Observations on the heart, kidney, and aorta, Atherosclerosis *14*, 203–218.

Henry, J. P., Stephens, P. M., Axelrod, J., Mueller, R. A. (1971): Effect of psychosocial stimulation on the enzymes involved in the biosynthesis and metabolism of noradrenaline and adrenaline, Psychosom. Med. *33*, 227–237.

Henry, J. P., Ely, D. L., and Stephens, P. M. (1972): Changes in catecholamine-controlling enzymes in response to psychosocial activation of defence and alarm reactions. In: Ciba

Foundation Symposium 8 *Physiology, Emotion & Psychosomatic Illness*, pp. 225–246, Ciba Foundation, Amsterdam.

Henry, J. P., Stephens, P. M., and Santisteban, G. A.: A model of psychosocial hypertension showing reversibility and progression of cardiovascular complications, Circ. Res. (*in press*).

Hinde, R. A. (1971): Development of social behavior. In: *Behavior of Non-Human Primates*, Vol. 3, eds. A. M. Schrier and F. Stollnitz, pp. 1–60, New York.

Kummer, H. (1971): *Primate Societies: Group Techniques of Ecological Adaptation*, Chicago.

Klüver, H., and Bucy, P. C. (1939): Preliminary analysis of functions of the temporal lobe in monkeys, AMA Arch. Neurol. Psychiatr. *42*, 979–1000.

Lapin, B., and Cherkovich, G. M. (1971): Environmental change causing the development of neuroses and corticovisceral pathology in monkeys. In: *Society, Stress and Disease: The Psychosocial Environment and Psychosomatic Diseases*, ed. L. Levi, pp. 266–280, London.

Lazarus, R. S. (1966): *Psychological Stress and the Coping Process*, New York.

MacLean, P. D. (1970a): The limbic brain in relation to the psychoses. In: *Physiological Correlates of Emotion*, ed. P. Black, pp. 130–144, New York.

MacLean, P. D. (1970b): The triune brain, emotion, and scientific bias. In: *The Neurosciences: Second Study Program*, ed. F. O. Schmitt, pp. 336–349, New York.

MacLean, P. D. (1972): Cerebral evolution and emotional processes: New findings on the striatal complex, Ann. N.Y. Acad. Sci. *193*, 137–149.

Meehan, J. P., Fineg, J., and Wheelwright, C. D. (1963): Results of the Project Mercury Ballistic and Orbital Chimpanzee Flights: Blood Pressure Instrumentation, NASA SP-39, Office of Scientific and Technical Information, National Aeronautics and Space Administration, Washington, D.C.

Miminoshvili, D. I. (1956): Experimental neuroses in monkeys. In: *Theoretical and Practical Problems in Experiments on Monkeys*, ed. I. Uttan, pp. 53–67, Oxford.

Nauta, W. (1971): The problem of the frontal lobe: A reinterpretation, J. Psychiatr. Res. *8*, 167–187.

Nemiah, J. C., and Sifneos, P. E. (1970): Affect and fantasy in patients with psychosomatic disorders. In: *Modern Trends in Psychosomatic Medicine*, ed. O. W. Hill, pp. 26–34, New York.

Papez, J. W. (1937): A proposed mechanism of emotion, AMA Arch. Neurol. Psychiatr. *38*, 725–743.

Ratcliffe, H. L. (1968): Environment, behavior and disease. In: *Progress in Physiological Psychology*, eds. E. Stellar and J. M. Sprague, pp. 161–229, New York.

Ratcliffe, H. L., Luginbuhl, H., Schnarr, W. R., and Chacko, K. (1969): Coronary arteriosclerosis in swine: Evidence of a relation to behavior, J. Comp. Physiol. Psychol. *68*, 385–392.

Reimer, J. D., and Petras, M. L. (1967): Breeding structure of the house mouse (*Mus musculus*) in a population cage, J. Mammal. *48*, 88–99.

Richter, C. P. (1957): On the phenomenon of sudden death in animals and man, Psychosom. Med. *19*, 191–198.

Rose, R. M., Holaday, J. W., and Bernstein, I. S. (1971): Plasma testosterone, dominance rank and aggressive behavior in male rhesus monkeys, Nature *231*, 366–368.

Rose, R. M., Gordon, T. P., and Bernstein, I. S. (1972): Plasma testosterone levels in the male rhesus; influences of sexual and social stimuli, Science *178*, 643–645.

Ruch, T. C. (1965): Neurophysiology of emotion. In: *Physiology and Biophysics*, eds. T. C. Ruch and H. D. Patton, Chap. 26, Philadelphia.

Sassenrath, E. N. (1970): Increased adrenal responsiveness related to social stress in rhesus monkeys, Hormones Behav. *1*, 283–298.

Senay, E. C. (1966): Toward an animal model of depression: A study of separation behavior in dogs, J. Psychiatr. Res. *4*, 65–71.

Van Lawick-Goodall, J. (1973): The behavior of chimpanzees in their natural habitat, Am. J. Psychiatr. *130*, 1–12.

Von Holst, D. (1969): Sozialer Stress bei Tupajas (*Tupaia belangeri*): Die Aktivierung des sympathischen Nervensystems und ihre Beziehung zu hormonal ausgelösten, ethologischen und physiologischen Veränderungen, Z. Vergl. Physiol. *63*, 1–58.

Von Holst, D. (1972): Renal failure as the cause of death in *Tupaia belangeri* (tree shrews) exposed to persistent social stress, J. Comp. Physiol. *78*, 236–273.

Washburn, S. L., and Hamburg, D. A. (1968): Aggressive behavior in old world monkeys and apes. In: *Primates: Studies in Adaptation and Variability,* ed. P. Jay, pp. 458–468, New York.

Welch, A. S., and Welch, B. L. (1971): Isolation reactivity and aggression: Evidence for an involvement of brain catecholamines and serotonin. In: *The Physiology of Aggression and Defeat,* eds. B. E. Eleftheriou and J. P. Scott, pp. 91–142, New York.

Emotions — Their Parameters and Measurement,
edited by L. Levi.
Raven Press, New York © 1975

Methodological Issues in the Assessment of Life Stress

Irwin G. Sarason, Cecily de Monchaux, and Tim Hunt

Department of Psychology, University of Washington, Seattle, Washington 98195; University College London; and University of Cambridge

INTRODUCTION

The idea of a possible relationship between life stress and the occurrence of physical illness has stimulated both speculation and research. Over the past decade, the amount of empirical inquiry has noticeably increased. The reason for this increase is not hard to identify. If there is a relationship between an individual's personal and social adjustment and his susceptibility to bodily breakdown, its delineation is clearly of great importance. The purpose of this chapter is to examine one particular recent research approach to the life stress-illness problem: namely that which interprets and measures life stress or life crisis in terms of *life changes*. This approach was initiated by the work of Holmes and his associates (Holmes and Rahe, 1967; Masuda and Holmes, 1967) and has been carried on and developed further by Rahe, Arthur, Gunderson, and others at the Navy Medical Neuropsychiatric Research Unit, San Diego, (Rahe, 1969, 1972; Rhae, Pugh, Erickson, Gunderson, and Rubin, 1971; Pugh, Erickson, Rubin, Gunderson, and Rahe, 1971; Rahe, Mahan, and Arthur, 1970).

The history of stress research has been bedeviled by the problem of establishing objective criteria to define both stressful stimuli (stressors) and stress responses. Too often, investigators have had to rely solely on subjective criteria in defining stressors and have failed, moreover to avoid circularity; aspects of the response to stress have been used in the identification of the stressor.

The work under scrutiny here is significant and valuable for its attempt to avoid these two pitfalls, and it is not surprising that it has aroused much interest in the field. Nor, since the measures employed are readily understandable by the layman, is it surprising that the work has already become well known outside specialist circles. We feel, therefore, that a review of this approach is especially timely.

The rationale and main features of what might be called the San Diego approach, are as follows:

(1) A significant contribution to life crisis or stress is made by life changes to which adaptation has to be made.

(2) Life changes may be defined objectively, and even if reported by the subject or patient rather than by an independent observer, should provide much more objective and verifiable indices of stressor variables than have hitherto been used in research in this area (e.g., asking the subject what he has been worried about lately).

(3) Life changes are defined in such a way as to include both desirable and undesirable events (e.g., marriage, illness, and bereavement) and both seemingly major and minor happenings (e.g., jail term and holiday).

(4) An objective estimate of the degree of adaptation needed to cope with specific life changes can be achieved by consensus ratings by large numbers of subjects representative of the population from which research samples will be drawn.

(5) Life change units are additive. Many molehills may make a mountain.

The two major measuring instruments used to operationalize life-change stimuli (thought of as independent variables) follow:

(1) *SRE: Schedule of recent experience.* This is a self-administered questionnaire listing 42 events (slight variations in item content being made to suit different groups of subjects) which the respondent is asked to check for their occurrence in his life over certain time-periods arbitrarily defined by the investigator and usually divided into 6-month periods.

(2) *SRRQ: Social readjustment rating questionnaire.* The 42 life event items of SRE were presented to large numbers of subjects of varying age, social class, race, religion, and occupation who were invited to rate them for degree of necessary adjustment by most people, against an arbitrary value or standard provided by the item "marriage." Average ratings for the 42 items provide values which enable quantification of the life events enumerated by subjects in response to the SRE. These values are called life-change units and are usually summed either for subgroups of events (e.g., health events, family events, work events, etc.) and/or for the total set of 42 items.

The dependent variable in much of the research in this area, particularly the San Diego studies, has been for the most part physical illness, although psychiatric illness and accidents have also been investigated (Rahe, 1969, 1972).

The general proposition tested with various samples, predominantly of naval personnel, is that recent life change is a necessary although not a sufficient predictor of illness. The theoretical rationale for this proposition has not been spelled out in any detail by the San Diego group, and need not in any case be discussed in this primarily methodological examination of the work. Suffice it to say at this point that the approach seems consonant with theories of nonspecific stress such as Selye's.

THE RELIABLE ASSESSMENT OF LIFE STRESS

A number of questions must be, at least, considered when a researcher presents a new assessment instrument. What is the instrument designed to measure? What operations are employed in making assessments? Would other operations yield comparable results? Why is the assessment procedure superior to alternative measurement procedures? What is the reliability of the assessment procedure?

Although all of these questions are important, let us look at the last one first. If an assessment instrument is not adequate, then at least partial answers to several of the earlier questions become available. A reliable instrument is one that yields similar scores on two or more test administrations. This assumes that major changes have not occurred in the subject's life between the two administrations. Other things being equal, the more reliable of two instruments is the one that shows the highest correlation between scores derived from the two administrations. What is the reliability of the instrument used by Rahe and his San Diego associates? Whereas reliabilities (Pearson r's) of 0.64 and 0.74 had been obtained for resident physicians (Casey, Masuda, and Holmes, 1967), the reliability for the population from which Rahe has drawn his samples (that is, from men in the Navy) has been reported to be $r = 0.55$ (Rahe, 1972). McDonald, Pugh, Gunderson, and Rahe (1972) examined the test-retest reliability of the SRE over a 6-month period and using four reporting periods in terms of four domains of life change: (1) the personal and social sphere, (2) the world of work, (3) marital relationships, and (4) disciplinary conditions. The correlations reported were 0.71, 0.69, 0.56, and 0.09, respectively.

It is generally agreed that test-retest reliabilities of about 0.80 are reasonably adequate and that r's of 0.75 or below raise serious questions about the success with which the assessor is accomplishing his measurement task. Few knowledgeable researchers would venture into an investigation of the validity of an assessment device in the absence of at least marginal reliability. By any reasonable standard the reliability of the SRE is low and, it seems, inadequate in the case of Navy personnel, the subjects in most of the recent studies. It is possible that through minor changes such as rewording items and instructions the test-retest reliabilities can be increased somewhat.

The fact that an instrument does not possess adequate reliability does not mean that the idea underlying it should be abandoned. It does indicate, however, the need for inquiry into the causes of the unreliability. One possibility that rather quickly comes to mind is the complexity of the task with which the subject is confronted in filling out the SRE. Much of the early work performed with the SRE used subjects of relatively high educational attainment. The naval research involved considerable heterogeneity in educational levels. The difficulty of the life-change-rating task for a sizeable subgroup (perhaps an absolute majority) within this population might well have contributed to the poor reported reliability.

Rahe and his colleagues have described the SRE as a self-administered instrument. This may be true for persons with university and professional backgrounds, but perhaps quite overoptimistic for populations that are not so well educated. Rahe (1972) has suggested using an increase in the number of items as a means of increasing the SRE reliability. While increasing the number of items does usually increase test reliability, this approach might not have much effect if the basic problem resides in the *nature* of the measuring instrument (for example, if it is of too great complexity). It is interesting that Komaroff, Masuda, and Holmes (1968) found it necessary in working with lower socioeconomic subjects both to reword items and to administer orally the instructions for the rating task.

INTERPRETING LIFE STRESS SCORES

When a self-administered questionnaire is the only source of information about the subject, and when the responses to the questionnaire itself are not further substantiated in any way, the interpretation of nil entries in particular is a hazardous enterprise. The subject may be consciously or unconsciously avoiding admission of an event. For instance, if a man has joined the Navy to escape family problems, it is quite possible that he is a "denier" who will "forget" to acknowledge events in the family sector of his life. Incumbent in an investigation in the area of assessment is the need to be aware of the factors that might influence scores obtained by subjects on a measuring instrument. Obviously, every assessment researcher hopes that the main factor influencing scores on his instrument is the variable he is seeking to measure. Yet, if he is realistic, he will feel called upon to explore the unwanted, less desirable relationships that might be obtained. We have already pointed out the cognitive task posed for the subject by the questionnaire administered to him. The task may be too complicated or perhaps not sufficiently meaningful for him. For example, might not one expect that sailors aboard a floating ship would interpret the "standard" life change of marriage differently from other groups, such as resident physicians and college students? This example illustrates another point: there may be important population differences.

Beyond these factors, other possible pitfalls cannot be ignored. Among these, the social psychology of the assessment situation looms large. A growing body of research shows that the conditions under which assessment is performed may significantly influence the scores obtained by subjects (Rosenthal, 1966). For example, someone who takes an intelligence test because it is required by a potential employer that he do so will approach his task in a quite different way than the person who takes the same test because he is serving as a volunteer subject in an experiment. It would not be surprising if these differences exerted a noticeable impact on actual performance. At the least, it must be expected that the researcher should spell out clearly what went on in his assessment sessions. In addition, he should point out how particular aspects of the testing conditions might influence subject's attitudes and expectations and how these, in turn, might influence the scores obtained on the measurement instrument. It is especially important to provide information about such matters as the status relationship that existed between the assessor and assessee. This information might provide valuable clues concerning both reliability and validity puzzles or inconsistencies that arise in the data.

How might the sailor on shipboard respond to an inquiry into his recent life changes? First of all, what reason is given to him for the assessment, and what is his interpretation of the rationale provided for him? For example, what might sailors bound for Vietnam or other actual or potential trouble spots think of the life-change-scaling task with which he is confronted? Might some sailors wonder about a possible connection between the assessment task and their present and future naval activities? What were the actual and implied operations involved in gathering information on life changes? Could the reported unreliability be due to heterogeneity in subject's interpretations of the assessment situation, some responding as if the task were personally relevant, others responding in conformity to the command of a superior officer, and still others responding derisively to what they regard as an unnecessary intrusion into their lives? These questions are, of course, speculative. They arise out of the ambiguity the reader of research reports experiences when the reports lack sufficient information concerning key points.

VALIDITY STUDIES

Thus far we have dealt primarily with possible uncontrolled sources of variation that might exert impacts on reported results, especially those pertaining to reliability. What of the validity of the results and the interpretation put on them?

The evidence is essentially correlational. Rahe and his associates have correlated magnitude of life changes as inferred from the SRE with illness. For naval populations the correlations have generally been around 0.11, which is, of course, on the border between tiny and small (Rahe, 1972). These correlations have been calculated in what have mainly been retrospective studies. However, some prospective data have been reported, and the results have been taken as meaning that correlations — albeit often small — exist between life stress and illness (Rahe, 1969, 1972). Assuming that the correlations are real, what do they mean? Even if in a prospective study positive correlations are obtained between SRE scores and illness rates, is it legitimate to conclude that the SRE played a predictive role?

Correlational data do not permit such an inference because correlations might be attributable either to a third, perhaps unknown, variable or some other source of confounding. For example, unfortunate early experiences might be implicated in the reported correlations. Earlier physical illness might be direct or indirect determiners of later illnesses and a high SRE score may simply be a correlate of these unfortunate events. Another possibility is that these early events contribute to inadequate social adjustment and that this is the factor being tapped by the SRE. The SRE may be as much a measure of certain personality characteristics as it is a measure of changes in life conditions.

There is a great need to identify and inquire into the seemingly tangential or irrelevant variables that may be involved in the determination of SRE scores. The term "plus getter" is used in research on personality assessment to refer to the person who obtains high scores on measures of psychopathology because he has, for whatever reason, the test-taking attitude or response set to attribute negative, undesirable personal characteristics to himself. When someone scores high on a measure of neuroticism is this because he actually possesses neurotic attributes or because he is motivated to attribute neurotic attributes to himself? This question is not a "how many angels can stand on the head of a pin?" type question. It is an unavoidable factual question whenever it is alleged that validity is being studied. The point to be stressed is that, while the SRE may be reflective of stressful life changes that are predictive of future physical illness, it may equally well be a measure of something else (e.g., the sequence of early childhood illness).

A study that suggests the importance of this point has been reported by Spilken and Jacobs (1971). These researchers studied a group of 92 college students who had been screened by an internist's examination as being free from disease. One year after these examinations, 79 of the students were recontacted and asked to describe the status of their health during the intervening period. Of the total number, 23 reported being ill and seeking medical treatment, whereas the remaining 42 did not feel the need to seek medical help. A careful analysis of the 23 treatment-seekers revealed that in three cases the physician did not give treatment; four were treated once by a physician; nine were treated twice; four were treated at least three times; and the remaining three began psychotherapy for symptoms of anxiety and depression. The treatment seekers were judged to fall into two groups: 11 who had emotional and behavioral complaints, and 12 who had experienced somatic distress.

Spilken and Jacobs correlated the life-crisis scores of subjects before and after the 1-year interval. The correlation was 0.47. It was found that presence of or absence of illness during the interval was not related in any systematic manner with changes in life-crisis scores. Spilken and Jacobs, distinguishing between behavioral and somatic dysfunction, made the following provocative point:

"We have no way of knowing from our data whether the actual symptoms were incidental, fortuitous or directly related to the behavioral processes observed (life stress and seeking help). One possibility which must be considered is that the S's became randomly ill at times when they were experiencing failures and disappointments, and sought professional help for the reasons given above. If life experiences had been pleasureable at that time, they might have ignored the symptoms or treated themselves. This view suggests that life stress leads not to illness, but to treatment-seeking behavior, and that the symptoms which are present are the ones which are used as calling cards" (pp. 260–261).

It is well recognized that receiving medical treatment may, in some cases, be more related to the way the individual presents his illness than to the seriousness of the symptoms in the traditional sense.

The problem of "plus getting" arises at an especially embarrassing point for Rahe and his associates. This is the point at which the criterion of illness is selected. In the Spilken and Jacobs article, the treatment-seeking subjects received careful medical attention. However, as physicians well know, unambiguously defining illness may, by no means, be a simple task. It is well known that a high percentage of patients who consult physicians have no identifiable physical malfunction or malformation. Placebos and a good bedside manner seem to be remarkably effective therapies with many people who come to physicians with medical problems. The implication of this well-established point is that just because a patient reports himself to be ill does not mean that he has a physical problem. It is perhaps precisely at this point that the work of Rahe and his associates is most deficient. While the criteria of illness reported in their studies varied somewhat, the most common one appears to have been report to sick call by sailors—that is, self-report of illness. Knowing that someone has reported to sick call on X occasions or that he has missed Y days of work because he says he is sick does not help us, in any reliable way, to define the status of his bodily condition.

It is noteworthy that one finds in the medical literature indications that "plus getting" is a factor in major physical disorders as well as in minor ones. Jenkins (1971) has recently reviewed research studies of life stress in the cardiac patient. He observed that several investigators have found patients with coronary disease to be high in the tendency to express dissatisfactions about their lives. Jenkins, noting the frequently retrospective character of these investigations, concluded that:

"These findings concerning dissatisfactions are almost entirely retrospective. Many of the findings could be simply the result of a greater tendency of patients with coronary or any other grave disease to be more critical and complaining" (p. 13).

The hypothesis that a significant percentage of cardiac patients have a low threshold for expressions of dissatisfaction merits inquiry. Inquiry is also needed into the possibilities that this low threshold is a concomitant of social mobility or status incongruity. Prospective studies of cardiac-prone persons have much to contribute in this area.

Researchers into problems of psychosomatic medicine seek to relate personal characteristics and social relationships with identifiable bodily conditions. What is the bodily condition of the sailor who reports to sick call? It might be satisfactory. It might be that his reporting to sick call reveals more about the state of his personality and his upbringing than it does about the state of his body. A "plus getter" attributes negative attributes and experiences to himself, and bodily attributes are not immune to "plus getting" tendencies. In the absence of reliable medical evidence (e.g., body-temperature elevations, congested bronchi), the patient who visits his physician may not have a physical problem. Sailors who report to sick call may do so for a variety of reasons, including a generalized "plus getting" tendency, a reaction to the anxiety or boredom of a prolonged voyage, and a desire to escape an uninteresting or dangerous assignment. In one study of life on a naval attack carrier, it was found that illness rates (apparently based on sailors' self-reports of illness) were significantly lower as the subjects eagerly awaited a "liberty" period at Hong Kong than at other times during their cruise (Rubin, Gunderson, and Doll, 1969).

Most of the work of Rahe and his associates has dealt with the reported minor illnesses of naval personnel. Not reported have been what are perhaps the most relevant comparisons, those between naval personnel who develop medically significant illnesses and those who do not. Medically significant illnesses are much more likely than are neurotically based illnesses to provide the necessary "hard" indices of bodily maladaptation. A certain number of the thousands of subjects studied by the San Diego group were seriously ill, received laboratory work-ups, and may even have been returned to the home base for more extensive diagnosis and therapy than would be possible on board a ship. Another interesting group of naval personnel, in addition to those who are judged to have serious physical problems, are those with psychiatric problems, and especially psychiatric problems which appear to have significant psychosomatic components.

It is difficult to escape the conclusion that the physical criteria of illness employed by the San Diego researchers are inadequate. In many cases they are nonexistent, since the sole measure was the sailor's description of his condition or the entry on a record form by a member of the sick bay staff. Although the description of the qualifications of the sick bay staff given by Rahe and his associates is not clear on this point, it seems likely that many or most staff members were not physicians but were rather workers supervised by physicians.

Let us summarize the points made thus far in the present chapter. Rahe and his associates have reported a numerically large number of studies of life crises and their relationship to illness. This relationship is of great importance, both for psychosomatic specialists and physicians engaged in general practice. Unfortunately the research reviewed here is defective in several ways and these defects make hazardous the drawing of conclusions from reported correlations. Both the measure of life stress and the criteria of physical illness are inadequate. The reliability of the measuring instrument, the SRE, appears to be too low for confident research, screening, or clinical use. The dependent measure of illness appears primarily to be self-reports and impressions by clinical workers who may or may not have been physicians and whose level of medical training and skill are often not described. Since seeking medical assistance (as distinct from having a reliably diagnosed condition) may reveal more about the patient's personality than the state of his bodily systems, conclusions based on the presently available information reflect a distressingly strong ingredient of speculation.

The links between methodology, theory, and application are important ones. Researchers have much to contribute in uncovering these links. But, unless the investigator follows accepted scientific guidelines, his "contribution" could be either obscurantistic or, worse, downright misleading. One outcome of this sort of situation is difficulty in interpreting research findings. An example of this is a study by Wyler, Masuda, and Holmes (1971). These investigators examined the relationship between SRE scores and the incidence of acute and chronic illnesses. Significant positive correlations were obtained between the seriousness of chronic illnesses and SRE scores. Negative correlations (although not statistically significant) were obtained between seriousness of acute illnesses and SRE scores. Might these diverging results be explicable in terms of differential "plus getting" tendencies among patients with chronic and acute illnesses?

It is our opinion that life changes do serve as stressors and that stressors may have profound psychophysiological outcomes. However, that is our opinion, not fact. Uncovering the needed facts will require resourceful research which utilizes reliable measures of life events and acceptable medical criteria. Before leaving this point, one further defect in the medical criteria of Rahe and associates should be mentioned. This pertains to the reliability of the medical judgments. Granted that the medical criteria typically were not physical measurements, would pairs of sick bay personnel show reliable agreement in describing and diagnosing cases? Not only have we not been provided with hard data (actual physical measurements) but the secondary data (presumably clinical accounts) are of unknown reliability.

WHERE DO WE GO FROM HERE?

Despite the critical tenor of the observations we have felt impelled to make in this chapter, we feel we can and should conclude on a hopeful note. The seminal ideas of Meyer and Wolf and the pioneering mensurational contribution of Holmes have facilitated progress from a purely speculative to a theoretically based empirical orientation. That man is continually involved in a process of adaptation is by now well established. It seems more than reasonable that events that interfere with normal, habitual activities will heighten the need for more adaptation. A challenging question for researchers interested in the effects of life changes on psychophysiological processes is the effects exerted on them by varying types and degrees of stimulation. Is there an optimal level of stimulation that maximizes the efficiency of these processes? Does man need a certain amount of life change occasionally in order to, as it were, keep him on his toes and protect him from the possible deleterious effects of boredom?

These are mammoth questions that will require painstaking investigation. If life changes have identifiable bodily and psychological consequences, what are the mechanisms that produce these consequences? There is a need for well-designed correlational studies relating life changes to illness, but there is also a need for experimental studies, with both humans and animals, of this relationship. While there are important limits to human research on this problem, intervention studies with people are possible. For example, can people who have experienced severe life stresses be helped to cope more effectively with the stresses? If so, might this type of intervention (e.g., through counseling) reduce the danger of bodily breakdown? Another perhaps enlightening area of study is that of the effects of cataclysmic events and natural disasters on the near-term and long-term illnesses of groups differing in certain personality characteristics, such as high scores on life stress measures.

But before these experimental questions can be approached in a meaningful way, measures of the frequency, amount, and clustering of life changes are required. In devising such measuring devices, it will be important to resist the temptation to fall back upon face validity, declaring that an instrument measures a particular variable simply because it *seems* to do so. Assessment and measurement are but first steps in empirical research—but they are important. Weak measurement devices can be misleading. They can lead investigators into blind alleys for long periods of time. We have dwelt on the inadequacies of one portion of the life stress literature not because we do not appreciate the work that has been done, but rather that we feel the methodologies employed in life stress research should be commensurate with the importance of the problem.

SUMMARY

This chapter reviews research on the assessment of life stress from the standpoint of psychometric properties. It points out the need to increase the test-retest reliability of instruments such as the Schedule of Recent Experience. It considers methodological issues that bear upon the interpretation of research relating life stress to physical illness. Among these is the role of "plus getting" as a factor contributing to high life-stress scores. Suggestions are made for needed directions in future research.

REFERENCES

Casey, R. L., Masuda, M., and Holmes, T. H. (1967): Quantitative study of recall of life events, J. Psychosom. Res. *11*, 239–247.

Holmes, T. H., and Rahe, R. H. (1967): The social readjustment rating scale, J. Psychosom. Res. *11*, 213–218.

Jenkins, C. D. (1971): Psychologic and social precursors of coronary disease, New Engl. J. Med. *284*, 244–255, 307–317.

Komaroff, A., Masuda, M., and Holmes, T. H. (1968): The social readjustment rating scale: A comparative study of Negro, Mexican and white Americans, J. Psychosom. Res. *12*, 121–128.

Masuda, M., and Holmes, T. H. (1967): The social readjustment rating scale: A cross-cultural study of Japanese and Americans, J. Psychosom. Res. *11*, 227–237.

McDonald, B. W., Pugh, W. M., Gunderson, E. K. E., and Rahe, R. H. (1972): Reliability of life change cluster scores, Br. J. Soc. Clin. Psychol. *11*, 407–409.

Pugh, W., Erickson, J. M., Rubin, R. T., Gunderson, E. K. E., Rahe, R. H. (1971): Cluster analyses of life changes. II. Method and replication in Navy subpopulations, Arch. Gen. Psych. *25*, 333–339.

Rahe, R. H. (1969): Life crisis and health change. In: *Psychotropic Drug Response: Advances in Prediction*, ed. Philip R. A. May and J. R. Wittenborn, pp. 92–125, Charles C. Thomas, Springfield, Ill.

Rahe, R. H. (1972): Temporal factors in the prediction of subjects' near-future illness reports, paper presented at NATO Conference on Life Stress and Illness, Beito, Norway.

Rahe, R. H., Mahan, J., and Arthur, R. J. (1970): Prediction of near-future health change from subjects' preceding life changes, J. Psychosom. Res. *14*, 401–406.

Rahe, R. H., Pugh, W., Erickson, J. M., Gunderson, E. K. E., and Rubin, R. T. (1971): Cluster analyses of life changes. I. Consistency of clusters across large Navy samples. Arch. Gen. Psych. *25*, 330–332.

Rubin, R. T., Gunderson, E. K. E., and Doll, R. E. (1969): Life stress and illness patterns in the U.S. Navy: I. Environmental variables and illness onset in an attack carrier's crew, Arch. Environ. Health *19*, 740–747.

Spilken, A. Z., and Jacobs, M. A. (1971): Prediction of illness from measures of life crisis, manifest distress and maladaptive coping, Psychosom. Med. *33*, 251–264.

Wyler, A. R., Masuda, M., and Holmes, T. H. (1971): Magnitude of life events and seriousness of illness, Psychosom. Med. *33*, 115–122.

Emotions—Their Parameters and Measurement,
edited by L. Levi.
Raven Press, New York © 1975

Life Changes and Near-Future Illness Reports*

R. H. Rahe

U.S. Navy Medical Neuropsychiatric Research Unit, San Diego, California 92152

INTRODUCTION

Man's constitutional endowment is of major importance in his resistance or vulnerability to many disease states, and such genetic and acquired traits operate over his entire life span. Life change events, on the other hand, are generally temporal in their occurrences and in their influence upon a person's life. For example, life changes, such as being fired from work or undergoing a change in residence, take place over relatively brief spans of an individual's total lifetime. The duration of psychological and physiological effects of a subject's recent life changes appear to vary from a few weeks to a year or more according to the relative intensities of the various life change events. Discourses on disease etiology often focus on man's constitutional predispositions for selected illness and omit consideration of temporally bound precipitants of illness onset. This review presents evidence for one important temporal precipitant of illness onset—life changes.

Research into life change events found to occur closely before the onset of illness has included such diverse medical entities as tuberculosis, diabetes, mental diseases, coronary heart disease, abdominal hernia, and the entire gamut of minor complaints generally recorded during "sick call" in military settings (1, 3, 6, 7, 26, 27, 31, 37). The wide variety of illnesses studied has been matched by the wide variety of life changes. These life change events have included personal, family, marital, occupational, recreational, economic, social, interpersonal, and religious changes in life adjustments.

Some researchers have studied the effects of just one or two recent life changes on illness susceptibility. Syme et al. has found that subjects with a past history of residential and/or job mobility have significantly higher prevalence rates for coronary heart disease than do persons who haven't altered these two areas of their life adjustment (36). Madison and Viola and Parkes et al. have found that widows and widowers show significantly increased illness rates, compared to control subjects, within a year following their bereavements (13, 18). Sheldon and Hooper have found that ill health

---

* Parts of this chapter were originally published in *Annals of Clinical Research*, Vol. 4, 1972.

tends to follow recent, poor, marital adjustment (33). Parens et al. and Cleghorn et al. found increased illness reporting in student nurses who had experienced a recent, poorly resolved, separation from home (3, 17). Kasl and Cobb found increased blood pressures in subjects who were experiencing job loss (11). Since, as shown in the above studies, subjects show increased illness rates following single, meaningful, life changes, it would appear to follow that a broader measurement of recent life changes would be of even greater value in arriving at predictions of near-future illness susceptibility.

There are several examples of studies of life situations prior to disease onset where the researchers have included several recent life changes in their protocols. Jacobs et al. has found that upper respiratory infections are significantly more common in male college students who have experienced a number of recent, distressing life changes (10). Mutter and Schleifer, in a study of children developing physical illnesses, found that the families of these children were more disorganized and had more recent (during the 6 months prior to the study) life changes than did the families of concurrently well children (15). Berkman has shown that several environmental "stress" factors seem to be important in explaining the increased illness rates seen in spouseless mothers (2). Myers et al. has used a scale of 60 recent life changes in his random sampling of subjects living in New Haven and found that persons with life changes of most any variety report closely following symptoms of mental distress (16). Thurlow et al. reported that recently preceding "subjective" life changes provided a significant predictor of illnesses reported over the following two years (38).

Substantial difficulties exist in obtaining valid life changes information when studying large samples. Questionnaire measurement might be seen as an approximation of recent life changes much in the same way that a casual blood pressure measurement is an approximation of a subject's hemodynamics. In my studies of over 600 subjects with coronary heart disease, where recent life changes are gathered both by interview as well as by questionnaire, interviewers have invariably been impressed that data obtained by questionnaire is a valid although conservative estimate of recent life changes. When interviewers probed into a respondent's answers, they rarely found that a subject listed life change events which had not happened. In validity studies spouses agree with their mate's recent life change information at correlations between 0.50 and 0.75 (25).

Reliability estimates of the questionnaire have varied from as high as 0.90 to as low as 0.26 (38). This dramatic variability in results seems chiefly related to the time interval between administration of the questionnaire, the education level, and probable intelligence level of the subjects, the time interval over which recent life changes are summed, the wording and format of the various life event questions, and the intercorrelations between various life change events. Over the past few years we have experimented with changes in the format of the schedule of recent experience (SRE) questionnaire and clarification of various questions, and have worked on a life change cluster scoring technique. Recently, a simplified format SRE achieved a test-retest correlation (over 1 month) of 0.90 for Navy enlisted men. Since a questionnaire is the only practical device for use in large-scale epidemiological investigations, it is important to realize that factors such as intelligence or lack of motivation to cooperate will always lend questionnaire results lower reliabilities than that achieved through solicitous interview.

METHODOLOGY

SRE Life Changes Questionnaire

Researchers at the University of Washington, Seattle, constructed the early editions of the SRE questionnaire in order to systematically document clinically observed life events reported by subjects during the years prior to their (respiratory) illnesses (6). The design of the SRE includes a broad spectrum of recent life changes, including personal, social, occupational, and family areas of life adjustment.

For many years no allowances were made for the relative degrees of life change inherent in the various life change events included in the SRE. One life change – such as death of a spouse, was counted the same as another life change – a residential move. In 1964 a scaling experiment for the various degrees of life change inherent in the various SRE life change events was carried out (9).

The 42 life change questions contained in the SRE were scaled according to the proportionate scaling method of Stevens (34, 35). A group of nearly 400 subjects, of both sexes and of differing ages, race, religion, education, social class, marital status, and generation American were selected. They were instructed that one of the life change events, marriage, had been arbitrarily assigned a life change unit (LCU) value of 500. The subjects then were instructed to assign LCU values for all of the remaining life change events in the SRE, using marriage as their module. These other LCU values were each to be in proportion with the 500 LCU arbitrarily assigned to marriage. For example, when a subject evaluated a life change event, such as change in residence, he was to ask himself: "Is a change in residence more, less, or perhaps equal to the amount and duration of life change and readjustment inherent in marriage?" If he decided it was more, he was to indicate how much more by choosing a proportionately larger LCU value than the 500 assigned to marriage. If he decided it was less, he was to indicate how much less by choosing a proportionately smaller number than 500. If he decided it was equal, he was to assign 500 LCU. This process was repeated for each of the remaining life change events in the SRE questionnaire.

Since this original scaling experiment, life change scaling studies have

TABLE 1. *Life change events*

	LCU values
Family:	
Death of spouse	100
Divorce	73
Marital separation	65
Death of close family member	63
Marriage	50
Marital reconciliation	45
Major change in health of family	44
Pregnancy	40
Addition of new family member	39
Major change in arguments with wife	35
Son or daughter leaving home	29
In-law troubles	29
Wife starting or ending work	26
Major change in family get-togethers	15
Personal:	
Detention in jail	63
Major personal injury or illness	53
Sexual difficulties	39
Death of a close friend	37
Outstanding personal achievement	28
Start or end of formal schooling	26
Major change in living conditions	25
Major revision of personal habits	24
Changing to a new school	20
Change in residence	20
Major change in recreation	19
Major change in church activities	19
Major change in sleeping habits	16
Major change in eating habits	15
Vacation	13
Christmas	12
Minor violations of the law	11
Work:	
Being fired from work	47
Retirement from work	45
Major business adjustment	39
Changing to different line of work	36
Major change in work responsibilities	29
Trouble with boss	23
Major change in working conditions	20
Financial:	
Major change in financial state	38
Mortgage or loan over $10,000	31
Mortgage foreclosure	30
Mortgage or loan less than $10,000	17

been performed in other locations in the United States and in several foreign countries. Results from all of these life change scaling experiments have been strikingly similar (21). Most divergent results have been found between a small sample of Mexican-Americans versus white, middle-class Americans, and between a sample of Swedish subjects living in Stockholm versus comparable Seattlites (12, 29).

The practical result of these LCU weightings has been that recent life change information can be given quantitative estimates in terms of the average degree of intensity of change inherent in the life change events. Arbitrary time intervals over which life changes (LCU) have been summed, in order to give incidence rates, have varied from 2 years, 1 year, 6 months, 3 months, 1 week, and 1 day (in order to find the most appropriate time interval for illness prediction (6, 8, 23, 27, 31, 37). For convenience in handling, originally determined LCU values were divided by 10 (Table 1).

RESULTS

Early Retrospective Studies

Pilot studies performed by the author while he was at the University of Washington (1962 to 1965) were generally retrospective in nature. Subjects studied were requested to review their life changes and illness histories over the 10 preceding years and record these data on the SRE. There appeared to be little falloff of recording due to difficulty in remembering events or illness occurring several years prior to the study compared to those years more recent in occurrence. In these retrospective studies there was an apparent increase in LCU values during the year or two prior to their reported illnesses (22).

A wide variety of illnesses were experienced — infections, accidents, metabolic disease, even exacerbations of congenital maladies. The observed build-up in subjects' life change intensity (LCU) prior to their reported health changes appeared to be a nonspecific finding, without regard to type of ensuing health change. There did appear to be a positive relationship between the LCU intensity recorded by subjects during the year or two prior to illness and the severity of the subsequent illness (22).

It was from this pilot study that the first quantitative estimate of how many LCU a subject might experience and still remain healthy was made. The majority of the physician-subjects recording up to 150 LCU a year also reported good health for the succeeding year. When yearly LCU values ranged between 150 and 300 LCU, an illness was reported during the following year in approximately half the instances. Finally, for the relatively few subjects who registered over 300 LCU per year, an illness was recorded during the following year in 70% of the cases. It was also noted that illnesses which followed yearly LCU values over 300 LCU tended to be multiple.

This tendency was not seen for illnesses following lesser yearly LCU totals. Therefore, not only was an association noted between the magnitude of yearly LCU totals and the likelihood of subsequent illness, but also between yearly LCU total and likelihood of experiencing multiple near-future illnesses.

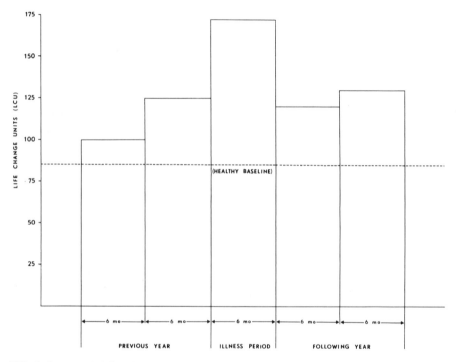

FIG. 1. Bar graph LCU data from 1,711 subjects showing 6-month totals over the year prior and the year following a 6-month interval in which they reported a single illness. The healthy base line was established from a grand mean 6-month LCU total for 1,554 subjects who were healthy over the same time span.

Beginning in 1965 a large scale Navy retrospective study of life changes and illness was performed utilizing nearly 2,500 U.S. Navy officers and enlisted men, virtually the entire ship's company aboard three cruisers. Subjects were given the SRE questionnaire and requested to report both their life changes and illness experience over the previous 4 years. These 4 years were divided into eight 6-month intervals. LCU totals were based on 6-month intervals, rather than over 1 year's time as was done in previous studies (23).

Whenever an illness was reported by a subject during the 4 years under study, the 6-month interval in which it occurred was labeled the "illness period." Subjects' (n = 1,711) LCU totals for all illness periods were examined along with their LCU totals for the two 6-month intervals immediately prior to their illness period and the two 6-month intervals immediately following their illness period, provided that they were in good health during these peri-illness intervals. For comparative purposes, all subjects (n = 1,554) who were healthy over the entire 4 years under investigation provided a grand mean, 6-month, LCU value, which was considered the best estimate of the "healthy base line" LCU value.

Figure 1 presents the results of the above retrospective investigation. The mean 6-month LCU total for the illness period was seen to be 174 LCU. Six months prior to the illness period, the subsequently ill subjects reported a mean LCU total of 125 LCU. Six months prior to this, these subjects had a mean LCU total of 100 LCU. Therefore, a gradual build-up in 6-month LCU total was seen over the 1½ years leading to their illness experience. The ill subjects' 6-month LCU magnitudes for the two 6-month intervals following their illness period were 120 LCU and 130 LCU. It appeared, therefore, that ill subjects' 6-month LCU totals remained relatively elevated over the year following their illness. In comparison, the 6-month LCU healthy base line value derived for all subjects reportedly in good health over the 4 year time-span was 85 LCU (23).

Perhaps the best retrospective study done on subjects' life changes and subsequent illness, as far as eliminating researcher bias, was a small study of 50 Navy and Marine Corps personnel discharged from service for psychiatric illness incurred while on active duty. In this study the life change data, as well as the men's health records, had been compiled 5 years earlier by social workers and physicians who knew nothing of our research. Each change of duty station, marriage, combat experience, childbirth, divorce, severe financial difficulty was recorded in the personnel records or elicited by interview at the time of his psychiatric evaluation prior to establishing his disability. Some of the health records extended over 30 years. All life changes which we thought were symptomatic of an illness, or a direct result of an illness were omitted from our analyses. Hence, yearly LCU totals could be given for each subject during each year he was in the military and these data could then be compared with his illness experiences up to his time of discharge (31).

Illnesses were scaled as to their severity, on a scale of 1 to 5, reflecting the risk of death or permanent disability of each illness after a method devised by Hinkle (31). Figure 2 presents in graph form life changes and illness data for a single subject whose case history is summarized below.

The subject, a Negro male, joined the U.S. Navy in 1941 at the age of 20 years. He was stationed aboard ship in Pearl Harbor when the Japanese attacked. He was transferred to another ship which subsequently was torpedoed and sunk. In 1943 he went to sick call for tension headaches; a few months later he had a circumcision. The following year he experienced two more changes of duty station and received a promotion to Steward, First Class. Late that year his tension symptoms returned and he also contracted mumps. At the end of the war he married; subsequently he developed low back pain symptoms. In 1947, at 26 years of age, he experienced a dramatic clustering of life changes. He was transferred, his first child was born, he reenlisted, he received two further transfers, and his wife became pregnant again. The following year he contracted gonorrhea, developed tonsillitis, and injured his wrist and knee. From 1951 through 1955 the subject's life changes were at a minimum. The only illnesses recorded over that period were two minor ones in 1955. In 1958, when the subject was 37 years old, he experienced a calamitous number of life changes. His wife developed a depressive illness while he was on a cruise. He returned home to find that she had moved out with all of his household effects, including $5,000 from their savings account. He located her in another city, living with another man. He was unable to recover any of his belongings. One week after returning to ship, while working in the galley, he received a severe electrical shock and almost died. His recovery was delayed by the development of aphonia which was thought to be on the basis of a conversion reaction. He gained a divorce and took charge of his two children. Subsequently, however, he entered into a chronic neurotic depressive reaction for which he received discharge and disability. Around this time his tension symptoms, headaches, and gastric distress returned.

In this study of 50 Navy and Marine Corps subjects, we found that mean LCU yearly total for the year prior to illness minor in severity was 130 LCU. Mean LCU total recorded for the year prior to health changes of major severity was 164 LCU. In comparison, mean year LCU value for all years studied was 72 LCU. A significant increase in usual yearly LCU total was therefore evidenced the year prior to recorded health changes. In addition, a positive relationship was seen between LCU magnitude the year prior to an illness and the severity of that illness. Two instances of high yearly LCU magnitude seen prior to death were also presented (31).

All these early retrospective studies complemented one another. For all samples it appeared that around 150 LCU per year (85 LCU per 6-month period) was a LCU total reported by people who subsequently remained healthy over the following year. When a subject reported an illness, his concomitant LCU total was often seen to be twice this healthy base line value, more than 300 LCU per year. LCU totals the year prior to illness, as well as the year following illness, were significantly elevated over the healthy base line LCU magnitude estimates. It was also seen that the LCU build-up over the year prior to illness, generally between 150 to 300 LCU/year, was particularly noticeable during the final 6-month interval (Fig. 1). Thus, for

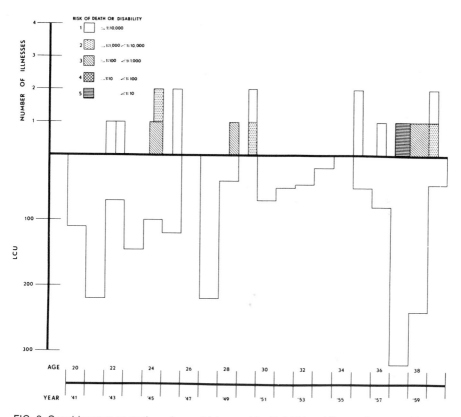

FIG. 2. Graphic representation of case history subject's LCU and illness data over 20 years of Navy experience.

purposes of illness prediction, most recent (6-month) LCU totals appeared to be the optimum ones to use.

Early and Recent Prospective Studies

In the original pilot study a small prospective experiment was built into the research design (22). Eighty-four of the 88 physician-subjects were contacted 9 months following their completion of the life change questionnaire and queried about their health change experiences over the 9-month interval. Forty-one of the 84 subjects had indicated at the time of their completion of the SRE questionnaire that they had experienced at least 250 LCU over the preceding year's time. Twenty-four of these 41 subjects, or 49%, reported a health change over the 9-month follow-up interval. Thirty-two subjects had indicated that for the year prior to SRE examination they had accumulated between 150 and 250 LCU. Eight of this group of

32 subjects, or 25%, reported a subsequent health change over the 9-month follow-up interval. Of the 11 remaining subjects who reported less than 150 LCU for the year prior to their completion of the SRE questionnaire, only one, or 9%, reported a health change during the follow-up interval.

Navy Shipboard Studies

Large-scale prospective studies of subjects' recent life change data and their near-future illness reporting were obtained with the three U.S. Navy cruisers shipboard populations (5, 26, 30). Aboard ship there is only one medical facility and health records are kept on all hands. Thus it was possible to collect the medical criterion data without having to ask the subjects to recall their recent illnesses as done with the resident physician sample. In addition, naval ships form a natural ecologic unit and the crews tend to be homogeneous in terms of age, education, and social backgrounds. The men, as a whole, encounter nearly identical environmental conditions, temporal stresses, food source, and even water supply.

Nearly 2,500 U.S. Navy enlisted men aboard the three large cruisers provided recent life change information and were followed for their reported health changes over the ensuing 6-month cruise period. Gastrointestinal, genitourinary, musculoskeletal, and dermal disorders accounted for 80% of all reported illnesses throughout the cruise (5). These illnesses tended to be minor in severity. Hence, this prospective study ultimately determined whether or not life change information for 6 months prior to going to sea could predict their reporting of minor illnesses while on their cruise.

The results were examined by first grouping the subjects into SRE deciles according to their relative LCU scores for the 6-month period prior to the cruise. Neighboring SRE deciles of men with similar mean illness rates for the 6-month follow-up period were then combined. The final grouping of subjects, according to their precruise LCU data, resulted in approximate quartile divisions of the total sample. Specifically, deciles 1 and 2, deciles 3 to 5, deciles 6 to 8, and deciles 9 and 10 made up the four divisions of the sample which best differentiated the men in terms of the follow-up period illness incidence rates. The illness rates for these four SRE divisions of the men ranged from 1.4 illnesses per man per 6 months for SRE deciles 1 and 2, to 2.1 illnesses per man per 6 months for deciles 9 and 10 (Table 2). Analysis of variance showed this progression of illness rates to be significant at the 0.01 level.

A companion analysis of the results of this large scale prospective experiment divided the men according to their ranges of total LCU scores for the year prior to their cruises. In other words, all men who registered less than 100 LCU for the year prior to the cruise were included in one group, those men who recorded between 101 and 200 LCU units were in the second group, those who recorded between 201 and 300 LCU were in the

TABLE 2. *Mean number of illnesses, standard deviations and analysis of variance for subjects aboard combined cruisers divided into LCU deciles*

SRE deciles	N	Mean	SD
1–2	526	1.4	1.7
3–5	797	1.5	1.8
6–8	803	1.7	1.9
9–10	538	2.1	2.1
Source	df	MS	F
Treatments	3	149.51	43.31[a]
Experimental error	2,660	3.45	–

[a] $p < 0.01$.
df = degrees of freedom; MS = means squared; F =
analysis of variance.

third group, and so forth, up to those few individuals who recorded between
601 and 1,000 life change units for the year prior to the cruise. The mean
illness rates for these LCU groups are plotted in Fig. 3. A positive and
linear relationship was seen between the recent LCU magnitude and the
cruise period mean illness rate of the men. For the few individuals who
registered between 601 LCU and 1,000 LCU the year prior to the cruise,
their mean illness rate for the cruise period fell below the projected regression line.

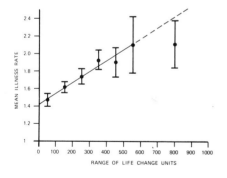

FIG. 3. Mean number of illnesses, per man,
per (6 months) cruise for subjects recording
0 to 100 LCU, for subjects recording 101 to
200 LCU, and so forth, up to subjects recording 601 to 1,000 LCU. Standard errors of the
means are indicated by brackets. Previously
published as Fig. 1 in Rahe, R. H., Mahan, J.,
and Arthur, R. J. (1970): Prediction of near-
future health change from subjects' preceding life changes, *J. Psychosom. Res. 14,* 404.

LCU Scores and Immediacy of Illness

Extrapolating from retrospective findings, it appeared that the higher a
recent (6-month) LCU total, the "closer" a possible illness. To examine
the prospective data for evidence of such a relationship between LCU magnitude and immediacy of illness, our shipboard subjects' first illnesses were
considered separately.

When first illnesses were tabulated for the men in SRE deciles 9 and 10, and compared to first illnesses for men in SRE deciles 1 and 2, the high LCU (SRE deciles 9 and 10) group developed nearly twice as many first illnesses as the low LCU (SRE deciles 1 and 2) group during the first follow-up month, and 60% more first illnesses during the second follow-up month. There were no significant differences in first illnesses between these high and low LCU groups for each of the remaining 4 months of the cruise, but, of course, the men most vulnerable to illness had already become ill (20).

Interaction of Selected Demographic Characteristics of the Men with Their LCU Totals in Modifying Their Cruise Period Illness Reports

The results of the SRE questionnaire and the cruise period illness reporting for all senior Navy enlisted men in a combined sample (n = 2,079) of Navy shipboard subjects were examined according to their age and marital status (19). (Similar results were seen for the junior enlisted men, but because of their younger age and their, in general, single marital status, they were not well distributed along these two dimensions.) For the entire group of senior enlisted men, a cruise period illness was reported by nearly three-quarters of the subjects. The percent deviations from this 75% illness incidence rate for particular subgroups of men is shown in the various cells in Table 3.

TABLE 3. *Recent life changes and age and marital status divisions for senior Navy enlisted men*

	SRE deciles			
	1 and 2	3–5	6–8	9 and 10
Age (yr):				
17–21	−3% (n = 87)	−2% (n = 168)	+3% (n = 186)	+9% (n = 112)
22–23	+7% (n = 52)	+7% (n = 119)	+6% (n = 119)	+6% (n = 69)
24–29	−22% (n = 47)	−18% (n = 88)	+2% (n = 83)	+1% (n = 71)
30+	−17% (n = 52)	−5% (n = 78)	+8% (n = 83)	−2% (n = 34)
Marital status:				
Single	−4% (n = 157)	+2% (n = 268)	+7% (n = 240)	+8% (n = 77)
Married	−16% (n = 81)	−11% (n = 183)	+1% (n = 231)	+4% (n = 209)

n = 1,446. Each cell's percent deviation in near-future illness rate from that for the group as a whole.

Table 3 is divided into quarters to facilitate inspection of the data. For example, the older men who reported least recent life changes had between 5 and 22% fewer sick men than that found for the groups as a whole. In contrast, younger men with the most recent life changes registered between 3 and 9% more ill personnel than was seen for the entire group. In the marital status and SRE deciles division of the table, married men with least recent life changes had between 11 and 16% fewer ill men than the entire group, whereas single subjects with highest recent life changes registered between 7 and 8% more sick individuals than that registered for the group as a whole.

Royal Norwegian Navy Cross-Cultural Comparison

In 1969 psychologists in the Royal Norwegian Navy administered the SRE to slightly more than 1,000 enlisted men, and followed the illness reports of these men over the next 13 months (25). This represents the longest follow-up period used to date to assess the predictive power of life change information. LCU scores were those for their final 6 months *prior* to Navy service.

The illness criterion data is still being collected on approximately one-quarter of the men. Preliminary analyses, however, show that the SRE and near-future illness results are very similar to those of the U.S. Navy study. Grouping subjects into approximate LCU quartiles, from lowest to highest recent LCU scores, near-future illness rates were 2.7, 2.9, 3.5, and 3.3 illnesses per man per year. Analysis of variance shows this progression of illness rates to be statistically significant at the 0.01 level.

Specificity of Particular Life Change Events for Particular Subsamples of Men

The Navy samples above dealt with only males and these men were drawn from a restricted age range (17 to 30 years) with a mean age of 22 years. The usual kinds of life change events of these young men (ceasing school, residential moves, financial problems, troubles with superiors, traffic violations) are characterized by their unspectacular nature, reflected in their generally low LCU values. Only when the enlisted men are slightly older and become married do relatively high LCU events, such as marriage, birth of children, illness of family member, buying a home, become applicable. Hence, a high LCU score for a young, single sailor is based on distinctly different life change events than a high LCU score for an older, married, senior enlisted man. We have found that the older married man's illnesses are more predictable by his LCU score than are illnesses for the young, single sailor.

This specificity of life change events for particular subgroups of subjects was examined by regression analysis of SRE data for all shipboard subjects aboard the three cruisers divided into various age and marital status subgroups (28). Results showed that the three to five recent life events which significantly correlated with the various subgroups of illness reports during cruise were rather specific for each subgroup—only recent disciplinary problems showed an overlap between subgroups. Further, even though multiple correlations of 0.36 could be achieved in particular subgroups of older, married subjects between their significant life change events and their cruise period illnesses, cross-validation of these same life change events upon illness reporting aboard other ships, led to low positive correlations around 0.10.

Recent Applications of the SRE

A recent study of 247 Underwater Demolition Team (UDT) trainees attacked a particular problem for SRE prediction of illness reporting as more than 75% of these men were young, single enlisted men, the group that has proved most difficult in the past to predict illness from their recent life changes information. The following study was of 194 young, single UDT enlisted trainees. By paying particular attention to the kinds of illness, particularly their severities, that these men developed, it was seen that their SRE information best predicted their relatively severe illnesses but not their minor ones (24).

UDT training is an extremely stressful 4-month training program where trainees undergo prolonged physical conditioning of running and swimming punctuated by periodic psychological and physical challenges, such as learning to be dropped into the ocean from helicopters. Illness reports are extremely high during UDT training. In those subjects who pass the course, their illness reporting rate is 10 times higher than that seen for shipboard subjects. For UDT subjects who drop from training, and this can range from 30 to 70% of a class, their illness reporting rate can be as high as 50 times the shipboard rate (22).

The sample of 194 men was divided into two random halves in order to utilize a validation, cross-validation methodology. As mentioned in the section on life changes specificity for subgroups of subjects, the entire list of 42 life change events were separately correlated with illness reports in the first, or validation, half of subjects. Six life change events were seen to have significant and positive correlations with the illness criterion. The SRE scores of subjects in the validation sample correlated 0.42 with their illness reports ($p < 0.001$). In the cross-validation sample, these same six life change events correlated significantly, and in the predicted direction, with cross-validation illness reports (0.19, $p < 0.05$).

UDT trainees who drop from the stressful training do so in two ways. First, if they develop relatively severe and disabling illnesses, they are medically dropped from training. Second, if they find they have insufficient motivation to cope with the physical and psychological stresses of training, they can voluntarily drop from training. It is unusual, however, for voluntary drops not to have some illness report prior to their drop, although usually of a very minor nature. Medically and voluntarily dropped UDT subjects' SRE information showed an overall correlation with number of illness reports of 0.33 ($p < 0.01$). The correlation of medically dropped subjects' SRE results with their numbers of dispensary visits — some of which were medically disabling — was 0.50 ($p < 0.01$). The correlation of voluntarily dropped subjects' SRE results with their number of generally minor dispensary visits was 0.20 (nonsignificant) (9) (Table 4).

TABLE 4. *Correlations of medically or voluntarily dropped UDT subjects' recent life changes with their near-future illness reports*

Subjects	Illnesses	Correlation
All (n = 68)	Both major and minor severities	0.33[a]
Voluntary drop (n = 40)	Minor severity	0.20 (NS)
Medical drop (n = 28)	Many of major severity	0.50[a]

[a] $p = < 0.01$.
(NS) = nonsignificant.

DISCUSSION

It is important to emphasize that our subjects were males, and their mean age was 22 years. The life changes reported by these men proved to be rather specific to their age and sex. The illnesses reported by the shipboard subjects were judged to be of minor severity. Thus, these particular large samples of subjects provided a prospective test of their particular recent life change events in the prediction of their subsequent minor illness reports. For the men aboard three U.S. Navy cruisers and for the 1,000 Royal Norwegian Navy enlisted men sample, a significant but low order positive relationship was seen between recent LCU magnitude and near-future illness reports.

Recently published data on both U.S. Navy and Royal Norwegian Navy subjects have shown that correlations between the LCU data for the 6 months immediately prior to study and perceptions of body symptoms at the beginning of the study ranged between 0.22 and 0.36 ($p < 0.001$). These correlations are considerably higher than those seen between recent LCU data and follow-up period illness reports. Whether or not the subjects perceiving symptoms at the start of the follow-up period go on to report illnesses over the next 6 to 13 months seems to depend on a number of "illness role" factors. For example, quite young Navy subjects, with relatively low educational attainment, serving in unskilled positions, who are not satisfied with their work, tend to report illnesses more readily than do subjects with opposite qualities (25, 26).

When the large samples were broken down into subgroups of various ages and differing marital status, it was evident that although the young, single sailor was reporting the majority of the illness episodes, his near-future illness reports were least predictable by looking at his recent LCU magnitude. It was the older, and often married, subject, who showed relatively high correlation between recent LCU score and near-future illnesses. This may have been the case because the older, married subject could answer several more recent life change events in the SRE which were not applicable to the young, single, sailor, thereby allowing older, married subjects greater life change variance.

The older, married, shipboard subjects were a particularly interesting group of men in that those who recorded the lowest, precruise, LCU levels, had far less illness in their ranks than that seen for this group of men as a whole. Up to 22% fewer subjects reported a cruise period illness in these older, married, subjects with lowest LCU totals. It appeared, for this particular, subgroup of men, that a lack of recent life changes was an excellent predictor of health during the cruise period.

A word should be said concerning the problem of illness reporting in large scale studies. Since individuals had to report to sick bay in order for their illness to be recorded, the question always remains "How many subjects got sick but didn't come to sick bay?" This is a particularly valid question for older, senior enlisted men in the Navy who can more readily go to their own quarters with an illness than can junior enlisted men. The problem of illness reporting was satisfactorily handled in a prospective study of 134 military academy officer cadets' recent life changes and their future illness experience over the following year (4). All men were required to report for illness histories and physical exams 2 weeks later. A correlation of 0.22 ($p < 0.05$) was seen between their previous 6-month LCU scores and their number of illnesses encountered over their first 2 weeks of training. For at least half the subjects, health change data were collected, at 4-month intervals, over the following year. Correlations obtained between these LCU scores and total number of health changes were: 0.34 ($p < 0.01$) at 4 months, 0.30 ($p < 0.05$) for 8 months, and 0.37 ($p < 0.01$) for the entire year (excluding the initial 2 weeks).

Currently, our life change and illness research is directed toward small groups of men relatively uniform in their major demographic dimensions and who tend to experience rapidly occurring near-future illnesses. Our studies of UDT trainees have shown that recent life changes reports are similar enough between men that one can predict illness results for one group of men utilizing recent life changes and illness correlations derived from a different group of UDT trainees. (This was not the case for shipboard subjects aboard different ships.) Also, UDT trainees' illnesses tend to cluster in the first month or so of their 4-month training program. Shipboard studies showed that recent life change information was most predictive of these first and second month illness reports. Other small, homogeneous groups of men currently being studied include deep-sea divers, naval aviators, submariners, and Navy athletic teams.

When the severity of UDT trainees' illnesses were examined, which included several medically disabling ones, recent life changes were seen to best predict serious illnesses. Minor illnesses of UDT subjects were not seen to be significantly correlated with their recent life change scores. Therefore, the illness criterion itself must be defined for a dimension of severity in order to achieve optimum illness prediction from recent life change information.

Although the illness reports of the U.S. Navy and the Norwegian Navy subjects aboard ship were uniformly minor in severity, they were not insignificant medical entities. Illness reports were counted in which the subjects presented a standard symptom picture of a recognized illness entity, and in over 75% of the instances, subjects also presented objective signs of tissue pathology. Visits to sick bay that appeared to be motivated by a desire to avoid work, or other such nonmedical motivation, were not counted as illness reports. Common examples of these minor severity illness reports were: lacerations, sprains, upper respiratory infections, venereal disease, and gastrointestinal complaints (25, 26).

Finally, it should be said that the life change method only measures one dimension of recent life stress. The life change questionnaire simply documents changes in ongoing adjustments in central areas of concern. It does not measure long-standing life difficulties, such as chronic marital or financial problems. It does not measure anticipated life stresses, such as imminent final exams or ensuing job changes. Hence, the findings of this review support the etiologic importance of just one measurable aspect (recent life changes) of recent life stress in the determination of near-future disease onset.

ACKNOWLEDGMENT

This study report was supported by the Bureau of Medicine and Surgery, Department of the Navy, under Research Work Unit MF51.524.002-5011-DD5G. Opinions expressed are those of the authors and are not to be construed as necessarily reflecting the official view or endorsement of the Department of the Navy.

REFERENCES

1. Alexander, F. (1966): *The History of Psychiatry.* Harper and Row, New York.
2. Berkman, P. L. (1969): Spouseless motherhood, psychological stress, and physical morbidity, *J. Health Soc. Behav. 10,* 323.
3. Cleghorn, J. M. and Streiner, B. J. (1971): Prediction of illness behavior from measures of

life change and verbalized depressive themes. Presented at the Annual Meeting of the American Psychosomatic Society, Denver.

4. Cline, D. W. and Chosey, J. J. (1972): A prospective study of life changes and subsequent health changes, *Arch. Gen. Psychiatry 27,* 51.

5. Gunderson, E. K. E., Rahe, R. H., and Arthur, R. J. (1970): The epidemiology of illness in naval environments II. Demographic, social background, and occupational factors, *Milit. Med. 135, 453.*

6. Hawkins, N. G., Davies, R., and Holmes, T. H. (1957): Evidence of psychosocial factors in the development of pulmonary tuberculosis, *Am. Rev. Tuberc. Pulmon. Dis. 75,* 5.

7. Hinkle, L. E., Jr., Conger, G. B., and Wolf, S. (1950): Studies on diabetes mellitus. The relation of stressful life situations to the concentration of ketone bodies in the blood of diabetic and nondiabetic humans, *J. Clin. Invest. 29,* 754.

8. Holmes, T. S., and Holmes, T. H. (1970): Short-term intrusions into the life style routine, *J. Psychosom. Res. 14,* 121.

9. Holmes, T. H., and Rahe, R. H. (1967): The social readjustment rating scale, *J. Psychosom. Res. 11,* 213.

10. Jacobs, M. A., Spilken, A. Z., Norman, M. M., and Anderson, L. S. (1970): Life stress and respiratory illness, *Psychosom. Med. 32,* 233.

11. Kasl, S. V., and Cobb, S. (1970): Blood pressure changes in men undergoing job loss: A preliminary report, *Psychosom. Med. 32,* 19.

12. Komaroff, A. L., Masuda, M., and Holmes, T. H. (1968): The social readjustment rating scale: A comparative study of Negro, Mexican and white Americans, *J. Psychosom. Res. 12,* 121.

13. Maddison, D., and Viola, A. (1968): The health of widows in the year following bereavement, *J. Psychosom. Res. 12,* 297.

14. Masuda, M., and Holmes, T. H. (1967): The social readjustment rating scale: A cross-cultural study of Japanese and Americans, *J. Psychosom. Res. 11,* 227.

15. Mutter, A. Z., and Schleifer, M. J. (1966): The role of psychological and social factors in the onset of somatic illness in children, *Psychosom. Med. 28,* 333.

16. Myers, J. K., Pepper, M. P., and Marches, J. (1969): Assessing mental health needs of a community, *Public Health Serv. Report* No. 43–67–743; *personal communication.*

17. Parens, H., McConville, B. J., and Kaplan, S. M. (1966): The prediction of frequency of illness from the response to separation: A preliminary study and replication attempt, *Psychosom. Med. 28,* 162.

18. Parkes, C. M., Benjamin, B., and Fitzgerald, R. G. (1969): Broken heart: A statistical study of increased mortality among widowers, *Br. Med. J. 1,* 740.

19. Pugh, W., Gunderson, E. K. E., Erickson, J. M., Rahe, R. H., and Rubin, R. T. (1972): Variations of illness incidence in the Navy population, *Milit. Med. 137,* 224.

20. Rahe, R. H. (1968): Life change measurement as a predictor of illness, *Proc. R. Soc. Med. 61,* 1124.

21. Rahe, R. H. (1969): Multi-cultural correlations of life change scaling: America, Japan, Denmark, and Sweden, *J. Psychosom. Res. 13,* 191.

22. Rahe, R. H. (1969): Life crisis and health change. In: *Psychotropic Drug Response: Advances in Prediction,* ed. P. R. A. May and J. R. Wittenborn, Charles C Thomas, Springfield, Illinois.

23. Rahe, R. H., and Arthur, R. J. (1968): Life change patterns surrounding illness experience, *J. Psychosom. Res. 11,* 341.

24. Rahe, R. H., Biersner, R. J., Ryman, D. H., and Arthur, R. J. (1972): Psychosocial predictors of illness behavior and failure in stressful training, *J. Health Soc. Behav. 13,* 393–397.

25. Rahe, H., Fløistad, I., Bergen, T., Ringdahl, R., Gerhardt, R., Gunderson, E. K. E., and Arthur, R. J. (1974): A model for life changes and illness research: Cross-cultural data from the Norwegian Navy, *Arch. Gen. Psychiatry 31,* 172–177.

26. Rahe, R. H., Gunderson, E. K. E., and Arthur, R. J. (1970): Demographic and psychosocial factors in acute illness reporting, *J. Chronic Dis. 23,* 245.

27. Rahe, R. H., and Holmes, T. H. (1965): Social, psychologic and psychophysiologic aspects of inguinal hernia, *J. Psychosom. Res. 8,* 487.

28. Rahe, R. H., Jensen, P. D., and Gunderson, E. K. E. (1971): Illness prediction by regression analysis of subjects' life changes information, *Unit Report* No. 71–5, U.S. Navy Medical Neuropsychiatric Research Unit, San Diego.

29. Rahe, R. H., Lundberg, U., Bennett, L., and Theorell, T. (1971): The social readjustment rating scale: A comparative study of Swedes and Americans, *J. Psychosom. Res. 15*, 241.
30. Rahe, R. H., Mahan, J., and Arthur, R. J. (1970): Prediction of near-future health change from subjects' preceding life changes, *J. Psychosom. Res. 14*, 401.
31. Rahe, R. H., McKean, J., and Arthur, R. J. (1967): A longitudinal study of life change and illness patterns, *J. Psychosom. Res. 10*, 355.
32. Rosenman, R. H., and Friedman, M. (1963): Behavior patterns, blood lipids and coronary heart disease, *J A M A 185*, 934.
33. Sheldon, A., and Hooper, D. (1969): An inquiry into health and ill health adjustment in early marriage, *J. Psychosom. Res. 13*, 95.
34. Stevens, S. S. (1966): A metric for the social consensus, *Science 151*, 530.
35. Stevens, S. S., and Galanter, E. H. (1957): Ratio scales and category scales for a dozen perceptual continua, *J. Exp. Psychol. 54*, 377.
36. Syme, S. L., Hyman, M. M., and Enterline, P. E. (1968): Some social and cultural factors associated with the occurrence of coronary heart disease, *J. Chronic Dis. 17*, 277.
37. Theorell, T., and Rahe, R. H. (1971): Psychosocial factors and myocardial infarction I: An inpatient study in Sweden, *J. Psychosom. Res. 15*, 25.
38. Thurlow, H. J. (1971): Illness in relation to life situation and sickrole tendency, *J. Psychosom. Res. 15*, 73.

Emotions—Their Parameters and Measurement,
edited by L. Levi.
Raven Press, New York © 1975

Epidemiology, Disease, and Emotion

Aubrey Kagan

Laboratory for Clinical Stress Research, S-10401 Stockholm 60, Sweden

The words of this title are used in different ways and so, as a contribution to discussion of concepts, I will first give some working definitions of "epidemiology" and "disease" and consider possible parameters of "emotion" and the way in which they might be defined.

The consequences of this for measurement and assessment of the roles of emotion in health and disease will be briefly considered and some hypotheses requiring investigation will be mentioned.

EPIDEMIOLOGY

Epidemiology may be used to signify the "science of studying disease in groups of people." A group is anything more than one person and may consist of, e.g., a family, a parish, a school, the army, the country, the nation, the world.

DISEASE

Disease is "disability or failure in performance of a task." The latter definition must always include tasks considered to be essential, might include tasks considered "normal," and, when enough is known, will include tasks considered optimal. Because, by this definition, disease differs according to the biological hierarchical level, e.g., cell, organ, organism, family, community, it is always necessary to state the level at which health is being considered.

EMOTION

As an epidemiologist I may look upon physiological, psychological, and sociological views of emotion without the bias peculiar to these particular disciplines although with some bias due to personal experience in real life or through literature.

From the practical point of view of prevention of disease it seems to be useful to consider emotion as consisting of three elements: emotional feeling, social action or behavior, and physiological changes. These elements are interrelated to each other and also markedly affected by a fourth element "intellectual symbolization."

Emotional Feeling

My earlier definition of emotional feeling was "pleasant or unpleasant sensation shorn of intellectual symbolization." This fits with MacLean *(this volume)* who puts emotional feelings on an "agreeable — disagreeable" continuum and points out that the neutral point (of a U-shaped continuum) is zero emotion. The notion also fits with Brady's *(this volume)* appetitive (pleasant) and aversive (unpleasant) stimuli, and also with the old idea that pleasant emotional feelings are associated in general with the effect of going toward and unpleasant emotional feeling with moving away.

There is little doubt, in the human at any rate, that intellection may both stimulate, and be stimulated by, emotional feeling; diminish or enhance emotional feeling; modify accompanying "social action" and "physiological change." Emotional feeling is often described as felt or thought of as joy, desire, affection, sorrow, anger, or fear (MacLean, *this volume*) as opposed to a vague feeling of pleasure or displeasure. In the former instance I would say that intellection had taken place and may have altered the pattern of response.

Since intellectual symbolization is highly likely to vary from time to time in the same individual or between individuals for the same stimulus and degree of pleasantness or unpleasantness, it will often be desirable to assess both factors separately — emotional feeling as I have defined it on a subjective quantitative pleasant/unpleasant scale and intellectual symbolization on a subjective multiqualitative scale. For practical purposes I would therefore retain the definition of emotional feeling given above.

Intellectual symbolization of emotional feeling should be regarded as an interacting variable and fourth parameter that must be taken into account in the study of emotion.

MacLean *(this volume)* distinguishes between "sensation" which ceases with the incoming signal that produces it and "emotion" which continues afterward.

"Passion" could then be defined as a short lasting emotional feeling of great intensity, and "mood" as a sustained emotional feeling. "Sentiment" could be defined as mood plus intellectual content and would thus be more than emotional feeling.

Social Action

The term social action is used to refer to "those physical and mental acts which accompany emotional feeling" and are the common outward behavioral signs of emotion, e.g., crying, laughing, running away, running toward. Social actions that are "emotion" based but may include considerable intellectual symbolization in man are described variously (*cf.* MacLean, *this volume*) as "searching," "aggressive," "protective," "dejective," "gratifying," "caressive." It is notable that what appear to be identical emotional feelings may be accompanied on different occasions or in different people by different social actions, e.g., laughter *or* tears may accompany unpleasant emotional feelings.

Physiological Change

The most studied physiological changes considered to be aspects of emotion are those mediated by the hypophyseal-adrenocortical and the sympathoadrenomedullary systems. Increased catecholamine and corticosteroid excretion has been demonstrated (see Levi, *this volume*) as an accompaniment of pleasant and unpleasant emotional feeling. Physiological accompaniments, such as, rise in blood pressure, redistribution of circulating blood, glucosemia, diminished thrombus time, which under some circumstances could be protective and others might be precursors of disease are well documented. They have been regarded as preparation of the organism for the social action of "flight or fight," but occur in many situations in which in modern life neither flight nor fight is the correct or the usual social response.

Physiological changes mediated by the hypophyseal-adrenocortical and sympathomedullary systems have always been found *when sought* in emotional situations. For this reason they are regarded by Levi and others as nonspecific or general physiological response. However the pattern may differ according to the situation; for example, increased epinephrine excretion is usually found in ambiguous situations but not when ambiguity is absent. Mason points out that to claim nonspecificity it would be necessary to demonstrate these changes *in all* situations and that has yet to be done. His own investigations of a large variety of endocrine changes in emotional situations lead him to suggest two broad patterns of endocrine change: catabolic, characterized perhaps by increased activity of adrenal medulla and cortex, thyroid, and growth hormone; and anabolic, characterized by increased secretion of insulin, testosterones, and estrones. He also speculates, and provides some evidence to support the idea, that there is a different pattern of enzyme activity for each of several emotional situations. This would be of great importance if it were true and it would seem advisable to include in some studies of emotion a battery of tests to cover the large number of enzyme changes that *might* be parameters.

It seems clear that emotional feeling, social action, and physiological change are strongly associated, but clarification is needed on whether emotional feeling causes physiological change or vice versa (see Lader, *this volume*) and whether feeling and physiological change can occur independently.

There is some evidence that emotional feeling is accompanied by phasic hypothalamic or limbic stimulation and that mood is accompanied by tonic stimulation. The notion that pleasant emotional feelings are accompanied by parasympathetic activity and unpleasant feelings by sympathetic activity is probably nearly true under the circumstances of Cannon's experiments (strong acute life-threatening situations), but the situation is likely to be more complex under less severe everyday circumstances (*cf.*, Wolf, *this volume*).

Composite Definition

A composite definition of "emotion" for practical purposes might then be: activity in the limbic-endocrine system accompanied by a feeling of pleasantness or unpleasantness and associated with behavior characterized by going toward or away from a person, place, thing, or idea.

FUNCTIONS AND DYSFUNCTIONS OF EMOTION

Functions

It seems highly likely from animal experimentation, that emotion type neuroendocrine changes give flexibility and increase the range of activity of many organ systems, and it is well known that under the influence of emotion humans can exert physical activity beyond their powers when not emotionally stirred.

It is also clear from animal and human experience that associative learning is speeded and reinforced under conditions of emotional stimulation as compared with unemotional situations.

On the basis of the nature of physiological change associated with emotion, it has been suggested that the latter's main function is to prepare the organism for fight or flight and, perhaps through another system or a special development of the latter, for mating, breeding, and rearing the young. These are undoubtedly fundamental survival activities in which limbic mediated physiological change plays an important role. Perhaps the emotional feeling associated with this has developed as a feedback system, or a compass, by which the organism knows whether the whole of its activities are being directed to the same purpose.

Under conditions in which change is more likely to be harmful than beneficial and strangers are more likely to be dangerous than friendly, emotional reactions to the new or unknown, based on well-established cultural attitudes, are likely to be of benefit to the individual and the community.

Dysfunctions

The above are all useful functions but too much or too little emotion may inhibit physical action when it is most required. Excess emotion may cause forgetfulness ranging from mild absent mindedness to a complete memory block. Anyone who has driven a car under the influence of a deep emotion will recall that his driving has been more dangerous due to failure to concentrate on the task and probably also due to diminished judgment and excessive speed. Many who are unexpectedly called upon to speak in public will recall the inability to do so through emotional block.

Studies on humans have shown that the same stereotyped emotional physiological changes that occur in circumstances for which the appropriate social action is flight, fight, or reproductive and breeding activities may occur in circumstances for which these social actions are not correct or not allowed, e.g., public speaking, inadequacy of creativity at work, expressed dissatisfaction of supervisor or someone in authority, personal dissatisfaction, tension during car driving, pressure of events.

Since many of the bodily changes associated with emotion are similar to precursors of a large variety of diseases (e.g., anxiety, indigestion, hypertension, decreased clotting time, diminished immunoreaction), it has been postulated that some aspect of emotion may in the long term cause or predispose to many diseases. Whether this is so and if so how it occurs is a high priority area for research.

MacLean *(this volume)* points out that the human brain is three brains (triune brain) each with its own sense of time and space, some neurological and biochemical independence, and some interdependence. The paleomammalian or limbic system is the "emotional brain" but it impinges upon the "reptilian" brain (corpus striatum, globus pallidus, peripallidal structures, responsible for autonomic function) and the neomammalian brain (neocortical, responsible for perceived and intellectualized function) and is in turn impinged upon by them.

Examples of how "limbic-endocrine" connections may affect the functions of the "reptilian" brain are given above. Methods of learning to influence this through training (biophysiological feedback) are beginning to emerge and may prove to be of practical use.

Through the neocortical interconnections, experience or education may increase or decrease emotional feeling and modify physiological activity and social action in response to stressors (see Hamburg and Lazarus on coping, *this volume*). This may be advantageous to the individual or the community but, when experience or education is inadequate to the situation, the neocortical effect on the emotions may lead to individual or community harm, e.g., unnecessary fear, diminution of alertness, mass hysteria, mob rule.

It is likely that developments in our understanding of how education and experience can influence emotional responses through the neocortical-limbic endocrine connections may be our most fruitful approach to controlling "emotion" to the advantage of individual and community.

PARAMETERS OF EMOTION

The three aspects of emotion—feeling, social action, physiological change—are associated but not completely dependent on each other. To measure one is not to know the other. Lack of complete dependence may be due to: some fundamental property; individual variation in biological processes; interacting intellectual symbolization; or some mixture of these. It follows that, in discussion or study of the influence of emotion on health or disease, it is likely to be necessary to take into account or assess these three aspects of emotion and also some interacting variables.

Emotional Feeling

This has to be measured in a subjective manner and, if the definition given is accepted, on a pleasant-unpleasant scale. One approach to this is to assess the difference between what a person expects and what he thinks he receives from a given situation (subjective person—environment fit).

Since intellectualized or symbolized feelings are almost certain to accompany and modify the effect of such "emotional feelings," the effect needs to be understood. Scales for this are needed. They will also, by definition, be subjective and multiple and will try to assess the "desire, anger, fear, sorrow, joy, affection" elements.

Even more important to evaluate is the interacting variable of "coping." To what extent is a rationalization process interacting with the stressor? This effect is best understood by introducing graded "amounts" of "coping" into an experimental study design.

Social Actions

Whereas observations on "feeling" are based on the subjects report of himself, observations on social action are based on observable activity. Sometimes such activities can be assessed in an objective way and sometimes the observer's subjective bias may intervene. Generally speaking, the more objective the assessment, the better, but in all cases estimates of bias and precision of observations need to be made.

The nature of the social actions studied will depend on the purpose. Generally speaking it is necessary to make observations on the qualitative nature of the actions and their duration, frequency, and intensity. Thus in a study of two kinds of day care for preschool children, that the Laboratory for Clinical Stress Research is now completing, the qualitative nature of the childrens' interactions and conflicts with each other and with adults is observed as well as the proportion of time spent in interaction, activity, or expression of emotional behavior.

Physiological Change

It is unlikely that direct assessment of limbic activity will be made in population studies for many years but the effects on the adrenal cortex and medulla is well reflected in the excretion of catecholamine and 17-OH corticosteroids. These may be measured over particular periods of a "test" day or in response to a load test, i.e., after exposure to a standard stimulus. Mason *(this volume)* has drawn attention to the importance of assessing other hormones, e.g., thyroid, growth, insulin, testosterone, estrone.

Although observations on hormones are objective, there is still great need to establish precision and bias and to make the observations and the tests under comparable conditions of study so that the effects of interacting confusing variables can be avoided or neutralized.

These tests are expensive and time consuming whereas obtaining the material on which they are made and storing it is comparatively inexpensive. For some studies where only a small proportion of the material needs to be examined, the identity of which will not be known until after a "subsequent event," it may pay to store material until it is clear which needs to be examined. For instance, in the day care study referred to above a urine specimen was collected from each of approximately 100 children twice a day for a period of roughly 100 days.

Only specimens in which some unusual event subsequently takes place in a child and for several days before and after and similar specimens for controls need to be examined. By storing the material, we may be able to reduce the number of specimens to be examined from about 20,000, which would have been impossible, to about 2,000 which will be possible and which will give nearly as much information.

In many studies it will be desirable to assess physiological and biochemical changes that are potential precursors of disease, e.g., heart rate, blood pressure, glucose tolerance, thrombus time, serum cholesterol, immune reactions.

HYPOTHESES TO BE TESTED AND A STRATEGY FOR RESEARCH

I have considered this subject in some detail elsewhere (Kagan, 1974). Here I will only mention that from the point of view of prevention of disease and promotion of health there are two types of hypotheses that should be given priority for test. The first relates to the mechanism or mechanisms whereby emotion arising from social situations may predispose to disease and promote health. A great deal of evidence supports the notion that one ıch mechanism is "some degree of intensity, duration, or frequency of 'Selye stress' or 'Selye stress' in the absence of physical activity." The second, for which there is also much supporting evidence, is that "the psychological stimulus most likely to trigger a pathogenic mechanism is the stimulus due to difference between expectation and perception of what has happened."

It can be seen in Fig. 1, which represents a concept of the system "social environment, emotion, disease," that if one or another of such hypotheses were shown to be true it would open up our understanding of the "system"

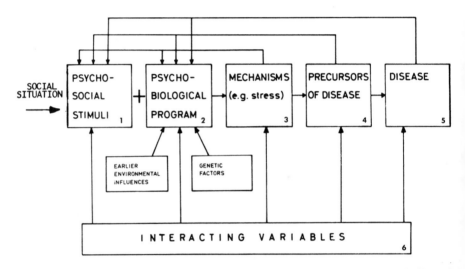

FIG. 1. A theoretical model of psychosocially mediated disease. The combined effect of psychosocial stimuli (1) and man's psychobiological program (2) determines the psychological and physiological reactions (mechanisms) (3), e.g., "stress (Selye)" of each individual. These may, under certain circumstances, lead to precursors of disease (4) and to disease itself (5). This sequence of events can be promoted or counteracted by interacting variables (6). The sequence is not a one-way process but constitutes part of a cybernetic system with continuous feedback (adapted from Kagan and Levi, *Stress Lab. Reports, 27* 1971).

and facilitate ways of: judging whether a social situation, psychological stimulus, or interacting factor was likely to be harmful or beneficial; estimating which subjects were at high risk; making the evaluation of health or social actions less difficult.

Such studies for testing hypotheses demand an experimental prospective study design. I have reviewed the ethics and technical problems involved and supplied references in a previous publication (Kagan, 1974). In order to establish the limits of such hypotheses it would be desirable to investigate a wide variety of subjects (e.g., age and sex) and a wide variety of social situations. It would be expensive and time consuming to carry out such studies and the immediate practical value would be limited if the hypotheses were shown to be wrong.

But in the framework of such studies it would be possible with little or no additional cost to evaluate health or social actions of immediate importance to the community studied. There are many communities in which administrators feel bound to take some health or social action and which the community feels bound to accept, and yet the safety and efficacy of the action is not known. It may be that the action will do as much or more harm than good. All that is generally known beforehand is that something must be done and the preferred action is costly.

The strategy that I propose is that in such a situation, where the community and administrators welcome the idea, to design a study which will show whether the health action is effective, how much and to whom; whether it is dangerous, how much and to whom; and to compare this and the costs with alternative actions.

In the same study, at no additional cost, key hypotheses could be evaluated and information quantifying the interrelationships of other parts of the system depicted in Fig. 1 will be obtained in order to give a broader understanding of the whole system.

REFERENCE

Kagan, A. (1974): *Life Stress and Illness,* edited by E. K. E. Gunderson and R. H. Rahe, Charles C Thomas, Springfield, Illinois.

Emotions—Their Parameters and Measurement,
edited by L. Levi.
Raven Press, New York © 1975

Certain Biochemical Parameters of Psychogenias

N. A. Ivanov

Biochemical Laboratory, Serbsky Research Institute of Forensic Psychiatry, Moscow, U.S.S.R.

Emotional stress produces a complex of changes in the organism: in the nervous system, in the endocrine system, and in the metabolic processes.

In psychiatric practice we encounter cases in which factors of emotional stress act over a long period, i.e., a stress situation is present. An emotional stress situation may be a cause of mental disturbances of varying persistence: from mild, transient forms to psychoses, which sometimes become durative. This depends upon the premorbid personality as well as upon the type of psychic trauma.

Forms of psychic pathology, conditioned by a mentally traumatic situation, have been classified into a group of psychogenias or reactive states ["psychogenic reaction," according to Braun (1928), and "abnormal," by Schneider (1955)].

Many clinicians (Ganser, 1904; Kirn, 1899; Krepelin, 1906; Korsakoff, 1901; Vvedensky, 1938; Buneyev, 1950; Felinskaya, 1965; Morozov, 1971) have thoroughly studied the main clinical features of psychogenias, defined the rules of their development, and formulated the general principles of pathogenesis. Psychogenias have been investigated not only by clinicians, but also by psychologists, pathophysiologists, psychopharmacologists, and biochemists.

This chapter concerns the results of a study in the field of psychogenias, performed with the aid of clinical chemistry.

Well-known publications by Cannon (1927) demonstrated a connection between mental activity and catecholamine metabolism; strong emotions (anger, fury, fear) stimulated the sympathetic nervous system and increased the excretion of epinephrine by the adrenal glands. Studies by Gelhorn (1966) demonstrated a relationship between emotions and the higher centers of the sympathetic nervous system.

The findings of Euler (1962) revealed that emotional stress produces marked changes in the metabolism of catecholamines. Recent studies exposed an important role of catecholamines in the organization of stress reactions via an influence upon certain parts of the hypothalamic area and reticular formations of the brain. Catecholamines are both hormones and mediators, regulating physiological functions, in some cases activating and in others inhibiting the activity of organs and tissues. These findings stimulated great interest in catecholamine metabolism in various forms of mental pathology, but progress was hampered by a lack of sufficiently accurate and specific methods for detecting catecholamines in biological fluids.

A great achievement of Euler and co-workers was the development of an accurate fluorometric method for the detection of epinephrine and norepinephrine.

When studying the metabolism of catecholamines, many investigators, instead of defining the level of catecholamines in the blood, prefer to estimate their excretion with the urine. Nor is this simply because the very low catecholamine concentration in the blood plasma makes accurate detection difficult. The advantage of studying diurnal urinary catecholamine excretion is that more precise and comprehensive information can be obtained concerning the type of catecholamine metabolism and the functional state of the sympathoadrenal system over a long period. Information on the catecholamine level in the blood refers to the moment of investigation only.

We studied a series of biochemical indices, reflecting the metabolism of catecholamines, in 89 patients (87 males and two females) with psychogenias of different clinical forms and various types of course. We assessed the diurnal urinary excretion of 3,4-dioxiphenilalanine (DOPA), dopamine, epinephrine, norepinephrine, and 3-metoxy-4-hydroxy-D (mandelic acid). Epinephrine and norepinephrine excretion were estimated by the method of Euler and Lishajko (1959, 1961), which had come into widespread use on account of its high sensitivity, specificity, and preciseness. The estimation of DOPA and dopamine was undertaken according to Matlina and Kiseleva (1966). The method of electrophoresis on paper, developed by Menshikov and Bolshakova (1963), was used to identify mandelic acid.

The study of catecholamine metabolism in psychogenias uncovers numerous problems which cannot be solved in a single investigation.

In the present study we aimed to discover: (a) differences in the metabolism of catecholamines between a group of patients with psychogenias and a normal group; (b) any particular features of catecholamine metabolism that are related to different forms of psychogenias; (c) the influence of the course of psychogenia upon catecholamine metabolism.

The comparison of average indices of diurnal excretion of catecholamines and their metabolites revealed certain differences between patients with psychogenias and normals. In patients the average indices of diurnal adrenal excretion were lower and the indices of diurnal DOPA and dopamine excretion were higher than in the normals. The excretion of the final metabolite — mandelic acid — was on the same level in the patients as in the normals.

Although the differences in average indices were statistically significant only for DOPA, the dissociation of excretion indices in patients with psychogenias is of some interest. This dissociation takes the form of decreased excretions of epinephrine and norepinephrine combined with elevated excretions of DOPA and dopamine. It may reflect a weakening of fermentative systems that participate in the transformation of DOPA and dopamine into epinephrine and norepinephrine, or an augmented rate of epinephrine and norepinephrine destruction in the organism. In the latter case, however, there would be an increased excretion of the final product of epinephrine and norepinephrine decay—mandelic acid. Since this was not observed (the average index of diurnal excretion of mandelic acid was not increased), it seems reasonable to assume a weakening of fermentative system activity, catalyzing the transformation of DOPA and dopamine into epinephrine.

An analysis of catecholamine metabolism indices by groups revealed a number of differences between the main clinical forms of psychogenias (psychogenic depression, hallucinatory-paranoid syndrome, stuporous states, hysterical psychoses). The group with psychogenic depression showed a decreased epinephrine excretion together with increased indices of DOPA and dopamine excretion; the group with stuporous states had the lowest indices of all groups for the excretion of epinephrine, norepinephrine, DOPA, and dopamine; the group with hallucinatory-paranoid syndrome had the highest norepinephrine and the lowest mandelic acid excretion; the group with hysterical psychoses had the highest epinephrine excretion and the highest excretion of mandelic acid.

The differences in the quantities of excreted catecholamines were not generally great between the groups of patients with different clinical forms of psychogenia, and most of them were not statistically significant. In fact it was only the decreased diurnal excretion of epinephrine and norepinephrine in the group of stuporous patients that showed statistical significance and even here it reflected a prevalence of patients with a protracted illness course in this group, a low excretion of catecholamines being characteristic for such patients.

Thus we failed to find significant differences in the metabolism of catecholamines between groups of patients with the main clinical forms of psychogenia. Clear-cut differences were found, on the other hand, between patients with subacute and protracted development respectively. These differences were traced in all the indices characterizing the metabolism of catecholamines. In patients with a protracted development of reactive psychoses the average excretion indices for epinephrine, norepinephrine, DOPA, dopamine, and mandelic acid were all significantly lower than they were in patients with a subacute course (*in* every case they were about twice as low), all the differences being statistically significant ($p < 0.01$).

Thus it seems to be the type of illness course (subacute or protracted) that largely determines the type of catecholamine metabolism in psychogenias. The impact of the illness course is displayed in activating the metabolism of catecholamines in subacute development and inhibiting it in protracted development of psychogenia. Proof of an activated metabolism is the increased diurnal excretion of epinephrine, norepinephrine, DOPA, dopamine, and mandelic acid, compared with similar indices in normals (the rise was statistically significant for all indices, except epinephrine). An inhibition of catecholamine metabolism in protracted development of psychogenia is seen in the markedly lower diurnal excretion of epinephrine, norepinephrine, DOPA, dopamine, and mandelic acid, compared to normals; this lower excretion was statistically significant for all indices, without exception.

It is interesting that the dynamic investigation of catecholamine metabolism in patients with subacute development has shown that, when the patients improve under treatment (aminazine therapy, barbamyl-coffein disinhibition), the diurnal excretion of catecholamines and their metabolites tends to decrease and approach the normal level. These observations support the assumption of an activated catecholamine metabolism in the subacute development of psychogenia.

The second part of the study concerned a series of biochemical indices that characterize the carbohydrate-phosphoric metabolism in patients with psychogenias. This approach was chosen to investigate the regulatory influence of the sympathoadrenal system and its mediators (catecholamines) on the character of the carbohydrate-phosphoric metabolism.

To estimate the carbohydrate-phosphoric metabolism in psychogenias we assessed the sugar level in blood on an empty stomach, the type of glycemic curves, and the blood concentrations of a number of phosphoric combinations: inorganic phosphorus, phosphorus of adenozintriphosphoric acid (ATP), phosphorus of diphosphoglyceric acid, acid soluble phosphorus, and general phosphorus. The concentrations of these phosphoric combinations in the blood and their ratio change according to the level of glycolic processes and, consequently, according to the state of the carbohydrate-phosphoric metabolism in the body.

It was noticed that patients had lower indices of glycemia on an empty stomach, compared to normals, but the difference was not significant. The study included 116 patients with psychogenia; only 57 displayed normal glycemic curves, the rest having abnormal glycemic curves of the hyperglycemic or hypoglycemic types, or torpid curves.

The study of carbohydrate metabolism in patients with main clinical forms of psychogenia (psychogenic depression, hallucinatory-paranoid syndrome, stupor, hysterical psychoses) revealed a maximal difference in the level of glycemia on an empty stomach between the group with psychogenic depression (the lowest index) and the groups with hallucinatory-paranoid syndrome and hysterical psychoses (the highest index). This difference was statistically significant ($p < 0.01$).

The glycemic curves differed between the groups with the main clinical forms of psychogenias. The group of stuporous patients had the biggest proportion of torpid glycemic curves; in the group with psychogenic depressions, hypoglycemic curves were in the majority and there were no hyperglycemic curves; the curves in the group with hysterical psychoses were mostly hyperglycemic. Nevertheless, these differences between the groups with the main clinical forms of psychogenias, testifying to an influence of the clinical form on the carbohydrate metabolism, do not form a system; thus one cannot assume that the clinical form has a determining influence on the metabolism of carbohydrates.

Clear-cut differences were revealed in carbohydrate metabolism between the groups of patients with subacute and protracted courses of illness. In patients with a subacute development the sugar level in the blood reached 97.9 mg%, whereas in patients with a protracted development it was 89.9 mg% (a statistically significant difference, $p < 0.01$).

Furthermore, in patients with a protracted development the proportion of abnormal glycemic curves was about twice that in patients with a subacute development of psychogenia; in the former patients, moreover, the abnormal curves were predominantly hypoglycemic, whereas in the patients with a subacute development they tended to be hyperglycemic.

The type of changes observed suggests that the course of psychogenia has a determining influence on the carbohydrate metabolism.

A comparison of the average contents of phosphoric combinations in the blood of 42 patients with psychogenias and the corresponding indices in normals revealed no significant difference, except for the ATP content, which was significantly higher in the patients.

Certain differences were found in the blood contents of phosphoric combinations between groups with the main clinical forms. Stuporous patients had the lowest indices of inorganic phosphorus and phosphorus of hexose phosphates and the highest index of ATP phosphorus; patients with psychogenic depression displayed the highest indices of phosphorus of diphosphoglyceric acid and general phosphorus; patients with hallucinatory-paranoid syndrome were characterized by the lowest indices of ATP and acid soluble phosphorus; patients with hysterical psychoses showed the highest indices of inorganic phosphorus, phosphorus of hexose phosphates, and acid soluble phosphorus.

In only two cases, however, were the differences statistically significant: (1) the difference in ATP phosphorus content in stuporous patients and patients with hallucinatory-paranoid syndromes; and (2) the difference in the content of hexose phosphate phosphorus between the stuporous patients and those with hysterical psychoses.

The groups with subacute and protracted types of psychogenia development were characterized by marked differences in the average contents of phosphorus combinations in the blood. The differences were due to an increase of inorganic phosphorus, hexose phosphate phosphorus, phosphorus of diphosphoglyceric acid, and acid soluble phosphorus in the blood of patients with a subacute development and a decrease of the same indices in patients with a protracted course.

It should be noted that the differences in indices between the groups with subacute and protracted courses were statistically significant in all cases ($p < 0.05$).

Evidently, the type of course by which a psychogenia develops determines the character of the carbohydrate-phosphoric metabolism: an activation of the process of anaerobic destruction of carbohydrates in the subacute course and a corresponding decrease in the protracted course of psychogenia.

CONCLUSION

The study of a series of biochemical tests, characterizing the metabolism of catecholamines and the state of the carbohydrate-phosphoric metabolism in patients with psychogenias, demonstrated that in these states, produced by a stress situation, marked changes occur in the complex of metabolic processes.

In the subacute course of a psychogenia the level of catecholamine metabolism increases, as evidenced by an elevated diurnal excretion of catecholamines and their metabolites; in a protracted course there is an inhibition of catecholamine metabolism. These changes also influence the carbohydrate-phosphoric metabolism, which is regulated by the sympathoadrenal system.

REFERENCES

Braun, E. (1928): Psychogene Reaktionen. In: *Handbuch der Geistes krankheiten*, Vol. 5, Berlin.

Buneyev, A. N. (1950): The reactive states. In: *The Forensic Psychiatry*, Moscow.

Cannon, W. B. (1927): The James-Lange theory of emotion, *Am. J. Psychol. 39*, 106–124.

Euler, U. S., Von (1962): Physiology of catecholamines. In: *Neurochemistry*, Springfield.

Euler, U. S., von, and Lishajko, F. (1959): The estimation of catecholamines in urine, *Acta Physiol. Scand. 45*, 122–132.

Euler, U. S., Von, and Lishajko, F. (1961): Improved technique for the fluorimetric estimation of catecholamines, *Acta Physiol. Scand. 51*, 348–356.

Felinskaya, N. I. (1965): The reactive states. In: *The Forensic Psychiatry*, Moscow.

Ganser, (1904): Zur Lehre vom hysterischen dämmerzustand, *Arch. Psychol. 38*, 32–46.

Gelhorn, E. (1966): *Emotions and Emotional Disorders*, Moscow.

Kirn (1899): Die Psychosen in der Strafanstalt, *Allg. Z. Psychiat. 45*, 1–97.

Korsakoff, S. S. (1901): *The Handbook of Psychiatry*, Moscow.

Krepelin, E. (1906): Über hysterische Schwindel. *Z. Gesamte Neurol. Psychiatr.*

Matlina, E. S., and Kiseleva, Z. M. (1966): The estimation of adrenaline, noradrenaline, DOPA and dopamine in urine. *Problems of endocrinology and hormonotherapeutics*, Moscow, *12*, 111–116.

Menshikov, V. V., and Bolshakova, T. D. (1963): The modification of the method of estimation of 3-metoxy-4-hydroxy-D (mandelic acid) in urine. *Cardiology*, Moscow, *3*, 91–92.

Morozov, G. V. (1971): On the differential diagnostics of schizophrenia and reactive states. *Vestn. Akad. Med. Sciences USSR 5*, 23–26.

Schneider, K. (1955): Abnorme Erlebnis-reaktionen. *Klin. Psychopathol.* Stuttgart, 47–73.

Vvedensky, Y. N. (1938): *The Forensic Psychiatry*, Moscow.

Emotions—Their Parameters and Measurement,
edited by L. Levi.
Raven Press, New York © 1975

Measurement of Emotion: Transcultural Aspects

Paolo Pancheri

Institute of Psychiatry, Rome, Italy

Although considerable progress has been made in recent years in the measurement of the physiological, psychophysiological, and behavioral correlates of the emotional states, little has been done to check the validity of the data obtained and of the instruments used in populations notably different for racial, cultural, and social reasons. One of the reasons why the results of many experimental studies, even when carried out correctly on the methodological level, lack confirmation when they are repeated by other investigators in other populations is probably the undervaluation of the variable constituted by the different intrinsic nature of the object of the experiment. The serious methodological problem created by the sampling of the subjects of the experiment is well known to any investigator of human behavior; even when the samples are taken at random and the number of subjects seems sufficiently large, the results are hardly applicable to populations different from that on which the sampling was made.

If this is true when one works on simple psychophysiological parameters such as the measurement of reaction times or the power spectrum of cerebral electric activity, the problem becomes particularly dramatic when one passes to the measurement of behavioral variables supposedly correlated to emotional states. In order to get information about those particular internal states that we call emotional, the only two methods actually available on the methodological level are the measurement of some physiological variables correlated to them (cardiac frequency, skin electric conductance) and the observation of spontaneous or experimentally elicited behavior. The "physiological" method could appear ideal from the point of view of the "transcultural" study of the emotional states. Because of the fundamental identity of the anatomophysiological structure of man, the somatic variables correlated to the emotional states seem less likely to be influenced by environmental factors of sociocultural type. The serious disadvantage of the method is nevertheless the limited information that it can give. At the present state of knowledge it is difficult to go much beyond generic information about the presence or not of a deviation from the base line. The extent of such a deviation can of course be measured, but qualitative information is almost completely lacking and one cannot reach the level of content analysis. The observation and measurement of behavior make information available about structure and content, but for transcultural study they have the disadvantage of being strongly influenced by socioenvironmental factors. When planning a study of the similarities and differences of emotional states in different sociocultural contexts, the main problem is therefore methodological and can be reduced to the search for a set of instruments and methods which can put aside sociocultural influences or at least suggest correction factors or "keys of interpretation" for the data obtained in different populations.

Looking at the problem from a general standpoint, we see that every behavioral measurement of emotional states, whether carried out on a nominal scale (absence of emotion/presence of emotion, normality/pathology, etc.) or with more complex scales (for example, measurement of anxiety or depression), is the resultant of an interaction between the observer and the observed (Fig. 1).

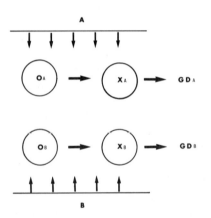

FIG. 1. Two observers (O_A, O_B) from different cultures (A, B), if asked to make a diagnostic judgment upon subjects of the population to which they belong (X_A, X_B), will give answers conditioned by their cultural and linguistic differences (GD_A, GD_B).

If two observers (O_A and O_B), belonging to different sociocultural contexts, make a judgment (qualitative or quantitative) upon any subject of the population to which they belong (X_A and X_B), they will produce two diagnostic judgments which, if similar criteria of reference have been used, can be compared with each other.

Whatever the result of such a comparison, it is quite unlikely that any useful information can be obtained about the similarity, the difference, or the quantity of the difference of the emotional states of the two subjects belonging to the two separate populations. For example, the same diagnostic judgment of "depression" for both subjects can be correlated to a marked difference of emotional states, since the interpretative criteria for the existence or not of a depressive condition can vary considerably from observer to observer. Since both observer and observed are conditioned in their judgments and in their behavior by the particular sociocultural context in which they developed and in which they live, it follows that the judgment (measurement) of an emotional state will be the resultant of three variables:

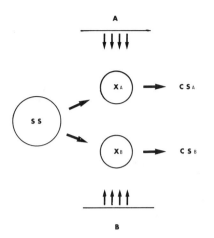

FIG. 2. When a set of standardized stimuli (SS) are administered to two subjects or two populations of subjects (X_A, X_B) different from the sociocultural point of view, they produce two sets of responses (CS_A, CS_B) which can give information about the emotional state of the subjects.

emotional state of the observed, criteria of reference of the observer, and sociocultural influences upon them both.

A possible way of reducing the variables involved and simplifying the experimental design is to use standardized stimuli not influenced by sociocultural differences (Fig. 2).

When the stimulus or the set of standardized stimuli (SS) are administered to two subjects or two populations of subjects (X_A, X_B) who differ from the sociocultural point of view, they produce two sets of responses (CS_A, CS_B) which, if the set of stimuli has been correctly selected, can give information about the emotional state of the subjects.

The method, widely used in psychometrics, nevertheless has the disadvantage in transcultural research of giving limited information about the influence of the sociocultural determinants, since the response to the standardized stimulus acquires a predictive meaning only if correlated with external criteria that almost always consist of clinical-behavioral observation (diagnostic judgment).

A vicious circle is thus created, with two possibilities of "error of transcultural diagnostic." In the first case, two observers who work in their own respective populations can make the same "diagnostic judgment" even when the emotional states, expressed by the responses to a standardized stimulus, are different (Fig. 3). In the second case, a different "diagnostic

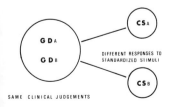

FIG. 3. First error in transcultural diagnostic: two observers who work in their own respective populations make the same diagnostic judgment even when the emotional states, expressed by the responses to a standardized stimulus, are different.

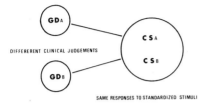

FIG. 4. Second error in transcultural diagnostic: a different diagnostic judgment is
made even in the case of identical emotional
states.

judgment" can be made even in the case of identical emotional states
(Fig. 4).

It follows that just comparing data gathered on different populations does
not seem sufficient to get information about the sociocultural determinants
of the emotional states; at the same time, the data obtained from one population are difficult to apply to another.

Therefore, the fundamental requirements when setting up a method for
correct transcultural research in the measurement of emotional states are
the following:

(a) Use of an instrument with which one can obtain a description of the
emotional state of the subject by administering a set of standardized stimuli.
Besides the characteristics common to any mental test, the following features are required: a measurement of the emotional variables by means of
numerical scales, availability of translations into the languages of the populations to be investigated, as well as the relative national norms.

(b) Availability of behavioral ratings or classifications (diagnostic judgments) based on criteria generally accepted by observers of different
linguistic or cultural areas. For example, general agreement is needed on
the definition of depression, anxiety, and excitement.

(c) Use of a statistical instrument that makes it possible to compare the
existing differences, from the standpoint of the objective data obtained from
the test, between two populations classified as identical from the point of
view of the observation of behavior and vice versa.

The purpose of the following study is to demonstrate the feasibility of a
transcultural investigation that avoids the two above-mentioned possibilities of error by the use of an appropriate methodology.

METHOD

Comparison of Populations

Two populations showing such ethnic, linguistic, and cultural differences
as to make possible a psychometric investigation according to the previously
stated conditions were compared. The first population consisted of subjects
of Italian language and nationality, living in Rome. The second consisted
of German-speaking subjects of Swiss nationality, living in Bern.

From each of the two populations, two groups were selected which differed quantitatively and qualitatively with respect to a parameter of emotional measurement evaluated by observers of the same nationality. The groups had the following characteristics:

(1) *Normal group*— Age between 20 and 30; at least 8 years of education; approximately equal number of male and female subjects; no previous psychiatric illness nor presence of behavioral changes suggestive of any psychopathological alteration.

(2) *Depressed group*—The same characteristics as the preceding group with respect to age, education and sex; diagnosis of "neurotic depression," made at the University clinic of psychiatry in the city of residence, on the basis of the case history and status data in the normal diagnostic routine of the institute to which the subjects were referred for psychodiagnostic evaluation and possible treatment.

The "neurotic depression" group was chosen because characteristics which are very useful for our investigation happen to converge in such a category: quantitative and qualitative alterations of a normal emotional state (depression), and probable impairment of the diagnostic judgment of the observer by factors dependent on the particular sociocultural context (neurotic characteristics of the depression). The four groups of subjects were thus: (1) depressed neurotic Swiss, 30; (2) depressed neurotic Italians, 69; (3) normal Swiss, 76; (4) normal Italians, 127.

The MMPI (complete form) was administered in the standard way to every subject. The MMPI was chosen as an objective instrument for the measurement of the subjects' emotional state both in view of characteristics of this test and for reasons connected with the type of research set up by us. Apart from its documented characteristics of validity, reliability, and sensitiveness to the variations of emotional states, the MMPI permitted a precise qualitative and quantitative evaluation of the emotional variable taken into consideration by us (depression) through numerical values which could be processed statistically. In addition, the availability of translations in the relevant languages and of the relative national norms rendered the instrument particularly suitable for a transcultural study.

The K-correct values, in T scores, for the 10 clinical scales and for the three control scales were obtained from the answer sheet. The T scores were calculated using the relative national norms. The MMPI versions used were the official ones in the respective countries, translated and adapted into Italian and German, and sold by the distributors of the test authorized by the Psychological Corporation (O.S. in Italy, Hans Huber in Switzerland).

The four groups were compared by means of a multiple discriminant analysis, as being the most suitable statistical instrument for testing the "emotional" differences (measured by the 13 MMPI scales) among the four groups defined *a priori* on the basis of diagnostic criteria presumptively influenced by socioenvironmental factors.

The analysis was carried out by means of the Anal program of the statistical program library of H. Barker, modified by A. Morgana. The subroutine of Overall and Klett was also used to calculate the test-vector projections in discriminant-function space. All programs were written in Fortran IV; the computer was the Univac 1108 of the computer center of the University of Rome.

Content Analysis

The MMPI was used again for the content analysis, in the forms, and with the methodology of administration described above. An item frequency endorsement was carried out on two groups of normal subjects, Italian and Swiss. The characteristics of the two groups were identical to those of the normal groups used for the preceding analysis, but the numerical consistency was higher (164 Swiss; 210 Italians), and the age range wider (18 to 45 years). For every item of the test the frequencies of response for the two groups were calculated; the significance of the differences was tested with the chi square ($p < 0.01$).

RESULTS

Comparison of Populations

Table 1 and Figs. 5 and 6 show the means and the SD of the four groups. It is clear that the average profiles for the two "normal" groups are prac-

TABLE 1. *MMPI basic scales for the four groups*

Scale	1. Depressed neurotic Swiss		2. Depressed neurotic Italians		3. Normal Swiss		4. Normal Italians	
	X̄	SD	X̄	SD	X̄	SD	X̄	SD
L	52.46	11.10	48.60	9.55	48.03	9.58	48.58	8.46
F	58.03	9.50	63.26	14.22	49.02	8.27	46.14	10.44
K	47.56	7.60	49.04	9.52	54.60	9.37	53.22	9.71
1	60.53	8.38	76.44	12.00	48.32	8.40	51.50	9.98
2	66.50	11.64	76.68	14.90	50.01	8.97	49.95	9.47
3	66.33	10.67	74.97	14.23	55.35	8.74	51.32	10.34
4	60.33	11.53	63.57	13.32	51.19	8.40	51.70	10.07
5	49.46	11.92	54.27	11.86	51.01	12.34	52.75	10.98
6	60.26	11.27	61.53	9.94	47.52	9.60	46.90	9.40
7	62.30	11.60	67.24	15.55	50.11	9.16	47.04	8.74
8	58.96	10.07	70.92	16.12	49.13	7.15	47.91	11.38
9	51.40	12.75	54.44	11.66	49.98	8.70	45.21	9.81
10	57.93	10.84	58.73	10.57	48.81	10.15	55.00	9.57

X̄ = mean.
SD = standard deviation.

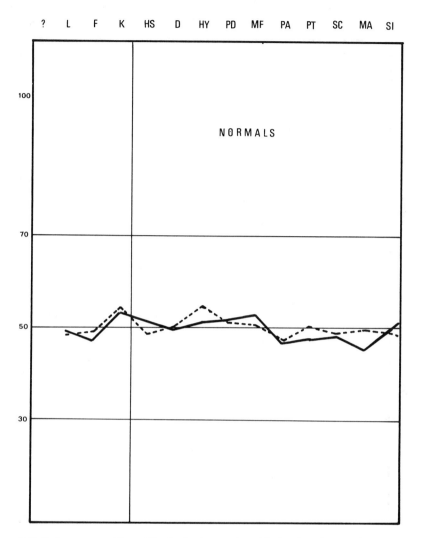

FIG. 5. Average profiles of the Swiss (– – –) and Italian (———) normal groups.

tically the same, both in the scores and in the general shape of the profile (no significant difference between the scales for $p < 0.05$). The "neurotic" profiles, on the other hand, display a fundamental similarity in their general shape but differ considerably in the elevation of the scales; the average Italian profile scores higher than 70 T scores in four scales (1–2–3–8) at a statistically significant level.

Table 2 shows the results of the multiple discriminant analysis applied to the four groups. It will be seen that the first two discriminant variables

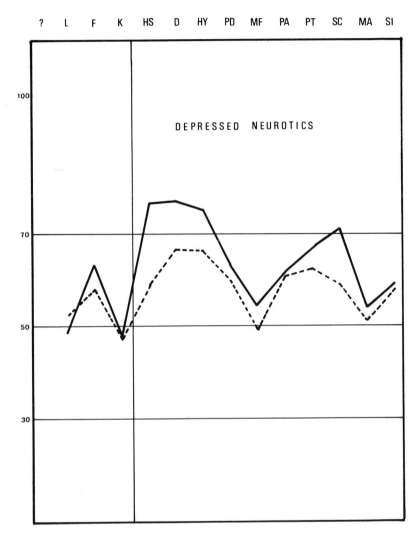

FIG. 6. Average profiles for the Italian (——) and Swiss (– – –) depressed groups.

calculated account for 94.36% of the total variance and can consequently be used for plotting in the discriminant space the centroids relative to the four groups. Figure 7 reports such data, together with the vectors of the original variables in the discriminant space.

Since the length of the vector represents its power as discriminator among the four groups, it follows that the most powerful discriminating variables are Hs and D. As regards the direction of the vectors, all except the vector K point toward the pathological groups, and within the two pathological

TABLE 2. *Discriminant function analysis on the four groups*

Cntr	1	2	3
1	69.95	36.02	8.60
2	86.20	28.63	15.04
3	48.70	33.01	16.41
4	50.75	27.22	12.49

Wilks lambda = 0.256.
D.F. = 39. and 848.
F-Ratio = 12.705 $p = 0.0000$.
Root 1 81.01 Pct. variance.
Chi-square = 293. 629 D.F.
= 15. $p = 0.0000$.
Root 2 13.34 Pct. variance.
Chi-square = 73.176 D.F. =
13. $p = 0.0000$.
Root 3 5.65 Pct. variance.
Chi-square = 33.243 D.F. =
11. $p = 0.0008$.

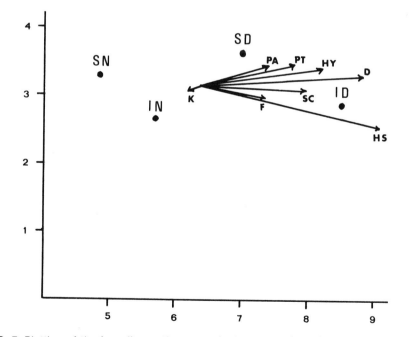

FIG. 7. Plotting of the four diagnostic groups in the space of the first two discriminant variables. IN: Italian normals. SN: Swiss normals. ID: Italian depressed. SD: Swiss depressed.

groups the vector Hs is nearest to the Italian group, whereas the vector Pa is nearest to the Swiss group.

Looking at the classification of the single cases on the basis of the maximum probability of their belonging to the four groups, it can be seen that the latter are discriminated at a good level of significance (Table 3).

TABLE 3. *Bayesan classification of the subjects in the four diagnostic groups according to the discriminant scores*

Actual	Predicted				% Subjects correctly classified
	1	2	3	4	
1. Depressed neurotic Swiss	17	3	5	5	56.6
2. Depressed neurotic Italians	2	58	0	9	84.0
3. Normal Swiss	2	2	52	20	70.2
4. Normal Italians	1	5	19	102	80.3

As can be noted, the percentage of cases correctly classified is higher in the two Italian groups. Looking instead at the overall number of subjects in every group who are classified either as depressed or as normal, in agreement with both the Italian and the Swiss models, we see that of 30 "depressed Swiss" subjects only 20 (66.6%) are classified as depressed, whereas of 69 "depressed Italians" 60 (86.9%) are classified likewise (Table 4). No appreciable difference can be found in the classification of the normal subjects.

TABLE 4. *Overall subjects classified as depressed or normals in every group*

Group	Depressed		Normals	
	No.	%	No.	%
1	20	66.6	10	33.3
2	60	86.9	9	13.1
3	4	5.2	72	94.7
4	6	4.7	119	93.7

Chi square group 1 vs. group 1 ($p < 0.05$).
Chi square group 3 vs. group 4 (n.s.).

Item Frequency Endorsement

Table 5 and Fig. 8 show the values relative to the means and to the SD of the group in which the item frequency endorsement was carried out. The average profiles do not seem to differ at a significant level in any of the

TABLE 5. Means and standard deviations for the 13 MMPI basic scales in the Italian and Swiss normal groups used in the item frequency endorsement

| Scale | Italians | | Swiss | |
	$\overline{X}$	SD	$\overline{X}$	SD
L	47.35	8.89	50.81	12.30
F	57.05	20.40	53.74	10.92
K	48.16	11.16	51.19	9.93
1	55.86	14.30	52.18	11.34
2	53.80	12.83	50.96	10.57
3	52.86	12.66	54.05	12.94
4	54.05	12.93	51.54	9.74
5	49.97	11.07	50.04	11.23
6	53.84	14.15	48.26	11.51
7	51.64	11.68	52.49	11.48
8	56.73	19.08	52.52	10.81
9	51.21	11.91	52.96	9.06
10	64.64	13.74	49.81	10.14

scales, except scale O (Si). A look at the results of the item frequency endorsement shows, however, that 289 items out of 566 show a different style of response in the two populations (Table 6).

Table 7 gives the results of the content analysis carried out on the first category (affect-depression) and on the 16th (affect-manic) of the original group of 26 content categories described by the authors of the MMPI. The 1st and 16th categories were selected since they seemed most relevant to a differential evaluation of the emotional contents.

The first column of Table 7 shows the number and the text of the item discriminating between the two groups; the second column reports the Italian "type" response, and the third column the Swiss "type" response.

DISCUSSION

The purpose of our research was essentially methodological, but the results deserve a short comment.

The data for the comparison between "normal" and "depressed" groups of different populations showed that the criteria of psychiatric classification can vary considerably with reference to the different contexts in which the diagnostic judgment, the classification, or the "measurement" is made. In fact, our study shows that the same judgment of pathological deviation as regards a parameter of measurement of emotions (depression) may be correlated to different emotional states and that this depends on the different sociocultural environment in which the judgment is made. In our two populations such a difference appears to be quantitative rather than qualitative;

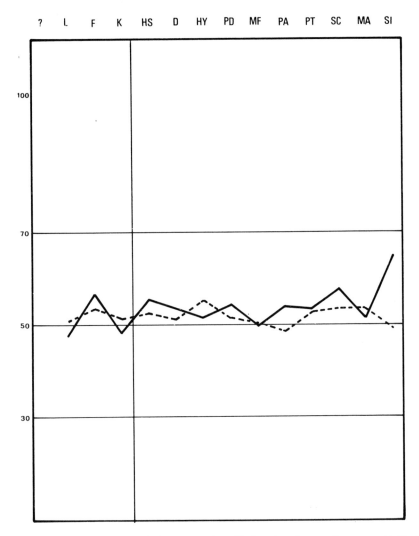

FIG. 8. Average profiles of the Swiss (– – –) and Italian (——) normal groups used in the item frequency endorsement study.

the profiles of the two groups of depressed neurotics were fundamentally similar in shape but the average Italian profile was very much higher than the average Swiss. Furthermore, the discriminant analysis showed that, even in the normal subjects whose average profiles are almost the same, differences exist that are not discernible in the average values. In fact, the position of the centroids in the space of the first two discriminant variables showed that a first variable permits a distinction between normality and depression apart from the ethnocultural composition of the groups, whereas

TABLE 6. Item frequency endorsement: Number and percentage of items discriminating, in each MMPI scale, between the two normal groups

Scale	Number of items discriminating at the 0.01 level	Total number of items in the scale	%
L	6	15	40
F	28	64	43
K	13	30	43
1	9	33	27
2	30	60	50
3	28	60	46
4	17	50	34
5	18	60	30
6	16	40	40
7	30	48	62
8	42	78	53
9	25	46	54
10	27	70	38

TABLE 7. Item analysis on the "affect-depression" and "affect-manic" content categories

Categories	Italians	Swiss
8. My daily life is full of things that keep me interested.	false	true
41. I have had periods of days, weeks, or months when I couldn't take care of things. I couldn't "get going."	true	false
67. I wish I could be as happy as others seem to be.	true	false
76. Most of the time I feel blue.	true	false
79. My feelings are not easily hurt.	false	true
88. I usually feel that life is worthwhile.	false	true
104. I don't seem to care what happens to me.	false	true
106. Much of the time I feel as if I have done something wrong or evil.	true	false
134. At times my thoughts have raced ahead faster than I could speak them.	false	true
145. At times I feel like picking a fist fight with someone.	true	false
202. I believe I am a condemned person.	true	false
209. I believe my sins are unpardonable.	false	true
234. I get mad easily and then get over it soon.	true	false
236. I brood a great deal.	false	true
238. I have periods of such great restlessness that I cannot sit long in a chair.	false	true
266. Once a week or oftener I become very excited.	false	true
272. At times I am all full of energy.	false	true
337. I feel anxiety about something or someone almost all the time.	true	false
339. Most of the time I wish I were dead.	true	false
342. I forget right away what people say to me.	true	false
372. I tend to be interested in several different hobbies rather than to stick to one of them for a long time.	true	false
374. At periods my mind seems to work more slowly than usual.	true	false
439. It makes me nervous to have to wait.	true	false
487. I feel like giving up quickly when things go wrong.	true	false

The first column shows the number and the text of the item discriminating between the two groups. The second column reports the Italian "type" response and the third column the Swiss "type" response.

the second variable permits a distinction between culturally different populations without making allowance for the presence or absence of a psychopathological condition. The calculation of the probability for every case to be classified in the four groups showed it to be much more probable that a subject diagnosed as depressed neurotic in Switzerland would be considered normal by an Italian psychiatrist, rather than the contrary. In other words, the diagnostic criteria of depressed neurotic psychopathology seem to be much stricter in a Swiss population than in an Italian one. It would actually seem that some manifestations of anxiety and depressive reactivity are tolerated more easily in an Italian context than in a Swiss.

The results of the content analysis make it possible to interpret the data from the discriminant analysis; in the two normal populations characteristic differential data appear when the analysis is carried out on the category of the affective contents selected according to the depression-excitement parameter.

In the Italian population there is a clear prevalence of basic traits of anxious depressive type: feelings of sadness, a pessimistic view of the future, psychomotor retardation, restlessness, and irritability seem to be more characteristic of the normal Italian population than of the normal Swiss population. Such a result is very interesting, since it appears in two populations unanimously defined as normal by observers of the same nationality, with average MMPI profiles within normal limits, with the same general shape, and without significant differences in the single scales, but where the discriminant analysis showed considerable differences.

The content analysis consequently made it possible to explain the data relative to the comparison of two psychiatric populations: since the psychiatrist is actually exposed to the same social and cultural pressures and conditioning as his patient, he tends to apply the same criteria of "psychopathological tolerance" to him as he does to himself; it thus happens that affective manifestations of the type listed above will be judged more normal in an Italian context and more deviant in a Swiss. The same emotional manifestations will tend to be judged differently and vice versa, even when the judges, as in the case of psychiatrists at university clinics in two European capitals, think of applying the same criteria of evaluation and measurement. This was known and the importance of our data lies in the indication of an objective method for evaluating the type and extent of such differences in order to allow observers of different origin to make correct evaluations of subjects coming from other populations than their own.

The method of the discriminant function actually makes it possible to compare many groups at the same time, when an objective measurement of the emotional state is available, such as that obtained by the MMPI. The item frequency endorsement will then make it possible to explain the differences met on the quantitative level by the qualitative evaluation of the contents.

Emotions—Their Parameters and Measurement,
edited by L. Levi.
Raven Press, New York © 1975

Communication and Generation of Emotion Through Essentic Form

Manfred Clynes

Sentic Research Laboratory, University of California at San Diego, La Jolla, California 92037 and Biocybernetic Institute, La Jolla

INTRODUCTION

In this chapter we are concerned with some aspects of the dynamic inherent relations between the expression of emotion and the emotional state. Subjective experience of emotion includes aspects of specific experience of expression; in addition, expression itself has a feedback effect on the state, that is not itself directly implied by the experience of the state. Both the dynamic and communicative aspects of expression, however, appear to be capable of scientific treatment through the methods described herein. The emotional states and its expression are treated together as one system in these methods.

Production and recognition of dynamic communicative forms, which we call essentic forms, are seen to be biologically programmed complementary functions of our nervous system.

In previous work involving the electrical activity of the brain, biologic channels of communication, and the nature of physiologic code for sensory quality, we noted aspects of precision in brain function representative of specific sensory qualities (particularly in color and visual field structure) (Clynes, 1969a,b,c, 1968a, 1967). Distinct spatiotemporal forms of electrical activity, as stable sequences, were observed for a specific quality such as red. These findings, independent of but complementary to the work of Hubel and Wiesel in animal studies, combined with the concepts of rein control and unidirectional rate sensitivity (Clynes, 1961, 1969, 1968b), which showed how biologic design proceeded to create opposite qualities from a single measure by providing two channels in a rein-like configuration (e.g., hot—cold, dark—light) to lead us to consider the possibility that other qualities, not associated directly with external inputs to the nervous system, might also be shown to have design aspects of precision. This was reinforced by the fact that many individuals, particularly artists and musicians, have regarded these qualities as more precise than the words we use to denote them.

The elusive question has been how this precision might be represented.

Association of mere quantity and of the "mechanical" with the specific qualities of these inner experiences has generally seemed rightly abhorrent. It can readily be seen that by assigning a number to such a quality the inherent connection to its identity is lost.

In expressing the nature of these qualities as unique spatiotemporal entities, however, a connection remains to the uniqueness of the quality in its representation. It is then possible to ask questions concerning the source of the stability of form observed, as it is possible to ask this of the form of the kidney or of the configuration of a molecule. And one may note how natural design has used such forms in achieving the possibility of emotion communication (Clynes, 1968, 1973; Alland, 1970; Byers, 1971; Greenbie, 1971).

What do the phenomena belonging to the possible class "emotion" have in common? In natural language, words have developed to denote certain entities that we feel belong to the class of emotions. Such words are joy, anger, love, grief. What kind of entities do these words represent?

Traditionally, it has been customary to study emotions as states (Schacter, 1962; Arnold, 1970; Levi, 1972). It has also been recognized that these states may be communicated through what is called "expression" (Piderit, 1858; Klages, 1923, 1950; Ekman, 1969). The latter, however, was generally investigated separately from the study of the state itself (Allport, 1933; Davitz, 1959). Through this separation, several difficulties arose. A main one was the neglect of the interaction between expression and the emotion state: a serious omission, since it appears that this interaction is not fortuitous, but is part of the very nature of the entity considered. This chapter takes the view that a specific emotion state, such as anger, and its dynamic expression form one system entity. This view holds that the expression of anger is specific to anger and is included in the brain algorithm program pertaining to anger; the same thing is true with respect to other emotion entities.

The words "emotion" and "feeling" have often been used almost interchangeably — the most systematic distinction being to regard emotion as intense whereas a slight emotion could well be called a feeling. An emotion could become out of control, a feeling could not. Clearly, some redefinition in terms of brain function processes is required if one is ever to deal with the phenomena of emotion in a precise way.

In this biocybernetic approach we endeavor to define an entity by its system properties. We may distinguish a class of "emotion" states where the state inherently demands to be expressed, and there is a programmed link between the state and motor function.

A second criterion that permits one to make distinctions is the ability of an expression to recreate a corresponding state in another individual; that is, the contagion of emotional communication (Maranon, 1924, 1950). There is a class of entities which have this potential power as a built-in function of our nervous system organization. It is a property of the expression of such a state that it has a generating function not only with respect to another individual, but also with respect to the individual who is expressing.

We have been interested in studying states that are capable of being communicated through expression. In order to avoid the confusion of terms of uncertain usage, we have called these states *sentic states,* derived from the Latin root "sentire," and have studied their specific expressive dynamic forms which we call *essentic forms.*

In order to study the interaction between the expression and the sentic state, a means was devised that permits a standardized form of expression, which, moreover, is not a cultural element in any known society and is convenient to perform. In choosing a particular mode of expression it was supposed that the specific expressive form for a particular entity, or sentic state, would be implicit in any expressive output modality, regardless of the motor action utilized; that is, a gesture of the arm or the foot or even the tone of voice would contain the dynamic signature that is perceived as the quality of anger. If this is correct, then any arbitrary motor output of a sufficient degree of freedom might be chosen and would reveal essential aspects of the dynamic forms we seek to find. Such a supposition may be called a principle of equivalence.

One would want to choose a mode of action which is convenient to measure and which also has sufficient degree of freedom to match those demanded by the expression (movement by the eyebrow, for example, has insufficient degree of freedom). These requirements are met in the use of transient pressure of a finger in a sitting position.

Generation of Sentic States and Generalized Emotion

Generation of the sentic state is accomplished in a very simple manner in our studies through a specific method of repeated expression of that same state. In initial studies (Clynes, 1968b) it was found that, after some time, a subject could express and generate these states without reference to specific content. For example, although at first it may have been useful for a subject to imagine being angry at a specific person, after some practice, he could express and generate anger without a specific situational imagery or a specific recipient for that emotion. Similarly, for other sentic states. At a third stage, the subject may find new fantasies arising but could also voluntarily choose to generate and express the emotion without any specific imagery. We have called the experience and expression of such emotion states "generalized emotion." It is possible, through the expression of specific dynamic form, to generate a state which is in itself, in certain aspects, indistinguishable from a similar state with a content-bound fantasy "cause" or fantasy "recipient." It became evident that one does not have to feel a "reason" to experience an emotion in this manner, and that one may enjoy all the emotions that may be so generated and expressed, in a manner that is well known to musicians and composers. This is rather freeing and is a basis for the therapeutic use of sentic cycles, which is described later. Experience of content-free emotions has an aspect that frees one from a form of slavery to emotions whereby one must wait for external "reasons," "causes," and "recipients" to experience a particular emotion. For example, many individuals who have found little reason for joy or love are able to experience these repeatedly through the generation process to be described.

Precision of Spatiotemporal Forms

Being primarily visually oriented, man's natural language has been heavily biased toward the recognition of spatial forms. Although we may today see that the reality of temporal forms is not inferior to that of spatial forms, and that indeed an existence such as that of the photon is inconceivable without a specific temporal process, natural language has seldom dignified those temporal forms that exist with appropriate names. Words such as sigh and caress are exceptions rather than the rule. There are many spatiotemporal forms in our experience, however, that display an extraordinary high degree of precision. Such precision is particularly manifest in the elements of expressiveness in music, in the tone of voice, and in gestures where slight deviations from a particular form are significant. The nervous system is programmed to recognize these forms with a resolution exceeding 0.01 sec.

The studies of this report are designed to examine the nature of this precision and to determine whether it is of biologic or cultural origin. Precision is also an essential factor in the communication of these states (both for auto- and cross-communication). Although previous studies of expressive movements were largely confined to denoting end points and verbal description (Birdwhistell, 1968; Ekman, 1969), our studies constitute an attempt at measuring the precision of the specific dynamic form. Our measurement results have been sufficiently accurate to make it possible to establish a differential equation capable of generating specific essentic forms observed.

In addition to studying the precision of the interaction between motor expressive forms and the sentic state, physiologic changes of respiration, of the cardiovascular system, and of oxygen metabolism were observed. These changes are quite separate from the experience of certain characteristic body sensations, which we call *virtual body images,* specific to each sentic state (such as a sensation of "flow" for love). The specific projected virtual body images (which include the direction and magnitude of gravitation as part of their character) are seen also to belong to the system entity of that state. Some aspects of body position and its kinesthetic experience also relate to specific sentic state entities.

Studies show that the practice of sentic state generation by this method with a series of states, called sentic cycles, appears to have an effect on dream and sleep processes and on the sense of elapsed time. There are psychic effects related to the drives, in particular with respect to aggression and to satisfaction, and to the sense of well-being (French, 1972).

The application of measures of essentic form to musical communication and composers has been outlined in earlier publications and was found to be fruitful (Clynes, 1969, 1970). (The concept of the "inner pulse" of composers, measured sentographically through thinking music, is described in these.) Much of the approach described here was derived from the expression and thinking of music (see also, Becking, 1928; Sievers, 1875–1915). The power of music to transform a person's state as a process requiring explanation underlies the nature of the inquiry. It seems that essentic forms, as elements of music, function mostly directly, rather than as a "symbol." For the experience of essentic form there appears to be no exclusively preferred sensory modality: essentic form does not have to be "translated" from one sensory modality into another, before it can exercise its function.

We cannot attempt in this place even an inadequate review of the past efforts in the study of expression. The scientific study of the qualities of expression, in spite of excellent work by many careful workers, still remains largely to be developed. The early history of studies of expression has been well reviewed by Klages (1923, 1950). His own studies of the specific character of expression show great care and discrimination, and he was intuitively aware of their characteristic entities. He was less in a position to consider the system interaction between the expression and the state and had no quantitive measurement techniques available. In studies of facial expression as a cross-cultural recognition function, Ekman (1969) has found that there were apparently universal characteristics of models of facial expression that were readily recognized. Birdwhistell (1968) and his school analyzed movements and postures in terms of social significance. In these studies detailed dynamic forms could not be systematically measured. In the study of dance movement Laban (1947, 1958) has devised a remarkable approach to the notation and production of expressive movement. His concept of "effort-shape" recognized the different preprogramming basis of movement according to the type of muscular effort involved, but no rigorous attempt is made to relate this to specific states and their dynamic expression in a precise way. Acoustic studies of the tone of voice as expressive quality have been largely unsuccessful so far due to the rather unsuitable techniques of spectral harmonic analysis used, which tend to underestimate and neglect transient phenomena essential in the communicative process (Moses, 1954; Tembrock, 1959; Thorpe, 1957; Starkweather, 1961). But, in observing the muscular action patterns involved in the vocal sound production a basis may be found to see the production of the essentic form in the tone of voice through a muscular action pattern that may be compared with that of the finger transient pressure, for the expression of a similar sentic state.

The remarkable work of ethologists in animal behavior, in particular

Lorenz and Eibl-Eibelsfeldt (1970) as modification of the direction taken
by Darwin (1872), the study of the genetic character of innate release
mechanisms, appears to be complementary to our studies.

METHODOLOGY AND MEASUREMENT TECHNIQUES

The following techniques are aspects that contribute to the method:
1. instruments developed: the sentograph, 2. position of the subject, 3. instructions given to the subject, 4. the development of a temporal program
of initiating signals, 5. observation of physiologic changes.

Special Measuring Instruments

An instrument, the sentograph, was developed which is capable of measuring the vertical and horizontal vector components of finger pressure,
against time, with a resolution of better than 5 g and a linear dynamic range
of 2,500 g. The earlier versions of this instrument used independently
mounted force transducers. The new form of the instrument uses a cantilever
arm of square cross-section horizontally mounted in a left-right direction.
Near the point of suspension, strain gauges are mounted on each face of the
cantilever. On the free end of the cantilever, a finger rest is mounted. This
is made of a plastic material, "gray" to the touch, that is, neither too smooth
nor of any noticeable texture, in order to avoid a specific touch stimulus or
irritation. The pressure is measured in a plane at right angles to the direction
of the cantilever arm, that is, vertically and in a horizontal direction toward
and away from the body. The deflection of the cantilever is slight; enough
to avoid the sensation of complete inflexibility, but not so large as to provide
a marked sensation of "give." The deflection is typically 0.25 mm/kg. The
diameter of the finger rest is 1 inch. Strain gauges mounted on opposite
pairs of faces of the cantilever are connected so as to be arms of a bridge
circuit, from which a FET amplifier derives a signal proportional to the
pressure. Two such bridge circuits and FET amplifiers provide the vertical
and horizontal measures of pressure. The output has a range of 10 V. The
natural resonance of the cantilever is around 500 Hz, and the frequency
response of the system is flat from DC to 50 Hz. (In practice a response
flat up to 10 Hz for such an instrument is sufficient.) Noise is less than 2 g
referred to the input, and drift less than 10 g per hour under room temperature conditions. The output is recorded on chart recorders.

The output is also fed to an averaging computer, similar in operation to a
CAT computer, which stores individual transient responses, and adds these
up, to obtain an average form. The period of each measurement is initiated
by the timing signal that also initiates the subject's expression. The period
normally is 2 sec. After each period, there is an interval in which no data
enter the computer, until the next initiating timing signal occurs. Several

hundred transients may be added in this way; but in practice from 10 to 50 and occasionally 100 transients are commonly used. There are 128 digital ordinate points for each transient measure, and two independent channels of analogue-digital conversion as well as digital to analogue conversion. Integrated circuit memory is used and analogue to digital conversion resolution is 8 bits, whereas digital to analogue conversion has a resolution of 12 bits. The accumulation of transients may be interrupted at any time, and the progressive average recorded, or the average may also be recorded concurrently with the accumulation of data on a separate channel.

The purpose of averaging the transients is to obtain a precise and reliable shape free from accidental variations of each individual act of expression. As in any repeated voluntary motor act, such as an attempt to hit an object with a ball, some deviations of the motor action occur. By averaging one tends to eliminate some effects of fluctuations of attention and other extraneous influences. Averaging is often not necessary, however, once the stable specific essentic forms have been recognized. Deviations may then be noted as they occur, analyzed, and studied.

Position of the Subject

Several considerations determine the adopted choice of position of the subject. It is desirable to keep an erect position of the spine. This appears to increase attention and avoid sleepiness, but, more importantly, it seems to allow a more consistent, better integrated communication path between fantasy and motor expression of the arm. A reclining position introduces kinesthetic effects that seem to counter some of the emotions studied (e.g., anger would incline a subject to sit upright if he is in a reclining position). The subject sits on a straight-backed chair without arm rest. (The arm rest would interfere with the free action of the arm in producing pressure transients.) A straight-backed chair is required to provide support for the back during states such as anger, the expression of which has a strong component of pressure away from the body. Without such support, muscle strain tends to develop in the back.

The subject sits on the chair with thighs supported horizontally and the legs resting on the ground with feet parallel and flat on the ground. (Legs should not be crossed.) For tall individuals, the height of the seat should be adjusted by cushions or otherwise so that the thighs are supported horizontally and do not project upward. It is advisable, also, to place a cushion behind the back, 10 to 20 cm below the shoulder, between the back and the back of the chair.

The subject uses his right arm if he is right-handed and the left arm if he is left-handed. The finger rest is placed slightly to the right so that the arm is parallel to the thighs and at the level of the chair seat or a little higher (but not on the same chair). The upper arm is slightly forward (but not outward) and the forearm slopes about 10 degrees downward. The position of the hand is as in Fig. 1a. Only the middle finger touches the finger rest. The other fingers are relaxed and do not touch anything. To enable this, the finger rest projects about 1 inch above the surrounding surface. During the measurement process, the finger remains in continuous contact with the finger rest. The contralateral hand rests on the lap or on the contralateral thigh. The subject is made to sit well back on the seat of the chair, so that his spine is straight. During the measurement, this position tends to be very stable, the body becomes very quiet, and the only changes in position that tend to occur are some rather slight changes in the orientation of the head. The tilt of the head (which varies with the state, but does not change during each separate expressive action) is a spontaneous and significant phenomenon.

Instructions Given to the Subject

The subject, after he has been positioned, is given quite simple instructions. He is asked to listen to the tape and told he will hear one word denoting a particular emotion, such as, anger or joy. After the spoken word, he will hear a series of timing signals; each signal is a soft tap and occurs every few seconds but at unpredictable times. Whenever he hears such a tap, he is to express, as precisely as he can, the character or quality of the state denoted by the word with a single pressure action only. He is to wait for the next tap before commencing another expression and to continue to express that state for each tap until another word is announced or no more taps are heard. Subjects need not necessarily be told the specific directions in which they may press. Occasionally, left-right movements of expressions are initially attempted. If this happens, the subject may be instructed to press away and toward the body, rather than left to right. But after a short practice, subjects generally feel it natural to express within the up-down and backward-forward plane. It appears that the phenomenon of dynamic expression is well represented by the dimensionality of one temporal and two spatial dimensions. (An additional spatial dimension, if available, tends to call for idiosyncratic behavior.) The subject is also instructed to keep his finger in touch with the finger rest throughout the measurement.

Since the subject is asked to be ready to express and yet not to express until he hears the tap, there is a (variable) waiting period of a few seconds between a completed expression and the next. The nature of this is discussed further in the next section.

The Timing of Initiating Signals

The specific timing of the initiating signals occupies a centrally important position in our method. It was found in early studies, that in order to obtain the most effective generation of states, the repetitive execution of expres-

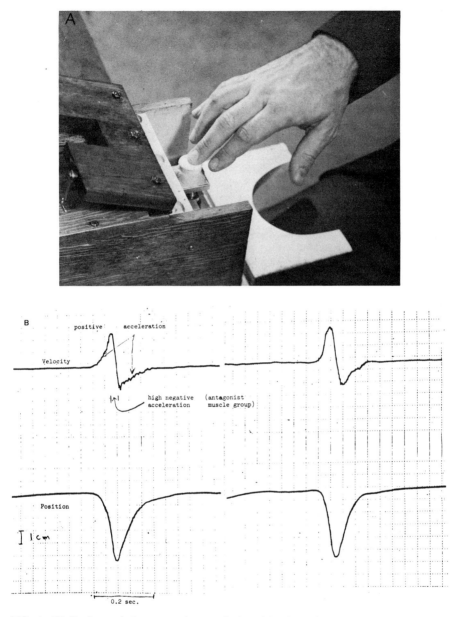

FIG. 1. (A) Sentograph for measuring vertical and horizontal components of transient pressure and touch transducer and arm position for the measurement of essentic form. Two strain-gauge transducers are mounted at right angles to one another on a square torsion bar of high stiffness, horizontally cantilevered in a left-right direction. The transducers are coupled into a FET high-impedance input state providing a frequency response essentially DC to 50 cycles. A special plastic touch surface is provided that is "gray" to the touch, i.e., does not itself cause tactile pleasure or irritability. (B) Impulse movement dynamics in a single nonexpressive movement of the finger. Note rapid switch from maximum positive to maximum negative velocity, a very significant aspect of preprogramming. Negative acceleration during this short phase is much larger than during the acceleration periods on either side (antagonist muscle group).

sion could not be "mechanical": a regular repetition rate was inimical to the generation of the state. Moreover, it was found that the degree of unexpectancy had to be within certain ranges to be effective. Too much variability would often become irritating, too little would stay in the range of expectancy. It was also found that the mean repetition rate would have to be different for each emotion state to be generated. Further, it turned out significantly that a repetition rate which appeared near optimal for one individual would also tend to be optimal for another individual.

Accordingly, considerable effort went into developing suitable sequences of timing signals. At first, it was thought that a purely random deviation from a mean would be the most consistently effective. Both Gaussian and Poisson distributions were tried. After several years, however, it was rather belatedly realized that random sequences in this mode of application are not really equivalent. Some random series start with shorter intervals and some with longer. It was clearly important how the first few expressions began. The development of a series became more like working on a sculpture or the work of a composer. The aim is to provide an unexpectedness without causing irritation, jolting, or excessive waiting.

In the development of sentic cycles, moreover, it was important to devise suitable bridges, at the beginning of each new state, of two or three expressions.

The sequence of signals is, in effect, a kind of biological tempo rubato and this function may not be unrelated to the requirement for deviations from strict metronomic timing in music. The rate of repetition allows for a pause between the completion of an expression and the beginning of the next. During this time, for a certain period, one tends to feel a mounting urgency or increase of the intensity of the state.

The converse of the above relationship can be used, as we have done recently, to devise an objective numerical index for the measurement of intensity. Since a strict or "mechanical" rhythmic repetition rate served to attenuate the intensity of the state at a given point, one may switch to such a pattern of timing signals at this point to gradually diminish the intensity until threshold is reached, at which time the subject indicates he no longer feels the state, the number of repetitions required for this being an index of intensity at the point in question.

Observations of Physiologic Changes

The method readily permits the measurement of various physiologic changes since the subject is sitting quietly. There is no difficulty in measuring such variables as respiration, heart rate, and EEG. We have measured respiration through transducers placed around the chest sensitive to stretch; a rubber tube filled with carbon powder attached to a bridge circuit has proved to be reliable. This is preferable to having the subject breathe into a mask or other device in front of his mouth as this tends to interfere with the spontaneity of expression. A similar transducer may be placed abdominally. Heart rate is measured from cardiographic leads. EEG electrodes have been used in various configurations both for measuring averaged potentials with CAT computers and for studying the ongoing EEG. Neurodata symmetry analyzers have also been used to test the correlation of left and right hemispheres, and front to back, and to investigate changes in these correlations with different states. The EEG has been analyzed for harmonic content and also for the presence of unusual patterns. In a few cases we have measured oxygen consumption by means of a mask leading to a standard Beckman respiration analyzer, measuring both oxygen and carbon dioxide.

Other physiologic changes may be observed visually if not instrumentally. These include crying or flushing. The position of the head and any unusual movements may be noted through a closed circuit TV monitor.

Muscle action patterns have been recorded from EMG electrodes on four pairs of muscles, on the forearm, an upper arm, shoulder, and at times from the back. The EMG's are rectified and integrated with a time constant of 0.01 sec. Muscle tension in the abdomen is also studied in some cases but not recorded in this manner.

The muscle tension variations are noted during the transients of expressive pressure (E-actons), but there are also aspects of steady muscular tension patterns related to the state.

The direction of gaze is also of significance and is noted.

Techniques are under development for measuring biochemical and hormonal changes, including lactate.

THEORETICAL CONSIDERATIONS

In the course development of sentic communication theory, a number of new concepts arose. As these studies progressed, these concepts in turn facilitated further development. We will briefly examine these concepts; they have been described more fully in the references cited.

Acton

A voluntary movement consists of a decision and its execution. Simple voluntary movements (such as, finger or eye movements) have clear beginnings and ends and a duration of approximately 0.2 sec (Fig. 1b). Such a movement is an example of organic system behavior incorporating both mental and physiologic processes. The execution of the act reflects the decision. The action together with its command decision constitutes an existential entity which we call an acton. During the execution of an acton the program governing the execution cannot be altered. It is preprogrammed by the brain before it begins, with appropriate instructions of where to stop.

The corresponding muscle systems are brought into play in a coordinated manner, so as to accelerate, decelerate, and stop the movement in the required manner. During the course of this preprogramming (0.2 sec) there is no time for feedback to affect the course of the movement. A separate decision altering the course of such a movement can only be made at the earliest 0.2 sec after a previous decision. Although the minimum duration of an acton is 0.2 sec, the preprogramming may be extended over a longer period of time than this (up to several seconds).

An expressive movement is considered to be modulated by the state that seeks to be expressed. The modulation process affects the dynamic course of the acton. We call such an acton an E-acton. The dynamic course appears to be particular to the state to be expressed and the duration is also different for each state.

Aspects of the neurophysiologic basis of the preprogramming of actons are known (especially through the study of eye movements), and involvement of the cerebellum in the computation process has been specially delineated by Eccles (1969).

Idiolog

In the execution of an acton the prerequisite for a clear execution is a clear idea. If one aims a ball at an object, unless one has a clear idea of what object one wishes to strike, the arm cannot be appropriately directed.

In the same way an expressive command to produce an E-acton presupposes an "idea" of the state to be expressed. Such an idea is not, in general, verbal. There is a high degree of precision with which one can imagine a particular quality entity, for example, the shade of a color or the quality combined with the specific brain processes that makes this an *idiolog* (as distinguished from the perception of it). Thus a person who imagines red creates an idiolog of red in his brain, and we will also say that a person who thinks of the quality of anger creates an idiolog of anger. An idiolog then is part of the process of imagination. We can have an idiolog of a movement, of a sensation, of a sentic state. The concept of an "image" as used by psychologists studying imaging is similar to this, in many respects.

In a voluntary action the precision of the action depends on the specificity of the idiolog. It seems that there exists what may be called a spectrum of emotions and that the precision of our expression is related to the clarity of our idiolog of these. Moreover, experimental evidence makes it appear that the greater this precision, the more effective is the communicative process. That is to say, the power of communication is a form function. The recognition process, as also in molecular biology, has aspects of key and lock functioning. Like a key in a lock, so does essentic form seem to fit data processing locks of our nervous system. The closer the essentic form produced is to the precise shape demanded by the state to be expressed, the more powerfully does it act to generate that state.

Elogize

It should be pointed out that the word "imagination" is biased toward the visual sense. A sound, an odor, or a taste may be imagined as readily as a visual quality. When we say to an individual to "imagine anger," he first tends to incorporate visual images. In part, this is the result of the visual bias of the word "imagine." It was found useful to use a word "elogize" to denote the process of imagination whereby a particular quality is imagined. A person may thus elogize a sound, a color, a taste, or the quality of a sentic state. Its use deemphasizes superfluous visual associations in "imagining" qualities.

Production of Essentic Form Is a Single Channel System

It was observed at an early stage that the expression of essentic form is a single channel system: only one sentic state could be expressed at any one time. It is not possible to use different parts of the body to express different sentic states and to experience them simultaneously. This also is in accord with the observations of Bull (1950), who under hypnosis tried to induce different affects simultaneously, without success.

E-ACTON PROPERTIES

Form

Through the method of transient finger pressure, one can observe for each state, a special dynamic form of expression. Some properties of these forms are illustrated in Figs. 2–5 and Table 1 and are typical for our observation of 80 adult subjects measured in this way.

It is noted that the essentic forms as observed in this manner have vector properties. There is a specific angle as well as magnitude of the pressure as a function of time. The direction of the vector is rather constant for each dynamic expression and, for most states, changes only slightly during the expression. The tangent of the angle is given by the instantaneous ratio of the vertical and horizontal components of pressure. Anger and hate have outward components of pressure toward the body. Reverence is slightly outward. (In hate, there tends to be a slight change in the angle during the course of the expression. This is related to the secondary, late muscular action characteristic for this state.)

Some actons display a late, secondary muscular action (see Fig. 3). These

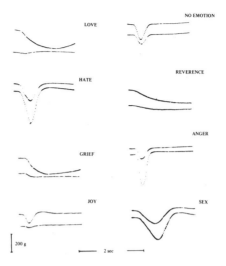

FIG. 2. Sentograms of the essentic forms of emotions: upper trace for each emotion is the vertical component of transient pressure, lower trace the horizontal component (at twice the scale). Each form is measured as the average of 50 actons. The subtle differences in the forms are as significant (e.g., between love and grief) as the more obvious ones.

late muscular actions occur approximately 0.7 sec after the beginning of the acton and are characteristic of certain "passionate" states in which there is a late developing tension in the acton. These actons contrast with the free character of other actons in which there is no late developing tension (e.g., joy, anger).

Duration

E-Actons of specific sentic states have characteristic durations. If we compare a "mechanical" impulse movement such as a single action on a typewriter, with the duration of an E-acton, we see that the duration of some of these is considerably extended. The duration of a love acton is at least 2.2 sec and may be considerably longer. Typical figures for minimum duration of E-actons are as follows: anger 0.7, joy 0.9, love 2.2, hate 1.2, grief 2.5 sec.

In the completion of the expressive act one is aware of a specific quality of that act, as a unit. There is also a minor sense of satisfaction.

Blocking

If an E-acton is not allowed to complete itself, we observe a phenomenon which we may call a *blocking* of the state. The experience of the state ceases quite abruptly and one experiences instead a sense of irritation or frustration. In a specific sense this blocking is also a kind of repression. An incom-

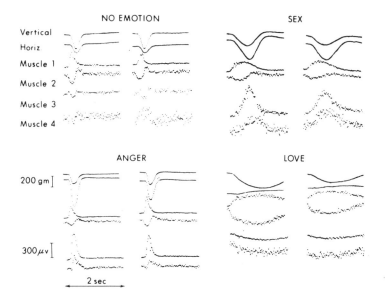

FIG. 3. Sentograms of essentic forms as vertical and horizontal components of finger pressure; also four groups of muscle potentials integrated and rectified with a time constant of 0.01 sec. Each group is the average of 50 actons. Muscle potentials are recorded from the forearm, upper arm, front shoulder, and back, respectively. Groups represent repeated recording from the same individual, showing the stability of the patterns. "No emotion" consists of a mechanical movement such as used for typewriting. In "anger" there is a marked accentuation of the horizontal component, indicating a tendency for the acton to be outward, away from the body. The type of anger illustrated here is more akin to irritability than to resentment. The "slow burning" type of anger has a different pattern which is not illustrated here. The characteristic shape for "love" (not sexual) shows a longer curved acton, often with a slightly reversed horizontal component indicating a pulling inward or embracing mode of behavior. The muscle actions reflect the differences of the essentic form. The preprogrammed time of the acton for love is considerably longer. The characteristic form for sex shows a strong secondary thrust with emphasized late muscle activity. This secondary thrust is a characteristic of the purely sexual expression and is analogous to the vocalized expressive effect of the syllable ur*nh*.

plete acton tends to result in an unpleasant sensation, regardless of the nature of the state expressed. It is as frustrating to interrupt an anger or hate acton, as a joy or love acton.

In a succession of expressive actons an ongoing E-acton must be completed before another may be started without blocking.

Predictions of Acton Theory

If we combine this last property with the principle that only one sentic state can be expressed at any one time, we can predict some interesting properties of E-actons. If we consider the possibility of expression of a sentic state with more than one motor output, then we could predict that an additional output modality could only begin a new expression of an

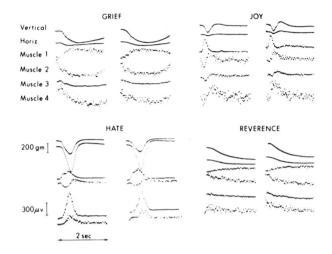

FIG. 4. Typical sentograms of the essentic form of grief, joy, hate, and reverence, respectively: Note the strong outward (negative horizontal) component of hate, the late muscle acceleration in muscle 2, indicating a secondary thrust, a characteristic of passion. The response to grief has similarity to the love form but is flatter and slightly outward. Muscular action of grief is related to an induced general lassitude, and the subject does not actively lift the released pressure, the opposite of joy. In joy there is rebound with overshoot, related to a floating sensation, a "jumping for joy" effect. Reverence has general similarity to love, but on a longer time scale and less toward the body. The preprogramming of the acton is extended in time. Respiration is slowed and the acton is preferably carried out on expiration. The latter is also true of hate and grief, but not of joy, which may be frequently done on inspiration.

E-acton, after completion of a previous E-acton begun in another output modality. There can be no phase overlap of actons executed with different modalities, even of the same sentic state.

Such a prediction, in fact, is easily confirmed. For example, if one attempts to express an E-acton with the other arm, while executing an E-acton with one arm, blocking invariably occurs. It is necessary to wait for the completion of the E-acton begun with one arm before another can be started with the other arm.

This is also true for the "tone of voice" as a distinct output modality.

One may, however, join an ongoing E-acton with additional output modalities, provided that these join at the current phase of the acton, so that the remaining fraction of the ongoing E-acton is completed together. The additional modality completes only a fraction of the acton and ends together in phase with the first modality. The tone of voice used needs to have a very different course if it begins during an ongoing acton than if it starts with the acton and corresponds to whatever fraction of the acton remains. In this aspect it behaves somewhat like a voice in a piece of music which enters after a rest.

In changing the sentic state, a substantial change can take place only

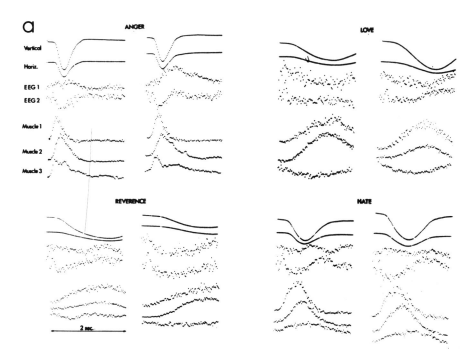

FIG. 4a. Examples of essentic form production on two occasions of another subject (F, 24 yrs.) showing also averaged EEG potentials, in addition to pressure transients and rectified EMGs. EEG traces are left parietal-frontal and parietal-occipital leads. (Average of 50 transients.)

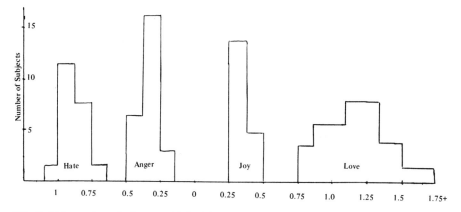

FIG. 5. Values of peak time multiplied by vertical/horizontal ratio for 30 subjects aged 20–47 (15 male, 15 female) showing separation without overlap for the four emotions hate, anger, joy, and love. This graph illustrates that it is easily possible to find simple measures that will discriminate specific emotion curves. However, this type of analysis does not do justice to the specific forms of the curves (i.e., the quality of the data). The parameters of the differential equation define the curve characteristics.

TABLE 1. *Correlation of vertical components of essentic forms of E-actons*

Essentic forms	MC2/MC1	EN/MC1	GB/MC1
Anger	0.927	−0.224	0.928
Hate	0.824	0.973	0.779
Grief	0.769	0.815	0.775
Love	0.951	0.827	0.702
Sex	0.966	0.779	0.867
Joy	0.994	0.827	0.917

Same individual on two separate occasions (MC2/MC1) and between two subjects (EN/MC1 and GB/MC1). Note the generally high correlations. Levels of significance are at the $p < 0.0001$ level. Note the small correlation of anger in the second column. This subject displayed a different form of anger—which we may call "slow burning type" as compared with irritability—a different essentic form, but commonly described by the same word. Cross correlations between different essentic forms were generally lower than 0.300.

after the completion of an acton. A change experienced during an acton appears to relate primarily to the intensity of its respective state.

The property or tendency for the state to continue in its quality during the expression of an E-acton plays a role in the continued generation and experience of a particular state.

Prediction of a New Form of Laughter

The coherence between dynamic expressive form and subjective experience of which these properties are also aspects finds a rather remarkable confirmation in the predictions that sentic theory is able to make concerning laughter (Clynes, 1974).

Laughter is readily seen to have two dynamic components: a voice component and a breathing component. But, according to sentic theory, the voice output may be regarded as one of a number of possible motor output modalities. The sentic theory predicts therefore that it should be possible to replace the voice component by a similar dynamic expression using finger pressure, as long as one does not change the breathing dynamic component. That is, one would produce the same "chopped" breathing as one produces during laughter, and not accompany this with the usual chopped voice sound, but instead of the voice sounds, a repeated pressure exertion with the finger (in an up and down direction) would accompany the breathing pattern, at a rate similar to the frequency of the chopped voice pattern, i.e., approximately five per second. In fact, it is readily confirmed that when one combines such repeated finger pressure simultaneously with the chopped breathing pattern corresponding to laughter, we can indeed experience laughter—even to the extent of paroxysms of laughter. (Either the breathing pattern or the finger pressure pattern alone does not provide the sensation of laughter.)

The coherence between the expressive pattern in this case and the sensation of "funniness" is direct and immediate. Sentic theory has made it possible to predict a new form of laughter (a voiceless laughter) and at the same time, demonstrate the coherence between the expressive output form and inner experience, in a new, convincing, and unambiguous way. Also, the angle of finger pressure appears to be related to the quality of the laughter, e.g., vertically up-down—merry; down and outward—malicious; toward the body—sardonic. These angles can be compared to the angle for joy—vertical.

Generating Function

In examining the manner in which a sentic state is produced, maintained, and discharged in our method consider the function of the word that indicates the state and is announced at the beginning of each sentic state. The word sets the stage. This is more than an arbitrary metaphor. The concept underlying the word continues to exercise a function after it is spoken. This function is by itself not usually sufficient to maintain or generate the state to any marked degree. When combined, however, with the expression of E-actons, a self-centering (in control system terminology) process appears to occur in which there is a continuing focus on the quality of the state.

Consider the behavior of an individual who decides to go to a certain place in a building. He will go through the appropriate paths, turns, elevators, without constantly repeating to himself his initial decision. In the production of a sentence, too, a succession of processes and phenomena takes place through generative processes that are not directed in conscious detail and yet derive from an "idea." The word denoting the emotion which is spoken casts a kind of shadow, and we may say, in good part, an unconscious shadow. The form of expression appears to function as a mold into which associations may readily fall; but it also acts as a filter which will attract only a particular type of association.

The concept of the word, combined with the repeated expression, and the variable waiting periods between successive expressions, acts through feedback in a self-steering manner that results in the experience becoming more specific rather than more diffuse. As the state becomes more intense with repeated expression, it also becomes more centered. The state acquires an inertia.

This course, however, does not continue indefinitely. A degree of satiety sets in after some time. There occurs a decay of the intensity, and we observe what appears to be a refractive period for that specific sentic state.

One "has had enough of it." The duration after which this occurs varies with the state but is of the order of 3 to 5 min.

Although one is satiated with one state, one is nevertheless quite fresh for another, different sentic state. This is an interesting phenomenon in itself. It can be considered, also, as an indication of the separateness of the components of the emotional spectrum.

Change of State: Sentic Fluidity

A change to a new sentic state is accomplished by the announcement of another word denoting that state. This is best done from an outside source, rather than by the subject himself. In order to initiate the state himself, he would have to monitor the timing and experience of his previous state in a way that interferes with its experience. The ability to shift to another state with ease, which we call "sentic fluidity," is a significant function. In subjects of good mental health there tends to be a high degree of sentic fluidity. Individuals with certain emotional problems tend, at time, to get "stuck" in a particular sentic state and have relative difficulty in leaving it. With practice, however, the sentic fluidity improves, and there occurs an evening of the emotional spectrum in this respect. It is found with subjects, in general, that the ease of switching sentic states is progressively increased with practice of the method. This ability is experienced as an enjoyable and constructive one. In some ways one may regard this as a kind of emotional training.

Mathematical Equations for Essentic Form

The essentic forms determined experimentally may be described by a single generating differential equation of physiologic significance, with different parameters determining specific essentic forms. The equation was devised with the aid of analogue computer simulation. The differential equation whose solutions for impulse function inputs are the various essentic forms is given in Laplace transform notation as:

$$\frac{U(s)}{I} = b\left(\frac{\tau_1\tau_2\tau_3 s}{(1 + \tau_1 s)(1 + \tau_2 s)(1 + \tau_3 s)}\right)\left(\frac{\tau_4 s}{1 + \tau_4 s} + \Omega k \frac{\tau_5}{(1 + \tau_5 s)}\right)$$

where s is the Laplace transform; $U(s)$ is the Laplace transform of $u(t)$, the essentic form; I is an input impulse; τ_1, τ_2, etc. are time constants, parameters that have characteristic or eigenvalues for each specific emotion; k_p is "passion coefficient" (positive for hate, sex; zero for love, joy, reverence); Ω is the unidirectionally rate-sensitive operator (Clynes, 1961, 1969) that has the value 1 for $du/dt \geq 0$; 0 for $du/dt < 0$.

The input to the equation is an impulse function. This appears to be the most natural form of input to use and on a certain level corresponds in form to the idea of an "impulse" to express an emotion. The input impulse function results in the various output essentic forms according to specific solutions of the differential equations. The equation contains two parts. The second part of the equation, invoked for the "passionate" states, provides the late secondary muscular effort described before. It has the form of a unidirectionally rate-sensitive operator channel. Its action begins at a point near the maximum excursion of the first term of the equation.

The set of parameters for all emotions may also be thought of as eigenvalues of a determining equation whose vector space has a number of properties to be described.

Vector Space of Parameters

The multidimensional vector space of the parameters of equation 1 determining the separate emotions is found to have a butterfly-type configuration. In each multidimensional region a combination of certain vectors is possible according to a certain general division into positive and negative classes, e.g., joy belonging to the positive class will not mix with anger belonging to the negative class; grief will mix with either love or anger. The positive and negative class is in accordance with the experimentally determined horizontal component of pressure strongly away from the body, as in anger and hate, and negative-infolding toward the body, or only slightly outward, as in love. In the vector space, combinations appear to be possible within each region, but not across. To proceed from one region to the other one must traverse through the region of the origin.

A part of the equation turns out to be similar to the physiologically determined "human operator" transfer function

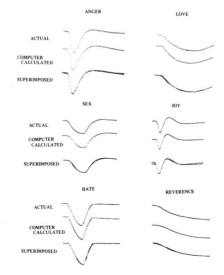

FIG. 6. Measured and computed essentic forms.

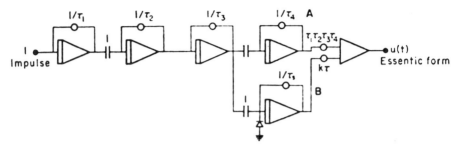

FIG. 7. Analogue computer simulation circuit for realizing essentic forms for the expression of different emotions according to equation 1.

$$K \frac{se^{-\tau_3 s}}{(1 + \tau_1 s)(1 + \tau_2 s)}$$

as determined for tracking tasks, for example, with an additional time constant. The second part is the sum of an adaptive and a unidirectionally rate-sensitive term.

The generating function is nonlinear and multiplication is noncommutative. That means the input to the transfer function in the second bracket must be considered the output of the transfer function in the first bracket and not the reverse.

The decision to express, or the act of will, is represented in this model by the input impulse function. Analytically, the output of the linear portion of the equation is represented by a sum of four exponentials as functions of time, with $t = 0$ at the time of the input (these have independent time constants but interdependent amplitude coefficients, since the input is always an impulse function). The nonlinear aspect of the equation has no known analytic solution but is easily determined on a computer (Fig. 6–8).

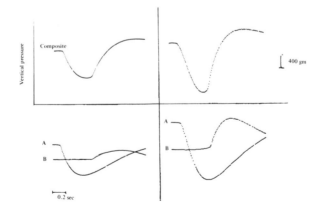

FIG. 8. Components of computer essentic form simulation showing separate contribution of portions A and B of transfer function. B represents effects of late acting muscle group.

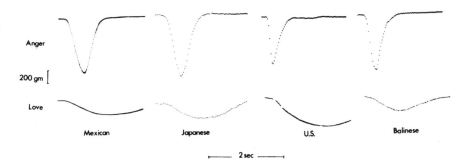

Anger

200 gm

Love

Mexican   Japanese   U.S.   Balinese

—— 2 sec ——

FIG. 9. Comparison of the essentic forms of love and anger in four cultures, Mexican, Japanese, American and Balinese. (Vertical component shown.) Similarities of the sentograms are apparent. Differences between individuals are typically of about the same order as variation between cultures.

Anthropologic Studies

In order to test the question of biologic versus cultural influence on the determination of the essentic form, studies were carried out on 60 subjects in Bali, Indonesia, Kyoto, Japan, and a preliminary study in Mexico, using the same techniques. These studies showed that the individuals in these

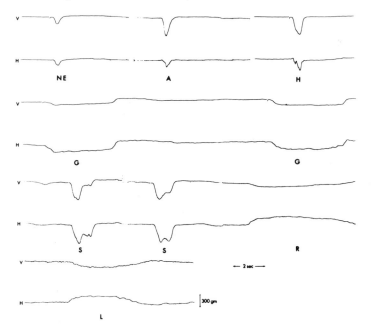

FIG. 10. Examples of single E-actons of various emotions recorded by a Balinese subject, female, age 24. Tape-recorded data were replayed on a strip chart recorder. These selected examples show the character of the raw data before averaging. Initials below actons stand for emotions expressed: no emotion, anger, hate, grief, sex, reverence, and love.

cultures had no difficulty in carrying out the method and obtained essentially similar results. An example of the results is shown in Figs. 9 and 10. Variations between cultures were of the same order as those within a group. Some interesting observations were gained in respect to the precise nature of the words denoting emotion in common usage: the Balinese language has no word for hate. The anthropologic studies can not be considered in detail here, however.

"Mechanical" Is Found to Be a Cultural Concept

A "no emotion" phase of 50 actons is first used in an attempt to obtain a base line. In this we have normally instructed the subject to act "mechanically" (as if typing, say). The speed with which a subject naturally executed a "mechanical" action was by no means constant across cultures. We found Mexicans considerably slower than Americans, Japanese as fast or faster, and, surprisingly, the Balinese seemed to have no available concept of "mechanical" at all. I suppose this is surprising only to the ignorant, but it was remarkable that we have become so culturally impregnated by the concept of "mechanical" that we did not notice in our original formulation that although "mechanical" is par excellence not a natural essentic form, it also is culturally conditioned! Hence here the cross-cultural results were quite different (except for the similarity between Japanese and Americans). This seemed in a minor way a rather nice, if unexpected, confirmation of our approach.

Attempts at Retraining of Essentic Form

Another way to test the nature of essentic form and its programming by the brain is to attempt to retrain the essentic form so that the form of anger is used to express love, and vice versa, for example. It is found that such attempts invariably fail.

These various considerations tend to be in accordance with the view that there appears to be a symbiotic functioning of the nervous system in producing and recognizing essentic form, similar to the symbiosis between the production and recognition of syllables of speech, but probably, in large part, of earlier evolutionary origin.

Effectiveness of Generation of Emotion

How effective is the present method in its emotion-generating function? And how do these states correspond to emotions in real life situations? As a general comment, it is remarkable how effective the method of generating emotions is. Subjects are all able to experience at least some of the emotions of the sentic cycle on first trial. After three trials the effectiveness, as reported by the subject in terms of which emotions they could feel, is well over 90%. Subjects who may have had difficulties with one or two of the states at first find that this difficulty diminishes with subsequent trials. Self-scoring indices, in which a subject scores himself $\frac{1}{2}$ hr after the completion of the cycle concerning the intensity of the separate emotions experienced on a scale from 0 to 5, give an average intensity of emotions from 400 subjects as 3.8. Subjects on the average tend to have least problems with anger, rarely with grief and sex, more with hate, love, and joy in that order. Difficulties are most often experienced with reverence, an emotion that perhaps half the subjects are "out of touch" with. It is usual in these subjects, however, to find scores for this rising from 0 or 1 to 3 or 4 after three trials. If instructions are misunderstood and subjects do not modulate their touch, they also report that they do not experience the states, but they feel boredom instead. Near optimal mean time between initiating signals was 4.8 sec for anger, 5.3 for hate, 8.2 for grief, 7.4 for love, 4.9 for sex, 5.2 for joy, 9.8 for reverence. Standard deviation of successive times of initiating ranges from 0.6 to 0.9 sec and is proportionately somewhat less for the longer periods.

The method of measuring intensity of a state at a given point by switching to a repetitive mode of initiation (which decreases the intensity progressively) and counting the number of repetitions required to reach threshold is being used now to round or supplement the theory, which until now had no objective criterion for the intensity of a state.

Point of View

In the process of imagination or of elogizing as we should say now, the "point of view" is an important functional aspect. It may be differentiated according to whether idiologs are viewed (1) from the point of view of "actor" or of "spectator." This difference is particularly clear in dreams, where we may sometimes be actors and sometimes spectators. Idiologs are experienced differently as a part of an acting or of a spectator phase. Depending on this, the process of fantasy is different. (2) As action in the present, or not. We may have idiologs dealing with action in the present, those of reminiscences of the past, or those of a future time. These distinctions are also of special significance in the meaning and experience of music.

Sentic cycles' special method of fantasizing and expression with actons is conducive to the point of view of "action in the present." But, as a subject becomes more activated, the various emotions may then be elogized with a measure of empathic detachment. (Note that the "spectator point of view" does not refer to inaction but to a "knowing," "viewed" mode of action.) Generally, a subject, in the course of an hour of sentic cycles, undergoes a change in point of view from actor toward spectator. The change is subtle, and the detachment does not tend toward indifference but toward empathy.

We may differentiate among three extreme modes of sources of acton modulation: detached mimicry, sentically involved action, and empathic spectator.

In the process of experiencing sentic cycles one may tend to begin as mimic, proceed to the action phase, and end as "empathic spectator," as a natural transformation of the "point of view" that occurs in the process.

In this transformation the sentic drive first becomes connected to the output modality, and then becomes "viewed" while at the same time one is aware of its quality—i.e., one becomes a "spectator" within oneself. To be a spectator in this way also implies a point of rest, of sentic freedom from which this is possible.

This shift is also parallel to the distinction between the Dionysian and Apollonian experience of emotion, a distinction that has had repercussions throughout history, in the history of the study of emotion and feeling as well as in the history of music.

In life there is constant interplay between degrees of sympathy, in the sense of emotional contagion and empathy. Sympathetic resonance alone without empathy often tends toward sentimentality, if not brutality. Empathy elogizes the total individual, even while a specific emotion is expressed and recognized. It requires an element of the "spectator" point of view. These differences are experienced with increasing clarity in the course of sentic cycle experience. How these differences are reflected in aspects of different physiological changes remains to be determined. There are many different types of crying, for example. At this time, however, we must content ourselves with the observation that some 23% of subjects cry during the phase of grief, the very first time they experience sentic cycles.

Virtual Body Images

As a subject generates a state with repeated expression of E-actons, he also experiences continuing sensations apart from the experience of the separate expressive acts. These continuing sensations (which may be called steady-state sensations), in contrast with the transient expression, are of characteristic (quasi)-kinesthetic quality. The sensations are quite different for each state. They cannot be described in detail in this chapter, but brief descriptions will be given. Thus, for love there is a sensation of flow appearing to come from within the torso, flowing outward to the limbs and through the neck. There is a steady sensation of such flow, without a sense of diminution of any substance at the region from which the flow appears to originate. There appears to be no actual physiologic process giving rise to this body image; changes in blood flow do not correspond to this feeling. Of course, there is no substance that actually flows in the way that is felt.

Similarly, joy produces a specific sense of lightness and floating, anger has a characteristic sensation that feels as if the body is tending to be torn apart, grief induces a sensation of heaviness, a state of collapse of the motor system. In reverence there is some sense of loss of boundary of the body.

These are not physiologic visceral processes, yet they are very specific and consistent. Our method of repeatedly generating these states makes it readily possible to observe these body images with a special focus, since the rest of the body, apart from the pressure exertion, becomes very quiet. We conclude from these observations that these images are projections of the nervous system. They project a sensation into space, such as accomplished by the sense of hearing and of vision (we do not sense at the retina, or normally at the eardrum), a capacity which is available to other sense modalities under certain circumstances, as has been demonstrated by Bekesy (1967). Bekesy was able to produce a sensation of touch 5 to 8 feet away from the body by phasing two vibrators placed on the chest some distance apart in a manner similar to stereophonic hearing of the two ears. (He could make the sensation of touch move about outside the body in space, depending on the relative phases of the two vibrators.)

We propose that the above mentioned sensation of flow, and other specific qualities characteristic of each separate sentic state are virtual body images, specifically programmed into the nervous system. These images in fact, include the direction of gravitation.

In addition to these virtual body images there may of course be sensations of actual physiologic change, such as, abdominal tension in anger and hate, crying, changes in the sexual organs. Some of these changes are perceived in a different characteristic manner, depending on the sentic state within which they occur. (For example, tears during the state of grief have a very different sensation from the tears produced by an irritation of the eye. But, as has been pointed out by the critics of the James-Lange theory, they are not synchronized in time with the initial emotion state and cannot in themselves be taken to represent the nature of the emotion.)

Corresponding to the actor or spectator point of view (or Dionysian and Apollonian expression) there appear to be also distinct corresponding virtual body images for each state.

The theory of virtual body images for specific sentic states in some ways appears to reconcile some aspects of the different viewpoint of traditional theories of emotion, as represented by the polar opposites of the James-Lange and Cannon theories and their offshoots.

The ability to generate emotion through initially focusing on a concept may be regarded in the perspective of the studies on cognitive labeling undertaken by Schacter and Singer (1962). These studies have indicated that injection of epinephrine, producing an arousal state, will tend to predispose an individual to be in an emotional state, without specifying what state, and that an additional influence is required to induce a specific emotion state, an influence they have called labeling. Our studies show that it is possible to begin by "labeling" and to produce sentic states which may in turn have hormonal consequences.

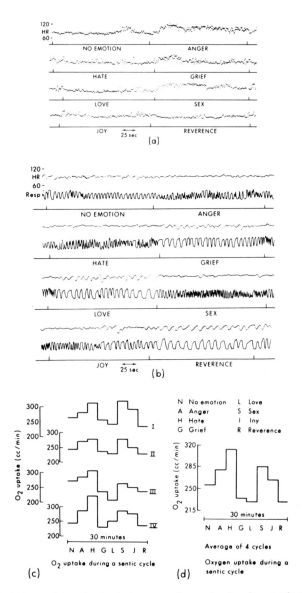

FIG. 11. (a) Variations of heart rate during a sentic cycle showing marked increases in heart rate, especially during anger and sex. Markers indicate the time when each new state is announced to the subject. (b) Changes in respiration and heart rate during a sentic cycle. Respiration accelerates during anger and hate. During grief, the respiration has a gasping character, with rest periods at the expiratory end of the cycle. Respiration slows during love and speeds up markedly for sex. It is particularly noteworthy that during reverence there is a marked slowing down of respiration with resting phases at the inspiratory phases of the cycle (*cf.* at the expiration phases for grief). Heart rate cycles in the subject are related to respiration. This subject shows otherwise less deviation in heart rate than the subject in the lower figure. (c) Oxygen consumption for four sentic cycles of the same subject show consistent changes in oxygen consumption between the various sentic states. Changes in all four cycles are in the same direction for corresponding states, except for one step between grief and oxygen consumption. Respiration rate and oxygen consumption are related. (d) Average of the four cycles shown in part c.

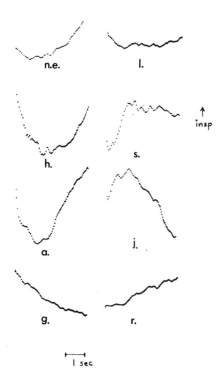

FIG. 12. Typical average transient respiration forms during E-actons for no emotion, love, hate, sex, anger, joy, grief, and reverence, respectively. Average of 20 actons. (Averaging began 0.5 sec after click.)

Respiration Patterns

Interestingly, in the respiration patterns during sentic state phases we may discern a relationship both with the state and with the specific expression. Respiration is a special motor system and presents a seemingly unique combination of voluntary and involuntary action. Figure 11 illustrates the changes in respiratory patterns with different sentic states. Figure 12 illustrates the preferred respiratory transient forms for the expression of each E-acton.

In so far as respiration is a motor output modality, one may also try to use it as a mode of expression in the place of finger pressure (Clynes, 1973).

Sentic Correlates in the Electric Activity of the Brain

In examining the electric activity as recorded from scalp electrodes, there are three kinds of phenomena that may be investigated. One is the change in electric activity occurring at the time of expression; this, like sensory-evoked potentials, needs to be averaged in order to be measured. Second, there are changes of the ongoing electric activity, i.e., the EEG, during various sentic states in sentic cycles. Some of these changes are very large and may be detected clearly by the eye.

love   n.e.

——— 2sec ———

FIG. 13. Average changes in brain potentials during the expressions of love and also during "no emotion." Essentic form of love is reflected in the top trace, representing the left frontal lead, which other occipital and frontal leads do not show this form. Early activity (especially notable in the occipital leads) includes auditory response to the click. Note that the form bears a resemblance to the essentic form of love as measured through the finger pressure transducer. Such a similarity of form does not appear to be maintained for other emotions. The significance of this needs to be studied further. The response on the right is shown for comparison, with the absence of the love-modulated E-acton. Leads are left frontal, left occipital, right occipital, and right frontal. All leads are referred to a common vertex lead. Average of 100 actons.

In most of our studies we used four leads, two frontal and two occipital, symmetrically spaced and connected to a common vertex lead. Figure 13 illustrates the average wave form that is observed with the expression of "love" and "no emotion," respectively. Figure 14 shows a comparison of the same essentic form expressed with the usual finger pressure and also with the pressure of the right leg. The forms of electric activity are remarkably similar. This is a rather nice demonstration of the independence of essentic form from the output mode. Note that the expressive form appears only in one lead and comes from an asymmetric distribution.

The average form as measured in this way has a resemblance to the essentic form as measured through finger-pressure transducer. Slow waves (Figs. 15 and 16) appear associated with the phases of reverence, sometimes love, and more rarely during grief. The most sustained slow waves, as illustrated in Fig. 15, appear in reverence and seem to correlate with a particularly deep state. These waves sometimes occur during experiments with eyes either open or closed. Their period seems to be from 4 to 5 or 5.5 sec. They are not correlated with respiration. The amplitude of these waves is very large (100 μV), yet the action is limited to specific regions and is asymmetric. These waves, of course, are unique and are not encountered in the

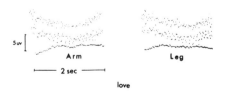

Arm   Leg

——— 2 sec ———

love

FIG. 14. Similar response as in Fig. 13 in another subject but comparing this time essentic form produced by the finger pressure with that through pressure of the foot. The similarity of the shapes observed illustrates the independence of essentic form from the output modality. (Three leads.)

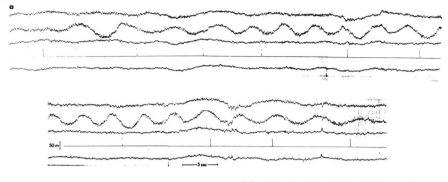

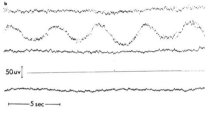

FIG. 15. (a). Very large slow waves observed in the right occipital lead only, during the phase of reverence. These waves persisted for more than 1 min, and have a period of 4 to 5.5 sec per cycle and an amplitude of over 100 μV. Leads are, from top to bottom, left occipital, right occipital, left frontal, right frontal. Pulses on fourth trace are the soft clicks initiating the E-actons. Respiration was considerably slower than these waves. (b). Same as Fig. 15a, but shown in greater detail.

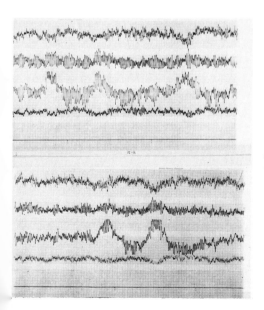

FIG. 16. Selective presence of large, slow waves, on right occipital lead during "love" phase.

normal EEG, either in the waking state or during stages of sleep. The possibility that they arise from a local scalp skin reflex specific to the emotion cannot be entirely ruled out. This would also be of interest in itself.

Another remarkable phenomenon is the appearance of burst shifts. These are sudden shifts accompanied by alpha burst of specific type and are seen in the faster states, predominantly in anger, occasionally also in "no emotion." These burst shifts mostly occur in one but may also be seen as occurring simultaneously in several leads (Fig. 17). Of course, artifacts such as eye blinks, eye movements, tongue and head movements have been ruled out as causes. These burst shifts are rarely seen in the phases of love or reverence, if at all.

The third large aspect of change is the absence of alpha activity during anger and hate and its prevalence during love, reverence, and grief. These changes are observed also in experiments with eyes open and involve in-

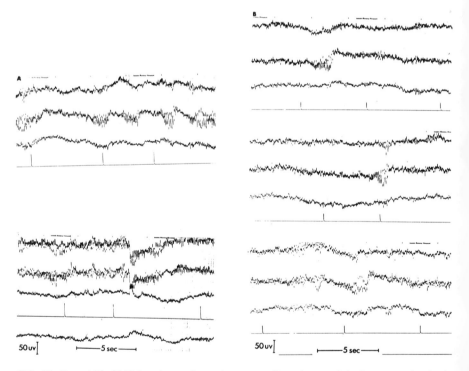

FIG. 17. (A and B). Shift bursts as shown here are often observed during anger in single leads and sometimes in two or more leads at a time. The bursts appear in a repetitive way such as shown in the top, or sometimes in single instances, as in Fig. 17B. There is a shift in the DC level of the EEG of considerable magnitude that persists for some time after the burst associated with it. This type of behavior is observed quite frequently and sometimes at a regular periodicity. The bursts do not seem to be phase related to the individual actons. Leads as in Fig. 15.

creases in alpha of as much as several hundred percent compared with anger and hate in some subjects.

Further, one may observe changes in the correlation of the EEG between symmetrically opposite leads of the hemispheres and between frontal and occipital leads. Using neurodata symmetry analyzers, we find indications of correlation changes with the experience of sentic cycles. Averaged potentials during the expression of specific sentic states display differed spatial orientations; that is, they indicate that different regions of the brain are involved for different states.

Partial Reciprocity

There is, in general, a parallel between the inner experience and movements of expression, but this parallel is by no means necessarily "instantaneous" point by point. This is implicit in the fact that the brain preprograms the acton. The sensations of touch arriving some milliseconds later are integrated into the experience of the acton, so that we are witnessing a phenomenon rather similar to that of hearing and thinking of a syllable as a unit. The one-to-one correspondence between the sentic experience and the produced essentic form does not happen without considerable temporal integration of the nervous system.

What happens if the same individual is asked to retrace an established essentic form without knowing what affect this form had measured? Can we expect a reciprocity: will the particular sentic state represented by the form being traced by the individual be produced in himself?

The act of tracing a form is different from perceiving such a form produced by another individual or from being touched by another individual according to such a form. This is generally recognized without difficulty. In tracing the form one is producing an acton; in perceiving the form no motor decisions are made. Yet, the process of tracing a given essentic form does provide an input to the individual that is similar to at least a subsystem of his sensory experience when expressing such an acton. It is important to realize why only a subsystem may be involved. In actual expression, the sentic state itself acts as a driving impetus, and the kinesthetic experience interacts with this. This interaction is integrated into the present moment through the activity of the nervous system.

When an essentic form is retraced by an individual, the experience is the kinesthetic experience without the driving force of the sentic state.

To test the effect of reciprocity, we draw an experimentally determined essentic form (both vertical and horizontal components) on the face of an oscilloscope. The two beam dots on the oscilloscope sweep the face in two seconds, in a triggered mode. Vertical and horizontal finger pressures deflect the two beams, respectively. The subject is asked to press on the transducer in such a way as to follow the essentic forms with both dots simultaneously. This means he has to press inwardly or outwardly as the form demands in the correct transient manner. The question is, does this, repeatedly done, recreate the sentic state? And what other effects does it produce?

It is found that there does in fact exist a partial reciprocity. The essentic form of love when repeatedly traced through an experimental setup where the form drawn on an oscilloscope is traced through finger pressure induces a calm state. Small variations in this essentic form do detract from the observed effect. Other emotions, such as anger, however, may be traced without generating anger. One observes rather a form of mimicry in which the appropriate actons are mimicked as movement, only without the driving force of passion behind it. Such experiments are particularly interesting in illustrating the difference between genuinely felt emotions and mimicry. (The sentic domain is disconnected when movements are merely reproduced rather than produced.) During such experiments there is also a tendency for the disconnectedness of the sentic domain to disappear through prolonged repetition of reproduced form. It is as if at times one forgets to disconnect the sentic domain and allows the appropriate sentic state to become the driving force. As this occurs, one may then gradually and spontaneously increase the sentic connection.

During an experiment, we noted that a subject suddenly did remarkably well in following the essentic form of love on the oscilloscope: when we looked closer, we saw he had his eyes closed! It seemed he had switched on his own essentic form, and appeared entranced in it: his own form corresponded more closely to the form drawn on the scope than when he was consciously trying to trace it!

"Mixed" Emotions

The selection of sentic state studies in our experiments has been largely arbitrary, although it was attempted to select what appeared to be basic emotions. Fear was initially included in our series of emotions. However, it soon became clear that fear involves a withdrawing, not readily measured by our method for technical reasons and is generally associated with inhibition of expression. We do not know the number of such basic emotions. Continuing studies of the essentic forms, however, over a range and combination of emotions may gradually lead us to a better understanding of this.

There are some emotions, however, that appear to be clearly "mixed," that is, contain elements of several other emotions. (In this respect also, we find a resemblance to the spectrum of colors. Although red and yellow are not analyzable in terms of color sensation, orange is clearly sensed as being a combination of red and yellow.) There are emotions such as melancholy or envy which seem to be clearly compounded from several others. How does the essentic form of these states represent their components? It is relatively easy to rule out an algebraic summation as a possibility. Such a combination would be unsuitable to the demodulating process that appears to function on a recognition principle of a key-lock manner. An algebraic combination would also obscure the separation between quality and intensity.

The component process is solved in the biologic design, however, by the rather elegant method of combination of phase-shifted actons. Thus, for example, melancholy, which may be regarded as a combination of love and sadness, appears to be expressed by an E-acton which begins as a love acton and after approximately 0.8 sec changes into a sadness acton. The combined form is the result of a single preprogramming and does not involve a separate decision of stopping and starting of the acton in midstream (which we have seen, would result in blocking.)

The component love phase at the beginning of the acton is sufficiently long to be recognized as such, and the termination of the acton in sadness is also recognized, although the acton is expressed and recognized as a single entity.

It appears that compound, "mixed" emotions may be expressed by a telescoped sequence of the component essentic forms, combined into a single acton. This process, if examined in more detail, may shed light on which emotions are single or compound emotions.

Orientation: Cognitive Attitude Component of Generalized Emotion

Although a sentic state may be experienced sui generis, without a specific fantasy situational context (such as being angry at a specific person), it is observed that such sentic state nevertheless seems to imply an attitude, which we may call an attitude of relationship. The implied relationship has some cognitive aspects, and it appears that perhaps in a specific way emotion and knowledge are not as mutually exclusive as is commonly supposed. Knowledge of emotions is more than an acquaintance with their special character. Each sentic state seems to imply almost a world view as part of its nature. Although such a view may not be formulated in specific terms, it seems nevertheless to be implicit. One of the factors that contribute toward the special experience of sentic cycles is that the succession of attitudes that it includes has a cognitive value. To know these attitudes intimately and clearly is to be conscious of aspects of human nature which we usually call "intuitive." The processes which we are studying may help to clarify some aspects of this kind of "intuitive" process. The attitudes and distinctions implied are not based on specific situational content but seem to be part of the nature of the quality itself, as experienced in the generalized form. We cannot refrain here from mentioning early interest (Engels, 1785; Schiller, 1793; Bell, 1806; Piderit, 1858) in these matters which has served as raw material for creative works, e.g., the cognitive relationship implicit in joy described poetically by Schiller in his "Ode to Joy"; the experience of brotherhood is seen to be a result of joy — not the other way around, as is often presumed. Some of these distinctions may be observed as related to the nature of the horizontal component of the essentic form. The horizontal component may be strongly away from the body, or only slightly, or may be toward the body. Rejection and acceptance and what lies behind these words may be considered in terms of this aspect of essentic form.

Other aspects of interest resulting from essentic form measurements that involve attitudes of relationship include the observation that the essentic form of hate does not find its formal opposite in the essentic form of love, but in that of hope: the opposite of hate in terms of essentic form is not love but hope. In considering this juxtaposition we may recognize that there is a sense of destroying life or killing in hate, but hope implies an engendering and nurturing of life. Another example is the essentic form of guilt; which generally has a strongly aggressive component directed toward the body. (It appears somewhat like anger directed inward.)

THE SENTIC PERSONAL RELATIONSHIP PROFILE: PRP

Having found essentic forms specific for each emotion, it is now possible, as a second generation approach, to apply the method to the measurement of a person's relationship with aspects of his environment (Fig. 18), and to the personal relationship profile of an individual at a particular time, as a matrix of his highly distinctive sentic responses to a number of suggested persons with whom he has a relationship, such as, mother, father, wife, children, girlfriend, enemy. Ten sentic responses, obtained a few seconds apart, are averaged for each repeatedly verbally suggested person.

The sentic personality relationship profile provides a stable collection of sentograms giving a picture of the individual's total relationship matrix and attitudes (Fig. 19). *The sentograms are interpretable in terms of the pre-*

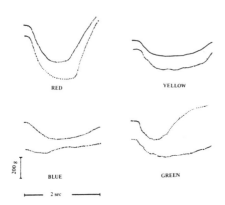

FIG. 18. Sentic reaction to colors as measured with the sentograph. Note the distinctive forms for each color. The excitement of red is shown by a strong outer-directed response. The color of blue is reflected by a small inverted horizontal component, i.e., the absence of an outward thrust. Yellow has a more sustained response form than red and is outward with a sustained energy. Green shows a compound motion outward and also upward in the second phase. Because of this response, it was necessary to use a modified transducer setup that permitted a negative vertical pressure to be recorded. Curves shown are valid for the particular subject and particular hue only. Shapes are relatively sensitive to minor changes in hue and saturation.

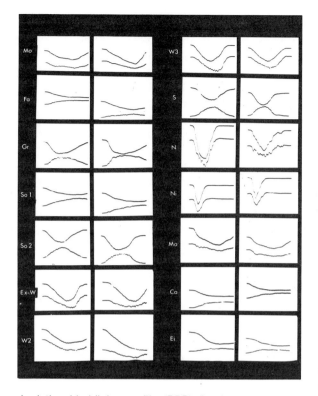

FIG. 19. Personal relationship idiolog profile. (PRP). Sentic responses to person idiologs from one subject (male, 45 years old) on two occasions. Sentograms shown are the average of 10 actons in response to such words as mother, father, etc. Each name is repeatedly pronounced a few seconds apart by the experimenter, 10 times in succession. Note the characteristic shapes introduced on two separate occasions (2 weeks apart), (left and right columns, for each person idiolog). These can be related to the emotion shapes previously measured, giving an indication of feelings toward that person. Such a "sentographic profile" appears to be a useful psychologic test. Vertical and horizontal trace patterns show a resemblance to love, anger, hate, and sex patterns, but also some compound stable forms. The nature of these is of special interest. They may be the expression of either a combination of sentic states measured already, or other sentic states that we have not yet measured, or both. Note for example the resemblance of the sentogram for "father" to the essentic form of love. "Mother," on the other hand, has a horizontal component in the same direction as the vertical. In fact, all female sentograms in this PRP show an outward angle of pressure, whereas sentograms to grandfather, son 2, and male friend (S) show marked inward horizontal component. Sentogram for woman 3 may be compared with the essentic form for sex. The sentogram to Richard Nixon is similar to the essentic form of anger. The sentogram for "business enemy" (N) is suggestive of essentic form of hate. Other sentograms are clearly different from the simple essentic forms so far measured. The element of "inscrutability" present in this subject's reaction to "Mao Tse Tung" confirmed by the interview is also subtly reflected in his attitude toward "mother." In the interview the subject indicated being awed by his mother and not really understanding her.

viously measured essentic forms of specific emotions. Visual comparison shows many specific emotion forms. Other stable forms observed in the sentogram profile may be recognized as compound and/or as emotion forms not previously measured in sentographic studies. Automated computer analysis of the personality relationship profile may be done, but is not usually necessary, since visual inspection is adequate and perhaps preferable. Recognition programs for compound forms are not linear.

The sentographic profile is stable—it appears to change only when the relationship changes. As a quantitative measure of an individual's relationship matrix, the PRP has diagnostic and prognostic function and indicates changes in relationships, in the course of treatment. It is also of value as a research tool, to investigate the spectrum of emotions and their essentic form. It is being used to chart the course of psychoanalysis.

Taking a PRP is itself an emotional experience for a subject that often leads to insights about the subject's relationships.

PROPERTIES OF SENTIC CYCLES

A sequence of sentic states produced by the method described was found to produce effects in addition to those of each separate state. These effects are dependent on the order in which the states are experienced. Sentic cycles may be experienced without measurement of the essentic forms produced; it is only necessary to sit in the correct position, express on a finger rest placed at the right height, and play the tape of the initiating signals (sentic cycles tape).[1]

One expects the order to have an effect for at least three reasons. (1) The effect of memory: of the remembered qualities experienced in the preceding phases of the cycle; associations. (2) The effects of hormonal and biochemical changes that would persist, and to some extent be cumulative. (3) Factors inherent in the relationship between the qualities themselves. A half-hour sequence found to be effective in producing a cumulative, in certain ways beneficial, effect consists of no emotion, anger, hate, grief, love, sex, joy, reverence.

The cycle may be repeated twice and the repeated experience will tend to be somewhat different from the first. Some modification of the timing signals for the second cycle is also called for. The aftereffect of sentic cycles is a specific state in itself (one could almost call it an emotion). Some persons have been able to elogize that state. To some extent the state also communicates itself.

The experience is in some ways like meditation; the body becomes very quiet but is more focused on emotion and involves continuing action. The

---

[1]Sentic cycle tapes may be obtained from the Secretary, American Sentic Association, Box 65, Palisades, N.Y. 10964.

aftereffects last for 3 to 24 hr and may be described as tending to have the following properties: calmness, absence of anxiety; reduction of hostile expression; de-stressing, absence of unpleasant nervous tension; frequently an increase of psychic energy; frequently improved quality of sleep; non-habituating; a feeling of well-being; enjoyment of being in itself. These observations are based on the some 1,200 subjects who have experienced sentic cycles at this time. For details, we refer to references cited.

Sentic cycles have been found useful also in psychoanalysis, to bring individuals in touch with their emotions and memories, and to induce a greater number of reported dreams; and in psychotherapy, as an integrating force.

The reduction of hostility makes it possible to use them to improve human relationships, for example, of couples, who can discuss their problems in a quite different atmosphere after the experience of sentic cycles. Increased knowledge and experience of generalized emotion appear to offer some promise toward altering human relationship, in several ways.

CONCLUSION

Studies of brain function have changed the relationship between the objective and subjective; subjective experience may be seen as partaking of natural order. As objective observers man has tried to cast out superstition and false belief. But he and his role are changing as he begins to observe himself as part of nature, that it is both his prison and his home. To put it differently, in a very stumbling way, we are trying to see a little of the reality in fantasy and of the fantasy in reality.

REFERENCES

Alland, A. (1970): Cross cultural aspects of Clynes' sentic cycles. In: *A. A. A. S. Symposium, Biocybernetics of the Dynamic Communication of Emotions and Qualities,* American Sentic Association, Palisades, New York.

Allport, G. W., and Vernon, P. E. (1933): *Studies in Expressive Movement.* Macmillan Co., New York.

Arnold, M. B. (1970): Brain function in emotion: A phenomenological analysis. In: *Physiological Correlates of Emotion,* ed. P. Black, Little Brown, Boston.

Ax, A. F. (1953): Physiological differentiation between fear and anger in humans, *Psychosom. Med. 15,* 433–442.

Becking, G. (1928): *Der musikalische Rhythmus als Erkenntnisquelle. B. Filser.* Ausberg, Germany.

Bekesy, G. (1967): *Sensory Inhibition,* Princeton University Press, Princeton, N.J.

Bell, C. (1806): *Essays on the Anatomy and Philosophy of Expressions,* London.

Birdwhistell, R. L. (1968): Communication as a multi-channel system. In: *International Encyclopedia of the Social Sciences,* Macmillan Co., New York.

Bruell, H. H. (1970): Heritability of emotional behavior. In: *Physiological Correlates of Emotion,* ed. P. Black, Little Brown, Boston.

Byers, P. (1971): Anthropologic implications of sentic research. In: *A. A. A. S. Symposium, Sentics, Brain Function and Human Values,* American Sentic Association, Palisades, New York.

Bull, N., and Frank, L. (1950): Emotions induced and studies in hypnotic subjects, *J. Nerv. Ment. Dis. 3*, 97–118.

Clynes, M. (1974): A new laughter homologue, predicted by sentic theory. Abstract, Society for Neuroscience, Oct. 1974, New Orleans.

Clynes, M. (1973a): Sentography: Dynamic forms of communication of emotion and qualities, *Comput. Biol. Med. 3*, 119–130.

Clynes, M. (1973b): Sentics: Biocybernetics of Emotion Communication. *Ann. N.Y. Acad. Sci. 220*, 55–131.

Clynes, M. (1972): Sentography: Dynamic measure of personal relationship profile. In: *Proceedings of 25th ACEMB Conference.*

Clynes, M. (1973c): Essentic form: E-Actons as programmed communication space time forms in the nervous system. IFAC Congress, Rochester, N.Y. In Regulation and Control in Physiologic Systems ed. Iberall and Guyton 604–607, Inst. Soc. America, Pittsburgh, Pa.

Clynes, M. (1970): Toward a view of man. In: *Biomedical Engineering Systems,* eds. M. Clynes and J. H. Milsum, McGraw-Hill, New York.

Clynes, M. (1970): Biocybernetics of space-time forms in the genesis and communication of emotion. In: *A. A. A. S. Symposium, Biocybernetics of the Dynamic Communication of Emotion,* American Sentic Association, Palisades, New York.

Clynes, M. (1971): Sentics: Precision of direct emotion communication. In: *A. A. A. S. Symposium, Sentics, Brain Function and Human Values,* American Sentic Association, Palisades, New York.

Clynes, M. (1970): Biocybernetics of the dynamic communication of emotions and qualities, *Science 170*, 764–765.

Clynes, M. (1969a): Toward a theory of man: Precision of essentic form in living communication. In: *Information Processing in the Nervous System,* eds. K. M. Leibovic and J. C. Eccles, Springer-Verlag, New York.

Clynes, M. (1969b): Cybernetic implications of rein control in perceptual and conceptual organization, *Ann. N.Y. Acad. Sci. 156*, 629–670.

Clynes, M. (1968a): Biocybernetic principles of dynamic assymetry: Unidirectional rate sensitivity, rein control (or how to create opposites from a single measure). In: *Biokybernetik 1,* eds. H. Drischel and N. Tiedt, Leipzig.

Clynes, M. (1969c): Rein control or unidirectional rate sensitivity, a fundamental dynamic and organizing function in biology, *Ann. N.Y. Acad. Sci. 156*, 627–968.

Clynes, M. (1968b): Recognition of visual stimuli from the electric response of the Brain. In: *Computers and Electronic Devices in Psychiatry,* eds. N. S. Kline and E. Laska, Grune and Stratton, Inc., New York.

Clynes, M. (1968c): Essentic form-aspects of control, function and measurement. In: *Proceedings of 21st ACEMB Conference.*

Clynes, M., and Kohn, M. (1967): Spatial visual evoked potentials as physiologic language elements of color and field structure, *Electroencephalogr. Clin. Neurophysiol.,* Suppl. *26,* 82–96.

Clynes, M. (1961): Unidirectional rate sensitivity, a biocybernetic law of reflex and humoral systems as physiologic channels of control and communication, *Ann. N.Y. Acad. Sci. 92,* 946–969.

Currier, R. (1971): Sentic communication in a Greek island culture. In: *A. A. A. S. Symposium, Sentics, Brain Function and Human Values,* American Sentic Association, Palisades, New York.

Darwin, C. (1872): *The Expression of the Emotions in Man and Animals,* Murray, London.

Davitz, J., and Davitz, L. (1959): The communication of feelings by content-free speech, *J. Commun. 9,* 6–13.

Engel, J. J. (1785–86): *Ideen zu einer Mimik.*

Eccles, J. C. (1969): The dynamic loop hypothesis of movement control. In: *Information Processing in the Nervous System,* eds. K. M. Leibovic and J. C. Eccles, Springer-Verlag, New York.

Eibl-Eibesfeldt, I. (1970): *Ethology: The Biology of Behavior.* Holt, Rinehart and Winston, New York.

Ekman, P., Sorenson, E. R., and Firensen, W. V. (1969): Pan-cultural elements of facial display of emotions, *Science 164,* 86–88.

Esser, A. H. (1970): Evolving neurologic substrates of essentic form. In: *A. A. A. S. Symposium, Biocybernetics of the Dynamic Communication of Emotions and Qualities*, American Sentic Association, Palisades, New York.

Fagan, J. (1971): Practice with sentic cycles and accuracy in the perception of emotions. In: *A. A. A. S. Symposium, Sentic, Brain Function and Human Values*, American Sentic Association, Palisades, New York.

French, A. P., Russell, P. L., and Tupin, J. P. (1972): Subjective changes with the sentic cycles of Clynes, *Dis. Nerv. Syst. 33*, 598–602.

French, A. P., and Tupin, J. (1971): Psychometic investigation of sentic cycles. In: *A. A. A. S. Symposium, Sentics, Brain Function and Human Values*, American Sentic Association, New York.

Gastaut, H., Regis, H., Lyagoubi, S., Mano, T., and Simon, L. (1967): Comparison of the potentials recorded from the occipital, temporal and central regions of the human scalp, evoked by visual, auditory and somatosensory stimuli, *Electroencephalogr. Clin. Neurophysiol.*, Suppl. *16*, 19–28.

Greenbie, B. B. (1971): Sentics and biocybernetics in the search for an optimum human habitat. In: *A. A. A. S. Symposium, Sentics, Brain Function and Human Values*, American Sentic Association, Palisades, New York.

Harlow, H. F., and Harlow, M. K. (1970): Developmental aspects of emotional behavior. In: *Physiological Correlates of Emotion*, ed. P. Black, Little Brown, Boston.

Hohmann, G. W. (1962): The effect of dysfunctions of the autonomic nervous system on experienced feelings and emotions. *Conference on Emotions and Feelings at New School for Social Research*, New York.

Jakobsen, R. (1968): *Child Language, Aphasia and Phonological Universals*, Trans. by A. R. Keiler. The Hague, Netherlands.

John, E. R. et. al. (1967): Effects of visual form on the evoked response, *Science 155*, 1939–1442.

Kety, S. S. (1970): Neurochemical aspects of emotional behavior. In: *Physiological correlates of Emotion*, ed. P. Black, Little Brown, Boston.

Klages, L. (1923): *Ausdrucksbewegung und Gestaltungskraft*. Barth, Leipzig.

Klages, V. L. (1950): *Grundlegung der Wissenschaft vom Ausdruck*. Barth, Bonn.

Laban, R. (1947): *Effort*, MacDonald and Evans, London.

Laban, R. (1958): *The Mastery of Movement*, MacDonald and Evans, London.

Lenneberg, E. H. (1967): *Biological Foundation of Language*. John Wiley, New York.

Levi, L. (1972): *Stress and Distress in Response to Psychosocial Stimuli*, Pergamon, New York.

Maranon, G. (1924): *Rev. Fran. Endocrinol. 2*, 301–325.

Maranon, G. (1950): The psychology of gesture, *J. Nerv. Ment. Dis. 112*, 485–486.

Meyer, G. (1898): *Graphisch Fixierte Ausdrucksbewegungen*.

Moses, P. (1954): *The Voice of Neuroses*. Grune & Stratton, Inc., New York.

Osgood, C. E., Suci, G. J., and Tannenbaum, P. (1957): *The Measurement of Meaning*. University of Illinois Press, Urban.

Piderit, T. (1858): *Mimik und Physiognomik*.

Ploog, D., Hopf, S., and Winter, P. (1967): Ontogenese des Verhaltens von Totenkopf-Affen (Saimiri sciureus), *Psychol. Forsch. 31*, 1–41.

Reiss, B. (1970): Use of sentic cycle tapes in psychotherapy. In: *A. A. A. S. Symposium, Biocybernetics of the Dynamic Communication of Emotions and Qualities*, American Sentic Association, Palisades, New York.

Schacter, S. (1962): *Advances in Experimental Social Psychology*. Vol. 1. The Interaction of Cognitive and Physiological Determinants of Emotional State.

Schacter, S., and Singer, J. (1962): *Psychol. Rev. 69*, 379–399.

Schiller, F. (1793): *Uber Anmut und Wurde*.

Seelig, E. (1927): Die Registrierung unwillkurlicher Ausdrucksbewegungen als forensisch-psychodiagnostische Methode, *Z. Psychol. 28*, 45–84.

Shevrin, H. (1971): Forms of feeling: The role of idiologs in empathy and dream imagery. In: *A. A. A. S. Sympsoium, Sentics, Brain Function and Human Values*, American Sentic Association, New York.

Sievers, E. (1875–1915): *Collected Works*, Stuttgart, Germany.

Starkweather, J. A. (1961): Vocal communication of personality and human feelings, *J. Commun. 11*, 63–72.

Tembrock, G. (1959): *Tierstimmen-Eine Einfuhrung in die Bioakustik,* Wittenberg, Lutherstadt.

Thorpe, W. H. (1957): Animal vocalization and communication. In: *Brain Mechanisms Underlying Speech and Language,* eds. C. H. Milliken and F. L. Darley, New York.

Tomkins, S. S., and McCarter, R. (1964): What and where are the primary affects? Some evidence for a theory. *Percept. Mot. Skills* A. T. 119–158.

Wolff, W. (1929): Gestaltidentität in der Charakterologie. *Psychol. Med. 4,* 32–44.

Emotions—Their Parameters and Measurement,
edited by L. Levi.
Raven Press, New York © 1975

Components of State and Trait Anxiety as Related to Personality and Arousal

D. Schalling, B. Cronholm, and M. Åsberg

Department of Psychiatry, Karolinska Hospital, S-104 01 Stockholm 60, Sweden

The definition of anxiety is equivocal—the term is used with widely varying implications and connotations (for a discussion, see Spielberger, 1972a,b). From a phenomenological point of view, the core manifestations of anxiety are feelings, introspectively characterized as uneasiness, distress, tenseness, nervousness, anguish, apprehension, panic, or fright. There is a diffuse over-arousal but no clear cognitive clues as to the source and no interpretation readily available (Lader, 1972). According to Lazarus and Averill (1972) and many other anxiety theorists, anxiety is triggered by a vague perception of threat evoked by internal or external stimuli. In morbid anxiety, and to some extent in normal anxiety, the threat is assumed to emanate from or be related to unresolved intrapsychic conflicts, ejected from consciousness by various defense mechanisms. Thus, the anxious person feels frightened but does not know why. Different coping processes may be instigated in this situation. There may be a reinforcement of repression: the triggering threat remains unconscious and what the person experiences is only the inner turmoil and its physiological and behavioral concomitants, e.g., autonomic disturbances and difficulties in concentrating. Another coping strategy may be a vigilant scanning of the environment for cues and possible explanations. This may lead to a different labeling of the feelings (e.g., anger) or to the choosing of only accidentally present, innocuous stimuli as "causes" of the distress and as "problems" about which the individual worries.

An important element in this model of the genesis of anxiety is the association between physiological over-arousal and anxiety. Such an association was early suggested by Malmo (1957, 1966) and is emphasized in some later anxiety models (Epstein, 1972; Lader, 1972).

ANXIETY, AROUSAL, AND PERSONALITY

The analysis of anxiety in terms of over-arousal meets with certain conceptual and practical difficulties. The early activation theorists' unitary concept of arousal as one dimension ranging from restful sleep to over-vigilance is difficult to reconcile with empirical findings. Lacey (1967) suggested that electrocortical, autonomic, and behavioral arousal are different forms of arousal, which are intimately related but dissociated mechanisms. A "two-arousal" model, postulating two different arousal systems in the brain, was presented by Routtenberg (1968). Arousal system I is related to the ascending reticular activating system (ARAS) and provides for organization of responses and maintains vigilance. Arousal system II is related to the limbic system and provides control of responses through incentive-related stimuli. A similar conceptual subdivision has been applied by Eysenck (1967), using *activation* as the term for autonomic arousal and *arousal* for cortical arousal. Activation is supposed to be mediated by the "visceral brain" and arousal by the reticular system; stimulation of ARAS leads to widespread cortical excitation. Eysenck assumes independence between these two systems, although very high activation is supposed to lead to high arousal, e.g., in strong emotion.

According to Eysenck, susceptibility to activation and arousal varies between individuals and is genetically determined. This variation is the physiological substrate for the two important personality dimensions of neuroticism and introversion-extraversion. Individuals high in neuroticism have a habitually high activation. High arousal and consequently efficiency in conditioning is assumed to characterize introverts. If an introvert is also high in neuroticism, he tends to react with high activation to an ever increasing range of stimuli, due to efficient conditioning. According to Eysenck (1961), this is the basis for one kind of anxiety, conditioned anxiety, which may correspond to what has been denoted "psychic anxiety" by Hamilton (1959). But what about anxiety in extraverts who are also high in neuroticism? As these individuals have a *low* level of (cortical) arousal accompanied by a *high* level of (autonomic) activation, somatic features of anxiety may be more prominent (Eysenck, 1961). We will analyze these assumptions in greater detail later.

ANXIETY—STATE AND TRAIT

Basically anxiety refers to a temporary emotional *state*. In English, however, the term anxiety is also often used to denote habitual anxiousness or anxiety-proneness, i.e., the *trait* of anxiety. The failure to distinguish between anxiety as a state and as a trait has led to some confusion. An example is the measuring of changes in state anxiety by means of the Taylor manifest anxiety scale (MAS), which is clearly a trait measure as has been recently emphasized by its author (Taylor-Spence, 1971). In the last few years the necessity to separate state and trait has been cogently emphasized by Spielberger (1966, 1972a,b).

ANXIETY COMPONENTS

Another issue in anxiety research is whether anxiety (state or trait) should be treated as a unitary concept, or whether a subdivision into qualitatively different components is warranted. MAS has in general been used to obtain a single anxiety score, although factor analytic studies have given support for separating groups of items as at least partly independent trait anxiety factors (O'Connor, Lorr, and Stafford, 1956; Fenz and Epstein, 1965). In clinical studies of ratings, Hamilton (1959, 1969), Buss (1962), and de Bonis (1968) have obtained factor analytic results suggesting two main components of state anxiety — psychic anxiety and somatic anxiety.

We will report on the empirical relations obtained between state and trait measures of psychic and somatic anxiety and their relationships to some personality constructs. The constructs of autonomic and cortical arousal will be used in a theoretical analysis of the findings. The data were obtained from a group of nonpsychotic, nonbrain-injured, psychiatric patients and clients from a rehabilitation institution. The group and the general procedure are described in Schalling, Cronholm, Åsberg, and Espmark (1973b). A modified version of the Buss anxiety rating scale (Buss, Wiener, Durkee, and Baer, 1955) was used to assess state anxiety on the basis of a psychiatric interview. Components of trait anxiety were assessed by means of the multi-component anxiety (MCA) inventory, a self-report instrument constructed by Schalling and Åsberg (Schalling, Åsberg, and Tobisson, 1973a). The patients were also given a battery of cognitive tests, and their behavior during the test situation was rated. Personality inventories were used to assess the constructs of neuroticism and introversion-extraversion. The Rorschach was given in a separate session. For reasons discussed above, both state and trait anxiety measures were assumed to be positively related to neuroticism variables. Extravert and impulsive patients were assumed to have higher somatic anxiety than introvert patients and, intraindividually, a higher proportion of somatic anxiety.

PERSONALITY VARIABLES

The Eysenck personality inventory (EPI) and the Marke-Nyman temperament (MNT) inventory were given. The *trait* character of the assessment was emphasized by adding to each inventory form a note reminding the patient that the questions pertained to his *habitual* feelings and behavior and not to the present illness period. EPI was given in a Swedish translation (Bederoff-Peterson, Jägtoft, and Åström, 1968). MNT is a Swedish personality inventory constructed on the basis of a personality model by Sjöbring (see Nyman and Marke, 1962; Coppen, 1966; Segraves, 1971). It includes three scales: validity (psychasthenia, neuroticism versus energy, dominance), stability (extraversion-sociability versus introversion, low emotional involvement, low sociability) and solidity (extraversion-impulsiveness versus introversion, impulse control, restraint). It should be noted that the MNT scales have a reversed scoring as compared to the EPI scales so that *low* scores in validity correspond to *high* neuroticism and *low* scores in stability and solidity to *high* extraversion. The above description and interpretation of the MNT variables are based on results of a series of studies on relations between various inventory scales, including the MNT scales (Schalling, 1970; Schalling and Holmberg, 1970), and are thus not identical with the original meaning of these variables, as proposed by Sjöbring.

RATINGS OF COMPONENTS OF STATE ANXIETY

The Buss anxiety (BA) rating scale (Buss et al., 1955; Buss, 1962), a measure of state anxiety, was translated by the present authors and slightly modified. The items included are listed in Table 1. The core content of the items was the same as that described by Buss et al. Distractability, autonomic disturbances, and muscular tension were rated both on the basis of observations during the interview (observed) and on the basis of the patient's answers (reported). Slight changes were made in the definitions of three items: muscular tension (according to Buss referring to reports of restlessness, agitation, tremor and tics, *and* to a feeling of internal tension),

TABLE 1. *Modified version of the Buss anxiety rating scale*

Observed symptoms
  Distractability (S)
    Performance in the task of subtracting sevens from the hundred.
    Inattentiveness during the interview.
  Autonomic disturbances (S)
    Perspiration, flushing, breathing disturbance, excessive swallowing.
  Muscular tension (P)
    Restlessness, tremor, tics, constrained, stiff posture.

Reported symptoms
  Distractability (S)
    Difficulties in concentrating.
  Autonomic disturbances (S)
    As in item no. 2. Also including palpitations, frequent micturition, nausea, vertigo.
  Somatic complaints (S)
    Pains, aches, disturbing bodily sensations, without apparent physical illness.
  Disquietude and mental discomfort (S)
    Uneasiness. Distress, not associated with specific cues. Feelings of inner tenseness.
    Panic attacks.
  Muscular tension (P)
    As in item no. 3. Awareness of muscular tension or contraction, difficulties in muscular relaxation.
  Worry (P)
    Anxiousness, apprehension, ruminations. Worrying in advance.

Global rating of anxiety
  Clinical impression of general anxiety level

S = included in the group of somatic anxiety items.
P = included in the group of psychic anxiety items.

subjective feeling of tenseness (referring to the patient's report of feeling upset or panicky), and worry (referring to apprehension). It was felt that the original definitions and delineations of these self-reported symptoms might present difficulties for the patient as well as for the rater. Hence the definitions of these three items were made more explicit and the content was slightly modified to fit our conceptions of these anxiety components (Schalling, 1970). In our version of the Buss scale, muscular tension referred exclusively to reports of tense muscles and difficulties to relax in a physical sense. Subjective feeling of tenseness was renamed disquietude and mental discomfort and was taken to mean vague, diffuse feelings of uneasiness, distress, inner tenseness, and panic. Worry was interpreted to mean anxiousness and was concerned with apprehensions attached to a cognitive content, ruminations, and worrying in advance. These distinctions appeared to be more in line with clinical experience and are appreciated in French psychiatry, where *angoisse* and *anxiéte* have connotations corresponding to disquietude and mental discomfort, and worry, respectively (Marchais, 1970).

A global rating was made at the end of the item ratings, based on the general clinical impressions. A 5-point scale was used. A score of one would correspond to a fairly normal state with no or only very slight occasional appearance of the symptom during the interview or during the last few days. A preliminary classification of the Buss scale items into two groups (Table 1) was made in agreement with the results by Buss. The sums of items were denoted somatic and psychic anxiety in accordance with the terminology of Buss and others, e.g., Hamilton (1959) and de Bonis (1968).

The ratings were based on a 20 to 30 min interview, during which three raters, one psychologist and two psychiatrists, were present. Certain relevant topics of direct concern for the items were always touched upon, but the procedure was flexible and adapted to the individual patient. The questions always pertained to the state of the patient during the last few days, not his habitual reactions. No questions were concerned with the case history. The type of questions included was based on a series of discussions among the raters concerning the meaning and range of each item in the scale. Before this study, some patients were interviewed for training purposes, which gave the raters a further possibility to discuss the implications and cues for each item.

The ratings were made immediately after the interview, independently by the three raters. After the independent ratings, the case was discussed and *joint ratings* decided upon. The ratings were thus simultaneous, i.e., the raters used the same basis for their ratings, which is not always the case in rating studies. Simultaneous ratings are however appropriate in the examination of a momentary affective state (Cronholm, Schalling, and Åsberg, 1974). The interrater reliability for the three raters measured by the intraclass correlation coefficient was high (Schalling et al., 1973b).

As may be expected, many items in the Buss anxiety scale were highly correlated. Among the exceptions may be noted a rather weak relation between observed distractability and most other items, including reported distractability. It is probable that the reported symptom is more pertinent, since it is based on a wider range of situations.

There was a high correlation ($p < 0.001$) between the total score (the sum of all items) and the global rating, based explicitly on clinical intuition. The same result was obtained by Buss et al. (1955), who remarked that "there is little difference between arithmetic and clinical integration." However, global ratings could probably not replace the ratings of separate items. The careful consideration of different aspects of anxiety which preceded the global rating may be decisive for the high correlations obtained.

A cluster analysis of the Buss anxiety scale item correlations, using McQuitty's (1957) technique, yielded two item clusters corresponding to the *a priori* groupings of somatic anxiety and psychic anxiety, respectively, with one exception, *observed* autonomic disturbances, which in the cluster analysis was placed in the psychic anxiety cluster together with worry and muscular tension. The results of this cluster analysis were on the whole in line with the findings by Buss. Despite some uncertainty as to the applicability of factor analysis on clinical ratings, a principal component factor analysis was also performed on the present data. Two factors were obtained, one with its highest loadings in observed and reported muscular tension, worry, and *observed* autonomic disturbances, and the second with the highest loadings in reported and observed distractability, reported autonomic disturbances, and somatic complaints. Thus, again *observed* autonomic disturbances fell out of the expected groupings. One reason may be that the observations were made in an interpersonal interview situation in which insecurity and lack of self-confidence (assumedly psychic anxiety components) may be accompanied by, e.g., blushing. Further, disquietude, which in the typal analysis was placed in the somatic anxiety cluster, had equally high loadings in both factors in the principal component analysis. These findings should not be overemphasized, however, since preconceived ideas of the raters may well have influenced the outcome of the multivariate analysis (a drawback common to all ratings, *cf.* Kendell, 1968). According to our view, conceptual subdivisions in this domain should not be based on single empirical findings, e.g., factor analysis, but should be integrated in a broader network of observations and interpreted in the light of theory. Thus, we have retained the *a priori* classification of Buss scale items into somatic anxiety and psychic anxiety groups. The sums of scores in these groups were significantly correlated in the present group ($r = 0.63$, $p < 0.001$). However, the shared variance is less than 40% and thus differences may be obtained in their relationships to external criteria, e.g., personality variables. Certainly, the concepts of somatic and psychic anxiety will need modification, once a coherent theory of "types of anxiety" is developed.

STATE ANXIETY MEASURES AND PERSONALITY

Correlations between somatic and psychic anxiety scores from the Buss anxiety rating scale and the personality inventory scales are given in Table 2. As expected, both anxiety scores showed highly significant correlations with the EPI neuroticism and the MNT validity scales. This finding implies that patients whose trait self-reports indicate a strong habitual tendency to react in a "neurotic" or "psychasthenic" way receive higher scores in the clinical ratings of state anxiety. In the light of the Eysenckian theory, the finding indicates an association between autonomic lability and habitually high activation (underlying neuroticism) and state anxiety.

TABLE 2. *Correlations between state anxiety scores from the Buss anxiety (BA) rating scale and trait anxiety scores from the multi-component anxiety (MCA) inventory and personality inventory scores*

	MNT			EPI	
	V	St	So	N	E
BA state anxiety rating scores					
Sum of somatic anxiety scores	−0.33[a]	0.04	−0.37[a]	0.58[c]	−0.01
Sum of psychic anxiety scores	−0.47[b]	−0.01	−0.17	0.54[c]	−0.08
Total BA scores	−0.42[b]	−0.02	−0.32[a]	0.62[c]	−0.04
MCA trait anxiety inventory scores					
Somatic anxiety scores (SA)	−0.58[c]	0.05	−0.58[c]	0.90[c]	−0.22
Psychic anxiety scores (PA)	−0.77[c]	0.23	−0.17	0.70[c]	−0.50[b]
Total MCA scores	−0.71[c]	0.15	−0.39[a]	0.84[c]	−0.38[a]

[a] $p < 0.05$, [b] $p < 0.01$, [c] $p < 0.001$.
N = 37. Marke-Nyman temperament (MNT) inventory scales: V = validity (neuroticism-psychasthenia vs. energy), St = stability (extraversion-sociability vs. introversion), So = solidity (extraversion-impulsiveness vs. introversion). Eysenck personality inventory (EPI) scales: N = neuroticism, E = introversion-extraversion. (Form B)

No significant correlations were obtained between the anxiety ratings and two of the extraversion variables, the EPI extraversion and the MNT stability scales. In contrast, MNT solidity was significantly negatively related to the somatic anxiety score and the total anxiety score. Anxiety rating score profiles in low and high solidity patients are illustrated in Fig. 1. The low solidity group had significantly higher ratings in disquietude and mental discomfort, in reported distractability, and autonomic disturbances. Thus the present findings indicate a higher level of *somatic anxiety* in low solidity (extravert-impulsive) patients than in high solidity patients.

In order to test the Eysenck hypothesis that extravert neurotics have predominantly somatic anxiety, i.e., that the proportion of their somatic

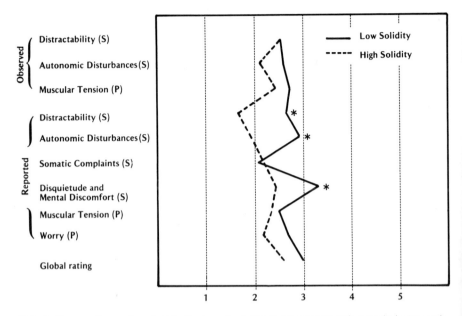

FIG. 1. Mean ratings of anxiety indicators from the Buss anxiety rating scale in two sub-groups of patients differing in solidity. High solidity = patients with scores above median in solidity (introvert). Mean solidity scores = 14.61, n = 18. Low solidity = patients with scores below median in solidity (extravert). Mean solidity scores = 6.28, n = 18. * $p < 0.05$.

anxiety scores to their total anxiety scores is greater than the corresponding proportion in introvert neurotics, certain indices were computed for the higher and lower third of the group with regard to extraversion and solidity scores. A correction was made for the fact that the Buss scale comprises twice as many somatic anxiety as psychic anxiety items. The proportion $SA/2\Sigma PA + \Sigma SA$ was computed both for observed and reported and for reported symptoms only. There were no significant differences between the extreme groups in any of these indices, except one marginally significant difference in the proportion of somatic anxiety for reported symptoms (0.54 for the low solidity versus 0.47 for the high solidity group). However, all differences between the solidity groups were in the expected direction, indicating a slightly higher proportion of somatic anxiety in low solidity (extravert-impulsive) patients. The high and low EPI extraversion groups did not differ in these indices. The results are thus in line with Eysenck's hypothesis, but only for the impulsiveness component of extraversion.

SELF-REPORT MEASURES OF SOMATIC AND PSYCHIC TRAIT ANXIETY

The multi-component anxiety (MCA) inventory was developed on the basis of preliminary work with the Buss rating scale, results of factor analytic studies of MAS and other anxiety inventories, and a series of interviews with patients suffering from anxiety (Schalling et al., 1973a). The first version, used in the present study, consists of two subscales with 20 items each, called somatic anxiety and psychic anxiety scales. The somatic anxiety scale included items concerning autonomic disturbances (n = 9), disquietude and mental discomfort of a diffuse kind, and panic attacks (n = 9), concentration difficulties and distractability (n = 2). Thus the main content of the Buss somatic anxiety items was covered with the exception of somatic complaints. The psychic anxiety scale included items referring to worrying and pronounced anticipatory reactions as well as prolonged post-stress reactions (n = 10) and increased muscular tension (n = 4), covering the main content of the Buss psychic anxiety items. The remaining six items concerned nervousness and lack of self-confidence in social situations, i.e., traits belonging to the same sphere (*cf.* de Bonis, 1970). The item choice was later controlled by a series of item analyses, in which the correlations between each item and the subscale to which it belongs were studied (Schalling et al., 1973a).

In the group of psychiatric patients described above, there was an intercorrelation of 0.81 ($p < 0.001$) between the two MCA subscales. Thus, in this group of patients, there was a strong association between self-reported tendency to experience disquietude and autonomic and cognitive disturbances, and self-reported tendency to worry, be tense, and feel insecure. However, as will be shown, the subscales may still display interesting differences in their relationships to other variables. The mean score in the MCA somatic anxiety scale was 8.32 (SD 5.38) and in the psychic anxiety scale 9.97 (SD 5.65). These means are significantly higher than those obtained in a group of students. The reliability of the total MCA scores as estimated by the Kuder-Richardson formula was 0.94. For the somatic anxiety and psychic anxiety subscales, both coefficients were 0.91.

TRAIT ANXIETY MEASURES AND PERSONALITY

The correlations between the MCA trait anxiety measures and scores in the personality inventory scales are given in Table 2. As expected, both MCA scales correlated strongly with EPI neuroticism and MNT validity. The correlations were higher than those obtained for the Buss anxiety scores, which is to be expected as they are trait measures, obtained by similar methods. The somatic anxiety scale was more associated with neuroticism and the psychic anxiety scale with validity.

Two interesting findings may be noted. There was a highly significant negative correlation between psychic anxiety and EPI extraversion. This result is in line with the anxiety model described above, implying that psychic (conditioned) anxiety should be lower in extravert patients, assumedly deficient in conditioning, than in introvert patients. There was also a highly significant negative correlation between the somatic anxiety scores and MNT solidity (more extravert-impulsive patients had *higher* somatic anxiety scores).

The proportion of somatic anxiety in the MCA inventory scores was tested on the extreme groups in extraversion and solidity, as was done for the Buss ratings. The results were in line with those obtained for the ratings, giving a significantly higher proportion of somatic anxiety scores in the low solidity group (t = 3.29, $p < 0.01$) than in the high solidity group. No significant differences were obtained for high and low extraversion groups. Thus, again, Eysenck's hypothesis of a more somatic type of anxiety in extravert subjects received some support, but again only with regard to the impulsiveness component of extraversion, as reflected in solidity scores.

RELATIONSHIPS BETWEEN STATE AND TRAIT ANXIETY MEASURES

The correlations between the Buss *state* anxiety measures and the MCA *trait* anxiety measures were all highly significant ($p < 0.001$). The highest correlation (r = 0.68) was obtained between the total Buss and the total MCA scores. Thus ratings of anxiety based on interviews concerning anxiety experience during the last few days and on observations during the interview proved to be highly related to the patient's own report of habitual anxiety reactions in this group of psychiatric patients. The coefficients are unusually high for measures obtained independently and with different methods (self-report versus expert ratings), but, on the other hand, state

TABLE 3. *Correlations between state anxiety scores from the BA rating scale and trait anxiety scores from the MCA inventory, and Rorschach ratings of anxiety and of coping with anxiety in terms of under- vs. overcontrol*

	Rorschach ratings	
	Anxiety	Coping with anxiety (overcontrol)
BA state anxiety scores		
Sum of somatic anxiety scores	0.23	−0.32[a]
Sum of psychic anxiety scores	0.35[a]	−0.04
Total BA scores	0.30	−0.23
MCA trait anxiety scores		
Somatic anxiety scores	0.40[a]	−0.34[a]
Psychic anxiety scores	0.37[a]	−0.14
Total MCA scores	0.40[a]	−0.25

[a] $p < 0.05$.
N = 37.

TABLE 4. *Correlations between ratings of autonomic indicators of state anxiety and scores in inventory scales of trait anxiety and neuroticism*

Ratings	MCA		EPI	MNT
	SA	PA	N	V
Autonomic disturbances observed during a psychiatric interview	0.30	0.31	0.33[a]	−0.08
Autonomic disturbances observed during cognitive testing	0.48[b]	0.55[c]	0.32[a]	−0.50[b]
Autonomic disturbances during the last few days, as reported by the patients	0.71[c]	0.62[c]	0.68[c]	−0.52[c]

[a] $p < 0.05$, [b] $p < 0.01$, [c] $p < 0.001$.
Multi-component anxiety (MCA) inventory: Somatic anxiety (SA) and psychic anxiety (PA) scales; Eysenck personality inventory (EPI): Neuroticism (N) scale; Marke-Nyman temperament (MNT) inventory: Validity (V) scale. N = 37.

and trait anxiety measures may be expected to be associated in a group of hospitalized psychiatric patients.

On the basis of Rorschach protocols, two clinical psychologists jointly made blind ratings (using 5-point scales) of two separate aspects of anxiety as it is manifested in Rorschach responses: degree of anxiety which was defined as the presence of accepted anxiety signs in the protocols and coping with anxiety in terms of under- versus overcontrol (undercontrol corresponding to free-floating anxiety). Table 3 shows the relationships between these Rorschach ratings, the Buss state anxiety measures, and the MCA trait anxiety measures. The Rorschach anxiety measure was significantly related to the patient's self-report of trait anxiety, both somatic and psychic, which is of interest in view of the wide methodological differences between the Rorschach and the inventory technique. It is in line with theoretical and clinical expectations that the overcontrol coping measure was *negatively* (consistently although weakly) related to somatic anxiety indicants, both state and trait.

Table 4 shows the relationships between trait anxiety and neuroticism variables, on one hand, and, on the other hand, autonomic disturbances, as *observed* during the interview (i.e., a short observation in an interpersonal situation), as *observed* during a long testing session (involving of course some ego-threat), and as *reported* by the patient (based on self-observation for some days). In line with expectation, the correlations with the trait anxiety and neuroticism measures increase with increasing observation time.

GENERAL DISCUSSION AND SUMMARY

The anxiety research reported above was based on some general conceptions briefly outlined in the introduction. First, the arguments by Spielberger and others emphasizing the necessity to use separate measures for *state* and *trait* anxiety were taken into account. As a state measure, the Buss anxiety rating scale was chosen. This scale contains items from the five main types of indicators: introspective (feeling), autonomic, muscular, somatic, and behavioral (distractability).

We used the Buss grouping of these items into two groups or clusters: *psychic anxiety* including muscular tension and worry, and *somatic anxiety* including autonomic disturbances, somatic complaints, distractability, and a "feeling" component, disquietude and mental distress. Disquietude was conceptualized as "uneasiness, distress not associated with specific cues, feelings of inner tenseness, and panic attacks." The distinction between somatic and psychic anxiety was accepted as it seemed to be in line with earlier research as well as clinical experience. Our results tend to confirm the validity of the distinction. The multivariate analyses were largely consistent with the Buss grouping. However, before deciding on the typing problem in anxiety research, we consider it necessary to apply the method to new and more heterogenous groups of subjects, attempting to establish a nomological network for both constructs.

The concept of two types or components of anxiety was the starting point for the construction of a new trait anxiety inventory, the multi-component anxiety inventory, including two subscales, somatic and psychic anxiety scales. A preliminary form of this inventory was used in the study reported.

Two kinds of relations were assumed to exist between the anxiety measures and the personality variables. Both state and trait anxiety measures of both somatic and psychic anxiety were assumed to be related to neuroticism scales in the personality inventories. This implies, according to Eysenck, that individuals with high habitual autonomic arousal (activation) are supposed to have high anxiety. The results were consistent with these expectations: there were highly significant correlations between the anxiety measures and the EPI neuroticism scale and the MNT validity scale. The correlations were consistently higher for the trait anxiety measures (MCA) as might be expected also from the methodological similarities between MCA and the personality inventories.

The second hypothesized personality relationship concerned the extraversion variables. According to Eysenck, the EPI extraversion is related to low cortical arousal. The same assumption was made for the MNT solidity scale on the basis of results in a series of studies (Schalling, 1970, 1971), indicating that low solidity (extravert-impulsive) subjects have a lower cortical arousal than high solidity subjects.

Many years ago, Eysenck suggested that extravert patients might have predominantly somatic anxiety. Introverts, assumed to be easily conditioned, were supposed to have predominantly psychic anxiety, that is, anxiety attached to many different cues by means of learning.

On the whole, the findings of the present study were in line with these hypotheses. A higher proportion of somatic anxiety in extraverts was found in low solidity (extravert-impulsive) patients significant for the trait anxiety measures. Further, the low solidity patients tended to have *higher* somatic anxiety (state) ratings and *higher* somatic anxiety (trait) MCA scores than high solidity patients. The psychic anxiety MCA scores were related in the opposite direction with the EPI extraversion scores, more extravert patients thus reporting *lower* psychic anxiety. This negative correlation between the psychic anxiety scale in MCA and extraversion has been confirmed in a series of studies on normal subjects (Schalling et al., 1973*a*).

Thus, the results were in line with the proposed model, implying that *intensity and frequency* of anxiety is related to susceptibility to high autonomic arousal (high neuroticism) in an individual, and that *type* of anxiety is related to whether the high autonomic arousal tends to occur in combination with low cortical arousal (as in extravert-impulsive individuals) or with high cortical arousal (as in introvert individuals).

It was further found that degree of anxiety, rated on the basis of the Rorschach, was related to both types of self-reported (MCA) anxiety, but that coping with anxiety in terms of under- versus overcontrol, according to Rorschach assessment, was related only to somatic anxiety; low control was associated with high somatic anxiety. This confirms the importance of taking into account coping styles in anxiety measurement, as suggested by Lazarus and Averill (1972). It appears possible that coping mechanisms, and perceptual or cognitive styles are among the mediators in the present findings. Extravert-impulsive individuals tend to view the world in a vague diffuse way (Shapiro, 1965) and are prone to denial and repression (Forrest, 1963; Blackburn, 1965), which may be related to the predominance of somatic anxiety manifestations, including diffuse disquietude and uneasiness. The higher psychic anxiety in introvert patients may be related to their tendency to intellectualize and rationalize. These patients may be more efficient not only in conditioning, learning to associate distress with new stimuli, but also in scanning the environment for plausible reasons for the distress felt in the anxiety state, i.e., objects of worry.

ACKNOWLEDGMENTS

This research has been financially supported by grants from the Swedish Medical Research Council (21X-5473 and 14P-3647) and from the Swedish Council for Social Science Research (588/72). The assistance of Sonja Levander, Ph.D., and Ulf Brinck, Ph.D., who performed the Rorschach ratings, is gratefully acknowledged.

REFERENCES

Bederoff-Peterson, A., Jägtoft, K., and Åström, I. (1968): Eysenck personality inventory (EPI). Den svenska versionen (The Swedish version). Skandinaviska Testförlaget, Stockholm.

Blackburn, R. (1965): Denial-admission tendencies and the Maudsley personality inventory, *Br. J. Soc. Clin. Psychol. 4*, 241–243.

de Bonis, M. (1968): Etude factorielle de la symptomatologie subjective de l'anxiété pathologique, *Rev. Psychol. Appl. 18*, 177–187.

de Bonis, M. (1970): Anxiétés pathologiques et anxiété normale, *Rev. Psychol. Appl. 20*, 1–25.

Buss, A. H. (1962): Two anxiety factors in psychiatric patients, *J. Abn. Soc. Psychol. 65*, 426–427.

Buss, A. H., Wiener, M., Durkee, A., and Baer, M. (1955): The measurement of anxiety in clinical situations, *J. Consult. Psychol. 19*, 125–129.

Coppen, A. (1966): The Marke-Nyman temperament scale: An English translation, *Br. J. Med. Psychol. 39*, 55–59.

Cronholm, B., Schalling, D., and Åsberg, M. (1974): Development of a rating scale for depressive illness, *Mod. Probl. Pharmacopsychiatry 7*, 139–150.

Epstein, S. (1972): The nature of anxiety with emphasis upon its relationship to expectancy. In: *Anxiety, Current Trends in Theory and Research*, Vol. 2, ed. C. D. Spielberger, Academic Press, New York.

Eysenck, H. J. (1961): Classification and the problem of diagnosis. In: *Handbook of Abnormal Psychology*, ed. H. J. Eysenck, Basic Books, New York.

Eysenck, H. J. (1967): *The Biological Basis of Personality*, Thomas, Springfield, Ill.

Fenz, W. D., and Epstein, S. (1965): Manifest anxiety: Unifactorial or multifactorial composition? *Percept. Motor Skills 20*, 773–780.

Forrest, D. W. (1963): Relationship between sharpening and extraversion, *Psychol. Rep. 13*, 564.

Hamilton, M. (1959): The assessment of anxiety states by rating, *Br. J. Med. Psychol. 32*, 50–55.

Hamilton, M. (1969): Diagnosis and ratings of anxiety. In: *Studies of Anxiety, Br. J. Psychiat.*, Special Publication, No. 3, ed. M. H. Lader, Headley Brothers, Ashford, Kent.

Kendell, R. E. (1968): *The Classification of Depressive Illness*, Maudsley Monograph Series, No. 18, Oxford University Press.

Lacey, J. I. (1967): Somatic response patterning and stress: Some revisions of activation theory. In: *Psychological Stress*, eds. M. H. Appley and R. Trumbull, Appleton-Century-Crofts, New York.

Lader, M. H. (1972): The nature of anxiety, *Br. J. Psychiat. 121*, 481–491.

Lazarus, R. S., and Averill, J. R. (1972): Emotion and cognition: With special reference to anxiety. In: *Anxiety, Current Trends in Theory and Research*, Vol. 2, ed. C. D. Spielberger, Academic Press, New York.

Malmo, R. B. (1957): Anxiety and behavioral arousal, *Psychol. Rev. 64*, 276–287.

Malmo, R. B. (1966): Studies of anxiety: Some clinical origins of the activation concept. In: *Anxiety and Behavior*, ed. C. D. Spielberger, Academic Press, New York.

Marchais, P. (1970): *Glossaire de Psychiatrie*, Masson, Paris.

McQuitty, L. L. (1957): Elementary linkage analysis for isolating orthogonal and oblique types and typal relevancies, *Educ. psychol. Measurem. 17*, 207–229.

Nyman, G. E., and Marke, S. (1962): *Sjöbrings Differentiella Psykologi, (The Differential Psychology of Sjöbring)*, Gleerups, Malmö.

O'Connor, J. P., Lorr, M., and Stafford, J. W. (1956): Some patterns of manifest anxiety, *J. Clin. Psychol. 12*, 160–163.

Routtenberg, A. (1968): The two-arousal hypothesis: Reticular formation and limbic system, *Psychol. Rev. 75*, 51–80.

Schalling, D. (1970): Contributions to the validation of some personality concepts, *Rep. Psychol. Lab., Univer. Stockholm*, Suppl. 1.

Schalling, D. (1971): Tolerance for experimentally induced pain as related to personality, *Scand. J. Psychol. 12*, 271–281.

Schalling, D., Åsberg, M., and Tobisson, B. (1973a): Components of trait anxiety (*in preparation*).

Schalling, D., Cronholm, B., Åsberg, M., and Espmark, S. (1973b): Ratings of psychic and somatic anxiety indicants, *Acta psychiat. Scand. 49*, 353–368.

Schalling, D., and Holmberg, M. (1970): Extraversion in criminals and the "dual nature" of extraversion. Comments based on results obtained by inventories, *Rep. Psychol. Lab., Univer. Stockholm*, No. 306.

Segraves, R. T. (1971): Intercorrelations between the Sjöbring and Eysenckian personality dimensions, *Acta Psychiat. Scand. 47*, 288–294.

Shapiro, D. (1965): *Neurotic Styles*, Basic Books, New York.

Spielberger, C. D. (1966): Theory and research on anxiety. In: *Anxiety and Behavior*, ed. C. D. Spielberger, Academic Press, New York.

Spielberger, C. D. (1972a): Anxiety as an emotional state. In: *Anxiety, Current Trends in Theory and Research*, Vol. 1, ed. C. D. Spielberger, Academic Press, New York.

Spielberger, C. D. (1972b): Conceptual and methodological issues in anxiety research. In: *Anxiety, Current Trends in Theory and Research*, ed. C. D. Spielberger, Academic Press, New York.

Taylor-Spence, J. (1971): What can you say about a twenty-year old theory that won't die? *J. Motor Behav. 3*, 193–203.

Emotions—Their Parameters and Measurement,
edited by L. Levi.
Raven Press, New York © 1975

Regulatory Mechanisms and Tissue Pathology

Stewart Wolf

Marine Biomedical Institute, University of Texas Medical Branch at Galveston, Galveston, Texas 77550

INTRODUCTION

Progress to date has brought us to the point of general acceptance of evidence linking stressful life experiences to certain diseases manifest by tissue pathology. The length of the list of diseases varies with the bias of the author. Drawn up in order ranging from the greatest to the least concensus it would include some forms of the following: duodenal ulcer, hives, eczema, asthma, phlyctenular keratitis, glaucoma, ulcerative colitis, myocardial infarction, hypertension, and others (Wolf and Goodell, 1968; Levi, 1971). While genetic predisposition is doubtless of great significance, as are other factors in the algebra of multifactorial disease processes, it is probable that a potential contribution of psychosomatic mechanisms can be postulated for almost any disease process.

The main assumption required is that not only visceral behavior but tissue integrity depends on smooth operation of visceral, vascular, and glandular regulatory mechanisms. In the case of local vasoconstriction and the consequences of tissue ischemia this is obvious enough, as is overebullient repair of injury as seen in keloid and perhaps in arteriosclerosis (Wolf, 1971). The effects of mast cell release of histamine are, perhaps, less obvious. Also somewhat recondite are the renal glomerular and other small vessel changes consequent upon sustained arterial hypertension.

TOO MUCH OR TOO LITTLE—THE NATURE OF DISEASE

The concept that emerges from all this is that the tissue changes characteristic of disease are the result of basically normal bodily processes gone wrong, exaggerated, insufficient, or inappropriate in some way. Health is manifested by a behavior of bodily systems that achieves and maintains a comfortable interaction or relationship with the environment. Haldane and Priestley (1935) stated this principle when they said that progress in medicine depends on understanding how the human organism adapts to changes in the environment. Thus, the healthy person increases his red-blood count when living at a high altitude but not at sea level. Polycythemia developed at sea level spells disease. The bodily mechanisms required to increase the number of circulating red-blood cells, however, are identical in health and disease. So it is with other bodily systems. For example, the difference between infection and mere exposure to microbes depends on a neat balance of activation and restraint of immunological and other defense mechanisms. Inadequate modulation of immunological function appears to be responsible for the exaggerated immune behavior of certain connective-tissue diseases. Disease, then, may reflect too much or too little of certain adaptive functions, resulting in essentially inappropriate physiological behavior.

Virtually every disease becomes a disease, then, on the basis of quantitative considerations. Cancer, for example, is a matter of cell replication that will not quit. Graves disease consists of the excessive elaboration of a normal, indeed an essential, hormone.

As for cardiovascular disorders, rheumatic fever is basically an excess of tissue immunity. Arteriosclerosis begins with an overebullient intimal proliferation. Hypertension consists of the excessive use of a normal mechanism for the adaptive constriction of arterioles.

In the gastrointestinal tract, whether etiologic or not, peptic ulcer is clearly associated with an excessive secretion of acid and pepsin. Ulcerative colitis is associated with an unduly sustained posture of transport on the part of the colon. The diabetic state, the substitution of a ketone for a glucose metabolism, is a healthy bodily response in the face of starvation. In the well-fed subject the same process constitutes potentially fatal disease.

THE NATURE OF THE REGULATORY PROCESS

Visceral adaptations, sometimes called functional and sometimes organic, result from activity in autonomic regulatory neurons with or without the interposition of endocrine secretions. That is to say what we all know well, namely that all endocrine secretions are ultimately under the control of the central nervous system (CNS).

A distorted balance of regulatory functions can at times be attributable to a genetic error, particularly the failure of appearance of certain enzymes, or an incorrect sequence of amino acids in the molecule. Likewise, nutritional disturbances may impair the development of proper visceral controls. So may a wide variety of experiences, including overload of the system, as from climatic extremes, injury, infection or perhaps social and psychological pressures, especially during periods of growth and development (Levi, 1972). Attention, therefore, is drawn to the responsible regulatory mechanisms, especially the neural and neuroendocrine pathways.

AUTONOMIC ORGANIZATION

We have been slow in learning that autonomic responses are usually not generalized discharges in which one or the other system predominates, but rather are discrete patterned reactions, many of which involve simultaneous activity of specific cholinergic and adrenergic nerves. Thus the original concept of Eppinger and Hess (1910) that responses or even individuals are either vagotonic or sympathotonic has become misleading. The frequent coexistence of essential hypertension with peptic ulcer, cold hands with bradycardia and fainting, or tachycardia with urinary frequency is everyday evidence against the oversimplified notion of sympathetic versus parasympathetic predominance. Each so-called psychosomatic pattern is indeed recognizable as a quasipurposeful adaption either exaggerated, insufficient, or invoked under inappropriate circumstances.

The patterns themselves gain meaning when they are seen as anticipatory adjustments to circumstances that do not actually materialize. Thus the hypersecreting victim of peptic ulcer is behaving "as if" he were about to be fed or ready to devour. The peripheral vasoconstriction of the hypertensive is an appropriate adjustment to blood loss. In fact it is often seen in an individual about to donate blood prior to venapuncture (Wolf, Cardon, Shepard, and Wolff, 1955).

Dozens of such quasipurposeful, "as if" responses involving a variety of discrete patterns of organ function accompany anxiety (Wolf and Goodell, 1968). Some are characteristic of specific situations, others of certain types of individuals. The matter of organ choice thus becomes a matter of individual makeup.

Physicians and researchers have often been blinded to the importance of visceral nerve connections by the remarkable intrinsic capability of the various internal organs. The heart will continue to beat, the kidney will continue to make urine, and the liver will persist in its metabolic conversions after all nerve connections have been severed. The range of visceral adaptability is restricted, however, and the ability to react in anticipation is lost in the absence of innervation.

In recent years it has been necessary to rethink our whole concept of the autonomic nervous system. The earlier focus of interest was on peripheral connections and automatic responses accomplished without awareness. It is now clear that the central connections of the autonomic nerves are as rich and complex as are those of the nerves that supply skeletal muscles. In fact, there is a great deal of interaction between the two at hindbrain, midbrain, and forebrain levels.

The number of central interactions that may be involved in the elaborate circuitry that regulates and modulates visceral behavior is probably so great as to be almost inconceivable. Levi's cybernetic system gives a helpful clue to the possible connections.

REGULATORY INHIBITION

Any regulatory system requires the interaction of activating and restraining forces with a feedback of some sort. The graceful movements of a ballerina, a pianist, or a champion athlete depend more on the modulating restraint of inhibitory neurons from cerebellum, red nucleus, and basal ganglia than they do on the activation of the Betz cells, the prime movers of the corticospinal tract. As the painful, useless skeletal-muscle contractions of tetanus infection or strychnine poisoning are attributable to blocking or inactivation of the normal modulating influence of an inhibitory network, so the almost ceaseless gastric secretion of HCl and proteolytic enzymes characteristic of duodenal ulcer or the sustained elevation of blood pressure by initially normal arterioles may reflect the failure of the normal balance of autonomic excitatory and inhibitory influence (Wolf, 1970).

Inhibitory pathways in the CNS have only recently come under serious scrutiny. Much has been learned through study of the inhibitory neurotransmitters, glycine and GABA. The latter has been identified, not only in association with Purkinje cells of the cerebellum (Fonnum, Storm-Mathisen, and Walberg, 1970), the sole output of that organ, but elsewhere in the CNS (Curtis and Felix, 1971; Nicol, 1971) and even peripherally in the walls of arteries and arterioles (Kuriyama, Haber, and Roberts, 1970). One may infer from this and other work an elaborate inhibitory network responsible for the modulation of visceral behavior as it is for the function of skeletal muscles (Wolf, 1970; Clemente, 1968; Livingston, 1972).

When Charles Richet, in 1894, first combined chloral hydrate and glucose to make what he called chloralose he noted that, while it dulled consciousness, it enhanced visceral responsiveness. Neurophysiologists have taken advantage of this property of the drug to identify autonomic pathways in anesthetized animals.

As more and more has been learned about excitatory and inhibitory influences, about facilitatory and inhibitory regulation of synaptic transmission, the concept of the reflex nature of bodily regulation has given way to a concept of neural interaction in which virtually all parts of the nervous system are interconnected so that local perturbations may have widespread effects. Rich interconnections among somatic sensory, visceral sensory, and the effector neurons of all sorts have been discovered that link many zones of the CNS, including thalamus, hypothalamus, and limbic cortex, with the frontal lobes (Hockman, 1972). The extent of interrelatedness of all of these structures in the formulation of organismal behavior not only has led to the discarding of the too simplistic reflex concept of regulation but has made it clear that the somatic and visceral pathways are not two systems after all but a single system with different kinds of neuronal hookup in a state of continuous dynamic interaction.

THE INTEGRATIVE PROCESS

With the newer knowledge of the vast central ramifications of the autonomic system and the fact that visceral effector neurons can be found as "high" in the cerebral hemispheres as those that activate skeletal muscles, the principal difference between somatic and autonomic effector nerves is evident only after they leave the cord, where autonomic nerves synapse before acting on the effector organ while somatic motor nerves do not. Furthermore, peripheral neural plexuses, such as are found in the gut and other viscera, are uniquely characteristic of autonomic innervation. The peripheral synapse of autonomic nerves seemed to have very little functional significance until the recent discovery of interneurons in mammalian autonomic ganglia (Williams and Palay, 1969). The implication of this discovery is that further visceral and vascular regulatory activity is possible peripheral to the CNS.

The neural plexuses that invest many visceral and vascular structures endow them with greater versatility and range of function than the skeletal muscles and enable them to perform and to adapt within limits even when isolated from the body and suspended in an artificial medium. Doubtless a capacity for automaticity and autoregulation in various organs was in part responsible for the fact that the widely ramified representation of autonomic nerves in the CNS was overlooked for so long a time.

Recent studies with the techniques of operant conditioning have shown that both somatic and visceral function can be modulated through "learning." Perhaps doors have been opened to new therapeutic measures through training maneuvers.

GOALS AND PURPOSEFUL ADAPTATIONS: PHYSIOLOGY VERSUS PATHOLOGY

A practical clinical objective may be the Cohnheim-Welch hypothesis that was proposed nearly 100 years ago, and which recently was elaborated by Jokl (1971). The hypothesis is based on the concept of "the wisdom of the body," and holds that adjustments in the function of skeletal muscles, viscera, vasculature, and glands reflect the purposes of the organism and react to perturbations with a tendency to re-establish the normal circumstances and to challenges and demands with a pattern of healthy adaptation. In certain pathological conditions, it was pointed out that the adaptations themselves may indeed make matters worse, so that proper medical practice would call for interfering with the natural process, draining abcesses, for example, or cutting away granulation tissue. At that time, nearly 100 years ago, inflammation itself was seen as a nonadaptive behavior. This was, of course, before it was realized that bringing leukocytes, immune globulins, and other combatants of infection is basically protective and therefore purposeful.

DISCUSSION

We are gradually learning that what we call health and disease reflects a balance of particular physiologic regulatory processes that operate through pathways that are enormously complex. The circuitry contains excitatory and inhibitory neurons that are subject to a variety of feedback and other influences at several levels of organization in the nervous system and in relation to locally elaborated or circulating humors. When the regulatory processes are comfortably balanced and adaptive, we speak of health. Disease occurs when there is too much or too little of some adaptive element. For example, a heart rate of 120 in a track man immediately after a 100-yard dash would be considered a sign of health, but in a bedridden or even sedentary patient the same pulse rate would be a clear evidence of illness. Similarly, the various manifestations of psychopathology are healthy when they assist the individual in coping with his life experiences. Otherwise they are evidence of illness. The classical grief reaction without an antecedent loss would be considered abnormal, but so would its absence following the death of a loved one. In the healthy subject, therefore, we speak of responses such as changes in blood pressure, body temperature, and a host of other indicators including emotional and cognitive changes as being "within normal limits." These same bodily processes become abnormal or pathological when in relation to the exciting situation they are excessive, insufficient, or inappropriate.

The basic element of psychosomatic medicine is the fact that the autonomic excitatory and inhibitory pathways that regulate visceral function are subject to influence by circuits in the forebrain, neuronal interactions that subserve the interpretation of life experience.

The rapidly growing understanding of the way the nervous system relates to all bodily structures has made it increasingly attractive to consider such disorders as pathological aggressiveness, alcoholism, epilepsy, and hemolytic anemia as resulting from a defective balance of excitatory and inhibitory mechanisms. At present it appears that the fault lies most often with inadequacy of smoothly regulatory inhibition.

The quality and quantity of visceral regulatory activity depends heavily on the prevailing state of the whole organism, his previous experience and attitudinal set. Conversely the state of the organism depends upon the character of the inputs. The inputs shape ourselves and our behavior. Lucretius once said, "I am a part of all that I have seen." This may be true, but it is much more certain that "all that I have seen is a part of me."

It follows that investigations at the molecular, cellular, and tissue level that have contributed so much to the rapid progress of our understanding must be followed now by a greater emphasis on studies at the organismal level, studies of the whole conscious behaving organism, preferably man. There will then evolve a clearer understanding of what we know now, that all parts of the organism are interdependent and that the adaptive behavior of the viscera, like that of skeletal muscles, becomes ultimately a matter of the needs, goals and purposes of the individual.

SUMMARY

As our knowledge and understanding increase, it appears more and more evident that all bodily responses are purposeful. Sometimes the requirements for adaptation are conflicting, and sometimes the bodily response is either insufficient or exaggerated, hence an imbalance with the potential of tissue damage, disability, and even death. It follows that treatment must be directed toward modulating wide swings of autonomic and somatic effector activity. How that is to be achieved is a problem. Perhaps some of the newer so-called autogenic techniques may be helpful.

REFERENCES

Clemente, C. D. (1968): Forebrain mechanisms related to internal inhibition and sleep, Cond. Reflex *3*, 145–174.

Curtis, D. R., and Felix, D. (1971): The effects of bicuculline upon synaptic inhibition in the cerebral and cerebellar cortices of the cat, Brain Res. *34*, 301–321.

Eppinger, H., and Hess, L. (1910): *Vagotonie, Klinische Studie,* Hirschwald, Berlin.

Fonnum, F., Storm-Mathisen, J., and Walberg, F. (1970): Glutamate decarboxylase in inhibitory neurons: A study of the enzyme in Purkinje cell axons and boutons, Brain Res. *20*, 259–275.

Haldane, J. B. S., and Priestley, J. G. (1935): *Respiration,* Oxford University Press, London.

Hockman, C. H. (1972): *Limbic System Mechanisms and Autonomic Function,* Charles C Thomas, Springfield, Ill.

Jokl, E. (1971): *The Clinical Physiology of Physical Fitness and Rehabilitation,* Charles C Thomas, Springfield, Ill.

Kuriyama, K., Haber, B., and Roberts, E. (1970): An L-glutamic acid decarboxylase in several blood vessels of the rabbit, Brain Res. *23*, 121–123.

Levi, L. (1971): *Society, Stress and Disease,* Oxford University Press, New York.

Levi, L. (1972): *Stress and Distress in Response to Psychosocial Stimuli,* Pergamon, Oxford.

Livingston, R. B. (1972): Neural integration. In: *Pathophysiology, Altered Regulatory Mechanisms in Disease,* ed. E. D. Frohlich, Lippincott, Philadelphia.

Nicol, R. A. (1971): Pharmacological evidence for GABA as the transmitter in granule cell inhibition in the olfactory bulb, Brain Res. *35*, 137–149.

Richet, C., Sr. (1894): Le chloralose dans l'experimentation physiologique, Arch. Ital. Biol. *21*, 266–271.

Williams, T. H., and Palay, S. L. (1969): Ultrastructure of small neurons in the superior cervical ganglia, Brain Res. *15*, 17–34.

Wolf, S. (1970): Evidence on inhibitory control of autonomic function, Int. J. Psychobiol. *1*, 27–33.

Wolf, S. (1971): *The Artery and the Process of Arteriosclerosis,* Plenum, New York.

Wolf, S., Cardon, P. V., Jr., Shepard, E. M., and Wolff, H. G. (1955): *Life Stress and Essential Hypertension: A Study of Circulatory Adjustments in Man,* Williams and Wilkins, Baltimore.

Wolf, S., and Goodell, H. (1968): In: *Stress and Disease,* ed. H. G. Wolff, Charles C Thomas, Springfield, Ill.

Emotions—Their Parameters and Measurement,
edited by L. Levi.
Raven Press, New York © 1975

On the Measurement of Happiness and Its Implications for Welfare

Roy Yensen*

Department of Psychology and Sociology, Massey University, Palmerston North, New Zealand

INTRODUCTION

No attempt will be made in this chapter to offer an overall definition of the concept of welfare. However, it is assumed that this concept ought to include, *inter alia,* aspects of both positive and negative emotional experience. For example, when a high level of welfare is present in a community, then the individuals in general in that community ought to experience a higher level of positive emotional feelings and a lower level of negative emotional feelings than when a lower level of welfare is present.

Most of the work that has been done in the general area of mental health and welfare has been concerned with aspects of maladjustment and negative emotional experiences with relatively little emphasis on the positive emotional experiences of the individual.

Positive emotional experiences include both the more transient feelings of joy, pleasure, elation, etc., and the deeper more pervasive and longer lasting feelings of happiness, which are associated with experiences of satisfaction in life or a general worthwhileness in living. Happiness, used in this sense,[1] is a very significant component of the positive emotional experiences included in the concept of welfare. Hence any discussion of welfare should include a consideration of the happiness of the individuals concerned and of the factors influencing happiness.

I will discuss some of the problems inherent in attempts to measure happiness and to uncover the nature of the factors contributing to overall happiness in life. Procedures aimed at overcoming some of these problems are developed, and, finally, some implications for social planning and welfare are discussed.

As yet there are no physiological or other objective ways of measuring happiness. Nor are observations or records of the objective conditions and

---

* This chapter was prepared while the author was at the Laboratory for Clinical Stress Research, Stockholm, in 1973, during Sabbatical Leave from Massey University, New Zealand.

[1] This term is further discussed in the section on "Theoretical Considerations of Happiness."

circumstances of life likely to be very helpful in this area, although they are sometimes cited as evidence of the relative level of welfare.

For it is not the objective conditions and circumstances per se that are important, but rather the way in which the individual perceives and reacts to his environment. For example, Hinkle et al. (1957) and Hinkle and Wolff (1958) compared groups of subjects who had experienced a high incidence of illness episodes over the past 20 years of their life, with similar groups of subjects who had experienced a low incidence of illness episodes. They could not find any significant differences between these groups in terms of their objective conditions and circumstances, as these were judged by objective observers. They did report, however, that there were significant differences between the groups in terms of the ways in which the individual subjects *perceived and reacted to* their environments. As Hinkle, et al. (1957, p. 218) state: ". . . the great majority of the clusters of illness which have occurred in the lives of our informants have occurred during life situations which the informant, himself, perceived as stressful, even though this situation might appear benign to an "objective" observer; conversely, when "objectively" difficult life situations are not associated with illness the informants usually did not perceive these life situations as difficult, even though the observer might expect them to do so."

In the absence, then, of any objective methods of assessing happiness, we must concentrate on the experiences or subjective states and feelings of the individual, even though there are considerable hazards associated with this type of approach, especially with respect to questions of the validity and reliability of one's data.

EARLIER STUDIES

A number of studies on happiness using a self-rating type of approach have been reported.

Wilson (1967), in a fairly comprehensive review article "Correlates of avowed happiness," discusses much of this work, but does not consider in detail the methods used in the various studies. As Wilson states: "Most of the studies of happiness have used some type of direct, self-report, questionnaire-type measure" (p. 294), but within this degree of similarity quite a number of differences exist.

These range from (a) a single scale (e.g., Fellows, 1956; Wilson, 1965; Symonds, 1937; Bradburn and Caplovitz, 1965) to (b) an additive combination of various items or scales (e.g., Watson, 1930), six main items with subscales in some, and nine scales (Goldings, 1954), to (c) factor analytic studies (e.g., Veroff et al., 1962), based on 22 indices for males and 19 indices for females, 16 scales (Wessman and Ricks, 1966), and 8 scales (Wilson, 1960).

The type of items or scales on which the S's were requested to indicate their degree of happiness and the way in which they were administered also varied. Graphic or linear type scales were used by Watson (1930), five reference points; Goldings (1954), six segments; and Wilson (1965), 11 points. Checklists were used by Symonds (1937), seven categories; Fellows (1956), five categories; and Veroff et al. (1962) and Bradburn and Caplovitz (1965), three categories. Interview techniques were used by Veroff, et al. (1962) and by Bradburn and Caplovitz (1965), for some S's only. Some type of self-administered questionnaire was used in the other studies. As would be expected, the age and background characteristics of the S's used also varied considerably.

In those studies adopting a composite approach to happiness, the number of items or scales, the life areas to which they related, and the scoring methods used all varied.

Watson (1930) used six main questions, with some subitems, relating to general happiness, health, vocation, love, friends, hobbies, religion, and happiness at earlier stages of life. "The happiness score was computed by assigning values to each question in an arbitrary fashion, as a result of discussion by a committee who had examined and tabulated the responses" (p. 82). No further rationale is offered for the weightings used.

Goldings (1954) used nine scales relating to family relations, health, intellectual activity, physical exercise, solitary leisure time, larger-group relations, sex relations, personal friendships, and general overall satisfaction. An arbitrary weighting of 5 times was assigned to the rating on overall satisfaction, and each of the other eight ratings were weighted 1, 2, or 3 times depending on the relative importance that the S had assigned to each area as contributing to his general satisfaction.

For their male S's, Veroff et al. (1962) used 22 indices relating to six areas, general feelings of distress, attitudes towards self, marital adjustment, adjustment as a parent, psychological and psychosomatic symptom complaints, and job adjustment; and for their female S's 19 indices, relating to the first five areas for males. Equal weights were used in scoring.

The studies also vary greatly in their treatments of reliability and validity. Some offer evidence relating to these very important aspects, but others do not mention them.

Watson (1930) reports correlations of 0.83 and 0.85 for male and female S's respectively between two composite scores, each derived from approximately half of the six main items used. He also reports a correlation of 0.81 between self-ratings on general happiness and the total happiness scores.

Wilson (1960) reports a split-half reliability of 0.87 for 16 dichotomous items.

Wessman and Ricks (1966) report that "questionnaire items indicative of *avowed happiness-unhappiness,* collected 2 years before" (p. 103), correlated 0.67 with the mean daily average scores, taken over a 6-week period, on their elation-depression scale which was used as a measure of happiness-unhappiness. A correlation of 0.71 is reported between scores on the latter scale and "a prior composite clinical rank order on happiness-unhappiness made by six of the staff psychologists after 2 years' assessment" of 17 male S's (p. 247).

Hartmann (1934) reports a test-retest reliability over a 2-month period of 0.70. He also reports a correlation of 0.34 between the self-ratings of some 200 college sophomores and the average estimates by four associates of each S's happiness.

Neither Symonds (1937) nor Fellows (1956) mention either reliability or validity in their reports. Wilson (1965) relied on earlier studies for reliability and validity, even though he used a happiness scale which was quite different from those used in the earlier studies.

Goldings (1954) also relied on earlier studies for reliability, even though his happiness scale differed considerably from those used in the earlier studies. However, he reports rank-order correlations ranging from 0.23 to 0.64 between self-ratings from 20 S's and the independent rank-order ratings made by five experimenters on the S's "general happiness and over-all satisfaction." The rank-order ratings were based on "the experimenter's subjective, clinical judgment" (p. 35).

Because of the numerous variations in methods used in the above studies, it is extremely difficult to draw any conclusions about their findings. [The actual findings are amply reviewed in Wilson (1967) and so will not be repeated here.] Of course, a very charitable point of view might see the differences in methods as examples of "systematic replication" (Sidman, 1960), but I seriously doubt this.

Nevertheless, these studies do suggest that to ask an individual to indicate how happy he is in a particular area of life, is not a meaningless question, and that depending on how this is done, one may get responses that have an acceptable level of reliability, and some rather lower level of validity.

Before leaving these studies there are two other shortcomings in many of them that need to be noted, namely,

(a) the use of an arbitrary set of life areas on which an overall happiness score is based, and

(b) the use of an arbitrary system of weighting the S's ratings of happiness in these various life areas, when these ratings are combined to yield an overall happiness score.

The use of an arbitrary list may result in the inadvertent omission of areas that are relevant to some S's, since there appear to be individual differences in the life areas that contribute to overall happiness. (e.g., Watson, 1930), Table III, p. 85). This problem could be solved by the use of a very extensive list, but this may induce some S's to respond to areas which, in fact, are not relevant to them. Asking the S to state the areas which are relevant to him could overcome this difficulty.

When the arbitrary system of weighting of the various life areas involves equal weighting (e.g., Veroff et al., 1962), the assumption is made that the various life areas contribute equally to overall happiness, and that this applies to all S's. When unequal weighting is used (e.g., Watson, 1930), it is assumed that

(a) some areas contribute more than others to overall happiness,
(b) the investigator knows which are the more important areas, and
(c) these are the same for all S's.

However, it would appear (see below under "Theoretical Considerations of Happiness") that the only one of these assumptions that is correct is that some areas contribute more to overall happiness than others. The degree of contribution depends on the relative importance of the area to the S. Of the studies reviewed only Goldings (1954) used a differential weighting based on the relative importance of an area to the S. He used an arbitrary list of eight life areas, and had each S rate the importance of each one "in contributing to his general satisfaction . . . . The 'importance' scores for the life areas were broken down to a three-point scale and assigned as multipliers to the value for the linear scale to which they referred" (p. 35).

THEORETICAL CONSIDERATIONS OF HAPPINESS

As Hall and Lindzey (1970) observe in their discussion of theories of personality: "In one form or the other . . . *the self* occupies a prominent role in most current personality formulations" (p. 590, italics by present author). Many theorists (e.g., Mead, 1934; Rogers, 1959; and Symonds, 1951), include within their concept of self an aspect which may be referred to as a self-image, or a composite overall "picture" of the self as seen by the individual.

The self-image is formed during the early life experiences of the individual and is subsequently modified in terms of his current experiences, his values and attitudes, and his hopes and aspirations for himself as an individual who is living in what he perceives to be a particular constellation of objective conditions and circumstances of life.

It is a composite overall "picture" of the individual as he sees himself and of how he thinks he would like to be. It has a number of facets, or aspects, some of which are more central, or salient, than others.

At a particular stage of his life the individual "sees" some, but not necessarily all, of his current experiences in various areas of his life as relevant to (in the sense of potentially or actually supporting or threatening) some, or all aspects of his self-image, depending on the nature and composition of that self-image.

These areas of his life, in which he has experiences that are "seen" as relevant to aspects of his self-image, will themselves be "seen" as areas of his life which are important to him.

Areas of his life, in which he has experiences that are "seen" as relevant to more salient aspects of his self-image, will themselves be "seen" as areas of his life that are more important, or salient, *to him* than other areas that are "seen" as relevant to less salient aspects of his self-image.

Areas of his life in which he has experiences which are *not* "seen" as relevant to aspects of his self-image will themselves be "seen" as areas of his life which are *not* important to him.

In a particular life area that he "sees" as important, the individual will have a multiplicity and variety of experiences, including both positive and negative emotional feelings. Insofar as the individual evaluates the overall outcome of these experiences as confirming and/or supporting some aspects of his self-image, so he will experience a relatively deep, pervasive, and long-lasting feeling of happiness in this area of his life. The degree of happiness is a function of the degree of support, as evaluated by the individual. It is not the individual or separate experiences per se, but rather the overall evaluation of them as confirming and/or supporting aspects of the self-image, which is important here in giving rise to happiness.

If the overall outcome of the multiplicity and variety of experiences arising from an important life area is such that it is evaluated as disconfirming some aspects of the self-image, then the individual will not experience happiness in this life area.

So each area of life that the individual "sees" as important has a potential to contribute to his overall happiness, and the greater the importance, the greater the potential. Areas of life that are "seen" by the individual as *not* important to him at this stage of his life do not have this potential. They may, of course, become important at some later stage of his life.

Hence, the actual contribution to overall happiness of an important life area is not only a function of the degree of happiness experienced in that area, but also of the relative salience of that area. To illustrate this point: Suppose an individual reports that he feels that his "relations with his wife" and his "work" are areas in his life that are important to him. He rates himself as "moderately happy" in each of these areas. He also reports that his "relations with his wife" are much more important to him than his "work." Then his "relations with his wife" will contribute much more than his "work" to his total or overall happiness in life, despite equal ratings of happiness in both areas.

If the individual does not experience happiness in an important life area, then his lack of happiness in that area will detract from his potential overall happiness, and the extent to which it does so will be a function of the relative salience of that area (see below).

These processes of evaluation, etc., do not necessarily go forward at a conscious level, but the individual is usually aware of their outcomes. Hence, he most probably can indicate those areas of his life that he "sees" as important to him, how happy he feels in each of these areas, and the relative salience of each area.

In conclusion, it is suggested that the overall happiness of the individual is made up of the sum of the feelings of happiness that he experiences in each important life area, when these feelings of happiness are suitably weighted in accordance with the relative salience of each area.

On the basis of the above the following hypothesis is advanced:

A meaningful index of overall happiness in life can be gained from summing the self-rated happiness in all areas of his life that the individual "sees" as important to him, when each rating is weighted by a factor derived from the individual's own estimate of the relative salience of that area.

A METHOD FOR MEASURING HAPPINESS

The following steps are proposed as a way to:

(a) develop an index of overall happiness in life, and

(b) gain some understanding of the nature of the factors that contribute to overall happiness.

At this stage only a broad indication is given, since no pilot work has been done to check the practicality of these suggestions, and to refine them to specific research procedures.

Collection of the Data

The data required include:

(a) objective information regarding the S's prior and present objective conditions and circumstances of life—age, sex, marital status, health, work, leisure activities, etc.;

(b) a list of all the areas in life which the S "sees" as important to him in his life at present;

(c) the S's estimates of the relative salience or degree of importance to him of each of the areas in (b);

(d) the S's estimates of the degree of happiness which he experiences in each of the areas in (b).

This information would be collected from recorded, extensive, open-ended, depth interviews, conducted by highly skilled interviewers. (A structured interview and, perhaps, a self-administered questionnaire would be developed later.)

The gleaning of information relating to (a) is relatively straightforward. For (b) an indirect approach, such as that used by Kornhauser (1965), when seeking similar information, could be used. By nondirective, probing questions, the S is encouraged to talk freely about himself, his activities, hopes and worries, problems and satisfactions. Subsequently, this information is analyzed and classified into life areas that are important to the S.

À more direct approach would probably be more efficient and more likely to ensure that all areas of importance to the S are elicited, although great care would be necessary to avoid "leading" the S. Direct questioning as to what the S "saw" as important to him in his life, would be used. This information would be classified into important life areas by follow-up probing and discussion between the interviewer and the S.

For (c) the S is asked to indicate from the areas in (b) an area which is not the most important area to him, but one which is fairly important, and to assign a value to this area. He is then asked to estimate the relative importance of each of the other areas as a proportion of that value.

For (d), taking each area separately, the S would be asked to assign a value of 10 to the feelings of happiness that he felt he would experience if he were completely and perfectly happy in this life area. Then, in terms of this value of 10, he would be asked to estimate the value of his present degree of happiness in this area.

Treatment and Analysis of the Data

From the data derived from the procedures listed above, we now have:

(a) objective background information about the S. This could provide a basis for the grouping or classifying of S's according to sex, marital status, socio-economic status, etc.;

(b) a list of all the life areas "seen" as important by the S, and proportionate ratings of the relative salience of each of these areas to him. Grouping or classifying of S's could also be done on the basis of this information in conjunction with, or independent of, the objective background data; and

(c) a self-rating of the degree of happiness in each life area that the S considers is important to him.

A composite overall happiness score (COHS) for each S is then calculated in the following way:

(a) The proportionate rating of relative salience for each important life area is converted to a percentage value to yield a salience score for that area. For example, suppose the S has listed a total of three life areas, x, y, and z, as being all of the life areas that are important to him. He assigns an arbitrary value of 15 to area y, then a value of 30 to area x, and 5 to area z, i.e., the ratio of areas $x:y:z = 6:3:1$. Since these three areas represent, by definition, all (i.e., 100%) of the life areas that are important to S, they are then given salience scores of 60, 30, and 10 respectively.

(b) For each area, the self-rating of happiness in that area is weighted in terms of its salience score (i.e., happiness score × salience score) to yield a value representing the contribution which each area makes to the overall happiness of the S. (This value is shown as the "Weighted Happiness Score" in the following tables.)

(c) The "Weighted Happiness Scores" are summed. This sum is then divided by 10 to yield a composite overall happiness score (COHS).

The composite overall happiness score (COHS) can range from 0 to 100. A COHS of 0 would indicate an individual who is, overall, *not happy,* and who, in fact, *may* be *unhappy,* but this latter condition would not necessarily follow or be implied by a score of zero. A COHS of 100 would indicate an individual who is, overall, perfectly and completely happy.

Two hypothetical cases are set out in Table 1, subjects A and B, to illustrate the application of this method. The COHS comprises the sum of the degree of happiness in each and every life area that is important to the S, where each area is weighted in accordance with its relative salience. So, if

TABLE 1. *Composite overall happiness scores (COHS) derived from hypothetical data for two subjects*

Important life areas	Happiness rating ×/10 (a)	Salience		Weighted happiness score (a) × (b)
		Ratio rating	Score % (b)	
1. Subject A				
Relations with wife	8	40	20	160
Relations with children	8	60	30	240
Club membership	6	30	15	90
Work	7	45	22	154
Golf	6	25	13	78
				722
$COHS = \dfrac{722}{10} \simeq \underline{\underline{72}}$				
2. Subject B				
Relations with wife	7	60	55	385
Hobby of painting	5	30	27	135
Work	3	20	18	54
				574
$COHS = \dfrac{574}{10} \simeq \underline{\underline{57}}$				
3. Subject B Decrease in COHS due to adding another important life area with a zero happiness rating.				
Relations with wife	7	60	40	280
Relations with son	0	40	27	0
Hobby of painting	5	30	20	100
Work	3	20	13	39
				419
$COHS = \dfrac{419}{10} \simeq \underline{\underline{42}}$				

the S is not happy in a particular area that is important to him (i.e., gives it a happiness rating of zero), then that area

(a) does not contribute to his overall happiness;

(b) reduces, in proportion to its relative salience, the potential and the actual contributions to overall happiness of the other important areas in which the S experiences some degree of happiness; and

(c) so reduces his COHS.

Suppose subject B in Table 1, included another area, "relations with son" in his list of life areas that are important to him, and gave it a happiness rating of zero. Then both his salience scores for the three important life areas shown in Table 1, subject B, and his derived COHS would be reduced, as shown in Table 1–3.

Reliability and Validity

To establish adequate reliability and validity of procedures aimed at the assessment of subjective states is an essential, although extremely difficult aspect of the development of such procedures. Some suggested approaches to this problem are outlined below, although no claims as to a complete solution are thereby implied.

First, let us consider the reliability and validity of the actual data, and then the reliability and validity of the COHS.

Reliability and Validity of the Data

To some extent the degree of reliability and validity of the data collected will depend on the skill and ability of the interviewer to obtain data that are not contaminated by the "social desirability" and/or the "yea saying" tendencies of the S, and which do, in fact, validly reflect the relevant experiences of the S.

If the S is agreeable, then data from reinterviewing after a short-term lag may be used to establish a short-term test-retest reliability. Since changes may occur over time in the self-image and/or in the nature of the areas considered important by the S, in their relative salience and in their rated happiness, long-term reliability checks are virtually excluded. However, this does not matter, provided an adequate degree of validity can be established.

Some indication of the internal consistency of the data and also, perhaps, of its validity may be gained from the following data, which would be collected in an independent interview conducted by another interviewer. The S would be asked to indicate how he spent his time, effort, money, and thoughts, over, say, the past month. Follow-up probing would be used to ensure a full cover of the time period. One would expect a pattern to emerge that reflected the important areas in S's life and their relative salience. For example, if no time, effort, etc., were devoted to a particular area, providing there were no peculiar circumstances, then this would suggest that the area was of little importance, if any, to the S.

The S would also be asked to indicate those areas of his life, in which he would like to see some changes, and the nature of such changes. Follow-up probing would be used to ensure that all relevant areas were considered by the S. Again, one would expect some patterns to emerge. If the S stated that he would not like to see any change in a particular area, then this would suggest either that he was completely happy in this area, or that this area was not important to him. Also, it is probable that the greater the degree of change desired in a particular area, the smaller the degree of happiness is in that area.

Another approach to the problem of validity lies in the development and use of independent criteria for areas of importance, their relative salience, and the degree of happiness experienced in each area.

It may be possible to use some of the existing value and/or attitude scales, or to develop new ones, to assess whether given life areas are important, and what their relative salience is to the S.

It should be possible to design experimental situations in which the independent variables are the S's rating of "important" or "not important," the degree of relative salience, and the degree of happiness in particular life areas. For example, the nature and content of verbal associations to the verbal and/or pictorial presentation of material relating to particular life areas would probably vary as a function of the above independent variables.

Objective measures of the physiological reactions of the S to the presentation of visual and/or verbal material relating to particular life areas may also reveal differential reactions as a function of these independent variables. For example, one would expect that many of the components of the orienting reflex would be greater to material relating to highly salient areas than to material relating to areas that were not important to the S. Likewise, there may be differences in the rates of habituation to the repeated presentation of such material.

Recognition thresholds of material presented tachistoscopically, and judgments of the apparent size and/or apparent brightness of appropriate visual material may vary as a function of these independent variables.

Reliability and Validity of the COHS

If adequate reliability and/or validity is established for the data collected, then the reliability of the COHS is ensured. This, however, does not necessarily apply to the question of the validity of the COHS.

The COHS should bear a close relationship to the S's self-report of overall happiness, provided adequate reliability and validity has been established for the latter. Wilson (1967) considers that these have been established: "It is already established that avowed happiness can be determined reliably" (p. 294) and "these facts would seem, if anything, to support the validity of self-ratings" (p. 295), but the present author is not quite so optimistic (see earlier discussion). However, if a valid self-rating of overall happiness were available, then this could be used to establish a validity coefficient for the COHS.

Another approach would be to follow the procedures used by Wessman and Ricks (1966), and by Kornhauser (1965), both of whom compared their "happiness scores" with the overall judgments of groups of "experts" (i.e., psychiatrists and/or clinical psychologists). When using this method, it is essential that the clinical judgments are made completely independent of the procedures used to assess the COHS.

A further approach that may yield evidence relating to validity stems from a suggestion by Wilson (1967), when he writes: ". . . it seems peculiar that avowed happiness as such has not been studied in relation to the effect of psychotherapy. It is not inconceivable that other manipulations could be attempted that might noticeably influence happiness" (p. 305).

The procedures on which the COHS is based, are such that predictions can be made concerning the influences on overall happiness of changes in all, or any, of the three components[2] of overall happiness. It should be possible to arrange experimental-clinical-intervention studies in which the independent variables are specific aspects of these components, and the dependent variable is overall happiness independently assessed by self-rating methods, or by clinical judgments of "experts." The results of such experiments could then be used to evaluate the validity of the predictions based on the procedures underlying the COHS. Some of these predictions are listed below:

(a) *Increase in degree of happiness in a particular area.* The influence on overall happiness of an increase in the degree of happiness experienced in a particular area of life, will depend not only on the degree of increase in happiness per se, in that area, but also on the relative salience of that area. If it is an area of low salience, then the increase in overall happiness will be smaller than if the salience is higher (see Table 2).

(b) *Increase in relative salience of a particular area.* The influence on overall happiness of an increase in the relative salience of a particular area will depend on the degree of happiness experienced in that area relative to the degree of happiness in each of the other important areas. If the degree of happiness is relatively low in the area in which the relative salience is increased, then there will be a decrease in overall happiness. If the degree of happiness is relatively high in the area in which the relative salience is increased, then there will be an increase in overall happiness (see Table 3).

---

[2] (a) whether the S "sees" a given life area as "important" or "not important," (b) the relative salience of the areas which are "seen" as "important," and (c) the degree of happiness experienced by the S in each important area.

TABLE 2. *Hypothetical data showing the influences on the COHS of an increase in the happiness rating of (1) an area with low salience, and (2) an area with high salience*

Important life areas	Happiness rating ×/10 (a)	Salience score % (b)	Weighted happiness score (a) × (b)
Base data			
x	2	10	20
y	2	60	120
z	6	30	180
			320
$\text{COHS} = \dfrac{320}{10} = 32$			
1. Increase in happiness rating of low salience area x from 2 to 6			
x	6	10	60
y	2	60	120
z	6	30	180
			360
$\text{COHS} = \dfrac{360}{10} = 36$			
2. Increase in happiness rating of high salience area y from 2 to 6			
x	2	10	20
y	6	60	360
z	6	30	180
			560
$\text{COHS} = \dfrac{560}{10} = 56$			

(c) *Further predictions.* In a similar manner further predictions could be made from the following manipulations:

(a) a decrease in happiness experienced in a particular area of life;
(b) a decrease in the relative salience of a particular area of life;
(c) a change (increase or decrease) in the number of areas in life that are considered to be important;
(d) various combinations of some of the above.

SOME IMPLICATIONS FOR SOCIAL PLANNING AND WELFARE

It is obvious that this work would require considerable research facilities. Nevertheless, I think that the time and effort involved would be justified. From a pure research point of view, our knowledge and understanding of overall happiness and of the factors contributing to it would undoubtedly increase, and considerable benefits could accrue from an applied point of view.

TABLE 3. *Hypothetical data showing the influences on the COHS of an increase in the salience of (1) an area with a low happiness rating, and (2) an area with a high happiness rating (note: A change in the ratio rating of the salience of one area results in a change in the salience scores of all areas)*

Important life areas	Happiness rating ×/10 (a)	Salience		Weighted happiness score (a) × (b)
		Ratio rating	Score % (b)	
Base data				
x	1	10	20	20
y	5	30	60	300
z	8	10	20	160
				480
$COHS = \dfrac{480}{10} = \underline{48}$				
1. Increase in the salience ratio rating of low happiness area x to equal that of y				
x	1	30	43	43
y	5	30	43	215
z	8	10	14	112
				370
$COHS = \dfrac{370}{10} = \underline{37}$				
2. Increase in the salience ratio rating of high happiness area z to equal that of y				
x	1	10	14	14
y	5	30	43	215
z	8	30	43	344
				573
$COHS = \dfrac{573}{10} \approx \underline{57}$				

Much time and effort is expended nowadays in the planning and implementation of broad social policies aimed at improving the general level of mental health and welfare in various communities. However, as noted in the introduction of this paper, most attempts at the evaluation of such planning have tended to concentrate either on the objective conditions and circumstances of life, or on aspects of maladjustment and the negative emotional experiences of the individuals concerned. An improvement in the objective conditions and/or a decrease in the negative emotional experiences do not necessarily imply an increase in overall happiness. In fact, very little appears to have been done in an endeavor to find out whether such planning and its implementation do, in fact, result in an increase in the overall happiness of the individuals concerned.

In saying this, it is not meant to imply that increased happiness should be the sole aim of social planning. However, I think it is the case that very few people would consider such planning as successful if it did not, *inter alia,* at least preserve the existing levels of overall happiness, and hopefully, result in some increase for the majority of the individuals concerned.

In most Western societies, social planning, in principle at least, usually includes an emphasis on the rights of the individual as an individual. It follows from this that the individual should be allowed, within certain limits, to gain his happiness from life areas of his own choosing. One would expect to find similarities as well as differences in the patterns of life areas seen as important by individuals from the same subcultural group. A knowledge of these areas, and the degree to which the happiness derived from them contributes to the overall happiness of the individual, as well as some basis for predicting the probable influence of changes in these areas on the future overall happiness, is essential for informed planning of social changes.

Similar knowledge is required for adequate evaluation of the results of the implementation of such planning. This knowledge could be gained from the use of the COHS and the procedures outlined earlier in this paper, provided they were adequately standardized and validated.

These procedures would also provide a meaningful basis for the comparison of the relative effectiveness, in terms of overall happiness, of different social plans and/or ways of life in various cultural groups, since they are designed to reveal the nature of the life areas that contribute, and the degree to which each area contributes, to the overall happiness of the individual.

At present, the goals of most of the psychiatric and psychological services that are available to the public, are concerned with the treatment of individuals who are currently maladjusted and/or are subject to disturbing negative emotional feelings. Surely the time is ripe for the establishment of such services that have the specific goal of increasing the overall happiness of "more or less normal" individuals. The theoretical model on which the COHS is based could prove useful in such therapy, since it allows the prediction of the probable outcomes, in terms of overall happiness, of certain kinds of changes in the experiences of the individual. In this connection it is worth noting that the theory implies that it is possible to increase overall happiness by effecting changes in those life areas which the individual himself currently "sees" as important. In other words, the overall happiness of the individual can be increased without imposing on him new standards or values that may only be subscribed to by some rather restricted group in the community.

A further point worth noting here is that this theory implies that positive emotional feelings experienced in connection with aspects of life which are *not* "seen" as important by the individual do *not* contribute to his overall happiness. Hence, induced positive emotional experiences, such as may be effected by intracranial self-stimulation (Heath, 1964), or by other means, would not lead to increases in overall happiness, unless they were "seen"

TABLE 4. *Hypothetical data showing the influence on the COHS of increasing the salience of the "work" area of an individual, when the low happiness rating of that area remains the same* (note: A change in the ratio rating of the salience of one area results in a change in the salience scores of all areas)

| Important life areas | Happiness rating $\times/10$ (a) | Salience | | Weighted happiness score (a) $\times$ (b) |
		Ratio rating	Score % (b)	
1. Base data				
Work	2	20	10	20
Relations with wife	7	40	20	140
Relations with son	6	80	40	240
Recreation (sailing)	5	60	30	150
				550
$COHS = \dfrac{550}{10} = 55$				
2. Salience of "Work" increased to most important of all areas				
Work	2	100	36	72
Relations with wife	7	40	14	98
Relations with son	6	80	29	174
Recreation (sailing)	5	60	21	105
				449
$COHS = \dfrac{449}{10} \simeq 45$				

by the individual as a relevant part of the experiences in an important life area, or became an important life area per se.

Finally, suppose we had recorded the data shown in Table 4,1 from a given individual.

This table indicates that our S "sees" his work as a life area that is important — but not very important — to him, and that he is somewhat happy in it. Now suppose that the value system of some people in the society in which the S lives states that work ought to be a very important life area, and that pressures are put on the S to increase the salience of this area.[3] If the S yields to these pressures, and comes to consider his work as, say, the most important area in his life, and concomitant with this his happiness rating for this area remains the same (since no changes have occurred in his overall work situation), then his overall happiness would, in fact, decrease (see Table 4, 2).

This example has some practical implications: If the degree of happiness

---

[3] For example, Gardell (1971): "Due to the influences exerted by the Protestant ethic and other culturally conditioned factors, it is probable that most people look upon work as a socially necessary, and hence positively sanctioned, act. These factors, moreover, make it probable that most people perceive work to be one of the most important life areas for the individual's general satisfaction" (p. 149).

derived from work cannot or is not increased, then it is better, in terms of overall happiness, to maintain the relative salience of work at a lower rather than a higher level. Much of the work in modern industrialized societies appears to be such, that the individuals employed therein do not experience a high degree of happiness in their work. It also appears that it would be extremely difficult and/or costly to change the nature of much of this work, so that the individuals employed therein could, in fact, derive high degrees of happiness from it. In this case, then, it would surely be much better if the emphasis on the work ethic were relaxed and more emphasis were placed on increasing the relative importance of other areas in life from which the individual can derive a higher degree of happiness, for in these areas some effective action is probably possible.

There is an old saying that, I think, sums up this point rather well: "Do not itch where you cannot scratch!" However, I do think that it is necessary to add "but do try to make your arms longer!"

SUMMARY

Happiness, in the sense of a relatively deep, pervasive, and long-lasting positive emotional experience, is considered to be a significant aspect of welfare. Problems inherent in previous attempts to measure happiness and to uncover the nature of the factors contributing to overall happiness in life are discussed. Procedures are presented for the development of a scale that yields a composite overall happiness score (COHS) and that gives some indication of the nature of the factors contributing to overall happiness. Some implications of this for social planning and welfare are presented.

REFERENCES

Bradburn, N. M., and Caplovitz, D. (1965): *Reports on Happiness,* Aldine Publishing Co., Chicago, Ill.

Fellows, E. W. (1956): A study of factors related to a feeling of happiness, J. Educ. Res. *50,* 231–234.

Gardell, B. (1971): Alienation and mental health in the modern industrial environment. In: *Society, Stress, and Disease,* Vol. 1, pp. 148–180, The Psychosocial Environment and Psychosomatic Diseases (ed., L. Levi) Oxford University Press, London.

Goldings, H. J. (1954): On the avowal and projection of happiness, J. Personal. *23,* 30–47.

Hall, C. S., and Lindzey, G. (1970): *Theories of Personality,* 2nd ed., Wiley, New York.

Hartmann, G. W. (1934): Personality traits associated with variations in happiness, J. Abn. Soc. Psychol. *29,* 202–212.

Heath, R. G. (1964): Pleasure response of human subjects to direct stimulation of the brain: physiologic and psychodynamic considerations. In: *The Role of Pleasure in Behavior,* pp. 219–243 (ed., R. G. Heath), Harper & Row, New York.

Hinkle Jr., L. E., Plummer, N., Metraux, R., et al. (1957): Studies in human ecology—factors relevant to the occurrence of bodily illness and disturbances in mood, thought and behavior in three homogenous population groups, Amer. J. Psychiat. *114,* 212–220.

Hinkle Jr., L. E., and Wolff, H. G. (1958): Ecological investigations of the relationship between illness, life experiences and the social environment, Amer. Intern. Med. *49,* 1374–1388.

Kornhauser, A. (1965): *Mental Health of the Industrial Worker—A Detroit Study,* Wiley, New York.

Mead, G. H. (1934): *Mind, Self, and Society,* University of Chicago Press, Chicago, Ill.

Rogers, C. R. (1959): A theory of therapy, personality, and interpersonal relationships, as developed in the client-centered framework. In: *Psychology: A Study of a Science,* Vol. 3, pp. 184–256 (ed. S. Koch), McGraw-Hill, New York.

Sidman, M. (1960): *Tactics of Scientific Research: Evaluating Experimental Data in Psychology,* Basic Books, New York.

Symonds, P. M. (1937): Happiness as related to problems and interests, J. Educ. Psychol. *28,* 290–294.

Symonds, P. M. (1951): *The Ego and the Self,* Appleton-Century-Crofts, New York.

Veroff, J., Feld, S., and Gurin, G. (1962): Dimensions of subjective adjustment, *J. Abn. Soc. Psychol. 64,* 192–205.

Watson, G. (1930): Happiness among adult students of education, J. Educ. Psychol. *21,* 79–109.

Wessman, A. E., and Ricks, D. F. (1966): *Mood and Personality,* Holt, Rinehart & Winston, New York.

Wilson, W. R. (1960): An attempt to determine some correlates and dimensions of hedonic tone, unpublished doctoral dissertation, Northwestern University, Evanston, Ill.

Wilson, W. R. (1965): Relation of sexual behaviors, values, and conflicts to avowed happiness, Psychol. Rep. *17,* 371–378.

Wilson, W. R. (1967): Correlates of avowed happiness, Psychol. Bull. *67,* 294–306.

Emotions—Their Parameters and Measurement,
edited by L. Levi.
Raven Press, New York © 1975

Manipulation of Emotion:
Electrophysiological and Surgical Methods

C. W. Sem-Jacobsen and O. B. Styri

EEG Research Institute Gaustad Sykehus, Gaustad Oslo 3, Norway

INTRODUCTION

Emotional changes in man triggered by head traumas or tumors have been well recognized for centuries. Intoxication by various drugs has been used extensively, not only to produce pleasure, but also to produce hallucinations in religious rites from the time of the Stone Age.

From neurosurgical treatment of patients, we have gained information on how neurosurgery in certain regions of the human brain may produce temporary or lasting changes in emotion and behavior. The many observations led Egas Moniz to investigate the possibility of neurosurgical treatment of psychiatric patients.

Moniz's classic paper "How I came to perform prefrontal leukotomy" illustrated not only the Pavlovian principles but also what he had learned from the chimpanzees operated on by Fulton, who presented his results at the First International Neurological Congress in London in 1935. The first prefrontal leukotomy was performed at the insistence of Moniz in 1936 by Almeida Lima.

At the International Symposium on the Reticular Formation of the Brain in Detroit in 1957, papers were presented dealing with electrical manipulation of emotions in animals. The papers from work with animals presented by Olds (1958b), Brady (1958), and Lilly (1958) are of great value and special interest for the interpretation of the results obtained by stimulation in the depth of the human brain.

At that meeting, one of the authors (Sem-Jacobsen, 1958) discussed electrical manipulation of emotion in man. We quote from the discussion of depth electrographic stimulation in the brain of human patients. In carrying out these studies we have had certain advantages in working with conscious humans. The patient is able to express desire for or dislike of further stimulation and also to define in detail the feelings evoked by such stimulation.

It has been possible to divide the positive responses described by the previous authors into different groups. Feelings of ease and relaxation, feelings of joy with smiling, and feelings of great satisfaction have been elicited from different areas in the positive system. It has been possible to divide the negative-response areas into those for anxiety, restlessness, depression, fright, and horror, to mention only a few.

As for the positive or pleasant areas, patients have repeatedly expressed desire for more stimulation. In the past year, a number of patients, after repeated stimulation of the ventromedial region of the frontal lobe, relaxed and were seemingly relieved of their psychotic symptoms. The clinical effects of the stimulations were temporary, but could last for more than a week.

STUDIES WITH IMPLANTED ELECTRODES IN MAN

Although Berger had already carried out depth recording in human brains (1931), Hess's observations, together with similar studies by others (Hunter and Jasper, 1949), led many clinical investigators to record electrical activity from the human brain during neurosurgical procedures, but inherent difficulties in obtaining good recordings in the operating room were discouraging. Consequently, certain expectations regarding the possibility of observing basic brain mechanisms and mental processes failed to materialize.

By the beginning of the 1950s, prefrontal leucotomy and neurosurgical treatment for mental disorders were being extensively employed. The success of thorough animal experimentation eventually prompted workers to weigh the anticipated benefits of using depth electroencephalography to limit and improve the accuracy of frontal-lobe surgery.

A number of conscientious physicians became concerned about the increased use of prefrontal leucotomy and particularly the associated gross inaccuracies and extensive brain damage inherent in the technique. Consequently, workers began to seek more accurate means of localization through refinements of the old technique. Their aim was to confine any interruption of fibers in the brain to the pathways involved in the disease. One goal, therefore, was to find a way to localize tracts that might be significant to the disease and to limit the surgery to focal lesions within them.

In the preliminary cases, using depth EEG as a guide, physicians observed positive results like those previously obtained by conventional prefrontal leucotomy. As the depth-EEG technique underwent refinements, the number of successful operations increased, complications decreased, and undesirable side effects such as postoperative convulsions were abolished (Petersen, Dodge, Sem-Jacobsen, Lazarte, and Holman, 1955).

The new technique included the placement of the electrodes in tissue already destined to be destroyed or excised. This permitted detailed observations without causing additional trauma to the patient. The information derived from such investigations threw more light on the procedure and facilitated the development of improved techniques, which would minimize the brain damage necessary during psychosurgery.

Between 1951 and 1952, the above mentioned idea led to additional clinical studies by several investigators. Each contributed to the development of appropriate techniques, including those for implanting multiple electrode leads. Of consequence were studies at Yale University by Delgado, Hamlin, and Chapman (1952), at Tulane University under the guidance of Heath (Heath, Peacock, Monroe, and Miller, 1954), and at the Mayo Clinic with a team led by Petersen, Bickford, Dodge, and Sem-Jacobsen (Woltman, Dodge, Holman, Sem-Jacobsen, Bickeford, Petersen, Faulconer, Schnugg, Bahley, Miller, and Craig, 1953).

The three centers, working independently, had the same basic objective: to improve the psychosurgical operation — leucotomy — by studying before the actual operation the electrical activity of tissue. This was an attempt to find an electrophysiological guide for psychosurgery.

The techniques developed — all outgrowths of earlier animal studies — were amazingly similar in their final refinement. One of the differences in technical detail was the Mayo team's technique of placing the electrodes inside their introducer, which was a needle. The two other groups, with the aid of a solid introducer, placed their arrays of electrodes beside the introducer. It was thought then that the latter technique introduced a risk of damaging or ripping small vessels near the tip of the lead, but the hazard has proved to be more theoretical than practical. Nevertheless, most workers today recommend and use an introducing needle.

The Mayo group published the results of its preliminary studies in the *Proceedings of the Staff Meetings of the Mayo Clinic,* March 1953 (Woltman et al., 1953). In June of the following year, the American EEG society held its first Symposium on Depth Electrography (1954) from the human brain. The meeting provided useful guidelines for subsequent depth-EEG studies, and served to establish friendly cooperation between various teams of investigators.

CLINICAL USE OF DEPTH-EEG IN THERAPY

From the studies presented at the 1953 symposium, one of the first practical results was improved treatment through the discovery of the delta activity, localized in the ventromedial area of the frontal lobe. By limiting prefrontal leucotomy to this region, some of the undesirable side effects were avoided (Petersen et al. 1955).

In the studies by the Mayo team, preliminary electrical stimulation in these same areas with the Type S-J stimulus improved the patient immensely. Sometimes the beneficial effect lasted several weeks.

In 1958, the Neurosurgical Congress in Copenhagen discussed the inaccuracies of stereotactic localization and the inherent risks of damaging the patient's mental processes while rendering successful neurosurgical treatment, and urged the use of preliminary depth-EEG studies in parkinsonian patients (Sem-Jacobsen and Torkildsen, 1958; Sem-Jacobsen, 1958). The new technique was refined so that it could be used for both psychosurgery and neurosurgery in Parkinson's disease.

JUSTIFICATION AND ETHICS FOR STUDIES WITH IMPLANTED ELECTRODES IN MAN

In the course of applying new diagnostic and therapeutic techniques, the physician must observe the patient closely. Most observations are directly pertinent to the information necessary for the diagnosis and treatment of the patient involved. The physician often finds it possible to make a number of additional observations of patients, as by-products of the main examination, while still following the rules of ethics outlined above.

Similarly, in the course of treating patients by depth electrography it is possible to record many additional observations without introducing unwarranted risks or discomfort to the patient. The physician records some observations with the full participation and cooperation of the patient in describing responses or following directions. Others he records by a complete biomedical monitoring of the patient. The former demands more detailed scrutiny of the patient, the latter only requires the use of more, although innocuous, sensors.

Today, the advantages of depth-EEG recording prior to the placement of permanent therapeutic lesions are well recognized. *Stereotactic lesions should not be made in the brain without a thorough preliminary testing of the potential effect of the lesion.* Depth-EEG recording provides a reliable tool for this purpose.

In a monograph (Sem-Jacobsen, 1968), one of the authors attempted to bridge the gap between physiology and clinical medicine by analyzing the voluminous data obtained in the course of diagnostic and therapeutic procedures. The major findings, which have been substantiated in one or more instances, are presented as much from the neurophysiological point of view as from the clinical.

The many ethically obtained observations already made in the course of placing electrodes for diagnosis and treatment of diseases have contributed significantly to current physiological concepts of the human forebrain.

INHERENT PROBLEMS IN THE INTERPRETATION OF RESPONSES TO ELECTRICAL STIMULATION

Most patients are at ease, cooperative, and eager to provide good descriptions of their reactions to electrical stimulation. They understand that the test results will enable the doctor to localize the site and render better treatment.

Cooperation with the Patient

Motivation is a crucial factor in the success of the examination. If the patient is uncooperative, overly cooperative, or even too cautious, the responses may not be accurately registered.

A case in point is an experience one of the authors had with an individual in whom the stimulation elicited visual phenomena. This was a rather quiet, uncooperative patient who withheld information because he thought it was ridiculous. In fact, he was hesitant to mention seeing things for fear the doctor might think he was hallucinating.

When questioned directly, the patient denied seeing anything.

Suddenly, after 2 weeks, the patient's curiosity served to clarify the situation. One day he asked, "Doctor, please, would you tell me how do you know that I see colored balls in front of my eyes? And how do you know when they appear and when they disappear? I have tested myself, with eyes closed and eyes open, and I am one hundred percent sure that you, yourself, can't see these colored balls. They are not put on the wall. It is something that only appears before my eyes."

An overly cooperative patient may present another type of problem. He might, for example, smile or report a fabricated experience simply because he thinks the doctor will be interested or is anticipating a response to the stimulus. In his eagerness to help out when questioned, he may honestly believe he experiences something that he does not. This is usually due to a high degree of autosuggestion. Sometimes an overly cooperative patient may assume that the examiner is pleased when he describes a certain response. In order to continue to please, he might repeat the same, or a similar, story on stimulation of a number of contacts. To overcome this difficulty, in some instances it has been necessary to carry out entire stimulation sessions using only "placebo" stimulation.

One patient was stimulated repeatedly while a senior visiting colleague was studying depth electrography in our laboratory. The patient noticed that the visiting physician became quite alert and interested in his smiles and general behavior following stimulation in a rewarding area. In gratitude for the interest we had shown him and his long-term crippling disease, this patient wanted very much to please. Thus, to be kind he started smiling during stimulation of contacts which previously had not rendered responses.

Cautioning the patient against false responses proved unsuccessful, and we had to carry out an entire session with placebo stimulation to keep him from smiling every time the master button was pressed. Following this, in a few sessions this patient did not smile, even when stimulated in mildly rewarding areas, because he was afraid we might think he was giving false responses again. Later, however, when he was stimulated in a strongly positive area, his responses were entirely convincing.

Context and Language

Often the patient must describe sensations that he may not have experienced before in the same form or within any similar context. He is forced, then, to relate the new experiences to his old concepts or frame of reference. The patient may need help in overcoming this difficulty, but it must be given without directly misleading him with suggestions.

In one of the author's first patients, one electrode was placed in the olfactory bulb. An attempt was made to map the ventromedial area of the frontal lobe in the plane of the coronal sutures. Electrical stimulation of this electrode elicited a sensation of a pleasant odor, but according to the patient, it was not like any she had ever perceived before.

This patient, a young girl about 20 years old, found it extremely hard to describe the odor. She had had some education after grade school, but despite a fairly good vocabulary, she was unable to render a satisfactory description of an experience clearly outside her former frame of reference. Although she experienced difficulty in comparing it with odors familiar to her in a large battery of odors, she always recognized the identical odor on stimulation of the same electrode. During later sessions, upon stimulation of this contact, she frequently said, "Now I smell that nice odor again." Although one might think it rather simple to describe a new odor, in this instance it proved impossible for the patient.

The problems of language and semantics are greater when stimulations give more diffuse, inner sensations and "feelings" or changes of mood. Even simple experiences may be difficult to describe if the patient's frame of reference or vocabulary is inadequate.

At first it seemed helpful, also, for patients to discuss their experiences with one another. In retrospect, however, this might have been a fallacy had any of the patients been influenced by another's leadership, the desire to describe a normal, or "correct," response, or by the urge to describe a response more interesting or unusual than his fellow patients'.

Atmosphere in the Examining Room

The general atmosphere in the examining room may affect the patient's mood and cause misleading results. In contrast to the very marked responses that are completely uninfluenced by what is going on around the patient, mild changes in mood are highly sensitive to the general environment in the examining room. If the examiner or the technicians are smiling (or worse, laughing) during the examination their moods may be transferred to the patient and cause him to start laughing in the middle of a stimulation. Conversely, too serious an atmosphere may affect the mood of the patient in the opposite way.

Prolonged indoctrination and training of the group participating in the stimulation is necessary to achieve an atmosphere of indifference in the examining room. Intermittently a planned change in the atmosphere is carried out in order to evaluate properly the effect of the environment on the stimulation responses.

Suppression

At times a response to an electrical stimulation of an electrode may depend upon the general susceptibility of the brain. In our experience, a response failed to occur now and then upon electrical stimulation although repeatable responses were observed in both earlier and later sessions.

In one patient, for instance, we observed repeatedly a movement of the left leg in response to stimulation of a certain electrode. The patient had been at ease during the stimulation session. While the author and a visiting colleague were examining this patient, we asked him to relax so completely that he did not move. He then closed his eyes, and his muscles were completely relaxed. This time, when stimulated, no response was obtained nor did the patient feel anything. When stimulating him the next time, we asked if he could feel anything, and the patient became alert and the usual response of muscle contraction in the leg reappeared.

This phenomenon is seen not only in responses like the contraction of the skeleton muscles, but also in the other modalities, such as moods.

Misinterpretation of Behavior

Misinterpretation of responses is another serious pitfall. For instance, frequently a patient will smile in response to electrical stimulation either because he likes it or because he is projected into a pleasant, happy mood. If the patient does not elaborate, however, it may be hard to tell whether the smile is interpreted correctly. He may volunteer the remark that he likes the response, but if, for example, it is a sexual pleasure, the patient may be embarrassed and fail to relay such additional information.

On the other hand, the smile may not be due to actual pleasure: rather, it may be triggered by a memory of something pleasant or funny. Occasionally, a smile may be only coincidental: at the time of the stimulation the patient may have been thinking or seeing something that appeared funny to him but was unrelated to the stimulation.

The coincidental smile is the easiest to verify because electrical stimulation of only eight to 10 contacts each day at irregular intervals is carried out in random order. Hence, the patient does not remember the response from one time to the next except when a contact produces a very marked response. A coincidental smile will not generally accompany subsequent stimulation of the same contact.

A smile might also represent a secondary response to a tickling sensation.

The patient, in this case, will continue to smile if he likes it and if the tickling is limited. It is difficult to determine, however, whether the smile is a genuine emotional response or is due to tickling in a "pleasure area." Distinction of the reason for the smile is definitely necessary and may demand thorough questioning and reexamination of the patient. The stimulus might also produce a smile and a tickling sensation caused by a rhythmic contraction of certain muscles.

Self-Stimulation and Reward

Self-stimulation is an extremely valuable tool for studying a response to electrical stimulation. The stimulators may be so adjusted that a continuous train of electrical stimuli is given as long as the patient presses the button. On the other hand, the stimulators may be set so that the pressed button triggers a train of stimuli of a certain duration. If additional stimulation is desired, the button must be pressed again after the original train is completed.

Self-stimulation in animals is the "bar pressing" resulting in an electrical stimulation of an electrode in its brain, especially when used to obtain a pleasurable stimulus. The frequency of the self-stimulation, i.e., the rate at which the animal will press the bar, has sometimes been regarded as an indication of how much the animal likes or dislikes the stimulus. Many authors (Brady, 1955, 1957; Olds, 1958a) have described the technique and phenomena associated with self-stimulation in work with animals.

In human patients, self-stimulation has been used in the authors' work for the past 20 years. The patients occasionally are asked to try self-stimulation; at other times they are just handed the button. In the latter case, without being asked, they have the opportunity for self-stimulation if they so desire.

In contrast to what has been described in animals (Brady, 1961; Olds, 1961), the author has found the rate of self-stimulation only of limited value in evaluating the desire for self-stimulation. The patient usually will not press the button more often than once per second. The only occasions on which the author has observed rates appreciably above this rate have been when after-discharges occurred. Then an extremely rapid rate of self-stimulation was maintained for as long as after-discharges were seen in the recording.

In such instances the patient's level of consciousness also appears to be definitely impaired and the patient will continue the rapid button-pressing (without effect) until the after-discharges cease and he becomes sufficiently alert to realize that the button is turned off.

An emotional reward often has been designated as an explanation or motivation for self-stimulation; an unpleasant response is thought to cause the patient to avoid stimulation. In humans, however, other incentives are also very strong and can sometimes be more potent than the simple pleasure received. The reasons given by patients for continuing self-stimulation seem as complex as man himself.

In man, curiosity is probably the most dominant causative factor in initiating self-stimulation. If a patient feels "something," he might wonder: "Precisely what is the nature of this sensation? What am I feeling? Let me try it once more. Once more! Is it tickling? Is it real pleasure?"

Other motivating factors include obedience and the desire to cooperate. Most patients want to be helpful to the examiner and do what he asks of them. Many patients will stimulate themselves upon the slightest suggestion even when the stimulus gives an unpleasant or punishing response. This is another pitfall one must avoid in interpreting motivation.

Self-stimulation also may be continued by the patient because he likes it, and if left alone, he will continue to stimulate himself for a long period. If the circuit breaker is used, he will stop very quickly when the stimulus is turned off. The response to the stimulus in this instance is a motivating factor in itself.

General Remarks

Certain types of responses are somewhat sensitive to the strength of stimulus to the extent that a response within a major group can be switched from one subcategory to another. The strength of stimulus will not, however, alter the response from one major group to another, e.g., from speech changes to visual changes.

Placebo stimulation is necessary to verify the reliability of the responses.

Summation effects and delayed recognition of the stimulus by the patients are other aspects of the problems. Evidently there are many pitfalls which may invalidate otherwise carefully collected information. Only a few are outlined above. The problems have been extensively dealt with in earlier monographs (Sem-Jacobsen, 1968, 1971; Sem-Jacobsen and Styri, 1971).

MATERIAL AND ANALYSIS

The main purpose of the detailed analysis of the data collected by the author on depth electrography is to further, in whatever way possible, the general understanding of the brain function and behavior. It is logical, consequently, for the analysis of the types of responses to be described in appropriate detail.

In so doing, it will be necessary to consider the material from both the detailed analysis of each of the major groups of responses and the interrelationships of the responses of the major groups.

In the 82 patients, 1,594 of the 2,659 electrodes tested yielded responses whereas no responses were elicited from 1,065. Table 1 indicates that approximately half of the electrodes (805) gave single responses (listed only

TABLE 1. Stimulation responses from intracerebral electrodes

Category	Total elect.	Single resp.	Mult. resp.	Total assoc. resp.	Motor	Tremor	Rigidity	Speech	Visual	Odor	Taste	Audio	Vestib-ular	Sensory	Mood	Memory	Aphasia	Conscious-ness	Cardio-vasc.	Vegeta-tive	Sex
Motor resp.	205	35	170	368	—	46	20	19	21	3		2	5	127	52		1	26	21	25	1
Tremor	138	31	107	230	46	—	14	9	2	1	1		1	71	38			16	17	14	
Rigidity	24	1	23	74	20	14	—	5	3					19	2			6	3	2	
Chgs. in speech	83	10	73	193	19	9	5	—	4				6	38	37	1		30	22	22	
Visual chgs.	104	42	62	124	21	2	3	4	—	1			2	39	28	1		7	7	10	
Olfact. resp.	15	6	9	27	3	1			1	—				9	5			1	3	5	
Taste	4	2	2	3							—			2	2						
Audit. resp.	6	6		13	2							—		5				3		1	
Vestibular chgs.	29	6	23	44	5			6				5	—	5	10			8	2	5	
Periph. sens.	655	259	396	745	127	71	19	38	30	9		5	5	—	193	2	1	77	80	76	
Chgs. in mood	643	285	358	656	52	38	2	37	28	5	2	2	10	193	—	6	1	108	89	83	2
Elicit. of memory	8	1	7	14				1						2	6	—		1	2	2	
Aphasia	1		1	4	1									1	1		—				
Chgs. in consc.	247	72	175	384	26	16	6	30	7	1		3	8	77	108	1	1	—	48	53	1
Cardiovasc. chgs.	187	34	153	349	21	17	3	22	7	3			2	80	89	2		48	—	53	2
Vegetative chgs.	163	21	142	352	25	14	2	22	10	5		1	5	76	83	2		53	53	—	1
Sexual resp.	2		2	6		1								1	2				1	1	—

Total no. of responses: 2514, single responses: 805, multiple responses: 1709.

in one group), and the other half of the electrodes (798) gave multiple simultaneous responses (listed in several groups).

It is necessary to grade the general reliability of these responses indicating the degree of accuracy with which a response may be observed. Those responses that could be measured objectively had a higher reliability than those dependent on a subjective description. This was especially true of a new phenomenon lacking a familiar frame of reference.

Sometimes the strength of the stimulus changed the response from one category to another (e.g., from arrest of speech II to arrest of speech III). It requires an increase in the voltage to switch these categories of responses equivalent to 0.1 and 0.3 V at the electrode level. On the other hand, the response was never switched from one group to another by a change in stimuli characteristics.

There seems to be no difference in the responses obtained from the right or left hemispheres. This is remarkable, particularly in regard to changes in speech, since none of the patients with speech responses was left-handed.

The analyses show that there is a general representation of nearly all groups of responses in the four sections of the brain studied. However, as expected there is an overrepresentation of mood and consciousness in the frontal lobe, motor and peripheral sensory responses in the central area around the third ventricle, and visual phenomena in the posterior part of the brain. Changes in speech are more heavily represented in the central area around the third ventricle and neighboring parts of the temporal lobe.

No response was obtained from 1,065 electrodes. At first, the locations of the electrodes in the different sections in the brain were thought to have a major influence in eliciting a response. However, no responses varied from 26 to 45% of the electrodes in the different sections of the brain.

The lower rate (26%) in, i.e., the central area around the third ventricle which contains the midline nuclei and the internal capsule, is not significantly different from the 31% in the posterior section of the brain, i.e., the occipital lobe. The higher number (45%) of no responses from the frontal lobe is, in part, related to the clinical diagnosis of the patients.

About half of the electrodes (805 out of 1,594) gave only a single response while the remainder of the electrodes (789) yielded more complex responses. From these electrodes a total of 1,709 responses was listed, constituting an average of 2.2 responses for each electrode. The actual number of responses listed for any electrode in this study ranges from one to seven.

From a physiological point of view, it might have been of greater interest to separate the orders of occurrence had the number of multiple responses increased with higher voltages. But since clinical consideration dictated careful use of stimulus voltage and limited the stimulus strength, in most instances, only early responses were obtained.

Motor responses include responses ranging from the contraction of single muscles to complex movements of head, body, and extremities. These were seen from 205 electrodes, whereas 138 electrodes caused changes in tremor. The muscular rigidity was affected by stimulation of 24 contacts.

Under speech are listed all responses affecting the highly complex motor and ideational mechanism of speech. Stimulation of 83 different electrodes interfered with this function in one way or another.

The visual function was altered by electrical stimulation of 104 contacts.

Olfactory (15) and gustatory (4) responses, as well as auditory (6) responses, resulted from a total of only 25 electrodes in these groups. The vestibular system was disrupted by electrical stimulation of 29 electrodes. The largest number of responses (655) were peripheral sensory changes.

The second largest (643) were related to changes in mood. Memory of past experiences and aphasia were encountered infrequently. Stimulation of 247 contacts caused changes in the level of alertness or consciousness. Cardiovascular and vegetative responses were elicited from 187 and 163 electrodes, respectively.

Responses related to sexual sensation or sexual behavior were described from stimulation of only two electrodes.

In 176 instances, the electrical stimulus triggered electrical after-discharge around certain electrodes. These phenomena, which lasted from 1 sec to as long as 5 min, were particularly valuable in forewarning us against impending seizures so that seizures from electrical stimulation were greatly minimized.

The after-discharges most often appeared to be localized to the tissue surrounding the electrode stimulated. They intermittently also appeared in the neighboring electrode on the same array of leads. However, as described in earlier publications the after-discharges infrequently spread to areas such as the ventromedial area of the frontal lobe, the central part of the temporal lobe, and the posterior part of the limbic area.

CHANGES IN MOOD PRODUCED BY ELECTRICAL STIMULATION

Patient Material

In response to electrical stimulation, changes in mood were elicited from 643 electrodes in 66 patients (Table 2). Although a majority of the patients were males, this merely reflects the distribution of sex in the total patient material.

Twenty-six patients suffered from schizophrenia and nine from other mental disorders. Twenty-six were being treated for Parkinson's disease, two for epilepsy, two for cerebral palsy, and one for phantom limb pain.

Electrode Location

Table 3, indicating the location of the electrodes affecting mood, illustrates that the same response is obtained from right (327) and left (316) sides with no significant difference.

TABLE 2. *Patients*

Total	Sex	Age	Mental dis.	Age	Misc.[a]	Age	Parkin-sonism	Age
16	F	21–63	7	21–57	1	55	8	41–63
50	M	15–70	28	19–54	4	15–46	18	37–70
66		15–70	35	19–57	5	15–55	26	37–70

[a] Misc. two cerebral palsy, age 15–17; one phantom limb, age 46; two epilepsy, age 26–55.

TABLE 3. *Location and reliability*

| Category | Pat | Elect | Location | | Reliability | | | | |
			R	L	Q	O	V	U	A-D
(1) Positive I	64	360	172	188	25	114	113	108	46
(2) Positive II	20	31	18	13		6	25		9
(3) Positive III	7	8	3	5			7	1	2
(4) Negative I	41	162	94	68	8	42	35	77	15
(5) Negative II	9	17	10	7		2	6	9	3
(6) Negative III	4	4	4				3	1	
(7) Emotional b.	15	20	10	10		5	9	6	6
(8) Ambivalent	17	38	16	22	1	2	33	2	7
(9) Orgastic resp.	3	3		3			3		
Total	66	643	327	316	34	171	234	204	88

Q, questionable; O, once of several; V, verified; U, unrepeated.

The majority of contacts (379) were located in the anterior part of the brain; whereas only a few (29) were located in the posterior head region. Thus there is a marked overrepresentation in the frontal lobe. This conforms with other general findings that mood and behavior are strongly represented in this area of the brain.

Neither emotional outbursts nor ambivalence was elicited from the occipital part of the brain.

Figures 1 and 2 show the plotting of the responses in the brain. Each diagram illustrates the location in the sagittal plane in slices 1 cm thick. For clarity, the responses have been consolidated into positive, negative, ambivalent, and orgastic groups. Again, the plottings indicate a concentration of electrodes in the ventromedial area of the forebrain and in or near the limbic system.

Reliability of Response

The authenticity of the responses was verified by repeated stimulation from 234 electrodes. From 204 other electrodes, convincing responses

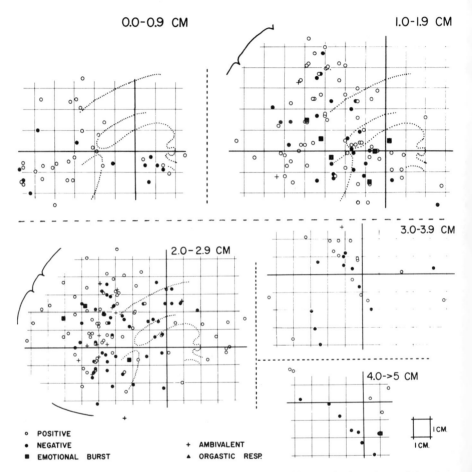

FIG. 1. Section of right hemisphere. Plottings in 1-cm-thick sagittal sections of the electrodes on which electrical stimulation produced emotional changes.

were observed once but, for clinical reasons, the stimulus was not repeated. Only from 34 electrodes were there any questions regarding the validity of the response (Reliability Q). Thirty-three of these responses, which were positive or negative grade 1, when compared with the anatomical locations and the types of responses of 148 other electrodes from which similar responses were verified, appeared to be valid.

MOOD

LEFT HEMISPHERE

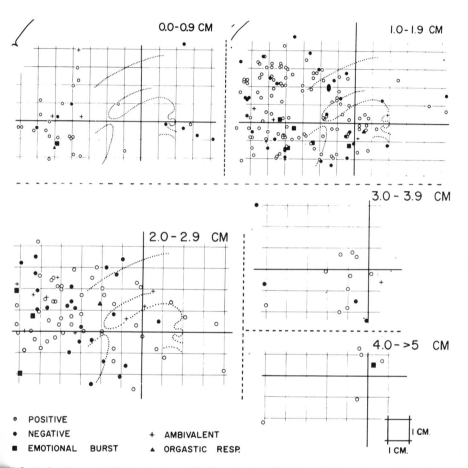

FIG. 2. Sections of left hemisphere. Plotting in 1-cm-thick sagittal sections of the electrodes on which electrical stimulation produced emotional changes.

Classification of Groups and Categories

The existence of areas within the brain in which electrical stimulation alter the patient's mood and behavior has long been recognized in the treatment of psychiatric disorders. The investigator's depth-electrographic examinations of patients also enabled him to localize areas in the brain, where the emotional state of the patient could be manipulated with electrical stimulation.

The observations of changes in mood were grouped according to the following nine categories:

(1) The patient becomes relaxed, at ease, has a feeling of well-being, and/or may be a little sleepy. Positive I.

(2) The patient is definitely changed, is in a good mood, and feels good. He is relaxed, at ease, and enjoying himself. He frequently smiles. There is slight euphoria, but the behavior is within normal limits. He may want more stimulations. Positive II.

(3) The euphoria is definitely beyond normal limits. The patient laughs out loud, enjoys himself, positively likes the stimulation, and wants more. Positive III.

(4) The patient gets restless, anxious, tense, or sad. Negative I.

(5) Irritability may be combined with a mild depression. The patient is unhappy and definitely uncomfortable. Negative II.

(6) The patient is depressed, irritable, nasty, or even angry, afraid, sometimes scared, sometimes crying. Negative III.

(7) Sudden emotional outbursts either in a positive or negative direction.

(8) Ambivalence. The patient sometimes likes it, sometimes does not. Definite ambivalence is expressed.

(9) Orgastic type response, orgastic mood reversal. The patient at first expresses a positive response, then suddenly is so completely satisfied that he does not want more stimulation for a shorter or longer period. Continued stimulation at this time may even be definitely unpleasant.

Problems in Classifying Responses

As in many other responses to electrical stimulation, some of the categories are easy to define and distinguish. For two reasons, however, it may be difficult to differentiate among various degrees of positivity or negativity: (a) The normal degree of happiness for a patient following a successful operation has not been defined. (b) Changes in the strength of the stimulus may alter the response from one degree to another, although an increase in the stimulus strength generally is not enough to switch the response from the first to the third degree.

The investigator must rely largely upon the patient's subjective evaluation of the effect of the stimulus, but if the response is marked, certain facial expressions or behavior, or both will often reflect the change in mood. These accompanying changes such as smiling, relaxation, tense restlessness, depression, laughing, or sobbing may often be observed by the investigating team. Self-stimulation, or even the desire to carry out self-stimulation at some electrodes, is often more revealing than at patient's verbal descriptions

For the less marked responses such as positive I and negative I the over- and undercooperative patients, described earlier, cause considerable problems, so that responses must be verified by repeated stimulation to avoid any doubt.

Pitfalls for the examiner in the interpretation of responses can be pronounced in regard to changes in mood. To illustrate, we tested a rather withdrawn 50-year-old female patient who responded to a stimulus by smiling. Sometimes she even laughed and seemed to enjoy the stimulation of a certain contact. The striking effect was repeated at irregular intervals and at different times of the day with the patient basically in various moods. The result was always the same. This phenomenon was demonstrated to several colleagues, and all were convinced that the electrode being tested was in a strong, positive "pleasure region."

Because of the patient's uniform reactions in repeated sessions, the author took it for granted that she liked it and discussed the significance of this response in her presence without eliciting any comment from her. Suddenly one day the patient became angry and told us that she was "fed up" and "did not enjoy these stimulations at all." She asked us to stop and refrain from any further stimulation of this contact. She said she "had had enough!"

The stimulus did not give the patient any pleasure. Instead it created in some of her pelvic muscles a rhythmic contraction which tickled her and caused the laughter. It was evident that the author had not been stimulating either a "pleasure center," nor a center dealing with sensation. He had simply been stimulating muscles that contracted and caused the tickling and, in turn, forced the patient to smile and laugh.

Type of Stimuli Used

The Type L and the Type S-J stimulus were employed (Sem-Jacobsen, 1968). As already pointed out, the Type S-J stimulus in the ventromedial area of the frontal lobe intermittently produced an ambivalent response or opposite response to that of the Type L, e.g., a positive response produced by the Type L would produce a negative or ambivalent response when the Type S-J was applied to the same electrode.

Single and Complex Responses

Changes in mood were the first responses noted from 617 of the 643 contacts. Other changes appeared prior to such responses in only 26 instances.

After-discharges occurred during stimulation of 88 electrodes, and in most instances were found in combination with the mild-positive or mild-negative response.

The frequency of single and multiple responses is indicated in Table 4. Single responses were elicited from 285 electrodes in this group. The pro-

TABLE 4. Responses associated with emotional changes

Category	Total elect.	Single resp.	Mult. resp.	Total assoc. resp.	Motor	Tremor	Rigidity	Speech	Visual	Odor	Audio	Vestibular	Sensory	Memory	Aphasia	Consciousness	Cardio-vascular	Vegetative	Sex
(1) Positive I	360	172	188	322	22	14	1	17	14	3	2	6	93	6		59	49	36	
(2) Positive II	31[a]	5	26	55	7	2		4	5			1	17			6	6	6	1
(3) Positive III	8	1	7	19	3	1			1	1		2	5			1	4	3	
(4) Negative I	162	77	85	148	12	15	1	6	3				47			25	15	21	
(5) Negative II	17	7	10	17	1	1		1	2				5			3	1	3	
(6) Negative III	4	1	3	4	1			1	1				1						
(7) Emotional burst	20	7	13	33	4	3		2	1			1	5			8	5	4	
(8) Ambivalent	38	14	24	51	2	2		5	1				18			5	8	9	
(9) Orgastic resp.	3	1	2	7				1		1			2		1	1	1	1	1
Total	643	285	358	656	52	38	2	37	28	5	2	10	193	6	1	108	89	83	2

[a] Three went to sleep.

portion, however, is not significantly different from that for the overall total number of single (805) and multiple (789) responses. From more than half of the electrodes, other types of responses were elicited simultaneously with the changes in mood. Both major categories, positive I and negative I, show a slightly higher number of multiple responses than the number of multiple responses in Categories 2 and 3, positive II and III.

Considering the large number of electrodes from which changes in mood were elicited, 643 out of a total of 1,594, it is evident that the number of associated responses would appear by chance. A discussion of the absolute number of associated responses without simultaneously giving their mathematical significance could therefore easily be misleading. In this study, fortunately, mathematical analysis gives the exact significance of the associating responses.

Interrelationship of Responses: Significance

The multitude of observations from the electrodes provides opportunity to study the brain and its functions further. *Is there a significant cross-correlation between the category of responses obtained from the various electrodes?*

Mathematical calculations of the correlations were carried out. First we treated all our responses and the whole brain as a single entity. We cross-correlated our electrodes divided on the basis of the 99 categories of response obtained.

The correlation coefficients have been calculated for each pair of categories by the formula:

$$R = \frac{ad - bc}{\sqrt{(a + b)(a + c)(b + d)(c + d)}}$$

Here a, b, c, and d are the numbers of cases with responses in both categories, in only one of the two categories or in neither category respectively. $R \cdot \sqrt{N}$ has a normal distribution with standard deviation equal to 1. Here N, equal to $a + b + c + d$, is the total number of electrodes giving a response in any of the 99 categories.

The limits of significance used are:

$R \sqrt{N}$	p
2.576	0.01
2.807	0.005
3.291	0.001
3.89	0.0001

This means that the probability of getting a correlation coefficient numerically greater than the observed one, by chance, is p. We mean "by chance" that there is no underlying correlation between the responses. The result is illustrated in Fig. 3.

The same cross-correlations were also carried out between the various groups.

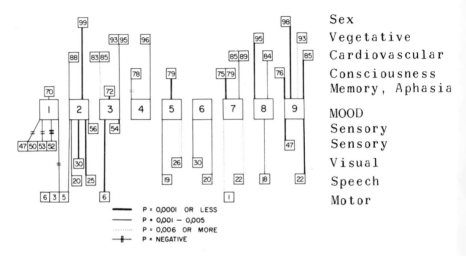

FIG. 3. Correlation between categories of mood and other categories, with significances. Categories in group mood: (1) positive I, (2) positive II, (3) positive III, (4) negative I, (5) negative II, (6) negative III, (7) emotional burst, (8) ambivalent, (9) orgastic response. Key to categories 1 to 99: (1) Head-face, cont., (3) Upper ext., (5) Complex with head, (6) Complex without h., (18) Change in voice, (19) Stutter, (20) Arrest I, (22) Arrest II, (25) Vocalization, (26) Colored balls, (30) Vibrations, (47) Current, body, (50) Funny, body and ext., (52) Unspecific, (53) Mixed and diffuse, (54) Warm, (56) Tickling, (70) Recollective memory, (72) Aphasia, (75) Confused, chewing, (76) Reduced alertness, (78) Alerting/waking, (79) Floating away, (83) Pulse, decrease, (84) Flushing, (85) Turning pale, (88) Extra systole, (89) Unst. flush/pale, (93) Perspiring, (95) Nausea, grade II, (96) Tears in eyes, (98) Sexual sensation, (99) Orgasm.

In Fig. 4 the heavy black lines between the blocks indicate the computed positive correlation. For $p = 0.0001$ the line is 10 mm wide. For $p = 0.001$ the line is 3 mm and for $p = 0.005$ the line is 1 mm wide. The computed negative correlation is indicated in the same way by the size of the black blocks on the connecting thin lines, using the same scale for the width of the black blocks as for the width of the heavy black lines just described.

Figure 3 is the graphic illustration, based on a more detailed mathematical correlation, and shows how the categories within mood are associated with the categories ( ) within the other major groups.

Change in mood positive I (1) shows a marked negative correlation with peripheral sensory sensations in body (47,50) and unspecific, diffuse sensations (52,53) as well as with movements in the body and extremities (3,5,6). Change in mood positive II (2), in contrast, has a positive correlation with

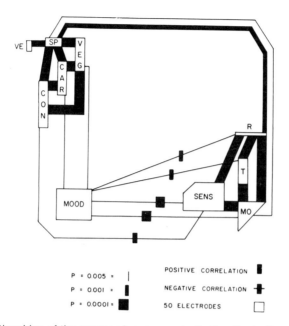

FIG. 4. Interrelationships of the groups of responses to E-stim. Key to figure: (R) Rigidity, (T) tremor, (Sens) sensory, (Mo) motor, (Sp) speech, (Ve) vestibular, (Veg) vegetative, (Car) cardiovascular, (Con) consciousness.

arrest of speech I (20) and vocalization (25), as well as the visual phenomenon of vibration (30).

Change in mood positive III (3) is correlated both with aphasia (72) and complex motor movements (6) with a significance of $p = 0.0001$. While the mood changes, negative grade I (4) and negative grade III (6) have rather weak correlations; negative grade II (5) has a positive correlation with a sense of floating in the air (79). It should be noted that negative grade I (4) has a negative correlation with alerting, waking up (78), while emotional outbursts (7) are positively correlated with the confused, chewing (75), and floating away (79).

Ambivalence (8), on the other hand, has a positive correlation with nausea grade II (95).

In contrast to the rest of the group, orgastic type responses (9) have significant positive correlations with arrest of speech III (22), current in body (47), reduced alertness (76), turning pale (85), and sexual sensations (98). The latter correlation may be a reason to seriously question the extent to which the orgastic response is really "nonsexual."

Figure 3 illustrates that the individual categories in change in mood have high correlations with different categories in the other groups. The group as a whole has no significant positive correlation with any of the other groups as a whole (Fig. 4).

MEMORY

Memory is closely related to emotional changes. It is therefore felt necessary to describe in more detail memory changes produced by electrical stimulation. The electrophysiological mechanisms and the associated neuronal processes underlying memory have been studied by a number of investigators (Penfield, 1952; Penfield and Roberts, 1959; Scoville and Milner, 1957).

Impairments in memory, frequently noticed in patients suffering from mental disorders, Parkinson's disease, and other neurological diseases, may be due to a primary disturbance of the memory mechanism or to a secondary phenomenon resulting from lack of perception, alertness, or ability to express one's self. A deterioration of the memory function often follows psychosurgery, thalamotomy, and other neurosurgical procedures.

As demonstrated in earlier publications (Scoville and Milner, 1957), memory responses may be elicited from electrodes in the same general region in which therapeutic lesions for Parkinson's disease are made. This emphasizes the necessity for thorough testing prior to the placement of a lesion.

The memory patterns elicited in response to electrical stimulation as reported by the patient were of two types:

(1) Recollection, i.e., a simple memory in which the patient suddenly and vividly remembers a certain past episode. [Identical with the term "recollective memory" used by Penfield and Roberts (1959)].

(2) Flash-back memory, i.e., a sudden transfer back in time, always to the same specific point or moment. [Identical with the term "flash-back memory" used by Penfield and Roberts (1959)].

In no instance was there a problem in distinguishing between these two types of responses. However, it is sometimes difficult to distinguish between recollection and hallucinations.

The elicitation of recollective and flash-back memories is a phenomenon that can be evaluated only on the basis of information volunteered by the patient. The observer may sometimes detect a change in behavior and/or the patient's expression, which is helpful in alerting him to the possibility that the patient is experiencing some type of response that he should report. This is especially true in regard to the flash-back type memory, since the associated facial and behavioral changes are more vivid and may prompt loud spontaneous comments. Three of the eight electrodes were in the right hemisphere and five in the left.

In one patient we elicited one recollection from the right temporal lobe and another by stimulating an electrode to the left of the third ventricle. In a second patient, a recollection was evoked from the anterior part of the frontal lobe on the left side whereas a flash-back memory was elicited from the right side, in the posterior part of the frontal lobe, medial to the tip of the temporal lobe.

Two memory responses were obtained from an area of the brain in which lesions for Parkinson's disease are generally made. These studies demonstrate a similar vulnerability of the frontal and parietal lobes in this respect.

Stimulation of seven of the electrodes elicited recollections. Recollection was the only symptom elicited from one contact, but from four of the contacts producing simple recollection, relaxation was also associated. The recollection evoked by two others was associated with more complex responses, including sensory phenomena, arrest of speech, altered levels of consciousness, as well as cardiovascular and vegetative changes.

From another electrode a flash-back memory was elicited. This primary response, associated with after-discharge, was verified a number of times.

After-discharges occurred on each occasion and the flash-back memory took the form of an outpouring of thoughts. That is, in response to each stimulation the past experiences seemed to be "played back" to the patient as from a tape recorder. He described the experience as though he was in a certain room where some people, indifferent to him, came walking by. When the stimulus was maintained for a prolonged period, the sequence continued, uninterrupted, until the stimulus was removed. When the stimulus was applied again, the flash-back was repeated, starting at the same point in time. The next time the stimulus was turned on, the patient exclaimed, "Here we go again. Here we are again." Then he described how his memory returned to the same point in time; yet he also realized he was in the examining room. This complex response was associated with cardiovascular and mood changes.

Many workers believe that the memories elicited during an epileptic aura, or through electrical stimulation, have special significance for the patient. However, the memory episode described here appeared to have no such significance. This was verified, through psychiatric interviews, by the psychiatrist at Gaustad Sykehus under whose care the patient had remained for several years. Additionally, the psychiatrist was able to verify the response as a memory of an experience and not a hallucination.

APHASIA

Aphasia usually has a strong impact on the patient's behavior. Because agraphia may also be considered a form of aphasia, four responses listed as arrest of speech with agraphia are included in this section. These were elicited in two patients whose simultaneous counting and writing of numbers was interrupted during electrical stimulation.

Although they are not discussed in detail here, a number of other responses listed as "confused" or "chewing," under consciousness, might also have been listed as aphasia inasmuch as the patients were unable to express themselves, or to express themselves correctly.

It should be noted that the four electrodes evoking agraphia with arrest of speech are located so closely together that they may actually be in the same minute structure. The fifth electrode, eliciting aphasia, is also located nearby, lateral to the third ventricle in the left hemisphere.

CORRELATION OF CEREBRAL RESPONSES
TO ELECTRICAL STIMULATION

In the preceding section, the multitude of the responses has been described in detail. The mathematical significance of the correlation between the categories has also been studied and illustrated with diagrams for each group.

This section, on the other hand, is devoted to determining the significance of correlations between one major group of responses and another. Those ten major groups in which there was a significant positive or negative correlation of $p = 0.005$, or less, are represented in Fig. 4. The figure shows the significance of the correlation as well as the number of responses in each group. The other seven groups in which the correlation was less significant statistically will not be discussed.

This analysis indicates that the group of motor responses has a significant correlation ($p = 0.0001$) with the tremor, rigidity, and peripheral sensory groups.

On the left side of the diagram (Fig. 4) is shown the strong intercorrelations among vegetative changes, cardiovascular responses, and changes in consciousness. All of these groups are part of the autonomic nervous system.

The two remaining groups, mood and speech distinguish themselves in special ways. In contrast to the other groups, changes in mood have only two meager, positive correlations (with the vegetative and cardiovascular groups); and have several strong negative correlations. The negative correlations relate to the peripheral sensory and motor groups with a significance of $p = 0.0001$ and to tremor and rigidity to a lesser degree, $p = 0.001$.

These findings illustrate a high degree of independence exercised by changes in mood.

The changes in speech represent an opposite situation. This group carries a highly significant correlation with rigidity, vestibular changes, and motor responses, as well as alterations, consciousness, cardiovascular, and vegetative changes.

These findings indicate the central role and importance of speech in human behavior and brain function. Speech is used to express ideas and memories (idential expressions) or crude input from the sensory (sensory expressions) to description of surroundings or reading (environmental expressions).

Interference of speech may be produced by changes in any of these spheres mentioned.

One is at the group level "missing" a correlation between speech and mood. This exists only at the level of the categories between changes in mood, positive II (62) and orgastic sensation (69) in the group of mood changes and arrest of speech (20) and vocalization (25) in the speech changes.

In the next step the material was divided into four parts according to the four sections of the brain; the anterior, the posterior, the temporal-parietal, and the block around the third ventricle.

Mathematical analysis of these data from each section revealed that the interrelationships described above are evident in each of the four sections (Sem-Jacobsen, 1966).

This latter analysis, however, shows also an overrepresentation of mood and consciousness in the anterior section, of visual phenomenon in the posterior section, and of somatosensory responses in the area around the third ventricle.

The data and their mathematical handling appear promising in substantiating old observations and in advancing new knowledge about the functioning of the whole brain as a network of closely interrelated and interacting systems.

SURGICAL MANIPULATION OF EMOTION

Mental disturbances are found in a number of patients suffering from Parkinson's disease, and may often be regarded as part of their illness. On the other hand, in some patients the development of changes in their mood or behavior, often complex in nature, is first *seen following neurosurgery.*

In spite of an excellent neurological result, for example, some patients develop depression to such a degree that the operation must be considered unsuccessful. Others may become euphoric, happy, and satisfied, despite an unsuccessful operation. Unfortunately, in some instances the euphoria that follows the operation may be extensive and create major problems in the subsequent care of the patient. Frequently the patients become emotionally unstable. For no apparent reason, they may suddenly burst into tears or laughter; yet, their change in mood is not based on any identifiable experience.

These general observations and earlier findings in depth recordings were discussed in 1958 at the Neurosurgical Congress in Copenhagen as well as at the Second International Symposium on Psychosurgery in Copenhagen in 1970 (Sem-Jacobsen, 1958; Sem-Jacobsen and Torkildsen, 1958, 1960; Hitchcock, 1972).

The recordings of the electrical activity in the brain have revealed paroxysmal delta activity and theta activity clearly associated with changes in the patient's clinical mood and behavior. These paroxysmal waves appear as synchronous activity, from the ventromedial part of the frontal lobes, parts of the temporal lobes, parts of the parietal lobes, and the region of the hypothalamus, indicating connections between these regions (Sem-Jacobsen, Petersen, Lazarte, Dodge, and Holman, 1955*b*; Sem-Jacobsen, Petersen, Dodge, Lazarte, and Holman, 1956).

These activity-in-depth recordings from the frontal, temporal, and parietal lobes are illustrated in Fig. 5. Electrodes 1, 3, and 4 are in the frontal lobe. The lower part of electrode 5 is in the temporal lobe. Electrodes 7 and 8 are in the parietal lobe.

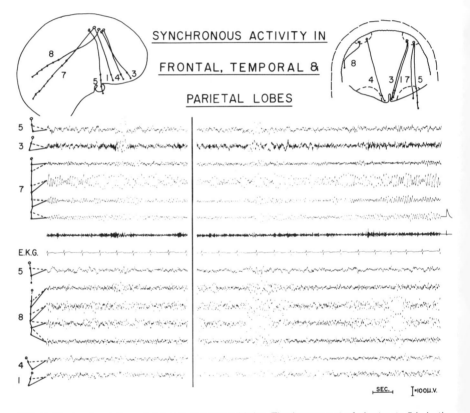

FIG. 5. Electrodes 1, 3, and 4 are in the frontal lobe. The lower part of electrode 5 is in the temporal lobe. Electrodes 7 and 8 are in the parietal lobe.

Profound changes in the electrical activity in these areas, as well as the areas lateral to the third ventricle during acute episodes of agitation and hallucination have been observed in more than 18 chronic schizophrenic patients. Figures 6 and 7 illustrate the profound changes as they appeared in one patient. The patients from whom these episodes have been recorded,

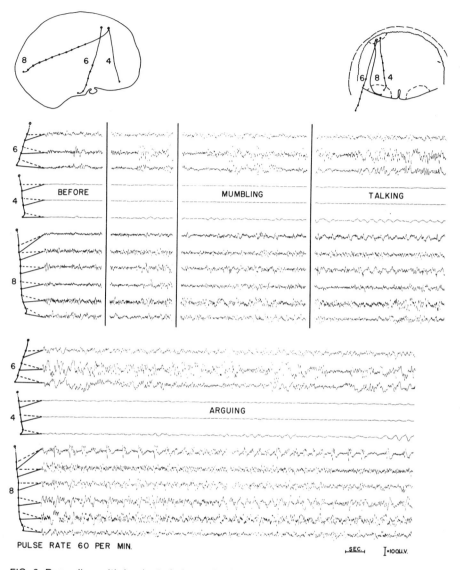

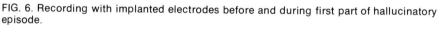

FIG. 6. Recording with implanted electrodes before and during first part of hallucinatory episode.

have, on an average, been observed in hospitals for more than 9 years, with no prior indication of any convulsive seizures (Sem-Jacobsen, Petersen, Lazarte, Dodge, and Holman, 1955a).

Figure 8 is intracerebral recording from another patient during acute episodes.

LSD and mescaline given orally, elicit a spike focus in the same region

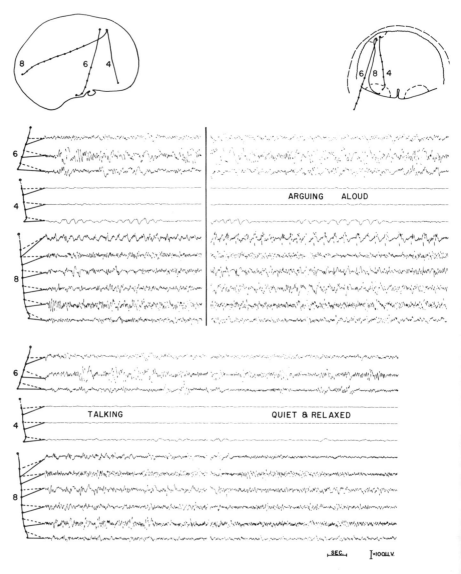

FIG. 7. Recording with implanted electrodes during last part of hallucinatory episode and afterward.

lateral to the posterior part of the third ventricle as was seen during the acute psychotic episode (Schwarz, Sem-Jacobsen, and Petersen, 1956).

The stimulation revealed the presence of a "positive" and a "negative" rewarding system in the ventromedial part of the frontal lobes, the central part of the temporal lobes as well as in the region around the third ventricle. The areas mentioned appear to contain a system, probably a part of the

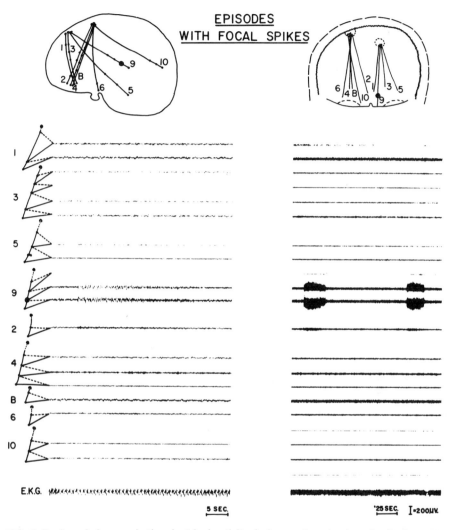

FIG. 8. Profound changes in the electrical activity during acute episodes of agitation with hallucination.

limbic system, where electrical stimulation may elicit all modalities of emotions (Sem-Jacobsen et al., 1955*b;* Sem-Jacobsen, 1968).

As already described, with intracerebral electrical stimulation it is possible (a) to localize the target in the frontal lobes and in the region around the third ventricle and (b) to avoid undesirable side effects and even evaluate and predict the result of the lesion before it is made. The lesion can be made in steps and enlarged in case of relapse as long as the electrodes are in place.

No lesion should be made before the effect on the intended spot in the brain has been thoroughly studied, fully evaluated, and no undesirable side effects encountered (Sem-Jacobsen et al. 1956; Sem-Jacobsen, 1965).

Lesions made both in the frontal lobes as well as lateral to the third ventricle in the areas mentioned above have given beneficial, lasting therapeutic results. Recent results indicate that it may be possible to treat some of the patients with compulsive disorders with a lesion 50 to 100 mm³ in size, *unilaterally in the region lateral to the third ventricle.* In the frontal lobe it appears that the lesion has to be slightly larger and bilateral.

With hyperoxia and hypoxia it is also possible to manipulate emotions. In our work with measurement of blood-flow (Sem-Jacobsen, Styri, and Mohn, 1971) in the brain, and particularly in work with pilots, scuba-divers, and aquanauts, it has been striking to see the way in which hyperoxia produces responses ranging from elevation of mood to vivid euphoria. This may be the future way of treating depressions.

SUMMARY

With electrical stimulation of the human brain it is possible to manipulate emotional behavior. The stimulation produces transient changes that may be made of a more permanent nature by stereotactic depth-electrographic interruption of pathways in the brain.

The method makes it possible to test and evaluate, in advance, the therapeutic effect of psychosurgery before the lesion is made.

Complications, such as mental impairment, seizure activity, and others, associated with the standard leucotomy have not been encountered over the past 20 years.

The procedure has greatly increased the therapeutic value of psychosurgery and decreased the risk to the patient.

The development has made human emotions accessible to neurophysiological measurement and evaluation.

REFERENCES

Berger, H. (1931): Über das Elektrenkephalogramm des Menschen, Arch. Psychiat. *94*, 16–60.

Brady, J. V. (1955): Motivational-emotional factors and intracranial self-stimulation, Amer. Psychol. *10*, 396.

Brady, J. V. (1957): A comparative approach to the experimental analysis of emotional behaviour. In: *Experimental Psychopathology,* eds. P. Hoch and J. Zubin, Grune and Stratton, New York.

Brady, J. V. (1958): Temporal and emotional factors related to electrical self-stimulation of the limbic system. *International Symposium on Reticular Formation of the Brain,* Henry Ford Hospital, March 1957, Toronto, pp. 689–703, Little, Boston.

Brady, J. V. (1961): Motivational-emotional factors and intracranial self-stimulation. In: *Electrical Stimulation of the Brain,* ed. Daniel E. Sheer, pp. 413–430, The Hogg Foundation, Univ. of Texas Press, Houston.

Delgado, J. M. R., Hamlin, H., and Chapman, W. P. (1952): Technique of intracranial electrode implacement for recording and stimulation and its possible therapeutic value in psychotic patients, Confin. Neurol. *12*, 315–319.

Fulton, J. F., and Jacobsen, F. (1935): The functions of the frontal lobes. A comparative study in monkey, chimpanzee and man. *II Int. Neurological Congress*, pp. 70–71. London.

Heath, R. G., Peacock, S. M., Jr., Monroe, R. R., and Miller, W. H., Jr. (1954): Electroencephalograms and subcorticograms recorded since the June 1952 meetings. In: *Studies in Schizophrenia*, Harvard Univ. Press, Cambridge, Mass.

Hitchcock, E., ed. (1972): Second International Symposium on Psychosurgery, Copenhagen, 1970, pp. 76–81 Charles C Thomas, Springfield, Ill.

Hunter, J., and Jasper, H. H. (1949): Effects of thalamic stimulation in unanesthetized animals; arrest, reaction, and petit mal-like seizures, activation patterns and generalized convulsions, Electroenceph. Clin. Neurophysiol. *1*, 305–324.

Lilly, J. C. (1958): Learning motivated by subcortical stimulation: The start and stop patterns of behavior. *International Symposium on Reticular Formation of the Brain*, Henry Ford Hospital, March 1957, Toronto, pp. 705–721, Little, Boston.

Olds, J. (1958a): Self-stimulation of the brain, Science, *127*, 315–324.

Olds, J. (1958b): Self-stimulation experiments and differentiated reward systems. *International Symposium on Reticular Formation of the Brain*, Henry Ford Hospital, March 1957, Toronto, pp. 671–687, Little, Boston.

Olds, J. (1961): Differential effects of drivers and drugs on self-stimulation at different brain sites. In: *Electrical Stimulation*, ed. Daniel E. Sheer, pp. 350–366, The Hogg Foundation, Univ. of Texas Press, Houston.

Penfield, W. (1952): Memory mechanisms, Arch. Neurol. Psychiat. *67*, 178–198.

Penfield, W., and Roberts, L. (1959): *Speech and Brain-Mechanisms*, p. 8, pp. 38–55, p. 286, Princeton Univ. Press, Princeton, N.J.

Petersen, M. C., Dodge, H. W., Jr., Sem-Jacobsen, C. W., Lazarte, J. A., and Holman, C. B. (1955): Clinical results of selective leucotomy based on intracerebral electrography, JAMA *159*, 774–775.

Schwarz, B. E., Sem-Jacobsen, C. W., and Petersen, M. C. (1956): Effects of mescaline d-lysergic acid diethylamid and adrenochrome on the depth electrogram of the human, AMA Arch. Neurol. Psychiat. *75*, 579–587.

Scoville, W. B., and Milner, B. (1957): Loss of recent memory after bilateral hippocampal lesions, J. Neurol. Neurosurg. Psychiat. *20*, 11–22.

Sem-Jacobsen, C. W., Petersen, M. C., Lazarte, J. A., Dodge, H. W., Jr., and Holman, C. B. (1955a): Intracerebral electrographic recordings from psychotic patients during agitation and hallucinations, J. Psychiat. *112*, 278–288.

Sem-Jacobsen, C. W., Petersen, M. C., Lazarte, J. A., Dodge, H. W., and Holman, C. B. (1955b): Electroencephalographic rhythms from the depth of the frontal lobe in 60 psychotic patients, J. EEG Clin. Neurophysiol. *7*, 193–210.

Sem-Jacobsen, C. W., Petersen, M. C., Dodge, H. W., Jr., Lazarte, J. A., and Holman, C. B. (1956): Electroencephalographic rhythms from the depth of the parietal, occipital and temporal lobes in man, J. EEG Clin. Neurophysiol. *8*, 263–278.

Sem-Jacobsen, C. W. (1958): "Positive" and "negative" rewarding system in humans. *International Symposium on Reticular Formation of the Brain*, Henry Ford Hospital, March 1957, Toronto, pp. 725–726, Little. Boston.

Sem-Jacobsen, C. W., and Torkildsen, A. (1958): The importance of localizing "positive" and "negative" emotional regions in the midbrain in the treatment of Parkinson's disease, presented at the Neurosurgical Congress in Copenhagen.

Sem-Jacobsen, C. W., and Torkildsen, A. (1960): Depth recording and electrical stimulation in the human brain. In: *Electrical Studies on the Unanesthetized Brain*, eds. E. R. Ramey and D. S. O'Dohery, pp. 275–290, Hoeber, New York.

Sem-Jacobsen, C. W. (1965): Depth electrographic stimulation and treatment of patients with Parkinson's disease including neurosurgical technique, Acta Neurol. Scand. *41*, Suppl. 13.

Sem-Jacobsen, C. W. (1966): Depth electrographic observations related to Parkinson's disease: Recording and electrical stimulation in the area around the third ventricle, J. Neurosurg. *24*, 388–402.

Sem-Jacobsen, C. W. (1968): *Depth-Electrographic Stimulation of the Human Brain and Behavior*, Charles C Thomas, Springfield, Ill.

Sem-Jacobsen, C. W. (1971): Pitfalls in technique and interpretation of behavioral changes in response to electrical stimulation. In: *Neuro-Electric Research*, eds. D. V. Reynolds and A. E. Sjöberg, chap. 2, pp. 15–24, Charles C Thomas, Springfield, Ill.

Sem-Jacobsen, C. W., Styri, O. B., and Mohn, E. (1971): Measurements in man of focal intra-cerebral blood flow around depth-electrodes with hydrogen gas. In: *Cerebral Blood Flow. Progress in Brain Research,* eds. J. S. Meyer and J. P. Shade, Vol. 35, pp. 105–113, Elsevier, Amsterdam.

Sem-Jacobsen, C. W., and Styri, O. B. (1971): Electrical stimulation of the human brain—Pitfalls and results. *Symposium on Neurophysiology Studied in Man,* Paris July 20–22, pp. 27–36, Excerpta Medica, Amsterdam.

Symposium on Depth Electrography with discussions (1954): Eighth Annual Meeting, Amer. EEG Soc. Introduction by (1) Spiegel, E. A., and Wycis, H. T., (2) Heath, R. G., Monroe, R. R., and Mickle, W. A., (3) Delgado, J. M. R., and Hamlin, H., and (4) Sem-Jacobsen, C. W., Petersen, M. C., Lazarte, J. A., Dodge, H. W., Jr., and Holman, C. B.: Electroen-ceph. Clin. Neurophysiol. 6, 702–706.

Woltman, H. W., Dodge, H. W., Jr., Holman, C. B., Sem-Jacobsen, C. W., Bickeford, R. G., Petersen, M. C., Faulconer, A., Jr., Schnugg, F. J., Bahley, A. A., Miller, R. H., and Craig, W. McK. (1953): Symposium on intracerebral electrography, Proc. Mayo Clin. 28, 145–192.

Emotions—Their Parameters and Measurement,
edited by L. Levi.
Raven Press, New York © 1975

Psychological and Pharmacological Manipulations

David M. Rioch

Institute for Behavioral Research, 2429 Linden Lane, Silver Spring, Maryland 20910

How all the other passions fleet to air,
As doubtful thoughts; and rash embrac'd despair;
And shuddering fear; and green-ey'd jealousy;
O love! be moderate; allay thy ecstasy;
In measure rain they joy; scant this excess;
I feel too much thy blessing; make it less,
For fear I surfeit!

Shakespeare: *The Merchant of Venice*

Doubt, despair, fear, jealousy, love, joy, hate, anger, grief, and scores, or possibly, hundreds of other states of being traditionally are included in the term emotion. The necessary implication of such a category of behavior patterns is that all these conditions are linked into a single class by some common denominator or denominators. The designation of the class by the term emotion indicates that the common factor is "agitation" or "disturbance," which may be sought or avoided.

The traditional concept of emotions seems to have been based on the postulate that all persons have minds or psyches which are separate from the body and of a different nature. With this assumption the emotions have been conceived of as mysterious forces or feelings and affects which cause the agitation and disturbance of the mind or psyche. In turn, the latter expresses itself through overt behavior. The mind and the psyche are hypothetical constructs, although commonly reified as actual things with their own functions, energies, etc., and they are unnecessary and misleading for investigative operations. Adolf Meyer (1957), the pioneer dynamic psychiatrist in America, showed that the phenomena from which these constructs were derived could be more operationally dealt with as levels or modes of central nervous functions, which he called mental (forebrain) and symbolic (forebrain including language—which is social) integration. MacKay (1962) regarded sensations, feelings, and affects as aspects of the phenomenon known as a person. Other aspects are the overt behavior and the mediating mechanisms. However, feelings and affects cannot be directly communicated and can only be inferred from behavior, including verbal behavior. Hence, they cannot be studied, except as inferences, in anyone other than oneself.

Nature is conservative. As the brain matures and, through memory processes, it stores simple, part responses which are used in several, more complex patterns; it continues to use these as long as they are effective. Many of these part responses or subroutines are reflexive or instinctual in nature although considerably modified by experience. Thus, the alternating movements of the legs — as in walking — are a reflex, but the posture, the distance between the feet, the pointing of the toes, and other characteristics of the gait are learned from the social group. The autonomic system is strongly involved in such patterns as is the respiratory. In general, these subroutines — postural, locomotor, autonomic, humoral, or sensory — are supportive, communicative, or informatory. Their facilitation or inhibition is learned to a greater extent than has been customarily thought.

Under a variety of situations — organic, functional, or combined — the interaction of the organism with the environment becomes more difficult, the load of information is increased, and the more delicate complexity of the organization of behavior begins to break down. Simpler, less adequate patterns of interaction take over. Planning and critical differential behavior are probably most vulnerable. Fewer factors in the situation are identified and they tend to be treated as though constant, rather than as continually changing during the interaction. Behavior comes under the control of more immediately associated events and consequences. One might say that both the spatial and temporal horizons shrink. With further disorganization, interaction is guided only by that which immediately impinges on the organism. At any stage of disorganization and disorientation one or other of the part reactions, or subroutines, may be activated, not infrequently increasing the load further. For example, a significant proportion of people, in stressful or emotional situations, experience fainting, involuntary micturition, nausea, difficulty in speaking, and so on. In the extreme, hyper- or hypoactivity of autonomic patterns may result in death. Richter (1957) described experiments on rats in which "fear" led to death from vagal block of the heart. He speculated on the possible equivalence of *voodoo* death. Death of young, vigorous men in P.O.W. camps from "hopelessness" has been also reported (Nardini, 1952).

The situations under which the complexity and adequacy of behavior breaks down include those in which there are high rates of sensory input, or hyper-alerting with increased excitation in the brain. Commonly both occur together. Whether one calls the resulting state stress or emotion is behaviorally immaterial, although socially significant. As with all central nervous activity, the threshold for breakdown, its course, and its accompanying symptoms are modified by learning, either through instruction, training, or life experiences.

Dr. Harry Stack Sullivan once told briefly of a woman, the wife of a politician from the prairie region, who consulted him on account of her tendency to blush. This was embarrassing as she was beyond the age at which women in her Washington subculture were positively reinforced for blushing. After a few interviews, in which the history of the blushing, the accompanying contingencies and consequences were reviewed, the blushing was not noticeable. Attending her first party wearing a low-cut dinner dress a few days later, she was most embarrassed by feeling a blush start and sweep upward to stop at a sharp line around her neck. This was the level of the high-necked dress she usually wore to Sullivan's office. In a few more interviews this response also stopped.

Under ordinary circumstances, a great deal of informal and intimate communication in our culture uses the verbal behavior of feelings, affects, and emotions. The expression "I know exactly how you feel" is not uncommon. That this verbal behavior is effective indicates a remarkable degree of learning, as it metaphorically refers to recognition of the preceding course of events, of the environmental contingencies, and of the usual consequences. Such verbal behavior reinforces the cohesiveness of the group. It is used to excuse or justify acts and attitudes not socially approved and to increase or reinforce desirable feelings, acts, and attitudes. In striking contrast, under conditions of continuous danger, as on and near the front lines in the Korean War, feelings and affects were never mentioned (Rioch, 1955). All verbal behavior was in terms of action. For example, a man at a support position close to the front related an episode which had recently occurred further forward. At one point in the narration, he said, "And then I felt like hitting him." He stopped, turned to me and said in a softer voice, "My God! I must have been angry." After a short pause, he returned to his narration. In contrast with this attitude, verbal, gestural, mimetic, and otherwise acted out or communicated expressions of fear, guilt, disorientation, hopelessness, etc. were used by psychiatric casualties, often with conventional explanations in terms of overwhelming feelings, lack of sleep, bad news from home, and so on.

Colonel Albert J. Glass, MC (Retired) (1957), studied the epidemiology of psychiatric casualties in World War II and Korea. He found that when a division went into combat for the first time the psychiatric casualties showed such bizarre symptomatology that no classification or diagnosis was possible. In about 6 weeks, however, they began showing one or another of four or five syndromes which remained conventional for the unit. Later, when replacements without previous experience in combat joined the unit, it only required some 2 weeks for them to learn the approved symptoms, even without having seen any. In the troops of the Republic of Korea, psychotic, but practically no neurotic, reactions occurred, possibly due to no facilities for psychiatric treatment other than base hospitals. When Koreans were taken into American units, however, occasional men suffered emotional disturbances similar to those in the American troops.

The importance of training for the performance of necessary tasks and for reducing emotional disturbance is well documented by military experience. S. L. A. Marshall (1965) records the maintenance of controlled, adequate behavior in a well-trained unit of professional Ethiopian soldiers under heavy attack while they were out on patrol. Their performance and maintenance of effective organization contrasted with that of minimally trained drafted men. Much of the effect of training and experience is to provide information on the probable environmental contingencies and events relevant to the consequences of the ongoing interaction. It also provides a relatively wide repertoire of programs to meet different contingencies. Training and experience also increase the probability that behavior will remain under the control of relevant environmental and remembered instructions. The danger of control by irrelevant contingencies, such as, feelings, imagining being hit, or of losing control, is reduced.

Equivalent effects of experience and training are seen in everyday life. People 15 to 25 years old are more readily and dramatically involved in social movements, love affairs, grieving over loss than are people in their fifth decade of life. The younger group is also quicker to change to other patterns. Some youngsters, however, with cultural training or occasionally, with personal experience in tasks for the consequences of which they are responsible, will respond more in the manner of the older group.

Over a period of time, whole cultural patterns of interaction may change. Not so long ago, an upper-class woman in our culture was more or less expected to swoon or actually faint with love, sorrow, surprise, anger, or any emotion socially considered to be strong. Smelling salts were frequently in use. Copious weeping with sorrow or sentiment was also socially reinforced. These grossly communicative emotional expressions have virtually disappeared. In World War I there were a large number of cases of neuro-circulatory asthenia — also called "soldier's" or "irritable heart." The symptoms were rapid pulse, pallor, weakness, shortness of breath, tremor, and other signs of clinical anxiety. Medically, they were considered "organic" by some physicians, "functional" by others. Many were treated by cardiologists, and most were evacuated home. Many of these continued to have repeated attacks for years, with only moderate amelioration. In World War II all anxiety symptoms were managed psychiatrically with reassurance, a few days of rest, and return to duty. Irritable heart proved not to be a problem. Very few, if any, cases occurred in Korea after the psychiatric service had been established.

The role of verbal behavior in controlling the course of a person's interaction with his environment is well illustrated by the studies of Bourne (1970) on men in combat situations in Vietnam. He gained the confidence of several helicopter ambulance crews by flying dangerous missions with them and was able to get more private information on attitudes and thoughts than was otherwise possible. Seven aid men were studied in considerable detail, and 24-hr urine specimens were collected for a week for measurement of the 17-hydroxycorticosteroids. The hormones were consistently excreted at a rate approximately 20% less than the normal calculated for the body weight of the men. The amount excreted did not correlate in any way with the danger they were exposed to but remained low whether they were on dangerous missions or around the base during a cease fire period. One man, however, showed a rise the day after he received a scalp wound in a brawl in a Saigon bar. Two of the men felt they were "invulnerable," one of these on religious grounds. Another had calculated the probabilities of being hit on any particular mission and found they were so small he could disregard them. Two—whom the helicopter pilots preferred to have with them, as they were the most effective—seemed to enjoy the excitement. They were young, vigorous, and always returned with very tall stories— some obviously prevaricated—of the dangers, near misses they had experienced and the feats they had performed. The seventh man used an interesting formula. From the time of getting into the helicopter he rehearsed the exact moves he would make on arriving in the combat zone and exactly how he would handle the litters, the wounded to be evacuated, and so on. On arrival, he followed the different steps of his program, being controlled by each segment only during its performance. The completion of one segment was the signal for the next. This method of maintaining behavior under the control of the relevant environmental stimuli is not common, but also not rare. It has the great advantage that it can be taught and practiced. Basically, it is one of the underlying principles of military training, although to be effective the training needs to give details of the environmental contingencies available only in the proximity of the combat. Bourne (1970) also studied a 12-man team of the Special Warfare Forces which manned an isolated outpost with a Vietnamese and Montagnard company they were training. Here the reputation of the SWF for personal competence, self-reliance, and aggressiveness played a critical role.

The manipulation of emotions by psychological means is an ancient art. Stirring up the young men to demand war on some neighboring group by reciting, singing, or chanting the great feats of the past heroes to the accompaniment of drums and other music is still used in technologically unsophisticated tribes. Funeral dirges are used in emphasizing grief. In some cultures, wedding ceremonies are accompanied by bawdy songs and dances. Not too different from these are the uses in modern advertising of good-looking girls or of men dressed like wealthy bankers in pictures of automobiles, of summer cruises, of vacation resorts, of jewelry. The stimulus to immediate feelings of attraction and social status is used to reduce the likelihood of behavior being controlled by the long-term requirements of daily life and increases the likelihood that the prospective buyer will commit himself at once.

Serious study of manipulating and changing emotional behavior has been conducted chiefly in the course of clinical treatment of patients with so-called emotional disturbance, mental illness, and disorders of behavior. It is not feasible to review here the enormous amount of work which has been carried on in the various schools of psychotherapy. The beginnings go back to Mesmer and his theories of "animal magnetism" in the early 19th Century. A surgeon, Braid, later called it "hypnotism" and it was made famous by Charcot for the treatment of hysteria. However, it was Bernheim who showed the role of suggestion in the process and introduced the term "psychoneurosis." Janet developed an important school of thought and recognized so-called unconscious phenomena. Freud studied under Charcot and used hypnosis for treating psychoneuroses. Breuer pointed out the correlation of neurotic symptoms with earlier events in the patient's life. Freud found that, if a patient was allowed to talk freely, he gradually remembered early events and his symptoms often stopped with discussion and understanding of their origins. This led to the technique of "free association" and laid the basis for "insight-therapy" as opposed to "suggestion" and "supportive advice." Freud called his method "psychoanalysis" and devoted the rest of his life to its development. The psychoanalytic movement grew as a revolt against the increasingly experimental and mechanistic approach in general medicine. It offered explanations for psychological phenomena using a complex system of hypothetical constructs and postulates derived from the way patients talked about their lives, experiences, and problems. It also supported the revolt against middle-class prudery which was in its early stages at that time. The psychoanalytic movement underwent several schisms: Jung, Adler, Horney, Sullivan, Fromm, Thompson, and others split off from the main group and established schools and followers of their own. Munroe (1955) has written a careful comparative summary and critique of the differences in practice and theory of these workers. Sullivan is important in that he made a remarkably successful effort to describe the phenomena of the patient-therapist interaction in operational terms, rather than using inferences and postulates to "explain" what he observed. In this respect he was closer to Adolf Meyer than to the psychoanalysts. Meyer was contemporaneous with Freud and developed a dynamic psychiatry based on long, very careful study of the life history of patients. He demonstrated the life course of the patterns of reaction the patient showed and spoke of these as habits. He emphasized the need for learning more effective habits. He was rigorous in differentiating data from interpretation but did not recognize behavior as interaction. Like Freud's but unlike Sullivan's his theory attempted to account for behavior by characteristics of the patient. For Meyer, those characteristics were the learned habits, for Freud they were the instincts, emotions, and complexes of the patient and their traumata and immaturities as well as interactions between his ego, id, and superego. Meyer's work, however, prepared the medical profession in America to accept the more popular dynamic psychiatry of Freud. The latter expanded rapidly during the period before World

War II but has since changed considerably. Its major appeal—namely a system for dealing with the patient as a person—has been increasingly adequately met in other ways.

The basic operations in all types of psychotherapy based on dynamic psychiatric principles whether Meyerian, Freudian, or Sullivanian consist in an agreement between the therapist and the patient to make a serious effort to collaborate in an intimate study of the patient's life and his problems, with the objective of improving the patient's manner of living, his emotions, and feelings. The *experience* of such a collaborative exercise needs to be differentiated from the verbal *content* in which it is conducted or the verbal *explanation* which may be arrived at. This type of experience has been found to be effective in reducing emotional disturbance and other symptoms to a sufficient degree that the practice of the dynamic psychiatric disciplines has not only been maintained but has increased. In other words, study together with another, unrejecting person of how one lives leads, in a high proportion of cases, to learning to live more effectively under the relevant, prevailing conditions. It may result in greater ability to deal with new situations as they arise, provided the novelty and the rate of situational change is not too great. The experience with one or another therapist differs, as do also the particular aspects of life experience emphasized by different therapists, in the course of the work. Unfortunately, no objective criteria have been standardized by which one might measure or estimate the changes in behavior resulting from these manipulations of emotional disturbance. The relief of symptoms and the subject's verbalization of an improved sense of well-being are the major clinical criteria.

The significance of learning in the therapeutic process has been approached from different points of view. For example, Margaret Rioch (1970a,b,c) recommended that the term "education" be used instead of "therapy" as being more accurately descriptive. Ferster (1972) has recently shown that Freudian clinical procedures can be readily formulated in the terminology of operant conditioning—a learning model. Many investigators in psychiatry have similarly expressed themselves in personal communication.

Not only does the patient learn about living more satisfactorily, but the therapist learns about treating (or educating) patients. Fiedler (1950) and, particularly, Strupp (1955) have looked into this aspect of psychotherapy. The great difficulties of studying the process called dynamic psychotherapy arise chiefly from two aspects. The interview data are confidential and there are few records of what goes on. Retrospective reports are necessarily colored by the theory held by the reporter. The other difficulty is the mass of data, most of which are of only marginal significance. Not infrequently critical events are alluded to in passing, while hours are spent repetitiously. However, using indirect methods, it has been found that experienced therapists of different schools of thought resemble each other more closely than they resemble novices in their own school. Somewhat slowly, but surely, patients will "shape a doctor up" (to use an operant conditioning term) to give them what they can use.

A case in point was a man in his early twenties who already had had two attacks diagnosed "manic psychosis" in another hospital. I was able to follow much of his further course through discussions with his therapist. He proceeded to have six more attacks with hospitalizations of 5 to 18 months and brief periods between the attacks living out of the hospital. Each attack started with a "love affair," of an infatuational pattern involving one or another girl who was seriously neurotic. These affairs built up rapidly to an unsatisfactory climax and separation, followed by the patient's hospitalization. The onset and course had been studied and hours spent on early life and subsequent experiences. In the last attack the patient's friends noted increased activity, more rapid talking, and flight of ideas a month before the break, requiring hospitalization. The therapist had noted a change in the same direction starting some 6 weeks earlier and gradually increasing. The patient reported that about 10 days before that he had been at a party and noticed a girl sitting off by herself, looking lonely. He felt "pity" for her and began talking to her. She responded well to his attention and they began seeing each other occasionally. He found he "liked" her and then "fell in love." On this occasion the therapist and I looked back further in the record and found that some 2 weeks before the party the patient had spent three or four treatment hours seriously discussing his desire to "be well," "leave therapy," and "have a career of his own." He was out of the hospital at the time and working at an undemanding job. The therapist took no decisive position but did not advise against the proposal. The patient, however, spoke of his concern and uncertainty and dropped the subject. On reviewing the case history it was found that each of the infatuational attacks and their following manic episodes had been preceded by the patient undertaking some task requiring continuing personal responsibility, such as, starting courses in college, or moving into an apartment by himself for the first time. When the manic attack had sufficiently subsided, the therapist laid out these data for the patient to consider. After thinking silently for some time, the patient agreed with the significance of the data and at intervals discussed its implications. Some 2 weeks later, he commented, "You know, my attitude toward girls has changed completely. I no longer get jealous if they go out with somebody else. I always used to. Of course, when a girl goes out with me, I want her to pay attention to me." He also demonstrated a reasonable self-assertion in other ways and shortly left treatment to live in another city. Unfortunately, the patient was killed in an automobile accident (another man driving) some 3 years later, but had no infatuations or manic attacks during that period. The same pattern was found in the life histories of several other patients with various neurotic or behavioral symptoms. Infatuations that seriously interfered with the progress of treatment were stopped with similar, although less dramatic results, in two other patients by careful review of the sequence of the prodromal events. (The doctor had learned enough to at least test the usefulness of the maneuver.) The "June weddings" (as men leave college and start work) and the frequent marriage of men in the army about to leave for war are probably related to the same pattern. One may note that the "love affair" provides at least temporary attention and supportive acceptance and also provides personal orientation in a socially accepted role when the subject is faced with uncertainty.

Most people use their feelings as indicators to guide behavior. For average persons under average conditions, this works well enough, so that few people seriously study their subjective responses and learn to correlate them with different aspects of the course of behavior. Just as with hearing and seeing, we tend to respond in the area of somatic feelings and affects in the manner that has earlier been reinforced. The uncertainty produced by novel "feelings" can be very disorganizing, especially if no conventional role to direct behavior and no bland term with which to "catalogue" the private phenomena come readily to hand. The patient in the foregoing paragraph overtly seemed to brush aside the uncertainty evoked by "wanting" to assume responsibility for his life career. The succeeding behavior, however, resulted in hospitalization and external control. The disturbance expressed in the course of the infatuation was platitudinous and more resembled the "recoil symptoms" which follow the "impact" of a disaster (Tyhurst, 1951) and which continue until reconstruction is underway. Sullivan's concept of "anxiety" (Sullivan, 1953) is probably equivalent to the "impact" in disaster studies and the succeeding symptoms — which are commonly called anxiety — are equivalent to the "recoil symptoms."

In addition to the techniques for manipulating emotional disturbance based on the classical theories of dynamic psychiatry, a host of others have been developed. These include some carefully studied methods, such as, client-centered therapy (Rogers, 1951), existential psychiatry and psychology (Frankel, 1951; May, 1961), Gestalt therapy (Perls, Hefferline, and Goodman, 1951), synthesis and reconstruction of Vittoz (1967), and others (*cf*. Patterson, 1973). During the past decade, a considerable degree of interest has developed in the theories of conditioning and the data on learning developed in experimental laboratories on animal behavior. Wolpe (1958) published a method for modifying phobias, sexual disturbances, and so forth. At first the underlying theory was considered to be Pavlovian or *respondent,* since the reduction of symptoms was gradual, associated with very slowly increasing the strength of the stimuli which evoked them. However, as the patient controlled the rate of increase and had to stimulate himself, as it were, by imagination, by looking at pictures, and by other active behavior, the procedure was regarded more as operant conditioning developed originally by B. F. Skinner (1938).

The operant techniques have come to be increasingly widely applied in teaching, training, and therapy. Goldiamond and Dyrud (1968) have presented the theory and its application to modifying personal problems; Cohen and Filipczak (1971) described a long-term experiment in a penal institution and Colman (1971) another on a ward for men with character and behavior disorders. Azrin (Foxx and Azrin, 1972) has been one of the most productive workers in this field and has applied the theory successfully to several problem areas.

The methods of modifying emotional disturbance based on conditioning theory are in general called behavioral therapy or behavior modification. This includes a considerable number of procedures, such as, nonreinforcement leading to extinction of disturbing emotional behavior; direct instruction to correct misinformation (such as sexual, Masters and Johnson, 1966); education and training in necessary skills, such as, speaking clearly, carrying on a conversation, and reading; desensitization or extinction of the undesired response; analyzing behavior and noting the external and internal (feelings, attitudes) contingencies and the consequences; and "implosion" and "flooding" techniques (Ayer, 1972). There is, of course, nothing in this that is not known and used in the ordinary course of life. In therapy, however, punishment is seldom used. Learning is guided by giving or withholding positive reinforcement. Lazarus (1971) found that in many cases the application of a single behavioral technique — such as desensitization — without attention to other than the patient's presenting symptom, was not infrequently followed by relapse in a relatively short time. He is now developing a multimodal method, systematically identifying all obvious problems the patient presents, and prescribing a variety of behavioral methods for correcting them. This strategy has led to greatly improved results.

Goldiamond has extended his study of psychotherapy and has developed an approach to the modification of emotional disturbance which has promising theoretical as well as practical significance. It is based on experimental observations (Azrin, Hake, Holz et al., 1965) that, if reinforcement (food) is given to a pigeon at intervals as a consequence of pecking a colored disc which is always accompanied by a moderately painful shock to the feet, the pigeon continues to peck the disc even when the food is withheld for long periods. If another colored disc is provided, pecking of which discontinues the shocks, the latter will always be pecked before the food disc is. Generalizing from these and related observations, one may say that if the only access to a needed response from the environment is "punished" the behavior will be maintained (as a patient's disturbing symptom is maintained). If another method with no punishment becomes available, however, the "punished" method will not be used. If a patient learns or develops a method the consequences of which fulfill his needs — whether physical or social — without the aversive results of his former symptomatic performance he will give up the latter and adopt the new method. This approach avoids the danger of depriving the patient, by *implied* social pressure or threat, of a symptom whose consequences were important but not obvious. (An acute paranoid episode may follow the "cure" of an hysterical conversion symptom by hypnotic suggestion.) The use of Goldiamond's approach to manipulating emotional behavior should provide data on the basic requirements of a person in our culture.

Nearly all the psychotherapeutic schools of thought have been applied to work with groups as well as with individual persons. Originally this departure from individual treatment was introduced on account of the shortage of psychiatrists. Later many therapists preferred group work. Also, the income from groups is higher than from individual therapy. Necessarily, the techniques had to be modified for application to groups, but the general principles and theory remained the same.

Ruitenbeek (1969) recently edited a book summarizing several classical and currently developing group methods for modifying emotions. Among the current methods he includes Perl's work in Gestalt therapy, group systematic desensitization, and self-confrontation groups. Another type of group work for reducing anxiety and providing experience is Moreno's technique of psychodrama (Moreno, 1963). It can, of course, be combined with other psychotherapy. Group methods for more limited purposes have also been developed, such as, Alcoholics Anonymous, for treating alcoholism, and "Synanon" and "Eupsychia" for drug addiction. A considerable variety of group methods have recently been used based in general on counteracting the anomie and loneliness assumed to be imposed by conventional city life. In these groups emphasis is placed on freedom of self-expression, being honest, saying whatever one thinks or feels at the time, being oneself honestly. A further extension includes increasing the time of a group session (to 30 or 50-odd hr in so-called marathon groups) and also includes various unconventional procedures, such as touching each other and gazing into each other's eyes. The National Training Laboratories of the National Education Association developed several types of group work based originally on Kurt Lewin's theories, to increase member's sensitivities to other persons, their attitudes and feelings, to reduce tension in work groups, and to train leaders. In some of this work a good deal of emphasis has been placed on open verbalization of feelings and attitudes (Bradford, Gibb, and Benne, 1964).

A different type of group work was developed by A. K. Rice (1965) at the Centre for Applied Social Research of the Tavistock Institute of Human Relations. Based on Bion's analysis of groups (M. J. Rioch, 1970a), this represents a rigorous educational endeavor to provide experience in group behavior under controlled conditions and to study leadership, the relations of groups with authority, and also the behavior of groups as functional units apart from the incidental behavior of individual members (M. J. Rioch, 1970b).

A quite different approach to controlling emotions has come to be recognized and has spread widely in Western culture relatively recently. Meditation, which has long been practiced in the Orient, is now a subject of study and is rapidly coming to be extensively used (Benoit, 1955; Watts, 1957). In contrast with Western thinking and procedures (directed primarily toward interaction with and control of the social and other environmental factors) meditation provides training in "maintaining attention" on an image, an imagined sound, a formula, a body sensation, or a repetitive act such as breathing. This is often formulated as, "make the mind a blank," incorrectly introducing the implication of "do something." It would be better to say, "let becoming blank occur." The training in maintaining attention, that is, in inhibiting other mental behavior, can generalize to other mental activity so that irrelevant intrusions are more readily excluded and behavior remains under the control of the task in hand. In studies of physiological functions of men during Zen meditation Kasamatus and Hirai (1966) found slowing of respiratory, cardiac, and metabolic rates together with a continuous alpha rhythm (8 to 12 per sec) in the electroencephalogram. There was no habituation of alpha blocking of the EEG by a continuing click at one per second. The extent to which these objective signs can be used to measure the process has yet to be determined. Recently an Indian, Maharishi Mahesh Yogi (1966), formerly a physicist, developed a method called transcendental meditation which has attracted a large number of people. It is said to be effective within a short period of training and does not require the long hours of the other systems.

Public interest in manipulating emotions by psychological means is only equaled, if not exceeded, by interest in using pharmacological agents for the same purpose. It is as though a member of an affluent society should be able to have a sense of well-being on demand, whether he needed his anxiety calmed or his jaded appetite stimulated. The medical profession, aided and abetted by the pharmaceutical industry, must assume much of the responsibility for the growth of the "pill" and "injection" fashion of life which was developed since the vitamins were first popularized. After the vitamins came the antibiotics, followed by the tranquilizers — now manufactured by the ton, although sold by prescription. However, when some neurotic people and rebellious students began a fashion of helping themselves to drugs, the fashion was called drug abuse and considerable effort made to control it. The story is pertinent of the politician saying to the doctor, "This drug abuse is terrible! Why don't you fellows do something about it?" The doctor replies, "Well, we're working on an anti-drug-abuse pill, but it isn't ready yet." Persons in all walks of life have become involved in one or another aspect of the drug problem and research has been stimulated by specific financial support. Only a few of the many recent developments will be referred to in this chapter, however, on account of obvious limitations.

It is a common observation that people respond differently to alcohol on different occasions. A man under treatment for alcoholism several years ago was of interest. He occasionally went to a party, was pleasant, friendly and entertaining, and could drink a dozen or more whiskey and sodas without showing any signs of inebriation. More frequently, however, he became antagonistic, critical, and sarcastic with one or two drinks, wandered off by himself with three or four, and was staggering and belligerent with five — following which he stayed in bed, drinking, until taken to a hospital to sober up. The nature of his response to taking alcohol correlated with his dominant mood preceding drinking. This, in turn, was a function of his relationships with several people of importance to him. The effects of drugs appear to vary very widely if one looks at the responses to the whole episode of taking the drug.

Schachter (1964) postulated that a vague somatic sensation would be interpreted very differently by human experimental subjects if the environment provided strong "instructions" for such interpretations. Experimental subjects were paired with stooges and were asked to fill out a questionnaire after an injection in an experiment which they were told was designed to determine the effects of a new compound on the emotions. They received saline or a dose of epinephrine sufficient to give the usual symptoms of increased blood pressure, fast pulse, etc. The stooges expressed euphoria or anger in different degrees. The experimental subjects were much more influenced by the behavior of the stooges than by the injection they received. Most of the subjects responded in the same pattern the stooge presented, regardless of whether they received the drug or saline. Schachter also referred to the observations of Becker (1953) on novices learning to recognize the symptoms of marijuana smoking. The novices not only learned the symptoms but also learned to enjoy them. Fisher (1970) recently discussed this problem of nonspecific and specific drug effects from a theoretical viewpoint. He pointed out that the more the responses to taking a drug concern awareness, different aspects of consciousness, subjective sensations, affects and so forth the greater the possibility of nonspecific factors influencing the responses. As the dose of the drug is increased, the effects of the specific drug factors tend to take precedence and the nonspecific symptoms become less apparent. The preferred use of drugs is to take advantage of the synergistic effects of the environmental contingencies to enhance the specific effects of the drug. With some drugs that have a wide range of effect (from the earliest symptoms with low dosage to incapacitation with high dosage), the environment may be a determining factor except at the highest doses. Thus, with lysergic acid diethylamide (LSD) small doses may evoke little more than alerting and a sense of clarity, brightness, and colorfulness of the visual scene. They may result in a sense of power, mysticism, and awe, or in acute anxiety, fear and dread as with nightmares. Such differences depend chiefly on the subject's expectations, on the instructions given him, and on the implications of the environment. Some subjects, however, recognize no changes in their awareness at all at these levels of the drug and show no change in behavior. With high doses all subjects show gross incoordination and clouding of consciousness. Even so, a subject alone in a room after a high dose of LSD may not be able to stand but must crawl or simply lie down. The same subject on the same dose placed in a group engaged in some simple manual task—such as, scrubbing the floor—and being repeatedly ordered to keep working will do so, although in a slow, clumsy, inadequate manner. In general terms one may say that stimulus control of behavior can be demonstrated over a much wider range of drug intoxication than would appear possible from observations made under a more limited set of circumstances.

Another aspect of drugs which modify emotions and affects needs also to be considered. This is the effect on the social group as a whole following the drug effect on a subgroup. For example, when reserpin and chlorpromazine were introduced and were being tested in clinical trials, the favorable responses of a proportion of the patients had a very strong effect on the nurses and attendants. They developed a new hope for and interest in the patients and began to respond to them as *persons* to be treated rather than as *cases* for custodial care. This change reinforced the effectiveness of the antipsychotic drugs. Indeed, in occasional situations in which drugs were not used the change in the attitudes of doctors, nurses, and attendants accomplished very much the same changes in hospitals as the use of the drugs did, although not as consistently. It is also of interest to note that physicians prescribe a combination of drugs for a high proportion of patients. Lithium, in manic episodes, and chlorpromazine or another antipsychotic, in acute schizophrenic episodes, are often prescribed alone. For most patients, including the majority of depressed patients, mixtures of drugs—antidepressant, anxiolytic, and antipsychotic—are frequently given. Mixtures of antipsychotic or anxiolytic and depressant drugs are common for patients with chronic anxiety. In these areas one finds fashions among hospitals and practitioners, with different preferences for particular drugs or mixtures at different times and places (*cf*. Overall and Henry, 1973). These preferences and the confidence they give the practitioner are probably not the least important among the factors that influence the patients.

Considering the availability in nature of drugs that modify emotions, affects, and other subjective phenomena, it is not surprising that the record of human utilization of such agents should extend back essentially as far as recorded history (*cf*. Blum, 1969). The use of alcohol probably antedated agriculture and chewing coca leaves and smoking or chewing tobacco probably started not long after man entered the Western continents. That the pharmacological agents available to Stone Age man had the same chemical characteristics they have today seems inevitable, but that the *feelings* and the *behavior* they evoked were similar to modern expressions is unlikely. Periods of increased usage of drugs and intervening periods of decreased usage have been recognized. Just what social factors play a role in greater drug use is not clear, although wars, their attendant uncertainties, and the socioeconomic changes that have accompanied them have been important in drug epidemics in recent decades.

In the current pandemic of drug taking and drug prescribing, there seem to be two major psychological factors as well as the practical factor of drug availability. The latter, namely drug availability, is basically economic and organizational. Buying the raw materials, transporting and processing them, and, finally, distributing them is big business without the controls which can be applied to legitimate businesses. Such operations are of course supported by the current value placed by our culture on economic rather than on human development. One of the major psychological factors influencing users appears to affect an adolescent and young adult age group. Drugs offer a thrilling and exciting way to express their revolt against conventions. In this sense, drugs have taken over the role that sexual experimentation played earlier. Much has always been excused as "sowing one's wild oats" — excepting that modern educational-industrial civilization is not as resilient in the face of deviance as were the earlier, more personal mores. The other psychological factor is more conventional. There has always been an unfortunate group of persons with neurotic and with so-called character and behavior disorders who use alcohol and drugs for the occasional thrills and ecstasies, and for deadening unpleasant or painful feelings in the intervening periods. This group is increased in size and also becomes more evident in periods of rapid cultural change.

Several observers have commented on the use of drugs in the American troops in Vietnam. It has also been noted that the incidence of the condition known as combat exhaustion or combat fatigue was low. Of course, the rapid movement and intermittent nature of guerilla warfare, the absence of heavy shelling, and the availability of almost uninterrupted transportation by air (providing ample supplies and quick medical evacuation) all tended to reduce the incidence of psychiatric casualties. In addition, the general medical officers with the combat units used tranquilizers to a considerable extent. The ready availability of other drugs, including narcotics, possibly also played a role in counteracting symptoms that in other wars were sent to the psychiatrist, although data on this aspect of the problem are lacking.

A considerable variety of drugs have been used for their nonmedicinal psychological effects. They may be classified as follows: stimulants (such as, amphetamine and cocaine), depressants and hypnotics (alcohol and the barbiturates), hallucinogens (LSD, mescaline, bufotonene, psilocybin), narcotics (morphine and its derivatives, methadone), and volatile chemicals (such as, toluene and other solvents used in glue). It is of interest that ether, which was a popular intoxicant when first produced, has only been used in isolated instances since. These drugs have been reviewed in considerable detail in recent conferences and monographs (Costa and Garattini, 1970; Clouet, 1971; Thompson and Pickens, 1971; Vinař, Votava, and Bradley,

1971; Brecher, 1972; Kopin, 1972; Ray, 1972; Zarafonetis, 1972; Chambers and Brill, 1973; Garattini and Randall, 1973; Nahas, 1973; Sabelli, 1973; Sankar, 1973). It is of interest that methadone, which was developed as a treatment for narcotic addiction, has now joined the rankś of abused drugs. Also, at the time of the International Conference on Drug Abuse (Zarafonetis, 1972), cocaine was not considered a problem drug. During the past 4 years, its availability from illegal sources has increased rapidly and it has become a serious problem. A very useful review of the pharmaceutical agents used for manipulating emotions and affects is provided in the *Clinical Handbook of Psychopharmacology* (DiMascio and Shader, 1970). DiMascio classifies these drugs into the following three major groups of agents as follows: Antipsychotic (the phenothiazines, the thiozanthenes, the butyrophenones, and the rauwolfia alkaloids), antidepressant (the iminodibenzyls, the dibenzocycloheptenes, the dibenzoxepin derivatives, and the monoamine oxidase inhibitors), and the antianxiety (the benzodiazepines and substituted propanediols). He includes the amphetamines as well as lithium under the heading antidepressants. These drugs should probably be separately classified. Amphetamine resembles norepinephrine and dopamine in structure and acts differently than the other antidepressant drugs. Lithium is only effective in reducing manic episodes and does not influence depressive reactions unless they form a part of a manic-depressive syndrome. In the latter case, the depressive phase may be much less severe if treatment has been maintained prophylactically.

In contrast with the wide variety of effects drugs may have on the behavior of persons and groups, their specific effects on neurons and neuronal and synaptic transmission of messages are much more precise. Research in all fields concerned with drugs and behavior has been strongly reinforced both by financial rewards for new pharmaceuticals and by the need for more effective methods of counteracting drug abuse. The volume of publications in these areas has threatened to become overwhelming. It may be that the curtailment of medical research and training funds proposed by the present administration in the U.S. Government is the expression of a general response antagonistic to the high rate of change in the culture that research produces. However, a comprehensive review of the field is not possible here. Attention will be paid, therefore, to some of the directions of recent studies that give promise for contributing to basic knowledge of the brain and behavior.

The early work of Elliott (1907), Otto Loewi (1921), and Cannon and Uridil (1921) laid the foundations for study of the neurotransmitters that now is a major field of interest (von Euler, 1971). Acetylcholine, norepinephrine, dopamine, and serotinin are now accepted as important neurotransmitters in the central nervous system and several other chemicals — particularly the amino acids glycine, gamma-aminobutyric acid, glutamic acid, and aspartic acid — are considered possible transmitters in mammals.

Each transmitter must be produced, must reach a target chemical in the neuron to be stimulated, must combine with it, and, finally, the combination must depolarize the neuronal membrane and so set up a propagated impulse. Further, the neurotransmitters must be rapidly removed from their sites of action in order appropriately to stop their effect and so keep the activity under the control of the input system. Drugs in therapeutic dosage may interfere with this system of transmission at any one of the steps. Thus, alcohol and the volatile anesthetics are thought to affect the neuronal membranes and prevent synaptic and axonal transmission. The barbiturates are also depressants and affect all the membranes. Atropine and scopolamine are similarly thought to prevent acetylcholine reaching its receptor. This neurotransmitter is very rapidly removed from its site of action by cholinesterase. The latter can be blocked briefly by eserine and for long periods by diisopropyl-fluro-phosphate, resulting in greatly increased acetylcholine activity. Serotonin, norepinephrine, and dopamine are removed relatively slowly by the action of the enzyme monoamino oxidase. Blocking this enzyme by the use of nialamide, pargyline, or another such agent increases the amount and activity of these neurotransmitters in the brain. The rapid removal of norepinephrine and dopamine is probably accomplished by re-uptake into the nerve terminals from which they are excreted. Inside the nerve terminal they are inactive and may be stored. It is thought that cocaine and amphetamine block this reuptake and the activity of these neurotransmitters is consequently greatly increased. LSD also acts on the adrenergic system, possibly stimulating the serotonin receptors at low dosage and, at higher dosage, stimulating those for norepinephrine also (*cf.* Porter, 1970; Ray, 1972). Pert and Snyder (1973) have recently studied the distribution of specific receptors for morphine and other opiates by the use of tritiated naloxone, which specifically binds to opiate receptors. They found receptors chiefly in the striatum, considerably less in the cortex and brainstem, and negligibly in the cerebellum. This distribution parallels the distribution of acetylcholine more closely than that of any other neurotransmitter. These findings suggest that the opiates act on the cholinergic transmission system.

An important effect of amphetamine has also recently been described by Taylor and Snyder (1970) and Snyder, Taylor, Horn, and Coyle (1972). These workers found that the activities of dopamine and of norepinephrine could be differentiated by the use of the D- and L-isomers of amphetamine. Whereas D-amphetamine, probably by blocking the reuptake of dopamine and of norepinephrine, increased the activities of both of these transmitters, L-amphetamine only affected the dopamine system. From studies of the effect of these isomers on the behavior of rats, the authors concluded that the hyperactivity and excitement evoked by amphetamine is due to norepinephrine and the stereotyped compulsive behavior (sniffing, licking, and gnawing in the rat) is due to dopamine, possibly acting in the region of the nucleus accumbens and tuberculum olfactorium.

Research interests in the psychotropic drugs have recently centered largely around the neurotransmitters associated with a number of phylogenetically old fiber systems which interconnect the fore-, mid-, and hindbrains. The work of Moruzzi and Magoun (1949) on the reticulo-thalamo-cortical activating system and the description of the systems of cells and nonmyelinated fibers connecting the midbrain with the thalamo-cortical arousal system by Nauta and Kuypers (1958) laid much of the ground work for the broad attack on the problem of the brain and emotional behavior which has developed in the past few years.

A major contribution toward the clarification of this problem has been made in Swedish laboratories by the use of the formaldehyde florescence histochemical method of Falck and Hillarp (1959). This work has recently been reviewed by Hökfelt and Ljungdahl (1972). The method visualizes the cell bodies and fibers of neurons containing serotonin, norepinephrine, and dopamine. Ungerstedt (1971) studied the rat brain and found a serotonin system to arise in nuclei of the raphe of the mesencephalon and medulla. From the former, fibers went through the medial forebrain bundle to the septum and cortex, and another component turned laterally to the amygdala. He found two norepinephrine pathways. A ventral tract from cells in four groups in the medulla, which gave off fibers to structures in the hind- and midbrains and distributed largely in the hypothalamus. A dorsal norepinephrine system which arose from cells in the locus ceruleus and ran dorsally to the cerebellar cortex and rostrally to distribute widely through the whole cerebral cortex and hippocampus. Both the serotonin and norepinephrine systems sent fibers to the lower brainstem and the former also to the cord. There were three dopamine systems. The well-known nigrostriatal system arose in the substantia nigra, ran through the globus pallidus to the whole caudate and putamen with some fibers to the amygdala. The mesolimbic dopamine system ran from cell bodies above the nucleus interpeduncularis to the nucleus accumbens to the dorsal part of the interstitial nucleus of the stria terminalis and to the region of the tuberculum olfactorium. The tubero-infundibular system arose in the arcuate nucleus of the hypothalamus, their axons terminating on cells in the median eminence of the hypothalamus.

There is no doubt but that these systems are important in many types of emotional behavior, including sleep and wakefulness (Jouvet, 1969), aggressive behavior (Reis, 1972), sexual behavior (Perez-Cruet, Tagliamonte, Tagliamonte, and Gessa, 1971; Benkert, 1972), and learning (Kety, 1972). Central control of hunger and thirst by d- and b-receptors in the hypothalamus, operating through norepinephrine transmission systems, has also been described (Leibowitz, 1972). It is, of course, not presumed that these behaviors are mediated entirely through the noradrenergic systems. Rather, these systems are thought to play key roles in evoking and maintaining the respective behavior patterns.

The "self-stimulation" phenomenon (Olds and Milner, 1954) in animals is a dramatic form of response which involves the adrenergic systems as well as others. This phenomenon is proving also to be very useful in analyzing the mechanisms that mediate the effects of the psychotropic drugs on behavior. Electrodes can be implanted in the brain in a manner permitting particular areas to be discretely stimulated. Animals (and humans) tolerate this procedure very well and the electrodes can be used to stimulate the structures in which they are implanted for months after the operation. With the weak currents used, only the cells and fibers in the immediate neighborhood of the electrodes are stimulated. Different brain systems can thus be stimulated during the course of ordinary behavior, and their effects observed and measured (Steiner, 1973). From a large number of sites in the limbic system or in fiber tracts and lower centers associated with it, stimulation immediately following a particular behavior soon results in the animal repeating that behavior. If the apparatus is arranged so the animal receives an appropriate stimulus when it presses a lever, it will continue repeatedly pressing. From some electrode placements, this activity may continue at very high rates and be maintained in preference to food or water until the animal collapses if the experiment is not discontinued. Other placements are much less positively reinforcing. Still other sites have been found that are negatively reinforcing, so that the animal will work to discontinue stimulation when that is given by the experimenter (Miller, 1958). These negative sites are not in the so-called pain tracts or "centers," and stimulation is not accompanied by the usual responses of withdrawal, shrinking, or flight associated with stimulation of peripheral or central "pain" fibers of systems. Finally, there are some sites at which stimulation may at first be positively reinforcing, but after a period of self-stimulation quite suddenly change to being negatively reinforcing. It may be noted here that the locus ceruleus, the medial forebrain bundle, and the septum are among the strongest and most reliable of the positively reinforcing sites in the brain, suggesting that the norepinephrine system is important in this behavior.

Naturally the positively and negatively reinforcing qualities of electrical stimulation of brainstem structures has given rise to interpretations of "pleasure" and "pain" centers. There are electrode placements in humans, stimulation of which evokes reports of "liking" or "not liking" or other equivalent responses, as Sem-Jacobsen has already reported. However, the stereotyped behavior and the rigid control exerted by the stimulus in animals have not been found. Indeed, if one watches the animal working for positive reinforcement, one does not get the impression of "pleasure." It gives the impression more of being "tense" and "determined" to carry on its activity. (One is reminded of the young narcotic addict hustling at his business of getting enough money to buy his shots. However, there are no indications of addiction in the self-stimulating animal. When the stimulus is discontinued, the animal presses the functionless lever a few times and turns to other activities.)

It may well be that these positive and negative reactions, when embedded in the total complex of organized living, are interpreted in awareness as one or another of the various desirable and undesirable feelings or affects, to be obtained and continued, or to be avoided or escaped. In states of disorganization of the organism's or person's interaction with the environment, with the associated disorientation, the positive and negative patterns come under control of relatively immediate environmental responses and hence become largely dissociated from their usual subjective nature and significance. They become more imperative and play more dominant roles. At the extreme, as in panic, one or the other reaction could "take over," as it were, and, in the form of little more than "Yes" or "No," become the sole occupant of awareness.

Steiner (1973) pointed out that the self-stimulation phenomenon gives promise of being very useful for analyzing both the sites of action of the psychotropic drugs in the brain and also the effects of the action, whether positively or negatively reinforcing. For example, high rates of self-stimulation are reliably maintained when the stimulating electrodes are implanted in the locus ceruleus, the medial forebrain bundle, or the septum. These are areas of cell bodies, fibers, and synapses of the norepinephrine system, particularly that part which distributes to the cerebral cortex. Steiner (1968) and Steiner and Stokely (1973) also found that with low intensities of stimulating current through electrodes in the septum of rats amphetamine increased the rate of self-stimulation, but with high intensities of stimulation amphetamine decreased it. In contrast several workers have found chlorpromazine reduces the rate of self-stimulation evoked from the septum and other structures. The rate at which self-stimulation is maintained under given conditions of current intensity, drug dose, and time of day is sufficiently constant to compare drugs and their sites of action and also to study the interaction of drugs at any one site.

The study of drugs, which not so long ago was relegated to pharmacologists, has come to be a genuinely multidisciplinary study, involving all the medical and behavioral sciences. A striking example of the significance of basic research data from diverse fields of study is provided in a recent paper by Snyder (1972) in which he proposed amphetamine psychosis as a model for schizophrenia. Starting with the similarity between the clinical symptomatology of the paranoid schizophrenic and the amphetamine psychotic reactions, he reviews much of the data on the norepinephrine and dopamine systems and their functions and presents a strong argument implicating dopamine as the neurotransmitter responsible for the psychotic manifestations. Snyder thus provides a mechanism through which some chemical agent could evoke the schizophrenic reaction pattern. The possibility may be noted that subliminal stimulation of the dopamine system by the hypothetical chemical could summate with stimulation of the system by stress to become supraliminal. Such summation of the effects would also account for the well-established observation that schizophrenic episodes occurring in adolescents and adults are preceded by stressful situations and that lack of skills in dealing with personal and social interactions (thus increasing the frequency of stress) is likely to lead to chronicity.

Much has been said about the dangers of the control of people and their emotions by the use of psychological or pharmacological means. Actually, this danger appears to be vastly less now that it has been at any time during recorded history, if indeed it ever existed. The brain's decisions are made on the basis of previous experience. Knowledge of the consequences of the current contingencies is sufficient to change the decisions and the behavior. The more complete our knowledge of behavior the greater the number of choices we have of programs of behavior that will have probably successful outcomes. One of the elements of human life that confuses this issue is the universal desire to have most decisions made by someone else. We have conventions and mores in part for the organization of the group but largely because life would be intolerable if we had to make decisions on all our behavior. There is a relatively narrow margin in which a man wants to be the decision-maker for himself. This is in the area of his personal expertise. Outside of this area he wants to be told what to do. With the increase in knowledge, we are better protected from control which we do not seek than ever before. A major threat, however would be physical control of the channels for disseminating knowledge.

REFERENCES

Ayer, W. A. (1972): Implosive therapy, *Psychotherapy 9*, 242.

Azrin, N. H., Hake, D. F., Holz, W. C., and Hutchinson, R. R. (1965): Motivational aspects of escape from punishment, *J. Exp. Anal. Behav. 8*, 31–44.

Becker, H. S. (1953): Becoming a marihuana user, *Am. J. Sociol. 59*, 235–242.

Benkert, O. (1972): L-Dopa treatment of impotence. In: *L-Dopa and Behavior*, ed. S. Malitz, Raven Press, New York.

Benoit, H. (1955): *The Supreme Doctrine*, Pantheon Books, New York.

Blum, R. H. (1969): *Society and Drugs. Drugs I. Social and Cultural Observations*, Jossey-Bass, San Francisco.

Bourne, P. C. (1970): *Men, Stress and Vietnam*, Little, Brown & Company, Boston.

Bradford, L. P., Gibb, J. F., and Benne, K. D., ed. (1964): *T-Group Theory and Laboratory Method*, John Wiley and Son, New York.

Brecher, E. M. (1972): *Licit and Illicit Drugs: The Consumers Union Report on Narcotics, Depressants, Inhalants, Hallucinogens, and Marihuana, Including Caffeine, Nicotine and Alcohol*, Little, Brown & Company, Boston.

Cannon, W. B., and Uridil, J. E. (1921): Studies on the conditions of activity in endocrine glands. VIII. Some effects on the denervated heart on stimulating the nerves of the liver, *Am. J. Physiol. 58*, 353–364.

Chambers, C. D., and Brill, L., ed. (1973): *Methadone: Experiences and Issues*, Behavioral Publications, New York.

Clouet, D. H., ed. (1971): *Narcotic Drugs: Biochemical Pharmacology*, Plenum Press, New York.

Cohen, H. L., and Filipczak, J. (1971): *A New Learning Environment: A Case for Learning*, Jossey-Bass, San Francisco.

Colman, A. D. (1971): *The Planned Environment in Psychiatric Treatment: A Manual for Ward Design*, Thomas, Springfield, Illinois.

Costa, E., and Garattini, S. (1970): *Amphetamines and Related Compounds*, Raven Press, New York.

DiMascio, A., and Shader, R. I., ed. (1970): *Clinical Handbook of Psychopharmacology*, Science House, New York.

Elliott, T. R. (1907): The innervation of the bladder and urethra, *J. Physiol. 35*, 367–445.

Falck, B., and Hillarp, N. Å. (1959): On the cellular localization of cateholamines and related compounds condensed with formaldehyde, *Acta Anat. 38*, 277–279.

Ferster, C. B. (1972): An experimental analysis of clinical phenomena, *Psychol. Rec. 22*, 1–16.

Fiedler, F. E. (1950): A comparison of therapeutic relationships in psychoanalytic, non-directive and Adlerian therapy, *J. Consult. Psychol. 14*, 436–445.

Fisher, S. (1970): Nonspecific factors as determinants of behavioral response to drugs. In: *Clinical Handbook of Psychopharmacology*, ed., A. DiMascio and R. I. Shader, Jossey-Bass, New York.

Foxx, R. M., and Azrin, N. H. (1972): Restitution: A method of eliminating aggressive-disruptive behavior of retarded and brain damaged patients, *Behav. Res. Ther. 10*, 15–27.

Frankel, V. E. (1951): *Logos and Existenze*, Ammandus-Verlag, Vienna.

Garattini, S., and Randall, L. O., ed. (1973): *The Benzodiazepines*, Raven Press, New York.

Glass, A. J. (1957): Observations upon the epidemiology of mental illness in troops during warfare, in Walter Reed Army Institute of Research. In: *Symposium on Preventive and Social Psychiatry*, U.S. Government Printing Office, Washington, D.C.

Goldiamond, I., and Dyrud, J. (1968): Some applications and implications of behavioral analysis for psychotherapy, *Res. Psychotherap. 3*, 54–89.

Hökfelt, T. G. M., and Ljungdahal, A. S. (1972): Histochemical determination of neurotransmitter distribution. In: *Neurotransmitters*, ed. I. J. Kopin, Williams & Wilkins, Baltimore.

Jouvet, M. (1969): Biogenic amines and the states of sleep, *Science 163*, 32–41.

Kasamatsu, A., and Hirai, T. (1966): An electroencephalographic study on the Zen meditation (Zazen), *Folia Psychiat. Neurolog. Jap. 20*, 315–336.

Kety, S. S. (1972): The possible role of adrenergic systems of the cortex in learning. In: *Neurotransmitters*, ed. I. J. Kopin, Williams & Wilkins, Baltimore.

Kopin, I. J., ed. (1972): *Neurotransmitters, Res. Publ. Assoc. Nerv. Ment. Dis.*, Vol. 50, Williams & Wilkins, Baltimore.

Lazarus, A. A. (1971): Notes on behavior therapy, *Psychotherapy 8*, 192–196.

Leibowitz, S. F. (1972): Central adrenergic receptors and the regulation of hunger and thirst. In: *Neurotransmitters*, ed. I. J. Kopin, Williams & Wilkins, Baltimore.

Loewi, O. (1921): Über humorale Übertragbarkeit der Herzennervenwirkung, *Pflügers Arch. ges. Physiol. 189*, 239–242.

MacKay, D. M. (1962): The use of behavioral language to refer to mechanical processes, *Br. J. Philos. Sci. 13*, 89–103.

Maharishi Mahesh Yogi (1966): *The Science of Being and the Art of Living*, International Spiritual Regeneration Movement, London.

Marshall, S. L. A. (1955): *Pork Chop Hill*, William Morrow, New York.

Masters, W. H., and Johnson, V. E. (1966): *Human Sexual Response*, Little, Brown and Company, Boston.

May, R., ed. (1961): *Existential Psychology*, Random House, New York.

Meyer, A. (1957): *Psychobiology, a Science of Man*, C. C. Thomas, Springfield, Illinois.

Miller, N. E. (1958): Central stimulation and other new approaches to motivation and reward, *Am. Psychol. 13*, 100–108.

Moreno, J. L. (1963): *New Introduction to Psychodrama*, Psychodrama and Group Psychotherapy Monographs, No. 39, Beacon House, New York.

Moruzzi, G., and Magoun, H. W. (1949): Brain stem reticular formation and activation of the EEG, *Electroencephalogr. Clin. Neurophysiol. 1*, 445.

Munroe, R. L. (1955): *Schools of Psychoanalytic Thought*, Holt, Rinehart & Winston, New York.

Nahas, G. H. (1973): *Marihuana—Deceptive Weed*, Raven Press, New York.

Nauta, W. J. H., and Kuypers, H. G. J. M. (1958): Some ascending pathways in the brain stem reticular formation. In: *Reticular Formation of the Brain*, ed. H. H. Jaspers, L. D. Proctor, R. S. Knighton, W. C. Noshay, and R. T. Cortello, Little, Brown and Company, Boston.

Olds, J., and Milner, P. (1954): Positive reinforcement produced by electrical stimulation of septal area and other regions of the rat brain, *J. Comp. Physiol. Psychol. 47*, 419–427.

Overall, J. E., and Henry, B. W. (1973): Decisions about drug therapy, *Arch. Gen. Psychiatry 28*, 81–89.

Patterson, C. H. (1973): *Theories of Counseling and Psychotherapy,* Harper & Row, New York.

Perez-Cruet, J., Tagliamonte, A., Tagliamonte, P., and Gessa, G. L. (1971): Differential effect of p-chlorophenylalanine (PCPA) on sexual behavior and on sleep patterns of male rabbits, *Riv. Farmacol. Terap. 11,* 27–34.

Perls, F. S., Hefferline, R. F., and Goodman, P. (1951): *Gestalt Therapy,* Julian Press, New York.

Pert, C. B., and Snyder, S. H. (1973): Opiate receptor: Demonstration in nervous tissue, *Science 179,* 1011–1014.

Porter, C. C. (1970): *Chemical Mechanisms of Drug Action,* Thomas, Springfield, Ill.

Ray, O. S. (1972): *Drugs, Society and Human Behavior,* C. V. Mosby, St. Louis.

Reis, D. J. (1972): The relationship between brain norepinephrine and aggressive behavior. In: *Neurotransmitters,* ed. I. J. Kopin, Williams & Wilkins, Baltimore.

Rice, A. K. (1965): *Learning for Leadership,* Tavistock Publications, London.

Richter, C. P. (1957): On the phenomenon of sudden death in animals and man, *Psychosom. Med. 19,* 191–198.

Rioch, D. M. (1955): Problems of preventive psychiatry in war. In: *Psychopathology of Childhood,* ed. P. H. Hoch and J. Zubin, Grune & Stratton, New York.

Rioch, M. J. (1970*a*): The work of Wilfred Bion on groups, *Psychiatry 33,* 56–65.

Rioch, M. J. (1970*b*): Group relations: Rationale and technique, *Int. J. Group Psychother. 20,* 340–355.

Rioch, M. J. (1970*c*): Should psychotherapists do psychotherapy? *J. Contemp. Psychother. 3,* 61–64.

Rogers, C. R. (1951): *Client-centered Therapy,* Houghton Mifflin Company, Boston.

Ruitenbeek, H. M., ed. (1969): *Group Therapy Today: Styles, Methods and Techniques,* Atherton Press, New York.

Sabelli, H. C., ed. (1973): *Chemical Modulation of Brain Function,* Raven Press, New York.

Sankar, D. V. S. (1973): *LSD–A Total Study,* PJD Publications, Westbury, N.Y.

Schachter, S. (1964): On the assumption of "identity" in psychopharmacology. In: *Walter Reed Army Institute of Research, Symposium on Medical Aspects of Stress in the Military Climate,* U.S. Government Printing Office, Washington, D.C.

Shakespeare, W. *The Merchant of Venice,* Act 3; Scene 2.

Skinner, B. F. (1938): *The Behavior of Organisms: (An Experimental Analysis),* Appleton-Century-Crofts, New York.

Snyder, S. H. (1973): Amphetamine psychosis: A "model" schizophrenia mediated by catecholamines, *Am. J. Psychiatry 130,* 61–67.

Snyder, S. H., Taylor, K. M., Horn, A. S., and Coyle, J. T. (1972): Psychoactive drugs and neurotransmitters: Differentiating dopamine and norepinephrine neuronal functions with drugs. In: *Neurotransmitters,* ed. I. J. Kopin, Williams & Wilkins, Baltimore.

Steiner, S. S. (1968): Effects of metamphetamine HCL on intracranial self-stimulation. Paper presented at the meetings of the Eastern Psychological Association, Washington, D.C., April 1968.

Steiner, S. S. (1973): Measurement of self-stimulation. In: *Methods for Assessing Psychoactive Drugs,* ed. S. Irwin (in press).

Steiner, S. S., and Stokely, S. N. (1973): Metamphetamine lowers self-stimulation thresholds, *Physiol. Psychol. 1,* 161–164.

Strupp, H. A. (1955): Psychotherapeutic technique, professional affiliation, and experience level, *J. Consult. Psychol. 19,* 97–102.

Sullivan, H. S. (1953): *The Interpersonal Theory of Psychiatry,* Norton, New York.

Taylor, K. M., and Snyder, S. H. (1970): Amphetamine: Differentiation by d- and l-isomers of behavior involving norepinephrine or dopamine, *Science 168,* 1487–1489.

Thompson, T. and Pickens, R., ed. (1971): *Stimulus Properties of Drugs,* Appleton-Century Crofts, New York.

Tyhurst, J. S. (1951): Individual reactions to community disaster. The natural history of psychiatric phenomena, *Am. J. Psychiatry 107,* 764.

Ungenstedt, U. (1971): Stereotoxic mapping of the monoamine pathways in the rat brain, *Acta Physiol. Scand.* Suppl. 367, 1–48.

Vinăr, O., Votava, Z., and Bradley, P. B., ed. (1971): *Advances in Neuropsychopharmacology: Proceedings of the Symposia held at the VII Congress of the Collegium Internationale Neuro-Psychopharmacologicum, Prague, August 11–15, 1970,* North-Holland Publishing Company, Amsterdam.

Vittoz, R. (1967): *Traitement des Psychonevroses par la Reeducation du controle Cerebrale,* Baillière, Paris.

von Euler, U. S. (1971): Adrenergic neurotransmitter functions, *Science 173,* 202–206.

Watts, A. W. (1957): *The Way of Zen,* Pantheon, New York.

Wolpe, J. (1958): *Psychotherapy by Reciprocal Inhibition,* University Press, Stanford.

Zarafonetis, C. J. D., ed. (1972): *Drug Abuse: Proceedings of the International Conference,* Lea & Febiger, Philadelphia.

Emotions—Their Parameters and Measurement,
edited by L. Levi.
Raven Press, New York © 1975

Session 4: Discussion

Chairman: Richard S. Lazarus

Lazarus: Most of the researchers use one parameter. What relationship might there be between this and other indicators and other response parameters? Are we dealing with emotion? In what sense are we dealing with emotion? Are we dealing with it in the same way as other approaches?

Wolf: With respect to the way in which emotions are reflected, I think the effort to tie a particular bodily response to an emotion is going to fail for two reasons: one, the work of the Levi group showing the numerous circumstances that elicit increased measurable catecholamines in the urine, and, two, the fact that ordinary life, as well as experimental work, can show you that two people experiencing the same emotion will behave in opposite ways. Although, one can associate a particular response to an emotion, it may be possible to relate patterned responses more clearly. We have plenty of evidence that most sympathetic responses to stressful experience are parasympathetic responses.

Frankenhaeuser: I agree that we have paid much too little attention to these internal mechanisms, as you call them. And what makes this a very hopeful strategy for future research is that we find, among what we call normal, healthy people, these large differences between individuals in the rate in which they turn off their responses. This is one of the lines of research that we are very much interested in continuing. We do not have much data so far, but at least we know at this stage that there seems to be a relation to what can be called the well-adjusted individual if we measure adjustment in terms of performance efficiency, or if we use a rating scale of some kind. We have used, for instance, questionnaires such as Eysenck's neuroticism scales. We find that the rapid turn off people have lower neuroticism scores. It seems that this time patterning may be very relevant to this whole question of disease and psychosomatic disorder.

Sarason: I reviewed the literature on genius and creativity and discovered that the two most outstanding characteristics of highly creative people are (1) that they tended to move around a lot, their parents moved a lot, and they were forced to adjust to many different environments, and (2) many of them had been sick as children. These two indices from life stress measure not only seem not to have negative effects but to have positive effects on people. A better concept might be how do people adapt to various types of situations.

Levi: Primarily Dr. Sarason described the positive effects as opposed to the negative ones, namely disease, and he posed that genius is clearly something rather positive and obviously the same characteristics applied to those exhibiting this characteristic as those exhibiting disease afterward; there is no contradiction. It might well be that we are stimulated by certain life events, that our accomplishment is greatly improved, but that we have to pay a medical price for it by increased disease in the long run. Second, life change unit measures no doubt have to be refined. The original idea of measuring or trying to quantify the psychosocial influences is a good one. It is a crude measure, but at least it is a beginning.

Mason: To tie in the endocrine system a little more closely with the point brought up by Dr. Wolf and Dr. Frankenhaeuser, we might look for not so much sympathetic versus parasympathetic but a balance between the two. Maybe the psychophysiological machinery when it is effective is not always able to hold them perfectly at equilibrium. It may be that somatic illnesses develop from overcompensatory suppression of repression or prevention of arousal as from excessive or inappropriate or prolonged arousals.

Lazarus: I would like to shift to the question of reported affects and emotionality as another response parameter. I think especially interesting are the implications of Pancheri's work with Swiss and Italian subjects on the expression of emotion via the MMPI. Would you draw out some of those implications for us?

Pancheri: Do you put the same label to the same behavior in different cultures? This is, I think, the main problem we have to face. And in my opinion it is a very important problem because there are many researchers who correlate their empirical results, neurophysiology, biochemistry, etc. with behavioral correlates. The problem is how can we compare the results coming from different social cultural contexts. We use the MMPI as an instrument for the measurements of emotions. The MMPI has to be seen like a set of stimuli that given to the patient or the normal person generates a pattern of reactions. Obviously it is a verbal stimulus, but I would like to underline the fact that here we are really in an experimental area. Then the MMPI gives us the possibility to have the description of a personality and of emotions with a set of variables that can be treated with statistical analysis. We compared four groups of people coming from different cultures, two groups of normals and two groups of depressed neurotic patients. We looked for any significant difference between these groups. In the normal groups the profiles were almost the same. But with the depressed patients they were quite different, not in terms of the shape of the profile, but in the height of the profile. Part of our research was dedicated to why we find these differences. We made an item frequency endorsement and found that almost one-half of the items on the test were discriminating between the two populations with normal profiles and average profiles at the same level and with the same shape. When we went into the analysis of the depressive items that discriminated between the two groups, we saw, in fact, that in the Italian population most of the items related to depressed mood, psychomotor retardation, and anxiety were responded to as positive. The Italian in the test showed a significantly higher tendency to respond to the test in this way. I think that the item endorsement frequency is the explanation of the results of the discriminant function of the comparison of the profiles. And this is because the diagnosis of depression or the diagnosis of normality was made in Italy by Italian psychiatrists and in Switzerland by Swiss psychiatrists. Both of them are obviously influenced by their social environment. For instance, the Italian psychiatrist is more likely to accept as a normal manifestation a complaint of "I am sad today; I don't want to go to work." In Switzerland the average psychiatrist will not be so tolerant.

Groen: These transcultural studies illustrate actually what has already been stated: these people express in different words their signs and symptoms, their feelings, and therefore the language communication does not enable us to make a diagnosis. The verbalization of the emotions is very much culturally dependent.

Lazarus: Dr. Yensen, in what sense is happiness an emotion?

Yensen: This is a very difficult question to answer, and some people have even suggested that perhaps it is not a very fruitful question. Perhaps we should ask questions about what are the outcomes of the existence of this sort of state. I feel intuitively that happiness, used in the sense of a satisfaction with life, a rather long-lasting state as compared with the more transient positive "emotions," is an emotion rather than a sentiment. I have suggested a predominately verbal report system, investigated by interview because I think that at this stage an interview is the best technique to test the reliability and perhaps validity of the verbal reports of the subject. It is reasonable to suggest that the individual gets satisfaction or happiness from those areas of life that are important to him, provided his evaluation of his experiences in those areas of life do in fact support his self image.

Sem-Jacobson: Following a stereotactic operation, you sometimes see that patients become highly euphoric and it may last. I have frequently been asked to what extent an operation has been successful. The patient is happy, but where is the border between happiness and euphoria?

Yensen: Firstly, I would suggest that, in terms of the theoretical model, the transient feelings of joys and pleasures, including induced euphoria, are not necessarily transient at all. I would see happiness as deriving from evaluation of the experiences in those areas of life which the individual deems important. The euphoric state might in fact in and of itself come to be an important part of the patient's life. When it does, I think it may contribute to what I would call happiness or satisfaction.

Frankenhaeuser: Dr. Yensen, since you discuss the implications of your measurement of happiness for social welfare and for social planning and you emphasize giving advice to politicians, I think that there is one class of investigations that I do not find in your chapter. I wanted to draw your attention to it because I think it is highly relevant. This is the area of the whole quality of life research which is now coming into fashion, the quality of life concept as different from the level of living concept. These quality of life measurements usually take off from the traditional social indicators, such as, education, housing, family relations, recreation, and then somehow link the satisfactions experienced in these different areas to the external level of living components.

Lader: I have been rather puzzled by the way in which some people talk about positive and negative emotions. I can conceive of an emotion being pleasant or unpleasant, but I can no more conceive of a negative emotion than I can of a negative idea, and I suspect that this is not a very useful concept.

Yensen: It is a loose usage, and one perhaps should endeavor to be more specific, but I think that there is a sense in which the positive emotions are those psychological states which most individuals would endeavor to prolong and the negative ones are those which most individuals would endeavor to terminate.

Lader: Dr. Yensen says that, as I understand it, happiness occurs when people find satisfaction in the areas of life which they regard as important. One could argue equally as well that the areas of life in which they find satisfaction they then regard as important.

Groen: I would like to make a remark about the cultural aspects of studies such as Dr. Clynes described. The human being, especially in his communication with others, expresses himself by skeletal-muscular movement. Some of these movements are verbalizations, muscles of speech, some of them are gesticulations, mimical like Darwin described in the animals, and some are movements like in fighting, running, and dancing. It is by these movements that we communicate to each other. In the Western culture if one compares this to some other cultures, the poverty of our skeletal-muscular expressions of emotions is very striking.

Sem-Jacobsen: In regard to this culture research I think the great difference in behavior even within the western culture, for instance, between Norway and southern Europe cannot be emphasized enough. It is not only language but it is basic behavior.

Emotions – Their Parameters and Measurement,
edited by L. Levi.
Raven Press, New York © 1975

Parameters of Emotion: An Evolutionary and Ecological Approach

Lennart Levi

WHO Psychosocial Center, S-104 01 Stockholm 60, Sweden

The main objectives of this volume are to clarify (a) major theoretical *concepts* of emotion, (b) some general principles and problems in *measuring emotion, (c) relationships* between emotion and events in organ systems, and (d) specific strategies and problems in measuring psychological and physiological *parameters* of emotion, and to discuss some (e) clinical and (f) ethical *implications* of emotion measurement and modification.

SOME DEFINITIONS

What is emotion? The expression is derived from Latin: *exmovere,* to move out, disturb, stir up, excite. Clearly, this original meaning comes rather close to today's psychological concepts of activation and arousal. However, THE definition or THE theory of emotion does not exist. It may even be advisable to stick to the everyday meaning of the word. Dorland's *Medical Dictionary* defines emotion as "a state of mental excitement, characterized by alteration of feeling tone." The *American Heritage Dictionary of the English Language* similarly defines emotion as "agitation of the passions or sensibilities" or as "any strong feeling, as of joy, sorrow, reverence, hate, or love, arising subjectively rather than through conscious mental effort."

Clearly, these definitions, like the more scientific formulations presented by a number of the authors in this volume, imply that emotions are subjective reactions or states. They further imply physiological phenomena in the brain and elsewhere in the organism and behavioral components. Avoiding the probably insoluble mind-body controversy, we may choose to measure psychological or physiological *parameters* of emotion, without attempting to trace the evasive "das Ding an sich" that may underly these parameters.

The preceding, technical part of this volume focuses to a high degree on theoretical, conceptual, and methodological issues. Instead of trying to summarize and review each contribution, I will try to apply what has been said so far to *human ecology,* i.e., to total man's interrelation with his total environment, and to the clinical practice of psychiatry and internal medicine.

STONE AGE REACTIONS

This approach is justified by the fact that emotions constitute important phenomena in the complex ecosystem comprising man and his environment. In general, whenever exposed to environmental change, the human organism reacts with a set of processes which are phylogenetically old and which presumably were adaptive in the dawn of the history of mankind. These processes seem to comprise a preparation for coping with the environment. The nonspecific *subjective* elements of this response may be labeled psychological "arousal" or "activation."

From the evolutionary point of view, *unpleasant* emotional reactions may have been adaptive by promoting the self-preservation of the living organism. Correspondingly, those perceived as predominantly *pleasant* may have promoted the development of the organism, and the maintenance of the species.

Similarly, the *physiological concomitants* of these subjective reactions can be seen as adaptive originally, namely by preparing the organism for muscular activity, e.g., fight, flight, sex. This rather nonspecific physiological reaction pattern in response to almost any type of environmental change is closely related to Selye's stress construct (Selye, 1971; Levi, 1972).

The past 500,000 years have seen dramatic changes in the human environment. These changes, however, do not seem to have been accompanied by any substantial modification of man's genetically determined "psychobiological program" and, accordingly, of his basic psychophysiological reaction patterns.

Anxiety and physiological stress reactions were probably promoting the survival of the individual and of the species when Stone Age man was confronting a wolf pack, but hardly so when modern man is confronting his boss or his spouse. Pleasurable emotional reactions and their physiological concomitants were presumably promoting the development and maintenance of the individual and the species, e.g., when Stone Age man got oral and general satisfaction when ingesting delicious vegetables or animals, but not when modern man ingests sweets, alcoholic beverages, or narcotic drugs.

Briefly, then, however, purposeful these psychophysiological "Stone Age reactions" may have been in the dawn of the history of mankind, they do not appear to be appropriate in the adaptation of modern man to a great number of the socioeconomic and psychosocial changes, conflicts and threats confronting him in a highly industrialized, urban society.

PSYCHOPHYSIOLOGICAL DISCREPANCIES

Furthermore, for social reasons, modern man often has to repress many of his emotional outlets and motor activities. This creates a situation that might very well involve a discrepancy between the subjective elements of emotion, the neuroendocrine concomitants of emotion, and the psychomotor activities likely to accompany such emotion. For example, modern man may feel anxiety or aggression in a marital or occupational setting without showing it in his facial expression or verbal or gross motor behavior. Or man feels obliged to exhibit emotional expressions (e.g., joy) and to perform physically or verbally in a way that is grossly incongruous with his actual neuroendocrine and subjective emotional state. It has been hypothesized that this "stress" or "arousal" pattern of response to psychosocial stimuli and/or this psychophysiological discrepancy, if it persists, and coping is unsuccessful, may become pathogenic. The question now is: how.

AN ECOLOGICAL MODEL

To discuss possible answers, let us return to the interaction between environmental factors and the individual as presented in the following theoretical ecological model (Fig. 1). Before discussing the model, some of the key terms must be defined (Kagan and Levi, 1974).

Psychosocial stimuli (1): These are stimuli, suspected of being able to cause disease, that originate in social relationships or arrangements (i.e., the environment) and affect the organism through the medium of higher nervous processes.

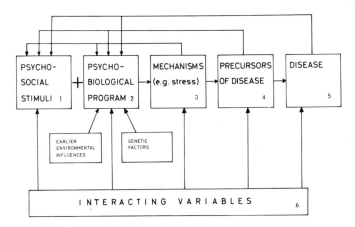

FIG. 1. An ecological model for psychosocially mediated disease. A variety of social structures and processes produce a relatively small number of psychosocial stimuli (1). The combined effect of such stimuli and the psychobiological program (2) determines the psychological and physiological reactions (mechanisms, 3) of each individual. These may, under certain circumstances, lead to precursors of disease (4) and to disease itself (5). This sequence of events can be promoted or counteracted by interacting variables (6). The sequence is not a one-way process but constitutes part of a cybernetic system with continuous feedback (Levi, 1972; Kagan and Levi, 1974).

Psychobiological program (2): By this we mean a propensity to react in accordance with a certain psychophysiological pattern, e.g., when solving a problem or adapting to an environment. Determinants of this program in an organism are genetic factors and earlier environmental influences.

Mechanisms (3): These are reactions in the organism (e.g., anxiety, increased activity in the sympathoadrenomedullary system) induced by psychosocial stimuli that, under some conditions of intensity, frequency, or duration, and in the presence or absence of certain interacting variables, can lead to disease.

Precursors of disease (4): These are malfunctions in mental or physical systems that have not resulted in disability but which, if continued, will do so.

Disease (5): Disease is disability caused by mental or somatic malfunction. Disability is failure in performance of a task. This must always include tasks considered essential, might include tasks considered normal, and, when more is known, will include tasks that are considered optimal. In applying this it is necessary to state the level of the biological hierarchy to which it refers. Disease as defined is different at the cell, organ, and organism level.

Interacting variables (6): These are intrinsic or extrinsic factors, mental or physical, that alter the action of "causative" factors at the mechanism, precursor, or disease stage. By "alter" we mean that they promote or prevent the process that might lead to disease.

ROLE OF EMOTIONS IN PATHOGENIC PROCESSES

Let us return to our ecological model to see where parameters of emotion come in. The model is cybernetic, with continuous feedback. Suppose we take an example. Certain environmental stimuli (1) provoke in certain, say, anxiety-prone individuals (2) an emotional response, say, anxiety (3). This response implies central and peripheral physiological concomitants, part of which, say, tachycardia and palpitations, may generate proprioceptive signals. If perceived and interpreted by the individual as something unpleasant and/or dangerous, this may augment his anxiety reaction.

In some individuals and under certain circumstances, even perfectly "normal" proprioceptive signals may be interpreted by the individual as a threat or as symptoms of disease, as in the case of *hypochondriasis*. If the environmental stimulation becomes pronounced, prolonged, or often repeated, or if the organism is predisposed to react, or because of the presence or absence of certain interacting variables, the result may be a prolonged or often repeated hyper-, hypo-, or dysfunction in one or more organs and organ systems, i.e., a *functional disorder* (cf., Levi, 1971, 1972; Levi and Andersson, 1974). This may be accompanied by or secondarily generate feelings of anxiety, depression, etc. If such functional disturbances become prolonged, or often repeated, it has been claimed that eventually they may even lead to *structural damage* in the organ or organ system involved. Again, disease characterized by such damage may be accompanied by or secondarily generate emotional reactions.

Briefly, then, unpleasant emotional reactions can be generated directly, i.e., in response to environmental stimuli, but also secondarily, in response to proprioceptive or cognitive stimuli arising from mechanisms, precursors of disease, or disease itself. The reactions are heavily influenced and conditioned by the individual's psychobiological program and by various interacting variables.

Accordingly, parameters of emotion may be of interest to us because of their possible role in etiological and pathogenetic processes; as symptoms, indices, or predictors of disease; as a target area for therapeutic intervention and preventive social and medical action.

MAN – ENVIRONMENT FIT

In Fig. 2, the man in a box serves as an example of a human ecosystem, i.e., of total man in his total environment. Clearly, our way of finding out the degree of "man-environment fit" lies in the study of individual and environmental characteristics and of man's reactions to his environment, including as they do various parameters of emotion. A bad "man-environment fit" may be due exclusively to characteristics of the environment, as is probable in this case. It may also be due mainly to characteristics of the individual, for example, in the case of anxiety-prone, phobic, obsessive-compulsive, or paranoid individuals.

When it comes to *improving* a certain man-environment fit, there are several alternatives. We may adapt the environment to man's abilities, needs, and expectations, or we may remove him from a noxious environment. We may further try to change his psychobiological program, i.e., his propensity to react in a certain manner. Theoretically, we can do this by modifying his pathological but occasionally also his normal reactions using pharmaco-, physio-, or psychotherapeutic methods. In this way we can (but in some cases perhaps should not) make him accept or at least tolerate a certain "box," a certain environment without suffering too much or getting ill.

As a necessary basis for any decision concerning measurement, modification or prevention of certain types of emotional response, we need to identify, *inter alia*, those at risk, the risks they run, mechanisms in the pathogenetic processes, efficiency of possible countermeasures, and "side-effects" of such countermeasures. As very little is known on all these points, we need research.

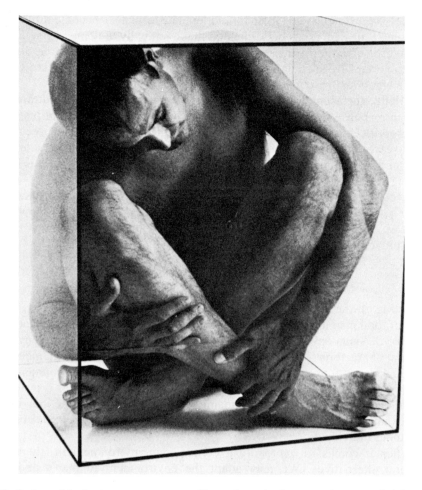

FIG. 2. A model of a human ecosystem, illustrating a bad man-environment fit (photo: courtesy Asbjörn Habberstad).

EPIDEMIOLOGICAL RESEARCH STRATEGIES

Research strategies can follow the traditional transsectional, descriptive epidemiological model, relating the interaction of stimuli (1) and individual characteristics (2) to morbidity (5), in some cases as modified by interacting variables (6). Such studies inform us about associations between various factors but give no definite answers about possible *causal* relationships.

Additional information can be obtained from longitudinal epidemiological studies, retrospective or prospective. Here, the *temporal* relationship may give some hints as to which is the chicken and which the egg. Additional evidence is provided if such studies include psychological and physiological mechanisms (3). This may be so, if some form of environmental exposure is found to be followed by, say, a high incidence of depressive reactions, or by increases in plasma lipids, and urinary catecholamines, which in turn may be found to precede increased rates of, say, suicide or an increased morbidity in myocardial infarction, respectively.

A further development of research strategy is represented by what can be called *experimental epidemiology*. This is taken to mean experimental modification either of environmental conditions (i.e., stimuli – 1) or of some of the reactions (i.e., mechanisms – 3). For ethical reasons these modifications and interventions should *always* focus on high risk groups and be assumed to be of a therapeutic and/or health-promoting and protecting nature.

Researchers and practitioners in the fields of psychiatry, psychology, sociology, and social engineering have presented numerous *hypotheses* on how to prevent psychiatric and psychosomatic disorders and how to promote and preserve what the World Health Organization refers to as the highest possible physical, mental, and social well-being. These hypotheses *need to be tested (cf.,* Levi, 1973).

Today, *social policy* is based, to a high degree, not on research, but on anecdotal evidence and wishful thinking. The time has come to start a fruitful dialogue between society planners, social engineers, and decision makers on the one hand and life and behavioral scientists on the other. In such a context, research on parameters of emotion will be of central importance.

This brings us to our last two problems: (1) under what conditions, if any, is it justifiable to measure and monitor parameters of emotion in a certain subject or group of subjects, and (2) under what conditions, if any, is it justifiable to interfere with emotional reactions, e.g., by behavioral modification or psychopharmacological agents. This will be the subject of later chapters.

REFERENCES

Kagan, A. R., and Levi, L. (1974): Health and environment – Psychosocial stimuli, *Soc. Sci. Med. 8*, 225–241.

Levi, L. (ed.) (1971): *Society, Stress and Disease – The Psychosocial Environment and Psychosomatic Diseases.* Oxford University Press, London.

Levi, L. (1972): *Stress and Distress in Response to Psychosocial Stimuli. Laboratory and Real Life Studies on Sympathoadrenomedullary and Related Reactions.* Pergamon Press, Oxford (also published as Supplement No. 528 to *Acta Med. Scand.*).

Levi, L. (1973): Humanökologie – psychosomatische Gesichtspunkte und Forschungsstrategien, *Psychosomatische Medizin 5*, 92–107.

Levi, L., and Andersson, L. (1974): *Population, Environment and Quality of Life. A Contribution to the United Nations' Population Conference.* Royal Ministry for Foreign Affairs, Stockholm (Allmänna Förlaget).

Selye, H. (1971): The evolution of the stress concept – Stress and cardiovascular disease. In: *Society, Stress and Disease – The Psychosocial Environment and Psychosomatic Diseases,* ed. L. Levi, Oxford University Press, London.

Emotions—Their Parameters and Measurement,
edited by L. Levi.
Raven Press, New York © 1975

The Measurement of State and Trait Anxiety: Conceptual and Methodological Issues*

Charles D. Spielberger

College of Social and Behavioral Sciences, Department of Psychology, University of South Florida, Tampa, Florida 33620

INTRODUCTION

My goal in this chapter is to discuss, in general terms, theoretical and methodological issues that are encountered in the measurement of anxiety. I will also describe, in some detail, the development of the state-trait anxiety inventory (STAI). Several examples of the use of the STAI in the assessment of anxiety in research and clinical contexts will also be reported. Before proceeding to these tasks, some popular conceptions of anxiety will be examined, and the evolution of anxiety as a scientific psychological concept will be reviewed.

POPULAR CONCEPTIONS OF ANXIETY

The 20th century has been called the "age of anxiety," but concern with anxiety phenomena is as old as the history of mankind. The concept of fear, for example, was clearly represented in ancient Egyptian hieroglyphs. James Kritzcek, of the Department of Oriental Studies at Princeton University, has noted a central concern with anxiety in medieval Arab philosophy. In a treatise entitled *A Philosophy of Character and Conduct,* written in the 11th century, the universality of anxiety as a basic condition of human existence is asserted by Ala ibn Hazm of Cordova.

In his investigations, Ibn Hazm writes, he had constantly tried to single out "one end in human actions which all men unanimously hold as good and which they all seek. I have found only this: the aim of escaping anxiety. . . . Not only have I discovered that all humanity considers this good and desirable, but also . . . no one is moved to act or moved to speak a single word who does not hope by means of this action or word to release anxiety from his spirit (Kritzcek, 1956, p. 573).

---

* This chapter is based in part on the author's chapters in *Anxiety and Behavior* (1966) and *Anxiety: Current Trends in Theory and Research,* Vols. 1 and 2 (1972), and is reprinted here with the kind permission of Academic Press, Inc., New York and London.

The importance of anxiety as a powerful influence in contemporary life is also widely recognized. Concern with anxiety phenomena is reflected in many facets of our culture, including literature, the arts, and religion, as well as in psychology and psychiatry. Consider for example, the following passage from a popular American periodical, *Time Magazine* (March 31, 1961, p. 44).

Anxiety seems to be the dominant fact – and is threatening to become the dominant cliche – of modern life. It shouts in the headlines, laughs nervously at cocktail parties, nags from advertisements, speaks suavely in the board room, whines from the stage, clatters from the Wall Street ticker, jokes with fake youthfulness on the golf course and whispers in privacy each day before the shaving mirror and the dressing table. Not merely the black statistics of murder, suicide, alcoholism and divorce betray anxiety (or that special form of anxiety which is guilt), but almost any innocent, everyday act: the limp or overhearty handshake, the second pack of cigarettes or the third martini, the forgotten appointment, the stammer in mid-sentence, the wasted hour before the TV set, the spanked child, the new car unpaid for.

THE EVOLUTION OF ANXIETY AS A SCIENTIFIC PSYCHOLOGICAL CONCEPT

Anxiety is currently considered a fundamental explanatory concept in most theories of personality and psychopathology, and it is generally regarded as the central problem in psychoneurosis. Anxiety is also widely regarded as a principal causative agent for such diverse behavioral consequences as insomnia, debilitating psychological and psychosomatic symptoms, immoral and sinful acts, and even instances of creative self-expression.

According to Rollo May (1950), in his classic book *The Meaning of Anxiety*, the historical roots of contemporary scientific conceptions of anxiety are to be found in the philosophical and theological views of Pascal in the 17th century and Kierkegaard in the 19th century. In *The Expression of Emotions in Man and Animals*, first published in 1872, Darwin described in perceptive detail a number of manifestations of fear such as rapid palpitation of the heart, trembling, dilation of the pupils, erection of the hair, dryness of the mouth, increased perspiration, peculiar facial expression, and changes in voice quality. The potential for experiencing fear was regarded by Darwin as an inherent characteristic of both animals and men that had evolved over countless generations through the process of natural selection. Significantly, Darwin also noted an important characteristic of fear, namely, that it varies in intensity – from mild apprehension or surprise to what he termed an extreme "agony of terror."

Whatever the historical forerunners, it was Freud (1924, 1933, 1936) who first attempted to explain the meaning of fear or anxiety within the context of psychological theory. He regarded anxiety as "something felt" – a fundamental, unpleasant affective (emotional) state or condition. This state, as Freud observed it in his patients, was characterized by subjective feelings of tension, nervousness, apprehension, and worry, and by physiological and behavioral manifestations such as heart palpitations or tachycardia, disturbances of respiration, sweating, tremor and shuddering, nausea, and vertigo.

Anxiety was distinguishable from other unpleasant affective states, such as anger or depression, by its unique combination of phenomenological and physiological qualities. The subjective, phenomenological qualities of anxiety — the feelings of apprehension, tension and dread — were emphasized by Freud in his theoretical formulations. While the physiological discharge phenomena were considered to be essential characteristics of anxiety states, these were of little theoretical interest to Freud.

In his early formulations, Freud believed that anxiety resulted from the discharge of repressed, somatic sexual tensions which he called libido. When libidinal energy was blocked from normal expression, it accumulated and was automatically transferred into free-floating anxiety, or into symptoms that were anxiety equivalents. Freud subsequently modified this view in favor of a more general conception of anxiety as a signal indicating the presence of a danger situation. The perceived presence of danger, either from the environment or from some internal source, evoked an unpleasant emotional state, and this served to warn the individual that some form of adjustment was necessary. Thus, Freud's second theory emphasized the adaptive, functional utility of anxiety in helping the ego to cope with danger.

In his second theory, Freud identified three kinds of anxiety, depending on whether the source of danger was from the external world or from internal impulses or conflicts. Objective anxiety, which was synonymous with fear, was evoked by real dangers in the external world; the intensity of objective anxiety reactions was proportional to the actual danger. Neurotic anxiety was evoked by unacceptable sexual and aggressive impulses that had been severely and consistently punished in childhood. The experience of these impulses in adolescence or adulthood elicited an anxiety state that warned against further punishment if the impulses were expressed. Moral anxiety or guilt resulted when an individual's behavioral acts violated the dictates of his conscience.

Freud's earliest conceptual statements on anxiety date back to a paper that he published in 1895. In this paper, he identified and described anxiety neurosis as a separate and distinct psychopathological syndrome to be differentiated from neurasthenia. In his *New Introductory Lectures,* published in 1933, near the end of his productive career, Freud noted that an understanding of anxiety was ". . . the most difficult task that has been set us, — a task whose solution requires the introduction of the right abstract ideas, and their application to the raw material of observation so as to bring order and lucidity to it" (1933, p. 113). The complexity of this task and Freud's personal commitment to it are reflected in the fact that his theoretical views on the subject of anxiety evolved over a period of nearly 50 years, were continually modified, and were never regarded by him as complete.

Despite the brilliance of Freud's conceptual contributions, he never got around to developing objective measures of anxiety and he has been justifiably criticized for this shortcoming. One of his most vocal critics, Raymond B. Cattell (Cattell and Scheier, 1961), has consistently pointed out that our understanding of anxiety cannot advance beyond the prescientific level until operational procedures are developed for the assessment of anxiety. The remainder of this chapter will be devoted to considering several approaches to the measurement of anxiety. It will be noted that the development of new procedures for the assessment of anxiety has generally followed clarification of the nature of anxiety as a scientific concept.

THE MEASUREMENT OF ANXIETY

The development of measurement procedures should be guided by a precise conceptual definition of the dimensions or variables that are to be measured, but this ideal is seldom realized in psychology and psychiatry. One of the earliest measures of anxiety, and, until recently, the most widely used, is the Taylor (1953) manifest anxiety scale (TMAS). The TMAS first appeared around 1950 and has been used subsequently to measure anxiety in more than 2,000 studies (Spielberger, 1966a). The TMAS was not originally intended to be a measure of anxiety. Rather, this scale was developed to provide a measure of motivation or drive level as this concept is defined in Hullian learning theory.

The rationale for the development of the TMAS was based on the assumption that nervous or emotional individuals operate at higher levels of motivation or drive, and that individual differences in motivation would influence performance on learning tasks. In the typical learning experiment the TMAS is used to select subjects who are presumed to differ in drive level, and the performance of high and low drive subjects on various learning tasks is then evaluated. While it is beyond the scope of this chapter to consider the vast literature on anxiety and learning, it should be noted that interest in learning phenomena, rather than concern with personality or psychopathology, stimulated the construction of the first, widely used anxiety scale.

It will be instructive to examine the test construction procedures used in the development of the TMAS. Taylor presented 200 items from the Minnesota multiphasic personality inventory to five clinical psychologists along with Norman Cameron's definition of manifest anxiety as observed in anxiety neurotics. The clinicians were instructed to identify, according to Cameron's definition, those items that described symptoms of manifest anxiety. An initial group of 66 items was selected on the basis of agreement among 4 of the 5 judges. Item analysis procedures were then employed to reduce the scale to 50 items.

In the administration of the TMAS the patient or subject is instructed to respond, either true or false, to each of the 50 items, according to whether or not the item describes how they generally feel. Examples of the TMAS items are indicated below. Items answered as noted in the parentheses contribute one point to the patient's anxiety score.

I work under a great deal of strain (True).
I blush as often as others (False).
I worry quite a bit over possible troubles (True).
At times I loose sleep over worry (True).
I am a nervous person (True).

Cattell and his colleagues have pioneered the application of multivariate techniques to the definition and measurement of anxiety. In their research a large number of questionnaires and physiological variables presumed to be related to anxiety have been studied with factor analytic procedures. Out of this multivariate approach, which permits investigation of the covariation of a number of different measures over time, "state" and "trait" anxiety factors have consistently emerged as principal personality dimensions (Cattell and Scheier, 1958).

The IPAT anxiety scale was developed by Cattell and Scheier to measure trait anxiety. Their main concern was to assess anxiety in clinical situations in a rapid, standardized manner. When compared with the test construction procedures employed by Taylor, Cattell, and Scheier, IPAT (a) employed a different definition of anxiety and had quite different goals for the application of their scale, (b) used multiple choice in contrast to true-false items, and (c) employed factor analytic procedures, whereas Taylor selected her items on the basis of content validity and internal consistency. Some sample items from the IPAT anxiety scale are listed below. The high anxiety alternative is underlined. (Cattell and Scheier, 1963).

1. As a child I was afraid of the dark
   (a) often   (b) sometimes   (c) never

2. Most people are a little queer mentally although they do not like to admit it
   (a) true   (b) uncertain   (c) false

3. In discussions with most people, I get so annoyed that I can hardly trust myself to speak.
   (a) sometimes   (b) rarely   (c) never

4. If I had my life to live over again, I would
   (a) plan very differently   (b) in-between   (c) want it the same

Despite differences in goals, definitions of anxiety, item format, and method of test construction, the IPAT anxiety scale correlates between 0.80 and 0.85 with the TMAS. Since the correlation among the scales approaches the reliabilities of the individual scales, it is reasonable to conclude that the TMAS and the IPAT anxiety scale can be considered as alternative measures of trait anxiety.

The IPAT 8-parallel form anxiety battery (8-PF) was developed by Scheier and Cattell (1960) for the "repeated measurement of changes in anxiety level over time." Each of the eight forms of this battery consists of subtests for which high loadings on a state-anxiety factor were demonstrated in differential-R and P-technique factor analysis. It should be noted, however, that a number of subtests in the 8-PF anxiety battery were taken from Cattell's objective-analytic (O-A) anxiety battery which measures trait anxiety. Furthermore, there is little empirical evidence of the construct validity of the 8-PF as a measure of state anxiety.

Zuckerman and his associates (Zuckerman, 1960; Zuckerman and Biase, 1962; Zuckerman and Lubin, 1965) developed the affect adjective check list (AACL) to measure both state and trait anxiety. State anxiety is assessed with the "today" version of the AACL, which requires the subject to check adjectives such as tense, nervous, and calm, that describe how he feels on the particular day the test is given. However, the instructions may be modified to require the subject to indicate how he feels at a particular moment or a specified time. Trait anxiety is assessed by asking the subject to check those adjectives that describe how he generally feels.

Zuckerman and Lubin (1968) have recently published an extensive bibliography of studies in which the AACL was used to evaluate changes in anxiety states as a function of a variety of stress-producing and stress-reducing conditions. Although evidence for the validity of the AACL as a measure of state anxiety is impressive, the general form of the AACL typically shows substantially lower correlations with other standard measures of trait anxiety, such as the TMAS and the IPAT anxiety scale, than these measures correlate with one another.

THE STATE-TRAIT ANXIETY INVENTORY

The state-trait anxiety inventory (STAI) was developed to provide reliable, relatively brief self-report measures of both state (A-state) and trait (A-trait) anxiety (Spielberger, Gorsuch, and Lushene, 1970). It was initially assumed that items with demonstrated concurrent validity in relationship to other measures of anxiety would be most useful in an inventory designed to measure both A-state and A-trait. Since most anxiety scales measure trait anxiety, a large number of items embodying content of proven relationship to the most widely used A-trait scales were rewritten so that each item could be administered with different instructions to measure either A-state or A-trait. It was discovered, however, that the connotations of key words in these items conveyed meanings that interfered with their use as measures of both A-state and A-trait. For example, "I feel upset" turned out to be a good A-state item, but a relatively poor measure of A-trait in that responses to this item were unstable over time.

The test construction strategy for the STAI was subsequently modified to develop separate scales for the measurement of A-state and A-trait. The STAI A-trait scale consists of 20 statements that ask people to describe how they generally feel. Subjects respond to each scale item by checking: "almost never," "sometimes," "often," "almost always." Thus, the subject is asked to report the frequency that he has experienced a symptom of trait anxiety.

Individual items were selected for the STAI A-trait scale on the basis of significant correlations with the two most widely accepted A-trait measures, the TMAS and the IPAT anxiety scale. Each A-trait item was also determined to be impervious to situational stress and relatively stable over time. Several representative items from the STAI A-trait scale are indicated below:

I feel that difficulties are piling up so that I cannot overcome them.

I worry too much over something that really doesn't matter.

I lack self-confidence.

I feel secure.

I take disappointments so keenly that I can't put them out of my mind.

I become tense and upset when I think about my present concerns.

State anxiety (A-state) may be conceptualized as a transitory emotional condition or feeling state that is characterized by subjective, consciously perceived feelings of tension and apprehension and heightened autonomic nervous system activity. A-States may vary in intensity and fluctuate over time. Three important characteristics determined the test construction strategy for the development of the STAI A-state scale:

(a) Validity of individual items was the major criterion for inclusion in the A-state scale. When the scale was given with instructions to report present feelings ("Indicate how you feel right now"), each item was expected to reflect the subject's level of anxiety (A-state) at that particular moment in time. Those items retained for the final scale showed higher means in *a priori* stressful situations than in nonstressful (neutral) or relaxed situations.

(b) A second characteristic that was sought in the development of the STAI A-state scale was a high degree of internal consistency. This was measured by item-remainder correlations and alpha coefficients.

(c) To maximize its usefulness in psychological research, a third characteristic that was desired in the STAI A-state scale was ease and brevity of administration. Since rapid fluctuations in A-state may occur in a changing environment, a long test would be less sensitive to such variations. Furthermore, in investigations of the effects of emotional states on performance, a long involved test is unsuitable for experimental tasks in which taking the test might interfere with performance on the task.

The essential qualities that should be measured by an A-state scale involve feelings of tension, nervousness, worry, and apprehension. In developing the STAI A-state scale, it was discovered empirically that such feelings were highly correlated with the absence of feelings of calmness, security, contentedness, and the like. Therefore, items designed to measure these feelings were included to produce a balanced A-state scale; half of the items relate to the presence of apprehension, worry, or tension, and the remaining items reflect the absence of such states.

The STAI A-state scale defines a continuum of increasing levels of A-state intensity. Low scores indicate states of calmness and serenity, intermediate scores indicate moderate levels of tension and apprehensiveness, and high scores reflect states of intense apprehension and fearfulness that approach panic. The published form of the STAI A-state scale consists of 20 statements that ask people to describe how they feel at a particular moment in time; subjects respond to each A-state item by rating themselves on the following four point scale: (1) not at all, (2) somewhat, (3) moderately so, (4) very much so. The following are representative items from the STAI A-state scale.

I feel calm
I am tense
I feel upset
I feel nervous

When administered for research purposes, the STAI A-state scale may be given with instructions that focus upon a particular time period. A subject may be instructed, for example, to respond according to how he felt while performing an experimental task that he has just completed. If the task is a long one, it may be useful to instruct the subject to respond according to how he felt early in the task or while working on the final portion of the task. In clinical research a patient may be asked to report the feelings he experienced in therapy interviews or how he felt while he visualized a specific stimulus situation in a behavior therapy session.

To measure changes in the intensity of transitory anxiety over time, the STAI A-state scale may be given on each occasion for which an A-state measure is needed. In research in which repeated measurements of A-state are desired during performance on an experimental task, very brief scales consisting of as few as five STAI A-state items may be used to provide valid measures of A-state (Spielberger, O'Neil, and Hansen, 1972). Responding to these brief scales does not seem to interfere with performance on an experimental task.

Multiple repeated measures of A-state may also be obtained either with the same or with different instructions as to the time period for which the subject's reports are desired. For example, a subject may be asked to report how he feels immediately before he begins to work on an experimental task. Then, after he completes the task, he may be asked to indicate how he felt while he was working on it.

Correlations with other measures of A-state, such as the Zuckerman today form, provide evidence of the concurrent validity of the STAI A-state scale (Spielberger et al., 1970). More important, however, is the demonstration that scores on the STAI A-state scale increase in response to various kinds of stress and decrease as a result of relaxation training, which provides evidence of the construct validity of the scale.

Self-report measures such as the STAI may be criticized on many grounds. It may be argued, for example, that the items are ambiguous and mean different things to different people, or that people do not know themselves well enough to give truthful answers, or that many people are unwilling to admit negative things about themselves. Administration of the STAI A-state scale for clinical and research purposes has shown, however, that adolescents and adults with at least dull–normal intelligence are capable of describing how they feel at a particular moment in time. Most people are willing to reveal how they feel while performing on an experimental task or during a therapy hour, provided they are asked specific questions about their feelings, and the feelings were recently experienced. Of course, the clinician or experimenter who uses self-report scales to measure anxiety, or any other emotional state, must endeavor to motivate his patients or subjects to provide accurate information about themselves.

THE ASSESSMENT OF ANXIETY WITH THE STAI
IN RESEARCH AND CLINICAL PRACTICE

Although the STAI was not generally available until 1969, the scale has been used to measure state and trait anxiety in more than 200 studies.[1] Current research with the STAI indicates that the A-trait scale is highly correlated with other measures of trait anxiety, and that the A-state scale provides a valid measure of changes in transitory anxiety in response to laboratory and real life stress. Several representative studies that illustrate how the STAI has been employed to measure anxiety will be briefly described.

Hodges (1967) exposed undergraduate college students to two different stress conditions: failure-threat and shock-threat. In the failure-threat condition the subjects were told they were not performing as well as other students. The subjects in the shock-threat condition were told that they had

---

[1] A bibliography of research studies in which the STAI was used to measure anxiety has been compiled by the author and will be sent to interested colleagues upon request. Please write to Professor C. D. Spielberger, Department of Psychology, University of South Florida, Tampa, Florida 33620, USA.

done well but would receive several "strong but safe" electric shocks (no shock was given). Both stress conditions produced marked increases in STAI A-state scores. The magnitude of the increase in A-state scores in the failure-threat condition was greater for subjects with high levels of A-trait (as measured by the TMAS) than for low A-trait subjects. While there was marked increase in A-state in the shock-threat condition, changes in A-state were unrelated to A-trait.

Lamb (1969) investigated the effects of stress on measures of state and trait anxiety for undergraduate college students in a public speaking class. Both heart rate and STAI A-state scores increased markedly from a pre-speech rest period to the period in which the subjects gave a 2-min speech that was videotaped (ego threat). Both A-state measures returned to pre-speech resting levels immediately after the speech and subsequently increased when the subjects were required to blow up a balloon until it burst (physical threat). The mean STAI A-state scores obtained by Lamb in his four experimental periods were: rest, 38.1; during speech, 43.8; after speech, 37.8; and balloon burst, 47.1. Similar changes were observed in heart rate as measured continuously by telemetric procedures.

Hodges and Felling (1970) administered the STAI A-state and A-trait scales and a "stressful situation questionnaire" (SSQ) to undergraduate college students. The SSQ described 40 stressful situations (e.g., "taking a test that you expect to fail," "going on a blind date," "riding an airplane in a storm"). The subjects were required to rate themselves on the degree of apprehensiveness or concern they believed they would feel in each situation. Correlations among the ratings for the different situations were computed and four factors were extracted from the resulting matrix: apprehension about classroom participation, concern about social and academic failure, apprehension in dating situations, and concern over pain and physical danger. The STAI A-trait scale correlated significantly with the first three factors, which involved psychological stress or threats to self-esteem (ego threats), but showed no relationship to the factor involving pain and physical danger.

The STAI was used by O'Neil, Spielberger, and Hansen (1969) to evaluate the relationship between A-state and performance in computer-assisted learning. STAI A-state scores and systolic blood pressure increased while students worked on difficult learning materials and decreased when they responded to easy materials. This pattern of change was observed on 5-item A-state scales embedded within the learning materials, and on the 20-item STAI A-state scale given before and after each task. Students with high A-state scores made more errors on the difficult materials and fewer errors on the easy materials than low A-state students. On the assumption that level of A-state is a linear function of drive level as this concept is defined in Hull's (1943) learning theory, the findings of O'Neil et al. are consistent with Spence-Taylor drive theory (Spence and Spence, 1966).

Taylor, Wheeler, and Altman (1968) used the STAI A-state scale to evaluate changes in anxiety level as a function of variations in experimentally induced stress for young sailors confined in isolation for periods of up to 8 days. Groups given instructions to expect simulated missions that would require them to remain in isolation for 20 days, and who "aborted" the mission before it was completed, reported more anxiety (higher levels of A-state) than unsuccessful groups given instructions to expect 4-day missions. Similarly, groups with long-mission expectations who successfully completed the assigned mission reported more anxiety (A-state) than successful groups with short-mission expectations.

Graham (1969) conducted a series of interviews with two groups of newly committed schizophrenic patients at a state psychiatric hospital. One group of patients (P group) was presented a series of pictures of two persons interacting; the second group (D group) was asked to respond to standardized verbal descriptions of these same pictures. The major goal of the study was to determine if there was any difference between these groups in anxiety level immediately following the interview. The mean STAI A-state scores of patients in the P group were significantly higher than those of patients in the D group. These results suggest that the STAI A-state scale may be useful for evaluating the amount of anxiety experienced by patients when they respond to tests such as the TAT and the Rorschach.

Edwards (1969) investigated emotional and attitudinal factors associated with pregnancy and obstetric complications in 53 primiparous, unmarried women. Following delivery, each subject was classified as either "normal" or "abnormal" on the basis of the medical records, including developmental abnormalities observed in the infants. An abbreviated form of the Holtzman inkblot technique (HIT) was administered to each subject and scored for anxiety (Holtzman, Thorpe, Swartz, and Herron, 1961). For the 7-week period immediately prior to delivery, the STAI A-state scale was given at the same time each week. Behavioral ratings of anxiety were also made during this period. Although the STAI A-state scale was uncorrelated with either the HIT or judge's ratings of anxiety, the serial assessment of A-state scores for the 7-week period suggested that the pattern of anxiety differed for the normal and abnormal groups. While no overall differences in level of anxiety were found for the two groups, the A-state scores of the normal group first decreased and remained at a relatively low level until a point near delivery, at which time they increased markedly. For the abnormal group, level of A-state began to increase approximately 4 weeks prior to delivery and then decreased markedly during the week immediately prior to delivery.

Parrino (1969) investigated the effects of different kinds of pretherapy information on therapeutic outcome for snake-phobic psychiatric patients. The patients who were chosen for the study were required, upon voluntarily consenting to participate, to attend nine sessions — three testing sessions in which they were confronted with the phobic object, three pretherapy information sessions, and three therapy sessions. The STAI scales were given to each patient immediately before he entered the fear-producing situation and the A-state scale was given immediately after the patient left the situation. Posttherapy STAI A-state scores were significantly lower (42.32) than pretherapy A-state scores (51.72). In contrast, mean A-trait scores were unchanged as a function of the therapeutic intervention.

SUMMARY

The evolution of anxiety as a scientific concept was shaped by the observations and theoretical conceptions of Darwin and Freud. Clarification of the meaning of anxiety was not possible until intensive effort was devoted to its measurement. The rationale and test construction procedures that guided the development of a number of anxiety scales were briefly considered in this chapter, and the construction of the state-trait anxiety inventory was reviewed in some detail.

The findings of studies that have employed the STAI to measure anxiety suggest that it is meaningful to distinguish between anxiety as a transitory state and as a relatively stable personality trait. Anxiety states are characterized by subjective, consciously perceived feelings of apprehension and tension and activation or arousal of the autonomic nervous system. Trait anxiety refers to anxiety proneness, that is, to individual differences in the disposition to perceive a wide range of circumstances as threatening and to respond to such situations with A-state reactions that are disproportionate in intensity to the magnitude of the objective danger.

It has been demonstrated that the STAI is a useful instrument for the assessment of anxiety in both laboratory and real-life situations. Research with the STAI appears to confirm that situations or circumstances in which personal adequacy is threatened, evoke higher levels of A-state in high A-trait individuals than in persons who were low in A-trait.

REFERENCES

Cattell, R. B., and Scheier, I. H. (1958): The nature of anxiety: a review of thirteen multivariate analyses comprising 814 variables, Psychol. Rep. 4, 351–388.

Cattell, R. B., and Scheier, I. H. (1961): *The Meaning and Measurement of Neuroticism and Anxiety*, Ronald Press, New York.

Cattell, R. B., and Scheier, I. H. (1963): *Handbook for the IPAT Anxiety Scale*, 2nd ed., Institute for Personality and Ability Testing, Champaign, Ill.

Darwin, C. (1965): *The Expression of Emotions in Man and Animals*, University of Chicago Press, Chicago, Ill.

Edwards, K. R., Jr. (1969): Psychological changes associated with pregnancy and obstetric complications, unpublished doctoral dissertation, University of Miami, Florida.

Freud, S. (1924): *Collected papers*, Vol. 1, Hogarth Press, London.

Freud, S. (1933): *New Introductory Lectures in Psychoanalysis*, Norton, New York.

Freud, S. (1936): *The Problem of Anxiety*, Norton, New York.

Graham, S. B. (1969): The effects of two types of initial interviews upon the state anxiety of newly admitted schizophrenic patients, unpublished manuscript, University of Pennsylvania.

Hodges, W. F. (1967): The effects of success, failure and threat of shock on physiological and phenomenological indices of state anxiety, unpublished dissertation, Vanderbilt University.

Hodges, W. F., and Felling, J. P. (1970): Types of stressful situations and their relation to trait anxiety and sex, J. Consulting Clin. Psychol. *34*, 333–337.

Holtzman, W. H., Thorpe, J. S., Swartz, J. D., and Herron, E. W. (1961): *Inkblot Perception and Personality: Holtzman Inkblot Technique*, University of Texas Press, Austin, Texas.

Hull, C. L. (1943): *Principles of Behavior*, Appleton-Century, New York.

Kritzeck, J. (1955): Philosophers of anxiety, *Commonweal 63*, 572–574.

Lamb, D. H. (1969): The effects of public speaking on self-report, physiological and behavioral measures of anxiety, unpublished doctoral dissertation, Florida State University.

May, R. (1950): *The Meaning of Anxiety*, Ronald Press, New York.

O'Neil, H. F., Spielberger, C. D., and Hansen. D. N. (1969): The effects of state-anxiety and task difficulty on computer-assisted learning, J. Educ. Psychol. *60*, 343–350.

Parrino, J. J. (1969): The effects of pretherapy information on learning in psychotherapy, unpublished doctoral dissertation, Louisiana State University.

Scheier, I. H., and Cattell, R. B. (1960): *Handbook and Test Kit for the IPAT 8 Parallel Form Anxiety Battery,* Institute for Personality and Ability Testing, Champaign, Ill.

Spence, J. T., and Spence, K. W. (1966): The motivational components of manifest anxiety: Drive and drive stimuli. In: *Anxiety and Behavior* (ed. C. D. Spielberger), pp. 291–326, Academic Press, New York.

Spielberger, C. D. (1966*a*): Theory and research on anxiety. In: *Anxiety and Behavior* (ed. C. D. Spielberger), pp. 3–20. Academic Press, New York.

Spielberger, C. D. (ed.) (1966*b*): *Anxiety and Behavior*, Academic Press, New York.

Spielberger, C. D. (1972): *Anxiety: Current Trends in Theory and Research*, Academic Press, New York.

Spielberger, C. D., Gorsuch, R. L., and Lushene, R. E. (1970): *Manual for the State-Trait Anxiety Inventory (Self-Evaluation Questionnaire)*, Consulting Psychologists Press, Palo Alto, Cal.

Spielberger, C. D., O'Neil, H. F., and Hansen, D. N. (1972): Anxiety, drive theory, and computer assisted learning. In: *Progress in Experimental Personality Research* (ed. B. A. Maher), Vol. 6, pp. 109–148. Academic Press, New York.

Taylor, D. A., Wheeler, L., and Altman, I. (1968): Stress reactions in socially isolated groups, J. Personal. Social Psychol. *9*, 369–376.

Taylor, J. A. (1953): A personality scale of manifest anxiety. *J. Abnorm. Social Psychol. 48*, 285–290.

Time (March 31, 1961): p. 44.

Zuckerman, M. (1960): The development of an Affect Adjective Check List for the measurement of anxiety, J. Consult. Psychol. *24*, 457–462.

Zuckerman, M., and Biase, D. V. (1962): Replication and further data on the validity of the Affect Adjective Check List measure of anxiety, J. Consult. Psychol. *26*, 291.

Zuckerman, M., and Lubin, B. (1965): *Manual for the Multiple Affect Adjective Check List,* Educational and Industrial Testing Service, San Diego, Cal.

Zuckerman, M., and Lubin, B. (1968): *Bibliography for the Multiple Affect Adjective Check List.* Educational and Industrial Testing Service, San Diego, Cal.

Emotions—Their Parameters and Measurement,
edited by L. Levi.
Raven Press, New York © 1975

The Measurement of Emotion and Arousal in the Clinical Physiological Laboratory and in Medical Practice

J. J. Groen

Psychiatrische Kliniek, Rijksuniversiteit Leiden "Jelgersma-Kliniek," Oegstgeest, The Netherlands

INTRODUCTION

It is still widely held in medical circles that emotions, because we experience them subjectively as irrational, cannot be rationally studied. It is also generally believed that emotions cannot be measured and therefore many doctors, even those who consider themselves "scientific thinkers," regard emotions as phenomena which, because they belong to the domain of the "mind" or "spirit," should be eliminated from scientific research. These negative *a priori* concepts are one of the main reasons why the study of emotions has lagged behind so much in medical research, to the detriment of patients who apply to doctors for understanding and treatment of emotional disturbances. Yet it is already 300 years since Spinoza pointed a way toward the objective study of the emotions when he wrote in the introduction to the third part of *Ethics* that he would "consider human actions and desires in exactly the same manner, as though I were concerned with lines, planes and solids. Nature's laws and ordinances, whereby all things come to pass, . . . are everywhere and always the same: so that there should be one and the same method of understanding the nature of all things whatsoever. . . . Thus the passions of hatred, anger, envy, and so on . . . follow from this same necessity and efficacy of nature: they answer to certain definite causes, through which they are understood. . . . I shall therefore treat of the nature and strength of the emotions according to the same method as I employed heretofore."

The method that he referred to was the logical deduction based on unprejudiced empirical observations. In later centuries emotions became the object of interest of early psychologists such as James, of biologists such as Darwin, of psychiatrists such as Freud, of physiologists such as Cannon, of neurobiochemists such as von Euler, and lately of neurophysiologists and psychologists of different "schools." With this shift of interest from the philosophical to the biological and physiological aspects has also come about a different methodological approach, which is now scientific throughout.

It is impossible to survey the research that has been done, especially during the last decades, on emotions and that has now reached a level that satisfies rigid scientific criteria. It will be my purpose in this chapter to describe a few of the recent achievements and try to illustrate their importance for medical practice.

DEFINITIONS AND BASIC CONCEPTS

Over the years, several definitions have been proposed for emotions. A purely psychological definition, starting out from everyday language, understands by emotions certain feeling states which every adult human can recognize in himself by introspection and, by extrapolation, presumes to be present in other human beings and in higher animals. Emotions are characterized by a more or less clearly associated sensation of pleasantness or unpleasantness. A further characteristic is that the individual perceives them "inwardly" and, having learned to speak and communicate about them in language with his fellow humans, learns to recognize them and designate them by certain words such as fear, anxiety, rage, guilt, shame, depression, happiness, and love. These emotions are analogous to the feeling states experienced in immediate connection with the stimulation of certain of the sense organs, like the pleasant feelings associated with being gently touched or the pain of being hurt, like orgasm on genital stimulation, vertigo on being turned around, disgust on smelling certain odors, or the feelings of hunger or thirst as a result of deprivation of food or fluid.

Some emotions, such as hunger, thirst, satiety, nausea, or vertigo, are experienced as more of a bodily nature, although it may be difficult to localize them. Other emotions, such as happiness, love, hate, or depression, are experienced by most humans as not so directly of a bodily nature. This subjective experience of some emotions as "spiritual" and others as more bodily feelings has contributed to the concept of dualism, namely that man consists of two separate areas, body and mind. Modern research has not supported the distinction between somatic and spiritual emotions and the whole dualistic concept is now regarded by most researchers as operationally not useful anyway.

Emotions can occur in immediate association with certain life events, but they may also be evoked by the memory of previous experiences or the anticipation of possible future (not necessarily real) events.

The recognition of his emotions by the individual and their translation into words is a typical human function. As no other animal can learn to speak and think in a word language, we assume from their behavior that animals experience emotions although they cannot be "conscious" of them as we are, that is to say they cannot express them to themselves in verbal thoughts or to their conspecifics by verbal communication. Instead their mutual communication takes place only by motoric (mimic) and vocalization behavior.

Another characteristic of the emotions is that, apart from being experienced with a connotation of pleasant or unpleasant, they are more or less specific: fear or rage, happiness or depression, love or hate, and hunger or satiety are characterized by their specific subjective experience by the individual. In addition, these specific subjective emotional feeling states manifest themselves in more or less specific behavior patterns. These behavior patterns are partly motoric (fight, flight, submission, vigilance, exploration, play), mimic (gesticulations), vocal (in the human, also verbal), and visceral (changes in the circulation, digestion, and external and internal secretion).

The more or less specific behavior patterns that accompany the experience of the emotions give the investigator an opportunity to study emotions not only by introspection but also by the objective observation of the behavior of human beings and animals during different emotional states. In other words, if a certain type of observable behavior is highly correlated with the subjective experience of certain emotions, we can try to measure this behavior under different circumstances and draw conclusions (formulate hypotheses) about the underlying emotions. This principle is one of the basic methodological concepts underlying the modern objectivistic approach to the study of emotion.

Another methodological stride ahead has been the study of emotions in animals and man after stimulation or lesions of circumscript areas of the central nervous system, the registration of electrical phenomena in the brain during emotional states, the study of chemical phenomena in the brain, and the effect of drugs and hormones on emotions and behavior. It is from the correlation of such studies of the functions of the brain with the behavior of the organism in its environment during the different emotions that we are beginning to acquire a scientific "psychobiological" understanding of the nature and function of the emotions.

From a large body of work of this kind has emerged the concept that all emotions have a substrate in the central nervous system and its connections with the sense organs and certain peripheral effector systems. *Emotions are now regarded as activations of special feedback systems which have their cognition (scanning) center in the central nervous system.* This concept is more or less a synthesis of the two main theories which existed about the nature of the emotions until relatively recently. One theory, advocated mainly by James (1890) and often called the James-Lange theory, held that emotions were nothing but the perception by the individual of certain bodily changes, for instance, in his pulse rate, sweat secretion, and stomach and bowel activity. Against this, Cannon (1953) maintained that all emotions had their physiological substrate specifically in the central nervous system. The new concept that the central nervous system is fundamentally a co-ordinating center linked between the sense organs and peripheral effector systems and serving incoming information, stored experiences, outgoing impulses and behavior has also contributed to the idea that emotions are activations of certain linked systems within the total individual; the experience of an emotion sets in motion and consists of both central and peripheral activations and behavior which may enforce or inhibit each other.

A large part of the modern studies is therefore concerned with the elucidation of exactly which structures function in relation with certain emotions and which are the physiological and chemical changes that take place in these systems. We seek, in other words, to find the morphological localization and physiological and chemical substrates of the different emotions. It is only during the last few years that we have begun to understand, e.g., where and how the typical distinction of the emotions as pleasant or unpleasant takes place. The fundamental work of Olds (1962), MacLean (1955), and others has furnished important evidence that this cognition of pleasant or unpleasant, of gratification or frustration, both in relation to the environmental situation and to internal sensations, is one of the functions of the septal area of the limbic system. Activation of this area is experienced as gratifying and thereby strongly reinforces the learning of certain "rewarding" patterns of behavior; other areas of the hippocampus, when activated, produce feelings of frustration and thereby decondition or inhibit nonrewarding ("punished") behavior. It is obvious how important this insight is in one of the fundamental "steering systems" of the central nervous system which plays a role in all forms of *learning,* especially of how to behave in contacts with other members of ones own species or group.

Another result of recent investigation is the insight that certain emotions, especially those of rage and anxiety, that is to say, the feeling states associated with the behavior of fight or flight, are accompanied or induced by activation of the ascending reticular arousal system (ARAS). The function of this system seems to be the regulation of the state of alertness of the cortex; for successful fight or flight a high degree of alertness is biologically necessary and socially useful. The amygdalae also play a role in flight or fight behavior, but there is still controversy about the exact mechanism. Activation of the ascending reticular arousal system appears to activate in its turn the autonomic nervous system and especially the sympathetic part of it.

Another system recently described by Margules and Stein (1969) which seems to be activated during other emotions is situated in the central gray matter of the third ventricle in the median line in the diencephalic region, where the ventromedial nuclei of the hypothalamus are situated. Activation of this system is associated in experimental animals with so-called punishment avoidance behavior, which in the human seems to be analogous to certain forms of behavior by which the individual manipulates his environment by other activities than flight or fight. It is too often thought that the organism has at its disposal in response to stress only two forms of motoric behavior, namely fight or flight. Actually, although these behavior forms are of great biological and social importance, the organism reacts to many signals from the environment by neither fight nor flight but by other adaptative responses that it has learned and utilizes to obtain a desired object, such as food, or to protect itself from unpleasant situations causing pain or defeat.

What the neurophysiologists call punishment avoidance in their experimentally conditioned animals appears to resemble a form of behavior that can be designated *conflict-avoidance* in an ethological system of reference. It includes, e.g., submissive behavior, which is another biologically useful response to aggression from a conspecific, or the finding and arrangement of a secure shelter or nest outside the territory of a competitor or predator. Conflict-avoiding behavior is just as efficient and necessary a form of coping behavior, as fight or flight. Actually both in the social contacts between animals in free-living groups and between people in human society, conflict avoiding forms of behavior occur much more frequently than fight-flight interactions. Moreover, in both animal and human social groups, one form of behavior may substitute for the other. This is made possible by extensive interconnections between the different nervous systems. This intensive interconnection (also with the different parts of the neocortex) also explains why it is possible to experience different combinations of emotions and behavior at the same time.

BIOCHEMICAL REGULATIONS OF EMOTIONS AND BEHAVIOR

Some synapses in the central nervous system, like those in the ascending reticular arousal system, are (nor)adrenergic, and those in the periventricular ventromedial hypothalamic system are cholinergic. Others use serotonin or dopamine as transmitters. It is interesting to speculate that the organism of the higher animals thus has at its disposal different neurophysiological *and neurobiochemical* feedback mechanisms, which serve to cope by different ways of behavior with the environment and especially with conspecifics. Some of the best studied of these are:

(a) Fight or flight (with arousal), which is largely norepinephrine and epinephrine mediated, both in the central arousal and visceral sympathetic nervous systems and via the adrenal medulla, also via the bloodstream;

(b) Conflict avoiding (submissive) behavior, in which acetylcholine mediated activations in the central and visceral parasympathetic nervous system are the predominant mechanisms.

(c) Depressive (defeat) behavior, which is supposed to be a result of (or associated with) a diminished secretion of one or more of the catecholamine or indolamine transmitters.

Present knowledge does not allow us more than this speculation on the existence of other neurochemical systems that correspond to different "patterns of life" and we should be aware of the probably highly simplified nature of this speculation. The scheme would, however, make understandable to us, as another example of the "wisdom of the body," why the circulatory system is predominantly regulated by adrenergic sympathetic impulses, because the motoric efforts of fight or flight require a hyperkinetic response of the heart and vessels. The processes of conflict avoidance and digestion, on the other hand, require much less motor muscular activity but rather muscular rest and peaceful relations with the environment. Optimal digestion requires a copious secretion of the digestive juices and activity of the smooth musculature of the stomach and bowel, which are mainly regulated by the parasympathetic.

The exact role of serotonin-mediated activations has not yet been defined satisfactorily. Dopamine, the mediator of extrapyramidal movements, may play a role in emotional behavior; possibly it mediates mimic and gesticulations.

A quite different system is the hypothalamus-anterior pituitary-adrenal cortex feedback mechanism, which is regulated by releasing factors, ACTH, cortisol, and cortisone. Its role in a general form of adaptation to stress was first described by Selye. It has received widespread attention and, although still not elucidated in every respect, is recognized as an essential feedback system for the survival of the organism, especially under circumstances that require unusually intense defense and adaptation mechanisms.

The different phases of sexual behavior and reproduction are under the influence of both adrenergic and cholinergic activations and internal secretions. The genital system is therefore intensely doubly innervated and under the influence of a hormonal feedback system in which the hypothalamic-releasing factors, FSH, LH, prolactin, and the female and male sex hormones, fulfill an interrelated function. Lately the influence of sex hormones on the limbic system and thereby on behavior has also been established.

ANXIETY

Of all emotions, anxiety has been the most extensively studied, and it can be used, therefore, as a model to illustrate both the problems and the methodology of the modern psychobiological approach to emotion in general. Purely psychologically anxiety can be defined as a peculiar, unpleasant feeling, characterized by the anticipation of a threatening or dangerous event that might happen in the future. When this future event is clear to both the subject and the investigator, the emotion is usually called fear; when the individual and the investigator are not quite conscious of the cause, the terms apprehension, anxiety *per se,* or "free-floating anxiety" are used.

The tendency of predisposition, which is present in some individuals more than in others, to react with anxiety to the perception of certain future events is called the *anxiety trait;* this is considered to be one of the characteristics of the individual personality. The emotion itself is designated as the *anxiety state* (Spielberger, 1966).

Thus a complete psychological definition of anxiety can be given: as a characteristic, unpleasant emotion, induced by the anticipation of a danger or frustration which threatens the security, homeostasis, or life of the individual or the biosocial group to which he belongs.

An important point should be made here. As no individual can perceive his environment "objectively" but perceives it from information reaching the central nervous system through the sense organs, and as the central nervous system scans this information according to its hereditary and acquired programmation, the effect of any environmental event on the individual is determined just as much by the objective event itself as by the significance attached to it by the individual. The organism, as von Uexküll has expressed it, does not live in and behave to an objective outer world but in a subjective "Umwelt." Thus an event is not necessarily anxiety producing in itself but only in so far as the individual recognizes it as such. This anxiety trait depends largely on previous experience, conditioning, and learning of the individual. This may mean, for instance, that an event to which one individual reacts by anxiety may induce in another aggressivity, in others depression, and in others no more than curiosity; consequently it depends mainly on previous programming whether an individual will react by fight, flight, submission, or some other form of coping behavior.

Anxiety is usually accompanied by certain somatic changes that are present more frequently among individuals who describe their feeling state as anxious than in others who describe themselves as being quiet or relaxed. In the same individual, moreover, these changes are more pronounced during periods when anxiety is present than when it is absent. These bodily correlates of anxiety are increased motoric activity ("restlessness"), e.g., pacing up and down, flight or fight, vivid gesticulations, tremors, and increased starting reactions to external stimuli. This anxious motoric behavior requires ethological methods of measurement, such as have been used up until now mostly in animals. The introduction of audiovisual techniques enables us to register behavior in a reproducible form and this may prove a great advance for the future ethological study and measurement of human behavior.

In animals anxiety is vocalized, in men verbalized. This opens the possibility of measurement, e.g., by speech analysis. Many psychiatrists use scales or questionnaires in which patients record their verbal interpretations of their feelings. These methods have a limited usefulness for the measurement of anxiety or depression, but they measure more what people think and verbalize under the circumstances of the tests, than what they actually experience.

During anxiety, sleep is absent or disturbed. This can be measured by registering eye movements and EEG during sleep, the hours of sleep versus waking, or the movements of the subject on a special bed to which a registration apparatus is attached.

Most investigators have used the autonomic changes for measurement of anxiety. Extensive work has been done on the measurement of the increased pulse rate, increased cardiac output, increased systolic and pulse pressure (sometimes also of diastolic pressure), increased forearm flow (due to increased perfusion of the muscles), diminished splanchnic and renal blood-flow, pounding apex beat, as parameters of the hyperkinetic circulatory state during anxiety.

Another variable is increased sweat secretion, especially on the tips of the fingers, the palms of the hands, and the axillae. This is measured mostly indirectly via the electrical resistance of the skin. The galvanic skin response is caused by a short spurt of sweat pushed out of the sweat glands, followed by a retraction of the sweat into the pores. The magnitude of the response is supposed to correlate with the emotion induced by a tactile, auditory, or optic stimulus. The electrical resistance of the skin can also be registered continually for the measurement of the continuous emotional state, e.g., during an interview.

Other concomitants of anxiety include widening of the palpebral fissure and the pupils, increased respiration, both in depth and in frequency, increased oxygen consumption (especially of the heart), increased diuresis, diminished secretion of saliva and (at least according to most authors) gastric juice, increased frequency of defecation or diarrhea, sometimes an increase in blood glucose and (more constantly) of free fatty acids.

Electroencephalography during anxiety and several other emotional states reveals a diminution of alpha- and an increase in beta-rhythm, sometimes also in slow theta-rhythm.

Most of these changes, as already stated, are caused by increased sympathetic stimulation and liberation of norepinephrine at the sympathetic nerve endings, for instance, in the heart muscle and vessels, in situations of severe anxiety, and also by an increased secretion of epinephrine from the adrenal medulla. By ingenious methods this increased liberation of catecholamines can be measured via an increased excretion of these substances and their metabolites in the urine and recently also by an increased level in the blood.

These autonomic changes have enabled scientists to study the intensity of anxiety quantitatively by the determination of the magnitude of these variables by exact physiological or biochemical methods. A large number of such studies have been published and the techniques are becoming part of the standard examination of patients with emotional disorders. Some of these variables have been shown to correlate so closely with the subjective experience of anxiety that they can indeed be accepted as reliable objective parameters of the anxiety state. For the clinician these laboratory determinations are acquiring more and more importance because they provide, in addition to the verbal information and clinical observation of motor behavior and simple counting of the pulse, more reliable quantitative data.

These data can be used not only to evaluate the presence and degree of anxiety in patients, but they can also serve as objective indicators of the effect of treatment.

In this connection two fundamental questions have kept investigators busy for many years:

(1) Are these physiological parameters the *result* of certain brain processes which form the physiological substrates of the subjective feeling of anxiety? Or are they part of a psychophysiological "syndrome" of anxiety which is conceived as an activation of a feedback system comprising both the central nervous system and the peripheral organs? The difference in concept boils down to the simple question of whether one can feel anxiety without manifesting tachycardia, palmar sweating, increased motoric behavior etc. There is no certain answer to this question. Under most conditions anxiety is indeed experienced and acted out by activation of a feedback mechanism which comprises the central and sympathetic autonomic systems and certain sense and skeletomuscular effector organs. But in other situations this need not be so, e.g., under acquired self-control (inhibition) of the motoric activities or during a very acute fright ("startle reaction") when there may occur, by reciprocal inhibition of two opposite behavior patterns, immobilization, slowing of respiration, bradycardia and even fainting, with persistence of subjective anxiety. Drugs may also inhibit some of the peripheral phenomena but incompletely relieve the feeling of anxiety. Apparently the positive feedback in the system can be interfered with and in those situations the "anxiety syndrome" becomes incomplete or complicated.

(2) Are the autonomic phenomena *specific* for anxiety *per se,* or do they occur in other emotional states? There are indeed a few other emotions which are accompanied by the same autonomic syndrome, e.g., rage (aggressivity), sexual excitement, and, to a minor degree, the emotional state associated with the solving of a mathematical task in an experimental situation or the "embarrassment" associated with having to answer a question pertaining to one's personal life situation (although it has been argued by some that these two examples are not valid because such situations can be assumed to be anxiety inducing). Above all, however, intense bodily exercise, even if not associated with anxiety or aggressivity, produces the same hyperkinetic effects on the circulation. In contrast, other emotional states, such as nausea, unhappiness, depression, and humiliation, manifest themselves in other motoric and autonomic behavior. In other words, there is some specificity in the autonomic behavior during certain emotional states but the specificity is not exclusively limited to anxiety. In particular it cannot be held that the hyperkinetic cardiovascular pattern that occurs in association with anxiety is characteristic for the anxiety state *only*. Most authors now agree that the hyperkinetic circulatory syndrome is more a

manifestation of increased activation of the arousal system than of anxiety *per se*. Increased arousal is part of, or more appropriately, very closely associated with anxiety. When an individual on certain environmental signals experiences anxiety, this sets in motion complicated feedback mechanisms which involve arousal, i.e., increased activation of certain areas of the cortex, the limbic and ascending reticular system; these in turn activate the sympathetic system and its peripheral effector organs and by positive feedback the experience of anxiety.

This means that in measuring autonomic changes during anxiety we are actually measuring manifestations of arousal. The work of Levi (1971, 1972) has substantiated this. He found an increase in urinary excretion of catecholamines not only when normal subjects watched movies that aroused feelings of aggressivity or sexual excitement but also when a pleasant movie was shown which induced attentive watching (like executing a mathematical calculation). Only while watching "bland" natural scenery films did the excretion drop to low levels.

Because the association between arousal and anxiety is very close, the autonomic changes can still be used as parameters of the degree of anxiety in most situations. But we must remain aware that the correlation is only indirect and that other emotions, which also activate the central reticular arousal system, may produce the same or similar changes. This holds especially for the emotions of aggressivity and sexual excitement and the behavior that *Pavlov* called "orientation" and that includes curiosity, approach, and exploration, where increased arousal is obviously equally useful biologically.

Related to the problem of the specificity of the autonomic response is the question of whether the same emotion, e.g., anxiety, manifests itself in some individuals predominantly by a cardiovascular hyperkinetic syndrome, in others by increased bowel activity, and in others again by both. The anxiety induced by examinations has confronted most doctors during their student days. Some had palpitations and sweating, others diarrhea, others had both. The issue is complicated by the fact that the same external or experimental situation may be differently interpreted and experienced by different individuals, depending on heredity, previous learning experiences, and repertoire of coping, so that it may result in different *degrees* of the same emotion and in different *combinations* of several emotions.

Most investigators have concluded that there exists *both* a specificity in the autonomic manifestations of the different types of emotions and in the personal response type of an individual. However, Lacey and co-workers have concluded from their experiments that the relative degree of change shown in each of a set of autonomic-somatic variables, that is, the pattern of autonomic reactions, is characteristic and constant for any given individual, regardless of the stimulus; this they termed the "relative response specificity." However, it can be held against this one-sided conclusion that the range of stimuli that they used in their work was not wide enough to produce different emotions in the same subject.

In addition to the factors already mentioned, we have to consider that many spontaneous and experimental situations induce in the subjects simultaneously with the emotion a certain degree of *inhibition* (in humans: self-control), which tends to prevent motoric activity in the form of fight, flight, or vocalization. This inhibition of motor activity may either reinforce or inhibit, via a feedback mechanism to the CNS, the autonomic reactions. This effect of inhibition on autonomic behavior has been compared to the phenomenon of *displacement* in animals when subject to different "drives" at the same time. Under such circumstances, either a gross change in behavior or an entirely new pattern of behavior may ensue.

It has been shown, e.g., that individuals who suffer from certain psychosomatic disorders (hypertension, peptic ulcer, asthma, diabetes), when asked not to speak and not to move in an unfamiliar laboratory setting show a rise in electrical skin resistance which drops to the initial level when they are instructed to make a fist or answer a simple question. This indicates that during the induced immobilization and silence the normal continuous outpouring of sweat stopped temporarily and that the accumulated sweat poured out all at once as soon as the inhibition was released (Van der Valk and Groen, 1950). Lacey and Lacey (1970) have described similar measurable effects of inhibition on sweat secretion, respiration, and heart rate in relation to the contingent negative variation response in the EEG.

HYPERVENTILATION: THE ROLE OF LACTATE

An interesting factor which may influence the measurement of certain parameters of emotion is hyperventilation. When normal individuals (and even more so patients suffering from so-called anxiety neurosis) breathe deeply and rapidly for a few minutes, the pulse rate rises and the pulse pressure increases; there is an increase in palmar sweat and in a few other physiological variables which have been described as signs of circulatory hyperkinesis through increased arousal. Some subjects (and especially those who suffer from anxiety neurosis) when asked to hyperventilate also experience the subjective emotion of anxiety without knowing what they are afraid of. Apparently hyperventilation (via acapnia, respiratory alkalosis of the tissue fluids, diminished ionization of serum calcium and possibly other effects) activates the anxiety-arousal feedback system in such a way that it can produce both the central (subjective) and the peripheral (objective) phenomena of the anxiety-arousal syndrome. There appears to be a large variability in the sensitivity with which different subjects react in this way to hyperventilation and the sensitivity seems to be increased by having experienced (learned) this type of anxiety in previous situations. The biochemical or neurophysiological basis of this individual variability is not known; apparently it can be influenced by conditioning or deconditioning. It is interesting that hyperventilation also causes slow wave activity in the EEG in some individuals more than in others.

A similar activation of the anxiety-arousal mechanism can be produced in some people by injection of epinephrine (Schachter, 1971) and, as described by Pitts (1969), by intravenous infusion of sodium lactate (which produces metabolic alkalosis). In contrast, the hyperventilation associated with severe exercise, which is generally accompanied by a carbon dioxide and lactic acid induced acidosis, produces the peripheral signs of arousal but not necessarily the subjective emotion of anxiety. It is difficult to say whether this is due to a specific difference in physiological effect between alcalosis or acidosis on the ARAS or to the fact that anybody who exercises and notices his increased respiration and hyperkinetic circulation knows what this is due to, whereas during induced hyperventilation this is unclear to the subject, and thereby anxiety arousing.

Biologically this positive feedback effect of hyperventilation on the arousal system (like that of epinephrine) is useful. Many subjects (human and animal) hyperventilate when faced with a threatening situation; the activation of the arousal system prepares them for more intense fight and flight. In other words, the feeling of anxiety itself is an "internal reinforcer" of arousal and, provided it is not too intense, plays a biologically useful role in the defense of the organism, promoting homeostasis and integrity within its environment. The observations of several workers that a low level of anxiety (by its activation of arousal) promotes learning also fit into this concept of the useful role of anxiety in a neurophysiological feedback system. However, in interhuman situations, when fight or flight do not ensue, the arousal is mostly useless. Its cause is unclear to the individual and this may be experienced as disturbing and the anxiety is interpreted as a panic, as in what is known clinically as the hyperventilation "syndrome."

EMOTIONS IN PSYCHOSOMATIC MEDICINE

Many doctors believe, on the basis of their clinical impressions, that emotional disturbances play an important role in the causation of functional disorders such as the cardiac arrhythmias and tachycardias, Raynaud's disease, migraine and tension headaches, the hyperventilation syndrome, functional diarrhea, habitual constipation, dysmenorrhea, ejaculatio praecox, vaginismus, and impotence. A similar "psychogenic" etiology has been hypothesized for the so-called psychosomatic disorders: peptic ulcer, ulcerative colitis, essential hypertension, bronchial asthma, anorexia nervosa, and obesity (voracity). It is claimed that these patients suffer from emotional problems due to conflicting, for them frustrating communications in their family and work situations. As they do not speak or act out their emotions in verbal or motoric behavior, the autonomic discharges are reinforced or disturbed, which ultimately gives rise to clinical disease. As these hypotheses are mostly based on the verbal communications of patients and their relatives with doctors, there is a great need for objective methods to test them and this is why the measurement and registration of suitable parameters of emotions have found widespread application in psychosomatic medicine.

One of the difficulties confronting the investigator in this field is the fact that the majority of these patients deny that they experience abnormally strong, disturbed, or inhibited emotions. On the contrary they insist, even with more emphasis than normal controls, that they are emotionally well-balanced and that their life situations are either normal or, even when difficult, do not affect them emotionally. The clinical impression of doctors that, in spite of this verbal denial, their diseases might be due to insufficient cognition and consciousness, and thereby to insufficient verbalization or acting out of their emotions, accordingly cannot be tested by routine interview, "scales," or questionnaires, which are all verbal techniques.

The possibility of testing the psychosomatic etiology hypothesis by objective physiological registrations has proved a great advance in psychosomatic research. In essence the method consists in the registration and measurement of suitable physiological parameters, associated with the disease during an acute observation or experiment. The method was introduced about 30 years ago by Wolff and Wolf (1950) in their classic study of a man, named Tom, with a gastric fistula. Wolff and Wolf used this anatomical opportunity to study the thickness of the folds and the color (vascularity) of the mucous membrane of the stomach, the secretion of gastric juice and mucus not only during fasting and digestion but also during life situations when Tom was relaxed or when he was "tense," "excited," "apprehensive," or "depressed." Later, with Mittelmann, they performed similar observations on normal individuals and patients with peptic ulcer, who were involved in different conversations while the gastric juice was sampled via an indwelling tube. In the course of these conversations the investigator tried to make the subject re-experience his real life events by bringing up either a neutral topic or the conflict situations about which the patient had spoken on previous occasions. The same approach was applied by other workers to patients with ulcerative colitis who, after an operative anus preternaturalis, presented their colonic mucosa for direct observation during different experimentally induced emotional situations. The nasal mucous membrane and the skin offer similar opportunities.

Others have registered and measured physiological variables such as heart rate, blood pressure, and cardiac output during emotional states in patients with essential hypertension and in controls during arterial catheterization. Others again have subjected asthmatic patients to emotional situations in the laboratory and have measured their vital capacity or expiratory peak flow rates in order to test the theory that asthmatic breathing could be the result of emotional factors. Using a chemical technique, several workers have determined in healthy individuals and in patients under different experimental or spontaneous life situations, the excretion of catecholamines, corticoid hormones or their metabolites in the urine or their blood levels. The modern microtechniques for the determination of practically all hormones in the blood make it possible to carry out similar studies to find out whether during certain emotional states certain hormones are secreted into the bloodstream in increased amounts and whether this happens more in patients with certain endocrine disorders than in normal individuals. Such studies have also been started in patients with diabetes mellitus, where blood glucose, keto-acids, free fatty acids, and other lipids can be followed either during a more or less quiet, relaxed state or during the discussion of the patient's interhuman conflicts. It is through these registrations and measurements that psychosomatic medicine has developed from a speculative field in which no other instrument of investigation was available than the subjective interpretation of the patient's verbal behavior, to an area of exact scientific clinical investigation. It can safely be predicted that this methodological development will expand in the coming years, especially when, in addition, refined techniques for the registration of electrical and chemical processes in circumscript areas of the brain will become available for studies in the human.

In view of what has been said in previous sections of this review, a general remark must be made here about the nature of the emotions which play a role in the life situations of patients with psychosomatic disorders. Only in relatively few of these conditions has it been possible to designate the pertinent emotional states in the simple terms of, e.g., anxiety, rage, or depression. In most cases there appeared to exist combinations of emotions, to which, also because they were partly inhibited, it was difficult, both for the patient and the investigator, to give a simple name. In hypertensive patients, for instance, there was a combination of anxiety and aggression, which inhibited each other from being acted out.

Peptic ulcer and colitis patients appeared to suffer from frustration because their conflict-avoiding behavior patterns had failed to induce from their key figures the expected reward behavior but still inhibited them from reacting aggressively. Asthmatic patients appeared to react by attacks of wheezing during an emotional state which was best characterized by a combination of aggressivity, helplessness, and grief toward a key figure. These emotions, when occurring together, normally induce crying, but this was inhibited.

In all these situations the common denominator seemed to be the simultaneous occurrence of partly contradictory emotions and it seemed as if the psychosomatic disorder was a result of *displacement* by mutual inhibition of the motoric behavior patterns, normally associated with each of these emotions separately. It appears therefore not justified to equate each of the psychosomatic disorders with one specific emotion. It is hoped that future research will give us a better *physiological understanding* of the psychobiological processes during *different types of frustration,* which for lack of a better classification, we now designate by *psychological* terms.

ANXIETY-AROUSAL SYNDROME AND HYPERVENTILATION; ANTIADRENERGIC THERAPY

In 1871 Da Costa described a functional syndrome in soldiers of breathlessness, palpitations, and motoric insufficiency. In 1895 Freud (1952) wrote a classic paper on anxiety neurosis in which he described a syndrome of irregular respiration, pain, and pressure sensations in the chest, tachycardia, sweating, tingling in hands and feet, vertigo, and a tendency to faint, associated with anxiety. Because the syndrome had no anatomical substrate he designated it as a neurosis and because he considered anxiety as the cause, as *anxiety neurosis.* The name is still used in most psychiatric classifications; the syndrome is very common in psychiatric practice.

During World War I Sir Thomas Lewis (1919) rediscovered Da Costa's syndrome and named it effort syndrome, soldier's heart, or disordered action of the heart. It was a frequent reason for the rejection of recruits for military service. A number of years later a group of Harvard workers under the cardiologist P. D. White and the psychiatrist Mandel Cohen described more or less the same syndrome, this time not in soldiers but in civilians; they called it *neurocirculatory asthenia* (White, Cobb, Chapman, and Cohen, 1944; Cohen, White, and Johnson, 1948). Most of their patients were women but they made the important observation that a similar syndrome occurred among men who were alcoholics. They also drew attention to the frequent occurrence of the syndrome among members of the same family.

In the following years cardiologists recognized more and more different types of so-called *cardiac neuroses.* These patients suffered from either pressure or pain in the precordium without clinical or electrocardiographic signs of angina pectoris or myocardial ischemia. In another type of patient the main symptoms and signs were tachycardia and different arrhythmias for which no organic cause could be found and which were ascribed to an impulse-emitting focus somewhere in the heart, although the nature of such a hypothetical remained a mystery. Recently Gorlin, Brachfeld, Tumer, Messer, and Salazar (1959) measured the cardiac output in this type of patient and found it to be greatly increased in the resting condition. They therefore proposed the diagnostic term of *hyperkinetic heart syndrome.* In some of their cases the blood pressure was increased intermittently but not permanently. The syndrome in these cases resembles what has been described by Von Uexküll and Wick (1962) as *situational hypertension* in medical students during examinations. In these cardiological descriptions, attention is focused on the circulatory phenomena; anxiety is hardly mentioned or regarded as a result of the disordered action of the heart, whereas in the psychiatric literature anxiety is seen as the main feature of the syndrome.

Independent of either the psychiatric literature on anxiety neurosis or the cardiological diagnoses, the term *hyperventilation syndrome* came into being. This diagnosis was mostly used by chest physicians who recognized that some patients who were referred to them with a presumptive diagnosis of asthma had none or very few signs of the bronchial expiratory obstruction that characterize this disease, but instead suffered from an irregular, deep, and often rapid respiration. These patients, much more frequently than true asthmatics, complain about anxiety, fear of dying, vertigo, pressure on the chest, sweating, and tachycardia. In short, they manifest the same clinical picture as had been described under other names by the psychiatrists and cardiologists, but it was only recently discovered that the syndrome was either caused or made much worse by the hyperventilation to which the other authors had paid insufficient attention. This hyperventilation at rest had no organic cause and was apparently induced by an emotional state, of which the patients were not aware. In fact, most of the patients do not know that they are hyperventilating before their attacks, although this can be confirmed by simple observation of their breathing. In an apparently disagreeable or threatening situation, these patients try to control shrieking or crying; it seems as if the hyperventilation is a displacement phenomenon, a substitute behavior for the increased respiration associated with flight, fight, or crying.

Some of these hyperventilating patients, because of the ensuing hypocapnia and alkalosis, develop tingling in the hands or fingers and even typical attacks of tetany and carpopedal spasms, which in turn greatly increase their anxiety.

It is amazing and characteristic for the lack of integrated thinking in medicine that it should take such a long time before it was realized that all these syndromes, described under different names, are only slightly different manifestations of one and the same disorder, in which anxiety, arousal, and hyperventilation are the main mutually reinforcing factors of a feedback system which produces signs and symptoms in different effector organs.

This realization is important not only from a diagnostic point of view. It has also born fruit in treatment. Until recently, treatment varied with the specialist caring for the patient. The cardiologist had little to offer apart from the "reassurance" that the heart was normal. The chest physician prescribed rebreathing in a plastic bag. The psychiatrist tried to practice psychotherapy. All prescribed so-called anxiolytic drugs (an euphemistic term!). The results were generally disappointing.

On the assumption that the manifestations of the *anxiety-arousal syndrome* (as we would now prefer to call it) are partly caused by sympathetic noradrenergic discharges, several workers have now begun to treat such patients with so-called beta-blocking sympathicolytic drugs. Most of them, including ourselves, have found that this block removes from the syndrome the cardiovascular phenomena. It is a great advantage that patients under this treatment cease to suffer from the palpitations and sweating which formerly reinforced their anxiety. As a result some patients are clinically cured if they take the drugs in sufficient quantity, occasionally supplemented by small amounts of anxiolytics. Not only do the palpitations and sweating disappear, but the tendency to hyperventilate and occasional hyperventilation does not result in reappearance of the syndrome. However, in the majority of cases, mental symptoms, although alleviated or modified, persist. The advantage in these cases is that, as the disagreeable somatic symptoms of the anxiety are relieved, the mental disturbances and interhuman conflicts are easier to treat by psychotherapy. The drugs, in other words, cannot replace psychotherapy but they complement and facilitate it.

Lately we have extended this work to other groups of patients. With Professor Barendregt and Dr. Ramsay at Amsterdam, we have treated a number of patients with different forms of phobia by the same drugs, combined with behavior therapy. We were induced to do so by the finding that such patients in the phobia-producing situation develop tachycardia, sweating, and hyperventilation. By suppressing this part of the syndrome, the phobia was made less disturbing and easier to treat by the behavior therapists.

In another series of observations we have treated alcoholics. It has long been known that in alcoholics a syndrome occurs, when they temporarily stop drinking, which is characterized by tachycardia, sweating, flushing of the face, tremors, and motoric restlessness. Presuming that this abstinence syndrome is likewise caused by increasing arousal and noradrenergic discharges, we have used beta-blocking agents in the treatment. It seems that these patients need very high amounts, often between 800 mg and 1.2 g of propranolol per day, to bring their pulse rate back to normal. Why they need such high dosages is the subject of further investigation. The treatment has been a definitely valuable adjunct in our therapy for alcoholism. Again, it cannot replace the psychosocial approach but supports it. This opens a new road to the treatment of abstinence phenomena in users or abusers of other drugs.

Recently Atzmon, Blum, Wysenbeek, Maoz, Steiner, and Zeigelman (1971) have advocated the use of very high quantities of beta-blocking agents in the treatment of acute psychoses, in which they also found high pulse rates and other signs of a hyperkinetic circulatory state. Trials are also under way to determine whether adrenergic discharges, in connection with hyperventilation, play a role in the abnormal behavior and excitation states of certain patients with temporal epilepsy and hysteria.

This advance in therapy, built on modern clinical, neurophysiological, and pharmacological insights and on the scientific measurement of emotion, may serve as a first example of the therapeutic gains afforded by these modern methods.

REFERENCES

Adey, W. R., and Tokizane, T., editors (1967): *Structure and Function of the Limbic System,* Elsevier, Amsterdam.

Arnold, M., editor (1970): *Feelings and Emotions,* Academic Press, New York.

Atsmon, A., Blum, I., Wysenbeek, A., Maoz, B., Steiner, M., and Ziegelman, G. (1971): Shorttime efforts of adrenergic blocking agents in psychotic patients, *Psychiatr. Neurol. Neurochir. 74,* 251.

Bastiaans, J., and Groen, J. (1954): Psychogenesis and psychotherapy of bronchial asthma. In: *Progress in Psychosomatic Medicine,* edited by D. O'Neill, Butterworth, London.

Black, P. (1970): *Physiological Correlates of Emotion,* Academic Press, New York and London.

Brachfeld, N., and Gorlin, R. (1960): Idiopathic hyperkinetic state; A new clinical syndrome. *Br. Heart J. 22,* 353.

Brod, J. (1970): Haemodynamics and emotional stress. In: *Psychosomatics in Essential Hypertension,* edited by Koster, M., Musaph, H., and Visser, P. S. Karger, Basel.

Cannon, W. B. (1953): *Bodily Changes in Pain, Hunger, Fear and Rage,* Charles Branford, Boston.

Ciba Symposium (1972): *New Perspectives in Beta-blockade,* Scanticon, Aarhus.

Ciba Foundation (1972): *Physiology, Emotion and Psychosomatic Illness,* Elsevier, Excerpta Medica-North Holland, Amsterdam.

Cohen, M. E., White, P. D., and Johnson, E. (1948): Neurocirculatory asthenia, anxiety neurosis and effort syndrome. *Arch. Intern. Med. 81,* 260.

Da Costa, J. M. (1871): quoted by Pitts (1969).

Delgado, J. M. R. (1960): Emotional behaviour in animals and humans, *Psychiatr. Res. Rep. 12,* 259.

Delgado, J. M. R. (1967): Limbic system and free behaviour, *Prog. Brain Res. 27,* 48.

Darwin, C. (1872): *Expression of the Emotions in Man and Animals,* John Murray, London.

Epstein, S. E., and Breunwald, E. (1966): Beta adrenergic receptor blocking drugs, *N. Engl. J. Med. 275,* 1106, 1175.

von Euler, U. S., Gemrell, C. A., Uri, C., and Ström, G. (1959): Cortical and medullary adrenal activity in emotional stress, *Acta Endocrinol. 30,* 567.

Eysenck, H. J. (1969): Psychological aspects of anxiety. In: *Studies of Anxiety,* edited by M. H. Lader, Headly Bros Ltd., Ashford.

Freud, S. (1952): Ueber die Berechtigung von der Neurasthenie einen Symptomencomplex als "Angstneurose" abzutrennen (1894). In: *Gesammelte Werke* I, 315. Imago Publ., London.

Gorlin, R., Brachfeld, N., Tumer, J. D., Messer, J. V., and Salazar, E. (1959): The idiopathic high cardiac output state. *J. Clin. Invest. 38,* 2144.

Grace, W. J., Wolf, S., and Wolff, H. G. (1951): *The Human Colon,* Paul Hoeber, New York.

Granville-Grosman, K. C., and Turner, P. (1966): Effect of propranolol on anxiety, *Lancet 1,* 788.

Groen, J. J. (1972): The mechanism of the disturbance of respiration during the asthmatic attack, physiotherapy, *J. Chartered Soc. Physiotherap. 58,* 371.

Groen, J. J. (1957): Psychosomatic disturbances as a form of substituted behaviour. Presidential address Second European Conference on Psychosomatic Research, Amsterdam, April 1956. *J. Psychosom. Res. 2,* 85.

Groen, J. J. (1971): The psychosomatic specificity hypothesis for the etiology of peptic ulcer, *Psychother. Psychosom. 19,* 295.

Groen, J., and Bastiaans, J. (1954): Studies on ulcerative colitis; Personality structure, emotional conflict situations and results of psychotherapy. In: *Progress in Psychosomatic Medicine,* edited by D. O'Neill, Butterworth, London.

Groen, J. J., Bastiaans, J., Barendregt, J. T., Dekker, E., Pelser, H. E., and van der Valk, J. M. (1964): *Psychosomatic Research,* Pergamon Press, Oxford.

Groen, J. J., and van der Valk, J. M. (1956): Ulcerative colitis, *Gastro-Enterologica, 86,* 591, and *Practitioner, 117,* 572.

Groen, J. J., van der Valk, J. M., Welner, A., and Ben Ishay, D. (1971): Psychobiological factors in the pathogenesis of essential hypertension. *Psychother. Psychosom. 19,* 1.

Henry, J. P., and Cassel, J. C. (1969): Psychosocial factors in essential hypertension, *Am. J. Epidemiol. 90,* 171.

Hess, W. R. (1954): *Das Zwischenhirn,* B. Schwalbe, Basel.

Hill, O. W., editor (1970): *Modern Trends in Psychosomatic Medicine,* Vol. 2, Butterworth, London.

Izard, C. E. (1972): *Patterns of Emotion,* Academic Press, New York and London.

James, W. (1890): *The Principles of Psychology,* Henry Holt, New York.

Kimmel, H. D. (1971): *Experimental Psychopathology,* Academic Press, New York and London.

Lacey, J. I., and Lacey, B. C. (1970): Autonomic-central nervous system interrelationships. In: *Physiological Correlates of Emotion,* edited by P. Black, Academic Press, New York.

Lader, M. H. (1969): Psychophysiological aspects of anxiety. In: *Studies of Anxiety,* edited by M. H. Lader, World Psych. Assoc. and Royal Medico-Psychological Assoc.; Headley Bros. Ltd., Ashford.

Levi, L., editor (1971): *Society, Stress and Disease, Vol. 1, The Environment and Psychosomatic Disease,* Oxford University Press, London.

Levi, L. (1972): Stress and distress in response to psychosocial stimuli, *Acta Med. Scand.* [Suppl.] 528.

Lewis, T. (1919): *The Soldiers Heart and the Effort Syndrome,* Hoeber, New York.

MacLean, P. D. (1955): The limbic system, *Psychosom. Med. 17,* 355.

Margules, D. L., and Stein, L. (1969): Cholinergic synapses of a periventricular punishment system in the medial hypothalamus, *Am. J. Physiol. 217,* 476.

Marks, I. M. (1969): *Fears and Phobias,* Heinemann Medical Books Ltd., London.

McGaugh, Weinberger, N. M., and Whalen, R. E. (1967): *Psychobiology,* W. H. Freeman, San Francisco.

Michaelis, R. (1970): *Das Herzangst Syndrom,* S. Karger, Basel.

Murray, C. D. (1930): A brief psychological analysis of a patient with ulcerative colitis, *J. Nerv. Ment. Dis. 72,* 617.

Offerhaus, L. (1973): De klinische toepassing van Beta-Blokkeerders, *Ned. Tijdschr. Geneeskd. 117,* 814.

Olds, J. (1962): Hypothalamic substrates of reward, *Physiol. Rev. 42,* 554.

Olds, J., and Milner, P. (1954): Reinforcement produced by electrical stimulation of the septal area, *J. Comp. Physiol. Psychol. 47,* 419.

Pitts, F. N. (1969): The biochemistry of anxiety, *Sci. Am. 43,* 69.

Porter, R., and Birch, J., editors (1971): *Identification of Asthma, A Ciba Foundation Symposium,* Churchill and Livingstone, Edinburgh and London.

Renout, W., and Vreeke, B. M. (1970): Autonome Respons Specificiteit bij Stress, Student thesis, Amsterdam University (Dept. of Psychology).

Reymert, M. L., edited (1950): *Feelings and Emotions,* McGraw-Hill Book Company, New York.

Schachter, S. (1971): *Emotion, Obesity and Crime,* Academic Press, New York and London.

Schachter, S., and Singer, J. E. (1962): Cognitive, social and physiological determinants of emotional state, *Psychol. Rev. 69,* 379.

van Sichem, P. (1972): Application of Propanolol in Psychiatry, A Survey of the Literature, Student Thesis, Leiden University, (Dept. of Psychobiology).

Spielberger, C. D., editor (1966): *Anxiety and Behaviour,* Academic Press, New York.

Spinoza, B. de: *Ethics,* Vol. 3.

Suzman, M. M. (1971): The use of beta adrenergic blockade with propanolol in anxiety syndromes. *Postgrad. Med. J. 47,* Suppl. 104.

Turner, P., and Granville-Grosman, K. L. (1965): Effect of adrenergic receptor blockade on the tachycardia of anxiety states, *Lancet 2,* 1316.

von Uexküll, T., and Wick, E. (1962): Die Situationshypertonie, *Arch. Kreislaufforsch. 39,* 236.

van der Valk, J. M., and Groen, J. J. (1950): Electrical resistance of the skin during induced emotional stress, *Psychosom. Med. 12,* 303.

Weinmann, G. (1968): *Das Hyperventilations — Syndrom.* Urban und Schwarzenberg, München.

White, P. D., Cobb, S., Chapman, W. P., and Cohen, M. E. (1944): Neurocirculatory asthenia. *Trans. Assoc. Am. Physicians, 58,* 129.

Wolff, H. G., and Wolf, S. (1950): Life stress and bodily disease, *Proc. Assoc. Res. Nerv. Ment. Dis. 29.*

Wolff, H. G. (1952): *Stress and Disease,* Charles Thomas, Springfield, Ill.

Wolf, S. (1967): Stress and the gut, *Gastroenterology 59,* 288.

Wolf, S. (1965): *The Stomach.* Oxford University Press, New York.

Emotions—Their Parameters and Measurement,
edited by L. Levi.
Raven Press, New York © 1975

Psychopharmacology Measurement of Emotion in Medical Practice

Paul Kielholz

Psychiatrische Universitätsklinik, CH-4052 Basle, Switzerland

By emotions we understand such feeling processes as joy, sorrow, fear, and anxiety. Emotions manifest the personal way in which an individual responds to the contents of his experience. Emotions possess three main qualities: *subjectivity,* in so far as the feelings are not bound to objective perceptions but are experienced solely as states of the ego; *universality,* in so far as the feelings are not bound to specific provoking stimuli, such as, sensations, or to special sensory organs but can be generally experienced; *the attendant somatic symptoms* which are prominent to a degree, depending on somatization, or which may appear as feeling equivalents in the physical sphere. Emotion thus refers both to the *coloring of experience* and to the *attendant physical symptoms* and at the same time to the response of the autonomic, endocrine, and neuromuscular apparatus to these psychophysical processes.

If protracted frames of mind are involved, we speak of mood. If the feelings are brief and intense, we call them affects. Needless to say, there are many nuances and the dividing lines are fluid. I will briefly give examples of these explanatory definitions by reference to fear and anxiety.

Fear and anxiety are primary emotions, i.e., specifically personal responses of the individual to the threatening content of his experience. In popular German usage no distinction is made between *Angst* (anxiety) and *Furcht* (fear) and the one is frequently substituted for the other. Often *Angst* and *Furcht* are not named as such, but instead reference is made symbolically merely to their physical accompaniments. We may say "it fairly took his breath away," "his heart was in his boots," or "he's got the wind up." It is remarkable how often popular expressions accurately reflect psychophysical facts.

Scientifically anxiety can be described in Jasper's terms as an elementary, unadapted emotional reaction which is inappropriate to the threatening danger and therefore cannot be countered by rational, purposive behavior. All anxiety is bound up with gestures and facial expression along with symptoms of autonomic stimulation of the ergotropic, adrenergic nervous system (Table 1). Anxiety may sometimes be manifested only at a physical

TABLE 1. *Physical accompaniments of anxiety*

Expressive features of gesture and facial expression
Symptoms due to stimulation of the sympathetic, adrenergic nervous system
    dilated pupils — psychogenic pupil reflex
    fine tremor
    dry mouth
    facial pallor, attacks of sweating
    tachycardia, precordial oppression, extrasystoles
    anorexia, gastric trouble, intestinal spasms, diarrhea
    tachypnea, nervous respiratory syndrome, choking feeling in the throat
    increased blood pressure
    increased blood sugar
    insomnia

level. These symptoms are then known as anxiety equivalents (Table 2).

It is apparent, then, that emotions may be manifested predominantly at a psychic, psychomotor, or autonomic-endocrine level, or at all three at the same time. This enables us to formulate the first *principle* for measuring emotions. In order to quantify feelings, all three possible forms of manifestation, namely, motor disturbances, autonomic-endocrine changes, and psychic effects, must be measured and correlated.

In contrast to anxiety, which represents an inappropriate reaction that is not adapted to the magnitude of the danger or controllable by reason and action, we have fear. According to Kierkegaard, fear is always distinguished from anxiety by the fact that it is invariably objective and reflects the magnitude of the threatening danger. Those affected can therefore meet the threat by rational and appropriate action. Let us take fear of examinations as an example. It is a spur to work, and the better the student is prepared the more readily can he master his fear, and even acquire a feeling of security through the acquisition of a sufficient stock of knowledge.

The position is quite different with examination anxiety. In spite of the most assiduous study, the anxiety grows more acute as the examination

TABLE 2. *Anxiety equivalents*

Headaches, lack of concentration, rapid fatigability
Psychomotor agitation, pseudoactivity
Inner disquiet and tensions
Aggression and forward flight
Self-aggression with suicidal impulses
Fugue, blind impulsion to flee, poriomania
Psychomotor inhibition, stupor
Cardiac, respiratory, gastrointestinal complaints
Pavor nocturnus
Accesses of ravenous appetite
Trembling fits
Diarrhea
Pollakiuria

approaches and, on the examination day, turns into an examination stupor with total failure as the outcome. The same holds true of sorrow and depression; sorrow engenders development and maturation of the character whereas depression leads to despair and suicidal impulses. From this the *second principle* for measuring emotions can be derived. Its methodology must be selective enough to allow a distinction to be made between appropriate and inappropriate reactions. Only abnormal emotions call for psychopharmacological treatment whereas appropriate reactions serve to deepen and mature the personality and require no treatment.

If we find that a person displays anxiety and its physical accompaniments, we have merely diagnosed a *syndrome* which may be referable to quite different causes, and the etiological factors must be clarified. Wherever an anxiety syndrome is diagnosed, the patient must undergo not only a psychological but also a medical and neurological examination, for it is important to ascertain whether the manifestation of anxiety is due to an existential anxiety, pure anxiety, or psychogenic or psychotic anxiety. Apart from the phobias, a pathogenetic distinction is made between five anxiety syndromes (Fig. 1).

In *existential anxiety* the danger originates from the patient's own body. However, constitutional and dispositional factors, together with environmental situations, also play a crucial role. Jores has found, for example, that only 50% of myocardial infarctions give rise to anxiety syndromes and that there is no correlation between the degree of anxiety and the severity of the infarction.

In *pure anxiety* the danger is extraneous in origin and the person affected

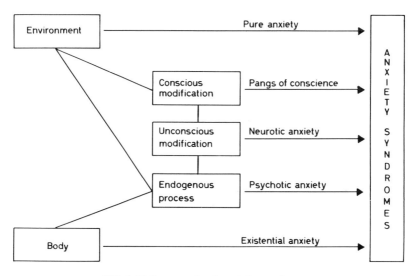

FIG. 1. Pathogenesis of anxiety syndromes.

need not recognize the link between the danger and his anxiety. We are concerned here with inappropriate feeling reactions to existential threats that may actually exist or be present only in the patient's imagination. How inappropriate such reactions may be is illustrated by the severe anxiety syndromes that are elicited by the sight of a mouse or a spider, whereas it is obvious enough that it is the mouse or spider which is under an existential threat.

The most common form of anxiety consists of pangs of conscience. Here the threat lies within the patient's own psyche in a conflict between the spheres of conscience and impulse or as a signal of a threat to satisfactory interpersonal relations.

An extreme form of anxiety is found in psychotic anxiety, which is elicited by the disintegration of the ego and the severe threat to it constituted by schizophrenia or endogenous depression. Similarly a nosological classification is also requisite in the depressive syndrome, for again in depressive conditions a distinction must be made between organic endogenous depressions and those of psychogenic origin (Fig. 2).

The *third principle* in the measurement of emotions is that any quantification of a feeling must be preceded by a precise diagnostic classification, for only emotions of the same etiology can be compared both psychologically and psychopharmacologically. An analysis of the etiology of the syndromes and symptoms and a diagnosis of the greatest possible accuracy are there-

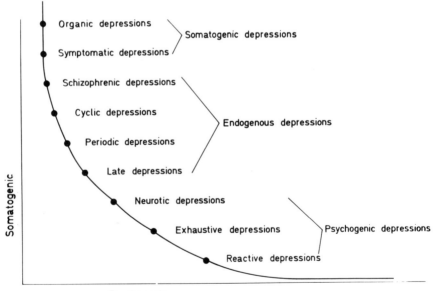

FIG. 2. Nosological classification of depressive states.

fore conditions which must be fulfilled before emotions are quantified if any comparable parameters at all are to be obtained.

The expressive phenomena of anxiety were already known to the founder of modern physiognomics. As early as 1780 Lavater described the fearful eye in his physiognomic vade mecum *How to Judge Men by Their Facial Features* (Fig. 3). In this connection he wrote "Wide-open eyes and dilated

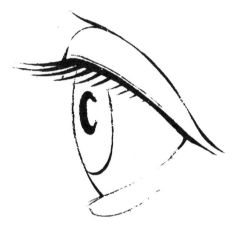

FIG. 3. Fearful eye.

pupils indicate fear." He also depicted the facial expression of fear (Fig. 4). He characterized the facial expression of fear as follows: "These eyes cast earthwards, the seams along the cheeks and forehead, the compressed lips, the dry mouth, the pale, bilious, tense facial expression and the dark-ringed eyes proclaim fear." He also intimated that fear can be qualified by the intensity of the facial expression and of the frightened gaze.

From this we can derive the *fourth principle* for measuring emotion. The methods used must mediate objective parameters and be repeatable at any time. The measurements must always be made under the same conditions. It was possible to demonstrate the difficulty and complexity of measuring the emotions by the example of anxiety and depression.

For measurements to be comparable four principles must be satisfied. (1) The definition of the symptoms, syndromes, and diagnoses must be standardized in order to obtain comparable data. (2) The methodology of examination must be sufficiently selective to allow a distinction to be made between average and morbid manifestations of emotion. (3) The psychological, psychometric, and autonomic parameters must be recorded and correlated in longitudinal studies because there is a large interindividual dispersion in cross-sectional studies. (4) The examination technique must be repeatable and always performed under the same conditions.

FIG. 4. Facial expression of fear.

FACIAL EXPRESSION AND ITS QUANTIFICATION

Heimann has measured the width of the palpebral fissure on films in anxious and depressive patients. He was able to show that the decreases in the width of the fissure and the corresponding values on the Hamilton scale are parallel and that in states of acute anxiety the movements of the eyelids diminish. With the abatement of anxiety he also found a significant increase at the 5% level of the movement quotient he had calculated from pictures as the measure of the distance moved by the left and right angles of the mouth. Again, the *asymmetry quotient,* i.e., a measure of distance obtained by adding the deviations of the left and right angles of the mouth, shows that as anxiety decreases the asymmetry of the movements increases in a highly significant way (Fig. 5).

Measurements of the *width of the palpebral fissures,* of the *movements of the eyelids,* of the *angles of the mouth,* and of *asymmetry of the face* allowed Heimann to express in numbers the changes of facial expression induced by anxiety and depression which had hitherto been assessed only

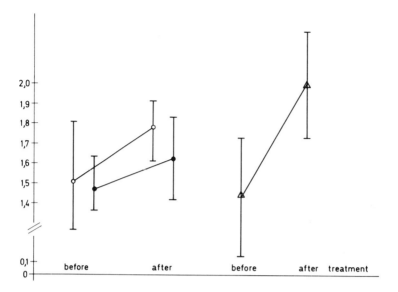

FIG. 5. Indices of the mouth angle movements in facial expression (200 frames, 24 frames/sec). Mean values and dispersions from 10 series of measurement: open circles— left, filled circles—right movement quotient; open triangles—asymmetry quotient.

on the basis of impression. This example is intended merely to serve as an illustration of the way in which facial expressions can be quantified and what connections can be established between expressive behavior and emotions.

QUANTIFICATION OF AUTONOMIC PARAMETERS

The following are results of studies by the Department for Research in Depression of the Psychiatric Clinic of the University of Basle.

Pupillometry

Measurements of photographs of pupils taken under standardized lighting conditions revealed very large interindividual differences of pupil diameter. No significant results could be obtained in cross-sectional studies because of the wide dispersion. In longitudinal studies inhibited depressives show an increase of pupil diameter ($p < 0.05$; n = 54) after clinical improvement.

Salivation

Quantitative measurements of the saliva revealed significant correlations between subjective dryness of the mouth and salivation rate. Salivation inhibition increases with the degree of anxiety and the depth of the depression. There is a negative correlation between fear and the quantity of salivation ($r = -0.39$) and between the depth of depression and the quantity of saliva ($r = -0.21$; n = 94). Examinations by Malcolm Lader yielded analogous results.

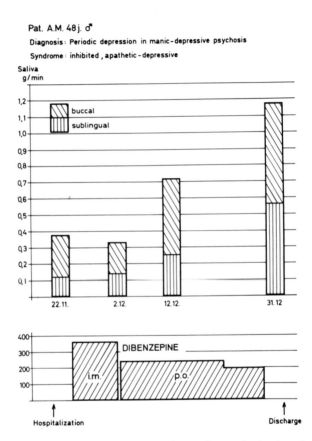

FIG. 6. Salivation and depth of depression under treatment.

Skin Temperature and Rewarming

The subjective feeling of "cold hands" can be made objective by the measurement of the skin temperature ($p < 0.001$; n=63). The skin temperature shows no differences between nosological and syndrome categories since the dispersion is too great. In longitudinal studies, however, there is a definite trend toward an improvement in rewarming as the depression is relieved.

Circulation

There are significant relations between "subjective vertigo" and "pathological orthostasis reaction" ($p < 0.001$; n = 63). In longitudinal studies the decrease in the pathological orthostasis reaction is parallel to the relieving of the depression.

Psychomotor Disturbances and Drive

A large number of methods are available for quantifying psychomotor disturbances. In our clinic we use writing speed, the measurement of optical illusions with the Necker cube, the determination of reaction time, and a driving simulator. In inhibited endogenous depressives there is a definite slowing down in the rate of writing. The rate of perceptive reversal with the Necker cube is held to be a measure of vigilance and drive, and there may be a significant increase in the average reversal rate as clinical improvement of the depression is observed ($p < 0.025$; n = 63).

Psychological Methods of Measurement

There are five possible approaches to the psychological measurement of emotions in man: (1) self-assessment by the patient, (2) assessment by the doctor and nurse, (3) quantification with rating scales, (4) multidimensional personality inventory, (5) objective measurements — performance, reactive behavior, modification of perception, fatigue (Fig. 7).

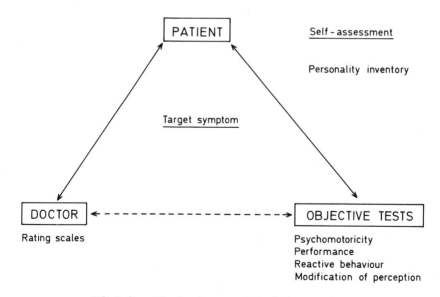

FIG. 7. Quantification by s psychological parameters.

Self-assessment by the patient and external assessment by the doctor yielded significant correlations as regards the state of mind at the time on an itemized basis. The state of mind (von Zerssen) and habitual aspects of personality (Fahrens-Berger personality inventory) showed a high degree of agreement (r = −0.75 −0.85) and at the same time high reliability (r = −0.70 −0.90).

There was also a significant correlation between the depth of the depression and autonomic parameters. Objective psychological measurements had formerly yielded significant relations only between self-assessments by the patients and objective measurements. The poor correlation previously obtained between rating scales and objective measurements may be partly due to inadequate rater training and lack of standardization in the classification and definition of individual symptoms. With *rater training,* adequate rater correlations can be obtained: Beck inventory 0.84, Hamilton scale 0.90.

Biochemical Parameters

The aim of biochemical research is to enable both a new classification and also a causal therapy to be established on the basis of biochemical criteria. Investigations of the metabolism and the physiology of biogenic amines in patients suffering from depressive conditions have recently centered on the catecholamines (norepinephrine, epinephrine, and dopamine) or on the indoleamines (serotonin and tryptophan). Results of these tests to date suggest that endogenous depressions in particular are associated with an absolute or relative diminution of the catecholamines, particularly norephedrine and/or indoleamine, and more especially serotonin, as important receptors in the brain. The manias are probably associated with the increase of these monamines. Levi has shown that various emotional reactions are accompanied by important biochemical functional changes which in turn influence the functions of numerous organs. In stress situations of long duration and strong emotional reactions there are pronounced increases in the excretion of epinephrine in the urine.

In view of the disparity of the results of biochemical studies in regard to both methodology and the classification of the depressions, a group of WHO advisers has recommended: (1) WHO should establish a network of centers for biological research in affective disorders. (2) Collaborative research should immediately be initiated to test some of the important hypotheses relevant to biogenic amines. (3) A standard methodology of work should be elaborated for the above collaborative research. (4) For the assessment and classification of the disorders to be investigated in such collaborative studies, the methods of procedure are being developed in the WHO study on standardized assessment of affective disorders.

It was also suggested that this collaborative research should include studies on sleep disorders, disturbances of the circadian rhythm, psychic daily fluctuations in the 24-hr rhythm of biochemical processes such as Levi has revealed. Particular importance was also attached to pressing on with the efforts to throw light on the role of the transmitters and of mineral, enzyme, and hormone metabolism.

We have found that quantification of the emotions must be approached from both the psychic and the somatic side. With research into depression as an illustration, I will show the great importance of the measurement of the emotions for psychopharmaco- and psychotherapy (Fig. 8).

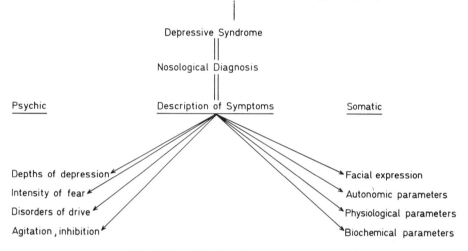

FIG. 8. Quantification of depressive states.

For the quantification of emotions it is essential always to carry out longitudinal studies which allow intraindividual comparisons to be made and reflect the course of the disease, for interindividual variations are too great to yield significant results. All the parameters shown in the figure must therefore be recorded longitudinally and correlated with one another. It is only in longitudinal studies of depressions that the depth of the depression, the disorders of drive, and the anxiety can be correlated with autonomic and facial expressive parameters. In individual patients it is possible to record the changes in the various parameters under the action of psychopharmacotherapy and psychotherapy or a combination of the two methods of treatment, and in this way the course of the disease can be objectified. Thus the *indications* and the onset of the action of the *psychopharmacological agents* can be elucidated and the necessary length of the treatment determined (Fig. 9).

By comparing the action of the psychopharmacological agents on the various symptoms, it is possible to determine the spectrum of action and thus the indications of these drugs. It was also found that in the treatment of

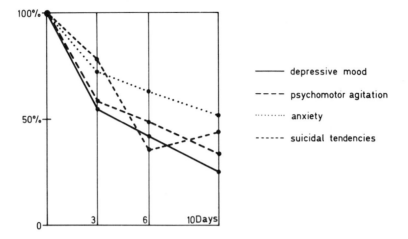

FIG. 9. Remission quotients of the individual symptoms during treatment with an anti-depressant.

depression the success of therapy depends on the choice of the antidepressant with the correct spectrum of action. The choice of the antidepressant to be used is determined by the target symptoms: *inhibited drive, basic feeling of sadness,* or *anxiety.* The various antidepressants influence the target symptoms in different ways. Hence, depending on the prevailing symptomatology, an antidepressant is indicated that primarily *increases drive, enhances mood,* or *suppresses anxiety.* In the light of their primary spectrum of action it has been possible to arrange the antidepressants in a reference system (Fig. 10).

The spectra of action which were first determined on the basis of clinical experience and observation have meanwhile been confirmed by quantification of the psychic parameters and comparative tests. In animal experiments involving tetrabenazine catalepsy in the cat and inhibition of the arousal reaction in electrical stimulation of the rabbit, Stille found a similar series of action spectra of the tricyclic antidepressants. If the depressive state is dominated by deficient drive and psychomotor inhibitions, antidepressants with drive-increasing, thymeretic effects, such as, protriptyline (Concordin ®), nortriptyline (Nortrilen ®, Aventyl ®), or desipramine (Pertofrane ®), are indicated. If sadness and oppression are in the foreground, mood-enhancing thymoleptic antidepressants, such as, imipramine (Tofranil ®), clomipramine (Anafranil ®), or dibenzepine (Noveril ®), should be given. If anxiety or anxious agitation are prominent features of the depressive state, then antidepressants with anxiolytic effect, such as, amitriptyline (Laroxyl ®, Saroten ®), trimeprimine (Surmontil ®), or doxepin (Sinequan ®), are indicated.

It has been found time and again that therapy in the clinic and medical

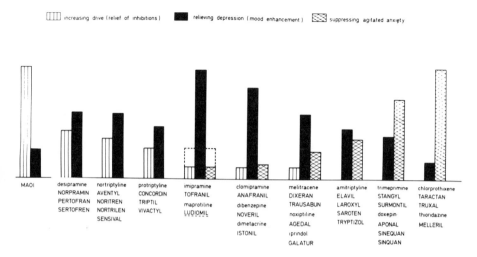

FIG. 10. Diagrammatic representation of spectrum of action of antidepressants.

practice depends for its success on the prescription of antidepressants with the correct spectrum of action. Thus an attempt has been made at the Bechterev Institute in Leningrad to ascertain the spectra of action of the antidepressants on the basis of a quantification of anxiety and depressive mood, and, although an entirely different methodology was adopted, the same spectra of action were obtained. In depressive states involving anxiety, drive-increasing antidepressants may have a disastrous effect by increasing drive and thereby aggravating the anxiety and also, by reducing motor inhibition, increasing the risk of suicide. The spectra of action of the psychopharmacological agents and their onset of action can only be elucidated if the emotions and their physical accompaniments are quantified.

Standardized methodology and diagnosis, interdisciplinary cooperation, and international collaborative research must be accomplished if, in work extending over a number of years, the many problems of measuring the emotions are to be brought nearer a solution.

SUMMARY

Our emotions are to be understood as the personal attitude of the individual to the content of his experience. They are very difficult to quantify because of their subjectivity and universality. Each emotion has its own manifold physical accompaniments. In order to obtain comparable results, four conditions must be fulfilled. (1) Only emotions of the same pathogenesis can be compared. The symptoms, syndromes and diagnosis must be uniformly defined and standardized. (2) The psychic, motor, and somatic parameters must be quantified and correlated. (3) The measurements must be as objective as possible, repeatable, and always be carried out at the same time of day. (4) The parameters must be recorded in longitudinal studies in order to establish possibilities of intraindividual comparison since cross-sectional studies show too large interindividual dispersions.

Various results of quantification obtained on the basis of longitudinal studies of the facial expression, pupil diameter, salivation, rewarming of the skin, the circulation, psychomotor disturbances, and psychological tests are discussed in brief.

With reference to the biochemical parameters, a summary is presented of the leading hypotheses, and the recommendations of the WHO for collaborative research are supported. The example of the antidepressants is used to show that is is possible today to determine the spectrum of action and thus the onset and indications of antidepressant substances on the basis of the results of psychological and somatic parameters. Many problems concerning the terminology, standardization, and quantification of the emotions are still unsolved and could be most rapidly brought nearer a solution by international, interdisciplinary collaborative research.

REFERENCES

Beck, D. (1962): Vegetative Untersuchungen, Therapie und Prognose der Erschöpfungs-depression, *Schweiz. Arch. Neurol. Neurochir. Psychiat. 90*, 370.

Fahrenberg, J., and Selg, H. (1970): *Das Freiburger Persönlichkeitsinventar*, FPI. Göttingen.

Hamilton, M. (1960): A rating scale for depression, *J. Neurol. Neurosurg. Psychiatry 23*, 50–62.

Heimann, H. (1973): Psychobiologie der Depression. In: *Die larvierte Depression*, pp. 35–54, Verl. Hans Huber Bern, Stuttgart und Wien.

Hole, G., Gehring, A., and Blaser, P. (1972): Vegetativum, Psychomotorik und Selbstbeurteilung in Längsschnittuntersuchungen depressiver Patienten, *Fortschr. Neurol. Psychiatr. 40*, 69–82.

Lavater, J. C. (1775–1778): *Physiognomische Fragmente zur Beförderung der Menschen-kenntnis und Menschenliebe*, Versuch I–IV. Weidmanns Erben und Reich und Heinrich Steiner & Cie, Leipzig und Winterthur.

Levi, L. (1964): *Stress, Körper, Seele und Krankheit*. Musterschmidt-Verlag Göttingen, Berlin, Frankfurt, Zürich.

Levi, L. (1967): Biochemische Reaktionen bei verschiedenen experimentell hervorgerufenen Gefühlszuständen. In: *Angst*, Verlag Hans Huber, Bern und Stuttgart.

Kielholz, P. (1965): *Psychiatrische Pharmakotherapie in Klinik und Praxis*. Hans Huber Verlag, Bern und Stuttgart.

Kielholz, P. (1971): Diagnose und Therapie der Depressionen für den Praktiker. 3. Auflage München. J. F. Lehmann.

Kielholz, P., and Hole, G. (1969): Differentialdiagnostik der endogenen Depressionen, Dysthymien und Schizophrenien. In: *Schizophrenie und Zyklothymie*, Hersg. G. Huber, S. 78–86. Georg Thieme Verlag, Stuttgart.

Stille, G., Lauener, H., and Eichenberger, E. (1965): Ein pharmakologischer Vergleich klinisch gebräuchlicher Antidepressiva unter besonderer Berücksichtigung von Noveril, *Schweiz. Med. Wochenschr. 25*, 366.

Zerssen, D. von (1973): Selbstbeurteilungs-Skalen zur Abschätzung des subjektiven Befindens in psychopathologischen Querschnitt- und Längsschnitt-Untersuchungen, *Arch. Psychiatr. Nervenkr. 217*, 299–314.

Emotions — Their Parameters and Measurement,
edited by L. Levi.
Raven Press, New York © 1975

Session 5: Discussion

Chairman: H. J. Eysenck

Eysenck: Many of the problems facing psychiatrists, of course, arise from the violent and inappropriate emotions which are so characteristic of psychiatric illness. And much of what has been said at this meeting is obviously extremely relevant to the kind of work they do. Clinicians are often very suspicious of pure research which they consider irrelevant and sometimes esoteric. I do not believe this is necessarily so; I think research is in fact the lifeline of psychiatry as it is of general medicine, and the four chapters in this session are designed to demonstrate the relevance of the kind of research that we have been discussing to psychiatric practice.

Quite generally there have been two revolutions in psychiatry which have dramatically changed the picture for the better and which have originated in the kind of research that we have been discussing. The first revolution, of course, is the drug treatment of psychosis. The outlook was pretty hopeless 20 years ago, but now the phenothiazines and the antidepressants have changed the outlook completely and very much for the better. We can restore countless sufferers from schizophrenia, from manic-depressive illness, to an active, useful and happy life.

The other revolution, of course, has been the advent of behavior therapy. Again 20 years ago, there was no effective treatment of the neurotic disorders. All that was available at the time was psychoanalysis and psychotherapy based on Freudian principles. And even then it was beginning to be realized by the leaders of the field that these methods were, in effect, largely useless. It was demonstrated that the spontaneous remission rate in neurosis was at least as high as the rate of recovery after several years of psychoanalytic treatment.

There is no evidence of any kind for the clinical and therapeutic effectiveness of psychoanalysis. It is here that behavior therapy has come in, which is based on modern learning theory, modern conditioning theories, and the study of the emotions, very much along the line of this volume. A development based on Pavlov rather than on Freud, it has already demonstrated its tremendous potential in the treatment of anxiety states, phobic states, obsessive-compulsive disorders, sexual dysfunctioning, and many other types of neurotic illness.

Both these revolutions really have already demonstrated very effectively their value in psychiatry. In this conference, we have heard the beginnings of another revolution which is still to come. We have been vouchsafed a glimpse into the future by Dr. Delgado, who has shown that by the use of implanted electrodes in specific brain areas joined to sophisticated telemetric devices you can treat incurable pain, epileptic seizures, antisocial and uncontrollable aggression, through a very simple application of electric current to these implanted electrodes.

Both drug treatment and behavior therapy depend very intimately on a better understanding of the emotions, the way they are generated, the way they become conditioned, and the way they can become extinguished, and a knowledge of the parameters which control these emotions. The conference has been extremely successful in throwing some light on the psychological, neurological, physiological, and pharmaceutical conditions and aspects of this problem.

Delgado: I am a neurophysiologist, and we have the opportunity to have some of our patients implanted with the long-term electrodes in the brain that can be stimulated transferably. In this way we have an ideal situation, not only for therapy, but perhaps also for some research about emotionality and emotions. Naturally, we have a battery of tests; the conversation with the patient is tape recorded, we also have videotape and a battery of tests, including free association and the Rorschach test, administered for 45 min two or three times a week, during or without brain stimulation that provides some idea of the situation, to really understand the different areas of the brain that play a role in emotionality. How would you suggest getting a broad coverage for testing emotions and at the same time some depth in this standard testing situation that is repeatable several times, two or three times per week for months or perhaps years?

Spielberger: I have one test in mind that I would like to recommend. I think that with regard to the state of anxiety, at least, we can with a five-item scale which takes 20 sec to administer get at changes within the individual that might prove very interesting. And your situation is such that the individual can serve as his own control. It would be extremely interesting to me if you would consider using our scale as a measure of state anxiety. I wish that there were measures available for other emotional states that were psychometrically adequate to assist in the task. There is a desperate need for a measure of anger and depression, as well. I think that the kinds of measures you need are state measures rather than trait measures. State measures, measures of changing personality states as a function of stimulation, might give us a better idea of what areas of the brain underlie these experiences.

Levi: Dr. Eysenck, you mentioned the alternative which is said to be a very effective one, namely behavioral therapy. Would you mind saying something more to that effect; giving some data?

Eysenck: As you know, Freud was one of the first people to put forward a theory of neurosis which was essentially a medical one, in the sense that he treated symptoms as symptoms and insisted on there being a true cause for these symptoms, namely by complex. And his therapy, essentially, consisted in trying to remove this complex. The evidence shows fairly conclusively that this method does not work. And the alternative hypothesis is one which is based on conditioning theory and which says, essentially, that the neurotic symptoms are not symptoms at all; they are in fact the disease, that all you are dealing with is conditioned emotional reactions and the verbal and motor consequences of these conditioned emotional reactions. Consequently the treatment should consist not in looking for nonexistent complexes supposedly underlying the disorder, but rather that you should extinguish the conditioned response using the methods introduced by Pavlov and widely studied in our laboratories. There is a great deal of evidence that this can be done very effectively and very quickly, and that none of the aftereffects feared by Freudians, namely, relapses and symptom substitutions, occurs.

MacLean: I think it would be unfortunate if the impression were given that there was any enthusiasm for psychosurgery or implantation of electrodes in the human being in our country. On the contrary, the last year has seen many demonstrations against these procedures, particularly among the thinking young people of our country.

Delgado: I think that Dr. MacLean is probably right, but I do not think that his comment should go without a comment. I think that it is true that there is some prejudice against this new kind of therapy, but we must remember that in history people who were right were burned by the Church. And let us hope that the new science is not like the old Church, trying to burn down new ideas. What I would say also is that against some of these feelings that Dr. MacLean is right about, I think that we must consider these new possibilities to deal with the brain not as harmful or aggressive procedures, but as far more conservative procedures than psychosurgery. In other words, when we destroy the brain in lobotomy, the brain is destroyed forever. When we electrically stimulate the brain, we have a more confined control, and the worst harm that we can do is that we do nothing, i.e., the procedures are not effective. But I think that with these new technologies we have a far more refined, far more conservative, and, therefore, far more medical methodology to deal with the disturbances of the brain.

Emotions — Their Parameters and Measurement,
edited by L. Levi.
Raven Press, New York © 1975

Drugs, Science, and People

Arne Engström

Department of Medical Biophysics, Karolinska Institutet, Stockholm, Sweden

INCREASE IN DRUG CONSUMPTION

With the advancement of standards of living and the introduction of national health systems, the consumption of what we generally call drugs has increased markedly. First, some illustrations to this point. In Sweden, to take an example, drug sales increased from 380 million kronor in 1960 to 1,484 million in 1972. As a percentage of the Swedish GNP, drug sales increased from 0.52 in 1960 to 0.71 in 1971. On the Swedish market the fraction of drugs manufactured abroad has increased steadily. For example in 1962 about 30% of the drugs sold were of foreign origin, while estimates in 1973 indicate that about 50% were manufactured abroad. The introduction and marketing of drugs in a country such as Sweden are thus of considerable economic importance and part of an advanced international network.

From an international point of view, the drug industry, although its major output consists of technically relatively simple products, is research intensive compared with other industrial activities. About 10 to 15% of the revenue from sales are set aside for research purposes. Globally this means that about 7,000 million Swedish kronor are utilized for research and development.

The major pharmaceutical developments naturally take place in the large pharmaceutical companies. For example, in the period 1958 to 1970, nearly half of the new pharmaceutical chemical compounds introduced on the world market originated in the United States with its large corporations. Switzerland and Great Britain introduced about 12% each, Germany 8%, and France 4%. Sweden and a number of smaller countries each had a share of about 2%. The costs for drugs in one city hospital in Stockholm amounts to 4.2% of the total budget. Costs for drugs amount to about 4 to 10% of the total expenditures for health and medical care in the developed countries and it is obvious that the world mechanism for producing pharmaceuticals is of a considerable economic size. In 1970, world sales (excluding the communist countries) amounted to 7,200 million pounds sterling. About 30% of these sales took place in North America and roughly another 30% in the European Community countries. It is equally obvious that the major consumption of drugs takes place in the developed parts of the world; only $\frac{1}{5}$ of the world consumption takes place in the developing countries, which have $\frac{4}{5}$ of the world's population.

SOME MAJOR PROBLEMS

These are some features of the present pattern of drug production and consumption. A number of questions could be raised, such as the following:

(a) Are we producing the right kind of drugs or is there an overmarketing and nonuseful consumption of certain compounds or mixtures, both pharmacologically active and nonactive?

(b) What will be the consequences for the affluent society of increased availability and use of drugs affecting basic biological mechanisms?

(c) How will the widespread consumption of drugs affect the future disease panorama, especially diseases with a long induction period?

(d) Are the present testing procedures for harmful side effects of and the registration procedures for drugs satisfactory and is the general public safeguarded?

(e) How is the risk–benefit complex going to be handled with the introduction of new, highly potent drugs engineered from the results of the dramatic advances in biochemistry and molecular biology research?

(f) Are enough research efforts being devoted to the development of therapeutically useful copies of the active substances in the organism itself (biological drugs, gene therapy)?

FUTURISTIC PROJECTIONS

In order to comment on the questions raised it may be of interest to look ahead and try to get some idea of future social and medical developments in the rapidly growing health sector. The world population will increase, although the futuristic projections vary. The age distribution of the population is shifting, with an increase in the fraction over 65 years of age, which will become a considerable part of the total population, at least in certain countries. Furthermore, a majority of the population will tend to live in urban areas. Economic expansion will most probably continue, with the consequence that the rhythm and abundance of social transformations will increase, not only in the industrial sector and labor market, but also in the service sectors, taken in a broad sense. Adaptation to such changes will impose extra stress on people, particularly individuals in the higher-age groups and those with less tolerance, due to biochemical individuality. The increased rate of change will cause the susceptible portion of the population to grow, with increasing health problems as a consequence. Such a development prompts new attitudes to our value systems and will have substantial ethical and economic consequences.

The physical environment is changing rapidly with pollution of water, air, and soil and possibly worldwide climatic changes. These aspects were fully reviewed during the UN environment conference in Stockholm, 1972. Sulfur dioxide in air, nitrates in water, chlorinated hydrocarbons in various media, to take a few examples, add to the stress of man. Some scientists even contend that the desertization now manifest in the West African Sahelian zone is man-made. Although active environmental-protection measures are being taken around the world, the size of future industrial and social operations could lead to still further deterioration if no drastic countermeasures are introduced. To the serious problems of the polluted physical environment should be added the whole sphere of adulteration of foodstuffs. We are clearly moving away from natural foodstuffs and various types of additives will be used, whose long-term effects on man are little known.

Thus we can expect that the pollution of the physical environment, the action of unnatural food additives, and the greater mental stress inherent in living conditions will result in the space below what might be termed the "clinical horizon" becoming more and more used up, so that an extra load on the individual will be more liable to produce a signal above this horizon, in other words, be manifested as a disease condition. The whole set of conditions mentioned will most probably have the effect of making therapy with several kinds of drugs more complicated, due to unwanted synergistic effects with respect to environmental pollution.

DISEASE PANORAMA

In the field of medicine itself, mortality causes have changed drastically during this century. The former high death rate from infectious diseases has dropped radically in the developed countries, where the main cause of death is now the degenerative and chronic diseases, such as cancer and cardiovascular disorders. Regarding infections, it seems that chronic recurrent infections, such as those that trigger off chronic bronchitis and a whole number of chronic kidney troubles, are increasing. There seem to be indications that toxic elements and compounds in the environment could be harmful to the kidneys and give similar damage.

The increase in the incidence of neuroses is considered to be serious, reflecting difficulties in adapting to an increasingly complex society.

Finally in this sketchy presentation, one could mention that diseases or abnormalities of genetic origin are likely to increase with the progress of therapy, which allows those affected to reach reproductive ages. But also the occurrence of toxic mutagenic compounds in the environment and in food may well have a similar effect, as may the side effects of a widespread use of drugs, i.e., increasing genetic malformations and teratogenecity.

AREAS FOR MEDICAL ACTION

In summary, the major future areas for medical action will be in prevention and in the handling of chronic diseases, including the diseases of old age. This trend will necessitate the development of new therapeutic means, but what it really implies is that we need more basic knowledge on the biological mechanisms such as growth and differentiation, biological control mechanisms, and control substances, including the biological mechanism underlying the process of aging. There is no doubt that we are well under way, especially thanks to recent advances in biochemistry and molecular biology, including immunology. The social and human urgency of making available still more effective tools in the hands of expanding health systems necessitates considerable increases in the allocation of resources to fundamental biological and medical research as well as to applied research and development in the fields of medicine and environment.

In general, there has been an annual increase in drug consumption of 3 to 5% in developed countries. In one particular case, France, it is estimated that 4 to 5% of household expenditure will be on medicaments by the year 1985. The conflicting trends became more disparate, with the medical profession and the public calling for more effective drugs and the consumer, i.e., government and individuals, calling for lower prices. If the present pattern continues, the price of drugs will increase at least threefold within 20 years. Price reductions can be achieved through lower production costs and reduced profits, which implies larger production units with large markets. The rocketing cost of research will probably have to be met by government participation. This is not a unique development; governments are already responsible for high-cost research such as space, high energy physics, and nuclear power.

It is however not only the processing of new types of drugs and their beneficial effects that must be backed up by fundamental new knowledge. It becomes equally necessary to sharpen the tools for testing and evaluation before a drug is marketed. The latter may become increasingly difficult for two reasons: one is that, due to an increased general toxic background from environmental pollution, tests must be conducted to ensure that the synergistic effects are insignificant. Secondly, when drugs for the prevention and treatment of chronic diseases are to be evaluated, the time constant is very long and one wonders whether it will ever be possible to market a product as free from side effects as one would like.

So the problem of specifying test conditions for drugs becomes one of defining an acceptable risk in relation to the beneficial effects. It is a serious matter that the definition of risk is highly susceptible to economic arguments, producers' profits, and the possible reduction of health-service costs. It is the task of scientists to define the risk and the responsibility of politicians to set the acceptable limits.

In the United States, the introduction of new drugs (new chemical entities and other new drugs) numbered about 240 per year in the period 1951 to 1962. For the period 1963 to 1970 the corresponding figure was 110. In 1962, the amendments to the Food, Drug, and Cosmetic Act came into force, requiring more vigorous control especially regarding the introduction of patented "socially wasteful" pharmaceutical products. The lower figure for new drugs has several causes, one being that the number of synonymous drugs is decreasing. In Sweden, studies are under way to further decrease the number of drugs with identical action.

The relatively new interest in the effect of toxic chemicals in the environment has led to proposals for an international registry and an international pooling of resources for toxicity testing. These efforts have much to learn from well-developed toxicology and pharmacology but it appears that a happy symbiosis may be created for certain aspects in the evaluation of long-term adverse effects on the human population. It may well be that specifications for the intake of certain chemical compounds (whether prescribed or acquired unintentionally) that have an effect on the genetic system will have to incorporate concepts like those employed for radiation, that is a concept analogous to "total dose commitment." In other words, consideration for the genetic state of future generations will be brought into the overall assessment.

ETHICAL PROBLEMS

But let us return for a moment to the problem of testing drugs. Obviously, short-term curative effects can be ascertained relatively easily but the adverse effects are more difficult to estimate. If a new drug such as chloramphenicol, which has a definite curative effect on several diseases but can induce a disease such as aplastic anemia, is held for testing for a long time, what is the human and economic balance between those who are saved in a high mortality condition and the fewer who acquire a serious disease? The desire of the individual in a critical situation to gain access to any conceivable form of treatment conflicts with the overall considerations for large-scale use. This classic conflict, which has been described dramatically in *Martin Arrowsmith*, highlights the inability of our value systems to deal with problems of this kind in a truly humanistic sense.

New, complicated drugs with very precise actions are being developed all the time for the treatment of serious diseases. Such specific drugs require a complicated means of delivery into the organism, with a continuous check on the concentration of the drug itself as well as its metabolites in the body fluids. Such advanced drug therapy can be given to only a limited number of patients, even in the developed countries. The resemblance to the ethical and moral problems connected with the transplantation of the kidney and heart is striking. Only a few of the many who should receive such treatment can obtain it.

LIMITS TO STRESS TOLERANCE

Today, when so much discussion is focused on the limits to growth and the outer limits for human existence, it is interesting to observe that the debate is influenced mainly by economists and systems analysts, who among other things predict that limits will be set by various types of more or less homemade, egoistic energy crises, the shortage of nonrenewable resources, pollution, and other more physical factors. The individual and the protoplasm are assumed to have an almost infinite tensile strength. However, the cumulative effects on the human germ plasm of the products of modern living and the cumulative attacks on mental and physical well-being by changes that recur many times in the lifespan of man are problems which deserve much interest and research. It may well be that we find reactions in man and society that are more important than the presently much discussed availability and control of nonrenewable natural resources. However, man's knowledge and capacity today offer unique possibilities, never experienced before, of creating a society with great opportunity for all. Our hope is not only for new and better drugs but also that all people in the world will have equal access to them.

ACKNOWLEDGMENT

This chapter was originally published in *Acta Pharmaceutica Suecica* 10:353 (1973). The permission for reprinting is gratefully acknowledged. Some minor changes have been introduced.

Emotions—Their Parameters and Measurement,
edited by L. Levi.
Raven Press, New York © 1975

Ethical and Social Implications

Talcott Parsons

William James Hall 558, Harvard University, Cambridge, Massachusetts 02138

INTRODUCTION

The title "Ethical and Social Implications" contains a possible critical ambiguity. I would like to begin this commentary with a brief discussion of this ambiguity. The terms "ethical" and "social" are at least on a first-stage level not strikingly difficult. The term "implications," however, raises problems. We are dealing with implications of the findings of research endeavors, which cover a rather wide range of considerations. They extend in reference all the way from the most definitely "biological" problems about structure and process in the organic world with reference to both individual organism and species. Many of the contributions to this volume could be said to have been more contributions to biology and its subdiscipline of physiology than anything else.

From this "biological base" the concerns of this volume extended into another very controversial range, what is often called that of "the psychology of personality." The drawing of the boundaries, or, indeed, the question of whether any boundaries are relevant has been a perennially controversial question among people who have identified themselves as psychologists. There is, however, an important school of thought that considers the level of personality to be analytically distinct from the purely organic level. However this may be, it is some time since there have been serious and influential voices asserting that the study of human culture and society should be considered to be branches of biology, if that concept is defined in a traditional sense. A good example is linguistics. The study of language clearly roots in, in a certain sense, that of phonetics, namely, the organic processes of the production of oral sounds in complex combinations. Very few linguists, however, would contend today that the "really fundamental" things to know for the linguistic scientist are phonetics, and that semantics, grammar, and syntax can either safely be bypassed or can rigorously be derived from phonetic considerations.

It is clear that my assignment is to discuss a few aspects of ethical and social implications at the human cultural-social level, and I will assume that this is analytically distinct from what has traditionally been a biological level.

It is on this background that I should like to try to state what I have felt to be the ambiguity of the term "implications." One primary possible meaning of that word concerns the *cognitive* implications of the findings of research in the various aspects of the topic of this volume. The other concerns the implication of these findings for human *action* in a sense that goes beyond the acquisition of knowledge to concern questions: "what should be *done* about it?" I would like to stress the importance of the analytical distinction between these two possible meanings of the word "implication." The problem of the meaning of the distinction and its relation to the conception of the role of scientists in the modern world, and particularly of their ethical and social responsibilities, is a very critical one. I also think that it is a problem that initially should be clarified at the level of the social and cultural sciences, rather than immediately and directly at the level of the biological sciences.

This is emphatically not to say that biological considerations are irrelevant. It is almost obvious that findings in the field of this volume at biological levels are highly relevant. More generally, however, I would assume a basic continuity, which should be understood in an evolutionary perspective, between what are frequently called the organic and the cultural-social realms. A few highlights of this continuity will be of central importance to the rest of the present statement. I would, however, like to suggest the centrality of the position of man, and rather definitely man as scientist, in this larger picture. Although there is not reason to deny cognitive capacities to subhuman species; indeed this is a very central concern of comparative psychology. Very few students of that subject would use the term "scientist" to characterize their animal subjects, be they rats or even chimpanzees. The particular level of cognitive capacity we associate with the term "scientist" seems to be a distinctly human level.

It follows from this consideration that our *knowledge* of the behavior of organisms is a function of human capacities, which I would define to be basically dependent on cultural and human-level social factors, and indeed this is true of knowledge of the physical world. In the sciences, the "observer" is always human, and since Einstein, we have come to appreciate that the more general and abstract forms of scientific knowledge in whatever field must always take account of what has come to be called "the position of the observer." In all human knowledge, then, and that considers notions of its social and ethical implications, there is an inherent circular factor. Humans, to be sure, observe and interpret many phenomena of the nonhuman world, but there is a fundamental sense in which they are incapable of doing so in anything except human terms, that is, humanly relevant terms in some sense. We think that this fact has much to do with the nature of the responsibilities of scientists and of course of their vulnerabilities. Some of the latter may be at the primarily cognitive level, but even here it is only the critical views of their fellow humans that can serve as a source of the correction of scientific error and bias. Human science is a matter of social organization, not merely of inborn capacity to understand the "external world." Considerations of this sort apply even more cogently when we think of not merely the validity and cognitive significance of scientific propositions and assertions, but also of their "implications" in the second sense outlined above for the larger human situation.

THE "HUMAN" SCIENCES

Let us step a little further into the complicated realm of the nature and implications of the attempt to study human social and cultural phenomena by essentially the methods of science or of cognitive rationality. It seems to me that the problems covered in this volume should be regarded as centrally involved in this area. Again, if we adopt for the moment the term emotion, human students of both human and animal emotions can scarcely avoid in some sense or other involving their own emotions. One aspect of this involvement might be illustrated by the related problems of vivisection and the ethics of experimentation with human subjects. I doubt if many students of animal phenomena dissect and perhaps destroy an organism at the evolutionary level of a cat without some feelings about their intervention in the world of life. The ethical problems of experimentation on human subjects have been much discussed in recent times (see, Freund, 1969, 1970; Barber, Laley, Lughlin, Makarushka, and Sullivan, 1973).

Another principal aspect, however, concerns the problem area which seems to have a bewildering combination of continuities and similarities on the one hand, differences on the other, as we pass along the spectrum from the "purely" organic to the "purely" cultural-social levels. At the conspicuously subhuman-animal level such as the classic study of the learning behavior of rats there is no lack of concern with phenomena that most psychologists do not hesitate to label "cognitive." A case significant to me was the view of the late E. C. Tolman on the role of what he called "cognitive maps." At the same time students of animal behavior have, as is exemplified in many of the chapters in this volume, been concerned with the emotional components of animal behavior. If we stick to the example of classical learning theory, the involved discussions of the nature and significance of "reward" lead the investigator into something that is by no means in a simple sense a set of problems about cognition.

If we are to recognize an analytically independent psychological-personality level, it is clear that a parallel set of problems has been exceedingly prominent at that level. An excellent example is furnished by Professor Lazarus *(this volume)*. Specifically in discussing the role of emotions in self-regulation of behavior as he spoke of it, if I understand him correctly, Lazarus also pointed to the indispensability of a process he called "cognitive appraisal," without which, he contended, the self-regulative functions of emotional processes could not operate effectively. In my opinion, the Lazarus point of view was particularly congenial because he stressed the role of emotion not merely as a phenomenon of adaptive crises at human or animal levels, but as an ongoing equilibrating process that should be conceived to operate in all types of behavioral phases and situations.

To those conversant with the world of social science it is saliently evident that a parallel preoccupation is of paramount significance there as well. The problem of the role of what is usually called "rationality" in social affairs, its consequences, and the limitations of "rationalistic" paradigms for understanding social action have been intensively discussed at the very least from the Age of the Enlightenment on. A landmark in this discussion was constituted by the views of the great sociologist Max Weber some two generations ago, which centered around his conception of "the process of rationalization" and its role in the social and cultural historical development. In these disciplines there has been a growing recent concern with the phenomena of nonrational, noncognitive determinants of cultural and social developments and specifically how they were to be related to the rational or cognitive. Some have adopted essentially a "zero-sum" point of view alleging that with the increase of rationality, the significance of nonrational factors *ipso facto* declined. This is a position to which I cannot subscribe. In any case there has also been an intensive search for ways of conceptualizing the nonrational or noncognitive components and the concept emotion has figured prominently in these attempts. Another, however, which I would like to discuss briefly is that of affect, which I understand in more than an individual-psychological sense.

It seems to me that affect, the term of course being borrowed from psychology, can and should be used to designate a generalized medium of interchange in the sense in which I and a number of associates have in recent years been talking about such media at the level of the general system of action and of the social system. Money is the prototypical medium of exchange as it operates in the economic concerns of social systems, but there are others such as political power and influence, which have been discussed in special technical meanings. Affect, I think, should be treated as a generalized medium at the level of the general system of action, which includes both the personality and organic aspects of individuals as well as social and cultural systems, which we conceive to articulate and interchange with each other. Among the media at the general-action-system level in which list I would include intelligence in a special technical meaning and something I call performance capacity, it seems to me that affect should be anchored in the social system, not the personality of the individual. I mean anchored in the sense in which money is anchored in the economy as a functionally defined sector of a society. Its use, however, is by no means confined to the economy, but it is a medium of interchange with other subsystems, notably the consuming household. The household, however, is not primarily in modern societies an agency of economic production. Affect thus mediates relations between social systems, the personalities of individuals who participate in them, and the cultural systems that are essential to action.

I would like to suggest that the concept emotion be treated as that of another generalized medium of interchange, but one internal to the personality of the individual. Emotion at its own level would be conceived to have functions cognate for the personality to those of affect for the general system of action, namely, integrative functions. It seems to me that this conception is consistent with various views, but I think particularly those put forward by Lazarus.

INTERNAL AND EXTERNAL ENVIRONMENTS

There are two further sets of considerations that need to be discussed briefly before coming around to the main climax of my analysis. Dr. John Mason *(this volume)* strongly emphasized the distinction between the external and the internal environments in a context that particularly focused on the organism and its functioning using the concept internal environment in the sense of its originator Claude Bernard. I think that this basic distinction is applicable also to social phenomena. The concept of social facts in the technical sense used by Emile Durkheim seems to me to designate essentially what Durkheim also called the social environment as the environment in which individual members of a society act. From the point of view of human action as a system, I would consider the social environment essentially to be the environment of action in general. It is clearly not the external environment to which, for example, technology is oriented and which figures so prominently in biological thinking. Like the internal environment of the organism in Bernard's sense, however, it has the very important property of a higher order of stability than characterizes the external environment of action. Both processes of social action development analogous to the embryological development of the individual organism and processes of control are necessary to bring about this special order of stability, which of course is not absolute, but neither is the internal environment of the organism absolutely stable.

With respect to both categories of internal environment there is now quite general agreement that stabilization operates through what have come to be called cybernetic or feedback mechanisms. At the physiological level such conceptions have figured prominently in this volume, and I think essentially parallel use of such concepts is parallel to the level of action and notably within that of social system with which I am particularly concerned. The symbolic structures of what we call the cultural system are particularly central to the nature and operation of such mechanisms of self-regulation, which I take to be synonymous with cybernetic control.

What I have referred to above as generalized media of interchange are centrally important in the processes of self-regulation as is illustrated by the role of money in market systems. Influence seems to me to be the most important medium with primarily integrative functions in the social system. I might illustrate this by a case that is particularly familiar to students of Anglo-American law, namely, the role of judicial opinions written by judges of appelate courts. Whether or not they are the opinions that justify the binding majority decision or are written by dissident members of the court to justify their unwillingness to join the majority, such opinions justify judicial decisions, but do much more than that in that through their impact on members of the legal profession and the future actions of courts of law, they play a very important role in shaping the development of the law and in producing a far higher level of consistency in the decisions of many different courts and in the advice given by legal counsel than could otherwise be obtained. The importance of phenomena of this type at the social level explains why I was so particularly interested in Lazarus' chapter with its development of the conception of self-regulation in the individual personality and the role of emotion in these processes.

CONCLUSION

The study of emotions at biopsychological levels, of affect at the level of general action, and, indeed, of social influence has a special importance to the theme with which I began the present statement. It is the use of methods of cognitive rationality to attempt to understand the nonrational components that influence human functioning and behavior at all of the levels that I have sketched, from the purely organic to the purely cultural. Freud's analysis of the unconscious was, of course, one of the great pioneering steps in developing such methods. And it is particularly important to be explicitly aware of the complex duality of the relations between rational and nonrational in the case of Freud and in many other cases. This problem area, furthermore, includes the task of not merely using rational methods to study the nonrational, but coming to understand how the two sets of components are related to each other. Again, I thought that Lazarus's discussion of the phenomenon he called "cognitive appraisal" was a very important statement of this relationship and I have been working quite intensively on the parallel problem for the level of social systems and general systems of action. The operation of nex*us* of social relationships which have the property of solidarity involves such delicate balances of rational and nonrational aspects. The affective components I think of as mainly nonrational, but the system clearly will not operate in a stable and effective manner without some equivalent of the cognitive appraisal of which Lazarus speaks. It is this integration of the rational and the nonrational that must provide the answer to the people who think of them as antithetical tendencies in human affairs standing in a zero-sum relation to each other.

Scientific research is from the point of view of the operation of social and cultural systems a peculiarly important and complex phenomenon. One of the main reasons for the prevalence of deep ambivalences about it is the fact that it is inherently a mode of bringing about change. Successful research is always a way of strengthening the rational cognitive component of action. This, however, cannot occur without repercussions on the nonrational components and the balances between the rational and the nonrational. The impact of these changes and their repercussions can clearly be highly disturbing to the stability and equilibrium of the cultural and social systems. The possibility of such disturbances seems to me to lie at the center of the topic on which I have been speaking. Change and disturbance always involve some combination of destructive and constructive potentialities. Whatever may be our conception of the responsibilities of the individual research scientist, the magnitude of the changes that modern science has been introducing is such that there is an imperative need for adequate mechanisms for the responsible management of the disturbances of which I speak.

Like the unconscious, which Freud studied with such pioneering originality, the social disturbances generated by the impact of new scientific knowledge can only be responsibly managed if there is adequate cognitive understanding of them. This, to me, is perhaps the most fundamental reason why a society in which physical and biological science has been making great progress has an imperative need for, I would say, an equally high level of scientific work in the social and cultural fields. The cognitive understanding of social disturbances is not by itself an adequate basis for their control in constructive directions. It is, however, an indispensible factor in such control. Social scientists have many other responsibilities than to lay cognitive foundations for this kind of control, but it seems to me that this is one of the most important of their responsibilities.

REFERENCES

Barber, B., Laley, J., Lughlin, J., Makarushka, and Sullivan, D. (1973): *Research on Human Subjects: Problems of Social Control in Medical Experimentation*, Russel Sage Foundation, New York.

Freund, P. A., ed. (1969) and (1970): *Experimentation with Human Subjects*, The Daedalus Library, George Braziller, New York.

Emotions—Their Parameters and Measurement,
edited by L. Levi.
Raven Press, New York © 1975

Ethical Problems Created by Commercial Psychopharmacology

Sven Britton

Immunobiology Group, Wallenberg Laboratory, Lilla Frescati, S-104 05 Stockholm 50, Sweden

THE MYTH OF THE OBJECTIVE DOCTOR

Most doctors believe that their choice of drugs in medical practice is uninfluenced by any other forces than the very rational and professional ones, such as, scientific papers, medical experience, education. They look upon the advertising and sales promotion activities of the drug industry with a feeling of superiority which they — at least in Sweden — often express when confronted personally with the representatives of this industry. This idea of doctors may be explained on the basis of their relative ignorance of the forces ruling economic life in most western societies.

In Sweden the drug industry spends each year very roughly $2,500 per doctor in order to make him prescribe drugs costing approximately $25,000. As the drug industry, like all other industries in Western society, operates with a view to obtaining maximal profits, it would be very unlikely to incur unnecessary expenditure. In point of fact, I think it is essential for the drug industry that doctors keep their dream of not being influenced by commercial arguments because otherwise they could be expected to react against its sales promotion methods.

The financial interests of the drug industry are not in natural opposition to the health of people. A good drug which makes ill persons healthy is easy to sell. However, more essential for the drug industry than the curative effects of a drug is its selling effects. The prime goal of the drug industry is therefore to make a drug which can be used against a very common disease or — still better — many common diseases. (Rationalization, resulting in an increasingly narrow production spectrum and industrialized mass production, has made it uneconomic and therefore uninteresting to produce drugs, however effective, against very rare diseases, a situation which may soon create difficulties for people with such diseases for which pharmacological remedies are available at present.)

EMOTIONS AND DRUGS–A SCHLARAFFENLAND
FOR THE DRUG INDUSTRY

The ideal drug for the industry, as far as profits are concerned, is one which can be prescribed for an ill-defined category of diseases with floating borders against the healthy state and thus likely to strike all individuals. This is where emotions come in so handy for the drug industry. The greatest explorer of this field—where much more exploration is to be expected—is the financial supporter of this volume on parameters of emotion, Hoffmann la Roche.

Emotions are ill-defined, difficult to measure but easy to sense, and thus an ideal outlet for drugs. Fatigue, anxiety, and sadness are emotional entities which have been opened for drug treatment. Within a very short time, drugs against these feelings have been willingly mass-distributed to people by doctors.

The ease with which such drugs are sold has many explanations. First, these drugs are good in so far as they cut the expression of some emotions. It has been claimed continuously that they are nontoxic, with little risk for addiction, without considering that the development of addictional habits to a family of drugs may take a long time. They cater to almost all doctors, as patients displaying these emotional reactions and seeking advice can now be seen to the door more easily, without impairing the doctor's professional image.

Since we have decided that emotional reactions are physiological responses to environmental stimuli, the question is whether they should be interfered with by drugs at all. *Is it in the interest of the individual—or society—for emotional reactions to be muted by drugs?* Apart from its medical aspects, this question has wide social, psychological, and political implications. These have not been discussed and we can hardly blame the drug industry, which has not tried to hide its intentions.

A PLEA TO LIMIT THE EMOTIONAL ENTITY
REQUIRING DRUG TREATMENT

No, the ones to blame are those prescribing these pills, playing this game. And as long as we have a drug industry working with the same ideals as the cosmetics or cartoon industry, we doctors must act as an effective—from the point of view of national and individual health—filter between producer and consumer.

This is a formidable task. To my mind it is natural that society should care for the development and fabrication of drugs, just as it cares for other health problems. Medical and social needs, not the accumulation of profits, must guide the production of drugs. In my country, society only pays for the drugs, via almost total subsidies, while their manufacture is still in private hands. Thus, I think the prime task in this respect is to work for society to take over the drug industry. At the same time, I think doctors must practice their ambitions to keep people healthy by preventing the distribution of drugs for which there is no real medical need. This know-how may still prove useful in a future when society owns the drug industry.

One means of doing this is to require that the illness against which pharmacological aid is claimed be distinguished from other illnesses and, more importantly, from health. This is varyingly difficult with somatic diseases but consistently difficult or impossible with psychiatric and psychosomatic disorders. We must therefore expect that this is where the drug industry will concentrate its forces and we, accordingly, must strengthen our resistance.

I hope this volume has helped in developing methods for measuring emotional reactions and also considered what should be regarded as a pathological reaction to an emotional stimuli. As an immunologist working with infectious diseases I am certainly not an expert in this field although I, like all kinds of doctors, encounter patients who seek advice for emotional problems. I still wish to emphasize that in my view there are at least two parameters to consider when defining emotional reactions as pathological. One is the social impact of the reaction — whether the patient can fulfill his duties to his macro and, to a lesser extent, micro society, i.e., work and perform the expected family role. The other is whether the reaction will upset his inner psychological balance. These parameters are admittedly interrelated but the traditional ambition of the doctor is to cover the former, because this is where the disabilities are most clearly seen and where they have the greatest social impact. But with this attitude the doctor is serving the prevailing system in that, to the best of his ability, he sees to it that the wheels of society keep turning.

While writing down these thoughts I realize that it will be difficult — and dangerous — for any group or institution to set out to define what is pathological and what is not in the field of emotional reactions. I certainly do not want to call for a society in which a bureaucratic institution sets these limits. I merely want doctors and behavioral scientists to challenge the invisible borders drawn up by the commercial drug industry and accepted without thorough discussion by the present and past generations of doctors. In opposition to the drug industry I urge great generosity in what is to be regarded as healthy with respect to emotional reactions, thus allowing people to face emotional signals with brain and sensory organs unpoisoned by drugs. With such an attitude medical practice will certainly be a bit heavier to run but it should leave a clearer conscience.

Emotions – Their Parameters and Measurement,
edited by L. Levi.
Raven Press, New York © 1975

Session 6: Discussion

Chairmen: Arne Engström and Stewart Wolf

Parsons: I would like to speak of the ethical aspect more implicitly than explicitly because of the extraordinarily close way in which ethical and social considerations are interwoven. To quote the great French sociologist Emil Dercant, "society is a very central moral phenomenon. Its structure is deeply organized about values and moral norms." The distinction between looking at society from a predominently analytical, in that sense objective, point of view and looking at it from the point of view of the guidance of action, that is trying to establish what ought to happen and to give guidelines how to achieve what it is felt ought to happen, are two distinct questions. Nevertheless, I would prefer to concentrate on the former and leave it to you to draw your inferences in the other context.

This involves the very complicated problems of the relation in general between knowledge and action on the one hand and the use of human subjects in the pursuit of knowledge, on the other. When we are studying human phenomena as such, we can rely only in part on nonhuman subjects. The student of human society, almost in the nature of the case, confines himself to human subjects in relation to a variety of artifacts.

I would like to really start with the very commonplace observation that research done by human agents, whatever the subject matter of the research, is always in the pursuit of some human interest. The rats, monkeys, and other animals that have been described in this volume as research subjects were not particularly interested in what the investigator was trying to do with them. The interest was the human interest of the investigating team, and, as such, all research is part of the system of human activity even if conducted by individuals who are isolated for a certain part of their work. It is fundamentally a social enterprise. Otherwise, researchers would not try to communicate with each other as we have here. This is another way of saying the point that has been made so often in discussions of science, especially since Einstein, of the fundamental importance to science and knowledge of the position of the observer. And even where it is astronomy, the observer is one or more human beings with some kind of location in the universe being studied. That is just as true but with varying emphasis and combinations of factors when you move from the very remote celestial bodies to the study of some human beings by other human beings in their own sociocultural settings. If we call it research, of course, we assert a kind of primacy of the cognitive aspect of interest in the objects of research. We speak of research as the pursuit of knowledge. We are less concerned with other aspects of man's relation to the things he studies than we are with knowledge about them. But if they are living beings, we must learn about the subjects including what they know, how they learn, what noncognitive aspects of their life, organism, personality are significant. And I think you could say in the study of human phenomena that there has been a tendency to move steadily further into the realm of the nonrational aspects of the behavior motivation of human beings. But, it is not, in my mind, an epistemological paradox that we develop rational methods to study the nonrational. No matter what the spectrum of opinion about Freud may be, he embarked on one relatively advanced phase of that great adventure to use the methods of rational analysis to try to understand the nonrational aspects of the human personality or human motivation. When you go into the interconnections between the subjectively personal and the organic, of which behaving subjects are very generally not even aware, you are pursuing the same kind of line, it seems to me.

In the sciences dealing primarily with human beings, one must take the analytical distinction between, on the one hand, concrete human beings and concrete nonhuman organisms, and, on the other, those aspects of the concrete human entity, which are distinctively human, as distinct from the aspects which are shared with nonhuman species in the organic world. That very subtle boundary line is important.

If we take certain great principles which came into our thinking through the biological sciences, we must connect these to things having continuity within this whole range of principles having to do with living systems. One of the great principles in that case is adaptation, in the sense it was originally formulated by Darwin. The concept has a longer history than that, but a particularly salient and influential form was proposed by Darwin which has been very substantially advanced since then. It has not only advanced within the biological sense but also extended into what we usually think of as the behavioral or sociocultural sciences. I think adaptation is as fundamental a concept in those areas as in the organic aspect, and it is a very essential concept.

There are two aspects of adaption I would like to mention. One is that I think in what you might call the first post-Darwinian era use of the concept the tendency was to think of adaptation in a more or less passive sense. The organism, the species, whatever the living system of reference was adapted *to* the environment. There was very little thinking of adaptation *of* the environment by active intervention of the living systems. Active intervention is by no means confined to man, although he has carried that mode of adaptation much further than any evolutionary predecessor, but beavers, after all, build dams and change the course of streams. There are many examples of changing of the environment by what living species do in that environment. The more active the species, the more this change is likely to be significant.

Man has outdone all other species by a very large margin. So much so that we hear cries suggesting that he ought to stop having an impact on the environment and adapt himself to his nonhuman environment. But man is different in a set of respects that came a little bit into our previous discussion. Man is not only a social animal, but a culture-bearing and culture-making animal, and as such quantitatively unique. There are protocultures at nonhuman levels but there is nothing that sociologists or anthropologists would call a full-blown culture at nonhuman levels. We have discussed language as an especially important phenomenon in the cultural area. And linguistics as a recently very rapidly developing science has had to develop a sophisticated understanding of certain physical phenomena, namely in the field of phonology, the processes by which the human vocal apparatus can form variant but precisely definable combinations of sounds and utter those sounds in a way that is not only audible to other human beings but also intelligible. The intelligibility extends to extremely complicated matters, even in the speech of ordinary "uneducated" people. I have never learned the language of a nonliterate people, but I am assured that it is not an easy task. For example, the famous Navaho language in the American Southwest is a very difficult and complicated language. Anthropologists have made grammars and dictionaries of the Navaho language, but even at its early stages of evolution language is an extremely complicated symbolic phenomenon.

The social cultural system is part of the human condition. We have discussed the background and history of psychological science; Dr. Groen mentioned the mind-body problem which has played such a role in the history of psychology. I would like to suggest that we who deal with living systems at the human level have to go beyond that; our system is a pluralistic system far beyond any single duality, because culture is not mind in the older psychological sense. It is an analytically independent set of entities. A language is not part of one living organism; it is a part of culture. It is internalized in many millions of living organisms who know the particular language. The English language is not a psychological entity in any ordinary sense of the term psychological. I can say it is my language, but it is no more my language than the language of millions of other English-speaking people. And it is the same language that they all speak. But if I have a fantasy or an idea or an emotion, that is my fantasy or idea or emotion. It may be similar to those held by many other persons.

Society is an intermediate or a social system, as I prefer to say because I think of a society as one particular kind of social system, as a system constituted by the interaction, when we stick to the human level, of a plurality of individuals who may or may not be in direct interactive contact with every other. If you take what is often called Western society, there are millions upon millions of members of Western society whom not one of the people here has ever directly interacted with. But to say that we are not fellow members of the same society, does not make sense, in my opinion. I think the concept of society is very close, in its logical nature and structure, to the concept of species, at the organic level. It is not identical with species; there is only one human species, organically speaking, but there are many human societies. It is cognate with the concept, species, with an indefinite number of individual phenotypic organisms at any given time in any given generation, and with a nonphenotypic, temporally continuing heritage which is essentially what we call culture. There is a very close relationship between the genetic constitution of species, on the one hand, and the cultural constitution of societies, on the other.

One specific problem has concerned social scientists intimately for a long time, but acutely in recent years, that is, the categories which are variously termed the cognitive aspect of the organization of human behavior. In some sense they are adaptive relative to environments, not only of the individual but also of larger aggregates of living beings. There is a long heritage, with what is sometimes called the affective aspect. Although the official term used for this symposium has been the parameters of emotion, I have noticed that the term "affect" has appeared in the discussions rather frequently, and some people use it almost as a synonym for emotion. There may be some important problems from my kind of point of view concealed under these common terms, but there will not be an opportunity to go into them. I would like to suggest that such categories as cognition and its related concepts are categories which are appropriate to use beginning with the completely nonverbal or nonsymbolic. If you take the usage of "cognitive" by a behavior psychologist like the late Edward Tolman and the concept cognitive map he created with reference to the behavior of rats and the usage of humanists and sociologists when they are talking about knowledge, technical competence and things of that sort should be sufficiently similar so that they belong in the same series. I would think that any radical dissociation that said what concepts are used in analyzing the learning behavior of rats has absolutely nothing to do with what concepts are used to analyze the behavior of human individuals who are students in a university or investigators in a research laboratory. These are common elements for which such terms as "cognitive" seem to me to be appropriate.

What we have got to do if we are going to have a comprehensive analysis of things human is to follow the continuities and variabilities of these syndromes all the way through the world of living systems. Of course, they vary at different levels, but this does not mean that there is sheer and absolute discontinuity between those levels. I would say much the same thing for the other syndrome area. At the level from which I speak, affect is a more congenial word than emotion. But however this is conceptually clarified, it seems to me that it is essential that it should be done in a way which can bring out the combination of continuities and variations that apply throughout what are essentially evolutionary levels. That is, there are plenty of living species that do not have what could be called a brain at all. And there seems to have been a very important evolutionary development by which the mammalian brain emerged. From this point of view culture is an evolutionary emergence which has come as part of an evolutionary process which is fundamentally part of the general process of evolution. But it can be as different from what any subhuman species has as the human brain is from a worm's brain. I dissected worms in college biology: they have a paraganglion and virtually nothing more. I wanted to emphasize that continuity. If this continuity has fundamental significance and there is relevance of what is done at physiological levels for cultural levels and vice versa, then the work you have been doing may be a contribution to the solution of certain acute problems of human society at this time. The problem I particularly refer to is the wide-spread impression that the cognitively governed elements of human society and culture have tended to get out of hand relative to the noncognitive elements. If the noncognitive elements are to be brought into place and into the proper balance and articulation with the cognitive, it seems to me they must be cognitively understood. But the many differences to which I have been referring between the levels may be very dangerous to extrapolate in too simple a sense from physiological levels to human sociocultural levels, and to say: we have found this to be true of the autonomic nervous system relative to what you have been referring to as emotion, therefore let us apply it immediately to the organization of human governments. I think there are a good many intermediate steps on which the physiologist needs the help of the social scientist. We social scientists do not know what we ought to know and certainly what we hope the future generations of our craft will come to know, but we know something that is way beyond the common sense of nonsocial sciences.

There has been much discussion of the environment in this volume. From my perspective, in order to work out the social and ethical consequences, you have got to have more than two environments, not only the internal environment of the organism and external environment of a particular organism, but also what we call society which is culturally structured as an internal environment. It is not the general environment of Darwinian theory which includes the whole physical environment and all other species than the species of reference, but it is a special, bounded, stabilized environment within which human action takes place and which is constituted by these two sets of components we call cultural and social which must be, at the human level, distinguished from the physical environment, from the nonhuman, organic environment. We must think not in terms of a duality of body and mind, but in the total human condition of pluralism that involves at least four major subsystems.

Britton: I have been asked to take part in this discussion because I have been writing in the Swedish daily press about the ethical aspects of using certain drugs or in using drugs as such. I think that most doctors believe that they make their choice of drugs unaffected by the sales promotion methods used by the drug industry. Most doctors believe that they make their choice on a rather more objective basis, such as scientific papers and what they have learned during their medical training. Why do I bring this up in this context? I do so because I think that emotion is an ideal tool for the drug industry in so far as it is a field where there are many undefined entities that can be treated with drugs. Furthermore, I think that emotions have wide political impact, and the treatment of them has wide political impact. Time is ripe for a discussion of whether emotions should be treated with drugs at all. We have not had this discussion. This discussion can not take place without discussing other nonmedical means of interfering with emotions, such as, alcohol and narcotics. This discussion is not at all exclusively a medical one, as these questions have perhaps even stronger cultural, political, social, and psychological impact. If we come to the conclusion that some emotions should be treated with drugs, then we must rapidly try to define what emotions should be treated with drugs, and, or rather, what emotions should be regarded as pathological because we must realize that it is in the interest of the drug industry not to have any borders between the state of health and the state of disease in this respect, because, by not having any borders, the drug industry has an unlimited amount of people to use these drugs. I believe that most of you here understand that a system of profit is actually guaranteeing progress and happiness in society. I hope that less of you here think that a system of profits is actually a guarantee for a good and medically motivated drug industry.

Wolf: Dr. Britton pointed out that emotions are an ideal medium for the drug company because they are ill-defined. One finds oneself treating an ill-defined syndrome with a drug and I think the implication was that that is bad, but, of course, that is the history of medicine, the history of the development of most drug treatments.

Kagan: Some time ago, I tried to look at the great discoveries that medical science had made in the last 50 years, and I came to the conclusion that probably the most consistent area of practical discovery was pharmacology. I think the drug houses have made considerable contribution to that. One particularly recent example and relevant to our debate here is the psychopharmacological drugs and the policy of reducing duration of stay in mental hospitals. But all health actions which have a chance of doing good also have a chance of doing harm, and it is therefore necessary to evaluate them in terms of safety, efficacy, and cost. Failure to evaluate is unethical. But who is responsible for evaluation? I think it is those who are responsible for treatment. Evaluation is the doctor's responsibility and so is the application of treatment. We have to decide how this will be done in conjunction with the wishes of the community in which we live. I think that it would be surprising if we were to ask the drug houses to evaluate drugs. This is rather like asking you to be the judge in your own trial. Nevertheless they have a better record in doing so than many other branches of medicine, e.g., psychiatry. Before deciding to take the profit motive out of invention of new drugs, you should look at the situations, and there are many, in the world today, where this has been done, and compare what the output is of new and valuable drugs when there is no profit motive, and what the output is when there is a profit motive. Perhaps, when this epidemiological comparison is made and evaluated you may find a good way of removing the profit motive and maintaining the output.

Lader: I agree with Dr. Kagan that one should state where one stands and declare one's interest. What interested me about Dr. Britton's polemic — and I think he has to be polemical here because the case needs stating — was that for all the advertisements of drugs he could have put up a package of corn flakes. Food is essential. People make profit out of food. And, indeed, in a package of corn flakes, the raw material comes to about 10 percent of the final price that you pay in the shop. The argument is not so much against the drug companies in particular; it is against capitalism in general. And the reason that we get so excited about drug companies is that we, as doctors, really feel the brunt of the capitalist process. We are the consumers, in the sense that we control the commercial aspect of drug prescribing, certainly in England where it is on the national health service and almost free to the patient.

There are two ways out of this. One way, which has been taken in the socialist countries and is a perfectly logical way, is to take the profit motive completely away and to nationalize the production of drugs. This is a political question. We can as doctors provide the information upon which political decisions are made, and we can as individuals have our own political beliefs, but we cannot as doctors make political decisions. If, therefore, we do not accept this outcome, then we have to think of ways of safeguarding both ourselves and, of course, our patients within the capitalist system.

The first point I would like to emphasize is that one cannot talk about drugs, the drug industry, and emotions. These are not homogeneous entities. The drug industry ranges from small, back street manufacturing companies who produce one almost unethical product which is full of contaminants and which they try to sell through the bulk of the drug industry, to a few drug companies which are not even working on a drug in the usual way with a profit motive. One cannot talk about the homogeneity of the drug industry. Secondly, one cannot talk about the homogeneity of drugs. Drugs vary from important compounds for trying to combat diseases such as cancer, to patent remedies purporting to prevent dandruff. The balance between the effects which the drug is being sold for and its dangerous effects will vary according to this. If a drug for cancer is effective but yet kills 5 percent of the patients, one would still use it. If a drug for dandruff did that, one would not use it. So one cannot talk about the homogeneity of drugs. Thirdly, one cannot talk about the homogeneity of emotions. The psychiatrist confronted with a patient will deal very differently with a patient with mild complaints of anxiety and depression, than a patient with a pathological, morbid genesis syndrome who could become homicidal the next day and kill his wife. Again, one cannot talk about the homogeneity of emotions, either.

Why do drug companies feel the need to make large profits? The general answer to this is to recoup their developmental and research costs on that drug. This is not so. The reason the drug companies feel the need to make large profits is so that they have the money in hand to develop their next drug. One has seen this in league tables of drug companies; a company can be first or second or third in the league table in 1952 and it can be 25th in 1972. It is a very competitive industry and very often even large drug companies are relying on two or three drugs. The reason they feel they need such large profits is in order to maintain their research for their next drug.

Here is where there is a very definite criticism of the drug industry: they use those profits in the wrong way. What they try to do is to produce drugs which are very similar to other drugs in their own range or to other drugs in the same line which they then introduce in a purely commercial way to try to corner a part of the market. The second thing they do is market a drug for many uses.

It is not all black and white because the problem very often lies with the patent laws. By the time a drug company has developed a drug sufficiently to market it, it may only have 5 years of patent left. We have, in many countries, regulating agencies. And these agencies have set themselves the difficult task of licensing the introduction of new drugs. We have heard that what they have to do is to convince themselves that the safety of the drug is commensurate with the effectiveness of the drug. What I would propose as a way of dealing with this would be for these regulating agencies to only license drugs which were shown to be more effective than the existing remedies. In this way the number of new drugs introduced would drop dramatically, and the drug companies would themselves be protected knowing that if they have introduced a drug for a certain condition then they will have the profits from that drug until a better drug is developed and introduced, not merely an equivalent drug.

Who comes for treatment? As a psychiatrist, the definition of illness is in fact a very easy one. It is an operational definition of the patient who cares sufficiently to put himself into medical care. This is the definition of illness. It is a sociological definition. It is unfortunately the only one that we have. If people, therefore, feel that there are treatments available which will help them, they will come for treatment, and this is why there is such a large problem with conditions like anxiety. We know very well that people in fact do not always come to doctors for treatment for their symptoms. The incidence of alcoholism in many countries exemplifies this. This is, in fact, caused by self-administered drugs, and it is a very large problem. However, I would like to wish Dr. Britton well because some of the points he makes are perfectly valuable ones. And I think that overstatement is one of the few weapons which the consumer has. I also know that the drug industry is well able to take care of itself.

Wolf: I would like to say for the participants in this symposium that it has been a real privilege for us to come to such a fine, well-organized symposium. And I know I speak for the group as a whole in expressing gratitude to Dr. Lennart Levi, who has done this so superbly.

Levi: It is my privilege to thank all of you for the attention you have shown. It is not correct to thank me because this is certainly not a one-man job; it is an entire team who has arranged this. We have done our best, it is up to you to judge if it has been successful or not. It is always a good policy to listen to both sides and that is why we have invited people who have quite different attitudes to quite a number of problems. People have been discussing, rather vigorously in a lively discussion, and that was the intention. Thank you very much, and thank you to the participants and to the staff that has made this possible.

SUBJECT INDEX

A

Acetylcholine, 109, 692-693
Action parameters and measuring
emotions, 421-438
Adaptive behavior, 236
Addison's disease, 256, 289
Adolescent behavior, 242-246
Adrenal medulla, 149, 210-234,
469-497
Adrenocorticosteroids, 245-278,
732
Affect and the subjective state,
73-74, 80, 93
Aggressive behavior, 241-246, 485-
488, 491-494
Agraphia, 667-668
Alimentary inhibition, 191, 430
Alpha rhythm, 286-287
Amitriptyline, 758
Aminergic pathways, 108-109
Amizil, 425
Amphetamines, 263-264, 387-388,
692-697
Amygdala, 100-108, 184, 189, 406,
430, 694
Androgens, 150-181
Anger, 235-278
evolutionary perspective, 236-
242
genetic aspects, 265-268
Antianxiety drugs, 692
Antidepressant drugs, 692, 757-758
Antipsychotic drugs, 692
Antithesis
principle of, 7
Anxiety, 603-617, 713-725, 732-
737, 741-744
autonomic signs of, 734-737
components of, 604-605

conditioned response, 311-340
existential, 749
measurement of, 716-718
physical accompaniments of, 748
popular conceptions of, 713-714
pure, 749-750
state, 609-610, 718-724
trait, 611-612, 718-724
Aphasia, 667-668
Appetitive-aversive behavior, 21, 326-
340
Appraisal, 47-67, 239
Arousal
hyperventilation and, 741-743
measurement of, 341-367, 727-744
Arteriosclerosis, 479-482, 619
Atropine, 134, 693
Auditory stimulation, 84-85
Autonomic nervous system, 11-14, 29-
32, 369-378
responses by, 311-340, 620-621,
753-759
Averaged evoked potential (AEP), 405-
420
Avoidance behavior, 318-340, 380-385

B

Barbiturates, 111-112, 380, 387, 693
Bard theory of emotion, 126-128
Behavior
adolescent, 242-246
aggressive, 241-246, 485-488, 491-
494
anger, 235-278
depression, 235-278
emotion and, 17-45, 547-560